The Writer's Presence
A Pool of Readings

The Writer's Presence

A Pool of Readings
Fifth Edition

EDITED BY

DONALD McQUADE
University of California, Berkeley

ROBERT ATWAN
Series Editor, The Best American Essays
Director, The Blue Hills Writing Institute at Curry College

Bedford / St. Martin's   Boston   ◆   New York

For Bedford/St. Martin's

Senior Developmental Editor: Carolyn Lengel
Senior Production Editor: Shuli Traub
Senior Production Supervisor: Joe Ford
Senior Marketing Manager: Rachel Falk
Art Director: Lucy Krikorian
Copy Editor: Sally Scott
Photo Research: Robin Raffer
Cover Designer: Donna L. Dennison
Cover Art: Robert Frame, *Evening Terrace*, oil on canvas, 54″×60″. Courtesy of George Stern Fine Art, Los Angeles, California.
Composition: Macmillan India Ltd.
Printing and Binding: Haddon Craftsmen, Inc., an R.R. Donnelley & Sons Company

President: Joan E. Feinberg
Editorial Director: Denise B. Wydra
Editor in Chief: Nancy Perry
Director of Marketing: Karen Melton Soeltz
Director of Editing, Design, and Production: Marcia Cohen
Managing Editor: Erica T. Appel

Library of Congress Control Number: 2005928580

Manufactured in the United States of America.

1 0 9 8 7 6
f e d c b a

For information, write: Bedford/St. Martin's, 75 Arlington Street, Boston, MA 02116   (617-399-4000)

ISBN: 0-312-43386-7

EAN: 978-0-312-43386-4

Acknowledgments

Preface for Instructors _____

At the center of our work on this new edition of *The Writer's Presence* is our commitment to creating an effective tool for teaching critical reading and writing. This commitment is reflected in our efforts to design *The Writer's Presence* to achieve three fundamental objectives: to introduce students to a wide range of prose genres emphasizing a strong authorial presence and voice; to allow writing instructors maximum flexibility in assigning reading materials and writing models; and to support composition teachers and students as effectively as possible with helpful, though unobtrusive, editorial and pedagogical features. We are confident that the readings we have selected, the ways we have chosen to arrange that material, and the instructional resources we have provided both in the book and in the comprehensive instructor's manual will make this a uniquely useful collection that will satisfy the requirements of most first-year writing programs.

The Writer's Presence combines eminently readable—and teachable—writing with a simple organization and minimal editorial apparatus. Each selection showcases a writer's unique voice and provides students with accessible models they can use to develop their own voices in the writing they produce. Engaging readings arranged alphabetically by author and by five types of writing—informal, personal, expository, and argumentative essays, as well as short fiction—offer instructors the freedom to explore a wide range of pedagogical options, readily adaptable to the specific abilities and needs of particular students.

ESTABLISHED FEATURES OF *THE WRITER'S PRESENCE*

We continue to work diligently to ensure that the book's enduring features are as useful to instructors and as helpful to students as possible. (For information on features new to this edition, see page viii.)

Diverse Selections with a Strong Writer's Presence

Each of the selections in *The Writer's Presence* displays the distinctive signature that characterizes memorable prose: the presence of a lively individual imagination attempting to explore the self, shape information into meaning, or contend with issues.

The 119 essays, 3 graphic selections, 8 short stories, and 22 writer's commentaries offer an array of voices, genres, and styles from different times and cultures. Women and writers of color are strongly represented. Ranging widely across subjects, methods of development, and stylistic patterns, the selections also illustrate both the expectations and the uncertainties that surface when a writer attempts to create a memorable presence in prose. We have built the book—like previous editions—out of first-rate teaching material proven to work in the writing classroom.

We continue to feature a large number of authors whose works instructors have repeatedly enjoyed teaching over the years. These classroom favorites include such respected writers as Maya Angelou, James Baldwin, Joan Didion, Annie Dillard, Ralph Ellison, Edward Hoagland, Langston Hughes, Zora Neale Hurston, Jamaica Kincaid, George Orwell, Adrienne Rich, Scott Russell Sanders, Jonathan Swift, Mark Twain, Virginia Woolf, Alice Walker, and E. B. White. In fact, as this list of writers clearly indicates, *The Writer's Presence* could be used as an introduction to the essay or to literary nonfiction in general. For instructors with even more literary ambitions, we have included paired selections so that certain writers can be shown working in two different genres. These writers are Virginia Woolf, Raymond Carver, Gish Jen, Jamaica Kincaid, Sherman Alexie, Joyce Carol Oates, George Orwell, Langston Hughes, and John Updike.

Flexible Organization

The organization of *The Writer's Presence* displays a broad range of private, personal, expository, argumentative, and creative writing without imposing an order or specifying an instructional context in which to work with individual selections. In that sense, the contents of *The Writer's Presence* can truly be called "a pool of readings." The nonfiction selections that constitute the first four parts are divided into the four most commonly taught types of nonfiction—informal writing, personal essays, exposition, and argumentation. That is the extent of the book's overarching structure. Within each part, we present the writers in alphabetical order to make the selections easy to retrieve, assign, analyze, and interpret, regardless of instructional emphasis. To make it even easier to explore different approaches, *The Writer's Presence* includes alternate tables of contents that allow the book to be used as a thematic reader, a rhetorical reader, or a contemporary argument reader, with each selection carefully chosen to play multiple roles.

Helpful and Unobtrusive Apparatus

As in previous editions, we continue to keep instructional apparatus to a minimum, striving for a middle ground between too much and too little. Student readers profit from brief headnotes that provide useful and accessible information about a particular writer's background and relevant publications. Many selections provide provocative glimpses of lives and places, and readers naturally want to know when a selection was written and how and where it originally appeared. The headnotes in *The Writer's Presence* provide important biographical data and publication lists, along with intriguing quotations, and are as attentive as possible to a selection's original source. We don't want readers to infer mistakenly that an excerpt is actually an essay; this distorts their approach to the selection and may be unfair to the author. For example, we want readers to know at the outset that Maya Angelou's "'What's Your Name, Girl?'" is taken from her award-winning autobiography, *I Know Why the Caged Bird Sings*, and was not originally intended to stand alone as an essay.

It is our experience that many students can be guided in their assessment or rereading of a selection by carefully constructed follow-up questions. In this edition we have retained "The Reader's Presence," the small collection of questions after each selection. These questions can be used by student readers and writers to enhance their understanding of the selection, or the questions can stimulate productive analysis and group discussion in the classroom. We have designed "The Reader's Presence" to cover some of the dominant features of the selection and to refer to matters of content, style, and structure. As the title indicates, the questions will often draw attention to the specific ways in which readers are present in a piece of writing—either as an implied reader (the reader imagined by the writer) or as an actual reader. The concept of presence—both the writer's and the reader's—is discussed more fully in the "Introduction for Students."

Uniquely Extensive Instructor's Manual

While the amount of instructional apparatus in *The Writer's Presence* is carefully managed, a wealth of specific instructional activities appear in *Resources for Teaching* THE WRITER'S PRESENCE, the most comprehensive instructor's manual available for any composition reader.

The resources in this guide to *The Writer's Presence* include the following four parts in each entry:

- "Approaching the Essay" provides a thorough overview of pedagogically effective ways to work with the essay in the classroom.
- "Additional Activities" offers imaginative classroom activities, connections to other essays in the book, and collaborative projects.

- "Generating Writing" includes a range of writing exercises — from suggestions for informal writing to essay assignments and ideas for research papers.
- "The Reader's Presence" addresses the questions that follow each selection in the text, pointing to illuminating passages in the selection and anticipating possible responses from students.

FEATURES NEW TO THIS EDITION

For the fifth edition of *The Writer's Presence*, while we have retained the book's key features — its flexible format and its emphasis on authorial presence — we have also introduced new features that we believe will enhance the book's appeal to teachers and students as well as improve its use in and beyond the classroom.

Fifty-Two New Selections

These compelling new essays include works by such well-known contemporary authors as Gerald Early, Jonathan Franzen, Malcolm Gladwell, Pico Iyer, Gish Jen, Joyce Carol Oates, and John Updike, and fresh pieces from such classic writers as James Agee, James Baldwin, and W. E. B. Du Bois. New fiction selections include stories by Sherman Alexie, Raymond Carver, Gish Jen, and Joyce Carol Oates.

Authors Relatively New to Anthologies

In addition to many established and frequently anthologized authors, this edition features the work of many writers who are now finding their way into major collections: Amanda Hesser, Sebastian Junger, Randall Kennedy, Laura Kipnis, and Marjane Satrapi, to name a few. Included here are Azar Nafisi discussing the impact of a liberal-arts education on students in a fundamentalist society, Danielle Ofri describing the odds facing an impoverished young acquaintance struggling to return to school, and Lauren Slater examining the downside of self-esteem. We hope that readers will be as delighted as we are with the selections from these outstanding authors. We've also made an effort to include authors who, though more established, are not often included in composition readers; in this edition, we are pleased to include essays by such well-known writers as religious historian Karen Armstrong, columnist David Brooks, cultural geographer Jared Diamond, poet Charles Simic, and novelist Scott Turow.

New Attention to Visual Texts

The Writer's Presence now includes selections from the best contemporary graphic writing—a newly appreciated literary genre with cross-generational appeal. Joe Sacco's examination of how Israeli and Palestinian perspectives differ and Marjane Satrapi's illustration of her rebellious youth within the highly circumscribed religious culture of Iran will intrigue instructors and students alike. *The Writer's Presence* also offers a new focus on writing that analyzes accompanying visuals. Among the new selections of this kind are Zadie Smith's "Scenes from the Smith Family Christmas," Nora Ephron's "The Boston Photographs," James Agee's "America, Look at Your Shame!" and Jonathan Franzen's "The Comfort Zone."

More Attention to Connections among Readings

At the request of instructors, we have strengthened the interconnection questions following each reading—questions aimed at helping students see the many thematic and stylistic links between and among selections. In addition to these questions and to the connections identified in the alternate tables of contents, *The Writer's Presence* now offers a "Connections" feature on the companion Web site to enable students and instructors to find selections in the book linked by theme, rhetorical mode, contemporary issue, or any combination of these attributes. Each fiction selection is also connected to at least one nonfiction piece on a related theme, usually by the same writer.

New "Writer at Work" Selections

These twenty-two readings, five of which are new, include excerpts from interviews and essays in which authors discuss their writing processes and their identities as writers or in which a writer's work or development process is usefully analyzed. We chose each to show students that good writing is thoughtful work done by real people. This popular feature now includes such new selections as Joyce Carol Oates on turning a short story into a film, Abraham Lincoln's "Hay Draft" of the Gettysburg Address, and graphic novelist Ho Che Anderson on Martin Luther King Jr.'s "I Have a Dream."

A Revised Writer's Presence Web Site with a Searchable List of Selections

The companion site for the fifth edition of *The Writer's Presence*, available at **bedfordstmartins.com/writerspresence**, offers biographies and research links for every author in the book, providing students with starting points for their research. For the first time, the Web site allows students and instructors to search for a selection by theme, rhetorical mode, current issue, or all of these characteristics — or to search for selections that share a chosen theme, mode, and/or issue.

ACKNOWLEDGMENTS

Each revision of *The Writer's Presence* has developed from correspondence and conversations — on the phone, in person, in letters, and on the Internet — with the many teachers and an appreciable number of students who have worked with *The Writer's Presence* in their writing classes. We continue to learn a great deal from these discussions, and we are grateful to the colleagues and friends who graciously have allowed us into their already crowded lives to seek advice and encouragement. Since its inception, *The Writer's Presence* has been and continues to be a truly collaborative enterprise.

In the same way we originally developed *The Writer's Presence*, this revision has emerged from spirited discussions with instructors. We are grateful to these colleagues across the country who took the time to tell us about what did — and did not — work well when they used the fourth edition: Helen Barnes, Boise State University; Deborah Burnham, University of Pennsylvania; Susan Cannata, University of North Carolina–Pembroke; Kimberly Connor, University of San Francisco; Todd Fox, California State University, Long Beach; Sharon Gerring, Buffalo State College; Lee Harrison, Houston Community College; Tim Hohmann, Arizona State University; Susanna Horng, New York University; Matthew Kelley, University of Michigan; Kate Kessler, James Madison University; Laura Kjosen, Arapahoe Community College; Mary Ann Lee, Longview Community College; Terri Long, Boston College; Debra Matier, College of Southern Idaho; Robert Mayer, College of Southern Idaho; Barbara Ohrstrom, University of Michigan; Jesse Peters, University of North Carolina–Pembroke; Erin Scott, Illinois College; Andrew Sidle, Northern Illinois University; Mary Robin Whitney, John Jay College, City University of New York; and Sallie Wolf, Arapahoe Community College.

We would also like to acknowledge those instructors who offered thoughtful responses and suggestions for improvement to previous editions: James Adams, Boston College; Susan J. Allspaw, Boston College; Lisa Altomari, Vermont Technical College; Linda Baker, Portland Community College; Maurice H. Barr, Spokane Community College; Bette Bauer, College of Saint Mary; Todd W. Bersley, California State University, Northridge; Gerri Black, Stockton State College; Scott Brookman, Virginia Commonwealth University; Ann Lightcap Bruno, Boston College; Larry Brunt, Highline Community College; Jennifer Buckley, John Carroll University; Irene

Burgess, SUC Cortland; Ruth Elizabeth Burks, Tufts University; Dolores M. Burton, Boston University; Susan M. Cannata, University of North Carolina at Pembroke; Diane Challis, Virginia Commonwealth University; Jimmy Cheshire, Wright State University; Chet Childress, Virginia Commonwealth University; Alice Cleveland, College of Mareu; Rosanne Colosi, Boston College; Michel S. Connell, University of Iowa; Chase Crossingham, University of South Carolina; Ruth Y. Davidson, Pennsylvania State University Schuylkill; Ellen Davis, Boston University; Michael G. Davros, University of Illinois at Chicago; Peggy C. de Broux, Peninsula College; Jessica Deforest, Michigan State University; Mary Devaney, Rutgers University–Newark; Emily Dial-Driver, Rogers State University; Debra DiPiazza, Bernard M. Baruch College, City University of New York; Trevor Dodge, Boise State University; Jamye Doerfler, Virginia Commonwealth University; Maria Rowena P. Dolorico, Bristol Community College; Eileen Donovan-Kranz, Boston College; Susan M. Eisenthal, University of Massachusetts–Boston; Alex Fagan, Virginia Commonwealth University; Grace Farrell, Butler University; Joan Gabriele, University of Colorado; Christie Anderson Garcia, Spokane Falls Community College; Jane Gatewood, Mary Washington College; Rae Greiner, Radford University; Brian Hale, University of South Carolina; Sarah Hanselman, Tufts University; Lori Harrison-Kahan, Boston College; Dave Hendrickson, Virginia Commonwealth University; Curtis W. Herr, Kutztown University; Benjamin Hoffman, Boston College; Jack Jacobs, Auburn University; Goldie Johnson, Winona State University; Nancy B. Johnson, Pace University; Ronald L. King, Virginia Commonwealth University; Elizabeth Klem, Atlantic Cape Community College; Donna Levy, University of Richmond and J. Sargeant Reynolds Community College; Anthony W. Lilly II, Tufts University; Genoveva Llosa, Boston College; Harriet Malinowitz, Hunter College, City University of New York; Barbara Mallonee, Loyola College; Denice Martone, New York University; Ilene Miele, Moorpark College; Andrew Mossin, Temple University; Cathryn A. Myers, Virginia Commonwealth University; Lolly Ockerstrom, Virginia Commonwealth University; Jean Pace, Emerson College; Cheryl Pallant, Virginia Commonwealth University; Marty Patton, University of Missouri–Columbia; Gary D. Pratt, Brandeis University; Catherine S. Quick, University of Missouri–Columbia; Colleen Richmond, George Fox College; Larry Rodgers, Kansas State University; Robert Rogan, University of North Carolina Wilmington; Jan Zlotnick Schmidt, State University of New York, New Paltz; Lissa Schneider, University of Miami; Marilyn S. Scott, California State University Hayward; Larry Severeid, College of Eastern Utah; Joanne Sibicky, Virginia Commonwealth University; Robert Singleton, State University of New York, New Paltz; Constance Fletcher Smith, Mary Washington College; Nancy Sorenson, California State University; Roger Sorkin, University of Massachusetts–Dartmouth; Robert L. Stapleton, Long Beach City College; J. F. Stenerson, Pace University; Chad R. Stockton, Emerson College; Steven

Strang, Massachusetts Institute of Technology; Pamela Topping, Long Island University–Southampton College; Mary Turnbull, University of Puget Sound; Donna M. Turner, University of North Dakota; Sandra Urban, Loyola University of Chicago; Jennifer Lynne Von Ammon, Florida State University; Michael M. Walker, Palomar College; Kathleen G. White, Bellevue Community College; Mary Robin Whitney, John Jay College of Criminal Justice, City University of New York; and Ed Wiltse, Tufts University.

We would especially like to acknowledge our colleagues in the Expository Writing Program at New York University—Lisa Altomari, Karen Boiko, Darlene Forrest, Alfred Guy, Mary Helen Kolisnyk, Jim Marcall, Denice Martone, and Will McCormack—for taking the time to talk with us and for sharing their ideas during the planning stages of the first edition of this book.

We also extend our thanks to the professional staff at Bedford/St. Martin's for their innumerable contributions to this revision. We are grateful for the unfailing support and imaginative and convincing recommendations we received from our thoughtful and gracious editor, Carolyn Lengel. She strengthened this book in every imaginable way. She never hesitated to urge us to explore an idea or an instructional feature of the book if it might make our purposes clearer and more useful to teachers and students.

We are also grateful to Stephanie Butler, who did so much to bring together all the inevitable loose ends as we neared the publication date. Many thanks, too, to Shuli Traub for skillfully moving an enormous manuscript through production and to Erica Appel for managing the entire process with great attentiveness and intelligence.

As ever, Joan Feinberg, the president of Bedford/St. Martin's, offered us spirited encouragement and first-rate and rigorous advice, as well as engaging suggestions for improving the project. When our conversations veered occasionally toward uncertainty, we relied on her steady editorial presence to help us convert pedagogical principle into sound instructional practice.

The comprehensive instructor's guide that accompanies this collection, *Resources for Teaching THE WRITER'S PRESENCE*, was prepared for this edition by Joanna Imm of the University of Arizona and by Kate Silverstein, who also supplied many of "The Reader's Presence" questions and linked these closely to the entries in the manual. We appreciate their intelligent contributions and their remarkable ability to assess the classroom potential of such a wide variety of texts. We continue to be grateful to Cassandra Cleghorn of Williams College; Shelley Salamensky of University of California, Los Angeles; Alfred Guy of Yale University; Jon Roberts of St. Thomas Aquinas College; and Alix Schwartz of University of California, Berkeley; their very helpful suggestions are still amply evident in the instructor's manual. The new headnote research and writing for this edition was handled by Jan Weber; we are enormously grateful to her for all of her efforts. We extend our thanks, too, to Elisabeth

Gehrlein, who adroitly managed the challenging process of securing reprint permissions.

Finally, we hope that Hélène, Gregory, and Emily Atwan, along with Susanne, Christine, and Marc McQuade, will once again share our satisfaction in seeing this project in print and our pleasure in continuing our productive collaboration.

Donald McQuade
Robert Atwan
August 2005

Contents

I. THE INFORMAL VOICE: Diaries, Journals, Notebooks, Letters, Lists, Bumper Stickers, and Testimony   11

Christopher Columbus, *Land! October 12–14, 1492*   13

"They ought to be good servants and of good skill, for I see that they repeat very quickly whatever was said to them. I believe that they would easily be made Christians, because it seemed to me that they belonged to no religion. I, please Our Lord, will carry off six of them at my departure to Your Highnesses, that they may learn to speak. I saw no animal of any kind in this island, except parrots."

Toi Derricotte, from *The Black Notebooks*   17

"I let the tension stay in my body. I go home and sit with myself for an hour, trying to grasp the feeling—the odor of self-hatred, the biting stench of shame."

Joan Didion, *On Keeping a Notebook*   21

"My first notebook was a Big Five tablet, given to me by my mother with the sensible suggestion that I stop whining and learn to amuse myself by writing down my thoughts."

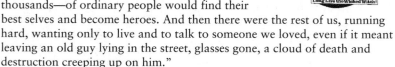

"What sort of diary should I like mine to be? Something loose knit and yet not slovenly, so elastic that it will embrace anything, solemn, slight or beautiful that comes into my mind. I should like it to resemble some deep old desk, or capacious hold-all, in which one flings a mass of odds and ends without looking them through."

II. PERSONAL WRITING: Exploring Our Own Lives   71

"A smart Indian is a dangerous person, widely feared and ridiculed by Indians and non-Indians alike. I fought with my classmates on a daily basis. They wanted me to stay quiet when the non-Indian teacher asked for answers, for volunteers, for help. We were Indian children who were expected to be stupid."

"Every person I knew had a hellish horror of being 'called out of his name.' It was a dangerous practice to call a Negro anything that could be loosely construed as insulting because of the centuries of their having been called niggers, jigs, dinges, blackbirds, crows, boots, and spooks."

"The day of my father's funeral had also been my nineteenth birthday. As we drove him to the graveyard, the spoils of injustice, anarchy, discontent, and hatred were all around us. It seemed to me that God himself had devised, to mark my father's end, the most sustained and brutally dissonant of codas. And it seemed to me, too, that the violence which rose all about us as my father left the world had been devised as a corrective for the pride of his eldest son."

"The brutal truth is that the bulk of white people in America never had any interest in educating black people, except as this could serve white purposes. It is not the black child's language that is in question, it is not his language that is despised: It is his experience."

"My Dad walked, hitched rides, and rode in empty boxcars when he went from Arkansas to Washington State in 1934, looking for work. I don't know whether he was pursuing a dream when he went out to Washington. I doubt it. I don't think he dreamed much."

French town of Avignon and brought to England by the Huguenots, but I could not have known that at the time), and it was made for me by my mother."

"First, the matter of semantics. I am a cripple. I choose this word to name me. I choose from among several possibilities, the most common of which are 'handicapped' and 'disabled.' I made the choice a number of years ago, without thinking, unaware of my motives for doing so."

"The question I am most often asked when I speak to students and others interested in writing is, How did you find your voice?"

"I spent my first month in town with my mouth hanging open. The sharp-dressed young 'cats' who hung on the corners and in the poolrooms, bars and restaurants, and who obviously didn't work anywhere, completely entranced me. I couldn't get over marveling at how their hair was straight and shiny like white men's hair; Ella told me this was called a 'conk.' "

"We were raking the lawn, my sister and I. I was raking, and she was stuffing the leaves into a bag. I loathed the job, and my muscles and my mind rebelled, and I was viciously angry, and my sister said something, and I turned and threw the rake at her and it hit her in the face."

"My early 'creative' experience evolved not from printed books, but from coloring books, predating my ability to read. I did not learn to read until I was in first grade, and six years old, though by this time I had already produced numerous 'books' of a kind by drawing, coloring, and scribbling in tablets, in what I believed to be a convincing imitation of adults."

"When I pulled the trigger I did not hear the bang or feel the kick—one never does when a shot goes home—but I heard the devilish roar of glee that went up from the crowd."

"Sometimes I feel I have seen too long from too many disconnected angles: white, Jewish, anti-Semite, racist, anti-racist, once-married, lesbian, middle-class, feminist, exmatriate southerner, *split at the root*—that I will never bring them whole."

"She cast back a worried glance. To her, the youngish black man—a broad six feet two inches with a beard and billowing hair, both hands shoved into the pockets of a bulky military jacket—seemed menacingly close. After a few more quick glimpses, she picked up her pace and was soon running in earnest."

▶ THE WRITER AT WORK
Another Version of *Just Walk on By* *287*
"She looked back at me once, then again, and picked up her pace. She looked back again and started to run. I stopped where I was and looked up at the surrounding windows. What did this look like to people peeking out through their blinds?"

"Lately, I've been giving more thought to the kind of English my mother speaks. Like others, I have described it to people as 'broken' or 'fractured' English. But I wince when I say that. It has always bothered me that I can think of no way to describe it other than 'broken,' as if it were damaged and needed to be fixed, as if it lacked a certain wholeness and soundness."

"For the rest of my days, I shall be a recovering short person. Even from my lofty perch of something over six feet (as if I don't know within a micron), I have the soul of a shrimp."

"In certain lights, your face looks passable; in slightly different other lights, not. Shaving mirrors and rearview mirrors in automobiles are merciless, whereas the smoky mirrors in airplane bathrooms are especially flattering and soothing: one's face looks as tawny as a movie star's."

"Where the BB pellet struck there is a glob of whitish scar tissue, a hideous cataract, on my eye. Now when I stare at people—a favorite pastime, up to now—they will stare back. Not at the 'cute' little girl, but at her scar."

"Summertime, oh, summertime, pattern of life indelible, the fadeproof lake, the woods unshatterable, the pasture with the sweetfern and the juniper forever and ever, summer without end."

▶ THE WRITER AT WORK
E. B. White on the Essayist *317*
"There is one thing the essayist cannot do . . . he cannot indulge himself in deceit or in concealment, for he will be found out in no time."

III. EXPOSITORY WRITING:
Shaping Information 319

"Words form the backbone of what we think. So, although it is possible to have thought without words, it's rarely possible to know what one thinks without bronzing it in words. Otherwise, the thoughts seem to float away. Refine the words, and you refine the thought. But that sometimes means squishing a square thought into a round hole and saying what you can instead of what you mean."

"If you want to be American, speak 'American.' If you don't like it, go back to Mexico, where you belong."

"Fundamentalists seek to drag God and religion from the sidelines to which they have been relegated in a secular polity and pull them back to center stage. Every fundamentalist movement I have studied, in Judaism, Christianity and Islam, is rooted in a profound fear of annihilation— a conviction that the liberal, secularist establishment wants to wipe out religion."

"It is appalling that Americans know so little about one another. It is appalling that many of us are so narrow-minded that we can't tolerate a few people with ideas significantly different from our own. It's appalling that evangelical Christians are practically absent from entire professions, such as academia, the media, and filmmaking. It's appalling that people should be content to cut themselves off from everyone unlike themselves."

"The first point to understand about the difference between honesty and integrity is that a person may be entirely honest without ever engaging in the hard work of discernment that integrity requires; she may tell us quite truthfully what she believes without ever taking the time to figure out whether what she believes is good and right and true."

"Smiles are associated with joy, relief, and amusement. But smiles are by no means limited to the expression of positive emotions: People of many different cultures smile when they are frightened, embarrassed, angry, or miserable."

an anatomist, or (especially) the coach of a women's softball team is that there is no structural reason why men and women should throw in different ways."

"I think of myself as a good American. I follow current events, come to a complete stop at stop signs, show up for jury duty, vote. When the government tells me to shop, as it's been doing recently, I shop.
Over the last few months, patriotically, I've bought all kinds of stuff I have no use for."

". . . one may have to think of celebrity in an entirely new way—not as a status that is conferred by publicity, but as a narrative form, written in the medium of life, that is similar to narratives in movies, novels, and television."

"We live in an age, after all, that is strangely fixated on the idea of helplessness: we're fascinated by hurricanes and terrorist acts and epidemics like SARS—situations in which we feel powerless to affect our own destiny. In fact, the risks posed to life and limb by forces outside our control are dwarfed by the factors we can control. Our fixation with helplessness distorts our perceptions of risk."

"The minute I set foot upon the island I could feel all that it stood for: insecurity, obedience, anxiety, dehumanization, the terrified and careful deference of the displaced."

"My greatest unhappiness with most popular presentations of science concerns their failure to separate fascinating claims from the methods that scientists use to establish the facts of nature."

"My daydreams were full of places I longed to be, shelters and solitudes. I wanted a room apart from others, a hidden cabin to rest in. I wanted to be in a redwood forest with trees so tall that the owls called out in the daytime."

"Mess is a state of mind. Or rather, messiness is a particular relation between the state of arrangement of a collection of things and a state of mind that contemplates it in its containing space."

". . . I am an example, perhaps, of an entirely new breed of people, a transcontinental tribe of wanderers that is multiplying as fast as IDD lines and IATA flights. We are the Transit Loungers, forever heading to the departure gate, forever orbiting the world. We buy our interests duty-free, we eat our food on plastic plates, we watch the world through borrowed headphones. We pass through countries as through revolving doors, resident aliens of the world, impermanent residents of nowhere."

"Life in modern society is designed to eliminate as many unforeseen events as possible, and as inviting as that seems, it leaves us hopelessly under-utilized. And that is where the idea of 'adventure' comes in. The word comes from the Latin *adventura*, meaning 'what must happen.' An adventure is a situation where the outcome is not entirely within your control."

"That's right. I know it sounds like an ad for some sleazy writers' school, but I really am going to tell you everything you need to pursue a successful and financially rewarding career writing fiction, and I really am going to do it in ten minutes, which is exactly how long it took me to learn."

"Whenever she had to warn us about life, my mother told stories that ran like this one, a story to grow up on. She tested our strength to establish realities."

   "I wanted to write directly what I was thinking and feeling, not imagining fictional other people. I wanted to write myself."

"The world will little note, nor long remember what we say here, but it can never forget what they did here."

"With malice toward none; with charity for all; with firmness in the right, as God gives us to see the right, let us strive on to finish the work we are in; to bind up the nation's wounds; to care for him who shall have borne the battle, and for his widow, and his orphan—to do all which may achieve and cherish a just, and a lasting peace, among ourselves, and with all nations."

"It was hot weather when they tried the infidel Scopes at Dayton, Tenn., but I went down there very willingly, for I was eager to see something of evangelical Christianity as a going concern."

"Loneliness is an aspect of the land. All things in the plain are isolate; there is no confusion of objects in the eye, but *one* hill or *one* tree or *one* man. To look upon that landscape in the early morning, with the sun at your back, is to lose the sense of proportion. Your imagination comes to life, and this, you think, is where Creation was begun."

"Teaching in the Islamic Republic, like any other vocation, was subservient to politics and subject to arbitrary rules. Always, the joy of teaching was marred by diversions and considerations forced on us by the regime—how well could one teach when the main concern of university officials was not the quality of one's work but the color of one's lips, the subversive potential of a single strand of hair?"

"If this were a movie, he'd score a perfect 1600 and be off to Princeton on full scholarship. But Harlem isn't Hollywood, and the challenges in real life are infinitely more complex."

"Political language—and with variations this is true of all political parties, from Conservatives to Anarchists—is designed to make lies sound truthful and murder respectable, and to give an appearance of solidity to pure wind."

"Putting aside the need to earn a living, I think there are four great motives for writing, at any rate for writing prose."

"Instead of looking at kids to 'prove' that differences in behavior by sex are innate, we can look at the ways we raise kids as an index to how unfinished the feminist revolution really is, and how tentatively it is embraced even by adults who fully expect their daughters to enter previously male-dominated professions and their sons to change diapers."

will have increased exponentially. We need to develop a new form of media literacy: readership skills for the culture of simulation."

"I was walking toward Market Street one afternoon when I saw it, a background of brilliant sky blue, with writing on it in airy white letters, which said: *now the world really does revolve around you.* The letters were lowercase, soft-edged, spaced irregularly, as if they'd been skywritten over a hot August beach and were already drifting off into the air. The message they left behind was a child's secret wish, the ultimate baby-world narcissism we are all supposed to abandon when we grow up: the world really does revolve around me."

"Let us consider television viewing in the light of the conditions that define serious addictions."

" 'Hooking up' was a term known in the year 2000 to almost every American child over the age of nine, but to only a relatively small percentage of their parents, who, even if they heard it, thought it was being used in the old sense of 'meeting' someone. Among the children, hooking up was always a sexual experience, but the nature and extent of what they did could vary widely."

"It was as if someone had taken a tiny bead of pure life and decking it as lightly as possible with down and feathers, had set it dancing and zigzagging to show us the true nature of life."

IV. ARGUMENTATIVE WRITING:
Contending with Issues   623

"The word cut across my solar plexus like a cold knife, and the whole bus, except for those two voices and the comments of their friends, was suddenly almost exploded by an immensely thick quietness."

"I think that using art to provoke uncertainty is what great writing and inspired images do most brilliantly. Art should provoke more questions than answers and, most of all, should make us think about what we rarely want to think about at all."

"Watching the news reports, it is often hard to tell whether there are real living and breathing women in conflict-stricken places like Haiti. The evening news broadcasts only allow us a brief glimpse of presidential coups, rejected boat people, and sabotaged elections. The women's stories never manage to make the front page. However they do exist."

   "Writing was a dangerous activity. Perhaps it was that danger that attracted me, the feeling of doing a high-wire act between stretching the limits of silence and telling the whole truth."

"Asteroids hurtling at us beyond our control don't figure high on our list of imminent dangers. To save ourselves, we don't need new technology: we just need the political will to face up to our problems of population and the environment."

"We can live any way we want. People take vows of poverty, chastity, and obedience—even of silence—by choice. The thing is to stalk your calling in a certain skilled and supple way, to locate the most tender and live spot and plug into that pulse. This is yielding, not fighting."

   "One of the few things I know about writing is this: spend it all, shoot it, play it, lose it, all, right away, every time. Do not hoard what seems good for a later place in the book, or for another book; give it, give it all, give it now."

"It is a peculiar sensation, this double-consciousness, this sense of always looking at one's self through the eyes of others, of measuring one's soul by the tape of a world that looks on in amused contempt and pity. One ever feels his two-ness,—an American, a Negro; two souls, two thoughts, two unreconciled strivings; two warring ideals in one dark body, whose dogged strength alone keeps it from being torn asunder."

"In the fairly near future, a standard item in the trunks of American police cruisers—perhaps even on each officer's belt—may be a DNA analyzer. As a suspect is arrested, police will quickly swipe the inside of his cheek with a cotton swab and pop the results into the scanner."

which gives you rest, so you wake up feeling good. I am black. I feel very good this evening."

▶ THE WRITER AT WORK
Martin Luther King Jr. on Self-Importance   *754*

"This is the prayer I pray to God every day, 'Lord help me to see M. L. King as M. L. King in his true perspective.' Because if I don't see that, I will become the biggest fool in America."

Laura Kipnis, *Against Love*   755

"As love has increasingly become the center of all emotional expression in the popular imagination, anxiety about obtaining it in sufficient quantities—and for sufficient duration—suffuses the population. Everyone knows that as the demands and expectations on couples escalated, so did divorce rates. And given the current divorce statistics (roughly 50 percent of all marriages end in divorce), all indications are that whomever you love today—your beacon of hope, the center of all your optimism—has a good chance of becoming your worst nightmare tomorrow."

Bill McKibben, *Worried? Us?*   763

". . . people think about 'global warming' in the way they think about 'violence on television' or 'growing trade deficits,' as a marginal concern to them, if a concern at all. Enlightened governments make smallish noises and negotiate smallish treaties; enlightened people look down on America for its blind piggishness. Hardly anyone, however, has fear in their guts."

Martha Nussbaum, *Can Patriotism Be Compassionate?*   768

"Compassion for our fellow Americans can all too easily slide over into an attitude that wants America to come out on top, defeating or subordinating other peoples or nations. Anger at the terrorists themselves is perfectly appropriate; so is the attempt to bring them to justice. But 'us versus them' thinking doesn't always stay focused on the original issue; it too easily becomes a general call for American supremacy, the humiliation of 'the other.' "

Bertrand Russell, *Why I Am Not a Christian*   773

"A good world needs knowledge, kindliness, and courage; it does not need a regretful hankering after the past or a fettering of the free intelligence by the words uttered long ago by ignorant men."

Scott Russell Sanders, *The Men We Carry in Our Minds*   786

"Here I met for the first time young men who had assumed from birth that they would lead lives of comfort and power. And for the first time I met women who told me that men were guilty of having kept all the joys and privileges of the earth for themselves. I was baffled. What privileges? What joys?"

imagined. Hollywood isn't going to make movies that are class-conscious, or antiwar, or conscious of the need for racial equality or gender equality."

V. THE VOICES OF FICTION: Eight Short Stories   883

Sherman Alexie, *This Is What It Means to Say Phoenix, Arizona*   885

"Victor didn't have any money. Who does have money on a reservation, except the cigarette and fireworks salespeople? His father had a savings account waiting to be claimed, but Victor needed to find a way to get to Phoenix. Victor's mother was just as poor as he was, and the rest of his family didn't have any use at all for him."

Raymond Carver, *The Bath*   895

"Of course, the birthday party never happened. The birthday boy was in the hospital instead. The mother sat by the bed. She was waiting for the boy to wake up. The father hurried over from his office. He sat next to the mother. So now the both of them waited for the boy to wake up. They waited for hours, and then the father went home to take a bath."

Nathaniel Hawthorne, *Young Goodman Brown*   901

"He had taken a dreary road, darkened by all the gloomiest trees of the forest, which barely stood aside to let the narrow path creep through, and closed immediately behind. It was all as lonely as could be; and there is this peculiarity in such a solitude, that the traveler knows not who may be concealed by the innumerable trunks and the thick boughs overhead; so that with lonely footsteps he may yet be passing through an unseen multitude."

Gish Jen, *Who's Irish?*   912

"My daughter thought this Amy very creative—another word we do not talk about in China. In China, we talk about whether we have difficulty or no difficulty. We talk about whether life is bitter or not bitter. In America, all day long, people talk about creative."

Jamaica Kincaid, *Girl*   921

"Wash the white clothes on Monday and put them on the stone heap; wash the color clothes on Tuesday and put them on the clothesline to dry; don't walk barehead in the hot sun."

▶ THE WRITER AT WORK
  Jamaica Kincaid on *Girl*   924
  "This mother in 'Girl' was really just giving the girl an idea about the things she
  would need to be a self-possessed woman in the world."

Alternate Tables of Contents

Selections Arranged by Theme

CHILDHOOD AND FAMILY

A SENSE OF PLACE

PSYCHOLOGY AND HUMAN BEHAVIOR

ETHICS AND MORALITY

PHILOSOPHY, SPIRITUALITY, AND RELIGION

THE NATURAL ENVIRONMENT

HISTORY AND BIOGRAPHY

EDUCATION

SCIENCES AND TECHNOLOGY

LAW, POLITICS, AND SOCIETY

RACIAL AND ETHNIC IDENTITY

GENDER ROLES

Selections Arranged by Common Rhetorical Modes and Patterns of Development

CONSTRUCTING NARRATIVES

Narratives That Lead to a Sudden Insight or a Decision

Narratives That Report Facts and Historical Events

Narratives That Illustrate a Position or a Philosophical Perspective

Narratives That Recount Other Lives

WRITING DESCRIPTION: PERSONS, PLACES, THINGS

USING COMPARISONS

DEFINING WORDS AND CONCEPTS

SUPPLYING INSTANCES AND EXAMPLES

CLASSIFYING IDEAS

ANALYZING AND DESCRIBING PROCESSES

ANALYZING AND DESCRIBING IMAGES

ESTABLISHING CAUSES AND EFFECTS

FORMING ANALOGIES

FASHIONING ARGUMENTS: EIGHT METHODS

Arguing from Personal Experience

Arguing from Factual Evidence

Correcting Popular Misconceptions

Countering Other Arguments

Arguing from Personal Authority and Expertise

Arguing with Humor, Irony, and Satire

Urging Changes in Public Policy

Finding Common Ground

The Writer's Presence
A Pool of Readings

Introduction for Students:
The Writer's Presence

Presence is a word — like *charisma* — that we reserve for people who create powerful and memorable impressions. Many public figures and political leaders are said to "have presence" — Martin Luther King Jr. and Eleanor Roosevelt were two superb examples — as well as many athletes, dancers, and musicians. In fact, the quality of presence is found abundantly in the performing arts, where top entertainers and actors self-consciously fashion — through style, costume, and gesture — an instantly recognizable public presence. Clearly, people with presence are able to command our attention. How do they do it?

Presence is far easier to identify than it is to define. We recognize it when we see it, but how do we capture it in words? Virtually everyone would agree, for example, that when Michael Jordan stepped onto a basketball court, he displayed an exceptional degree of presence; we acknowledge this whether or not we are basketball fans. But what is it about such individuals that commands our attention? How can we begin to understand this elusive characteristic known as presence?

On one level, *presence* simply means "being present." But the word is more complex than that; it suggests much more than the mere fact of being physically present. Most dictionaries define *presence* as an ability to project a sense of self-assurance, poise, ease, or dignity. We thus speak of someone's "stage presence" or "presence of mind." But the word is also used today to suggest an impressive personality, an individual who can make his or her presence felt. As every college student knows, to be present in a classroom is not the same thing as *having a presence* there. We may be present in body, but not in spirit. In that sense, presence is also a matter of individual energy and exertion, of putting something of ourselves into whatever it is we do.

Presence is especially important in writing, which is what this book is about. Just as we notice individual presence in sports, or music, or conversation, so too we discover it in good writing. If what we read seems dreary, dull, or dead, it's usually because the writer forgot to include an important ingredient: *personal presence*. That doesn't mean that your essays should be written *in* the first-person singular (this book contains many exceptional essays that aren't) but that your essays should be written *by* the first-person singular—by *you*. Interesting essays are produced by a real and distinct person, not an automaton following a set of mechanical rules and abstract principles.

PRESENCE IN WRITING

How can someone be present in writing? How can you project yourself into an essay so that it seems that you're personally there, even though all your reader sees are words on a piece of paper?

The Writer's Presence shows you how this is done. It shows how a wide variety of talented writers establish a distinct presence in many different kinds of writing and for many different purposes and audiences. Although the book offers numerous examples of methods for establishing presence, several are worth pointing out at the start. Let's examine four of the chief ways an experienced writer can be present in an essay.

1. Through Personal Experience. One of the most straightforward ways for the writer to make his or her presence felt in an essay is to include appropriate personal experiences. Of course, many assignments may call for a personal essay, and in those cases you will naturally be putting episodes from your own life at the center of your writing. But writers also find ways to build their personal experiences into essays that are basically informative or argumentative, essays on topics other than oneself. They do this to show their close connection with a subject, to offer testimony, or to establish their personal authority on a subject. Many of the essays in this collection offer clear illustrations of how writers incorporate personal experience into an essay on a specific topic or issue.

Look, for example, at the essay by Amy Cunningham, "Why Women Smile" (page 355). This essay is primarily an explanation of a cultural phenomenon—the way women are socially conditioned to maintain a smiling attitude. But Cunningham begins the essay not with a general observation but with a personal anecdote: "After smiling brilliantly for nearly four decades, I now find myself trying to quit." Although her essay is not "personal," her opening sentence, besides establishing her own connection with the topic, provides readers with a personal motive for her writing.

One of the first places to look for the writer's presence is in the motive, the purpose, for putting words down on paper or on the computer screen. The extent of your success in making clear your motive for writing will largely depend on your interest both in the subject and in your ideas about the subject. It is extremely difficult for any writer to establish a presence when he or she is either bored with—or simply uninterested in—the subject at hand. But a writer who demonstrates what Virginia Woolf calls a "fierce attachment to an idea" can create a presence that attracts and holds a reader's attention.

2. *Through Voice*. Another way a writer makes his or her presence felt is through creating a distinctive and identifiable *voice*. All words are composed of sounds, and language itself is something nearly all of us originally learned through *hearing*. Any piece of writing can be read aloud, though many readers have developed such ingrained habits of silent reading that they no longer *hear* the writing. Good writers, however, want their words to be heard. They want their sentences to have rhythm, cadence, and balance. Experienced authors revise a great deal of their writing just to make sure the sentences *sound* right. They're writing for the reader's ear as well as the reader's mind.

In many respects, voice is the writer's "signature," what finally distinguishes the work of one writer from another. Consider how quickly we recognize voice. We've *heard* only the opening lines of a comedy routine on television, yet we instantly recognize the speaker. So, too, whenever we read a piece of writing, we ought to think of it as an experience similar to listening to someone speak aloud. Doing so adds drama to writing and reading. Here is what the poet Robert Frost has to say on the subject:

> Everything written is as good as it is dramatic. . . . A dramatic necessity goes deep into the nature of the sentence. Sentences are not different enough to hold the attention unless they are dramatic. No ingenuity of varying structure will do. All that can save them is the speaking tone of voice somehow entangled in the words and fastened to the page for the ear of the imagination. That is all that can save poetry from singing, all that can save prose from itself. (Preface to *A Way Out*, in *Selected Prose of Robert Frost*)

Frost spent a good portion of his celebrated public life encouraging people to cultivate what he called "the hearing imagination."

A more specific dimension of voice is *tone*, which refers not only to the implied relationship of the writer to the reader, but also to the manner the writer adopts in addressing the reader. Tone suggests not the writer's attitudes themselves but the way those attitudes are revealed. In either projecting or analyzing tone, writers and readers ought to consider its intensity, the force with which the writer's attitudes are expressed. The strength of the writer's tone depends on such factors as the seriousness of the situation, the nature and extent of the writer's involvement in the situation, and the control the writer exercises over expression. In practical terms, tone is usually a matter of diction and individual word choice.

A writer's voice is usually fairly consistent from essay to essay and can be detected quickly by an experienced reader who pays attention to "the hearing imagination." To be distinctive and effective, a writer's voice need not be strange, artificial, or self-consciously literary. Many essayists develop a casual, familiar, flexible tone of voice that allows them to range easily from the intimate to the intellectual. Sentence rhythm and word choice play a large part in determining a writer's tone of voice. Observe how Raymond Carver begins an essay about his father (page 103):

> My dad's name was Clevie Raymond Carver. His family called him Raymond and friends called him C.R. I was named Raymond Clevie Carver, Jr. I hated the "Junior" part. When I was little my dad called me Frog, which was okay. . . .

Carver's voice here is casual and almost childlike, a quality he is striving for in an essay intended to be candid, intimate, and low-key. Throughout the essay, for example, he rarely uses the word *father* but always the more colloquial *dad*. If you read this passage aloud, you will get the feeling that someone is speaking directly to you.

   3. *Through Point of View*. Another sure way for writers to establish presence is through the point of view they adopt toward a subject. In this sense, point of view comprises the "where" of the writer's presence. Sometimes a point of view can be a literal reality, an actual place or situation in which writers physically locate themselves. This occurs most frequently in autobiographical essays in which the writer is present both as the narrator and as a character. For example, in "A Clack of Tiny Sparks: Remembrances of a Gay Boyhood" (page 121), Bernard Cooper is always meticulous about telling us his actual location at any given moment in his writing. The essay begins, "Theresa Sanchez sat behind me in ninth-grade algebra."

   Or consider the tremendous importance of point of view — this time in terms of perspective — to another essayist in the volume, Brent Staples, in "Just Walk on By: A Black Man Ponders His Power to Alter Public Space" (page 283). This is how Staples opens his essay:

> My first victim was a woman — white, well dressed, probably in her early twenties. I came upon her late one evening on a deserted street in Hyde Park, a relatively affluent neighborhood in an otherwise mean, impoverished section of Chicago. As I swung onto the avenue behind her, there seemed to be a discreet, uninflammatory distance between us. Not so. She cast back a worried glance. To her, the youngish black man — a broad six feet two inches with a beard and billowing hair, both hands shoved into the pockets of a bulky military jacket — seemed menacingly close. After a few more quick glimpses, she picked up her pace and was soon running in earnest. Within seconds she disappeared into a cross street.

In order to see why he frightens people, Staples needs to see himself in the stereotypical ways that others see him. Thus, by the middle of this opening paragraph (in the sentence beginning "To her"), he literally switches the point of view from his own perspective to that of the young and terrified white woman, describing his appearance as she would perceive it.

Point of view is not always a matter of a specific location or position. Writers are not always present in their essays as dramatic characters. In many reflective, informative, or argumentative essays, the point of view is determined more by a writer's intellectual attitude or opinions—an angle of vision—than by a precise physical perspective. As an example of how a writer establishes a personal perspective without a dominant first-person narrator, consider the following passage from John Taylor Gatto's "Against School" (page 688), an argumentative essay against America's traditional school system. Although Gatto from time to time introduces his own personal background, he makes his point of view—opposition to modern education—clear to the reader without ever referring directly to himself. Note his comparison between how schools train children and how concerned parents might better handle the job:

> Now for the good news. Once you understand the logic behind modern schooling, its tricks and traps are fairly easy to avoid. School trains children to be employees and consumers; teach your own to be leaders and adventurers. School trains children to obey reflexively; teach your own to think critically and independently. Well-schooled kids have a low threshold for boredom; help your own to develop an inner life so that they'll never be bored. Urge them to take on the serious material, the *grown-up* material, in history, literature, philosophy, music, art, economics, theology—all the stuff schoolteachers know well enough to avoid. Challenge your kids with plenty of solitude so that they can learn to enjoy their own company, to conduct inner dialogues.

There is no first person singular here, nor a dramatically rendered self. Yet this passage conveys a very distinct point of view.

4. Through Verbal Patterns. A writer can also be present in an essay as a *writer*—that is, as a person consciously crafting and shaping his or her work. This artistic presence is not always obvious. Yet when we begin to detect in our reading certain kinds of repeated elements—a metaphor or an image, a twist on an earlier episode, a conclusion that echoes the opening—we become aware that someone is deliberately shaping experience or ideas in a special manner. We often find this type of presence in imaginative literature—especially in novels and poems—as well as in essays that possess a distinct literary flavor.

To see an example of creating a presence through verbal patterns, look at the opening paragraph of E. B. White's now-classic essay, "Once More to the Lake" (page 311).

> One summer, along about 1904, my father rented a camp on a lake in Maine and took us all there for the month of August. We all got ringworm from some kittens and had to rub Pond's Extract on our arms and legs night and morning, and my father rolled over in a canoe with all his clothes on; but outside of that the vacation was a success and from then on none of us ever thought there was any place in the world like that lake in Maine. We returned summer after summer—always on August 1st for one month. I have since become a salt-water man, but sometimes

in summer there are days when the restlessness of the tides and the fearful cold of the sea water and the incessant wind that blows across the afternoon and into the evening make me wish for the placidity of a lake in the woods. A few weeks ago this feeling got so strong I bought myself a couple of bass hooks and a spinner and returned to the lake where we used to go, for a week's fishing and to revisit old haunts.

If, in rereading this opening, you circle every use of the word *and*, you will clearly see a pattern of repetition. *And*, of course, is a very unobtrusive word, and you may not notice right away how White keeps it present throughout the passage. This repetition alone may strike you at first as of no special importance, but as you read through the essay and see how much of White's central theme depends on the idea of return and repetition, you will get a better sense of why the little word *and*—a word that subtly reinforces the idea of repetition itself—is so significant.

E. B. White is present in his essay in more obvious ways—he is both telling the story and appearing in it as a character. But he is also present to us as a writer, someone consciously shaping the language and form of his essay. We are dealing here with three levels of presence (which might also be described as three levels of "I"). If this sounds confusing, just think of a movie in which a single person directs, stars, and perhaps plays one or more other roles in the making of the film. It's not that uncommon. If you watch the 2004 film *Million Dollar Baby*, for example, you can observe the multiple presences of Clint Eastwood. Not only is Eastwood visibly present in the film as one of the main characters, but we also can detect his creative and shaping presence as the director and as a producer (roles for which he won two Oscars), and as the composer of the film's score. The audience can directly see him on the screen as an actor; the audience can also infer his presence as a composer, a producer, and especially as a director—presences that, though less directly observable, are still original and powerful.

THE SELECTIONS IN THIS BOOK

Many of the selections in this book feature the first-person point of view directly. These selections appear mostly in the first two parts, "The Informal Voice: Diaries, Journals, Notebooks, Letters, Lists, Bumper Stickers, Testimony" and "Personal Writing: Exploring Our Own Lives." In most of these selections, the writer will appear as both narrator and main character, and the writer's presence will be quite observable.

But private and personal writing provide only a fraction of the different types of nonfiction that appear regularly in books, newspapers, and magazines. Many essays are written on specific topics and deal with specific issues. Most of the essays appearing in America's dominant periodicals, for example, are intended to be either informative or persuasive; the author wants to convey information about a particular subject (a Civil War battle, for example) or wants to express an opinion about a particular issue (such as how to deal with terrorism). The book's third and fourth parts, "Expository Writing: Shaping Information" and "Argumentative Writing: Contending with Issues," contain a large number of selections that illustrate writing intended to inform, argue, and persuade.

You'll notice, however, a strong writer's presence in many of the informative and persuasive essays. This is deliberate. To write informatively or persuasively about subjects other than yourself doesn't mean that you have to disappear as a writer. Sometimes you will want to insert your own experiences and testimony into an argumentative essay; at other times you will want to assume a distinct viewpoint concerning a piece of information; and at still other times — though you may not introduce the first-person singular — you will make your presence strongly felt in your tone of voice or simply in the way you arrange your facts and juxtapose details (see the Gatto passage above). At the heart of the word *information* is *form*. Writers don't passively receive facts and information in a totally finished format; they need to shape their information, to give it form. This shaping or patterning is something the writer *contributes*. A large part of the instructional purpose of this collection is to encourage you to pay more attention to the different ways writers are present in their work.

Presence in Fiction

An individual writer's presence and voice are perhaps more easily discerned in nonfiction than in fiction. The reason for this is that a novelist or short, story writer invents and gives voices to numerous characters who should not be confused with the author. Sometimes, a story is told by an invented character who also should not be closely identified with his or her author. A good example of this technique can be found in John Updike's "A & P" (page 959), in which a story is narrated in the distinctive voice of its main character, Sammy, a teenager who is working at a small suburban supermarket. Although the story is written in the first-person singular — exactly like most personal essays — the character and voice are fictional and do not correspond to any real person. Sammy is not John Updike, nor does he necessarily speak like John Updike would if we met him.

To further complicate matters, this biographical gap between narrator and author remains even when a story that is told in the third person appears to be written in the voice of the author. The third-person narrator is also invented, and the narrative voice and presence may have little to do with the life of the author who created it. So in what ways can the writer's presence be observed in a story if we cannot attach to its teller any biographical connection with its author? In fiction, we often find a writer's presence in a distinctive style of writing, in certain repeated patterns, in the dynamics of structure and plot, and of course in the ethical, spiritual, or intellectual values a story may be intended to illustrate. In certain stories, to be sure, a particular character may clearly represent the author's own values, and in those cases we might argue that the writer becomes "present" in that character. As can be seen in Part V, "The Voices of Fiction: Eight Short Stories," an author may refuse to locate his or her moral and psychological values within a particular character but will expect instead that the reader will derive these values from the overall perspective of the story itself. Unlike essayists, short story writers rarely state their ethical or aesthetic values directly and explicitly. As the novelist D. H. Lawrence aptly put it, in fiction we must trust the tale and not the teller. We have included in this book several examples of fiction and nonfiction by the same author (Sherman Alexie, Raymond Carver, Gish Jen, Jamaica Kincaid, Joyce Carol Oates, and John Updike) so that readers can explore the different ways a writer's values are conveyed in different genres.

THE READER'S PRESENCE

Because almost all writing (and *all* published writing) is intended to be read, we can't dismiss the importance of the reader. Just as we find different levels of a writer's presence in a given piece of writing, so too can we detect different ways in which a reader can be present.

An author writes a short essay offering an opinion about gun control. The author herself has been the victim of a shooting, and her piece, though it includes her personal experiences, is largely made up of a concrete plan to eliminate all guns—even hunting rifles—from American life. She would like lawmakers to adopt her plan. Yet, in writing her essay, she imagines that there will be a great deal of resistance to her argument. In other words, she imagines a reader who will most likely disagree with her and who needs to be won over. Let's imagine she gets her essay published in *Newsweek*.

Now imagine three people in a dentist's office who within the same afternoon pick up this issue of *Newsweek* and read the essay. One of them has also been victimized by guns (her son was accidentally wounded by a hunter), and she reads the essay with great sympathy and conviction. She understands perfectly what this woman has gone through and believes in her plan completely. The next reader, a man who has never once in his life committed a crime and has no tolerance for criminals, is outraged by the essay. He was practically brought up in the woods and loves to hunt. He could never adopt a gun control plan that would in effect criminalize hunting. He's ready to fire off a letter attacking this woman's plan. The third reader also enjoys hunting and has always felt that hunting rifles should be exempt from any government regulation of firearms. But he finds the writer's plan convincing and feasible. He spends the rest of the day trying to think of counterarguments.

Obviously, these are only three of many possibilities. But you can see from this example the differences between the reader imagined by the writer and some actual readers. The one person who completely agreed with the writer was not the kind of reader the author had originally imagined or was trying to persuade; she was already persuaded. And though the other two readers were part of her intended audience, one of them could never be persuaded to her point of view, whereas the other one might.

The differences briefly outlined here are distinctions between what can be called *implied readers* and *actual readers*. The implied reader is the reader imagined by the writer for a particular piece of writing. In constructing arguments, for example, it is usually effective to imagine readers we are *trying* to win over to our views. Otherwise, we are simply asking people who already agree with us to agree with us—what's commonly known as "preaching to the converted" or "preaching to the choir."

In informative or critical essays, a writer also needs to be careful about the implied reader. For example, it's always important to ask how much your intended audience may already know about your subject. Here's a practical illustration. If you were asked to write a review of a recent film for your college newspaper, you would assume your readers had not yet seen it (or else you might annoy them by giving away some surprises). On the other hand, if you were asked to write a critical essay about the same movie for a film course, you could assume your readers had seen it. It's the same movie, and you have the same opinions about it, but your two essays have two different purposes, and in the process of writing them you imagine readers with two different levels of knowledge about the film.

Actual readers, of course, differ from implied readers in that they are real people who read the writing—not readers intended or imagined by the writer. As you read the essays in this collection, you should be aware of at least two readers—(1) the reader you think the writer imagines for the essay, and (2) the reader you are in actuality. Sometimes you will seem very close to the kind of reader the writer is imagining. In those cases, you might say that you "identify" with a particular writer, essay, or point of view. At other times, however, you will notice a great deal of distance between the reader the author imagines and you as an actual reader. For example, you may feel excluded by the author on the basis of race, gender, class, or expected knowledge and educational level. Or you may feel you know more than the author does about a particular topic.

To help you get accustomed to your role as a reader, each selection in the book is followed by a set of questions, "The Reader's Presence." These questions are designed to orient you to the various levels of reading suggested by the selection. Some of the questions will ask you to identify the kind of reader you think the author imagines; other questions will prompt you to think about specific ways you may differ from the author's intended reader; others will help you to make connections between and among the selections and authors. In general, the questions are intended to make you more deeply aware of your *presence* as a reader.

In this brief introduction, we covered only two levels of readers (imagined and actual), but some literary essays, such as Jonathan Swift's "A Modest Proposal" (page 825), demand more complex consideration. Whenever we think more than these two types of readers need to be identified in an essay, we will introduce this information in the questions.

We hope you will find *The Writer's Presence* a stimulating book to read and think about. To make our presence felt as writers is as much a matter of self-empowerment as it is of faith. It requires the confidence that we can affect others, or determine a course of action, or even surprise ourselves by new ideas or by acquiring new powers of articulation.

Part of the enduring pleasure of writing is precisely that element of surprise, of originality—that lifelong pleasure of discovering new resources of language, finding new means of knowing ourselves, and inventing new ways to be present in the world.

Part I

The Informal Voice: Diaries, Journals, Notebooks, Letters, Lists, Bumper Stickers, Testimony

Christopher Columbus
Land! October 12–14, 1492

Christopher Columbus (1451–1506) landed in the Bahamas on October 12, 1492, seven weeks after setting off to sea in three small boats with a crew of about ninety men. The journal of his first voyage (1492–1493) describes the land and peoples of the Bahamas, Cuba, Haiti, and the Dominican Republic. The original journal notes were lost; much of what we know today as Columbus's journals consists of later transcriptions made by Fray Bartolomé de las Casas. The first printed version of the journal appeared in 1825 and was translated into English in 1827. This translation is by Samuel Eliot Morison, a noted biographer of Columbus.

These journal entries describe the arrival of Columbus (here called "the Admiral") and his first encounters with native people on the island he names San Salvador, or "Holy Savior." Erecting two flags in honor of his patrons, the Spanish monarchs Ferdinand and Isabella, he claims possession.

Friday, 12 October [1492]

At two hours after midnight appeared the land,[1] at a distance of 2 leagues. They handed all sails and set the *treo*, which is the mainsail without bonnets, and lay-to waiting for daylight Friday, when they arrived at an island of the Bahamas that was called in the Indians' tongue *Guanahaní*. Presently they saw naked people, and the Admiral went ashore in his barge, and Martín Alonso Pinzón and Vicente Yáñez, his brother, who was captain of the *Niña*, followed. The Admiral broke out the royal standard, and the captains [displayed] two banners of the Green Cross, which the Admiral flew on all the vessels as a signal, with an F and a Y,[2] one at one arm of the cross and the other on the other, and over each letter his or her crown. Once ashore they saw very green trees, many streams, and fruits of different kinds. The Admiral called to the two captains and to the others who

---

[1]*the land:* San Salvador. — Eds.
[2]*an F and a Y:* For Ferdinand and Isabella, the king and queen of Spain.

jumped ashore and to Rodrigo de Escobedo, secretary of the whole fleet, and to Rodrigo Sánchez of Segovia, and said that they should bear faith and witness how he before them all was taking, as in fact he took, possession of the said island for the King and Queen, their Lord and Lady, making the declarations that are required, as is set forth at length in the testimonies which were there taken down in writing. Presently there gathered many people of the island. What follows are the formal words of the Admiral, in his Book of the First Navigation and Discovery of these Indies:[3]

"I," says he, "in order that they might develop a very friendly disposition towards us, because I knew that they were a people who could better be freed and converted to our Holy Faith by love than by force, gave to some of them red caps and to others glass beads, which they hung on their necks, and many other things of slight value, in which they took much pleasure. They remained so much our [friends] that it was a marvel, later they came swimming to the ships' boats in which we were, and brought us parrots and cotton thread in skeins and darts and many other things, and we swopped them for other things that we gave them, such as little glass beads and hawks' bells.[4] Finally they traded and gave everything they had, with good will; but it appeared to me that these people were very poor in everything. They all go quite naked as their mothers bore them; and also the women, although I didn't see more than one really young girl. All that I saw were young men, none of them more than 30 years old, very well built, of very handsome bodies and very fine faces; the hair coarse, almost like the hair of a horse's tail, and short, the hair they wear over their eyebrows, except for a hank behind that they wear long and never cut. Some of them paint themselves black (and they are of the color of the Canary Islanders, neither black nor white), and others paint themselves white, and some red, and others with what they find. And some paint their faces, others the body, some the eyes only, others only the nose. They bear no arms, nor know thereof; for I showed them swords and they grasped them by the blade and cut themselves through ignorance. They have no iron. Their darts are a kind of rod without iron, and some have at the end a fish's tooth and others, other things. They are generally fairly tall and good looking, well built. I saw some who had marks of wounds on their bodies, and made signs to them to ask what it was, and they showed me that people of other islands which are near came there and wished to capture them, and they defended themselves. And I believed and now believe that people do come here from the mainland to take them as slaves. They ought to be good servants and of good skill, for I see that they repeat very quickly whatever was said to them. I believe that they would easily be made Christians, because it seemed to me that

---

[3]***Book of . . . these Indies:*** Title of Columbus's original journal. — EDS.
   [4]***hawks' bells:*** Tiny bells used in falconry; these had proved, along with other trifles, popular with African natives. — EDS.

they belonged to no religion. I, please Our Lord, will carry off six of them at my departure to Your Highnesses, that they may learn to speak. I saw no animal of any kind in this island, except parrots." All these are the words of the Admiral.

Saturday, 13 October [1492]

"At the time of daybreak there came to the beach many of these men, all young men, as I have said, and all of good stature, very handsome people. Their hair is not kinky but straight and coarse like horsehair; the whole forehead and head is very broad, more so than [in] any other race that I have yet seen, and the eyes very handsome and not small. They themselves are not at all black, but of the color of the Canary Islanders; nor should anything else be expected, because this is on the same latitude as the island of Ferro in the Canaries. The legs of all, without exception, are very straight and [they have] no paunch, but are very well proportioned. They came to the ship in dug-outs which are fashioned like a long boat from the trunk of a tree, and all in one piece, and wonderfully made (considering the country), and so big that in some came 40 or 50 men, and others smaller, down to some in which but a single man came. They row with a thing like a baker's peel and go wonderfully, and if they capsize all begin to swim and right it and bail it out with calabashes[5] that they carry. They brought skeins of spun cotton, and parrots, and darts, and other trifles that would be tedious to describe, and give all for whatever is given to them. And I was attentive and worked hard to know if there was any gold, and saw that some of them wore a little piece hanging from a thing like a needle case which they have in the nose; and by signs I could understand that, going to the S, or doubling the island to the S, there was a king there who had great vessels of it and possessed a lot. I urged them to go there, and later saw that they were not inclined to the journey. I decided to wait until tomorrow afternoon and then depart to the SW, since, as many of them informed me, there should be land to the S, SW, and NW, and that they of the NW used to come to fight them many times; and so also to go to the SW to search for gold and precious stones. This island is very big and very level; and the trees very green, and many bodies of water, and a very big lake in the middle, but no mountain, and the whole of it so green that it is a pleasure to gaze upon, and this people are very docile, and from their longing to have some of our things, and thinking that they will get nothing unless they give something, and not having it, they take what they can, and soon swim off. But all that they have, they give for whatever is given to them, even bartering for pieces of broken crockery and glass. I even saw 16 skeins of cotton given

---

[5]*calabashes:* Gourds. — EDS.

for three *ceitis* of Portugal, which is [equivalent to] a *blanca* of Castile,[6] and in them there was more than an *arroba*[7] of spun cotton. This I should have forbidden and would not have allowed anyone to take anything, except that I had ordered it all taken for Your Highnesses if there was any there in abundance. It is grown in this island; but from the short time I couldn't say for sure; and also here is found the gold that they wear hanging from the nose. But, to lose no time, I intend to go and see if I can find the Island of Çipango.[8] Now, as it was night, all went ashore in their dugouts."

Sunday, 14 October [1492]

"When day was breaking I ordered the ship's gig and the caravels'   5
barges to be readied, and I went along the coast of the island to the NNE, to see the other side, which was the eastern side, what there was there, and also to see the villages; and soon I saw two or three, and the people who all came to the beach, shouting and giving thanks to God. Some brought us water, others, other things to eat. Others, when they saw that I didn't care to go ashore, plunged into the sea swimming, and came out, and we understood that they asked us if we had come from the sky. And one old man got into the boat, and others shouted in loud voices to all, men and women, 'Come and see the men who come from the sky, bring them food and drink.' Many came and many women, each with something, giving thanks to God, throwing themselves on the ground, they raised their hands to the sky, and then shouted to us to come ashore; but I was afraid to, from seeing a great reef of rocks which surrounded the whole of this island, and inside it was deep water and a harbor to hold all the ships in Christendom, and the entrance of it very narrow. It's true that inside this reef there are some shoal spots, but the sea moves no more than within a well. In order to see all this I kept going this morning, that I might give an account of all to Your Highnesses, and also [to see] where there might be a fortress; and I saw a piece of land which is formed like an island, although it isn't one (and on it there are six houses), the which could in two days be made an island, although I don't see that it would be necessary, because these people are very unskilled in arms, as Your Highnesses will see from the seven that I caused to be taken to carry them off to learn our language and return; unless Your Highnesses should order them all to be taken to Castile or held captive in the same island, for with 50 men they could all be subjected and made to do all that one wished. And, moreover, next to said islet are groves of trees the most beautiful that I have seen, and as green and leafy as those of Castile in the months of April and May; and much water. I inspected all that harbor, and then returned to the ship and made sail, and saw so many islands that I could not decide where

---

[6]*three ceitis . . . blanca of Castile:* Fractions of a cent. —EDS.
[7]*arroba:* About twenty-five pounds. —EDS.
[8]*Çipango:* Japan; following Marco Polo's report, Columbus thought the island of Japan was approximately fifteen hundred miles from the Asian continent. —EDS.

to go first; and those men whom I had captured made signs to me that they were so many that they could not be counted, and called by their names more than a hundred. Finally I looked for the biggest, and decided to go there, and so I did, and it is probably distant from this island of San Salvador 5 leagues, and some of them more, some less. All are very level, without mountains, and very fertile, and all inhabited, and they make war on one another, although these are very simple people and very fine figures of men."

The Reader's Presence

1. A ship's log is the captain's legal record of everything that happens on a voyage. What does this portion of Columbus's log emphasize? Why do you think the author focuses on this information? Columbus's original journals were lost; this version was transcribed (and perhaps changed) by Bartolomé de las Casas, who had seen the original log. Does knowing this fact change the way you view the journals' contents? Why or why not?

2. What observations in the log point to misunderstandings between the native people and Columbus's crew? What does each group's overall impression of the other people seem to have been?

3. Compare the perspective in Columbus's logs with George Orwell's description of his feelings about the Burmese in "Shooting an Elephant" (page 221). How much resemblance do you see between the descriptions of native people? How does the "outsider's perspective" differ in these two selections?

Toi Derricotte

From *The Black Notebooks*

In the 1970s Toi Derricotte, a well-known and award-winning African American poet, moved with her husband and young son to an upscale, all-white New Jersey suburb. She soon began keeping a sketchy yet intimate journal of her experiences with friends, neighbors, and family as complex and unpleasant tensions developed. As she wrote, she realized that her disclosures were bringing her face to face with her own shame, her own "internalized racism." She worked at the notebooks for twenty-five years, slowly revising them until they captured "the language of self-hate, the pain of re-emerging thought and buried memory and consciousness." The Black Notebooks: An Interior Journey, *from which the following selections were extracted, was published in 1997. It won a number of awards and was a* New York Times *Notable Book of the Year. "October" recounts an episode that took place while Derricotte and her husband were house-hunting in New Jersey; the incident in "July" occurred after they had moved to the all-white community.*

Born in Detroit, Michigan, in 1941, Derricotte is also the author of four collections of poetry: Natural Birth, The Empress of the Death House, Captivity, *and* Tender. *She currently teaches at the University of Pittsburgh.*

OCTOBER

It's the overriding reality I must get through. Each time I drive down the streets and see only whites, each time I notice no blacks in the local supermarket or walking on the streets, I think, *I'm not supposed to be here.* When I go into real estate agents' offices, I put on a mask. At first they hope you are in for a quick sell. They show you houses they want to get rid of. But if you stick around, and if you are the "right kind," they show you ones just newly listed, and sometimes not even on the market. There are neighborhoods that even most white people are not supposed to be in.

I make myself likable, optimistic. I am married, a woman who belongs to a man. Sometimes I reveal I am Catholic, if it might add a feeling of connection. It is not entirely that I am acting. I am myself but slightly strained, like you might strain slightly in order to hear something whispered.

Yesterday an agent took me into the most lily-white neighborhood imaginable, took me right into the spotless kitchen, the dishwasher rumbling, full of the children's dishes. I opened the closets as if I were a thief, as if I were filthying them, as if I believe about myself what they believe: that I'm "passing," that my silence is a crime.

The first woman I knew about who "passed" was the bronze-haired daughter of insurance money, one of the wealthiest black families in the United States. I remember my mother telling me stories of her white roadster, how she wrote plays and opened a theater. She had directed several of the plays in which my mother and father had acted. She went to New York to "make it" and was published in the *New York Times.* I was seven when my father went down to meet the midnight train that brought her home: people said she had confessed to her rich fiancé that she was black and he had jilted her. They dressed her in a long bronze dress, a darkened tone of her long auburn hair. She looked like Sleeping Beauty in a casket made especially for her with a glass top.

My mother told me how, when she was young, her mother used to get great pleasure when she would seat her daughter in the white part of the train and then depart, as if she were her servant. She said her mother   5 would stand alongside the train and wave good-bye with a smile on her face, like a kid who has gotten away with the cookies. And my father told how, during the Detroit riots of 1943, when black men were being pulled off the buses and beaten to death, he used to walk down East Grand Boulevard as a dare.

Of course, we are never caught; it is absolutely inconceivable that we could go unrecognized, that we are that much like them. In fact, we are the same.

When Bruce and I first got married, I had been looking for an apartment for months. Finally, I found a building in a nice neighborhood with a playground nearby, and a school that was integrated. I rang the bell and was relieved when the supervisor who came to the door was black. I loved the apartment. Then I became terrified. Should I tell *him* we're black? Would that make my chances of getting the apartment greater? I wondered if he would be glad to have another black family in the building, or if maybe his job was dependent on his keeping us out. I decided to be silent, to take the chance that he liked me.

When I left, sailing over the George Washington Bridge, I had my first panic attack. I thought I might drive my car right over the edge. I felt so high up there, so disconnected, so completely at my own mercy. Some part of me doesn't give a fuck about boundaries — in fact, sees the boundaries and is determined to dance over them no matter what the consequences are. I am so precarious, strung out between two precipices, that even when I get to the other side, I am still not down, still not so low I can't harm myself.

I could hardly control my car, my heart pounding, my hands sweaty on the wheel. I had to pull off the West Side Highway as soon as I could, and I went into the first place I could find, a meat-packing house. The kind white man let me use the phone to call Bruce before he took me in a big meat truck to the nearest hospital. The doctor said it was anxiety, and I should just go home and rest. For days I was afraid to come out of my house, and even now, though I push myself to do it, every time I go over a high place, or am in a strange territory, I fear I will lose control, that something horrible and destructive will come out of me.

Each night Bruce and I don't talk about it, as if there were no cost to   10
what I'm doing, or as if whatever the cost is I've got to pay.

JULY

This morning I put my car in the shop. The neighborhood shop. When I went to pick it up I had a conversation with the man who had worked on it. I told him I had been afraid to leave the car there at night with the keys in it. "Don't worry," he said. "You don't have to worry about stealing as long as the niggers don't move in." I couldn't believe it. I hoped I had heard him wrong. "What did you say?" I asked. He repeated the same thing without hesitation.

In the past, my anger would have swelled quickly. I would have blurted out something, hotly demanded he take my car down off the rack immediately, though he had not finished working on it, and taken off in a blaze. I love that reaction. The only feeling of power one can possibly have in a situation in which there is such a sudden feeling of powerlessness is to "do" something, handle the situation. When you "do" something, everything is clear. But this is the only repair shop in the city. Might I have to come back here someday in an emergency?

Blowing off steam is supposed to make you feel better. But in this situation it *doesn't*! After responding in anger, I often feel sad, guilty, frightened, and confused. Perhaps my anger isn't just about race. Perhaps it's like those rapid-fire responses to Bruce — a way of dulling the edge of feelings that lie even deeper.

I let the tension stay in my body. I go home and sit with myself for an hour, trying to grasp the feeling — the odor of self-hatred, the biting stench of shame.

The Reader's Presence

1. In what ways does Derricotte try to fit into a white community? What features of an all-white community does she appear to find desirable? What features worry her? What does she mean by "passing"? How does she feel about the act of "passing"?

2. Why doesn't Derricotte express her anger to the auto mechanic? What explanations does she offer? What feelings does her silence lead to?

3. Compare Derricotte's growing awareness of "the odor of self-hatred, the biting stench of shame" (paragraph 14) to Malcolm X's insights at the end of "Homeboy" (page 194). How do the tones of the two pieces compare? What does this comparison tell you about the differences between a journal entry and an essay?

Joan Didion

On Keeping a Notebook

The author of novels, short stories, screenplays, and essays, Joan Didion (b. 1934) began her career in 1956 as a staff writer at Vogue *magazine in New York. In 1963 she published her first novel,* Run River, *and the following year returned to her native California. Didion's essays have appeared in periodicals ranging from* Mademoiselle *to the* National Review. *Her essay "On Keeping a Notebook" can be found in her collection of essays,* Slouching Towards Bethlehem *(1968). Didion's other nonfiction publications include* The White Album *(1979),* Salvador *(1983),* Miami *(1987),* After Henry *(1992),* Political Fictions *(2001),* Fixed Ideas: America since 9.11 *(2003), and* Where I Was From *(2003).*

Didion has defined a writer as "a person whose most absorbed and passionate hours are spent arranging words on pieces of paper. I write entirely to find out what's on my mind, what I'm thinking, what I'm looking at, what I'm seeing and what it means, what I want and what I'm afraid of." She has also said that "all writing is an attempt to find out what matters, to find the pattern in disorder, to find the grammar in the shimmer. Actually I don't know whether you find the grammar in the shimmer or you impose a grammar on the shimmer, but I am quite specific about the grammar — I mean it literally. The scene that you see in your mind finds its own structure; the structure dictates the arrangement of the words. . . . All the writer has to do really is to find the words." However, she warns, "You have to be alone to do this."

"'That woman Estelle,'" the note reads, "'is partly the reason why George Sharp and I are separated today.' *Dirty crepe-de-Chine wrapper, hotel bar, Wilmington RR, 9:45 a.m. August Monday morning."*

Since the note is in my notebook, it presumably has some meaning to me. I study it for a long while. At first I have only the most general notion of what I was doing on an August Monday morning in the bar of the hotel across from the Pennsylvania Railroad station in Wilmington, Delaware (waiting for a train? missing one? 1960? 1961? why Wilmington?), but I do remember being there. The woman in the dirty crepe-de-Chine wrapper had come down from her room for a beer, and the bartender had heard before the reason why George Sharp and she were separated today. "Sure," he said, and went on mopping the floor. "You told me." At the other end of the bar is a girl. She is talking, pointedly, not to the man beside her but to a cat lying in the triangle of sunlight cast through the open door. She is wearing a plaid silk dress from Peck & Peck, and the hem is coming down.

Here is what it is: The girl has been on the Eastern Shore, and now she is going back to the city, leaving the man beside her, and all she can see ahead are the viscous summer sidewalks and the 3 A.M. long-distance calls that will make her lie awake and then sleep drugged through all the steaming mornings left in August (1960? 1961?). Because she must go directly from the train to lunch in New York, she wishes that she had a safety pin for the hem of the plaid silk dress, and she also wishes that she could forget about the hem and the lunch and stay in the cool bar that smells of disinfectant and malt and make friends with the woman in the crepe-de-Chine wrapper. She is afflicted by a little self-pity, and she wants to compare Estelles. That is what that was all about.

Why did I write it down? In order to remember, of course, but exactly what was it I wanted to remember? How much of it actually happened? Did any of it? Why do I keep a notebook at all? It is easy to deceive oneself on all those scores. The impulse to write things down is a peculiarly compulsive one, inexplicable to those who do not share it, useful only accidentally, only secondarily, in the way that any compulsion tries to justify itself. I suppose that it begins or does not begin in the cradle. Although I have felt compelled to write things down since I was five years old, I doubt that my daughter ever will, for she is a singularly blessed and accepting child, delighted with life exactly as life presents itself to her, unafraid to go to sleep and unafraid to wake up. Keepers of private notebooks are a different breed altogether, lonely and resistant rearrangers of things, anxious malcontents, children afflicted apparently at birth with some presentiment of loss.

My first notebook was a Big Five tablet, given to me by my mother   5
with the sensible suggestion that I stop whining and learn to amuse myself by writing down my thoughts. She returned the tablet to me a few years ago; the first entry is an account of a woman who believed herself to be freezing to death in the Arctic night, only to find, when day broke, that she had stumbled onto the Sahara Desert, where she would die of the heat before lunch. I have no idea what turn of a five-year-old's mind could have prompted so insistently "ironic" and exotic a story, but it does reveal a certain predilection for the extreme which has dogged me into adult life; perhaps if I were analytically inclined I would find it a truer story than any I might have told about Donald Johnson's birthday party or the day my cousin Brenda put Kitty Litter in the aquarium.

So the point of my keeping a notebook has never been, nor is it now, to have an accurate factual record of what I have been doing or thinking. That would be a different impulse entirely, an instinct for reality which I sometimes envy but do not possess. At no point have I ever been able successfully to keep a diary; my approach to daily life ranges from the grossly negligent to the merely absent, and on those few occasions when I have tried dutifully to record a day's events, boredom has so overcome me that the results are mysterious at best. What is this business about "shopping, typing piece, dinner with E, depressed"? Shopping for what? Typing what piece? Who is E? Was this "E" depressed, or was I depressed? Who cares?

In fact I have abandoned altogether that kind of pointless entry; instead I tell what some would call lies. "That's simply not true," the members of my family frequently tell me when they come up against my memory of a shared event. "The party was *not* for you, the spider was *not* a black widow, *it wasn't that way at all.*" Very likely they are right, for not only have I always had trouble distinguishing between what happened and what merely might have happened, but I remain unconvinced that the distinction, for my purposes, matters. The cracked crab that I recall having for lunch the day my father came home from Detroit in 1945 must certainly be embroidery, worked into the day's pattern to lend verisimilitude; I was ten years old and would not now remember the cracked crab. The day's events did not turn on cracked crab. And yet it is precisely that fictitious crab that makes me see the afternoon all over again, a home movie run all too often, the father bearing gifts, the child weeping, an exercise in family love and guilt. Or that is what it was to me. Similarly, perhaps it never did snow that August in Vermont; perhaps there never were flurries in the night wind, and maybe no one else felt the ground hardening and summer already dead even as we pretended to bask in it, but that was how it felt to me, and it might as well have snowed, could have snowed, did snow.

How it felt to me: that is getting closer to the truth about a notebook. I sometimes delude myself about why I keep a notebook, imagine that some thrifty virtue derives from preserving everything observed. See enough and write it down, I tell myself, and then some morning when the world seems drained of wonder, some day when I am only going through the motions of doing what I am supposed to do, which is write— on that bankrupt morning I will simply open my notebook and there it will all be, a forgotten account with accumulated interest, paid passage back to the world out there: dialogue overheard in hotels and elevators and at the hatcheck counter in Pavillon (one middle-aged man shows his hat check to another and says, "That's my old football number"); impressions of Bettina Aptheker and Benjamin Sonnenberg and Teddy ("Mr. Acapulco") Stauffer; careful *aperçus*[1] about tennis bums and failed fashion models and Greek shipping heiresses, one of whom taught me a significant lesson (a lesson I could have learned from F. Scott Fitzgerald, but perhaps we all must meet the very rich for ourselves) by asking, when I arrived to interview her in her orchid-filled sitting room on the second day of a paralyzing New York blizzard, whether it was snowing outside.

---

[1]*aperçus:* Summarizing glimpse or insight (French).—EDS.

I imagine, in other words, that the notebook is about other people. But of course it is not. I have no real business with what one stranger said to another at the hatcheck counter in Pavillon; in fact I suspect that the line "That's my old football number" touched not my own imagination at all, but merely some memory of something once read, probably "The Eighty-Yard Run."[2] Nor is my concern with a woman in a dirty crepe-de-Chine wrapper in a Wilmington bar. My stake is always, of course, in the unmentioned girl in the plaid silk dress. *Remember what it was to be me:* that is always the point.

It is a difficult point to admit. We are brought up in the ethic that   10 others, any others, all others, are by definition more interesting than ourselves; taught to be diffident, just this side of self-effacing. ("You're the least important person in the room and don't forget it," Jessica Mitford's[3] governess would hiss in her ear on the advent of any social occasion; I copied that into my notebook because it is only recently that I have been able to enter a room without hearing some such phrase in my inner ear.) Only the very young and the very old may recount their dreams at breakfast, dwell upon self, interrupt with memories of beach picnics and favorite Liberty lawn dresses and the rainbow trout in a creek near Colorado Springs. The rest of us are expected, rightly, to affect absorption in other people's favorite dresses, other people's trout.

And so we do. But our notebooks give us away, for however dutifully we record what we see around us, the common denominator of all we see is always, transparently, shamelessly, the implacable "I." We are not talking here about the kind of notebook that is patently for public consumption, a structural conceit for binding together a series of graceful *pensées*;[4] we are talking about something private, about bits of the mind's string too short to use, an indiscriminate and erratic assemblage with meaning only for its maker.

And sometimes even the maker has difficulty with the meaning. There does not seem to be, for example, any point in my knowing for the rest of my life that, during 1964, 720 tons of soot fell on every square mile of New York City, yet there it is in my notebook, labeled "FACT." Nor do I really need to remember that Ambrose Bierce liked to spell Leland Stanford's[5] name "£eland $tanford" or that "smart women almost always wear black in Cuba," a fashion hint without much potential for practical application. And does not the relevance of these notes seem marginal at best?:

---

[2] *"The Eighty-Yard Run":* Popular short story by Irwin Shaw.—EDS.

[3] *Jessica Mitford* (1917–1996): British satirical writer.—EDS.

[4] *pensées:* Thoughts or reflections (French).—EDS.

[5] *Bierce . . . Stanford's:* Ambrose Bierce (1842–1914?), American journalist and short story writer known for his savage wit; Leland Stanford (1824–1893), wealthy railroad builder who was a governor of California and the founder of Stanford University.—EDS.

In the basement museum of the Inyo County Courthouse in Independence, California, sign pinned to a mandarin coat: "This MANDARIN COAT was often worn by Mrs. Minnie S. Brooks when giving lectures on her TEAPOT COLLECTION."

Redhead getting out of car in front of Beverly Wilshire Hotel, chinchilla stole, Vuitton bags with tags reading:

> MRS. LOU FOX
> HOTEL SAHARA
> VEGAS

Well, perhaps not entirely marginal. As a matter of fact, Mrs. Minnie S. Brooks and her MANDARIN COAT pull me back into my own childhood, for although I never knew Mrs. Brooks and did not visit Inyo County until I was thirty, I grew up in just such a world, in houses cluttered with Indian relics and bits of gold ore and ambergris and the souvenirs my Aunt Mercy Farnsworth brought back from the Orient. It is a long way from that world to Mrs. Lou Fox's world, where we all live now, and is it not just as well to remember that? Might not Mrs. Minnie S. Brooks help me to remember what I am? Might not Mrs. Lou Fox help me to remember what I am not?

But sometimes the point is harder to discern. What exactly did I have in mind when I noted down that it cost the father of someone I know $650 a month to light the place on the Hudson in which he lived before the Crash? What use was I planning to make of this line by Jimmy Hoffa:[6] "I may have my faults, but being wrong ain't one of them"? And although I think it interesting to know where the girls who travel with the Syndicate have their hair done when they find themselves on the West Coast, will I ever make suitable use of it? Might I not be better off just passing it on to John O'Hara?[7] What is a recipe for sauerkraut doing in my notebook? What kind of magpie keeps this notebook? "*He was born the night the* Titanic *went down.*" That seems a nice enough line, and I even recall who said it, but is it not really a better line in life than it could ever be in fiction?

But of course that is exactly it: not that I should ever use the line, but that I should remember the woman who said it and the afternoon I heard it. We were on her terrace by the sea, and we were finishing the wine left from lunch, trying to get what sun there was, a California winter sun. The woman whose husband was born the night the *Titanic* went down wanted to rent her house, wanted to go back to her children in Paris. I remember wishing that I could afford the house, which cost $1,000 a

15

---

[6]*Jimmy Hoffa* (1913–1975?): Controversial leader of the Teamsters Union who disappeared in the mid-seventies.—EDS.

[7]*John O'Hara* (1905–1970): American novelist who wrote several books about gangsters.—EDS.

month. "Someday you will," she said lazily. "Someday it all comes." There in the sun on her terrace it seemed easy to believe in someday, but later I had a low-grade afternoon hangover and ran over a black snake on the way to the supermarket and was flooded with inexplicable fear when I heard the checkout clerk explaining to the man ahead of me why she was finally divorcing her husband. "He left me no choice," she said over and over as she punched the register. "He has a little seven-month-old baby by her, he left me no choice." I would like to believe that my dread then was for the human condition, but of course it was for me, because I wanted a baby and did not then have one and because I wanted to own the house that cost $1,000 a month to rent and because I had a hangover.

It all comes back. Perhaps it is difficult to see the value in having one's self back in that kind of mood, but I do see it; I think we are well advised to keep on nodding terms with the people we used to be whether we find them attractive company or not. Otherwise they turn up unannounced and surprise us, come hammering on the mind's door at 4 A.M. of a bad night and demand to know who deserted them, who betrayed them, who is going to make amends. We forget all too soon the things we thought we could never forget. We forget the loves and the betrayals alike, forget what we whispered and what we screamed, forget who we were. I have already lost touch with a couple of people I used to be; one of them, a seventeen-year-old, presents little threat, although it would be of some interest to me to know again what it feels like to sit on a river levee drinking vodka-and-orange-juice and listening to Les Paul and Mary Ford[8] and their echoes sing "How High the Moon" on the car radio. (You see I still have the scenes, but I no longer perceive myself among those present, no longer could even improvise the dialogue.) The other one, a twenty-three-year-old, bothers me more. She was always a good deal of trouble, and I suspect she will reappear when I least want to see her, skirts too long, shy to the point of aggravation, always the injured party, full of recriminations and little hurts and stories I do not want to hear again, at once saddening me and angering me with her vulnerability and ignorance, an apparition all the more insistent for being so long banished.

It is a good idea, then, to keep in touch, and I suppose that keeping in touch is what notebooks are all about. And we are all on our own when it comes to keeping those lines open to ourselves: your notebook will never help me, nor mine you. "*So what's new in the whiskey business?*" What could that possibly mean to you? To me it means a blonde in a Pucci bathing suit sitting with a couple of fat men by the pool at the Beverly Hills Hotel. Another man approaches, and they all regard one another in silence for a while. "So what's new in the whiskey business?" one of the fat men finally says by way of welcome, and the blonde stands up, arches one foot

---

[8]*Les Paul and Mary Ford:* Husband-and-wife musical team of the forties and fifties who had many hit records.—EDS.

and dips it in the pool, looking all the while at the cabaña where Baby Pignatari is talking on the telephone. That is all there is to that, except that several years later I saw the blonde coming out of Saks Fifth Avenue in New York with her California complexion and a voluminous mink coat. In the harsh wind that day she looked old and irrevocably tired to me, and even the skins in the mink coat were not worked the way they were doing them that year, not the way she would have wanted them done, and there is the point of the story. For a while after that I did not like to look in the mirror, and my eyes would skim the newspapers and pick out only the deaths, the cancer victims, the premature coronaries, the suicides, and I stopped riding the Lexington Avenue IRT because I noticed for the first time that all the strangers I had seen for years—the man with the seeing-eye dog, the spinster who read the classified pages every day, the fat girl who always got off with me at Grand Central—looked older than they once had.

It all comes back. Even that recipe for sauerkraut: even that brings it back. I was on Fire Island when I first made that sauerkraut, and it was raining, and we drank a lot of bourbon and ate the sauerkraut and went to bed at ten, and I listened to the rain and the Atlantic and felt safe. I made the sauerkraut again last night and it did not make me feel any safer, but that is, as they say, another story.

The Reader's Presence

1. Notice that Didion begins her essay not with a general comment about notebooks but with an actual notebook entry. What does the entry sound like at first? What effect do you think Didion wants it to have on you as a reader?

2. Consider the comparison Didion makes in paragraph 6 between a notebook and a diary. How do they differ? Why is she fond of one and not the other? How does her example of a diary entry support her distinction?

3. Didion's notebook entries were never intended to have an audience. How is that apparent from the entries themselves? Compare Didion's ideas about keeping a notebook to Virginia Woolf's diary entries on the writing process (page 66). Focus especially on the first paragraph, in which Woolf discusses the advantages of a form of writing that is for "[her] own eye only." Where do you fit in as a reader of Didion's work? of Woolf's work? Do you think the two writers would agree about the uses of private diaries?

Anne Frank

From *The Diary of a Young Girl*

On her thirteenth birthday (June 12, 1942), and as World War II raged on, Anne Frank began a diary that she called "Kitty." Less than a month later, she and her family went into hiding in a cramped attic in Amsterdam, Holland, in hopes of escaping the Nazis. She continued to keep her diary, addressing it in the form of letters that candidly and freely expressed her most personal thoughts and feelings. Living in conditions that allowed for little privacy, she cherished the secrecy her diary provided: "Who besides me will ever read these letters?" she writes, never dreaming that after her death her intimate diary would be found, published, and read by millions throughout the world.

In August 1944 the Frank family's hiding place was discovered by the Nazis and in March 1945, three months before her sixteenth birthday, Anne died in the concentration camp at Bergen-Belsen. As they searched the attic for valuables and important documents, the Nazis left behind on the floor an insignificant-looking little red-checkered cloth book. Anne Frank: The Diary of a Young Girl *was first published in 1952.*

THINGS THAT LIE BURIED DEEP IN MY HEART

Saturday, June 20, 1942

I haven't written for a few days, because I wanted first of all to think about my diary. It's an odd idea for someone like me to keep a diary; not only because I have never done so before, but because it seems to me that neither I—nor for that matter anyone else—will be interested in the unbosomings of a thirteen-year-old schoolgirl. Still, what does that matter? I want to write, but more than that, I want to bring out all kinds of things that lie buried deep in my heart.

There is a saying that "paper is more patient than man"; it came back to me on one of my slightly melancholy days, while I sat chin in hand, feeling too bored and limp even to make up my mind whether to go out or stay at home. Yes, there is no doubt that paper is patient and as I don't intend to show this cardboard-covered notebook, bearing the proud name of "diary," to anyone, unless I find a real friend, boy or girl, probably nobody cares. And now I come to the root of the matter, the reason for my starting a diary: it is that I have no such real friend.

Let me put it more clearly, since no one will believe that a girl of thirteen feels herself quite alone in the world, nor is it so. I have darling parents and a sister of sixteen. I know about thirty people whom one might call friends—I have strings of boy friends, anxious to catch a glimpse of me and who, failing that, peep at me through mirrors in class. I have relations, aunts and uncles, who are darlings too, a good home, no — I don't seem to lack anything. But it's the same with all my friends, just fun and joking, nothing more. I can never bring myself to talk of anything outside the common round. We don't seem to be able to get any closer, that is the root of the trouble. Perhaps I lack confidence, but anyway, there it is, a stubborn fact and I don't seem to be able to do anything about it.

Hence, this diary. In order to enhance in my mind's eye the picture of the friend for whom I have waited so long, I don't want to set down a series of bald facts in a diary like most people do, but I want this diary itself to be my friend, and I shall call my friend Kitty. No one will grasp what I'm talking about if I begin my letters to Kitty just out of the blue, so albeit unwillingly, I will start by sketching in brief the story of my life.

My father was thirty-six when he married my mother, who was then   5
twenty-five. My sister Margot was born in 1926 in Frankfurt-on-Main, I followed on June 12, 1929, and, as we are Jewish, we emigrated to Holland in 1933, where my father was appointed Managing Director of Travies N.V. This firm is in close relationship with the firm of Kolen & Co. in the same building, of which my father is a partner.

The rest of our family, however, felt the full impact of Hitler's anti-Jewish laws, so life was filled with anxiety. In 1938 after the pogroms, my two uncles (my mother's brothers) escaped to the U.S.A. My old grandmother came to us, she was then seventy-three. After May 1940 good times rapidly fled: first the war, then the capitulation, followed by the arrival of the Germans, which is when the sufferings of us Jews really began. Anti-Jewish decrees followed each other in quick succession. Jews must wear a yellow star, Jews must hand in their bicycles, Jews are banned from trains and are forbidden to drive. Jews are only allowed to do their shopping between three and five o'clock and then only in shops which bear the placard "Jewish shop." Jews must be indoors by eight o'clock and cannot even sit in their own gardens after that hour. Jews are forbidden to visit theaters, cinemas, and other places of entertainment. Jews may not take part in public sports. Swimming baths, tennis courts, hockey fields, and other sports grounds are all prohibited to them. Jews may not visit Christians. Jews must go to Jewish schools, and many more restrictions of a similar kind.

So we could not do this and were forbidden to do that. But life went on in spite of it all. Jopie[1] used to say to me, "You're scared to do anything, because it may be forbidden." Our freedom was strictly limited. Yet things were still bearable.

Granny died in January 1942; no one will ever know how much she is present in my thoughts and how much I love her still.

[1]*Jopie:* A girlfriend. — Eds.

In 1934 I went to school at the Montessori Kindergarten and continued there. It was at the end of the school year, I was in form 6B, when I had to say good-by to Mrs. K. We both wept, it was very sad. In 1941 I went, with my sister Margot, to the Jewish Secondary School, she into the fourth form and I into the first.

So far everything is all right with the four of us and here I come to the   10
present day.

I ALWAYS COME BACK TO MY DIARY

Saturday, November 7, 1942

Dear Kitty,

Mummy is frightfully irritable and that always seems to herald unpleasantness for me. Is it just chance that Daddy and Mummy never rebuke Margot and that they always drop on me for everything? Yesterday evening, for instance: Margot was reading a book with lovely drawings in it; she got up and went upstairs, put the book down ready to go on with it later. I wasn't doing anything, so picked up the book and started looking at the pictures. Margot came back, saw "her" book in my hands, wrinkled her forehead and asked for the book back. Just because I wanted to look a little further on, Margot got more and more angry. Then Mummy joined in: "Give the book to Margot; she was reading it," she said. Daddy came into the room. He didn't even know what it was all about, but saw the injured look on Margot's face and promptly dropped on me: "I'd like to see what you'd say if Margot ever started looking at one of your books!" I gave way at once, laid the book down, and left the room—offended, as they thought. It so happened I was neither offended nor cross, just miserable. It wasn't right of Daddy to judge without knowing what the squabble was about. I would have given Margot the book myself, and much more quickly, if Mummy and Daddy hadn't interfered. They took Margot's part at once, as though she were the victim of some great injustice.

It's obvious that Mummy would stick up for Margot; she and Margot always do back each other up. I'm so used to that that I'm utterly indifferent to both Mummy's jawing and Margot's moods.

I love them; but only because they are Mummy and Margot. With Daddy it's different. If he holds Margot up as an example, approves of what she does, praises and caresses her, then something gnaws at me inside, because I adore Daddy. He is the one I look up to. I don't love anyone in the world but him. He doesn't notice that he treats Margot differently from me. Now Margot is just the prettiest, sweetest, most beautiful girl in the world. But all the same I feel I have some right to be taken seriously too. I have always been the dunce, the ne'er-do-well of the family, I've always had to pay double for my deeds, first with the scolding and then again because of the way my feelings are hurt. Now I'm not satisfied with this apparent favoritism any more. I want something from Daddy that he is not able to give me.

I'm not jealous of Margot, never have been. I don't envy her good looks or her beauty. It is only that I long for Daddy's real love: not only as his child, but for me — Anne, myself.

I cling to Daddy because it is only through him that I am able to retain   15
the remnant of family feeling. Daddy doesn't understand that I need to give vent to my feelings over Mummy sometimes. He doesn't want to talk about it; he simply avoids anything which might lead to remarks about Mummy's failings. Just the same, Mummy and her failings are something I find harder to bear than anything else. I don't know how to keep it all to myself. I can't always be drawing attention to her untidiness, her sarcasm, and her lack of sweetness, neither can I believe that I'm always in the wrong.

We are exact opposites in everything; so naturally we are bound to run up against each other. I don't pronounce judgment on Mummy's character, for that is something I can't judge. I only look at her as a mother, and she just doesn't succeed in being that to me; I have to be my own mother. I've drawn myself apart from them all; I am my own skipper and later on I shall see where I come to land. All this comes about particularly because I have in my mind's eye an image of what a perfect mother and wife should be; and in her whom I must call "Mother" I find no trace of that image.

I am always making resolutions not to notice Mummy's bad example. I want to see only the good side of her and to seek in myself what I cannot find in her. But it doesn't work; and the worst of it is that neither Daddy nor Mummy understands this gap in my life, and I blame them for it. I wonder if anyone can ever succeed in making their children absolutely content.

Sometimes I believe that God wants to try me, both now and later on; I must become good through my own efforts, without examples and without good advice. Then later on I shall be all the stronger. Who besides me will ever read these letters? From whom but myself shall I get comfort? As I need comforting often, I frequently feel weak, and dissatisfied with myself; my shortcomings are too great. I know this, and every day I try to improve myself, again and again.

My treatment varies so much. One day Anne is so sensible and is allowed to know everything; and the next day I hear that Anne is just a silly little goat who doesn't know anything at all and imagines that she's learned a wonderful lot from books. I'm not a baby or a spoiled darling any more, to be laughed at, whatever she does. I have my own views, plans, and ideas, though I can't put them into words yet. Oh, so many things bubble up inside me as I lie in bed, having to put up with people I'm fed up with, who always misinterpret my intentions. That's why in the end I always come back to my diary. That is where I start and finish, because Kitty is always patient. I'll promise her that I shall persevere, in spite of everything, and find my own way through it all, and swallow my tears. I only wish I could see the results already or occasionally receive encouragement from someone who loves me.

Don't condemn me; remember rather that sometimes I too can reach   20 the bursting point.

Yours, Anne

A SWEET SECRET

Wednesday, January 5, 1944

Dear Kitty,

I have two things to confess to you today, which will take a long time. But I must tell someone and you are the best one to tell, as I know that, come what may, you always keep a secret.

The first is about Mummy. You know that I've grumbled a lot about Mummy, yet still tried to be nice to her again. Now it is suddenly clear to me what she lacks. Mummy herself has told us that she looked upon us more as her friends than her daughters. Now that is all very fine, but still, a friend can't take a mother's place. I need my mother as an example which I can follow, I want to be able to respect her. I have the feeling that Margot thinks differently about these things and would never be able to understand what I've just told you. And Daddy avoids all arguments about Mummy.

I imagine a mother as a woman who, in the first place, shows great tact, especially towards her children when they reach our age, and who does not laugh at me if I cry about something—not pain, but other things—like "Mums" does.

One thing, which perhaps may seem rather fatuous, I have never forgiven her. It was on a day that I had to go to the dentist. Mummy and Margot were going to come with me, and agreed that I should take my bicycle. When we had finished at the dentist, and were outside again, Margot and Mummy told me that they were going into the town to look at something or buy something—I don't remember exactly what. I wanted to go, too, but was not allowed to, as I had my bicycle with me. Tears of rage sprang into my eyes, and Mummy and Margot began laughing at me. Then I became so furious that I stuck my tongue out at them in the street just as an old woman happened to pass by, who looked very shocked! I rode home on my bicycle, and I know I cried for a long time.

It is queer that the wound that Mummy made then still burns, when I   25 think of how angry I was that afternoon.

The second is something that is very difficult to tell you, because it is about myself.

Yesterday I read an article about blushing by Sis Heyster. This article might have been addressed to me personally. Although I don't blush very easily, the other things in it certainly all fit me. She writes roughly something like this — that a girl in the years of puberty becomes quiet within and begins to think about the wonders that are happening to her body.

I experience that, too, and that is why I get the feeling lately of being embarrassed about Margot, Mummy, and Daddy. Funnily enough, Margot, who is much more shy than I am, isn't at all embarrassed.

I think what is happening to me is so wonderful, and not only what can be seen on my body, but all that is taking place inside. I never discuss myself or any of these things with anybody; that is why I have to talk to myself about them.

Each time I have a period — and that has only been three times — I   30
have the feeling that in spite of all the pain, unpleasantness, and nastiness, I have a sweet secret, and that is why, although it is nothing but a nuisance to me in a way, I always long for the time that I shall feel that secret within me again.

Sis Heyster also writes that girls of this age don't feel quite certain of themselves, and discover that they themselves are individuals with ideas, thoughts, and habits. After I came here, when I was just fourteen, I began to think about myself sooner than most girls, and to know that I am a "person." Sometimes, when I lie in bed at night, I have a terrible desire to feel my breasts and to listen to the quiet rhythmic beat of my heart.

I already had these kinds of feelings subconsciously before I came here, because I remember that once when I slept with a girl friend I had a strong desire to kiss her, and that I did do so. I could not help being terribly inquisitive over her body, for she had always kept it hidden from me. I asked her whether, as proof of our friendship, we should feel one another's breasts, but she refused. I go into ecstasies every time I see the naked figure of a woman, such as Venus, for example. It strikes me as so wonderful and exquisite that I have difficulty in stopping the tears rolling down my cheeks.

If only I had a girl friend!

Yours, Anne

The Reader's Presence

1. Why do you think the thirteen-year-old Frank feels compelled to write? Does she have a purpose for keeping a diary?

2. Speculate why her diary is addressed to "Kitty." What is the effect of personalizing her diary in this way? What does that personalization allow her to do as a person and as a writer?

3. Frank wrote during wartime, but the bulk of her diary is devoted to her relationships with family and friends, and to her experiences

as a teenager whose mind and body are changing. Walt Whitman (page 60), Virginia Woolf (page 66), and Michihiko Hachiya (page 34) also kept journals during wartime. How do these writers deal with what is going on around them? How do they deal with their feelings? How do their ways of expressing context and feelings compare to Frank's?

Michihiko Hachiya

From *Hiroshima Diary*

On August 6, 1945, the United States dropped an atomic bomb on the Japanese city of Hiroshima and introduced a new, devastating weapon into modern war. Two days later, the military dropped another bomb on Nagasaki, forcing the Japanese government into an unconditional surrender. For years, the Japanese survivors of the blasts suffered from unhealing burns, radiation poisoning, cancers, and a score of other illnesses. At first, the Japanese had no idea what had hit them, though rumors of a new secret weapon circulated rapidly. Most Americans today know of the bombing mainly through repeated images of the mushroom cloud itself; rarely do they see photographs or footage of the destruction and casualties. One of the most vivid accounts of the bombing and its immediate aftermath can be found in a diary kept by a Hiroshima physician, Michihiko Hachiya, who, though severely injured himself, miraculously found the time to record both his professional observations of a medical nightmare and his human impressions of an utterly destroyed community. Published on the tenth anniversary of the bombing of Hiroshima, Hiroshima Diary *(1955) gained widespread attention. The diary runs only for some two months, from the moment of the blast on the sunny morning of August 6 to the end of September, when the American occupation was well under way.*

WHAT HAD HAPPENED?
August 6, 1945

Badly injured from the blast, Dr. Hachiya managed to make his way to the hospital where he served as director and which, fortunately, was quite near his house. He spent several days in bed and did not begin writing his diary until August 8. As we can see from the following passage, however, the events were still fresh in his mind.

The hour was early; the morning still, warm, and beautiful. Shimmering leaves, reflecting sunlight from a cloudless sky, made a pleasant contrast with shadows in my garden as I gazed absently through wide-flung doors opening to the south.

Clad in drawers and undershirt, I was sprawled on the living room floor exhausted because I had just spent a sleepless night on duty as an air warden in my hospital.

Suddenly, a strong flash of light startled me — and then another. So well does one recall little things that I remember vividly how a stone lantern in the garden became brilliantly lit and I debated whether this light was caused by a magnesium flare or sparks from a passing trolley.

Garden shadows disappeared. The view where a moment before all had been so bright and sunny was now dark and hazy. Through swirling dust I could barely discern a wooden column that had supported one corner of my house. It was leaning crazily and the roof sagged dangerously.

Moving instinctively, I tried to escape, but rubble and fallen timbers   5
barred the way. By picking my way cautiously I managed to reach the *rōka*[1] and stepped down into my garden. A profound weakness overcame me, so I stopped to regain my strength. To my surprise I discovered that I was completely naked. How odd! Where were my drawers and undershirt?

What had happened?

All over the right side of my body I was cut and bleeding. A large splinter was protruding from a mangled wound in my thigh, and something warm trickled into my mouth. My cheek was torn, I discovered as I felt it gingerly, with the lower lip laid wide open. Embedded in my neck was a sizable fragment of glass which I matter-of-factly dislodged, and with the detachment of one stunned and shocked I studied it and my blood-stained hand.

Where was my wife?

Suddenly thoroughly alarmed, I began to yell for her: "Yaeko-san! Yaeko-san! Where are you?"

Blood began to spurt. Had my carotid artery been cut? Would I bleed   10
to death? Frightened and irrational, I called out again: "It's a five-hundred-ton bomb! Yaeko-san, where are you? A five-hundred-ton bomb has fallen!"

Yaeko-san, pale and frightened, her clothes torn and blood-stained, emerged from the ruins of our house holding her elbow. Seeing her, I was reassured. My own panic assuaged, I tried to reassure her.

"We'll be all right," I exclaimed. "Only let's get out of here as fast as we can."

---

[1]*rōka:* A narrow outside hall. — EDS.

She nodded, and I motioned for her to follow me.

The shortest path to the street lay through the house next door so through the house we went—running, stumbling, falling, and then running again until in headlong flight we tripped over something and fell sprawling into the street. Getting to my feet, I discovered that I had tripped over a man's head.

"Excuse me! Excuse me, please!" I cried hysterically.   15

There was no answer. The man was dead. The head had belonged to a young officer whose body was crushed beneath a massive gate.

We stood in the street, uncertain and afraid, until a house across from us began to sway and then with a rending motion fell almost at our feet. Our own house began to sway, and in a minute it, too, collapsed in a cloud of dust. Other buildings caved in or toppled. Fires sprang up and whipped by a vicious wind began to spread.

It finally dawned on us that we could not stay there in the street, so we turned our steps towards the hospital. Our home was gone; we were wounded and needed treatment; and after all, it was my duty to be with my staff. This latter was an irrational thought—what good could I be to anyone, hurt as I was.

We started out, but after twenty or thirty steps I had to stop. My breath became short, my heart pounded, and my legs gave way under me. An overpowering thirst seized me and I begged Yaeko-san to find me some water. But there was no water to be found. After a little my strength somewhat returned and we were able to go on.

I was still naked, and although I did not feel the least bit of shame, I   20
was disturbed to realize that modesty had deserted me. On rounding a corner we came upon a soldier standing idly in the street. He had a towel draped across his shoulder, and I asked if he would give it to me to cover my nakedness. The soldier surrendered the towel quite willingly but said not a word. A little later I lost the towel, and Yaeko-san took off her apron and tied it around my loins.

Our progress towards the hospital was interminably slow, until finally, my legs, stiff from drying blood, refused to carry me farther. The strength, even the will, to go on deserted me, so I told my wife, who was almost as badly hurt as I, to go on alone. This she objected to, but there was no choice. She had to go ahead and try to find someone to come back for me.

Yaeko-san looked into my face for a moment, and then, without saying a word, turned away and began running towards the hospital. Once, she looked back and waved and in a moment she was swallowed up in the gloom. It was quite dark now, and with my wife gone, a feeling of dreadful loneliness overcame me.

I must have gone out of my head lying there in the road because the next thing I recall was discovering that the clot on my thigh had been dislodged and blood was again spurting from the wound. I pressed my hand to the bleeding area and after a while the bleeding stopped and I felt better.

Could I go on?

I tried. It was all a nightmare—my wounds, the darkness, the road   25
ahead. My movements were ever so slow; only my mind was running at
top speed.

In time I came to an open space where the houses had been removed
to make a fire lane. Through the dim light I could make out ahead of me
the hazy outlines of the Communications Bureau's big concrete building,
and beyond it the hospital. My spirits rose because I knew that now
someone would find me; and if I should die, at least my body would be
found.

I paused to rest. Gradually things around me came into focus. There
were the shadowy forms of people, some of whom looked like walking
ghosts. Others moved as though in pain, like scarecrows, their arms held
out from their bodies with forearms and hands dangling. These people
puzzled me until I suddenly realized that they had been burned and were
holding their arms out to prevent the painful friction of raw surfaces rubbing together. A naked woman carrying a naked baby came into view. I
averted my gaze. Perhaps they had been in the bath. But then I saw a
naked man, and it occurred to me that, like myself, some strange thing
had deprived them of their clothes. An old woman lay near me with an
expression of suffering on her face; but she made no sound. Indeed, one
thing was common to everyone I saw—complete silence. . . .

PIKADON
August 9, 1945

*As the wounded poured into Dr. Hachiya's hospital, the physicians tried to
make sense of the symptoms and injuries, which did not resemble those of ordinary
bombings. Because many of the patients with horrible symptoms showed no obvious signs of injuries, Dr. Hachiya could only speculate about what might have occurred. He had no idea as yet what type of weapon had been used against them.*

Today, Dr. Hanaoka's[2] report on the patients was more detailed. One
observation particularly impressed me. Regardless of the type of injury,
nearly everybody had the same symptoms. All had a poor appetite, the
majority had nausea and gaseous indigestion, and over half had vomiting.

Not a few had shown improvement since yesterday. Diarrhea, though,
continued to be a problem and actually appeared to be increasing. Distinctly alarming was the appearance of blood in the stools of patients who
earlier had only diarrhea. The isolation of these people was becoming increasingly difficult.

One seriously ill man complained of a sore mouth yesterday, and   30
today, numerous small hemorrhages began to appear in his mouth and

[2]*Dr. Hanaoka:* Head of Internal Medicine. —EDS.

under his skin. His case was the more puzzling because he came to the hospital complaining of weakness and nausea and did not appear to have been injured at all.

This morning, other patients were beginning to show small subcutaneous hemorrhages, and not a few were coughing and vomiting blood in addition to passing it in their stools. One poor woman was bleeding from her privates. Among these patients there was not one with symptoms typical of anything we knew, unless you could excuse those who developed signs of severe brain disease before they died.

Dr. Hanaoka believed the patients could be divided into three groups:

1. Those with nausea, vomiting, and diarrhea who were improving.
2. Those with nausea, vomiting, and diarrhea who were remaining stationary.
3. Those with nausea, vomiting, and diarrhea who were developing hemorrhage under the skin or elsewhere.

Had these patients been burned or otherwise injured, we might have tried to stretch the logic of cause and effect and assume that their bizarre symptoms were related to injury, but so many patients appeared to have received no injury whatsoever that we were obliged to postulate an insult heretofore unknown.

The only other possible cause for the weird symptoms observed was a sudden change in atmospheric pressure. I had read somewhere about bleeding that follows ascent to high altitudes and about bleeding in deep sea divers who ascend too rapidly from the depths. Having never seen such injury I could not give much credence to my thoughts.

Still, it was impossible to dismiss the thought that atmospheric pressure had had something to do with the symptoms of our patients. During my student days at Okayama University, I had seen experiments conducted in a pressure chamber. Sudden, temporary deafness was one symptom everyone complained of if pressure in the chamber was abruptly altered.

Now, I could state positively that I heard nothing like an explosion when we were bombed the other morning, nor did I remember any sound during my walk to the hospital as houses collapsed around me. It was as though I walked through a gloomy, silent motion picture. Others whom I questioned had had the same experience.

Those who experienced the bombing from the outskirts of the city characterized it by the word: *pikadon*.[3]

[3]*pikadon: Pika* means a glitter, sparkle, or bright flash of light, like a flash of lightning. *Don* means a boom! or loud sound. Together, the words came to mean to the people of Hiroshima an explosion characterized by a flash and a boom. Hence: "flash-boom!" Those who remember the flash only speak of the *"pika"*; those who were far enough from the hypocenter to experience both speak of the *"pikadon."* —EDS.

How then could one account for my failure and the failure of others to hear an explosion except on the premise that a sudden change in atmospheric pressure had rendered those nearby temporarily deaf: Could the bleeding we were beginning to observe be explained on the same basis?

Since all books and journals had been destroyed, there was no way to corroborate my theories except by further appeal to the patients. To that end Dr. Katsube[4] was asked to discover what else he could when he made ward rounds.

It was pleasing to note my scientific curiosity was reviving, and I lost no opportunity to question everyone who visited me about the bombing of Hiroshima. Their answers were vague and ambiguous, and on one point only were they in agreement: a new weapon had been used. *What* the new weapon was became a burning question. Not only had our books been destroyed, but our newspapers, telephones, and radios as well. . . .

The Reader's Presence

1. In many ways it is fortunate that one of the diaries kept immediately after the atomic blast was written by a medical doctor. Why? How does it contribute to the diary's historical value? Could this be a disadvantage? Would you have preferred to read a patient's diary instead? If so, why?

2. Hachiya's first entry on August 6 was written a few days after the events it depicts. What indications do you receive from the writing that the entry was predated? Can you detect any differences from the second entry (August 9), which was apparently composed on the stated day?

3. Hachiya's confusion reveals itself in his writing in many ways: short paragraphs, multiple questions, and unconfirmed guesses. Throughout, his matter-of-fact language belies his panic. How does Hachiya's characterization of the bombing of Hiroshima compare with Don DeLillo's account of the attack on the World Trade Center (page 361)? Is a survivor's account necessarily more vivid than that of a firsthand witness?

[4]***Dr. Katsube:*** Chief of Surgery. —EDS.

Amanda Hesser

Shop Write

Amanda Hesser (b. 1971) has been called "one of the best—if not the best—young food writers." After graduating in 1993 from Bentley College in Waltham, Massachusetts, with a major in economics and finance, she began to study food and cuisine seriously, interning at restaurants in France and Italy, and finally earning her culinary degree from a renowned French cooking school in 1997. Joining the New York Times *as a staff writer that year, she is now the food editor at the* New York Times Magazine *and editor of the magazine's* Living *supplement, which features lifestyle and entertainment trends and reports on the latest in food and wine. Hesser has written two books,* The Cook and the Gardener *(1999) and* Cooking for Mr. Latte *(2003), based on her "Food Diary" column in the* Times.*

Hesser has said that her writing has tried "to capture that real-life slice of how we live and how we really eat, how we really cook, with all the flaws and sort of satisfaction bundled into one." "Shop Write" appeared in the New York Times Magazine *on October 10, 2004.*

If you are what you eat, then you are also what you buy to eat. And mostly what people buy is scrawled onto a grocery list, those ethereal scraps of paper that record the shorthand of where we shop and how we feed ourselves. Most grocery lists end up in the garbage. But if you live in St. Louis, they might have a half-life you never imagined: as a cultural document, posted on the Internet.

For the past decade, Bill Keaggy, 33, the features photo editor at *The St. Louis Post-Dispatch*, has been collecting grocery lists and since 1999 has been posting them online at www.grocerylists.org. The collection, which now numbers more than 500 lists, is strangely addictive.

The lists elicit twofold curiosity—about the kind of meal the person was planning and the kind of person who would make such a meal. What was the shopper with vodka, lighters, milk and ice cream on his list planning to do with them? In what order would they be consumed? Was it a he or a she? Who had written "Tootie food, kitten chow, bird food stick, toaster scrambles, coffee drinks"? Some shoppers organize their lists by aisle; others start with dairy, go to cleaning supplies and then back to dairy before veering off to Home Depot. A few meticulous ones note the price of every item. One shopper had written in large letters on an envelope, simply, "Milk."

The thin lines of ink and pencil jutting and looping across crinkled and torn pieces of paper have a purely graphic beauty. One of life's most banal duties, viewed through the curatorial lens, can somehow seem pregnant with possibility. It can even appear poetic, as in the list that reads "meat, cigs, buns, treats."

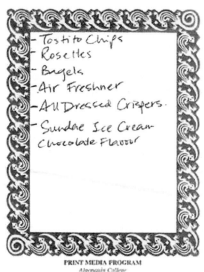

PRINT MEDIA PROGRAM
Algonquin College

One thing Keaggy discovered is that Dan Quayle is not alone—few people can spell bananas and bagels, let alone potato.[1] One list calls for "suchi" and "strimp." "Some people pass judgment on the things they buy," Keaggy says. At the end of one list, the shopper wrote "Bud Light" and then "good beer." Another scribbled "good loaf of white bread." Some pass judgment on themselves, like the shopper who wrote "read, stay home or go somewhere, I act like my mom, go to Kentucky, underwear, lemon."

People send messages to one another, too. Buried in one list is this statement: "If you buy more rice, I'll punch you." And plenty of shoppers, like the one with both ice cream and diet pills on the list, reveal their vices.

Keaggy has always been a collector and recorder. When he was young, it was rocks and key chains. As a teenager, he published zines on freestyle biking and punk rock. These were just a warm-up. His collection of rocks in the shapes of shoes has been featured at the St. Louis Artists' Guild. And in addition to his grocery-list Web site, he has an extensive personal Web site, www.keaggy.com (the grocery lists can be found from here). At keaggy.com, there is a segment called "What's for Dinner?" Every time you click on it, a new dining haiku appears. There is a sandwich Web log, to which he adds photos of the sandwiches he eats every day during National Sandwich Month (August). A page called "mageirevo" features "incredibly vague recipes," including one for "happy fun pork time," and a page called "found in the

---

[1] *potato:* In 1992, Vice president Dan Quayle made headlines when he spelled *potato* wrong (he spelled it *potatoe*) while visiting a New Jersey sixth-grade classroom. — EDS.

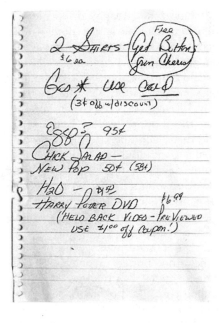

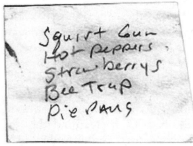

"street" is dedicated to junk (not what he calls it) that he found when he biked to work from May 1 to May 31. And in "age: 30," Keaggy posts photos he took of himself every day of his 31st year, along with a brief description of what he was doing that day, which is almost as addictive as the grocery lists.

Keaggy finds most of his grocery lists at Schnucks, a regional chain with a branch down the street from his home. (Some lists have been sent in by a cashier at a grocery store in Iowa and someone in Tucson who once collected grocery lists.) Keaggy spots the lists in grocery carts, mostly, and sometimes in the checkout line or on shelves. "The funny thing is you never find them on the ground," he says. "On the best day, I'll find two or three, and on a bad day I'll find zero."

As a group, the lists are an enlightening barometer of eating and shopping trends, as well as of attitudes toward food. Almost none of them include fresh herbs, but cumin is surprisingly common. Evaporated milk is still popular, and feta is increasingly so. . . . Many shoppers are brand loyal: Swiffer, the disposable floor-mopping sheet, is doing a bang-up business in the heartland. And Parkay and Cool Whip are alive and well.

Except for one list, which includes everything from pigs in a blanket   10 and "block cheese" to salmon and anchovy fillets, most lists fall into one of two categories. They seem to have been compiled either by foodies or by convenience junkies. This growing divide has been discussed in the food industry for nearly a decade, but no statistics have measured it. In these lists, however, the gap is as clear as day. A number of people simply write "food," as if it were like getting gas or picking up dry cleaning.

"You can see their lives from these lists even if you haven't been in their houses," Keaggy says.

Which bodes poorly for the the individual who wrote: "Shell corn, bind holder, belt, knife, coolers, map, cellphone, hunting license, say goodbye to wife, kill deer, Mt. View Motel, kill deer."

The Reader's Presence

1. What meaning does Hesser say can be read from people's grocery lists? What value does Keaggy's collection of lists have? How do the lists themselves function as a kind of journal or diary entry?

2. According to Hesser, what do the grocery lists reveal about American food habits? What kinds of shoppers do the lists exemplify? What might the lists in the essay tell you about the shoppers?

3. Read "On Dumpster Diving" by Lars Eighner (page 379). Do you think the discarded food that Eighner finds reveals information about the people who threw it away? Which would you expect to be more revealing, the items people purchase or the items they discard? Why?

Adam Mayblum

The Price We Pay

Adam Mayblum, the 35-year-old managing director of the May Davis Group private investment firm, was in his office on the eighty-seventh floor of the North Tower of the World Trade Center when one of the hijacked planes struck on September 11, 2001. He escaped just before the tower's collapse. The following day, at his home in New Rochelle, New York, Mayblum composed a terse, harrowing e-mail describing his experience and sent the 2,100-word piece out to friends and family. This e-mail quickly circulated throughout the world, bringing Mayblum more than 1,000 responses from strangers offering thanks, sympathy, and prayers. One woman wrote, "The fact that you survived . . . helped to lift the terrible weight from my heart." Mayblum, who disclaims the label of "hero" by pointing out that firefighters and police officers were the ones who rushed in to save lives, attributes the enormous outpouring of support to the fact that his e-mail "helped a lot of people understand what was going on inside the building at the same time they had seen what was going on outside."

My name is Adam Mayblum. I am alive today. I am committing this to "paper" so I never forget. SO WE NEVER FORGET. I am sure that this is one of thousands of stories that will emerge over the next several days and weeks.

I arrived as usual a little before 8 A.M. My office was on the eighty-seventh floor of 1 World Trade Center, aka: Tower 1, aka: the North Tower. Most of my associates were in by 8:30 A.M. We were standing around, joking around, eating breakfast, checking e-mails, and getting set for the day when the first plane hit just a few stories above us. I must stress that we did not know that it was a plane. The building lurched violently and shook as if it were an earthquake. People screamed. I watched out my window as the building seemed to move ten to twenty feet in each direction. It rumbled and shook long enough for me to get my wits about myself and grab a coworker and seek shelter under a doorway. Light fixtures and parts of the ceiling collapsed. The kitchen was destroyed. We were certain that it was a bomb. We looked out the windows. Reams of paper were flying everywhere, like a ticker tape parade. I looked down at the street. I could see people in Battery Park City looking up. Smoke started billowing in through the holes in the ceiling. I believe that there were thirteen of us.

We did not panic. I can only assume that we thought that the worst was over. The building was standing and we were shaken but alive. We checked the halls. The smoke was thick and white and did not smell like I imagined smoke should smell. Not like your BBQ or your fireplace or even a bonfire. The phones were working. My wife had taken our nine-month-old for his checkup. I called my nanny at home and told her to page my wife, tell her that a bomb went off, I was O.K., and on my way out, I grabbed my laptop. Took off my T-shirt and ripped it into three pieces. Soaked it in water. Gave two pieces to my friends. Tied my piece around my face to act as an air filter. And we all started moving to the staircase. One of my dearest friends said that he was staying until the police or firemen came to get him. In the halls there were tiny fires and sparks. The ceiling had collapsed in the men's bathroom. It was gone along with anyone who may have been in there. We did not go in to look. We missed the staircase on the first run and had to double back. Once in the staircase we picked up fire extinguishers just in case. On the eighty-fifth floor a brave associate of mine and I headed back up to our office to drag out my partner who stayed behind. There was no air, just white smoke. We made the rounds through the office calling his name. No response. He must have succumbed to the smoke. We left defeated in our efforts and made our way back to the stairwell. We proceeded to the seventy-eighth floor where we had to change over to a different stairwell. Seventy-eight is the main junction to switch to the upper floors. I expected to see more people. There were some fifty to sixty more. Not enough. Wires and fires all over the place. Smoke too. A brave man was fighting a fire with the emergency hose. I stopped with friends to make sure that everyone from our office was accounted for. We ushered them and confused people into the stairwell. In retrospect, I recall seeing Harry, my head trader, doing the same several yards behind me. I am only thirty-five. I have known him for over fourteen years. I headed into the stairwell with two friends.

We were moving down very orderly in Stairwell A. Very slowly. No panic. At least not overt panic. My legs could not stop shaking. My heart was pounding. Some nervous jokes and laughter. I made a crack about ruining a brand new pair of Merrells. Even still, they were right, my feet felt great. We all laughed. We checked our cell phones. Surprisingly, there was a very good signal, but the Sprint network was jammed. I heard that the BlackBerry two-way e-mail devices worked perfectly. On the phones, one out of twenty dial attempts got through. I knew I could not reach my wife so I called my parents. I told them what happened and that we were all O.K. and on the way down. Soon, my sister-in-law reached me. I told her we were fine and moving down. I believe that was about the sixty-fifth floor. We were bored and nervous. I called my friend Angel in San Francisco. I knew he would be watching. He was amazed I was on the phone. He told me to get out, that there was another plane on its way. I did not know what he was talking about. By now the second plane had struck Tower 2. We were so deep into the middle of our building that we did not hear or feel anything. We had no idea what was really going on. We kept making way for wounded to go down ahead of us. Not many of them, just a few. No one seemed seriously wounded. Just some cuts and scrapes. Everyone cooperated. Everyone was a hero yesterday. No questions asked. I had coworkers in another office on the seventy-seventh floor. I tried dozens of times to get them on their cell phones or office lines. It was futile. Later I found that they were alive. One of the many miracles on a day of tragedy.

On the fifty-third floor we came across a very heavyset man sitting on the stairs. I asked if he needed help or was he just resting. He needed help. I knew I would have trouble carrying him because I have a very bad back. But my friend and I offered anyway. We told him he could lean on us. He hesitated, I don't know why. I said do you want to come or do you want us to send help for you. He chose for help. I told him he was on the fifty-third floor in Stairwell A and that's what I would tell the rescue workers. He said O.K. and we left.

On the forty-fourth floor my phone rang again. It was my parents. They were hysterical. I said relax, I'm fine. My father said get out, there is a third plane coming. I still did not understand. I was kind of angry. What did my parents think? Like I needed some other reason to get going? I couldn't move the thousand people in front of me any faster. I know they love me, but no one inside understood what the situation really was. My parents did. Starting around this floor the firemen, policemen, WTC K-9 units without the dogs, anyone with a badge, started coming up as we were heading down. I stopped a lot of them and told them about the man on Fifty-three and my friend on Eighty-seven. I later felt terrible about this. They headed up to find those people and met death instead.

On the thirty-third floor I spoke with a man who somehow knew most of the details. He said two small planes hit the building. Now we

5

all started talking about which terrorist group it was. Was it an internal organization or an external one? The overwhelming but uninformed opinion was Islamic fanatics. Regardless, we now knew that it was not a bomb and there were potentially more planes coming. We understood.

On the third floor the lights went out and we heard and felt this rumbling coming towards us from above. I thought the staircase was collapsing upon itself. It was 10 A.M. now and that was Tower 2 collapsing next door. We did not know that. Someone had a flashlight. We passed it forward and left the stairwell and headed down a dark and cramped corridor to an exit. We could not see at all. I recommended that everyone place a hand on the shoulder of the person in front of them and call out if they hit an obstacle so others would know to avoid it. They did. It worked perfectly. We reached another stairwell and saw a female officer emerge soaking wet and covered in soot. She said we could not go that way, it was blocked. Go up to Four and use the other exit. Just as we started up she said it was O.K. to go down instead. There was water everywhere. I called out for hands on shoulders again and she said that was a great idea. She stayed behind instructing people to do that. I do not know what happened to her.

We emerged into an enormous room. It was light but filled with smoke. I commented to a friend that it must be under construction. Then we realized where we were. It was the second floor. The one that overlooks the lobby. We were ushered out into the courtyard, the one where the fountain used to be. My first thought was of a TV movie I saw once about nuclear winter and fallout. I could not understand where all of the debris came from. There was at least five inches of this gray pasty dusty drywall soot on the ground as well as a thickness of it in the air. Twisted steel and wires. I heard there were bodies and body parts as well, but I did not look. It was bad enough. We hid under the remaining overhangs and moved out to the street. We were told to keep walking towards Houston Street. The odd thing is that there were very few rescue workers around. Less than five. They all must have been trapped under the debris when Tower 2 fell. We did not know that and could not understand where all of that debris came from. It was just my friend Kern and I now. We were hugging but sad. We felt certain that most of our friends ahead of us died and we knew no one behind us.

We came upon a post office several blocks away. We stopped and   10
looked up. Our building, exactly where our office is (was), was engulfed in flame and smoke. A postal worker said that Tower 2 had fallen down. I looked again and sure enough it was gone. My heart was racing. We kept trying to call our families. I could not get in touch with my wife. Finally I got through to my parents. Relieved is not the word to explain their feelings. They got through to my wife, thank G–d, and let her know I was alive. We sat down. A girl on a bike offered us some water. Just as she took the cap off her bottle we heard a rumble. We looked up and our building, Tower 1, collapsed. I did not note the time but I am told it was 10:30 A.M. We had been out less than fifteen minutes.

We were mourning our lost friends, particularly the one who stayed in the office, as we were now sure that he had perished. We started walking towards Union Square. I was going to Beth Israel Medical Center to be looked at. We stopped to hear the president speaking on the radio. My phone rang. It was my wife. I think I fell to my knees crying when I heard her voice. Then she told me the most incredible thing. My partner who had stayed behind called her. He was alive and well. I guess we just lost him in the commotion. We started jumping and hugging and shouting. I told my wife that my brother had arranged for a hotel in midtown. He can be very resourceful in that way. I told her I would call her from there. My brother and I managed to get a gypsy cab to take us home to Westchester instead. I cried on my son and held my wife until I fell asleep. As it turns out, my partner, the one who I thought had stayed behind, was behind us with Harry Ramos, our head trader. This is now secondhand information. They came upon Victor, the heavyset man on the fifty-third floor. They helped him. He could barely move. My partner bravely/stupidly tested the elevator on the fifty-second floor. He rode it down to the sky lobby on Forty-four. The doors opened, it was fine. He rode it back up and got Harry and Victor. I don't yet know if anyone else joined them. Once on Forty-four they made their way back into the stairwell. Someplace around the thirty-ninth to thirty-sixth floors they felt the same rumble I felt on the third floor. It was 10 A.M. and Tower 2 was coming down. They had about thirty minutes to get out. Victor said he could no longer move. They offered to have him lean on them. He said he couldn't do it. My partner hollered at him to sit on his butt and scooch down the steps. He said he was not capable of doing it. Harry told my partner to go ahead of them. Harry once had a heart attack and was worried about this man's heart. It was his nature to be this way. He was/is one of the kindest people I know. He would not leave a man behind. My partner went ahead and made it out. He said he was out maybe ten minutes before the building came down. This means that Harry had maybe twenty-five minutes to move Victor thirty-six floors. I guess they moved one floor every 1.5 minutes. Just a guess. This means Harry was around the twentieth floor when the building collapsed. As of now twelve of thirteen people are accounted for. As of 6 P.M. yesterday his wife had not heard from him. I fear that Harry is lost. However, a short while ago I heard that he may be alive. Apparently there is a Web site with survivor names on it and his appears there. Unfortunately, Ramos is not an uncommon name in New York. Pray for him and all those like him.

With regards to the firemen heading upstairs, I realize that they were going up anyway. But it hurts to know that I may have made them move quicker to find my friend. Rationally, I know this is not true and that I am not the responsible one. The responsible ones are in hiding somewhere on this planet and damn them for making me feel like this. But they should know that they failed in terrorizing us. We were calm. Those men and women that went up were heroes in the face of it all. They must have known what was going on and they did their jobs. Ordinary people were heroes, too. Today the images that people around the world equate with power and democracy are gone, but "America" is not an image, it is a concept. That concept is only strengthened by our pulling together as a team. If you want to kill us, leave us alone because we will try to do it by ourselves. If you want to make us stronger, attack and we unite. This is the ultimate failure of terrorism against the United States and the ultimate price we pay to be free, to decide where we want to work, what we want to eat, and when and where we want to go on vacation. The very moment the first plane was hijacked, democracy won.

The Reader's Presence

1. Whom does Mayblum talk to as he moves down the stairs? What subject(s) do they discuss? Whom did you talk to following the attacks on the World Trade Center? To what extent do these conversations confirm Mayblum's claim that "If you want to make us stronger, attack and we unite" (paragraph 12)?

2. As Mayblum mentions the floors he passes in his descent, how does the countdown affect his overall story? Point to specific parts of his story that are more hurried than other parts. What about the moments in which he pauses? How do these moments affect your reading?

3. Compare Mayblum's account with Tim Townsend's in "The First Hours" (page 51). How does each person think of his actions after the disaster? Which account do you find more moving? Why?

Sparrow and Art Chantry

My Career in Bumper Stickers

Sparrow—writer, street poet, social commentator, and gossip columnist— lives and works in the small town of Phoenicia, New York. His columns appear in two local newspapers, the Phoenicia Times *and the* Olive Press, *and in the regional publication* Chronogram. *Though far from the mainstream in content, his work has also been published in and reviewed by such publications as the* Village Voice, Grist Online, *and the* New Yorker. *His books include* Republican like Me *(1998), in which he describes his run for president on the "Pajama Party" ticket, and* Yes, You ARE a Revolutionary! *(2002), a blend of "gonzo poetry" and self-help advice.*

Art Chantry *is the American underground's leading graphic artist–designer. His work has had a profound impact on the history of graphic design in the United States and is found on the covers of hundreds of 45s, LPs, and CDs, and in ads, logos, and various other commercial and not-so-commercial venues. His posters are the subject of numerous books, including* Some People Can't Surf: The Graphic Design of Art Chantry *by Julie Lasky and* 45 RPM *by Spencer Drate and Charles L. Granata.*

"My Career in Bumper Stickers" appeared in the Op-Ed section of the New York Times *in February 2005.*

Like many people (most people?), I have always wanted to write bumper stickers. However, I was not willing to invest the money and effort to print my messages, so my ambition languished.

Then, several years ago, I took a new job as a gossip columnist for my local newpaper. In this role, I was to invent fake gossip (as actual gossip might offend the townsfolk). In my column, which is called "Heard by a Bird," I began to transcribe amusing bumper stickers I saw on Main Street, like this.

Stop Global Whining.

One day it struck me that I could write my own messages, and pretend they were real—just as Jorge Luis Borges suggested it was superior to write reviews of imaginary books, rather than actually write the books. I would create, if not true bumper stickers, then the *rumor* of bumper stickers.

My early bumper stickers were often rural. Phoenicia is a center of   5
fly-fishing, which led me to invent slogans like *If Fishing Is a Religion, I'm a Bishop* and *I've Been Fishing So Long, My Worm Gets Social Security*. Gradually I ventured into politics, hiding behind the anonymity of my form: *Stupidity + Rage = War*. I also began reading the Northern Sun catalog, which sells "T-shirts, bumper stickers, buttons, posters, etc., covering a wide variety of issues." Many of its slogans, I noticed, are parodies of other slogans. I began to play this game, too:

If Thought Is Outlawed, Only Outlaws Will Have Thoughts. Warning: I Brake for Chinese Restaurants. Don't Blame Me—I Voted for Britney Spears. This Bumper Sticker Is Covering Up My Last Bumper Sticker.

Eventually I realized: bumper stickers are the haiku of the American highway. Could one such slogan actually be a haiku? I turned this thought itself into a haiku:

Why Can't a Bumper
Sticker Be a Haiku? No
One Can Quite Explain.

I am proudest of my one attempt to spread goodness through the world:

I Transferred Out of the School of Hard Knocks   10
Into the School of Soft Rubs.

Above are a few other bumper stickers I have written over the years. I encourage everyone to become one of the proud, nameless writers of adhesive rectangular wisdom. It's easy: just write down your entire philosophy of life—then remove everything but nine words.

The Reader's Presence

1. What techniques does Sparrow use to turn ordinary phrases into bumper sticker parodies? Examine a few examples and try to explain each example in full. What is the object of the parody? What is gained by limiting the idea to just a few words?

2. Traditionally, a haiku—a Japanese poetic form consisting of three lines with five, seven, and five syllables—refers to a season. How are bumper stickers "the haiku of the American highway" (paragraph 7)? In what ways does Sparrow's example serve as a haiku? In what ways might it fall short?

3. Compare Chantry's illustration with Ho Che Anderson's image, consisting of photographs, graphics, and words, to depict Martin Luther King Jr.'s "I Have a Dream" speech (page 723). Why do you think these artists chose a collage style for their images? Does this style help each artist make an effective point? Why or why not?

Tim Townsend

The First Hours

Tim Townsend is a 32-year-old financial reporter. He was only a few blocks away from his office at the World Financial Center when the first hijacked plane crashed into the World Trade Center tower on September 11, 2001. The following selection, which appeared in Rolling Stone *(October 25, 2001), is based on notes he wrote immediately following the attack.*

The first thing I saw in the parking lot across Liberty Street from the South Tower was luggage. Burned luggage. A couple of cars were on fire. Half a block east, a man who'd been working out in a South Tower fitness club was walking barefoot over shards of glass, wearing only a white towel around his waist; he still had shaving cream on the left side of his face. Bits of glass were falling to the ground like hail. I ventured a block south, away from the towers, and that's when I started seeing body parts. At first, just scattered lumps of mangled flesh dotting the road and the sidewalks, then a leg near the gutter. Someone mentioned a severed head over by a fire hydrant. Hunks of metal—some silver and the size of a fist, others green and as big as toasters—were strewn for blocks south of the building. Shoes were everywhere.

"Oh, Jesus," I heard someone say. "They're jumping." Every few moments a body would fall from the North Tower, from about ninety floors up. The jumpers all seemed to come from the floors that were engulfed in flames. Sometimes they jumped in pairs—one just after the other. They were up so high, it took ten to twelve seconds for each of them to hit the ground. I counted.

What must have been going through their minds, to choose certain death? Was it a decision between one death and another? Or maybe it wasn't a decision at all, their bodies involuntarily recoiling from the heat, the way you pull your hand off a hot stove.

Moments later, a low metallic whine, quickly followed by a high-pitched whoosh, came out of the south. I looked up to see the white belly of an airplane much closer than it should have been. The South Tower of the Trade Center seemed to suck the plane into itself. For an instant it looked like there would be no trauma to the building — it was as if the plane just slipped through a mail slot in the side of the tower, or simply vanished. But then a fireball ballooned out of the top of the building just five blocks from where we stood.

People were running south down West Street toward Battery Park —   5
the southern tip, the end, of Manhattan — and west toward the Hudson River. I ran with the crowd that veered toward the river, looking back over my shoulder at the new gash in the Trade Center. Once relatively safe among the tree-lined avenues of Battery Park City, people hugged each other and some cried.

After about ten minutes, a wave of calm returned to the streets. Police were trying to get the thousands of people south of the World Trade Center off the West Street, east to the FDR Drive, over the Brooklyn Bridge. And still people were throwing themselves out of the North Tower: You could see suit jackets fluttering in the wind and women's dresses billowing like failed parachutes.

But about five minutes later, a sharp cracking sound momentarily replaced the shrill squeal of sirens, and the top half of the South Tower imploded, bringing the entire thing down. It was the most frightened I've ever been. Screaming and sprinting south toward Battery Park, we all flew from the dark cloud that was slowly funneling toward us. At that moment I believed two things about this cloud. One, that it was made not just of ash and soot, but of metal, glass and concrete; and two, that soon this shrapnel would be whizzing by — and perhaps through — my head. A woman next to me turned to run. Her black bag came off her shoulder and a CD holder went flying, sending bright silver discs clattering across the ground. An older man to my right tripped and took a face-first dive across the pavement, glasses flying off his face.

In the seconds, minutes, and hours following the World Trade Center attacks, hundreds — maybe thousands — of ordinary people would find their best selves and become heroes. And then there were the rest of us, running hard, wanting only to live and to talk to someone we loved, even if it meant leaving an old guy lying in the street, glasses gone, a cloud of death and destruction creeping up on him.

I'd always wondered what I'd do in a life-or-death situation. Until that moment, I'd believed I'd do the right thing, would always help the helpless, most likely without regard for my own well-being. All across lower Manhattan at that moment, people were making similar decisions, so many of them so much more critical than mine. September 11th, 2001, at 9:45 A.M. was not my finest moment. As I turned back to help, I saw two younger guys scoop the fallen man up, and we all continued running south.

After about three blocks, I hid for a moment behind a large Dumpster   10 on the west side of the street. But when I looked back toward the towers, I could see that my Dumpster was no match for the cloud, and I took off again. I ran the last few blocks into Battery Park, where the cloud finally did catch up with the thousands of us fleeing it. I could see only a few feet in front of me, and so I followed the silhouettes I could make out. Because Battery Park is the tip of the island, it wasn't much of a surprise that the crowd would wind up dead-ending at the water. When it happened, the people in the front panicked. So they turned around, screamed and ran back toward us in a stampede. We had nowhere to go — there were thousands of people behind us and hundreds coming back the other way.

As the crowd doubled back on itself, I jumped over a wrought-iron fence and landed in a flower bed. I stayed down for a second, thinking I'd wait out the panic low to the ground. But then I felt other people jumping the fence and landing near me. Thinking I was about to be trampled, I got up and ran behind a nearby tree. In a minute or two the panic subdued, and I hopped back over the fence and onto a park path. But now the air was heavier with debris and there was no clear path out of the park. I took off my tie and wrapped it around my face. People were coughing and stumbling. Some were crying, others screaming. It was difficult to breathe or even keep my eyes open.

Soon, there was another wave of calm and quiet, and the ash that fell from the sky and settled on the grass and trees gave the park the peaceful feel of a light evening snowfall. Eventually, I found a path that led me out to the east side of the Battery area, and I followed a crowd to the FDR. Thousands participated in the exodus up the highway and into Brooklyn. It was now just past ten, and we looked like refugees. In a way, we were. My tie wasn't doing much good against the ash, so I took off my shirt and tied it around my head. We walked in the falling gray dust for fifteen minutes, still hacking, and rubbing our eyes. Then the cloud broke, and, covered in soot, we were in the sunlight again. There wasn't a lot of talking. Some walked in groups, desperately trying to stay together. Others walked alone, crying out the names of friends, co-workers, or loved ones from whom they'd been separated.

At 10:25, as I was getting ready to cross the bridge, another cracking sound came out of the west. We looked behind us and to the left to see the remaining tower collapse. Soon, that ash reached the Manhattan foot of the Brooklyn Bridge, and the bridge was closed. Three hours later, I was finally back in my apartment in Brooklyn. It was nearly one o'clock. There was a thin layer of ash all over my kitchen from the blast. I made my phone calls and cried with my fiancée. Then I called some friends who'd left messages, checking on me. I called my friend Sully in Boston, and we went through the list of names of our friends who worked in the financial district. I was one of the last to be accounted for. When we'd gotten through most of the names—Sims, Kane, T-Bone, Molloy—Sully said, "It's not all good news. Beezo called his wife from high up in the second building to say he was OK, but she hasn't heard from him since it fell." Beezo—Tom Brennan to those he didn't go to high school or college with—still hasn't been heard from.

As it turns out, when I was watching that tower fall, I was watching my friend die. His wife was at home, in their brand-new house in Westchester County, amid their still boxed-up life. She'd already turned off the TV when Beezo's building collapsed. Their seventeen-month-old daughter is too young to have seen the images of her father's death, but someday—maybe on a distant anniversary of September 11th when each network commemorates the tragedy—I'm sure she'll be able to see it, along with her little brother or sister who is due in two months.

I hung up with Sully and turned on the television to see what I had   15
seen. Places where I once ate lunch or shopped for a sweater or bought stamps were now buried under piles of concrete and metal, as were thousands of people—some of whom I probably rode the subway with every day. One of whom was my friend.

Since then, I've been freakishly fine, given what I'd seen. Maybe it's because I realize how lucky I was—my experience was like Christmas morning compared to what other people went through. Maybe it's because I lack the imagination, or the will, to realize the scope of what I'd seen. But sadness works in bizarre ways. The second night after the attack, I sat in front of the news, alone with my eighth or ninth beer, and I listened to a report about NFL officials considering a postponement of the second week of games. I thought about what a nice gesture that would be, and I cried and cried.

The Reader's Presence

1. How would you characterize Townsend's actions after the World Trade Center disaster? To what extent do you agree with his assessment that he didn't find his best self or act heroically like so many others? What did he do, or not do, that showed him at less than his best? Townsend describes his movements and thoughts step by step—what would you have done differently? What would you have thought differently?

2. Examine the structure of the first paragraph carefully. What significance can you find in the order in which Townsend presents details or in how he describes relatively mundane sights ("[b]urned luggage") compared to how he describes gruesome sights ("mangled flesh")? Does he seem more affected by some things than others, or does each thing he encounters seem to affect him similarly? What indicates his level of emotion or detachment throughout the essay? Townsend reports twice during the narrative that he cried: the first time, when he talked to his fiancée, he "cried" (paragraph 13); the second time, when he heard that the NFL was considering canceling games, he "cried and cried" (paragraph 16). What effect(s) does he produce by repeating "cried" in the second instance? What was it about the more trivial instance that makes him emphasize how much he cried?

3. Compare Townsend's account with Michihiko Hachiya's in the except from *Hiroshima Diary* (page 34). What writing strategies do these writers adopt to mark the passing of time? What are the similarities and differences in how they interact with other people trying to escape? How does each person think of his actions after the disaster?

Marine Staff Sergeant Aaron Dean White, Army Pfc. Diego Fernando Rincon, Army Specialist Brett T. Christian

Last Letters Home

Even in an age of instant electronic communication, soldiers continue to put pen or pencil to paper as they write to people far from the war zone. These final letters from American soldiers who died in Iraq in 2003 poignantly indicate both the pain and the banality of war. In the first year of the fighting in Iraq, the average age of the American soldiers killed there was twenty-six. The soldiers—men and women of all races and ethnicities—came from all over the United States and from all kinds of backgrounds. The following letters were written by twenty-seven-year-old Marine Staff Sergeant Aaron Dean White of Shawnee, Oklahoma; nineteen-year-old Army Pfc. Diego Fernando Rincon of Conyers, Georgia; and twenty-seven-year-old Army Specialist Brett T. Christian of North Royalton, Ohio. "Last Letters Home" is excerpted from letters published in Esquire *magazine in February 2004.*

MARINE STAFF SERGEANT AARON DEAN WHITE

20 Mar 03

Dear Mom + Dad

Its the 20th of March here so you can probably guess what my day has been like. We heard first thing this morning about the initial strikes on Iraq. It was somewhat anti-climactic since we were seeing nothing here. Around 11 A.M. we got our first air-raid alarm. It was a Mopp 0[1] alarm, so we only had our flak vest and helmets on. After the all clear was given 3 of us took a Humvee to chow and to get part of our paycheck.

We ate uneventfully and was on our way back to work, almost out of the tent compound where we live. Bet you can guess what happened next. We got an "Alarm Red" with "Bunker Now" orders and MOPP 4 instructions. That meant we hauled ass to the nearest bunker while trying to put on our gas mask and chem suits. It was funny as hell to watch while at the same time I was scared to death. Breathing so hard my mask was sucking up to my face. While in the bunker we felt the impacts of at least two inbound rounds. They were far off. You guys would have been amazed. We were laughing and joking like we were camping or something. After about 45 minutes we were again released as All Clear. We made it out to our Humvee and we're getting in when . . . You guessed it! Another "Alarm Red." I made record time for 40 yards. This time we had more company in the Bunker. I was again joking around until some guy started praying. That ruined the mood for me. I wanted to ask him to stop but I guess it was doing him good. Me on the other hand, well it was making me nervous. Like he knew something I didn't. That was the only time I felt fear. After 20 or so minutes we came out and returned to our work area. A few other Alarms were sounded but it became routine before the end of the day.

So here we are, sitting halfway in our mopp gear, letting the adrenaline leave our bodies. And, you know what, here comes a letter from you two. Made my day. I can't wait to get out of this airbase. It sucks just sitting here waiting for scuds to hit.

Please know that I'm not scared and that I am not alone. Keeping my   5
Marines in line and motivated keeps me occupied and helps me keep a good perspective. The news makes it seem worse than it is. We are all

[1]*Mopp:* Mission-Oriented Protection Posture levels that indicate the protective gear and defensive action required in response to an alarm.—EDS.

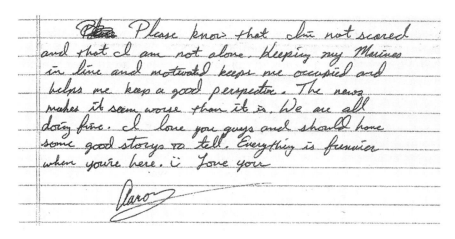

doing fine. I love you guys and should have some good storys to tell. Everything is funnier when you're here. ☺ Love you, Aaron

Staff Sergeant White was killed in a helicopter crash on May 19, 2003.

ARMY PFC. DIEGO FERNANDO RINCON

February 22, 2003

Hola Mother,

How are you doing? Good I hope. I'm doing OK I guess. I won't be able to write anymore starting the 28th of this month. We are moving out. We are already packed and ready to move to a tactical Alpha-Alpha (in Iraq). Once that happens, there will not be any mail sent out. We will only receive mail that is less than 12 ounces. At least that's what they said. I'm not sure where exactly we're going to be at yet, but it is said to be a 20-hour drive in the Bradleys.

So I guess the time has finally come for us to see what we are made of, who will crack when the stress level rises and who will be calm all the way through it. Only time will tell. We are at the peak of our training and it's time to put it to the test.

I just want to tell everybody how much you all mean to me and how much I love you all. Mother, I love you so much! I'm not going to give up! I'm living my life one day at a time, sitting here picturing home with a small tear in my eyes, spending time with my brothers who will hold my life in their hands.

I try not to think of what may happen in the future, but I can't stand seeing it in my eyes. There's going to be murders, funerals and tears

10

rolling down everybody's eyes. But the only thing I can say is, keep my head up and try to keep the faith and pray for better days. All this will pass. I believe God has a path for me.

Whether I make it or not, it's all part of the plan. It can't be changed, only completed.

Mother will be the last word I'll say. Your face will be the last picture that goes through my eyes. I'm not trying to scare you, but it's reality. . . .

I don't know what I'm talking about or why I'm writing it down. Maybe I just want someone to know what goes through my head. . . .

I just hope that you're proud of what I'm doing and have faith in my   15 decisions. I will try hard and not give up. I just want to say sorry for anything I have ever done wrong. And I'm doing it all for you mom. I love you.

Your son, Diego Rincon

Pfc. Rincon was killed by a car bomb in central Iraq on March 29, 2003. A Colombian citizen, he was posthumously granted American citizenship.

ARMY SPECIALIST BRETT T. CHRISTIAN

Dear Grandma and Grandpa,

I received the care package you sent, I greatly appreciate it. I shared some of the items with my platoon, so thanks from them too. I hope you both are doing well, as well as my mom and brothers, and Aunt and uncle, if you guys even ever see each other. I've tried to reach you, as well as my mother by phone, with no luck, the numbers I have won't connect for some reason. The phones are pretty bad here, and the mail system is even worse. I'm not sure you'll even receive this letter. I guess the art of delivering mail was lost by the military after the last war. I would appreciate it if you could console my mom, and ask her not to send any red cross messages unless there is an emergency. I have received no mail from her as of yet, and I know I've given her my address. I don't have an address for her, though. No news is good news here, there are worse things that can happen than not hearing from me.

Our living conditions are meager at best. My unit (HHC 2/502 INF of the 101st Airborne Division) is currently occupying the city of Mosul, Iraq, which is in the northern part of the country close to Syria. We are also jointly occupying the city of Falusia (I'm uncertain of the proper spelling) along with 3rd Division. We have occupied other towns in the past, such as Najaf (where the 502nd commandeered the Kufa Cola factory, supplying us with a lifetime supply of soda—its actually pretty good) and the muslim holy city of Kerbela, as well as Baghdad. The closest way I could describe this place is if you could imagine what hell must be like. The days are unbearably hot, and filled with flies. The nights are also hot, but with swarms of mosquitoes instead of flies. The streets are covered with garbage and sewage, which the livestock enjoys grazing in, and wild packs of dogs seem to run things around here. You can tell these cities were once beautiful, but are now overgrown with weeds and left to decay under years of Saddam's regime. The people are generally pretty nice and seem appreciative of us, no one more than the Kurds. I've been to Kurdistan, and its quite the contrast to here. Its very clean, and there are no beggars or looters there.

This place is still very dangerous. I have been in plenty of fire fights   20
to prove it. As for what you saw on T.V., that wasn't me. Most of the Iraqi military either laid down their weapons, or has been destroyed. We are currently believed to be fighting against members of the former Baath party, and the Fedeeyin militia. They are a difficult enemy because they use hit and run tactics, as they would never face us head on. Hopefully some semblance of order will be returned to this area, but regardless of when that happens, we should be returning in September, when I look forward to my first real hamburger in six months. Please give everyone my love, and I hope to see you one day soon.

Love, Brett

Specialist Christian was killed on July 23, 2003, in Mosul, when his convoy came under attack by rocket-propelled grenades. He was posthumously promoted to sergeant.

The Reader's Presence

1. What are the different reasons these soldiers express for communicating with their families? What are their concerns? What do they ask for? How important is it for their families to understand where they are and what they are experiencing?

2. In what ways do the soldiers explicitly or implicitly acknowledge the risks they face? What are their feelings about the danger? How prepared do they seem to be for the possibility of facing injury or death?

3. To what extent do these letters serve as a record of the war in Iraq? How much description do the men give of their daily duties? Compare these letters to the historical accounts of war experiences given by Walt Whitman in the excerpt from *Specimen Days* (page 60) and by Anne Frank in the excerpt from her diary (page 28). How do the various perspectives differ? How does the writer's role (as civilian, nurse, or soldier) affect the story he or she tells?

Walt Whitman

From *Specimen Days:*
Civil War Diary

If the United States can be said to have a national poet, it would be Walt Whitman (1819–1892). No other American poet has represented the national experience more fully and has had a deeper influence on the shape of our litera-ture. His major work, Leaves of Grass, is almost universally considered a world masterpiece, though when it first appeared in 1855, it was loudly condemned as incoherent and obscene. Born into a working-class family near Huntington, Long Island, Whitman grew up in Brooklyn, New York, where he attended public schools until he dropped out at the age of eleven to start work as an of-fice boy and later as a printer's apprentice. Whitman enjoyed a successful career in newspaper journalism but by the late 1840s decided to concentrate on more literary endeavors, while supporting himself with various jobs and freelance writing. In 1862, as the Civil War intensified, Whitman visited the front in Virginia, where his brother had been wounded. Feeling great sympathy for the average soldier, he settled in Washington, D.C., to perform volunteer work nursing the wounded in military hospitals. He kept notes of this experience and years later included them (with some slight revision) in a volume of reminis-cence, Specimen Days (1882), from which the following few passages have been taken.

DOWN AT THE FRONT
*Falmouth, Va., opposite Fredericksburgh,
December 21, 1862*

Whitman kept a diary of his Civil War experiences among the sick and wounded. It now represents one of our literature's most moving on-the-spot ac-counts of the war's human devastation. Whitman, however, did not intend to compose a literary work when he recorded his entries, which were often written in a hurry and during a pause from emergency duties. When he returned to this diary years later, he sometimes added information in parentheses (his titles, too, are later additions), as you will note in the following passages, but he never al-lowed himself to edit out the immediacy of his observations and feelings of the moment.

Begin my visits among the camp hospitals in the army of the Po-tomac. Spend a good part of the day in a large brick mansion on the banks of the Rappahannock, used as a hospital since the battle — seems to have receiv'd only the worst cases. Out doors, at the foot of a tree, within ten yards of the front of the house, I notice a heap of amputated

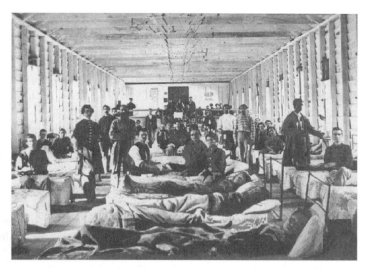

Wounded soldiers in a Civil War hospital

feet, legs, arms, hands, &c., a full load for a one-horse cart. Several dead bodies lie near, each cover'd with its brown woolen blanket. In the door-yard, towards the river, are fresh graves, mostly of officers, their names on pieces of barrel-staves or broken boards, stuck in the dirt. (Most of these bodies were subsequently taken up and transported north to their friends.) The large mansion is quite crowded upstairs and down, every-thing impromptu, no system, all bad enough, but I have no doubt the best that can be done; all the wounds pretty bad, some frightful, the men in their old clothes, unclean and bloody. Some of the wounded are rebel soldiers and officers, prisoners. One, a Mississippian, a captain, hit badly in leg, I talk'd with some time; he ask'd me for papers, which I gave him. (I saw him three months afterward in Washington, with his leg amputated, doing well.) I went through the rooms, downstairs and up. Some of the men were dying. I had nothing to give at that visit, but wrote a few letters to folks home, mothers, &c. Also talk'd to three or four, who seem'd most susceptible to it, and needing it.

FIFTY HOURS LEFT WOUNDED ON THE FIELD
[undated; most likely late January 1863]

One of the horrors of the war that especially disturbed Whitman was the army's inability to rescue wounded soldiers quickly. Many died unnecessarily in the field on both sides because of inadequate first aid. Whitman noted the following ex-ample shortly after he went to the front. Though Whitman was fiercely committed to the Union cause, the entry shows his unwillingness to demonize the Confederate soldier, whom he frequently refers to in his diary as a "secesh" (secessionist).

Here is a case of a soldier I found among the crowded cots in the Patent-office. He likes to have some one to talk to, and we will listen to him. He got badly hit in his leg and side at Fredericksburgh that eventful Saturday, 13th of December. He lay the succeeding two days and nights helpless on the field, between the city and those grim terraces of batteries; his company and regiment had been compell'd to leave him to his fate. To make matters worse, it happen'd he lay with his head slightly down hill, and could not help himself. At the end of some fifty hours he was brought off, with other wounded, under a flag of truce. I ask him how the rebels treated him as he lay during those two days and nights within reach of them — whether they came to him — whether they abused him? He answers that several of the rebels, soldiers and others, came to him at one time and another. A couple of them, who were together, spoke roughly and sarcastically, but nothing worse. One middle-aged man, however, who seem'd to be moving around the field, among the dead and wounded, for benevolent purposes, came to him in a way he will never forget; treated our soldier kindly, bound up his wounds, cheer'd him, gave him a couple of biscuits and a drink of whiskey and water; asked him if he could eat some beef. This good secesh, however, did not change our soldier's position, for it might have caused the blood to burst from the wounds, clotted and stagnated. Our soldier is from Pennsylvania; has had a pretty severe time; the wounds proved to be bad ones. But he retains a good heart, and is at present on the gain. (It is not uncommon for the men to remain on the field this way, one, two, or even four or five days.)

ABRAHAM LINCOLN
August 12, 1863

Whitman was a fervent supporter and great admirer of Lincoln, and throughout his later years often lectured on the assassinated president. His poem on the assassination, "When Lilacs Last in the Dooryard Bloom'd," remains one of America's finest elegies. While in Washington, Whitman saw Lincoln on numerous occasions, though the two never met. In this entry, Whitman obtains a close glimpse of a somber leader.

I see the President almost every day, as I happen to live where he passes to or from his lodgings out of town. He never sleeps at the White House during the hot season, but has quarters at a healthy location some three miles north of the city, the Soldiers' home, a United States military establishment. I saw him this morning about 8½ coming in to business, riding on Vermont avenue, near L street. He always has a company of twenty-five or thirty cavalry, with sabres drawn and held upright over their shoulders. They say this guard was against his personal wish, but he let his counselors have their way. The party makes no great show in uniform or horses. Mr. Lincoln on the saddle generally rides a good-sized, easy-going gray horse, is dress'd in plain black, somewhat rusty and dusty, wears a black stiff hat, and looks about as ordinary in attire, &c., as the commonest man. A lieutenant, with yellow straps, rides at his left, and following behind, two by two, come the cavalry men, in their yellow-striped jackets. They are generally going at a slow trot, as that is the pace set them by the one they wait upon. The sabres and accoutrements clank, and the entirely unornamental *cortège* as it trots towards Lafayette square arouses no sensation, only some curious stranger stops and gazes. I see very plainly Abraham Lincoln's dark brown face, with the deep-cut lines, the eyes, always to me with a deep latent sadness in the expression. We have got so that we exchange bows, and very cordial ones. Sometimes the President goes and comes in an open barouche. The cavalry always accompany him, with drawn sabres. Often I notice as he goes out evenings — and sometimes in the morning, when he returns early — he turns off and halts at the large and handsome residence of the Secretary of War, on K street, and holds conference there. If in his barouche, I can see from my window he does not alight, but sits in his vehicle, and Mr. Stanton comes out to attend him. Sometimes one of his sons, a boy of ten or twelve, accompanies him, riding at his right on a pony. Earlier in the summer I occasionally saw the President and his wife, toward the latter part of the afternoon, out in a barouche, on a pleasure ride through the city. Mrs. Lincoln was dress'd in complete black, with a long crape veil. The equipage is of the plainest kind, only two horses, and they nothing extra. They pass'd me once very close, and I saw the President in the face fully, as they were moving slowly, and his look, though abstracted, happen'd to be directed steadily in my eye. He bow'd and smiled, but far beneath his smile I noticed well the expression I have alluded to. None of the artists or pictures has caught the deep, though subtle and indirect expression of this man's face. There is something else there. One of the great portrait painters of two or three centuries ago is needed.

TWO BROTHERS, ONE SOUTH, ONE NORTH
May 28–29, 1865

Whitman stayed on to help with the wounded after the South surrendered. In the following entry he personally experiences one of the war's distressing incidents — the way it sometimes resulted in brother battling brother.

I staid to-night a long time by the bedside of a new patient, a young Baltimorean, aged about 19 years, W. S. P., (2d Maryland, southern,) very feeble, right leg amputated, can't sleep hardly at all — has taken a great deal of morphine, which, as usual, is costing more than it comes to. Evidently very intelligent and well bred — very affectionate — held on to my hand, and put it by his face, not willing to let me leave. As I was lingering, soothing him in his pain, he says to me suddenly, "I hardly think you know who I am — I don't wish to impose upon you — I am a rebel soldier." I said I did not know that, but it made no difference. Visiting him daily for about two weeks after that, while he lived, (death had mark'd him, and he was quite alone,) I loved him much, always kiss'd him, and he did me. In an adjoining ward I found his brother, an officer of rank, a Union soldier, a brave and religious man, (Col. Clifton K. Prentiss, sixth Maryland infantry, Sixth corps, wounded in one of the engagements at Petersburgh, April 2 — linger'd, suffer'd much, died in Brooklyn, Aug. 20, '65.) It was in the same battle both were hit. One was a strong Unionist, the other Secesh; both fought on their respective sides, both badly wounded, and both brought together here after a separation of four years. Each died for his cause.

THE REAL WAR WILL NEVER GET IN THE BOOKS
[undated]

As he reviewed the page proofs of Specimen Days, *Whitman worried that his "diary would prove, at best, but a batch of convulsively written reminiscences." Yet he decided to leave it that way, for the notes "are but parts of the actual distraction, heat, smoke, and excitement of those times." The war itself, he realized, could only be described by the word* convulsiveness. *In other words, the real war — as he suggests in this famous passage from* Specimen Days — *will never properly be seen by writers or historians in retrospect. It can perhaps best be conveyed by the spontaneous and fragmentary jottings of a diary.*

And so good-bye to the war. I know not how it may have been, or   5
may be, to others — to me the main interest I found, (and still, on recollection, find,) in the rank and file of the armies, both sides, and in those specimens amid the hospitals, and even the dead on the field. To me the points illustrating the latent personal character and eligibilities of these States, in the two or three millions of American young and middle-aged men, North and South, embodied in those armies — and especially the one-third or one-fourth of their number, stricken by wounds or disease at some time in the course of the contest — were of more significance even than the political interests involved. (As so much of a race depends on how it faces death, and how it stands personal anguish and sickness. As, in the glints of emotions under emergencies, and the indirect traits and asides in Plutarch, we get far profounder clues to the antique world than all its more formal history.)

Future years will never know the seething hell and the black infernal background of countless minor scenes and interiors, (not the official surface-courteousness of the Generals, not the few great battles) of the Secession war; and it is best they should not — the real war will never get in the books. In the mushy influences of current times, too, the fervid atmosphere and typical events of those years are in danger of being totally forgotten. I have at night watch'd by the side of a sick man in the hospital, one who could not live many hours. I have seen his eyes flash and burn as he raised himself and recurr'd to the cruelties of his surrender'd brother, and mutilations of the corpse afterward. . . .

Such was the war. It was not a quadrille in a ball-room. Its interior history will not only never be written — its practicality, minutiæ of deeds and passions, will never be even suggested. The actual soldier of 1862–'65, North and South, with all his ways, his incredible dauntlessness, habits, practices, tastes, language, his fierce friendship, his appetite, rankness, his superb strength and animality, lawless gait, and a hundred unnamed lights and shades of camp, I say, will never be written — perhaps must not and should not be.

The preceding notes may furnish a few stray glimpses into that life, and into those lurid interiors, never to be fully convey'd to the future. The hospital part of the drama from '61 to '65, deserves indeed to be recorded. Of that many-threaded drama, with its sudden and strange surprises, its confounding of prophecies, its moments of despair, the dread of foreign interference, the interminable campaigns, the bloody battles, the mighty and cumbrous and green armies, the drafts and bounties — the immense money expenditure, like a heavy-pouring constant rain — with, over the whole land, the last three years of the struggle, an unending, universal mourning-wail of women, parents, orphans — the marrow of the tragedy concentrated in those Army Hospitals — (it seem'd sometimes as if the whole interest of the land, North and South, was one vast central hospital, and all the rest of the affair but flanges) — those forming the untold and unwritten history of the war — infinitely greater (like life's) than the few scraps and distortions that are ever told or written. Think how much, and of importance, will be — how much, civic and military, has already been — buried in the grave, in eternal darkness.

The Reader's Presence

1. In your opinion, what aspects of Whitman's Civil War diary help make the experience of the war vivid and realistic? How are these aspects captured in Whitman's writing?

2. Formulate in your own words what Whitman means by his expression "the real war will never get in the books" (paragraph 6). What sort of book is he thinking about? Do you think he means that it could never be conveyed in language at all?

3. Whitman's poetry is characterized by long lines in which he incorporates the speech of real Americans, or what he called "the blab of the pave." Do you see these stylistic features in his prose? Compare

Whitman's long last sentence (paragraph 8) to one of Jamaica
Kincaid's long sentences in "Biography of a Dress" (page 175) or
"Girl" (page 921). Does the stylistic similarity produce similar effects? If not, why not? How do the two writers work pauses into
their prose?

Virginia Woolf
From *A Writer's Diary*

*At the time of her death, Virginia Woolf (1882–1941), one of modern litera-
ture's outstanding creative voices, left twenty-six volumes of a handwritten diary
that she had started in 1915. Her diary records her daily activities, social life,
reading, and, most important, her thoughts about the writing process. In 1953,
her husband, Leonard Woolf, extracted her remarks about writing and published
them in a separate volume called* A Writer's Diary. *The following diary entries are
taken from this edition. They show Virginia Woolf struggling with creative
doubts and aesthetic demands, as well as with social obligations, depression, and,
with the onset of World War II, the Nazi bombing of Britain. For more information on Virginia Woolf, see page 619.*

THIS LOOSE, DRIFTING MATERIAL OF LIFE
Easter Sunday, April 20, 1919

*One of the pleasures of keeping a diary is rereading what we've written. Here,
just having completed a newspaper article on the novelist Daniel Defoe, Woolf decides to take a break and think about the different ways she composes when she
writes in her diary as opposed to when she writes more formally for publication.*

In the idleness which succeeds any long article, and Defoe is the second leader this month, I got out this diary and read, as one always does
read one's own writing, with a kind of guilty intensity. I confess that the
rough and random style of it, often so ungrammatical, and crying for a
word altered, afflicted me somewhat. I am trying to tell whichever self it is
that reads this hereafter that I can write very much better; and take no
time over this; and forbid her to let the eye of man behold it. And now I
may add my little compliment to the effect that it has a slapdash and

vigour and sometimes hits an unexpected bull's eye. But what is more to
the point is my belief that the habit of writing thus for my own eye only is
good practice. It loosens the ligaments. Never mind the misses and the
stumbles. Going at such a pace as I do I must make the most direct and instant shots at my object, and thus have to lay hands on words, choose them
and shoot them with no more pause than is needed to put my pen in the
ink. I believe that during the past year I can trace some increase of ease in
my professional writing which I attribute to my casual half hours after tea.
Moreover there looms ahead of me the shadow of some kind of form which
a diary might attain to. I might in the course of time learn what it is that
one can make of this loose, drifting material of life; finding another use for
it than the use I put it to, so much more consciously and scrupulously, in
fiction. What sort of diary should I like mine to be? Something loose knit
and yet not slovenly, so elastic that it will embrace anything, solemn, slight,
or beautiful that comes into my mind. I should like it to resemble some
deep old desk, or capacious hold-all, in which one flings a mass of odds and
ends without looking them through. I should like to come back, after a year
or two, and find that the collection had sorted itself and refined itself and
coalesced, as such deposits so mysteriously do, into a mould, transparent
enough to reflect the light of our life, and yet steady, tranquil compounds
with the aloofness of a work of art. The main requisite, I think on rereading my old volumes, is not to play the part of censor, but to write as
the mood comes or of anything whatever; since I was curious to find how I
went for things put in haphazard, and found the significance to lie where I
never saw it at the time. But looseness quickly becomes slovenly. A little effort is needed to face a character or an incident which needs to be
recorded. . . .

CHAINED TO MY ROCK
Thursday, August 18, 1921

*In 1919, Virginia and Leonard (referred to throughout the diaries as L.) pur-
chased a small country house in Sussex. For many years, they divided their time
between there and London. In 1921, Virginia Woolf suffered a bout of nervous
depression and was advised by a local doctor (who, she wrote, thought of her as a
"chronic invalid") to rest and do nothing for a while. In an irritable state of mind,
the day after the doctor's visit, she wrote the following entry in which she com-
pares herself to Prometheus, the Greek mythic hero who was chained to a rock by
Zeus as punishment for stealing fire from the gods and giving it to human beings.*

Nothing to record; only an intolerable fit of the fidgets to write away.
Here I am chained to my rock; forced to do nothing; doomed to let every
worry, spite, irritation, and obsession scratch and claw and come again.
This is a day that I may not walk and must not work. Whatever book I
read bubbles up in my mind as part of an article I want to write. No one

in the whole of Sussex is so miserable as I am; or so conscious of an infinite capacity of enjoyment hoarded in me, could I use it. The sun streams (no, never streams; floods rather) down upon all the yellow fields and the long low barns; and what wouldn't I give to be coming through Firle woods, dirty and hot, with my nose turned home, every muscle tired and the brain laid up in sweet lavender, so sane and cool, and ripe for the morrow's task. How I should notice everything—the phrase for it coming the moment after and fitting like a glove; and then on the dusty road, as I ground my pedals, so my story would begin telling itself; and then the sun would be down; and home, and some bout of poetry after dinner, half read, half lived, as if the flesh were dissolved and through it the flowers burst red and white. There! I've written out half my irritation. I hear poor L. driving the lawn mower up and down, for a wife like I am should have a latch to her cage. She bites! And he spent all yesterday running round London for me. Still if one is Prometheus, if the rock is hard and the gadflies pungent, gratitude, affection, none of the nobler feelings have sway. And so this August is wasted.

Only the thought of people suffering more than I do at all consoles; and that is an aberration of egotism, I suppose. I will now make out a time table if I can to get through these odious days. . . .

THEY GET CLOSER EVERY TIME
Wednesday, October 2, 1940

The Woolfs lost their London house during the Nazi bombing raids in 1940. But even in their Sussex house they experienced the incessant raids. They often witnessed air battles above their home. On one occasion, having watched an enemy plane being shot down, Woolf wrote that it "would have been a peaceful matter of fact death to be popped off on the terrace . . . this very fine cool sunny August evening." The thought of death returned during another bombing raid in October. Six months later, on March 28, 1941, she took her own life.

Ought I not to look at the sunset rather than write this? A flush of red in the blue; the haystack on the marsh catches the glow; behind me, the apples are red in the trees. L. is gathering them. Now a plume of smoke goes from the train under Caburn. And all the air a solemn stillness holds. Till 8:30 when the cadaverous twanging in the sky begins; the planes going to London. Well it's an hour still to that. Cows feeding. The elm tree sprinkling its little leaves against the sky. Our pear tree swagged with pears; and the weathercock above the triangular church tower above it. Why try again to make the familiar catalogue, from which something escapes. Should I think of death? Last night a great heavy plunge of bomb under the window. So near we both started. A plane had passed dropping this fruit. We went on to the terrace. Trinkets of stars sprinkled and glittering. All quiet. The bombs dropped on Itford Hill. There are two by the river, marked with white wooden crosses, still unburst. I said to L.: I don't want to die yet. The chances are against it. But they're aiming at the railway and the power works. They get closer every time. Caburn was crowned with what looked like a settled moth, wings extended—a Messerschmitt it was, shot down on Sunday. . . . Oh I try to imagine how one's killed by a bomb. I've got it fairly vivid—the sensation: but can't see anything but suffocating nonentity following after. I shall think—oh I wanted another 10 years—not this—and shan't, for once, be able to describe it. It—I mean death; no, the scrunching and scrambling, the crushing of my bone shade in on my very active eye and brain: the process of putting out the light—painful? Yes. Terrifying. I suppose so. Then a swoon; a drain; two or three gulps attempting consciousness—and then dot dot dot.

The Reader's Presence

1. In the first excerpt from Woolf's diaries, what positive qualities does she discover about her diary as she rereads it? Does she note any negative tendencies? In what ways does her diary offer her a means of self-discovery?

2. Woolf observed that one of the problems with diaries is that we usually turn to them only in certain moods (for example, loneliness, depression) and that therefore they provide only a limited view of someone's personality. Do you think, from the three excerpts reprinted here, that this observation would pertain to her own diaries? Can you apply her observation to some of the other diary entries in this chapter?

3. In the "Writer at Work" selection on page 161, Edward Hoagland characterizes the essay as "serendipitous or domestic satire or testimony, tongue-in-cheek or wail of grief." What do Woolf's criteria for diaries share with Hoagland's criteria for essays? What possible relationships exist between the "raw material" of an event recorded in a diary and an account of that same event offered in an essay?

Part II

Personal Writing: Exploring Our Own Lives

Sherman Alexie

The Joy of Reading and Writing: Superman and Me

Sherman Alexie (b. 1966) is a Spokane/Coeur d'Arelene Indian who grew up on the Spokane Indian Reservation in Wellpinit, Washington. He was born hydrocephalic and underwent a brain operation at the age of six months, which he was not expected to survive. As a youth, Alexie left the reservation for a public high school where he excelled in academics and became a star player on the basketball team. He attended Gonzaga University in Spokane on a scholarship and then transferred to Washington State University, where his experience in a poetry workshop encouraged him to become a writer. Soon after graduation he received the Washington State Arts Commission Poetry Fellowship and a National Endowment for the Arts Poetry Fellowship. His first collection of short stories, The Lone Ranger and Tonto Fistfight in Heaven *(1993), received both a PEN/Hemingway Award for Best First Book of Fiction and a Lila Wallace–Reader's Digest Writer's Award. He was subsequently named one of* Granta's *Best Young American Novelists and published a novel titled* Reservation Blues *(1995), followed the next year by* Indian Killer *(1996). Since 1997 Alexie has written for the screen; his screenplay for the movie* Smoke Signals, *based on his short story "This Is What It Means to Say Phoenix, Arizona" (page 885), received the Christopher Award in 1999. He has published fifteen books; his most recent collection of short stories is* Ten Little Indians *(2003).*

Sherman Alexie has commented on his own work, "I'm a good writer who may be a great writer one day. I'm harder on myself than anybody."

I learned to read with a Superman comic book. Simple enough, I suppose. I cannot recall which particular Superman comic book I read, nor can I remember which villain he fought in that issue. I cannot remember the plot, nor the means by which I obtained the comic book. What I can remember is this: I was 3 years old, a Spokane Indian boy living with his family on the Spokane Indian Reservation in eastern Washington state. We were poor by most standards, but one of my parents usually managed to find some minimum-wage job or another, which made us middle-class

73

by reservation standards. I had a brother and three sisters. We lived on a combination of irregular paychecks, hope, fear, and government surplus food.

My father, who is one of the few Indians who went to Catholic school on purpose, was an avid reader of westerns, spy thrillers, murder mysteries, gangster epics, basketball player biographies, and anything else he could find. He bought his books by the pound at Dutch's Pawn Shop, Goodwill, Salvation Army, and Value Village. When he had extra money, he bought new novels at supermarkets, convenience stores, and hospital gift shops. Our house was filled with books. They were stacked in crazy piles in the bathroom, bedrooms, and living room. In a fit of unemployment-inspired creative energy, my father built a set of bookshelves and soon filled them with a random assortment of books about the Kennedy assassination, Watergate, the Vietnam War, and the entire 23-book series of the Apache westerns. My father loved books, and since I loved my father with an aching devotion, I decided to love books as well.

I can remember picking up my father's books before I could read. The words themselves were mostly foreign, but I still remember the exact moment when I first understood, with a sudden clarity, the purpose of a paragraph. I didn't have the vocabulary to say "paragraph," but I realized that a paragraph was a fence that held words. The words inside a paragraph worked together for a common purpose. They had some specific reason for being inside the same fence. This knowledge delighted me. I began to think of everything in terms of paragraphs. Our reservation was a small paragraph within the United States. My family's house was a paragraph, distinct from the other paragraphs of the LeBrets to the north, the Fords to our South, and the Tribal School to the west. Inside our house, each family member existed as a separate paragraph but still had genetics and common experiences to link us. Now, using this logic, I can see my changed family as an essay of seven paragraphs: mother, father, older brother, the deceased sister, my younger twin sisters, and our adopted little brother.

At the same time I was seeing the world in paragraphs, I also picked up that Superman comic book. Each panel, complete with picture, dialogue, and narrative was a three-dimensional paragraph. In one panel, Superman breaks through a door. His suit is red, blue, and yellow. The brown door shatters into many pieces. I look at the narrative above the picture. I cannot read the words, but I assume it tells me that "Superman is breaking down the door." Aloud, I pretend to read the words and say, "Superman is breaking down the door." Words, dialogue, also float out of Superman's mouth. Because he is breaking down the door, I assume he says, "I am breaking down the door." Once again, I pretend to read the words and say aloud, "I am breaking down the door." In this way, I learned to read.

This might be an interesting story all by itself. A little Indian boy teaches himself to read at an early age and advances quickly. He reads "Grapes of   5

Wrath" in kindergarten when other children are struggling through "Dick and Jane." If he'd been anything but an Indian boy living on the reservation, he might have been called a prodigy. But he is an Indian boy living on the reservation and is simply an oddity. He grows into a man who often speaks of his childhood in the third person, as if it will somehow dull the pain and make him sound more modest about his talents.

A smart Indian is a dangerous person, widely feared and ridiculed by Indians and non-Indians alike. I fought with my classmates on a daily basis. They wanted me to stay quiet when the non-Indian teacher asked for answers, for volunteers, for help. We were Indian children who were expected to be stupid. Most lived up to those expectations inside the classroom but subverted them on the outside. They struggled with basic reading in school but could remember how to sing a few dozen powwow songs. They were monosyllabic in front of their non-Indian teachers but could tell complicated stories and jokes at the dinner table. They submissively ducked their heads when confronted by a non-Indian adult but would slug it out with the Indian bully who was 10 years older. As Indian children, we were expected to fail in the non-Indian world. Those who failed were ceremonially accepted by other Indians and appropriately pitied by non-Indians.

I refused to fail. I was smart. I was arrogant. I was lucky. I read books late into the night, until I could barely keep my eyes open. I read books at recess, then during lunch, and in the few minutes left after I had finished my classroom assignments. I read books in the car when my family traveled to powwows or basketball games. In shopping malls, I ran to the bookstores and read bits and pieces of as many books as I could. I read the books my father brought home from the pawnshops and secondhand. I read the books I borrowed from the library. I read the backs of cereal boxes. I read the newspaper. I read the bulletins posted on the walls of the school, the clinic, the tribal offices, the post office. I read junk mail. I read auto-repair manuals. I read magazines. I read anything that had words and paragraphs. I read with equal parts joy and desperation. I loved those books, but I also knew that love had only one purpose. I was trying to save my life.

Despite all the books I read, I am still surprised I became a writer. I was going to be a pediatrician. These days, I write novels, short stories, and poems. I visit schools and teach creative writing to Indian kids. In all my years in the reservation school system, I was never taught how to write poetry, short stories, or novels. I was certainly never taught that Indians wrote poetry, short stories, and novels. Writing was something beyond Indians. I cannot recall a single time that a guest teacher visited the reservation. There must have been visiting teachers. Who were they? Where are they now? Do they exist? I visit the schools as often as possible. The Indian kids crowd the classroom. Many are writing their own poems, short stories, and novels. They have read my books. They have read many other books. They look at me with bright eyes and arrogant wonder. They are trying to save their lives. Then there are the sullen and already defeated Indian kids who sit in the back rows and ignore me with theatrical precision. The pages of their notebooks are empty. They carry neither pencil nor pen. They stare out the window. They refuse and resist. "Books," I say to them. "Books," I say. I throw my weight against their locked doors. The door holds. I am smart. I am arrogant. I am lucky. I am trying to save our lives.

The Reader's Presence

1. What does literacy mean to Alexie? What are his associations with reading? with writing? How does he use his reading and his writing to establish his ties to the community? What aspects of his identity are bound up with reading and writing?

2. How did the young Alexie use popular culture to educate himself? What did comic books teach him? How does Alexie use the figure of Superman, and aspects of action-hero stories more generally, to give structure and coherence to his essay?

3. Alexie uses the metaphor of "breaking down the door" to describe the act of learning to read. What are the connotations of this metaphor? How does it compare with Frederick Douglass's account of his acquisition of literacy in "Learning to Read and Write" (page 129) in which he says that he sometimes felt as though "learning to read had been a curse rather than a blessing"? As he encountered arguments for and against slavery in the books he read, Douglass felt that reading deepened his already vivid experience of slavery: "It had given me a view of my wretched condition, without the remedy" (paragraph 6). Is literacy a means to freedom for Alexie as it was, ultimately, for Douglass? If so, freedom from what and/or freedom to do what?

Maya Angelou

"What's Your Name, Girl?"

Maya Angelou (b. 1928) grew up in St. Louis, Missouri, and in Stamps, Arkansas, a victim of poverty, discrimination, and abuse. Angelou confronts the pain and injustice of her childhood in I Know Why the Caged Bird Sings *(1969), from which the selection "'What's Your Name, Girl?'" is taken. James Baldwin, who suggested she write about her childhood, praised this book as the mark of the "beginning of a new era in the minds and hearts of all black men and women." Angelou, who has received more than a hundred honorary degrees, is currently Reynolds Professor of American Studies at Wake Forest University. In addition to the several volumes of her autobiography, she is the author of articles, short stories, and poetry. Her most recent publications are a collection of essays,* Hallelujah! The Welcome Table *(2004) and a series of children's picture books in 2001. Her first feature-length film,* Down in the Delta, *was released in 1998, and she won a 2002 Grammy for her recording of her autobiographical work* A Song Flung Up to Heaven.*

Angelou describes a typical day in her life as a writer in this way: "When I'm writing, everything shuts down. I get up about five. . . . I get in my car and drive off to a hotel room: I can't write in my house, I take a hotel room and ask them to take everything off the walls so there's me, the Bible, Roget's Thesaurus, and some good, dry sherry and I'm at work by 6:30. I write on the bed lying down— one elbow is darker than the other, really black from leaning on it—and I write in longhand on yellow pads. Once into it, all disbelief is suspended, it's beautiful. I hate to go, but I've set for myself 12:30 as the time to leave, because after that it's an indulgence, it becomes stuff I am going to edit out anyway. . . . After dinner I re-read what I have written . . . if April is the cruellest month, then 8:00 at night is the cruellest hour because that's when I start to edit and all that pretty stuff I've written gets axed out. So if I've written ten or twelve pages in six hours, it'll end up as three or four if I'm lucky."

Recently a white woman from Texas, who would quickly describe herself as a liberal, asked me about my hometown. When I told her that in Stamps[1] my grandmother had owned the only Negro general merchandise store since the turn of the century, she exclaimed, "Why, you were a debutante." Ridiculous and even ludicrous. But Negro girls in small Southern towns, whether poverty-stricken or just munching along on a few of life's necessities, were given as extensive and irrelevant preparations for adulthood as rich white girls shown in magazines. Admittedly the training was not the same. While white girls learned to waltz and sit gracefully with a teacup balanced on their knees, we were lagging behind, learning the mid-Victorian values with very little money to indulge them. (Come and see

---

[1] *Stamps:* A town in southwestern Arkansas. —EDS.

Edna Lomax spending the money she made picking cotton on five balls of ecru tatting thread. Her fingers are bound to snag the work and she'll have to repeat the stitches time and time again. But she knows that when she buys the thread.)

We were required to embroider and I had trunkfuls of colorful dish-towels, pillowcases, runners, and handkerchiefs to my credit. I mastered the art of crocheting and tatting, and there was a lifetime's supply of dainty doilies that would never be used in sacheted dresser drawers. It went without saying that all girls could iron and wash, but the finer touches around the home, like setting a table with real silver, baking roasts, and cooking vegetables without meat, had to be learned elsewhere. Usually at the source of those habits. During my tenth year, a white woman's kitchen became my finishing school.

Mrs. Viola Cullinan was a plump woman who lived in a three-bedroom house somewhere behind the post office. She was singularly un-attractive until she smiled, and then the lines around her eyes and mouth which made her look perpetually dirty disappeared, and her face looked like the mask of an impish elf. She usually rested her smile until late after-noon when her women friends dropped in and Miss Glory, the cook, served them cold drinks on the closed-in porch.

The exactness of her house was inhuman. This glass went here and only here. That cup had its place and it was an act of impudent rebellion to place it anywhere else. At twelve o'clock the table was set. At 12:15 Mrs. Cullinan sat down to dinner (whether her husband had arrived or not). At 12:16 Miss Glory brought out the food.

It took me a week to learn the difference between a salad plate, a   5
bread plate, and a dessert plate.

Mrs. Cullinan kept up the tradition of her wealthy parents. She was from Virginia. Miss Glory, who was a descendant of slaves that had worked for the Cullinans, told me her history. She had married beneath her (according to Miss Glory). Her husband's family hadn't had their money very long and what they had "didn't 'mount to much."

As ugly as she was, I thought privately, she was lucky to get a hus-band above or beneath her station. But Miss Glory wouldn't let me say a thing against her mistress. She was very patient with me, however, over the housework. She explained the dishware, silverware, and servants' bells.

The large round bowl in which soup was served wasn't a soup bowl, it was a tureen. There were goblets, sherbet glasses, ice-cream glasses, wine glasses, green glass coffee cups with matching saucers, and water glasses. I had a glass to drink from, and it sat with Miss Glory's on a sep-arate shelf from the others. Soup spoons, gravy boat, butter knives, salad forks, and carving platter were additions to my vocabulary and in fact al-most represented a new language. I was fascinated with the novelty, with the fluttering Mrs. Cullinan and her Alice-in-Wonderland house.

Her husband remains, in my memory, undefined. I lumped him with all the other white men that I had ever seen and tried not to see.

On our way home one evening, Miss Glory told me that Mrs. Cullinan couldn't have children. She said that she was too delicate-boned. It was hard to imagine bones at all under those layers of fat. Miss Glory went on to say that the doctor had taken out all her lady organs. I reasoned that a pig's organs included the lungs, heart, and liver, so if Mrs. Cullinan was walking around without these essentials, it explained why she drank alcohol out of unmarked bottles. She was keeping herself embalmed.

When I spoke to Bailey[2] about it, he agreed that I was right, but he also informed me that Mr. Cullinan had two daughters by a colored lady and that I knew them very well. He added that the girls were the spitting image of their father. I was unable to remember what he looked like, although I had just left him a few hours before, but I thought of the Coleman girls. They were very light-skinned and certainly didn't look very much like their mother (no one ever mentioned Mr. Coleman).

My pity for Mrs. Cullinan preceded me the next morning like the Cheshire cat's smile. Those girls, who could have been her daughters, were beautiful. They didn't have to straighten their hair. Even when they were caught in the rain, their braids still hung down straight like tamed snakes. Their mouths were pouty little cupid's bows. Mrs. Cullinan didn't know what she missed. Or maybe she did. Poor Mrs. Cullinan.

For weeks after, I arrived early, left late, and tried very hard to make up for her barrenness. If she had had her own children, she wouldn't have had to ask me to run a thousand errands from her back door to the back door of her friends. Poor old Mrs. Cullinan.

Then one evening Miss Glory told me to serve the ladies on the porch. After I set the tray down and turned toward the kitchen, one of the women asked, "What's your name, girl?" It was the speckled-face one. Mrs. Cullinan said, "She doesn't talk much. Her name's Margaret."

"Is she dumb?"

"No. As I understand it, she can talk when she wants to but she's usually quiet as a little mouse. Aren't you, Margaret?"

I smiled at her. Poor thing. No organs and couldn't even pronounce my name correctly.[3]

"She's a sweet little thing, though."

"Well, that may be, but the name's too long. I'd never bother myself. I'd call her Mary if I was you."

I fumed into the kitchen. That horrible woman would never have the chance to call me Mary because if I was starving I'd never work for her. I

10

15

20

---

[2]*Bailey:* Her brother.—Eds.
[3]*couldn't even pronounce my name correctly:* Angelou's first name is actually Marguerite.—Eds.

decided I wouldn't pee on her if her heart was on fire. Giggles drifted in off the porch and into Miss Glory's pots. I wondered what they could be laughing about.

Whitefolks were so strange. Could they be talking about me? Everybody knew that they stuck together better than the Negroes did. It was possible that Mrs. Cullinan had friends in St. Louis who heard about a girl from Stamps being in court and wrote to tell her. Maybe she knew about Mr. Freeman.[4]

My lunch was in my mouth a second time and I went outside and relieved myself on the bed of four-o'clocks. Miss Glory thought I might be coming down with something and told me to go on home, that Momma would give me some herb tea, and she'd explain to her mistress.

I realized how foolish I was being before I reached the pond. Of course Mrs. Cullinan didn't know. Otherwise she wouldn't have given me the two nice dresses that Momma cut down, and she certainly wouldn't have called me a "sweet little thing." My stomach felt fine, and I didn't mention anything to Momma.

That evening I decided to write a poem on being white, fat, old, and without children. It was going to be a tragic ballad. I would have to watch her carefully to capture the essence of her loneliness and pain.

The very next day, she called me by the wrong name. Miss Glory and   25
I were washing up the lunch dishes when Mrs. Cullinan came to the doorway. "Mary?"

Miss Glory asked, "Who?"

Mrs. Cullinan, sagging a little, knew and I knew. "I want Mary to go down to Mrs. Randall's and take her some soup. She's not been feeling well for a few days."

Miss Glory's face was a wonder to see. "You mean Margaret, ma'am. Her name's Margaret."

"That's too long. She's Mary from now on. Heat that soup from last night and put it in the china tureen and, Mary, I want you to carry it carefully."

Every person I knew had a hellish horror of being "called out of   30
his name." It was a dangerous practice to call a Negro anything that could be loosely construed as insulting because of the centuries of their having been called niggers, jigs, dinges, blackbirds, crows, boots, and spooks.

Miss Glory had a fleeting second of feeling sorry for me. Then as she handed me the hot tureen she said, "Don't mind, don't pay that no mind. Sticks and stones may break your bones, but words . . . You know, I been working for her for twenty years."

---

[4]**Mr. Freeman:** A friend of Angelou's mother; he was convicted of raping Angelou when she was a child. —EDS.

She held the back door open for me. "Twenty years; I wasn't much older than you. My name used to be Hallelujah. That's what Ma named me, but my mistress give me 'Glory,' and it stuck. I likes it better too."

I was in the little path that ran behind the houses when Miss Glory shouted. "It's shorter too."

For a few seconds it was a tossup over whether I would laugh (imagine being named Hallelujah) or cry (imagine letting some white woman rename you for her convenience). My anger saved me from either outburst. I had to quit the job, but the problem was going to be how to do it. Momma wouldn't allow me to quit for just any reason.

"She's a peach. That woman is a real peach." Mrs. Randall's maid 35 was talking as she took the soup from me, and I wondered what her name used to be and what she answered to now.

For a week I looked into Mrs. Cullinan's face as she called me Mary. She ignored my coming late and leaving early. Miss Glory was a little annoyed because I had begun to leave egg yolk on the dishes and wasn't putting much heart in polishing the silver. I hoped that she would complain to our boss, but she didn't.

Then Bailey solved my dilemma. He had me describe the contents of the cupboard and the particular plates she liked best. Her favorite piece was a casserole shaped like a fish and the green glass coffee cups. I kept his instructions in mind, so on the next day when Miss Glory was hanging out clothes and I had again been told to serve the old biddies on the porch, I dropped the empty serving tray. When I heard Mrs. Cullinan scream, "Mary!" I picked up the casserole and two of the green glass cups in readiness. As she rounded the kitchen door I let them fall on the tiled floor.

I could never absolutely describe to Bailey what happened next, because each time I got to the part where she fell on the floor and screwed up her ugly face to cry, we burst out laughing. She actually wobbled around on the floor and picked up shards of the cups and cried, "Oh, Momma. Oh, dear Gawd. It's Momma's china from Virginia. Oh, Momma, I sorry."

Miss Glory came running in from the yard and the women from the porch crowded around. Miss Glory was almost as broken up as her mistress. "You mean to say she broke our Virginia dishes? What we gone do?"

Mrs. Cullinan cried louder. "That clumsy nigger. Clumsy little black 40 nigger."

Old speckled-face leaned down and asked, "Who did it, Viola? Was it Mary? Who did it?"

Everything was happening so fast I can't remember whether her action preceded her words, but I know that Mrs. Cullinan said, "Her name's Margaret, goddamn it, her name's Margaret!" And she threw a wedge of the broken plate at me. It could have been the hysteria which put her aim off, but the flying crockery caught Miss Glory right over her ear and she started screaming.

I left the front door wide open so all the neighbors could hear.

Mrs. Cullinan was right about one thing. My name wasn't Mary.

The Reader's Presence

1. At the center of this autobiographical episode is the importance of people's names in African American culture. Where does Angelou make this point clear? If she hadn't explained the problem of names directly, how might your interpretation of the episode be different? To what extent do the names of things also play an important role in the essay? What does it mean to be "called out of [one's] name" (paragraph 30)?

2. Consider Marguerite's final act carefully. What turns her sympathetic feelings for Mrs. Cullinan to anger? Why does she respond by deliberately destroying Mrs. Cullinan's china? What else could she have done? Why was that act especially appropriate? What does the china represent? How does Angelou establish our sympathy, or lack thereof, for Marguerite in the final paragraphs?

3. Many coming-of-age stories involve an account of the child's acquisition of language, but also, and perhaps more important, of the importance of social context to communication. Miss Glory's training of Marguerite as a maid involves "additions to [her] vocabulary and in fact almost represented a new language" (paragraph 8). How does her education compare to that of Malcolm X in "Homeboy" (page 194) when he arrives in the Roxbury ghetto (paragraph 15 and following)? What is the relation between language and power in each essay?

James Baldwin

Notes of a Native Son

James Baldwin (1924–1987) grew up in New York City but moved to France in 1948 because he felt personally and artistically stifled as a gay African American man in the United States. His first novels, Go Tell It on the Mountain *(1956) and* Giovanni's Room *(1956), and his first collection of essays,* Notes of a Native Son *(1955), were published during Baldwin's first stay abroad, where he was able to write critically about race, sexual identity, and social injustice in America. "Once I found myself on the other side of the ocean," he told an interviewer, "I could see where I came from very clearly, and I could see that I carried myself, which is my home, with me. You can never escape that. I am the grandson of a slave, and I am a writer. I must deal with both."*

After nearly a decade in France, he returned to New York and became a national figure in the civil rights movement. After Baldwin's death, Henry Louis Gates Jr. eulogized him as the conscience of the nation, for he "educated an entire generation of Americans about the civil-rights struggle and the sensibility of Afro-Americans as we faced and conquered the final barriers in our long quest for civil rights." Baldwin continues to educate through his essays, collected in The Price of the Ticket: Collected Nonfiction *(1985).*

When asked if he approached the writing of fiction and nonfiction in different ways, Baldwin responded, "Every form is different, no one is easier than another. . . . An essay is not simpler, though it may seem so. An essay is clearly an argument. The writer's point of view in an essay is always absolutely clear. The writer is trying to make the readers see something, trying to convince them of something. In a novel or a play you're trying to show them something. The risks, in any case, are exactly the same."

The title essay of the book Notes of a Native Son *first appeared in* Harper's *magazine in 1955. In it, Baldwin recounts the death of his father, whose funeral took place on Baldwin's nineteenth birthday—the same day a bloody race riot broke out in Harlem.*

ONE

On the twenty-ninth of July, in 1943, my father died. On the same day, a few hours later, his last child was born. Over a month before this, while all our energies were concentrated in waiting for these events, there had been, in Detroit, one of the bloodiest race riots of the century. A few hours after my father's funeral, while he lay in state in the undertaker's chapel, a race riot broke out in Harlem. On the morning of the third of August, we drove my father to the graveyard through a wilderness of smashed plate glass.

The day of my father's funeral had also been my nineteenth birthday. As we drove him to the graveyard, the spoils of injustice, anarchy, discontent, and hatred were all around us. It seemed to me that God himself had devised, to mark my father's end, the most sustained and brutally dissonant of codas. And it seemed to me, too, that the violence which rose all about us as my father left the world had been devised as a corrective for the pride of his eldest son. I had declined to believe in that apocalypse which had been central to my father's vision; very well, life seemed to be saying, here is something that will certainly pass for an apocalypse until the real thing comes along. I had inclined to be contemptuous of my father for the conditions of his life, for the conditions of our lives. When his life had ended I began to wonder about that life and also, in a new way, to be apprehensive about my own.

I had not known my father very well. We had got on badly, partly because we shared, in our different fashions, the vice of stubborn pride. When he was dead I realized that I had hardly ever spoken to him. When he had been dead a long time I began to wish I had. It seems to be typical of life in America, where opportunities, real and fancied, are thicker than anywhere else on the globe, that the second generation has no time to talk to the first. No one, including my father, seems to have known exactly how old he was, but his mother had been born during slavery. He was of the first generation of free men. He, along with thousands of other Negroes, came North after 1919 and I was part of that generation which had never seen the landscape of what Negroes sometimes call the Old Country.

He had been born in New Orleans and had been a quite young man there during the time that Louis Armstrong, a boy, was running errands for the dives and honky-tonks of what was always presented to me as one of the most wicked of cities — to this day, whenever I think of New Orleans, I also helplessly think of Sodom and Gomorrah. My father never mentioned Louis Armstrong, except to forbid us to play his records; but there was a picture of him on our wall for a long time. One of my father's strong-willed female relatives had placed it there and forbade my father to take it down. He never did, but he eventually maneuvered her out of the house and when, some years later, she was in trouble and near death, he refused to do anything to help her.

He was, I think, very handsome. I gather this from photographs and   5 from my own memories of him, dressed in his Sunday best and on his way to preach a sermon somewhere, when I was little. Handsome, proud, and ingrown, "like a toenail," somebody said. But he looked to me, as I grew older, like pictures I had seen of African tribal chieftains: he really should have been naked, with warpaint on and barbaric mementos, standing among spears. He could be chilling in the pulpit and indescribably cruel in his personal life and he was certainly the most bitter man I have ever met; yet it must be said that there was something else in him, buried in him, which lent him his tremendous power and, even, a rather crushing charm. It had something to do with his blackness, I think—he was very black—with his blackness and his beauty, and with the fact that he knew that he was black but did not know that he was beautiful. He claimed to be proud of his blackness but it had also been the cause of much humiliation and it had fixed bleak boundaries to his life. He was not a young man when we were growing up and he had already suffered many kinds of ruin; in his outrageously demanding and protective way he loved his children, who were black like him and menaced, like him; and all these things sometimes showed in his face when he tried, never to my knowledge with any success, to establish contact with any of us. When he took one of his children on his knee to play, the child always became fretful and began to cry; when he tried to help one of us with our homework the absolutely unabating tension which emanated from him caused our minds and our tongues to become paralyzed, so that he, scarcely knowing why, flew into a rage and the child, not knowing why, was punished. If it ever entered his head to bring a surprise home for his children, it was, almost unfailingly, the wrong surprise and even the big watermelons he often brought home on his back in the summertime led to the most appalling scenes. I do not remember, in all those years, that one of his children was ever glad to see him come home. From what I was able to gather of his early life, it seemed that this inability to establish contact with other people had always marked him and had been one of the things which had driven him out of New Orleans. There was something in him, therefore, groping and tentative, which was never expressed and which was buried with him. One saw it most clearly when he was facing new people and hoping to impress them. But he never did, not for long. We went from church to smaller and more improbable church, he found himself in less and less demand as a minister, and by the time he died none of his friends had come to see him for a long time. He had lived and died in an intolerable bitterness of spirit and it frightened me, as we drove him to the graveyard through those unquiet, ruined streets, to see how powerful and overflowing this bitterness could be and to realize that this bitterness now was mine.

When he died I had been away from home for a little over a year. In that year I had had time to become aware of the meaning of all my father's bitter warnings, had discovered the secret of his proudly pursed lips and rigid carriage: I had discovered the weight of white people in the world. I saw that this had been for my ancestors and now would be for me an awful thing to live with and that the bitterness which had helped to kill my father could also kill me.

He had been ill a long time—in the mind, as we now realized, reliving instances of his fantastic intransigence in the new light of his affliction and endeavoring to feel a sorrow for him which never, quite, came true. We had not known that he was being eaten up by paranoia, and the discovery that his cruelty, to our bodies and our minds, had been one of the symptoms of his illness was not, then, enough to enable us to forgive him. The younger children felt, quite simply, relief that he would not be coming home anymore. My mother's observation that it was he, after all, who had kept them alive all these years meant nothing because the problems of keeping children alive are not real for children. The older children felt, with my father gone, that they could invite their friends to the house without fear that their friends would be insulted or, as had sometimes happened with me, being told that their friends were in league with the devil and intended to rob our family of everything we owned. (I didn't fail to wonder, and it made me hate him, what on earth we owned that anybody else would want.)

His illness was beyond all hope of healing before anyone realized that he was ill. He had always been so strange and had lived, like a prophet, in such unimaginably close communion with the Lord that his long silences which were punctuated by moans and hallelujahs and snatches of old songs while he sat at the living-room window never seemed odd to us. It was not until he refused to eat because, he said, his family was trying to poison him that my mother was forced to accept as a fact what had, until then, been only an unwilling suspicion. When he was committed, it was discovered that he had tuberculosis and, as it turned out, the disease of his mind allowed the disease of his body to destroy him. For the doctors could not force him to eat, either, and, though he was fed intravenously, it was clear from the beginning that there was no hope for him.

In my mind's eye I could see him, sitting at the window, locked up in his terrors; hating and fearing every living soul including his children who had betrayed him, too, by reaching toward the world which had despised him. There were nine of us. I began to wonder what it could have felt like for such a man to have had nine children whom he could barely feed. He used to make little jokes about our poverty, which never, of course, seemed very funny to us; they could not have seemed very funny to him, either, or else our all too feeble response to them would never have caused such rages. He spent great energy and achieved, to our chagrin, no small amount of success in keeping us away from the people who surrounded us, people who had all-night rent parties[1] to which we listened when we should have been sleeping, people who cursed and drank and flashed razor blades on Lenox Avenue. He could not understand why, if they had so much energy to spare, they could not use it to make their lives better. He treated almost everybody on our block with a most uncharitable asperity and neither they, nor, of course, their children were slow to reciprocate.

The only white people who came to our house were welfare workers   10 and bill collectors. It was almost always my mother who dealt with them,

---

[1]*rent parties:* Part of a Harlem tradition; musicians were often hired and contributions taken to help pay the rent for needy tenants. —EDS.

for my father's temper, which was at the mercy of his pride, was never to be trusted. It was clear that he felt their very presence in his home to be a violation: this was conveyed by his carriage, almost ludicrously stiff, and by his voice, harsh and vindictively polite. When I was around nine or ten I wrote a play which was directed by a young, white schoolteacher, a woman, who then took an interest in me, and gave me books to read and, in order to corroborate my theatrical bent, decided to take me to see what she somewhat tactlessly referred to as "real" plays. Theater-going was forbidden in our house, but, with the really cruel intuitiveness of a child, I suspected that the color of this woman skin would carry the day for me. When, at school, she suggested taking me to the theater, I did not, as I might have done if she had been a Negro, find a way of discouraging her, but agreed that she should pick me up at my house one evening. I then, very cleverly, left all the rest to my mother, who suggested to my father, as I knew she would, that it would not be very nice to let such a kind woman make the trip for nothing. Also, since it was a schoolteacher, I imagine that my mother countered the idea of sin with the idea of "education," which word, even with my father, carried a kind of bitter weight.

Before the teacher came my father took me aside to ask *why* she was coming, what *interest* she could possibly have in our house, in a boy like me. I said I didn't know but I, too, suggested that it had something to do with education. And I understood that my father was waiting for me to say something—I didn't quite know what; perhaps that I wanted his protection against this teacher and her "education." I said none of these things and the teacher came and we went out. It was clear, during the brief interview in our living room, that my father was agreeing very much against his will and that he would have refused permission if he had dared. The fact that he did not dare caused me to despise him: I had no way of knowing that he was facing in that living room a wholly unprecedented and frightening situation.

Later, when my father had been laid off from his job, this woman became very important to us. She was really a very sweet and generous woman and went to a great deal of trouble to be of help to us, particularly during one awful winter. My mother called her by the highest name she knew: she said she was a "christian." My father could scarcely disagree but during the four or five years of our relatively close association he never trusted her and was always trying to surprise in her open, Midwestern face the genuine, cunningly hidden, and hideous motivation. In later years, particularly when it began to be clear that this "education" of mine was going to lead me to perdition, he became more explicit and warned me that my white friends in high school were not really my friends and that I would see, when I was older, how white people would do anything to keep a Negro down. Some of them could be nice, he admitted, but none of them were to be trusted and most of them were not even nice. The best thing was to have as little to do with them as possible.

I did not feel this way and I was certain, in my innocence, that I never would.

But the year which preceded my father's death had made a great change in my life. I had been living in New Jersey, working in defense plants, working and living among southerners, white and black. I knew about the south, of course, and about how southerners treated Negroes and how they expected them to behave, but it had never entered my mind that anyone would look at me and expect *me* to behave that way. I learned in New Jersey that to be a Negro meant, precisely, that one was never looked at but was simply at the mercy of the reflexes the color of one's skin caused in other people. I acted in New Jersey as I had always acted, that is as though I thought a great deal of myself — I had to *act* that way — with results that were, simply, unbelievable. I had scarcely arrived before I had earned the enmity, which was extraordinarily ingenious, of all my superiors and nearly all my co-workers. In the beginning, to make matters worse, I simply did not know what was happening. I did not know what I had done, and I shortly began to wonder what *anyone* could possibly do, to bring about such unanimous, active, and unbearably vocal hostility. I knew about Jim Crow but I had never experienced it. I went to the same self-service restaurant three times and stood with all the Princeton boys before the counter, waiting for a hamburger and coffee; it was always an extraordinarily long time before anything was set before me; but it was not until the fourth visit that I learned that, in fact, nothing had ever been set before me: I had simply picked something up. Negroes were not served there, I was told, and they had been waiting for me to realize that I was always the only Negro present. Once I was told this, I determined to go there all the time. But now they were ready for me and, though some dreadful scenes were subsequently enacted in that restaurant, I never ate there again.

It was the same story all over New Jersey, in bars, bowling alleys, diners, places to live. I was always being forced to leave, silently, or with mutual imprecations. I very shortly became notorious and children giggled behind me when I passed and their elders whispered or shouted — they really believed that I was mad. And it did begin to work on my mind, of course; I began to be afraid to go anywhere and to compensate for this I went places to which I really should not have gone and where, God knows, I had no desire to be. My reputation in town naturally enhanced my reputation at work and my working day became one long series of acrobatics designed to keep me out of trouble. I cannot say that these acrobatics succeeded. It began to seem that the machinery of the organization I worked for was turning over, day and night, with but one aim: to eject me. I was fired once, and contrived, with the aid of a friend from New York, to get back on the payroll; was fired again, and bounced back again. It took a while to fire me for the third time, but the third time took. There were no loopholes anywhere. There was not even any way of getting back inside the gates.

That year in New Jersey lives in my mind as though it were the year   15
during which, having an unsuspected predilection for it, I first contracted some dread, chronic disease, the unfailing symptom of which is
a kind of blind fever, a pounding in the skull and fire in the bowels.
Once this disease is contracted, one can never be really carefree again,
for the fever, without an instant's warning, can recur at any moment.
It can wreck more important things than race relations. There is not
a Negro alive who does not have this rage in his blood—one has
the choice, merely, of living with it consciously or surrendering to it. As
for me, this fever has recurred in me, and does, and will until the day
I die.

My last night in New Jersey, a white friend from New York took me
to the nearest big town, Trenton, to go to the movies and have a few
drinks. As it turned out, he also saved me from, at the very least, a violent
whipping. Almost every detail of that night stands out very clearly in my
memory. I even remember the name of the movie we saw because its title
impressed me as being so patly ironical. It was a movie about the German
occupation of France, starring Maureen O'Hara and Charles Laughton
and called *This Land Is Mine*. I remember the name of the diner we
walked into when the movie ended: it was the "American Diner." When
we walked in the counterman asked what we wanted and I remember answering with the casual sharpness which had become my habit: "We want
a hamburger and a cup of coffee, what do you think we want?" I do not
know why, after a year of such rebuffs, I so completely failed to anticipate
his answer, which was, of course, "We don't serve Negroes here." This
reply failed to discompose me, at least for the moment. I made some sar-
donic comment about the name of the diner and we walked out into the
streets.

This was the time of what was called the "brownout," when the
lights in all American cities were very dim. When we reentered the streets
something happened to me which had the force of an optical illusion, or
a nightmare. The streets were very crowded and I was facing north. People were moving in every direction but it seemed to me, in that instant,
that all of the people I could see, and many more than that, were moving
toward me, against me, and that everyone was white. I remember how
their faces gleamed. And I felt, like a physical sensation, a *click* at the
nape of my neck as though some interior string connecting my head to
my body had been cut. I began to walk. I heard my friend call after me,
but I ignored him. Heaven only knows what was going on in his mind,
but he had the good sense not to touch me—I don't know what would
have happened if he had—and to keep me in sight. I don't know what
was going on in my mind, either; I certainly had no conscious plan. I
wanted to do something to crush these white faces, which were crushing

me. I walked for perhaps a block or two until I came to an enormous, glittering, and fashionable restaurant in which I knew not even the intercession of the Virgin would cause me to be served. I pushed through the doors and took the first vacant seat I saw, at a table for two, and waited.

I do not know how long I waited and I rather wonder, until today, what I could possibly have looked like. Whatever I looked like, I frightened the waitress who shortly appeared, and the moment she appeared all of my fury flowed toward her. I hated her for her white face, and for her great, astounded, frightened eyes. I felt that if she found a black man so frightening I would make her fright worthwhile.

She did not ask me what I wanted, but repeated, as though she had learned it somewhere, "We don't serve Negroes here." She did not say it with the blunt, derisive hostility to which I had grown so accustomed, but, rather, with a note of apology in her voice, and fear. This made me colder and more murderous than ever. I felt I had to do something with my hands. I wanted her to come close enough for me to get her neck between my hands.

So I pretended not to have understood her, hoping to draw her closer.   20
And she did step a very short step closer, with her pencil poised incongruously over her pad, and repeated the formula: ". . . don't serve Negroes here."

Somehow, with the repetition of that phrase, which was already ringing in my head like a thousand bells of a nightmare, I realized that she would never come any closer and that I would have to strike from a distance. There was nothing on the table but an ordinary watermug half full of water, and I picked this up and hurled it with all my strength at her. She ducked and it missed her and shattered against the mirror behind the bar. And, with that sound, my frozen blood abruptly thawed, I returned from wherever I had been, I *saw*, for the first time, the restaurant, the people with their mouths open, already, as it seemed to me, rising as one man, and I realized what I had done, and where I was, and I was frightened. I rose and began running for the door. A round, potbellied man grabbed me by the nape of the neck just as I reached the doors and began to beat me about the face. I kicked him and got loose and ran into the streets. My friend whispered, *"Run!"* and I ran.

My friend stayed outside the restaurant long enough to misdirect my pursuers and the police, who arrived, he told me, at once. I do not know what I said to him when he came to my room that night. I could not have said much. I felt, in the oddest, most awful way, that I had somehow betrayed him. I lived it over and over and over again, the way one relives an automobile accident after it has happened and one finds oneself alone and safe. I could not get over two facts, both equally difficult for the imagination to grasp, and one was that I could have been murdered. But the other was that I had been ready to commit murder. I saw nothing very clearly but I did see this: that my life, my *real* life, was in danger, and not from anything other people might do but from the hatred I carried in my own heart.

TWO

I had returned home around the second week in June — in great haste because it seemed that my father's death and my mother's confinement were both but a matter of hours. In the case of my mother, it soon became clear that she had simply made a miscalculation. This had always been her tendency and I don't believe that a single one of us arrived in the world, or has since arrived anywhere else, on time. But none of us dawdled so intolerably about the business of being born as did my baby sister. We sometimes amused ourselves, during those endless, stifling weeks, by picturing the baby sitting within in the safe, warm dark, bitterly regretting the necessity of becoming a part of our chaos and stubbornly putting it off as long as possible. I understood her perfectly and congratulated her on showing such good sense so soon. Death, however, sat as purposefully at my father's bedside as life stirred within my mother's womb and it was harder to understand why he so lingered in that long shadow. It seemed that he had bent, and for a long time, too, all of his energies toward dying. Now death was ready for him but my father held back.

All of Harlem, indeed, seemed to be infected by waiting. I had never before known it to be so violently still. Racial tensions throughout this country were exacerbated during the early years of the war, partly because the labor market brought together hundreds of thousands of ill-prepared people and partly because Negro soldiers, regardless of where they were born, received their military training in the south. What happened in defense plants and army camps had repercussions, naturally, in every Negro ghetto. The situation in Harlem had grown bad enough for clergymen, policemen, educators, politicians, and social workers to assert in one breath that there was no "crime wave" and to offer, in the very next breath, suggestions as to how to combat it. These suggestions always seemed to involve playgrounds, despite the fact that racial skirmishes were occurring in the playgrounds, too. Playground or not, crime wave or not, the Harlem police force had been augmented in March, and the unrest grew — perhaps, in fact, partly as a result of the ghetto's instinctive hatred of policemen. Perhaps the most revealing news item, out of the steady parade of reports of muggings, stabbings, shootings, assaults, gang wars, and accusations of police brutality, is the item concerning six Negro girls who set upon a white girl in the subway because, as they all too accurately put it, she was stepping on their toes. Indeed she was, all over the nation.

I had never before been so aware of policemen, on foot, on horse- 25 back, on corners, everywhere, always two by two. Nor had I ever been so aware of small knots of people. They were on stoops and on corners and in doorways, and what was striking about them, I think, was that they did not seem to be talking. Never, when I passed these groups, did the usual sound of a curse or a laugh ring out and neither did there seem to be any hum of gossip. There was certainly, on the other hand, occurring between them communication extraordinarily intense. Another thing that was striking was the unexpected diversity of the people who made up these groups. Usually, for example, one would see a group of sharpies standing on the street corner, jiving the passing chicks; or a group of older men, usually, for some reason, in the vicinity of a barber shop, discussing baseball scores, or the numbers, or making rather chilling observations about women they had known. Women, in a general way, tended to be seen less often together — unless they were church women, or very young girls, or prostitutes met together for an unprofessional instant. But that summer I saw the strangest combinations: large, respectable, churchly matrons standing on the stoops or the corners with their hair tied up, together with a girl in sleazy satin whose face bore the marks of gin and the razor, or heavy-set, abrupt, no-nonsense older men, in company with the most disreputable and fanatical "race" men,[1] or these same "race" men with the sharpies, or these sharpies with the churchly women. Seventh Day Adventists and Methodists and Spiritualists seemed to be hobnobbing with Holyrollers and they were all, alike, entangled with the most flagrant disbelievers; something heavy in their stance seemed to indicate that they had all, incredibly, seen a common vision, and on each face there seemed to be the same strange, bitter shadow.

The churchly women and the matter-of-fact, no-nonsense men had children in the Army. The sleazy girls they talked to had lovers there, the sharpies and the "race" men had friends and brothers there. It would have demanded an unquestioning patriotism, happily as uncommon in this country as it is undesirable, for these people not to have been disturbed by the bitter letters they received, by the newspaper stories they read, not to have been enraged by the posters, then to be found all over New York, which described the Japanese as "yellow-bellied Japs." It was only the "race" men, to be sure, who spoke ceaselessly of being revenged — how this vengeance was to be exacted was not clear — for the indignities and dangers suffered by Negro boys in uniform; but everybody felt a directionless, hopeless bitterness, as well as that panic which can scarcely be suppressed when one knows that a human being one loves is beyond one's reach, and in danger. This helplessness and this gnawing uneasiness does something, at length, to even the toughest mind. Perhaps the best way to sum all this up is to say that the people I knew felt, mainly, a peculiar kind of relief when they knew that their boys were being shipped out of the south, to do battle overseas. It was, perhaps, like feeling that the most dangerous part of a dangerous journey had been passed and that

---

[1] *"race" men:* Baldwin seems to be thinking of self-appointed spokesmen for racial consciousness and not serious black leaders. — EDS.

now, even if death should come, it would come with honor and without the complicity of their countrymen. Such a death would be, in short, a fact with which one could hope to live.

It was on the twenty-eighth of July, which I believe was a Wednesday, that I visited my father for the first time during his illness and for the last time in his life. The moment I saw him I knew why I had put off this visit so long. I had told my mother that I did not want to see him because I hated him. But this was not true. It was only that I *had* hated him and I wanted to hold on to this hatred. I did not want to look on him as a ruin: it was not a ruin I had hated. I imagine that one of the reasons people cling to their hates so stubbornly is because they sense, once hate is gone, that they will be forced to deal with pain.

We traveled out to him, his older sister and myself, to what seemed to be the very end of a very Long Island. It was hot and dusty and we wrangled, my aunt and I, all the way out, over the fact that I had recently begun to smoke and, as she said, to give myself airs. But I knew that she wrangled with me because she could not bear to face the fact of her brother's dying. Neither could I endure the reality of her despair, her unstated bafflement as to what had happened to her brother's life, and her own. So we wrangled and I smoked and from time to time she fell into a heavy reverie. Covertly, I watched her face, which was the face of an old woman; it had fallen in, the eyes were sunken and lightless; soon she would be dying, too.

In my childhood—it had not been so long ago—I had thought her beautiful. She had been quick-witted and quick-moving and very generous with all the children and each of her visits had been an event. At one time one of my brothers and myself had thought of running away to live with her. Now she could no longer produce out of her handbag some unexpected and yet familiar delight. She made me feel pity and revulsion and fear. It was awful to realize that she no longer caused me to feel affection. The closer we came to the hospital the more querulous she became and at the same time, naturally, grew more dependent on me. Between pity and guilt and fear I began to feel that there was another me trapped in my skull like a jack-in-the-box who might escape my control at any moment and fill the air with screaming.

She began to cry the moment we entered the room and she saw him   30
lying there, all shriveled and still, like a little black monkey. The great, gleaming apparatus which fed him and would have compelled him to be still even if he had been able to move brought to mind, not beneficence, but torture; the tubes entering his arm made me think of pictures I had seen when a child, of Gulliver, tied down by the pygmies on that island. My aunt wept and wept, there was a whistling sound in my father's throat; nothing was said; he could not speak. I wanted to take his hand, to say something. But I do not know what I could have said, even if he could have heard me. He was not really in that room with us, he had at last really embarked on his journey; and though my aunt told me that he said he was going to meet Jesus, I did not hear anything except that

whistling in his throat. The doctor came back and we left, into that unbearable train again, and home. In the morning came the telegram saying
that he was dead. Then the house was suddenly full of relatives, friends,
hysteria, and confusion and I quickly left my mother and the children to
the care of those impressive women, who, in Negro communities at least,
automatically appear at times of bereavement armed with lotions, proverbs,
and patience, and an ability to cook. I went downtown. By the time I returned, later the same day, my mother had been carried to the hospital
and the baby had been born.

THREE

For my father's funeral I had nothing black to wear and this posed a
nagging problem all day long. It was one of those problems, simple, or
impossible of solution, to which the mind insanely clings in order to
avoid the mind's real trouble. I spent most of that day at the downtown
apartment of a girl I knew, celebrating my birthday with whisky and
wondering what to wear that night. When planning a birthday celebration one naturally does not expect that it will be up against competition
from a funeral and this girl had anticipated taking me out that night, for
a big dinner and a night club afterwards. Sometime during the course of
that long day we decided that we would go out anyway, when my father's
funeral service was over. I imagine I decided it, since, as the funeral hour
approached, it became clearer and clearer to me that I would not know
what to do with myself when it was over. The girl, stifling her very lively
concern as to the possible effects of the whisky on one of my father's chief
mourners, concentrated on being conciliatory and practically helpful. She
found a black shirt for me somewhere and ironed it and, dressed in the
darkest pants and jacket I owned, and slightly drunk, I made my way to
my father's funeral.

The chapel was full, but not packed, and very quiet. There were,
mainly, my father's relatives, and his children, and here and there I saw
faces I had not seen since childhood, the faces of my father's one-time
friends. They were very dark and solemn now, seeming somehow to suggest that they had known all along that something like this would happen. Chief among the mourners was my aunt, who had quarreled with
my father all his life; by which I do not mean to suggest that her mourning was insincere or that she had not loved him. I suppose that she was
one of the few people in the world who had, and their incessant quarrel-
ing proved precisely the strength of the tie that bound them. The only
other person in the world, as far as I knew, whose relationship to my father rivaled my aunt's in depth was my mother, who was not there.

It seemed to me, of course, that it was a very long funeral. But it was,
if anything, a rather shorter funeral than most, nor, since there were no
overwhelming, uncontrollable expressions of grief, could it be called—if I

dare to use the word—successful. The minister who preached my father's funeral sermon was one of the few my father had still been seeing as he neared his end. He presented to us in his sermon a man whom none of us had ever seen—a man thoughtful, patient, and forbearing, a Christian inspiration to all who knew him, and a model for his children. And no doubt the children, in their disturbed and guilty state, were almost ready to believe this; he had been remote enough to be anything and, anyway, the shock of the incontrovertible, that it was really our father lying up there in that casket, prepared the mind for anything. His sister moaned and this grief-stricken moaning was taken as corroboration. The other faces held a dark, noncommittal thoughtfulness. This was not the man they had known, but they had scarcely expected to be confronted with *him*; this was, in a sense deeper than questions of fact, the man they had not known, and the man they had not known may have been the real one. The real man, whoever he had been, had suffered and now he was dead: this was all that was sure and all that mattered now. Every man in the chapel hoped that when his hour came he, too, would be eulogized, which is to say forgiven, and that all of his lapses, greeds, errors, and strayings from the truth would be invested with coherence and looked upon with charity. This was perhaps the last thing human beings could give each other and it was what they demanded, after all, of the Lord. Only the Lord saw the midnight tears, only He was present when one of His children, moaning and wringing hands, paced up and down the room. When one slapped one's child in anger the recoil in the heart reverberated through heaven and became part of the pain of the universe. And when the children were hungry and sullen and distrustful and one watched them, daily, growing wilder, and further away, and running headlong into danger, it was the Lord who knew what the charged heart endured as the strap was laid to the backside; the Lord alone who knew what one *would* have said if one had had, like the Lord, the gift of the living word. It was the Lord who knew of the impossibility every parent in that room faced: how to prepare the child for the day when the child would be despised and how to *create* in the child—by what means?—a stronger antidote to this poison than one had found for oneself. The avenues, side streets, bars, billiard halls, hospitals, police stations, and even the playgrounds of Harlem—not to mention the houses of correction, the jails, and the morgue—testified to the potency of the poison while remaining silent as to the efficacy of whatever antidote, irresistibly raising the question of whether or not such an antidote existed; raising, which was worse, the question of whether or not an antidote was desirable; perhaps poison should be fought with poison. With these several schisms in the mind and with more terrors in the heart than could be named, it was better not to judge the man who had gone down under an impossible burden. It was better to remember: *Thou knowest this man's fall; but thou knowest not his wrassling.*

While the preacher talked and I watched the children—years of changing their diapers, scrubbing them, slapping them, taking them to school, and scolding them had had the perhaps inevitable result of making me love them, though I am not sure I knew this then—my mind was busily breaking out with a rash of disconnected impressions. Snatches of popular songs, indecent jokes, bits of books I had read, movie sequences, faces, voices, political issues—I thought I was going mad; all these impressions suspended, as it were, in the solution of the faint nausea produced in me by the heat and liquor. For a moment I had the impression that my alcoholic breath, inefficiently disguised with chewing gum, filled the entire chapel. Then someone began singing one of my father's favorite songs and, abruptly, I was with him, sitting on his knee, in the hot, enormous, crowded church which was the first church we attended. It was the Abyssinian Baptist Church on 138th Street. We had not gone there long. With this image, a host of others came. I had forgotten, in the rage of my growing up, how proud my father had been of me when I was little. Apparently, I had had a voice and my father had liked to show me off before the members of the church. I had forgotten what he had looked like when he was pleased but now I remembered that he had always been grinning with pleasure when my solos ended. I even remembered certain expressions on his face when he teased my mother—had he loved her? I would never know. And when had it all begun to change? For now it seemed that he had not always been cruel. I remembered being taken for a haircut and scraping my knee on the footrest of the barber's chair and I remembered my father's face as he soothed my crying and applied the stinging iodine. Then I remembered our fights, fights which had been of the worst possible kind because my technique had been silence.

I remembered the one time in all our life together when we had really   35
spoken to each other.

It was on a Sunday and it must have been shortly before I left home. We were walking, just the two of us, in our usual silence, to or from church. I was in high school and had been doing a lot of writing and I was, at about this time, the editor of the high school magazine. But I had also been a Young Minister and had been preaching from the pulpit. Lately, I had been taking fewer engagements and preached as rarely as possible. It was said in the church, quite truthfully, that I was "cooling off."

My father asked me abruptly, "You'd rather write than preach, wouldn't you?"

I was astonished at his question—because it was a real question. I answered, "Yes."

That was all we said. It was awful to remember that that was all we had *ever* said.

The casket now was opened and the mourners were being led up the   40
aisle to look for the last time on the deceased. The assumption was that the family was too overcome with grief to be allowed to make this journey alone and I watched while my aunt was led to the casket and, muffled in black, and shaking, led back to her seat. I disapproved of forcing the children to look on their dead father, considering that the shock of his

death, or, more truthfully, the shock of death as a reality, was already a little more than a child could bear, but my judgment in this matter had been overruled and there they were, bewildered and frightened and very small, being led, one by one, to the casket. But there is also something very gallant about children at such moments. It has something to do with their silence and gravity and with the fact that one cannot help them. Their legs, somehow, seem *exposed*, so that it is at once incredible and terribly clear that their legs are all they have to hold them up.

I had not wanted to go to the casket myself and I certainly had not wished to be led there, but there was no way of avoiding either of these forms. One of the deacons led me up and I looked on my father's face. I cannot say that it looked like him at all. His blackness had been equivocated by powder and there was no suggestion in that casket of what his power had or could have been. He was simply an old man dead, and it was hard to believe that he had ever given anyone either joy or pain. Yet, his life filled that room. Further up the avenue his wife was holding his newborn child. Life and death so close together, and love and hatred, and right and wrong, said something to me which I did not want to hear concerning man, concerning the life of man.

After the funeral, while I was downtown desperately celebrating my birthday, a Negro soldier, in the lobby of the Hotel Braddock, got into a fight with a white policeman over a Negro girl. Negro girls, white policemen, in or out of uniform, and Negro males—in or out of uniform—were part of the furniture of the lobby of the Hotel Braddock and this was certainly not the first time such an incident had occurred. It was destined, however, to receive an unprecedented publicity, for the fight between the policeman and the soldier ended with the shooting of the soldier. Rumor, flowing immediately to the streets outside, stated that the soldier had been shot in the back, an instantaneous and revealing invention, and that the soldier had died protecting a Negro woman. The facts were somewhat different—for example, the soldier had not been shot in the back, and was not dead, and the girl seems to have been as dubious a symbol of womanhood as her white counterpart in Georgia usually is, but no one was interested in the facts. They preferred the invention because this invention expressed and corroborated their hates and fears so perfectly. It is just as well to remember that people are always doing this. Perhaps many of those legends, including Christianity, to which the world clings began their conquest of the world with just some such concerted surrender to distortion. The effect, in Harlem, of this particular legend was like the effect of a lit match in a tin of gasoline. The mob gathered before the doors of the Hotel Braddock simply began to swell and to spread in every direction, and Harlem exploded.

The mob did not cross the ghetto lines. It would have been easy, for example, to have gone over Morningside Park on the west side or to have crossed the Grand Central railroad tracks at 125th Street on the east side, to wreak havoc in white neighborhoods. The mob seems to have been mainly interested in something more potent and real than the white face, that is, in white power, and the principal damage done during the riot of the summer of 1943 was to white business establishments in Harlem. It might have been a far bloodier story, of course, if, at the hour the riot began, these establishments had still been open. From the Hotel Braddock the mob fanned out, east and west along 125th Street, and for the entire length of Lenox, Seventh, and Eighth avenues. Along each of these avenues, and along each major side street—116th, 125th, 135th, and so on—bars, stores, pawnshops, restaurants, even little luncheonettes had been smashed open and entered and looted—looted, it might be added, with more haste than efficiency. The shelves really looked as though a bomb had struck them. Cans of beans and soup and dog food, along with toilet paper, corn flakes, sardines and milk tumbled every which way, and abandoned cash registers and cases of beer leaned crazily out of the splintered windows and were strewn along the avenues. Sheets, blankets, and clothing of every description formed a kind of path, as though people had dropped them while running. I truly had not realized that Harlem *had* so many stores until I saw them all smashed open; the first time the word *wealth* ever entered my mind in relation to Harlem was when I saw it scattered in the streets. But one's first, incongruous impression of plenty was countered immediately by an impression of waste. None of this was doing anybody any good. It would have been better to have left the plate glass as it had been and the goods lying in the stores.

It would have been better, but it would also have been intolerable, for Harlem had needed something to smash. To smash something is the ghetto's chronic need. Most of the time it is the members of the ghetto who smash each other, and themselves. But as long as the ghetto walls are standing there will always come a moment when these outlets do not work. That summer, for example, it was not enough to get into a fight on Lenox Avenue, or curse out one's cronies in the barber shops. If ever, indeed, the violence which fills Harlem's churches, pool halls, and bars erupts outward in a more direct fashion, Harlem and its citizens are likely to vanish in an apocalyptic flood. That this is not likely to happen is due to a great many reasons, most hidden and powerful among them the Negro's real relation to the white American. This relation prohibits, simply, anything as uncomplicated and satisfactory as pure hatred. In order really to hate white people, one has to blot so much out of the mind—and the heart—that this hatred itself becomes an exhausting and self-destructive pose. But this does not mean, on the other hand, that love comes easily: the white world is too powerful, too complacent, too ready with gratuitous humiliation, and, above all, too ignorant and too innocent for that. One is absolutely forced to make perpetual qualifications and one's own reactions are always canceling each other out. It is this, really, which has driven so many people mad, both white and black. One is always in the position of having to decide between amputation and gangrene. Amputation is swift but time may prove that the amputation was not necessary—or one may delay the amputation too long. Gangrene is slow, but it is impossible to be sure that one is reading one's symptoms right. The idea of going through life as a cripple is more than one can bear, and equally unbearable is the risk of swelling up slowly, in agony, with poison. And the trouble, finally, is that the risks are real even if the choices do not exist.

"But as for me and my house," my father had said, "we will serve the 45 Lord." I wondered, as we drove him to his resting place, what this line had meant for him. I had heard him preach it many times. I had preached it once myself, proudly giving it an interpretation different from my father's. Now the whole thing came back to me, as though my father and I were on our way to Sunday school and I were memorizing the golden text: *And if it seem evil unto you to serve the Lord, choose you this day whom you will serve; whether the gods which your fathers served that were on the other side of the flood, or the gods of the Amorites, in whose land ye dwell: but as for me and my house, we will serve the Lord.* I suspected in these familiar lines a meaning which had never been there for me before. All of my father's texts and songs, which I had decided were meaningless, were arranged before me at his death like empty bottles, waiting to hold the meaning which life would give them for me. This was his legacy: nothing is ever escaped. That bleakly memorable morning I hated the unbelievable streets and the Negroes and whites who had, equally, made them that way. But I knew that it was folly, as my father would have said, this bitterness was folly. It was necessary to hold on to the things that mattered. The dead man mattered, the new life mattered; blackness and whiteness did not matter; to believe that they did was to acquiesce in one's own destruction. Hatred, which could destroy so much, never failed to destroy the man who hated and this was an immutable law.

It began to seem that one would have to hold in the mind forever two ideas which seemed to be in opposition. The first idea was acceptance, the acceptance, totally without rancor, of life as it is, and men as they are: in the light of this idea, it goes without saying that injustice is a commonplace. But this did not mean that one could be complacent, for the second idea was of equal power: that one must never, in one's own life, accept these injustices as commonplace but must fight them with all one's strength. This fight begins, however, in the heart and it now had been laid to my charge to keep my own heart free of hatred and despair. This intimation made my heart heavy and, now that my father was irrecoverable, I wished that he had been beside me so that I could have searched his face for the answers which only the future would give me now.

The Reader's Presence

1. Why does Baldwin open with three events: his father's death, his youngest sibling's birth, and the race riots in Detroit and Harlem? How did the death of his father serve to change Baldwin's thinking

about how he would deal with racism in his life? How does Baldwin make peace with his father's memory?

2. At the end of the essay, Baldwin remembers a biblical passage his father used to quote. How does Baldwin reinterpret the passage after his father's death? What does it mean in the context of being his father's son? How does it help him make sense of the race riots in Harlem?

3. Examine Baldwin's description of the Harlem riots in the third section of his essay. How does he approach the riots as a native of Harlem and as an African American? What explanations does he give for the violence? How does he use the riots to explain the relations between white and black America? Compare Baldwin's discussion of the Harlem race riots to the description of the Detroit riots in James Agee's "America, Look at Your Shame!" (page 625). How do their discussions of the riots differ, and why? What concerns do the two men share?

THE WRITER AT WORK

James Baldwin on Black English

In the following piece, Baldwin takes up a subject that is periodically scrutinized by the American mass media: Is black English a language and, if so, what kind of language is it? Whatever its current status in the eyes of the dominant society, black English is an indisputable fact of everyday life for many Americans. When Baldwin writes that blacks have "endured and transcended" American racism by means of language, he echoes William Faulkner's belief that our compulsion to talk is what will save the human race.

Since Baldwin wrote this piece in 1979, the language he so ardently defends as necessary to African American strength in the face of "brutal necessity" (that is, in defense against racism) has entered the mainstream through the spread of hip-hop culture. What might Baldwin say about white speakers of Black English? Are they simply another example of the appropriation of subcultural forms by the dominant culture, a means of containing or defusing resistance? The "rules of the language are dictated by what the language must convey," Baldwin writes. Who is using black English today? For what purposes?

The argument concerning the use, or the status, or the reality, of black English is rooted in American history and has absolutely nothing to do with the question the argument supposes itself to be posing. The argument has nothing to do with language itself but with the *role* of language. Language, incontestably, reveals the speaker. Language, also, far more dubiously, is meant to define the other—and, in this case, the other is refusing to be defined by a language that has never been able to recognize him.

People evolve a language in order to describe and thus control their circumstances, or in order not to be submerged by a reality that they cannot articulate. (And, if they cannot articulate it, they *are* submerged.) A Frenchman living in Paris speaks a subtly and crucially different language from that of the man living in Marseilles; neither sounds very much like a man living in Quebec; and they would all have great difficulty in apprehending what the man from Guadeloupe, or Martinique, is saying, to say nothing of the man from Senegal—although the "common" language of all these areas is French. But each has paid, and is paying, a different price for this "common" language, in which, as it turns out, they are not saying, and cannot be saying, the same things: They each have very different realities to articulate, or control.

What joins all languages, and all men, is the necessity to confront life, in order, not inconceivably, to outwit death: The price for this is the acceptance, and achievement, of one's temporal identity. So that, for example, though it is not taught in the schools (and this has the potential of becoming a political issue) the south of France still clings to its ancient and musical Provençal, which resists being described as a "dialect." And much of the tension in the Basque countries, and in Wales, is due to the Basque and Welsh determination not to allow their languages to be destroyed. This determination also feeds the flames in Ireland, for among the many indignities the Irish have been forced to undergo at English hands is the English contempt for their language.

It goes without saying, then, that language is also a political instrument, means, and proof of power. It is the most vivid and crucial key to identity: It reveals the private identity, and connects one with, or divorces one from, the larger, public, or communal identity. There have been, and are, times, and places, when to speak a certain language could be dangerous, even fatal. Or, one may speak the same language, but in such a way that one's antecedents are revealed, or (one hopes) hidden. This is true in France, and is absolutely true in England: The range (and reign) of accents on that damp little island make England coherent for the English and totally incomprehensible for everyone else. To open your mouth in England is (if I may use black English) to "put your business in the street": You have confessed your parents, your youth, your school, your salary, your self-esteem, and, alas, your future.

Now, I do not know what white Americans would sound like if there 5 had never been any black people in the United States, but they would not sound the way they sound. *Jazz*, for example, is a very specific sexual term, as in *jazz me, baby*, but white people purified it into the Jazz Age. *Sock it to me*, which means, roughly, the same thing, has been adopted by Nathaniel Hawthorne's descendants with no qualms or hesitations at all, along with *let it all hang out* and *right on! Beat to his socks* which was once the black's most total and despairing image of poverty, was transformed into a thing called the Beat Generation, which phenomenon was, largely, composed of *uptight*, middle-class white people, imitating poverty, trying to *get down*, to get *with it*, doing their *thing*, doing their despairing best to be *funky*, which we, the blacks, never dreamed of doing—we *were* funky, baby, like *funky* was going out of style.

Now, no one can eat his cake and have it, too, and it is late in the day to attempt to penalize black people for having created a language that permits the nation its only glimpse of reality, a language without which the nation would be even more *whipped* than it is.

I say that the present skirmish is rooted in American history, and it is. Black English is the creation of the black diaspora. Blacks came to the United States chained to each other, but from different tribes: Neither could speak the other's language. If two black people, at that bitter hour of the world's history, had been able to speak to each other, the institution of chattel slavery could never have lasted as long as it did. Subsequently, the slave was given, under the eye, and the gun, of his master, Congo Square, and the Bible—or in other words, and under these conditions, the slave began the formation of the black church, and it is within this unprecedented tabernacle that black English began to be formed. This was not, merely, as in the European example, the adoption of a foreign tongue, but an alchemy that transformed ancient elements into a new language: *A language comes into existence by means of brutal necessity, and the rules of the language are dictated by what the language must convey.*

There was a moment, in time, and in this place, when my brother, or my mother, or my father, or my sister, had to convey to me, for example, the danger in which I was standing from the white man standing just behind me, and to convey this with a speed, and in a language, that the white man could not possibly understand, and that, indeed, he cannot understand, until today. He cannot afford to understand it. This understanding would reveal to him too much about himself, and smash that mirror before which he has been frozen for so long.

Now, if this passion, this skill, this (to quote Toni Morrison) "sheer intelligence," this incredible music, the mighty achievement of having brought a people utterly unknown to, or despised by "history"—to have brought this people to their present, troubled, troubling, and unassailable and unanswerable place—if this absolutely unprecedented journey does not indicate that black English is a language, I am curious to know what definition of language is to be trusted.

A people at the center of the Western world, and in the midst of so hostile a population, has not endured and transcended by means of what is patronizingly called a "dialect." We, the blacks, are in trouble, certainly, but we are not doomed, and we are not inarticulate because we are not compelled to defend a morality that we know to be a lie.

The brutal truth is that the bulk of white people in America never had any interest in educating black people, except as this could serve white purposes. It is not the black child's language that is in question, it is not his language that is despised: It is his experience. A child cannot be taught by anyone who despises him, and a child cannot afford to be fooled. A child cannot be taught by anyone whose demand, essentially, is that the child repudiate his experience, and all that gives him sustenance, and enter a limbo in which he will no longer be black, and in which he knows that he can never become white. Black people have lost too many black children that way.

And, after all, finally, in a country with standards so untrustworthy, a country that makes heroes of so many criminal mediocrities, a country unable to face why so many of the nonwhite are in prison, or on the needle, or standing, futureless, in the streets — it may very well be that both the child, and his elder, have concluded that they have nothing whatever to learn from the people of a country that has managed to learn so little.

Raymond Carver

My Father's Life

Son of a laborer and a homemaker in Clatskanie, Oregon, Raymond Carver (1938–1988) resembled the characters in the short stories for which he is widely acclaimed. Once a manual laborer, a gas station attendant, and a janitor himself, Carver acquired his vision of the working class and the desperate lives of ordinary folk through direct experience. The Pacific Northwest of Carver's writing is peopled with types such as "the waitress, the bus driver, the mechanic, the hotel keeper" — people Carver feels are "good people." First published in Esquire *in 1984, "My Father's Life," Carver's account of his father's hardships during the Great Depression, puts a biographical spin on these "good people." Carver's short story collections,* Will You Please Be Quiet, Please? *(1976),* Cathedral *(1984), and* Where I'm Calling From *(1988), were all nominated for the National Book Critics Circle Award. The latter two collections were also nominated for the Pulitzer Prize for fiction in 1985 and 1989, respectively. Carver's poetry is collected in* Where Water Comes Together with Other Water *(1985), recipient of the 1986 Los Angeles Times Book Prize;* Ultramarine *(1986); and* A New Path to the Waterfall *(1989).*

In his essay "On Writing," Carver states, "Writers don't need tricks or gimmicks or even necessarily to be the smartest fellows on the block. At the risk of appearing foolish, a writer sometimes needs to be able to just stand and gape at this or that thing — a sunset or an old shoe — in absolute and simple amazement."

For an example of Carver's fiction, see "The Bath" (page 895).

My dad's name was Clevie Raymond Carver. His family called him Raymond and friends called him C. R. I was named Raymond Clevie Carver, Jr. I hated the "Junior" part. When I was little my dad called me

Frog, which was okay. But later, like everybody else in the family, he began calling me Junior. He went on calling me this until I was thirteen or fourteen and announced that I wouldn't answer to that name any longer. So he began calling me Doc. From then until his death, on June 17, 1967, he called me Doc, or else Son.

When he died, my mother telephoned my wife with the news. I was away from my family at the time, between lives, trying to enroll in the School of Library Science at the University of Iowa. When my wife answered the phone, my mother blurted out, "Raymond's dead!" For a moment, my wife thought my mother was telling her that I was dead. Then my mother made it clear *which* Raymond she was talking about and my wife said, "Thank God. I thought you meant *my* Raymond."

My dad walked, hitched rides, and rode in empty boxcars when he went from Arkansas to Washington State in 1934, looking for work. I don't know whether he was pursuing a dream when he went out to Washington. I doubt it. I don't think he dreamed much. I believe he was simply looking for steady work at decent pay. Steady work was meaningful work. He picked apples for a time and then landed a construction laborer's job on the Grand Coulee Dam. After he'd put aside a little money, he bought a car and drove back to Arkansas to help his folks, my grandparents, pack up for the move west. He said later that they were about to starve down there, and this wasn't meant as a figure of speech. It was during that short while in Arkansas, in a town called Leola, that my mother met my dad on the sidewalk as he came out of a tavern.

"He was drunk," she said. "I don't know why I let him talk to me. His eyes were glittery. I wish I'd had a crystal ball." They'd met once, a year or so before, at a dance. He'd had girlfriends before her, my mother told me. "Your dad always had a girlfriend, even after we married. He was my first and last. I never had another man. But I didn't miss anything."

They were married by a justice of the peace on the day they left for Washington, this big, tall country girl and a farmhand-turned-construction worker. My mother spent her wedding night with my dad and his folks, all of them camped beside the road in Arkansas.   5

In Omak, Washington, my dad and mother lived in a little place not much bigger than a cabin. My grandparents lived next door. My dad was still working on the dam, and later, with the huge turbines producing electricity and the water backed up for a hundred miles into Canada, he stood in the crowd and heard Franklin D. Roosevelt when he spoke at the construction site. "He never mentioned those guys who died building that dam," my dad said. Some of his friends had died there, men from Arkansas, Oklahoma, and Missouri.

He then took a job in a sawmill in Clatskanie, Oregon, a little town alongside the Columbia River. I was born there, and my mother has a picture of my dad standing in front of the gate to the mill, proudly holding me up to face the camera. My bonnet is on crooked and about to come untied. His hat is pushed back on his forehead, and he's wearing a big grin.

Was he going in to work or just finishing his shift? It doesn't matter. In either case, he had a job and a family. These were his salad days.

In 1941 we moved to Yakima, Washington, where my dad went to work as a saw filer, a skilled trade he'd learned in Clatskanie. When war broke out, he was given a deferment because his work was considered necessary to the war effort. Finished lumber was in demand by the armed services, and he kept his saws so sharp they could shave the hair off your arm.

After my dad had moved us to Yakima, he moved his folks into the same neighborhood. By the mid-1940s the rest of my dad's family—his brother, his sister, and her husband, as well as uncles, cousins, nephews, and most of their extended family and friends—had come out from Arkansas. All because my dad came out first. The men went to work at Boise Cascade, where my dad worked, and the women packed apples in the canneries. And in just a little while, it seemed—according to my mother—everybody was better off than my dad. "Your dad couldn't keep money," my mother said. "Money burned a hole in his pocket. He was always doing for others."

The first house I clearly remember living in, at 1515 South Fifteenth   10
Street, in Yakima, had an outdoor toilet. On Halloween night, or just any night, for the hell of it, neighbor kids, kids in their early teens, would carry our toilet away and leave it next to the road. My dad would have to get somebody to help him bring it home. Or these kids would take the toilet and stand it in somebody else's backyard. Once they actually set it on fire. But ours wasn't the only house that had an outdoor toilet. When I was old enough to know what I was doing, I threw rocks at the other toilets when I'd see someone go inside. This was called bombing the toilets. After a while, though, everyone went to indoor plumbing until, suddenly, our toilet was the last outdoor one in the neighborhood. I remember the shame I felt when my third-grade teacher, Mr. Wise, drove me home from school one day. I asked him to stop at the house just before ours, claiming I lived there.

I can recall what happened one night when my dad came home late to find that my mother had locked all the doors on him from the inside. He was drunk, and we could feel the house shudder as he rattled the door. When he'd managed to force open a window, she hit him between the eyes with a colander and knocked him out. We could see him down there on the grass. For years afterward, I used to pick up this colander—it was as heavy as a rolling pin—and imagine what it would feel like to be hit in the head with something like that.

It was during this period that I remember my dad taking me into the bedroom, sitting me down on the bed, and telling me that I might have to go live with my Aunt LaVon for a while. I couldn't understand what I'd done that meant I'd have to go away from home to live. But this, too—whatever prompted it—must have blown over, more or less, anyway, because we stayed together, and I didn't have to go live with her or anyone else.

I remember my mother pouring his whiskey down the sink. Sometimes she'd pour it all out and sometimes, if she was afraid of getting caught, she'd only pour half of it out and then add water to the rest. I tasted some of his whiskey once myself. It was terrible stuff, and I don't see how anybody could drink it.

After a long time without one, we finally got a car, in 1949 or 1950, a 1938 Ford. But it threw a rod the first week we had it, and my dad had to have the motor rebuilt.

"We drove the oldest car in town," my mother said. "We could have had a Cadillac for all he spent on car repairs." One time she found someone else's tube of lipstick on the floorboard, along with a lacy handkerchief. "See this?" she said to me. "Some floozy left this in the car."   15

Once I saw her take a pan of warm water into the bedroom where my dad was sleeping. She took his hand from under the covers and held it in the water. I stood in the doorway and watched. I wanted to know what was going on. This would make him talk in his sleep, she told me. There were things she needed to know, things she was sure he was keeping from her.

Every year or so, when I was little, we would take the North Coast Limited across the Cascade Range from Yakima to Seattle and stay in the Vance Hotel and eat, I remember, at a place called the Dinner Bell Cafe. Once we went to Ivar's Acres of Clams and drank glasses of warm clam broth.

In 1956, the year I was to graduate from high school, my dad quit his job at the mill in Yakima and took a job in Chester, a little sawmill town in northern California. The reasons given at the time for his taking the job had to do with a higher hourly wage and the vague promise that he might, in a few years' time, succeed to the job of head filer in this new mill. But I think, in the main, that my dad had grown restless and simply wanted to try his luck elsewhere. Things had gotten a little too predictable for him in Yakima. Also, the year before, there had been the deaths, within six months of each other, of both his parents.

But just a few days after graduation, when my mother and I were packed to move to Chester, my dad penciled a letter to say he'd been sick for a while. He didn't want us to worry, he said, but he'd cut himself on a saw. Maybe he'd got a tiny sliver of steel in his blood. Anyway, something had happened and he'd had to miss work, he said. In the same mail was an unsigned postcard from somebody down there telling my mother that my dad was about to die and that he was drinking "raw whiskey."

When we arrived in Chester, my dad was living in a trailer that belonged to the company. I didn't recognize him immediately. I guess for a moment I didn't want to recognize him. He was skinny and pale and looked bewildered. His pants wouldn't stay up. He didn't look like my dad. My mother began to cry. My dad put his arm around her and patted her shoulder vaguely, like he didn't know what this was all about, either. The three of us took up life together in the trailer, and we looked after him as best we could. But my dad was sick, and he couldn't get any better. I worked with him in the mill that summer and part of the fall. We'd   20 get up in the mornings and eat eggs and toast while we listened to the radio, and then go out the door with our lunch pails. We'd pass through the gate together at eight in the morning, and I wouldn't see him again until quitting time. In November I went back to Yakima to be closer to my girlfriend, the girl I'd made up my mind I was going to marry.

He worked at the mill in Chester until the following February, when he collapsed on the job and was taken to the hospital. My mother asked if I would come down there and help. I caught a bus from Yakima to Chester, intending to drive them back to Yakima. But now, in addition to being physically sick, my dad was in the midst of a nervous breakdown, though none of us knew to call it that at the time. During the entire trip back to Yakima, he didn't speak, not even when asked a direct question. ("How do you feel, Raymond?" "You okay, Dad?") He'd communicate, if he communicated at all, by moving his head or by turning his palms up as if to say he didn't know or care. The only time he said anything on the trip, and for nearly a month afterward, was when I was speeding down a gravel road in Oregon and the car muffler came loose. "You were going too fast," he said.

Back in Yakima a doctor saw to it that my dad went to a psychiatrist. My mother and dad had to go on relief, as it was called, and the county paid for the psychiatrist. The psychiatrist asked my dad, "Who is the President?" He'd had a question put to him that he could answer. "Ike," my dad said. Nevertheless, they put him on the fifth floor of Valley Memorial Hospital and began giving him electroshock treatment. I was married by then and about to start my own family. My dad was still locked up when my wife went into this same hospital, just one floor down, to have our first baby. After she had delivered, I went upstairs to give my dad the news. They let me in through a steel door and showed me where I could find him. He was sitting on a couch with a blanket over his lap. *Hey,* I thought. *What in hell is happening to my dad?* I sat down next to him and told him he was a grandfather. He waited a minute and then he said, "I feel like a grandfather." That's all he said. He didn't smile or move. He was in a big room with a lot of other people. Then I hugged him, and he began to cry.

Somehow he got out of there. But now came the years when he couldn't work and just sat around the house trying to figure what next and what he'd done wrong in his life that he'd wound up like this. My mother went from job to crummy job. Much later she referred to that time he was in the hospital, and those years just afterward, as "when Raymond was sick." The word *sick* was never the same for me again.

In 1964, through the help of a friend, he was lucky enough to be hired on at a mill in Klamath, California. He moved down there by himself to see if he could hack it. He lived not far from the mill, in a one-room cabin not much different from the place he and my mother had started out living in when they went west. He scrawled letters to my mother, and if I called she'd read them aloud to me over the phone. In the letters, he said it was touch and go. Every day that he went to work, he felt like it was the most important day of his life. But every day, he told her, made the next day that much easier. He said for her to tell me he said hello. If he couldn't sleep at night, he said, he thought about me and the good times we used to have. Finally, after a couple of months, he regained some of his confidence. He could do the work and didn't think he had to worry that he'd let anybody down ever again. When he was sure, he sent for my mother.

He'd been off from work for six years and had lost everything in that   25
time — home, car, furniture, and appliances, including the big freezer that had been my mother's pride and joy. He'd lost his good name too — Raymond Carver was someone who couldn't pay his bills — and his self-respect was gone. He'd even lost his virility. My mother told my wife, "All during that time Raymond was sick we slept together in the same bed, but we didn't have relations. He wanted to a few times, but nothing happened. I didn't miss it, but I think he wanted to, you know."

During those years I was trying to raise my own family and earn a living. But, one thing and another, we found ourselves having to move a lot. I couldn't keep track of what was going down in my dad's life. But I did have a chance one Christmas to tell him I wanted to be a writer. I might as well have told him I wanted to become a plastic surgeon. "What are you going to write about?" he wanted to know. Then, as if to help me out, he said, "Write about stuff you know about. Write about some of those fishing trips we took." I said I would, but I knew I wouldn't. "Send me what you write," he said. I said I'd do that, but then I didn't. I wasn't writing anything about fishing, and I didn't think he'd particularly care about, or even necessarily understand, what I was writing in those days. Besides, he wasn't a reader. Not the sort, anyway, I imagined I was writing for.

Then he died. I was a long way off, in Iowa City, with things still to say to him. I didn't have the chance to tell him goodbye, or that I thought he was doing great at his new job. That I was proud of him for making a comeback.

My mother said he came in from work that night and ate a big supper. Then he sat at the table by himself and finished what was left of a bottle of whiskey, a bottle she found hidden in the bottom of the garbage under some coffee grounds a day or so later. Then he got up and went to bed, where my mother joined him a little later. But in the night she had to get up and make a bed for herself on the couch. "He was snoring so loud I couldn't sleep," she said. The next morning when she looked in on him, he was on his back with his mouth open, his cheeks caved in. *Graylooking*, she said. She knew he was dead — she didn't need a doctor to tell her that. But she called one anyway, and then she called my wife.

Among the pictures my mother kept of my dad and herself during those early days in Washington was a photograph of him standing in front of a car, holding a beer and a stringer of fish. In the photograph he is wearing his hat back on his forehead and has this awkward grin on his face. I asked her for it and she gave it to me, along with some others. I put it up on my wall, and each time we moved, I took the picture along and put it up on another wall. I looked at it carefully from time to time, trying to figure out some things about my dad, and maybe myself in the process. But I couldn't. My dad just kept moving further and further away from me and back into time. Finally, in the course of another move, I lost the photograph. It was then that I tried to recall it, and at the same time make an attempt to say something about my dad, and how I thought that in some important ways we might be alike. I wrote the poem when I was living in an apartment house in an urban area south of San Francisco, at a time when I found myself, like my dad, having trouble with alcohol. The poem was a way of trying to connect up with him.

PHOTOGRAPH OF MY FATHER IN HIS TWENTY-SECOND YEAR

October. Here in this dank, unfamiliar kitchen
I study my father's embarrassed young man's face.
Sheepish grin, he holds in one hand a string
of spiny yellow perch, in the other
a bottle of Carlsberg beer.

In jeans and flannel shirt, he leans
against the front fender of a 1934 Ford.
He would like to pose brave and hearty for his posterity,
wear his old hat cocked over his ear.
All his life my father wanted to be bold.

But the eyes give him away, and the hands
that limply offer the string of dead perch
and the bottle of beer. Father, I love you,
yet how can I say thank you, I who can't hold my liquor either
and don't even know the places to fish.

The poem is true in its particulars, except that my dad died in June and not October, as the first word of the poem says. I wanted a word with more than one syllable to it to make it linger a little. But more than that, I wanted a month appropriate to what I felt at the time I wrote the poem — a month of short days and failing light, smoke in the air, things perishing. June was summer nights and days, graduations, my wedding anniversary, the birthday of one of my children. June wasn't a month your father died in.

After the service at the funeral home, after we had moved outside, a woman I didn't know came over to me and said, "He's happier where he is now." I stared at this woman until she moved away. I still remember the little knob of a hat she was wearing. Then one of my dad's cousins — I didn't know the man's name — reached out and took my hand. "We all miss him," he said, and I knew he wasn't saying it just to be polite.

I began to weep for the first time since receiving the news. I hadn't been able to before. I hadn't had the time, for one thing. Now, suddenly,

30

I couldn't stop. I held my wife and wept while she said and did what she could do to comfort me there in the middle of that summer afternoon.

I listened to people say consoling things to my mother, and I was glad that my dad's family had turned up, had come to where he was. I thought I'd remember everything that was said and done that day and maybe find a way to tell it sometime. But I didn't. I forgot it all, or nearly. What I do remember is that I heard our name used a lot that afternoon, my dad's name and mine. But I knew they were talking about my dad. *Raymond*, these people kept saying in their beautiful voices out of my childhood. *Raymond*.

The Reader's Presence

1. You may have noticed that Carver begins and ends his essay with a reference to his and his father's name. Of what importance is this information at the opening? What do we learn about his relationship with his father through their names? How do names matter in the final paragraph?

2. Try rereading the essay with particular attention to the conversations between father and son. How many reported conversations can you find? What do the conversations sound like? Can you find any pattern to them? To what extent do these conversations help you understand Carver's relationship with his father?

3. Carver includes one of his own poems in his essay, as do Alice Walker in "Beauty: When the Other Dancer Is the Self" (page 304) and Gloria Anzaldúa in "How to Tame a Wild Tongue" (page 324). How do these writers explore the margins between poetry and prose? What do you think a poem communicates that a passage of prose may not?

Judith Ortiz Cofer

Silent Dancing

Born in Puerto Rico in 1952, Judith Ortiz Cofer moved to New Jersey in 1955. Her poetry has appeared in numerous literary magazines, and several collections of her poems have been published. Her first novel, The Line of the Sun *(1989), was nominated for the Pulitzer Prize. "Silent Dancing" is from Cofer's 1990 essay collection,* Silent Dancing: A Partial Remembrance of a Puerto Rican

Childhood, *which won a PEN/Martha Albrand special citation for nonfiction.
Among her notable books are* The Latin Deli: Prose and Poetry *(1993),* An Island
like You: Stories of the Barrio *(1995),* Woman in Front of the Sun *(2000), and*
The Meaning of Consuelo *(2003).*

*Reflecting on her life as a writer, Cofer has said, "The 'infinite variety' and
power of language interest me. I never cease to experiment with it. As a native
Puerto Rican, my first language was Spanish. It was a challenge, not only to learn
English, but to master it enough to teach it and—the ultimate goal—to write po-
etry in it." Cofer is professor of English and creative writing at the University of
Georgia.*

*We have a home movie of this party. Several times my mother and I
have watched it together, and I have asked questions about the silent rev-
elers coming in and out of focus. It is grainy and of short duration, but it's
a great visual aid to my memory of life at that time. And it is in color—the
only complete scene in color I can recall from those years.*

We lived in Puerto Rico until my brother was born in 1954. Soon
after, because of economic pressures on our growing family, my father
joined the United States Navy. He was assigned to duty on a ship in
Brooklyn Yard—a place of cement and steel that was to be his home
base in the States until his retirement more than twenty years later. He
left the Island first, alone, going to New York City and tracking down his
uncle who lived with his family across the Hudson River in Paterson,
New Jersey. There my father found a tiny apartment in a huge tenement
that had once housed Jewish families but was just being taken over and
transformed by Puerto Ricans, overflowing from New York City. In 1955
he sent for us. My mother was only twenty years old, I was not quite
three, and my brother was a toddler when we arrived at *El Building*, as
the place had been christened by its newest residents.

My memories of life in Paterson during those first few years are all in
shades of gray. Maybe I was too young to absorb vivid colors and details, or
to discriminate between the slate blue of the winter sky and the darker hues
of the snow-bearing clouds, but that single color washes over the whole period. The building we lived in was gray, as were the streets, filled with slush
the first few months of my life there. The coat my father had bought for me
was similar in color and too big; it sat heavily on my thin frame.

I do remember the way the heater pipes banged and rattled, startling
all of us out of sleep until we got so used to the sound that we automatically shut it out or raised our voices above the racket. The hiss from the
valve punctuated my sleep (which has always been fitful) like a nonhuman
presence in the room—a dragon sleeping at the entrance of my childhood.
But the pipes were also a connection to all the other lives being lived
around us. Having come from a house designed for a single family back in
Puerto Rico—my mother's extended-family home—it was curious to
know that strangers lived under our floor and above our heads, and that

the heater pipe went through everyone's apartments. (My first spanking in Paterson came as a result of playing tunes on the pipes in my room to see if there would be an answer.) My mother was as new to this concept of bee-hive life as I was, but she had been given strict orders by my father to keep the doors locked, the noise down, ourselves to ourselves.

It seems that Father had learned some painful lessons about prejudice 5 while searching for an apartment in Paterson. Not until years later did I hear how much resistance he had encountered with landlords who were panick-ing at the influx of Latinos into a neighborhood that had been Jewish for a couple of generations. It made no difference that it was the American phe-nomenon of ethnic turnover which was changing the urban core of Paterson, and that the human flood could not be held back with an accusing finger.

"You Cuban?" one man had asked my father, pointing at his name tag on the Navy uniform—even though my father had the fair skin and light-brown hair of his northern Spanish background, and the name Ortiz is as common in Puerto Rico as Johnson is in the United States.

"No," my father had answered, looking past the finger into his ad-versary's angry eyes. "I'm Puerto Rican."

"Same shit." And the door closed.

My father could have passed as European, but we couldn't. My brother and I both have our mother's black hair and olive skin, and so we lived in El Building and visited our great-uncle and his fair children on the next block. It was their private joke that they were the German branch of the family. Not many years later that area too would be mainly Puerto Rican. It was as if the heart of the city map were being gradually colored brown—*café con leche*[1] brown. Our color.

The movie opens with a sweep of the living room. It is "typical" immi- 10 *grant Puerto Rican decor for the time: The sofa and chairs are square and hard-looking, upholstered in bright colors (blue and yellow in this instance), and covered with the transparent plastic that furniture salesmen then were so adept at convincing women to buy. The linoleum on the floor is light blue; if it had been subjected to spike heels (as it was in most places), there were dime-sized indentations all over it that cannot be seen in this movie. The room is full of people dressed up: dark suits for the men, red dresses for the women. When I have asked my mother why most of the women are in red that night, she has shrugged, "I don't remember. Just a coincidence." She doesn't have my obsession for assigning symbolism to everything.*

The three women in red sitting on the couch are my mother, my eighteen-year-old cousin, and her brother's girlfriend. The novia is just up from the Island, which is apparent in her body language. She sits up for-mally, her dress pulled over her knees. She is a pretty girl, but her posture

---

[1]*café con leche:* Coffee with cream. In Puerto Rico it is sometimes prepared with boiled milk. —Eds.

makes her look insecure, lost in her full-skirted dress, which she has care-fully tucked around her to make room for my gorgeous cousin, her future sister-in-law. My cousin has grown up in Paterson and is in her last year of high school. She doesn't have a trace of what Puerto Ricans call la mancha *(literally, the stain: the mark of the new immigrant—something about the posture, the voice, or the humble demeanor that makes it obvi-ous to everyone the person has just arrived on the mainland). My cousin is wearing a tight, sequined, cocktail dress. Her brown hair has been lightened with peroxide around the bangs, and she is holding a cigarette expertly between her fingers, bringing it up to her mouth in a sensuous arc of her arm as she talks animatedly. My mother, who has come up to sit between the two women, both only a few years younger than herself, is somewhere between the poles they represent in our culture.*

It became my father's obsession to get out of the barrio, and thus we were never permitted to form bonds with the place or with the people who lived there. Yet El Building was a comfort to my mother, who never got over yearning for *la isla*. She felt surrounded by her language: The walls were thin, and voices speaking and arguing in Spanish could be heard all day. *Salsas* blasted out of radios, turned on early in the morning and left on for company. Women seemed to cook rice and beans perpetually—the strong aroma of boiling red kidney beans permeated the hallways.

Though Father preferred that we do our grocery shopping at the super-market when he came home on weekend leaves, my mother insisted that she could cook only with products whose labels she could read. Consequently, during the week I accompanied her and my little brother to *La Bodega*—a hole-in-the-wall grocery store across the street from El Building. There we squeezed down three narrow aisles jammed with various products. Goya's and Libby's—those were the trademarks that were trusted by *her mamá*, so my mother bought many cans of Goya beans, soups, and condiments, as well as little cans of Libby's fruit juices for us. And she also bought Colgate toothpaste and Palmolive soap. (The final *e* is pronounced in both these products in Spanish, so for many years I believed that they were manufac-tured on the Island. I remember my surprise at first hearing a commercial on television in which Colgate rhymed with "ate.") We always lingered at La Bodega, for it was there that Mother breathed best, taking in the familiar aromas of the foods she knew from Mamá's kitchen. It was also there that she got to speak to the other women of El Building without violating out-right Father's dictates against fraternizing with our neighbors.

Yet Father did his best to make our "assimilation" painless. I can still see him carrying a real Christmas tree up several flights of stairs to our apartment, leaving a trail of aromatic pine. He carried it formally, as if it were a flag in a parade. We were the only ones in El Building that I knew of who got presents on both Christmas day and *dia de Reyes*, the day when the Three Kings brought gifts to Christ and to Hispanic children.

Our supreme luxury in El Building was having our own television set. 15
It must have been a result of Father's guilt feelings over the isolation he
had imposed on us, but we were among the first in the barrio to have one.
My brother quickly became an avid watcher of Captain Kangaroo and
Jungle Jim, while I loved all the series showing families. By the time I
started first grade, I could have drawn a map of Middle America as exem-
plified by the lives of characters in "Father Knows Best," "The Donna Reed
Show," "Leave It to Beaver," "My Three Sons," and (my favorite) "Bachelor Father," where John Forsythe treated his adopted teenage daughter like
a princess because he was rich and had a Chinese houseboy to do everything for him. In truth, compared to our neighbors in El Building, *we* were
rich. My father's Navy check provided us with financial security and a standard of life that the factory workers envied. The only thing his money could
not buy us was a place to live away from the barrio—his greatest wish,
Mother's greatest fear.

In the home movie the men are shown next, sitting around a card table
set up in one corner of the living room, playing dominoes. The clack of the
ivory pieces was a familiar sound. I heard it in many houses on the Island
and in many apartments in Paterson. In "Leave It to Beaver," the Cleavers
played bridge in every other episode; in my childhood, the men started
every social occasion with a hotly debated round of dominoes. The women
would sit around and watch, but they never participated in the games.

Here and there you can see a small child. Children were always
brought to parties and, whenever they got sleepy, were put to bed in the
host's bedroom. Babysitting was a concept unrecognized by the Puerto
Rican women I knew: A responsible mother did not leave her children
with any stranger. And in a culture where children are not considered in-
trusive, there was no need to leave the children at home. We went where
our mother went.

Of my preschool years I have only impressions: the sharp bite of the
wind in December as we walked with our parents toward the brightly lit
stores downtown; how I felt like a stuffed doll in my heavy coat, boots,
and mittens; how good it was to walk into the five-and-dime and sit at the
counter drinking hot chocolate. On Saturdays our whole family would
walk downtown to shop at the big department stores on Broadway.
Mother bought all our clothes at Penney's and Sears, and she liked to buy
her dresses at the women's specialty shops like Lerner's and Diana's. At
some point we'd go into Woolworth's and sit at the soda fountain to eat.

We never ran into other Latinos at these stores or when eating out,
and it became clear to me only years later that the women from El Building shopped mainly in other places—stores owned by other Puerto Ricans
or by Jewish merchants who had philosophically accepted our presence in
the city and decided to make us their good customers, if not real neighbors and friends. These establishments were located not downtown but in

the blocks around our street, and they were referred to generically as *La Tienda, El Bazar, La Bodega, La Botánica*. Everyone knew what was meant. These were the stores where your face did not turn a clerk to stone, where your money was as green as anyone else's.

One New Year's Eve we were dressed up like child models in the Sears catalogue: my brother in a miniature man's suit and bow tie, and I in black patent-leather shoes and a frilly dress with several layers of crinoline underneath. My mother wore a bright red dress that night, I remember, and spike heels; her long black hair hung to her waist. Father, who usually wore his Navy uniform during his short visits home, had put on a dark civilian suit for the occasion: We had been invited to his uncle's house for a big celebration. Everyone was excited because my mother's brother Hernan—a bachelor who could indulge himself with luxuries—had bought a home movie camera, which he would be trying out that night.

Even the home movie cannot fill in the sensory details such a gathering left imprinted in a child's brain. The thick sweetness of women's perfumes mixing with the ever-present smells of food cooking in the kitchen: meat and plantain *pasteles*, as well as the ubiquitous rice dish made special with pigeon peas—*gandules*—and seasoned with precious *sofrito*[2] sent up from the Island by somebody's mother or smuggled in by a recent traveler. *Sofrito* was one of the items that women hoarded, since it was hardly ever in stock at La Bodega. It was the flavor of Puerto Rico.

The men drank Palo Viejo rum, and some of the younger ones got weepy. The first time I saw a grown man cry was at a New Year's Eve party: He had been reminded of his mother by the smells in the kitchen. But what I remember most were the boiled *pasteles*—plantain or yucca rectangles stuffed with corned beef or other meats, olives, and many other savory ingredients, all wrapped in banana leaves. Everybody had to fish one out with a fork. There was always a "trick" pastel—one without stuffing—and whoever got that one was the "New Year's Fool."

There was also the music. Long-playing albums were treated like precious china in these homes. Mexican recordings were popular, but the songs that brought tears to my mother's eyes were sung by the melancholy Daniel Santos, whose life as a drug addict was the stuff of legend. Felipe Rodríguez was a particular favorite of couples, since he sang about faithless women and brokenhearted men. There is a snatch of one lyric that has stuck in my mind like a needle on a worn groove: *De piedra ha de ser mi cama, de piedra la cabezera . . . la mujer que a mi me quiera . . . ha de quererme de veras. Ay, Ay, Ay, corazón, porque no amas.*[3] . . . I must have

20

---

[2]*sofrito:* A cooked condiment. A sauce composed of a mixture of fatback, ham, tomatoes, and many island spices and herbs. It is added to many Puerto Rican dishes for a distinctive flavor.—EDS.

[3]*De piedra ha de ser . . . amas:* Lyrics from a popular romantic balled (called a *bolero* in Puetro Rico). Freely translated: "My bed will be made of stone, of stone also my headrest (or pillow), the woman who (dares to) loves me, will have to love me for real. Ay, Ay, Ay, my heart, why can't you (let me) love. . . ."—EDS.

heard it a thousand times since the idea of a bed made of stone, and its connection to love, first troubled me with its disturbing images.

The five-minute home movie ends with people dancing in a circle— the creative filmmaker must have set it up, so that all of them could file past him. It is both comical and sad to watch silent dancing. Since there is no justification for the absurd movements that music provides for some of us, people appear frantic, their faces embarrassingly intense. It's as if you were watching sex. Yet for years I've had dreams in the form of this home movie. In a recurring scene, familiar faces push themselves forward into my mind's eyes, plastering their features into distorted close-ups. And I'm asking them: "Who is *she*? Who is the old woman I don't recognize? Is she an aunt? Somebody's wife? Tell me who she is."

"See the beauty mark on her cheek as big as a hill on the lunar landscape of her face—well, that runs in the family. The women on your father's side of the family wrinkle early; it's the price they pay for that fair skin. The young girl with the green stain on her wedding dress is *La Novia*—just up from the Island. See, she lowers her eyes when she approaches the camera, as she's supposed to. Decent girls never look at you directly in the face. *Humilde*, humble, a girl should express humility in all her actions. She will make a good wife for your cousin. He should consider himself lucky to have met her only weeks after she arrived here. If he marries her quickly, she will make him a good Puerto Rican–style wife; but if he waits too long, she will be corrupted by the city—just like your cousin there."

"She means me. I do what I want. This is not some primitive island I live on. Do they expect me to wear a black mantilla on my head and go to mass every day? Not me. I'm an American woman, and I will do as I please. I can type faster than anyone in my senior class at Central High, and I'm going to be a secretary to a lawyer when I graduate. I can pass for an American girl anywhere—I've tried it. At least for Italian, anyway—I never speak Spanish in public. I hate these parties, but I wanted the dress. I look better than any of these *humildes* here. My life is going to be different. I have an American boyfriend. He is older and has a car. My parents don't know it, but I sneak out of the house late at night sometimes to be with him. If I marry him, even my name will be American. I hate rice and beans—that's what makes these women fat."

"Your *prima*[4] is pregnant by that man she's been sneaking around with. Would I lie to you? I'm your *Tía Política*,[5] your great-uncle's common-law wife—the one he abandoned on the Island to go marry your cousin's mother. *I* was not invited to this party, of course, but I came anyway. I came to tell you that story about your cousin that you've always wanted to hear. Do you remember the comment your mother made to a neighbor that has always haunted you? The only thing you heard was your cousin's name, and then you saw your mother pick up your doll from the couch and say: 'It was as big as this doll when they flushed it down the

[4]*prima:* Female cousin. —EDS.
[5]*Tía Política:* Aunt by marriage. —EDS.

toilet.' This image has bothered you for years, hasn't it? You had night-mares about babies being flushed down the toilet, and you wondered why anyone would do such a horrible thing. You didn't dare ask your mother about it. She would only tell you that you had not heard her right, and yell at you for listening to adult conversations. But later, when you were old enough to know about abortions, you suspected.

"I am here to tell you that you were right. Your cousin was growing an *Americanito* in her belly when this movie was made. Soon after she put something long and pointy into her pretty self, thinking maybe she could get rid of the problem before breakfast and still make it to her first class at the high school. Well, *Niña*,[6] her screams could be heard downtown. Your aunt, her mamá, who had been a midwife on the Island, managed to pull the little thing out. Yes, they probably flushed it down the toilet. What else could they do with it—give it a Christian burial in a little white casket with blue bows and ribbons? Nobody wanted that baby—least of all the father, a teacher at her school with a house in West Paterson that he was filling with real children, and a wife who was a natural blonde.

"Girl, the scandal sent your uncle back to the bottle. And guess where your cousin ended up? Irony of ironies. She was sent to a village in Puerto Rico to live with a relative on her mother's side: a place so far away from civilization that you have to ride a mule to reach it. A real change in scenery. She found a man there—women like that cannot live without male company—but believe me, the men in Puerto Rico know how to put a saddle on a woman like her. *La Gringa*,[7] they call her. Ha, ha, ha. *La Gringa* is what she always wanted to be. . . ."

The old woman's mouth becomes a cavernous black hole I fall into. And as I fall, I can feel the reverberations of her laughter. I hear the echoes of her last mocking words: *La Gringa, La Gringa!* And the conga line keeps mov-ing silently past me. There is no music in my dream for the dancers.

When Odysseus visits Hades to see the spirit of his mother, he makes an   25 offering of sacrificial blood, but since all the souls crave an audience with the living, he has to listen to many of them before he can ask questions. I, too, have to hear the dead and the forgotten speak in my dream. Those who are still part of my life remain silent, going around and around in their dance. The others keep pressing their faces forward to say things about the past.

My father's uncle is last in line. He is dying of alcoholism, shrunken and shriveled like a monkey, his face a mass of wrinkles and broken ar-teries. As he comes closer I realize that in his features I can see my whole family. If you were to stretch that rubbery flesh, you could find my fa-ther's face, and deep within *that* face—my own. I don't want to look into those eyes ringed in purple. In a few years he will retreat into silence, and take a long, long time to die. *Move back, Tio*, I tell him. *I don't want to hear what you have to say. Give the dancers room to move. Soon it will be midnight. Who is the New Year's Fool this time?*

[6]***Niña***: Girl. —Eds.
[7]***La Gringa***: Derogatory epithet used here to ridicule a Puerto Rican girl who wants to look like a blonde North American. —Eds.

The Reader's Presence

1. "Silent Dancing" explores the personal, familial, and communal transformations that resulted from moving in the 1950s to Paterson, New Jersey—to "a huge tenement that had once housed Jewish families," and to a new community that emerged from the sprawling barrio that Puerto Ricans "overflowing from New York City" called home. Reread the essay carefully, and summarize the transformations that occurred in the life of the narrator, her family, and their larger Puerto Rican community.

2. Cofer uses an account of a home movie to create a structure for her essay. What are the specific advantages and disadvantages of this strategy? How, for example, does the home movie serve as "a great visual aid" to recounting life in the barrio of Paterson, New Jersey? What effect does the fact that the home movie is in color have on what she notices? on how she writes?

3. Because Cofer's essay is built around the occasion of watching a home movie, the narrator assumes the position of an observer of the scenes and people she describes. What specific strategies as a writer does Cofer use to establish a presence for herself in this narrative and descriptive account of growing up?

4. In his attempt to aid the family's "assimilation" into American culture, Cofer's father forbids his relatives from making friends in "El Building." Cofer and her mother were expected "to keep the doors locked, the noise down, ourselves to ourselves" (paragraph 4). How do the father's strategies and goals compare with those of Adrienne Rich's father in "Split at the Root: An Essay on Jewish Identity" (page 228)? How do the two essays become part of the writers' responses to their fathers? Cofer at times feels alienated from her own relatives. How does her situation compare to that of the narrator of Maxine Hong Kingston's "No Name Woman" (page 485)?

THE WRITER AT WORK

Judith Ortiz Cofer on Memory and Personal Essays

In setting out to write essays recounting her family history, Judith Ortiz Cofer found in Virginia Woolf a brilliant mentor and guide who taught her how to release the creative power of memory. In the following preface to Silent Dancing: A Partial Remembrance of a Puerto Rican Childhood, *she pays tribute to Woolf, who "understood that the very act of reclaiming her memories could provide a writer with confidence in the power of art to discover meaning and truth in ordinary events." How do Cofer's remarks in the preface (which she called "Journey to a Summer's Afternoon"), along with Woolf's "The Death of the Moth" (page 619), help illuminate the artistry of Cofer's own essay, "Silent Dancing"?*

As one gets older, childhood years are often conveniently consolidated into one perfect summer's afternoon. The events can be projected on a light blue screen; the hurtful parts can be edited out, and the moments of joy brought in sharp focus to the foreground. It is our show. But with all that on the cutting room floor, what remains to tell?

Virginia Woolf, whose vision guided my efforts as I tried to recall the faces and words of the people who are a part of my "summer's afternoon," wrote of the problem of writing truth from memory. In "A Sketch of the Past" she says, "But if I turn to my mother, how difficult it is to single her out as she really was; to imagine what she was thinking, to put a single sentence into her mouth." She accepts the fact that in writing about one's life, one often has to rely on that combination of memory, imagination, and strong emotion that may result in "poetic truth." In preparing to write her memoirs Woolf said, "I dream, I make up pictures of a summer's afternoon."

In one of her essays from her memoir *Moments of Being*, Woolf recalls the figure of her beautiful and beloved mother who died while the author was still a child, leaving her a few precious "moments of being" from which the mature woman must piece together a childhood. And she does so not to showcase her life, extraordinary as it was, but rather out of a need most of us feel at some point to study ourselves and our lives in retrospect; to understand what people and events formed us (and, yes, what and who hurt us, too).

From "A Sketch of the Past": "Many bright colors; many distinct sounds; some human beings, caricatures; several violent moments of being, always including a circle of the scene they cut out: and all surrounded by a vast space—that is a rough visual description of childhood. This is how I shape it; and how I see myself as a child . . ."

This passage illustrates the approach that I was seeking in writing 5 about my family. I wanted the essays to be, not just family history, but also creative explorations of known territory. I wanted to trace back through scenes based on my "moments of being" the origins of my creative imagination. As a writer, I am, like most artists, interested in the genesis of ideas: How does a poem begin? Can the process be triggered at will? What compels some of us to examine and re-examine our lives in poems, stories, novels, memoirs?

Much of my writing begins as a meditation on past events. But memory for me is the "jumping off " point; I am not, in my poetry and my fiction writing, a slave to memory. I like to believe that the poem or story contains the "truth" of art rather than the factual, historical truth that the journalist, sociologist, scientist—most of the rest of the world—must adhere to. Art gives me that freedom. But in writing these "essays" (the Spanish word for essay, *ensayo*, suits my meaning here better—it can mean "a rehearsal," an exercise or practice), I faced the possibility that the past is mainly a creation of the imagination also, although there are facts one can research and confirm. The biographer's time-honored task can be employed on one's own life too. There are birth, marriage, and death certificates on file, there are letters and family photographs in someone's desk or attic; and there are the relatives who have assigned themselves the role of genealogist or family bard, recounting at the least instigation the entire history of your clan. One can go to these sources and come up with a *Life* in several volumes that will make your mother proud and give you the satisfaction of having "preserved" something. I am not interested in merely "canning" memories, however, and Woolf gave me the focus that I needed to justify this work. Its intention is not to chronicle my life—which in my case is still very much "in-progress," nor are there any extraordinary accomplishments to showcase; neither is it meant to be a record of public events and personal histories (in fact, since most of the characters in these essays are based on actual, living persons and real places, whenever I felt that it was necessary to protect their identities, I changed names, locations, etc.). Then, what is the purpose of calling this collection non-fiction or a memoir? Why not just call it fiction? Once again I must turn to my literary mentor for this project, Virginia Woolf, for an answer: like her, I wanted to try to connect myself to the threads of lives that have touched mine and at some point converged into the tapestry that is my memory of childhood. Virginia Woolf understood that the very act of reclaiming her memories could provide a writer with confidence in the power of art to discover meaning and truth in ordinary events. She was a time-traveler who saw the past as a real place one could return to by following the tracks left by strong emotions: "I feel that strong emotion must leave its trace; and it is only a question of discovering how we can get ourselves attached to it, so that we shall be able to live our lives through from the start."[1]

It was this winding path of memory, marked by strong emotions, that I followed in my *ensayos* of a life.

---

[1]All quotes by Virginia Woolf are from *Moments of Being* (Harcourt Brace Jovanovich, Inc.).—COFER'S NOTE.

Bernard Cooper

A Clack of Tiny Sparks: Remembrances of a Gay Boyhood

Born (1951), raised, and still residing in Los Angeles, Bernard Cooper received his B.F.A. and M.F.A. from the California Institute of the Arts. He has taught at the Otis/Parsons Institute of Art and Design and Southern California Institute of Architecture, Los Angeles, and at the UCLA writing program; he is now an art critic for Los Angeles Magazine. *His collection of essays,* Maps to Anywhere *(1990), covers a wide range of topics as varying as the aging of his father, the extinction of the dinosaur, and the future of American life and culture. Cooper contributes to various periodicals such as* Harper's, *where "A Clack of Tiny Sparks: Remembrances of a Gay Boyhood" first appeared in January 1991. His most recent collection of short stories is* Guess Again *(2000).*

Commenting on his 1993 novel, A Year of Rhymes, *Cooper notes, "One of the reasons why there is so much detail in my work is that I'm a person that essentially shies away from abstractions, from Large Issues and Big Ideas. The world only seems real and vivid and meaningful to me in the smaller details, what's heard and felt and smelled and tasted."*

Theresa Sanchez sat behind me in ninth-grade algebra. When Mr. Hubbley faced the blackboard, I'd turn around to see what she was reading; each week a new book was wedged inside her copy of *Today's Equations*. The deception worked; from Mr. Hubbley's point of view, Theresa was engrossed in the value of *X*, but I knew otherwise. One week she perused *The Wisdom of the Orient*, and I could tell from Theresa's contemplative expression that the book contained exotic thoughts, guidelines handed down from high. Another week it was a paperback novel whose title, *Let Me Live My Life*, appeared in bold print atop every page, and whose cover, a gauzy photograph of a woman biting a strand of pearls, head thrown back in an attitude of ecstasy, confirmed my suspicion that Theresa Sanchez was mature beyond her years. She was the tallest girl in school. Her bouffant hairdo, streaked with blond, was higher than the flaccid bouffants of other girls. Her smooth skin, plucked eyebrows, and painted fingernails suggested hours of pampering, a worldly and sensual vanity that placed her within the domain of adults. Smiling dimly, steeped in daydreams, Theresa moved through the crowded halls with a languid, self-satisfied indifference to those around her. "You are merely children," her posture seemed to say. "I can't be bothered." The week Theresa hid *101 Ways to Cook Hamburger* behind her algebra book, I could stand it no longer and, after the bell rang, ventured a question.

"Because I'm having a dinner party," said Theresa. "Just a couple of intimate friends."

No fourteen-year-old I knew had ever given a dinner party, let alone used the word "intimate" in conversation. "Don't you have a mother?" I asked.

Theresa sighed a weary sigh, suffered my strange inquiry. "Don't be so naive," she said. "Everyone has a mother." She waved her hand to indicate the brick school buildings outside the window. "A higher education should have taught you that." Theresa draped an angora sweater over her shoulders, scooped her books from the graffiti-covered desk, and just as she was about to walk away, she turned and asked me, "Are you a fag?"

There wasn't the slightest hint of rancor or condescension in her   5
voice. The tone was direct, casual. Still I was stunned, giving a sidelong glance to make sure no one had heard. "No," I said. Blurted really, with too much defensiveness, too much transparent fear in my response. Octaves lower than usual, I tried a "Why?"

Theresa shrugged. "Oh, I don't know. I have lots of friends who are fags. You remind me of them." Seeing me bristle, Theresa added, "It was just a guess." I watched her erect, angora back as she sauntered out the classroom door.

She had made an incisive and timely guess. Only days before, I'd invited Grady Rogers to my house after school to go swimming. The instant Grady shot from the pool, shaking water from his orange hair, freckled shoulders shining, my attraction to members of my own sex became a matter I could no longer suppress or rationalize. Sturdy and boisterous and gap-toothed, Grady was an inveterate backslapper, a formidable arm wrestler, a wizard at basketball. Grady was a boy at home in his body.

My body was a marvel I hadn't gotten used to; my arms and legs would sometimes act of their own accord, knocking over a glass at dinner or flinching at an oncoming pitch. I was never singled out as a sissy, but I could have been just as easily as Bobby Keagan, a gentle, intelligent, and introverted boy reviled by my classmates. And although I had always been aware of a tacit rapport with Bobby, a suspicion that I might find with him a rich friendship, I stayed away. Instead, I emulated Grady in the belief that being seen with him, being like him, would somehow vanquish my self-doubt, would make me normal by association.

Apart from his athletic prowess, Grady had been gifted with all the trappings of what I imagined to be a charmed life: a fastidious, aproned mother who radiated calm, maternal concern; a ruddy, stoic father with a knack for home repairs. Even the Rogerses' small suburban house in Hollywood, with its spindly Colonial furniture and chintz curtains, was a testament to normalcy.

Grady and his family bore little resemblance to my clan of Eastern Eu-   10
ropean Jews, a dark and vociferous people who ate with abandon — matzo

and halvah and gefilte fish; foods the goyim couldn't pronounce — who cajoled one another during endless games of canasta, making the simplest remark about the weather into a lengthy philosophical discourse on the sun and the seasons and the passage of time. My mother was a chain-smoker, a dervish in a frowsy housedress. She showed her love in the most peculiar and obsessive ways, like spending hours extracting every seed from a watermelon before she served it in perfectly bite-sized, geometric pieces. Preoccupied and perpetually frantic, my mother succumbed to bouts of absentmindedness so profound she'd forget what she was saying midsentence, smile and blush and walk away. A divorce attorney, my father wore roomy, iridescent suits, and the intricacies, the deceits inherent in his profession, had the effect of making him forever tense and vigilant. He was "all wound up," as my mother put it. But when he relaxed, his laughter was explosive, his disposition prankish: "Walk this way," a waitress would say, leading us to our table, and my father would mimic the way she walked, arms akimbo, hips liquid, while my mother and I were wracked with laughter. Buoyant or brooding, my parents' moods were unpredictable, and in a household fraught with extravagant emotion it was odd and awful to keep my longing secret.

One day I made the mistake of asking my mother what a "fag" was. I knew exactly what Theresa had meant but hoped against hope it was not what I thought; maybe "fag" was some French word, a harmless term like "naive." My mother turned from the stove, flew at me, and grabbed me by the shoulders. "Did someone call you that?" she cried.

"Not me," I said. "Bobby Keagan."

"Oh," she said, loosening her grip. She was visibly relieved. And didn't answer. The answer was unthinkable.

For weeks after, I shook with the reverberations from that afternoon in the kitchen with my mother, pained by the memory of her shocked expression and, most of all, her silence. My longing was wrong in the eyes of my mother, whose hazel eyes were the eyes of the world, and if that longing continued unchecked, the unwieldy shape of my fate would be cast, and I'd be subjected to a lifetime of scorn.

During the remainder of the semester, I became the scientist of my own desire, plotting ways to change my yearning for boys into a yearning for girls. I had enough evidence to believe that any habit, regardless of how compulsive, how deeply ingrained, could be broken once and for all: The plastic cigarette my mother purchased at the Thrifty pharmacy — one end was red to approximate an ember, the other tan like a filtered tip — was designed to wean her from the real thing. To change a behavior required self-analysis, cold resolve, and the substitution of one thing for another: plastic, say, for tobacco. Could I also find a substitute for Grady? What I needed to do, I figured, was kiss a girl and learn to like it.

This conclusion was affirmed one Sunday morning when my father, seeing me wrinkle my nose at the pink slabs of lox he layered on a bagel, tried to convince me of its salty appeal. "You should try some," he said. "You don't know what you're missing."

"It's loaded with protein," added my mother, slapping a platter of sliced onions onto the dinette table. She hovered above us, cinching her housedress, eyes wet from onion fumes, the mock cigarette dangling from her lips.

My father sat there chomping with gusto, emitting a couple of hearty grunts to dramatize his satisfaction. And still I was not convinced. After a loud and labored swallow, he told me I may not be fond of lox today, but sooner or later I'd learn to like it. One's tastes, he assured me, are destined to change.

"Live," shouted my mother over the rumble of the Mixmaster. "Expand your horizons. Try new things." And the room grew fragrant with the batter of a spice cake.

The opportunity to put their advice into practice, and try out my plan   20
to adapt to girls, came the following week when Debbie Coburn, a member of Mr. Hubbley's algebra class, invited me to a party. She cornered me in the hall, furtive as a spy, telling me her parents would be gone for the evening and slipping into my palm a wrinkled sheet of notebook paper. On it were her address and telephone number, the lavender ink in a tidy cursive. "Wear cologne," she advised, wary eyes darting back and forth. "It's a make-out party. Anything can happen."

The Santa Ana wind blew relentlessly the night of Debbie's party, careening down the slopes of the Hollywood hills, shaking the road signs and stoplights in its path. As I walked down Beachwood Avenue, trees thrashed, surrendered their leaves, and carob pods bombarded the pavement. The sky was a deep but luminous blue, the air hot, abrasive, electric. I had to squint in order to check the number of the Coburns' apartment, a three-story building with glitter embedded in its stucco walls. Above the honeycombed balconies was a sign that read BEACHWOOD TERRACE in lavender script resembling Debbie's.

From down the hall, I could hear the plaintive strains of Little Anthony's "I Think I'm Going Out of My Head." Debbie answered the door bedecked in an Empire dress, the bodice blue and orange polka dots, the rest a sheath of black and white stripes. "Op art," proclaimed Debbie. She turned in a circle, then proudly announced that she'd rolled her hair in orange juice cans. She patted the huge unmoving curls and dragged me inside. Reflections from the swimming pool in the courtyard, its surface ruffled by wind, shuddered over the ceiling and walls. A dozen of my classmates were seated on the sofa or huddled together in corners, their whispers full of excited imminence, their bodies barely discernible in the dim light. Drapes flanking the sliding glass doors bowed out with every gust of wind, and it seemed that the room might lurch from its foundations and sail with its cargo of silhouettes into the hot October night.

Grady was the last to arrive. He tossed a six-pack of beer into Debbie's arms, barreled toward me, and slapped my back. His hair was slicked back with Vitalis, lacquered furrows left by the comb. The wind hadn't shifted a single hair. "Ya ready?" he asked, flashing the gap between his front teeth and leering into the darkened room. "You bet," I lied.

Once the beers had been passed around, Debbie provoked everyone's attention by flicking on the overhead light. "Okay," she called. "Find a partner." This was the blunt command of a hostess determined to have her guests aroused in an orderly fashion. Everyone blinked, shuffled about, and grabbed a member of the opposite sex. Sheila Garabedian landed beside me—entirely at random, though I wanted to believe she was driven by passion—her timid smile giving way to plain fear as the light went out. Nothing for a moment but the heave of the wind and the distant banter of dogs. I caught a whiff of Sheila's perfume, tangy and sweet as Hawaiian Punch. I probed her face with my own, grazing the small scallop of an ear, a velvety temple, and though Sheila's trembling made me want to stop, I persisted with my mission until I found her lips, tightly sealed as a private letter. I held my mouth over hers and gathered her shoulders closer, resigned to the possibility that, no matter how long we stood there, Sheila would be too scared to kiss me back. Still, she exhaled through her nose, and I listened to the squeak of every breath as though it were a sigh of inordinate pleasure. Diving within myself, I monitored my heartbeat and respiration, trying to will stimulation into being, and all the while an image intruded, an image of Grady erupting from our pool, rivulets of water sliding down his chest. "Change," shouted Debbie, switching on the light. Sheila thanked me, pulled away, and continued her routine of gracious terror with every boy throughout the evening. It didn't matter whom I held— Margaret Sims, Betty Vernon, Elizabeth Lee—my experiment was a failure; I continued to picture Grady's wet chest, and Debbie would bellow "change" with such fervor, it could have been my own voice, my own incessant reprimand.

Our hostess commandeered the light switch for nearly half an hour. Whenever the light came on, I watched Grady pivot his head toward the newest prospect, his eyebrows arched in expectation, his neck blooming with hickeys, his hair, at last, in disarray. All that shuffling across the carpet charged everyone's arms and lips with static, and eventually, between low moans and soft osculations, I could hear the clack of tiny sparks and see them flare here and there in the dark like meager, short-lived stars.

I saw Theresa, sultry and aloof as ever, read three more books—*North American Reptiles, Bonjour Tristesse, and MGM: A Pictorial History*— before she vanished early in December. Rumors of her fate abounded.

Debbie Coburn swore that Theresa had been "knocked up" by an older man, a traffic cop, she thought, or a grocer. Nearly quivering with relish, Debbie told me and Grady about the home for unwed mothers in the San Fernando Valley, a compound teeming with pregnant girls who had nothing to do but touch their stomachs and contemplate their mistake. Even Bobby Keagan, who took Theresa's place behind me in algebra, had a theory regarding her disappearance colored by his own wish for escape; he imagined that Theresa, disillusioned with society, booked passage to a tropical island, there to live out the rest of her days without restrictions or ridicule. "No wonder she flunked out of school," I overheard Mr. Hubbley tell a fellow teacher one afternoon. "Her head was always in a book."

Along with Theresa went my secret, or at least the dread that she might divulge it, and I felt, for a while, exempt from suspicion. I was, however, to run across Theresa one last time. It happened during a period of torrential rain that, according to reports on the six o'clock news, washed houses from the hillsides and flooded the downtown streets. The halls of Joseph Le Conte Junior High were festooned with Christmas decorations: crepe-paper garlands, wreaths studded with plastic berries, and one requisite Star of David twirling above the attendance desk. In Arts and Crafts, our teacher, Gerald (he was the only teacher who allowed us— *required* us—to call him by his first name), handed out blocks of balsa wood and instructed us to carve them into bugs. We would paint eyes and antennae with tempera and hang them on a Christmas tree he'd made the previous night. "Voilà," he crooned, unveiling his creation from a burlap sack. Before us sat a tortured scrub, a wardrobe-worth of wire hangers that were bent like branches and soldered together. Gerald credited his inspiration to a Charles Addams cartoon he's seen in which Morticia, grimly preparing for the holidays, hangs vampire bats on a withered pine. "All that red and green," said Gerald. "So predictable. *So boring.*"

As I chiseled a beetle and listened to rain pummel the earth, Gerald handed me an envelope and asked me to take it to Mr. Kendrick, the drama teacher. I would have thought nothing of his request if I hadn't seen Theresa on my way down the hall. She was cleaning out her locker, blithely dropping the sum of its contents—pens and textbooks and mimeographs—into a trash can. "Have a nice life," she sang as I passed. I mustered the courage to ask her what had happened. We stood alone in the silent hall, the reflections of wreaths and garlands submerged in brown linoleum.

"I transferred to another school. They don't have grades or bells, and you get to study whatever you want." Theresa was quick to sense my incredulity. "Honest," she said. "The school is progressive." She gazed into a glass cabinet that held the trophies of track meets and intramural spelling bees. "God," she sighed, "this place is so . . . barbaric." I was still trying to decide whether or not to believe her story when she asked me where I was headed. "Dear," she said, her exclamation pooling in the silence, "that's no ordinary note, if you catch my drift." The envelope was blank and white; I looked up at Theresa, baffled. "Don't be so naive," she muttered, tossing an empty bottle of nail polish into the trash can. It struck bottom with a resolute thud. "Well," she said, closing her locker and breathing deeply, "bon voyage." Theresa swept through the double doors and in seconds her figure was obscured by rain.

As I walked toward Mr. Kendrick's room, I could feel Theresa's in-   30
sinuation burrow in. I stood for a moment and watched Mr. Kendrick through the pane in the door. He paced intently in front of the class, handsome in his shirt and tie, reading from a thick book. Chalked on the blackboard behind him was THE ODYSSEY BY HOMER. I have no recollection of how Mr. Kendrick reacted to the note, whether he accepted it with pleasure or embarrassment, slipped it into his desk drawer or the pocket of his shirt. I have scavenged that day in retrospect, trying to see Mr. Kendrick's expression, wondering if he acknowledged me in any way as his liaison. All I recall is the sight of his mime through a pane of glass, a lone man mouthing an epic, his gestures ardent in empty air.

Had I delivered a declaration of love? I was haunted by the need to know. In fantasy, a kettle shot steam, the glue released its grip, and I read the letter with impunity. But how would such a letter begin? Did the common endearments apply? This was a message between two men, a message for which I had no precedent, and when I tried to envision the contents, apart from a hasty, impassioned scrawl, my imagination faltered.

Once or twice I witnessed Gerald and Mr. Kendrick walk together into the faculty lounge or say hello at the water fountain, but there was nothing especially clandestine or flirtatious in their manner. Besides, no matter how acute my scrutiny, I wasn't sure, short of a kiss, exactly what to look for—what semaphore of gesture, what encoded word. I suspected there were signs, covert signs that would give them away, just as I'd unwittingly given myself away to Theresa.

In the school library, a *Webster's* unabridged dictionary lay on a wooden podium, and I padded toward it with apprehension; along with clues to the bond between my teachers, I risked discovering information that might incriminate me as well. I had decided to consult the dictionary during lunch period, when most of the students would be on the playground. I clutched my notebook, moving in such a way as to appear both studious and nonchalant, actually believing that, unless I took precautions, someone would see me and guess what I was up to. The closer I came to the podium, the more obvious, I thought, was my endeavor; I felt like the model of The Visible Man in our science class, my heart's undulations, my overwrought nerves legible through transparent skin. A couple of kids riffled through the card catalogue. The librarian, a skinny woman whose perpetual whisper and rubber-soled shoes caused her to drift through the room like a phantom, didn't seem to register my presence. Though I'd looked up dozens of words before, the pages felt strange beneath my fingers. *Homer* was the first word I saw. *Hominid.* *Homogenize.* I feigned interest and skirted other words before I found the word I was after. Under the heading HO•MO•SEX•U•AL was the terse definition: *adj. Pertaining to, characteristic of, or exhibiting homo-sexuality.—n. A homosexual person.* I read the definition again and again, hoping the words would yield more than they could. I shut the dictionary, swallowed hard, and, none the wiser, hurried away.

As for Gerald and Mr. Kendrick, I never discovered evidence to prove or dispute Theresa's claim. By the following summer, however, I had over-heard from my peers a confounding amount about homosexuals: They wore green on Thursday, couldn't whistle, hypnotized boys with a piercing glance. To this lore, Grady added a surefire test to ferret them out.

"A test?" I said.   35

"You ask a guy to look at his fingernails, and if he looks at them like this"—Grady closed his fingers into a fist and examined his nails with manly detachment—"then he's okay. But if he does this"—he held out his hands at arm's length, splayed his fingers, and coyly cocked his head—"you'd better watch out." Once he'd completed his demonstration, Grady peeled off his shirt and plunged into our pool. I dove in after. It was early June, the sky immense, glassy, placid. My father was cooking spareribs on the barbecue, an artist with a basting brush. His apron bore the caricature of a frazzled French chef. Mother curled on a chaise lounge, plumes of smoke wafting from her nostrils. In a stupor of contentment she took an-other drag, closed her eyes, and arched her face toward the sun.

Grady dog-paddled through the deep end, spouting a fountain of chlo-rinated water. Despite shame and confusion, my longing for him hadn't diminished; it continued to thrive without air and light, like a luminous fish in the dregs of the sea. In the name of play, I swam up behind him, encircled his shoulders, astonished by his taut flesh. The two of us flailed, pretended to drown. Beneath the heavy press of water, Grady's orange hair wavered, a flame that couldn't be doused.

I've lived with a man for seven years. Some nights, when I'm half-asleep and the room is suffused with blue light, I reach out to touch the expanse of his back, and it seems as if my fingers sink into his skin, and I feel the pleasure a diver feels the instant he enters a body of water.

I have few regrets. But one is that I hadn't said to Theresa, "Of course I'm a fag." Maybe I'd have met her friends. Or become friends with her. Imagine the meals we might have concocted: hamburger Stroganoff, Swedish meatballs in a sweet translucent sauce, steaming slabs of Salisbury steak.

The Reader's Presence

1. Cooper's first stirrings of attraction for his friend Grady occur in a swimming pool. What importance does swimming play in Cooper's essay? How does it provide him with a cluster of images for sexual experience?

2. Why does Cooper attend the "make-out party"? What does he hope will happen? Why do you think he ends his description of the party with the observation of the "clack of tiny sparks"? Why do you think he used that image for his title?

3. In paragraph 15, Cooper writes that he became "the scientist of [his] own desire," as he tried to understand—and to resist—his "yearning for boys." Adrienne Rich determines as a young woman to understand her parents' seeming denial of her Jewish heritage: "I have to face the sources and the flickering presence of my own ambivalence as a Jew" (paragraph 2, "Split at the Root: An Essay on Jewish Identity," page 228). Both writers describe feeling shame and a sense of betrayal in their essays. What more do you find in common between the two? What are key differences between them? Children often turn to dictionaries to solve mysteries they are too shy to ask people about. How does Cooper's discovery of the definition of "homosexual" compare to Frederick Douglass's attempt to discover the meaning of "abolition" in "Learning to Read and Write"?

Frederick Douglass

Learning to Read and Write

Born into slavery, Frederick Douglass (1817?–1895) was taken from his mother as an infant and denied any knowledge of his father's identity. He escaped to the north at the age of twenty-one and created a new identity for himself as a free man. He educated himself and went on to become one of the most eloquent orators and persuasive writers of the nineteenth century. He was a national leader in the abolition movement and, among other activities, founded and edited the North Star *and* Douglass' Monthly. *His public service included appointments as United States marshal and consul general to the Republic of Haiti. His most lasting literary accomplishment was his memoirs, which he revised several times before they were published as the* Life and Times of Frederick Douglass *(1881 and 1892). "Learning to Read and Write" is taken from these memoirs.*

Douglass overcame his initial reluctance to write his memoirs because, as he put it, "not only is slavery on trial, but unfortunately, the enslaved people are also on trial. It is alleged that they are, naturally, inferior; that they are so low in the scale of humanity, and so utterly stupid, that they are unconscious of their wrongs, and do not apprehend their rights." Therefore, wishing to put his talents to work "to the benefit of my afflicted people," Douglass agreed to write the story of his life.

I lived in Master Hugh's family about seven years. During this time, I succeeded in learning to read and write. In accomplishing this, I was compelled to resort to various stratagems. I had no regular teacher. My mistress, who had kindly commenced to instruct me, had, in compliance with the advice and direction of her husband, not only ceased to instruct, but had set her face against my being instructed by anyone else. It is due, however, to my mistress to say of her, that she did not adopt this course of treatment immediately. She at first lacked the depravity indispensable to shutting me up in mental darkness. It was at least necessary for her to have some training in the exercise of irresponsible power, to make her equal to the task of treating me as though I were a brute.

My mistress was, as I have said, a kind and tender-hearted woman; and in the simplicity of her soul she commenced, when I first went to live with her, to treat me as she supposed one human being ought to treat another. In entering upon the duties of a slaveholder, she did not seem to perceive that I sustained to her the relation of a mere chattel, and that for her to treat me as a human being was not only wrong, but dangerously so. Slavery proved as injurious to her as it did to me. When I went there, she was a pious, warm, and tender-hearted woman. There was no sorrow or suffering for which she had not a tear. She had bread for the hungry, clothes for the naked, and comfort for every mourner that came within her reach. Slavery soon proved its ability to divest her of these heavenly qualities. Under its influence, the tender heart became stone, and the lamb-like disposition gave way to one of tiger-like fierceness. The first step in her downward course was in her ceasing to instruct me. She now commenced to practice her husband's precepts. She finally became even more violent in her opposition than her husband himself. She was not satisfied with simply doing as well as he had commanded; she seemed anxious to do better. Nothing seemed to make her more angry than to see me with a newspaper. She seemed to think that here lay the danger. I have had her rush at me with a face made all up of fury, and snatch from me a newspaper, in a manner that fully revealed her apprehension. She was an apt woman; and a little experience soon demonstrated, to her satisfaction, that education and slavery were incompatible with each other.

From this time I was most narrowly watched. If I was in a separate room any considerable length of time, I was sure to be suspected of having a book, and was at once called to give an account of myself. All this, however, was too late. The first step had been taken. Mistress, in teaching me the alphabet, had given me the *inch*, and no precaution could prevent me from taking the *ell*.

The plan which I adopted, and the one by which I was most successful, was that of making friends of all the little white boys whom I met in the street. As many of these as I could, I converted into teachers. With their kindly aid, obtained at different times and in different places, I finally succeeded in learning to read. When I was sent to errands, I always took my book with me, and by doing one part of my errand quickly, I found time to get a lesson before my return. I used also to carry bread with me, enough of which was always in the house, and to which I was always welcome; for I was much better off in this regard than many of the poor white children in our neighborhood. This bread I used to bestow upon the hungry little urchins, who, in return, would give me that more valuable bread of knowledge. I am strongly tempted to give the names of two or three of those little boys, as a testimonial of the gratitude and affection I bear them; but prudence forbids — not that it would injure me, but it might embarrass them; for it is almost an unpardonable offense to teach slaves to read in this Christian country. It is enough to say of the dear little fellows, that they lived on Philpot Street, very near Durgin and Bailey's ship-yard. I used to talk this matter of slavery over with them. I would sometimes say to them, I wished I could be as free as they would be when they got to be men. "You will be free as soon as you are twenty-one, *but I am a slave for life!* Have not I as good a right to be free as you have?" These words used to trouble them; they would express for me the liveliest sympathy, and console me with the hope that something would occur by which I might be free.

I was now about twelve years old, and the thought of being *a slave*   5 *for life* began to bear heavily upon my heart. Just about this time, I got hold of a book entitled *The Columbian Orator.* Every opportunity I got, I used to read this book. Among much of other interesting matter, I found in it a dialogue between a master and his slave. The slave was represented as having run away from his master three times. The dialogue represented the conversation which took place between them, when the slave was retaken the third time. In this dialogue, the whole argument in behalf of slavery was brought forward by the master, all of which was disposed of by the slave. The slave was made to say some very smart as well as impressive things in reply to his master — things which had the desired though unexpected effect; for the conversation resulted in the voluntary emancipation of the slave on the part of the master.

In the same book, I met with one of Sheridan's[1] mighty speeches on and in behalf of Catholic emancipation. These were choice documents to me. I read them over and over again with unabated interest. They gave tongue to interesting thoughts of my own soul, which had frequently flashed through my mind, and died away for want of utterance. The moral which I gained from the dialogue was the power of truth over the conscience of even a slaveholder. What I got from Sheridan was a bold denunciation of slavery, and a powerful vindication of human rights. The reading of these documents enabled me to utter my thoughts, and to meet

[1]*Sheridan's:* Richard Brinsley Butler Sheridan (1751–1816), Irish dramatist and orator. — EDS.

the arguments brought forward to sustain slavery; but while they relieved me of one difficulty, they brought on another even more painful than the one of which I was relieved. The more I read, the more I was led to abhor and detest my enslavers. I could regard them in no other light than a band of successful robbers, who had left their homes, and gone to Africa, and stolen us from our homes, and in a strange land reduced us to slavery. I loathed them as being the meanest as well as the most wicked of men. As I read and contemplated the subject, behold! that very discontentment which Master Hugh had predicted would follow my learning to read had already come, to torment and sting my soul to unutterable anguish. As I writhed under it, I would at times feel that learning to read had been a curse rather than a blessing. It had given me a view of my wretched condition, without the remedy. It opened my eyes to the horrible pit, but to no ladder upon which to get out. In moments of agony, I envied my fellow-slaves for their stupidity. I have often wished myself a beast. I preferred the condition of the meanest reptile to my own. Anything, no matter what, to get rid of thinking! It was this everlasting thinking of my condition that tormented me. There was no getting rid of it. It was pressed upon me by every object within sight or hearing, animate or inanimate. The silver trump of freedom had roused my soul to eternal wakefulness. Freedom now appeared, to disappear no more forever. It was heard in every sound, and seen in every thing. It was ever present to torment me with a sense of my wretched condition. I saw nothing without seeing it, I heard nothing without hearing it, and felt nothing without feeling it. It looked from every star, it smiled in every calm, breathed in every wind, and moved in every storm.

I often found myself regretting my own existence, and wishing myself dead; and but for the hope of being free, I have no doubt but that I should have killed myself, or done something for which I should have been killed. While in this state of mind, I was eager to hear anyone speak of slavery. I was a ready listener. Every little while, I could hear something about the abolitionists. It was some time before I found what the word meant. It was always used in such connections as to make it an interesting word to me. If a slave ran away and succeeded in getting clear, or if a slave killed his master, set fire to a barn, or did anything very wrong in the mind of a slaveholder, it was spoken of as the fruit of *abolition*. Hearing the word in this connection very often, I set about learning what it meant. The dictionary afforded me little or no help. I found it was "the act of abolishing"; but then I did not know what was to be abolished. Here I was perplexed. I did not dare to ask anyone about its meaning, for I was satisfied that it was something they wanted me to know very little about. After a patient waiting, I got one of our city papers, containing an account of the number of petitions from the North, praying for the abolition of slavery in the District of Columbia, and of the slave trade between the States. From this time I understood the words *abolition* and *abolitionist*, and always drew near when that word was spoken, expecting to hear something of importance to myself and fellow-slaves. The light broke in upon me by degrees. I went one day down on the wharf of Mr. Waters; and seeing two Irishmen unloading a scow of stone, I went, unasked, and helped them. When we had finished, one of them came to me and asked me if I were a slave. I told him I was. He asked, "Are ye a slave for life?" I told him that I was. The good Irishman seemed to be deeply affected by the statement. He said to the other that it was a pity so fine a little fellow as myself should be a slave for life. He said it was a shame to hold me. They both advised me to run away to the North; that I should find friends there, and that I should be free. I pretended not to be interested in what they said, and treated them as if I did not understand them; for I feared they might be treacherous. White men have been known to encourage slaves to escape, and then, to get the reward, catch them and return them to their masters. I was afraid that these seemingly good men might use me so; but I nevertheless remembered their advice, and from that time I resolved to run away. I looked forward to a time at which it would be safe for me to escape. I was too young to think of doing so immediately; besides, I wished to learn how to write, as I might have occasion to write my own pass. I consoled myself with the hope that I should one day find a good chance. Meanwhile, I would learn to write.

The idea as to how I might learn to write was suggested to me by being in Durgin and Bailey's ship-yard, and frequently seeing the ship carpenters, after hewing, and getting a piece of timber ready for use, write on the timber the name of that part of the ship for which it was intended. When a piece of timber was intended for the larboard side, it would be marked thus—"L." When a piece was for the starboard side, it would be marked thus—"S." A piece for the larboard side forward, would be marked thus—"L.F." When a piece was for starboard side forward, it would be marked thus—"S.F." For larboard aft, it would be marked thus—"L.A." For starboard aft, it would be marked thus—"S.A." I soon learned the names of these letters, and for what they were intended when placed upon a piece of timber in the shipyard. I immediately commenced copying them, and in a short time was able to make the four letters named. After that, when I met with any boy who I knew could write, I would tell him I could write as well as he. The next word would be, "I don't believe you. Let me see you try it." I would then make the letters which I had been so fortunate as to learn, and ask him to beat that. In this way I got a good many lessons in writing, which it is quite possible I should never have gotten in any other way. During this time, my copy-book was the board fence, brick wall, and pavement; my pen and ink was a lump of chalk. With these, I learned mainly how to write. I then commenced and continued copying the Italics in *Webster's Spelling Book*, until I could make them all without looking in the book. By this time, my little Master Thomas had gone to school, and learned how to write, and had written over a number of copy-books. These had been brought home, and shown to some of our near neighbors, and then laid aside. My mistress used to go to class meeting at the Wilk

Street meeting-house every Monday afternoon, and leave me to take care of the house. When left thus, I used to spend the time in writing in the spaces left in master Thomas's copy-book, copying what he had written. I continued to do this until I could write a hand very similar to that of Master Thomas. Thus, after a long, tedious effort for years, I finally succeeded in learning how to write.

The Reader's Presence

1. What sort of audience does Douglass anticipate for his reminiscence? How much does he assume his readers know about the conditions of slavery?

2. What books seem to matter most to Douglass? Why? What are his motives for wanting to read and write? For Douglass, what is the relationship between literacy and freedom? How does he move from curiosity to anguish to "eternal wakefulness" in paragraph 6? What is the relationship between learning to read and learning to write?

3. Read Azar Nafisi's "Reading *Lolita* in Tehran" (page 516) and consider Nafisi's students' challenges in obtaining an education. What obstacles do the girls overcome to join Nafisi's class? How do the difficulties Douglass faced in getting an education compare with those of Nafisi's students?

Jonathan Franzen

The Comfort Zone

Jonathan Franzen (b. 1959) grew up in a suburb of St. Louis, Missouri. After graduating from Swarthmore College, he attended the Free University in Berlin as a Fulbright Scholar. His first novel, The Twenty-Seventh City, *was published in 1988, followed by* Strong Motion *in 1992. His next novel,* The Corrections *(2001), won the 2001 National Book Award; in 2002, it won the James Tait Black Memorial Prize for fiction and was a finalist for both a Pulitzer Prize and the PEN/Faulkner Award. Franzen became both famous and infamous for refusing to appear on Oprah Winfrey's television show after she selected the novel for her book club. Franzen writes about the incident and other topics in his 2002 collection of essays,* How to Be Alone. *The collection also includes his well-known 1996 article about the precarious state of the American novel, "Perchance to Dream," and an essay about his father, who died of Alzheimer's disease in 1995. Franzen is a frequent contributor to magazines and journals, including the* New Yorker, *from which "The Comfort Zone" is taken.*

In a 2001 interview, Franzen said, "I think any artistic child of a businessman is prone to a sense of the slightness of what he or she is doing. Of the uselessness of art. This uselessness is intrinsic, of course, and that's part of art's charm. But it's useless nonetheless. And when you compound this . . . with the sense of being in one's father's shadow, well, you risk feeling like a little kid. My first response to this feeling of smallness was to try to Know Everything, to exude confidence and total command. But when the world refuses to be changed by what you're writing—when the world takes, essentially, no note of it—it gets harder and harder to persuade yourself that your desire for total control, and your head-on engagement with Big Issues, is meaningful."

In May, 1970, a few nights after the Kent State shootings, my father and my brother Tom, who was nineteen, started fighting. They weren't fighting about the Vietnam War, which both of them opposed. The fight was probably about a lot of different things at once. But the immediate issue was Tom's summer job. He was a good artist, with a meticulous nature, and my father had encouraged him (you could even say forced him) to choose a college from a short list of schools with strong programs in architecture. Tom had deliberately chosen the most distant of these schools, Rice University, and he had just returned from his second year in Houston, where his adventures in late-sixties youth culture were pushing him toward majoring in film studies, not architecture. My father, however, had found him a plum summer job with Sverdrup & Parcel, the big engineering firm in St. Louis, whose senior partner, General Leif Sverdrup, had been a United States Army Corps of Engineers hero in the Philippines. It couldn't have been easy for my father, who was shy and morbidly principled, to pull the requisite strings at Sverdrup. But the office gestalt was hawkish and buzz-cut and generally inimical to bell-bottomed, lefty film-studies majors; and Tom didn't want to be there.

Up in the bedroom that he and I shared, the windows were open and the air had the stuffy wooden-house smell that came out every spring. I preferred the make-believe no-smell of air-conditioning, but my mother, whose subjective experience of temperature was notably consistent with low gas and electric bills, claimed to be a devotee of "fresh air," and the windows often stayed open until Memorial Day.

On my night table was the *Peanuts Treasury*, a large, thick hardcover compilation of daily and Sunday funnies by Charles M. Schulz. My mother had given it to me the previous Christmas, and I'd been rereading it at bedtime ever since. Like most of the nation's ten-year-olds, I had an intense, private relationship with Snoopy, the cartoon beagle. He was a solitary not-animal animal who lived among larger creatures of a different species, which was more or less my feeling in my own house. My brothers, who are nine and twelve years older than I, were less like siblings than like an extra, fun pair of quasi-parents. Although I had friends and was a Cub Scout in good standing, I spent a lot of time alone with talking animals. I was an obsessive rereader of A. A. Milne and the Narnia and Doctor Dolittle novels, and my involvement with my collection of stuffed animals was on the verge of becoming age-inappropriate. It was another point of kinship with Snoopy that he, too, liked animal games. He impersonated tigers and vultures and mountain lions, sharks, sea monsters, pythons, cows, piranhas, penguins, and vampire bats. He was the perfect sunny egoist, starring in his ridiculous fantasies and basking in everyone's attention. In a cartoon strip full of children, the dog was the character I recognized as a child.

Tom and my father had been talking in the living room when I went up to bed. Now, at some late and even stuffier hour, after I'd put aside the *Peanuts Treasury* and fallen asleep, Tom burst into our bedroom. He was shouting with harsh sarcasm. "You'll get over it! You'll forget about me! It'll be so much easier! You'll get over it!"

My father was offstage somewhere, making large abstract sounds.   5
My mother was right behind Tom, sobbing at his shoulder, begging him to stop, to stop. He was pulling open dresser drawers, repacking bags he'd only recently unpacked. "You think you want me here," he said, "but you'll get over it."

What about me? my mother pleaded. *What about Jon?*

"You'll get over it!"

I was a small and fundamentally ridiculous person. Even if I'd dared sit up in bed, what could I have said? "Excuse me, I'm trying to sleep"? I lay still and followed the action through my eyelashes. There were further dramatic comings and goings, through some of which I may in fact have slept. Finally I heard Tom's feet pounding down the stairs and my mother's terrible cries, now nearly shrieks, receding after him: "Tom! Tom! Tom! Please! Tom!" And then the front door slammed.

Things like this had never happened in our house. The worst fight I'd ever witnessed was between Tom and our older brother, Bob, on the subject of Frank Zappa, whose music Tom admired and Bob one day dismissed with such patronizing disdain that Tom began to sneer at Bob's own favorite group, the Supremes, which led to bitter hostilities. But a scene of real wailing and doors slamming in the night was completely off the map. When I woke up the next morning, the memory of it already felt decades-old and semi-dreamlike and unmentionable.

My father had left for work, and my mother served me breakfast with-   10
out comment. The food on the table, the jingles on the radio, and the walk to school all were unremarkable; and yet everything about the day was soaked in dread. At school that week, in Miss Niblack's class, we were

rehearsing our fifth-grade play. The script, which I'd written, had a large number of bit parts and one very generous role that I'd created with my own memorization abilities in mind. The action took place on a boat, involved a taciturn villain named Mr. Scuba, and lacked the most rudimentary comedy, point, or moral. Not even I, who got to do most of the talking, enjoyed being in it. Its badness—my responsibility for its badness—became part of the day's general dread.

There was something dreadful about springtime itself, the way plants and animals lost control, the *Lord of the Flies* buzzing, the heat indoors. After school, instead of staying outside to play, I followed my dread home and cornered my mother in our dining room. I asked her about my upcoming class performance. Would Dad be in town for it? What about Bob? Would he be home from college yet? And what about Tom? Would Tom be there, too? This was quite plausibly an innocent line of questioning—I was a small glutton for attention, forever turning conversations to the subject of myself—and, for a while, my mother gave me plausibly innocent answers. Then she slumped into a chair, put her face in her hands, and began to weep.

"Didn't you hear anything last night?" she said.

"No."

"You didn't hear Tom and Dad shouting? You didn't hear doors slamming?"

"No!"   15

She gathered me in her arms, which was probably the main thing I'd been dreading. I stood there stiffly while she hugged me. "Tom and Dad had a terrible fight," she said. "After you went to bed. They had terrible fight, and Tom got his things and left the house, and we don't know where he went."

"Oh."

"I thought we'd hear from him today, but he hasn't called, and I'm frantic, not knowing where he is. I'm just frantic!"

I squirmed a little in her grip.

"But this has nothing to do with you," she said. "It's between him   20 and Dad and has nothing to do with you. I'm sure Tom's sorry he won't be here to see your play. Or maybe, who knows, he'll be back by Friday and he will see it."

"O.K."

"But I don't want you telling anyone he's gone until we know where he is. Will you agree not to tell anyone?"

"O.K.," I said, breaking free of her. "Can we turn the air-conditioning on?"

I was unaware of it, but an epidemic had broken out across the country. Late adolescents in suburbs like ours had suddenly gone berserk, running away to other cities to have sex and not attend college, ingesting every substance they could get their hands on, not just clashing with their parents but rejecting and annihilating everything about them. For a while, the parents were so frightened and so mystified and so ashamed that each family, especially mine, quarantined itself and suffered in isolation.

When I went upstairs, my bedroom felt like an overwarm sickroom.   25 The clearest remaining vestige of Tom was the "Don't Look Back" poster that he'd taped to a flank of his dresser where Bob Dylan's psychedelic hair style wouldn't always be catching my mother's censorious eye. Tom's bed, neatly made, was the bed of a kid carried off by an epidemic.

In that unsettled season, as the so-called generation gap was rending the cultural landscape, Charles Schulz's work was almost uniquely beloved. Fifty-five million Americans had seen *A Charlie Brown Christmas* the previous December, for a Nielsen share of better than fifty per cent. The musical *You're a Good Man, Charlie Brown* was in its second sold-out year on Broadway. The astronauts of Apollo X, in their dress rehearsal for the first lunar landing, had christened their orbiter and landing vehicle Charlie Brown and Snoopy. Newspapers carrying *Peanuts* reached more than a hundred and fifty million readers, *Peanuts* collections were all over the bestseller lists, and if my own friends were any indication there was hardly a kid's bedroom in America without a *Peanuts* wastebasket or *Peanuts* bedsheets or a *Peanuts* gift book. Schulz, by a luxurious margin, was the most famous living artist on the planet.

To the countercultural mind, a be-goggled beagle piloting a doghouse and getting shot down by the Red Baron was akin to Yossarian paddling a dinghy to Sweden. The strip's square panels were the only square thing about it. Wouldn't the country be better off listening to Linus Van Pelt than Robert McNamara? This was the era of flower children, not flower adults. But the strip appealed to older Americans as well. It was unfailingly inoffensive (Snoopy never lifted a leg) and was set in a safe, attractive suburb where the kids, except for Pigpen, whose image Ron McKernan of the Grateful Dead pointedly embraced, were clean and well spoken and conservatively dressed. Hippies and astronauts, the Pentagon and the anti-war movement, the rejecting kids and the rejected grownups were all of one mind here.

An exception was my own household. As far as I know, my father never in his life read a comic strip, and my mother's interest in the funnies was limited to a single-panel feature called *The Girls*, whose generic middle-aged matrons, with their weight problems and stinginess and poor driving skills and weakness for department-store bargains, she found just endlessly amusing.

I didn't buy comic books, or even *Mad* magazine, but I worshipped at the altars of Warner Bros. cartoons and the funnies section of the St. Louis *Post-Dispatch*. I read the section's black-and-white page first, skipping the dramatic features like *Steve Roper* and *Juliet Jones* and glancing at *Li'l Abner* only to satisfy myself that it was still trashy and repellent. On the full-color back page I read the strips strictly in reverse order of preference, doing my best to be amused by Dagwood Bumstead's midnight snacks and struggling to ignore the fact that Tiger and Punkin-head were the kind of messy, unreflective kids I disliked in real life, before treating myself to my favorite strip, *B.C.* The strip, by Johnny Hart, was caveman humor. Hart wrung hundreds of gags from the friendship be-tween a flightless bird and a long-suffering tortoise who was constantly attempting unturtlish feats of agility and flexibility. Debts were always paid in clams; dinner was always roast leg of something. When I was done with *B.C.*, I was done with the paper.

The comics in St. Louis's other paper, the *Globe-Democrat*, which   30 my parents didn't take, seemed bleak and foreign to me. *Broom Hilda* and *Animal Crackers* and *The Family Circus* were off-putting in the man-ner of the kid whose partially visible underpants, which had the name CUTTAIR hand-markered on the waistband, I'd stared at throughout my family's tour of the Canadian parliament. Although *The Family Circus* was resolutely unfunny, its panels clearly were based on some actual fam-ily's life and were aimed at an audience that recognized this life, which compelled me to posit an entire subspecies of humanity that found *The Family Circus* hilarious.

I knew very well, of course, why the *Globe-Democrat's* funnies were so lame: the paper that carried *Peanuts* didn't *need* any other good strips. Indeed, I would have swapped the entire *Post-Dispatch* for a daily dose of Schulz. Only *Peanuts*, the strip we didn't get, dealt with stuff that really mattered. I didn't for a minute believe that the children in *Peanuts* were re-ally children—they were so much more emphatic and cartoonishly *real* than anybody in my own neighborhood—but I nevertheless took their stories to be dispatches from a universe of childhood that was somehow more substantial and convincing than my own. Instead of playing kick-ball and foursquare, the way my friends and I did, the kids in *Peanuts* had real baseball teams, real football equipment, real fistfights. Their interactions with Snoopy were far richer than the chasings and bitings that constituted my own relationships with neighborhood dogs. Minor but incredible dis-asters, often involving new vocabulary words, befell them daily. Lucy was "blackballed from the Bluebirds." She knocked Charlie Brown's croquet ball so far that he had to call the other players from a phone booth. She gave Charlie Brown a signed document in which she swore not to pull the football away when he tried to kick it, but the "peculiar thing about this document," as she observed in the final frame, was that "it was never no-tarized." When Lucy smashed the bust of Beethoven on Schroeder's toy piano, it struck me as odd and funny that Schroeder had a closet full of identical replacement busts, but I accepted it as humanly possible, because Schulz had drawn it.

To the *Peanuts Treasury* I soon added two other equally strong hard-cover collections, *Peanuts Revisited* and *Peanuts Classics*. A well-meaning relative once also gave me a copy of Robert Short's national best-sellers, *The Gospel According to Peanuts*, but it couldn't have interested me less. *Peanuts* wasn't a portal to the Gospel. It was my gospel.

Chapter 1, verses 1–4, of what I knew about disillusionment: Charlie Brown passes the house of the Little Red-Haired Girl, the object of his eternal fruitless longing. He sits down with Snoopy and says, "I wish I had two ponies." He imagines offering one of the ponies to the Little Red-Haired Girl, riding out into the countryside with her, and sitting down with her beneath a tree. Suddenly, he's scowling at Snoopy and asking, "Why aren't you two ponies?" Snoopy, rolling his eyes, thinks, "I knew we'd get around to that."

Or Chapter 1, verses 26–32, of what I knew about the mysteries of etiquette: Linus is showing off his new wristwatch to everyone in the neighborhood. "New watch!" he says proudly to Snoopy, who, after a hesitation, licks it. Linus's hair stands on end. "YOU LICKED MY WATCH!" he cries. "It'll rust! It'll turn green! He's ruined it!" Snoopy is left looking mildly puzzled and thinking, "I thought it would have been impolite not to taste it."

Or Chapter 2, verses 6–12, of what I knew about fiction: Linus is an-   35
noying Lucy, wheedling and pleading with her to read him a story. To shut him up, she grabs a book, randomly opens it, and says, "A man was born, he lived and he died. The End!" She tosses the book aside, and Linus picks it up reverently. "What a fascinating account," he says. "It almost makes you wish you had known the fellow."

The perfect silliness of stuff like this, the koanlike inscrutability, entranced me even when I was ten. But many of the more elaborate sequences,

especially the ones about Charlie Brown's humiliation and loneliness, made only a generic impression on me. In a classroom spelling bee that Charlie Brown has been looking forward to, the first word he's asked to spell is "maze." With a complacent smile, he produces "M-A-Y-S." The class screams with laughter. He returns to his seat and presses his face into his desktop, and when his teacher asks him what's wrong he yells at her and ends up in the principal's office. *Peanuts* was steeped in Schulz's awareness that for every winner in a competition there has to be a loser, if not twenty losers, or two thousand, but I personally enjoyed winning and couldn't see why so much fuss was made about the losers.

In the spring of 1970, Miss Niblack's class was studying homonyms to prepare for what she called the Homonym Spelldown. I did some desultory homonym drilling with my mother, rattling off "sleigh" for "slay" and "slough" for "slew" the way other kids roped softballs into center field. To me, the only halfway interesting question about the Spelldown was who was going to come in second. A new kid had joined our class that year, a shrimpy black-haired striver, Chris Toczko, who had it in his head that he and I were academic rivals. I was a nice enough little boy as long as you didn't compete on my turf. Toczko was annoyingly unaware that I, not he, by natural right, was the best student in the class. On the day of the Spelldown, he actually taunted me. He said he'd done a lot of studying and he was going to beat me! I looked down at the little pest and did not know what to say. I evidently mattered a lot more to him than he did to me.

For the Spelldown, we all stood by the blackboard, Miss Niblack calling out one half of a pair of homonyms and my classmates sitting down as soon as they had failed. Toczko was pale and trembling, but he knew his homonyms. He was the last kid standing, besides me, when Miss Niblack called out the word "liar." Toczko trembled and essayed, "L . . . I . . ." And I could see that I had beaten him. I waited impatiently while, with considerable anguish, he extracted two more letters from his marrow: "E . . . R?"

"I'm sorry, Chris, that's not a word," Miss Niblack said.

With a sharp laugh of triumph, not even waiting for Toczko to sit down, I stepped forward and sang out, "L-Y-R-E! *Lyre*. It's a stringed instrument." 40

I hadn't really doubted that I would win, but Toczko had got to me with his taunting, and my blood was up. I was the last person in class to realize that Toczko was having a meltdown. His face turned red and he began to cry, insisting angrily that "lier" *was* a word, it *was* a word.

I didn't care if it was a word or not. I knew my rights. Toczko's tears disturbed and disappointed me, as I made quite clear by fetching the class-room dictionary and showing him that "lier" wasn't in it. This was how both Toczko and I ended up in the principal's office.

I'd never been sent down before. I was interested to learn that the principal, Mr. Barnett, had a Webster's International Unabridged in his office. Toczko, who barely outweighed the dictionary, used two hands to open it and to roll back the pages to the "L" words. I stood at his shoulder and saw where his tiny, trembling index finger was pointing: *lier, n., one that lies (as in ambush)*. Mr. Barnett immediately declared us co-winners of the Spelldown—a compromise that didn't seem quite fair to me, since I would surely have murdered Toczko if we'd gone another round. But his outburst had spooked me, and I decided it might be O.K., for once, to let somebody else win.

A few months after the Homonym Spelldown, just after summer vacation started, Toczko ran out into Grant Road and was killed by a car. What little I knew then about the world's badness I knew mainly from a camping trip, some years earlier, when I'd dropped a frog into a campfire and watched it shrivel and roll down the flat side of a log. My memory of that shrivelling and rolling was sui generis, distinct from my other memories. It was like a nagging, sick-making atom of rebuke in me. I felt similarly rebuked now when my mother, who knew nothing of Toczko's rivalry with me, told me that he was dead. She was weeping as she'd wept over Tom's disappearance some weeks earlier. She sat me down and made me write a letter of condolence to Toczko's mother. I was very much unaccustomed to considering the interior states of people other than myself, but it was impossible not to consider Mrs. Toczko's. Though I never met her, in the ensuing weeks I pictured her suffering so incessantly and vividly that I could almost see her: a tiny, trim, dark-haired woman who cried the way her son did.

"Everything I do makes me feel guilty," says Charlie Brown. He's at the beach, and he has just thrown a pebble into the water, and Linus has commented, "Nice going. . . . It took that stone four thousand years to get to shore, and now you've thrown it back."

I felt guilty about Toczko. I felt guilty about the little frog. I felt guilty about shunning my mother's hugs when she seemed to need them most. I felt guilty about the washcloths at the bottom of the stack in the linen closet, the older, thinner washcloths that we seldom used. I felt guilty for preferring my best shooter marbles, a solid-red agate and a solid-yellow agate, my king and my queen, to marbles farther down my rigid marble hierarchy. I felt guilty about the board games that I didn't like to play—Uncle Wiggily, U.S. Presidential Elections, Game of the States—and sometimes, when my friends weren't around, I opened the boxes and examined the pieces in the hope of making the games feel less forgotten. I felt guilty about neglecting the stiff-limbed, scratchy-pelted Mr. Bear, who had no voice and didn't mix well with my other stuffed animals. To avoid feeling guilty about them, too, I slept with one of them per night, according to a strict weekly schedule.

We laugh at dachshunds for humping our legs, but our own species is even more self-centered in its imaginings. There's no object so Other that it can't be anthropomorphized and shanghaied into conversation with us. Some objects are more amenable than others, however. The trouble with Mr. Bear was that he was more realistically bearlike than the other animals.

He had a distinct, stern, feral persona; unlike our faceless washcloths, he was assertively Other. It was no wonder I couldn't speak through him. An old shoe is easier to invest with comic personality than is, say, a photograph of Cary Grant. The blanker the slate, the more easily we can fill it with our own image.

Our visual cortexes are wired to quickly recognize faces and then quickly subtract massive amounts of detail from them, zeroing in on their essential message: Is this person happy? Angry? Fearful? Individual faces may vary greatly, but a smirk on one is a lot like a smirk on another. Smirks are conceptual, not pictorial. Our brains are like cartoonists — and cartoonists are like our brains, simplifying and exaggerating, subordinating facial detail to abstract comic concepts.

Scott McCloud, in his cartoon treatise "Understanding Comics," argues that the image you have of yourself when you're conversing is very different from your image of the person you're conversing with. Your interlocutor may produce universal smiles and universal frowns, and they may help you to identify with him emotionally, but he also has a particular nose and particular skin and particular hair that continually remind you that he's an Other. The image you have of your own face, by contrast, is highly cartoonish. When you feel yourself smile, you imagine a cartoon of smiling, not the complete skin-and-nose-and-hair package. It's precisely the simplicity and universality of cartoon faces, the absence of Otherly particulars, that invite us to love them as we love ourselves. The most widely loved (and profitable) faces in the modern world tend to be exceptionally basic and abstract cartoons: Mickey Mouse, the Simpsons, Tintin, and, simplest of all—barely more than a circle, two dots, and a horizontal line—Charlie Brown.

Schulz only ever wanted to be a cartoonist. He was born in St. Paul in   50
1922, the only child of a German father and a mother of Norwegian extraction. As an infant, he was nicknamed Sparky, after a horse in the then popular comic strip *Barney Google*. His father, who, like Charlie Brown's father, was a barber, bought six different newspapers on the weekend and read all the era's comics with his son. Schulz skipped a grade in elementary school and was the least mature kid in every class after that. Much of the existing Schulzian literature dwells on the Charlie Brownish traumas in his early life: his skinniness and pimples, his unpopularity with girls at school, the inexplicable rejection of a batch of his drawings by his high-school yearbook, and, some years later, the rejection of his marriage proposal by the real-life Little Red-Haired Girl, Donna Mae Johnson. Schulz himself spoke of his youth in a tone close to anger. "It took me a long time to become a human being," he told NEMO magazine in 1987.

> I was regarded by many as kind of sissyfied, which I resented because I really was not a sissy. I was not a tough guy, but . . . I was good at any sport where you threw things, or hit them, or caught them, or something like that. I hated things like swimming and tumbling and those kinds of things, so I was really not a sissy. [But] the coaches were so intolerant and there was no program for all of us. So I never regarded myself as being much and I never regarded myself as being good looking and I never had a date in high school, because I thought, who'd want to date me? So I didn't bother.

Schulz "didn't bother" going to art school, either—it would only have discouraged him, he said, to be around people who could draw better than he could. You could see a lack of confidence here. You could also see a kid who knew how to protect himself.

On the eve of Schulz's induction into the Army, his mother died of cancer. She was forty-eight and had suffered greatly, and Schulz later described the loss as an emotional catastrophe from which he almost did not recover. During basic training, he was depressed, withdrawn, and grieving. In the long run, though, the Army was good for him. He went into the service, he recalled later, as "a nothing person" and came out as a staff sergeant in charge of a machine-gun squadron. "I thought, By golly, if that isn't a man, I don't know what is," he said. "And I felt good about myself and that lasted about eight minutes, and then I went back to where I am now." After the war, Schulz returned to his childhood neighborhood, lived with his father, became intensely involved in a Christian youth group, and learned to draw kids. For the rest of his life, he virtually never drew adults. He avoided adult vices—didn't drink, didn't smoke, didn't swear—and, in his work, he spent more and more time in the imagined yards and sandlots of his childhood. But the world of *Peanuts* remained a deeply motherless place. Charlie Brown's dog may (or may not) cheer him up after a day of failures; his mother never does.

Although Schulz had been a social victim as a child, he'd also had the undivided attention of two loving parents. All his life, he was a prickly Minnesotan mixture of disabling inhibition and rugged self-confidence. In high school, after another student illustrated an essay with a watercolor drawing, Schulz was surprised when a teacher asked him why he hadn't done some illustrations himself. He didn't think it was fair to get academic credit for a talent that most kids didn't have. He never thought it was fair to draw caricatures. ("If somebody has a big nose," he said, "I'm sure that they regret the fact they have a big nose and who am I to point it out in gross caricature?") In later decades, when he had enormous bargaining power, he was reluctant to demand a larger or more flexible layout for "Peanuts," because he didn't think it was fair to the papers that had been his loyal customers. His resentment of the name *Peanuts*, which his editors had given the strip in 1950, was still fresh in the eighties, when he was one of the ten highest-paid entertainers in America (behind Bill Cosby, ahead of Michael Jackson). "They didn't know when I walked in there that here was a fanatic," he told NEMO. "Here was a kid totally dedicated to what he was going to do. And to label then something that was going to be a life's work with a name like *Peanuts* was really insulting." To the suggestion that thirty-seven years might have softened the insult, Schulz said, "No, no. I hold a grudge, boy."

I never heard my father tell a joke. Sometimes he reminisced about a business colleague who ordered a "Scotch and Coke" and a "flander" fillet in a Dallas diner in July, and he could smile at his own embarrassments, his impolitic remarks at the office and his foolish mistakes on home-improvement projects, but there wasn't a silly bone in his body. He responded to other people's jokes with a wince or a grimace. As a boy, I told him a story I'd made up about a trash-hauling company cited for "fragrant violations." He shook his head, stone-faced, and said, "Not plausible."

In another archetypal *Peanuts* strip, Violet and Patty are abusing Charlie Brown in vicious stereo: "GO ON HOME! WE DON'T WANT YOU AROUND HERE!" As he trudges away with his eyes on the ground, Violet remarks, "It's a strange thing about Charlie Brown. You almost never see him laugh."

My father only ever wanted not to be a child anymore. His parents were a pair of nineteenth-century Scandinavians caught up in a Hobbesian struggle to prevail in the swamps of north-central Minnesota. His popular, charismatic older brother drowned in a hunting accident when he was still a young man. His nutty and pretty and spoiled younger sister had an only daughter who died in a one-car accident when she was twenty-two. My father's parents also died in a one-car accident, but only after regaling him

with prohibitions, demands, and criticisms for fifty years. He never said a harsh word about them. He never said a nice word, either.

The few childhood stories he told were about his dog, Spider, and his gang of friends in the invitingly named little town, Palisade, that his father and uncles had constructed among the swamps. The local high school was eight miles from Palisade. To attend, my father lived in a boarding house for a year and later commuted in his father's Model A. He was a social cipher, invisible after school. The most popular girl in his class, Romelle Erickson, was expected to be the valedictorian, and the school's "social crowd" was "shocked," my father told me many times, when it turned out that "the country boy," "Earl Who," had claimed the title.

When he registered at the University of Minnesota, in 1993, his father went with him and announced, at the head of the registration line, "He's going to be a civil engineer." For the rest of his life, my father was restless. He was studying philosophy at night school when he met my mother, and it took her four years to persuade him to have children. In his thirties, he agonized about whether to study medicine; in his forties, he was offered a partnership in a contracting firm which he almost dared to accept; in his fifties and sixties, he admonished me not to waste my life working for a corporation. In the end, though, he spent fifty years doing exactly what his father had told him to do.

My mother called him "oversensitive." She meant that it was easy to hurt his feelings, but the sensitivity was physical as well. When he was young, a doctor gave him a pinprick test that showed him to be allergic to "almost everything," including wheat, milk, and tomatoes. A different doctor, whose office was at the top of five long flights of stairs, greeted him with a blood-pressure test and immediately declared him unfit to fight the Nazis. Or so my father told me, with a shrugging gesture and an odd smile (as if to say, "What could I do?"), when I asked him why he hadn't been in the war. Even as a teen-ager, I sensed that his social awkwardness and sensitivities and been aggravated by not serving. He came from a family of pacifist Swedes, however, and was very happy not to be a soldier. He was happy that my brothers had college deferments and good luck with the lottery. Among his patriotic colleagues and the war-vet husbands of my mother's friends, he was such an outlier on the subject of Vietnam that he didn't dare talk about it. At home, in private, he aggressively declared that, if Tom had drawn a bad number, he personally would have driven him to Canada.

Tom was a second son in the mold of my father. He got poison ivy so bad it was like measles. He had a mid-October birthday and was perennially the youngest kid in his classes. On his only date in high school, he was so nervous that he forgot his baseball tickets and left the car idling in the street while he ran back inside; the car rolled down the hill, punched through an asphalt curb, and cleared two levels of a terraced garden before coming to rest on a neighbor's front lawn.

To me, it simply added to Tom's mystique that the car was not only 60 still drivable but entirely undamaged. Neither he nor Bob could do any wrong in my eyes. They were expert whistlers and chess players, phenomenal wielders of tools and pencils, sole suppliers of whatever anecdotes and cultural data I was able to impress my friends with. In the margins of Tom's school copy of *A Portrait of the Artist*, he drew a two-hundred-page riffle-animation of a stick-figure pole-vaulter clearing a hurdle, landing on his head, and being carted away on a stretcher by stick-figure E.M.S. personnel; this seemed to me a masterwork of filmic art and science. But my father had told Tom: "You'd make a good architect, here are three schools to choose from." He said: "You're going to work for Sverdrup."

Tom was gone for five days before we heard from him. His call came on a Sunday after church. We were sitting on the screen porch, and my mother ran the length of the house to answer the phone. She sounded so ecstatic with relief I felt embarrassed for her. Tom had hitchhiked back to Houston and was doing deep-fry at a Church's Fried Chicken, hoping to save enough money to join his best friend in Colorado. My mother kept asking him when he might come home, assuring him that he was welcome and that he wouldn't have to work at Sverdrup; but there was something toxic about us now which Tom obviously wanted nothing to do with.

Charles Schulz was the best comic-strip artist who ever lived. When *Peanuts* débuted, in October, 1950 (the same month Tom was born), the funny pages were full of musty holdovers from the thirties and forties. Even with the strip's strongest precursors, George Herriman's *Krazy Kat* and Elzie Segar's *Popeye*, you were aware of the severe constraints under which newspaper comics operated. The faces of Herriman's characters were too small to display more than rudimentary emotion, and so, the burden of humor and sympathy came to rest on Herriman's language; his work read more like comic fable than like funny drawing. Popeye's face was proportionately larger than Krazy Kat's, but he was such a florid caricature that much of Segar's expressive budget was spent on nondiscretionary items, like Popeye's distended jaw and oversized nose; these were good jokes, but the same jokes every time. The very first *Peanuts* strip, by contrast, was all white space and big funny faces. It invited you right in. The minor character Shermy was speaking in neat letters and clear diction: "Here comes ol' Charlie Brown! Good ol' Charlie Brown . . . Yes, sir! Good ol' Charlie Brown . . . How I hate him!"

This first strip and the seven hundred and fifty-nine that immediately followed it have recently been published, completed and fully indexed, in a handsome volume from Fantagraphics Books. (This is the first in a series of twenty-five uniform volumes that will reproduce Schulz's entire daily œuvre.) Even in Schulz's relatively primitive early work, you can appreciate what a breakthrough he made in drawing characters with large, visually uncluttered heads. Long limbs and big landscapes and fully articulated facial features—adult life, in short—were unaffordable luxuries. By dispensing with them, and by jumping from a funnies world of five or ten facial expressions into a world of fifty or a hundred, Schulz introduced a new informational dimension to the newspaper strip.

Although he later became famous for putting words like "depressed" and "inner tensions" and "emotional outlets" in the mouths of little kids, only a tiny percentage of his strips were actually drawn in the mock-psychological vein. His most important innovations were visual—he was all about *drawing funny*—and for most of my life as a fan I was curiously unconscious of this fact. In my imagination, *Peanuts* was a narrative, a collection of locales and scenes and sequences. And, certainly, some comic strips do fit this description. Mike Doonesbury, for example, can be translated into words with minimal loss of information. Garry Trudeau is essentially a social novelist, his topical satire and intricate family dynamics and elaborate camera angles all serving to divert attention from the monotony of his comic expression. But Linus Van Pelt consists, first and foremost, of pen strokes. You'll never really understand him without seeing his hair stand on end. Translation into words inevitably diminishes Linus. As a cartoon, he's already a perfectly efficient vector of comic intention.

The purpose of a comic strip, Schulz liked to say, was to sell newspapers and to make people laugh. Although the formulation may look self-deprecating at first glance, in fact it is an oath of loyalty. When I. B. Singer, in his Nobel address, declared that the novelist's first responsibility is to be a storyteller, he didn't say "mere storyteller," and Schulz didn't say "merely make people laugh." He was loyal to the reader who wanted something funny from the funny pages. Just about anything—protesting

against world hunger; getting a laugh out of words like "nooky"; dispensing wisdom; dying—is easier than real comedy.

Schulz never stopped trying to be funny. Around 1970, though, he began to drift away from aggressive humor and into melancholy reverie. There came tedious meanderings in Snoopy-land with the unhilarious bird

Woodstock and the unamusing beagle Spike. Certain leaden devices, such as Marcie's insistence on calling Peppermint Patty "sir," were heavily recycled. By the late eighties, the strip had grown so quiet that younger friends of mine seemed baffled by my fandom. It didn't help that later *Peanuts* anthologies loyally reprinted so many Spike and Marcie strips. The volumes that properly showcased Schulz's genius, the three hardcover collections from the sixties, had gone out of print. There were a few critical appreciations, most notably by Umberto Eco, who argued for Schulz's literary greatness in an essay written in the sixties and reprinted in the eighties (when Eco got famous). But the praise of a "low" genre by an old semiotic soldier in the culture wars couldn't help carrying an odor of provocation.

Still more harmful to Schulz's reputation were his own kitschy spinoffs. Even in the sixties, you had to fight through cloying Warm Puppy paraphemalia to reach the comedy; the cuteness levels in latter-day *Peanuts* TV specials tied my toes in knots. What first made *Peanuts Peanuts* was cruelty and failure, and yet every *Peanuts* greeting card and tchotchke and blimp had to feature somebody's sweet, crumpled smile. (You should go out and buy the new Fantagraphics book just to reward the publisher for putting a scowling Charlie Brown on the cover.) Everything about the billion-dollar *Peanuts* industry, which Schulz himself helped create, argued against him as an artist to be taken seriously. Far more than Disney, whose studios were churning out kitsch from the start, Schulz came to seem an icon of art's corruption by commerce, which sooner or later paints a smiling sales face on everything it touches. The fan who wants to see an artist sees a merchant instead. Why isn't he two ponies?

It's hard to repudiate a comic strip, however, when your memories of it are more vivid than your memories of your own life. When Charlie Brown went off to summer camp, I went along in my imagination. I heard him trying to make conversation with the fellow-camper who sat on his bunk and refused to say anything but "Shut up and leave me alone." I watched when he finally came home again and shouted to Lucy "I'm back!" and Lucy gave him a bored look and said, "Have you been away?"

I went to camp myself, in the summer of 1970. But, aside from an alarming personal-hygiene situation that seemed to have resulted from my peeing in some poison ivy, and which, for several days, I was convinced was either a fatal tumor or puberty, my camp experience paled beside Charlie Brown's. The best part of it was coming home and seeing Bob's new yellow Karmann Ghia waiting for me at the Y.M.C.A.

Tom was also home by then. He'd managed to make his way to his   70
friend's house in Colorado, but the friend's parents weren't happy about harboring somebody else's runaway son, and so they'd sent Tom back to St. Louis. Officially, I was very excited that he was back. In truth, I was embarrassed to be around him. I was afraid that if I referred to his sickness and our quarantine I might trigger a relapse. I wanted to live in a *Peanuts* world where rage was funny and insecurity was lovable. The littlest kid in my *Peanuts* books, Sally Brown, grew older for a while and then hit a glass ceiling. I wanted everyone in my family to get along and nothing to change; but suddenly, after Tom ran away, it was as if the five of us looked around, asked why we should be spending time together, and failed to come up with many good answers.

For the first time, in the months that followed, my parents' conflicts became audible. My father came home on cool nights to complain about the house's "chill." My mother countered that the house wasn't cold if you were *doing housework all day*. My father marched into the dining room to adjust the thermostat and dramatically point to its "Comfort Zone," a pale-blue arc between 72 and 78 degrees. My mother said that she was *so hot*. And I decided, as always, not to voice my suspicion that the Comfort Zone referred to air-conditioning in the summer rather than heat in the winter. My father set the temperature at seventy-two and retreated to the den, which was situated directly above the furnace. There was a lull, and then big explosions. No matter what corner of the house I hid myself in, I could hear my father bellowing, "LEAVE THE GOD-DAMNED THERMOSTAT ALONE!"

"Earl, I didn't touch it!"

"You did! Again!"

"I didn't think I even moved it, I just *looked* at it, I didn't mean to change it."

"Again! You monkeyed with it again! I had it set where I wanted it.   75
And you moved it down to seventy!"

"Well, if I did somehow change it, I'm sure I didn't mean to. You'd be hot, too, if you worked all day in the kitchen."

"All I ask at the end of a long day at work is that the temperature be set in the Comfort Zone."

"Earl, it is so hot in the kitchen. You don't know, because you're never *in* here, but it is *so* hot."

"The *low end* of the Comfort Zone! Not even the middle! The low end! It is not too much to ask!"

I wonder why "cartoonish" remains such a pejorative. It took me 80 half my life to achieve seeing my parents as cartoons. And to become more perfectly a cartoon myself: what a victory that would be.

My father eventually applied technology to the problem of temperature. He bought a space heater to put behind his chair in the dining room, where he was bothered in winter by drafts from the bay window. Like so many of his appliance purchases, the heater was a pathetically cheap little thing, a wattage hog with a stertorous fan and a grining orange mouth which dimmed the lights and drowned out conversation and produced a burning smell every time it cycled on. When I was in high school, he bought a quieter, more expensive model. One evening, my mother and I started reminiscing about the old model, caricaturing my father's temperature sensitivities, doing cartoons of the little heater's faults, the smoke and the buzzing, and my father got mad and left the table. He thought we were ganging up on him. He thought I was being cruel, and I was, but I was also forgiving him.

The Reader's Presence

1. Why does Franzen open the essay with the scene of his brother and father fighting? Where else in the essay does Franzen refer back to the fight? Why do you think Franzen returns to this scene repeatedly rather than resolving it in the first section?

2. Franzen titles the essay "The Comfort Zone." Where in the essay does this phrase appear? How might other scenes or passages relate to the concept of a "comfort zone"? How does the "comfort zone" relate to how Franzen felt about *Peanuts* and about his parents?

3. Note that Franzen inserts sections that directly cover information about Charles M. Schulz's biography and art. Why do you think Franzen includes this material in an otherwise personal essay? In your opinion, does it add to Franzen's family story or interrupt it?

4. Franzen says, "The blanker the slate, the more easily we can fill it with our own image" (paragraph 47). How does he use *Peanuts* as evidence for this observation? Read Charles Simic's "The Life of Images" (page 570), in which Simic analyzes photographs by Berenice Abbott and "experience[s] nostalgia for a time and place [he] did not know" (paragraph 5). How does Simic's interest in anonymous people in old photos compare with Franzen's fascination with Charlie Brown and other *Peanuts* characters?

Henry Louis Gates Jr.

Rope Burn

The critic, educator, writer, and activist Henry Louis Gates Jr. (b. 1950) is perhaps the most recent in a long line of African American intellectuals who are also public figures. In 1979 he became the first African American to earn a Ph.D. from Cambridge University in its eight-hundred-year history. He has been the recipient of countless honors, including a Carnegie Foundation Fellowship, a Mellon Fellowship, a MacArthur "genius" grant for his work in literary theory, and the 1998 National Medal for the Humanities. Gates is currently the W. E. B. Du Bois Professor of the Humanities at Harvard University. He has been at the forefront of the movement to expand the literary canon that is studied in American schools to include the works of non-European authors. He is also known for his work as a "literary archaeologist," uncovering literally thousands of previously unknown stories, poems, and reviews written by African American authors between 1829 and 1940 and making those texts available to modern readers. Much of his writing, in particular for publications such as the New York Times, Newsweek, *and* Sports Illustrated, *is accessible to general audiences.*

Gates's publications include Figures in Black: Words, Signs, and the "Racial" Self *(1987),* The Signifying Monkey: A Theory of African-American Literary Criticism *(1988),* Loose Canons: Notes on the Culture Wars *(1992),* Colored People: A Memoir *(1994),* Back to Africa *(2002), and* America behind the Color Line: Dialogues with African Americans *(2004).*

"Rope Burn" was first published in the New Yorker *and later became part of the* PBS *television series* Wonders of the African World, *broadcast in 2000. "My attitudes when I first came to the African Continent in 1970 were as romantic as any; in my sophomore year I had read DuBois's account of his own first visit to the Continent in 1923, and it certainly had shaped my own expectations," Gates notes in a travel diary on the PBS Web site. "My quest to encounter the glories of Africa's past would be a journey of discovery, for the readers and viewers, of course, but for me as well."*

The link between the sacred and the profane is a tenuous one, but never more so than at Debra Damo, the oldest monastery in black Africa. The monastery sits at the edge of a fifty-foot cliff, right on top of a mountain in the Ethiopian highlands. For the past fifteen hundred years, the only thing that has connected it to the secular world below is a couple of leather ropes that dangle from its gatehouse.

Not long ago, I found myself at the base of the cliff, peering up and asking myself just how badly I wanted to make it up there. I'd had a life-long fascination with Africa — I had spent a year in rural Tanzania when I was a college student, had studied African cultures as an adult, and had recently begun making a series of documentaries about the continent. This time, I thought I'd explore some of Africa's less visited corners, and that's how I ended up contemplating the doubtful integrity of an extremely elderly piece of leather.

According to legend, the monastery was founded by Za-Mikael, one of the Nine Saints who spread the doctrine of Christianity through the region. Since there was no way to scale the mountain, he decided that its top would be a perfect place for worship, meditation, prayer, and penitence. But how to get there? God conveniently commanded a snake to coil its tail around Za-Mikael and lift him to the pinnacle. God also commanded the Archangel Gabriel to stand guard with a drawn sword as Za-Mikael ascended and insure that the snake would do him no harm, because — well, you never know with snakes. The monk shouted "Hallelujah!" when he arrived at the mountaintop, and thus the monastery gained one of its bynames, Debra Hallelujah.

Za-Mikael's miracle soon attracted the attention of a great king of the region, who granted the saint's request that a church be built on the site where the serpent had deposited him. In order to build the church, the king first had a ramp constructed. Then, once the church was completed, Za-Mikael uttered the word *dahmemo*, which means "take it off," and the ramp was destroyed. *Dahmemo* was eventually shortened to "*damo*," thereby giving the monastery its most common name.

As I stood at the base of the cliff — and just to get that far had taken   5
a twenty-minute climb past huge boulders and gnarled, ancient-looking tree roots — all I could see at the top was a doorlike frame. Before me were the two ropes, one made of plaited leather and the other of sewn-together strips of cowhide, swaying gently in the breeze. What I wanted was a little chair, strapped securely to a failsafe rope-and-pulley mechanism, and a few robust, youthful monks at the top, pulling me smoothly up the face of the mountain. But there was no chair; no harness; no system of pulleys; no robust monks at the top waiting to welcome the pilgrim home to Mother Africa. There was only one old monk, about my father's age, pretending that he could pull me up by that cowhide strap, which was so frayed and discolored that it might have dated back to the sixth century. He looked like a bronzed elf as he peered over the edge of the cliff, his snow-white goatee framed by what I imagined was the door to eternity.

The end of the strap was formed into a loop, and it slipped easily over my head and settled around my chest. Suddenly, I felt it go taut. My instructions now were to grasp hold of the plaited leather rope and, hand over hand, to walk my way up the precipice, my body parallel to the ground. My feet found their way into crevices worn into the cliff, and I began to scale it, like the human fly, or a cat burglar, or, anyway, someone who knew his way around the Ethiopian highlands. Then, when I was about halfway up, my feet lost their grip and, as the craggy, nearly vertical incline gave way to a sheer, smooth rockface, slipped off the side of the mountain. I was now dangling from the line, unanchored, like a side of beef. The strap constricted my chest like a noose, and I could scarcely breathe.

My abject terror settled on a question: Which vista would be less sickening—the view down or the view up? Should I contemplate the twenty-five-foot drop to the rocks below or the equivalently daunting distance that separated me from the sanctuary in the sky? It was onward and upward for me, and, with considerable difficulty, I summoned my breath to urge on the wizened monk: "Pull . . . pull . . . pull!" I couldn't swear he'd heard me, but I could see his face, and the strain of my dead weight was showing.

In Ethiopia, a monk has the legal status of a dead man. Monks pay no taxes, do not appear in censuses, and cannot vote. They are, in fact, known as "the Living Dead." They read scripture in the ancient ecclesiastical language of Geez. They dedicate their lives to preparing for Heaven. All in all, I wasn't convinced that this monk would handle what I now considered my lifeline in entirely the right spirit. If the rope snapped and I fell to my death, he might think I'd been done a favor. That wasn't the kind of salvation I was hoping for. Besides, the holy geezer scarcely seemed strong enough to raise me, and my body hung uselessly in midair, legs pumping like Wile E. Coyote's just before he realizes that he has overshot the cliff.

Then I noticed that I'd begun to move—slowly, inch by inch, but steadily, until the wooden stump to which the rope was tied came into my view. I reached out and grabbed it, and soon found myself dragged through the open door to safety. Hallelujah.

"You saved my life," I gasped pathetically. I was winded by the   10
grip of the leather around my chest, marks from which would be visible for several days. For a brief while, I lay there on the sacred earth, promising God and myself that I would try to be a better person, and wondering what grand act of charity I could embark upon to make things right with the order of the universe. Only then did I realize that within a few hours I would have to go through it all over again: there was no other way down. What if I stayed where I was—dedicating myself to the hereafter, taking a vow of poverty, joining the Living Dead in an existence of communal holiness? That prospect was, just at that moment, more pleasing than the alternative. My beard would grow snowy, my skin leathery from the highland rays, and my arms sinewy and strong. My eyes would acquire the faraway serenity of the truly sanctified. I wondered how long it would take me to become fluent in Geez.

The Reader's Presence

1. Why is Gates attempting to reach the monastery? In what ways is Gates's journey an act of pilgrimage? To what extent is his trip purely an intellectual pursuit? What do you think he is seeking in climbing to Debra Damo? How does his perspective change as he ascends?

2. "The link between the sacred and the profane is a tenuous one," begins Gates. What in the essay represents the sacred? What represents the profane? How do the two meet?

3. Compare Gates's essay to Langston Hughes's "Salvation" (page 162). What kind of "salvation" is each man hoping to gain? In what ways are the two men's experiences similar? How are they different?

THE WRITER AT WORK

Henry Louis Gates Jr. on the Writer's Voice

Skilled at critical and academic writing, Henry Louis Gates Jr. hoped to find ways to tell stories about his growing up in a small West Virginia community. In writing his memoir, Colored People, *Gates found the voice he wanted. The following comments appeared in a 1995 collection,* Swing Low: Black Men Writing, *edited by Rebecca Carroll.*

My father told stories all the time when I was growing up. My mother used to call them "lies." I didn't know that "lies" was the name for stories in the black vernacular, I just thought it was her own word that she had made up. I was inspired by those "lies," though, and knew that I wanted to tell some too one day.

When I was ten or twelve, I had a baseball column in the local newspaper. I was the scorekeeper for the minor-league games in my town—I would compile all of the facts, and then the editor and I would put together a narrative. I did that every week during the summer. The best part was seeing my name in print. After that, I was hooked—hooked to seeing my name in black and white on paper.

At fourteen or fifteen, I read James Baldwin's work and became fascinated with the idea of writing. When I started reading about black people through the writings of black people, suddenly I was seized by the desire to write. I was in awe of how writers were able to take words and create an illusion of the world that people could step into—a world where people opened doors and shut doors, fell in love and out of love, where people lived and died. I wanted to be able to create those worlds too. I knew I had a voice even before I knew what a "writer's voice" meant. I didn't know what it was, but I could hear it, and I knew when my rhythm was on—it was almost as if I could hear myself write. I thought I had a unique take on the world and trusted my sensibility. It struck me that perhaps it would be a good thing to share it with other people. . . .

I don't think that the prime reason for writing is to save the world, or to save black people. I do it because it makes me feel good. I want to record my vision and to entertain people. When I was writing reviews, although it was an intriguing way to discuss literature, I would have a lot of black people say to me, "I'm having a hard time understanding you, brother." I've always had two conflicting voices within me, one that wants to be outrageous and on the edge, always breaking new ground, and another that wants to be loved by the community for that outrageousness. It is very difficult to expect that people will let you have it both ways like that. Those who really care about a community are the ones who push the boundaries and create new definitions, but generally they get killed for doing that, which is what I mean when I refer to myself as a griot in the black community—the one who makes the wake-up call, who loves his people enough to truly examine the status quo.

The wonderful thing about *Colored People* is that everybody gets it   5
and can appreciate it because it is a universal story. It is my segue from nonfiction to fiction. I wrote it to preserve a world that has passed away, and to reveal some secrets—not for the shock value, but because I want to re-create a voice that black people use when there are no white people around. Oftentimes in black literature, black authors get all lockjawed in their writing because they are doing it for a white audience, and not for themselves. You don't hear the voice of black people when it's just us in the kitchen, talking out the door and down the road, and that is the voice that I am trying to capture in *Colored People*. Integration may have cost us that voice. We cannot take it for granted and must preserve it whenever possible. I don't know what kind of positive language and linguistic rituals are being passed down in the fragmented, dispossessed black underclass. I think it's very different from when and where I was raised, when there was a stronger sense of community, and that language was everywhere I turned.

Edward Hoagland

On Stuttering

Edward Hoagland (b. 1932) is an essayist, nature writer, and novelist. Before his graduation from Harvard University, his first novel, Cat Man *(1956), was accepted for publication and won the Houghton-Mifflin Literary Fellowship Award. He has received several other honors, including a Guggenheim Fellowship, an O. Henry Award, an award from the American Academy of Arts and Letters, and a Lannan Foundation Award, and he has taught for more than fifteen years at Bennington College in Vermont. Hoagland's essays cover a wide range of topics, such as personal experiences, wild animals, travels to other countries, and ecological crises. Among his many highly regarded books are* Walking the Dead Diamond River *(1973),* African Calliope *(1979),* Balancing Acts *(1992), and* Tigers and Ice *(1999). Hoagland also served as guest editor for* Best American Essays 1999. *In his memoir,* Compass Points *(2001), Hoagland writes: "Most of us live like stand-up comedians on a vaudeville stage—the way an essayist does—by our humble wits, messing up, swallowing an aspirin, knowing Hollywood won't call, thinking no one we love will die today, just another day of sunshine and rain."*

Stuttering is like trying to run with loops of rope around your feet. And yet you feel that you do want to run because you may get more words out that way before you trip: an impulse you resist so other people won't tell you to "calm down" and "relax." Because they themselves may stammer a little bit when jittery or embarrassed, it's hard for a real stutterer like me to convince a new acquaintance that we aren't perpetually in such a nervous state and that it's quite normal for us to be at the mercy of strangers. Strangers are usually civilized, once the rough and sometimes inadvertently hurtful process of recognizing what is wrong with us is over (that we're not laughing, hiccuping, coughing, or whatever) and in a way we plumb them for traces of schadenfreude. A stutterer knows who the good guys are in any crowded room, as well as the location of each mocking gleam, and even the St. Francis type, who will wait until he thinks nobody is looking to wipe a fleck of spittle off his face.

I've stuttered for more than 60 years, and the mysteries of the encumbrance still catch me up: being reminded every morning that it's engrained in my fiber, although I had forgotten in my dreams. Life can become a matter of measuring the importance of anything you have to say. Is it better to remain a pleasant cipher who ventures nothing in particular but chuckles immoderately at everyone else's conversation, or instead to subject your several companions to the ordeal of watching you struggle to expel opinions that are either blurred and vitiated, or made to sound too emphatic, by all the huffing and puffing, the facial contortions, tongue biting, blushing, and suffering? "Write it down," people often said to me in school; indeed I sold my first novel before I left college.

Self-confidence can reduce a stutter's dimensions (in that sense you do "outgrow" it), as will affection (received or felt), anger, sexual arousal, and various other hormonal or pheromonal states you may dip into in the shorter term. Yet it still lurks underfoot, like a trapdoor. I was determined not to be impeded and managed to serve a regular stint in the Army by telling the draft-board psychiatrist that I wanted to and was only stammering from "nervousness" with him. Later I also contrived to become a college professor, thanks to the patience of my early students. Nevertheless, through childhood and adolescence, when I was almost mute in public, I could talk without much difficulty to one or two close friends, and then to the particular girl I was necking with. In that case, an overlapping trust was then the lubricant, but if it began to evaporate as our hopes for permanence didn't pan out, I'd start regretfully, apologetically but willy-nilly, to stutter with her again. Adrenaline, when I got mad, operated in a similar fashion, though only momentarily. That is, if somebody made fun of me or treated me cavalierly and a certain threshold was crossed, a spurt of chemistry would suddenly free my mouth and—like Popeye grabbing a can of spinach—I could answer him. Poor Billy Budd didn't learn this technique (and his example frightened me because of its larger implications). Yet many stutterers develop a snappish temperament, and from not just sheer frustration but the fact that being more than ready to "lose one's temper" (as Billy wasn't) actually helps. As in jujitsu, you can trap an opponent by employing his strength and cruelty against him; and bad guys aren't generally smart enough to know that if they wait me out, I'll bog down helplessly all over again.

Overall, however, stuttering is not so predictable. Whether rested or exhausted, fibbing or speaking the Simon-pure truth, and when in the company of chums or people whom I don't respect, I can be fluent or tied in knots. I learned young to be an attentive listener, both because my empathy for others' worries was honed by my handicap and because it was in my best interest that they talk a lot. And yet a core in you will hemorrhage if you become a mere assenter. How many opinions can you keep to yourself before you choke on them (and turn into a stick of furniture for everybody else)? So, instead, you measure what's worth specifying. If you agree with two-thirds of what's being suggested, is it worth the labor of breathlessly elaborating upon the one-third where you differ? There were plenty of times when a subject might come up that I knew more about than the rest of the group, and it used to gall me if I had held my peace till maybe closeted afterward with a close friend. A stymieing bashfulness can also slide a stutterer into slack language because accurate words are so much harder to say than bland ones. You're tempted to be content with an approximation of what you mean in

order to escape the scourge of being exact. A sort of football game is
going on in your head—the tacklers live there too—and the very effort
of pausing to figure out the right way to describe something will alert
them to how to pull you down. Being glib and sloppy generates less
blockage.

But it's important not to err in the opposite direction, on the side of   5
tendentiousness, and insist on equal time only because you are a pain
in the neck with a problem. You can stutter till your tongue bleeds
and your chest is sore from heaving, but so what, if you haven't anything to say that's worth the humiliation? Better to function as a kind of
tuning fork, vibrating to other people's anguish or apprehensiveness, as
well as your own. A handicap can be cleansing. My scariest moments
as a stutterer have been (1) when my daughter was learning to talk and
briefly got the impression that she was supposed to do the same;
(2) once when I was in the woods and a man shot in my direction and I
had to make myself heard loud and fast; and (3) when anticipating
weddings where I would need either to propose a toast or say "I
do." Otherwise my impediment ceased to be a serious blight about the
time I lost my virginity: just a sort of cleft to step around—a squint and
gasp of hesitation that indicated to people I might want to be friends
with or interview that I wasn't perfect either and perhaps they could
trust me.

At worst, during my teens, when I was stuttering on vowels as well
as consonants and spitting a few words out could seem interminable, I
tried some therapies. But "Slow Speech" was as slow as the trouble itself; and repeatedly writing the first letter of the word that I was stuttering on with my finger in my pocket looked peculiar enough to attract
almost as much attention. It did gradually lighten with my maturity and
fatherhood, professional recognition, and the other milestones that traditionally help. Nothing "slew" it, though, until at nearly 60 I went
semiblind for a couple of years, and this emergency eclipsed—
completely trumped—the lesser difficulty. I felt I simply had to talk or
die, and so I talked. Couldn't do it gratuitously or lots, but I talked
enough to survive. The stutter somehow didn't hold water and ebbed
away, until surgery restored my vision and then it returned, like other
normalcies.

Such variations can make a stutter seem like a sort of ancillary eccentricity, or a personal Godzilla. But the ball carrier in your head is going to
have his good days too—when he can swivel past the tacklers, improvising a broken-field dash so that they are out of position—or even capture
their attention with an idea so intriguing that they stop and listen. Not
for long, however: The message underlying a stutter is rather like mortality, after all. Real reprieves and fluency are not for you and me. We blun-
der along, stammering—then not so much—through minor scrapes and
scares, but not unscathed. We're not Demosthenes, of course. And poor

Demosthenes, if you look him up, ended about as sadly as Billy Budd. People tend to.

The Reader's Presence

1. Why does Hoagland compare his stutter to a football game (paragraph 4)? Explore the metaphor fully. For example, what position does Hoagland play? Who are the tacklers who are trying to pull him down? How many touchdowns does he score in his life, according to his essay? What strategies does he develop to avoid anticipated blockers? Would you say he's winning or losing? Why?

2. In what specific ways do Hoagland's sentences and paragraphs begin and end as you might have anticipated? Can you detect written signs of his stutter? What kinds of verbal hesitations and restatements happen when someone stutters? Where—and with what effects—are there similar hesitations and restatements in Hoagland's essay? Imagine Hoagland speaking this essay. At which points do you think that he would hesitate? Rewrite a paragraph to include the imagined stuttering and compare it to the original paragraph. What changes in meaning occur in the rewritten version?

3. Read David Sedaris's "Me Talk Pretty One Day" (page 273) and compare the two authors' approaches to handling difficulties with speech. What strategies do they use to deal with being less than fluent? To what extent do their limitations affect their feelings about themselves? about the world around them? Who deals more effectively with not being able to communicate fluently? Why?

THE WRITER AT WORK

Edward Hoagland on What an Essay Is

Known as one of America's finest essayists, Edward Hoagland began his career writing fiction. In this passage from his Introduction to The Best American Essays 1999, *Hoagland describes how he thinks essays work and the idiosyncratic ways essayists—like himself—approach the act of writing them. Essays, he reminds us, are different from articles and documents: They don't necessarily offer objective information and they don't require their writers to be authorities about anything other than their own experiences. All good essays, he suggests, encapsulate their writer's presence. In these literary beliefs he is a direct descendent of Montaigne (1533–1592), whom many consider the inventor of the modern essay. Montaigne, too, was skeptical of authority and wrote essays that appear to follow the drifts of an interior dialogue carried on with himself. After reading Hoagland's brief but thoughtful passage, consider how it comments on his essay on stuttering.*

Essays are how we speak to one another in print—caroming thoughts not merely in order to convey a certain packet of information, but with a special edge or bounce of personal character in a kind of public letter. You multiply yourself as a writer, gaining height as though jumping on a trampoline, if you can catch the gist of what other people have also been feeling and clarify it for them. Classic essay subjects, like the flux of friendship, "On Greed," "On Religion," "On Vanity," or solitude, lying, self-sacrifice, can be major-league yet not require Bertrand Russell to handle them. A layman who has diligently looked into something, walking in the mosses of regret after the death of a parent, for instance, may acquire an intangible authority, even without being memorably angry or funny or possessing a beguiling equanimity. *He* cares; therefore, if he has tinkered enough with his words, we do too.

An essay is not a scientific document. It can be serendipitous or domestic, satire or testimony, tongue-in-cheek or a wail of grief. Mulched perhaps in its own contradictions, it promises no sure objectivity, just the condiment of opinion on a base of observation, and sometimes such leaps of illogic or superlogic that they may work a bit like magic realism in a novel: namely, to simulate the mind's own processes in a murky and incongruous world. More than being instructive, as a magazine article is, an essay has a slant, a seasoned personality behind it that ought to weather well. Even if we think the author is telling us the earth is flat, we might want to listen to him elaborate upon the fringes of his premise because the bristle of his narrative and what he's seen intrigues us. He has a cutting edge, yet balance too. A given body of information is going to be eclipsed, but what lives in art is spirit, not factuality, and we respond to Montaigne's human touch despite four centuries of technological and social change.

Langston Hughes

Salvation

One of the leading figures of the Harlem Renaissance, Langston Hughes (1902–1967) was a prolific writer. He started his career as a poet, but he also wrote fiction, autobiography, biography, history, and plays, and he worked at various times as a journalist. One of his most famous poems, "The Negro Speaks of Rivers," was written while he was in high school. Although Langston Hughes traveled widely, most of his writings are concerned with the lives of urban working-class African Americans.

Hughes used the rhythms of blues and jazz to bring to his writing a distinctive expression of black culture and experience. His work continues to be popular today, especially collections of short stories such as The Ways of White Folks *(1934), volumes of poetry such as* Montage of a Dream Deferred *(1951), and his series of vignettes on the character Jesse B. Simple, collected and published from 1950 to 1965 (see pages 707–710). Hughes published two volumes of autobiography; "Salvation" is taken from the first of these,* The Big Sea *(1940).*

Throughout his work, Hughes refused to idealize his subject. "Certainly," he said, "I personally knew very few people anywhere who were wholly beautiful and wholly good. Besides I felt that the masses of our people had as much in their lives to put into books as did those more fortunate ones who had been born with some means and the ability to work up to a master's degree at a Northern college." Expressing the writer's truism about writing about what one knows best, he continued, "Anyway, I didn't know the upper-class Negroes well enough to write much about them. I only knew the people I had grown up with, and they weren't the people whose shoes were always shined, who had been to Harvard, or who had heard of Bach. But they seemed to me good people too."

I was saved from sin when I was going on thirteen. But not really saved. It happened like this. There was a big revival at my Auntie Reed's church. Every night for weeks there had been much preaching, singing, praying, and shouting, and some very hardened sinners had been brought to Christ, and the membership of the church had grown by leaps and bounds. Then just before the revival ended, they held a special meeting for children, "to bring the young lambs to the fold." My aunt spoke of it for days ahead. That night I was escorted to the front row and placed on the mourners' bench with all the other young sinners, who had not yet been brought to Jesus.

My aunt told me that when you were saved you saw a light, and something happened to you inside! And Jesus came into your life! And God was with you from then on! She said you could see and hear and feel Jesus in your soul. I believed her. I had heard a great many old people say the same thing and it seemed to me they ought to know. So I sat there calmly in the hot, crowded church, waiting for Jesus to come to me.

The preacher preached a wonderful rhythmical sermon, all moans and shouts and lonely cries and dire pictures of hell, and then he sang a song about the ninety and nine safe in the fold, but one little lamb was left out in the cold. Then he said: "Won't you come? Won't you come to Jesus? Young lambs, won't you come?" And he held out his arms to all us young sinners there on the mourners' bench. And the little girls cried. And some of them jumped up and went to Jesus right away. But most of us just sat there.

A great many old people came and knelt around us and prayed, old women with jet-black faces and braided hair, old men with work-gnarled hands. And the church sang a song about the lower lights are burning, some poor sinners to be saved. And the whole building rocked with prayer and song.

Still I kept waiting to *see* Jesus.   5

Finally all the young people had gone to the altar and were saved, but one boy and me. He was a rounder's son named Westley. Westley and I were surrounded by sisters and deacons praying. It was very hot in the church, and getting late now. Finally Westley said to me in a whisper: "God damn! I'm tired o' sitting here. Let's get up and be saved." So he got up and was saved.

Then I was left all alone on the mourners' bench. My aunt came and knelt at my knees and cried, while prayers and song swirled all around me in the little church. The whole congregation prayed for me alone, in a mighty wail of moans and voices. And I kept waiting serenely for Jesus, waiting, waiting—but he didn't come. I wanted to see him, but nothing happened to me. Nothing! I wanted something to happen to me, but nothing happened.

I heard the songs and the minister saying: "Why don't you come? My dear child, why don't you come to Jesus? Jesus is waiting for you. He wants you. Why don't you come? Sister Reed, what is this child's name?"

"Langston," my aunt sobbed.

"Langston, why don't you come? Why don't you come and be saved?   10
Oh, Lamb of God! Why don't you come?"

Now it was really getting late. I began to be ashamed of myself, holding everything up so long. I began to wonder what God thought about Westley, who certainly hadn't seen Jesus either, but who was now sitting proudly on the platform, swinging his knickerbockered legs and grinning down at me, surrounded by deacons and old women on their knees praying. God had not struck Westley dead for taking his name in vain or for lying in the temple. So I decided that maybe to save further trouble, I'd better lie, too, and say that Jesus had come, and get up and be saved.

So I got up.

Suddenly the whole room broke into a sea of shouting, as they saw me rise. Waves of rejoicing swept the place. Women leaped in the air. My aunt threw her arms around me. The minister took me by the hand and led me to the platform.

When things quieted down, in a hushed silence, punctuated by a few ecstatic "Amens," all the new young lambs were blessed in the name of God. Then joyous singing filled the room.

That night, for the first time in my life but one—for I was a big boy   15
twelve years old—I cried. I cried, in bed alone, and couldn't stop. I buried my head under the quilts, but my aunt heard me. She woke up and told my uncle I was crying because the Holy Ghost had come into my life, and because I had seen Jesus. But I was really crying because I couldn't bear to tell her that I had lied, that I had deceived everybody in the

church, that I hadn't seen Jesus, and that now I didn't believe there was a Jesus anymore, since he didn't come to help me.

The Reader's Presence

1. Pay close attention to Hughes's two opening sentences. How would you describe their tone? How do they suggest the underlying pattern of the essay? How do they introduce the idea of deception right from the start? Who is being deceived in the essay? Is it the congregation? God? Hughes's aunt? the reader?

2. Hughes's essay is full of hyperbole, much of it expressing the heightened emotion of religious conversion. What is the purpose of the exclamation points Hughes uses in paragraph 2? Who is speaking these sentences? Where are other examples of overstatement? How does Hughes incorporate lyrics from songs into his prose (see especially paragraph 3)? Why not simply quote from the songs directly? How do these stylistic decisions affect your sense of the scene? Do you feel aligned with Hughes? Why or why not?

3. How does Hughes use the character of Westley? Is he essential to the narrative? If so, why? How does his role compare to secondary characters in other essays—for example, Theresa in Bernard Cooper's "A Clack of Tiny Sparks" (page 121) or Shorty in Malcolm X's "Homeboy" (page 194)?

THE WRITER AT WORK

Langston Hughes on *How to Be a Bad Writer (in Ten Easy Lessons)*

Established authors are frequently asked for tips on writing. Here Langston Hughes reverses the practice and offers young writers some memorable advice on how to write poorly. "How to Be a Bad Writer" first appeared in the Harlem Quarterly *(Spring 1950). Some of his suggestions no longer seem applicable today, thanks in part to his own literary efforts. But which lessons do you think are still worth paying attention to?*

1. Use all the clichés possible, such as "He had a gleam in his eye," or "Her teeth were white as pearls."

2. If you are a Negro, try very hard to write with an eye dead on the white market—use modern stereotypes of older stereotypes—big burly Negroes, criminals, low-lifers, and prostitutes.

3. Put in a lot of profanity and as many pages as possible of near-pornography and you will be so modern you pre-date Pompei in your

lonely crusade toward the best seller lists. By all means be misunderstood, unappreciated, and ahead of your time in print and out, then you can be felt-sorry-for by your own self, if not the public.

4. Never characterize characters. Just name them and then let them go for themselves. Let all of them talk the same way. If the reader hasn't imagination enough to make something out of cardboard cut-outs, shame on him!

5. Write about China, Greece, Tibet, or the Argentine pampas — anyplace you've never seen and know nothing about. Never write about anything you know, your home town, or your home folks, or yourself.

6. Have nothing to say, but use a great many words, particularly high-sounding words, to say it.

7. If a playwright, put into your script a lot of hand-waving and spirituals, preferably the ones everybody has heard a thousand times from Marion Anderson to the Golden Gates.

8. If a poet, rhyme June with moon as often and in as many ways as possible. Also use *thee*'s and *thou*'s and *'tis* and *o'er*, and invert your sentences all the time. Never say, "The sun rose, bright and shining." But, rather, "Bright and shining rose the sun."

9. Pay no attention to spelling or grammar or the neatness of the manuscript. And in writing letters, never sign your name so anyone can read it. A rapid scrawl will better indicate how important and how busy you are.

10. Drink as much liquor as possible and always write under the influence of alcohol. When you can't afford alcohol yourself, or even if you can, drink on your friends, fans, and the general public.

If you are white, there are many more things I can advise in order to be a bad writer, but since this piece is for colored writers, there are some things I know a Negro just will not do, not even for writing's sake, so there is no use mentioning them.

Zora Neale Hurston

How It Feels to Be Colored Me

Born in Eatonville, Florida, in a year that she never remembered the same way twice, Zora Neale Hurston (1901?–1960) entered Howard University in 1923. In 1926 she won a scholarship to Barnard College, where she was the first black woman to be admitted. There Hurston developed an interest in anthropology, which was cultivated by Columbia University's distinguished anthropologist Franz Boas. From 1928 to 1931 she collected voodoo folklore in the South and published her findings in Mules and Men *(1935). Two successive Guggenheim Fellowships allowed her to do field work in the Caribbean, resulting in another anthropological study,* Tell My Horse *(1938). She also collected folklore about Florida for the Work Projects Administration and published the two novels for which she is justly famous,* Jonah's Gourd Vine *(1934), and* Their Eyes Were Watching God *(1937).*

Langston Hughes said that "she was always getting scholarships and things from wealthy white people." But when the economy collapsed and brought the famous Harlem Renaissance down with it, Hurston's patrons all but disappeared. She managed to publish two more books, Moses, Man of the Mountain *(1939) and* Seraph on the Suwanee *(1948), and her autobiography,* Dust Tracks on a Road *(1942), before her reputation suffered a serious decline during the 1950s. After working as a librarian, part-time teacher, and maid near the end of her life, Hurston died in a county welfare home in Florida in virtual obscurity. The rediscovery of her work is largely attributed to Alice Walker, who edited a collection of Hurston's writings,* I Love Myself When I'm Laughing *(1975). "How It Feels to Be Colored Me" originally appeared in* The World Tomorrow *in 1928.*

Hurston said, "I regret all my books. It is one of the tragedies of life that one cannot have all the wisdom one is ever to possess in the beginning. Perhaps, it is just as well to be rash and foolish for a while. If writers were too wise, perhaps no books would be written at all. It might be better to ask yourself 'Why?' afterwards than before. Anyway, the force from somewhere in Space which commands you to write in the first place, gives you no choice. You take up the pen when you are told, and write what is commanded. There is no agony like bearing an untold story inside you."

I am colored but I offer nothing in the way of extenuating circumstances except the fact that I am the only Negro in the United States whose grandfather on the mother's side was *not* an Indian chief.

I remember the very day that I became colored. Up to my thirteenth year I lived in the little Negro town of Eatonville, Florida. It is exclusively a colored town. The only white people I knew passed through the town going to or coming from Orlando. The native whites rode dusty horses, the Northern tourists chugged down the sandy village road in automobiles. The town knew the Southerners and never stopped cane chewing[1] when they passed. But the Northerners were something else again. They were peered at cautiously from behind curtains by the timid. The more venturesome would come out on the porch to watch them go past and got just as much pleasure out of the tourists as the tourists got out of the village.

The front porch might seem a daring place for the rest of the town, but it was a gallery seat for me. My favorite place was atop the gate-post. Proscenium box for a born first-nighter. Not only did I enjoy the show, but I didn't mind the actors knowing that I liked it. I usually spoke to them

---

[1]*cane chewing:* Chewing on sugar cane. —EDS.

in passing. I'd wave at them and when they returned my salute, I would say something like this: "Howdy-do-well-I-thank-you-where-you-goin'?" Usually automobile or the horse paused at this, and after a queer exchange of compliments, I would probably "go a piece of the way" with them, as we say in farthest Florida. If one of my family happened to come to the front in time to see me, of course negotiations would be rudely broken off. But even so, it is clear that I was the first "welcome-to-our-state" Floridian, and I hope the Miami Chamber of Commerce will please take notice.

During this period, white people differed from colored to me only in that they rode through town and never lived there. They liked to hear me "speak pieces" and sing and wanted to see me dance the parse-me-la,[2] and gave me generously of their small silver for doing these things, which seemed strange to me for I wanted to do them so much that I needed bribing to stop. Only they didn't know it. The colored people gave no dimes. They deplored any joyful tendencies in me, but I was their Zora nevertheless. I belonged to them, to the nearby hotels, to the county — everybody's Zora.

But changes came in the family when I was thirteen, and I was sent to school in Jacksonville. I left Eatonville, the town of the oleanders, as Zora. When I disembarked from the river-boat at Jacksonville, she was no more. It seemed that I had suffered a sea change. I was not Zora of Orange County any more, I was now a little colored girl. I found it out in certain ways. In my heart as well as in the mirror, I became a fast brown — warranted not to rub nor run.

But I am not tragically colored. There is no great sorrow dammed up in my soul, nor lurking behind my eyes. I do not mind at all. I do not belong to the sobbing school of Negrohood who hold that nature somehow has given them a lowdown dirty deal and whose feelings are all hurt about it. Even in the helter-skelter skirmish that is my life, I have seen that the world is to the strong regardless of a little pigmentation more or less. No, I do not weep at the world — I am too busy sharpening my oyster knife.

Someone is always at my elbow reminding me that I am the granddaughter of slaves. It fails to register depression with me. Slavery is sixty years in the past. The operation was successful and the patient is doing well, thank you. The terrible struggle that made me an American out of a potential slave said "On the line!" The Reconstruction[3] said "Get set!"; and the generation before said "Go!" I am off to a flying start and I must not halt in the stretch to look behind and weep. Slavery is the price I paid for civilization, and the choice was not with me. It is a bully adventure and worth all that I have paid through my ancestors for it. No one on

---

[2]*parse-me-la:* Probably an old dance song. — EDS.
[3]*Reconstruction:* The period of rebuilding and reorganizing immediately following the Civil War. — EDS.

earth ever had a greater chance for glory. The world to be won and nothing to be lost. It is thrilling to think — to know that for any act of mine, I shall get twice as much praise or twice as much blame. It is quite exciting to hold the center of the national stage, with the spectators not knowing whether to laugh or to weep.

The position of my white neighbor is much more difficult. No brown specter pulls up a chair beside me when I sit down to eat. No dark ghost thrusts its leg against mine in bed. The game of keeping what one has is never so exciting as the game of getting.

I do not always feel colored. Even now I often achieve the unconscious Zora of Eatonville before the Hegira.[4] I feel most colored when I am thrown against a sharp white background.

For instance at Barnard. "Beside the waters of the Hudson" I feel my   10
race. Among the thousand white persons, I am a dark rock surged upon, and overswept, but through it all, I remain myself. When covered by the waters, I am; and the ebb but reveals me again.

Sometimes it is the other way around. A white person is set down in our midst, but the contrast is just as sharp for me. For instance, when I sit in the drafty basement that is The New World Cabaret with a white person, my color comes. We enter chatting about any little nothing that we have in common and are seated by the jazz waiters. In the abrupt way that jazz orchestras have, this one plunges into a number. It loses no time in circumlocutions, but gets right down to business. It constricts the thorax and splits the heart with its tempo and narcotic harmonies. This orchestra grows rambunctious, rears on its hind legs and attacks the tonal veil with primitive fury, rending it, clawing it until it breaks through to the jungle beyond. I follow those heathen — follow them exultingly. I dance wildly inside myself; I yell within, I whoop; I shake my assegai[5] above my head, I hurl it true to the mark *yeeeeoeoww*! I am in the jungle and living in the jungle way. My face is painted red and yellow and my body is painted blue. My pulse is throbbing like a war drum. I want to slaughter something — give pain, give death to what, I do not know. But the piece ends. The men of the orchestra wipe their lips and rest their fingers. I creep back slowly to the veneer we call civilization with the last tone and find the white friend sitting motionless in his seat, smoking calmly.

"Good music they have here," he remarks, drumming the table with his fingertips.

Music. The great blobs of purple and red emotion have not touched him. He has only heard what I felt. He is far away and I see him but dimly across the ocean and the continent that have fallen between us. He is so pale with his whiteness then and I am *so* colored.

---

[4]*Hegira:* A journey to safety. Historically it refers to Mohammed's flight from Mecca in A.D. 622. — EDS.

[5]*assegai:* A hunting spear. — EDS.

At certain times I have no race, I am *me*. When I set my hat at a certain angle and saunter down Seventh Avenue, Harlem City, feeling as snooty as the lions in front of the Forty-Second Street Library, for instance. So far as my feelings are concerned, Peggy Hopkins Joyce[6] on the Boule Mich[7] with her gorgeous raiment, stately carriage, knees knocking together in a most aristocratic manner, has nothing on me. The cosmic Zora emerges. I belong to no race nor time. I am the eternal feminine with its string of beads.

I have no separate feeling about being an American citizen and col-   15
ored. I am merely a fragment of the Great Soul that surges within the boundaries. My country, right or wrong.

Sometimes, I feel discriminated against, but it does not make me angry. It merely astonishes me. How *can* any deny themselves the pleasure of my company? It's beyond me.

But in the main, I feel like a brown bag of miscellany propped against a wall. Against a wall in company with other bags, white, red, and yellow. Pour out the contents, and there is discovered a jumble of small things priceless and worthless. A first-water diamond, an empty spool, bits of broken glass, lengths of string, a key to a door long since crumbled away, a rusty knife-blade, old shoes saved for a road that never was and never will be, a nail bent under the weight of things too heavy for any nail, a dried flower or two still a little fragrant. In your hand is the brown bag. On the ground before you is the jumble it held—so much like the jumble in the bags, could they be emptied, that all might be dumped in a single heap and the bags refilled without altering the content of any greatly. A bit of colored glass more or less would not matter. Perhaps that is how the Great Stuffer of Bags filled them in the first place—who knows?

The Reader's Presence

1. How much does being "colored" inform Hurston's identity? Does it seem to matter throughout the essay? At what points does color seem deeply important to Hurston? When does it seem less important? What do you think the reasons are for these differences?

2. Consider Hurston's startling image in the final paragraph: "But in the main, I feel like a brown bag of miscellany propped against a wall." Try rereading the essay with this image in mind. In what ways does it help you understand Hurston's sense of personal identity? In what ways can it be said to describe the form and style of the essay itself?

3. Hurston uses an extended description of jazz at The New World Cabaret to illustrate the claim: "I feel most colored when I am

[6]*Peggy Hopkins Joyce:* A fashionable American who was a celebrity in the 1920s. —EDS.
[7]*Boule Mich:* The Boulevard Saint-Michel in Paris. —EDS.

thrown against a sharp white background" (paragraph 9). Does Malcolm X's experience at the Roseland State Ballroom in Boston teach him the same lesson in "Homeboy" (page 194)? How might Malcolm X respond to Hurston's claim that at times she has "no race" (paragraph 14)? What might he say to her statement, "I do not belong to the sobbing school of Negrohood" (paragraph 6)? What are Hurston's and Malcolm X's definitions of "race"? How do these definitions compare to that of Richard Rodriguez, who says that he has been "liberated . . . from the black-and-white checkerboard" (page 239)?

Gish Jen

Name Dropping

Lillian Jen (b. c. 1956), who writes under the name Gish Jen, is a second-generation Chinese American, born of immigrant parents, raised in the largely Jewish community of Scarsdale, New York, and educated at Harvard University. As a writer, she takes on the subject of ethnic identity, but shies away from being identified simply as an Asian American writer. "Of course I'm interested in the Asian American experience," she told an interviewer in 1999. "But I'm also interested in architecture; I'm interested in religion. I'm very interested in the different realities, not just my own ethnic group." Known for both her sensitive treatment of diverse cultural and ethnic themes, and for her handling of these serious issues with great humor, Jen has been described as "a writer who moves and entertains us as she updates the American Dream." Her books include Typical American *(1991),* Mona in the Promised Land *(1996), and* The Love Wife *(2004). The title story from her collection* Who's Irish? *(1999) appears on page 912. Her stories have appeared in the* New Yorker, *the* New Republic, *and the* New York Times, *as well as in a variety of anthologies, including* The Best American Short Stories of the Century.*

Jen's essay "Name Dropping" appeared in the July 1996 issue of Allure. *In it she explains that she took on the pseudonym "Gish" as a way of "inventing" herself, of joining a long, enduring list of writers—from Mark Twain to Jamaica Kincaid—who have "named themselves into existence."*

Not all people are name changers. We all know people named Hogette or Winifred or Barbarella who have suffered through life without doing anything to better their plight. On the other hand, we also all know people with perfectly nice names who have felt compelled to do something about them for no good reason other than that they felt like it; and I, I confess, am one of them. I am not sure why this is. However, I have long suspected that an outsider looking at me might have known I would be the type to change my name by the number of times I changed my hairstyle.

This is not to say that I was a hair experimenter per se. I was not a person who knew how to do hair curlers and home perms, though I did once try some black henna. But I have only to look at my photo albums to behold undeniable pictorial evidence that I was more open than usual to the suggestions of hairdressers. I have left salon chairs with bangs, with frizz, with spikes. Once I discovered my hair so much lighter as a result of perm chemicals that I looked like a Dolly Parton impersonator who hadn't put on her bust yet. Blond at last! (That's when I bought the henna.)

But of course, all this was mere warm-up for the less photo-worthy but finally more radical act of rebaptizing myself—to understand which you would first have to know that I was given two complicated names when I was born, neither of which was Gish. The first was Bi Lian, my Chinese name, which was my name to sigh over. " 'Bi' means jade," my mom would explain to me, "and 'Lian' means lotus flower." And then she would explain how the lotus was a kind of water lily, and how it symbolizes purity because it grows up out of the mud but opens clean and white. I would listen to this while privately rehashing certain fascinating exchanges of glances in homeroom; and that's when she would sigh the kind of sigh of which mothers are such consummate masters—the kind of sigh whose economy of expression takes one's breath away. The upshot of hers, for example, being that the events of the twentieth century had truly been a nuisance. For if it hadn't been for the Chinese Revolution and so on, she would have had a real Jade Lotus, and how unlike her daughter she would have been! For Jade Lotuses did not wear eye shadow, and Jade Lotuses did not pierce their ears, and Jade Lotuses did not grow their hair to a length that made them look like Cousin Itt. Jade Lotuses did not wear miniskirts so short they had to be sure their underwear was clean. No—Jade Lotuses made straight A's, even in Conduct, and wore their hair in braids and never considered the length of their eyelashes. They did not feel doomed because their bra brand was "AA-OK," and when asked what they most wanted in life, Jade Lotuses answered that they wanted to make their parents happy.

It says something that my parents never actually called me by that name. Maybe they used it when I was an infant; but for the most part, Bi Lian was a name they informed me about. It was a name they took down off the shelf, dusted off, and admired in a pointed sort of way, then put back, like an overfancy wedding present that I might think they ought to just give to Salvation Army but that they meant to hand down to me in their will. After all, the twentieth century was happening, like it or not;

they were now living in America — for good it seemed. And so they pinned all their immigrant hopes on my English name instead.

Lillian Constance Jen. Today I think it's not so bad as names go. "Lillian Constance" kind of tumbles along, and then there's that nice punctuating "Jen" at the end, neat as an ace gymnast nailing her landing. But of course, growing up, I hated it. Not the Jen part, I liked that. And not the Constance part so much — one's middle name is one of life's most easily ignored intimate facts. However, I hated "Lillian." As far as I was concerned, it was a totally weird name that nobody else I knew was afflicted with. I thought it distinctly out-of-date and maybe even fusty, whatever that meant. It seemed to me most naturally prefaced with the words "my maiden aunt," and it put me in mind of half-glasses on a chain and support stockings. It put me in mind of sensible shoes and accordion rain bonnets with little snap sacks and the kind of wardrobe where you not only have the same number of tops as bottoms but everything goes with everything else, so that if you wanted to you could make some sort of math problem out of it. You know, if T = Tops and B = Bottoms and T = B, then how many looks do you gain if you buy yourself one more tweed skirt and one more navy sweater? The answer would no doubt have something to do with factorials.

But for all of this, I never told my parents how I felt until long after I'd turned myself into Gish. My parents thought Lillian a very nice name; indeed, they were outright proud of it. For in picking Lillian, they had followed the rules of English name picking then fashionable and come up with a rather beautiful solution. I hear that nowadays even first-generation Chinese-Americans choose names like Michelle and Ashley for their girls, the sort of names one associates more with mint green carpeting and coordinating wallpaper than with symbolic complexity and nobility of aspiration. My own cousin from China asked me to call her Cyndy — a name that seemed to me surprising for a chemical engineer and one that had nothing whatsoever to do with her Chinese name. Whereas my parents chose Lillian expressly because it not only sounded like Bi Lian — Bi Lian, Lillian — but because Lillian also had as a word root "water lily." How elegant! In Lillian, their dreams of a daughter seemed to survive. Real translation seemed possible.

I got the name Gish when I was in high school. It was not the first nickname I'd had; I had at various times been called Professor and Lily Two-shoes and, in one of my periods of hair wildness, Coconut. Also it was not the first time I'd adopted a name. When I was confirmed in fourth grade, I took for myself the name that seemed the most opposite possible from the one I had: Mary. But as soon as I began to be Gish, I knew this was more serious than any other name change I'd been involved in, because it seemed to be associated not with a change of hair but, even more portentously, with a change of handwriting. "Lillian Constance" I continued to write the way I'd always written everything — with a reasonably slanting script that was, for all its illegibility, a clear corruption of the Palmer method. (This is the handwriting in which I still sign checks and

Visa card charges and tax returns.) "Gish," on the other hand, I write in a more upright script, with gaps between the letters. I do not know how it was that I suddenly started writing this way, but this is the handwriting I use every day now and for signing books.

It is easier to say how I got the name Gish. A bunch of friends and I were in an arty phase, the kind of phase in which you go to films instead of movies and start preferring profundity in poetry. And as part of that phase, we all got arty nicknames. Thus my friend Maddy Hausman became A.E. after that poet; and I became Gish after the actress Lillian Gish. Never mind that we had never read any of Housman's poetry or seen any of Gish's movies. We assumed the names for a week, after which, Maddy went back to being Maddy. I, though, went shortly after that to a summer National Science Foundation archaeological dig; and it was there, as my fellow diggers and I were going around the circle introducing ourselves, that I first gave my name as Gish. It was a strange moment. There was a hurricane going on, similar to a storm that occurred on the day I was born; and the building had just been hit by lightning, which perhaps reminded me of hair dryers and, by association, hair salons. I don't know. I didn't plan to do it. But there I was, nonchalantly acting as if Gish were a name everyone called me all of the time instead of a name a few people had called me a couple of times; and all summer, this was a secret delight to me. I listened for my name avidly — partly because I didn't want to fail to respond when someone said it — and I did other things too that Lillian did not do. I snuck out of the dorm at night, propping a certain door open; I returned at dawn. I drank beer. I stopped wearing a bra. I wore itty-bitty cutoffs instead of the twill midthigh camp shorts with cuffs my mother had insisted I pack. And I made fun of a boy who was in love with me as if I were too used to being adored to be touched by him in the least. Indeed, I mooed when he made eyes at me, that my friends might laugh and see how he did look exactly like a cow.

Of course, today I know how very normal all this is, even the name changing. Today I know an Irwin who, his first day of college, introduced himself to everyone as Richard. I know a Becky who, once she got to grad school, asked even her oldest friends to call her Rebecca. Names matter to us; and as for whether the world cares, I think it does much more than it realizes. My friend Karen, for example, seems to pick marriage partners whose names resemble her maiden name, Smoler; the first was Parker, the second, Heller. And if you look up and down the line in my husband's family, every female except one has married an Irishman named John.

For myself, though, I think that choosing the name Gish had less to   10
do with how I wanted to be perceived than it did with a desire to lead, not a received life, but an authentic one. I wanted to invent myself; and in this I turned out, of course, to be like many, many writers before me. George Eliot, Mark Twain, Tennessee Williams. T. Coraghessan Boyle was formerly Tom Boyle; Jamaica Kincaid was Elaine Potter Richardson.

All these writers have named themselves into existence and, tickled by what they've gotten away with, gone on to try for more. I was not thinking about any of them in particular, though, when I decided to become Gish. Indeed, I was not thinking at all. I did it because I felt like it, and because I was just beginning to realize that I could do all kinds of things if I felt like it. I was realizing that I could go around bald if I wanted to; and that I could become a writer if I wanted to; and that if I did become a writer, I could write whatever I wanted to write, if I wanted to.

The Reader's Presence

1. Compile a list of all the names Jen has had. What was the association or meaning of each of them? Why does Jen eventually dispose of them all and choose "Gish"? What do you think it means for her to have many names and to choose one for herself?

2. How is Jen's choice a symbol of her "desire to lead, not a received life, but an authentic one" (paragraph 10)?

3. Consider the importance of names in Maya Angelou's "'What's Your Name, Girl?'" (page 77) and Maxine Hong Kingston's "No Name Woman" (page 485). How does the importance of Gish Jen's name compare to the importance of names in these other essays?

Jamaica Kincaid

Biography of a Dress

Jamaica Kincaid was born in Antigua in 1949 and came to the United States at the age of seventeen to work for a New York family as an au pair. Her novel Lucy *(1990) is an imaginative account of her experience of coming into adulthood in a foreign country and continues the narrative of her personal history begun in the novel* Annie John *(1985). She has also published a collection of short stories,* At the Bottom of the River *(1983), a collection of essays,* A Small Place *(1988), and a third novel,* The Autobiography of My Mother *(1995). Her most recent publications include* My Brother *(1997), which was a National Book Award Finalist for Nonfiction,* My Favorite Plant: Writers and Gardeners on the Plants

They Love *(1998),* My Garden *(2001), and* Mr. Potter *(2002). Her writing also appears in national magazines, especially the* New Yorker, *where she worked as a staff writer until 1995. Her well-known story "Girl" appears on page 921.*

   "I'm someone who writes to save her life," Kincaid says, "I mean, I can't imagine what I would do if I didn't write. I would be dead or I would be in jail because—what else could I do? I can't really do anything but write. All the things that were available to someone in my position involved being a subject person. And I'm very bad at being a subject person."

   The dress I am wearing in this black-and-white photograph, taken when I was two years old, was a yellow dress made of cotton poplin (a fabric with a slightly unsmooth texture first manufactured in the French town of Avignon and brought to England by the Huguenots, but I could

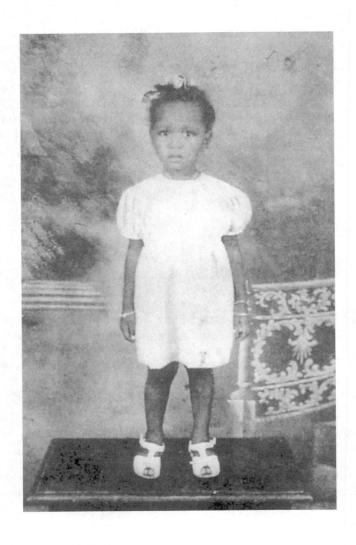

not have known that at the time), and it was made for me by my mother. This shade of yellow, the color of my dress that I am wearing when I was two years old, was the same shade of yellow as boiled cornmeal, a food that my mother was always eager for me to eat in one form (as a porridge) or another (as fongie, the starchy part of my midday meal) because it was cheap and therefore easily available (but I did not know that at the time), and because she thought that foods bearing the colors yellow, green or orange were particularly rich in vitamins and so boiled cornmeal would be particularly good for me. But I was then (not so now) extremely particular about what I would eat, not knowing then (but I do now) of shortages and abundance, having no consciousness of the idea of rich and poor (but I know now that we were poor then), and would eat only boiled beef (which I required my mother to chew for me first and, after she had made it soft, remove it from her mouth and place it in mine), certain kinds of boiled fish (doctor or angel), hard-boiled eggs (from hens, not ducks), poached calf's liver and the milk from cows, and so would not even look at the boiled cornmeal (porridge or fongie). There was not one single thing that I could isolate and say I did not like about the boiled cornmeal (porridge or fongie) because I could not isolate parts of things then (though I can and do now), but whenever I saw this bowl of trembling yellow substance before me I would grow still and silent, I did not cry, that did not make me cry. My mother told me this then (she does not tell me this now, she does not remember this now, she does not remember telling me this now): she knew of a man who had eaten boiled cornmeal at least once a day from the time he was my age then, two years old, and he lived for a very long time, finally dying when he was almost one hundred years old, and when he died he had looked rosy and new, with the springy wrinkles of the newborn, not the slack pleats of skin of the aged; as he lay dead his stomach was cut open, and all his insides were a beautiful shade of yellow, the same shade of yellow as boiled cornmeal. I was powerless then (though not so now) to like or dislike this story; it was beyond me then (though not so now) to understand the span of my lifetime then, two years old, and it was beyond me then (though not so now), the span of time called almost one hundred years old; I did not know then (though I do now) that there was such a thing as an inside to anybody, and that this inside would have a color, and that if the insides were the same shade of yellow as the yellow of boiled cornmeal my mother would want me to know about it.

On a day when it was not raining (that would have been unusual, that would have been out of the ordinary, ruining the fixed form of the day), my mother walked to one of the Harneys stores (there were many Harneys who owned stores, and they sold the same things, but I did not know then and I do not know now if they were all of the same people) and bought one-and-a-half yards of this yellow cotton poplin to make a dress for me, a dress I would wear to have my picture taken on the day I turned two years old. Inside, the store was cool and dark, and this was a good thing because outside was hot and overly bright. Someone named Harney did not wait on my mother, but someone named Miss Verna did and she was very nice still, so nice that she tickled my cheek as she spoke to my mother, and I reached forward as if to kiss her, but when her cheek met my lips I opened my mouth and bit her hard with my small child's teeth. Her cry of surprise did not pierce the air, but she looked at me hard, as if she knew me very, very well; and later, much later, when I was about twelve years old or so and she was always in and out of the crazy house, I would pass her on the street and throw stones at her, and she would turn and look at me hard, but she did not know who I was, she did not know who anyone was at all, not at all. Miss Verna showed my mother five flat thick bolts of cloth, white, blue (sea), blue (sky), yellow and pink, and my mother chose the yellow after holding it up against the rich copper color that my hair was then (it is not so now); she paid for it with a one-pound note that had an engraving of the king George Fifth on it (an ugly man with a cruel, sharp, bony nose, not the kind, soft, fleshy noses I was then used to), and she received change that included crowns, shillings, florins, and farthings.

My mother, carrying me and the just-bought piece of yellow poplin wrapped in coarse brown paper in her arms, walked out of Mr. Harney's store, up the street a few doors away, and into a store called Murdoch's (because the family who owned it were the Murdochs), and there my mother bought two skeins of yellow thread, the kind used for embroidering and a shade of yellow almost identical to the yellow poplin. My mother not only took me with her everywhere she went, she carried me, sometimes in her arms, sometimes on her back; for this errand she carried me in her arms; she did not complain, she never complained (but later she refused to do it anymore and never gave an explanation, at least not one that I can remember now); as usual, she spoke to me and sang to me in French patois (but I did not understand French patois then and I do not now and so I can never know what exactly she said to me then). She walked back to our house on Dickenson Bay Street, stopping often to hold conversations with people (men and women) she knew, speaking to them sometimes in English, sometimes in French; and if after they said how beautiful I was (for people would often say that about me then but they do not say that about me now), she would laugh and say that I did not like to be kissed (and I don't know if that was really true then but it is not so now). And that night after we had eaten our supper (boiled fish in a butter-and-lemon-juice sauce) and her husband (who was not my father but I did not know that at the time, I know that now) had gone for a walk (to the jetty), she removed her yellow poplin from its brown wrapper and folded and made creases in it and with scissors made holes (for the arms and neck) and slashes (for an opening in the back and the shoulders); she then placed it along with some ordinary thread (yellow), the thread for embroidering, the scissors and a needle in a basket that she had brought with her from her home in Dominica when she first left it at sixteen years of age.

For days afterward, my mother, after she had finished her usual chores (clothes washing, dish washing, floor scrubbing, bathing me, her only child, feeding me a teaspoon of cod-liver-oil), sat on the sill of the doorway, half in the sun, half out of the sun, and sewed together the various parts that would make up altogether my dress of yellow poplin; she gathered and hemmed and made tucks; she was just in the early stages of teaching herself how to make smocking and so was confined to making straight stitches (up-cable, down-cable, outline, stem, chain); the bodice of the dress appeared simple, plain, and the detail and pattern can only be seen close up and in real life, not from far away and not in a photograph; and much later, when she grew in confidence with this craft, the bodice of my dresses became overburdened with the stitches, chevron, trellis, diamonds, Vandyke, and species of birds she had never seen (swan) and species of flowers she had never seen (tulip) and species of animals she had never seen (bear) in real life, only in a picture in a book.

My skin was not the color of cream in the process of spoiling, my 5 hair was not the texture of silk and the color of flax, my eyes did not gleam like blue jewels in a crown, the afternoons in which I sat watching my mother make me this dress were not cool, and verdant lawns and pastures and hills and dales did not stretch out before me; but it was the picture of such a girl at two years old—a girl whose skin was the color of cream in the process of spoiling, whose hair was the texture of silk and the color of flax, a girl whose eyes gleamed like blue jewels in a crown, a girl whose afternoons (and mornings and nights) were cool, and before whom stretched verdant lawns and pastures and hills and dales—that my mother saw, a picture on an almanac advertising a particularly fine and scented soap (a soap she could not afford to buy then but I can now), and this picture of this girl wearing a yellow dress with smocking on the front bodice perhaps created in my mother the desire to have a daughter who looked like that or perhaps created the desire in my mother to try and make the daughter she already had look like that. I do not know now and I did not know then. And who was that girl really? (I did not ask then because I could not ask then but I ask now.) And who made her dress? And this girl would have had a mother; did the mother then have some friends, other women, did they sit together under a tree (or sit somewhere else) and compare strengths of potions used to throw away a child, or weigh the satisfactions to be had from the chaos of revenge or the smooth order of forgiveness; and this girl with skin of cream on its way to spoiling and hair the color of flax, what did her insides look like, what did she eat? (I did not ask then because I could not ask then and I ask now but no one can answer me, really answer me.)

My second birthday was not a major event in anyone's life, certainly not my own (it was not my first and it was not my last, I am now forty-three years old), but my mother, perhaps because of circumstances (I would not have known then and to know now is not a help), perhaps only because of an established custom (but only in her family, other people didn't do this), to mark the occasion of my turning two years old had my ears pierced. One day, at dusk (I would not have called it that then), I was taken to someone's house (a woman from Dominica, a woman who was as dark as my mother was fair, and yet they were so similar that I am sure now as I was then that they shared the same tongue), and two thorns that had been heated in a fire were pierced through my earlobes. I do not now know (and could not have known then) if the pain I experienced resembled in any way the pain my mother experienced while giving birth to me or even if my mother, in having my ears bored in that way, at that time, meant to express hostility or aggression toward me (but without meaning to and without knowing that it was possible to mean to). For days afterward my earlobes were swollen and covered with a golden crust (which might have glistened in the harsh sunlight, but I can only imagine that now), and the pain of my earlobes must have filled up all that made up my entire being then and the pain of my earlobes must have been unbearable, because it was then that was the first time that I separated myself from myself, and I became two people (two small children then, I was two years old), one having the experience, the other observing the one having the experience. And the observer, perhaps because it was an act of my own will (strong then, but stronger now), my first and only real act of self-invention, is the one of the two I most rely on, the one of the two whose voice I believe to be the true voice; and of course it is the observer who cannot be relied on as the final truth to be believed, for the observer has woven between myself and the person who is having an experience a protective membrane, which allows me to see but only feel as much as I can handle at any given moment. And so . . .

. . . On the day I turned two years old, the twenty-fifth of May 1951, a pair of earrings, small hoops made of gold from British Guiana (it was called that then, it is not called that now), were placed in the bored holes in my earlobes (which by then had healed); a pair of bracelets made of silver from someplace other than British Guiana (and that place too was called one thing then, something else now) was placed one on each wrist; a pair of new shoes bought from Bata's was placed on my feet. That afternoon, I was bathed and powdered, and the dress of yellow poplin, completed, its seams all stitched together with a certainty found only in the natural world (I now realize), was placed over my head, and it is quite possible that this entire act had about it the feeling of being draped in a shroud. My mother, carrying me in her arms (as usual), took me to the studio of a photographer, a man named Mr. Walker, to have my picture taken. As she walked along with me in her arms (not complaining), with the heat of the sun still so overwhelming that it, not gravity, seemed to be the force that kept us pinned to the earth's surface, I placed my lips against one side of her head (the temple) and could feel the rhythm of the blood pulsing through her body; I placed my lips against her throat and could hear her swallow saliva that had collected in her mouth; I placed my face against her neck and inhaled deeply a scent that I could not identify then (how could I, there was nothing to compare it to) and cannot now, because it is not of animal or place or thing, it was (and is) a scent unique to her, and it left a mark of such depth that it eventually became a part of my other senses, and even now (yes, now) that scent is also taste, touch, sight, and sound.

And Mr. Walker lived on Church Street in a house that was mysterious to me (then, not now) because it had a veranda (unlike my own house) and it had many rooms (unlike my own house, but really Mr. Walker's house had only four rooms, my own house had one) and the windows were closed (the windows in my house were always open). He spoke to my mother, I did not understand what they said, they did not share the same tongue. I knew Mr. Walker was a man, but how I knew that I cannot say (now, then, sometime to come). It is possible that because he touched his hair often, smoothing down, caressing, the forcibly straightened strands, and because he admired and said that he admired my dress of yellow poplin with its simple smocking (giving to me a false air of delicacy), and because he admired and said that he admired the plaid taffeta ribbon in my hair, I thought that he perhaps wasn't a man at all, I had never seen a man do or say any of those things, I had then only seen a woman do or say those things. He (Mr. Walker) stood next to a black box which had a curtain at its back (this was his camera but I did not know that at the time, I only know it now) and he asked my mother to stand me on a table, a small table, a table that made me taller, because the scene in the background, against which I was to be photographed, was so vast, it overwhelmed my two-year-old frame, making me seem a mere figurine, not a child at all; and when my mother picked me up, holding me by the armpits with her hands, her thumb accidentally (it could have been deliberate, how could someone who loved me inflict so much pain just in passing?) pressed deeply into my shoulder, and I cried out and then (and still now) looked up at her face and couldn't find any reason in it, and could find no malice in it, only that her eyes were full of something, a feeling that I thought then (and am convinced now) had nothing to do with me; and of course it is possible that just at that moment she had realized that she was exhausted, not physically, but just exhausted by this whole process, celebrating my second birthday, commemorating an event, my birth, that she may not have wished to occur in the first place and may have tried repeatedly to prevent, and then, finally, in trying to find some beauty in it, ended up with a yard and a half of yellow poplin being shaped into a dress, teaching herself smocking and purchasing gold hoops from places whose names never remained the same and silver bracelets from places whose names never remained the same. And Mr. Walker, who was not at all interested in my mother's ups and downs and would never have dreamed of taking in the haphazard mess of her life (but there was nothing so unusual about that, every life, I now know, is a haphazard mess), looked on for a moment as my mother, belying the look in her eyes, said kind and loving words to me in a kind and loving voice, and he then walked over to a looking glass that hung on a wall and squeezed with two of his fingers a lump the size of a pinch of sand that was on his cheek; the lump had a shiny white surface and it broke, emitting a tiny plap sound, and from it came a long ribbon of thick, yellow pus that curled on Mr. Walker's cheek imitating, almost, the decoration on the birthday cake that awaited me at home, and my birthday cake was decorated with a series of species of flora and fauna my mother had never seen (and still has not seen to this day, she is seventy-three years old).

After that day I never again wore my yellow poplin dress with the smocking my mother had just taught herself to make. It was carefully put aside, saved for me to wear to another special occasion; but by the time another special occasion came (I could say quite clearly then what the special occasion was and can say quite clearly now what the special occasion was but I do not want to), the dress could no longer fit me, I had grown too big for it.

The Reader's Presence

1. Kincaid's prose style is unusual. Read the first few sentences of the essay aloud. How does Kincaid use repetition? What is the relation of the parenthetical phrases to the main sentences? Are Kincaid's sentences "run-on" sentences? What is the effect of their length and sweep? Summarize the essay's "plot." What details beyond simple actions matter to Kincaid? Compare Kincaid's style in this essay to her style in the short story "Girl" (page 921).

2. The writer's early surroundings are evoked through objects and sensations; she never identifies the locale nor explicitly describes it. The reader is forced to absorb potentially unfamiliar background material in the course of following the plot. How might this experience parallel that of the young Kincaid, navigating a world full of alien images? How might Kincaid's stylistic approach serve to challenge traditional colonial hierarchies?

3. Kincaid interrupts her primary story, set in the past, with parenthetical references to the present. How does the writer's adult perspective enhance or detract from the story of childhood? What does Kincaid think of her younger self? Do the interjections interpret the earlier story, or simply add another layer of narrative? Can you infer how memory works for Kincaid? How does Kincaid's essay compare to E. B. White's meditation upon memory in "Once More to the Lake" (page 311)?

Nancy Mairs

On Being a Cripple

Nancy Mairs (b. 1943) has contributed poetry, short stories, articles, and essays to numerous journals. "On Being a Cripple" comes from Plaintext, *which was published in 1986. More recent publications include* Remembering the Bone House: An Erotics of Time and Space *(1989),* Carnal Acts *(1990),* Ordinary Time: Cycles in Marriage, Faith, and Renewal *(1993), and* A Troubled Guest: Life and Death Stories *(2001). From 1983 to 1985 she served as assistant director of the Southwest Institute for Research on Women, and she has also taught at the University of Arizona and at UCLA.*

In Voice Lessons: On Becoming a (Woman) Writer *(1994), she writes, "I want a prose that is allusive and translucent, that eases you into me and embraces you, not one that baffles you or bounces you around so that you can't even tell where I am. And so I have chosen to work, very, very carefully, with the language we share, faults and all, choosing each word for its capacity, its ambiguity, the space it provides for me to live my life within it, relating rather than opposing each word to the next, each sentence to the next, 'starting on all sides at once . . . twenty times, thirty times, over': the stuttering adventure of the essay."*

> To escape is nothing. Not to escape is nothing.
>
> —Louise Bogan

The other day I was thinking of writing an essay on being a cripple. I was thinking hard in one of the stalls of the women's room in my office building, as I was shoving my shirt into my jeans and tugging up my zipper. Preoccupied, I flushed, picked up my book bag, took my cane down from the hook, and unlatched the door. So many movements unbalanced me, and as I pulled the door open I fell over backward, landing fully clothed on the toilet seat with my legs splayed in front of me: the old beetle-on-its-back routine. Saturday afternoon, the building deserted, I was free to laugh aloud as I wriggled back to my feet, my voice bouncing off the yellowish tiles from all directions. Had anyone been there with me, I'd have been still and faint and hot with chagrin. I decided that it was high time to write the essay.

First, the matter of semantics. I am a cripple. I choose this word to name me. I choose from among several possibilities, the most common of which are "handicapped" and "disabled." I made the choice a number of years ago, without thinking, unaware of my motives for doing so. Even now, I'm not sure what those motives are, but I recognize that they are complex and not entirely flattering. People—crippled or not—wince at the word "cripple," as they do not at "handicapped" or "disabled."

Perhaps I want them to wince. I want them to see me as a tough customer, one to whom the fates/gods/viruses have not been kind, but who can face the brutal truth of her existence squarely. As a cripple, I swagger.

But, to be fair to myself, a certain amount of honesty underlies my choice. "Cripple" seems to me a clean word, straightforward and precise. It has an honorable history, having made its first appearance in the Lindisfarne Gospel in the tenth century. As a lover of words, I like the accuracy with which it describes my condition: I have lost the full use of my limbs. "Disabled," by contrast, suggests any incapacity, physical or mental. And I certainly don't like "handicapped," which implies that I have deliberately been put at a disadvantage, by whom I can't imagine (my God is not a Handicapper General), in order to equalize chances in the great race of life. These words seem to me to be moving away from my condition, to be widening the gap between word and reality. Most remote is the recently coined euphemism "differently abled," which partakes of the same semantic hopefulness that transformed countries from "undeveloped" to "underdeveloped," then to "less developed," and finally to "developing" nations. People have continued to starve in those countries during the shift. Some realities do not obey the dictates of language.

Mine is one of them. Whatever you call me, I remain crippled. But I don't care what you call me, so long as it isn't "differently abled," which strikes me as pure verbal garbage designed, by its ability to describe anyone, to describe no one. I subscribe to George Orwell's thesis that "the slovenliness of our language makes it easier for us to have foolish thoughts."[1] And I refuse to participate in the degeneration of the language to the extent that I deny that I have lost anything in the course of this calamitous disease; I refuse to pretend that the only differences between you and me are the various ordinary ones that distinguish any one person from another. But call me "disabled" or "handicapped" if you like. I have long since grown accustomed to them; and if they are vague, at least they hint at the truth. Moreover, I use them myself. Society is no readier to accept crippledness than to accept death, war, sex, sweat, or wrinkles. I would never refer to another person as a cripple. It is the word I use to name only myself.

I haven't always been crippled, a fact for which I am soundly grateful. To be whole of limb is, I know from experience, infinitely more pleasant and useful than to be crippled: and if that knowledge leaves me open to bitterness at my loss, the physical soundness I once enjoyed (though I did not enjoy it half enough) is well worth the occasional stab of regret. Though never any good at sports, I was a normally active child and young adult. I climbed trees, played hopscotch, jumped rope, skated,

5

---

[1]*Orwell:* From his essay "Politics and the English Language" (page 533). —EDS.

swam, rode my bicycle, sailed. I despised team sports, spending some of the wretchedest afternoons of my life, sweaty and humiliated, behind a field-hockey stick and under a basketball hoop. I tramped alone for miles along the bridle paths that webbed the woods behind the house I grew up in. I swayed through countless dim hours in the arms of one man or another under the scattered shot of light from mirrored balls, and gyrated through countless more as Tab Hunter and Johnny Mathis gave way to the Rolling Stones, Creedance Clearwater Revival, Cream. I walked down the aisle. I pushed baby carriages, changed tires in the rain, marched for peace.

When I was twenty-eight I started to trip and drop things. What at first seemed my natural clumsiness soon became too pronounced to shrug off. I consulted a neurologist, who told me that I had a brain tumor. A battery of tests, increasingly disagreeable, revealed no tumor. About a year and a half later I developed a blurred spot in one eye. I had, at last, the episodes "disseminated in space and time" requisite for a diagnosis: multiple sclerosis. I have never been sorry for the doctor's initial misdiagnosis, however. For almost a week, until the negative results of the tests were in, I thought that I was going to die right away. Every day for the past nearly ten years, then, has been a kind of gift. I accept all gifts.

Multiple sclerosis is a chronic degenerative disease of the central nervous system, in which the myelin that sheathes the nerves is somehow eaten away and scar tissue forms in its place, interrupting the nerves' signals. During its course, which is unpredictable and uncontrollable, one may lose vision, hearing, speech, the ability to walk, control of bladder and/or bowels, strength in any or all extremities, sensitivity to touch, vibration, and/or pain, potency, coordination of movements—the list of possibilities is lengthy and, yes, horrifying. One may also lose one's sense of humor. That's the easiest to lose and the hardest to survive without.

In the past ten years, I have sustained some of these losses. Characteristic of MS are sudden attacks, called exacerbations, followed by remissions, and these I have not had. Instead, my disease has been slowly progressive. My left leg is now so weak that I walk with the aid of a brace and a cane; and for distances I use an Amigo, a variation on the electric wheelchair that looks rather like an electrified kiddie car. I no longer have much use of my left hand. Now my right side is weakening as well. I still have the blurred spot in my right eye. Overall, though, I've been lucky so far. My world has, of necessity, been circumscribed by my losses, but the terrain left me has been ample enough for me to continue many of the activities that absorb me: writing, teaching, raising children and cats and plants and snakes, reading, speaking publicly about MS and depression, even playing bridge with people patient and honorable enough to let me scatter cards every which way without sneaking a peek.

Lest I begin to sound like Pollyanna, however, let me say that I don't like having MS. I hate it. My life holds realities—harsh ones, some of them—that no right-minded human being ought to accept without grumbling. One of them is fatigue. I know of no one with MS who does not complain of bone-weariness; in a disease that presents an astonishing variety of symptoms, fatigue seems to be a common factor. I wake up in the morning feeling the way most people do at the end of a bad day, and I take it from there. As a result, I spend a lot of time *in extremis* and, impatient with limitation, I tend to ignore my fatigue until my body breaks down in some way and forces rest. Then I miss picnics, dinner parties, poetry readings, the brief visits of old friends from out of town. The offspring of a puritanical tradition of exceptional venerability, I cannot view these lapses without shame. My life often seems a series of small failures to do as I ought.

I lead, on the whole, an ordinary life, probably rather like the one I   10
would have led had I not had MS. I am lucky that my predilections were already solitary, sedentary, and bookish—unlike the world-famous French cellist I have read about, or the young woman I talked with one long afternoon who wanted only to be a jockey. I had just begun graduate school when I found out something was wrong with me, and I have remained, interminably, a graduate student. Perhaps I would not have if I'd thought I had the stamina to return to a full-time job as a technical editor; but I've enjoyed my studies.

In addition to studying, I teach writing courses. I also teach medical students how to give neurological examinations. I pick up freelance editing jobs here and there. I have raised a foster son and sent him into the world, where he has made me two grandbabies, and I am still escorting my daughter and son through adolescence. I go to Mass every Saturday. I am a superb, if messy, cook. I am also an enthusiastic laundress, capable of sorting a hamper full of clothes into five subtly differentiated piles, but a terrible housekeeper. I can do italic writing and, in an emergency, bathe an oil-soaked cat. I play a fiendish game of Scrabble. When I have the time and the money, I'd like to sit on my front steps with my husband, drinking Amaretto and smoking a cigar, as we imagine our counterparts in Leningrad and make sure that the sun gets down once more behind the sharp childish scrawl of the Tucson Mountains.

This lively plenty has its bleak complement, of course, in all the things I can no longer do. I will never run again, except in dreams, and one day I may have to write that I will never walk again. I like to go camping, but I can't follow George and the children along the trails that wander out of a campsite through the desert or into the mountains. In fact, even on the level I've learned never to check the weather or try to hold a coherent conversation: I need all my attention for my wayward feet. Of late, I have begun to catch myself wondering how people can propel themselves without canes. With only one usable hand, I have to select my clothing with care not so much for style as for ease of ingress and egress, and even so, dressing can be laborious. I can no longer do fine stitchery, pick up babies, play the piano, braid my hair. I am immobilized by acute attacks of depression, which may or may not be physiologically related to MS but are certainly its logical concomitant.

These two elements, the plenty and the privation, are never pure, nor are the delight and wretchedness that accompany them. Almost every pickle that I get into as a result of my weakness and clumsiness—and I get into plenty—is funny as well as maddening and sometimes painful. I recall one May afternoon when a friend and I were going out for a drink after finishing up at school. As we were climbing into opposite sides of my car, chatting, I tripped and fell, flat and hard, onto the asphalt parking lot, my abrupt departure interrupting him in mid-sentence. "Where'd you go?" he called as he came around the back of the car to find me hauling myself up by the door frame. "Are you all right?" Yes, I told him, I was fine, just a bit rattly, and we drove off to find a shady patio and some beer. When I got home an hour or so later, my daughter greeted me with "What have you done to yourself?" I looked down. One elbow of my white turtleneck with the green froggies, one knee of my white trousers, one white kneesock were blood-soaked. We peeled off the clothes and inspected the damage, which was nasty enough but not alarming. That part wasn't funny: The abrasions took a long time to heal, and one got a little infected. Even so, when I think of my friend talking earnestly, suddenly, to the hot thin air while I dropped from his view as though through a trap door, I find the image as silly as something from a Marx Brothers movie.

I may find it easier than other cripples to amuse myself because I live propped by the acceptance and the assistance and, sometimes, the amusement of those around me. Grocery clerks tear my checks out of my checkbook for me, and sales clerks find chairs to put into dressing rooms when I want to try on clothes. The people I work with make sure I teach at times when I am least likely to be fatigued, in places I can get to, with the materials I need. My students, with one anonymous exception (in an end-of-the-semester evaluation), have been unperturbed by my disability. Some even like it. One was immensely cheered by the information that I paint my own fingernails; she decided, she told me, that if I could go to such trouble over fine details, she could keep on writing essays. I suppose I became some sort of bright-fingered muse. She wrote good essays, too.

The most important struts in the framework of my existence, of course, 15 are my husband and children. Dismayingly few marriages survive the MS test, and why should they? Most twenty-two- and nineteen-year-olds, like George and me, can vow in clear conscience, after a childhood of chicken pox and summer colds, to keep one another in sickness and in health so long as they both shall live. Not many are equipped for catastrophe: the dismay, the depression, the extra work, the boredom that a degenerative disease can insinuate into a relationship. And our society, with its emphasis on fun and its association of fun with physical performance, offers little encouragement for a whole spouse to stay with a crippled partner. Children experience similar stresses when faced with a crippled parent, and they are more helpless, since parents and children can't usually get divorced. They hate, of course, to be different from their peers, and the child whose mother is tacking down the aisle of a school auditorium packed with proud parents like a Cape Cod dinghy in a stiff breeze jolly well stands out in a crowd. Deprived of legal divorce, the child can at least deny the mother's disability, even her existence, forgetting to tell her about recitals and PTA meetings, refusing to accompany her to stores or church or the movies, never inviting friends to the house. Many do.

But I've been limping along for ten years now, and so far George and the children are still at my left elbow, holding tight. Anne and Matthew vacuum floors and dust furniture and haul trash and rake up dog droppings and button my cuffs and bake lasagna and Toll House cookies with just enough grumbling so I know that they don't have brain fever. And far from hiding me, they're forever dragging me by racks of fancy clothes or through teeming school corridors, or welcoming gaggles of friends while I'm wandering through the house in Anne's filmy pink babydoll pajamas. George generally calls before he brings someone home, but he does just as many dumb thankless chores as the children. And they all yell at me, laugh at some of my jokes, write me funny letters when we're apart—in short, treat me as an ordinary human being for whom they have some use. I think they like me. Unless they're faking. . . .

Faking. There's the rub. Tugging at the fringes of my consciousness always is the terror that people are kind to me only because I'm a cripple. My mother almost shattered me once, with that instinct mothers have—blind, I think, in this case, but unerring nonetheless—for striking blows along the fault-lines of their children's hearts, by telling me, in an attack on my selfishness, "We all have to make allowances for you, of course, because of the way you are." From the distance of a couple of years, I have to admit that I haven't any idea just what she meant, and I'm not sure that she knew either. She was awfully angry. But at the time, as the words thudded home, I felt my worst fear, suddenly realized. I could bear being called selfish: I am. But I couldn't bear the corroboration that those around me were doing in fact what I'd always suspected them of doing, professing fondness while silently putting up with me because of the way I am. A cripple. I've been a little cracked ever since.

Along with this fear that people are secretly accepting shoddy goods comes a relentless pressure to please—to prove myself worth the burdens I impose, I guess, or to build a substantial account of good will against which I may write drafts in times of need. Part of the pressure arises from social expectations. In our society, anyone who deviates from the norm had better find some way to compensate. Like fat people, who are expected to be jolly, cripples must bear their lot meekly and cheerfully. A grumpy cripple isn't playing by the rules. And much of the pressure is self-generated. Early on I vowed that, if I had to have MS, by God I was going to do it well. This is a class act, ladies and gentlemen. No tears, no recriminations, no faint-heartedness.

One way and another, then, I wind up feeling like Tiny Tim,[2] peering over the edge of the table at the Christmas goose, waving my crutch, piping down God's blessing on us all. Only sometimes I don't want to play Tiny Tim; I'd rather be Caliban,[3] a most scurvy monster. Fortunately, at home no one much cares whether I'm a good cripple or a bad cripple as long as I make vichyssoise with fair regularity. One evening several years ago, Anne was reading at the dining-room table while I cooked dinner. As I opened a can of tomatoes, the can slipped in my left hand and juice spattered me and the counter with bloody spots. Fatigued and infuriated, I bellowed, "I'm so sick of being crippled!" Anne glanced at me over the top of her book. "There now," she said, "do you feel better?" "Yes," I said, "yes, I do." She went back to her reading. I felt better. That's about all the attention my scurviness ever gets.

Because I hate being crippled, I sometimes hate myself for being a crip-   20
ple. Over the years I have come to expect—even accept—attacks of violent self-loathing. Luckily, in general our society no longer connects deformity and disease directly with evil (though a charismatic once told me that I have MS because a devil is in me) and so I'm allowed to move largely at will, even among small children. But I'm not sure that this revision of attitude has been particularly helpful. Physical imperfection, even freed of moral disapprobation, still defies and violates the ideal, especially for women, whose confinement in their bodies as objects of desire is far from over. Each age, of course, has its ideal, and I doubt that ours is any better or worse than any other. Today's ideal woman, who lives on the glossy pages of dozens of magazines, seems to be between the ages of eighteen and twenty-five; her hair has body, her teeth flash white, her breath smells minty, her underarms are dry; she has a career but is still a fabulous cook, especially of meals that take less than twenty minutes to prepare; she does not ordinarily appear to have a husband or children; she is trim and deeply tanned; she jogs, swims, plays tennis, rides a bicycle, sails, but does not bowl; she travels widely, even to out-of-the-way places like Finland and Samoa, always in the company of the ideal man, who possesses a nearly identical set of characteristics. There are a few exceptions. Though usually white and often blonde, she may be black, Hispanic, Asian, or Native American, so long as she is unusually sleek. She may be old, provided she is selling a laxative or is Lauren Bacall. If she is selling a detergent, she may be married and have a flock of strikingly messy children. But she is never a cripple.

Like many women I know, I have always had an uneasy relationship with my body. I was not a popular child, largely, I think now, because I was peculiar: intelligent, intense, moody, shy, given to unexpected actions

[2]*Tiny Tim:* Crippled boy in Charles Dicken's *A Christmas Carol.*—EDS.
[3]*Caliban:* A character in William Shakespeare's play *The Tempest.*—EDS.

and inexplicable notions and emotions. But as I entered adolescence, I believed myself unpopular because I was homely; my breasts too flat, my mouth too wide, my hips too narrow, my clothing never quite right in fit or style. I was not, in fact, particularly ugly, old photographs inform me, though I was well off the ideal; but I carried this sense of self-alienation with me into adulthood, where it regenerated in response to the depredations of MS. Even with my brace I walk with a limp so pronounced that, seeing myself on the videotape of a television program on the disabled, I couldn't believe that anything but an inchworm could make progress humping along like that. My shoulders droop and my pelvis thrusts forward as I try to balance myself upright, throwing my frame into a bony S. As a result of contractures, one shoulder is higher than the other and I carry one arm bent in front of me, the fingers curled into a claw. My left arm and leg have wasted into pipe-stems, and I try always to keep them covered. When I think about how my body must look to others, especially to men, to whom I have been trained to display myself, I feel ludicrous, even loathsome.

At my age, however, I don't spend much time thinking about my appearance. The burning egocentricity of adolescence, which assures one that all the world is looking all the time, has passed, thank God, and I'm generally too caught up in what I'm doing to step back, as I used to, and watch myself as though upon a stage. I'm also too old to believe in the accuracy of self-image. I know that I'm not a hideous crone, that in fact, when I'm rested, well dressed, and well made up, I look fine. The self-loathing I feel is neither physically nor intellectually substantial. What I hate is not me but a disease.

I am not a disease.

And a disease is not—at least not singlehandedly—going to determine who I am, though at first it seemed to be going to. Adjusting to a chronic incurable illness, I have moved through a process similar to that outlined by Elisabeth Kübler-Ross in *On Death and Dying*. The major difference—and it is far more significant than most people recognize—is that I can't be sure of the outcome, as the terminally ill cancer patient can. Research studies indicate that, with proper medical care, I may achieve a "normal" life span. And in our society, with its vision of death as the ultimate evil, worse even than decrepitude, the response to such news is, "Oh well, at least you're not going to *die*." Are there worse things than dying? I think that there may be.

I think of two women I know, both with MS, both enough older than I to have served me as models. One took to her bed several years ago and has been there ever since. Although she can sit in a high-backed wheelchair, because she is incontinent she refuses to go out at all, even though incontinence pants, which are readily available at any pharmacy, could protect her from embarrassment. Instead, she stays at home and insists that her husband, a small quiet man, a retired civil servant, stay there with her except for a quick weekly foray to the supermarket. The other woman, whose illness was diagnosed when she was eighteen, a nursing

25

student engaged to a young doctor, finished her training, married her doctor, accompanied him to Germany when he was in the service, bore three sons and a daughter, now grown and gone. When she can, she travels with her husband; she plays bridge, embroiders, swims regularly; she works, like me, as a symptomatic-patient instructor of medical students in neurology. Guess which woman I hope to be.

At the beginning, I thought about having MS almost incessantly. And because of the unpredictable course of the disease, my thoughts were always terrified. Each night I'd get into bed wondering whether I'd get out again the next morning, whether I'd be able to see, to speak, to hold a pen between my fingers. Knowing that the day might come when I'd be physically incapable of killing myself, I thought perhaps I ought to do so right away, while I still had the strength. Gradually I came to understand that the Nancy who might one day lie inert under a bedsheet, arms and legs paralyzed, unable to feed or bathe herself, unable to reach out for a gun, a bottle of pills, was not the Nancy I was at present, and that I could not presume to make decisions for that future Nancy, who might well not want in the least to die. Now the only provision I've made for the future Nancy is that when the time comes—and it is likely to come in the form of pneumonia, friend to the weak and the old—I am not to be treated with machines and medications. If she is unable to communicate by then, I hope she will be satisfied with these terms.

Thinking all the time about having MS grew tiresome and intrusive, especially in the large and tragic mode in which I was accustomed to considering my plight. Months and even years went by without catastrophe (at least without one related to MS), and really I was awfully busy, what with George and children and snakes and students and poems, and I hadn't the time, let alone the inclination, to devote myself to being a disease. Too, the richer my life became, the funnier it seemed, as though there were some connection between largesse and laughter, and so my tragic stance began to waver until, even with the aid of a brace and a cane, I couldn't hold it for very long at a time.

After several years I was satisfied with my adjustment. I had suffered my grief and fury and terror, I thought, but now I was at ease with my lot. Then one summer day I set out with George and the children across the desert for a vacation in California. Part way to Yuma I became aware that my right leg felt funny. "I think I've had an exacerbation," I told George. "What shall we do?" he asked. "I think we'd better get the hell to California," I said, "because I don't know whether I'll ever make it again." So we went on to San Diego and then to Orange, up the Pacific Coast Highway to Santa Cruz, across to Yosemite, down to Sequoia and Joshua Tree, and so back over the desert to home. It was a fine two-week trip, filled with friends and fair weather, and I wouldn't have missed it for the world, though I did in fact make it back to California two years later. Nor would there have been any point in missing it, since in MS, once the symptoms have appeared, the neurological damage has been done, and there's no way to predict or prevent that damage.

The incident spoiled my self-satisfaction, however. It renewed my grief and fury and terror, and I learned that one never finishes adjusting to MS. I don't know now why I thought one would. One does not, after all, finish adjusting to life, and MS is simply a fact of my life—not my favorite fact, of course—but as ordinary as my nose and my tropical fish and my yellow Mazda station wagon. It may at any time get worse, but no amount of worry or anticipation can prepare me for a new loss. My life is a lesson in losses. I learn one at a time.

And I had best be patient in the learning, since I'll have to do it like it   30
or not. As any rock fan knows, you can't always get what you want. Particularly when you have MS. You can't, for example, get cured. In recent years researchers and the organizations that fund research have started to pay MS some attention even though it isn't fatal; perhaps they have begun to see that life is something other than a quantitative phenomenon, that one may be very much alive for a very long time in a life that isn't worth living. The researchers have made some progress toward understanding the mechanism of the disease: It may well be an autoimmune reaction triggered by a slow-acting virus. But they are nowhere near its prevention, control, or cure. And most of us want to be cured. Some, unable to accept incurability, grasp at one treatment after another, no matter how bizarre: megavitamin therapy, gluten-free diet, injections of cobra venom, hypothermal suits, lymphocytopharesis, hyperbaric chambers. Many treatments are probably harmless enough, but none are curative.

The absence of a cure often makes MS patients bitter toward their doctors. Doctors are, after all, the priests of modern society, the new shamans, whose business is to heal, and many an MS patient roves from one to another, searching for the "good" doctor who will make him well. Doctors too think of themselves as healers, and for this reason many have trouble dealing with MS patients, whose disease in its intransigence defeats their aims and mocks their skills. Too few doctors, it is true, treat their patients as whole human beings, but the reverse is also true. I have always tried to be gentle with my doctors, who often have more at stake in terms of ego than I do. I may be frustrated, maddened, depressed by the incurability of my disease, but I am not diminished by it, and they are. When I push myself up from my seat in the waiting room and stumble toward them, I incarnate the limitation of their powers. The least I can do is refuse to press on their tenderest spots.

This gentleness is part of the reason that I'm not sorry to be a cripple. I didn't have it before. Perhaps I'd have developed it anyway—how could I know such a thing?—and I wish I had more of it, but I'm glad of what I have. It has opened and enriched my life enormously, this sense that my frailty and need must be mirrored in others, that in searching for and shaping a stable core in a life wrenched by change and loss, change and loss, I must recognize the same process, under individual conditions, in the lives around me. I do not deprecate such knowledge, however I've come by it.

All the same, if a cure were found, would I take it? In a minute. I may be a cripple, but I'm only occasionally a loony and never a saint. Anyway, in my brand of theology God doesn't give bonus points for a limp. I'd take a cure; I just don't need one. A friend who also has MS startled me once by asking, "Do you ever say to yourself, 'Why me, Lord?'" "No, Michael, I don't," I told him, "because whenever I try, the only response I can think of is 'Why not?'" If I could make a cosmic deal, who would I put in my place? What in my life would I give up in exchange for sound limbs and a thrilling rush of energy? No one. Nothing. I might as well do the job myself. Now that I'm getting the hang of it.

The Reader's Presence

1. Mairs's approach to her multiple sclerosis may come across as ironic, jaunty, or tough. Near the beginning of the essay she assumes that her reader is fundamentally alienated from her: "I refuse to pretend that the only differences between you and me are the various ordinary ones that distinguish any one person from another" (paragraph 4). What are those differences? How does the essay attempt to move the reader away from awkwardness or suspicion or hostility? Does it succeed?

2. What does the epigraph from Louise Bogan mean to you? What might it signify in relation to Mairs's essay? What is "escape," in Mairs's context? What meanings might the word *nothing* have?

3. "Lest I begin to sound like Polyanna, however, let me say that I don't like having MS. I hate it" (paragraph 9). Discuss Mairs's admission of hatred for the disease—and for herself (paragraph 20)—in relation to Alice Walker's "abuse" of her injured eye (paragraph 30) in "Beauty: When the Other Dancer Is the Self" (page 304). What is the role of self-loathing in personal growth?

THE WRITER AT WORK

Nancy Mairs on Finding a Voice

In writing workshops and lectures, the essayist Nancy Mairs is often asked what appears to be a simple question: How did you find your voice as a writer? Yet is the question truly an easy one? In the following passage from her book "on becoming a (woman) writer," Voice Lessons, Mairs closely examines the question and suggests a way it might be answered. You might want to compare her concern about finding a voice to that of Henry Louis Gates Jr. on page 156.

The question I am most often asked when I speak to students and others interested in writing is, How did you find your voice? I have some trouble with this locution because "find" always suggests to me the discovery, generally fortuitous, of some lack or loss. I have found an occasional four-leaf clover. I have found a mate. I have, more than once, found my way home. But is a voice susceptible of the same sort of revelation or retrieval? Hasn't mine simply always been there, from my earliest lallation to the "I love you" I called after my husband on his way to school several hours ago?

But of course, I remind myself, the question doesn't concern *my* voice at all but the voice of another woman (also named Nancy Mairs, confusingly enough) whose "utterances" are, except for the occasional public reading, literally inaudible: not, strictly speaking, a voice at all, but a fabrication, a device. And when I look again at the dictionary, I see that "find" can indeed also mean "devise." The voice in question, like the woman called into being to explain its existence, is an invention.

But of whom? For simplicity's sake, we assume that the voice in a work is that of the writer (in the case of nonfiction) or one invented by her (in the case of fiction). This assumption describes the relationship between writer (the woman in front of a luminous screen) and persona (whoever you hear speaking to you right now) adequately for most readers. And maybe for most writers, too. Until that earnest student in the second row waves a gnawed pencil over her head and asks, timidly as a rule because hers is the first question, "How did you find your voice?"

As though "you" were a coherent entity already existing at some original point, who had only to open her mouth and agitate her vocal chords—or, to be precise, pick up her fingers and diddle the keys—to call the world she had in mind into being. Not just a writer, an Author. But I've examined this process over and over in myself, and the direction of this authorial plot simply doesn't ring true. In the beginning, remember, was the *Word*. Not me. And the question, properly phrased, should probably be asked of my voice: How did you find (devise, invent, contrive) your Nancy?

Malcolm X
Homeboy

Malcolm X (1925–1965) is regarded as one of the most influential figures in the struggle for racial equality. Born Malcolm Little in Omaha, Nebraska, his family was frequently the target of racist violence: white supremacists burned their home, and his father, a Baptist minister, was horribly murdered. After his father's death, his mother was hospitalized for mental illness, and he and his seven brothers and sisters were placed in foster homes. Although a gifted student, Malcolm was discouraged by a racist teacher and quit high school. He lived for a while in Lansing, Michigan, and later moved to Boston, where he engaged in various illegal activities, became addicted to narcotics, and was imprisoned for robbery. While in jail Malcolm made extensive use of the prison library and studied philosophy, politics, and the teachings of the Black Muslims' Nation of Islam. After his release from prison, Malcolm worked with Elijah Muhammad, founder and leader of the Nation of Islam, and changed his name to Malcolm X. He became known as an outspoken and articulate minister, championing racial separatism, faith in Allah, and rejection of white society, and he quickly rose to a position of prominence within the organization. While on a pilgrimage to Mecca in 1964, Malcolm X became an orthodox Muslim, adopted the name El-Hajj Malik El-Shabazz, and formed his own religious organization. Hostilities grew between his followers and the Black Muslims, and in 1965 Malcolm X was assassinated in a Harlem ballroom. The Autobiography of Malcolm X *(1965), from which "Homeboy" is taken, was written with Alex Haley and was published posthumously.*

I looked like Li'l Abner. Mason, Michigan, was written all over me. My kinky, reddish hair was cut hick style, and I didn't even use grease in it. My green suit's coat sleeves stopped above my wrists, the pants legs showed three inches of socks. Just a shade lighter green than the suit was my narrow-collared, three-quarter length Lansing department store topcoat. My appearance was too much for even Ella.[1] But she told me later she had seen countrified members of the Little family come up from Georgia in even worse shape than I was.

Ella had fixed up a nice little upstairs room for me. And she was truly a Georgia Negro woman when she got into the kitchen with her pots and pans. She was the kind of cook who would heap up your plate with such as ham hock, greens, black-eyed peas, fried fish, cabbage, sweet potatoes, grits and gravy, and cornbread. And the more you put away, the better she felt. I worked out at Ella's kitchen table like there was no tomorrow.

Ella still seemed to be as big, black, outspoken, and impressive a woman as she had been in Mason and Lansing. Only about two weeks before I arrived, she had split up with her second husband—the soldier, Frank, whom I had met there the previous summer; but she was taking it right in stride. I could see, though I didn't say, how any average man would find it almost impossible to live for very long with a woman whose every instinct was to run everything and everybody she had anything to do with—including me. About my second day there in Roxbury, Ella told me that she didn't want me to start hunting for a job right away, like most newcomer Negroes did. She said that she had told all those she'd brought North to take their time, to walk around, to travel the buses and the subway, and get the feel of Boston, before they tied themselves down

---

[1]*Ella:* Malcolm's older sister. He left Lansing, Michigan, and moved to her house in the Roxbury section of Boston in 1948. —EDS.

working somewhere, because they would never again have the time to re-ally see and get to know anything about the city they were living in. Ella said she'd help me find a job when it was time for me to go to work.

So I went gawking around the neighborhood—the Waumbeck and Humboldt Avenue Hill section of Roxbury, which is something like Harlem's Sugar Hill, where I'd later live. I saw those Roxbury Negroes acting and liv-ing differently from any black people I'd ever dreamed of in my life. This was the snooty-black neighborhood; they called themselves the "Four Hundred," and looked down their noses at the Negroes of the black ghetto, or so-called "town" section where Mary, my other half-sister, lived.

What I thought I was seeing there in Roxbury were high-class, edu-cated, important Negroes, living well, working in big jobs and positions. Their quiet homes sat back in their mowed yards. These Negroes walked along the sidewalks looking haughty and dignified, on their way to work, to shop, to visit, to church. I know now, of course, that what I was really seeing was only a big-city version of those "successful" Negro bootblacks and janitors back in Lansing. The only difference was that the ones in Boston had been brainwashed even more thoroughly. They prided them-selves on being incomparably more "cultured," "cultivated," "dignified," and better off than their black brethren down in the ghetto, which was no further away than you could throw a rock. Under the pitiful misappre-hension that it would make them "better," these Hill Negroes were break-ing their backs trying to imitate white people.

Any black family that had been around Boston long enough to own the home they lived in was considered among the Hill elite. It didn't make any difference that they had to rent out rooms to make ends meet. Then the native-born New Englanders among them looked down upon recently migrated Southern home-owners who lived next door, like Ella. And a big percentage of the Hill dwellers were in Ella's category— Southern strivers and scramblers, and West Indian Negroes, whom both the New Englanders and the Southerners called "Black Jews." Usually it was the Southerners and the West Indians who not only managed to own the places where they lived, but also at least one other house which they rented as income property. The snooty New Englanders usually owned less than they.

In those days on the Hill, any who could claim "professional" status— teachers, preachers, practical nurses—also considered themselves supe-rior. Foreign diplomats could have modeled their conduct on the way the Negro postmen, Pullman porters, and dining car waiters of Roxbury acted, striding around as if they were wearing top hats and cutaways.

I'd guess that eight out of ten of the Hill Negroes of Roxbury, despite the impressive-sounding job titles they affected, actually worked as me-nials and servants. "He's in banking," or "He's in securities." It sounded as though they were discussing a Rockefeller or a Mellon—and not some grayheaded, dignity-posturing bank janitor, or bond-house messenger. "I'm with an old family" was the euphemism used to dignify the professions

5

of white folks' cooks and maids who talked so affectedly among their own kind in Roxbury that you couldn't even understand them. I don't know how many forty- and fifty-year-old errand boys went down the Hill dressed like ambassadors in black suits and white collars, to downtown jobs "in government," "in finance," or "in law." It has never ceased to amaze me how so many Negroes, then and now, could stand the indignity of that kind of self-delusion.

Soon I ranged out of Roxbury and began to explore Boston proper. Historic buildings everywhere I turned, and plaques and markers and statues for famous events and men. One statue in the Boston Commons astonished me: a Negro named Crispus Attucks, who had been the first man to fall in the Boston Massacre. I had never known anything like that.

I roamed everywhere. In one direction, I walked as far as Boston University. Another day, I took my first subway ride. When most of the people got off, I followed. It was Cambridge, and I circled all around in the Harvard University campus. Somewhere, I had already heard of Harvard — though I didn't know much more about it. Nobody that day could have told me I would give an address before the Harvard Law School Forum some twenty years later.

I also did a lot of exploring downtown. Why a city would have *two* big railroad stations — North Station and South Station — I couldn't understand. At both of the stations, I stood around and watched people arrive and leave. And I did the same thing at the bus station where Ella had met me. My wanderings even led me down along the piers and docks where I read plaques telling about the old sailing ships that used to put into port there.

In a letter to Wilfred, Hilda, Philbert, and Reginald back in Lansing, I told them about all this, and about the winding, narrow, cobblestoned streets, and the houses that jammed up against each other. Downtown Boston, I wrote them, had the biggest stores I'd ever seen, and white people's restaurants and hotels. I made up my mind that I was going to see every movie that came to the fine, air-conditioned theaters.

On Massachusetts Avenue, next door to one of them, the Loew's State Theater, was the huge, exciting Roseland State Ballroom. Big posters out in front advertised the nationally famous bands, white and Negro, that had played there. "COMING NEXT WEEK," when I went by that first time, was Glenn Miller.[2] I remember thinking how nearly the whole evening's music at Mason High School dances had been Glenn Miller's records. What wouldn't that crowd have given, I wondered, to be standing where Glenn Miller's band was actually going to play? I didn't know how familiar with Roseland I was going to become.

Ella began to grow concerned, because even when I had finally had enough sight-seeing, I didn't stick around very much on the Hill. She kept dropping hints that I ought to mingle with the "nice young people my

10

---

[2]**Miller:** One of America's most popular band leaders of the 1940s. — EDS.

age" who were to be seen in the Townsend Drugstore two blocks from her house, and a couple of other places. But even before I came to Boston, I had always felt and acted toward anyone my age as if they were in the "kid" class, like my younger brother Reginald. They had always looked up to me as if I were considerably older. On weekends back in Lansing where I'd go to get away from the white people in Mason, I'd hung around in the Negro part of town with Wilfred's and Philbert's set. Though all of them were several years older than me, I was bigger, and I actually looked older than most of them.

I didn't want to disappoint or upset Ella, but despite her advice, I began   15 going down into the town ghetto section. That world of grocery stores, walk-up flats, cheap restaurants, poolrooms, bars, storefront churches, and pawnshops seemed to hold a natural lure for me.

Not only was this part of Roxbury much more exciting, but I felt more relaxed among Negroes who were being their natural selves and not putting on airs. Even though I did live on the Hill, my instincts were never—and still aren't—to feel myself any better than any other Negro.

I spent my first month in town with my mouth hanging open. The sharp-dressed young "cats" who hung on the corners and in the poolrooms, bars and restaurants, and who obviously didn't work anywhere, completely entranced me. I couldn't get over marveling at how their hair was straight and shiny like white men's hair; Ella told me this was called a "conk." I had never tasted a sip of liquor, never even smoked a cigarette, and here I saw little black children, ten and twelve years old, shooting craps, playing cards, fighting, getting grown-ups to put a penny or a nickel on their number for them, things like that. And these children threw around swear words I'd never heard before, even, and slang expressions that were just as new to me, such as "stud" and "cat" and "chick" and "cool" and "hip." Every night as I lay in bed I turned these new words over in my mind. It was shocking to me that in town, especially after dark, you'd occasionally see a white girl and a Negro man strolling arm in arm along the sidewalk, and mixed couples drinking in the neon-lighted bars—not slipping off to some dark corner, as in Lansing. I wrote Wilfred and Philbert about that, too.

I wanted to find a job myself, to surprise Ella. One afternoon, something told me to go inside a poolroom whose window I was looking through. I had looked through that window many times. I wasn't yearning to play pool; in fact, I had never held a cue stick. But I was drawn by the sight of the cool-looking "cats" standing around inside, bending over the big, green, felt-topped tables, making bets and shooting the bright-colored balls into the holes. As I stared through the window this particular afternoon, something made me decide to venture inside and talk to a dark, stubby, conk-headed fellow who racked up balls for the pool-players, whom I'd heard called "Shorty." One day he had come outside and seen me standing there and said "Hi, Red," so that made me figure he was friendly.

As inconspicuously as I could, I slipped inside the door and around the side of the poolroom, avoiding people, and on to the back, where Shorty was filling an aluminum can with the powder that pool players dust on their hands. He looked up at me. Later on, Shorty would enjoy teasing me about how with that first glance he knew my whole story. "Man, that cat still *smelled* country!" he'd say, laughing. "Cat's legs was so long and his pants so short his knees showed—an' his head looked like a briar patch!"

But that afternoon Shorty didn't let it show in his face how "coun-   20
try" I appeared when I told him I'd appreciate it if he'd tell me how could somebody go about getting a job like his.

"If you mean racking up balls," said Shorty, "I don't know of no pool joints around here needing anybody. You mean you just want any slave you can find?" A "slave" meant work, a job.

He asked what kind of work I had done. I told him that I'd washed restaurant dishes in Mason, Michigan. He nearly dropped the powder can. "My homeboy! Man, gimme some skin! I'm from Lansing!"

I never told Shorty—and he never suspected—that he was about ten years older than I. He took us to be about the same age. At first I would have been embarrassed to tell him, later I just never bothered. Shorty had dropped out of first-year high school in Lansing, lived a while with an uncle and aunt in Detroit, and had spent the last six years living with his cousin in Roxbury. But when I mentioned the names of Lansing people and places, he remembered many, and pretty soon we sounded as if we had been raised in the same block. I could sense Shorty's genuine gladness, and I don't have to say how lucky I felt to find a friend as hip as he obviously was.

"Man, this is a swinging town if you dig it," Shorty said. "You're my homeboy—I'm going to school you to the happenings." I stood there and grinned like a fool. "You got to go anywhere now? Well, stick around until I get off."

One thing I liked immediately about Shorty was his frankness. When   25
I told him where I lived, he said what I already knew—that nobody in town could stand the Hill Negroes. But he thought a sister who gave me a "pad," not charging me rent, not even running me out to find "some slave," couldn't be all bad. Shorty's slave in the poolroom, he said, was just to keep ends together while he learned his horn. A couple of years before, he'd hit the numbers and bought a saxophone. "Got it right in there in the closet now, for my lesson tonight." Shorty was taking lessons "with some other studs," and he intended one day to organize his own small band. "There's a lot of bread to be made gigging right around here in Roxbury," Shorty explained to me. "I don't dig joining some big band, one-nighting all over just to say I played with Count or Duke or some-body." I thought that was smart. I wished I had studied a horn; but I never had been exposed to one.

All afternoon, between trips up front to rack balls, Shorty talked to me out of the corner of his mouth: which hustlers—standing around, or playing at this or that table—sold "reefers," or had just come out of prison, or were "second-story men." Shorty told me that he played at least a dollar a day on the numbers. He said as soon as he hit a number, he would use the winnings to organize his band.

I was ashamed to have to admit that I had never played the numbers. "Well, you ain't never had nothing to play with," he said, excusing me, "but you start when you get a slave, and if you hit, you got a stake for something."

He pointed out some gamblers and some pimps. Some of them had white whores, he whispered. "I ain't going to lie—I dig them two-dollar white chicks," Shorty said. "There's a lot of that action around here, nights: you'll see it." I said I already had seen some. "You ever had one?" he asked.

My embarrassment at my inexperience showed. "Hell, man," he said, "don't be ashamed. I had a few before I left Lansing—them Polack chicks that used to come over the bridge. Here, they're mostly Italians and Irish. But it don't matter what kind, they're something else! Ain't no different nowhere—there's nothing they love better than a black stud."

Through the afternoon, Shorty introduced me to players and loungers.   30
"My homeboy," he'd say, "he's looking for a slave if you hear anything." They all said they'd look out.

At seven o'clock, when the night ball-racker came on, Shorty told me he had to hurry to his saxophone lesson. But before he left, he held out to me the six or seven dollars he had collected that day in nickel and dime tips. "You got enough bread, homeboy?"

I was okay, I told him—I had two dollars. But Shorty made me take three more. "Little fattening for your pocket," he said. Before we went out, he opened his saxophone case and showed me the horn. It was gleaming brass against the green velvet, an alto sax. He said, "Keep cool, homeboy, and come back tomorrow. Some of the cats will turn you up a slave."

When I got home, Ella said there had been a telephone call from somebody named Shorty. He had left a message that over at the Roseland State Ballroom, the shoeshine boy was quitting that night, and Shorty had told him to hold the job for me.

"Malcolm, you haven't had any experience shining shoes," Ella said. Her expression and tone of voice told me she wasn't happy about my taking that job. I didn't particularly care, because I was already speechless thinking about being somewhere close to the greatest bands in the world. I didn't even wait to eat any dinner.

The ballroom was all lighted when I got there. A man at the front   35
door was letting in members of Benny Goodman's band. I told him I wanted to see the shoeshine boy, Freddie.

"You're going to be the new one?" he asked. I said I thought I was, and he laughed, "Well, maybe you'll hit the numbers and get a Cadillac, too." He told me that I'd find Freddie upstairs in the men's room on the second floor.

But downstairs before I went up, I stepped over and snatched a glimpse inside the ballroom. I just couldn't believe the size of that waxed floor! At the far end, under the soft, rose-colored lights, was the bandstand with the Benny Goodman musicians moving around, laughing and talking, arranging their horns and stands.

A wiry, brown-skinned, conked fellow upstairs in the men's room greeted me. "You Shorty's homeboy?" I said I was, and he said he was Freddie. "Good old boy," he said. "He called me, he just heard I hit the big number, and he figured right I'd be quitting." I told Freddie what the man at the front door had said about a Cadillac. He laughed and said, "Burns them white cats up when you get yourself something. Yeah, I told them I was going to get me one — just to bug them."

Freddie then said for me to pay close attention, that he was going to be busy and for me to watch but not get in the way, and he'd try to get me ready to take over at the next dance, a couple of nights later.

As Freddie busied himself setting up the shoeshine stand, he told me,   40
"Get here early . . . your shoeshine rags and brushes by this footstand . . . your polish bottles, paste wax, suede brushes over here . . . everything in place, you get rushed, you never need to waste motion. . . ."

While you shined shoes, I learned, you also kept watch on customers inside, leaving the urinals. You darted over and offered a small white hand towel. "A lot of cats who ain't planning to wash their hands, sometimes you can run up with a towel and shame them. Your towels are really your best hustle in here. Cost you a penny apiece to launder — you always get at least a nickel tip."

The shoeshine customers, and any from the inside rest room who took a towel, you whiskbroomed a couple of licks. "A nickel or a dime tip, just give 'em that," Freddie said. "But for two bits, Uncle Tom a little — white cats especially like that. I've had them to come back two, three times a dance."

From down below, the sound of the music had begun floating up. I guess I stood transfixed. "You never seen a big dance?" asked Freddie. "Run on awhile, and watch."

There were a few couples already dancing under the rose-colored lights. But even more exciting to me was the crowd thronging in. The most glamorous-looking white women I'd ever seen — young ones, old ones, white cats buying tickets at the window, sticking big wads of green bills back into their pockets, checking the women's coats, and taking their arms and squiring them inside.

Freddie had some early customers when I got back upstairs. Between   45
the shoeshine stand and thrusting towels to me just as they approached the wash basin, Freddie seemed to be doing four things at once. "Here, you can take over the whiskbroom," he said, "just two or three licks — but let 'em feel it."

When things slowed a little, he said, "You ain't seen nothing tonight. You wait until you see a spooks' dance! Man, our own people carry *on*!"

Whenever he had a moment, he kept schooling me. "Shoelaces, this drawer here. You just starting out, I'm going to make these to you as a present. Buy them for a nickel a pair, tell cats they need laces if they do, and charge two bits."

Every Benny Goodman record I'd ever heard in my life, it seemed, was filtering faintly into where we were. During another customer lull, Freddie let me slip back outside again to listen. Peggy Lee was at the mike singing. Beautiful! She had just joined the band and she was from North Dakota and had been singing with a group in Chicago when Mrs. Benny Goodman discovered her, we had heard some customers say. She finished the song and the crowd burst into applause. She was a big hit.

"It knocked me out, too, when I first broke in here," Freddie said, grinning, when I went back in there. "But, look, you ever shined any shoes?" He laughed when I said I hadn't excepting my own. "Well, let's go to work. I never had neither." Freddie got on the stand and went to work on his own shoes. Brush, liquid polish, brush, paste wax, shine rag, lacquer sole dressing . . . step by step, Freddie showed me what to do.

"But you got to get a whole lot faster. You can't waste time!" Freddie showed me how fast on my own shoes. Then, because business was tapering off, he had time to give me a demonstration of how to make the shine rag pop like a firecracker. "Dig the action?" he asked. He did it in slow motion. I got down and tried it on his shoes. I had the principle of it. "Just got to do it faster," Freddie said. "It's a jive noise, that's all. Cats tip better, they figure you're knocking yourself out!"

By the end of the dance, Freddie had let me shine the shoes of three   50
or four stray drunks he talked into having shines, and I had practiced picking up my speed on Freddie's shoes until they looked like mirrors. After we had helped the janitors to clean up the ballroom after the dance, throwing out all the paper and cigarette butts and empty liquor bottles, Freddie was nice enough to drive me all the way home to Ella's on the Hill in the second-hand maroon Buick he said he was going to trade in on his Cadillac. He talked to me all the way. "I guess it's all right if I tell you, pick up a couple of dozen packs of rubbers, two-bits apiece. You notice some of those cats that came up to me around the end of the dance? Well, when some have new chicks going right, they'll come asking you for rubbers. Charge a dollar, generally you'll get an extra tip."

He looked across at me. "Some hustles you're too new for. Cats will ask you for liquor, some will want reefers. But you don't need to have nothing except rubbers—until you can dig who's a cop.

"You can make ten, twelve dollars a dance for yourself if you work everything right," Freddie said, before I got out of the car in front of Ella's. "The main thing you got to remember is that everything in the world is a hustle. So long, Red."

The next time I ran into Freddie I was downtown one night a few weeks later. He was parked in his pearl gray Cadillac, sharp as a tack, "cooling it."

"Man, you sure schooled me!" I said, and he laughed; he knew what I meant. It hadn't taken me long on the job to find out that Freddie had done less shoeshining and towel-hustling than selling liquor and reefers, and putting white "Johns" in touch with Negro whores. I also learned that white girls always flocked to the Negro dances — some of them whores whose pimps brought them to mix business and pleasure, others who came with their black boy friends, and some who came in alone, for a little free-lance lusting among a plentiful availability of enthusiastic Negro men.

At the white dances, of course, nothing black was allowed, and that's where the black whores' pimps soon showed a new shoeshine boy what he could pick up on the side by slipping a phone number or address to the white Johns who came around the end of the dance looking for "black chicks." 55

Most of Roseland's dances were for whites only, and they had white bands only. But the only white band ever to play there at a Negro dance to my recollection, was Charlie Barnet's. The fact is that very few white bands could have satisfied the Negro dancers. But I know that Charlie Barnet's "Cherokee" and his "Redskin Rhumba" drove those Negroes wild. They'd jampack that ballroom, the black girls in way-out silk and satin dresses and shoes, their hair done in all kinds of styles, the men sharp in their zoot suits and crazy conks, and everybody grinning and greased and gassed.

Some of the bandsmen would come up to the men's room at about eight o'clock and get shoeshines before they went to work. Duke Ellington, Count Basie, Lionel Hampton, Cootie Williams, Jimmie Lunceford were just a few of those who sat in my chair. I would really make my shine rag sound like someone had set off Chinese firecrackers. Duke's great alto sax-man, Johnny Hodges — he was Shorty's idol — still owes me for a shoeshine I gave him. He was in the chair one night, having a friendly argument with the drummer, Sonny Greer, who was standing there, when I tapped the bottom of his shoes to signal that I was finished. Hodges stepped down, reaching his hand in his pocket to pay me, but then snatched his hand out to gesture, and just forgot me, and walked away. I wouldn't have dared to bother the man who could do what he did with "Day-dream" by asking him for fifteen cents.

I remember that I struck up a little shoeshine-stand conversation with Count Basie's great blues singer, Jimmie Rushing. (He's the one famous for "Sent For You Yesterday, Here You Come Today" and things like that.) Rushing's feet, I remember, were big and funny-shaped — not long like most big feet, but they were round and roly-poly like Rushing. Anyhow, he even introduced me to some of the other Basie cats, like Lester Young, Harry Edison, Buddy Tate, Don Byas, Dickie Wells, and Buck Clayton. They'd walk in the rest room later, by themselves. "Hi, Red." They'd be up there in my chair, and my shine rag was popping to the beat of all of their records, spinning in my head. Musicians never have had, anywhere, a greater shoeshine-boy fan than I was. I would write to Wilfred and Hilda and Philbert and Reginald back in Lansing, trying to describe it.

I never got any decent tips until the middle of the Negro dances, which is when the dancers started feeling good and getting generous. After the white dances, when I helped to clean out the ballroom, we would throw out perhaps a dozen empty liquor bottles. But after the Negro dances, we would have to throw out cartons full of empty fifth bottles—not rotgut, either, but the best brands, and especially Scotch.

During lulls up there in the men's room, sometimes I'd get in five   60
minutes of watching the dancing. The white people danced as though somebody had trained them—left, one, two; right, three, four—the same steps and patterns over and over, as though somebody had wound them up. But those Negroes—nobody in the world could have choreographed the way they did whatever they felt—just grabbing partners, even the white chicks who came to the Negro dances. And my black brethren today may hate me for saying it, but a lot of black girls nearly got run over by some of those Negro males scrambling to get at those white women; you would have thought God had lowered some of his angels. Times have sure changed; if it happened today, those same black girls would go after those Negro men—and the white women, too.

Anyway, some couples were so abandoned—flinging high and wide, improvising steps and movements—that you couldn't believe it. I could feel the beat in my bones, even though I had never danced.

"*Showtime!*" people would start hollering about the last hour of the dance. Then a couple of dozen really wild couples would stay on the floor, the girls changing to low white sneakers. The band now would really be blasting, and all the other dancers would form a clapping, shouting circle to watch that wild competition as it began, covering only a quarter or so of the ballroom floor. The band, the spectators and the dancers, would be making the Roseland Ballroom feel like a big rocking ship. The spotlight would be turning, pink, yellow, green, and blue, picking up the couples lindy-hopping as if they had gone mad. "*Wail, man, wail!*" people would be shouting at the band; and it *would* be wailing, until first one and then another couple just ran out of strength and stumbled off toward the crowd, exhausted and soaked with sweat. Sometimes I would be down there standing inside the door jumping up and down in my gray jacket with the whiskbroom in the pocket, and the manager would have to come and shout at me that I had customers upstairs.

The first liquor I drank, my first cigarettes, even my first reefers, I can't specifically remember. But I know they were all mixed together with my first shooting craps, playing cards, and betting my dollar a day on the numbers, as I started hanging out at night with Shorty and his friends. Shorty's jokes about how country I had been made us all laugh. I still was country, I know now, but it all felt so great because I was accepted. All of us would be in somebody's place, usually one of the girls', and we'd be turning on, the reefers making everybody's head light, or the whiskey aglow in our middles. Everybody understood that my head had to stay kinky a while longer, to grow long enough for Shorty to conk it for me. One of these nights, I remarked that I had saved about half enough to get a zoot.

"*Save?*" Shorty couldn't believe it. "Homeboy, you never heard of credit?" He told me he'd call a neighborhood clothing store the first thing in the morning, and that I should be there early.

A salesman, a young Jew, met me when I came in. "You're Shorty's 65 friend?" I said I was; it amazed me—all of Shorty's contacts. The salesman wrote my name on a form, and the Roseland as where I worked, and Ella's address as where I lived. Shorty's name was put down as recommending me. The salesman said, "Shorty's one of our best customers."

I was measured, and the young salesman picked off a rack a zoot suit that was just wild: sky-blue pants thirty inches in the knee and angle-narrowed down to twelve inches at the bottom, and a long coat that pinched my waist and flared out below my knees.

As a gift, the salesman said, the store would give me a narrow leather belt with my initial "L" on it. Then he said I ought to also buy a hat, and I did—blue, with a feather in the four-inch brim. Then the store gave me another present: a long, thick-lined, gold-plated chain that swung down lower than my coat hem. I was sold forever on credit.

When I modeled the zoot for Ella, she took a long look and said, "Well, I guess it had to happen." I took three of those twenty-five-cent sepia-toned, while-you-wait pictures of myself, posed the way "hipsters" wearing their zoots would "cool it"—hat dangled, knees drawn close together, feet wide apart, both index fingers jabbed toward the floor. The long coat and swinging chain and the Punjab pants were much more dramatic if you stood that way. One picture, I autographed and airmailed to my brothers and sisters in Lansing, to let them see how well I was doing. I gave another one to Ella, and the third to Shorty, who was really moved: I could tell by the way he said, "Thanks, homeboy." It was part of our "hip" code not to show that kind of affection.

Shorty soon decided that my hair was finally long enough to be conked. He had promised to school me in how to beat the barbershops' three- and four-dollar price by making up congolene, and then conking ourselves.

I took the little list of ingredients he had printed out for me, and went 70 to a grocery store, where I got a can of Red Devil lye, two eggs, and two medium-sized white potatoes. Then at a drugstore near the poolroom, I asked for a large jar of vaseline, a large bar of soap, a large-toothed comb and a fine-toothed comb, one of those rubber hoses with a metal spray-head, a rubber apron, and a pair of gloves.

"Going to lay on that first conk?" the drugstore man asked me. I proudly told him, grinning, "Right!"

Shorty paid six dollars a week for a room in his cousin's shabby apartment. His cousin wasn't at home. "It's like the pad's mine, he spends so much time with his woman," Shorty said. "Now, you watch me — "

He peeled the potatoes and thin-sliced them into a quart-sized Mason fruit jar, then started stirring them with a wooden spoon as he gradually poured in a little over half the can of lye. "Never use a metal spoon; the lye will turn it black," he told me.

A jelly-like, starchy-looking glop resulted from the lye and potatoes, and Shorty broke in the two eggs, stirring real fast — his own conk and dark face bent down close. The congolene turned pale-yellowish. "Feel the jar," Shorty said. I cupped my hand against the outside, and snatched it away. "Damn right, it's hot, that's the lye," he said. "So you know it's going to burn when I comb it in — it burns *bad*. But the longer you can stand it, the straighter the hair."

He made me sit down, and he tied the string of a new rubber apron   75
tightly around my neck, and combed up my bush of hair. Then, from the big vaseline jar, he took a handful and massaged it hard all through my hair and into the scalp. He also thickly vaselined my neck, ears and forehead. "When I get to washing out your head, be sure to tell me anywhere you feel any little stinging," Shorty warned me, washing his hands, then pulling on the rubber gloves, and tying on his own rubber apron. "You always got to remember that any congolene left in burns a sore into your head."

The congolene just felt warm when Shorty started combing it in. But then my head caught fire.

I gritted my teeth and tried to pull the sides of the kitchen table together. The comb felt as if it was raking my skin off.

My eyes watered, my nose was running. I couldn't stand it any longer; I bolted to the washbasin. I was cursing Shorty with every name I could think of when he got the spray going and started soap-lathering my head.

He lathered and spray-rinsed, lathered and spray-rinsed, maybe ten or twelve times, each time gradually closing the hot-water faucet, until the rinse was cold, and that helped some.

"You feel any stinging spots?"   80

"No," I managed to say. My knees were trembling.

"Sit back down, then. I think we got it all out okay."

The flame came back as Shorty, with a thick towel, started drying my head, rubbing hard. "*Easy, man, easy!*" I kept shouting.

"The first time's always worst. You get used to it better before long. You took it real good, homeboy. You got a good conk."

When Shorty let me stand up and see in the mirror, my hair hung   85
down in limp, damp strings. My scalp still flamed, but not as badly; I could bear it. He draped the towel around my shoulders, over my rubber apron, and began again vaselining my hair.

I could feel him combing, straight back, first the big comb, then the fine-tooth one.

Then, he was using a razor, very delicately, on the back of my neck. Then, finally, shaping the sideburns.

My first view in the mirror blotted out the hurting. I'd seen some pretty conks, but when it's the first time, on your *own* head, the transformation, after the lifetime of kinks, is staggering.

The mirror reflected Shorty behind me. We both were grinning and sweating. And on top of my head was this thick, smooth sheen of shining red hair — real red — as straight as any white man's.

How ridiculous I was! Stupid enough to stand there simply lost in admiration of my hair now looking "white," reflected in the mirror in Shorty's room. I vowed that I'd never again be without a conk, and I never was for many years.   90

This was my first really big step toward self-degradation: when I endured all of that pain, literally burning my flesh to have it look like a white man's hair. I had joined that multitude of Negro men and women in America who are brainwashed into believing that the black people are "inferior" — and white people "superior" — that they will even violate and mutilate their God-created bodies to try to look "pretty" by white standards.

Look around today, in every small town and big city, from two-bit catfish and soda-pop joints into the "integrated" lobby of the Waldorf-Astoria, and you'll see conks on black men. And you'll see black women wearing these green and pink and purple and red and platinum-blond wigs. They're all more ridiculous than a slapstick comedy. It makes you wonder if the Negro has completely lost his sense of identity, lost touch with himself.

You'll see the conk worn by many, many so-called "upper class" Negroes, and, as much as I hate to say it about them, on all too many Negro entertainers. One of the reasons that I've especially admired some of them, like Lionel Hampton and Sidney Poitier, among others, is that they have kept their natural hair and fought to the top. I admire any Negro man who has never had himself conked, or who has had the sense to get rid of it — as I finally did.

I don't know which kind of self-defacing conk is the greater shame — the one you'll see on the heads of the black so-called "middle class" and "upper class," who ought to know better, or the one you'll see on the heads of the poorest, most downtrodden, ignorant black men. I mean the legal-minimum-wage ghetto-dwelling kind of Negro, as I was when I got my first one. It's generally among these poor fools that you'll see a black kerchief over the man's head, like Aunt Jemima; he's trying to make his conk last longer, between trips to the barbershop. Only for special occasions is this kerchief-protected conk exposed — to show off how "sharp" and "hip" its owner is. The ironic thing is that I have never heard any woman, white or black, express any admiration for a conk. Of course, any white woman with a black man isn't thinking about his hair. But I don't see how on earth a black woman with any race pride could walk down the street with any black man wearing a conk—the emblem of his shame that he is black.

To my own shame, when I say all of this I'm talking first of all about   95
myself—because you can't show me any Negro who ever conked more faithfully than I did. I'm speaking from personal experience when I say of any black man who conks today, or any white-wigged black woman, that if they gave the brains in their heads just half as much attention as they do their hair, they would be a thousand times better off.

The Reader's Presence

1. The young Malcolm resists Ella's pressure to imitate white lifestyles in order to get ahead. Instead, he seeks the company of his brethren in the black ghetto (paragraph 15) from whom he learns that "everything in the world is a hustle" (paragraph 52). What might this resistance signify politically? What relation might it bear to his later name changes, from Malcolm Little to Malcolm X and, finally, to El-Hajj Malik El-Shabazz? What elements of African American identity appeal to the young Malcolm Little?

2. The writer, of course, was a courageous African American leader who was assassinated in 1965, when he was only forty years old. How does this knowledge affect your reading of this account of his early years? How does Malcolm himself indicate the difference in time between the events he is relating and the time at which he is writing?

3. In "People Like Us" (page 344) David Brooks notes, "Human beings are capable of drawing amazingly subtle social distinctions and then shaping their lives around them." What kinds of social distinctions does Malcolm X draw about the neighborhoods he describes in Boston? How does he seek to fit in where he most wants to belong?

David Mamet

The Rake: A Few Scenes from My Childhood

David Mamet (b. 1947) is a playwright, screenwriter, and director whose work is appreciated for the attention he pays to language as it is spoken by ordinary people in the contemporary world. His Pulitzer Prize–winning play, Glengarry Glen Ross, *explores the psychology of ambition, competition, failure, and despair among a group of Chicago real estate agents who are driven to sell worthless property to unsuspecting customers.*

Mamet has said that "playwriting is simply showing how words influence actions and vice versa. All my plays attempt to bring out the poetry in the plain, everyday language people use. That's the only way to put art back in the theater." Mamet's sensitivity to working-class language and experience is due in part to his own work experience in factories, at a real estate agency, and as a window washer, office cleaner, and taxi driver. More recently, he has taught theater at several leading universities and has published two collections of essays. His most recent publications include two plays, Ricky Jay: On the Stem *(2002) and* Dr. Faustus *(2004); a collection of essays,* Jafsie and John Henry *(1999); and several nonfiction books, including* True and False: Heresy and Common Sense for the Actor *(1997) and* Three Uses of the Knife *(1998). He has written and directed several films, including* State and Main *(2000) and* Heist *(2001). "The Rake: A Few Scenes from My Childhood" appeared in* Harper's *in 1992.*

There was the incident of the rake and there was the incident of the school play, and it seems to me that they both took place at the round kitchen table.

The table was not in the kitchen proper but in an area called "the nook," which held its claim to that small measure of charm by dint of a waist-high wall separating it from an adjacent area known as the living room.

All family meals were eaten in the nook. There was a dining room to the right, but, as in most rooms of that name at the time and in those surroundings, it was never used.

The round table was of wrought iron and topped with glass; it was noteworthy for that glass, for it was more than once and rather more than several times, I am inclined to think, that my stepfather would grow so angry as to bring some object down on the glass top, shattering it, thus giving us to know how we had forced him out of control.

And it seems that most times when he would shatter the table, as 5 often as that might have been, he would cut some portion of himself on the glass, or that he or his wife, our mother, would cut their hands on picking up the glass afterward, and that we children were to understand, and did understand, that these wounds were our fault.

So the table was associated in our minds with the notion of blood.

The house was in a brand-new housing development in the southern suburbs. The new community was built upon, and now bordered, the remains of what had once been a cornfield. When our new family moved in, there were but a few homes in the development completed, and a few more under construction. Most streets were mud, and boasted a house here or there, and many empty lots marked out by white stakes.

The house we lived in was the development's Model Home. The first time we had seen it, it had signs plastered on the front and throughout the interior telling of the various conveniences it contained. And it had a lawn, and was one of the only homes in the new community that did.

My stepfather was fond of the lawn, and he detailed me and my sister to care for it, and one fall afternoon we found ourselves assigned to rake the leaves.

Why this chore should have been so hated I cannot say, except   10
that we children, and I especially, felt ourselves less than full members of this new, cobbled-together family, and disliked being assigned to the beautification of a home that we found unbeautiful in all respects, and for which we had neither natural affection nor a sense of proprietary interest.

We went to the new high school. We walked the mile down the open two-lane road on one side of which was the just-begun suburban community and on the other side of which was the cornfield.

The school was as new as the community, and still under construction for the first three years of its occupancy. One of its innovations was the notion that honesty would be engendered by the absence of security, and so the lockers were designed and built both without locks and without the possibility of attaching locks. And there was the corresponding rash of thievery and many lectures about the same from the school administration, but it was difficult to point with pride to any scholastic or community tradition supporting the suggestion that we, the students, pull together in this new, utopian way. We were, in school, in an uncompleted building in the midst of a mud field in the midst of a cornfield. Our various sports teams were called The Spartans; and I played on those teams, which were of a wretchedness consistent with their novelty.

Meanwhile my sister interested herself in the drama society. The year after I had left the school she obtained the lead in the school play. It called for acting and singing, both of which she had talent for, and it looked to be a signal triumph for her in her otherwise unremarkable and unenjoyed school career.

On the night of the play's opening, she sat down to dinner with our mother and our stepfather. It may be that they ate a trifle early to allow her to get to the school to enjoy the excitement of opening night. But however it was, my sister had no appetite, and she nibbled a bit at her food, and then she got up from the table to carry her plate back to scrape it in the sink, when my mother suggested that she sit down, as she had not finished her food. My sister said she really had no appetite, but my mother insisted that, as the meal had been prepared, it would be good form to sit and eat it.

My sister sat down with the plate and pecked at her food and she   15
tried to eat a bit, and told my mother that, no, really, she possessed no appetite whatever, and that was due, no doubt, not to the food, but to her nervousness and excitement at the prospect of opening night.

My mother, again, said that, as the food had been cooked, it had to be eaten, and my sister tried and said that she could not; at which my mother nodded. She then got up from the table and went to the telephone and looked the number up and called the school and got the drama teacher and identified herself and told him that her daughter wouldn't be coming to school that night, that, no, she was not ill, but that she would not be coming in. Yes, yes, she said, she knew her daughter had the lead in the play, and, yes, she was aware that many children and teachers had worked hard for it, et cetera, and so my sister did not play the lead in her school play. But I was long gone, out of the house by that time, and well out of it. I heard that story, and others like, at the distance of twenty-five years.

In the model house our rooms were separated from their room, the master bedroom, by a bathroom and a study. On some weekends I would go alone to visit my father in the city and my sister would stay and sometimes grow frightened or lonely in her part of the house. And once, in the period when my grandfather, then in his sixties, was living with us, she became alarmed at a noise she had heard in the night; or perhaps she just became lonely, and she went out of her room and down the hall, calling for my mother, or my stepfather, or my grandfather, but the house was dark, and no one answered.

And, as she went farther down the hall, toward the living room, she heard voices, and she turned the corner, and saw a light coming from under the closed door in the master bedroom, and heard my stepfather crying, and the sound of my mother weeping. So my sister went up to the door, and she heard my stepfather talking to my grandfather and saying, "Jack. Say the words. Just say the words . . ." And my grandfather in his Eastern European accent, saying with obvious pain and difficulty, "No. No. I can't. Why are you making me do this? Why?" And the sound of my mother crying convulsively.

My sister opened the door, and she saw my grandfather sitting on the bed, and my stepfather standing by the closet and gesturing. On the floor of the closet she saw my mother, curled in a fetal position, moaning and crying and hugging herself. My stepfather was saying, "Say the words. Just say the words." And my grandfather was breathing fast and repeating, "I can't. She knows how I feel about her. I can't." And my stepfather said, "Say the words, Jack. Please. Just say you love her." At which my mother would moan louder. And my grandfather said, "I can't."

My sister pushed the door open farther and said—I don't know what she said, but she asked, I'm sure, for some reassurance, or some explanation, and my stepfather turned around and saw her and picked up a hairbrush from a dresser that he passed as he walked toward her, and he hit her in the face and slammed the door on her. And she continued to hear "Jack, say the words."

She told me that on weekends when I was gone my stepfather ended every Sunday evening by hitting or beating her for some reason or other. He would come home from depositing his own kids back at their mother's house after their weekend visitation, and would settle down tired and angry, and, as a regular matter on those evenings, would find out some intolerable behavior on my sister's part and slap or hit or beat her.

Years later, at my mother's funeral, my sister spoke to our aunt, my mother's sister, who gave a footnote to this behavior. She said when they were young, my mother and my aunt, they and their parents lived in a small flat on the West Side. My grandfather was a salesman on the road from dawn on Monday until Friday night. Their family had a fiction, and that fiction, that article of faith, was that my mother was a naughty child. And each Friday, when he came home, his first question as he climbed the stairs was, "What has she done this week . . . ?" At which my grandmother would tell him the terrible things that my mother had done, after which she, my mother, was beaten.

This was general knowledge in my family. The footnote concerned my grandfather's behavior later in the night. My aunt had a room of her own, and it adjoined her parents' room. And she related that each Friday, when the house had gone to bed, she, through the thin wall, heard my grandfather pleading for sex. "Cookie, please." And my grandmother responding, "No, Jack." "Cookie, please." "No, Jack." "Cookie, please."

And once, my grandfather came home and asked, "What has she done this week?" and I do not know, but I imagine that the response was not completed, and perhaps hardly begun; in any case, he reached and grabbed my mother by the back of the neck and hurled her down the stairs.

And once, in our house in the suburbs there had been an outburst by my stepfather directed at my sister. And she had, somehow, prevailed. It was, I think, that he had the facts of the case wrong, and had accused her of the commission of something for which she had demonstrably had no

20

25

opportunity, and she pointed this out to him with what I can imagine, given the circumstances, was an understandable, and, given my prejudice, a commendable degree of freedom. Thinking the incident closed she went back to her room to study, and, a few moments later, saw him throw open her door, bat the book out of her hands, and pick her up and throw her against the far wall, where she struck the back of her neck on the shelf.

She was told, the next morning, that her pain, real or pretended, held no weight, and that she would have to go to school. She protested that she could not walk, or, if at all, only with the greatest of difficulty and in great pain; but she was dressed and did walk to school, where she fainted, and was brought home. For years she suffered various headaches; an X ray taken twenty years later for an unrelated problem revealed that when he threw her against the shelf he had cracked her vertebrae.

When we left the house we left in good spirits. When we went out to dinner, it was an adventure, which was strange to me, looking back, because many of these dinners ended with my sister or myself being banished, sullen or in tears, from the restaurant, and told to wait in the car, as we were in disgrace.

These were the excursions that had ended, due to her or my intolerable arrogance, as it was explained to us.

The happy trips were celebrated and capped with a joke. Here is the joke: My stepfather, my mother, my sister, and I would exit the restaurant, my stepfather and mother would walk to the car, telling us that they would pick us up. We children would stand by the restaurant entrance. They would drive up in the car, open the passenger door, and wait until my sister and I had started to get in. They would then drive away.

They would drive ten or fifteen feet, and open the door again, and we would walk up again, and they would drive away again. They sometimes would drive around the block. But they would always come back, and by that time the four of us would be laughing in camaraderie and appreciation of what, I believe, was our only family joke.

We were raking the lawn, my sister and I. I was raking, and she was stuffing the leaves into a bag. I loathed the job, and my muscles and my mind rebelled, and I was viciously angry, and my sister said something, and I turned and threw the rake at her and hit her in the face.

The rake was split bamboo and metal, and a piece of metal caught her lip and cut her badly.

We were both terrified, and I was sick with guilt, and we ran into the house, my sister holding her hand to her mouth, and her mouth and her hand and the front of her dress covered in blood.

We ran into the kitchen where my mother was cooking dinner, and my mother asked what happened.

Neither of us, myself out of guilt, of course, and my sister out of a de-   35
sire to avert the terrible punishment she knew I would receive, neither of
us would say what occurred.

My mother pressed us, and neither of us would answer. She said that
until one or the other answered, we would not go to the hospital; and so
the family sat down to dinner where my sister clutched a napkin to her
face and the blood soaked the napkin and ran down onto her food, which
she had to eat; and I also ate my food and we cleared the table and went
to the hospital.

I remember the walks home from school in the frigid winter, along the
cornfield that was, for all its proximity to the city, part of the prairie. The
winters were viciously cold. From the remove of years, I can see how
the area might and may have been beautiful. One could have walked in the
stubble of the cornfields, or hunted birds, or enjoyed any of a number of
pleasures naturally occurring.

The Reader's Presence

1. Interwoven through Mamet's essay are descriptions of suburban
   developments and model homes; he even uses the word "utopian"
   (paragraph 12). What is Mamet's attitude toward these ideals?
   What is his tone in discussing them? Mamet says that he and his
   sister hate doing chores, in part because they "had neither natural
   affection nor a sense of proprietary interest" (paragraph 10) toward their house. What does this mean?

2. Near the end of the essay, Mamet recalls a "joke" that his family
   shared. How does he present the joke to the reader? Do you think
   Mamet wants the reader to think the joke is funny? Would the
   joke seem different if Mamet had told it at the beginning of
   the essay? How does he connect this joke back to the story about
   the rake?

3. Mamet says that "the table was associated in our minds with the
   notion of blood" (paragraph 6). Do you think the rake also has
   symbolic value? If so, what does it represent? How does Mamet's
   use of symbolic objects compare to George Orwell's treatment of
   the gun and the elephant in "Shooting an Elephant" (page 221)?
   How does Mamet's account of his relationship with his sister
   compare to Alice Walker's account of her brothers' role in the
   "accident" in which she lost an eye in "Beauty: When the Other
   Dancer Is the Self" (page 304)?

Joyce Carol Oates

District School #7, Niagara County, New York

Joyce Carol Oates (b. 1938) has published more than a hundred works of fiction and nonfiction in every genre, including novels, short stories, essays, poetry, screenplays, and a libretto — frequently publishing several projects simultaneously while working and reworking the manuscript for the next. Describing herself as a "chronicler of the American experience," Oates often explores violent behavior "in a nation prone to violence" and its effect on the lives of ordinary people, particularly women and children. Among her long list of novels are A Garden of Earthly Delights *(1967) and* them *(1969), which won the National Book Award for fiction in 1970. Her most recent works of fiction include* The Tattooed Girl *(2003),* Rape: A Love Story *(2003),* The Falls *(2004), and* Sexy *(2005). Oates's interests and versatility are also reflected in her nonfiction prose, which includes* The Profane Art *(1983),* On Boxing *(1987),* Where I've Been, and Where I'm Going *(1999), and her latest,* Uncensored: Views and (Re)views *(2005). "District School #7, Niagara Country, New York" comes from her 2003 collection,* The Faith of a Writer: Life, Craft, Art.*

The skill with which she handles diverse topics and writing styles make it clear that Oates knows what it takes to write well in any situation. She has this advice for aspiring writers: "Remember that writing is a craft; it's not an experience like an emotion. It's not like going to a psychiatrist and delivering yourself of emotions. It's made up of text, the text has paragraphs, the paragraphs have sentences, and all of this has to be coherent and as beautifully composed as you can make it."

For additional information on Joyce Carol Oates, see page 925.

As a child I took for granted what seems wonderful to me now: that, from first through fifth grades, during the years 1943–1948, I attended the same single-room schoolhouse in western New York that my mother, Carolina Bush, had attended twenty years before. Apart from the introduction of electricity in the early 1940s, and a few minor improvements, not including indoor plumbing, the school had scarcely changed in the intervening years. It was a rough-hewn, weatherworn, uninsulated woodframe building on a crude stone foundation, built around the turn of the century near the crossroads community of Millersport, twenty-five miles north of Buffalo and seven miles south of Lockport. *I loved my first school!* — so I have often said, and possibly this is true.

In late August, in anticipation of school beginning immediately after Labor Day in September, I would walk the approximate mile from our house, carrying my new pencil box and lunch pail, to sit on the front, stone step of the school building. Just to sit there, dreamy in anticipation of school starting; possibly to enjoy the solitude and quiet, which would not prevail once school started.

(Perhaps no one recalls pencil boxes? They were of about the size of a lunch pail, with several drawers that, slid out, revealed freshly sharpened yellow "lead" pencils, Crayola crayons, erasers, compasses. Lunch pails, which perhaps no one recalls either, were of about the size of pencil boxes but, unlike pencil boxes, which smelled wonderfully of Crayolas, lunch pails quickly came to smell awfully of milk in Thermos bottles, overripe bananas, baloney sandwiches, and waxed paper.)

The school, more deeply imprinted in my memory than my own child-face, was set approximately thirty feet back from a pebble-strewn unpaved road, Tonawanda Creek Road; it had six tall, narrow windows in its side walls, and very small windows in its front wall; a steeply slanting shingleboard roof that often leaked in heavy rain; and a shadowy, smelly, shed-like structure at the front called the "entry"; nothing so romantic as a cupola with a bell to be rung, to summon pupils inside. (Our teacher Mrs. Dietz, standing Amazon-like in the entry doorway, rang a hand bell. This was a sign of her adult authority, the jarring noise of the bell, the thrusting, hacking gesture of her muscled right arm as she vigorously shook it.) Behind the school, down a slope of briars and jungle-like vegetation, was the "crick" — the wide, often muddy, fast-moving Tonawanda Creek, where pupils were forbidden to play or explore; on both sides of the school were vacant, overgrown fields; "out back" were crudely built wooden outhouses, the boys' to the left and the girls' to the right, with drainage, raw sewage, virulently fetid in warm weather, seeping out into the creek. (Elsewhere, off the creek bank, children, mostly older boys, swam. There was not much consciousness of "polluted" waters in those days and yet less fastidiousness on the part of energetic farm boys.)

At the front of the school, and to the sides, was an improvised playground of sorts, where we played such improvised games as "May I?" — which involved "baby-" and "giant-steps" — and "Pom-Pom-Pullaway" which was more raucous, and rougher, where one might be dragged across an expanse of cinders, even thrown down into the cinders. And there was "Tag" which was my favorite game, at which I excelled since I could run, even at a young age, out of necessity, fast.

Joyce runs like a deer! certain of the boys, chasing me, as they chased other younger children, to bully and terrorize us, and for fun, would say, admiring.

Inside, the school smelled smartly of varnish and wood smoke from the potbellied stove. On gloomy days, not unknown in upstate New York in this region south of Lake Ontario and east of Lake Erie, the windows emitted a vague, gauzy light, not much reinforced by ceiling lights. We squinted at the blackboard, that seemed far away since it was on a small platform, where Mrs. Dietz's desk was also positioned, at the front, left of the room. We sat in rows of seats, smallest at the front, largest at the rear, attached at their bases by metal runners, like a toboggan; the wood of these desks seemed beautiful to me, smooth and of the red-burnished hue of horse chestnuts. The floor was bare wooden planks. An American flag hung limply at the far left of the blackboard and above the black-board, running across the front of the room, designed to draw our eyes to it avidly, worshipfully, were paper squares showing that beautifully shaped script known as Parker Penmanship.

Mrs. Dietz, of course, had mastered the art of penmanship. She wrote our vocabulary and spelling lists on the blackboard, and we learned to imitate her. We learned to "diagram" sentences with the solemn preci-sion of scientists articulating chemical equations. We learned to read by reading aloud, and we learned to spell by spelling aloud. We memorized, and we recited. Our textbooks were rarely new, but belonged to the school district and were passed on, year after year until they wore out entirely. Our "library" was a shelf or two of books including a Web-ster's dictionary, which fascinated me: a book containing *words!* A trea-sure of secrets this seemed to me, available to anyone who cared to look into it.

My earliest reading experiences, in fact, were in this dictionary. We had no dictionary at home until, winner of a spelling bee sponsored by the *Buffalo Evening News*, when I was in fifth grade, I was given a dictio-nary like the one at school. This, like the prized *Alice* books, remained with me for decades.

My early "creative" experiences evolved not from printed books,   10
but from coloring books, predating my ability to read. I did not learn to read until I was in first grade, and six years old, though by this time I had already produced numerous "books" of a kind by drawing, color-ing, and scribbling in tablets, in what I believed to be a convincing imita-tion of adults. My earliest fictional characters were zestfully if crudely drawn, upright chickens and cats engaged in various dramatic con-frontations; the title of my first full-length novel, on tablet paper, was *The Cat House*. (Somewhere, *The Cat House* still exists. Through my life, I seem to have been an unlikely combination of precocity and naiveté.)

After I learned to read, most of my reading was related to school, ex-cept for a few books we had at home, including the daunting *The Gold Bug and Other Stories* by Edgar Allan Poe, my father's book. What I could make of this, I can't imagine. Though Poe's classic tales would seem to move, in our memories, with the nightmare ease of horror films, yet the prose in which Poe cast these tales is highly formal, tortuous, turgid if not opaque. Yet, somehow, I persevered; I "read" Edgar Allan

Poe as a young child, and who knows what effect that experience has had upon me? (No wonder my immediate kinship with Paul Bowles, whose first story collection, *The Delicate Prey*, is addressed to his mother, who had read him the tales of Poe as a young boy.)

My child's logic, which was not corrected by any adult because it would not have occurred to me to mention it to any adult, was that the mysterious world of books was divided into two types: those for children, and those for adults. Reading for children, in our grade-school textbooks, was simple-minded in its vocabulary, grammar, and content; it was usually about unreal, improbable, or unconditionally fantastic situations, like fairy tales, comic books, Disney films. It might be amusing, it might even be instructive, but it was not *real*. Reality was the province of adults, and though I was surrounded by adults, as an only child for five years, it was not a province I could enter, or even envision, from the outside. To enter that reality, to find a way *in*, I read books.

Avidly, ardently! As if my life depended upon it.

One of the earliest books I read, or tried to read, was an anthology from our school library, an aged *Treasury of American Literature* that had probably been published before World War II. Mixed with writers who are mostly forgotten today (James Whitcomb Riley, Eugene Field, Helen Hunt Jackson) were our New England classics—though I was too young to know that Hawthorne, Emerson, Poe, Melville, et al. were "classics" or even to know that they spoke out of an America that no longer existed, and would never have existed for families like my own. I believed that these writers, who were exclusively male, were in full possession of *reality*. That their *reality* was so very different from my own did not discredit it, or even disqualify it, but confirmed it: adult writing was a form of wisdom and power, difficult to comprehend, but unassailable. These were no children's easy-reading fantasies but the real thing, voices of adult authenticity. I forced myself to read for long minutes at a time, finely printed prose on yellowed, dog-eared pages, retaining very little but utterly captivated by the strangeness of another's voice sounding in my ear. I tackled such a book as I would tackle a tree (a pear tree, for instance) difficult to climb. I must have felt almost physically challenged by lengthy, near-impenetrable paragraphs so unlike the American-English language spoken in Millersport, New York, and unlike the primer sentences of our schoolbooks. The writers were mere names, words. And these words were exotic: "Washington Irving"—"Benjamin Franklin"—"Nathaniel Hawthorne"—"Herman Melville"—"Ralph Waldo Emerson"—"Henry David Thoreau"—"Edgar Allan Poe"—"Samuel Clemens." There was no Emily Dickinson in this anthology, I would not read Dickinson until high school. I did not think of these exalted individuals as actual men, human beings like my father and grandfather who might have lived and breathed; the writing attributed to them was them. If I could not always make sense of what I read, I knew at least that it was true.

It was the first-person voice, the (seemingly) unmediated voice, that   15
struck me as *truth-telling*. For some reason, very few books for children
are in the first-person voice; Lewis Carroll's Alice is always seen from a
little distance, as "Alice." But many of the adult writers whom I struggled to read wrote in the first person, and very persuasively. I could not
have distinguished between the (nonfiction) voices of Thoreau and Emerson and the (wholly fictional) voices of Irving and Poe; even today, I
have to think to recall whether "The Imp of the Perverse" is a confessional essay, as it sets itself up to be, or one of the *Tales of the Grotesque*.
I may have absorbed from Poe the predilection for moving fluidly
through genres, and grounding the surreal in the seeming "reality" of an
earnest, impassioned voice. Poe was a master of, among other things, the
literary trompe l'oeil, in which speculative musings upon human psychology shift into fantastic narratives while retaining the same first-person
voice.

I would one day wonder why the earliest, most "primitive" forms of
art seem to have been fabulist, legendary, and surreal, populated not by
ordinary, life-sized men and women but by gods, giants, and monsters?
Why was reality so slow to evolve? It's as if, looking into a mirror, our
ancestors shrank from seeing their own faces in the hope of seeing something other—exotic, terrifying, comforting, idealistic, or delusional—but
distinctly *other*.

Of Mrs. Dietz, I think: how heroic she must have been! Underpaid,
undervalued, overworked. Not only was it the task of a one-room schoolteacher to lead eight disparate grades through their lessons, but to maintain discipline in the classroom where most of the older boys attended
school grudgingly, waiting for their sixteenth birthdays when they were
legally released from attending school and could work with their fathers
on family farms; these boys were taught by their fathers to hunt and kill
animals, and they were without mercy in "teasing" (the term "harassing"
hadn't yet been coined) younger children. (Some of this "teasing" could
become very cruel. Certainly, out of Mrs. Dietz's earshot, it shaded into
what would be called in a more civil environment "assault" and "sexual
molestation"—but that's another story, at odds with the romance of
childhood nostalgia.) Mrs. Dietz was also in charge of maintaining our
woodburning stove, the school's only source of heat, in that pitiless up-
state New York climate in which below-zero temperatures weren't uncommon on gusty winter mornings, and we had to wear mittens, hats,
and coats through the day, stamping our booted feet against the drafty
plank floor to keep our toes from going numb. . . . I can only imagine the
physical as well as the emotional and psychological difficulties poor Mrs.
Dietz endured, and feel now a belated kinship with her, who had seemed
to me a very giantess of my childhood. No other teacher looms as archetypal in my memory, for no other teacher taught me the fundamental skills
of reading, writing, and "doing" arithmetic, that seem to me as natural as
breathing. I am grateful to Mrs. Dietz for not (visibly) breaking down,

and for maintaining a certain degree of good cheer in the classroom. The schoolhouse for all its shortcomings and dangers became for me a kind of sanctuary: a precious counter-world to the chaotic and unbookish roughness that existed outside it.

For a long time vacant and boarded-up, District #7 school was finally razed about twenty years ago. And for a long time afterward, when I returned to Millersport to visit my parents, I would make a sentimental pilgrimage to the site, where a wrecked stone foundation and a mound of rubble were all that remained. Soon such one-room schoolhouses will be recalled, if at all, only in photographs: links with a mythopoetic "American frontier past" that, when it was lived, seemed to us, who lived it, simply life.

The Reader's Presence

1. What does the single-room schoolhouse symbolize to Oates? How does she understand and appreciate it today? What parts of her childhood memories does she suggest do not fit into her nostalgic picture of her early schooling?

2. How does Oates represent her early understandings of literature? What does she suggest is a naïve misunderstanding of the role of books and writing?

3. How does Oates characterize her early reading experiences? What are her assumptions about books and fiction? How does she characterize the difference between children's and adult's books? Compare Oates's early reading experiences to Sherman Alexie's in "The Joy of Reading and Writing: Superman and Me" (page 73). How does each writer's early schooling reflect his or her cultural background? How do these early experiences shape each writer's understanding of reading and writing?

George Orwell

Shooting an Elephant

    George Orwell (1903–1950) was born Eric Arthur Blair in Bengal, India, the son of a colonial administrator. He was sent to England for his education and attended Eton on a scholarship, but rather than go on to university in 1922 he returned to the East and served with the Indian Imperial Police in Burma. Orwell hated his work and the colonial system; published posthumously, the essay "Shooting an Elephant" was based on his experience in Burma and is found in Shooting an Elephant and Other Essays *(1950). In 1927 Orwell returned to England and began a career as a professional writer. He served briefly in the Spanish Civil War until he was wounded and then settled in Hertfordshire. Best remembered for his novels* Animal Farm *(1945) and* Nineteen Eighty-Four *(1949), Orwell also wrote articles, essays, and reviews, usually with a political point in mind. In 1969 Irving Howe honored Orwell as "the best English essayist since Hazlitt, perhaps since Dr. Johnson. He was the greatest moral force in English letters during the last several decades: craggy, fiercely polemical, sometimes mistaken, but an utterly free man."*

    In his 1946 essay "Why I Write," Orwell said that from a very early age "I knew that when I grew up I should be a writer." At first he saw writing as a remedy for loneliness, but as he grew up his reasons for writing expanded: "Looking back through my work, I see it is invariably when I lacked a political *purpose that I wrote lifeless books." In his mature work, he relied on simple, clear prose to express his political and social convictions: "Good prose," he once wrote, "is like a windowpane."*

In Moulmein, in Lower Burma, I was hated by large numbers of people—the only time in my life that I have been important enough for this to happen to me. I was subdivisional police officer of the town, and in an aimless, petty kind of way anti-European feeling was very bitter. No one had the guts to raise a riot, but if a European woman went through the bazaars alone somebody would probably spit betel juice over her dress. As a police officer I was an obvious target and was baited whenever it seemed safe to do so. When a nimble Burman tripped me up on the football field and the referee (another Burman) looked the other way, the crowd yelled with hideous laughter. This happened more than once. In the end the sneering yellow faces of young men that met me everywhere, the insults hooted after me when I was at a safe distance, got badly on my nerves. The young Buddhist priests were the worst of all. There were several thousands of them in the town and none of them seemed to have anything to do except stand on street corners and jeer at Europeans.

All this was perplexing and upsetting. For at that time I had already made up my mind that imperialism was an evil thing and the sooner I

chucked up my job and got out of it the better. Theoretically—and secretly, of course—I was all for the Burmese and all against the oppressors, the British. As for the job I was doing, I hated it more bitterly than I
can perhaps make clear. In a job like that you see the dirty work of Empire at close quarters. The wretched prisoners huddling in the stinking
cages of the lockups, the grey, cowed faces of the long-term convicts, the
scarred buttocks of the men who had been flogged with bamboos—all
these oppressed me with an intolerable sense of guilt. But I could get
nothing into perspective. I was young and ill-educated and I had had to
think out my problems in the utter silence that is imposed on every Englishman in the East. I did not even know that the British Empire is dying,
still less did I know that it is a great deal better than the younger empires
that are going to supplant it. All I knew was that I was stuck between my
hatred of the empire I served and my rage against the evil-spirited little
beasts who tried to make my job impossible. With one part of my mind
I thought of the British Raj[1] as an unbreakable tyranny, as something
clamped down, *in saecula saeculorum*,[2] upon the will of prostrate peoples; with another part I thought that the greatest joy in the world would
be to drive a bayonet into a Buddhist priest's guts. Feelings like these are
the normal by-products of imperialism; ask any Anglo-Indian official, if
you can catch him off duty.

One day something happened which in a roundabout way was enlightening. It was a tiny incident in itself, but it gave me a better glimpse
than I had had before of the real nature of imperialism—the real motives
for which despotic governments act. Early one morning the subinspector
at a police station the other end of town rang me up on the phone and
said that an elephant was ravaging the bazaar. Would I please come and
do something about it? I did not know what I could do, but I wanted to
see what was happening and I got on to a pony and started out. I took my
rifle, an old .44 Winchester and much too small to kill an elephant, but I
thought the noise might be useful *in terrorem*.[3] Various Burmans stopped
me on the way and told me about the elephant's doings. It was not, of
course, a wild elephant, but a tame one which had gone "must."[4] It had
been chained up, as tame elephants always are when their attack of
"must" is due, but on the previous night it had broken its chain and escaped. Its mahout,[5] the only person who could manage it when it was in
that state, had set out in pursuit, but had taken the wrong direction and
was now twelve hours' journey away, and in the morning the elephant
had suddenly reappeared in the town. The Burmese population had no
weapons and were quite helpless against it. It had already destroyed
somebody's bamboo hut, killed a cow, and raided some fruit stalls and

[1]*Raj:* The British administration.—Eds.
[2]*in saecula saeculorum:* Forever and ever (Latin).—Eds.
[3]*in terrorem:* As a warning (Latin).—Eds.
[4]*"must":* Sexual arousal.—Eds.
[5]*mahout:* Keeper (Hindi).—Eds.

devoured the stock; also it had met the municipal rubbish van and, when the driver jumped out and took to his heels, had turned the van over and inflicted violence upon it.

The Burmese subinspector and some Indian constables were waiting for me in the quarter where the elephant had been seen. It was a very poor quarter, a labyrinth of squalid bamboo huts, thatched with palm-leaf, winding all over a steep hillside. I remember that it was a cloudy, stuffy morning at the beginning of the rains. We began questioning the people as to where the elephant had gone and, as usual, failed to get any definite information. That is invariably the case in the East; a story always sounds clear enough at a distance, but the nearer you get to the scene of events the vaguer it becomes. Some of the people said that the elephant had gone in one direction, some said that he had gone in another, some professed not even to have heard of any elephant. I had almost made up my mind that the whole story was a pack of lies, when we heard yells a little distance away. There was a loud, scandalized cry of "Go away, child! Go away this instant!" and an old woman with a switch in her hand came round the corner of a hut, violently shooing away a crowd of naked children. Some more women followed, clicking their tongues and exclaiming; evidently there was something that the children ought not to have seen. I rounded the hut and saw a man's dead body sprawling in the mud. He was an Indian, a black Dravidian[6] coolie, almost naked, and he could not have been dead many minutes. The people said that the elephant had come suddenly upon him round the corner of the hut, caught him with its trunk, put its foot on his back, and ground him into the earth. This was the rainy season and the ground was soft, and his face had scored a trench a foot deep and a couple of yards long. He was lying on his belly with arms crucified and head sharply twisted to one side. His face was coated with mud, the eyes wide open, the teeth bared and grinning with an expression of unendurable agony. (Never tell me, by the way, that the dead look peaceful. Most of the corpses I have seen looked devilish.) The friction of the great beast's foot had stripped the skin from his back as neatly as one skins a rabbit. As soon as I saw the dead man I sent an orderly to a friend's house nearby to borrow an elephant rifle. I had already sent back the pony, not wanting it to go mad with fright and throw me if it smelled the elephant.

The orderly came back in a few minutes with a rifle and five cartridges, and meanwhile some Burmans had arrived and told us that the elephant was in the paddy fields below, only a few hundred yards away. As I started forward practically the whole population of the quarter flocked out of the houses and followed me. They had seen the rifle and were all shouting excitedly that I was going to shoot the elephant. They had not shown much interest in the elephant when he was merely ravaging their

[6]*Dravidian:* A populous Indian group. —EDS.

homes, but it was different now that he was going to be shot. It was a bit of fun to them, as it would be to an English crowd; besides, they wanted the meat. It made me vaguely uneasy. I had no intention of shooting the elephant—I had merely sent for the rifle to defend myself if necessary—and it is always unnerving to have a crowd following you. I marched down the hill, looking and feeling a fool, with the rifle over my shoulder and an ever-growing army of people jostling at my heels. At the bottom, when you got away from the huts, there was a metalled road and beyond that a miry waste of paddy fields a thousand yards across, not yet ploughed but soggy from the first rains and dotted with coarse grass. The elephant was standing eight yards from the road, his left side towards us. He took not the slightest notice of the crowd's approach. He was tearing up bunches of grass, beating them against his knees to clean them and stuffing them into his mouth.

I had halted on the road. As soon as I saw the elephant I knew with perfect certainty that I ought not to shoot him. It is a serious matter to shoot a working elephant—it is comparable to destroying a huge and costly piece of machinery—and obviously one ought not to do it if it can possibly be avoided. And at that distance, peacefully eating, the elephant looked no more dangerous than a cow. I thought then and I think now that his attack of "must" was already passing off; in which case he would merely wander harmlessly about until the mahout came back and caught him. Moreover, I did not in the least want to shoot him. I decided that I would watch him for a little while to make sure that he did not turn savage again, and then go home.

But at that moment, I glanced round at the crowd that had followed me. It was an immense crowd, two thousand at the least and growing every minute. It blocked the road for a long distance on either side. I looked at the sea of yellow faces above the garish clothes—faces all happy and excited over this bit of fun, all certain that the elephant was going to be shot. They were watching me as they would watch a conjuror about to perform a trick. They did not like me, but with the magical rifle in my hands I was momentarily worth watching. And suddenly I realized that I should have to shoot the elephant after all: The people expected it of me and I had got to do it; I could feel their two thousand wills pressing me forward, irresistibly. And it was at this moment, as I stood there with the rifle in my hands, that I first grasped the hollowness, the futility of the white man's dominion in the East. Here was I, the white man with his gun, standing in front of the unarmed native crowd—seemingly the leading actor of the piece; but in reality I was only an absurd puppet pushed to and fro by the will of those yellow faces behind. I perceived in this moment that when the white man turns tyrant it is his own freedom that he destroys. He becomes a sort of hollow, posing dummy, the conventionalized figure of a sahib. For it is the condition of his rule that he shall spend his life in trying to impress the "natives," and so in every crisis he has got to do what the "natives" expect of him. He wears a mask, and his face grows to fit it. I had got to shoot the elephant. I had committed myself to doing it when I sent for the rifle. A sahib has got to act like a sahib; he has got to appear resolute, to know his own mind and do definite things. To come all that way, rifle in hand, with two thousand people marching at my heels, and then to trail feebly away, having done nothing—no, that was impossible. The crowd would laugh at me. And my whole life, every white man's life in the East, was one long struggle not to be laughed at.

But I did not want to shoot the elephant. I watched him beating his bunch of grass against his knees, with that preoccupied grandmotherly air that elephants have. It seemed to me that it would be murder to shoot him. At that age I was not squeamish about killing animals, but I had never shot an elephant and never wanted to. (Somehow it always seems worse to kill a *large* animal.) Besides, there was the beast's owner to be considered. Alive, the elephant was worth at least a hundred pounds; dead, he would only be worth the value of his tusks, five pounds, possibly. But I had got to act quickly. I turned to some experienced-looking Burmans who had been there when we arrived, and asked them how the elephant had been behaving. They all said the same thing: He took no notice of you if you left him alone, but he might charge if you went too close to him.

It was perfectly clear to me what I ought to do. I ought to walk up to within, say, twenty-five yards of the elephant and test his behavior. If he charged, I could shoot; if he took no notice of me, it would be safe to leave him until the mahout came back. But also I knew that I was going to do no such thing. I was a poor shot with a rifle and the ground was soft mud into which one would sink at every step. If the elephant charged and I missed him, I should have about as much chance as a toad under a steamroller. But even then I was not thinking particularly of my own skin, only of the watchful yellow faces behind. For at that moment, with the crowd watching me, I was not afraid in the ordinary sense, as I would have been if I had been alone. A white man mustn't be frightened in front of "natives"; and so, in general, he isn't frightened. The sole thought in my mind was that if anything went wrong those two thousand Burmans would see me pursued, caught, trampled on, and reduced to a grinning corpse like that Indian up the hill. And if that happened it was quite probable that some of them would laugh. That would never do. There was only one alternative. I shoved the cartridges into the magazine and lay down on the road to get a better aim.

The crowd grew very still, and a deep, low, happy sigh, as of people who see the theatre curtain go up at last, breathed from innumerable throats. They were going to have their bit of fun after all. The rifle was a beautiful German thing with cross-hair sights. I did not then know that in shooting an elephant one would shoot to cut an imaginary bar running from ear-hole to ear-hole. I ought, therefore, as the elephant was sideways on, to have aimed straight at his ear-hole; actually I aimed several inches in front of this, thinking the brain would be further forward.

10

When I pulled the trigger I did not hear the bang or feel the kick — one never does when a shot goes home — but I heard the devilish roar of glee that went up from the crowd. In that instant, in too short a time, one would have thought, even for the bullet to get there, a mysterious, terrible change had come over the elephant. He neither stirred nor fell, but every line of his body had altered. He looked suddenly stricken, shrunken, immensely old, as though the frightful impact of the bullet had paralyzed him without knocking him down. At last, after what seemed a long time — it might have been five seconds, I dare say — he sagged flabbily to his knees. His mouth slobbered. An enormous senility seemed to have settled upon him. One could have imagined him thousands of years old. I fired again into the same spot. At the second shot he did not collapse but climbed with desperate slowness to his feet and stood weakly upright, with legs sagging and head drooping. I fired a third time. That was the shot that did for him. You could see the agony of it jolt his whole body and knock the last remnant of strength from his legs. But in falling he seemed for a moment to rise, for as his hind legs collapsed beneath him he seemed to tower upward like a huge rock toppling, his trunk reaching skywards like a tree. He trumpeted, for the first and only time. And then down he came, his belly towards me, with a crash that seemed to shake the ground even where I lay.

I got up. The Burmans were already racing past me across the mud. It was obvious that the elephant would never rise again, but he was not dead. He was breathing very rhythmically with long rattling gasps, his great mound of a side painfully rising and falling. His mouth was wide open. I could see far down into caverns of pale pink throat. I waited a long time for him to die, but his breathing did not weaken. Finally, I fired my two remaining shots into the spot where I thought his heart must be. The thick blood welled out of him like red velvet, but still he did not die. His body did not even jerk when the shots hit him, the tortured breathing continued without a pause. He was dying, very slowly and in great agony, but in some world remote from me where not even a bullet could damage him further. I felt I had got to put an end to that dreadful noise. It seemed dreadful to see the great beast lying there, powerless to move and yet powerless to die, and not even to be able to finish him. I sent back for my small rifle and poured shot after shot into his heart, and down his throat. They seemed to make no impression. The tortured gasps continued as steadily as the ticking of a clock.

In the end I could not stand it any longer and went away. I heard later that it took him half an hour to die. Burmans were bringing dahs[7] and baskets even before I left, and I was told they had stripped his body almost to the bones by the afternoon.

Afterwards, of course, there were endless discussions about the shooting of the elephant. The owner was furious, but he was only an Indian and could do nothing. Besides, legally I had done the right thing, for a mad elephant has to be killed, like a mad dog, if its owner fails to control

---

[7]*dahs:* Large knives. — EDS.

it. Among the Europeans opinion was divided. The older men said I was right, the younger men said it was a damn shame to shoot an elephant for killing a coolie, because the elephant was worth more than any damn Coringhee coolie. And afterwards I was very glad that the coolie had been killed; it put me legally in the right and it gave me sufficient pretext for shooting the elephant. I often wondered whether any of the others grasped that I had done it solely to avoid looking a fool.

The Reader's Presence

1. At the end of paragraph 2, Orwell gives the perfect expression of ambivalence, the simultaneous holding of two opposed feelings or opinions: "With one part of my mind . . . with another part . . ." How would you describe Orwell's dilemma? How would you react in such a situation? Is Orwell recommending that readers see his behavior as a model of what to do in such a conflict? To what extent is Orwell responsible for the situation in which he finds himself? What does he mean when he says that his conflicted feelings "are the normal by-products of imperialism"?

2. Some literary critics doubt that Orwell really did shoot an elephant in Burma. No external historical documentation has ever been found to corroborate Orwell's account. Yet what *internal* elements in the essay—what details or features—suggest that the episode is fact and not fiction? In other words, what makes this piece seem to be an essay and not a short story?

3. Orwell's essay describes a state of extreme personal self-consciousness, even vigilance, in a situation in which one's behavior feels somehow "scripted" by society. Orwell writes, "in reality I was only an absurd puppet pushed to and fro by the will of those yellow faces behind" (paragraph 7). How does Orwell's essay compare with Brent Staples's essay "Just Walk on By" (page 283)? Compare especially Orwell's use of the word *fool* in his last paragraph and Staples's use of the same word in the second paragraph of the alternate version of his essay. Do you believe both authors?

Adrienne Rich

Split at the Root: An Essay on Jewish Identity

Adrienne Rich (b. 1929) has published numerous volumes of poetry and her work has appeared in many anthologies. She received her first award for poetry, a Yale Series of Younger Poets Award, while a student at Radcliffe College in 1951. Since then Rich has received many other professional honors, including a National Institute of Art and Letters Award (1961), a National Book Award (1974), a Fund for Human Dignity Award from the National Gay Task Force (1981), and the Lenore Marshall Nation *Poetry Prize for her 1991 book,* An Atlas of the Difficult World. *In 1999, she received the Lannan Foundation Lifetime Achievement Award. Her most recent books of poems are* Midnight Salvage *(1999),* Fox *(2001), and* The School among the Ruins *(2004). Rich's poetics are informed by her political work in support of equal rights for women and for gays and lesbians.*

Besides poetry, Rich has published five prose collections, including Blood, Bread and Poetry *(1986), from which "Split at the Root" is excerpted;* What Is Found There: Notebooks on Poetry and Politics *(1993); and* Arts of the Possible *(2001). She has taught at many colleges and universities, most recently as a professor of English and feminist studies at Stanford University and as the Marjorie Kouler Visiting Fellow at the University of Chicago.*

Rich has written about a pivotal moment in her life as a writer, "To write directly and overtly as a woman, out of a woman's body and experience, to take women's existence seriously as theme and source for art, was something I had been hungering to do, needing to do, all my writing life. It placed me nakedly face to face with both terror and anger; it did indeed imply the breakdown of the world as I had always known it, the end of safety, *to paraphrase Baldwin. . . . But it released tremendous energy in me, as in many other women, to have that way of writing affirmed and validated in a growing political community. I felt for the first time the closing of the gap between poet and woman."*

For about fifteen minutes I have been sitting chin in hand in front of the typewriter, staring out at the snow. Trying to be honest with myself, trying to figure out why writing this seems to be so dangerous an act, filled with fear and shame, and why it seems so necessary. It comes to me that in order to write this I have to be willing to do two things: I have to claim my father, for I have my Jewishness from him and not from my gentile mother, and I have to break his silence, his taboos; in order to claim him I have in a sense to expose him.

And there is, of course, the third thing: I have to face the sources and the flickering presence of my own ambivalence as a Jew; the daily, mundane anti-Semitisms of my entire life.

These are stories I have never tried to tell before. Why now? Why, I asked myself sometime last year, does this question of Jewish identity float so impalpably, so ungraspably around me, a cloud I can't quite see the outlines of, which feels to me to be without definition?

And yet I've been on the track of this longer than I think.

In a long poem written in 1960, when I was thirty-one years old, I described myself as "Split at the root, neither Gentile nor Jew, / Yankee nor Rebel."[1] I was still trying to have it both ways: to be neither/nor, trying to live (with my Jewish husband and three children more Jewish in ancestry than I) in the predominantly gentile Yankee academic world of Cambridge, Massachusetts.

But this begins, for me, in Baltimore, where I was born in my father's workplace, a hospital in the black ghetto, whose lobby contained an immense white marble statue of Christ.

My father was then a young teacher and researcher in the department of pathology at the Johns Hopkins Medical School, one of the very few Jews to attend or teach at that institution. He was from Birmingham, Alabama; his father, Samuel, was Ashkenazic,[2] an immigrant from Austria-Hungary, and his mother, Hattie Rice, a Sephardic[3] Jew from Vicksburg, Mississippi. My grandfather had had a shoe store in Birmingham, which did well enough to allow him to retire comfortably and to leave my grandmother income on his death. The only souvenirs of my grandfather, Samuel Rich, were his ivory flute, which lay on our living-room mantel and was not to be played with; his thin gold pocket watch, which my father wore; and his Hebrew prayer book, which I discovered among my father's books in the course of reading my way through his library. In this prayer book there was a newspaper clipping about my grandparents' wedding, which took place in a synagogue.

My father, Arnold, was sent in adolescence to a military school in the North Carolina mountains, a place for training white southern Christian gentlemen. I suspect that there were few, if any, other Jewish boys at Colonel Bingham's, or at "Mr. Jefferson's university" in Charlottesville, where he studied as an undergraduate. With whatever conscious forethought, Samuel and Hattie sent their son into the dominant southern WASP culture to become an "exception," to enter the professional class. Never, in describing these experiences, did he speak of having suffered—from loneliness, cultural alienation, or outsiderhood. Never did I hear him use the word *anti-Semitism*.

---

[1]Adrienne Rich, "Readings of History," in *Snapshots of a Daughter-in-Law* (New York: W. W. Norton, 1967), pp. 36–40.

[2]*Ashkenazic:* Descendants of the Jews, generally Yiddish-speaking, who settled in middle and northern Europe.—EDS.

[3]*Sephardic:* Descendants of the Jews who settled for the most part in Spain, Portugal, and northern Africa.—EDS.

It was only in college, when I read a poem by Karl Shapiro beginning "To hate the Negro and avoid the Jew / is the curriculum," that it flashed on me that there was an untold side to my father's story of his student years. He looked recognizably Jewish, was short and slender in build with dark wiry hair and deep-set eyes, high forehead, and curved nose.

My mother is a gentile. In Jewish law I cannot count myself a Jew. If   10
it is true that "we think back through our mothers if we are women" (Virginia Woolf)—and I myself have affirmed this—then even according to lesbian theory, I cannot (or need not?) count myself a Jew.

The white southern Protestant woman, the gentile, has always been there for me to peel back into. That's a whole piece of history in itself, for my gentile grandmother and my mother were also frustrated artists and intellectuals, a lost writer and a lost composer between them. Readers and annotators of books, note takers, my mother a good pianist still, in her eighties. But there was also the obsession with ancestry, with "background," the southern talk of family, not as people you would necessarily know and depend on, but as heritage, the guarantee of "good breeding." There was the inveterate romantic heterosexual fantasy, the mother telling the daughter how to attract men (my mother often used the word "fascinate"); the assumption that relations between the sexes could only be romantic, that it was in the woman's interest to cultivate "mystery," conceal her actual feelings. Survival tactics of a kind, I think today, knowing what I know about the white woman's sexual role in the southern racist scenario. Heterosexuality as protection, but also drawing white women deeper into collusion with white men.

It would be easy to push away and deny the gentile in me—that white southern woman, that social christian. At different times in my life I have wanted to push away one or the other burden of inheritance, to say merely *I am a woman; I am a lesbian.* If I call myself a Jewish lesbian, do I thereby try to shed some of my southern gentile white woman's culpability? If I call myself only through my mother, is it because I pass more easily through a world where being a lesbian often seems like outsiderhood enough?

According to Nazi logic, my two Jewish grandparents would have made me a *Mischling, first-degree*—nonexempt from the Final Solution.[4]

The social world in which I grew up was christian virtually without needing to say so—christian imagery, music, language, symbols, assumptions everywhere. It was also a genteel, white, middle-class world in which "common" was a term of deep opprobrium. "Common" white people might speak of "niggers"; *we* were taught never to use that word—*we* said

---

[4]***Final Solution:*** The Nazi plan to exterminate the Jews.—EDS.

"Negroes" (even as we accepted segregation, the eating taboo, the assumption that black people were simply of a separate species). Our language was more polite, distinguishing us from the "rednecks" or the lynch-mob mentality. But so charged with negative meaning was even the word "Negro" that as children we were taught never to use it in front of black people. We were taught that any mention of skin color in the presence of colored people was treacherous, forbidden ground. In a parallel way, the word *Jew* was not used by polite gentiles. I sometimes heard my best friend's father, a Presbyterian minister, allude to "the Hebrew people" or "people of the Jewish faith." The world of acceptable folk was white, gentile (christian, really), and had "ideals" (which colored people, white "common" people, were not supposed to have). "Ideals" and "manners" included not hurting someone's feelings by calling her or him a Negro or a Jew—naming the hated identity. This is the mental framework of the 1930s and 1940s in which I was raised.

(Writing this, I feel dimly like the betrayer: of my father, who did not speak the word; of my mother, who must have trained me in the messages; of my caste and class; of my whiteness itself.) 15

Two memories: I am in a play reading at school of *The Merchant of Venice*. Whatever Jewish law says, I am quite sure I was *seen* as Jewish (with a reassuringly gentile mother) in that double vision that bigotry allows. I am the only Jewish girl in the class, and I am playing Portia. As always, I read my part aloud for my father the night before, and he tells me to convey, with my voice, more scorn and contempt with the word *Jew*: "Therefore, Jew . . ." I have to say the word out, and say it loudly. I was encouraged to pretend to be a non-Jewish child acting a non-Jewish character who has to speak the word *Jew* emphatically. Such a child would not have had trouble with the part. But *I* must have had trouble with the part, if only because the word itself was really taboo. I can see that there was a kind of terrible, bitter bravado about my father's way of handling this. And who would not dissociate from Shylock in order to identify with Portia? As a Jewish child who was also a female, I loved Portia—and, like every other Shakespearean heroine, she proved a treacherous role model.

A year or so later I am in another play, *The School for Scandal*, in which a notorious spendthrift is described as having "many excellent friends . . . among the Jews." In neither case was anything explained, either to me or to the class at large, about this scorn for Jews and the disgust surrounding Jews and money. Money, when Jews wanted it, had it, or lent it to others, seemed to take on a peculiar nastiness; Jews and money had some peculiar and unspeakable relation.

At the same school—in which we had Episcopalian hymns and prayers, and read aloud through the Bible morning after morning—I gained the impression that Jews were in the Bible and mentioned in English literature, that they had been persecuted centuries ago by the wicked Inquisition, but that they seemed not to exist in everyday life. These were the 1940s, and we were told a great deal about the Battle of Britain, the noble French Resistance fighters, the brave, starving Dutch—but I did not learn of the resistance of the Warsaw ghetto until I left home.

I was sent to the Episcopal church, baptized and confirmed, and attended it for about five years, though without belief. That religion seemed to have little to do with belief or commitment; it was liturgy that mattered, not spiritual passion. Neither of my parents ever entered that church, and my father would not enter *any* church for any reason—wedding or funeral. Nor did I enter a synagogue until I left Baltimore. When I came home from church, for a while, my father insisted on reading aloud to me from Thomas Paine's *The Age of Reason*—a diatribe against institutional religion. Thus, he explained, I would have a balanced view of these things, a choice. He—they—did not give me the choice to be a Jew. My mother explained to me when I was filling out forms for college that if any question was asked about "religion," I should put down "Episcopalian" rather than "none"—to seem to have no religion was, she implied, dangerous.

But it was white social christianity, rather than any particular christ- 20
ian sect, that the world was founded on. The very word *Christian* was used as a synonym for virtuous, just, peace-loving, generous, etc., etc.[5] The norm was christian: "Religion: none" was indeed not acceptable. Anti-Semitism was so intrinsic as not to have a name. I don't recall exactly being taught that the Jews killed Jesus—"Christ killer" seems too strong a term for the bland Episcopal vocabulary—but certainly we got the impression that the Jews had been caught out in a terrible mistake, failing to recognize the true Messiah, and were thereby less advanced in moral and spiritual sensibility. The Jews had actually allowed *moneylenders in the Temple* (again, the unexplained obsession with Jews and money). They were of the past, archaic, primitive, as older (and darker) cultures are supposed to be primitive; christianity was lightness, fairness, peace on earth, and combined the feminine appeal of "The meek shall inherit the earth" with the masculine stride of "Onward, Christian Soldiers."

Sometime in 1946, while still in high school, I read in the newspaper that a theater in Baltimore was showing films of the Allied liberation of the Nazi concentration camps. Alone, I went downtown after school one afternoon and watched the stark, blurry, but unmistakable newsreels. When I try to go back and touch the pulse of that girl of sixteen, growing up in many ways so precocious and so ignorant, I am overwhelmed by a memory of despair, a sense of inevitability more enveloping than any I had ever known. Anne Frank's diary and many other personal narratives

[5]In a similar way the phrase *That's white of you* implied that you were behaving with the superior decency and morality expected of white but not of black people.

of the Holocaust were still unknown or unwritten. But it came to me that every one of those piles of corpses, mountains of shoes and clothing had contained, simply, individuals, who had believed, as I now believed of myself, that they were intended to live out a life of some kind of meaning, that the world possessed some kind of sense and order; yet *this* had happened to them. And I, who believed my life was intended to be so interesting and meaningful, was connected to those dead by something—not just mortality but a taboo name, a hated identity. Or was I—did I really have to be? Writing this now, I feel belated rage that I was so impoverished by the family and social worlds I lived in, that I had to try to figure out by myself what this did indeed mean for me. That I had never been taught about resistance, only about passing. That I had no language for anti-Semitism itself.

When I went home and told my parents where I had been, they were not pleased. I felt accused of being morbidly curious, not healthy, sniffing around death for the thrill of it. And since, at sixteen, I was often not sure of the sources of my feelings or of my motives for doing what I did, I probably accused myself as well. One thing was clear: There was nobody in my world with whom I could discuss those films. Probably at the same time, I was reading accounts of the camps in magazines and newspapers; what I remember were the films and having questions that I could not even phrase, such as *Are those men and women "them" or "us"?*

To be able to ask even the child's astonished question *Why do they hate us so?* means knowing how to say "we." The guilt of not knowing, the guilt of perhaps having betrayed my parents or even those victims, those survivors, through mere curiosity—these also froze in me for years the impulse to find out more about the Holocaust.

1947: I left Baltimore to go to college in Cambridge, Massachusetts, left (I thought) the backward, enervating South for the intellectual, vital North. New England also had for me some vibration of higher moral rectitude, of moral passion even, with its seventeenth-century Puritan self-scrutiny, its nineteenth-century literary "flowering," its abolitionist righteousness, Colonel Shaw and his black Civil War regiment depicted in granite on Boston Common. At the same time, I found myself, at Radcliffe, among Jewish women. I used to sit for hours over coffee with what I thought of as the "real" Jewish students, who told me about middle-class Jewish culture in America. I described my background—for the first time to strangers—and they took me on, some with amusement at my illiteracy, some arguing that I could never marry into a strict Jewish family, some convinced I didn't "look Jewish," others that I did. I learned the names of holidays and foods, which surnames are Jewish and which are "changed names"; about girls who had had their noses "fixed," their hair straightened. For these young Jewish women, students in the late 1940s, it was acceptable, perhaps even necessary, to strive to look as gentile as possible; but they stuck proudly to being Jewish, expected to marry a Jew, have children, keep the holidays, carry on the culture.

I felt I was testing a forbidden current, that there was danger in these   25 revelations. I bought a reproduction of a Chagall portrait of a rabbi in striped prayer shawl and hung it on the wall of my room. I was admittedly young and trying to educate myself, but I was also doing something that is dangerous: I was flirting with identity.

One day that year I was in a small shop where I had bought a dress with a too-long skirt. The shop employed a seamstress who did alterations, and she came in to pin up the skirt on me. I am sure that she was a recent immigrant, a survivor. I remember a short, dark woman wearing heavy glasses, with an accent so foreign I could not understand her words. Something about her presence was very powerful and disturbing to me. After marking and pinning up the skirt, she sat back on her knees, looked up at me, and asked in a hurried whisper: "You Jewish?" Eighteen years of training in assimilation sprang into the reflex by which I shook my head, rejecting her, and muttered, "No."

What was I actually saying "no" to? She was poor, older, struggling with a foreign tongue, anxious; she had escaped the death that had been intended for her, but I had no imagination of her possible courage and foresight, her resistance — I did not see in her a heroine who had perhaps saved many lives, including her own. I saw the frightened immigrant, the seamstress hemming the skirts of college girls, the wandering Jew. But I was an American college girl having her skirt hemmed. And I was frightened myself, I think, because she had recognized me ("It takes one to know one," my friend Edie at Radcliffe had said) even if I refused to recognize myself or her, even if her recognition was sharpened by loneliness or the need to feel safe with me.

But why should she have felt safe with me? I myself was living with a false sense of safety.

There are betrayals in my life that I have known at the very moment were betrayals: this was one of them. There are other betrayals committed so repeatedly, so mundanely, that they leave no memory trace behind, only a growing residue of misery, of dull, accreted self-hatred. Often these take the form not of words but of silence. Silence before the joke at which everyone is laughing: the anti-woman joke, the racist joke, the anti-Semitic joke. Silence and then amnesia. Blocking it out when the oppressor's language starts coming from the lips of one we admire, whose courage and eloquence have touched us: *She didn't really mean that; he didn't really say that.* But the accretions build up out of sight, like scale inside a kettle.

1948: I come home from my freshman year at college, flaming with   30 new insights, new information. I am the daughter who has gone out into the world, to the pinnacle of intellectual prestige, Harvard, fulfilling my father's hopes for me, but also exposed to dangerous influences. I have already been reproved for attending a rally for Henry Wallace[6] and the Progressive party. I challenge my father: "Why haven't you told me that I am Jewish? Why do you never talk about being a Jew?" He answers measuredly, "You know that I have never denied that I am a Jew. But it's not important to me. I am a scientist, a deist. I have no use for organized religion. I choose to live in a world of many kinds of people. There are Jews I admire and others whom I despise. I am a person, not simply a Jew." The words are as I remember them, not perhaps exactly as spoken. But that was the message. And it contained enough truth — as all denial drugs itself on partial truth — so that it remained for the time being unanswerable, leaving me high and dry, split at the root, gasping for clarity, for air.

At that time Arnold Rich was living in suspension, waiting to be appointed to the professorship of pathology at Johns Hopkins. The appointment was delayed for years, no Jew ever having held a professional chair in that medical school. And he wanted it badly. It must have been a very bitter time for him, since he had believed so greatly in the redeeming power of excellence, of being the most brilliant, inspired man for the job. With enough excellence, you could presumably make it stop mattering that you were Jewish; you could become the *only* Jew in the gentile world, a Jew so "civilized," so far from "common," so attractively combining southern gentility with European cultural values that no one would ever confuse you with the raw, "pushy" Jews of New York, the "loud, hysterical" refugees from eastern Europe, the "overdressed" Jews of the urban South.

We — my sister, mother, and I — were constantly urged to speak quietly in public, to dress without ostentation, to repress all vividness or spontaneity, to assimilate with a world which might see us as too flamboyant. I suppose that my mother, pure gentile though she was, could be seen as acting "common" or "Jewish" if she laughed too loudly or spoke aggressively. My father's mother, who lived with us half the year, was a model of circumspect behavior, dressed in dark blue or lavender, retiring in company, ladylike to an extreme, wearing no jewelry except a good gold chain, a narrow brooch, or a string of pearls. A few times, within the family, I saw her anger flare, felt the passion she was repressing. But when Arnold took us out to a restaurant or on a trip, the Rich women were always tuned down to some WASP level my father believed, surely, would protect us all — maybe also make us unrecognizable to the "real Jews" who wanted to seize us, drag us back to the *shtetl*, the ghetto, in its many manifestations.

For, yes, that *was* a message — that some Jews would be after you, once they "knew," to rejoin them, to re-enter a world that was messy, noisy,

---

[6]*Henry Wallace* (1888–1965): American journalist, agriculturist, and politician, as well as the 1948 Progressive party's candidate for the presidency. — EDS.

unpredictable, maybe poor—"even though," as my mother once wrote me, criticizing my largely Jewish choice of friends in college, "some of them will be the most brilliant, fascinating people you'll ever meet." I wonder if that isn't one message of assimilation—of America—that the unlucky or the unachieving want to pull you backward, that to identify with them is to court downward mobility, lose the precious chance of passing, of token existence. There was always within this sense of Jewish identity a strong class discrimination. Jews might be "fascinating" as individuals but came with huge unruly families who "poured chicken soup over everyone's head" (in the phrase of a white southern male poet). Anti-Semitism could thus be justified by the bad behavior of certain Jews; and if you did not effectively deny family and community, there would always be a remote cousin claiming kinship with you who was the "wrong kind" of Jew.

I have always believed his attitude toward other Jews depended on who they were. . . . It was my impression that Jews of this background looked down on Eastern European Jews, including Polish Jews and Russian Jews, who generally were not as well educated. This from a letter written to me recently by a gentile who had worked in my father's department, whom I had asked about anti-Semitism there and in particular regarding my father. This informant also wrote me that it was hard to perceive anti-Semitism in Baltimore because the racism made so much more intense an impression: *I would almost have to think that blacks went to a different heaven than the whites, because the bodies were kept in a separate morgue, and some white persons did not even want blood transfusions from black donors.* My father's mind was predictably racist and misogynist; yet as a medical student he noted in his journal that southern male chivalry stopped at the point of any white man in a streetcar giving his seat to an old, weary black woman standing in the aisle. Was this a Jewish insight—an outsider's insight, even though the outsider was striving to be on the inside?

Because what isn't named is often more permeating than what is, I   35 believe that my father's Jewishness profoundly shaped my own identity and our family existence. They were shaped both by external anti-Semitism and my father's self-hatred, and by his Jewish pride. What Arnold did, I think, was call his Jewish pride something else: achievement, aspiration, genius, idealism. Whatever was unacceptable got left back under the rubric of Jewishness or the "wrong kind" of Jews—uneducated, aggressive, loud. The message I got was that we were really superior: Nobody else's father had collected so many books, had traveled so far, knew so many languages. Baltimore was a musical city, but for the most part, in the families of my school friends, culture was for women. My father was an amateur musician, read poetry, adored encyclopedic knowledge. He prowled and pounced over my school papers, insisting I use "grown-up" sources; he criticized my poems for faulty technique and gave me books on rhyme and meter and form. His investment in my intellect and talent was egotistical, tyrannical, opinionated, and terribly wearing. He taught me, nevertheless, to believe in hard work, to mistrust easy inspiration, to write and rewrite; to feel that I *was* a person of the book, even though a woman; to take ideas seriously. He made me feel, at a very young age, the power of language and that I could share in it.

The Riches were proud, but we also had to be very careful. Our behavior had to be more impeccable than other people's. Strangers were not to be trusted, nor even friends; family issues must never go beyond the family; the world was full of potential slanderers, betrayers, *people who could not understand*. Even within the family, I realize that I never in my whole life knew what my father was really feeling. Yet he spoke—monologued—with driving intensity. You could grow up in such a house mesmerized by the local electricity, the crucial meanings assumed by the merest things. This used to seem to me a sign that we were all living on some high emotional plane. It was a difficult force field for a favored daughter to disengage from.

Easy to call that intensity Jewish; and I have no doubt that passion is one of the qualities required for survival over generations of persecution. But what happens when passion is rent from its original base, when the white gentile world is softly saying "Be more like us and you can be almost one of us"? What happens when survival seems to mean closing off one emotional artery after another? His forebears in Europe had been forbidden to travel or expelled from one country after another, had special taxes levied on them if they left the city walls, had been forced to wear special clothes and badges, restricted to the poorest neighborhoods. He had wanted to be a "free spirit," to travel widely, among "all kinds of people." Yet in his prime of life he lived in an increasingly withdrawn world, in his house up on a hill in a neighborhood where Jews were not supposed to be able to buy property, depending almost exclusively on interactions with his wife and daughters to provide emotional connectedness. In his home, he created a private defense system so elaborate that even as he was dying, my mother felt unable to talk freely with his colleagues or others who might have helped her. Of course, she acquiesced in this.

The loneliness of the "only," the token, often doesn't feel like loneliness but like a kind of dead echo chamber. Certain things that ought to don't resonate. Somewhere Beverly Smith writes of women of color "inspiring the behavior" in each other. When there's nobody to "inspire the behavior," act out of the culture, there is an atrophy, a dwindling, which is partly invisible. . . .

Sometimes I feel I have seen too long from too many disconnected angles: white, Jewish, anti-Semite, racist, anti-racist, once-married, lesbian, middle-class, feminist, exmatriate southerner, *split at the root*—that I will never bring them whole. I would have liked, in this essay, to bring together the meanings of anti-Semitism and racism as I have experienced them and as I believe they intersect in the world beyond my life. But I'm not able to do this yet. I feel the tension as I think, make notes: *If you really look at the one reality, the other will waver and disperse.* Trying in one week to read Angela Davis and Lucy

Davidowicz,[7] trying to hold throughout to a feminist, a lesbian, perspective—what does this mean? Nothing has trained me for this. And sometimes I feel inadequate to make any statement as a Jew; I feel the history of denial within me like an injury, a scar. For assimilation has affected *my* perceptions; those early lapses in meaning, those blanks, are with me still. My ignorance can be dangerous to me and to others.

Yet we can't wait for the undamaged to make our connections for us;   40 we can't wait to speak until we are perfectly clear and righteous. There is no purity and, in our lifetimes, no end to this process.

This essay, then, has no conclusions: It is another beginning for me. Not just a way of saying, in 1982 Right-Wing America, *I, too, will wear the yellow star.* It's a moving into accountability, enlarging the range of accountability. I know that in the rest of my life, the next half century or so, every aspect of my identity will have to be engaged. The middle-class white girl taught to trade obedience for privilege. The Jewish lesbian raised to be a heterosexual gentile. The woman who first heard oppression named and analyzed in the black Civil Rights struggle. The woman with three sons, the feminist who hates male violence. The woman limping with a cane, the woman who has stopped bleeding are also accountable. The poet who knows that beautiful language can lie, that the oppressor's language sometimes sounds beautiful. The woman trying, as part of her resistance, to clean up her act.

The Reader's Presence

1. Why does Rich feel she needs to "claim" her father in order to come to terms with her identity? What does she mean by "claim"? How do we make such claims? Why is her father so closely tied to her sense of identity?

2. In rereading Rich's essay, pay close attention to her use of time. Try to construct a chronology for the essay. How does she organize that chronology in the essay itself? Can you think of some explanations for why Rich does not proceed in an orderly and straightforward manner? Can you discover any patterns in the procedure she chose to follow?

3. In paragraph 30, Rich writes that "all denial drugs itself on partial truth." What is Rich saying about her father? About herself? She writes in the previous paragraph about the danger of silence in the face of bigotry. Read Zora Neale Hurston's "How It Feels to Be Colored Me" (page 166) in the context of these statements. How do they affect the way you read Rich's self-protective denial?

[7]Angela Y. Davis, *Women, Race and Class* (New York: Random House, 1981); Lucy S. Davidowicz, *The War against the Jews 1933–1945* (New York: Bantam, 1979).

Richard Rodriguez

Aria: A Memoir of a Bilingual Childhood

Richard Rodriguez (b. 1944) has contributed articles to many magazines and newspapers, including Harper's, American Scholar, *the* Los Angeles Times, *and the* New York Times. *He is an editor at Pacific News Service and a contributing editor for* Harper's, U.S. News & World Report, *and the* Los Angeles Times. *He is also a regular essayist for the News Hour with Jim Lehrer, for which he received the 1997 George Foster Peabody Award. His most sensational literary accomplishment, however, is his intellectual autobiography,* Hunger of Memory: The Education of Richard Rodriguez *(1982). In it, Rodriguez outlines his positions on issues such as bilingualism, affirmative action, and assimilation, and he concludes that current policies in these areas are misguided and serve only to reinforce current social inequalities. Other books include* Days of Obligations: An Argument with My Mexican Father *(1992) and* Brown: The Last Discovery of America *(2002).*

About the experience of writing his autobiography, Rodriguez comments, "By finding public words to describe one's feelings, one can describe oneself to oneself. . . . I have come to think of myself as engaged in writing graffiti."

The following essay originally appeared in the American Scholar *(winter 1980/81) and later served as the opening chapter in his autobiography* Hunger of Memory *(1982).*

I remember, to start with, that day in Sacramento, in a California now nearly thirty years past, when I first entered a classroom—able to understand about fifty stray English words. The third of four children, I had been preceded by my older brother and sister to a neighborhood Roman Catholic school. But neither of them had revealed very much about their classroom experiences. They left each morning and returned each afternoon, always together, speaking Spanish as they climbed the five steps to the porch. And their mysterious books, wrapped in brown shopping-bag paper, remained on the table next to the door, closed firmly behind them.

An accident of geography sent me to a school where all my classmates were white and many were the children of doctors and lawyers and business executives. On that first day of school, my classmates must certainly have been uneasy to find themselves apart from their families, in the first institution of their lives. But I was astonished. I was fated to be the "problem student" in class.

The nun said, in a friendly but oddly impersonal voice: "Boys and girls, this is Richard Rodriguez." (I heard her sound it out: *Rich-heard*

Road-ree-guess.) It was the first time I had heard anyone say my name in English. "Richard," the nun repeated more slowly, writing my name down in her book. Quickly I turned to see my mother's face dissolve in a watery blur behind the pebbled-glass door.

Now, many years later, I hear of something called "bilingual education" — a scheme proposed in the late 1960s by Hispanic-American social activists, later endorsed by a congressional vote. It is a program that seeks to permit non-English-speaking children (many from lower class homes) to use their "family language" as the language of school. Such, at least, is the aim its supporters announce. I hear them, and am forced to say no: It is not possible for a child, any child, ever to use his family's language in school. Not to understand this is to misunderstand the public uses of schooling and to trivialize the nature of intimate life.

Memory teaches me what I know of these matters. The boy reminds   5
the adult. I was a bilingual child, but of a certain kind: "socially disadvantaged," the son of working-class parents, both Mexican immigrants.

In the early years of my boyhood, my parents coped very well in America. My father had steady work. My mother managed at home. They were nobody's victims. When we moved to a house many blocks from the Mexican-American section of town, they were not intimidated by those two or three neighbors who initially tried to make us unwelcome. ("Keep your brats away from my sidewalk!") But despite all they achieved, or perhaps because they had so much to achieve, they lacked any deep feeling of ease, of belonging in public. They regarded the people at work or in crowds as being very distant from us. Those were the others, *los gringos*. That term was interchangeable in their speech with another, even more telling: *los americanos*.

I grew up in a house where the only regular guests were my relations. On a certain day, enormous families of relatives would visit us, and there would be so many people that the noise and the bodies would spill out to the backyard and onto the front porch. Then for weeks no one would come. (If the doorbell rang, it was usually a salesman.) Our house stood apart — gaudy yellow in a row of white bungalows. We were the people with the noisy dog, the people who raised chickens. We were the foreigners on the block. A few neighbors would smile and wave at us. We waved back. But until I was seven years old, I did not know the name of the old couple living next door or the names of the kids living across the street.

In public, my father and mother spoke a hesitant, accented, and not always grammatical English. And then they would have to strain, their bodies tense, to catch the sense of what was rapidly said by *los gringos*. At home, they returned to Spanish. The language of their Mexican past sounded in counterpoint to the English spoken in public. The words would come quickly, with ease. Conveyed through those sounds was the pleasing, soothing, consoling reminder that one was at home.

During those years when I was first learning to speak, my mother and father addressed me only in Spanish; in Spanish I learned to reply. By contrast, English (*inglés*) was the language I came to associate with gringos, rarely heard in the house. I learned my first words of English overhearing my parents speaking to strangers. At six years of age, I knew just enough words for my mother to trust me on errands to stores one block away — but no more.

I was then a listening child, careful to hear the very different sounds   10 of Spanish and English. Wide-eyed with hearing, I'd listen to sounds more than to words. First, there were English (gringo) sounds. So many words still were unknown to me that when the butcher or the lady at the drugstore said something, exotic polysyllabic sounds would bloom in the midst of their sentences. Often the speech of people in public seemed to me very loud, booming with confidence. The man behind the counter would literally ask, "What can I do for you?" But by being so firm and clear, the sound of his voice said that he was a gringo; he belonged in public society. There were also the high, nasal notes of middle-class American speech — which I rarely am conscious of hearing today because I hear them so often, but could not stop hearing when I was a boy. Crowds at Safeway or at bus stops were noisy with the birdlike sounds of *los gringos*. I'd move away from them all — all the chirping chatter above me.

My own sounds I was unable to hear, but I knew that I spoke English poorly. My words could not extend to form complete thoughts. And the words I did speak I didn't know well enough to make distinct sounds. (Listeners would usually lower their heads to hear better what I was trying to say.) But it was one thing for *me* to speak English with difficulty; it was more troubling to hear my parents speaking in public: their high-whining vowels and guttural consonants; their sentences that got stuck with "eh" and "ah" sounds; the confused syntax; the hesitant rhythm of sounds so different from the way gringos spoke. I'd notice, moreover, that my parents' voices were softer than those of gringos we would meet.

I am tempted to say now that none of this mattered. (In adulthood I am embarrassed by childhood fears.) And, in a way, it didn't matter very much that my parents could not speak English with ease. Their linguistic difficulties had no serious consequences. My mother and father made themselves understood at the county hospital clinic and at government offices. And yet, in another way, it mattered very much. It was unsettling to hear my parents struggle with English. Hearing them, I'd grow nervous, and my clutching trust in their protection and power would be weakened.

There were many times like the night at a brightly lit gasoline station (a blaring white memory) when I stood uneasily hearing my father talk to a teenage attendant. I do not recall what they were saying, but I cannot forget the sounds my father made as he spoke. At one point his words slid together to form one long word—sounds as confused as the threads of blue and green oil in the puddle next to my shoes. His voice rushed through what he had left to say. Toward the end, he reached falsetto notes, appealing to his listener's understanding. I looked away at the lights of passing automobiles. I tried not to hear any more. But I heard only too well the attendant's reply, his calm, easy tones. Shortly afterward, headed for home, I shivered when my father put his hand on my shoulder. The very first chance that I got, I evaded his grasp and ran on ahead into the dark, skipping with feigned boyish exuberance.

But then there was Spanish: *español*, the language rarely heard away from the house; *español*, the language which seemed to me therefore a private language, my family's language. To hear its sounds was to feel myself specially recognized as one of the family, apart from *los otros*. A simple remark, an inconsequential comment could convey that assurance. My parents would say something to me and I would feel embraced by the sounds of their words. Those sounds said: *I am speaking with ease in Spanish. I am addressing you in words I never use with los gringos. I recognize you as someone special, close, like no one outside. You belong with us. In the family. Ricardo.*

At the age of six, well past the time when most middle-class children   15
no longer notice the difference between sounds uttered at home and words spoken in public, I had a different experience. I lived in a world compounded of sounds. I was a child longer than most. I lived in a magical world, surrounded by sounds both pleasing and fearful. I shared with my family a language enchantingly private—different from that used in the city around us.

Just opening or closing the screen door behind me was an important experience. I'd rarely leave home all alone or without feeling reluctance. Walking down the sidewalk, under the canopy of tall trees, I'd warily notice the (suddenly) silent neighborhood kids who stood warily watching me. Nervously, I'd arrive at the grocery store to hear there the sounds of the gringo, reminding me that in this so-big world I was a foreigner. But if leaving home was never routine, neither was coming back. Walking toward our house, climbing the steps from the sidewalk, in summer when the front door was open, I'd hear voices beyond the screen door talking in Spanish. For a second or two I'd stay, linger there listening. Smiling, I'd hear my mother call out, saying in Spanish, "Is that you, Richard?" Those were her words, but all the while her sounds would assure me: *You are home now. Come closer inside. With us.* "*Sí,*" I'd reply.

Once more inside the house, I would resume my place in the family. The sounds would grow harder to hear. Once more at home, I would grow less conscious of them. It required, however, no more than the blurt of the doorbell to alert me all over again to listen to sounds. The house would turn instantly quiet while my mother went to the door. I'd hear her hard English sounds. I'd wait to hear her voice turn to soft-sounding Spanish, which assured me, as surely as did the clicking tongue of the lock on the door, that the stranger was gone.

Plainly it is not healthy to hear such sounds so often. It is not healthy to distinguish public from private sounds so easily. I remained cloistered by sounds, timid and shy in public, too dependent on the voices at home. And yet I was a very happy child when I was at home. I remember many nights when my father would come back from work, and I'd hear him call out to my mother in Spanish, sounding relieved. In Spanish, his voice would sound the light and free notes that he never could manage in English. Some nights I'd jump up just hearing his voice. My brother and I would come running into the room where he was with our mother. Our laughing (so deep was the pleasure!) became screaming. Like others who feel the pain of public alienation, we transformed the knowledge of our public separateness into a consoling reminder of our intimacy. Excited, our voices joined in a celebration of sounds. *We are speaking now the way we never speak out in public—we are together*, the sounds told me. Some nights no one seemed willing to loosen the hold that sounds had on us. At dinner we invented new words that sounded Spanish, but made sense only to us. We pieced together new words by taking, say, an English verb and giving it Spanish endings. My mother's instructions at bedtime would be lacquered with mock-urgent tones. Or a word like *sí*, sounded in several notes, would convey added measures of feeling. Tongues lingered around the edges of words, especially fat vowels. And we happily sounded that military drum roll, the twirling roar of the Spanish *r*. Family language, my family's sounds: the voices of my parents and sisters and brother. Their voices insisting: *You belong here. We are family members. Related. Special to one another. Listen!* Voices singing and sighing, rising and straining, then surging, teeming with pleasure which burst syllables into fragments of laughter. At times it seemed there was steady quiet only when, from another room, the rustling whispers of my parents faded and I edged closer to sleep.

Supporters of bilingual education imply today that students like me miss a great deal by not being taught in their family's language. What they seem not to recognize is that, as a socially disadvantaged child, I regarded Spanish as a private language. It was a ghetto language that deepened and strengthened my feeling of public separateness. What I needed to learn in school was that I had the right, and the obligation, to speak the public language. The odd truth is that my first-grade classmates could have become bilingual, in the conventional sense of the word, more easily than I. Had they been taught early (as upper middle-class children often are taught) a "second language" like Spanish or French, they could have regarded it simply as another public language. In my case, such bilingualism could not have been so quickly achieved. What I did not believe was that I could speak a single public language.

Without question, it would have pleased me to have heard my teachers address me in Spanish when I entered the classroom. I would have felt much less afraid. I would have imagined that my instructors were somehow "related" to me; I would indeed have heard their Spanish as my family's language. I would have trusted them and responded with ease. But I would have delayed—postponed for how long?—having to learn the language of public society. I would have evaded—and for how long?—learning the great lesson of school: that I had a public identity.

Fortunately, my teachers were unsentimental about their responsibility. What they understood was that I needed to speak public English. So their voices would search me out, asking me questions. Each time I heard them I'd look up in surprise to see a nun's face frowning at me. I'd mumble, not really meaning to answer. The nun would persist. "Richard, stand up. Don't look at the floor. Speak up. Speak to the entire class, not just to me!" But I couldn't believe English could be my language to use. (In part, I did not want to believe it.) I continued to mumble. I resisted the teacher's demands. (Did I somehow suspect that once I learned this public language my family life would be changed?) Silent, waiting for the bell to sound, I remained dazed, diffident, afraid.

Because I wrongly imagined that English was intrinsically a public language and Spanish was intrinsically private, I easily noted the difference between classroom language and the language of home. At school, words were directed to a general audience of listeners. ("Boys and girls . . .") Words were meaningfully ordered. And the point was not self-expression alone, but to make oneself understood by many others. The teacher quizzed: "Boys and girls, why do we use that word in this sentence? Could we think of a better word to use there? Would the sentence change its meaning if the words were differently arranged? Isn't there a better way of saying much the same thing?" (I couldn't say. I wouldn't try to say.)

Three months passed. Five. A half year. Unsmiling, ever watchful, my teachers noted my silence. They began to connect my behavior with the slow progress my brother and sisters were making. Until, one Saturday morning, three nuns arrived at the house to talk to our parents. Stiffly they sat on the blue living-room sofa. From the doorway of another room, spying on the visitors, I noted the incongruity, the clash of two worlds, the faces and voices of school intruding upon the familiar setting of home. I overheard one voice gently wondering, "Do your children speak only Spanish at home, Mrs. Rodriguez?" While another voice added, "That Richard especially seems so timid and shy."

That Rich-heard!

With great tact, the visitors continued, "Is it possible for you and your husband to encourage your children to practice their English when they are home?" Of course my parents complied. What would they not do for their children's well-being? And how could they question the Church's authority which those women represented? In an instant they agreed to give up the language (the sounds) which had revealed and accentuated our family's closeness. The moment after the visitors left, the change was observed. "*Ahora*, speak to us only *en inglés*," my father and mother told us.

At first, it seemed a kind of game. After dinner each night, the family gathered together to practice "our" English. It was still then *inglés*, a language foreign to us, so we felt drawn to it as strangers. Laughing, we would try to define words we could not pronounce. We played with strange English sounds, often over-anglicizing our pronunciations. And we filled the smiling gaps of our sentences with familiar Spanish sounds. But that was cheating, somebody shouted, and everyone laughed.

In school, meanwhile, like my brother and sisters, I was required to attend a daily tutoring session. I needed a full year of this special work. I also needed my teachers to keep my attention from straying in class by calling out, "*Rich-heard!*"—their English voices slowly loosening the ties to my other name, with its three notes, *Ri-car-do*. Most of all, I needed to hear my mother and father speak to me in a moment of seriousness in "broken"—suddenly heartbreaking—English. This scene was inevitable. One Saturday morning I entered the kitchen where my parents were talking, but I did not realize that they were talking in Spanish until, the moment they saw me, their voices changed and they began speaking English. The gringo sounds they uttered startled me. Pushed me away. In that moment of trivial misunderstanding and profound insight, I felt my throat twisted by unsounded grief. I simply turned and left the room. But I had no place to escape to where I could grieve in Spanish. My brother and sisters were speaking English in another part of the house.

Again and again in the days following, as I grew increasingly angry, I was obliged to hear my mother and father encouraging me: "Speak to us *en inglés*." Only then did I determine to learn classroom English. Thus, sometime afterward it happened: one day in school, I raised my hand to volunteer an answer to a question. I spoke out in a loud voice and I did not think it remarkable when the entire class understood. That day I moved very far from being the disadvantaged child I had been only days earlier. Taken hold at last was the belief, the calming assurance, that I *belonged* in public.

Shortly after, I stopped hearing the high, troubling sounds of *los gringos*. A more and more confident speaker of English, I didn't listen to how strangers sounded when they talked to me. With so many English-speaking people around me, I no longer heard American accents. Conversations quickened. Listening to persons whose voices sounded eccentrically pitched, I might note their sounds for a few seconds, but then I'd concentrate on what they were saying. Now when I heard someone's tone of voice—angry or questioning or sarcastic or happy or sad—I didn't distinguish it from the words it expressed. Sound and word were thus tightly wedded. At the end of each day I was often bemused, and always relieved, to realize how "soundless," though crowded with words, my day in public had been. An eight-year-old boy, I finally came to accept what had been technically true since my birth: I was an American citizen.

But diminished by then was the special feeling of closeness at home.   30
Gone was the desperate, urgent, intense feeling of being at home among those with whom I felt intimate. Our family remained a loving family, but one greatly changed. We were no longer so close, no longer bound tightly together by the knowledge of our separateness from *los gringos*. Neither my older brother nor my sisters rushed home after school any more. Nor did I. When I arrived home, often there would be neighborhood kids in the house. Or the house would be empty of sounds.

Following the dramatic Americanization of their children, even my parents grew more publicly confident—especially my mother. First she learned the names of all the people on the block. Then she decided we needed to have a telephone in our house. My father, for his part, continued to use the word gringo, but it was no longer charged with bitterness or distrust. Stripped of any emotional content, the word simply became a name for those Americans not of Hispanic descent. Hearing him, sometimes, I wasn't sure if he was pronouncing the Spanish word *gringo*, or saying gringo in English.

There was a new silence at home. As we children learned more and more English, we shared fewer and fewer words with our parents. Sentences needed to be spoken slowly when one of us addressed our mother or father. Often the parent wouldn't understand. The child would need to repeat himself. Still the parent misunderstood. The young voice, frustrated, would end up saying, "Never mind"—the subject was closed. Dinners would be noisy with the clinking of knives and forks against dishes. My mother would smile softly between her remarks; my father, at the other end of the table, would chew and chew his food while he stared over the heads of his children.

My mother! My father! After English became my primary language, I no longer knew what words to use in addressing my parents. The old Spanish words (those tender accents of sound) I had earlier used—*mamá* and *papá*—I couldn't use any more. They would have been all-too-painful reminders of how much had changed in my life. On the other hand, the words I heard neighborhood kids call their parents seemed equally unsatisfactory. "Mother" and "father," "ma," "papa," "pa," "dad," "pop" (how I hated the all-American sound of that last word)—all these I felt were unsuitable terms of address for *my* parents. As a result, I never used them at home. Whenever I'd speak to my parents, I would try to get their attention by looking at them. In public conversations, I'd refer to them as my "parents" or my "mother" and "father."

My mother and father, for their part, responded differently, as their children spoke to them less. My mother grew restless, seemed troubled and anxious at the scarceness of words exchanged in the house. She would question me about my day when I came home from school. She smiled at my small talk. She pried at the edges of my sentences to get me to say something more. ("What . . . ?") She'd join conversations she overheard, but her intrusions often stopped her children's talking. By contrast, my father seemed to grow reconciled to the new quiet. Though his English somewhat improved, he tended more and more to retire into silence. At dinner he spoke very little. One night his children and even his wife helplessly giggled at his garbled English pronunciation of the Catholic "Grace Before Meals." Thereafter he made his wife recite the prayer at the start of each meal, even on formal occasions when there were guests in the house.

Hers became the public voice of the family. On official business it was she, not my father, who would usually talk to strangers on the phone or in stores. We children grew so accustomed to his silence that years later we would routinely refer to his "shyness." (My mother often tried to explain: Both of his parents died when he was eight. He was raised by an uncle who treated him as little more than a menial servant. He was never encouraged to speak. He grew up alone—a man of few words.) But I realized my father was not shy whenever I'd watch him speaking Spanish with relatives. Using Spanish, he was quickly effusive. Especially when talking with other men, his voice would spark, flicker, flare alive with varied sounds. In Spanish he expressed ideas and feelings he rarely revealed when speaking English. With firm Spanish sounds he conveyed a confidence and authority that English would never allow him. 35

The silence at home, however, was not simply the result of fewer words passing between parents and children. More profound for me was the silence created by my inattention to sounds. At about the time I no longer bothered to listen with care to the sounds of English in public, I grew careless about listening to the sounds made by the family when they spoke. Most of the time I would hear someone speaking at home and didn't distinguish his sounds from the words people uttered in public. I didn't even pay much attention to my parents' accented and ungrammatical speech—at least not at home. Only when I was with them in public would I become alert to their accents. But even then their sounds caused me less and less concern. For I was growing increasingly confident of my own public identity.

I would have been happier about my public success had I not recalled, sometimes, what it had been like earlier, when my family conveyed its intimacy through a set of conveniently private sounds. Sometimes in public, hearing a stranger, I'd hark back to my lost past. A Mexican farm worker approached me one day downtown. He wanted directions to some place. "*Hijito* . . . ," he said. And his voice stirred old longings. Another time I was standing beside my mother in the visiting room of a

Carmelite convent, before the dense screen which rendered the nuns shadowy figures. I heard several of them speaking Spanish in their busy, singsong, overlapping voices, assuring my mother that, yes, yes, we were remembered, all our family was remembered, in their prayers. Those voices echoed faraway family sounds. Another day a dark-faced old woman touched my shoulder lightly to steady herself as she boarded a bus. She murmured something to me I couldn't quite comprehend. Her Spanish voice came near, like the face of a never-before-seen relative in the instant before I was kissed. That voice, like so many of the Spanish voices I'd hear in public, recalled the golden age of my childhood.

Bilingual educators say today that children lose a degree of "individuality" by becoming assimilated into public society. (Bilingual schooling is a program popularized in the seventies, that decade when middle-class "ethnics" began to resist the process of assimilation—the "American melting pot.") But the bilingualists oversimplify when they scorn the value and necessity of assimilation. They do not seem to realize that a person is individualized in two ways. So they do not realize that, while one suffers a diminished sense of *private* individuality by being assimilated into public society, such assimilation makes possible the achievement of *public* individuality.

Simplistically again, the bilingualists insist that a student should be reminded of his difference from others in mass society, of his "heritage." But they equate mere separateness with individuality. The fact is that only in private—with intimates—is separateness from the crowd a prerequisite for individuality; an intimate "tells" me that I am unique, unlike all others, apart from the crowd. In public, by contrast, full individuality is achieved, paradoxically, by those who are able to consider themselves members of the crowd. Thus it happened for me. Only when I was able to think of myself as an American, no longer an alien in gringo society, could I seek the rights and opportunities necessary for full public individuality. The social and political advantages I enjoy as a man began on the day I came to believe that my name is indeed *Rich-heard Road-ree-guess*. It is true that my public society today is often impersonal; in fact, my public society is usually mass society. But despite the anonymity of the crowd, and despite the fact that the individuality I achieve in public is often tenuous—because it depends on my being one in a crowd—I celebrate the day I acquired my new name. Those middle-class ethnics who scorn assimilation seem to me filled with decadent self-pity, obsessed by the burden of public life. Dangerously, they romanticize public separateness and trivialize the dilemma of those who are truly socially disadvantaged.

If I rehearse here the changes in my private life after my Americanization, it is finally to emphasize a public gain. The loss implies the gain. The house I returned to each afternoon was quiet. Intimate sounds no longer greeted me at the door. Inside there were other noises. The telephone rang. Neighborhood kids ran past the door of the bedroom where I was   40 reading my schoolbooks—covered with brown shopping-bag paper. Once I learned the public language, it would never again be easy for me to hear intimate family voices. More and more of my day was spent hearing words, not sounds. But that may only be a way of saying that on the day I raised my hand in class and spoke loudly to an entire roomful of faces, my childhood started to end.

I grew up the victim of a disconcerting confusion. As I became fluent in English, I could no longer speak Spanish with confidence. I continued to understand spoken Spanish, and in high school I learned how to read and write Spanish. But for many years I could not pronounce it. A powerful guilt blocked my spoken words; an essential glue was missing whenever I would try to connect words to form sentences. I would be unable to break a barrier of sound, to speak freely. I would speak, or try to speak, Spanish, and I would manage to utter halting, hiccuping sounds which betrayed my unease. (Even today I speak Spanish very slowly, at best.)

When relatives and Spanish-speaking friends of my parents came to the house, my brother and sisters would usually manage to say a few words before being excused. I never managed so gracefully. Each time I'd hear myself addressed in Spanish, I couldn't respond with any success. I'd know the words I wanted to say, but I couldn't say them. I would try to speak, but everything I said seemed to me horribly anglicized. My mouth wouldn't form the sounds right. My jaw would tremble. After a phrase or two, I'd stutter, cough up a warm, silvery sound, and stop.

My listeners were surprised to hear me. They'd lower their heads to grasp better what I was trying to say. They would repeat their questions in gentle, affectionate voices. But then I would answer in English. No, no, they would say, we want you to speak to us in Spanish ("*en español*"). But I couldn't do it. Then they would call me *Pocho*. Sometimes playfully, teasing, using the tender diminutive—*mi pochito*. Sometimes not so playfully but mockingly, *pocho*. (A Spanish dictionary defines that word as an adjective meaning "colorless" or "bland." But I heard it as a noun, naming the Mexican-American who, in becoming an American, forgets his native society.) "*¡Pocho!*" my mother's best friend muttered, shaking her head. And my mother laughed, somewhere behind me. She said that her children didn't want to practice "our Spanish" after they started going to school. My mother's smiling voice made me suspect that the lady who faced me was not really angry at me. But searching her face, I couldn't find the hint of a smile.

Embarrassed, my parents would often need to explain their children's inability to speak fluent Spanish during those years. My mother encountered the wrath of her brother, her only brother, when he came up from Mexico one summer with his family and saw his nieces and nephews for the very first time. After listening to me, he looked away and said what a disgrace it was that my siblings and I couldn't speak Spanish, "*su propria idioma.*" He made that remark to my mother, but I noticed that he stared at my father.

One other visitor from those years I clearly remember: a long-time   45
friend of my father from San Francisco who came to stay with us for several days in late August. He took great interest in me after he realized that
I couldn't answer his questions in Spanish. He would grab me, as I started
to leave the kitchen. He would ask me something. Usually he wouldn't
bother to wait for my mumbled response. Knowingly, he'd murmur, "*¿Ay
pocho, pocho, donde vas?*" And he would press his thumbs into the
upper part of my arms, making me squirm with pain. Dumbly I'd stand
there, waiting for his wife to notice us and call him off with a benign
smile. I'd giggle, hoping to deflate the tension between us, pretending that
I hadn't seen the glittering scorn in his glance.

I recount such incidents only because they suggest the fierce power
that Spanish had over many people I met at home, how strongly Spanish was associated with closeness. Most of those people who called me
a *pocho* could have spoken English to me, but many wouldn't. They
seemed to think that Spanish was the only language we could use
among ourselves, that Spanish alone permitted our association. (Such
persons are always vulnerable to the ghetto merchant and the politician
who have learned the value of speaking their clients' "family language"
so as to gain immediate trust.) For my part, I felt that by learning English I had somehow committed a sin of betrayal. But betrayal against
whom? Not exactly against the visitors to the house. Rather, I felt I had
betrayed my immediate family. I knew that my parents had encouraged
me to learn English. I knew that I had turned to English with angry
reluctance. But once I spoke English with ease, I came to feel guilty.
I sensed that I had broken the spell of intimacy which had once held the
family so close together. It was this original sin against my family that
I recalled whenever anyone addressed me in Spanish and I responded,
confounded.

Yet even during those years of guilt, I was coming to grasp certain
consoling truths about language and intimacy — truths that I learned
gradually. Once, I remember playing with a friend in the backyard when
my grandmother appeared at the window. Her face was stern with suspicion when she saw the boy (the *gringo* boy) I was with. She called out to
me in Spanish, sounding the whistle of her ancient breath. My companion
looked up and watched her intently as she lowered the window and moved
(still visible) behind the light curtain, watching us both. He wanted to know
what she had said. I started to tell him, to translate her Spanish words
into English. The problem was, however, that though I knew how to
translate exactly what she had told me, I realized that any translation
would distort the deepest meaning of her message: it had been directed
only to me. This message of intimacy could never be translated because it
did not lie in the actual words she had used but passed through them. So
any translation would have seemed wrong; the words would have been
stripped of an essential meaning. Finally I decided not to tell my friend
anything — just that I didn't hear all she had said.

This insight was unfolded in time. As I made more and more friends outside my house, I began to recognize intimate messages spoken in English in a close friend's confidential tone or secretive whisper. Even more remarkable were those instances when, apparently for no special reason, I'd become conscious of the fact that my companion was speaking *only to me*. I'd marvel then, just hearing his voice. It was a stunning event to be able to break through the barrier of public silence, to be able to hear the voice of the other, to realize that it was directed just to me. After such moments of intimacy outside the house, I began to trust what I heard intimately conveyed through my family's English. Voices at home at last punctured sad confusion. I'd hear myself addressed as an intimate — in English. Such moments were never as raucous with sound as in past times, when we had used our "private" Spanish. (Our English-sounding house was never to be as noisy as our Spanish-sounding house had been.) Intimate moments were usually moments of soft sound. My mother would be ironing in the dining room while I did my homework nearby. She would look over at me, smile, and her voice sounded to tell me that I was her son. *Richard*.

Intimacy thus continued at home; intimacy was not stilled by English. Though there were fewer occasions for it — a change in my life that I would never forget — there were also times when I sensed the deep truth about language and intimacy: *Intimacy is not created by a particular language; it is created by intimates*. Thus the great change in my life was not linguistic but social. If, after becoming a successful student, I no longer heard intimate voices as often as I had earlier, it was not because I spoke English instead of Spanish. It was because I spoke public language for most of my day. I moved easily at last, a citizen in a crowded city of words.

As a man I spend most of my day in public, in a world largely devoid   50
of speech sounds. So I am quickly attracted by the glamorous quality of certain alien voices. I still am gripped with excitement when someone passes me on the street, speaking in Spanish. I have not moved beyond the range of the nostalgic pull of those sounds. And there is something very compelling about the sounds of lower-class blacks. Of all the accented versions of English that I hear in public, I hear theirs most intently. The Japanese tourist stops me downtown to ask me a question and I inch my way past his accent to concentrate on what he is saying. The eastern European immigrant in the neighborhood delicatessen speaks to me and, again, I do not pay much attention to his sounds, nor to the Texas accent of one of my neighbors or the Chicago accent of the woman who lives in the apartment below me. But when the ghetto black teenagers get on the city bus, I hear them. Their sounds in my society are the sounds of the outsider. Their voices annoy me for being so loud — so self-sufficient and unconcerned by my presence, but for the same reason they are glamorous: a romantic gesture against public acceptance. And as I listen to their

shouted laughter, I realize my own quietness. I feel envious of them—envious of their brazen intimacy.

I warn myself away from such envy, however. Overhearing those teenagers, I think of the black political activists who lately have argued in favor of using black English in public schools—an argument that varies only slightly from that of foreign-language bilingualists. I have heard "radical" linguists make the point that black English is a complex and intricate version of English. And I do not doubt it. But neither do I think that black English should be a language of public instruction. What makes it inappropriate in classrooms is not something in the language itself but, rather, what lower-class speakers make of it. Just as Spanish would have been a dangerous language for me to have used at the start of my education, so black English would be a dangerous language to use in the schooling of teenagers for whom it reinforces feelings of public separateness.

This seems to me an obvious point to make, and yet it must be said. In recent years there have been many attempts to make the language of the alien a public language. "Bilingual education, two ways to understand . . ." television and radio commercials glibly announce. Proponents of bilingual education are careful to say that above all they want every student to acquire a good education. Their argument goes something like this: Children permitted to use their family language will not be so alienated and will be better able to match the progress of English-speaking students in the crucial first months of schooling. Increasingly confident of their ability, such children will be more inclined to apply themselves to their studies in the future. But then the bilingualists also claim another very different goal. They say that children who use their family language in school will retain a sense of their ethnic heritage and their family ties. Thus the supporters of bilingual education want it both ways. They propose bilingual schooling as a way of helping students acquire the classroom skills crucial for public success. But they likewise insist that bilingual instruction will give students a sense of their identity apart from the English-speaking public.

Behind this scheme gleams a bright promise for the alien child: One can become a public person while still remaining a private person. Who would not want to believe such an appealing idea? Who can be surprised that the scheme has the support of so many middle-class ethnic Americans? If the barrio or ghetto child can retain his separateness even while being publicly educated, then it is almost possible to believe that no private cost need be paid for public success. This is the consolation offered by any of the number of current bilingual programs. Consider, for example, the bilingual voter's ballot. In some American cities one can cast a ballot printed in several languages. Such a document implies that it is possible for one to exercise that most public of rights—the right to vote—while still keeping oneself apart, unassimilated in public life.

It is not enough to say that such schemes are foolish and certainly doomed. Middle-class supporters of public bilingualism toy with the confusion of those Americans who cannot speak standard English as well as they do. Moreover, bilingual enthusiasts sin against intimacy. A Hispanic-American tells me, "I will never give up my family language," and he clutches a group of words as though they were the source of his family ties. He credits to language what he should credit to family members. This is a convenient mistake, for as long as he holds on to certain familiar words, he can ignore how much else has actually changed in his life.

It has happened before. In earlier decades, persons ambitious for social mobility, and newly successful, similarly seized upon certain "family words." Workingmen attempting to gain political power, for example, took to calling one another "brother." The word as they used it, however, could never resemble the word (the sound) "brother" exchanged by two people in intimate greeting. The context of its public delivery made it at best a metaphor; with repetition it was only a vague echo of the intimate sound. Context forced the change. Context could not be overruled. Context will always protect the realm of the intimate from public misuse. Today middle-class white Americans continue to prove the importance of context as they try to ignore it. They seize upon idioms of the black ghetto, but their attempt to appropriate such expressions invariably changes the meaning. As it becomes a public expression, the ghetto idiom loses its sound, its message of public separateness and strident intimacy. With public repetition it becomes a series of words, increasingly lifeless.

The mystery of intimate utterance remains. The communication of intimacy passes through the word and enlivens its sound, but it cannot be held by the word. It cannot be retained or ever quoted because it is too fluid. It depends not on words but on persons.

My grandmother! She stood among my other relations mocking me when I no longer spoke Spanish. *Pocho,* she said. But then it made no difference. She'd laugh, and our relationship continued because language was never its source. She was a woman in her eighties during the first decade of my life—a mysterious woman to me, my only living grandparent, a woman of Mexico in a long black dress that reached down to her shoes. She was the one relative of mine who spoke no word of English. She had no interest in gringo society and remained completely aloof from the public. She was protected by her daughters, protected even by me when we went to Safeway together and I needed to act as her translator. An eccentric woman. Hard. Soft.

When my family visited my aunt's house in San Francisco, my grandmother would search for me among my many cousins. When she found me, she'd chase them away. Pinching her granddaughters, she would warn them away from me. Then she'd take me to her room, where she had prepared for my coming. There would be a chair next to the bed, a dusty jellied candy nearby, and a copy of *Life en Español* for me to examine. "There," she'd say. And I'd sit content, a boy of eight. *Pocho,* her favorite. I'd sift through the pictures of earthquake-destroyed Latin-American cities

55

and blonde-wigged Mexican movie stars. And all the while I'd listen to the sound of my grandmother's voice. She'd pace around the room, telling me stories of her life. Her past. They were stories so familiar that I couldn't remember when I'd heard them for the first time. I'd look up sometimes to listen. Other times she'd look over at me, but she never expected a response. Sometimes I'd smile or nod. (I understood exactly what she was saying.) But it never seemed to matter to her one way or the other. It was enough that I was there. The words she spoke were almost irrelevant to that fact. We were content. And the great mystery remained: intimate utterance.

I learn nothing about language and intimacy listening to those social activists who propose using one's family language in public life. I learn much more simply by listening to songs on a radio, or hearing a great voice at the opera, or overhearing the woman downstairs at an open window singing to herself. Singers celebrate the human voice. Their lyrics are words, but, animated by voice, those words are subsumed into sounds. (This suggests a central truth about language: All words are capable of becoming sounds as we fill them with the "music" of our life.) With excitement I hear the words yielding their enormous power to sound, even though their meaning is never totally obliterated. In most songs, the drama or tension results from the way that the singer moves between words (sense) and notes (song). At one moment the song simply "says" something; at another moment the voice stretches out the words and moves to the realm of pure sound. Most songs are about love: lost love, celebrations of loving, pleas. By simply being occasions when sounds soar through words, however, songs put me in mind of the most intimate moments of life.

Finally, among all types of music, I find songs created by lyric poets   60
most compelling. On no other public occasion is sound so important for me. Written poems on a page seem at first glance a mere collection of words. And yet, without musical accompaniment, the poet leads me to hear the sounds of the words that I read. As song, a poem moves between the levels of sound and sense, never limited to one realm or the other. As a public artifact, the poem can never offer truly intimate sound, but it helps me to recall the intimate times of my life. As I read in my room, I grow deeply conscious of being alone, sounding my voice in search of another. The poem serves, then, as a memory device; it forces remembrance. And it refreshes; it reminds me of the possibility of escaping public words, the possibility that awaits me in intimate meetings.

The child reminds the adult: To seek intimate sounds is to seek the company of intimates. I do not expect to hear those sounds in public. I would dishonor those I have loved, and those I love now, to claim anything else. I would dishonor our intimacy by holding on to a particular language and calling it my family language. Intimacy cannot be trapped within words; it passes through words. It passes. Intimates leave the room. Doors close. Faces move away from the window. Time passes, and voices recede into the dark. Death finally quiets the voice. There is no way to deny it, no way to stand in the crowd claiming to utter one's family language.

The last time I saw my grandmother I was nine years old. I can tell you some of the things she said to me as I stood by her bed, but I cannot quote the message of intimacy she conveyed with her voice. She laughed, holding my hand. Her voice illumined disjointed memories as it passed them again. She remembered her husband — his green eyes, his magic name of Narcissio, his early death. She remembered the farm in Mexico, the eucalyptus trees nearby (their scent, she remembered, like incense). She remembered the family cow, the bell around its neck heard miles away. A dog. She remembered working as a seamstress, how she'd leave her daughters and son for long hours to go into Guadalajara to work. And how my mother would come running toward her in the sun — in her bright yellow dress — on her return. "MMMAAAAMMMMÁÁÁÁ," the old lady mimicked her daughter (my mother) to her daughter's son. She laughed. There was the snap of a cough. An aunt came into the room and told me it was time I should leave. "You can see her tomorrow," she promised. So I kissed my grandmother's cracked face. And the last thing I saw was her thin, oddly youthful thigh, as my aunt rearranged the sheet on the bed.

At the funeral parlor a few days after, I remember kneeling with my relatives during the rosary. Among their voices I traced, then lost, the sounds of individual aunts in the surge of the common prayer. And I heard at that moment what since I have heard very often — the sound the women in my family make when they are praying in sadness. When I went up to look at my grandmother, I saw her through the haze of a veil draped over the open lid of the casket. Her face looked calm — but distant and unyielding to love. It was not the face I remembered seeing most often. It was the face she made in public when the clerk at Safeway asked her some question and I would need to respond. It was her public face that the mortician had designed with his dubious art.

The Reader's Presence

1. The writer blames the intrusion of English into his family's private language, Spanish, for a breakdown of communication, and even of caring. How does the Spanish language appear in the essay? What associations does it have for the author? Why does Rodriguez end the essay with the scene of his dying grandmother followed by a glimpse of her corpse?

2. Rodriguez's rhetorical style alternates between persuasive argument and personal drama. Find examples of each. Do these

divergent tactics undercut or reinforce each other? Why? What is the purpose of the exclamation points at the beginning of paragraph 33?

3. Rodriguez opposes proposals to teach bilingual children in their native languages, wishing to keep native language "private" and fearing it will further contribute to the marginalization of minorities. In contrast, Gloria Anzaldúa, in "How to Tame a Wild Tongue" (page 324), considers Spanish one of America's native languages and wishes to see it publicly accepted and promoted. Whose argument do you find more persuasive, and why?

THE WRITER AT WORK

Richard Rodriguez on a Writer's Identity

How important is cultural or ethnic identity to a writer? Some writers clearly draw creative strength from their allegiances and affiliations, whereas others prefer to remain independent of groups, even those they are undeniably part of. In the following passage from a 1997 interview published in Sun Magazine, *Scott London asks Richard Rodriguez some tough questions about his various "identities." Could you have anticipated his responses based on his essay, "Aria: A Memoir of a Bilingual Childhood"?*

London: Many people feel that the call for diversity and multiculturalism is one reason the American educational system is collapsing.

Rodriguez: It's no surprise that at the same time that American universities have engaged in a serious commitment to diversity, they have been thought-prisons. We are not talking about diversity in any real way. We are talking about brown, black, and white versions of the same political ideology. It is very curious that the United States and Canada both assume that diversity means only race and ethnicity. They never assume it might mean more Nazis, or more Southern Baptists. That's diversity, too, you know.

London: What do *you* mean by diversity?

Rodriguez: For me, diversity is not a value. Diversity is what you find in Northern Ireland. Diversity is Beirut. Diversity is brother killing brother. Where diversity is *shared*—where I share with you my difference—that can be valuable. But the simple fact that we are unlike each other is a terrifying notion. I have often found myself in foreign settings where I became suddenly aware that I was not like the people around me. That, to me, is not a pleasant discovery.

London: You've said that it's tough in America to lead an intellectual   5
life outside the universities. Yet you made a very conscious decision to leave academia.

Rodriguez: My decision was sparked by affirmative action. There was a point in my life when affirmative action would have meant something to me—when my family was working-class, and we were struggling. But very early in life I became part of the majority culture and now don't think of myself as a minority. Yet the university said I was one. Anybody who has met a real minority—in the economic sense, not the numerical sense—would understand how ridiculous it is to describe a young man who is already at the university, already well into his studies in Italian and English Renaissance literature, as a minority. Affirmative action ignores our society's real minorities—members of the disadvantaged classes, no matter what their race. We have this ludicrous, bureaucratic sense that certain racial groups, regardless of class, are minorities. So what happens is those "minorities" at the very top of the ladder get chosen for everything.

London: Is that what happened to you?

Rodriguez: Well, when it came time for me to look for jobs, the jobs came looking for me. I had teaching offers from the best universities in the country. I was about to accept one from Yale when the whole thing collapsed on me.

London: What do you mean?

Rodriguez: I had all this anxiety about what it meant to be a minority. My professors—these same men who taught me the intricacies of language—just shied away from the issue. They didn't want to talk about it, other than to suggest I could be a "role model" to other Hispanics—when I went back to my barrio, I suppose. I came from a white, middle-class neighborhood. Was I expected to go back there and teach the woman next door about Renaissance sonnets? The embarrassing truth of the matter was that I was being chosen because Yale University had some peculiar idea about what my skin color or ethnicity signified. Who knows what Yale thought it was getting when it hired Richard Rodriguez? The people who offered me the job thought there was nothing wrong with that. I thought there was something very wrong. I still do. I think race-based affirmative action is crude and absolutely mistaken.

London: I noticed that some university students put up a poster outside the lecture hall where you spoke the other night. It said, "Richard Rodriguez is a disgrace to the Chicano community."

Rodriguez: I sort of like that. I don't think writers should be convenient examples. I don't think we should make people feel settled. I don't try to be a gadfly, but I do think that real ideas are troublesome. There should be something about my work that leaves the reader unsettled. I intend that. The notion of the writer as a kind of sociological sample of a community is ludicrous. Even worse is the notion that writers should provide an example of how to live. Virginia Woolf ended her life by putting a rock in her sweater one day and walking into a lake. She is not a model for how I want to live my life. On the other hand, the bravery of her syntax,

10

of her sentences, written during her deepest depression, is a kind of example for me. But I do not want to become Virginia Woolf. That is not why I read her.

London: What's wrong with being a role model?

Rodriguez: The popular idea of a role model implies that an adult's influence on a child is primarily occupational, that all a black child needs is to see a black doctor, and then this child will think, "Oh, I can become a doctor, too." I have a good black friend who is a doctor, but he didn't become a doctor because he saw other black men who were doctors. He became a doctor because his mother cleaned office buildings at night, and because she loved her children. She grew bowlegged from cleaning office buildings at night, and in the process she taught him something about courage and bravery and dedication to others. I became a writer not because my father was one — my father made false teeth for a living. I became a writer because the Irish nuns who educated me taught me something about bravery with their willingness to give so much to me.

London: There used to be a category for writers and thinkers and   15
intellectuals — "the intelligentsia." But not anymore.

Rodriguez: No, I think the universities have co-opted the intellectual, by and large. But there is an emerging intellectual set coming out of Washington think tanks now. There are people who are leaving the universities and working for the government or in think tanks, simply looking for freedom. The university has become so stultified since the sixties. There is so much you can't do at the university. You can't say this, you can't do that, you can't think this, and so forth. In many ways, I'm free to range as widely as I do intellectually precisely because I'm not at a university. The tiresome Chicanos would be after me all the time. You know: "We saw your piece yesterday, and we didn't like what you said," or, "You didn't sound happy enough," or, "You didn't sound proud enough."

London: You've drawn similar responses from the gay community, I understand.

Rodriguez: Yes, I've recently gotten in trouble with certain gay activists because I'm not gay enough! I am a morose homosexual. I'm melancholy. *Gay* is the last adjective I would use to describe myself. The idea of being gay, like a little sparkler, never occurs to me. So if you ask me if I'm gay, I say no.

After the second chapter of *Days of Obligation*, which is about the death of a friend of mine from AIDS, was published in *Harper's*, I got this rather angry letter from a gay-and-lesbian group that was organizing a protest against the magazine. It was the same old problem: political groups have almost no sense of irony. For them, language has to say exactly what it means. "Why aren't you proud of being gay?" they wanted to know. "Why are you so dark? Why are you so morbid? Why are you so sad? Don't you realize, we're all OK? Let's celebrate that fact." But that is not what writers do. We don't celebrate being "OK." If you want to be OK, take an aspirin.

London: Do you consider yourself more Mexican, or more American?   20

Rodriguez: In some ways I consider myself more Chinese, because I live in San Francisco, which is becoming a predominantly Asian city. I avoid falling into the black-and-white dialectic in which most of America still seems trapped. I have always recognized that, as an American, I am in relationships with other parts of the world; that I have to measure myself against the Pacific, against Asia. Having to think of myself in relationship to that horizon has liberated me from the black-and-white checkerboard.

Marjane Satrapi

The Socks

Writer-illustrator and graphic novelist Marjane Satrapi (b. 1969) was born in Iran and, after a sojourn in Europe and a return to Tehran, now lives and works in France. Her graphic memoir, Persepolis: The Story of a Childhood *(2003), recounts in comic-book form growing up in Iran from ages six to fourteen, years that saw the overthrow of the Shah, the triumph of the Islamic Revolution, and the devastating effects of war with Iraq. The book was an immediate hit in France, selling more than 150,000 copies, and has been translated into numerous languages. In the United States,* Persepolis *was named a* New York Times No-table Book *and one of* Time *magazine's "Best Comix of the Year." Spain recognized her work with the Fernando Buesa Blanco Peace Prize in 2003.* Persepolis 2: The Story of a Return *(2004), from which "The Socks" is excerpted, picks up her story with Satrapi's departure for Austria when she was fourteen and continues through her college years back in Tehran. Her most recent volume is* Embroideries *(2005), which she described as "one of those long afternoons in my grand-mother's living room with ten or eleven women of a different generation having tea." She has also written several children's books, and her commentary and comics appear in newspapers and magazines around the world, including the* New York Times *and the* New Yorker.

"The Socks" takes places after Satrapi's return to Tehran, where she was considered "too European" to fit back into the conservative Islamic society she had left. It tells the story of the consequences of the forced double lives led by many people, young and old, as they attempt to navigate the absurd and danger-ous world of fundamentalist Iran.

THE SOCKS

TO KEEP US FROM STRAYING OFF THE STRAIGHT PATH, OUR STUDIOS WERE SEPARATED FROM THOSE OF THE BOYS.

I'M YOUR ANATOMY PROFESSOR. IN THE PAST, WE DREW NUDES, BUT THINGS HAVE CHANGED. YOUR MODEL WILL BE COVERED. TRY TO MAKE THE BEST OF IT.

WE TRIED,

WE LOOKED...

...FROM EVERY DIRECTION...

...AND FROM EVERY ANGLE...

BUT NOT A SINGLE PART OF HER BODY WAS VISIBLE.

WE NEVERTHELESS LEARNED TO DRAW DRAPES.

THESE ABSURD SITUATIONS WERE QUITE FREQUENT. ONE DAY, FOR EXAMPLE, I WAS SUPPOSED TO GO SEE MY DENTIST, BUT CLASSES FINISHED LATER THAN EXPECTED.

SUDDENLY, I HEARD A VOICE OVER THE LOUDSPEAKER:

THE LADY IN THE BLUE COAT! DON'T RUN!

THE LADY IN THE BLUE COAT!!! STOP RUNNING!

??

HEY—BLUE COAT! STOP RUNNING!

???

ME?

MADAM, WHY WERE YOU RUNNING?

I'M VERY LATE! I WAS RUNNING TO CATCH MY BUS.

YES . . . BUT . . . WHEN YOU RUN, YOUR BEHIND MAKES MOVEMENTS THAT ARE . . . HOW DO YOU SAY . . . OBSCENE!

WELL THEN DON'T LOOK AT MY ASS!

I YELLED SO LOUDLY THAT THEY DIDN'T EVEN ARREST ME.

WE CONFRONTED THE REGIME AS BEST WE COULD.

IN 1990, THE ERA OF GRAND REVOLUTIONARY IDEAS AND DEMONSTRATIONS WAS OVER. BETWEEN 1980 AND 1983, THE GOVERNMENT HAD IMPRISONED AND EXECUTED SO MANY HIGH-SCHOOL AND COLLEGE STUDENTS THAT WE NO LONGER DARED TO TALK POLITICS.

OUR STRUGGLE WAS MORE DISCREET.

IT HINGED ON THE LITTLE DETAILS. TO OUR LEADERS, THE SMALLEST THING COULD BE A SUBJECT OF SUBVERSION.

SHOWING YOUR WRIST.

A LOUD LAUGH.

HAVING A WALKMAN.

IN SHORT . . . EVERYTHING WAS A PRETEXT TO ARREST US.

I EVEN REMEMBER SPENDING AN ENTIRE DAY AT THE COMMITTEE BECAUSE OF A PAIR OF RED SOCKS.

THE REGIME HAD UNDERSTOOD THAT ONE PERSON LEAVING HER HOUSE WHILE ASKING HERSELF:

ARE MY TROUSERS LONG ENOUGH?

IS MY VEIL IN PLACE?

CAN MY MAKE-UP BE SEEN?

ARE THEY GOING TO WHIP ME?

NO LONGER ASKS HERSELF:

WHERE IS MY FREEDOM OF THOUGHT?

WHERE IS MY FREEDOM OF SPEECH?

MY LIFE, IS IT LIVABLE?

WHAT'S GOING ON IN THE POLITICAL PRISONS?

IT'S ONLY NATURAL! WHEN WE'RE AFRAID, WE LOSE ALL SENSE OF ANALYSIS AND REFLECTION. OUR FEAR PARALYZES US. BESIDES, FEAR HAS ALWAYS BEEN THE DRIVING FORCE BEHIND ALL DICTATORS' REPRESSION.

SHOWING YOUR HAIR OR PUTTING ON MAKEUP LOGICALLY BECAME ACTS OF REBELLION.

I DIDN'T SAY EVERYTHING I COULD HAVE: THAT SHE WAS FRUSTRATED BECAUSE SHE WAS STILL A VIRGIN AT TWENTY-SEVEN! THAT SHE WAS FORBIDDING ME WHAT WAS FORBIDDEN TO HER! THAT TO MARRY SOMEONE THAT YOU DON'T KNOW, FOR HIS MONEY, IS PROSTITUTION. THAT DESPITE HER LOCKS OF HAIR AND HER LIPSTICK, SHE WAS ACTING LIKE THE STATE. THAT... ETC.... THAT DAY, HALF THE CLASS TURNED ITS BACK ON ME.

HAPPILY, THERE WAS STILL THE OTHER HALF. LITTLE BY LITTLE, I GOT TO KNOW THE STUDENTS WHO THOUGHT LIKE ME.

WE WOULD GO TO ONE ANOTHER'S HOUSES, WHERE WE POSED FOR EACH OTHER ... WE HAD AT LAST FOUND A PLACE OF FREEDOM.

AT FIRST THERE WERE ONLY FIVE OF US.

THEN ...

AND FINALLY ...

WE WERE MUCH MORE NUMEROUS THAN I WOULD HAVE BELIEVED.

OUR PROFESSOR WAS SO HAPPY TO SEE THE SKETCHES WE DID AT HOME.

BRAVO! AN ARTIST SHOULD DEFY THE LAW! I CONGRATULATE YOU!

THE MORE TIME PASSED, THE MORE I BECAME CONSCIOUS OF THE CONTRAST BETWEEN THE OFFICIAL REPRESENTATION OF MY COUNTRY AND THE REAL LIFE OF THE PEOPLE, THE ONE THAT WENT ON BEHIND THE WALLS.

TO FIND A SEMBLANCE OF EQUILIBRIUM, WE PARTIED ALMOST EVERY NIGHT ...

...BUT EVEN IN OUR HOMES, THEY DIDN'T LEAVE US ALONE.

I SAW A PATROL OF GUARDIANS OF THE REVOLUTION OUT THE WINDOW! I THINK THEY'RE COMING TO ARREST US!

COME ALONG YOU LITTLE BASTARD! YOU'RE ORGANIZING PARTIES! I'LL CURE YOU OF YOUR TASTE FOR PLEASURE!

THEY CARTED EVERYONE OFF TO PRISON. OBVIOUSLY, WE WERE VERY SCARED THE FIRST TIME.

...BUT WE QUICKLY GOT USED TO IT. WE WOULD EVEN ARRIVE LAUGHING.

OH BEARDED ONE, YOUR BEARD STINKS!

THEN CAME THE USUAL SPIEL ...

..AGAINST THE MORAL CODE... THE BLOOD OF MARTYRS .. TWENTY THOUSAND TUMANS ...

OUR PARENTS PAID AND WE WERE RELEASED.

...UNTIL THE NEXT TIME. TO BE ABLE TO PARTY, YOU HAD TO HAVE MEANS.

DAD, FARZAD IS...

I KNOW. I WAS SCARED... MAYBE YOU SHOULD...

BUT HE DIDN'T FINISH HIS SENTENCE. DESPITE THE DANGER, MY FATHER ALWAYS LET ME LIVE THE WAY I FELT WAS RIGHT.

THE NEXT DAY, WE GATHERED AT MY HOUSE.

POOR FARZAD. HE WAS SO HANDSOME. I CAN'T BELIEVE HE'S DEAD!

I COULD KILL THOSE BEARDED MEN WITH MY OWN HANDS.

I'M NOT COMING TO ANY MORE PARTIES. IT'S TOO FRIGHTENING!

YOU'RE WRONG. THAT'S EXACTLY WHAT THEY WANT! TO STOP US FROM LIVING! NOTHING BOTHERS THEM MORE THAN TO SEE US HAPPY!

ALI IS RIGHT!

THAT SAME NIGHT, ALI HAD A BIG PARTY AT HIS HOUSE.

I NEVER DRANK SO MUCH IN MY LIFE.

The Reader's Presence

1. What absurdities does Satrapi point out in the restrictions that the Revolutionary Guard places on her and her peers? Which of these does Satrapi represent graphically and which does she explain in writing? What seems to be the rationale behind these restrictions? What is Satrapi's argument against them?

2. Why is this selection entitled "The Socks"? What is the importance of the socks in this selection? What do the socks represent in the larger story?

3. Satrapi notes on page 265, "The more time passed, the more I became conscious of the contrast between the official representation of my country and the real life of the people, the one that went on behind the walls." How does Azar Nafisi's essay "Reading *Lolita* in Tehran" (page 516) express this contrast between the public and private lives of Iranians, especially women? To what degree would you say Nafisi and her students are "schizophrenic," as Satrapi puts it, because their public and private lives contradict each other?

David Sedaris

Me Talk Pretty One Day

David Sedaris was born in 1956 in Johnson City, New York, and raised in Raleigh, North Carolina. He is a dramatist whose plays, written in collaboration with his sister, Amy (one of which won an Obie Award), have been produced at La Mama and Lincoln Center. Sedaris launched his career as a wry, neurotically self-disparaging humorist on National Public Radio's Morning Edition, *when he read aloud from "The Santaland Diaries," an autobiographical piece about working as a Christmas elf at Macy's. He has since published a number of best-selling collections, including* Barrel Fever *(1994),* Naked *(1997),* Holiday on Ice *(1997),* Me Talk Pretty One Day *(2000) and his latest,* Dress Your Family in Corduroy and Denim *(2004). His essays appear regularly in the* New Yorker *and Esquire. In 2001, Sedaris was named Humorist of the Year by* Time *magazine and received the Thurber Prize for American Humor.* New York *magazine had dubbed Sedaris "the most brilliantly witty New Yorker since Dorothy Parker." He currently divides his time between France and New York City.*

Sedaris, who for two years taught writing at the Art Institute of Chicago, laments that the students in his writing classes "were ashamed of their middle-class background . . . they felt like unless they grew up in poverty, they had nothing to write about." Sedaris feels that "it doesn't really matter what your life was like, you can write about anything. It's just the writing of it that is the challenge."

At the age of forty-one, I am returning to school and have to think of myself as what my French textbook calls "a true debutant." After paying my tuition, I was issued a student ID, which allows me a discounted entry fee at movie theaters, puppet shows, and Festyland, a far-flung amusement park that advertises with billboards picturing a cartoon stegosaurus sitting in a canoe and eating what appears to be a ham sandwich.

I've moved to Paris with hopes of learning the language. My school is an easy ten-minute walk from my apartment, and on the first day of class I arrived early, watching as the returning students greeted one another in the school lobby. Vacations were recounted, and questions were raised concerning mutual friends with names like Kang and Vlatnya. Regardless of their nationalities, everyone spoke in what sounded to me like excellent French. Some accents were better than others, but the students exhibited an ease and confidence I found intimidating. As an added discomfort, they were all young, attractive, and well dressed, causing me to feel not unlike Pa Kettle trapped backstage after a fashion show.

The first day of class was nerve-racking because I knew I'd be expected to perform. That's the way they do it here — it's everybody into the language pool, sink or swim. The teacher marched in, deeply tanned from a recent vacation, and proceeded to rattle off a series of administrative announcements. I've spent quite a few summers in Normandy, and I took a monthlong French class before leaving New York. I'm not completely in the dark, yet I understood only half of what this woman was saying.

"If you have not *meimslsxp* or *lgpdmurct* by this time, then you should not be in this room. Has everyone *apzkiubjxow*? Everyone? Good, we shall begin." She spread out her lesson plan and sighed, saying, "All right, then, who knows the alphabet?"

It was startling because (a) I hadn't been asked that question in a   5
while and (b) I realized, while laughing, that I myself did *not* know the alphabet. They're the same letters, but in France they're pronounced differently. I know the shape of the alphabet but had no idea what it actually sounded like.

"Ahh." The teacher went to the board and sketched the letter *a*. "Do we have anyone in the room whose first name commences with an *ahh*?"

Two Polish Annas raised their hands, and the teacher instructed them to present themselves by stating their names, nationalities, occupations, and a brief list of things they liked and disliked in this world. The first Anna hailed from an industrial town outside of Warsaw and had front teeth the size of tombstones. She worked as a seamstress, enjoyed quiet times with friends, and hated the mosquito.

"Oh, really," the teacher said. "How very interesting. I thought that everyone loved the mosquito, but here, in front of all the world, you claim to detest him. How is it that we've been blessed with someone as unique and original as you? Tell us, please."

The seamstress did not understand what was being said but knew that this was an occasion for shame. Her rabbity mouth huffed for breath, and she stared down at her lap as though the appropriate come-back were stitched somewhere alongside the zipper of her slacks.

The second Anna learned from the first and claimed to love sunshine and detest lies. It sounded like a translation of one of those Playmate of the Month data sheets, the answers always written in the same loopy handwriting: "Turn-ons: Mom's famous five-alarm chili! Turnoffs: insecurity and guys who come on too strong!!!!"

The two Polish Annas surely had clear notions of what they loved and hated, but like the rest of us, they were limited in terms of vocabulary, and this made them appear less than sophisticated. The teacher forged on, and we learned that Carlos, the Argentine bandonion player, loved wine, music, and, in his words, "making sex with the womens of the world." Next came a beautiful young Yugoslav who identified herself as an optimist, saying that she loved everything that life had to offer.

The teacher licked her lips, revealing a hint of the saucebox we would later come to know. She crouched low for her attack, placed her hands on the young woman's desk, and leaned close, saying, "Oh yeah? And do you love your little war?"

While the optimist struggled to defend herself, I scrambled to think of an answer to what had obviously become a trick question. How often is one asked what he loves in this world? More to the point, how often is one asked and then publicly ridiculed for his answer? I recalled my mother, flushed with wine, pounding the tabletop late one night, saying, "Love? I love a good steak cooked rare. I love my cat, and I love . . ." My sisters and I leaned forward, waiting to hear our names. "Tums," our mother said. "I love Tums."

The teacher killed some time accusing the Yugoslavian girl of masterminding a program of genocide, and I jotted frantic notes in the margins of my pad. While I can honestly say that I love leafing through medical textbooks devoted to severe dermatological conditions, the hobby is beyond the reach of my French vocabulary, and acting it out would only have invited controversy.

When called upon, I delivered an effortless list of things that I detest: blood sausage, intestinal pâtés, brain pudding. I'd learned these words the hard way. Having given it some thought, I then declared my love for IBM typewriters, the French word for *bruise*, and my electric floor waxer. It was a short list, but still I managed to mispronounce *IBM* and assign the wrong gender to both the floor waxer and the typewriter. The teacher's reaction led me to believe that these mistakes were capital crimes in the country of France.

"Were you always this *palicmkrexis?*" she asked. "Even a *fiuscrzsa ticiwelmun* knows that a typewriter is feminine."

I absorbed as much of her abuse as I could understand, thinking—but not saying—that I find it ridiculous to assign a gender to an inanimate object incapable of disrobing and making an occasional fool of itself. Why refer to Lady Crack Pipe or Good Sir Dishrag when these things could never live up to all that their sex implied?

The teacher proceeded to belittle everyone from German Eva, who hated laziness, to Japanese Yukari, who loved paintbrushes and soap. Italian, Thai, Dutch, Korean, and Chinese—we all left class foolishly believing that the worst was over. She'd shaken us up a little, but surely that was just an act designed to weed out the deadweight. We didn't know it then, but the coming months would teach us what it was like to spend time in the presence of a wild animal, something completely unpredictable. Her temperament was not based on a series of good and bad days but, rather, good and bad moments. We soon learned to dodge chalk and protect our heads and stomachs whenever she approached us with a question. She hadn't yet punched anyone, but it seemed wise to protect ourselves against the inevitable.

Though we were forbidden to speak anything but French, the teacher would occasionally use us to practice any of her five fluent languages.

"I hate you," she said to me one afternoon. Her English was flawless. "I really, really hate you." Call me sensitive, but I couldn't help but take it personally.

After being singled out as a lazy *kfdtinvfm*, I took to spending four hours a night on my homework, putting in even more time whenever we were assigned an essay. I suppose I could have gotten by with less, but I was determined to create some sort of identity for myself: David the hard worker, David the cut-up. We'd have one of those "complete this sentence" exercises, and I'd fool with the thing for hours, invariably settling on something like "A quick run around the lake? I'd love to! Just give me a moment while I strap on my wooden leg." The teacher, through word and action, conveyed the message that if this was my idea of an identity, she wanted nothing to do with it.

My fear and discomfort crept beyond the borders of the classroom and accompanied me out onto the wide boulevards. Stopping for a coffee, asking directions, depositing money in my bank account: these things were out of the question, as they involved having to speak. Before beginning school, there'd been no shutting me up, but now I was convinced that everything I said was wrong. When the phone rang, I ignored it. If someone asked me a question, I pretended to be deaf. I knew my fear was getting the best of me when I started wondering why they don't sell cuts of meat in vending machines.

My only comfort was the knowledge that I was not alone. Huddled in the hallways and making the most of our pathetic French, my fellow students and I engaged in the sort of conversation commonly overheard in refugee camps.

"Sometime me cry alone at night."

"That be common for I, also, but be more strong, you. Much work and someday you talk pretty. People start love you soon. Maybe tomorrow, okay." 25

Unlike the French class I had taken in New York, here there was no sense of competition. When the teacher poked a shy Korean in the eyelid with a freshly sharpened pencil, we took no comfort in the fact that, unlike Hyeyoon Cho, we all knew the irregular past tense of the verb *to defeat*. In all fairness, the teacher hadn't meant to stab the girl, but neither did she spend much time apologizing, saying only, "Well, you should have been *vkkdyo* more *kdeynfulh*."

Over time it became impossible to believe that any of us would ever improve. Fall arrived and it rained every day, meaning we would now be scolded for the water dripping from our coats and umbrellas. It was mid-October when the teacher singled me out, saying, "Every day spent with you is like having a cesarean section." And it struck me that, for the first time since arriving in France, I could understand every word that someone was saying.

Understanding doesn't mean that you can suddenly speak the language. Far from it. It's a small step, nothing more, yet its rewards are intoxicating and deceptive. The teacher continued her diatribe and I settled back, bathing in the subtle beauty of each new curse and insult.

"You exhaust me with your foolishness and reward my efforts with nothing but pain, do you understand me?"

The world opened up, and it was with great joy that I responded, "I know the thing that you speak exact now. Talk me more, you, plus, please, plus." 30

The Reader's Presence

1. How did Sedaris take a potentially boring experience—auditing a beginner's language class—and turn it into a humorous essay? What were the funniest parts of the essay? An interviewer once wrote that Sedaris's signature is "deadpan" humor. What is deadpan humor? Identify—and characterize the effectiveness of— examples of it in "Me Talk Pretty One Day."

2. Which English words would you substitute for the nonsense words that represent Sedaris's difficulties understanding his teacher's French? Have a classmate tell you what he or she thinks such words as *meimslsxp* (paragraph 4), *palicmkrexis* (paragraph 16), or *kdeynfulh* (paragraph 26) might mean. Did he or she pick the same or similar words to the ones you picked? Point to the clues

Sedaris includes in the essay to hint at what such words mean. How would you rewrite the passage with different clues to indicate a different possible meaning for the nonsense words?

3. How surprised were you by the last line in the essay? To what extent did you expect that Sedaris would speak fluently because he understood his teacher's French perfectly? Look at some other unexpected last lines in essays that you've read in this collection. Choose two surprising last lines and identify how each author goes about setting up the surprise. When you look back, at what point in each essay should you have been expecting the unexpected? If there were clues beforehand, identify them.

Zadie Smith

Scenes from the Smith Family Christmas

Zadie Smith (b. 1975) was born in England and raised in the clamor of a richly multicultural north London neighborhood (where she still lives) to a British father and a Jamaican mother. At age 14, Smith changed her name from Sadie to Zadie because it seemed to her to be more "exotic" and reflective of her early desire, not to write, but to be a star dancer in movie musicals. "I tapped danced for ten years before I began to understand people don't make musicals anymore," she says. "Slowly but surely the pen became mightier than the double pick-up timestep with shuffle." By the time she reached 24, she had graduated from Cambridge University and had published her first novel, White Teeth *(2000), garnering numerous prizes, including the Whitbread First Book Award, the James Tait Black Memorial Prize for fiction, and the Commonwealth Writers Prize. Her second novel,* The Autograph Man, *came out in 2002.*

"I went to University to study English Literature. I never attended a creative writing class in my life," she told an interviewer. "The best, the only real training you can get is from reading other people's books. I spent three years in college and wrote three and a half stories but I read everything I could get my hands on." Besides her reading, Smith lists her city upbringing as a key influence. "If you grow up in London you hear a lot of different voices all the time. But I would say that's true of Paris, or New York, or any urban center. It would be very hard to get on a train and not notice that there are sometimes twenty-five or thirty different races. That seems to me a fairly normal experience if you live in a city."

In "Scenes from the Smith Family Christmas," a 2003 op-ed piece for the New York Times, Smith pays homage to her own diverse family as "the real gift beneath the wrapping."

This is a picture of my father and me, Christmas 1980 or thereabouts. Across his chest and my bottom there is the faint pink, inverted watermark of postal instructions—something about a card, and then "stamp here." Hanging from the tree like a decoration is yet more mirror-writing, this time from my own pen. Does it say "Nothing"? Or maybe "Letting"?

I've ruined this photo. I don't understand why I can't take better care of things like this. It's an original, I have no negative, yet I allowed it to sit for months in a pile of mail on my open windowsill. Finally the photo got soaked, imprinted with the text of phone bills and Post-it notes. I felt sick wedging it inside my O.E.D. to stop the curling.

But I also felt the weird relief which comes from knowing that the inevitable destruction of precious things, though done in your house, was not done by your hand. What is that? Christmas, childhood, the past, families, fathers, regret of all kinds—no one wants to be the Grinch who steals these things, but you leave the door open with the hope he might come in and relieve you of your heavy stuff. And my God, Christmas is heavy.

Anyway, it's done now. And this is me and my dad one Christmas past. I'm five and he's too old to have a five-year-old. At the time the Smiths lived in London in a half-English, half-Irish housing project called Athelston

Gardens, one black family squished between two tribes at war. It was confusing. I didn't understand why certain football games made people pour into Biddy Mulligan's pub and hit other people over the head with chairs and bottles, and I didn't get the thing about people pouring into the Prince Charles the next day and repeating the procedure. I didn't get the men who came round collecting for the I.R.A. on Christmas Eve, and I didn't have to give them anything either—once they saw my mum, with her exotic shift dress and her cornrows, they respectfully withdrew, thinking we had nothing to do with their particular argument.

In fact, my parents were friends with an Irishman who gave us a   5
homemade fruit bowl this same Christmas and then the following winter betrayed the spirit of Christmas by making a different kind of homemade gift with which he tried to blow up No. 11 Downing Street. We knew nothing about the bomb until years later, but we all knew about the ugly fruit bowl, ceramic and swirly and unable to stand straight on a tabletop. This was filled with nuts and laid on the carpet to limit the wobble. It's out of the frame in this photo, on the floor by Dad's feet. My brother Ben, a little fat thing back then, has it between his legs like Buddha with his lotus flower.

Ben was always on food detail in the war that is Christmas. I did, or overdid, the decorations (as you will note, the tree is bending to the left under the weight of Manga-eyed reindeer, chocolate Santas, swollen baubles, tinsel, three sets of lights and the presents I tastefully nestled in the branches). Dad cooked. Mum marked out television schedules with a pen. Ben ate the food. Just as Joseph tended to the Virgin Mary, we tended to Ben, making his comfort our first priority. He ate what he needed and whatever was left we ate.

I think it's Carole King's "Tapestry" on the record player. But which song? "It's Too Late" would make thematic sense—my dad's smile has the let's-just-get-through-this tension of a code-red marriage. As for the "Natural Woman" Christmas or the "You've Got a Friend" Christmas—these predate my consciousness. But they must have existed, what with Ben being a September baby and me October. Those were the sexy Noels, delivering babies like presents nine months later. By contrast, Luke, my youngest brother, came in July and is still unborn in this photo. He was clearly the result of a we-haven't-had-sex-in-five-years birthday treat (Dad's birthday is in late September), and by the time he turned up, "Blood on the Tracks" had replaced "Tapestry" as the family Christmas soundtrack.

Maybe you wonder about the black man in the pink hat. I wonder about him, too. I think he's an uncle of mine by the name of Denzil (spelling uncertain). My mother claims 36 siblings, most of them—in the Jamaican parlance—"outdoor children," meaning same father, different mother. Denzil must have been one of these, because he was 6-foot-7, whereas my mother is 5-foot-5 and shrinking, as my grandmother did before her.

This Christmas was the only time we ever met each other, Denzil and I. He was the gift that kept on giving, with his strange patois and his huge feet and the piggyback rides he conducted out on the balcony because the ceilings were too low. Outside was where he wanted to be anyway—you can tell that much from the look of infinite weariness he's giving my dad's left elbow.

Poor Denzil; off the plane from Jamaica into bitter England, and stuck in the most cultish, insular day in the nuclear-family calendar. Families speak in semaphore at Christmas; the falcons are the only ones to understand the falconer, and something dismal is slouching toward Bethlehem. It's called The Truth About What Happens to Your Family When No Member Is Allowed to Leave the House. Outsiders do best if they seeketh neither enlightenment nor the remote control.

Denzil found this out when he attempted, on this most sacred of days, to do the things we could not do because we'd always done them another way, our way—a way we all hated, to be sure, but could not change. Denzil wants to open a present on Christmas Eve—don't do that, Denzil. Denzil wants to go for a walk—I'm so sorry, Denzil, that's impossible. We'd like to, but we just can't swing it. Why not? Because, Denzil. Just because. Because like the two parts of Ireland, because like the Holy Trinity, because like nuclear proliferation, like men not wearing skirts, because like brandy butter.

Because that's the way we do things around here, Denzil. We don't eat till 4 o'clock, we open the smallest presents first, we have to watch two MGM musicals when we wake up, followed by a Jimmy Stewart movie, and then settle down in front of a feted sitcom's "Christmas special," which is also the time—read my lips—when we begin the search for batteries to go into the many things we have bought that require batteries we forgot to buy. Don't mess with us on this, Denzil. The Smiths are not for turning. It's our way or the highway. We want Christmas, dead or alive.

I make it sound bad. In truth, we had great times. As great as anybody's. Certainly better than Denzil's the year he got his own place and phoned us to say he'd killed a partridge in the backyard with a slingshot and just finished eating it like a proper English gentleman (it was a London pigeon, of course). Oh, we Smiths are ardent seekers after the spirit of Christmas, and we do not listen to Iris Murdoch's sensible analogical advice: "Good represents the reality of which God is the dream." We're chasing the dream, baby.

But we do sense the more difficult truth: that Family represents the reality of which Christmas is the dream. It is of course Family (messy, complex, miserable, happy, so many gradations of those last two words) which is the real gift, beneath the wrapping. Family is the daily miracle,

10

and Christmas is the enforcement of ideals which, in truth, do not matter. It would be tempting therefore to say "Well, then ditch Christmas!" the same way people say "Ditch God" or "Ditch marriage," but people find it hard to do these things because they feel that there is more than a ghost in these machines, there is an animating spirit.

Santa help me, but I believe this, too. You know you believe it when   15
you start your own little family with some person you met four years ago in a bar and then he tries to open the presents on Christmas Eve because that's what he did in his family and you have the strong urge to run screaming from the building holding your banner about the end and how it is nigh. It is a moving and comic thing—a Murdochian scuffle between the Real and the Dream—to watch a young couple as they teeter around the Idea of Christmas, trying to avoid internecine festive warfare.

Of course, sometimes the angel of history gets the better of you; one part of your family simply secedes from the other. When my parents divorced, seven years after this photo, the Christmas war became briefly more violent (which day, which house, which parent), and then grew subdued, because peace is what you want, in the end, at Christmas. On that one day you value it more than your life. Nowadays, we all get into a car with presents in the trunk, quietly drive to my father's in Felixstowe, and two people divorced 15 years ago rediscover that cycle whereby "It's Too Late" doubles back onto itself and becomes "You've Got a Friend." It's called a cease-fire.

Then, last year, out of nowhere hostilities resumed. Not with my dad, who is beyond such things now, but between mother and brood. That ancient battle poor Denzil couldn't understand, the one about not bloody leaving the house on Christmas Eve, which is the one day you're meant to spend with your family, the one day your mother asks for a little quality time, etc., hit the house like a grenade, and everybody yelled a lot and walked out and I spent Christmas Eve sleeping in my friend Adam's bath.

I see now the mistake we made. We thought that because we'd reached adulthood, Mum wouldn't mind if we ditched Christmas—the ritual, the dream, the animating spirit, the whole shebang—and just paraded around town at nightclubs and other people's dinner parties as if we were individuals living in the free world. Don't ever think that. Where women are concerned (mothers especially), Zora Neale Hurston had it right: the dream is the truth.

After all, for 364 days of the year you live in the Real. Your mother is asking you only for this one day. It's nothing, it says on my photo, nothing but letting; it's about letting Christmas in, letting go of that Kantian will of yours, getting freaky like Iris, giving it up to a beautiful, insane, mystical idea. So you damaged the photo of Christmas Past—well, let's try it again; Christmas Present, Christmas Future. "War is over, if you want it," sang John and Yoko. So let it happen.

The Reader's Presence

1. Smith opens the essay by admitting that the photo she describes has been ruined. How does Smith use the ruined photo to relieve herself of "heavy stuff" such as "Christmas, childhood, the past, families, fathers, and regrets of all kind"? In what way is a photograph the ultimate keeper of such memories? In the end, how does Smith reconcile her feelings about the ruined photograph?

2. How does Smith describe her position between cultures? In what ways does she negotiate between two different sides in the essay?

3. Smith refers to the photograph in her opening line: "This is a picture of my father and me, Christmas 1980 or thereabouts." How does she draw the reader into the essay by means of the accompanying image? How might the essay have been different if she had merely described the photograph? Compare Smith's use of the image to Jamaica Kincaid's in "Biography of a Dress" (page 175). To what extent does either writer rely on the inclusion of a photograph in her writing? Do Kincaid and Smith use the photographs in similar ways? Why or why not?

Brent Staples

Just Walk on By: A Black Man Ponders His Power to Alter Public Space

As he describes in Parallel Time: Growing Up in Black and White *(1994), Brent Staples (b. 1951) escaped a childhood of urban poverty through success in school and his determination to be a writer. Although Staples earned a Ph.D. in psychology from the University of Chicago in 1982, his love of journalism led him to leave the field of psychology and start a career that has taken him to his current position on the editorial board of the* New York Times. *Staples contributes to several national magazines, including* Harper's, *the* New York Times Magazine, *and* Ms., *in which "Just Walk on By" appeared in 1986.*

In his autobiography, which won the Anisfield Wolff Book Award, previously won by such writers as James Baldwin, Ralph Ellison, and Zora Neale Hurston, Staples remembers how in Chicago he prepared for his writing career by keeping a journal. "I wrote on buses, on the Jackson Park el—though only at the stops to keep the writing legible. I traveled to distant neighborhoods, sat on their curbs, and sketched what I saw in words. Thursdays meant free admission at the Art Institute. All day I attributed motives to people in paintings, especially people in Rembrandts. At closing time I went to a nightclub in The Loop and spied on patrons, copied their conversations and speculated about their lives. The journal was more than 'a record of my inner transactions.' It was a collection of stolen souls from which I would one day construct a book."

My first victim was a woman—white, well dressed, probably in her early twenties. I came upon her late one evening on a deserted street in Hyde Park, a relatively affluent neighborhood in an otherwise mean, impoverished section of Chicago. As I swung onto the avenue behind her, there seemed to be a discreet, uninflammatory distance between us. Not so. She cast back a worried glance. To her, the youngish black man—a broad six feet two inches with a beard and billowing hair, both hands shoved into the pockets of a bulky military jacket—seemed menacingly close. After a few more quick glimpses, she picked up her pace and was soon running in earnest. Within seconds she disappeared into a cross street.

That was more than a decade ago. I was twenty-two years old, a graduate student newly arrived at the University of Chicago. It was in the echo of that terrified woman's footfalls that I first began to know the unwieldy inheritance I'd come into—the ability to alter public space in ugly ways. It was clear that she thought herself the quarry of a mugger, a rapist, or worse. Suffering a bout of insomnia, however, I was stalking sleep, not defenseless wayfarers. As a softy who is scarcely able to take a knife to a raw chicken—let alone hold it to a person's throat—I was surprised, embarrassed, and dismayed all at once. Her flight made me feel like an accomplice in tyranny. It also made it clear that I was indistinguishable from the muggers who occasionally seeped into the area from the surrounding ghetto. That first encounter, and those that followed, signified that a vast, unnerving gulf lay between nighttime pedestrians—particularly women—and me. And I soon gathered that being perceived as dangerous is a hazard in itself. I only needed to turn a corner into a dicey situation, or crowd some frightened, armed person in a foyer somewhere, or make an errant move after being pulled over by a policeman. Where fear and weapons meet—and they often do in urban America—there is always the possibility of death.

In that first year, my first away from my hometown, I was to become thoroughly familiar with the language of fear. At dark, shadowy intersections in Chicago, I could cross in front of a car stopped at a traffic light and elicit the *thunk, thunk, thunk, thunk* of the driver—black, white, male, or female—hammering down the door locks. On less traveled streets after dark, I grew accustomed to but never comfortable with people who crossed to the other side of the street rather than pass me. Then there were the standard unpleasantries with police, doormen, bouncers,

cabdrivers, and others whose business is to screen out troublesome individuals *before* there is any nastiness.

I moved to New York nearly two years ago and I have remained an
avid night walker. In central Manhattan, the near-constant crowd cover
minimizes tense one-on-one street encounters. Elsewhere—visiting friends
in Soho,[1] where sidewalks are narrow and tightly spaced buildings shut
out the sky—things can get very taut indeed.

Black men have a firm place in New York mugging literature. Norman   5
Podhoretz[2] in his famed (or infamous) 1963 essay, "My Negro Problem—
And Ours," recalls growing up in terror of black males; they "were tougher
than we were, more ruthless," he writes—and as an adult on the Upper
West Side of Manhattan, he continues, he cannot constrain his nervousness
when he meets black men on certain streets. Similarly, a decade later, the
essayist and novelist Edward Hoagland extols a New York where once
"Negro bitterness bore down mainly on other Negroes." Where some see
mere panhandlers, Hoagland sees "a mugger who is clearly screwing up his
nerve to do more than just *ask* for money." But Hoagland has "the New
Yorker's quick-hunch posture for broken-field maneuvering," and the bad
guy swerves away.

I often witness that "hunch posture," from women after dark on the
warrenlike streets of Brooklyn where I live. They seem to set their faces
on neutral and, with their purse straps strung across their chests ban-
dolier style, they forge ahead as though bracing themselves against being
tackled. I understand, of course, that the danger they perceive is not a
hallucination. Women are particularly vulnerable to street violence, and
young black males are drastically overrepresented among the perpetrators
of that violence. Yet these truths are no solace against the kind of alienation that comes of being ever the suspect, against being set apart, a fearsome entity with whom pedestrians avoid making eye contact.

It is not altogether clear to me how I reached the ripe old age of
twenty-two without being conscious of the lethality nighttime pedestrians
attributed to me. Perhaps it was because in Chester, Pennsylvania, the
small, angry industrial town where I came of age in the 1960s, I was
scarcely noticeable against a backdrop of gang warfare, street knifings,
and murders. I grew up one of the good boys, had perhaps a half-dozen
fistfights. In retrospect, my shyness of combat has clear sources.

Many things go into the making of a young thug. One of those things
is the consummation of the male romance with the power to intimidate.
An infant discovers that random flailings send the baby bottle flying out
of the crib and crashing to the floor. Delighted, the joyful babe repeats
those motions again and again, seeking to duplicate the feat. Just so, I recall the points at which some of my boyhood friends were finally seduced
by the perception of themselves as tough guys. When a mark cowered and

---

[1]*Soho:* A district of lower Manhattan known for its art galleries.—EDS.
[2]*Podhoretz:* A well-known literary critic and editor of *Commentary* magazine.—EDS.

surrendered his money without resistance, myth and reality merged—and paid off. It is, after all, only manly to embrace the power to frighten and intimidate. We, as men, are not supposed to give an inch of our lane on the highway; we are to seize the fighter's edge in work and in play and even in love; we are to be valiant in the face of hostile forces.

Unfortunately, poor and powerless young men seem to take all this nonsense literally. As a boy, I saw countless tough guys locked away; I have since buried several, too. They were babies, really—a teenage cousin, a brother of twenty-two, a childhood friend in his midtwenties— all gone down in episodes of bravado played out in the streets. I came to doubt the virtues of intimidation early on. I chose, perhaps even unconsciously, to remain a shadow—timid, but a survivor.

The fearsomeness mistakenly attributed to me in public places often   10
has a perilous flavor. The most frightening of these confusions occurred in the late 1970s and early 1980s when I worked as a journalist in Chicago. One day, rushing into the office of a magazine I was writing for with a deadline story in hand, I was mistaken for a burglar. The office manager called security and, with an ad hoc posse, pursued me through the labyrinthine halls, nearly to my editor's door. I had no way of proving who I was. I could only move briskly toward the company of someone who knew me.

Another time I was on assignment for a local paper and killing time before an interview. I entered a jewelry store on the city's affluent Near North Side. The proprietor excused herself and returned with an enormous red Doberman pinscher straining at the end of a leash. She stood, the dog extended toward me, silent to my questions, her eyes bulging nearly out of her head. I took a cursory look around, nodded, and bade her good night. Relatively speaking, however, I never fared as badly as another black male journalist. He went to nearby Waukegan, Illinois, a couple of summers ago to work on a story about a murderer who was born there. Mistaking the reporter for the killer, police hauled him from his car at gunpoint and but for his press credentials would probably have tried to book him. Such episodes are not uncommon. Black men trade tales like this all the time.

In "My Negro Problem—And Ours," Podhoretz writes that the hatred he feels for blacks makes itself known to him through a variety of avenues—one being his discomfort with that "special brand of paranoid touchiness" to which he says blacks are prone. No doubt he is speaking here of black men. In time, I learned to smother the rage I felt at so often being taken for a criminal. Not to do so would surely have led to madness—via that special "paranoid touchiness" that so annoyed Podhoretz at the time he wrote the essay.

I began to take precautions to make myself less threatening. I move about with care, particularly late in the evening. I give a wide berth to nervous people on subway platforms during the wee hours, particularly when I have exchanged business clothes for jeans. If I happen to be entering a building behind some people who appear skittish, I may walk by, letting them clear the lobby before I return, so as not to seem to be following them. I have been calm and extremely congenial on those rare occasions when I've been pulled over by the police.

And on late-evening constitutionals along streets less traveled by, I employ what has proved to be an excellent tension-reducing measure: I whistle melodies from Beethoven and Vivaldi and the more popular classical composers. Even steely New Yorkers hunching toward nighttime destinations seem to relax, and occasionally they even join in the tune. Virtually everybody seems to sense that a mugger wouldn't be warbling bright, sunny selections from Vivaldi's *Four Seasons*. It is my equivalent of the cowbell that hikers wear when they know they are in bear country.

The Reader's Presence

1. Why does Staples use the word *victim* in his opening sentence? In what sense is the white woman a "victim"? How is he using the term? As readers, how might we interpret the opening sentence upon first reading? How does the meaning of the term change in rereading?

2. In rereading the essay, pay close attention to the way Staples handles points of view. When does he shift viewpoints or perspectives? What is his purpose in doing so? What are some of the connections Staples makes in this essay between the point of view one chooses and one's identity?

3. How does Staples behave on the street? How does he deal with the woman's anxiety? How has he "altered" his own public behavior? In what ways is his behavior on the street similar to his "behavior" as a writer? Compare this version of the essay to the alternate version that follows. What are the changes and how do those changes influence the essay's effect on the reader? How do you compare Staples's strategies—in both versions—to those of Zora Neale Hurston in "How It Feels to Be Colored Me" (page 166)?

THE WRITER AT WORK

Another Version of *Just Walk on By*

When he published his memoir, Parallel Time, *in 1994, Brent Staples decided to incorporate his earlier essay into the book. He also decided to revise it substantially. As you compare the two versions, note the passages Staples retained and those he chose not to carry forward into book form. Do you agree with his changes? Why in general do you think he made them? If you had been his editor, what revision strategy would you have suggested?*

At night, I walked to the lakefront whenever the weather permitted. I was headed home from the lake when I took my first victim. It was late fall, and the wind was cutting. I was wearing my navy pea jacket, the collar turned up, my hands snug in the pockets. Dead leaves scuttled in shoals along the streets. I turned out of Blackstone Avenue and headed west on 57th Street, and there she was, a few yards ahead of me, dressed in business clothes and carrying a briefcase. She looked back at me once, then again, and picked up her pace. She looked back again and started to run. I stopped where I was and looked up at the surrounding windows. What did this look like to people peeking out through their blinds? I was out walking. But what if someone had thought they'd seen something they hadn't and called the police. I held back the urge to run. Instead, I walked south to The Midway, plunged into its darkness, and remained on The Midway until I reached the foot of my street.

I'd been a fool. I'd been walking the streets grinning good evening at people who were frightened to death of me. I did violence to them by just being. How had I missed this? I kept walking at night, but from then on I paid attention.

I became expert in the language of fear. Couples locked arms or reached for each other's hand when they saw me. Some crossed to the other side of the street. People who were carrying on conversations went mute and stared straight ahead, as though avoiding my eyes would save them. This reminded me of an old wives' tale: that rabid dogs didn't bite if you avoided their eyes. The determination to avoid my eyes made me invisible to classmates and professors whom I passed on the street.

It occurred to me for the first time that I was big. I was 6 feet $1\frac{1}{2}$ inches tall, and my long hair made me look bigger. I weighed only 170 pounds. But the navy pea jacket that Brian had given me was broad at the shoulders, high at the collar, making me look bigger and more fearsome than I was.

I tried to be innocuous but didn't know how. The more I thought   5 about how I moved, the less my body belonged to me; I became a false character riding along inside it. I began to avoid people. I turned out of my way into side streets to spare them the sense that they were being stalked. I let them clear the lobbies of buildings before I entered, so they wouldn't feel trapped. Out of nervousness I began to whistle and discovered I was good at it. My whistle was pure and sweet — and also in tune. On the street at night I whistled popular tunes from the Beatles and Vivaldi's *Four Seasons*. The tension drained from people's bodies when they heard me. A few even smiled as they passed me in the dark.

Then I changed. I don't know why, but I remember when. I was walking west on 57th Street, after dark, coming home from the lake. The man and the woman walking toward me were laughing and talking but clammed up when they saw me. The man touched the woman's elbow, guiding her toward the curb. Normally I'd have given way and begun to whistle, but not this time. This time I veered toward them and aimed myself so that they'd have to part to avoid walking into me. The man stiffened, threw back his head and assumed the stare: eyes dead ahead, mouth open. His face took on a bluish hue under the sodium vapor streetlamps. I suppressed the urge to scream into his face. Instead I glided between them, my shoulder nearly brushing his. A few steps beyond them I stopped and howled with laughter. I called this game Scatter the Pigeons.

Fifty-seventh Street was too well lit for the game to be much fun; people didn't feel quite vulnerable enough. Along The Midway were heart-stopping strips of dark sidewalk, but these were so frightening that few people traveled them. The stretch of Blackstone between 57th and 55th provided better hunting. The block was long and lined with young trees that blocked out the streetlight and obscured the heads of people coming toward you.

One night I stooped beneath the branches and came up on the other side, just as a couple was stepping from their car into their town house. The woman pulled her purse close with one hand and reached for her husband with the other. The two of them stood frozen as I bore down on them. I felt a surge of power: these people were mine; I could do with them as I wished. If I'd been younger, with less to lose, I'd have robbed them, and it would have been easy. All I'd have to do was stand silently before them until they surrendered their money. I thundered, "Good evening!" into their bleached-out faces and cruised away laughing.

I held a special contempt for people who cowered in their cars as they waited for the light to change at 57th and Woodlawn. The intersection was always deserted at night, except for a car or two stuck at the red. *Thunk! Thunk! Thunk!* they hammered down the door locks when I came into view. Once I had hustled across the street, head down, trying to seem harmless. Now I turned brazenly into the headlights and laughed. Once across, I paced the sidewalk, glaring until the light changed. They'd made me terrifying. Now I'd show them how terrifying I could be.

Amy Tan

Mother Tongue

Amy Tan (b. 1952) was born in California several years after her parents im-
migrated to the United States from China. She started writing as a child and won
a writing contest at age eight. As an adult, Tan made her living as a freelance
business writer for many years. In 1989 she published a best-selling novel, The
Joy Luck Club, *followed by the novel* The Kitchen God's Wife *(1991); the chil-*
dren's books The Moon Lady *(1992) and* The Chinese Siamese Cat *(1994); and*
the novels The Hundred Secret Senses *(1995) and* The Bonesetter's Daughter
(2001). Her latest book, The Opposite of Fate *(2003), is a collection of autobio-*
graphical essays. "Mother Tongue" originally appeared in the Threepenny Review
in 1990.

Commenting on the art of writing, Tan has said, "I had a very unliterary
background, but I had a determination to write for myself." She believes that the
goal of every serious writer of literature is "to try to find your voice and your art,
because it comes from your own experiences, your own pain."

I am not a scholar of English or literature. I cannot give you much
more than personal opinions on the English language and its variations in
this country or others.

I am a writer. And by that definition, I am someone who has always
loved language. I am fascinated by language in daily life. I spend a great
deal of my time thinking about the power of language—the way it can
evoke an emotion, a visual image, a complex idea, or a simple truth. Language is the tool of my trade. And I use them all—all the Englishes I grew
up with.

Recently, I was made keenly aware of the different Englishes I do
use. I was giving a talk to a large group of people, the same talk I had
already given to half a dozen other groups. The nature of the talk was
about my writing, my life, and my book, *The Joy Luck Club*. The talk
was going along well enough, until I remembered one major difference
that made the whole talk sound wrong. My mother was in the room.
And it was perhaps the first time she had heard me give a lengthy
speech, using the kind of English I have never used with her. I was saying things like "The intersection of memory upon imagination" and
"There is an aspect of my fiction that relates to thus-and-thus"—a
speech filled with carefully wrought grammatical phrases, burdened, it
suddenly seemed to me, with nominalized forms, past perfect tenses,
conditional phrases, all the forms of standard English that I had learned
in school and through books, the forms of English I did not use at home
with my mother.

Just last week, I was walking down the street with my mother, and I again found myself conscious of the English I was using, the English I do use with her. We were talking about the price of new and used furniture and I heard myself saying this: "Not waste money that way." My husband was with us as well, and he didn't notice any switch in my English. And then I realized why. It's because over the twenty years we've been together I've often used that same kind of English with him, and sometimes he even uses it with me. It has become our language of intimacy, a different sort of English that relates to family talk, the language I grew up with.

So you'll have some idea of what this family talk I heard sounds like, 5 I'll quote what my mother said during a recent conversation which I videotaped and then transcribed. During this conversation, my mother was talking about a political gangster in Shanghai who had the same last name as her family's, Du, and how the gangster in his early years wanted to be adopted by her family, which was rich by comparison. Later, the gangster became more powerful, far richer than my mother's family, and one day showed up at my mother's wedding to pay his respects. Here's what she said in part:

"Du Yusong having business like fruit stand. Like off the street kind. He is Du like Du Zong — but not Tsung-ming Island people. The local people call putong, the river east side, he belong to that side local people. That man want to ask Du Zong father take him in like become own family. Du Zong father wasn't look down on him, but didn't take seriously, until that man big like become a mafia. Now important person, very hard to inviting him. Chinese way, came only to show respect, don't stay for dinner. Respect for making big celebration, he shows up. Mean gives lots of respect. Chinese custom. Chinese social life that way. If too important won't have to stay too long. He come to my wedding. I didn't see, I heard it. I gone to boy's side, they have YMCA dinner. Chinese age I was nineteen."

You should know that my mother's expressive command of English belies how much she actually understands. She reads the *Forbes* report, listens to *Wall Street Week*, converses daily with her stockbroker, reads all of Shirley MacLaine's books with ease — all kinds of things I can't begin to understand. Yet some of my friends tell me they understand 50 percent of what my mother says. Some say they understand 80 to 90 percent. Some say they understand none of it, as if she were speaking pure Chinese. But to me, my mother's English is perfectly clear, perfectly natural. It's my mother tongue. Her language, as I hear it, is vivid, direct, full of observation and imagery. That was the language that helped shape the way I saw things, expressed things, made sense of the world.

Lately, I've been giving more thought to the kind of English my mother speaks. Like others, I have described it to people as "broken" or "fractured" English. But I wince when I say that. It has always bothered me that I can think of no other way to describe it other than "broken," as if it were damaged and needed to be fixed, as if it lacked a certain wholeness and soundness. I've heard other terms used, "limited English," for example. But they seem just as bad, as if everything is limited, including people's perceptions of the limited English speaker.

I know this for a fact, because when I was growing up, my mother's "limited" English limited *my* perception of her. I was ashamed of her English. I believed that her English reflected the quality of what she had to say. That is, because she expressed them imperfectly her thoughts were imperfect. And I had plenty of empirical evidence to support me: the fact that people in department stores, at banks, and at restaurants did not take her seriously, did not give her good service, pretended not to understand her, or even acted as if they did not hear her.

My mother has long realized the limitations of her English as well.   10
When I was fifteen, she used to have me call people on the phone to pretend I was she. In this guise, I was forced to ask for information or even to complain and yell at people who had been rude to her. One time it was a call to her stockbroker in New York. She had cashed out her small portfolio and it just so happened we were going to go to New York the next week, our very first trip outside California. I had to get on the phone and say in an adolescent voice that was not very convincing, "This is Mrs. Tan."

And my mother was standing in the back whispering loudly, "Why he don't send me check, already two weeks late. So mad he lie to me, losing me money."

And then I said in perfect English, "Yes, I'm getting rather concerned. You had agreed to send the check two weeks ago, but it hasn't arrived."

Then she began to talk more loudly. "What he want, I come to New York tell him front of his boss, you cheating me?" And I was trying to calm her down, make her be quiet, while telling the stockbroker, "I can't tolerate any more excuses. If I don't receive the check immediately, I am going to have to speak to your manager when I'm in New York next week." And sure enough, the following week there we were in front of this astonished stockbroker, and I was sitting there red-faced and quiet, and my mother, the real Mrs. Tan, was shouting at his boss in her impeccable broken English.

We used a similar routine just five days ago, for a situation that was far less humorous. My mother had gone to the hospital for an appointment, to find out about a benign brain tumor a CAT scan had revealed a month ago. She said she had spoken very good English, her best English, no mistakes. Still, she said, the hospital did not apologize when they said they had lost the CAT scan and she had come for nothing. She said they did not seem to have any sympathy when she told them she was anxious to know the exact diagnosis, since her husband and son had both died of brain tumors. She

said they would not give her any more information until the next time and
she would have to make another appointment for that. So she said she
would not leave until the doctor called her daughter. She wouldn't budge.
And when the doctor finally called her daughter, me, who spoke in perfect
English—lo and behold—we had assurances the CAT scan would be
found, promises that a conference call on Monday would be held, and
apologies for any suffering my mother had gone through for a most regrettable mistake.

I think my mother's English almost had an effect on limiting my possi-   15
bilities in life as well. Sociologists and linguists probably will tell you that
a person's developing language skills are more influenced by peers. But I
do think that the language spoken in the family, especially in immigrant
families which are more insular, plays a large role in shaping the language
of the child. And I believe that it affected my results on achievement
tests, IQ tests, and the SAT. While my English skills were never judged as
poor, compared to math, English could not be considered my strong
suit. In grade school I did moderately well, getting perhaps B's, sometimes
B-pluses, in English and scoring perhaps in the sixtieth or seventieth percentile on achievement tests. But those scores were not good enough to
override the opinion that my true abilities lay in math and science, because
in those areas I achieved A's and scored in the ninetieth percentile or
higher.

This was understandable. Math is precise; there is only one correct
answer. Whereas, for me at least, the answers on English tests were always
a judgment call, a matter of opinion and personal experience. Those tests
were constructed around items like fill-in-the-blank sentence completion,
such as "Even though Tom was _____, Mary thought he was _____." And
the correct answer always seemed to be the most bland combinations of
thoughts, for example, "Even though Tom was shy, Mary thought he was
charming," with the grammatical structure "even though" limiting the
correct answer to some sort of semantic opposites, so you wouldn't get
answers like, "Even though Tom was foolish, Mary thought he was ridiculous." Well, according to my mother, there were very few limitations as
to what Tom could have been and what Mary might have thought of
him. So I never did well on tests like that.

The same was true with word analogies, pairs of words in which you
were supposed to find some sort of logical, semantic relationship—for
example, "*Sunset* is to *nightfall* as _____ is to _____." And here you
would be presented with a list of four possible pairs, one of which
showed the same kind of relationship: *red* is to *stoplight*, *bus* is to *arrival*,
chills is to *fever*, *yawn* is to *boring*. Well, I could never think that way. I
knew what the tests were asking, but I could not block out of my mind
the images already created by the first pair, "*sunset* is to *nightfall*"—and
I would see a burst of colors against a darkening sky, the moon rising, the
lowering of a curtain of stars. And all the other pairs of words—red, bus,

stoplight, boring—just threw up a mass of confusing images, making it impossible for me to sort out something as logical as saying: "A sunset precedes nightfall" is the same as "a chill precedes a fever." The only way I would have gotten that answer right would have been to imagine an associative situation, for example, my being disobedient and staying out past sunset, catching a chill at night, which turns into feverish pneumonia as punishment, which indeed did happen to me.

I have been thinking about all this lately, about my mother's English, about achievement tests. Because lately I've been asked, as a writer, why there are not more Asian Americans represented in American literature. Why are there few Asian Americans enrolled in creative writing programs? Why do so many Chinese students go into engineering? Well, these are broad sociological questions I can't begin to answer. But I have noticed in surveys—in fact, just last week—that Asian students, as a whole, always do significantly better on math achievement tests than in English. And this makes me think that there are other Asian-American students whose English spoken in the home might also be described as "broken" or "limited." And perhaps they also have teachers who are steering them away from writing and into math and science, which is what happened to me.

Fortunately, I happen to be rebellious in nature and enjoy the challenge of disproving assumptions made about me. I became an English major my first year in college, after being enrolled as pre-med. I started writing nonfiction as a freelancer the week after I was told by my former boss that writing was my worst skill and I should hone my talents toward account management.

But it wasn't until 1985 that I finally began to write fiction. And at   20
first I wrote using what I thought to be wittily crafted sentences, sentences that would finally prove I had mastery over the English language. Here's an example from the first draft of a story that later made its way into *The Joy Luck Club*, but without this line: "That was my mental quandary in its nascent state." A terrible line, which I can barely pronounce.

Fortunately, for reasons I won't get into today, I later decided I should envision a reader for the stories I would write. And the reader I decided upon was my mother, because these were stories about mothers. So with this reader in mind—and in fact she did read my early drafts—I began to write stories using all the Englishes I grew up with: the English I spoke to my mother, which for lack of a better term might be described as "simple"; the English she used with me, which for lack of a better term might be described as "broken"; my translation of her Chinese, which could certainly be described as "watered down"; and what I imagined to be her translation of her Chinese if she could speak in perfect English, her internal language, and for that I sought to preserve the essence, but neither an English nor a Chinese structure. I wanted to capture what language ability tests can never reveal: her intent, her passion, her imagery, the rhythms of her speech, and the nature of her thoughts.

Apart from what any critic had to say about my writing, I knew I had succeeded where it counted when my mother finished reading my book and gave me her verdict: "So easy to read."

The Reader's Presence

1. In her second paragraph, Tan mentions "all the Englishes" she grew up with. What were those "Englishes"? What is odd about the term? How does the oddity of the word reinforce the point of her essay?

2. In paragraph 20, Tan gives an example of a sentence that she once thought showed her "mastery" of English. What does she now find wrong with that sentence? What do you think of it? What would her mother have thought of it? What sort of reader does that sentence anticipate?

3. What exactly is Tan's "mother tongue"? What does the phrase usually mean? Would you call her mother's English "broken English"? What does that phrase imply? Why does Tan write with her mother in mind as her ideal reader? How does Tan's determination to keep her mother linked to her writing compare with Richard Rodriguez's profound sense of having irrecoverably lost a connection with his parents in "Aria: A Memoir of a Bilingual Childhood" (page 239)? Does Rodriguez's distinction between private and public languages hold true for Tan?

Garry Trudeau
My Inner Shrimp

Garry Trudeau (b. 1948), creator of the popular comic strip "Doonesbury," has also contributed articles to such publications as Harper's, Rolling Stone, *the* New Republic, *the* New Yorker, New York, *and the* Washington Post. *He received bachelor's and master's degrees from Yale University. Trudeau won a Pulitzer Prize in 1975 and in 1994 received the award for best comic strip from the National Cartoonists Society. For five years he was an occasional columnist for the* New York Times *opinion and editorial page. Currently, he is a contributing essayist for* Time *magazine. He lives in New York City with his wife, Jane Pauley, and their three children. This essay originally appeared in the* New York Times Magazine *for March 31, 1996.*

For the rest of my days, I shall be a recovering short person. Even from my lofty perch of something over six feet (as if I don't know within a micron), I have the soul of a shrimp. I feel the pain of the diminutive, irrespective of whether they feel it themselves, because my visit to the planet of the teenage midgets was harrowing, humiliating, and extended. I even perceive my last-minute escape to have been flukish, somehow unearned — as if the Commissioner of Growth Spurts had been an old classmate of my father.

My most recent reminder of all this came the afternoon I went hunting for a new office. I had noticed a building under construction in my neighborhood — a brick warren of duplexes, with wide, westerly-facing windows, promising ideal light for a working studio. When I was ushered into the model unit, my pulse quickened: The soaring, twenty-two-foot living room walls were gloriously aglow with the remains of the day. I bonded immediately.

Almost as an afterthought, I ascended the staircase to inspect the loft, ducking as I entered the bedroom. To my great surprise, I stayed ducked: The room was a little more than six feet in height. While my head technically cleared the ceiling, the effect was excruciatingly oppressive. This certainly wasn't a space I wanted to spend any time in, much less take out a mortgage on.

Puzzled, I wandered down to the sales office and asked if there were any other units to look at. No, replied a resolutely unpleasant receptionist, it was the last one. Besides, they were all exactly alike.

"Are you aware of how low the bedroom ceilings are?" I asked.   5

She shot me an evil look. "Of course we are," she snapped. "There were some problems with the building codes. The architect knows all about the ceilings.

"He's not an idiot, you know," she added, perfectly anticipating my next question.

She abruptly turned away, but it was too late. She'd just confirmed that a major New York developer, working with a fully licensed architect, had knowingly created an entire twelve-story apartment building virtually uninhabitable by anyone of even average height. It was an exclusive highrise for shorties.

Once I knew that, of course, I couldn't stay away. For days thereafter, as I walked to work, some perverse, unreasoning force would draw me back to the building. But it wasn't just the absurdity, the stone silliness of its design that had me in its grip; it was something far more compelling.

Like some haunted veteran come again to an ancient battlefield, I was revisiting my perilous past.

When I was fourteen, I was the third-smallest in a high school class   10
of one hundred boys, routinely mistaken for a sixth grader. My first
week of school, I was drafted into a contingent of students ignominiously dubbed the "Midgets," so grouped by taller boys presumably so
they could taunt us with more perfect efficiency. Inexplicably, some of
my fellow Midgets refused to be diminished by the experience, but I retreated into self-pity. I sent away for a book on how to grow tall, and
committed to memory its tips on overcoming one's genetic destiny — or
at least making the most of a regrettable situation. The book cited historical figures who had gone the latter route — Alexander the Great,
Caesar, Napoleon (the mind involuntarily added Hitler). Strategies for
stretching the limbs were suggested — hanging from door frames, sleeping on your back, doing assorted floor exercises — all of which I incorporated into my daily routine (get up, brush teeth, hang from door
frame). I also learned the importance of meeting girls early in the day,
when, the book assured me, my rested spine rendered me perceptibly
taller.

For six years, my condition persisted; I grew, but at nowhere near the
rate of my peers. I perceived other problems as ancillary, and loaded up
the stature issue with freight shipped in daily from every corner of my
life. Lack of athletic success, all absence of a social life, the inevitable run-ins with bullies — all could be attributed to the missing inches. The night I
found myself sobbing in my father's arms was the low point; we both
knew it was one problem he couldn't fix.

Of course what we couldn't have known was that he and my mother
already had. They had given me a delayed developmental timetable. In
my seventeenth year, I miraculously shot up six inches, just in time for
graduation and a fresh start. I was, in the space of a few months, reborn —
and I made the most of it. Which is to say that thereafter, all of life's disappointments, reversals, and calamities still arrived on schedule — but
blissfully free of subtext.

Once you stop being the butt, of course, any problem recedes, if only
to give way to a new one. And yet the impact of being literally looked
down on, of being *made* to feel small, is forever. It teaches you how to
stretch, how to survive the scorn of others for things that are beyond your
control. Not growing forces you to grow up fast.

Sometimes I think I'd like to return to a high-school reunion to surprise my classmates. Not that they didn't know me when I finally started
catching up. They did, but I doubt they'd remember. Adolescent hierarchies have a way of enduring; I'm sure I am still recalled as the Midget I
myself have never really left behind.

Of course, if I'm going to show up, it'll have to be soon. I'm starting   15
to shrink.

The Reader's Presence

1. It is said that "beauty is in the eye of the beholder"; Trudeau's testimony challenges this old saw. Does Trudeau's piece convince you that imagined shortcomings are nearly as ruinous as those apparent to others? Why or why not?

2. Locate examples of exaggeration or hyperbole in the essay. Does this descriptive technique support or weaken Trudeau's case, and why? What phrase does Trudeau's title intentionally echo? Why?

3. "Not growing forces you to grow up fast" (paragraph 13), Trudeau writes near the end of the essay—a general truth that can apply to any reader, tall or short. Compare this essay to Nancy Mairs's "On Being a Cripple" (page 183). Their respective subjects differ, of course, but both writers strive to make their essays speak to a wide audience. How do they do this?

John Updike

At War with My Skin

Over the course of his career as a novelist, short story writer, poet, essayist, and dramatist, John Updike (b. 1932) has been awarded every major American literary award; in 1998 he was awarded the National Book Foundation Medal for Distinguished Contribution to American Letters. For one novel alone, Rabbit Is Rich *(1981), he won the Pulitzer Prize, the American Book Award, and the National Book Critics Circle Award. Among more than a dozen published novels, his recurring themes include religion, sexuality, and middle-class experience. In his essays, Updike's concerns range widely over literary and cultural issues. One volume of his collected essays,* Hugging the Shore: Essays and Criticism *(1983), was also awarded a National Book Critics Circle Award. His most recent publications include* More Matter: Essays and Criticism *(1999),* Licks of Love: Short Stories and a Sequel *(2000), and* Gertrude and Claudius *(2000). "At War with My Skin," first published in 1985, appears in Updike's 1989 book* Self-Consciousness: Memoirs.

Updike has said, "I began my writing career with a fairly distinct set of principles which, one by one, have eroded into something approaching shapelessness." He does maintain one principle, however: "You should attempt to write things that you would like to read." Writing, he continues, is a process of rendering "your vision of reality into the written symbol. Out of this, living art will come."

My mother tells me that up to the age of six I had no psoriasis; it came on strong after an attack of measles in February of 1938, when I was in kindergarten. The disease — "disease" seems strong, for a condition that is not contagious, painful, or debilitating; yet psoriasis has the volatility of a disease, the sense of another presence coöccupying your body and singling you out from the happy herds of healthy, normal mankind — first attached itself to my memory while I was lying on the upstairs side porch of the Shillington house, amid the sickly, oleaginous smell of Siroil, on fuzzy sun-warmed towels, with my mother, sunbathing. We are both, in my mental picture, not quite naked. She would have been still a youngish woman at the time, and I remember being embarrassed by something, but whether by our being together this way or simply by my skin is not clear in this mottled recollection. She, too, had psoriasis; I had inherited it from her. Siroil and sunshine and not eating chocolate were our only weapons in our war against the red spots, ripening into silvery scabs, that invaded our skins in the winter. Siroil was the foremost medication available in the thirties and forties: a bottled preparation the consistency of pus, tar its effective ingredient and its drippy texture and bilious color and insinuating odor deeply involved with my embarrassment. Yet, as with our own private odors, those of sweat and earwax and even of excrement, there was also something satisfying about this scent, an intimate rankness that told me who I was.

One dabbed Siroil on; it softened the silvery scales but otherwise did very little good. Nor did abstaining from chocolate and "greasy" foods like potato chips and french fries do much visible good, though as with many palliations there was no knowing how much worse things would be otherwise. Only the sun, that living god, had real power over psoriasis; a few weeks of summer erased the spots from all of my responsive young skin that could be exposed — chest, legs, and face. Inspecting the many photographs taken of me as a child, including a set of me cavorting in a bathing suit in the back yard, I can see no trace of psoriasis. And I remember, when it rained, going out in a bathing suit with friends to play in the downpour and its warm puddles. Yet I didn't learn to swim, because of my appearance; I stayed away from "the Porgy," the dammed pond beyond the poorhouse, and from the public pool in West Reading, and the indoor pool at the Reading "Y," where my father in winter coached the high-school swimming team. To the travails of my freshman year at Harvard was added the humiliation of learning at last to swim, with my spots and my hydrophobia, in a class of quite naked boys. Recently the chunky, mild-spoken man who taught that class over thirty years ago came up to me at a party and pleasantly identified himself; I could scarcely manage politeness, his face so sharply brought back that old suppressed rich mix of chlorine and fear and brave gasping and naked, naked shame.

Psoriasis is a metabolic disorder that causes the epidermis, which normally replaces itself at a gradual, unnoticeable rate, to speed up the process markedly and to produce excess skin cells. The tiny mechanisms gone awry are beyond the precise reach of internally taken medicine; a derivative of vitamin A, etretinate, and an anticancer drug, methotrexate, are effective but at the price of potential side-effects to the kidneys and liver more serious than the disease, which is, after all, superficial—too much, simply, of a good thing (skin). In the 1970s, dermatologists at Massachusetts General Hospital developed PUVA, a controlled light treatment: fluorescent tubes radiate long-wave ultraviolet (UV-A) onto skin sensitized by an internal dose of methoxsalen, a psoralen (the "P" of the acronym) derived from a weed, *Ammi majus*, which grows along the river Nile and whose sun-sensitizing qualities were known to the ancient Egyptians. So a curious primitivity, a savor of folk-medicine, clings to this new cure, a refinement of the old sun-cure. It is pleasant, once or twice a week, to stand nearly naked in a kind of glowing telephone booth. It was pleasant to lie on the upstairs porch, hidden behind the jigsawed wooden balusters, and to feel the slanting sun warm the fuzzy towel while an occasional car or pack of children crackled by on Shilling Alley. One became conscious, lying there trying to read, of bird song, of distant shouts, of a whistle calling men back to work at the local textile factory, which was rather enchantingly called the Fairy Silk Mill.

My condition forged a hidden link with things elemental—with the seasons, with the sun, and with my mother. A tendency to psoriasis is inherited—only through the maternal line, it used to be thought. My mother's mother had had it, I was told, though I never noticed anything wrong with my grandmother's skin—just her false teeth, which slipped down while she was napping in her rocking chair. Far in the future, I would marry a young brunette with calm, smooth, deep-tanning skin and was to imagine that thus I had put an end to at least my particular avenue of genetic error. Alas, our fourth child inherited my complexion and, lightly, in her late teens, psoriasis. The disease favors the fair, the dry-skinned, the pallid progeny of cloud-swaddled Holland and Ireland and Germany. Though my father was not red-haired, his brother Arch was, and when I grew a beard, as my contribution to the revolutionary sixties, it came in reddish. And when I shaved it off, red spots had thrived underneath.

Psoriasis keeps you thinking. Strategies of concealment ramify, and   5
self-examination is endless. You are forced to the mirror, again and again; psoriasis compels narcissism, if we can suppose a Narcissus who did not like what he saw. In certain lights, your face looks passable; in slightly different other lights, not. Shaving mirrors and rearview mirrors in automobiles are merciless, whereas the smoky mirrors in airplane bathrooms are especially flattering and soothing: one's face looks as tawny as a movie star's. Flying back from the Caribbean, I used to admire my improved looks; years went by before I noticed that I looked equally good, in the

lavatory glow, on the flight down. I cannot pass a reflecting surface on the street without glancing in, in hopes that I have somehow changed. Nature and the self, the great moieties of earthly existence, are each cloven in two by a fascinated ambivalence. One hates one's abnormal, erupting skin but is led into a brooding, solicitous attention toward it. One hates the Nature that has imposed this affliction, but only this same Nature can be appealed to for erasure, for cure. Only Nature can forgive psoriasis; the sufferer in his self-contempt does not grant to other people this power. Perhaps the unease of my first memory has to do with my mother's presence; I wished to be alone with the sun, the air, the distant noises, the possibility of my hideousness eventually going away.

I recall remarkably few occasions when I was challenged, in the brute world of childhood, about my skin. In the second grade, perhaps it was, the teacher, standing above our obedient rows, rummaged in my hair and said aloud, "Good heavens, child, what's this on your head?" I can hear these words breaking into the air above me and see my mother's face when, that afternoon, I recounted them to her, probably with tears; her eyes took on a fanatic glare and the next morning, like an arrow that had fixed her course, she went to the school to "have it out" with the teacher who had heightened her defective cub's embarrassment. Our doctor, Doc Rothermel in his big grit-and-stucco house, also, eerily, had psoriasis; far from offering a cure out of his magical expanding black bag, he offered us the melancholy confession that he had felt prevented, by his scaly wrists, from rolling back his sleeves and becoming—his true ambition—a surgeon. " 'Physician, heal thyself,' they'd say to me," he said. I don't, really, know how bad I looked, or how many conferences among adults secured a tactful silence from above. My peers (again, as I remember, which is a choosing to remember) either didn't notice anything terrible about my skin or else neglected to comment upon it. Children are frank, as we know from the taunts and nicknames they fling at one another; but also they all feel imperfect and vulnerable, which works for mutual forbearance. In high school, my gym class knew how I looked in the locker room and shower. Once, a boy from a higher class came up to me with an exclamation of cheerful disgust, touched my arm, and asked if I had syphilis. But my classmates held their tongues, and expressed no fear of contagion.

I participated, in gym shorts and tank top, in the annual gym exhibitions. Indeed, as the tallest of the lighter boys, I stood shakily on top of "Fats" Sterner's shoulders to make the apex of our gymnastics pyramid. I braved it through, inwardly cringing, prisoner and victim of my skin. It was not really *me*, was the explanation I could not shout out. Like an obese person (like good-natured Fats so sturdy under me, a human rock, his hands gripping my ankles while I fought the sensation that I was about to lurch forward and fly out over the heads of our assembled audience of admiring parents), and unlike someone with a withered arm, say, or a port-wine stain splashed across his neck and cheek, I could change—every summer I *did* become normal and, as it were, beautiful. An overvaluation of the normal went with my ailment, a certain idealization of everyone who was not, as I felt myself to be, a monster.

Because it came and went, I never settled in with my psoriasis, never adopted it as, inevitably, part of myself. It was temporary and in a way illusionary, like my being poor, and obscure, and (once we moved to the farm) lonely—a spell that had been put upon me, a test, as in a fairy story or one of those divinely imposed ordeals in the Bible. "Where's my public?" I used to ask my mother, coming back from the empty mailbox, by this joke conjuring a public out of the future.

My last public demonstration of my monstrosity, in a formal social setting, occurred the day of my examination for the draft, in the summer of 1955. A year in England, with no sun, had left my skin in bad shape, and the examining doctor took one glance up from his plywood table and wrote on my form, "4-F: Psoriasis." At this point in my young life I had a job offer in New York, a wife, and an infant daughter, and was far from keen to devote two years to the national defense; I had never gone to summer camp, and pictured the Army as a big summer camp, with extra-rough bullies and extra-cold showers in the morning. My trepidation should be distinguished from political feelings; I had absolutely no doubts about my country's need, from time to time, to fight, and its right to call me to service. So suddenly and emphatically excused, I felt relieved, guilty, and above all ashamed at being singled out; the naked American men around me had looked at my skin with surprise and now were impressed by the exemption it had won me. I had not foreseen this result; psoriasis would handicap no killing skills and, had I reported in another season, might have been nearly invisible. My wife, when I got back to my parents' house with my news, was naturally delighted; but my mother, always independent in her moods, seemed saddened, as if she had laid an egg which, when candled by the government, had been pronounced rotten.

It pains me to write these pages. They are humiliating—"scab-   10
picking," to use a term sometimes leveled at modern autobiographical writers. I have written about psoriasis only twice before: I gave it to Peter Caldwell in *The Centaur*[1] and to an anonymous, bumptious ceramicist in the short story "From the Journal of a Leper." I expose it this third time only in order to proclaim the consoling possibility that whenever in my timid life I have shown some courage and originality it has been because of my skin. Because of my skin, I counted myself out of any of those jobs—salesman, teacher, financier, movie star—that demand being presentable. What did that leave? Becoming a craftsman of some sort, closeted and unseen—perhaps a cartoonist or a writer, a worker in ink who can hide himself and send out a surrogate presence, a signature that multiplies even while it conceals. Why did I marry so young? Because, having once

---

[1]*The Centaur:* Updike's 1963 novel. —Eds.

found a comely female who forgave me my skin, I dared not risk losing her and trying to find another. Why did I have children so young? Because I wanted to surround myself with people who did not have psoriasis. Why, in 1957, did I leave New York and my nice employment there? Because my skin was bad in the urban shadows, and nothing, not even screwing a sunlamp bulb into the socket above my bathroom mirror, helped. Why did I move, with my family, all the way to Ipswich, Massachusetts? Because this ancient Puritan town happened to have one of the great beaches of the Northeast, in whose dunes I could, like a sin-soaked anchorite of old repairing to the desert, bake and cure myself.

The Reader's Presence

1. Examine the ways that Updike characterizes psoriasis in the essay. What language does he use to describe his condition and his emotional state dealing with it? What does his diction say about the way he relates to his disease?

2. In what ways does psoriasis single Updike out "from the happy herds of healthy, normal mankind" (paragraph 1)? What examples does he give of times when his condition alienated him from others? What was the result of this alienation?

3. Updike uses the word "scabpicking" to describe the humiliating nature of his reflection on psoriasis. He defines "scabpicking" as "a term sometimes leveled at modern autobiographical writers" (paragraph 10). Does Updike accept the criticism inherent in this term? What does he claim is his larger purpose for writing about his condition? Do you think the term "scabpicking" applies to David Mamet's "The Rake" (page 209)? How does Mamet's work serve a larger purpose that could counter this criticism?

Alice Walker

Beauty: When the Other Dancer Is the Self

Alice Walker (b. 1944) was awarded the Pulitzer Prize and the American Book Award for her second novel, The Color Purple *(1982), which was made into a popular film. This novel helped establish Walker's reputation as one of America's most important contemporary writers. In both her fiction and nonfiction, she shares her compassion for the black women of America whose lives have long been largely excluded from or distorted in literary representation. Walker is also the author of other novels, short stories, several volumes of poetry, a children's biography of Langston Hughes, essays, and criticism. Her most recent books are* By the Light of My Father's Smile *(1998),* The Way Forward Is with a Broken Heart *(2000),* Now Is the Time to Open Your Heart *(2004), and a collection of poetry,* Absolute Trust in the Goodness of the Earth *(2003). "Beauty: When the Other Dancer Is the Self" comes from her 1983 collection,* In Search of Our Mothers' Gardens.*

When asked by an interviewer about her writing habits, Walker replied, "I think it was Hemingway who said that each day that you write, you don't try to write to the absolute end of what you feel and think. You leave a little, you know, so that the next day you have something else to go on. And I would take it a little further — the thing is being able to create out of fullness, and that in order to create out of fullness, you have to let it well up. . . . In creation you must always leave something. You have to go to the bottom of the well with creativity. You have to give it everything you've got, but at the same time you have to leave that last drop for the creative spirit or for the earth itself."

It is a bright summer day in 1947. My father, a fat, funny man with beautiful eyes and a subversive wit, is trying to decide which of his eight children he will take with him to the county fair. My mother, of course, will not go. She is knocked out from getting most of us ready: I hold my neck stiff against the pressure of her knuckles as she hastily completes the braiding and the beribboning of my hair.

My father is the driver for the rich old white lady up the road. Her name is Miss Mey. She owns all the land for miles around, as well as the house in which we live. All I remember about her is that she once offered to pay my mother thirty-five cents for cleaning her house, raking up piles of her magnolia leaves, and washing her family's clothes, and that my mother — she of no money, eight children, and a chronic earache — refused it. But I do not think of this in 1947. I am two-and-a-half years old. I want to go everywhere my daddy goes. I am excited at the prospect of riding in a car. Someone has told me fairs are fun. That there is room in the car for only three of us doesn't faze me at all. Whirling happily in my starchy frock, showing off my biscuit-polished patent-leather shoes and lavender socks, tossing my head in a way that makes my ribbons bounce, I stand, hands on hips, before my father. "Take me, Daddy," I say with assurance; "I'm the prettiest!"

Later, it does not surprise me to find myself in Miss Mey's shiny black car, sharing the back seat with the other lucky ones. Does not surprise me that I thoroughly enjoy the fair. At home that night I tell the unlucky ones all I can remember about the merry-go-round, the man who eats live chickens, and the teddy bears, until they say: that's enough, baby Alice. Shut up now, and go to sleep.

It is Easter Sunday, 1950. I am dressed in a green, flocked, scalloped-hem dress (handmade by my adoring sister, Ruth) that has its own smooth satin petticoat and tiny hot-pink roses tucked into each scallop. My shoes, new T-strap patent leather, again highly biscuit-polished. I am six years old and have learned one of the longest Easter speeches to be heard that day, totally unlike the speech I said when I was two: "Easter lilies / pure and white / blossom in / the morning light." When I rise to give my speech I do so on a great wave of love and pride and expectation. People in the church stop rustling their new crinolines. They seem to hold their breath. I can tell they admire my dress, but it is my spirit, bordering on sassiness (womanishness), they secretly applaud.

"That girl's a little *mess*," they whisper to each other, pleased.   5

Naturally I say my speech without stammer or pause, unlike those who stutter, stammer, or, worst of all, forget. This is before the word "beautiful" exists in people's vocabulary, but "Oh, isn't she the *cutest* thing!" frequently floats my way. "And got so much sense!" they gratefully add . . . for which thoughtful addition I thank them to this day.

It was great fun being cute. But then, one day, it ended.

I am eight years old and a tomboy. I have a cowboy hat, cowboy boots, checkered shirt and pants, all red. My playmates are my brothers, two and four years older than I. Their colors are black and green, the only difference in the way we are dressed. On Saturday nights we all go to the picture show, even my mother; Westerns are her favorite kind of movie. Back home, "on the ranch," we pretend we are Tom Mix, Hopalong Cassidy, Lash LaRue (we've even named one of our dogs Lash LaRue); we chase each other for hours rustling cattle, being outlaws, delivering damsels from distress. Then my parents decide to buy my brothers guns. These are not "real" guns. They shoot BBs, copper pellets my brothers say will kill birds. Because I am a girl, I do not get a gun. Instantly I am relegated to the position of Indian. Now there appears a

great distance between us. They shoot and shoot at everything with their
new guns. I try to keep up with my bow and arrows.

One day while I am standing on top of our makeshift "garage"—
pieces of tin nailed across some poles—holding my bow and arrow and
looking out toward the fields, I feel an incredible blow in my right eye. I
look down just in time to see my brother lower his gun.

Both brothers rush to my side. My eye stings, and I cover it with my   10
hand. "If you tell," they say, "we will get a whipping. You don't want that
to happen, do you?" I do not. "Here is a piece of wire," says the older
brother, picking it up from the roof; "say you stepped on one end of it
and the other flew up and hit you." The pain is beginning to start. "Yes,"
I say. "Yes, I will say that is what happened." If I do not say this is what
happened, I know my brothers will find ways to make me wish I had. But
now I will say anything that gets me to my mother.

Confronted by our parents we stick to the lie agreed upon. They
place me on a bench on the porch and I close my left eye while they examine the right. There is a tree growing from underneath the porch that
climbs past the railing to the roof. It is the last thing my right eye sees. I
watch as its trunk, its branches, and then its leaves are blotted out by the
rising blood.

I am in shock. First there is intense fever, which my father tries to
break using lily leaves bound around my head. Then there are chills: my
mother tries to get me to eat soup. Eventually, I do not know how, my
parents learn what has happened. A week after the "accident" they take
me to see a doctor. "Why did you wait so long to come?" he asks, looking into my eye and shaking his head. "Eyes are sympathetic," he says.
"If one is blind, the other will likely become blind too."

This comment of the doctor's terrifies me. But it is really how I look
that bothers me most. Where the BB pellet struck there is a glob of
whitish scar tissue, a hideous cataract, on my eye. Now when I stare at
people—a favorite pastime, up to now—they will stare back. Not at the
"cute" little girl, but at her scar. For six years I do not stare at anyone,
because I do not raise my head.

Years later, in the throes of a mid-life crisis, I ask my mother and sister whether I changed after the "accident." "No," they say, puzzled.
"What do you mean?"

What do I mean?   15

I am eight, and, for the first time, doing poorly in school, where I have
been something of a whiz since I was four. We have just moved to the
place where the "accident" occurred. We do not know any of the people
around us because this is a different county. The only time I see the friends
I knew is when we go back to our old church. The new school is the former state penitentiary. It is a large stone building, cold and drafty,
crammed to overflowing with boisterous, ill-disciplined children. On the
third floor there is a huge circular imprint of some partition that has been
torn out.

"What used to be here?" I ask a sullen girl next to me on our way past it to lunch.

"The electric chair," says she.

At night I have nightmares about the electric chair, and about all the people reputedly "fried" in it. I am afraid of the school, where all the students seem to be budding criminals.

"What's the matter with your eye?" they ask, critically.   20

When I don't answer (I cannot decide whether it was an "accident" or not), they shove me, insist on a fight.

My brother, the one who created the story about the wire, comes to my rescue. But then brags so much about "protecting" me, I become sick.

After months of torture at the school, my parents decide to send me back to our old community, to my old school. I live with my grandparents and the teacher they board. But there is no room for Phoebe, my cat. By the time my grandparents decide there *is* room, and I ask for my cat, she cannot be found. Miss Yarborough, the boarding teacher, takes me under her wing, and begins to teach me to play the piano. But soon she marries an African—a "prince," she says—and is whisked away to his continent.

At my old school there is at least one teacher who loves me. She is the teacher who "knew me before I was born" and bought my first baby clothes. It is she who makes life bearable. It is her presence that finally helps me turn on the one child at the school who continually calls me "one-eyed bitch." One day I simply grab him by his coat and beat him until I am satisfied. It is my teacher who tells me my mother is ill.

My mother is lying in bed in the middle of the day, something I have   25
never seen. She is in too much pain to speak. She has an abscess in her ear. I stand looking down on her, knowing that if she dies, I cannot live. She is being treated with warm oils and hot bricks held against her cheek. Finally a doctor comes. But I must go back to my grandparents' house. The weeks pass but I am hardly aware of it. All I know is that my mother might die, my father is not so jolly, my brothers still have their guns, and I am the one sent away from home.

"You did not change," they say.

Did I imagine the anguish of never looking up?

I am twelve. When relatives come to visit I hide in my room. My cousin Brenda, just my age, whose father works in the post office and whose mother is a nurse, comes to find me. "Hello," she says. And then she asks, looking at my recent school picture, which I did not want taken, and on which the "glob," as I think of it, is clearly visible, "You still can't see out of that eye?"

"No," I say, and flop back on the bed over my book.

That night, as I do almost every night, I abuse my eye. I rant and rave   30
at it, in front of the mirror. I plead with it to clear up before morning. I tell it I hate and despise it. I do not pray for sight. I pray for beauty.

"You did not change," they say.

I am fourteen and baby-sitting for my brother Bill, who lives in Boston. He is my favorite brother and there is a strong bond between us. Understanding my feelings of shame and ugliness he and his wife take me to a local hospital, where the "glob" is removed by a doctor named O. Henry. There is still a small bluish crater where the scar tissue was, but the ugly white stuff is gone. Almost immediately I become a different person from the girl who does not raise her head. Or so I think. Now that I've raised my head I win the boyfriend of my dreams. Now that I've raised my head I have plenty of friends. Now that I've raised my head classwork comes from my lips as faultlessly as Easter speeches did, and I leave high school as valedictorian, most popular student, and *queen*, hardly believing my luck. Ironically, the girl who was voted most beautiful in our class (and was) was later shot twice through the chest by a male companion, using a "real" gun, while she was pregnant. But that's another story in itself. Or is it?

"You did not change," they say.

It is now thirty years since the "accident." A beautiful journalist comes to visit and to interview me. She is going to write a cover story for her magazine that focuses on my latest book. "Decide how you want to look on the cover," she says. "Glamorous, or whatever."

Never mind "glamorous," it is the "whatever" that I hear. Suddenly all I can think of is whether I will get enough sleep the night before the photography session: If I don't, my eye will be tired and wander, as blind eyes will.   35

At night in bed with my lover I think up reasons why I should not appear on the cover of a magazine. "My meanest critics will say I've sold out," I say. "My family will now realize I write scandalous books."

"But what's the real reason you don't want to do this?" he asks.

"Because in all probability," I say in a rush, "my eye won't be straight."

"It will be straight enough," he says. Then, "Besides, I thought you'd made your peace with that."

And I suddenly remember that I have.   40

I remember:

I am talking to my brother Jimmy, asking if he remembers anything unusual about the day I was shot. He does not know I consider that day the last time my father, with his sweet home remedy of cool lily leaves, chose me, and that I suffered and raged inside because of this. "Well," he says, "all I remember is standing by the side of the highway with Daddy, trying to flag down a car. A white man stopped, but when Daddy said he needed somebody to take his little girl to the doctor, he drove off."

I remember:

I am in the desert for the first time. I fall totally in love with it. I am so overwhelmed by its beauty, I confront for the first time, consciously, the meaning of the doctor's words years ago: "Eyes are sympathetic. If one is blind, the other will likely become blind too." I realize I have dashed about the world madly, looking at this, looking at that, storing up images against the fading of the light. *But I might have missed seeing the desert!* The shock of that possibility — and gratitude for over twenty-five years of sight — sends me literally to my knees. Poem after poem comes — which is perhaps how poets pray.

ON SIGHT

I am so thankful I have seen
The Desert
And the creatures in the desert
And the desert Itself.

The desert has its own moon
Which I have seen
With my own eye.
There is no flag on it.

Trees of the desert have arms
All of which are always up
That is because the moon is up
The sun is up
Also the sky
The Stars
Clouds
None with flags.

If there were flags, I doubt
the trees would point.
Would you?

But mostly, I remember this: 45

I am twenty-seven, and my baby daughter is almost three. Since her birth I have worried about her discovery that her mother's eyes are different from other people's. Will she be embarrassed? I think. What will she say? Every day she watches a television program called *Big Blue Marble*. It begins with a picture of the earth as it appears from the moon. It is bluish, a little battered-looking, but full of light, with whitish clouds swirling around it. Every time I see it I weep with love, as if it is a picture of Grandma's house. One day when I am putting Rebecca down for her nap, she suddenly focuses on my eye. Something inside me cringes, gets ready to try to protect myself. All children are cruel about physical differences, I know from experience, and that they don't always mean to be is another matter. I assume Rebecca will be the same.

But no-o-o-o. She studies my face intently as we stand, her inside and me outside her crib. She even holds my face maternally between her dimpled little hands. Then, looking every bit as serious and lawyerlike as her father, she says, as if it may just possibly have slipped my attention: "Mommy, there's a *world* in your eye." (As in, "Don't be alarmed, or do anything crazy.") And then, gently, but with great interest: "Mommy, where did you *get* that world in your eye?"

For the most part, the pain left then. (So what, if my brothers grew up to buy even more powerful pellet guns for their sons and to carry real guns themselves. So what, if a young "Morehouse[1] man" once nearly fell off the steps of Trevor Arnett Library because he thought my eyes were blue.) Crying and laughing I ran to the bathroom, while Rebecca mumbled and sang herself to sleep. Yes indeed, I realized, looking into the mirror. There *was* a world in my eye. And I saw that it was possible to love it: that in fact, for all it had taught me of shame and anger and inner vision, I *did* love it. Even to see it drifting out of orbit in boredom, or rolling up out of fatigue, not to mention floating back at attention in excitement (bearing witness, a friend has called it), deeply suitable to my personality, and even characteristic of me.

That night I dream I am dancing to Stevie Wonder's song "Always" (the name of the song is really "As," but I hear it as "Always"). As I dance, whirling and joyous, happier than I've ever been in my life, another bright-faced dancer joins me. We dance and kiss each other and hold each other through the night. The other dancer has obviously come through all right, as I have done. She is beautiful, whole, and free. And she is also me.

The Reader's Presence

1. In her opening paragraph, Walker refers to her father's "beautiful eyes." How does that phrase take on more significance in rereading? Can you find other words, phrases, or images that do the same? For example, why might Walker have mentioned the pain of having her hair combed?

2. Note that Walker uses the present tense throughout the essay. Why might this be unusual, given her subject? What effect does it have for both writer and reader? Try rewriting the opening paragraph in the past tense. What difference do you think it makes?

3. What is the meaning of Walker's occasional italicized comments? What do they have in common? Whose comments are they? To whom do they seem addressed? What time frame do

---

[1] ***Morehouse:*** Morehouse College, a black men's college in Atlanta, Georgia. — EDS.

they seem to be in? What purpose do you think they serve? How do they compare to those of Judith Ortiz Cofer in "Silent Dancing" (page 110)?

E. B. White

Once More to the Lake

Elwyn Brooks White (1899–1985) started contributing to the New Yorker *soon after the magazine began publication in 1925, and in the "Talk of the Town" and other columns helped establish the magazine's reputation for precise and brilliant prose. Collections of his contributions can be found in* Every Day Is Saturday *(1934),* Quo Vadimus? *(1939), and* The Wild Flag *(1946). He also wrote essays for* Harper's *on a regular basis; these essays include "Once More to the Lake" and are collected in* One Man's Meat *(1941). In his comments on this work, the critic Jonathan Yardley observed that White is "one of the few writers of this or any century who has succeeded in transforming the ephemera of journalism into something that demands to be called literature."*

Capable of brilliant satire, White could also be sad and serious, as in his compilation of forty years of writing, Essays *(1977). Among his numerous awards and honors, White received the American Academy of Arts and Letters Gold Medal (1960), a Presidential Medal of Freedom (1963), and a National Medal for Literature (1971). He made a lasting contribution to children's literature with* Stuart Little *(1945),* Charlotte's Web *(1952), and* The Trumpet of the Swan *(1970).*

White has written, "I have always felt that the first duty of a writer was to ascend — to make flights, carrying others along if he could manage it." According to White, the writer needs not only courage, but also hope and faith to accomplish this goal: "Writing itself is an act of faith, nothing else. And it must be the writer, above all others, who keeps it alive — choked with laughter, or with pain."

One summer, along about 1904, my father rented a camp on a lake in Maine and took us all there for the month of August. We all got ringworm from some kittens and had to rub Pond's Extract on our arms and legs night and morning, and my father rolled over in a canoe with all his clothes on; but outside of that the vacation was a success and from then on none of us ever thought there was any place in the world like that lake in Maine. We returned summer after summer — always on August 1st for one month.

I have since become a salt-water man, but sometimes in summer there are days when the restlessness of the tides and the fearful cold of the sea water and the incessant wind that blows across the afternoon and into the evening make me wish for the placidity of a lake in the woods. A few weeks ago this feeling got so strong I bought myself a couple of bass hooks and a spinner and returned to the lake where we used to go, for a week's fishing and to revisit old haunts.

I took along my son, who had never had any fresh water up his nose and who had seen lily pads only from train windows. On the journey over to the lake I began to wonder what it would be like. I wondered how time would have marred this unique, this holy spot—the coves and streams, the hills that the sun set behind, the camps and the paths behind the camps. I was sure that the tarred road would have found it out and I wondered in what other ways it would be desolated. It is strange how much you can remember about places like that once you allow your mind to return into the grooves that lead back. You remember one thing, and that suddenly reminds you of another thing. I guess I remembered clearest of all the early mornings, when the lake was cool and motionless, remembered how the bedroom smelled of the lumber it was made of and the wet woods whose scent entered through the screen. The partitions in the camp were thin and did not extend clear to the top of the rooms, and as I was always the first up I would dress softly so as not to wake the others, and sneak out into the sweet outdoors and start out in the canoe, keeping close along the shore in the long shadows of the pines. I remembered being very careful never to rub my paddle against the gunwale for fear of disturbing the stillness of the cathedral.

The lake had never been what you would call a wild lake. There were cottages sprinkled about the shores, and it was in farming country although the shores of the lake were quite heavily wooded. Some of the cottages were owned by nearby farmers, and you would live at the shore and eat your meals at the farmhouse. That's what our family did. But although it wasn't wild, it was a fairly large and undisturbed lake and there were places in it which, to a child at least, seemed infinitely remote and primeval.

I was right about the tar: It led to within half a mile of the shore. But when I got back there, with my boy, and we settled into a camp near a farmhouse and into the kind of summertime I had known, I could tell that it was going to be pretty much the same as it had been before—I knew it, lying in bed the first morning, smelling the bedroom, and hearing the boy sneak quietly out and go off along the shore in a boat. I began to sustain the illusion that he was I, and therefore, by simple transposition, that I was my father. This sensation persisted, kept cropping up all the time we were there. It was not an entirely new feeling, but in this setting it grew much stronger. I seemed to be living a dual existence. I would be in the middle of some simple act, I would be picking up a bait box or laying down a table fork, or I would be saying something, and suddenly it would be not I but my father who was saying the words or making the gesture. It gave me a creepy sensation.

We went fishing the first morning. I felt the same damp moss covering the worms in the bait can, and saw the dragonfly alight on the tip of my rod as it hovered a few inches from the surface of the water. It was the arrival of this fly that convinced me beyond any doubt that everything was as it always had been, that the years were a mirage and there had been no years. The small waves were the same, chucking the rowboat under the chin as we fished at anchor, and the boat was the same boat, the same color green and the ribs broken in the same places, and under the floor-boards the same fresh-water leavings and debris — the dead hellgrammite, the wisps of moss, the rusty discarded fishhook, the dried blood from yesterday's catch. We stared silently at the tips of our rods, at the dragonflies that came and went. I lowered the tip of mine into the water, tentatively, pensively dislodging the fly, which darted two feet away, poised, darted two feet back, and came to rest again a little farther up the rod. There had been no years between the ducking of this dragonfly and the other one — the one that was part of memory. I looked at the boy, who was silently watching his fly, and it was my hands that held his rod, my eyes watching. I felt dizzy and didn't know which rod I was at the end of.

We caught two bass, hauling them in briskly as though they were mackerel, pulling them over the side of the boat in a businesslike manner without any landing net, and stunning them with a blow on the back of the head. When we got back for a swim before lunch, the lake was exactly where we had left it, the same number of inches from the dock, and there was only the merest suggestion of a breeze. This seemed an utterly enchanted sea, this lake you could leave to its own devices for a few hours and come back to, and find that it had not stirred, this constant and trustworthy body of water. In the shallows, the dark, watersoaked sticks and twigs, smooth and old, were undulating in clusters on the bottom against the clean ribbed sand, and the track of the mussel was plain. A school of minnows swam by, each minnow with its small individual shadow, doubling the attendance, so clear and sharp in the sunlight. Some of the other campers were in swimming, along the shore, one of them with a cake of soap, and the water felt thin and clear and unsubstantial. Over the years there had been this person with the cake of soap, this cultist, and here he was. There had been no years.

Up to the farmhouse to dinner through the teeming, dusty field, the road under our sneakers was only a two-track road. The middle track was missing, the one with the marks of the hooves and splotches of dried, flaky manure. There had always been three tracks to choose from in choosing which track to walk in; now the choice was narrowed down to two. For a moment I missed terribly the middle alternative. But the way led past the tennis court, and something about the way it lay there in the sun reassured me; the tape had loosened along the backline, the alleys were green with plantains and other weeds, and the net (installed in June and removed in September) sagged in the dry noon, and the whole place steamed with midday heat and hunger and emptiness. There was a choice of pie for dessert, and one was blueberry and one was apple, and the waitresses were the same country girls, there having been no passage of time, only the illusion of it as in a dropped curtain—the waitresses were still fifteen; their hair had been washed, that was the only difference—they had been to the movies and seen the pretty girls with the clean hair.

Summertime, oh summertime, pattern of life indelible, the fade-proof lake, the woods unshatterable, the pasture with the sweetfern and the juniper forever and ever, summer without end; this was the background, and the life along the shore was the design, the cottages with their innocent and tranquil design, their tiny docks with the flagpole and the American flag floating against the white clouds in the blue sky, the little paths over the roots of the trees leading from camp to camp and the paths leading back to the outhouses and the can of lime for sprinkling, and at the souvenir counters at the store the miniature birch-bark canoes and the post cards that showed things looking a little better than they looked. This was the American family at play, escaping the city heat, wondering whether the newcomers in the camp at the head of the cove were "common" or "nice," wondering whether it was true that the people who drove up for Sunday dinner at the farmhouse were turned away because there wasn't enough chicken.

It seemed to me, as I kept remembering all this, that those times and those summers had been infinitely precious and worth saving. There had been jollity and peace and goodness. The arriving (at the beginning of August) had been so big a business in itself, at the railway station the farm wagon drawn up, the first smell of the pine-laden air, the first glimpse of the smiling farmer, and the great importance of the trunks and your father's enormous authority in such matters, and the feel of the wagon under you for the long ten-mile haul, and at the top of the last long hill catching the first view of the lake after eleven months of not seeing this cherished body of water. The shouts and cries of the other campers when they saw you, and the trunks to be unpacked, to give up their rich burden. (Arriving was less exciting nowadays, when you sneaked up in your car and parked it under a tree near the camp and took out the bags and in five minutes it was all over, no fuss, no loud wonderful fuss about trunks).

Peace and goodness and jollity. The only thing that was wrong now, 10 really, was the sound of the place, an unfamiliar nervous sound of the outboard motors. This was the note that jarred, the one thing that would sometimes break the illusion and set the years moving. In those other summertimes all motors were inboard; and when they were at a little distance, the noise they made was a sedative, an ingredient of summer sleep. They were one-cylinder and two-cylinder engines, and some were make-and-break and some were jump-spark, but they all made a sleepy sound across the lake. The one-lungers throbbed and fluttered, and the twin-cylinder ones purred and purred, and that was a quiet sound too. But now the campers all had outboards. In the daytime, in the hot mornings, these motors made a petulant, irritable sound; at night, in the still evening when the afterglow lit the water, they whined about one's ears like mosquitoes. My boy loved our rented outboard, and his great desire was to achieve singlehanded mastery over it, and authority, and he soon learned the trick of choking it a little (but not too much), and the adjustment of the needle valve. Watching him I would remember the things you could do with the old one-cylinder engines with the heavy flywheel, how you could have it eating out of your hand if you got really close to it spiritually. Motor boats in those days didn't have clutches, and you would make a landing by shutting off the motor at the proper time and coasting in with a dead rudder. But there was a way of reversing them, if you learned the trick, by cutting the switch and putting it on again exactly on the final dying revolution of the flywheel, so that it would kick back against compression and begin reversing. Approaching a dock in a strong following breeze, it was difficult to slow up sufficiently by the ordinary coasting method, and if a boy felt he had complete mastery over his motor, he was tempted to keep it running beyond its time and then reverse it a few feet from the dock. It took a cool nerve, because if you threw the switch a twentieth of a second too soon you could catch the flywheel when it still had speed enough to go up past center, and the boat would leap ahead, charging bull-fashion at the dock.

We had a good week at the camp. The bass were biting well and the sun shone endlessly, day after day. We would be tired at night and lie down in the accumulated heat of the little bedrooms after the long hot day and the breeze would stir almost imperceptibly outside and the smell of the swamp drift in through the rusty screens. Sleep would come easily and in the morning the red squirrel would be on the roof, tapping out his gay routine. I kept remembering everything, lying in bed in the mornings — the small steamboat that had a long rounded stern like the lip of a Ubangi, and how quietly she ran on the moonlight sails, when the older boys played their mandolins and the girls sang and we ate doughnuts dipped in sugar, and how sweet the music was on the water in the shining night, and what it had felt like to think about girls then. After breakfast we would go up to the store and the things were in the same place — the minnows in a bottle, the plugs and spinners disarranged and pawed over by the youngsters from the boys' camp, the Fig Newtons and the Beeman's gum. Outside, the road was tarred and cars stood in front of the store. Inside, all was just as it had always been, except there was more Coca-Cola and not so much Moxie and root beer and birch beer and sarsaparilla. We would walk out with a bottle of pop apiece and sometimes the pop would backfire up our noses and hurt. We explored the streams, quietly, where the turtles slid off the sunny logs and dug their way into the soft bottom; and we lay on the town wharf and fed worms to the tame bass. Everywhere we went I had trouble making out which was I, the one walking at my side, the one walking in my pants.

One afternoon while we were there at that lake a thunderstorm came up. It was like the revival of an old melodrama that I had seen long ago with childish awe. The second-act climax of the drama of the electrical disturbance over a lake in America had not changed in any important respect. This was the big scene, still the big scene. The whole thing was so familiar, the first feeling of oppression and heat and a general air around camp of not wanting to go very far away. In midafternoon (it was all the same) a curious darkening of the sky, and a lull in everything that had made life tick; and then the way the boats suddenly swung the other way at their moorings with the coming of a breeze out of the new quarter, and the premonitory rumble. Then the kettle drum, then the snare, then the bass drum and cymbals, then crackling light against the dark, and the gods grinning and licking their chops in the hills. Afterward the calm, the rain steadily rustling in the calm lake, the return of light and hope and spirits, and the campers running out in joy and relief to go swimming in the rain, their bright cries perpetuating the deathless joke about how they were getting simply drenched, and the children screaming with delight at the new sensation of bathing in the rain, and the joke about getting drenched linking the generations in a strong indestructible chain. And the comedian who waded in carrying an umbrella.

When the others went swimming my son said he was going in too. He pulled his dripping trunks from the line where they had hung all through the shower, and wrung them out. Languidly, and with no thought of going in, I watched him, his hard little body, skinny and bare, saw him wince slightly as he pulled up around his vitals the small, soggy, icy garment. As he buckled the swollen belt suddenly my groin felt the chill of death.

The Reader's Presence

1. In paragraph 2, White begins to reflect on the way his memory works. How does he follow the process of remembering throughout the essay? Are his memories of the lake safely stored in the past? If not, why not?

2. Go through the essay and identify words and images having to do with the sensory details of seeing, hearing, touching, and so on. How do these details contribute to the overall effect of the essay? How do they anticipate White's final paragraph?

3. In paragraph 4, White refers to a "creepy sensation." What is the basis of that sensation? Why is it "creepy"? What is the "dual existence" White feels he is living? How does the essay build the

story of White's relationships with both his father and his son? Compare this account of intergenerational intimacy to Raymond Carver's essay "My Father's Life" (page 103).

THE WRITER AT WORK

E. B. White on the Essayist

For several generations, E. B. White has remained America's best known essayist, his works widely available and widely anthologized. Yet in the foreword to his 1977 collected essays, when he addresses the role of the essayist, he sounds wholly modest not only about his career but about his chosen genre: In the world of literature, he writes, the essayist is a "second-class citizen." Why do you think White thinks of himself that way, and how might that self-deprecation be reconciled with the claims of his final two paragraphs? Do you think White's description of himself as an essayist matches the actual essayist we encounter in "Once More to the Lake"? Also, do you think his persistent use of the male pronoun is merely for grammatical convenience (the essay was written in 1977) or reflects a gender bias on his part?

The essayist is a self-liberated man, sustained by the childish belief that everything he thinks about, everything that happens to him, is of general interest. He is a fellow who thoroughly enjoys his work, just as people who take bird walks enjoy theirs. Each new excursion of the essayist, each new "attempt," differs from the last and takes him into new country. This delights him. Only a person who is congenitally self-centered has the effrontery and the stamina to write essays.

There are as many kinds of essays as there are human attitudes or poses, as many essay flavors as there are Howard Johnson ice creams. The essayist arises in the morning and, if he has work to do, selects his garb from an unusually extensive wardrobe: he can pull on any sort of shirt, be any sort of person, according to his mood or his subject matter — philosopher, scold, jester, raconteur, confidant, pundit, devil's advocate, enthusiast. I like the essay, have always liked it, and even as a child was at work, attempting to inflict my young thoughts and experiences on others by putting them on paper. I early broke into print in the pages of *St. Nicholas*. I tend still to fall back on the essay form (or lack of form) when an idea strikes me, but I am not fooled about the place of the essay in twentieth century American letters — it stands a short distance down the line. The essayist, unlike the novelist, the poet, and the playwright, must be content in his self-imposed role of second-class citizen. A writer who has his sights trained on the Nobel Prize or other earthly triumphs had best write a novel, a poem, or a play, and leave the essayist to ramble about, content with living a free life and enjoying the satisfactions of a somewhat undisciplined existence. (Dr. Johnson called the essay "an irregular, undigested piece"; this happy practitioner has no wish to quarrel with the good doctor's characterization.)

There is one thing the essayist cannot do, though—he cannot indulge himself in deceit or in concealment, for he will be found out in no time. Desmond MacCarthy, in his introductory remarks to the 1928 E. P. Dutton & Company edition of Montaigne, observes that Montaigne "had the gift of natural candour. . . ." It is the basic ingredient. And even the essayist's escape from discipline is only a partial escape: the essay, although a relaxed form, imposes its own disciplines, raises its own problems, and these disciplines and problems soon become apparent and (we all hope) act as a deterrent to anyone wielding a pen merely because he entertains random thoughts or is in a happy or wandering mood.

I think some people find the essay the last resort of the egoist, a much too self-conscious and self-serving form for their tastes; they feel that it is presumptuous of a writer to assume that his little excursions or his small observations will interest the reader. There is some justice in their complaint. I have always been aware that I am by nature self-absorbed and egoistical; to write of myself to the extent I have done indicates a too great attention to my own life, not enough to the lives of others. I have worn many shirts, and not all of them have been a good fit. But when I am discouraged or downcast I need only fling open the door of my closet, and there, hidden behind everything else, hangs the mantle of Michel de Montaigne, smelling slightly of camphor.

Part III

Expository Writing: Shaping Information

Diane Ackerman

We Are Our Words

Diane Ackerman (b. 1948), poet, essayist, and naturalist, explores nature and human nature, science and art, and writes frequently about "that twilight zone" where these seemingly opposite spheres meet. The author of more than twenty volumes of poetry and nonfiction, Ackerman has received numerous awards and honors, including the Lavan Poetry Prize, the John Burroughs Nature Award, and a Guggenheim Fellowship; she was honored as a "Literary Lion" by the New York Public Library in 1994. Her books of poetry include The Planets *(1976),* Jaguar of Sweet Laughter *(1991),* I Praise My Destroyer *(1998),* The Senses of Animals *(2000), and* Origami Bridges *(2003). Her nonfiction includes* Twilight of the Tenderfoot *(1980);* On Extended Wings *(1987); and the best-selling* A Natural History of the Senses *(1990), which became the basis for a PBS series, "Mystery of the Senses," which she hosted in 1995. Ackerman's latest work is* An Alchemy of Mind: The Marvel and Mystery of the Brain *(2004), from which her essay "We Are Our Words" was adapted for publication in* Parade Magazine. *She is a contributing editor to* Parade *and a contributor of poems and nonfiction to literary journals, periodicals, and newspapers, including the* New Yorker, American Poetry Review, Paris Review, *and the* New York Times.*

Ackerman has explained why she does not write fiction: "I have enormous respect for fiction, but I consider it a very high class form of lying. I like it a lot. I admire it. I'm just not very good at it. It's not something that appeals to me to do myself. Which is not to say that nonfiction writing is any closer to the truth all the time because of course it's subjective and you choose what you're going to include. You can't lie about something, but you can choose. . . ."

Babies are citizens of the world, whether they're born into a world of high-rises or tundra, jackhammers or machine guns, Quechua or French. The ultimate immigrants, babies arrive ready to learn the language of their parents, with a brain flexible enough to adapt to any locale. Whatever language they hear becomes an indelible part of their lives, providing the words they'll use to know and be known.

If two languages are spoken at home, they'll become bilingual. One of my nieces is trilingual, because her Brazilian mother spoke Portuguese as well as English to her from birth, and then together they learned Italian. A bonus of bilingualism is that it forces a child to favor one set of rules while ignoring another, and that trains the brain early on to focus and discriminate, to ignore what's irrelevant and discover the arbitrariness of words.

Learning language can begin surprisingly early, at around 6 months, when babies start to identify the special sounds of their native tongues, like the umlauted ü of German that requires a little lip pucker or the squeaky e of American English's "street." Long before words make sense, babies learn a circus of familiar sounds—all the exotic vowels and leaping rhythms. Before their first birthday, they can recognize a foreign language, analyze word order and memorize sentence and sound patterns in their native language. Babies the world over babble alike at first, then gradually babble in their own language. Children born deaf can babble with their hands.

But we're not the planet's only babblers. Some monkeys babble, which suggests that babbling evolved long before language, perhaps as a plea for affection or to summon Mom. In that case, language may have bloomed from a natural urge to babble.

Human babies learn language the way most baby birds learn their songs—by imitating grown-ups. Like birds, we have a learning window. A bird or child raised in isolation, then introduced to its song or language later in life, won't be able to fully learn it.

There's a prime time—the first few years—during which the brain is so plastic, so busily restructuring itself, that one can almost inhale a language. Children acquire the basic rules of grammar before they enter school, and it doesn't matter which language or how complicated the rules. By puberty, the process requires active learning skills, repetition and hard work. Learning a language as a grown-up is heavy lifting. Language is so difficult, only children can master it.

How miraculous human language seems. But no more so than hummingbirds being born with the ability to navigate through jungles, over mountains and open seas; or bloodhounds with a talent for discriminating among thousands of odors. Because species evolve what serves them best, the ability to decipher complex rules of language is woven into our genetic suit.

We use words to label and categorize, to discern subtle differences, to group related things, to build endless lists. But also to create false divisions, false distinctions and false unities, which become possible the moment they're put into words.

Thanks to language, we have a verbal memory that allows us to learn and remember without physically experiencing something. Through writing and other technology, we no longer have to memorize the endless fine rubble that passes for everyday life. We make lists, we take notes, we file things away. Books invite one to view another's mind, self, suite of defining memories. Instead of straining to remember everything, we can deploy our attention (and many neurons and synapses) to toil at other jobs— coining new games and ideas, for instance.

Words can gap gushing emotions and trawl for memories. They can   10 highlight and name things when we need perspective, and they're excellent handles when we need to grip a slippery notion. As social beasts, we trade words with others, negotiate meanings, use words as currency.

Words form the backbone of what we think. So, although it is possible to have thought without words, it's rarely possible to know what one thinks without bronzing it in words. Otherwise, the thoughts seem to float away. Refine the words, and you refine the thought. But that sometimes means squishing a square thought into a round hole and saying what you can instead of what you mean.

We try to remedy that by piling up words like brushstrokes in what we call descriptions or explanations or by blending images (words, paint, brushstrokes) or by adding emotional sounds to what we say.

"Please do that for me" means altogether different things if you say it pleadingly or in separate jabs. How eager humans are to complicate things. Isn't language complicated enough? Apparently not. Every family invents its own dialect, as members bring home this or that expression from school or work and add televisionese or song lyrics to the general mix.

A separate lingo binds people, but I find another motive persuasive too: our endless need to express the sheer feel of being alive. How does the brain convey that to itself and others? Only through language, memory's accomplice.

The Reader's Presence

1. Why does Ackerman call babies "the ultimate immigrants"? What aspects of language that babies pick up easily through imitation prove difficult for older humans to learn?

2. Ackerman outlines a number of purposes for language. In what ways does our language define us as human beings?

3. Ackerman argues that bilingualism trains a child to "favor one set of rules while ignoring another . . . to focus and discriminate, to ignore what's irrelevant and discover the arbitrariness of words" (paragraph 2). Compare Ackerman's perspective on language and bilingualism to Richard Rodriguez's in "Aria: A Memoir of a Bilingual Childhood" (page 239). How does Rodriguez exemplify the difficulties of learning a language after infancy? What is the distinction he makes between a private and a public language?

Gloria Anzaldúa

How to Tame a Wild Tongue

> *Gloria Anzaldúa (1942–2004), a poet, cultural theorist, essayist, and editor, used her writings to explore issues such as racism, Chicano culture, lesbianism, and feminism. In addition to writing and editing, Anzaldúa taught creative writing, literature, and feminist studies at San Francisco State University, Oakes College at the University of California in Santa Cruz, and Norwich University. She coedited* This Bridge Called My Back: Writings by Radical Women of Color *(1981), which received the Before Columbus Foundation American Book Award. She was also the editor of* Making Face, Making Soul/Haciendo Caras: Creative and Critical Perspectives by Feminists of Color *(1990), and coeditor of* Cassell's Encyclopedia of Queer Myth, Symbol, and Spirit: Gay, Lesbian, Bisexual, and Transgender Lore *(1997). Anzaldúa coedited the collection* This Bridge We Call Home: Radical Visions for Transformation *(2002), for which she was named a 2002 Lambda Literary Award finalist. She was the author of three bilingual children's books,* Prietita Tiene un Amigo/Prietita Has a Friend *(1991),* Friends from the Other Side/Amigos del Otro Lado *(1993), and* Prietita and the Ghost Woman/Prietita y la Ilorona *(1995). Her last published writings were* La Prieta *(1997) and* Interviews/Entrevistas *(2000). Her first book,* Borderlands/La Frontera: The New Mestiza *(1987), from which "How to Tame a Wild Tongue" is taken, is a blend of poetry, memoir, and historical analysis. Anzaldúa, a native of South Texas, lived in Santa Cruz, California.*

"We're going to have to control your tongue," the dentist says, pulling out all the metal from my mouth. Silver bits plop and tinkle into the basin. My mouth is a motherlode.

The dentist is cleaning out my roots. I get a whiff of the stench when I gasp. "I can't cap that tooth yet, you're still draining," he says.

"We're going to have to do something about your tongue," I hear the anger rising in his voice. My tongue keeps pushing out the wads of cotton, pushing back the drills, the long thin needles. "I've never seen anything as strong or as stubborn," he says. And I think how do you tame a wild tongue, train it to be quiet, how do you bridle and saddle it? How do you make it lie down?

> "Who is to say that robbing a people of its language is less violent than war?"
>
> —Ray Gwyn Smith[1]

---

[1]Ray Gwyn Smith, *Moorland Is Cold Country*, unpublished book.

324

I remember being caught speaking Spanish at recess—that was good for three licks on the knuckles with a sharp ruler. I remember being sent to the corner of the classroom for "talking back" to the Anglo teacher when all I was trying to do was tell her how to pronounce my name. "If you want to be American, speak 'American.' If you don't like it, go back to Mexico where you belong."

"I want you to speak English. *Pa' hallar buen trabajo tienes que saber*   5
*hablar el inglés bien. Qué vale toda tu educación si todavía hablas inglés
con un* 'accent,'" my mother would say, mortified that I spoke English like a Mexican. At Pan American University, I, and all Chicano students were required to take two speech classes. Their purpose: to get rid of our accents.

Attacks on one's form of expression with the intent to censor are a violation of the First Amendment. *El Anglo con cara de inocente nos arrancó la lengua.* Wild tongues can't be tamed, they can only be cut out.

OVERCOMING THE TRADITION OF SILENCE

> *Ahogadas, escupimos el oscuro.*
> *Peleando con nuestra propia sombra*
> *el silencio nos sepulta.*

En boca cerrada no entran moscas. "Flies don't enter a closed mouth" is a saying I kept hearing when I was a child. *Ser habladora* was to be a gossip and a liar, to talk too much. *Muchachitas bien criadas*, well-bred girls don't answer back. *Es una falta de respeto* to talk back to one's mother or father. I remember one of the sins I'd recite to the priest in the confession box the few times I went to confession: talking back to my mother, *hablar pa' 'tras, repelar. Hocicona, repelona, chismosa*, having a big mouth, questioning, carrying tales are all signs of being *mal criada*. In my culture they are all words that are derogatory if applied to women—I've never heard them applied to men.

The first time I heard two women, a Puerto Rican and a Cuban, say the word *"nosotras,"* I was shocked. I had not known the word existed. Chicanas use *nosotros* whether we're male or female. We are robbed of our female being by the masculine plural. Language is a male discourse.

> And our tongues have become
> dry   the wilderness has
> dried out our tongues   and
> we have forgotten speech.
>
> —Irena Klepfisz[2]

---

[2]Irena Klepfisz, *"Di rayze aheym*/The Journey Home," in *The Tribe of Dina: A Jewish Women's Anthology*, Melanie Kaye/Kantrowitz and Irena Klepfisz, eds. (Montpelier, VT: Sinister Wisdom Books, 1986), 49.

Even our own people, other Spanish speakers *nos quieren poner candados en la boca*. They would hold us back with their bag of *reglas de academia*.

OYÉ COMO LADRA: EL LENGUAJE DE LA FRONTERA

Quien tiene boca se equivoca.

— Mexican saying

"*Pocho*, cultural traitor, you're speaking the oppressor's language by   10
speaking English, you're ruining the Spanish language," I have been accused by various Latinos and Latinas. Chicano Spanish is considered by the purist and by most Latinos deficient, a mutilation of Spanish.

But Chicano Spanish is a border tongue which developed naturally. Change, *evolución, enriquecimiento de palabras nuevas por invención o adopción* have created variants of Chicano Spanish, *un nuevo lenguaje. Un lenguaje que corresponde a un modo de vivir*. Chicano Spanish is not incorrect, it is a living language.

For people who are neither Spanish nor live in a country in which Spanish is the first language; for a people who live in a country in which English is the reigning tongue but who are not Anglo; for a people who cannot entirely identify with either standard (formal, Castillian) Spanish nor standard English, what recourse is left to them but to create their own language? A language which they can connect their identity to, one capable of communicating the realities and values true to themselves — a language with terms that are neither *español ni inglés*, but both. We speak a patois, a forked tongue, a variation of two languages.

Chicano Spanish sprang out of the Chicanos' need to identify ourselves as a distinct people. We needed a language with which we could communicate with ourselves, a secret language. For some of us, language is a homeland closer than the Southwest — for many Chicanos today live in the Midwest and the East. And because we are a complex, heterogeneous people, we speak many languages. Some of the languages we speak are:

1. Standard English
2. Working class and slang English
3. Standard Spanish
4. Standard Mexican Spanish
5. North Mexican Spanish dialect
6. Chicano Spanish (Texas, New Mexico, Arizona and California have regional variations)

7. Tex-Mex
8. *Pachuco* (called *caló*)

My "home" tongues are the languages I speak with my sister and brothers, with my friends. They are the last five listed, with 6 and 7 being closest to my heart. From school, the media, and job situations, I've picked up standard and working class English. From Mamagrande Locha and from reading Spanish and Mexican literature, I've picked up Standard Spanish and Standard Mexican Spanish. From *los recién llegados*, Mexican immigrants, and *braceros*, I learned the North Mexican dialect. With Mexicans I'll try to speak either Standard Mexican Spanish or the North Mexican dialect. From my parents and Chicanos living in the Valley, I picked up Chicano Texas Spanish, and I speak it with my mom, younger brother (who married a Mexican and who rarely mixes Spanish with English), aunts and older relatives.

With Chicanas from *Nuevo México* or *Arizona* I will speak Chicano   15
Spanish a little, but often they don't understand what I'm saying. With most California Chicanas I speak entirely in English (unless I forget). When I first moved to San Francisco, I'd rattle off something in Spanish, unintentionally embarrassing them. Often it is only with another Chicana *tejana* that I can talk freely.

Words distorted by English are known as anglicisms or *pochismos*. The *pocho* is an anglicized Mexican or American of Mexican origin who speaks Spanish with an accent characteristic of North Americans and who distorts and reconstructs the language according to the influence of English.[3] Tex-Mex, or Spanglish, comes most naturally to me. I may switch back and forth from English to Spanish in the same sentence or in the same word. With my sister and my brother Nune and with Chicano *tejano* contemporaries I speak in Tex-Mex.

From kids and people my own age I picked up *Pachuco*. *Pachuco* (the language of the zoot suiters) is a language of rebellion, both against Standard Spanish and Standard English. It is a secret language. Adults of the culture and outsiders cannot understand it. It is made up of slang words from both English and Spanish. *Ruca* means girl or woman, *vato* means guy or dude, *chale* means no, *simón* means yes, *churro* is sure, talk is *periquiar*, *pigionear* means petting, *que gacho* means how nerdy, *ponte águila* means watch out, death is called *la pelona*. Through lack of practice and not having others who can speak it, I've lost most of the *Pachuco* tongue.

---

[3]R. C. Ortega, *Dialectología del Barrio*, trans. Hortencia S. Alwan (Los Angeles, CA: R. C. Ortega Publisher & Bookseller, 1977), 132.

CHICANO SPANISH

Chicanos, after 250 years of Spanish/Anglo colonization have developed significant differences in the Spanish we speak. We collapse two adjacent vowels into a single syllable and sometimes shift the stress in certain words such as *maíz/maiz, cohete/cuete*. We leave out certain consonants when they appear between vowels: *lado/lao, mojado/majao*. Chicanos from South Texas pronounce *f* as *j* as in *jue (fue)*. Chicanos use "archaisms," words that are no longer in the Spanish language, words that have been evolved out. We say *semos, truje, haiga, ansina*, and *naiden*. We retain the "archaic" *j*, as in *jalar*, that derives from an earlier *h* (the French *halar* or the Germanic *halon* which was lost to standard Spanish in the 16th century), but which is still found in several regional dialects such as the one spoken in South Texas. (Due to geography, Chicanos from the Valley of South Texas were cut off linguistically from other Spanish speakers. We tend to use words that the Spaniards brought over from Medieval Spain. The majority of the Spanish colonizers in Mexico and the Southwest came from Extremadura — Hernán Cortés was one of them — and Andalucía. Andalucians pronounce *ll* like a *y*, and their *d*'s tend to be absorbed by adjacent vowels: *tirado* becomes *tirao*. They brought *el lenguaje popular, dialectos y regionalismos*.[4])

Chicanos and other Spanish speakers also shift *ll* to *y* and *z* to *s*.[5] We leave out initial syllables, saying *tar* for *estar, toy* for *estoy, hora* for *ahora* (*cubanos* and *puertorriqueños* also leave out initial letters of some words.) We also leave out the final syllable such as *pa* for *para*. The intervocalic *y*, the *ll* as in *tortilla, ella, botella*, gets replaced by *tortia* or *tortiya, ea, botea*. We add an additional syllable at the beginning of certain words: *atocar* for *tocar, agastar* for *gastar*. Sometimes we'll say *lavaste las vacijas*, other times *lavates* (substituting the *ates* verb endings for the *aste*).

We use anglicisms, words borrowed from English: *bola* from ball,   20
carpeta from carpet, *máchina de lavar* (instead of *lavadora*) from washing machine. Tex-Mex argot, created by adding a Spanish sound at the beginning or end of an English word such as *cookiar* for cook, *watchar* for watch, *parkiar* for park, and *rapiar* for rape, is the result of the pressures on Spanish speakers to adapt to English.

We don't use the word *vosotros/as* or its accompanying verb form. We don't say *claro* (to mean yes), *imagínate*, or *me emociona*, unless we picked up Spanish from Latinas, out of a book, or in a classroom. Other Spanish-speaking groups are going through the same, or similar, development in their Spanish.

---

[4]Eduardo Hernández-Chávez, Andrew D. Cohen, and Anthony F. Beltramo, *El Lenguaje de los Chicanos: Regional and Social Characteristics of Language Used By Mexican Americans* (Arlington, VA: Center for Applied Linguistics, 1975), 39.
[5]Hernández-Chávez, xvii.

LINGUISTIC TERRORISM

> *Deslenguadas. Somos los del español deficiente.* We are your lingistic nightmare, your linguistic aberration, your linguistic *mestisaje*, the subject of your *burla*. Because we speak with tongues of fire we are culturally crucified. Racially, culturally and linguistically *somos huérfanos*—we speak an orphan tongue.

Chicanas who grew up speaking Chicano Spanish have internalized the belief that we speak poor Spanish. It is illegitimate, a bastard language. And because we internalize how our language has been used against us by the dominant culture, we use our language differences against each other.

Chicana feminists often skirt around each other with suspicion and hesitation. For the longest time I couldn't figure it out. Then it dawned on me. To be close to another Chicana is like looking into the mirror. We are afraid of what we'll see there. *Pena.* Shame. Low estimation of self. In childhood we are told that our language is wrong. Repeated attacks on our native tongue diminish our sense of self. The attacks continue throughout our lives.

Chicanas feel uncomfortable talking in Spanish to Latinas, afraid of their censure. Their language was not outlawed in their countries. They had a whole lifetime of being immersed in their native tongue; generations, centuries in which Spanish was a first language, taught in school, heard on radio and TV, and read in the newspaper.

If a person, Chicana or Latina, has a low estimation of my native 25 tongue, she also has a low estimation of me. Often with *mexicanas y latinas* we'll speak English as a neutral language. Even among Chicanas we tend to speak English at parties or conferences. Yet, at the same time, we're afraid the others will think we're *agringadas* because we don't speak Chicano Spanish. We oppress each other trying to out-Chicano each other, vying to be the "real" Chicanas, to speak like Chicanos. There is no one Chicano language just as there is no one Chicano experience. A monolingual Chicana whose first language is English or Spanish is just as much a Chicana as one who speaks several variants of Spanish. A Chicana from Michigan or Chicago or Detroit is just as much a Chicana as one from the southwest. Chicano Spanish is as diverse linguistically as it is regionally.

By the end of this century, Spanish speakers will comprise the biggest minority group in the U.S., a country where students in high schools and colleges are encouraged to take French classes because French is considered more "cultured." But for a language to remain alive it must be used.[6] By the end of this century English, and not Spanish, will be the mother tongue of most Chicanos and Latinos.

---

[6]Irena Klepfisz, "Secular Jewish Identity: Yidishkayt in America," in *The Tribe of Dina*, Kaye/Kantrowitz and Klepfisz, eds., 43.

So, if you want to really hurt me, talk badly about my language. Ethnic identity is twin skin to linguistic identity—I am my language. Until I can take pride in my language, I cannot take pride in myself. Until I can accept as legitimate Chicano Texas Spanish, Tex-Mex and all the other languages I speak, I cannot accept the legitimacy of myself. Until I am free to write bilingually and to switch codes without having always to translate, while I still have to speak English or Spanish when I would rather speak Spanglish, and as long as I have to accommodate the English speakers rather than having them accommodate me, my tongue will be illegitimate.

I will no longer be made to feel ashamed of existing. I will have my voice: Indian, Spanish, white. I will have my serpent's tongue—my woman's voice, my sexual voice, my poet's voice. I will overcome the tradition of silence.

> My fingers
> move sly against your palm
> Like women everywhere, we speak in code. . . .
>   —Melanie Kaye/Kantrowitz[7]

"VISTAS," CORRIDOS, Y COMIDA: MY NATIVE TONGUE

In the 1960s, I read my first Chicano novel. It was *City of Night* by John Rechy, a gay Texan, son of a Scottish father and a Mexican mother. For days I walked around in stunned amazement that a Chicano could write and could get published. When I read *I Am Joaquín*[8] I was surprised to see a bilingual book by a Chicano in print. When I saw poetry written in Tex-Mex for the first time, a feeling of pure joy flashed through me. I felt like we really existed as a people. In 1971, when I started teaching High School English to Chicano students, I tried to supplement the required texts with works by Chicanos, only to be reprimanded and forbidden to do so by the principal. He claimed that I was supposed to teach "American" and English literature. At the risk of being fired, I swore my students to secrecy and slipped in Chicano short stories, poems, a play. In graduate school, while working toward a Ph.D., I had to "argue" with one advisor after the other, semester after semester, before I was allowed to make Chicano literature an area of focus.

Even before I read books by Chicanos or Mexicans, it was the Mexican movies I saw at the drive-in—the Thursday night special of $1.00 a   30

---

[7]Melanie Kaye/Kantrowitz, "Sign," in *We Speak in Code: Poems and Other Writings* (Pittsburgh, PA: Motheroot Publications, Inc., 1980), 85.

[8]Rodolfo Gonzales, *I Am Joaquín/Yo Soy Joaquín* (New York, NY: Bantam Books, 1972). It was first published in 1967.

carload—that gave me a sense of belonging. *"Vámonos a las vistas,"* my mother would call out and we'd all—grandmother, brothers, sister and cousins—squeeze into the car. We'd wolf down cheese and bologna white bread sandwiches while watching Pedro Infante in melodramatic tear-jerkers like *Nosotros los pobres*, the first "real" Mexican movie (that was not an imitation of European movies). I remember seeing *Cuando los hijos se van* and surmising that all Mexican movies played up the love a mother has for her children and what ungrateful sons and daughters suffer when they are not devoted to their mothers. I remember the singing-type "westerns" of Jorge Negrete and Miguel Aceves Mejía. When watching Mexican movies, I felt a sense of homecoming as well as alienation. People who were to amount to something didn't go to Mexican movies, or *bailes* or tune their radios to *bolero*, *rancherita*, and *corrido* music.

The whole time I was growing up, there was *norteño* music sometimes called North Mexican border music, or Tex-Mex music, or Chicano music, or *cantina* (bar) music. I grew up listening to *conjuntos*, three- or four-piece bands made up of folk musicians playing guitar, *bajo sexto*, drums and button accordion, which Chicanos had borrowed from the German immigrants who had come to Central Texas and Mexico to farm and build breweries. In the Rio Grande Valley, Steve Jordan and Little Joe Hernández were popular, and Flaco Jiménez was the accordian king. The rhythms of Tex-Mex music are those of the polka, also adapted from the Germans, who in turn had borrowed the polka from the Czechs and Bohemians.

I remember the hot, sultry evenings when *corridos*—songs of love and death on the Texas-Mexican borderlands—reverberated out of cheap amplifiers from the local *cantinas* and wafted in through my bedroom window.

Corridos first became widely used along the South Texas/Mexican border during the early conflict between Chicanos and Anglos. The *corridos* are usually about Mexican heroes who do valiant deeds against the Anglo oppressors. Pancho Villa's song, *"La cucaracha,"* is the most famous one. *Corridos* of John F. Kennedy and his death are still very popular in the Valley. Older Chicanos remember Lydia Mendoza, one of the great border *corrido* singers who was called *la Gloria de Tejas*. Her *"El tango negro,"* sung during the Great Depression, made her a singer of the people. The ever-present *corridos* narrated one hundred years of border history, bringing news of events as well as entertaining. These folk musicians and folk songs are our chief cultural myth-makers, and they made our hard lives seem bearable.

I grew up feeling ambivalent about our music. Country-western and rock-and-roll had more status. In the 50s and 60s, for the slightly educated and *agringado* Chicanos, there existed a sense of shame at being caught listening to our music. Yet I couldn't stop my feet from thumping to the music, could not stop humming the words, nor hide from myself the exhilaration I felt when I heard it.

There are more subtle ways that we internalize identification, espe-   35
cially in the forms of images and emotions. For me food and certain smells are tied to my identity, to my homeland. Woodsmoke curling up to an immense blue sky; woodsmoke perfuming my grandmother's clothes, her skin. The stench of cow manure and the yellow patches on the ground; the crack of a .22 rifle and the reek of cordite. Homemade white cheese sizzling in a pan, melting inside a folded *tortilla*. My sister Hilda's hot, spicy *menudo, chile colorado* making it deep red, pieces of *panza* and hominy floating on top. My brother Carito barbequing *fajitas* in the backyard. Even now and 3,000 miles away, I can see my mother spicing the ground beef, pork and venison with *chile*. My mouth salivates at the thought of the hot steaming *tamales* I would be eating if I were home.

SI LE PREGUNTAS A MI MAMÁ, "¿QUÉ ERES?"

> "Identity is the essential core of who we are as individuals, the conscious experience of the self inside."
>
> —Kaufman[9]

Nosotros los Chicanos straddle the borderlands. On one side of us, we are constantly exposed to the Spanish of the Mexicans, on the other side we hear the Anglos' incessant clamoring so that we forget our language. Among ourselves we don't say *nosotros los americanos, o nosotros los españoles, o nosotros los hispanos*. We say *nosotros los mexicanos* (by *mexicanos* we do not mean citizens of Mexico; we do not mean a national identity, but a racial one). We distinguish between *mexicanos del otro lado* and *mexicanos de este lado*. Deep in our hearts we believe that being Mexican has nothing to do with which country one lives in. Being Mexican is a state of soul—not one of mind, not one of citizenship. Neither eagle nor serpent, but both. And like the ocean, neither animal respects borders.

> *Dime con quien andas y te diré quien eres.*
> (Tell me who your friends are and I'll tell you who you are.)
>
> —Mexican saying

Si le preguntas a mi mamá, "¿Qué eres?" te dirá, "Soy mexicana." My brothers and sister say the same. I sometimes will answer *"soy mexicana"* and at others will say *"soy Chicana" o "soy tejana."* But I identified as "Raza" before I ever identified as *"mexicana"* or "Chicana."

[9]Gershen Kaufman, *Shame: The Power of Caring* (Cambridge, MA: Shenkman Books, 1980), 68.

As a culture, we call ourselves Spanish when referring to ourselves as a linguistic group and when copping out. It is then that we forget our predominant Indian genes. We are 70–80% Indian.[10] We call ourselves Hispanic[11] or Spanish-American or Latin American or Latin when linking ourselves to other Spanish-speaking peoples of the Western hemisphere and when copping out. We call ourselves Mexican-American[12] to signify we are neither Mexican nor American, but more the noun "American" than the adjective "Mexican" (and when copping out).

Chicanos and other people of color suffer economically for not acculturating. This voluntary (yet forced) alienation makes for psychological conflict, a kind of dual identity—we don't identify with the Anglo-American cultural values and we don't totally identify with the Mexican cultural values. We are a synergy of two cultures with various degrees of Mexicanness or Angloness. I have so internalized the borderland conflict that sometimes I feel like one cancels out the other and we are zero, nothing, no one. *A veces no soy nada ni nadie. Pero hasta cuando no lo soy, lo soy.*

When not copping out, when we know we are more than nothing, we   40
call ourselves Mexican, referring to race and ancestry; *mestizo* when affirming both our Indian and Spanish (but we hardly ever own our Black ancestry); Chicano when referring to a politically aware people born and/or raised in the U.S.; *Raza* when referring to Chicanos; *tejanos* when we are Chicanos from Texas.

Chicanos did not know we were a people until 1965 when César Chávez and the farmworkers united and *I Am Joaquín* was published and *la Raza Unida* party was formed in Texas. With that recognition, we became a distinct people. Something momentous happened to the Chicano soul—we became aware of our reality and acquired a name and a language (Chicano Spanish) that reflected that reality. Now that we had a name, some of the fragmented pieces began to fall together—who we were, what we were, how we had evolved. We began to get glimpses of what we might eventually become.

Yet the struggle of identities continues, the struggle of borders is our reality still. One day the inner struggle will cease and a true integration take place. In the meantime, *tenémos que hacer la lucha. ¿Quién está protegiendo los ranchos de mi gente? ¿Quién está tratando de cerrar la fisura entre la india y el blanco en nuestra sangre? El Chicano, si, el Chicano que anda como un ladrón en su propia casa.*

---

[10]John R. Chávez, *The Lost Land: The Chicano Image of the Southwest* (Albuquerque, NM: U of New Mexico P, 1984), 88–90.

[11]"Hispanic" is derived from *Hispanis* (*España*, a name given to the Iberian Peninsula in ancient times when it was a part of the Roman Empire) and is a term designated by the U.S. government to make it easier to handle us on paper.

[12]The Treaty of Guadalupe Hidalgo created the Mexican-American in 1848.

Los Chicanos, how patient we seem, how very patient. There is the quiet of the Indian about us.[13] We know how to survive. When other races have given up their tongue, we've kept ours. We know what it is to live under the hammer blow of the dominant *norteamericano* culture. But more than we count the blows, we count the days the weeks the years the centuries the eons until the white laws and commerce and customs will rot in the deserts they've created, lie bleached. *Humildes* yet proud, *quietos* yet wild, *nosotros los mexicanos-Chicanos* will walk by the crumbling ashes as we go about our business. Stubborn, persevering, impenetrable as stone, yet possessing a malleability that renders us unbreakable, we, the *mestizas* and *mestizos*, will remain.

The Reader's Presence

1. Anzaldúa links her dentist's literal use of the word *tongue* to a metaphorical meaning. What connotations do the two senses of the word share? How does the tongue-as-organ/tongue-as-language pun relate to the quotation from Ray Gwyn Smith and questions of cultural silencing?

2. Anzaldúa peppers her English prose with untranslated Spanish words and phrases. How does this formal innovation influence the reader's experience of the text? How does the reader's experience mirror Anzaldúa's own in English-speaking America? In what ways might this technique underline the writer's insistence on the importance of keeping different languages active and alive?

3. Anzaldúa champions Spanish as the language of Mexican Americans. Spanish, of course, was brought to native Mexicans by colonizing conquistadors. The writer also distinguishes numerous dialects of Spanish and "Spanglish" as tongues in their own right. Cultural identity, in Anzaldúa's formulation, seems at once a unified and a divided entity. How does this condition compare to the one suggested by Richard Rodriguez's "Aria: A Memoir of a Bilingual Childhood" (page 239)? For all their differences of politics and style, are there ideas held in common by these Spanish- and English-speaking Americans? Do you think these writers would agree with your assessment?

---

[13]Anglos, in order to alleviate their guilt for dispossessing the Chicano, stressed the Spanish part of us and perpetrated the myth of the Spanish Southwest. We have accepted the fiction that we are Hispanic, that is Spanish, in order to accommodate ourselves to the dominant culture and its abhorrence of Indians. Chávez, 88–91.

Karen Armstrong
Is a Holy War Inevitable?

Karen Armstrong (b. 1945), a noted expert on the world's religions, spent most of the turbulent 1960s as a cloistered nun in a strict Catholic convent. This experience inspired Through the Narrow Gate *(1981) and* The Spiral Staircase: My Climb Out of Darkness *(2004), both of which retrace her early life story. In between, Armstrong has written numerous books on religious themes, concepts, and conflicts, including* The Gospel According to Woman: Christianity's Creation of the Sex War in the West *(1986),* Holy War: The Crusades and Their Impact on Today's World *(1988),* Muhammad *(1992),* The Battle for God: Fundamentalism in Judaism, Christianity and Islam *(2000), and* Buddha *(2001). Armstrong's best-selling 1993 book,* A History of God, *is still widely read and has been translated into sixteen languages. She has written three television documentaries and collaborated with Bill Moyers on the television series* Genesis. *Since the terrorist attacks of September 11, 2001, Armstrong has frequently lectured and written about Islam.*

"An extraordinary thing happened after 9/11," Armstrong says. "The American people descended on the bookstores and swept everything on Islam off the shelves. That is very positive. . . . Americans are curious in that way, and when I went round lecturing, people impressed me with their tough-minded desire to try to come to terms with all this." Her article "Is a Holy War Inevitable?" — written for GQ *magazine in 2002 — delineates between the "intransigent and fundamentalist voices that fill us all with fear" and the voices of moderate Islamic thinkers.*

Although uncertainties remain about the causes and effects of the terror that has gripped the Western world since September 11, one fact is clear: We are feeling the onslaught of a nihilistic Muslim rage. How deep are its roots, and how far might it go? Many Western leaders and thinkers, struggling to distinguish between "good" and "bad" Muslims, see the rage rooted in Islamic cultures. Some feel a civilizational inevitability: that Islam is entirely incompatible with Western culture and that the West has long been heading for a major confrontation with the Islamic world.

The roots, first, are not as ancient as some of the pundits imagine. But they are substantive. Since the late 1960s, the Islamic world has been convulsed by a fundamentalism that seems to fill Muslims with an atavistic rage against the West in general and the United States in particular. During the Islamic Revolution in Iran (1978–79), we saw mass crowds clutching copies of the Koran and yelling "Death to America!" We heard the United States denounced as "the Great Satan." Though the level of enmity toward the West has decreased in Iran, in other circles it has become more intense, as the attacks of September 11 painfully show. Still, in the aftermath of that tragedy, the word *fundamentalism* has frequently been used imprecisely and in ways that are misleading. It is often equated with extremism and terror, but in fact only a tiny proportion of religious fundamentalists resort to violence. The vast majority are simply struggling to live truly religious lives in a world that seems increasingly inimical to faith.

Fundamentalism is often described as a Muslim phenomenon, but during the twentieth century this militant type of piety erupted in every major faith worldwide, so that we have not only Christian fundamentalism but also Jewish, Sikh, Hindu, Buddhist and even Confucian forms. The first fundamentalist movement developed in Christian circles in the United States at the turn of the twentieth century, whereas fundamentalism did not appear in the Muslim world until the late 1960s. This is not surprising, since fundamentalism is essentially a revolt against modern secular civilization. In almost every region where a Western-style society has established itself, a religious counterculture has grown alongside in conscious reaction. That is why fundamentalism appeared first in North America, the showcase of modernity, and could develop in the Middle East only after a degree of modernization had been achieved.

Fundamentalists seek to drag God and religion from the sidelines to which they have been relegated in a secular polity and pull them back to center stage. Every fundamentalist movement I have studied, in Judaism, Christianity and Islam, is rooted in a profound fear of annihilation — a conviction that the liberal, secularist establishment wants to wipe out religion. This is as true of militant Christian groups in the United States as it is of Muslim extremists in Egypt and Iran. Fundamentalists believe they are fighting for survival, and when people feel that their backs are to the wall, they can lash out violently like a wounded animal.

One thing we in the West have to learn to appreciate is that disenchantment with modern society is fairly widespread. Those of us who enjoy modern society and value its freedoms and privileges need to realize that not everybody shares our enthusiasm. We must reflect seriously on the ubiquity of this fundamentalist disaffection. In Britain, where there is little interest in traditional faith, there is virtually no fundamentalism, because people do not express their discontent in a religious manner. But British soccer hooliganism reveals the same brew of emotions that fuels many fundamentalist movements: pent-up rage, frustration, a desire to belong to a clearly defined group, burning humiliation and a sense of lost prestige that on occasion can erupt into shameful violence.

These fears may seem irrational, but the history of fundamentalism shows that this aggressive new religiosity is not going to go away. Attempts to suppress fundamentalism simply make it more extreme. September 11 showed that the people who feel compelled to take part in this battle for God are moved by a level of distress, anxiety and, sometimes, fury that no society, no government, can safely ignore.

It wasn't always like this. When Muslims first became fully aware of Western modernity, they seemed to "recognize" it at a profound level. During the nineteenth and early twentieth centuries, almost every single Muslim intellectual was full of admiration for the new West. Islamic thinkers of the day wanted their countries to be just like Britain and France. In 1906 many of the leading ulama (religious scholars) in Iran joined secularists in a revolution demanding a constitution and parliamentary rule modeled on those of Europe. Any system that could reduce the tyranny of the shahs was clearly compatible with Shiite Islam. The nineteenth-century Egyptian writer Rifa'ah al-Tahtawi was enthralled by the ideas of the European Enlightenment, which reminded him of the teachings of the great Muslim philosophers. He loved the way everything worked properly in Paris, was impressed by the systematic education of French children and the literacy of the common people. In India, Sayyid Ahmad Khan (1817–1898) tried to adapt the ideals of Islam to modern Western liberalism. He founded a college at Aligarh, where Muslims could study science and English alongside their traditional Islamic subjects. This would help Muslims live in a modernized society without becoming inferior copies of the British, since they would retain a sense of their own cultural identity.

In the Islamic world, however, disenchantment with the West and its accelerating form of modernity became more widespread during the twentieth century. What is it about modernity that fills so many people all over the world with visceral dread? Modernization, we are apt to forget, is a traumatic process. In Europe and the United States, it took us some 300 years to develop our secular and democratic institutions. Starting in the sixteenth century, we began creating a new form of civilization. Economically, it was based not on a surplus of agricultural produce, as all premodern civilizations had been, but on technology and the constant reinvestment of capital. This enabled us to reproduce our resources indefinitely and thus freed us from the constraints of the more vulnerable traditional agrarian cultures. But because this was such a major social undertaking, it required change in almost every sphere of life—political, social, economic, intellectual and religious—which was often accompanied by pain and bloodshed. Political institutions had to be altered to accommodate these new conditions. In the West, it was found, by trial and error, that a modern state had to be democratic, secular and tolerant—but this trial and error had grave costs. Europe and America both witnessed revolutions, which were sometimes succeeded by reigns of terror. As we made the painful rite of passage to modernity—which did not come into its own until the nineteenth century—we experienced fearful wars of religion, genocide, persecution of minorities, exploitation of workers in factories, despoliation of the countryside and anomie and spiritual disorientation in the slums of the newly industrialized cities. Today we are witnessing similar distress in developing countries that are now in the throes of this transformation.

In Europe and America, the emerging modern spirit had two main characteristics. The first was independence. Modernization was accompanied by declarations of independence on all fronts: political, religious, scientific and intellectual. People could no longer be constrained by coercive governments or churches; they had to have the freedom to follow their ideas and projects wherever they might lead, a luxury no previous society could afford. The second characteristic was innovation. The West also came to accept — even value — institutionalized change. In the more vulnerable premodern economies, it had always been more important to conserve what had been achieved. But now the people of the West came to find a virtue in the pace of change — we were always creating something fresh and breaking into uncharted realms, and despite the inherent difficulties, this gave our lives a wholly new excitement. Instead of looking back at past achievements, we were continually thrusting forward into the future.

The modernization process has been very different in the Muslim   10
world. Modernity came not with independence but with political and economic subjection. Muslim countries were colonized by the European powers, organized into mandates or protectorates and reduced to a dependent bloc. Instead of innovation, their modern experience was one of imitation, since Western countries were so far ahead that Muslim modernizers could only copy us. Lagging behind and endlessly trying to play catch-up, Muslim countries found their own way to modernity. Because the process has been so different, so too has been the end product. Democratic, liberal, secular societies could not automatically emerge in these more problematic circumstances.

Modernization has also been too rapid in the Muslim world, and inevitably, the new ideas have not been able to filter down gradually to all sectors of the population as they did in the West. Muslim countries have been split unhealthily into two camps: an elite, who have received a Western-style education and can understand the new norms and institutions, and the vast majority who have not. Because the process has been so accelerated, the secularization of society, the separation of religion and politics, has been experienced by religious people as a deadly assault. Thus when Atatürk (1881–1938), the founder of the Turkish republic, was creating modern secular Turkey, he closed all the madrasahs, the colleges of Islamic education, abolished the orders of Sufi mystics, which had played a crucial role in the social and spiritual lives of the people, and forced the Sufis underground. Men and women were compelled to wear Western dress, because Atatürk wanted the country to look modern. In

Iran the shahs had their soldiers go through the streets, taking off Muslim women's veils with their bayonets and tearing them to pieces. In 1935, Reza Shah Pahlavi gave his soldiers orders to shoot at hundreds of unarmed demonstrators at the holy shrine of Mashhad who were peacefully protesting against obligatory Western dress. His son Muhammad Reza shot down hundreds of madrasah students who dared to protest against his dictatorship, and leading clerics were tortured to death, imprisoned or exiled. In such forceful circumstances, secularism is not the liberating polity we have experienced in the West. It is invasive and frightening, an attack on one's way of life.

This has been keenly felt in Egypt. The Egyptian ideologue Sayyid Qutb (1906–1966) founded the most influential form of fundamentalism in Sunni Islam (the version of the faith followed by the majority of Muslims). Qutb had once greatly admired Western culture and secular politics, had been a moderate, eager to reform Egypt. In 1953 he joined the Muslim Brotherhood, a welfare society intent on religious and social reform, only to watch President Gamal Abdel Nasser imprison, torture and execute thousands of Brothers, often without trial and for doing nothing more incriminating than attending a meeting or handing out leaflets. Spending years in vile concentration camps made him a radical, determined to fight against the corrupt secularism of Nasser and his counterparts in the Muslim world. He was executed by Nasser in 1966, but his ideology has shaped most Sunni fundamentalists, including Osama bin Laden.

The case of Qutb shows us the path fundamentalism invariably takes. Fundamentalism always begins as an internal struggle. It is an intrareligious conflict, in that fundamentalists start by attacking their own coreligionists and fellow countrymen. Qutb was sickened by the colonial activities of the French and the British in North Africa and the Middle East, and he had been disillusioned by a visit to the United States, whose culture seemed to him trivial, decadent and materialistic. But Qutb did not become a fundamentalist until he saw his country overtaken by an ethos that seemed cruel, tyrannical and corrupt. Similarly, bin Laden's original targets were the so-called Muslim regimes of Saudi Arabia, Egypt, Jordan and Iran, which he regarded as defecting from the Islamic norm. It was only at a later stage that bin Laden turned his attention to the United States, which supports many of these regimes and which he now regards as the root of the problem.

So Muslim fundamentalism was not originally inspired by a hatred of America per se, but it has become increasingly disturbed by the role of the United States in Islamic countries. This was certainly the case in Iran. Americans were understandably shocked to hear their nation described as "the Great Satan." But Westerners—particularly Christian Westerners—misread that phrase. In Christianity, Satan is a figure of absolute, towering evil, and though the policy of the United States was often shortsighted, exploitative and self-interested, it did not deserve to be stigmatized in this way. But in popular Shiism, the Shaitan is a rather pathetic creature, incapable of appreciating spirituality. In one folk legend, he complains to God that humans are acquiring gifts that he wants for himself. He would like to have a scripture and beautifully illuminated manuscripts; God tells him to get himself a few tattoos. He wants to have a mosque, so God tells him to go to the bazaar. He wants prophets, and God fobs him off with fortune-tellers. And the Shaitan is quite happy with these inferior gifts. He is incurably trivial, trapped forever in the realm of the exterior and unable to see that there is a deeper and more important dimension to life. For many Iranians, America, the Great Shaitan, was "the Great Trivializer." The bars, casinos and the secularist ethos of north Tehran, the Americanized zone, seemed to be the abode of the superficial and materialistic Shaitan. The Great Satan was a joke, and its icons were often ridiculous: a giant figure of Ronald Reagan in an Uncle Sam outfit.

Furthermore, the word *Shaitan* means "tempter." America, it was   15
thought, had tempted the shah away from the true values of Islam to a life of unspiritual secularism. Rightly or wrongly, Iranians believed that the shah would not have behaved so tyrannically toward his people had he not been assured of the unconditional support of the United States. The image of the Great Satan, therefore, did not reflect a hatred of American culture in itself; Iranians simply did not want to see this materialism in their own country. Nor did they want their destinies to be controlled by the Great Tempter of the shah.

The same kind of precise symbolism underlay the capture of the American hostages in the United States embassy in Tehran. Since an embassy is considered native soil, the siege amounted to an invasion of American sovereignty. Yet to some Iranians, it seemed appropriate that American citizens should be held captive in their own embassy, because for decades, under the Pahlavi shahs, Iranians felt they had been held prisoner in their own country, with the connivance of the United States.

But this is revenge, not religion. Hostage taking is repugnant to Western values, and not unnaturally many Americans assumed Islam condones such behavior and must, therefore, be an immoral creed. But when he refused to return the hostages, Ayatollah Khomeini was violating clear legislation in the Koran. The Koran demands that Muslims treat their opponents humanely. It is unlawful to take prisoners, except during the fighting of a regular war. Prisoners must not be ill-treated and should be released after hostilities have come to an end. If no ransom is forthcoming, the prisoner must be allowed to earn money to pay the sum himself, and his captor is urged to help him out of his own pocket (Koran 8:68, 47:5, 24:34, 2:178). A tradition has preserved the Prophet's directions about the treatment of captives: "You must feed them as you feed yourselves, and clothe them as you clothe yourselves, and if you should set them a hard task, you must help them in it yourselves." This is the true teaching of Islam, and it is clearly close to the Western ideal.

This example reminds us that fundamentalism very often distorts the tradition it is trying to defend. Because fundamentalists believe they are facing a massive threat to their faith, they can accentuate the more intransigent elements of their scriptures and downplay those that speak of compassion and benevolence. It would be a great mistake to assume that fundamentalist discourse represents the rich and complex traditions of Islam or to imagine that the Muslim faith is adamantly opposed to our values. In fact, it shares most of the central tenets of the Judeo-Christian traditions that have shaped our culture. We are not speaking here about a clash of civilizations that are essentially opposed. We are much closer to Muslims than we imagine.

There are passages in the Koran that seem to give license to unfettered violence, and we have all heard bin Laden quoting these. But in the Koran, these verses are in almost every case followed by exhortations to peace and mercy. The Koran teaches that the only valid war is one of self-defense, which is clearly in line with the Western notion of the just war. War is always abhorrent and evil, but it is sometimes necessary to fight in order to preserve decent values or to defend oneself against persecution.

Nor would it be fair to say Muslims are incapable of separating religion and politics. For much of their history, Muslims effected a de facto separation of what we would call church and state. During the Abbasid caliphate (750–1258)—when Baghdad was the capital of the Islamic world—the court was ruled by an aristocratic ethos, which had little to do with Islam. Indeed the shari'a, the system of Islamic holy law, initially developed as a countercultural revolt against this ethos. The clerics and the ruling class thus operated according to entirely different norms. Though secularism as practiced in the West has since acquired sinister connotations, Islam is a realistic faith; it understands that politics is a messy business that can corrupt religion. In Shiite Islam, religion and politics were separated as a matter of sacred principle.

Nor is Islam inherently opposed to the democratic ideal. It is true that fundamentalists, be they Jewish, Christian or Muslim, have little time for democracy, since their militant beliefs are not typical of any of these faiths' traditions. It is also true that Muslims would have difficulty with the classic definition of democracy, as "government of the people, by the people and for the people." In Islam, God, not the people, gives a government legitimacy, and this elevation of humanity could seem a usurpation of God's sovereignty. But Muslim countries could well introduce representative governments without relying on this Western slogan. This is what is beginning to happen in Iran, which had never been permitted to have a fully functioning parliament before the Islamic Revolution. In fact, Muslim thinkers have pointed out that Islamic laws have principles that are eminently compatible with democracy. The notion of *shura*, for example, which decrees that there must be some form of "consultation" with the

20

people before new legislation can be passed, is clearly congenial to the democratic ideal, as is ijma, the "consensus" of the people, which gives legitimacy to a legal decision.

Even today, when so many Muslims feel alienated by American foreign policy, important and influential thinkers emphasize the kinship that exists between Islam and Western thought. President Mohammad Khatami of Iran is an obvious example; immediately after his landslide election victory in 1997, he made it clear that he wanted to build stronger links to the West, and that he represented a platform that stood for greater pluralism, more democracy and improved rights for women. The leading Iranian intellectual, Abdolkarim Sorush, who held office under Khomeini, argues that Iranians have a Western as well as an Iranian identity. He rejects the secularism of the West and insists that Iranians hold on to their Shiite identity. But he also believes that traditional Islamic law must evolve to embrace a philosophy of civil rights.

In the Sunni world, the Tunisian thinker Rashid al-Ghannouchi describes himself as a "democratic Islamist." Muslims, he believes, want modernity, but not one that has been imposed upon them by America, Britain or France. They admire the efficiency and technology of the West but want to hold on to their own religious and moral traditions while incorporating some of the best aspects of Western civilization. Similarly, Yusuf al-Qaradawi, currently at the University of Qatar, preaches moderation and is adamantly opposed to the extremism that has recently appeared in the Muslim world. This fundamentalist intolerance will impoverish the Muslim people, by depriving them of the insights and visions of other human beings.

Qaradawi argues, "It is better for the West that Muslims should be religious, hold to their religion and try to be moral." He makes an important point. Like any other great world religion, Islam has helped Muslims to cultivate decent values. The religion does not preach bigotry and hatred but justice, compassion and peace. The Koran has a pluralistic vision and respects other faiths. Constantly, it insists that Muhammad has not come to cancel out the revelations of such earlier prophets as Abraham, Moses and Jesus. God commands Muslims to "speak courteously" to Jews and Christians, "the People of the Book," and to tell them: "We believe what you believe; your God and our God is one" (Koran 29:46). Alongside the more intransigent and fundamentalist voices that fill us all with fear have always been Muslims such as Tahtawi, Sorush, Ghannouchi and Qaradawi, who recognize this relationship, even in these difficult days. Unlike the fundamentalists, these moderate Muslim thinkers, who are every bit as influential, if not more so, than bin Laden and his like, have not become repelled by our modern Western society but still see it as deeply compatible with the Islamic ideal.

The bedrock message of the Koran is that it is wrong for Muslims to stockpile their wealth selfishly and good to share their resources equally. Since the time of the Prophet Muhammad, Islamic piety and spirituality   25 have been inspired by the ideal of a just society, in which the poor and vulnerable are treated with respect. Such a goal is obviously close to Western aspirations, and the search for a more just and, therefore, safer world could bring us closer to Muslims today.

Both Qaradawi and Ghannouchi assume, however, that there is no religion in the secular West. As Ghannouchi said, Muslims see no light, no heart and no spirituality when they look at Western culture. But they are wrong. Many Europeans may have little interest in conventional faith, but the United States is a deeply religious country. Every time I land on American soil, I am struck anew by this fact. But the Muslim world sees the West at its worst. It sees the bars, nightclubs and materialism of "the Great Satan," which are alien to its culture. It has also experienced the West, led by the United States, as coercive and exploitative. Muslims find American policy difficult to square with true faith, which, according to the Koran, must go hand in hand with the pursuit of justice. At the time of the Iranian Revolution, the clerics were astonished that President Jimmy Carter, a religious man who was so passionate about human rights, supported the shah, who denied his people rights that most Americans take for granted.

All over the world, Muslims have been outraged by the carnage of September 11, which violates the essential principles of Islam. But many feel bitter about American policy in their region, and as we have seen, it is this, rather than a dislike for Western modernity and democracy, that fuels fundamentalist rage.

In all three monotheistic religions, fundamentalism is becoming more extreme. In the United States, the movements known as Reconstructionism and Christian Identity have left Jerry Falwell's Moral Majority far behind. They both, in different ways, look forward to the destruction of the democratic federal government and would not be too unhappy about the burning towers of the World Trade Center. As September 11 showed, Islamic fundamentalism has also entered a more radical phase, which has outstripped Sayyid Qutb and Ayatollah Khomeini and embraced a totally nihilistic vision.

This is a dangerous moment. It is crucial that we convince those millions of Muslims who abhor the September atrocities but have been alienated from the United States that Americans are indeed religious, because they share this monotheistic passion for a just world. The word *jihad* does not primarily mean "holy war." It means "struggle, effort." Muslims have to make a strenuous effort to implement God's will in a flawed and tragic world. It is a jihad that must be conducted on all fronts: political, spiritual, moral, intellectual and social. The Prophet Muhammad once said on returning from a battle: "We are returning from the lesser jihad [the battle] to the greater jihad," the far more difficult and crucial effort to reform our own hearts, our own attitudes and our own societies. In our present crisis, we have begun the lesser jihad in Afghanistan, but we must make sure we conduct a greater jihad and scrutinize our own conduct and our own policies, in the interests of peace.

The Reader's Presence

1. How does Armstrong define *fundamentalism*? Do you think that fundamentalists of different religions have more in common with each other than with moderates of their own faith? Why or why not?

2. Armstrong debunks many of the myths of vast differences between Islam and Christianity and puts Muslim disillusionment with Western modernization into context. Does Armstrong explicitly attempt to answer the question presented in the title, or is the answer implied? What do you think her answer is?

3. Look at H. L. Mencken's portrayal of Christians at a revival meeting in "The Hills of Zion" (page 504). Do their actions suggest the kind of reaction against modernity that Armstrong describes? Do these people meet Armstrong's definition of "fundamentalists"? Why or why not?

David Brooks

People Like Us

David Brooks (b. 1961) was born in Toronto and grew up in New York City and in a suburb of Philadelphia. A journalist, columnist, and self-described "comic sociologist," Brooks has authored two books of cultural commentary, Bobos in Paradise *(2001) and* On Paradise Drive: How We Live Now (and Always Have) in the Future Tense *(2004), and he edited the anthology* Backward and Upward: The New Conservative Writing *(1995). After graduating from the University of Chicago, Brooks worked as a reporter for the* Wall Street Journal. *Since that time, he has served as a senior editor at the* Weekly Standard *and as a contributing editor at the* Atlantic *and* Newsweek, *where the managing editor praised his "dead-on eye for the foibles of the Beltway—and his strong sense of how what happens in the capital's conservative circles affects the rest of the country." Brooks presents commentary on* National Public Radio *and on* The Newshour with Jim Lehrer. *In 2003 he joined the* New York Times *as an op-ed columnist.*

In a PBS interview in 2000, Brooks argued that people tend to gravitate to like-minded, like-cultured people—a "congealing pot" of people just like themselves: "Now if you look at the New York Times *wedding page, it's this great clash of resumés. . . . Harvard marries Yale. Princeton marries Stanford. Magna*

*cum laude marries magna cum laude. You never get a magna cum laude marrying
a summa cum laude because the tensions would be too great in that wedding."
"People Like Us" first appeared in the* Atlantic *in 2003.*

Maybe it's time to admit the obvious. We don't really care about diversity all that much in America, even though we talk about it a great
deal. Maybe somewhere in this country there is a truly diverse neighborhood in which a black Pentecostal minister lives next to a white anti-
globalization activist, who lives next to an Asian short-order cook, who
lives next to a professional golfer, who lives next to a postmodern-literature
professor and a cardiovascular surgeon. But I have never been to or heard
of that neighborhood. Instead, what I have seen all around the country is
people making strenuous efforts to group themselves with people who are
basically like themselves.

Human beings are capable of drawing amazingly subtle social distinctions and then shaping their lives around them. In the Washington, D.C.,
area Democratic lawyers tend to live in suburban Maryland, and Republican lawyers tend to live in suburban Virginia. If you asked a Democratic
lawyer to move from her $750,000 house in Bethesda, Maryland, to a
$750,000 house in Great Falls, Virginia, she'd look at you as if you had
just asked her to buy a pickup truck with a gun rack and to shove chewing tobacco in her kid's mouth. In Manhattan the owner of a $3 million
SoHo loft would feel out of place moving into a $3 million Fifth Avenue
apartment. A West Hollywood interior decorator would feel dislocated if
you asked him to move to Orange County. In Georgia a barista from
Athens would probably not fit in serving coffee in Americus.

It is a common complaint that every place is starting to look the
same. But in the information age, the late writer James Chapin once told
me, every place becomes more like itself. People are less often tied down
to factories and mills, and they can search for places to live on the basis
of cultural affinity. Once they find a town in which people share their
values, they flock there, and reinforce whatever was distinctive about the
town in the first place. Once Boulder, Colorado, became known as congenial to politically progressive mountain bikers, half the politically progressive mountain bikers in the country (it seems) moved there; they
made the place so culturally pure that it has become practically a parody
of itself.

But people love it. Make no mistake — we are increasing our happiness by segmenting off so rigorously. We are finding places where we are
comfortable and where we feel we can flourish. But the choices we make
toward that end lead to the very opposite of diversity. The United States
might be a diverse nation when considered as a whole, but block by block
and institution by institution it is a relatively homogeneous nation.

When we use the word "diversity" today we usually mean racial inte- 5
gration. But even here our good intentions seem to have run into the
brick wall of human nature. Over the past generation reformers have

tried heroically, and in many cases successfully, to end housing discrimi-nation. But recent patterns aren't encouraging: according to an analysis of the 2000 census data, the 1990s saw only a slight increase in the racial integration of neighborhoods in the United States. The number of middle-class and upper-middle-class African-American families is rising, but for whatever reasons—racism, psychological comfort—these families tend to congregate in predominantly black neighborhoods.

In fact, evidence suggests that some neighborhoods become more seg-regated over time. New suburbs in Arizona and Nevada, for example, start out reasonably well integrated. These neighborhoods don't yet have reputations, so people choose their houses for other, mostly economic reasons. But as neighborhoods age, they develop personalities (that's where the Asian live, and that's where the Hispanics live), and segmenta-tion occurs. It could be that in a few years the new suburbs in the South-west will be nearly as segregated as the established ones in the Northeast and the Midwest.

Even though race and ethnicity run deep in American society, we should in theory be able to find areas that are at least culturally diverse. But here, too, people show few signs of being truly interested in building diverse communities. If you run a retail company and you're thinking of opening new stores, you can choose among dozens of consulting firms that are quite effective at locating your potential customers. They can do this because people with similar tastes and preferences tend to congregate by ZIP code.

The most famous of these precision marketing firms is Claritas, which breaks down the U.S. population into sixty-two psycho-demographic clus-ters, based on such factors as how much money people make, what they like to read and watch, and what products they have bought in the past. For example, the "suburban sprawl" cluster is composed of young fami-lies making about $41,000 a year and living in fast-growing places such as Burnsville, Minnesota, and Bensalem, Pennsylvania. These people are almost twice as likely as other Americans to have three-way calling. They are two and a half times as likely to buy Light n' Lively Kid Yogurt. Members of the "towns & gowns" cluster are recent college graduates in places such as Berkeley, California, and Gainesville, Florida. They are big consumers of DoveBars and *Saturday Night Live*. They tend to drive small foreign cars and to read *Rolling Stone* and *Scientific American*.

Looking through the market research, one can sometimes be amazed by how efficiently people cluster—and by how predictable we all are. If you wanted to sell imported wine, obviously you would have to find places where rich people live. But did you know that the sixteen counties with the greatest proportion of imported-wine drinkers are all in the same three metropolitan areas (New York, San Francisco, and Washington, D.C.)? If you tried to open a motor-home dealership in Montgomery County, Pennsylvania, you'd probably go broke, because people in this ring of the Philadelphia suburbs think RVs are kind of uncool. But if you traveled just a short way north, to Monroe County, Pennsylvania, you would find yourself in the fifth motor-home-friendliest county in America.

Geography is not the only way we find ourselves divided from people   10
unlike us. Some of us watch Fox News, while others listen to NPR. Some like David Letterman, and others—typically in less urban neighborhoods— like Jay Leno. Some go to charismatic churches; some go to mainstream churches. Americans tend more and more often to marry people with education levels similar to their own, and to befriend people with backgrounds similar to their own.

My favorite illustration of this latter pattern comes from the first, noncontroversial chapter of *The Bell Curve*. Think of your twelve closest friends, Richard J. Herrnstein and Charles Murray write. If you had chosen them randomly from the American population, the odds that half of your twelve closest friends would be college graduates would be six in a thousand. The odds that half of the twelve would have advanced degrees would be less than one in a million. Have any of your twelve closest friends graduated from Harvard, Stanford, Yale, Princeton, Caltech, MIT, Duke, Dartmouth, Cornell, Columbia, Chicago, or Brown? If you chose your friends randomly from the American population, the odds against your having four or more friends from those schools would be more than a billion to one.

Many of us live in absurdly unlikely groupings, because we have organized our lives that way.

It's striking that the institutions that talk the most about diversity often practice it the least. For example, no group of people sings the diversity anthem more frequently and fervently than administrators at just such elite universities. But elite universities are amazingly undiverse in their values, politics, and mores. Professors in particular are drawn from a rather narrow segment of the population. If faculties reflected the general population, 32 percent of professors would be registered Democrats and 31 percent would be registered Republicans. Forty percent would be evangelical Christians. But a recent study of several universities by the conservative Center for the Study of Popular Culture and the American Enterprise Institute found that roughly 90 percent of those professors in the arts and sciences who had registered with a political party had registered Democratic. Fifty-seven professors at Brown were found on the voter-registration rolls. Of those, fifty-four were Democrats. Of the forty-two professors in the English, history, sociology, and political-science departments, all were Democrats. The results at Harvard, Penn State, Maryland, and the University of California at Santa Barbara were similar to the results at Brown.

What we are looking at here is human nature. People want to be around others who are roughly like themselves. That's called community. It probably would be psychologically difficult for most Brown professors to share an office with someone who was pro-life, a member of the National Rifle Association, or an evangelical Christian. It's likely that hiring committees would subtly—even unconsciously—screen out any such people they encountered. Republicans and evangelical Christians have sensed that they are not welcome at places like Brown, so they don't even consider working there. In fact, any registered Republican who contemplates a career in academia these days is both a hero and a fool. So, in a semi–self-selective pattern, brainy people with generally liberal social mores flow to academia, and brainy people with generally conservative mores flow elsewhere.

The dream of diversity is like the dream of equality. Both are based 15
on ideals we celebrate even as we undermine them daily. (How many times have you seen someone renounce a high-paying job or pull his child from an elite college on the grounds that these things are bad for equality?) On the one hand, the situation is appalling. It is appalling that Americans know so little about one another. It is appalling that many of us are so narrow-minded that we can't tolerate a few people with ideas significantly different from our own. It's appalling that evangelical Christians are practically absent from entire professions, such as academia, the media, and filmmaking. It's appalling that people should be content to cut themselves off from everyone unlike themselves.

The segmentation of society means that often we don't even have arguments across the political divide. Within their little validating communities, liberals and conservatives circulate half-truths about the supposed awfulness of the other side. These distortions are believed because it feels good to believe them.

On the other hand, there are limits to how diverse any community can or should be. I've come to think that it is not useful to try to hammer diversity into every neighborhood and institution in the United States. Sure, Augusta National should probably admit women, and university sociology departments should probably hire a conservative or two. It would be nice if all neighborhoods had a good mixture of ethnicities. But human nature being what it is, most places and institutions are going to remain culturally homogeneous.

It's probably better to think about diverse lives, not diverse institutions. Human beings, if they are to live well, will have to move through a series of institutions and environments, which may be individually homogeneous but, taken together, will offer diverse experiences. It might also be a good idea to make national service a rite of passage for young people in this country: it would take them out of their narrow neighborhood segment and thrust them in with people unlike themselves. Finally, it's probably important for adults to get out of their own familiar circles. If you live in a coastal, socially liberal neighborhood, maybe you should take out a subscription to *The Door*, the evangelical humor magazine; or maybe you should visit Branson, Missouri. Maybe you should stop in at a megachurch. Sure, it would be superficial familiarity, but it beats the iron curtains that now separate the nation's various cultural zones.

Look around at your daily life. Are you really in touch with the broad diversity of American life? Do you care?

The Reader's Presence

1. Brooks begins his argument by "admitting the obvious": Americans don't care about diversity, they just like to talk as if they do. What was your initial reaction to Brooks's "admission"? What is the effect of admitting something that many of his readers will instinctually reject? How is your opinion affected by his evidence? How well has he supported this assertion by the end of the essay?

2. Brooks claims that it is human nature for people to group together with those who have similar ideals and backgrounds. What might be the advantages of such grouping? What might be lost if Americans were truly integrated? What is lost by segregating by religion, politics, race, class, profession, and sexuality?

3. Compare Brooks's observations about how we prefer to be around "people like us" to Mary Gordon's discussion of looking for her ancestors' history in "The Ghosts of Ellis Island" (page 443). How does Gordon's discussion of her view that much of American history is "not mine" fit into Brooks's argument?

Stephen L. Carter

The Insufficiency of Honesty

Law professor and writer Stephen L. Carter (b. 1954) is an insightful and incisive critic of contemporary cultural politics. His first book, Reflections of an Affirmative Action Baby *(1992), criticizes affirmative action policies that reinforce racial stereotypes rather than break down structures of discrimination. Carter's critique emerges from his own experience as an African American student at Stanford University and at Yale University Law School. After graduating from Yale, he served as a law clerk for Supreme Court justice Thurgood Marshall and eventually joined the faculty at Yale as professor of law, where he has served since 1991 as the William Cromwell Professor of Law. Carter has published widely on legal and social topics, including his books* The Culture of Disbelief: How

American Law and Politics Trivialize Religious Devotion *(1993)*, The Confirma-
tion Mess *(1994)*, Civility: Manners, Morals, and the Etiquette of Democracy
(1998), The Dissent of the Governed: A Meditation on Law, Religion, and Loyalty *(1998)*, and God's Name in Vain *(2000)*.

Carter's most recent work is the best-selling novel The Emperor of Ocean
Park *(2002)*, *a work that took him four years to complete. Carter says, "One of
the best pieces of advice about writing I ever received was from a professor at law
school who said to me, 'Stephen, there's no piece of writing that can't be improved by spending more time on it. The discipline is to make yourself stop.' "*

"The Insufficiency of Honesty" first appeared in Integrity *in 1996.*

A couple of years ago I began a university commencement address by
telling the audience that I was going to talk about integrity. The crowd
broke into applause. Applause! Just because they had heard the word "integrity": that's how starved for it they were. They had no idea how I was
using the word, or what I was going to say about integrity, or, indeed,
whether I was for it or against it. But they knew they liked the idea of
talking about it.

Very well, let us consider this word "integrity." Integrity is like the
weather: everybody talks about it but nobody knows what to do about it.
Integrity is that stuff that we always want more of. Some say that we need
to return to the good old days when we had a lot more of it. Others say
that we as a nation have never really had enough of it. Hardly anybody
stops to explain exactly what we mean by it, or how we know it is a good
thing, or why everybody needs to have the same amount of it. Indeed, the
only trouble with integrity is that everybody who uses the word seems to
mean something slightly different.

For instance, when I refer to integrity, do I mean simply "honesty"?
The answer is no; although honesty is a virtue of importance, it is a different virtue from integrity. Let us, for simplicity, think of honesty as not
lying; and let us further accept Sissela Bok's definition of a lie: "any intentionally deceptive message which is *stated*." Plainly, one cannot have integrity without being honest (although, as we shall see, the matter gets
complicated), but one can certainly be honest and yet have little integrity.

When I refer to integrity, I have something very specific in mind. Integrity, as I will use the term, requires three steps: discerning what is right
and what is wrong; acting on what you have discerned, even at personal
cost; and saying openly that you are acting on your understanding of
right and wrong. The first criterion captures the idea that integrity requires a degree of moral reflectiveness. The second brings in the ideal of a
person of integrity as steadfast, a quality that includes keeping one's com-
mitments. The third reminds us that a person of integrity can be trusted.

The first point to understand about the difference between honesty   5
and integrity is that a person may be entirely honest without ever engaging in the hard work of discernment that integrity requires; she may tell
us quite truthfully what she believes without ever taking the time to figure
out whether what she believes is good and right and true. The problem

may be as simple as someone's foolishly saying something that hurts a friend's feelings; a few moments of thought would have revealed the likelihood of the hurt and the lack of necessity for the comment. Or the problem may be more complex, as when a man who was raised from birth in a society that preaches racism states his belief in one race's inferiority as a fact, without ever really considering that perhaps this deeply held view is wrong. Certainly the racist is being honest—he is telling us what he actually thinks—but his honesty does not add up to integrity.

TELLING EVERYTHING YOU KNOW

A wonderful epigram sometimes attributed to the filmmaker Sam Goldwyn goes like this: "The most important thing in acting is honesty; once you learn to fake that, you're in." The point is that honesty can be something one *seems* to have. Without integrity, what passes for honesty often is nothing of the kind; it is fake honesty—or it is honest but irrelevant and perhaps even immoral.

Consider an example. A man who has been married for fifty years confesses to his wife on his deathbed that he was unfaithful thirty-five years earlier. The dishonesty was killing his spirit, he says. Now he has cleared his conscience and is able to die in peace.

The husband has been honest—sort of. He has certainly unburdened himself. And he has probably made his wife (soon to be his widow) quite miserable in the process, because even if she forgives him, she will not be able to remember him with quite the vivid image of love and loyalty that she had hoped for. Arranging his own emotional affairs to ease his transition to death, he has shifted to his wife the burden of confusion and pain, perhaps for the rest of her life. Moreover, he has attempted his honesty at the one time in his life when it carries no risk; acting in accordance with what you think is right and risking no loss in the process is a rather thin and unadmirable form of honesty.

Besides, even though the husband has been honest in a sense, he has now twice been unfaithful to his wife: once thirty-five years ago, when he had his affair, and again when, nearing death, he decided that his own peace of mind was more important than hers. In trying to be honest he has violated his marriage vow by acting toward his wife not with love but with naked and perhaps even cruel self-interest.

As my mother used to say, you don't have to tell people everything you know. Lying and nondisclosure, as the law often recognizes, are not the same thing. Sometimes it is actually illegal to tell what you know, as, for example, in the disclosure of certain financial information by market insiders. Or it may be unethical, as when a lawyer reveals a confidence entrusted to her by a client. It may be simple bad manners, as in the case of a gratuitous comment to a colleague on his or her attire. And it may be subject to religious punishment, as when a Roman Catholic priest

10

breaks the seal of the confessional—an offense that carries automatic ex-communication.

In all the cases just mentioned, the problem with telling everything you know is that somebody else is harmed. Harm may not be the intention, but it is certainly the effect. Honesty is most laudable when we risk harm to ourselves; it becomes a good deal less so if we instead risk harm to others when there is no gain to anyone other than ourselves. Integrity may counsel keeping our secrets in order to spare the feelings of others. Sometimes, as in the example of the wayward husband, the reason we want to tell what we know is precisely to shift our pain onto somebody else—a course of action dictated less by integrity than by self-interest. Fortunately, integrity and self-interest often coincide, as when a politician of integrity is rewarded with our votes. But often they do not, and it is at those moments that our integrity is truly tested.

ERROR

Another reason that honesty alone is no substitute for integrity is that if forthrightness is not preceded by discernment, it may result in the expression of an incorrect moral judgment. In other words, I may be honest about what I believe, but if I have never tested my beliefs, I may be wrong. And here I mean "wrong" in a particular sense: the proposition in question is wrong if I would change my mind about it after hard moral reflection.

Consider this example. Having been taught all his life that women are not as smart as men, a manager gives the women on his staff less-challenging assignments than he gives the men. He does this, he believes, for their own benefit: he does not want them to fail, and he believes that they will if he gives them tougher assignments. Moreover, when one of the women on his staff does poor work, he does not berate her as harshly as he would a man, because he expects nothing more. And he claims to be acting with integrity because he is acting according to his own deepest beliefs.

The manager fails the most basic test of integrity. The question is not whether his actions are consistent with what he most deeply believes but whether he has done the hard work of discerning whether what he most deeply believes is right. The manager has not taken this harder step.

Moreover, even within the universe that the manager has constructed   15
for himself, he is not acting with integrity. Although he is obviously wrong to think that the women on his staff are not as good as the men, even were he right, that would not justify applying different standards to their work. By so doing he betrays both his obligation to the institution that employs him and his duty as a manager to evaluate his employees.

The problem that the manager faces is an enormous one in our practical politics, where having the dialogue that makes democracy work can seem impossible because of our tendency to cling to our views even when we have not examined them. As Jean Bethke Elshtain has said, borrowing from John Courtney Murray, our politics are so fractured and contentious that we often cannot reach *disagreement*. Our refusal to look closely at our own most cherished principles is surely a large part of the reason. Socrates thought the unexamined life not worth living. But the unhappy truth is that few of us actually have the time for constant reflection on our views—on public or private morality. Examine them we must, however, or we will never know whether we might be wrong.

None of this should be taken to mean that integrity as I have described it presupposes a single correct truth. If, for example, your integrity-guided search tells you that affirmative action is wrong, and my integrity-guided search tells me that affirmative action is right, we need not conclude that one of us lacks integrity. As it happens, I believe— both as a Christian and as a secular citizen who struggles toward moral understanding—that we *can* find true and sound answers to our moral questions. But I do not pretend to have found very many of them, nor is an exposition of them my purpose here.

It is the case not that there aren't any right answers but that, given human fallibility, we need to be careful in assuming that we have found them. However, today's political talk about how it is wrong for the government to impose one person's morality on somebody else is just mindless chatter. *Every* law imposes one person's morality on somebody else, because law has only two functions: to tell people to do what they would rather not or to forbid them to do what they would.

And if the surveys can be believed, there is far more moral agreement in America than we sometimes allow ourselves to think. One of the reasons that character education for young people makes so much sense to so many people is precisely that there seems to be a core set of moral understandings—we might call them the American Core—that most of us accept. Some of the virtues in this American Core are, one hopes, relatively noncontroversial. About 500 American communities have signed on to Michael Josephson's program to emphasize the "six pillars" of good character: trustworthiness, respect, responsibility, caring, fairness, and citizenship. These virtues might lead to a similarly noncontroversial set of political values: having an honest regard for ourselves and others, protecting freedom of thought and religious belief, and refusing to steal or murder.

HONESTY AND COMPETING RESPONSIBILITIES

A further problem with too great an exaltation of honesty is that it   20
may allow us to escape responsibilities that morality bids us bear. If honesty is substituted for integrity, one might think that if I say I am not planning to fulfill a duty, I need not fulfill it. But it would be a peculiar

morality indeed that granted us the right to avoid our moral responsibilities simply by stating our intention to ignore them. Integrity does not permit such an easy escape.

Consider an example. Before engaging in sex with a woman, her lover tells her that if she gets pregnant, it is her problem, not his. She says that she understands. In due course she does wind up pregnant. If we believe, as I hope we do, that the man would ordinarily have a moral responsibility toward both the child he will have helped to bring into the world and the child's mother, then his honest statement of what he intends does not spare him that responsibility.

This vision of responsibility assumes that not all moral obligations stem from consent or from a stated intention. The linking of obligations to promises is a rather modern and perhaps uniquely Western way of looking at life, and perhaps a luxury that the well-to-do can afford. As Fred and Shulamit Korn (a philosopher and an anthropologist) have pointed out, "If one looks at ethnographic accounts of other societies, one finds that, while obligations everywhere play a crucial role in social life, promising is not preeminent among the sources of obligation and is not even mentioned by most anthropologists." The Korns have made a study of Tonga, where promises are virtually unknown but the social order is remarkably stable. If life without any promises seems extreme, we Americans sometimes go too far the other way, parsing not only our contracts but even our marriage vows in order to discover the absolute minimum obligation that we have to others as a result of our promises.

That some societies in the world have worked out evidently functional structures of obligation without the need for promise or consent does not tell us what *we* should do. But it serves as a reminder of the basic proposition that our existence in civil society creates a set of mutual responsibilities that philosophers used to capture in the fiction of the social contract. Nowadays, here in America, people seem to spend their time thinking of even cleverer ways to avoid their obligations, instead of doing what integrity commands and fulfilling them. And all too often honesty is their excuse.

The Reader's Presence

1. If Carter intends his essay to be a discussion of honesty, why does he begin with a consideration of the concept of integrity? How are the terms related? In what important ways are they different? What does integrity involve that honesty doesn't?

2. Notice that in this essay Carter never once offers a dictionary definition of the words *honesty* and *integrity*. Look up each term in a standard dictionary. As a reader, do you think such definitions would have made Carter's distinctions clearer? Why do you think

he chose not to define the words according to their common dictionary meanings? How does he define them? How are his considerations of honesty and integrity related to his conclusion?

3. In "Why Women Smile," Amy Cunningham argues that women often "smile in lieu of showing what's really on our minds" (page 356). Would Carter classify this kind of smiling as insufficiently honest? Why or why not? Cunningham notes that she is "trying to quit" smiling; would not smiling show greater integrity, as Carter explains it?

Amy Cunningham

Why Women Smile

Amy Cunningham (b. 1955) has been writing on psychological issues and modern life for magazines such as Redbook, Glamour, *and the* Washington Post Magazine *since she graduated from the University of Virginia in 1977 with a bachelor's degree in English. Cunningham says that the essay reprinted here grew out of her own experience as an "easy to get along with person" who was raised by Southerners in the suburbs of Chicago. She also recalls that when writing it, "I was unhappy with myself for taking too long, for not being efficient the way I thought a professional writer should be—but the work paid off and now I think it is one of the best essays I've written." "Why Women Smile" originally appeared in* Lear's *in 1993.*

Looking back on her writing career, Cunningham notes, "When I was younger I thought if you had talent you would make it as a writer. I'm surprised to realize now that good writing has less to do with talent and more to do with the discipline of staying seated in the chair, by yourself, in front of the computer and getting the work done."

After smiling brilliantly for nearly four decades, I now find myself trying to quit. Or, at the very least, seeking to lower the wattage a bit.

Not everyone I know is keen on this. My smile has gleamed like a cheap plastic night-light so long and so reliably that certain friends and relatives worry that my mood will darken the moment my smile dims. "Gee," one says, "I associate you with your smile. It's the essence of you. I should think you'd want to smile more!" But the people who love me best agree that my smile—which springs forth no matter where

I am or how I feel—hasn't been serving me well. Said my husband recently, "Your smiling face and unthreatening demeanor make people like you in a fuzzy way, but that doesn't seem to be what you're after these days."

Smiles are not the small and innocuous things they appear to be: Too many of us smile in lieu of showing what's really on our minds. Indeed, the success of the women's movement might be measured by the sincerity—and lack of it—in our smiles. Despite all the work we American women have done to get and maintain full legal control of our bodies, not to mention our destinies, we still don't seem to be fully in charge of a couple of small muscle groups in our faces.

We smile so often and so promiscuously—when we're angry, when we're tense, when we're with children, when we're being photographed, when we're interviewing for a job, when we're meeting candidates to employ—that the Smiling Woman has become a peculiarly American archetype. This isn't entirely a bad thing, of course. A smile lightens the load, diffuses unpleasantness, redistributes nervous tension. Women doctors smile more than their male counterparts, studies show, and are better liked by their patients.

Oscar Wilde's old saw that "a woman's face is her work of fiction" is   5
often quoted to remind us that what's on the surface may have little connection to what we're feeling. What is it in our culture that keeps our smiles on automatic pilot? The behavior seems to be an equal blend of nature and nurture. Research has demonstrated that since females often mature earlier than males and are less irritable, girls smile more than boys from the very beginning. But by adolescence, the differences in the smiling rates of boys and girls are so robust that it's clear the culture has done more than its share of the dirty work. Just think of the mothers who painstakingly embroidered the words ENTER SMILING on little samplers, and then hung their handiwork on doors by golden chains. Translation: "Your real emotions aren't welcome here."

Clearly, our instincts are another factor. Our smiles have their roots in the greetings of monkeys, who pull their lips up and back to show their fear of attack, as well as their reluctance to vie for a position of dominance. And like the opossum caught in the light by the clattering garbage cans, we, too, flash toothy grimaces when we make major mistakes. By declaring ourselves nonthreatening, our smiles provide an extremely versatile means of protection.

Our earliest baby smiles are involuntary reflexes having only the vaguest connection to contentment or comfort. In short, we're genetically wired to pull on our parents' heartstrings. As Desmond Morris explains in *Babywatching*, this is our way of attaching ourselves to our caretakers, as truly as baby chimps clench their mothers' fur. Even as babies we're capable of projecting onto others (in this case, our parents) the feelings we know we need to get back in return.

Bona fide social smiles occur at two-and-a-half to three months of age, usually a few weeks after we first start gazing with intense interest into the faces of our parents. By the time we are six months old, we are smiling and laughing regularly in reaction to tickling, feedings, blown raspberries, hugs, and peekaboo games. Even babies who are born blind intuitively know how to react to pleasurable changes with a smile, though their first smiles start later than those of sighted children.

Psychologists and psychiatrists have noted that babies also smile and laugh with relief when they realize that something they thought might be dangerous is not dangerous after all. Kids begin to invite their parents to indulge them with "scary" approach-avoidance games; they love to be chased or tossed up into the air. (It's interesting to note that as adults, we go through the same gosh-that's-shocking-and-dangerous-but-it's-okay-to-laugh-and-smile cycles when we listen to raunchy stand-up comics.)

From the wilds of New Guinea to the sidewalks of New York, smiles   10 are associated with joy, relief, and amusement. But smiles are by no means limited to the expression of positive emotions: People of many different cultures smile when they are frightened, embarrassed, angry, or miserable. In Japan, for instance, a smile is often used to hide pain or sorrow.

Psychologist Paul Ekman, the head of the University of California's Human Interaction Lab in San Francisco, has identified 18 distinct types of smiles, including those that show misery, compliance, fear, and contempt. The smile of true merriment, which Dr. Ekman calls the Duchenne Smile, after the nineteenth-century French doctor who first studied it, is characterized by heightened circulation, a feeling of exhilaration, and the employment of two major facial muscles: the zygomaticus major of the lower face, and the orbicularis oculi, which crinkles the skin around the eyes. But since the average American woman's smile often has less to do with her actual state of happiness than it does with the social pressure to smile no matter what, her baseline social smile isn't apt to be a felt expression that engages the eyes like this. Ekman insists that if people learned to read smiles, they could see the sadness, misery, or pain lurking there, plain as day.

Evidently, a woman's happy, willing deference is something the world wants visibly demonstrated. Woe to the waitress, the personal assistant or receptionist, the flight attendant, or any other woman in the line of public service whose smile is not offered up to the boss or client as proof that there are no storm clouds—no kids to support, no sleep that's been missed—rolling into the sunny workplace landscape. Women are expected to smile no matter where they line up on the social, cultural, or economic ladder: College professors are criticized for not smiling, political spouses are pilloried for being too serious, and women's roles in films have historically been smiling ones. It's little wonder that men on the street still call out, "Hey, baby, smile! Life's not *that* bad, is it?" to women passing by, lost in thought.

A friend remembers being pulled aside by a teacher after class and asked, "What is wrong, dear? You sat there for the whole hour looking so sad!" "All I could figure," my friend says now, "is that I wasn't smiling. And the fact that *she* felt sorry for me for looking normal made me feel horrible."

Ironically, the social laws that govern our smiles have completely reversed themselves over the last two thousand years. Women weren't always expected to seem animated and responsive; in fact, immoderate laughter was once considered one of the more conspicuous vices a woman could have, and mirth was downright sinful. Women were kept apart, in some cultures even veiled, so that they couldn't perpetuate Eve's seductive, evil work. The only smile deemed appropriate on a privileged woman's face was the serene, inward smile of the Virgin Mary at Christ's birth, and even that expression was best directed exclusively at young children. Cackling laughter and wicked glee were the kinds of sounds heard only in hell.

What we know of women's facial expressions in other centuries comes   15
mostly from religious writings, codes of etiquette, and portrait paintings. In fifteenth century Italy, it was customary for artists to paint lovely, blank-faced women in profile. A viewer could stare endlessly at such a woman, but she could not gaze back. By the Renaissance, male artists were taking some pleasure in depicting women with a semblance of complexity, Leonardo da Vinci's Mona Lisa, with her veiled enigmatic smile, being the most famous example.

The Golden Age of the Dutch Republic marks a fascinating period for studying women's facial expressions. While we might expect the drunken young whores of Amsterdam to smile devilishly (unbridled sexuality and lasciviousness were *supposed* to addle the brain), it's the faces of the Dutch women from fine families that surprise us. Considered socially more free, these women demonstrate a fuller range of facial expressions than their European sisters. Frans Hals's 1622 portrait of Stephanus Geraerdt and Isabella Coymans, a married couple, is remarkable not just for the full, friendly smiles on each face, but for the frank and mutual pleasure the couple take in each other.

In the 1800s, sprightly, pretty women began appearing in advertisements for everything from beverages to those newfangled Kodak Land cameras. Women's faces were no longer impassive, and their willingness to bestow status, to offer, proffer, and yield, was most definitely promoted by their smiling images. The culture appeared to have turned the smile, originally a bond shared between intimates, into a socially required display that sold capitalist ideology as well as kitchen appliances. And female viewers soon began to emulate these highly idealized pictures. Many longed to be more like her, that perpetually smiling female. She seemed so beautiful. So content. So whole.

By the middle of the nineteenth century, the bulk of America's smile burden was falling primarily to women and African-American slaves, providing a very portable means of protection, a way of saying, "I'm harmless. I won't assert myself here." It reassured those in power to see signs of gratitude and contentment in the faces of subordinates. As long ago as 1963, adman David Ogilvy declared the image of a woman smiling approvingly at a product clichéd, but we've yet to get the message. Cheerful Americans still appear in ads today, smiling somewhat less disingenuously than they smiled during the middle of the century, but smiling broadly nonetheless.

Other countries have been somewhat reluctant to import our "Don't worry, be happy" American smiles. When McDonald's opened in Moscow not long ago and when EuroDisney debuted in France last year, the Americans involved in both business ventures complained that they couldn't get the natives they'd employed to smile worth a damn.

Europeans visiting the United States for the first time are often surprised at just how often Americans smile. But when you look at our history, the relentless good humor (or, at any rate, the pretense of it) falls into perspective. The American wilderness was developed on the assumption that this country had a shortage of people in relation to its possibilities. In countries with a more rigid class structure or caste system, fewer people are as captivated by the idea of quickly winning friends and influencing people. Here in the States, however, every stranger is a potential associate. Our smiles bring new people on board. The American smile is a democratic version of a curtsy or doffed hat, since, in this land of free equals, we're not especially formal about the ways we greet social superiors.   20

The civil rights movement never addressed the smile burden by name, but activists worked on their own to set new facial norms. African-American males stopped smiling on the streets in the 1960s, happily aware of the unsettling effect this action had on the white population. The image of the simpleminded, smiling, white-toothed black was rejected as blatantly racist, and it gradually retreated into the distance. However, like the women of Sparta and the wives of samurai, who were expected to look happy upon learning their sons or husbands had died in battle, contemporary American women have yet to unilaterally declare their faces their own property.

For instance, imagine a woman at a morning business meeting being asked if she could make a spontaneous and concise summation of a complicated project she's been struggling to get under control for months. She might draw the end of her mouth back and clench her teeth—Eek!—in a protective response, a polite, restrained expression of her surprise, not unlike the expression of a conscientious young schoolgirl being told to get out paper and pencil for a pop quiz. At the same time, the woman might be feeling resentful of the supervisor who sprang the request, but she fears taking that person on. So she holds back a comment. The whole performance resolves in a weird grin collapsing into a nervous smile that conveys discomfort and unpreparedness. A pointed remark by way of explanation or self-defense might've worked better for her—but her mouth was otherwise engaged.

We'd do well to realize just how much our smiles misrepresent us, and swear off for good the self-deprecating grins and ritual displays of deference. Real smiles have beneficial physiological effects, according to Paul Ekman. False ones do nothing for us at all.

"Smiles are as important as sound bites on television," insists producer and media coach Heidi Berenson, who has worked with many of Washington's most famous faces. "And women have always been better at understanding this than men. But the smile I'm talking about is not a cutesy smile. It's an authoritative smile. A genuine smile. Properly timed, it's tremendously powerful."

To limit a woman to one expression is like editing down an orchestra 25
to one instrument. And the search for more authentic means of expression isn't easy in a culture in which women are still expected to be magnanimous smilers, helpmates in crisis, and curators of everybody else's morale. But change is already floating in the high winds. We see a boon in assertive female comedians who are proving that women can *dish out* smiles, not just wear them. Actress Demi Moore has stated that she doesn't like to take smiling roles. Nike is running ads that show unsmiling women athletes sweating, reaching, pushing themselves. These women aren't overly concerned with issues of rapport; they're not being "nice" girls—they're working out.

If a woman's smile were truly her own, to be smiled or not, according to how the *woman* felt, rather than according to what someone else needed, she would smile more spontaneously, without ulterior, hidden motives. As Rainer Maria Rilke wrote in *The Journal of My Other Self*, "Her smile was not meant to be seen by anyone and served its whole purpose in being smiled."

That smile is my long-term aim. In the meantime, I hope to stabilize on the smile continuum somewhere between the eliciting grin of Farrah Fawcett and the haughty smirk of Jeane Kirkpatrick.

The Reader's Presence

1. Cunningham presents an informative précis of the causes and effects of smiling in Western culture. Consider the points of view from which she addresses this subject. Summarize and evaluate her treatment of smiling from a psychological, physiological, sociological, and historical point of view. Which do you find most incisive? Why? What other points of view does she introduce into her discussion of smiling? What effects do they create? What does she identify as the benefits (and the disadvantages) of smiling?

2. At what point in this essay does Cunningham address the issue of gender? Characterize the language she uses to introduce this issue. She distinguishes between the different patterns—and the consequences—experienced by men and women who smile. Summarize these differences and assess the nature and the extent of the evidence she provides for each of her points. What more general distinctions does she make about various kinds of smiles? What are their different purposes and degrees of intensity? What information does she provide about smiling as an issue of nationality and race? What is the overall purpose of this essay? Where—and how—does Cunningham create and sustain a sense of her own presence in this essay? What does she set as her personal goal in relation to smiling?

3. Cunningham presents an explanation of the causes of an activity that few of her readers think of in both scientific and historical terms. Compare her use of science and history to that of Vicki Hearne in "What's Wrong with Animal Rights" (page 699) and to that of Stephen Jay Gould in "Sex, Drugs, Disasters, and the Extinction of Dinosaurs" (page 448). How does each writer establish her or his authority in these fields? What is each writer's argument? To what extent does each argument depend upon factual evidence?

Don DeLillo

In the Ruins of the Future: Reflections on Terror, Loss and Time in the Shadow of September

Don DeLillo was born in the Bronx, New York, in 1936, the son of Italian immigrants, and grew up in an Italian-American neighborhood. He attended Cardinal Hayes High School and then majored in communication arts at Fordham University, graduating with a B.A. in 1958. During the 1960s, he worked as a copywriter for the renowned ad agency Ogilvy and Mather. He did not start writing his first novel, Americana, *until about 1967. But after it appeared in print in 1971, he continued to write prolifically, publishing five novels in only seven years:* End Zone *(1972),* Great Jones Street *(1973),* Ratner's Star *(1976),* Players

(1977), and Running Dog *(1978). Although popular with reviewers and a small but fanatical readership, DeLillo had difficulty reaching a wide audience until the publication of* White Noise *(1985), which won the National Book Award, and* Mao II *(1991), which won the PEN/Faulkner Award. DeLillo's work surveys recent history and portrays American culture since the 1950s, dealing with such themes as paranoia, terrorist violence, and consumerism. His novels include* Libra *(1988),* Underworld *(1997),* The Body Artist *(2001), and* Cosmopolitis *(2003).* Conversations with Don DeLillo, *edited by Thomas Depietro, was published in 2005. "In the Ruins of the Future" first appeared in* Harper's *magazine in December 2001.*

DeLillo once commented, "Writing is a concentrated form of thinking. I don't know what I think about certain subjects, even today, until I sit down and try to write about them."

In a 1997 essay, "The Power of History," DeLillo argued that ". . . the writer will reconfigure things the way his own history demands. He has his themes and biases and limitations. He has the small crushed pearl of his anger. He has his teaching job, his middling reputation, and the one radical idea that he has been waiting for all his life. The other thing he has is a flat surface that he will decorate, fitfully, with words. . . . Let language shape the world." DeLillo's work reflects a fascination with language—its power to free the writer and to shape narrative and history. "Language lives in everything it touches and can be an agent of redemption, the thing that delivers us, paradoxically, from history's flat, thin, tight, and relentless designs, its arrangement of stark pages, and that allows us to find an unconstraining otherness, a free veer from time and place and fate."

I

In the past decade the surge of capital markets has dominated discourse and shaped global consciousness. Multinational corporations have come to seem more vital and influential than governments. The dramatic climb of the Dow and the speed of the Internet summoned us all to live permanently in the future, in the utopian glow of cyber-capital, because there is no memory there and this is where markets are uncontrolled and investment potential has no limit.

All this changed on September 11. Today, again, the world narrative belongs to terrorists. But the primary target of the men who attacked the Pentagon and the World Trade Center was not the global economy. It is America that drew their fury. It is the high gloss of our modernity. It is the thrust of our technology. It is our perceived godlessness. It is the blunt force of our foreign policy. It is the power of American culture to penetrate every wall, home, life, and mind.

Terror's response is a narrative that has been developing over years, only now becoming inescapable. It is *our* lives and minds that are occupied now. This catastrophic event changes the way we think and act, moment to moment, week to week, for unknown weeks and months to come, and steely years. Our world, parts of our world, have crumbled into theirs, which means we are living in a place of danger and rage.

The protesters in Genoa, Prague, Seattle, and other cities want to decelerate the global momentum that seemed to be driving unmindfully toward a landscape of consumer-robots and social instability, with the chance of self-determination probably diminishing for most people in most countries. Whatever acts of violence marked the protests, most of the men and women involved tend to be a moderating influence, trying to slow things down, even things out, hold off the white-hot future.

The terrorists of September 11 want to bring back the past.   5

II

Our tradition of free expression and our justice system's provisions for the rights of the accused can only seem an offense to men bent on suicidal terror.

We are rich, privileged, and strong, but they are willing to die. This is the edge they have, the fire of aggrieved belief. We live in a wide world, routinely filled with exchange of every sort, an open circuit of work, talk, family, and expressible feeling. The terrorist, planted in a Florida town, pushing his supermarket cart, nodding to his neighbor, lives in a far narrower format. This is his edge, his strength. Plots reduce the world. He builds a plot around his anger and our indifference. He lives a certain kind of apartness, hard and tight. This is not the self-watcher, the soft white dangling boy who shoots someone to keep from disappearing into himself. The terrorist shares a secret and a self. At a certain point he and his brothers may begin to feel less motivated by politics and personal hatred than by brotherhood itself. They share the codes and protocols of their mission here and something deeper as well, a vision of judgment and devastation.

Does the sight of a woman pushing a stroller soften the man to her humanity and vulnerability, and her child's as well, and all the people he is here to kill?

This is his edge, that he does not see her. Years here, waiting, taking flying lessons, making the routine gestures of community and home, the credit card, the bank account, the post-office box. All tactical, linked, layered. He knows who we are and what we mean in the world—an idea, a righteous fever in the brain. But there is no defenseless human at the end of his gaze.

The sense of disarticulation we hear in the term "Us and Them" has   10
never been so striking, at either end.

We can tell ourselves that whatever we've done to inspire bitterness, distrust, and rancor, it was not so damnable as to bring this day down on our heads. But there is no logic in apocalypse. They have gone beyond the bounds of passionate payback. This is heaven and hell, a sense of armed martyrdom as the surpassing drama of human experience.

He pledges his submission to God and meditates on the blood to come.

III

The Bush Administration was feeling a nostalgia for the Cold War. This is over now. Many things are over. The narrative ends in the rubble, and it is left to us to create the counter-narrative.

There are a hundred thousand stories crisscrossing New York, Washington, and the world. Where we were, whom we know, what we've seen or heard. There are the doctors' appointments that saved lives, the cell phones that were used to report the hijackings. Stories generating others and people running north out of the rumbling smoke and ash. Men running in suits and ties, women who'd lost their shoes, cops running from the skydive of all that towering steel.

People running for their lives are part of the story that is left to us.   15

There are stories of heroism and encounters with dread. There are stories that carry around their edges the luminous ring of coincidence, fate, or premonition. They take us beyond the hard numbers of dead and missing and give us a glimpse of elevated being. For a hundred who are arbitrarily dead, we need to find one person saved by a flash of forewarning. There are configurations that chill and awe us both. Two women on two planes, best of friends, who die together and apart, Tower 1 and Tower 2. What desolate epic tragedy might bear the weight of such juxtaposition? But we can also ask what symmetry, bleak and touching both, takes one friend, spares the other's grief?

The brother of one of the women worked in one of the towers. He managed to escape.

In Union Square Park, about two miles north of the attack site, the improvised memorials are another part of our response. The flags, flower beds, and votive candles, the lamppost hung with paper airplanes, the passages from the Koran and the Bible, the letters and poems, the cardboard John Wayne, the children's drawings of the Twin Towers, the hand-painted signs for Free Hugs, Free Back Rubs, the graffiti of love and peace on the tall equestrian statue.

There are many photographs of missing persons, some accompanied by hopeful lists of identifying features. (Man with panther tattoo, upper right arm.) There is the saxophonist, playing softly. There is the sculptured flag of rippling copper and aluminum, six feet long, with two young people still attending to the finer details of the piece.

Then there are the visitors to the park. The artifacts on display represent the confluence of a number of cultural tides, patriotic and multidevotional and retro hippie. The visitors move quietly in the floating aromas   20 of candlewax, roses, and bus fumes. There are many people this mild evening, and in their voices, manner, clothing, and in the color of their skin they recapitulate the mix we see in the photocopied faces of the lost.

For the next fifty years, people who were not in the area when the attacks occurred will claim to have been there. In time, some of them will believe it. Others will claim to have lost friends or relatives, although they did not.

This is also the counter-narrative, a shadow history of false memories and imagined loss.

The Internet is a counter-narrative, shaped in part by rumor, fantasy, and mystical reverberation.

The cell phones, the lost shoes, the handkerchiefs mashed in the faces of running men and women. The box cutters and credit cards. The paper that came streaming out of the towers and drifted across the river to Brooklyn back yards: status reports, résumés, insurance forms. Sheets of paper driven into concrete, according to witnesses. Paper slicing into truck tires, fixed there.

These are among the small objects and more marginal stories in the   25
sifted ruins of the day. We need them, even the common tools of the terrorists, to set against the massive spectacle that continues to seem unmanageable, too powerful a thing to set into our frame of practiced response.

IV

Ash was spattering the windows. Karen was half dressed, grabbing the kids and trying to put on some clothes and talking with her husband and scooping things to take out to the corridor, and they looked at her, twin girls, as if she had fourteen heads.

They stayed in the corridor for a while, thinking there might be secondary explosions. They waited, and began to feel safer, and went back to the apartment.

At the next impact, Marc knew in the sheerest second before the shock wave broadsided their building that it was a second plane, impossible, striking the second tower. Their building was two blocks away, and he'd thought the first crash was an accident.

They went back to the hallway, where others began to gather, fifteen or twenty people.

Karen ran back for a cell phone, a cordless phone, a charger, water,   30
sweaters, snacks for the kids, and then made a quick dash to the bedroom for her wedding ring.

From the window she saw people running in the street, others locked shoulder to shoulder, immobilized, with debris coming down on them. People were trampled, struck by falling objects, and there was ash and paper everywhere, paper whipping through the air, no sign of light or sky.

Cell phones were down. They talked on the cordless, receiving information measured out in eyedrops. They were convinced that the situation outside was far more grave than it was here.

Smoke began to enter the corridor.

Then the first tower fell. She thought it was a bomb. When she talked to someone on the phone and found out what had happened, she felt a surreal relief. Bombs and missiles were not falling everywhere in the city. It was not all-out war, at least not yet.

Marc was in the apartment getting chairs for the older people, for the   35
woman who'd had hip surgery. When he heard the first low drumming rumble, he stood in a strange dead calm and said, "Something is happening." It sounded exactly like what it was, a tall tower collapsing.

The windows were surfaced with ash now. Blacked out completely, and he wondered what was out there. What remained to be seen and did he want to see it?

They all moved into the stairwell, behind a fire door, but smoke kept coming in. It was gritty ash, and they were eating it.

He ran back inside, grabbing towels off the racks and washcloths out of drawers and drenching them in the sink, and filling his bicycle water bottles, and grabbing the kids' underwear.

He thought the crush of buildings was the thing to fear most. This is what would kill them.

Karen was on the phone, talking to a friend in the district attorney's   40
office, about half a mile to the north. She was pleading for help. She begged, pleaded, and hung up. For the next hour a detective kept calling with advice and encouragement.

Marc came back out to the corridor. I think we *might* die, he told himself, hedging his sense of what would happen next.

The detective told Karen to stay where they were.

When the second tower fell, my heart fell with it. I called Marc, who is my nephew, on his cordless. I couldn't stop thinking of the size of the towers and the meager distance between those buildings and his. He answered, we talked. I have no memory of the conversation except for his final remark, slightly urgent, concerning someone on the other line, who might be sending help.

Smoke was seeping out of the elevator shaft now. Karen was saying goodbye to her father in Oregon. Not hello-goodbye. But goodbye-I-think-we-are-going-to-die. She thought smoke would be the thing that did it.

People sat on chairs along the walls. They chatted about practical   45
matters. They sang songs with the kids. The kids in the group were cooperative because the adults were damn scared.

There was an improvised rescue in progress. Karen's friend and a colleague made their way down from Centre Street, turning up with two policemen they'd enlisted en route. They had dust masks and a destination, and they searched every floor for others who might be stranded in the building.

They came out into a world of ash and near night. There was no one else to be seen now on the street. Gray ash covering the cars and pavement, ash falling in large flakes, paper still drifting down, discarded shoes, strollers, briefcases. The members of the group were masked and toweled, children in adults' arms, moving east and then north on Nassau Street, trying not to look around, only what's immediate, one step and then another, all closely focused, a pregnant woman, a newborn, a dog.

They were covered in ash when they reached shelter at Pace University, where there was food and water, and kind and able staff members, and a gas-leak scare, and more running people.

Workers began pouring water on the group. *Stay wet, stay wet.* This was the theme of the first half hour.

Later a line began to form along the food counter.   50

Someone said, "I don't want cheese on that."

Someone said, "I like it better not so cooked."

Not so incongruous really, just people alive and hungry, beginning to be themselves again.

                                    V

Technology is our fate, our truth. It is what we mean when we call ourselves the only superpower on the planet. The materials and methods we devise make it possible for us to claim our future. We don't have to depend on God or the prophets or other astonishments. We are the astonishment. The miracle is what we ourselves produce, the systems and networks that change the way we live and think.

But whatever great skeins of technology lie ahead, ever more complex,   55
connective, precise, micro-fractional, the future has yielded, for now, to medieval expedience, to the old slow furies of cutthroat religion.

Kill the enemy and pluck out his heart.

If others in less scientifically advanced cultures were able to share, wanted to share, some of the blessings of our technology, without a threat to their faith or traditions, would they need to rely on a God in whose name they kill the innocent? Would they need to invent a God who rewards violence against the innocent with a promise of "infinite paradise," in the words of a handwritten letter found in the luggage of one of the hijackers?

For all those who may want what we've got, there are all those who do not. These are the men who have fashioned a morality of destruction. They want what they used to have before the waves of Western influence. They surely see themselves as the elect of God whether or not they follow the central precepts of Islam. It is the presumptive right of those who choose violence and death to speak directly to God. They will kill and then die. Or they will die first, in the cockpit, in clean shoes, according to instructions in the letter.

Six days after the attacks, the territory below Canal Street is hedged with barricades. There are few civilians in the street. Police at some checkpoints, troops in camouflage gear at others, wearing gas masks, and a pair of state troopers in conversation, and ten burly men striding east in hard hats, work pants, and NYPD jackets. A shop owner tries to talk a cop into letting him enter his place of business. He is a small elderly man with a Jewish accent, but there is no relief today. Garbage bags are everywhere in high broad stacks. The area is bedraggled and third-worldish, with an air of permanent emergency, everything surfaced in ash.

It is possible to pass through some checkpoints, detour around others.   60 At Chambers Street I look south through the links of the National Rent-A-Fence barrier. There stands the smoky remnant of filigree that marks the last tall thing, the last sign in the mire of wreckage that there were towers here that dominated the skyline for over a quarter of a century.

Ten days later and a lot closer, I stand at another barrier with a group of people, looking directly into the strands of openwork facade. It is almost too close. It is almost Roman, I-beams for stonework, but not nearly so salvageable. Many here describe the scene to others on cell phones.

"Oh my god I'm standing here," says the man next to me.

The World Trade towers were not only an emblem of advanced technology but a justification, in a sense, for technology's irresistible will to realize in solid form whatever becomes theoretically allowable. Once defined, every limit must be reached. The tactful sheathing of the towers was intended to reduce the direct threat of such straight-edge enormity, a giantism that eased over the years into something a little more familiar and comfortable, even dependable in a way.

Now a small group of men have literally altered our skyline. We have fallen back in time and space. It is their technology that marks our moments, the small lethal devices, the remote-control detonators they fashion out of radios, or the larger technology they borrow from us, passenger jets that become manned missiles.

Maybe this is a grim subtext of their enterprise. They see something   65 innately destructive in the nature of technology. It brings death to their customs and beliefs. Use it as what it is, a thing that kills.

VI

Nearly eleven years ago, during the engagement in the Persian Gulf, people had trouble separating the war from coverage of the war. After the first euphoric days, coverage became limited. The rush of watching all that eerie green night-vision footage, shot from fighter jets in combat, had been so intense that it became hard to honor the fact that the war was still going on, untelevised. A layer of consciousness had been stripped away. People shuffled around, muttering. They were lonely for their war.

The events of September 11 were covered unstintingly. There was no confusion of roles on TV. The raw event was one thing, the coverage another. The event dominated the medium. It was bright and totalizing, and some of us said it was unreal. When we say a thing is unreal, we mean it is too real, a phenomenon so unaccountable and yet so bound to the power of objective fact that we can't tilt it to the slant of our perceptions. First the planes struck the towers. After a time it became possible for us to absorb this, barely. But when the towers fell. When the rolling smoke began moving downward, floor to floor. This was so vast and terrible that it was outside imagining even as it happened. We could not catch up to it. But it was real, punishingly so, an expression of the physics of structural limits and a void in one's soul, and there was the huge antenna falling out of the sky, straight down, blunt end first, like an arrow moving backward in time.

The event itself has no purchase on the mercies of analogy or simile. We have to take the shock and horror as it is. But living language is not diminished. The writer wants to understand what this day has done to us. Is it too soon? We seem pressed for time, all of us. Time is scarcer now. There is a sense of compression, plans made hurriedly, time forced and distorted. But language is inseparable from the world that provokes it. The writer begins in the towers, trying to imagine the moment, desperately. Before politics, before history and religion, there is the primal terror. People falling from the towers hand in hand. This is part of the counter-narrative, hands and spirits joining, human beauty in the crush of meshed steel.

In its desertion of every basis for comparison, the event asserts its singularity. There is something empty in the sky. The writer tries to give memory, tenderness, and meaning to all that howling space.

VII

We like to think America invented the future. We are comfortable with the future, intimate with it. But there are disturbances now, in large and small ways, a chain of reconsiderations. Where we live, how we travel, what we think about when we look at our children. For many people, the event has changed the grain of the most routine moment.

We may find that the ruin of the towers is implicit in other things. The new PalmPilot at fingertip's reach, the stretch limousine parked outside the hotel, the midtown skyscraper under construction, carrying the name of a major investment bank—all haunted in a way by what has happened, less assured in their authority, in the prerogatives they offer.

There is fear of other kinds of terrorism, the prospect that biological and chemical weapons will contaminate the air we breathe and the water we drink. There wasn't much concern about this after earlier terrorist acts. This time we are trying to name the future, not in our normally hopeful way but guided by dread.

What has already happened is sufficient to affect the air around us, psychologically. We are all breathing the fumes of lower Manhattan, where traces of the dead are everywhere, in the soft breeze off the river, on rooftops and windows, in our hair and on our clothes.

Think of a future in which the components of a microchip are the size of atoms. The devices that pace our lives will operate from the smart quantum spaces of pure information. Now think of people in countless thousands massing in anger and vowing revenge. Enlarged photos of martyrs and holy men dangle from balconies, and the largest images are those of a terrorist leader.

Two forces in the world, past and future. With the end of Communism, the ideas and principles of modern democracy were seen clearly to prevail, whatever the inequalities of the system itself. This is still the case. But now there is a global theocratic state, unboundaried and floating and so obsolete it must depend on suicidal fervor to gain its aims.

Ideas evolve and de-evolve, and history is turned on end.

VIII

On Friday of the first week a long series of vehicles moves slowly west on Canal Street. Dump trucks, flatbeds, sanitation sweepers. There are giant earthmovers making a tremendous revving sound. A scant number of pedestrians, some in dust masks, others just standing, watching, the indigenous people, clinging to walls and doorways, unaccustomed to traffic that doesn't bring buyers and sellers, goods and cash. The fire rescue car and state police cruiser, the staccato sirens of a line of police vans. Cops stand at the sawhorse barriers, trying to clear the way. Ambulances, cherry pickers, a fleet of Con Ed trucks, all this clamor moving south a few blocks ahead, into the cloud of sand and ash.

One month earlier I'd taken the same walk, early evening, among crowds of people, the panethnic swarm of shoppers, merchants, residents and passersby, with a few tourists as well, and the man at the curbstone doing acupoint massage, and the dreadlocked kid riding his bike on the sidewalk. This was the spirit of Canal Street, the old jostle and stir unchanged for many decades and bearing no sign of SoHo just above, with its restaurants and artists' lofts, or TriBeCa below, rich in architectural textures. Here were hardware bargains, car stereos, foam rubber and industrial plastics, the tattoo parlor and the pizza parlor.

Then I saw the woman on the prayer rug. I'd just turned the corner, heading south to meet some friends, and there she was, young and slender, in a silk headscarf. It was time for sunset prayer, and she was kneeling, upper body pitched toward the edge of the rug. She was partly concealed by a couple of vendors' carts, and no one seemed much to notice her. I think there was another woman seated on a folding chair near the curbstone. The figure on the rug faced east, which meant most immediately a storefront just a foot and a half from her tipped head but more distantly and pertinently toward Mecca, of course, the holiest city of Islam.

Some prayer rugs include a *mihrab* in their design, an arched element   80
representing the prayer niche in a mosque that indicates the direction of Mecca. The only locational guide the young women needed was the Manhattan grid.

I looked at her in prayer and it was clearer to me than ever, the daily sweeping taken-for-granted greatness of New York. The city will accommodate every language, ritual, belief, and opinion. In the rolls of the dead of September 11, all these vital differences were surrendered to the impact and flash. The bodies themselves are missing in large numbers. For the survivors, more grief. But the dead are their own nation and race, one identity, young or old, devout or unbelieving—a union of souls. During the *hadj*, the annual pilgrimage to Mecca, the faithful must eliminate every sign of status, income, and nationality, the men wearing identical strips of seamless white cloth, the women with covered heads, all recalling in prayer their fellowship with the dead.

Allahu akbar. God is great.

The Reader's Presence

1. From the title's linking of the past and the future to statements such as "history is turned on end" (paragraph 76), DeLillo's essay is absorbed with time. Trace the way time is used in the piece. How does the writer make schematic use of past and future to evoke the warring forces of the world? How does he vary tenses and points of view to report the events of September 11 and their aftermath? Why is time central to DeLillo's understanding of these events?

2. For the most part, DeLillo's discussion of the terrorists themselves is unspecific with respect to nationality, religion, or political affiliation. He first mentions Islam several pages into the essay, in section V. How does DeLillo build the reader's sense of "the enemy"? How is Islam woven through the essay? Why might DeLillo resist giving too narrow an articulation of "us" and "them"?

3. Compare DeLillo's account of the very recent past to Barbara Tuchman's history of the distant past in " 'This Is the End of the World': The Black Death" (page 579). Which sections of DeLillo's essay read like a historian's account and which read more like the primary accounts of the plague's disastrous effects? Compare section IV to Michihiko Hachiya's journal of the days immediately following the bombing of Hiroshima in "From *Hiroshima Diary*" (page 34). Why do you think DeLillo varies his style so dramatically from section to section? What are the advantages and disadvantages of writing about an event whose meaning is still being discovered?

Gerald Early

Fear and Fate in America

Gerald Early (b. 1952) is the director of the Center for the Humanities, the Merle Kling Professor of Modern Letters, and professor of English and African and Afro-American Studies at Washington University in St. Louis, where he has taught since 1982. His many books and publications reflect his broad and eclectic interests in literature, baseball, jazz, prizefighting, American culture, and African American history. He has edited numerous books, including My Soul's High Song: The Collected Works of Countee Cullen *(1991);* Lure and Loathing: Essays on Race, Identity, and the Ambivalence of Assimilation *(1992);* Body Language: Writers on Sport *(1998);* The Muhammad Ali Reader *(1998);* The Sammy Davis Jr. Reader *(2001); and* Miles Davis and American Culture *(2001). He has also published poetry and numerous collections of essays and criticism, including* Tuxedo Junction: Essays on American Culture *(1989);* Daughters: On Family and Fatherhood *(1994);* This Is Where I Came In: Black America in the '60s *(2003); and a study of Motown,* One Nation under a Groove *(1994). His 1992 book,* The Culture of Bruising: Essays on Prizefighting, Literature, and Modern American Culture, *won the 1994 National Book Critics Circle Award for criticism. Early has been a consultant for Ken Burns's PBS documentaries on baseball, jazz, and the boxer Jack Johnson.*

Early has explained his interest in sports and jazz as growing out of a search for role models: "As a kid, growing up, there were a lot of athletes I admired, particularly Ali, and guys like Wilt Chamberlain, Bill Russell, Jim Brown, Willie Mays, Hank Aaron. . . . These men became my models, not because I wanted to become an athlete, but because I wanted to be as good at something in life as they were as athletes. As I grew older, I became interested in jazz music . . . because I heard it and admired the ability of the people who played it. Once again, I sort of adopted them as role models, not because I wanted to be a musician, but because I wanted to be able to do as well in life as these people did, and exhibit the same level of dedication."

Early is a frequent contributor to speakeasy, *in which this essay appeared in 2004.*

I

When I saw *Dirty Harry*[1] for the first time in 1973, the year after its initial release, I knew little about film noir or how *Dirty Harry* made such stylized use of noir's weave of fear and fate or, more precisely, of noir's weave of fear as fate. But I did know that the Eastwood movie was, at

---

[1]*Dirty Harry:* A movie starring Clint Eastwood as a renegade policeman, which was directed by Don Siegel and released in 1972. — EDS.

the time, one of the most frightening films I had ever seen because it portrayed virtually every institution of urban life as threatened by the senseless violence that, as the film seemed to argue, only urban life could produce: courts (the killer is freed because his rights were violated, even though he is clearly guilty), schools (the children on the school bus are threatened by the maniac killer at the film's end), financial institutions (a bank is robbed early in the film), churches (Harry has a shootout with the killer near a church), recreational life (Harry tortures the killer in a sports stadium). In short, *Dirty Harry* depicted urban life as irrational. Other films of the period did something like this, such as blaxploitation movies, but they generally lacked the artistic power and technical coherence of a film like *Dirty Harry*.

Dirty Harry did not strike me then, and does not now, as a remake of a western but rather as a nihilistic vision of the end of culture as we know it. At the time I was living in Philadelphia and thought it a pretty awful place to be: teenage gang violence was high (my cousin was killed in a street gang war that year) and crime was everywhere, which, in turn, made it seem as if the police were everywhere. Their presence did not reassure, at least, it did not reassure me, but rather made one even more afraid of being in the wrong place at the wrong time. I had this twin terror in those days of, first, living in a world where everyone was at war with everyone else and so I seemed to have no side, but, strangely, everyone else did; and, second, feeling like a cipher drowning in demographics, sociological assumptions arising mostly from the ghastly combination of my skin color and my sex that were bound to get me killed. I felt I had no reality as a person, only as the representative idea of a type of person.

The city was dirty, broke, perverse, and cruel. The schools were bad, services were compromised by shrinking revenue, drugs were rampant, and everyone seemed to be trying to live somewhere else. Philadelphia had become one huge pathology of modern life. In fact, the city was modernity as pathology. I suppose its downfall began with the riots of the 1960s, or perhaps it began with school integration, which didn't seem to work, or perhaps it began with the creation of the interstate highway and the lawn which made the suburbs a place to live, a place to escape to.

When I saw *Dirty Harry*, all the horror and fear of living in the city in the early 1970s descended on me with such surreal vividness, with such compelling anguish, that it was all I could do not to rush from the theater in a delirium. (I saw the movie in downtown Philadelphia one spring afternoon in a run-down theater that had once been a pop culture palace when I was a child. No one was in the theater but derelicts and me. The setting augmented the depression and fear the film induced.)

When I left the theater and started walking home, I hadn't gone very far when I spotted a friend, a boy I had grown up with. I had not   5 seen him for a few years, and I was surprised to see him at that moment. He had been a fundamentalist Christian, a Jehovah's Witness, actually, and he nearly talked me into joining the group when I was about fourteen or fifteen and vulnerable to that sort of thing. His maturity, the assurance of his answers to all questions, the fact that he thought he had answers to all questions, his neat, disciplined appearance, quite impressed me in those days, and being a Jehovah's Witness or any sort of fundamentalist seemed a considerable hedge against the growing chaos of the city's culture. Indeed, I was spellbound and it took a strenuous effort on my part not to succumb to the romanticism of certainty.

When I saw him on that day in the spring of 1973, he was among a group of transvestites, dressed as one himself, wigged, made-up, in women's clothes. I was walking by a corner that had become something like Philadelphia's small-scale version of 1970s Times Square, an area of male and female prostitutes, drug pushers and junkies, pornographic theaters and strip joints. I was so taken aback to see him there, selling himself on a street corner, dressed as a woman, so different from how I remembered him, that I actually turned for a moment to stare at him. (It is an odd coincidence that I was to have nearly an identical experience with another boyhood friend a few years later.) He saw me, too. He looked almost amused when he recognized me—he even seemed to smile. I thought he was about to call my name. I turned and ran as fast as I could. I was disgusted by what I saw. My friend's new life, or hidden life that had now become open, shocked and shamed me, even worse, mocked me. I finally stopped running when I felt that I was far enough away.

I ran because I was afraid, but it took me several years to realize the exact nature of my fear. At first, I thought I was scared by what my friend had become, of how the corruption and filth of the city had overtaken his life, reduced his life, wrecked his life, destroyed his certainty and fundamentalism. But as I grew older and more sober (I was twenty when this happened), I realized that I was afraid of something else and something more: I was afraid that when I saw my friend, I was looking at myself. I was afraid, not because he was foreign, but because he was familiar; not because he was uninviting, but because he was seductive again—not in his literal imitation of a woman, which was completely unappealing to me, but in his willingness to be so brazenly what he was; not because of how he ended up, but because it seemed a fate that I could have had, a fate that someone could even want. How much, in the end, did I want to wallow in the mud? How much of myself did I not even want to face? That was the horror of the city, really, as a *Dirty Harry* vision: fates were anonymous, shockingly reversible, and interchangeable. Noir taught me that much about how absolutely unknowable fear really is, and how utterly accidental all fate is: we are, in varied and complex ways, what we fear.

II

September 11 is an odd, contradictory date in the history of American self-definition. On the one hand, we see ourselves, as a result of the terrorist attacks on the World Trade Center and the Pentagon, as having entered the community of nations, experiencing something that has become nearly commonplace in the world: mass murder as a political statement. We now know what the rest of the world feels like and the kind of uncertainty and insecurity that other people must accept as routine. On the other hand, the attacks seemed to have intensified our perception of our exceptionalism: how dare anyone attack the most powerful nation on earth, indeed, the most powerful nation in history? Or, expressed another way in our bewilderment over the attacks: how dare anyone attack the *best* nation on earth, a nation as good, kind, and generous as the United States? This combination of arrogance and innocence, our country being trapped in the clashing notions of seeing itself as an isolated fortress and as a holy redeemer, is the hallmark of our self-regard. It is the singular result of our geography, our grand fortune and good luck, our democratic institutions, our simplistic and implacable greed, our obsession with self-improvement, our provincial yet remarkably guileless sense of morality, and our complex sense of fear.

Of all of these elements that make up our national character, fear is perhaps the most astonishingly misunderstood. Many commentators, from historian Richard Hofstadter to filmmaker Michael Moore, have made much of American paranoia, particularly the conspiratorial fears of the right wing, from the John Birch Society[2] to the National Rifle Association, although the left has expressed an equal measure of paranoia, ranging from the incessant search of many African Americans to see racism every time something unfavorable or unfortunate or unfair happens to a black (not an unjustified tendency, but ultimately a debilitating, self-patronizing one) to Bill and Hillary Clinton's insistence that a "vast right-wing conspiracy" is out to get them.

Both the left and the right see the other as a cabal, plotting and scheming, a subversive network of disinformation and manipulation. Both sides want the certainty of orthodoxy and the constant reassurance that their enemies are real, undeterred by momentary defeat, corporately organized, and, indeed, evil (much like villains in Hollywood action movies, our latest cultural representation of paranoia as artistic catharsis). The objects of our paranoia must be worthy of it. September 11 intensified this paranoia on both sides because the stakes became bigger: Can the country be made secure, or will the right become even more authoritarian and compromise civil liberties (of course, many on the right are as concerned about civil liberties as liberals are)? Who are the traitors who made us

10

²*John Birch Society:* An ultra-right wing anti-Communist organization founded in 1958. — Eds.

vulnerable to such an attack? Was it the weak-willed, defense-slashing, anti-intelligence-gathering left (most defense slashing in the United States is bipartisan)? In this sense, patriotism becomes not simply a nationalistic expression of pride but a combative, psychological hedge against the fear that makes patriotism possible.

Chinese premier Chou En-lai was once asked what he thought the impact of the French Revolution on world politics had been, to which he replied, "It's too soon to tell." It was not entirely a tongue-in-cheek answer. To understand, in some measure, how complex fear is in the United States, it is necessary to think about perhaps the past sixty years, the scope of American history since the end of World War II, when the United States emerged as, unquestionably, the most powerful nation in the world. With great power comes not only great responsibility but also tremendous fear of losing that power or of misusing it in such a way as to compromise one's moral entitlement to it. (And Americans feel eminently entitled to the power they possess.) It may be too soon to conclude much from a period that is so recent, but we might learn a few tentative things.

Having been born during the Korean War, the military gambit that truly convened the post–World War II epoch in American history, and having grown into young adulthood during the Cold War, what was most striking to me about that era of our nation's confrontation with communism was not simply the fear but the character of that fear. If the United States was, as one famous historian put it, a country shaped by war, it had been culturally and psychologically shaped by fear. In its earlier years, there was fear of the wilderness (the Puritans referred to their journey here as "the errand in the wilderness"), a mirror reflecting the darkness and chaos of the human soul, that had to be tamed, controlled, and harnessed; and the fear of the inhabitants of that wilderness, the Indians, who had also had to be controlled, harnessed, tamed, if not eliminated entirely. There was fear of the African slaves, whose rebellion would have been justified in the eyes of many whites, including Thomas Jefferson, by the treatment they received. And in a market-driven economy, there was fear of failure, of not seizing or even recognizing the main chance when it came. In a highly individualistic society, there was a fear of conformity and not being sufficiently oneself, and in a society of joiners, there was a fear of being too individualistic and not belonging.

During the Cold War period, several threads of fear intertwined and perhaps even fed one another. As a result of atomic power, there was the fear of science as a destructive force. Most of the science fiction movies of the 1950s relied to some extent on this sort of Pandora's box theme. Even a noted children's book of the early 1960s, Madeleine L'Engle's *A Wrinkle in Time*, which was highly derivative of the science fiction films of the 1950s, made use of such an idea: the quest for knowledge had to be tempered and humanized, which seems to me, in retrospect, an obscurantist redundancy. Television shows like *The Twilight Zone* and *The Outer*

Limits, with their predictable bourgeois morality (nearly apotheosized in *A Wrinkle in Time*), also explored the fear of science in many of its episodes.

This fear of science was occurring at the same time as our obsession with communism had become a new national policy. But the focus on communism led not to a direct confrontation with it but rather to the idea of containment, that is, confining it and controlling it in some way, as if it were a communicable illness. Maintaining fear was important so that we as Americans never became complacent about containment. Science made the containment possible because each side, the United States and the Soviet Union, had sufficient nuclear weapons to destroy the other but also had something to lose in using them. (This deterrence would seem to exist for the United States even in dealing with "rogue" nations. Didn't a dictator like Saddam Hussein have as much to lose in using a nuclear weapon against the United States or supplying one to a terrorist group to use against the United States as any Soviet dictator in the 1960s or 1970s? Clearly, Hussein wanted more than anything else to stay in power, and wouldn't using some sort of weapon of mass destruction against the United States assure that he would not only lose power but that his country would probably be vaporized in retaliation? After all, so far, the only country in the world to have used nuclear weapons is the United States.) Containment, to be effective, had to breed paranoia. But this atmosphere of fear flourished during what Stanley Crouch has called "the Age of Redefinition," the civil rights era, a time that inspired the push for widespread human liberation in the United States. This challenge to the status quo naturally heightened the fear of change and the fear of a change in status for the social and political group being challenged. This apprehension, coupled with the general paranoia of the time, led some to the conviction that the communists were behind the civil rights movement. (The left, indeed, was, but Christianity was a much more central force.) The bug-eyed monster sci-fi art of the 1950s and 1960s was not only about fear of science but also about the challenge of otherness, the tolerance, or lack thereof, of difference. It is difficult to tell whether most of those symbolic representations of the civil rights struggle in science fiction movies, comic books, and television shows of the period endorsed the paranoia or mocked it—or, in fact, did both simultaneously, like Marvel comics.

It might be argued that the unease we feel in the United States today, post-9/11, is different in degree and kind from the paranoia of the Cold War. I am not sure this is true. Most of our Cold War concerns remain: fear of science in the form of modified foods, food additives, indeed of food itself, as we increasingly embrace "the natural" as something opposed to science. Our fear of otherness remains as well: the poor, as always, continue to be misunderstood and largely seen as a nuisance (why can't they be like us?) or a mission (let's make them into us!); homosexuals are the latest battleground of tolerance. Are they like us, fundamentally, or are

15

they really different? We have additional fears: of self-indulgence, of our own triviality, which perhaps helped to fuel the fear created by 9/11. We had lost our sense of mission, of purpose in the world, so 9/11 was somehow biblical, a cosmic wake-up call to honor our greatness. And who can say it wasn't that? Despite President Bush's pre-emption doctrine (not new in American political history), it is not likely that the United States, in the end, will adopt any other approach over the long haul but containment and co-optation. How can we eradicate Islam, fundamentalism, Arabs, radicalism, poverty, hatred, or terrorism as the warfare of the weak unless we eradicate the weak or weakness as a condition, both of which are impossible? And so we Americans will soldier on, part-swagger, part-jog, part-limp, wrestling with our devils and angels. Ah, the price that must be paid, the burden that must be borne, when, in Cole Porter's words, you're the tops.

The Reader's Presence

1. The essay is divided into two distinct halves. What is the relationship of the first half to the second? Why do you think Early begins the essay the way he does? Are the connections between the two sections explicit? If not, what evidence is presented about the relationship between the two sections? How would each section have functioned alone?

2. In what ways is fear a component of American identity and a recurring theme in our history? List the different ways that fear has influenced our culture and history. Would Early agree or disagree that the fear emanating from the events of 9/11 is a different fear than Americans have experienced before?

3. Early juxtaposes personal experience and discussion of a greater context of American identity and politics in his discussion of fear and fate. Compare the way Early uses structure to the way Don DeLillo does in "In the Ruins of the Future" (page 361). Why do you think each writer chose to make distinct section breaks between each segment? How do the two works compare in the way they juxtapose personal and general discussion?

Lars Eighner

On Dumpster Diving

Lars Eighner (b. 1948) was born in Texas and attended the University of Texas at Austin. An essayist and fiction writer, he contributes regularly to the Threepenny Review, Advocate Men, *the* Guide, *and* Inches. *He has published several collections of short stories, essays, and gay erotica. His most recent publications include a camp novel,* Pawn to Queen Four *(1995); a collection of essays,* Gay Cosmos *(1995); an erotic short story collection,* Whispered in the Dark *(1995); and* WANK: The Tapes *(1998).*

Eighner became homeless in 1988, after he lost his job as a mental-hospital attendant. "On Dumpster Diving" is Eighner's prize-winning essay based on this experience, later reprinted as part of his full-length book about homelessness, Travels with Lizbeth: Three Years on the Road and on the Streets *(1993). Eighner and Lizbeth, Eighner's dog, became homeless again in 1996. Friends organized a fund under the auspices of the* Texas Observer *and obtained an apartment for Eighner and Lizbeth in Austin. Lizbeth has since passed away.*

On what is required to find success as a writer, Eighner has said, "I was not making enough money to support myself as a housed person, but I was writing well before I became homeless. . . . A writer needs talent, luck, and persistence. You can make do with two out of three, and the more you have of one, the less you need of the others."

Long before I began Dumpster diving I was impressed with Dumpsters, enough so that I wrote the Merriam-Webster research service to discover what I could about the word "Dumpster." I learned from them that "Dumpster" is a proprietary word belonging to the Dempster Dumpster company.

Since then I have dutifully capitalized the word although it was lowercased in almost all of the citations Merriam-Webster photocopied for me. Dempster's word is too apt. I have never heard these things called anything but Dumpsters. I do not know anyone who knows the generic name for these objects. From time to time, however, I hear a wino or hobo give some corrupted credit to the original and call them Dipsy Dumpsters.

I began Dumpster diving about a year before I became homeless.

I prefer the term "scavenging" and use the word "scrounging" when I mean to be obscure. I have heard people, evidently meaning to be polite, using the word "foraging," but I prefer to reserve that word for gathering nuts and berries and such which I do also according to the season and the opportunity. "Dumpster diving" seems to me to be a little too cute and, in my case, inaccurate because I lack the athletic ability to lower myself into the Dumpsters as the true divers do, much to their increased profit.

I like the frankness of the word "scavenging," which I can hardly   5
think of without picturing a big black snail on an aquarium wall. I live from the refuse of others. I am a scavenger. I think it a sound and honorable niche, although if I could I would naturally prefer to live the comfortable consumer life, perhaps — and only perhaps — as a slightly less wasteful consumer owing to what I have learned as a scavenger.

While my dog Lizbeth and I were still living in the house on Avenue B in Austin, as my savings ran out, I put almost all my sporadic income into rent. The necessities of daily life I began to extract from Dumpsters. Yes, we ate from Dumpsters. Except for jeans, all my clothes came from Dumpsters. Boom boxes, candles, bedding, toilet paper, medicine, books, a typewriter, a virgin male love doll, change sometimes amounting to many dollars: I acquired many things from the Dumpsters.

I have learned much as a scavenger. I mean to put some of what I have learned down here, beginning with the practical art of Dumpster diving and proceeding to the abstract.

What is safe to eat?

After all, the finding of objects is becoming something of an urban art. Even respectable employed people will sometimes find something tempting sticking out of a Dumpster or standing beside one. Quite a number of people, not all of them of the bohemian type, are willing to brag that they found this or that piece in the trash. But eating from Dumpsters is the thing that separates the dilettanti from the professionals.

Eating safely from the Dumpsters involves three principles: using   10
the senses and common sense to evaluate the condition of the found materials, knowing the Dumpsters of a given area and checking them regularly, and seeking always to answer the question "Why was this discarded?"

Perhaps everyone who has a kitchen and a regular supply of groceries has, at one time or another, made a sandwich and eaten half of it before discovering mold on the bread or got a mouthful of milk before realizing the milk had turned. Nothing of the sort is likely to happen to a Dumpster diver because he is constantly reminded that most food is discarded for a reason. Yet a lot of perfectly good food can be found in Dumpsters.

Canned goods, for example, turn up fairly often in the Dumpsters I frequent. All except the most phobic people would be willing to eat from a can even if it came from a Dumpster. Canned goods are among the safest of foods to be found in Dumpsters, but are not utterly foolproof.

Although very rare with modern canning methods, botulism is a possibility. Most other forms of food poisoning seldom do lasting harm to a healthy person. But botulism is almost certainly fatal and often the first symptom is death. Except for carbonated beverages, all canned goods should contain a slight vacuum and suck air when first punctured. Bulging, rusty, dented cans and cans that spew when punctured should be avoided, especially when the contents are not very acidic or syrupy.

Heat can break down the botulin, but this requires much more cooking than most people do to canned goods. To the extent that botulism occurs at all, of course, it can occur in cans on pantry shelves as well as in cans from Dumpsters. Need I say that home-canned goods found in Dumpsters are simply too risky to be recommended.

From time to time one of my companions, aware of the source of my provisions, will ask, "Do you think these crackers are really safe to eat?" For some reason it is most often the crackers they ask about.

This question always makes me angry. Of course I would not offer my companion anything I had doubts about. But more than that I wonder why he cannot evaluate the condition of the crackers for himself. I have no special knowledge and I have been wrong before. Since he knows where the food comes from, it seems to me he ought to assume some of the responsibility for deciding what he will put in his mouth.

For myself I have few qualms about dry foods such as crackers, cookies, cereal, chips, and pasta if they are free of visible contaminates and still dry and crisp. Most often such things are found in the original packaging, which is not so much a positive sign as it is the absence of a negative one.

Raw fruits and vegetables with intact skins seem perfectly safe to me, excluding of course the obviously rotten. Many are discarded for minor imperfections which can be pared away. Leafy vegetables, grapes, cauliflower, broccoli, and similar things may be contaminated by liquids and may be impractical to wash.

Candy, especially hard candy, is usually safe if it has not drawn ants. Chocolate is often discarded only because it has become discolored as the cocoa butter de-emulsified. Candying after all is one method of food preservation because pathogens do not like very sugary substances.

All of these foods might be found in any Dumpster and can be evaluated with some confidence largely on the basis of appearance. Beyond these are foods which cannot be correctly evaluated without additional information.

I began scavenging by pulling pizzas out of the Dumpster behind a pizza delivery shop. In general prepared food requires caution, but in this case I knew when the shop closed and went to the Dumpster as soon as the last of the help left.

Such shops often get prank orders, called "bogus." Because help seldom stays long at these places pizzas are often made with the wrong topping, refused on delivery for being cold, or baked incorrectly. The products to be discarded are boxed up because inventory is kept by counting boxes: A boxed pizza can be written off; an unboxed pizza does not exist.

I never placed a bogus order to increase the supply of pizzas and I believe no one else was scavenging in this Dumpster. But the people in the shop became suspicious and began to retain their garbage in the shop overnight.

While it lasted I had a steady supply of fresh, sometimes warm pizza. Because I knew the Dumpster I knew the source of the pizza, and because I visited the Dumpster regularly I knew what was fresh and what was yesterday's.

The area I frequent is inhabited by many affluent college students. I   25
am not here by chance; the Dumpsters in this area are very rich. Students throw out many good things, including food. In particular they tend to throw everything out when they move at the end of a semester, before and after breaks, and around midterm when many of them despair of college. So I find it advantageous to keep an eye on the academic calendar.

The students throw food away around the breaks because they do not know whether it has spoiled or will spoil before they return. A typical discard is a half jar of peanut butter. In fact nonorganic peanut butter does not require refrigeration and is unlikely to spoil in any reasonable time. The student does not know that, and since it is Daddy's money, the student decides not to take a chance.

Opened containers require caution and some attention to the question "Why was this discarded?" But in the case of discards from student apartments, the answer may be that the item was discarded through carelessness, ignorance, or wastefulness. This can sometimes be deduced when the item is found with many others, including some that are obviously perfectly good.

Some students, and others, approach defrosting a freezer by chucking out the whole lot. Not only do the circumstances of such a find tell the story, but also the mass of frozen goods stays cold for a long time and items may be found still frozen or freshly thawed.

Yogurt, cheese, and sour cream are items that are often thrown out while they are still good. Occasionally I find a cheese with a spot of mold, which of course I just pare off, and because it is obvious why such a cheese was discarded, I treat it with less suspicion than an apparently perfect cheese found in similar circumstances. Yogurt is often discarded, still sealed, only because the expiration date on the carton had passed. This is one of my favorite finds because yogurt will keep for several days, even in warm weather.

Students throw out canned goods and staples at the end of semesters   30
and when they give up college at midterm. Drugs, pornography, spirits, and the like are often discarded when parents are expected—Dad's day, for example. And spirits also turn up after big party weekends, presumably

discarded by the newly reformed. Wine and spirits, of course, keep perfectly well even once opened.

My test for carbonated soft drinks is whether they still fizz vigorously. Many juices or other beverages are too acid or too syrupy to cause much concern provided they are not visibly contaminated. Liquids, however, require some care.

One hot day I found a large jug of Pat O'Brien's Hurricane mix. The jug had been opened, but it was still ice cold. I drank three large glasses before it became apparent to me that someone had added the rum to the mix, and not a little rum. I never tasted the rum and by the time I began to feel the effects I had already ingested a very large quantity of the beverage. Some divers would have considered this a boon, but being suddenly and thoroughly intoxicated in a public place in the early afternoon is not my idea of a good time.

I have heard of people maliciously contaminating discarded food and even handouts, but mostly I have heard of this from people with vivid imaginations who have had no experience with the Dumpsters themselves. Just before the pizza shop stopped discarding its garbage at night, jalapeños began showing up on most of the discarded pizzas. If indeed this was meant to discourage me it was a wasted effort because I am native Texan.

For myself, I avoid game, poultry, pork, and egg-based foods whether I find them raw or cooked. I seldom have the means to cook what I find, but when I do I avail myself of plentiful supplies of beef which is often in very good condition. I suppose fish becomes disagreeable before it becomes dangerous. The dog is happy to have any such thing that is past its prime and, in fact, does not recognize fish as food until it is quite strong.

Home leftovers, as opposed to surpluses from restaurants, are very often bad. Evidently, especially among students, there is a common type of personality that carefully wraps up even the smallest leftover and shoves it into the back of the refrigerator for six months or so before discarding it. Characteristic of this type are the reused jars and margarine tubs which house the remains.   35

I avoid ethnic foods I am unfamiliar with. If I do not know what it is supposed to look like when it is good, I cannot be certain I will be able to tell if it is bad.

No matter how careful I am I still get dysentery at least once a month, oftener in warm weather. I do not want to paint too romantic a picture. Dumpster diving has serious drawbacks as a way of life.

I learned to scavenge gradually, on my own. Since then I have initiated several companions into the trade. I have learned that there is a predictable series of stages a person goes through in learning to scavenge.

At first the new scavenger is filled with disgust and self-loathing. He is ashamed of being seen and may lurk around, trying to duck behind things, or he may try to dive at night.

(In fact, most people instinctively look away from a scavenger. By   40
skulking around, the novice calls attention to himself and arouses suspicion. Diving at night is ineffective and needlessly messy.)

Every grain of rice seems to be a maggot. Everything seems to stink.
He can wipe the egg yolk off the found can, but he cannot erase the
stigma of eating garbage out of his mind.

That stage passes with experience. The scavenger finds a pair of running shoes that fit and look and smell brand new. He finds a pocket calculator in perfect working order. He finds pristine ice cream, still frozen,
more than he can eat or keep. He begins to understand: People do throw
away perfectly good stuff, a lot of perfectly good stuff.

At this stage, Dumpster shyness begins to dissipate. The diver, after
all, has the last laugh. He is finding all manner of good things which
are his for the taking. Those who disparage his profession are the fools,
not he.

He may begin to hang onto some perfectly good things for which he
has neither a use nor a market. Then he begins to take note of the things
which are not perfectly good but are nearly so. He mates a Walkman
with broken earphones and one that is missing a battery cover. He picks
up things which he can repair.

At this stage he may become lost and never recover. Dumpsters are   45
full of things of some potential value to someone and also of things which
never have much intrinsic value but are interesting. All the Dumpster
divers I have known come to the point of trying to acquire everything
they touch. Why not take it, they reason, since it is all free.

This is, of course, hopeless. Most divers come to realize that they
must restrict themselves to items of relatively immediate utility. But in
some cases the diver simply cannot control himself. I have met several of
these pack-rat types. Their ideas of the values of various pieces of junk
verge on the psychotic. Every bit of glass may be a diamond, they think,
and all that glistens, gold.

I tend to gain weight when I am scavenging. Partly this is because I
always find far more pizza and doughnuts than water-packed tuna, non-
fat yogurt, and fresh vegetables. Also I have not developed much faith in
the reliability of Dumpsters as a food source, although it has been proven
to me many times. I tend to eat as if I have no idea where my next meal is
coming from. But mostly I just hate to see food go to waste and so I eat
much more than I should. Something like this drives the obsession to collect junk.

As for collecting objects, I usually restrict myself to collecting one
kind of small object at a time, such as pocket calculators, sunglasses, or
campaign buttons. To live on the street I must anticipate my needs to a
certain extent: I must pick up and save warm bedding I find in August because it will not be found in Dumpsters in November. But even if I had a
home with extensive storage space I could not save everything that might
be valuable in some contingency.

I have proprietary feelings about my Dumpsters. As I have suggested, it is no accident that I scavenge from Dumpsters where good finds are common. But my limited experience with Dumpsters in other areas suggests to me that it is the population of competitors rather than the affluence of the dumpers that most affects the feasibility of survival by scavenging. The large number of competitors is what puts me off the idea of trying to scavenge in places like Los Angeles.

Curiously, I do not mind my direct competition, other scavengers, so much as I hate the can scroungers.

People scrounge cans because they have to have a little cash. I have tried scrounging cans with an able-bodied companion. Afoot a can scrounger simply cannot make more than a few dollars a day. One can extract the necessities of life from the Dumpsters directly with far less effort than would be required to accumulate the equivalent value in cans.

Can scroungers, then, are people who *must* have small amounts of cash. These are drug addicts and winos, mostly the latter because the amounts of cash are so small.

Spirits and drugs do, like all other commodities, turn up in Dumpsters and the scavenger will from time to time have a half bottle of a rather good wine with his dinner. But the wino cannot survive on these occasional finds; he must have his daily dose to stave off the DTs. All the cans he can carry will buy about three bottles of Wild Irish Rose.

I do not begrudge them the cans, but can scroungers tend to tear up the Dumpsters, mixing the contents and littering the area. They become so specialized that they can see only cans. They earn my contempt by passing up change, canned goods, and readily hockable items.

There are precious few courtesies among scavengers. But it is a common practice to set aside surplus items: pairs of shoes, clothing, canned goods, and such. A true scavenger hates to see good stuff go to waste and what he cannot use he leaves in good condition in plain sight.

Can scroungers lay waste to everything in their path and will stir one of a pair of good shoes to the bottom of a Dumpster, to be lost or ruined in the muck. Can scroungers will even go through individual garbage cans, something I have never seen a scavenger do.

Individual garbage cans are set out on the public easement only on garbage days. On other days going through them requires trespassing close to a dwelling. Going through individual garbage cans without scattering litter is almost impossible. Litter is likely to reduce the public's tolerance of scavenging. Individual garbage cans are simply not as productive as Dumpsters; people in houses and duplexes do not move as often and for some reason do not tend to discard as much useful material. Moreover, the time required to go through one garbage can that serves one household is not much less than the time required to go through a Dumpster that contains the refuse of twenty apartments.

But my strongest reservation about going through individual garbage cans is that this seems to me a very personal kind of invasion to which I

would object if I were a householder. Although many things in Dumpsters are obviously meant never to come to light, a Dumpster is somehow
less personal.

I avoid trying to draw conclusions about the people who dump in the
Dumpsters I frequent. I think it would be unethical to do so, although I
know many people will find the idea of scavenger ethics too funny for
words.

Dumpsters contain bank statements, bills, correspondence, and other   60
documents, just as anyone might expect. But there are also less obvious
sources of information. Pill bottles, for example. The labels on pill bottles
contain the name of the patient, the name of the doctor, and the name of
the drug. AIDS drugs and antipsychotic medicines, to name but two
groups, are specific and are seldom prescribed for any other disorders.
The plastic compacts for birth control pills usually have complete label
information.

Despite all of this sensitive information, I have had only one apartment resident object to my going through the Dumpster. In that case it
turned out the resident was a university athlete who was taking bets and
who was afraid I would turn up his wager slips.

Occasionally a find tells a story. I once found a small paper bag containing some unused condoms, several partial tubes of flavored sexual lubricant, a partially used compact of birth control pills, and the torn pieces
of a picture of a young man. Clearly she was through with him and planning to give up sex altogether.

Dumpster things are often sad—abandoned teddy bears, shredded
wedding books, despaired-of sales kits. I find many pets lying in state in
Dumpsters. Although I hope to get off the streets so that Lizbeth can have
a long and comfortable old age, I know this hope is not very realistic. So I
suppose when her time comes she too will go into a Dumpster. I will have
no better place for her. And after all, for most of her life her livelihood
has come from the Dumpster. When she finds something I think is safe
that has been spilled from the Dumpster I let her have it. She already
knows the route around the best Dumpsters. I like to think that if she survives me she will have a chance of evading the dog catcher and of finding
her sustenance on the route.

Silly vanities also come to rest in the Dumpsters. I am a rather accomplished needleworker. I get a lot of materials from the Dumpsters. Evidently sorority girls, hoping to impress someone, perhaps themselves, with
their mastery of a womanly art, buy a lot of embroider-by-number kits,
work a few stitches horribly, and eventually discard the whole mess. I pull
out their stitches, turn the canvas over, and work an original design. Do
not think I refrain from chuckling as I make original gifts from these kits.

I find diaries and journals. I have often thought of compiling a book   65
of literary found objects. And perhaps I will one day. But what I find is
hopelessly commonplace and bad without being, even unconsciously,
camp. College students also discard their papers. I am horrified to discover

the kind of paper which now merits an A in an undergraduate course. I am grateful, however, for the number of good books and magazines the students throw out.

In the area I know best I have never discovered vermin in the Dumpsters, but there are two kinds of kitty surprise. One is alley cats which I meet as they leap, claws first, out of Dumpsters. This is especially thrilling when I have Lizbeth in tow. The other kind of kitty surprise is a plastic garbage bag filled with some ponderous, amorphous mass. This always proves to be used cat litter.

City bees harvest doughnut glaze and this makes the Dumpster at the doughnut shop more interesting. My faith in the instinctive wisdom of animals is always shaken whenever I see Lizbeth attempt to catch a bee in her mouth, which she does whenever bees are present. Evidently some birds find Dumpsters profitable, for birdie surprise is almost as common as kitty surprise of the first kind. In hunting season all kinds of small game turn up in Dumpsters, some of it, sadly, not entirely dead. Curiously, summer and winter, maggots are uncommon.

The worst of the living and near-living hazards of the Dumpsters are the fire ants. The food that they claim is not much of a loss, but they are vicious and aggressive. It is very easy to brush against some surface of the Dumpster and pick up half a dozen or more fire ants, usually in some sensitive area such as the underarm. One advantage of bringing Lizbeth along as I make Dumpster rounds is that, for obvious reasons, she is very alert to ground-based fire ants. When Lizbeth recognizes the signs of fire ant infestation around our feet she does the Dance of the Zillion Fire Ants. I have learned not to ignore this warning from Lizbeth, whether I perceive the tiny ants or not, but to remove ourselves at Lizbeth's first pas de bourrée.[1] All the more so because the ants are the worst in the months I wear flip-flops, if I have them.

(Perhaps someone will misunderstand the above. Lizbeth does the Dance of the Zillion Fire Ants when she recognizes more fire ants than she cares to eat, not when she is being bitten. Since I have learned to react promptly, she does not get bitten at all. It is the isolated patrol of fire ants that falls in Lizbeth's range that deserves pity. Lizbeth finds them quite tasty.)

By far the best way to go through a Dumpster is to lower yourself into it. Most of the good stuff tends to settle at the bottom because it is usually weightier than the rubbish. My more athletic companions have often demonstrated to me that they can extract much good material from a Dumpster I have already been over. 70

To those psychologically or physically unprepared to enter a Dumpster, I recommend a stout stick, preferably with some barb or hook at one end. The hook can be used to grab plastic garbage bags. When I find canned goods or other objects loose at the bottom of a Dumpster I usually

---

[1]*pas de bourrée:* A transitional ballet step. —EDS.

can roll them into a small bag that I can then hoist up. Much Dumpster diving is a matter of experience for which nothing will do except practice.

Dumpster diving is outdoor work, often surprisingly pleasant. It is not entirely predictable; things of interest turn up every day and some days there are finds of great value. I am always very pleased when I can turn up exactly the thing I most wanted to find. Yet in spite of the element of change, scavenging more than most other pursuits tends to yield returns in some proportion to the effort and intelligence brought to bear. It is very sweet to turn up a few dollars in change from a Dumpster that has just been gone over by a wino.

The land is now covered with cities. The cities are full of Dumpsters. I think of scavenging as a modern form of self-reliance. In any event, after ten years of government service, where everything is geared to the lowest common denominator, I find work that rewards initiative and effort refreshing. Certainly I would be happy to have a sinecure again, but I am not heartbroken not to have one anymore.

I find from the experience of scavenging two rather deep lessons. The first is to take what I can use and let the rest go by. I have come to think that there is no value in the abstract. A thing I cannot use or make useful, perhaps by trading, has no value however fine or rare it may be. I mean useful in a broad sense—so, for example, some art I would think useful and valuable, but other art might be otherwise for me.

I was shocked to realize that some things are not worth acquiring,   75
but now I think it is so. Some material things are white elephants that eat up the possessor's substance.

The second lesson is of the transience of material being. This has not quite converted me to a dualist, but it has made some headway in that direction. I do not suppose that ideas are immortal, but certainly mental things are longer-lived than other material things.

Once I was the sort of person who invests material objects with sentimental value. Now I no longer have those things, but I have the sentiments yet.

Many times in my travels I have lost everything but the clothes I was wearing and Lizbeth. The things I find in Dumpsters, the love letters and ragdolls of so many lives, remind me of this lesson. Now I hardly pick up a thing without envisioning the time I will cast it away. This I think is a healthy state of mind. Almost everything I have now has already been cast out at least once, proving that what I own is valueless to someone.

Anyway, I find my desire to grab for the gaudy bauble has been largely sated. I think this is an attitude I share with the very wealthy—we both know there is plenty more where what we have came from. Between us are the rat-race millions who have confounded their selves with the objects they grasp and who nightly scavenge the cable channels looking for they know not what.

I am sorry for them.   80

The Reader's Presence

1. At the center of "On Dumpster Diving" is Eighner's effort to bring out from the shadows of contemporary American life the lore and practices of scavenging, what he calls "a modern form of self-reliance." His essay also provides a compelling account of his self-education as he took to the streets for "the necessities of life." Outline the stages in this process, and summarize the ethical and moral issues and the questions of decorum that Eighner confronted along the way. Show how this process reflects the structure of his essay, "beginning with the practical art of Dumpster diving and proceeding to the abstract."

2. One of the most remarkable aspects of Eighner's essay is the tone (the attitude) he expresses toward his subject. Select a paragraph from the essay. Read it aloud. How would you characterize the sound of his voice? Does he sound, for example, tough-minded? polite? strident? experienced? cynical? something else? Consider, for example, paragraph 34, where he notes: "For myself, I avoid game, poultry, pork, and egg-based foods whether I find them raw or cooked." Where have you heard talk like this before? Do you notice any changes as the essay develops, or does Eighner maintain the same tone in discussing his subject? What responses does he elicit from his readers when he speaks of scavenging as a "profession" and a "trade"?

3. Consider Eighner's relationship with his readers. Does he consider himself fundamentally different from or similar to his audience? In what specific ways? Consider, for example, the nature of the information Eighner provides in the essay. Does he expect his readers to be familiar with the information? How does he characterize his own knowledgeability about this often-noticed but rarely discussed activity in urban America? Comment on his use of irony in presenting information about Dumpster diving and in anticipating his readers' responses to the circumstances within which he does the work of his trade.

4. Compare Eighner's description of trash to John Hollander's in his essay "Mess" (page 461). How do both writers work from lists to build their essays?

Ralph Ellison

What America Would Be Like without Blacks

Ralph Ellison (1914–1994), one of the most influential writers of the twenti-eth century, wrote novels, short stories, essays, and social criticism. His first novel, Invisible Man *(1952), about a black man's struggle for identity, received the National Book Award and is considered to be a landmark of modern fiction. Ellison was born in Oklahoma City and in his twenties moved to New York City. He began writing his second novel in 1954, but a large portion of the manuscript was destroyed in a fire in 1967. For the last forty years of his life, he rewrote hun-dreds and hundreds of pages in an effort to complete this second novel. With the help of editor John Callahan, this long-awaited book,* Juneteenth, *was finally published posthumously in 1999. "What America Would Be Like without Blacks" first appeared in* Time *in 1970.*

The fantasy of an America free of blacks is at least as old as the dream of creating a truly democratic society. While we are aware that there is something inescapably tragic about the cost of achieving our democratic ideals, we keep such tragic awareness segregated to the rear of our minds. We allow it to come to the fore only during moments of great national crisis.

On the other hand, there is something so embarrassingly absurd about the notion of purging the nation of blacks that it seems hardly a product of thought at all. It is more like a primitive reflex, a throwback to the dim past of tribal experience, which we rationalize and try to make respectable by dressing it up in the gaudy and highly questionable trappings of what we call the "concept of race." Yet, despite its absur-dity, the fantasy of a blackless America continues to turn up. It is a fan-tasy born not merely of racism but of petulance, of exasperation, of moral fatigue. It is like a boil bursting forth from impurities in the bloodstream of democracy.

In its benign manifestations, it can be outrageously comic — as in the picaresque adventures of Percival Brownlee who appears in William Faulkner's story "The Bear." Exasperating to his white masters because his aspirations and talents are for preaching and conducting choirs rather than for farming, Brownlee is "freed" after much resistance and ends up as the prosperous proprietor of a New Orleans brothel. In Faulkner's hands, the uncomprehending drive of Brownlee's owners to "get shut" of him is comically instructive. Indeed, the story resonates certain abiding, tragic themes of American history with which it is interwoven, and which are causing great turbulence in the social atmosphere today. I refer to the exasperation and bemusement of the white American with the black, the black American's ceaseless (and swiftly accelerating) struggle to escape the misconceptions of whites, and the continual confusing of the black American's racial background with his individual culture. Most of all, I refer to the recurring fantasy of solving one basic problem of American democracy by "getting shut" of the blacks through various wishful schemes that would banish them from the nation's bloodstream, from its social structure, and from its conscience and historical consciousness.

This fantastic vision of a lily-white America appeared as early as 1713, with the suggestion of a white "native American," thought to be from New Jersey, that all the Negroes be given their freedom and returned to Africa. In 1777, Thomas Jefferson, while serving in the Virginia legislature, began drafting a plan for the gradual emancipation and exportation of the slaves. Nor were Negroes themselves immune to the fantasy. In 1815, Paul Cuffe, a wealthy merchant, shipbuilder, and landowner from the New Bedford area, shipped and settled at his own expense thirty-eight of his fellow Negroes in Africa. It was perhaps his example that led in the following year to the creation of the American Colonization Society, which was to establish in 1821 the colony of Liberia. Great amounts of cash and a perplexing mixture of motives went into the venture. The slave owners and many Border-state politicians wanted to use it as a scheme to rid the country not of slaves but of the militant free Negroes who were agitating against the "peculiar institution." The abolitionists, until they took a lead from free Negro leaders and began attacking the scheme, also participated as a means of righting a great historical injustice. Many blacks went along with it simply because they were sick of the black and white American mess and hoped to prosper in the quiet peace of the old ancestral home.

Such conflicting motives doomed the Colonization Society to failure, but what amazes one even more than the notion that anyone could have believed in its success is the fact that it was attempted during a period when the blacks, slave and free, made up eighteen percent of the total population. When we consider how long blacks had been in the New World and had been transforming it and being Americanized by it, the scheme appears not only fantastic, but the product of a free-floating irrationality. Indeed, a national pathology.

Nevertheless, some of the noblest of Americans were bemused. Not only Jefferson but later Abraham Lincoln was to give the scheme credence. According to historian John Hope Franklin, Negro colonization seemed as important to Lincoln as emancipation. In 1862, Franklin notes, Lincoln called a group of prominent free Negroes to the White House and urged them to support colonization, telling them, "Your race suffers greatly, many of them by living among us, while ours suffers from your presence. If this is admitted, it affords a reason why we should be separated."

In spite of his unquestioned greatness, Abraham Lincoln was a man of his times and limited by some of the less worthy thinking of his times. This is demonstrated both by his reliance upon the concept of race in his analysis of the American dilemma and by his involvement in a plan of purging the nation of blacks as a means of healing the badly shattered ideals of democratic federalism. Although benign, his motive was no less a product of fantasy. It envisaged an attempt to relieve an inevitable suffering that marked the growing pains of the youthful body politic by an operation which would have amounted to the severing of a healthy and indispensable member.

Yet, like its twin, the illusion of secession, the fantasy of a benign amputation that would rid the country of black men to the benefit of a nation's health not only persists; today, in the form of neo-Garveyism, it fascinates black men no less than it once hypnotized whites. Both fantasies become operative whenever the nation grows weary of the struggle toward the ideal of American democratic equality. Both would use the black man as a scapegoat to achieve a national catharsis, and both would, by way of curing the patient, destroy him.

What is ultimately intriguing about the fantasy of "getting shut" of the Negro American is the fact that no one who entertains it seems ever to have considered what the nation would have become had Africans *not* been brought to the New World, and had their descendants not played such a complex and confounding role in the creation of American history and culture. Nor do they appear to have considered with any seriousness the effect upon the nation of having any of the schemes for exporting blacks succeed beyond settling some fifteen thousand or so in Liberia.

We are reminded that Daniel Patrick Moynihan,[1] who has recently aggravated our social confusion over the racial issue while allegedly attempting to clarify it, is co-author of a work which insists that the American melting pot didn't melt because our white ethnic groups have resisted all assimilative forces that appear to threaten their identities. The problem here is that few Americans know who and what they really are. That is why few of these groups — or at least few of the children of these groups — have been able to resist the movies, television, baseball, jazz, football, drum-majoretting, rock, comic strips, radio commercials, soap operas, book clubs, slang, or any of a thousand other expressions and carriers of our pluralistic and easily available popular culture. And it is here precisely that ethnic resistance is least effective. On this level the melting pot did indeed melt, creating such deceptive metamorphoses and blending of identities, values,

10

---

[1]*Moynihan:* Moynihan wrote extensively on issues of poverty and welfare; he retired as senator of New York in 2000 and died in 2003. — EDS.

and life-styles that most American whites are culturally part Negro American without even realizing it.

If we can resist for a moment the temptation to view everything having to do with Negro Americans in terms of their racially imposed status, we become aware of the fact that for all the harsh reality of the social and economic injustices visited upon them, these injustices have failed to keep Negroes clear of the cultural mainstream; Negro Americans are in fact one of its major tributaries. If we can cease approaching American social reality in terms of such false concepts as white and nonwhite, black culture and white culture, and think of these apparently unthinkable matters in the realistic manner of Western pioneers confronting the unknown prairie, perhaps we can begin to imagine what the United States would have been, or not been, had there been no blacks to give it — if I may be so bold as to say — color.

For one thing, the American nation is in a sense the product of the American language, a colloquial speech that began emerging long before the British colonials and Africans were transformed into Americans. It is a language that evolved from the king's English but, basing itself upon the realities of the American land and colonial institutions — or lack of institutions, began quite early as a vernacular revolt against the signs, symbols, manners, and authority of the mother country. It is a language that began by merging the sounds of many tongues, brought together in the struggle of diverse regions. And whether it is admitted or not, much of the sound of that language is derived from the timbre of the African voice and the listening habits of the African ear. So there is a *de'z* and *do'z* of slave speech sounding beneath our most polished Harvard accents, and if there is such a thing as a Yale accent, there is a Negro wail in it — doubtlessly introduced there by Old Yalie John C. Calhoun, who probably got it from his mammy.

Whitman viewed the spoken idiom of Negro Americans as a source for a native grand opera. Its flexibility, its musicality, its rhythms, free-wheeling diction, and metaphors, as projected in Negro American folklore, were absorbed by the creators of our great nineteenth-century literature even when the majority of blacks were still enslaved. Mark Twain celebrated it in the prose of *Huckleberry Finn*; without the presence of blacks, the book could not have been written. No Huck and Jim, no American novel as we know it. For not only is the black man a co-creator of the language that Mark Twain raised to the level of literary eloquence, but Jim's condition as American and Huck's commitment to freedom are at the moral center of the novel.[2]

In other words, had there been no blacks, certain creative tensions arising from the cross-purposes of whites and blacks would also not have

---

[2]*Mark Twain celebrated . . . moral center of the novel:* Ellison's observations on *Huckleberry Finn* became the basis of much subsequent literary criticism. For a different perspective on Twain's novel, see "Say It Ain't So, Huck," by Jane Smiley (page 815).—EDS.

existed. Not only would there have been no Faulkner; there would have been no Stephen Crane, who found certain basic themes of his writing in the Civil War. Thus, also, there would have been no Hemingway, who took Crane as a source and guide. Without the presence of Negro American style, our jokes, our tall tales, even our sports would be lacking in the sudden turns, the shocks, the swift changes of pace (all jazz-shaped) that serve to remind us that the world is ever unexplored, and that while a complete mastery of life is mere illusion, the real secret of the game is to make life swing. It is its ability to articulate this tragic-comic attitude toward life that explains much of the mysterious power and attractiveness of that quality of Negro American style known as "soul." An expression of American diversity within unity, of blackness with whiteness, soul announces the presence of a creative struggle against the realities of existence.

Without the presence of blacks, our political history would have been   15
otherwise. No slave economy, no Civil War; no violent destruction of the Reconstruction; no K.K.K. and no Jim Crow system. And without the disenfranchisement of black Americans and the manipulation of racial fears and prejudices, the disproportionate impact of white Southern politicians upon our domestic and foreign policies would have been impossible. Indeed, it is almost impossible to conceive of what our political system would have become without the snarl of forces—cultural, racial, religious— that make our nation what it is today.

Absent, too, would be the need for that tragic knowledge which we try ceaselessly to evade: that the true subject of democracy is not simply material well-being but the extension of the democratic process in the direction of perfecting itself. And that the most obvious test and clue to that perfection is the inclusion—*not* assimilation—of the black man.

Since the beginning of the nation, white Americans have suffered from a deep inner uncertainty as to who they really are. One of the ways that has been used to simplify the answer has been to seize upon the presence of black Americans and use them as a marker, a symbol of limits, a metaphor for the "outsider." Many whites could look at the social position of blacks and feel that color formed an easy and reliable gauge for determining to what extent one was or was not American. Perhaps that is why one of the first epithets that many European immigrants learned when they got off the boat was the term "nigger"—it made them feel instantly American. But this is tricky magic. Despite his racial difference and social status, something indisputably American about Negroes not only raised doubts about the white man's value system but aroused the troubling suspicion that whatever else the true American is, he is also somehow black.

Materially, psychologically, and culturally, part of the nation's heritage is Negro American, and whatever it becomes will be shaped in part by the Negro's presence. Which is fortunate, for today it is the black American who puts pressure upon the nation to live up to its ideals. It is he who gives creative tension to our struggle for justice and for the elimination of those factors, social and psychological, which make for slums and shaky suburban communities. It is he who insists that we purify the American language by demanding that there be a closer correlation between the meaning of words and reality, between ideal and conduct, our assertions and our actions. Without the black American, something irrepressibly hopeful and creative would go out of the American spirit, and the nation might well succumb to the moral slobbism that has ever threatened its existence from within.

When we look objectively at how the dry bones of the nation were hung together, it seems obvious that some one of the many groups that compose the United States had to suffer the fate of being allowed no easy escape from experiencing the harsh realities of the human condition as they were to exist under even so fortunate a democracy as ours. It would seem that some one group had to be stripped of the possibility of escaping such tragic knowledge by taking sanctuary in moral equivocation, racial chauvinism, or the advantage of superior social status. There is no point in complaining over the past or apologizing for one's fate. But for blacks, there are no hiding places down here, not in suburbia or in penthouse, neither in country nor in city. They are an American people who are geared to what *is* and who yet are driven by a sense of what it is possible for human life to be in this society. The nation could not survive being deprived of their presence because, by the irony implicit in the dynamics of American democracy, they symbolize both its most stringent testing and the possibility of its greatest human freedom.

The Reader's Presence

1. Ellison recounts little-known information about Abraham Lincoln. What might be Ellison's purpose in challenging the common view of history? How might he hope to influence the future by uncovering unsettling aspects of the past? He also argues that white people in America are culturally part black. Why might this notion have seemed radical at the time of this essay's writing?

2. What does Ellison mean by describing certain aspects of mainstream American culture as "jazz-shaped"? Where else does Ellison's writing venture from the literal to the figurative? Are Ellison's metaphors more or less effective than his straightforward

statements in advancing his argument? Why? Where does Ellison write from a basis of cool reason, and where does emotion seem to arise? Which style of expression do you find more effective? Why?

3. What connections can you find in the essay between cultural difference and invisibility? By what means, according to Ellison, do African American lives and their contributions to mainstream culture become and remain hidden? Does Ellison represent America's notion of itself as a great "melting-pot"? Why or why not? Compare this essay to Mary Gordon's "The Ghosts of Ellis Island" (page 443). How does Ellison's account of African Americans' place in American culture compare with that of Zora Neale Hurston in "How It Feels to Be Colored Me" (page 166)? Ellison makes a pun on the idea of "mainstream" America by saying that "Negro Americans are in fact one of its major tributaries" (paragraph 11). What is Hurston's central metaphor and how does it compare to Ellison's?

Joseph Epstein

The Perpetual Adolescent

A self-described "stickler for language," Joseph Epstein (b. 1937) has authored sixteen books of literary criticism, social commentary, personal essays, and fiction. His essays and articles are found in numerous publications, including Commentary, *the* New Yorker, Harper's, *the* New Republic, *and the* New York Review of Books. *He was a lecturer in English and writing at Northwestern University from 1974 to 2002 and editor of the Phi Beta Kappa magazine* American Scholar *for more than two decades. In his "Life and Letters" column in that magazine, Epstein declared his principles regarding the use and abuse of language: "Take out all language that is pretentious and imprecise, undereducated and over-intellectualized. Question all language that says more than it means, that leaves the ground but doesn't really fly. Question authority only after you have first seriously consulted it; it isn't always as stupid as it looks. Never forget that today's hot new phrase becomes tomorrow's cold dead cliché." Now retired from the magazine and teaching, he has continued to write; his most recent books are* Narcissus Leaves the Pool *(1999),* Snobbery *(2002),* Envy *(2003), and* Fabulous Small Jews *(2003).*

In a 2003 interview, Epstein described writing about people who are "caught in a cultural switch. That is to say they grew up with one set of values and now there is another. . . . I like to think of myself as a kind of chronicler of people caught in the switch." In his essay "The Perpetual Adolescent," Epstein comments on such a "cultural switch" in the United States since World War II. The essay is taken from the March 15, 2003, issue of the Weekly Standard, *to which Epstein is a regular contributor.*

Whenever anyone under the age of 50 sees old newsreel film of Joe DiMaggio's 56-game hitting streak of 1941, he is almost certain to be brought up by the fact that nearly everyone in the male-dominated crowds—in New York, Boston, Chicago, Detroit, Cleveland—seems to be wearing a suit and a fedora or other serious adult hat. The people in those earlier baseball crowds, though watching a boyish game, nonetheless had a radically different conception of themselves than most Americans do now. A major depression was ending, a world war was on. Even though they were watching an entertainment that took most of them back to their boyhoods, they thought of themselves as adults, no longer kids, but grown-ups, adults, men.

How different from today, when a good part of the crowd at any ballgame, no matter what the age, is wearing jeans and team caps and T-shirts; and let us not neglect those (one hopes) benign maniacs who paint their faces in home-team colors or spell out, on their bare chests, the letters of the names of star players: S-O-S-A.

Part of the explanation for the suits at the ballpark in DiMaggio's day is that in the 1940s and even '50s there weren't a lot of sport, or leisure, or casual clothes around. Unless one lived at what H.L. Mencken[1] called "the country-club stage of culture"—unless, that is, one golfed, played tennis, or sailed—one was likely to own only the clothes one worked in or better. Far from casual Fridays, in those years there weren't even casual Sundays. Wearing one's "Sunday best," a cliché of the time, meant wearing the good clothes one reserved for church.

Dressing down may first have set in on the West Coast, where a certain informality was thought to be a new way of life. In the 1960s, in universities casual dress became absolutely *de rigueur* among younger faculty, who, in their ardor to destroy any evidence of their being implicated in evil hierarchy, wished not merely to seem in no wise different from their students but, more important, to seem always young; and the quickest path to youthfulness was teaching in jeans, T-shirts, and the rest of it.

This informality has now been institutionalized. Few are the restaurants that could any longer hope to stay in business if they required men to wear a jacket and tie. Today one sees men wearing baseball caps—some worn backwards—while eating indoors in quite good restaurants. In an episode of *The Sopranos*, Tony Soprano, the mafia don, representing

5

---

[1]**Mencken:** For more on H. L. Mencken, see page 504.—EDS.

life of a different day, finds this so outrages his sense of decorum that, in a restaurant he frequents, he asks a man, in a quiet but entirely menacing way, to remove his goddamn hat.

Life in that different day was felt to observe the human equivalent of the Aristotelian unities: to have, like a good drama, a beginning, middle, and end. Each part, it was understood, had its own advantages and detractions, but the middle — adulthood — was the lengthiest and most earnest part, where everything serious happened and much was at stake. To violate the boundaries of any of the three divisions of life was to go against what was natural and thereby to appear unseemly, to put one's world somehow out of joint, to be, let us face it, a touch, and perhaps more than a touch, grotesque.

Today, of course, all this has been shattered. The ideal almost everywhere is to seem young for as long as possible. The health clubs and endemic workout clothes, the enormous increase in cosmetic surgery (for women and men), the special youth-oriented television programming and moviemaking, all these are merely the more obvious signs of the triumph of youth culture. When I say youth culture, I do not mean merely that the young today are transcendent, the group most admired among the various age groups in American society, but that youth is no longer viewed as a transitory state, through which one passes on the way from childhood to adulthood, but an aspiration, a vaunted condition in which, if one can only arrange it, to settle in perpetuity.

This phenomenon is not something that happened just last night; it has been underway for decades. Nor is it something that can be changed even by an event as cataclysmic as that of September 11, which at first was thought to be so sobering as to tear away all shreds of American innocence. As a generalization, it allows for a wide variety of exceptions. There still are adults in America; if names are wanted, I would set out those of Alan Greenspan, Jeane Kirkpatrick, Robert Rubin, Warren Buffett, Sol Linowitz,[2] and many more. But such men and women, actual grown-ups, now begin to appear a bit anomalous; they no longer seem representative of the larger culture.

The shift into youth culture began in earnest, I suspect, during the 10 or so years following 1951, the year of the publication of *Catcher in the Rye*. Salinger's novel exalts the purity of youth and locates the enemy — a clear case of Us versus Them — in those who committed the sin of having grown older, which includes Holden Caulfield's pain-in-the-neck parents, his brother (the sellout screenwriter), and just about everyone else who has passed beyond adolescence and had the rather poor taste to remain alive.

---

[2]*Alan Greenspan . . . Sol Linowitz:* Greenspan: Five-term chairman of the Federal Reserve System; Kirkpatrick: former Reagan cabinet member and United Nations representative; Rubin: Secretary of the Treasury under President Clinton; Buffet: world-famous multibillionaire; Linowitz (d. 2005): cofounder and chairman of Xerox, who also served in the Johnson and Carter administrations. — EDS.

The case for the exaltation of the young is made in Wordsworth's   10
"Intimation of Immortality," with its idea that human beings are born
with great wisdom from which life in society weans them slowly but inexorably. Plato promulgated this same idea long before: For him we all had
wisdom in the womb, but it was torn from us at the exact point that we
came into the world. Rousseau gave it a French twist, arguing that human
beings are splendid all-round specimens — noble savages, really — with
life out in society turning us mean and loutish, which is another way of
saying that the older we are, the worse we get. We are talking about romanticism here, friend, which never favors the mature, let alone the aged.

The triumph of youth culture has conquered perhaps nowhere more
completely than in the United States. The John F. Kennedy administration,
with its emphasis on youthfulness, beginning with its young president — the
first president routinely not to wear a serious hat — gave it its first public
prominence. Soon after the assassination of Kennedy, the Free Speech
Movement, which spearheaded the student revolution, positively enshrined
the young. Like Yeats's Byzantium, the sixties utopia posited by the student
radicals was "no country for old men"[3] or women. One of the many tenets
in its credo — soon to become a cliché, but no less significant for that — was
that no one over 30 was to be trusted. (If you were part of that movement
and 21 years old in 1965, you are 60 today. Good morning, Sunshine.)

Music was a key element in the advance of youth culture. The dividing moment here is the advent of Elvis. On one side were those who
thought Elvis an amusing and largely freakish phenomenon — a bit of a
joke — and on the other, those who took him dead seriously as a figure of
youthful rebellion, the musical equivalent of James Dean in the movie
Rebel Without a Cause [1955], another early winning entry in the
glorification-of-youth sweepstakes then forming. Rock 'n' roll presented a
vinyl curtain, with those committed to retaining their youth on one side,
those wanting to claim adulthood on the other. The Beatles, despite the
very real charms of their non-druggie music, solidified things. So much of
hard rock 'n' roll came down to nothing more than a way of saying bug-
ger off to adult culture.

Reinforcement for these notions — they were not yet so coherent as to
qualify as ideas — was to be found in the movies. Movies for some years
now have been made not only increasingly for the young but by the
young. I once worked on a movie script with a producer who one day announced to me that it was his birthday. When I wished him happy returns
of the day, he replied that it wasn't so happy for him; he was turning 41,
an uncomfortably old age in Hollywood for someone who hadn't many
big success-scalps on his belt.

Robert Redford, though now in his mid-sixties, remains essentially a
guy in jeans, a handsome graduate student with wrinkles. Paul Newman,

---

[3] ***"no country for old men":*** One of the most famous poems by Irish poet William Butler Yeats, "Sailing to Byzantium," begins: "That is no country for old men." — EDS.

now in his late seventies, seems uncomfortable in a suit. Hugh Grant, the English actor, may be said to be professionally boyish, and in a recent role, in the movie *About a Boy*, is described in the *New York Times* as a character who "surrounds himself with gadgets, videos, CDs, and other toys" and who "is doing everything in his power to avoid growing up." The actor Jim Carrey, who is 42, not long ago said of the movie *The Majestic*, in which he stars, "It's about manhood. It's about adulthood," as if italicizing the rarity of such movies. He then went on to speak about himself in standard self-absorbed adolescent fashion: "You've got that hole you're left with by whatever your parents couldn't give you." Poor baby.

Jim Carrey's roles in movies resemble nothing so much as comic-book characters come to life. And why, just now, does so much of contemporary entertainment come in the form of animation or comic-book cartooning? Such television shows as *The Simpsons* and *King of the Hill*, the occasional back page in the *New York Times Book Review* or the *New Yorker* and the comic-book novel, all seem to feel that the animated cartoon and comic-book formats are very much of the moment. They are of course right, at least if you think of your audience as adolescent, or, more precisely, as being unwilling quite to detach themselves from their adolescence.

Recent history has seemed to be on the side of keeping people from growing up by supplying only a paucity of stern tests of the kind out of which adulthood is usually formed. We shall never have another presidential candidate tested by the Depression or by his experience in World War II. These were events that proved crucibles for the formation of adult character, not to say manliness. Henceforth all future presidential—and congressional—candidates will come with a shortage of what used to pass for significant experience. Crises for future politicians will doubtless be about having to rethink their lives when they didn't get into Brown or found themselves unequipped emotionally for Stanford Business School.

Corporate talent these days feels no weightier. Pictures of heads of corporations in polo shirts with designer logos in the business section of the *New York Times*, fresh from yet another ephemeral merger, or acquiring an enormous raise after their company has recorded another losing year, do not inspire confidence. "The trouble with Enron," said an employee of the company in the aftermath of that corporation's appalling debacle, "is that there weren't any grown-ups."

The increasing affluence the United States enjoyed after World War II, extending into the current day, also contributed heavily to forming the character I've come to think of as the perpetual American adolescent. Earlier, with less money around, people were forced to get serious, to grow up—and fast. How quickly the Depression generation was required to mature! How many stories one used to hear about older brothers going to work at 18 or earlier, so that a younger brother might be allowed to go to college, or simply to help keep the family afloat! With lots of money around, certain kinds of pressure were removed. More and more people

15

nowadays are working, as earlier generations were not, with a strong safety net of money under them. All options opened, they now swim in what Kierkegaard[4] called "a sea of possibilities," and one of these possibilities in America is to refuse to grow up for a longer period than has been permitted any other people in history.

All this is reinforced by the play of market forces, which strongly encourage the mythical dream of perpetual youthfulness. The promise behind 95 percent of all advertising is that of recaptured youth, whose deeper promise is lots more sex yet to go. The ads for the $5,000 wristwatch, the $80,000 car, the khakis, the vodka, the pharmaceuticals to regrow hair and recapture ardor, all whisper display me, drive me, wear me, drink me, swallow me, and you stop the clock—youth, Baby, is yours.

The whole sweep of advertising, which is to say of market, culture   20 since soon after World War II has been continuously to lower the criteria of youthfulness while extending the possibility for seeming youthful to older and older people. To make the very young seem older—all those 10- and 12-year-old Britney Spears and Jennifer Lopez imitators, who already know more about brand-name logos than I do about English literature—is another part of the job. It's not a conspiracy, mind you, not six or eight international ad agencies meeting in secret to call the shots, but the dynamics of marketing itself, finding a way to make it more profitable all around by convincing the young that they can seem older and the old that they can seem a lot younger. Never before has it been more difficult to obey the injunction to act one's age.

Two of the great television sitcom successes of recent years, *Seinfeld* and *Friends*, though each is different in its comic tone, are united by the theme of the permanent adolescent loose in the big city. One takes the characters in *Seinfeld* to be in their middle to late thirties, those in *Friends* in their late twenties to early thirties. Charming though they may be, both sets of characters are oddly stunted. They aren't quite anywhere and don't seem to be headed anywhere, either. Time is suspended for them. Aimless and shameless, they are in the grip of the everyday *Sturm und Drang*[5] of adolescent self-absorption. Outside their rather temporary-looking apartments, they scarcely exist. Personal relations provide the full drama of their lives. Growth and development aren't part of the deal. They are still, somehow, in spirit, locked in a high school of the mind, eating dry cereal, watching a vast quantity of television, hoping to make ecstatic sexual scores. Apart from the high sheen of the writing and the comic skill of the casts, I wonder if what really attracts people to these shows—*Friends* still, *Seinfeld* in its reruns—isn't the underlying identification with the characters because of the audience's own longing for a

---

[4]*Kierkegaard:* Soren Kierkegaard (1813–1855), Danish philosopher.—EDS.
[5]*Sturm und Drang:* German for "storm and stress." The phrase refers to a literary movement in the late eighteenth century that emphasized the emotional conflicts of unconventional youth.—EDS.

perpetual adolescence, cut loose, free of responsibility, without the real pressures that life, that messy business, always exerts.

Time for the perpetual adolescents is curiously static. They are in no great hurry: to succeed, to get work, to lay down achievements. Perhaps this is partly because longevity has increased in recent decades—if one doesn't make it to 90 nowadays, one feels slightly cheated—but more likely it is that time doesn't seem to the perpetual adolescent the excruciatingly finite matter, the precious commodity, it indubitably is. For the perpetual adolescent, time is almost endlessly expandable. Why not go to law school in one's late thirties, or take the premed requirements in one's early forties, or wait even later than that to have children? Time enough to toss away one's twenties, maybe even one's thirties; 40 is soon enough to get serious about life; maybe 50, when you think about it, is the best time really to get going in earnest.

The old hunger for life, the eagerness to get into the fray, has been replaced by an odd patience that often looks more like passivity. In the 1950s, people commonly married in their twenties, which may or may not have been a good thing, but marriage did prove a forcing house into adulthood, for men and women, especially where children issued from the marriage, which they usually did fairly quickly. I had two sons by the time I was 26, which, among other things, made it impossible, either physically or spiritually, for me to join the general youth movement of the 1960s, even though I still qualified by age. It also required me to find a vocation. By 30, one was supposed to be settled in life: wife, children, house, job—"the full catastrophe," as Zorba the Greek[6] liked to say. But it was also a useful catastrophe. Today most people feel that they can wait to get serious about life. Until then one is feeling one's way, still deciding, shopping around, contributing to the formation of a new psychological type: the passive-nonaggressive.

Not everywhere is nonaggression the psychological mode of choice. One hears about the young men and women working the 14-hour days at low six-figure jobs in front-line law firms; others sacrificing to get into MBA programs, for the single purpose of an early financial score. But even here one senses an adolescent spirit to the proceedings. The old model for ambition was solid hard work that paid off over time. One began at a low wage, worked one's way up through genuine accomplishment, grew wealthier as one grew older, and, with luck, retired with a sense of financial security and pleasure in one's achievement. But the new American ambition model features the kid multimillionaire—the young man or woman who breaks the bank not long out of college. An element of adolescent impatience enters in here—I want it, *now!*—and also an element of continued youthfulness.

The model of the type may be the professional athlete. "The growth   25 of professional basketball over the past twenty-odd years, from a relatively

---

[6]***Zorba the Greek:*** Nikos Kazantzakis's *Zorba the Greek* was published in the United States in 1953 and became a major film in 1964.—EDS.

minor spectator sport to a mass-cultural phenomenon," notes Rebecca Mead, in the *New Yorker*, "is an example of the way in which all of American culture is increasingly geared to the tastes of teenage boys." Mead writes this in an article about Shaquille O'Neal, the 32-year-old center for the Los Angeles Lakers, who earns, with endorsements, 30-odd million dollars a year and lives the life of the most privileged possible junior high school boy: enjoying food fights, go-carts, motorcycles, the run of high rides at amusement parks. It may be a wonderful, but it's also a strange life.

And yet what is so wrong about any of this? If one wants to dress like a kid, spin around the office on a scooter, not make up one's mind about what work one wants to do until one is 40, be noncommittal in one's relationships—what, really, are the consequences? I happen to think that the consequences are genuine, and fairly serious.

"Obviously it is normal to think of oneself as younger than one is," W.H. Auden, a younger son, told Robert Craft, "but fatal to want to be younger." I'm not sure about fatal, but it is at a minimum degrading for a culture at large to want to be younger. The tone of national life is lowered, made less rich. The first thing lowered is expectations, intellectual and otherwise. To begin with education, one wonders if the dumbing down of culture one used to hear so much about and which continues isn't connected to the rise of the perpetual adolescent.

Consider contemporary journalism, which tends to play everything to lower and lower common denominators. Why does the *New York Times*, with its pretensions to being our national newspaper, choose to put on its front pages stories about Gennifer Flowers's career as a chanteuse in New Orleans, the firing of NFL coaches, the retirement of Yves Saint Laurent, the canceling of the singer Mariah Carey's recording contract? Slow-news days is a charitable guess; a lowered standard of the significant is a more realistic one. Since the advent of its new publisher, a man of the baby boomer generation, an aura of juvenilia clings to the paper. Frank Rich and Maureen Dowd, two of the paper's most-read columnists, seem not so much the type of the bright college student but of the sassy high-school student—the clever, provocative editor of the school paper out to shock the principal—even though both are in their early fifties.

Television comes closer and closer to being a wholly adolescent form of communication. Clicking the remote from major network news shows, one slides smoothly from superficiality to triviality. When Tom Brokaw announces that some subject will be covered "In Depth," what he really means is that roughly 90 seconds, perhaps two minutes, will be devoted to it. It's scarcely original to note that much of contemporary journalism, print and electronic, is pitched to the short attention span, the soundbite, photo-op, quickie take, the deep distaste for complexity—in short, so much is pitched to the adolescent temperament.

Political correctness and so many of the political fashions of our day— 30 from academic feminism to cultural studies to queer theory—could only be perpetrated on adolescent minds: minds, that is, that are trained to search out one thing and one thing only: Is my teacher, or this politician, or that public spokesman, saying something that is likely to be offensive to me or members of any other victim group? Only an adolescent would find it worthwhile to devote his or her attention chiefly to the hunting of offenses, the possibility of slights, real and imagined.

Self-esteem, of which one currently hears so much, is at bottom another essentially adolescent notion. The great psychological sin of our day is to violate the self-esteem of adolescents of all ages. One might have thought that such self-esteem as any of us is likely to command would be in place by the age of 18. (And what is the point of having all that much self-esteem anyhow, since its logical culminating point can only be smug complacence?) Even in nursing homes, apparently, patients must be guarded against a feeling of their lowered consequence in the world. Self-esteem has become a womb to tomb matter, so that, in contemporary America, the inner and the outer child can finally be made one in the form of the perpetual adolescent.

The coarsening of American culture seems part of the adolescent phenomenon. Television commercials have gotten grosser and grosser. The level of profanity on prime-time television shows has risen greatly over the years. Flicks known to their audiences as "gross-out movies," featuring the slimy and hideous, are part of the regular film menu. Florence King, writing about this phenomenon in her column in the *National Review*, noted: "Since arrested development is as American as apple pie, it is easy to identify the subconscious motivation of the adult male Ughs who produce all these revolting movies and commercials." What makes these things possible is what is known as "niche programming," or the aiming of entertainment at quite specific segments of the audience—African Americans, or teenagers, or the educated classes, or the beer brutes. But increasingly, apparently, we are all being forced into that largest of niches, the American adolescent mentality.

Consider now what must be taken as the most consequential adolescent act in American history during the past half century: the Bill Clinton–Monica Lewinsky relationship. I hesitate to call it an affair, because an affair implies a certain adult style: the good hotel room, the bottle of excellent wine, the peignoir, the Sulka pajamas. With Bill and Monica, you had instead the pizza, the canoodling under the desk, the cigar business, even the whole thing going without consummation. No matter what one's politics, one has to admit that our great national scandal was pure high school.

In a 1959 review of Iona and Peter Opie's *The Lore and Language of School Children*, the poet Philip Larkin[7] revealed first sensing a sharp waning of his interest in Christianity when he read the Bible verse that promises one will return to one's childish state upon entry into Heaven.

---

[7]***Larkin:*** A British poet (1922–1985) who was known for his witty formal verse.—Eds.

Larkin wanted nothing more to do with being a child or with the company of children. He looked forward to "money, keys, wallets, letters, books, long-playing records, drinks, the opposite sex, and other solaces of adulthood."

I wanted these things, too, and as soon as possible. From roughly the age of 14, I wanted to stay out all night, to dress like Fred Astaire, to drink and smoke cigarettes with the elegance of William Powell, to have the company of serious women like Susan Hayward and Ingrid Bergman.[8] As I grew older, I sadly began to realize it wasn't going to happen, at least not in the way I had hoped. What happened instead was the triumph of youth culture, with its adoration of youth, in and for itself, and as a time in one's life of purity and goodness always in danger of being despoiled by the corruption of growing older, which is also to say, of "growing up."

At a certain point in American life, the young ceased to be viewed as a transient class and youth as a phase of life through which everyone soon passed. Instead, youthfulness was vaunted and carried a special moral status. Adolescence triumphed, becoming a permanent condition. As one grew older, one was presented with two choices, to seem an old fogey for attempting to live according to one's own standard of adulthood, or to go with the flow and adapt some variant of pulling one's long gray hair back into a ponytail, struggling into the spandex shorts, working on those abs, and ending one's days among the Rip Van With-Its. Not, I think, a handsome set of alternatives.

The greatest sins, Santayana[9] thought, are those that set out to strangle human nature. This is of course what is being done in cultivating perpetual adolescence, while putting off maturity for as long as possible. Maturity provides a more articulated sense of the ebb and flow, the ups and downs, of life, a more subtly reticulated graph of human possibility. Above all, it values a clear and fit conception of reality. Maturity is ever cognizant that the clock is running, life is finite, and among the greatest mistakes is to believe otherwise. Maturity doesn't exclude playfulness or high humor. Far from it. The mature understand that the bitterest joke of all is that the quickest way to grow old lies in the hopeless attempt to stay forever young.

The Reader's Presence

1. What does Epstein believe caused the shift toward adolescent culture? When did it happen? What are some of the earliest examples he cites of youth culture triumphing over maturity? Do you agree that most Americans behave in an "adolescent" way? Why or why not?

[8]*Susan Hayward . . . Bergman:* Glamorous film stars of the 1940s and 1950s. —Eds.
[9]*Santayana:* Spanish-born George Santayana (1863–1952) was an influential American philosopher. —Eds.

2. What areas of life does Epstein believe have been negatively affected by our immaturity? What are the consequences of youth culture's triumph over adulthood? What does Epstein's interpretation suggest about what he values?

3. Read John Taylor Gatto's "Against School" (page 688). What does he suggest are the benefits of treating adults like children? Who benefits? How does Gatto's argument about Americans' immaturity differ from Epstein's?

Kai Erikson

The Witches of Salem Village

Kai Erikson (b. 1931), son of renowned psychoanalyst Erik Erikson, is professor emeritus of sociology and American studies at Yale University. A noted scholar, Erikson has published several books and received numerous professional awards. His interests in communities and the effects of human disasters are reflected in Everything in Its Path: Destruction of Community in the Buffalo Creek Flood *(1976) and* A New Species of Trouble: Explorations in Disaster, Trauma, and Community *(1994). Erikson edited* Sociological Visions *(1997), a collection of writings on social problems. "The Witches of Salem Village" is from his study of Puritan New England,* Wayward Puritans: A Study in the Sociology of Deviance *(1966).*

No one really knows how the witchcraft hysteria began, but it originated in the home of the Reverend Samuel Parris, minister of the local church. In early 1692, several girls from the neighborhood began to spend their afternoons in the Parris' kitchen with a slave named Tituba, and it was not long before a mysterious sorority of girls, aged between nine and twenty, became regular visitors to the parsonage. We can only speculate what was going on behind the kitchen door, but we know that Tituba had been brought to Massachusetts from Barbados and enjoyed a reputation in the neighborhood for her skills in the magic arts. As the girls grew closer together, a remarkable change seemed to come over them: perhaps it is not true, as someone later reported, that they went out into the forest to celebrate their own version of a black mass, but it is apparent that they began to live in a state of high tension and shared secrets with one another which were hardly becoming to quiet Puritan maidens.

Before the end of winter, the two youngest girls in the group succumbed to the shrill pitch of their amusements and began to exhibit a most
unusual malady. They would scream unaccountably, fall into grotesque
convulsions, and sometimes scamper along on their hands and knees making noises like the barking of a dog. No sooner had word gone around
about this extraordinary affliction than it began to spread like a contagious
disease. All over the community young girls were groveling on the ground
in a panic of fear and excitement, and while some of the less credulous
townspeople were tempted to reach for their belts in the hopes of strapping
a little modesty into them, the rest could only stand by in helpless horror as
the girls suffered their torments.

The town's one physician did what he could to stem the epidemic, but
he soon exhausted his meagre store of remedies and was forced to conclude that the problem lay outside the province of medicine. The Devil had
come to Salem Village, he announced; the girls were bewitched. At this
disturbing news, ministers from many of the neighboring parishes came to
consult with their colleague and offer what advice they might. Among the
first to arrive was a thoughtful clergyman named Deodat Lawson, and he
had been in town no more than a few hours when he happened upon a
frightening exhibition of the devil's handiwork. "In the beginning of the
evening," he later recounted of his first day in the village,

> I went to give Mr. Parris a visit. When I was there, his kinswoman,
> Abigail Williams, (about 12 years of age,) had a grievous fit; she was at
> first hurried with violence to and fro in the room, (though Mrs. Ingersoll
> endeavored to hold her,) sometimes making as if she would fly, stretch-
> ing up her arms as high as she could, and crying "whish, whish, whish!"
> several times. . . . After that, she run to the fire, and began to throw fire
> brands about the house; and run against the back, as if she would run up
> the chimney, and, as they said, she had attempted to go into the fire in
> other fits.[1]

Faced by such clear-cut evidence, the ministers quickly agreed that Satan's
new challenge would have to be met with vigorous action, and this meant
that the afflicted girls would have to identify the witches who were harassing them.

It is hard to guess what the girls were experiencing during those early
days of the commotion. They attracted attention everywhere they went and
exercised a degree of power over the adult community which would have
been exhilarating under the sanest of circumstances. But whatever else was
going on in those young minds, the thought seems to have gradually occurred to the girls that they were indeed bewitched, and after they had been
coaxed over and over again to name their tormentors, they finally singled
out three women in the village and accused them of witchcraft.

---

[1]Deodat Lawson, "A Brief and True Narrative of Witchcraft at Salem Village," 1692,
in *Narratives of the Witchcraft Cases, 1648–1706*, edited by George Lincoln Burr (New
York: Scribner's, 1914), p. 154.

Three better candidates could not have been found if all the gossips in   5
New England had met to make the nominations. The first, understandably, was Tituba herself, a woman who had grown up among the rich colors and imaginative legends of Barbados and who was probably acquainted with some form of voodoo. The second, Sarah Good, was a proper hag of a witch if Salem Village had ever seen one. With a pipe clenched in her leathery face she wandered around the countryside neglecting her children and begging from others, and on more than one occasion the old crone had been overheard muttering threats against her neighbors when she was in an unusually sour humor. Sarah Osburne, the third suspect, had a higher social standing than either of her alleged accomplices, but she had been involved in a local scandal a year or two earlier when a man moved into her house some months before becoming her husband.

A preliminary hearing was set at once to decide whether the three accused women should be held for trial. The girls were ushered to the front row of the meeting house, where they took full advantage of the space afforded them by rolling around in apparent agony whenever some personal fancy (or the invisible agents of the devil) provoked them to it. It was a remarkable show. Strange creatures flew about the room pecking at the girls or taunting them from the rafters, and it was immediately obvious to everyone that the women on trial were responsible for all the disorder and suffering. When Sarah Good and Sarah Osburne were called to the stand and asked why they sent these spectres to torment the girls, they were too appalled to say much in their defense. But when Tituba took the stand she had a ready answer. A lifetime spent in bondage is poor training for standing up before a bench of magistrates, and anyway Tituba was an excitable woman who had breathed the warmer winds of the Caribbean and knew things about magic her crusty old judges would never learn. Whatever the reason, Tituba gave her audience one of the most exuberant confessions ever recorded in a New England courtroom. She spoke of the creatures who inhabit the invisible world, the dark rituals which bind them together in the service of Satan; and before she had ended her astonishing recital she had convinced everyone in Salem Village that the problem was far worse than they had dared imagine. For Tituba not only implicated Sarah Good and Sarah Osburne in her own confession but announced that many other people in the colony were engaged in the devil's conspiracy against the Bay.

So the hearing that was supposed to bring a speedy end to the affair only stirred up a hidden hornet's nest, and now the girls were urged to identify other suspects and locate new sources of trouble. Already the girls had become more than unfortunate victims: in the eyes of the community they were diviners, prophets, oracles, mediums, for only they could see the terrible spectres swarming over the countryside and tell what persons had sent them on their evil errands. As they became caught up in the enthusiasm of their new work, then, the girls began to reach into every corner of the community in a search for likely suspects. Martha Corey was an upstanding woman in the village whose main mistake was to snort incredulously at the girls' behavior. Dorcas Good, five years old, was a daughter of the accused Sarah. Rebecca Nurse was a saintly old woman who had been bedridden at the time of the earlier hearings. Mary Esty and Sarah Cloyce were Rebecca's younger sisters, themselves accused when they rose in energetic defense of the older woman. And so it went—John Proctor, Giles Corey, Abigail Hobbs, Bridgit Bishop, Sarah Wild, Susanna Martin, Dorcas Hoar, the Reverend George Burroughs: as winter turned into spring the list of suspects grew to enormous length and the Salem jail was choked with people awaiting trial. We know nothing about conditions of life in prison, but it is easy to imagine the tensions which must have echoed within those grey walls. Some of the prisoners had cried out against their relatives and friends in a desperate effort to divert attention from themselves, others were witless persons with scarcely a clue as to what had happened to them, and a few (very few, as it turned out) were accepting their lot with quiet dignity. If we imagine Sarah Good sitting next to Rebecca Nurse and lighting her rancid pipe or Tituba sharing views on supernatural phenomena with the Reverend George Burroughs, we may have a rough picture of life in those crowded quarters.

By this time the hysteria had spread well beyond the confines of Salem Village, and as it grew in scope so did the appetites of the young

The Trial of George Jacobs for Witchcraft in 1692. *Painting by Tompkins H. Matteson, 1855.*

girls. They now began to accuse persons they had never seen from places they had never visited (in the course of which some absurd mistakes were made),[2] yet their word was so little questioned that it was ordinarily warrant enough to put respected people in chains.

From as far away as Charlestown, Nathaniel Cary heard that his wife had been accused of witchcraft and immediately traveled with her to Salem "to see if the afflicted did know her." The two of them sat through an entire day of hearings, after which Cary reported:

> I observed that the afflicted were two girls of about ten years old, and about two or three others, of about eighteen. . . . The prisoners were called in one by one, and as they came in were cried out of [at]. . . . The prisoner was placed about seven or eight feet from the Justices, and the accusers between the Justices and them; the prisoner was ordered to stand right before the Justices, with an officer appointed to hold each hand, lest they should therewith afflict them, and the prisoner's eyes must be constantly on the Justices; for if they looked on the afflicted, they would either fall into their fits, or cry out of being hurt by them. . . . Then the Justices said to the accusers, "which of you will go and touch the prisoner at the bar?" Then the most courageous would adventure, but before they had made three steps would ordinarily fall down as in a fit. The Justices ordered that they should be taken up and carried to the prisoner, that she might touch them; and as soon as they were touched by the accused, the Justices would say "they are well," before I could discern any alteration. . . . Thus far I was only as a spectator, my wife also was there part of the time, but no notice taken of her by the afflicted, except once or twice they came to her and asked her name.

After this sorry performance the Carys retired to the local inn for dinner, but no sooner had they taken seats than a group of afflicted girls burst into the room and "began to tumble about like swine" at Mrs. Cary's feet, accusing her of being the cause of their miseries. Remarkably, the magistrates happened to be sitting in the adjoining room — "waiting for this," Cary later decided — and an impromptu hearing took place on the spot.   10

> Being brought before the Justices, her chief accusers were two girls. My wife declared to the Justices that she never had any knowledge of them before that day; she was forced to stand with her arms stretched out. I did request that I might hold one of her hands, but it was denied me; then she desired me to wipe the tears from her eyes, and the sweat from her face, which I did; then she desired she might lean herself on me, saying she should faint. Justice Hathorne replied, she had strength enough to torment those persons, and she should have strength enough to stand. I speaking something against their cruel proceedings, they commanded me

---

[2]John Alden later reported in his account of the affair that the girls pointed their fingers at the wrong man when they first accused him of witchcraft and only realized their mistake when an obliging passer-by corrected them. See Robert Calef, "More Wonders of the Invisible World," Boston, 1701, in Burr, *Narratives*, p. 353.

to be silent, or else I should be turned out of the room. An Indian . . . was also brought in to be one of her accusers: being come in, he now (when before the Justices) fell down and tumbled about like a hog, but said nothing. The Justices asked the girls, "who afflicted the Indian?", they answered "she" (meaning my wife). . . . The Justices ordered her to touch him, in order of his cure . . . but the Indian took hold of her in a barbarous manner; then his hand was taken off, and her hand put on his, and the cure was quickly wrought. . . . Then her mittimus was writ.[3]

For another example of how the hearings were going, we might listen for a moment to the examination of Mrs. John Proctor. This record was taken down by the Reverend Samuel Parris himself, and the notes in parentheses are his. Ann Putnam and Abigail Williams were two of the most energetic of the young accusers.

> Justice: Ann Putnam, doth this woman hurt you?
> Putnam: Yes, sir, a good many times. (Then the accused looked upon them and they fell into fits.)
> Justice: She does not bring the book to you, does she?[4]
> Putnam: Yes, sir, often, and saith she hath made her maid set her hand to it.
> Justice: Abigail Williams, does this woman hurt you?
> Williams: Yes, sir, often.
> Justice: Does she bring the book to you?
> Williams: Yes.
> Justice: What would she have you do with it?
> Williams: To write in it and I shall be well.
> Putnam to Mrs. Proctor: Did you not tell me that your maid had written?
> Mrs. Proctor: Dear child, it is not so. There is another judgment, dear child. (Then Abigail and Ann had fits. By and by they cried out, "look you, there is Goody Proctor upon the beam." By and by both of them cried out of Goodman Proctor himself, and said he was a wizard. Immediately, many, if not all of the bewitched, had grievous fits.)
> Justice: Ann Putnam, who hurt you?
> Putnam: Goodman Proctor and his wife too. (Some of the afflicted cried, "there is Proctor going to take up Mrs. Pope's feet" — and her feet were immediately taken up.)
> Justice: What do you say Goodman Proctor to these things?
> Proctor: I know not. I am innocent.
> Williams: There is Goodman Proctor going to Mrs. Pope (and immediately said Pope fell into a fit).
> Justice: You see, the Devil will deceive you. The children could see what you was going to do before the woman was hurt. I would advise you to repentance, for the devil is bringing you out.[5]

---

[3]Reproduced in Calef, "More Wonders," in Burr, *Narratives*, pp. 350–352.
[4]The "book" refers to the Devil's registry. The girls were presumably being tormented because they refused to sign the book and ally themselves with Satan.
[5]Hutchinson, *History*, II, pp. 27–28.

This was the kind of evidence the magistrates were collecting in readiness for the trials; and it was none too soon, for the prisons were crowded with suspects. In June the newly arrived Governor of the Bay, Sir William Phips, appointed a special court of Oyer and Terminer to hear the growing number of witchcraft cases pending, and the new bench went immediately to work. Before the month was over, six women had been hanged from the gallows in Salem. And still the accused poured in.

As the court settled down to business, however, a note of uncertainty began to flicker across the minds of several thoughtful persons in the colony. To begin with, the net of accusation was beginning to spread out in wider arcs, reaching not only across the surface of the country but up the social ladder as well, so that a number of influential people were now among those in the overflowing prisons. Nathaniel Cary was an important citizen of Charlestown, and other men of equal rank (including the almost legendary Captain John Alden) were being caught up in the widening circle of panic and fear. Slowly but surely, a faint glimmer of skepticism was introduced into the situation; and while it was not to assert a modifying influence on the behavior of the court for some time to come, this new voice had become a part of the turbulent New England climate of 1692.

Meantime, the girls continued to exercise their extraordinary powers. Between sessions of the court, they were invited to visit the town of Andover and help the local inhabitants flush out whatever witches might still remain at large among them. Handicapped as they were by not knowing anyone in town, the girls nonetheless managed to identify more than fifty witches in the space of a few hours. Forty warrants were signed on the spot, and the arrest total only stopped at that number because the local Justice of the Peace simply laid down his pen and refused to go on with the frightening charade any longer—at which point, predictably, he became a suspect himself.

Yet the judges worked hard to keep pace with their young representatives in the field. In early August five persons went to the gallows in Salem. A month later fifteen more were tried and condemned, of which eight were hung promptly and the others spared because they were presumably ready to confess their sins and turn state's evidence. Nineteen people had been executed, seven more condemned, and one pressed to death under a pile of rocks for standing mute at his trial. At least two more persons had died in prison, bringing the number of deaths to twenty-two. And in all that time, not one suspect brought before the court had been acquitted.

At the end of this strenuous period of justice, the whole witchcraft mania began to fade. For one thing, the people of the Bay had been shocked into a mood of sober reflection by the deaths of so many persons. For another, the afflicted girls had obviously not learned very much from their experience in Andover and were beginning to display an ambition which far exceeded their credit. It was bad enough that they should accuse the likes of John Alden and Nathaniel Cary, but when they brought up the

15

name of Samuel Willard, who doubled as pastor of Boston's First Church and President of Harvard College, the magistrates flatly told them they were mistaken. Not long afterwards, a brazen finger was pointed directly at the executive mansion in Boston, where Lady Phips awaited her husband's return from an expedition to Canada, and one tradition even has it that Cotton Mather's mother was eventually accused.[6]

This was enough to stretch even a Puritan's boundless credulity. One by one the leading men of the Bay began to reconsider the whole question and ask aloud whether the evidence accepted in witchcraft hearings was really suited to the emergency at hand. It was obvious that people were being condemned on the testimony of a few excited girls, and responsible minds in the community were troubled by the thought that the girls' excitement may have been poorly diagnosed in the first place. Suppose the girls were directly possessed by the devil and not touched by intermediate witches? Suppose they were simply out of their wits altogether? Suppose, in fact, they were lying? In any of these events the rules of evidence used in court would have to be reviewed—and quickly.

Deciding what kinds of evidence were admissible in witchcraft cases was a thorny business at best. When the court of Oyer and Terminer had first met, a few ground rules had been established to govern the unusual situation which did not entirely conform to ordinary Puritan standards of trial procedure. In the first place, the scriptural rule that two eyewitnesses were necessary for conviction in capital cases was modified to read that any two witnesses were sufficient even if they were testifying about different events—on the interesting ground that witchcraft was a "habitual" crime. That is, if one witness testified that he had seen Susanna Martin bewitch a horse in 1660 and another testified that she had broken uninvited into his dreams twenty years later, then both were witnesses to the same general offense. More important, however, the court accepted as an operating principle the old idea that Satan could not assume the shape of an innocent person, which meant in effect that any spectres floating into view which resembled one of the defendants must be acting under his direct instruction. If an afflicted young girl "saw" John Proctor's image crouched on the window sill with a wicked expression on his face, for example, there could be no question that Proctor himself had placed it there, for the devil could not borrow that disguise without the permission of its owner. During an early hearing, one of the defendants had been asked: "How comes your appearance to hurt these [girls]?" "How do I know," she had answered testily, "He that appeared in the shape of Samuel, a glorified saint, may appear in anyone's shape."[7] Now this was no idle retort, for every man who read his Bible knew that the Witch of Endor had once caused the image of Samuel to appear before Saul, and this scriptural

---

[6]Burr, *Narratives*, p. 377.

[7]Cotton Mather, "Wonders of the Invisible World," in Drake, *The Witchcraft Delusion*, p. 176.

evidence that the devil might indeed be able to impersonate an innocent person proved a difficult matter for the court to handle. Had the defendant been able to win her point, the whole machinery of the court might have fallen in pieces at the magistrates' feet; for if the dreadful spectres haunting the girls were no more than free-lance apparitions sent out by the devil, then the court would have no prosecution case at all.

All in all, five separate kinds of evidence had been admitted by the court during its first round of hearings. First were trials by test, of which repeating the Lord's Prayer, a feat presumed impossible for witches to perform, and curing fits by touch were the most often used. Second was the testimony of persons who attributed their own misfortunes to the sorcery of a neighbor on trial. Third were physical marks like warts, moles, scars, or any other imperfection through which the devil might have sucked his gruesome quota of blood. Fourth was spectral evidence, of the sort just noted; and fifth were the confessions of the accused themselves.

Now it was completely obvious to the men who began to review the court's proceedings that the first three types of evidence were quite inconclusive. After all, anyone might make a mistake reciting the Lord's Prayer, particularly if the floor was covered with screaming, convulsive girls, and it did not make much sense to execute a person because he had spiteful neighbors or a mark upon his body. By those standards, half the people in Massachusetts might qualify for the gallows. This left spectral evidence and confessions. As for the latter, the court could hardly maintain that any real attention had been given to that form of evidence, since none of the executed witches had confessed and none of the many confessors had been executed. Far from establishing guilt, a well-phrased and tearfully delivered confession was clearly the best guarantee against hanging. So the case lay with spectral evidence, and legal opinion in the Bay was slowly leaning toward the theory that this form of evidence, too, was worthless.

In October, Governor Phips took note of the growing doubts by dismissing the special court of Oyer and Terminer and releasing several suspects from prison. The tide had begun to turn, but still there were 150 persons in custody and some 200 others who had been accused.

In December, finally, Phips appointed a new session of the Superior Court of Judicature to try the remaining suspects, and this time the magistrates were agreed that spectral evidence would be admitted only in marginal cases. Fifty-two persons were brought to trial during the next month, and of these, forty-nine were immediately acquitted. Three others were condemned ("two of which," a contemporary observer noted, "were the most senseless and ignorant creatures that could be found"),[8] and in addition death warrants were signed for five persons who had been condemned earlier. Governor Phips responded to these carefully reasoned judgments by signing reprieves for all eight of the defendants anyway, and at this, the

[8]Calef, "More Wonders," in Burr, *Narratives*, p. 382.

court began to empty the jails as fast as it could hear cases. Finally Phips ended the costly procedure by discharging every prisoner in the colony and issuing a general pardon to all persons still under suspicion.

The witchcraft hysteria had been completely checked within a year of the day it first appeared in Salem Village.

The Reader's Presence

1. This essay appears in a larger work on social deviance. What is social deviance, in Erikson's perspective? How has it been perceived and controlled? Why might Erikson view the long-past historical events of Salem as relevant to questions of deviance today?

2. Erikson retells a familiar American story in a deceptively straight-forward manner. Does his tone endorse or undercut the surface meaning of his tale? What position toward the events does the essay appear to encourage in the reader? By what means?

3. Erikson's essay has a neat timeline: The essay begins with the onset of the witchcraft hysteria in 1692, and concludes at the end of that year by which point the "hysteria had been completely checked." Barbara Tuchman's historical account of the Black Death (page 579) covers a similarly brief period. Reread the essays together and note how each historian paces the telling of the historical narrative. When is primary evidence included? What comment does the writer offer, or withhold, and why? How is each essay's sense of momentum established? What makes you keep reading?

4. Nathaniel Hawthorne's "Young Goodman Brown" (page 901) is a work of short fiction set in Salem at around the time of the witchcraft hysteria Erikson describes. How does Hawthorne address the fear of witches? Which aspects of Erikson's work give you insight into Hawthorne's characters? Why?

James Fallows

Throwing Like a Girl

James Fallows (b. 1949) is a defense reporter, economic theorist, and media critic. He attended Harvard University and received a diploma in economic development from Queen's College, Oxford. He has been editor of the Washington Monthly, Texas Monthly, and U.S. News & World Report. He is a national correspondent for the Atlantic and has written extensively about the war in Iraq; his cover story "The Fifty-First State?" (November 2002) won a National Magazine Award. In addition to National Defense, which won the National Book Award, he has written Looking at the Sun (1995), Breaking the News: How the Media Undermines American Democracy (1996), and Free Fight (2001). The following article first appeared in the Atlantic in August 1996.

Most people remember the 1994 baseball season for the way it ended — with a strike rather than a World Series. I keep thinking about the way it began. On opening day, April 4, Bill Clinton went to Cleveland and, like many Presidents before him, threw out a ceremonial first pitch. That same day Hillary Rodham Clinton went to Chicago and, like no First Lady before her, also threw out a first ball, at a Cubs game in Wrigley Field.

The next day photos of the Clintons in action appeared in newspapers around the country. Many papers, including the *New York Times* and the *Washington Post*, chose the same two photos to run. The one of Bill Clinton showed him wearing an Indians cap and warm-up jacket. The President throwing lefty, had turned his shoulders sideways to the plate in preparation for delivery. He was bringing the ball forward from behind his head in a clean-looking throwing action as the photo was snapped. Hillary Clinton was pictured wearing a dark jacket, a scarf, and an over-sized Cubs hat. In preparation for her throw she was standing directly facing the plate. A right-hander, she had the elbow of her throwing arm pointed out in front of her. Her forearm was tilted back, toward her shoulder. The ball rested on her upturned palm. As the picture was taken, she was in the middle of an action that can only be described as throwing like a girl.

The phrase "throwing like a girl" has become an embattled and offensive one. Feminists smart at its implication that to do something "like a girl" is to do it the wrong way. Recently, on the heels of the O. J. Simpson case, a book appeared in which the phrase was used to help explain why male athletes, especially football players, were involved in so

416

many assaults against women. Having been trained (like most American boys) to dread the accusation of doing anything "like a girl," athletes were said to grow into the assumption that women were valueless, and natural prey.

I grant the justice of such complaints. I am attuned to the hurt caused by similar broad-brush stereotypes when they apply to groups I belong to — "dancing like a white man," for instance, or "speaking foreign languages like an American," or "thinking like a Washingtonian."

Still, whatever we want to call it, the difference between the two Clintons in what they were doing that day is real, and it is instantly recognizable. And since seeing those photos I have been wondering, Why, exactly, do so many women throw "like a girl"? If the motion were easy to change, presumably a woman as motivated and self-possessed as Hillary Clinton would have changed it. (According to her press secretary, Lisa Caputo, Mrs. Clinton spent the weekend before opening day tossing a ball in the Rose Garden with her husband, for practice.) Presumably, too, the answer to the question cannot be anything quite as simple as, because they *are* girls.

A surprising number of people think that there is a structural difference between male and female arms or shoulders—in the famous "rotator cuff," perhaps—that dictates different throwing motions. "It's in the shoulder joint," a well-educated woman told me recently. "They're hinged differently." Someday researchers may find evidence to support a biological theory of throwing actions. For now, what you'll hear if you ask an orthopedist, an anatomist, or (especially) the coach of a women's softball team is that there is no structural reason why men and women should throw in different ways. This point will be obvious to any male who grew up around girls who liked to play baseball and became good at it. It should be obvious on a larger scale this summer, in broadcasts of the Olympic Games. This year, for the first time, women's fast-pitch softball teams will compete in the Olympics. Although the pitchers in these games will deliver the ball underhand, viewers will see female shortstops, center fielders, catchers, and so on pegging the ball to one another at speeds few male viewers could match.

Even women's tennis is a constant if indirect reminder that men's and women's shoulders are "hinged" the same way. The serving motion in tennis is like a throw—but more difficult, because it must be coordinated with the toss of the tennis ball. The men in professional tennis serve harder than the women, because they are bigger and stronger. But women pros serve harder than most male amateurs have ever done, and the service motion for good players is the same for men and women alike. There is no expectation in college or pro tennis that because of their anatomy female players must "serve like a girl." "I know many women who can throw a lot harder and better than the normal male," says Linda Wells, the coach of the highly successful women's softball team at Arizona State

University. "It's not gender that makes the difference in how they throw."

So what is it, then? Since Hillary Clinton's ceremonial visit to Wrigley Field, I have asked men and women how they learned to throw, or didn't. Why did I care? My impetus was the knowledge that eventually my sons would be grown and gone. If my wife, in all other ways a talented athlete, could learn how to throw, I would still have someone to play catch with. My research left some women, including my wife, thinking that I am some kind of obsessed lout, but it has led me to the solution to the mystery. First let's be clear about what there is to be explained.

At a superficial level it's easy to tick off the traits of an awkward-looking throw. The fundamental mistake is the one Mrs. Clinton appeared to be making in the photo: trying to throw a ball with your body facing the target, rather than rotating your shoulders and hips ninety degrees away from the target and then swinging them around in order to accelerate the ball. A throw looks bad if your elbow is lower than your shoulder as your arm comes forward (unless you're throwing sidearm). A throw looks really bad if, as the ball leaves your hand, your wrist is "inside your elbow" — that is, your elbow joint is bent in such a way that your forearm angles back toward your body and your wrist is closer to your head than your elbow is. Slow-motion film of big-league pitchers shows that when they release the ball, the throwing arm is fully extended and straight from shoulder to wrist. The combination of these three elements — head-on stance, dropped elbow, and wrist inside the elbow — mechanically dictates a pushing rather than a hurling motion, creating the familiar pattern of "throwing like a girl."

It is surprisingly hard to find in the literature of baseball a deeper explanation of the mechanics of good and bad throws. Tom Seaver's pitching for the Mets and the White Sox got him into the Hall of Fame, but his book *The Art of Pitching* is full of bromides that hardly clarify the process of throwing, even if they might mean something to accomplished pitchers. His chapter "The Absolutes of Pitching Mechanics," for instance, lays out these four unhelpful principles: "Keep the Front Leg Flexible!" "Rub Up the Baseball." "Hide the Baseball!" "Get it Out, Get it Up!" (The fourth refers to the need to get the ball out of the glove and into the throwing hand in a quick motion.)

A variety of other instructional documents, from *Little League's Official How-to-Play Baseball Book* to *Softball for Girls & Women*, mainly reveal the difficulty of finding words to describe a simple motor activity that everyone can recognize. The challenge, I suppose, is like that of writing a manual on how to ride a bike, or how to kiss. Indeed, the most useful description I've found of the mechanics of throwing comes from a man whose specialty is another sport: Vic Braden made his name as a

10

tennis coach, but he has attempted to analyze the physics of a wide variety of sports so that they all will be easier to teach.

Braden says that an effective throw involves connecting a series of links in a "kinetic chain." The kinetic chain, which is Braden's tool for analyzing most sporting activity, operates on a principle like that of crack-the-whip. Momentum builds up in one part of the body. When that part is suddenly stopped, as the end of the "whip" is stopped in crack-the-whip, the momentum is transferred to and concentrated in the next link in the chain. A good throw uses six links of chain, Braden says. The first two links involve the lower body, from feet to waist. The first motion of a throw (after the body has been rotated away from the target) is to rotate the legs and hips back in the direction of the throw, building up momentum as large muscles move body mass. Then those links stop — a pitcher stops turning his hips once they face the plate — and the momentum is transferred to the next link. This is the torso, from waist to shoulders, and since its mass is less than that of the legs, momentum makes it rotate faster than the hips and legs did. The torso stops when it is facing the plate, and the momentum is transferred to the next link — the upper arm. As the upper arm comes past the head, it stops moving forward, and the momentum goes into the final links — the forearm and wrist, which snap forward at tremendous speed.

This may sound arcane and jerkily mechanical, but it makes perfect sense when one sees Braden's slow-mo movies of pitchers in action. And it explains why people do, or don't, learn how to throw. The implication of Braden's analysis is that throwing is a perfectly natural action (millions and millions of people can do it) but not at all innate. A successful throw involves an intricate series of actions coordinated among muscle groups, as each link of the chain is timed to interact with the next. Like bike riding or skating, it can be learned by anyone — male or female. No one starts out knowing how to ride a bike or throw a ball. Everyone has to learn.

Readers who are happy with their throwing skills can prove this to themselves in about two seconds. If you are right-handed, pick up a ball with your left hand and throw it. Unless you are ambidextrous or have some other odd advantage, you will throw it "like a girl." The problem is not that your left shoulder is hinged strangely or that you don't know what a good throw looks like. It is that you have not spent time training your leg, hip, shoulder, and arm muscles on that side to work together as required for a throw. The actor John Goodman, who played football seriously and baseball casually when he was in high school, is right-handed. When cast in the 1992 movie *The Babe*, he had to learn to bat and throw left-handed, for realism in the role of Babe Ruth. For weeks before the filming began, he would arrive an hour early at the set of his TV show, *Roseanne*, so that he could practice throwing a tennis ball against a wall left-handed. "I made damn sure no one could see me," Goodman told me recently. "I'm hard enough on myself without the derisive laughter of my so-called friends." When *The Babe* was released, Goodman told a newspaper interviewer, "I'll never say something like 'He throws like a girl' again. It's not easy to learn how to throw."

What Goodman discovered is what most men have forgotten: that if   15
they know how to throw now, it is because they spent time learning at some point long ago. (Goodman says that he can remember learning to ride a bicycle but not learning to throw with his right hand.) This brings us back to the roots of the "throwing like a girl" phenomenon. The crucial factor is not that males and females are put together differently but that they typically spend their early years in different ways. Little boys often learn how to throw without noticing that they are learning. Little girls are more rarely in environments that encourage them to learn in the same way. A boy who wonders why a girl throws the way she does is like a Frenchman who wonders why so many Americans speak French "with an accent."

"For young boys it is culturally acceptable and politically correct to develop these skills," says Linda Wells, of the Arizona State softball team. "They are mentored and networked. Usually girls are not coached at all, or are coached by Mom—or if it's by Dad, he may not be much of an athlete. Girls are often stuck with the bottom of the male talent pool as examples. I would argue that rather than learning to 'throw like a girl,' they learn to throw like poor male athletes. I say that a bad throw is 'throwing like an old man.' This is not gender, its acculturation."

Almost any motor skill, from doing handstands to dribbling a basketball, is easier to learn if you start young, which is why John Goodman did not realize that learning to throw is difficult until he attempted it as an adult. Many girls reach adulthood having missed the chance to learn to throw when that would have been easiest to do. And as adults they have neither John Goodman's incentive to teach their muscles a new set of skills nor his confidence that the feat is possible. Five years ago, Joseph Russo, long a baseball coach at St. John's University, gave athletic-talent tests to actresses who were trying out for roles in *A League of Their Own*, a movie about women's baseball. Most of them were "well coordinated in general, like for dancing," he says. But those who had not happened to play baseball or softball when they were young had a problem: "It sounds silly to say it, but they kept throwing like girls." (The best ball-field talents, by the way, were Madonna, Demi Moore, and the rock singer Joan Jett, who according to Russo "can really hit it hard." Careful viewers of *A League of Their Own* will note that only in a fleeting instant in one scene is the star, Geena Davis, shown actually throwing a ball.)

I'm not sure that I buy Linda Wells' theory that most boys are "mentored" or "networked" into developing ball skills. Those who make the baseball team, maybe. But for a far larger number the decisive ingredient seems to be the hundreds of idle hours spent throwing balls, sticks, rocks, and so on in the playground or the back yard. Children on the playground, I think, demonstrate the moment when the kinetic chain begins to work. It is when a little boy tries to throw a rock farther than his friend can or to throw a stick over a telephone wire thirty feet up. A toddler's first, instinctive throw is a push from the shoulder, showing the essential traits of "throwing like a girl." But when a child is really trying to put some oomph into the throw, his natural instinct is to wind up his body and let fly with the links of the chain. Little girls who do the same thing—compete with each other in distance throwing—learn the same way, but whereas many boys do this, few girls do. Tammy Richards, a woman who was raised on a farm in central California, says that she learned to throw by trying to heave dried cow chips farther than her brother could. It may have helped that her father, Bob Richards, was a former Olympic competitor in the decathlon (and two-time Olympic champion in the pole vault) and that he taught all his sons and daughters to throw not only the ball but also the discus, the shotput, and the javelin.

Is there a way to make up for lost time if you failed to invest those long hours on the playground years ago? Of course. Adults may not be able to learn to speak unaccented French, but they can learn to ride a bike, or skate, or throw. All that is required for developing any of these motor skills is time for practice—and spending that time requires overcoming the sense of embarrassment and futility that adults often have when attempting something new. Here are two tips that may help.

One is a surprisingly valuable drill suggested by the Little League's 20 *How-to-Play* handbook. Play catch with a partner who is ten or fifteen feet away—but do so while squatting with the knee of your throwing side touching the ground. When you start out this low, you have to keep the throw high to get the ball to your partner without bouncing it. This encourages a throw with the elbow held well above the shoulder, where it belongs.

The other is to play catch with a person who can throw like an athlete but is using his or her off hand. The typical adult woman hates to play catch with the typical adult man. She is well aware that she's not looking graceful and reacts murderously to the condescending tone in his voice ("That's more like it, honey!"). Forcing a right-handed man to throw left-handed is the great equalizer. He suddenly concentrates his attention on what it takes to get hips, shoulder, and elbow working together. He is suddenly aware of the strength of character needed to ignore the snickers of onlookers while learning new motor skills. He can no longer be condescending. He may even be nervous, wondering what he'll do if his partner makes the breakthrough first and he's the one still throwing like a girl.

The Reader's Presence

1. Fallows acknowledges the objections of feminists to the phrase "throwing like a girl." What other activities are linked to one gender or the other? Which gender gathers more negative associations? Why might feminists challenge the phrase? In your opinion, does Fallows satisfactorily answer such objections?

2. As a reporter, Fallows has covered many serious issues. Where does his use of language indicate that this essay is a lighter piece? Where does Fallows use an exaggerated or self-mocking tone? How does his use of humor affect the reader's reception of his message?

3. Reread the essay, focusing your attention on Fallows's descriptions of physical movement, especially paragraphs 9 to 14. Is it possible to understand his idea of the "kinetic chain" just by reading a description of it or must the reader also enact it with her or his body? Compare Fallows's anatomically detailed account to George Orwell's description of the dying elephant in "Shooting an Elephant" (page 221). How does each writer integrate such "close focus" descriptions into his larger argument? Do these passages slow down the essays? If not, why not?

Ian Frazier

All-Consuming Patriotism

The journalist and essayist Ian Frazier (b. 1951) started his career on the staff of the New Yorker, *writing "Talk of the Town" pieces as well as signed essays. Many of these essays can be found in his first two books:* Dating Your Mom *(1986) and* Nobody Better, Better than Nobody *(1987). In the mid-1980s Frazier left his job in New York and embarked on a journey across the North American prairies to Montana. The book that emerged after several years spent exploring this region,* Great Plains *(1989), was a huge success with both critics and readers. In* Family *(1994), Frazier turned to a subject closer to home and tells the story of twelve generations of his family. His recent books include a collection of comic essays,* Coyote v. Acme *(1996);* On the Rez *(2000), an account of his return to the Great Plains; and a new collection of essays,* The Fish's Eye *(2002). Frazier co-edited* The Best American Essays 1997 *and* The Best American Travel Writing 2003.

In all of his writing Frazier pays close attention to detail and location. "If you know something about a place it can save your sanity," he says, and a writer can find that knowledge through observation. "With a lot of writing, what you see is the top, the pinnacle, and the rest is invisible—all of these observations are ways of keeping yourself from flying off into space." In "All-Consuming Patriotism," which appeared in Mother Jones *in 2002, Frazier observes the expression of patriotism in the post-9/11 world.*

I think of myself as a good American. I follow current events, come to a complete stop at stop signs, show up for jury duty, vote. When the government tells me to shop, as it's been doing recently, I shop. Over the last few months, patriotically, I've bought all kinds of stuff I have no use for. Lack of money has been no obstacle; years ago I could never get a credit card, due to low income and lack of a regular job, and then one day for no reason credit cards began tumbling on me out of the mail. I now owe more to credit card companies than the average family of four earns in a year. So when buying something I don't want or need, I simply take out my credit card. That part's been easy; for me, it's the shopping itself that's hard. I happen to be a bad shopper—nervous, uninformed, prone to grab the first product I see on the shelf and pay any amount for it and run out the door. Frequently, trips I make to the supermarket end with my wife shouting in disbelief as she goes through the grocery bags and immediately transfers one wrongly purchased item after another directly into the garbage can.

It's been hard, as I say, but I've done my duty—I've shopped and then shopped some more. Certain sacrifices are called for. Out of concern for the economy after the terror attacks, the president said that he wanted us to go about our business, and not stop shopping. On a TV commercial sponsored by the travel industry, he exhorted us to take the family for a vacation. The treasury secretary, financial commentators, leaders of industry—all told us not to be afraid to spend. So I've gone out of my comfort zone, even expanded my purchasing patterns. Not long ago I detected a look of respect in the eye of a young salesman with many piercings at the music store as he took in my heavy middle-aged girth and then the rap music CD featuring songs of murder and gangsterism that I had selflessly decided to buy. My life is usually devoid of great excitement or difficulty, knock wood and thank God, and I have nothing to cry about, but I've also noticed in the media recently a strong approval for uninhibited public crying. So now, along with the shopping, I've been crying a lot, too. Sometimes I cry and shop at the same time.

As I'm pushing my overfull shopping cart down the aisle, sobbing quietly, moving a bit more slowly because of the extra weight I've lately put on, a couple of troubling questions cross my mind. First, I start to worry about the real depth of my shopping capabilities. So far I have more or less been able to keep up with what the government expects of me. I'm at a level of shopping that I can stand. But what if, God forbid,

events take a bad turn and the national crisis worsens, and more shopping is required? Can I shop with greater intensity than I am shopping
now? I suppose I could eat even more than I've been eating, and order
additional products in the mail, and go on costlier trips, and so on. But
I'm not eager, frankly, to enter that "code red" shopping mode. I try to
tell myself that I'd be equal to it, that in a real crisis I might be surprised
by how much I could buy. But I don't know.

My other worry is a vague one, more in the area of atmospherics, in-
tangibles. I feel kind of wrong even mentioning it in this time of trial.
How can I admit that I am worried about my aura? I worry that my aura
is not . . . well, that it's not what I had once hoped it would be. I can explain this only by comparison, obliquely. On the top shelf of my book-
case, among the works vital to me, is a book called *Trials and Triumphs:
The Record of the Fifty-Fifth Ohio Volunteer Infantry*, by Captain
Hartwell Osborn. I've read this book many times and studied it to the
smallest detail, because I think the people in it are brave and cool and admirable in every way.

The Fifty-Fifth was a Union Army regiment, formed in the Ohio   5
town of Norwalk, that fought throughout the Civil War. My great-great-
grand-father served in the regiment, as did other relatives. The book lists
every mile the regiment marched and every casualty it suffered. I like
reading about the soldiering, but I can't really identify with it, having
never been in the service myself. I identify more with the soldiers' wives
and mothers and daughters, whose home-front struggles I can better
imagine. *Trials and Triumphs* devotes a chapter to them, and to an organization they set up called the Soldiers' Aid Society.

The ladies of the Soldiers' Aid Society worked for the regiment almost constantly from the day it began. They sewed uniforms, made pil-
lows, held ice-cream sociables to raise money, scraped lint for bandages,
emptied their wedding chests of their best linen and donated it all. To
provide the men with antiscorbutics while on campaign, they pickled
everything that would pickle, from onions to potatoes to artichokes.
Every other day they were shipping out a new order of home-made supplies. Some of the women spent so much time stooped over while packing
goods in barrels that they believed they had permanently affected their
postures. When the war ended the ladies of the Soldiers' Aid said that for
the first time in their lives they understood what united womanhood
could accomplish. The movements for prohibition and women's suffrage
that grew powerful in the early 1900s got their start among those who'd
worked in similar home-front organizations during the war.

I don't envy my forebears, or wish I'd lived back then. I prefer the
greater speed and uncertainty and complicatedness of now. But I can't
help thinking that in terms of aura, the Norwalk ladies have it all over me.
I study the pages with their photographs, and admire the plainness of their
dresses, the set of their jaws, the expression in their eyes. Next to them my
credit card and I seem a sorry spectacle indeed. Their sense of purpose

shames me. What the country needed from those ladies it asked for, and they provided, straightforwardly; what it wants from me it somehow can't come out and ask. I'm asked to shop more, which really means to spend more, which eventually must mean to work more than I was working before. In previous wars, harder work was a civilian sacrifice that the government didn't hesitate to ask. Nowadays it's apparently unwilling to ask for any sacrifice that might appear to be too painful, too real.

But I *want* it to be real. I think a lot of us do. I feel like an idiot with my tears and shopping cart. I want to participate, to do something—and shopping isn't it. Many of the donors who contributed more than half a billion dollars to a Red Cross fund for the families of terror attack victims became angry when they learned that much of the money would end up not where they had intended but in the Red Cross bureaucracy. People want to express themselves with action. In New York City so many have been showing up recently for jury duty that the courts have had to turn hundreds away; officials said a new surplus of civic consciousness was responsible for the upsurge. I'd be glad if I were asked to—I don't know—drive less or turn the thermostat down or send in seldom-used items of clothing or collect rubber bands or plant a victory garden or join a civilian patrol or use fewer disposable paper products at children's birthday parties. I'd be willing, if asked, just to sit still for a day and meditate on the situation, much in the way that Lincoln used to call for national days of prayer.

A great, shared desire to *do* something is lying around mostly untapped. The best we can manage, it seems, is to show our U.S.A. brand loyalty by putting American flags on our houses and cars. Some businesses across the country even display in their windows a poster on which the American flag appears as a shopping bag, with two handles at the top. Above the flag-bag are the words "America: Open for Business." Money and the economy have gotten so tangled up in our politics that we forget we're citizens of our government, not its consumers. And the leaders we elect, who got where they are by selling themselves to us with television ads, and who often are only on short loan from the corporate world anyway, think of us as customers who must be kept happy. There's a scarcity of ideas about how to direct all this patriotic feeling because usually the market, not the country, occupies our minds. I'm sure it's possible to transform oneself from salesman to leader, just as it is to go from consumer to citizen. But the shift of identity is awkward, without many precedents, not easily done. In between the two—between selling and leading, between consuming and being citizens—is where our leaders and the rest of us are now.

We see the world beyond our immediate surroundings mostly through television, whose view is not much wider than that of a security peephole in a door. We hear over and over that our lives have forever changed, but the details right in front of us don't look very different, for all that. The forces fighting in Afghanistan are in more danger than we are back home, but perhaps not so much more; everybody knows that when catastrophe comes it could hit anywhere, most likely someplace it isn't expected. 10

Strong patriotic feelings stir us, fill us, but have few means of expressing themselves. We want to be a country, but where do you go to do that? Surely not the mall. When Mayor Giuliani left office at the end of 2001, he said he was giving up the honorable title of mayor for the more honorable title of citizen. He got that right. Citizen is honorable; shopper is not.

The Reader's Presence

1. How does Frazier characterize shopping as an act of patriotism? What sacrifices does he make in the name of patriotic consumerism? What words and phrases exemplify the way he satirizes the call to shop?

2. Frazier discusses the sacrifices that patriotism asks of citizens. How is "sacrifice" defined in the first couple of paragraphs? Compare that definition to Frazier's discussion of sacrifice toward the end of the essay.

3. Frazier is known primarily as a humor writer. At what point did you recognize the humor in Frazier's writing? Where does his tone modulate and become more serious? Why? Compare Frazier's use of humor to Langston Hughes's in "Liberals Needs a Mascot" (page 707) and "That Word *Black*" (page 709).

Neal Gabler

Our Celebrities, Ourselves

Neal Gabler (b. c. 1950), a senior fellow at the Lear Center for the Study of Entertainment and Society at the University of Southern California, is a media critic and film commentator whose work focuses primarily on the impact of show business on mass culture. A former co-host of public television's Sneak Previews, *his books include* An Empire of Their Own: How the Jews Invented Hollywood *(1988),* Winchell: Gossip, Power, and the Culture of Celebrity *(1994), and* Life the Movie: How Entertainment Conquered Reality *(1998). Gabler contributes to numerous publications including* American Film, *the* New York Times Book Review, *and* Video Review.

Gabler sees entertainment as a "democratizing force." He notes, "You don't need gatekeepers to understand entertainment. You don't need elites or interpreters to gain the pleasure from entertainment. As I define it, entertainment is largely a function of sensation and emotion. It unseats reason. It's a kind of mass force, rather than an elitist force. Anybody can respond to it. It challenges social controls by its very nature and even psychological controls."

In "Our Celebrities, Ourselves," which appeared in the Chronicle of Higher Education *in 2003, Gabler looks at how the search for "sensation and emotion" in entertainment has given rise to a new cult of celebrity.*

It has been more than 40 years since the historian Daniel Boorstin, in a now famously clever turn of phrase, defined a celebrity as someone who is known for being well known. If he were writing about celebrity today, Boorstin might describe it less flippantly as one of America's most prominent cottage industries and one of television's fastest-growing genres—one in which spent entertainers can find an afterlife by turning their daily existence into real-life situation comedy or tragedy. Anyone caring to stargaze can see *The Osbournes, The Anna Nicole Smith Show, Star Dates, The Surreal Life,* and the network prime-time celebrity interviews conducted by Barbara Walters, Diane Sawyer, Jane Pauley, and others. A reality series for VH1 capturing the life of the former star Liza Minnelli was derailed by a spat between the network and the principals. Meanwhile, cable networks continue to troll for celebrities eager to expose their lives to the public. Programs on the drawing boards include one in which over-the-hill stars spend the weekend with typical families, and another in which stars return to their hometowns and revisit their roots.

When Boorstin was writing in the early '60s, celebrity was one of those absurdities of contemporary culture—a large and ever-growing class of public figures for which there had been no precedent. Celebrities existed not to entertain, though they usually were entertainers, but rather to be publicized. Their talent, as Boorstin put it, was to grab the spotlight, whether or not they had done anything to deserve it. Now they have not only become an entertainment themselves, a kind of ambulatory show, but are also a cultural force with tremendous appeal, though exactly what that appeal is has been hard to determine. Most conventional analysts, from the popular historian Barbara Goldsmith to the pundit Andrew Sullivan, find celebrity a form of transport—a vicarious fantasy that lifts audiences out of the daily grind. Others, like Joshua Gamson in *Claims to Fame: Celebrity in Contemporary America,* see celebrity-watching as a ritual of empowerment through deconstruction. The audience doesn't seek to be elevated; it seeks to bring the celebrities back to earth. Still others, notably the rulers of the media, attribute the rapid rise of celebrity to mundane financial considerations, like the cheapness of programming real-life celebrities as opposed to fictional stories, and to the power of celebrities to sell magazines and tabloids by appearing on the cover.

There is no doubt some truth to each of those explanations—particularly the last one—but none of them fully expresses the range and power of celebrity in contemporary America, or its rampant march through the culture. None really gets to the root of the matter. To do that, one may have to think of celebrity in an entirely new way—not as a status that is conferred by publicity, but as a narrative form, written in the medium of life, that is similar to narratives in movies, novels, and television.

The only difference, really, is that since it is written in the medium of life, it requires another medium, be it television or print, to bridge the gap between the narrative lived and the narrative watched. In fact, celebrity narratives are so pervasive, with so many being generated, that they have subordinated other narratives and commandeered other media, until one could argue that life itself has become the dominant medium of the new century, and celebrity its most compelling product. Though purists will blanch at the thought, celebrity may even be the art of the age.

When you think of celebrity as a form of narrative art—the romances   5 and divorces, the binges, the dysfunctions, the triumphs, the transgressions—you can immediately appreciate one of its primary appeals, which is the appeal of any good story. Boorstin was wrong: Celebrities aren't known for being well known. They are known for living out real-life melodramas, which is why anyone from Elizabeth Taylor to Joey Buttafuoco[1] can be a celebrity. All one needs is a good story and a medium in which to retail it, and the media, always in desperate need of a story, are only too happy to oblige. And so we get the saga of Ozzy Osbourne, one-time Goth-rock star now stumbling through life as an addled dad to his own teenagers, or Whitney Houston insisting that she isn't addicted to drugs even as she crumbles before our eyes, or Mariah Carey telling us how she has rebounded from a nervous breakdown (she was really just exhausted) and a series of career disasters.

Of course, conventional narratives can provide equally riveting tales, but celebrity has advantages over fiction, not the least of which is novelty. Traditional narrative forms are so familiar to us now, especially with the proliferation of television programs and the staggering number of books published—well over 100,000 each year—that they have become exhausted, attenuated, predictable. We feel as if we've seen it all before. Celebrity is an antidote to that sense of exhaustion. Though celebrity narratives themselves have certain conventions—already, the idea of a famous eccentric displaced into normal life, which *The Osbournes* introduced a year ago, has been stolen by Anna Nicole Smith—they also have a *frisson*[2] that so-called imaginative narratives lack.

Part of that *frisson* is the intensification of one of the staples of any form of storytelling: suspense. Readers or viewers always want to know what's going to happen next, and there are some readers for whom that

---

[1]*Buttafuoco:* A Long Island auto repairman who in 1989 received enormous media attention when his teenage lover, Amy Fisher, gravely wounded his wife by shooting her in the head. His name, like John Wayne Bobbitt's or Kato Kaelin's—both referred to later in the essay—has become synonymous with instant notoriety as a result of media saturation.—EDS.

[2]*frisson:* French term meaning a moment of excitement or intense thrill.—EDS.

tension is so excruciating that they race to the end of the book for the outcome so that they can then read comfortably and without anxiety. Celebrity, playing out in real time, obviously has suspense, since there is no author to imagine the finish, only life itself to devise the next scene. One never knows what will happen. Who knew that Sharon Osbourne would be diagnosed with cancer? Who knew that Michael Jackson would dangle his infant son from a hotel balcony, or that his nose would erode into a nub after multiple plastic surgeries? Who knew whether Winona Ryder would be convicted or acquitted of her shoplifting charges, or what the sentence would be? Who knows whether Jennifer Lopez and Ben Affleck will be wed or whether something will happen to spoil their idyll? No one knows. The scenes just keep unspooling, and we wait, like Dickens's 19th-century readers eagerly snatching the next installment of his new novel, or like the moviegoers in the '30s watching the weekly chapters of a serial—only it is not just the *what* that we anticipate, it is the *when* or even the *if*. Fictional narratives have closure. They end, and the characters are frozen in time. Celebrity narratives resist closure. They go on and on and on.

Celebrity has another advantage over conventional narratives. All narratives depend on our emotional connection to the material—not only on our anticipation of what will happen, but also on our caring about what happens. In the case of fictional tales, we must, in the timeworn phrase, suspend our disbelief, because we know that what we are watching or reading is not real, although to be conscious of the unreality would seriously undermine, if not destroy, our sense of engagement. We must believe that these are not fictional creations but people, and that there is something at stake in the outcome of their story. That is one reason Henry James insisted on "felt life" as his aesthetic standard.

Great works still compel us to suspend our disbelief and convince us that we are watching life itself, but that is a harder and harder sell at a time when many Americans, particularly younger ones, are aware of narrative manipulations and regard all imaginative fiction as counterfeit. Celebrity, on the other hand, doesn't require one to suspend disbelief, because it is real, or at least purports to be. The stakes are real, too. Sharon Osbourne may eventually die of her cancer. Kelly Clarkson would get a record contract if she won *American Idol*. The various celebrities who beam at us from the cover of *People* each week will find romance or will recover or will succeed—or they won't. Either way, something is at stake. There are consequences that we will be able to see down the road. It matters.

Finally, there is the appeal of voyeurism that is heightened precisely 10 because celebrity is unavoidably contrasted with the fictional narratives in which most celebrities find themselves. For many fans today, the roles that celebrities play, both on television and in movies, and the roles they assume as they project themselves in the media, operate as a kind of disguise. They obscure the real person. Celebrity purportedly allows us to peek behind the disguise and see the real person in real joy or torment. This has resulted in an odd reversal that further underscores the power of celebrity. There was a time when celebrities, with a few exceptions, interested us only because of the work they did; their movies, books, albums, TV shows piqued our curiosity. We wanted to know more. But the ratio of interest in the work to interest in the personalities within the work has changed. Now the work they do serves as a curtain that celebrity draws, but since celebrities almost always have a larger appeal than that work—more people certainly know about the Osbournes than buy Ozzy's albums, just as more people are following the exploits of J. Lo and Ben Affleck than watch their movies—the work is almost an excuse for the celebrity. In effect, you need a curtain so that you can reveal what is behind it. Celebrity, then, is the real narrative—the real achievement.

After the terrible events of 9/11, some predicted that the days of celebrity obsession were over, and that Americans would prefer the comforts of closure to the roilings of reality. It hasn't turned out that way. If anything, 9/11 itself delivered a narrative of such extraordinary impact that it was impossible for fictional narratives to equal or approximate it, and it may even have created a new aesthetic divide—not between good stories and formulaic ones, but between real stories and imagined ones. In that context, celebrity, for all its seeming triviality and irrelevance, survives and thrives because it still has the mark of authenticity.

That element of authenticity is critical in understanding the public's attraction not only to the text of celebrity, but also to its subtext, without which celebrity would just be a bundle of melodramatic, albeit real, stories. The deeper appeal of these narratives is that they address one of the central tensions in contemporary America: the tension between artifice and authenticity, between the image and the reality.

The celebrity narrative is especially well suited to reify that issue. One is likely to think of celebrities as creatures of artifice. They wear makeup and costumes (even when they are not before the cameras, the hottest ones are dressed by designers), they rely on public-relations stunts and gossip to promote themselves, and they play roles and affect attitudes. That isn't just the public's view. Celebrities often think of themselves in the same way. Cary Grant was once quoted, perhaps apocryphally, as having said that it wasn't easy being Cary Grant. Presumably he meant that the persona was vastly different from the person who inhabited it, and that the latter was always having to work to become the former.

That idea—of a distance between the celebrity as public figure and the person within the celebrity narrative—is, indeed, the basis for almost every celebrity narrative that features an entertainer, as opposed to narratives, like those of Joey Buttafuoco or John Wayne Bobbitt or Kato Kaelin, that create the celebrity in the first place, out of notoriety. As I wrote in *Life the Movie*, virtually every celebrity profile, be it in *People*, *Vanity Fair*, *The New Yorker*, or on *Entertainment Tonight* or *Access*

Hollywood, focuses on the celebrity's battle to find himself or herself, to achieve some genuineness, to understand what really constitutes happiness instead of settling for the Hollywood conception of happiness.

These stories are all chronicles of self-discovery. Now that she is rid 15 of Tom Cruise, Nicole Kidman can find herself. Having broken up with her boyfriend, Justin Timberlake, Britney Spears is flailing about trying to find herself. Winona Ryder's shoplifting was a cry for help to enable her to find herself. Whitney Houston is now in a state of denial, but she will eventually have to find herself or perish. Lost in romance, drugs, abuse, failure, breakdowns — you name it — celebrities must fight through the layers of image to discover who they really are. Whether that is just more public-relations blather or not, those are the stories we read and see every day.

It is the same process that is charted on the new celebrity television shows. Ozzy Osbourne may be brain-fried and distracted, but his life, for all its oddities and even freakishness, is touchingly ordinary in its emotional groundedness. Ozzy has found himself in his family, which makes the program remarkably old-fashioned and life-affirming. Next to the F-word, the word most often used on the program is "love." Similarly, Anna Nicole Smith, the former *Playboy* centerfold now overweight and bovine and searching for love, may be a moron, but there is something attractive in her almost pathetic ordinariness beneath all her attempts at grandeur. Watching her and Ozzy and the minor stars from old sitcoms now looking for love on *Star Dates*, one is reminded not how different these celebrities are from us but how similar they are once they have recognized the supposed falsity of the celebrity way of life.

All of that may seem a very long way from the lives of those who read and watch the celebrity narrative — us. Not many Americans, after all, have had to struggle with the sorts of things, like romantic whirligigs, drug detoxification, and sudden career spirals, that beset celebrities. And yet in many respects, celebrity is just ordinary American life writ large and more intense. In an image-conscious society, where nearly everyone has access to the tools of self-invention and self-promotion — makeup, designer clothes, status symbols, and quirks of behavior, language, and attitude — people are forced to opt for a persona or else to find out who they really are. That is the modern condition. Each of us, to a greater or lesser degree, is fighting the same battle as the celebrities, which is why celebrity, for all its obvious entertainment value, resonates psychically in a way that few modern fictional narratives do. Celebrity doesn't transport us from the niggling problems of daily life. It amplifies and refines them in an exciting narrative context.

And so we keep watching as we might watch any soap opera, engaged by the melodrama, or any sitcom, amused by the comedy. We watch not because, as Boorstin wrote, we are too benumbed by artifice to recognize the difference between celebrities and people of real accomplishment who are more deserving of our attention. Rather we watch

because we understand, intuitively or not, that these celebrities are enacting a kind of modern parable of identity, with all its ridiculousness and
all its tragedy. We watch because in their celebrity — Ozzy's and Anna
Nicole's and Whitney's and Winona's and J. Lo's and Mariah's and even
Jacko's — we somehow manage to find ourselves.

The Reader's Presence

1. How does Gabler seem to define "celebrity"? What different interpretations of our fascination with celebrity does he present? How
   have these interpretations changed since the terrorist attacks of
   September 11, 2001? Where do you think the changes are most
   clearly seen?

2. Do you agree with Gabler that audiences prefer celebrity narratives to traditional television comedy and dramas? Which do you
   prefer? Why?

3. Gabler suggests that Americans in the post–9/11 era are fulfilling
   their needs for authenticity in watching celebrity reality television.
   Read Marie Winn's "TV Addiction" (page 608). How would Winn
   judge this phenomenon? What might she say are the consequences
   of looking to television to fulfill such needs?

Malcolm Gladwell

Big and Bad

*Malcolm Gladwell was born in England in 1963 and grew up in Canada. He
graduated with a degree in history from the University of Toronto in 1984. From
1987 to 1996, he was a reporter for the* Washington Post, *first as a science writer
and then as New York City bureau chief. Since 1996, he has been a staff writer
for the* New Yorker. *He is known for writing clearly and engagingly on complex
topics; he described his best-selling book,* The Tipping Point (2001), *as "an intellectual adventure story . . . it takes theories and ideas from the social sciences and
shows how they can have real relevance to our lives." His most recent book is*
Blink (2004).

"Big and Bad" first appeared in the New Yorker *in 2004.*

In the summer of 1996, the Ford Motor Company began building the Expedition, its new, full-sized S.U.V., at the Michigan Truck Plant, in the Detroit suburb of Wayne. The Expedition was essentially the F-150 pickup truck with an extra set of doors and two more rows of seats—and the fact that it was a truck was critical. Cars have to meet stringent fuel-efficiency regulations. Trucks don't. The handling and suspension and braking of cars have to be built to the demanding standards of drivers and passengers. Trucks only have to handle like, well, trucks. Cars are built with what is called unit-body construction. To be light enough to meet fuel standards and safe enough to meet safety standards, they have expensive and elaborately engineered steel skeletons, with built-in crumple zones to absorb the impact of a crash. Making a truck is a lot more rudimentary. You build a rectangular steel frame. The engine gets bolted to the front. The seats get bolted to the middle. The body gets lowered over the top. The result is heavy and rigid and not particularly safe. But it's an awfully inexpensive way to build an automobile. Ford had planned to sell the Expedition for thirty-six thousand dollars, and its best estimate was that it could build one for twenty-four thousand—which, in the automotive industry, is a terrifically high profit margin. Sales, the company predicted, weren't going to be huge. After all, how many Americans could reasonably be expected to pay a twelve-thousand-dollar premium for what was essentially a dressed-up truck? But Ford executives decided that the Expedition would be a highly profitable niche product. They were half right. The "highly profitable" part turned out to be true. Yet, almost from the moment Ford's big new S.U.V.s rolled off the assembly line in Wayne, there was nothing "niche" about the Expedition.

Ford had intended to split the assembly line at the Michigan Truck Plant between the Expedition and the Ford F-150 pickup. But, when the first flood of orders started coming in for the Expedition, the factory was entirely given over to S.U.V.s. The orders kept mounting. Assembly-line workers were put on sixty- and seventy-hour weeks. Another night shift was added. The plant was now running twenty-four hours a day, six days a week. Ford executives decided to build a luxury version of the Expedition, the Lincoln Navigator. They bolted a new grille on the Expedition, changed a few body panels, added some sound insulation, took a deep breath, and charged forty-five thousand dollars—and soon Navigators were flying out the door nearly as fast as Expeditions. Before long, the Michigan Truck Plant was the most profitable of Ford's fifty-three assembly plants. By the late nineteen-nineties, it had become the most profitable factory of any industry in the world. In 1998, the Michigan Truck Plant grossed eleven billion dollars, almost as much as McDonald's made that year. Profits were $3.7 billion. Some factory workers, with overtime, were making two hundred thousand dollars a year. The demand for Expeditions and Navigators was so insatiable that even when a blizzard hit the Detroit region in January of

1999—burying the city in snow, paralyzing the airport, and stranding hundreds of cars on the freeway—Ford officials got on their radios and commandeered parts bound for other factories so that the Michigan Truck Plant assembly line wouldn't slow for a moment. The factory that had begun as just another assembly plant had become the company's crown jewel.

In the history of the automotive industry, few things have been quite as unexpected as the rise of the S.U.V. Detroit is a town of engineers, and engineers like to believe that there is some connection between the success of a vehicle and its technical merits. But the S.U.V. boom was like Apple's bringing back the Macintosh, dressing it up in colorful plastic, and suddenly creating a new market. It made no sense to them. Consumers said they liked four-wheel drive. But the overwhelming majority of consumers don't need four-wheel drive. S.U.V. buyers said they liked the elevated driving position. But when, in focus groups, industry marketers probed further, they heard things that left them rolling their eyes. As Keith Bradsher writes in "High and Mighty"—perhaps the most important book about Detroit since Ralph Nader's "Unsafe at Any Speed"—what consumers said was "If the vehicle is up high, it's easier to see if something is hiding underneath or lurking behind it." Bradsher brilliantly captures the mixture of bafflement and contempt that many auto executives feel toward the customers who buy their S.U.V.s. Fred J. Schaafsma, a top engineer for General Motors, says, "Sport-utility owners tend to be more like 'I wonder how people view me,' and are more willing to trade off flexibility or functionality to get that." According to Bradsher, internal industry market research concluded that S.U.V.s tend to be bought by people who are insecure, vain, self-centered, and self-absorbed, who are frequently nervous about their marriages, and who lack confidence in their driving skills. Ford's S.U.V. designers took their cues from seeing "fashionably dressed women wearing hiking boots or even work boots while walking through expensive malls." Toyota's top marketing executive in the United States, Bradsher writes, loves to tell the story of how at a focus group in Los Angeles "an elegant woman in the group said that she needed her full-sized Lexus LX 470 to drive up over the curb and onto lawns to park at large parties in Beverly Hills." One of Ford's senior marketing executives was even blunter: "The only time those S.U.V.s are going to be off-road is when they miss the driveway at 3 A.M."

The truth, underneath all the rationalizations, seemed to be that S.U.V. buyers thought of big, heavy vehicles as safe: they found comfort in being surrounded by so much rubber and steel. To the engineers, of course, that didn't make any sense, either: if consumers really wanted something that was big and heavy and comforting, they ought to buy minivans, since minivans, with their unit-body construction, do much better in accidents than S.U.V.s. (In a thirty-five-m.p.h. crash test, for instance, the driver of a Cadillac Escalade—the G.M. counterpart to the Lincoln Navigator—has a sixteen-per-cent chance of a life-threatening head injury, a twenty-per-cent chance of a life-threatening chest injury, and a thirty-five-per-cent chance of a leg injury. The same numbers in a Ford Windstar minivan—a vehicle engineered from the ground up, as opposed to simply being bolted onto a pickup-truck frame—are, respectively, two per cent, four per cent, and one per cent.) But his desire for safety wasn't a rational calculation. It was a *feeling*. Over the past decade, a number of major automakers in America have relied on the services of a French-born cultural anthropologist, G. Clotaire Rapaille, whose speciality is getting beyond the rational—what he calls "cortex"—impressions of consumers and tapping into their deeper, "reptilian" responses. And what Rapaille concluded from countless, intensive sessions with car buyers was that when S.U.V. buyers thought about safety they were thinking about something that reached into their deepest unconscious. "The No. 1 feeling is that everything surrounding you should be round and soft, and should give," Rapaille told me. "There should be air bags everywhere. Then there's this notion that you need to be up high. That's a contradiction, because the people who buy these S.U.V.s know at the cortex level that if you are high there is more chance of a rollover. But at the reptilian level they think that if I am bigger and taller I'm safer. You feel secure because you are higher and dominate and look down. That you can look down is psychologically a very powerful notion. And what was the key element of safety when you were a child? It was that your mother fed you, and there was warm liquid. That's why cupholders are absolutely crucial for safety. If there is a car that has no cupholder, it is not safe. If I can put my coffee there, if I can have my food, if everything is round, if it's soft, and if I'm high, then I feel safe. It's amazing that intelligent, educated women will look at a car and the first thing they will look at is how many cupholders it has." During the design of Chrysler's PT Cruiser, one of the things Rapaille learned was that car buyers felt unsafe when they thought that an outsider could easily see inside their vehicles. So Chrysler made the back window of the PT Cruiser smaller. Of course, making windows smaller—and thereby reducing visibility—makes driving *more* dangerous, not less so. But that's the puzzle of what has happened to the automobile world: feeling safe has become more important than actually being safe.

One day this fall, I visited the automobile-testing center of Consumers   5
Union, the organization that publishes *Consumer Reports*. It is tucked away in the woods, in south-central Connecticut, on the site of the old Connecticut Speedway. The facility has two skid pads to measure cornering, a long straightaway for braking tests, a meandering "handling" course that winds around the back side of the track, and an accident-avoidance obstacle course

made out of a row of orange cones. It is headed by a trim, white-haired Englishman named David Champion, who previously worked as an engineer with Land Rover and with Nissan. On the day of my visit, Champion set aside two vehicles: a silver 2003 Chevrolet TrailBlazer—an enormous five-thousand-pound S.U.V.—and a shiny blue two-seater Porsche Boxster convertible.

We started with the TrailBlazer. Champion warmed up the Chevrolet with a few quick circuits of the track, and then drove it hard through the twists and turns of the handling course. He sat in the bucket seat with his back straight and his arms almost fully extended, and drove with practiced grace: every movement smooth and relaxed and unhurried. Champion, as an engineer, did not much like the TrailBlazer. "Cheap interior, cheap plastic," he said, batting the dashboard with his hand. "It's a little bit heavy, cumbersome. Quiet. Bit wallowy, side to side. Doesn't feel that secure. Accelerates heavily. Once it gets going, it's got decent power. Brakes feel a bit spongy." He turned onto the straightaway and stopped a few hundred yards from the obstacle course.

Measuring accident avoidance is a key part of the Consumers Union evaluation. It's a simple setup. The driver has to navigate his vehicle through two rows of cones eight feet wide and sixty feet long. Then he has to steer hard to the left, guiding the vehicle through a gate set off to the side, and immediately swerve hard back to the right, and enter a second sixty-foot corridor of cones that are parallel to the first set. The idea is to see how fast you can drive through the course without knocking over any cones. "It's like you're driving down a road in suburbia," Champion said. "Suddenly, a kid on a bicycle veers out in front of you. You have to do whatever it takes to avoid the kid. But there's a tractor-trailer coming toward you in the other lane, so you've got to swing back into your own lane as quickly as possible. That's the scenario."

Champion and I put on helmets. He accelerated toward the entrance to the obstacle course. "We do the test without brakes or throttle, so we can just look at handling," Champion said. "I actually take my foot right off the pedals." The car was now moving at forty m.p.h. At that speed, on the smooth tarmac of the raceway, the TrailBlazer was very quiet, and we were seated so high that the road seemed somehow remote. Champion entered the first row of cones. His arms tensed. He jerked the car to the left. The TrailBlazer's tires squealed. I was thrown toward the passenger-side door as the truck's body rolled, then thrown toward Champion as he jerked the TrailBlazer back to the right. My tape recorder went skittering across the cabin. The whole maneuver had taken no more than a few seconds, but it felt as if we had been sailing into a squall. Champion brought the car to a stop. We both looked back: the TrailBlazer had hit the cone at the gate. The kid on the bicycle was probably dead. Champion shook his head. "It's very rubbery. It slides a lot. I'm not getting much communication back from the steering wheel. It feels really ponderous, clumsy. I felt a little bit of tail swing."

I drove the obstacle course next. I started at the conservative speed of thirty-five m.p.h. I got through cleanly. I tried again, this time at thirty-eight m.p.h., and that small increment of speed made a dramatic difference. I made the first left, avoiding the kid on the bicycle. But, when it came time to swerve back to avoid the hypothetical oncoming eighteen-wheeler, I found that I was wrestling with the car. The protests of the tires were jarring. I stopped, shaken. "It wasn't going where you wanted it to go, was it?" Champion said. "Did you feel the weight pulling you sideways? That's what the extra weight the S.U.V.s have tends to do. It pulls you in the wrong direction." Behind us was a string of toppled cones. Getting the TrailBlazer to travel in a straight line, after that sudden diversion, hadn't been easy. "I think you took out a few pedestrians," Champion said with a faint smile.

Next up was the Boxster. The top was down. The sun was warm on my forehead. The car was low to the ground; I had the sense that if I dangled my arm out the window my knuckles would scrape on the tarmac. Standing still, the Boxster didn't feel safe: I could have been sitting in a go-cart. But when I ran it through the handling course I felt that I was in perfect control. On the straightaway, I steadied the Boxster at forty-five m.p.h., and ran it through the obstacle course. I could have balanced a teacup on my knee. At fifty m.p.h., I navigated the left and right turns with what seemed like a twitch of the steering wheel. The tires didn't squeal. The car stayed level. I pushed the Porsche up into the mid-fifties. Every cone was untouched. "Walk in the park!" Champion exclaimed as we pulled to a stop.

Most of us think that S.U.V.s are much safer than sports cars. If you asked the young parents of America whether they would rather strap their infant child in the back seat of the TrailBlazer or the passenger seat of the Boxster, they would choose the TrailBlazer. We feel that way because in the TrailBlazer our chances of surviving a collision with a hypothetical tractor-trailer in the other lane are greater than they are in the Porsche. What we forget, though, is that in the TrailBlazer you're also much more likely to hit the tractor-trailer because you can't get out of the way in time. In the parlance of the automobile world, the TrailBlazer is better at "passive safety." The Boxster is better when it comes to "active safety," which is every bit as important.

Consider the set of safety statistics compiled by Tom Wenzel, a scientist at Lawrence Berkeley National Laboratory, in California, and Marc Ross, a physicist at the University of Michigan. The numbers are expressed in fatalities per million cars, both for drivers of particular models and for the drivers of the cars they hit. (For example, in the first case, for every million Toyota Avalons on the road, forty Avalon

10

drivers die in car accidents every year, and twenty people die in accidents involving Toyota Avalons.) The numbers below have been rounded:

Make/Model	Type	Driver Deaths	Other Deaths	Total
Toyota Avalon	large	40	20	60
Chrysler Town & Country	minivan	31	36	67
Toyota Camry	mid-size	41	29	70
Volkswagen Jetta	subcompact	47	23	70
Ford Windstar	minivan	37	35	72
Nissan Maxima	mid-size	53	26	79
Honda Accord	mid-size	54	27	82
Chevrolet Venture	minivan	51	34	85
Buick Century	mid-size	70	23	93
Subaru Legacy/ Outback	compact	74	24	98
Mazda 626	compact	70	29	99
Chevrolet Malibu	mid-size	71	34	105
Chevrolet Suburban	S.U.V.	46	59	105
Jeep Grand Cherokee	S.U.V.	61	44	106
Honda Civic	subcompact	84	25	109
Toyota Corolla	subcompact	81	29	110
Ford Expedition	S.U.V.	55	57	112
GMC Jimmy	S.U.V.	76	39	114
Ford Taurus	mid-size	78	39	117
Nissan Altima	compact	72	49	121
Mercury Marquis	large	80	43	123
Nissan Sentra	subcompact	95	34	129
Toyota 4Runner	S.U.V.	94	43	137
Chevrolet Tahoe	S.U.V.	68	74	141
Dodge Stratus	mid-size	103	40	143
Lincoln Town Car	large	100	47	147
Ford Explorer	S.U.V.	88	60	148
Pontiac Grand Am	compact	118	39	157
Toyota Tacoma	pickup	111	59	171
Chevrolet Cavalier	subcompact	146	41	186
Dodge Neon	subcompact	161	39	199
Pontiac Sunfire	subcompact	158	44	202
Ford F-Series	pickup	110	128	238

Are the best performers the biggest and heaviest vehicles on the road? Not at all. Among the safest cars are the midsize imports, like the Toyota Camry and the Honda Accord. Or consider the extraordinary performance of some subcompacts, like the Volkswagen Jetta. Drivers of the tiny Jetta die at a rate of just forty-seven per million, which is in the same range as drivers of the five-thousand-pound Chevrolet Suburban and almost half that of popular S.U.V. models like the Ford Explorer or the GMC Jimmy. In a head-on crash, an Explorer or a Suburban would crush a Jetta or a Camry. But, clearly, the drivers of Camrys and Jettas are finding a way to avoid head-on crashes with Explorers and Suburbans. The benefits of being nimble—of being in an automobile that's capable of staying out of trouble—are in many cases greater than the benefits of being big.

I had another lesson in active safety at the test track when I got in the TrailBlazer with another Consumers Union engineer, and we did three emergency-stopping tests, taking the Chevrolet up to sixty m.p.h. and then slamming on the brakes. It was not a pleasant exercise. Bringing five thousand pounds of rubber and steel to a sudden stop involves lots of lurching, screeching, and protesting. The first time, the TrailBlazer took 146.2 feet to come to a halt, the second time 151.6 feet, and the third time 153.4 feet. The Boxster can come to a complete stop from sixty m.p.h. in about 124 feet. That's a difference of about two car lengths, and it isn't hard to imagine any number of scenarios where two car lengths could mean the difference between life and death.

The S.U.V. boom represents, then, a shift in how we conceive of   15
safety—from active to passive. It's what happens when a larger number of drivers conclude, consciously or otherwise, that the extra thirty feet that the TrailBlazer takes to come to a stop don't really matter, that the tractor-trailer will hit them anyway, and that they are better off treating accidents as inevitable rather than avoidable. "The metric that people use is size," says Stephen Popiel, a vice-president of Millward Brown Goldfarb, in Toronto, one of the leading automotive market-research firms. "The bigger something is, the safer it is. In the consumer's mind, the basic equation is, If I were to take this vehicle and drive it into this brick wall, the more metal there is in front of me the better off I'll be."

This is a new idea, and one largely confined to North America. In Europe and Japan, people think of a safe car as a nimble car. That's why they build cars like the Jetta and the Camry, which are designed to carry out the driver's wishes as directly and efficiently as possible. In the Jetta, the engine is clearly audible. The steering is light and precise. The brakes are crisp. The wheelbase is short enough that the car picks up the undulations of the road. The car is so small and close to the ground, and so dwarfed by other cars on the road, that an intelligent driver is constantly reminded of the necessity of driving safely and defensively. An S.U.V. embodies the opposite logic. The driver is seated as high and far from the road as possible. The vehicle is designed to overcome its environment, not to respond to it. Even four-wheel drive, seemingly the most beneficial feature of the S.U.V., serves to reinforce this isolation. Having the engine provide power to all four wheels, safety experts point out, does nothing to improve braking, although many S.U.V. owners erroneously believe this to be the case. Nor does the feature necessarily make it safer to turn across a slippery surface: that is largely a function of how much friction is generated by the vehicle's tires. All it really does is improve what engineers call tracking—that is, the ability to accelerate without slipping in perilous conditions or in deep snow or mud. Champion says that one of the occasions when he came closest to death was a snowy day, many years ago, just after he had bought a new Range Rover. "Everyone around me was slipping, and I was thinking, *Yeahhh*. And I came to a stop sign on a major road, and I was driving probably twice as fast as I should have been, because I could. I had traction. But also weighed probably twice as much as most cars. And I still had only four brakes and four tires on the road. I slid right across a four-lane road." Four-wheel drive robs the driver of feedback. "The car driver whose wheels spin once or twice while backing out of the driveway knows that the road is slippery," Bradsher writes. "The SUV driver who navigates the driveway and street without difficulty until she tries to brake may not find out that the road is slippery until it is too late." Jettas are safe because they make their drivers feel unsafe. S.U.V.s are unsafe because they make their drivers feel safe. That feeling of safety isn't the solution; it's the problem.

Perhaps the most troublesome aspect of S.U.V. culture is its attitude toward risk. "Safety, for most automotive consumers, has to do with the notion that they aren't in complete control," Popiel says. "There are unexpected events that at any moment in time can come out and impact them—an oil patch up ahead, an eighteen-wheeler turning over, something falling down. People feel that the elements of the world out of their control are the ones that are going to cause them distress."

Of course, those things really aren't outside a driver's control: an alert driver, in the right kind of vehicle, can navigate the oil patch, avoid the truck, and swerve around the thing that's falling down. Traffic-fatality rates vary strongly with driver behavior. Drunks are 7.6 times more likely to die in accidents than non-drinkers. People who wear their seat belts are almost half as likely to die as those who don't buckle up. Forty-year-olds are ten times less likely to get into accidents than sixteen-year-olds. Drivers of minivans, Wenzel and Ross's statistics tell us, die at a fraction of the rate of drivers of pickup trucks. That's clearly because minivans are family cars, and parents with children in the back seat are less likely to get into accidents. Frank McKenna, a safety expert at the University of Reading, in England, has done experiments where he shows drivers a series of videotaped scenarios—a child running out the front door of his house and onto the street, for example, or a car approaching an intersection at too great a speed to stop at the red light—and asks people to press a button the minute they become aware of the potential for an accident. Experienced drivers press the button between half a second and a second faster than new drivers, which, given that car accidents are events measured in milliseconds, is a significant difference. McKenna's work shows that, with experience, we all learn how to exert some degree of control over what might otherwise appear to be uncontrollable events. Any conception of safety that revolves entirely around the vehicle, then, is incomplete. Is the Boxster safer than the TrailBlazer? It depends on who's behind the wheel. In the hands of, say, my very respectable and prudent middle-aged mother, the Boxster is by far the safer car. In my hands, it probably isn't. On the open road, my reaction to the Porsche's extraordinary road manners and the sweet, irresistible wail of its engine would be to drive much faster than I should. (At the end of my day at Consumers Union, I parked the Boxster, and immediately got into my own car to drive home. In my mind, I was still at the wheel of the Boxster. Within twenty minutes, I had a two-hundred-and-seventy-one-dollar speeding ticket.) The trouble with the S.U.V. ascendancy is that it excludes the really critical component of safety: the driver.

In psychology, there is a concept called learned helplessness, which arose from a series of animal experiments in the nineteen-sixties at the University of Pennsylvania. Dogs were restrained by a harness, so that they couldn't move, and then repeatedly subjected to a series of electrical shocks. Then the same dogs were shocked again, only this time they could easily escape by jumping over a low hurdle. But most of them didn't; they just huddled in the corner, no longer believing that there was anything they could do to influence their own fate. Learned helplessness is now thought to play a role in such phenomena as depression and the failure of battered women to leave their husbands, but one could easily apply it more widely. We live in an age, after all, that is strangely fixated on the idea of helplessness: we're fascinated by hurricanes and terrorist acts and epidemics like SARS—situations in which we feel powerless to affect our own destiny. In fact, the risks posed to life and limb by forces outside our control are dwarfed by the factors we can control. Our fixation with helplessness distorts our perceptions of risk. "When you feel safe, you can be passive," Rapaille says of the fundamental appeal of the S.U.V. "Safe means I can sleep. I can give up control. I can relax. I can take off my shoes. I can listen to music." For years, we've all made fun of the middle-aged man who suddenly trades in his sedate family sedan for a shiny red sports car. That's called a midlife crisis. But at least it involves some degree of engagement with the act of driving. The man who gives up his sedate family sedan for an S.U.V. is saying something far more troubling—that he finds the demands of the road to be overwhelming. Is acting out really worse than giving up?

On August 9, 2000, the Bridgestone Firestone tire company announced one of the largest product recalls in American history. Because of mounting 20 concerns about safety, the company said, it was replacing some fourteen million tires that had been used primarily on the Ford Explorer S.U.V. The cost of the recall—and of a follow-up replacement program initiated by Ford a year later—ran into billions of dollars. Millions more were spent by both companies on fighting and settling lawsuits from Explorer owners, who alleged that their tires had come apart and caused their S.U.V.s to roll over. In the fall of that year, senior executives from both companies were called to Capitol Hill, where they were publicly berated. It was the biggest scandal to hit the automobile industry in years. It was also one of the strangest. According to federal records, the number of fatalities resulting from the failure of a Firestone tire on a Ford Explorer S.U.V., as of September, 2001, was two hundred and seventy-one. That sounds like a lot, until you remember that the total number of tires supplied by Firestone to the Explorer from the moment the S.U.V. was introduced by Ford, in 1990, was fourteen million, and that the average life span of a tire is forty-five thousand miles. The allegation against Firestone amounts to the claim that its tires failed, with fatal results, two hundred and seventy-one times in the course of six hundred and thirty billion vehicle miles. Manufacturers usually win prizes for failure rates that low. It's also worth remembering that during that same ten-year span almost half a million Americans died in traffic accidents. In other words, during the nineteen-nineties hundreds of thousands of people were killed on the roads because they drove too fast or ran red lights or drank too much. And, of those, a fair proportion involved people in S.U.V.s who were lulled by their four-wheel drive into driving recklessly on slick roads, who drove aggressively because they felt invulnerable, who disproportionately killed those they hit because they chose to drive trucks with inflexible steel-frame architecture, and who crashed because they couldn't bring their five-thousand-pound vehicles to a halt in time. Yet, out of all those fatalities, regulators, the legal profession, Congress, and the media chose to highlight the .0005 per cent that could be linked to an alleged defect in the vehicle.

But should that come as a surprise? In the age of the S.U.V., this is what people worry about when they worry about safety—not risks, however commonplace, involving their own behavior but risks, however rare, involving some unexpected event. The Explorer was big and imposing. It was high above the ground. You could look down on other drivers. You could see if someone was lurking behind or beneath it. You could drive it up on someone's lawn with impunity. Didn't it seem like the safest vehicle in the world?

The Reader's Presence

1. According to Gladwell, how do automobile companies regard consumer safety? What evidence does he provide to support his

argument? Were you aware of any of the concerns Gladwell raises? Do you find his argument convincing? Why or why not?

2. Explain the terms "active safety" and "passive safety." What would be the priorities of a car buyer and driver interested in each? Do you agree with Gladwell that SUV drivers are giving up active safety for passive safety? What would be the consequences of such an exchange?

3. Gladwell points out that consumers' reasons for buying cars are frequently illogical. Read "Why McDonald's Fries Taste So Good" by Eric Schlosser (page 559). What basis do consumers have for choosing fast food over other options? Why do you think consumers sometimes make choices that are ultimately not in their best interests?

Mary Gordon

The Ghosts of Ellis Island

Mary Gordon (b. 1949) is a professor of English at Barnard College and frequently contributes articles and short stories to Harper's, Ladies' Home Journal, Virginia Quarterly Review, *and the* Atlantic. *Since her first novel,* Final Payments *(1978), earned her critical success, Gordon has published numerous books, including* The Company of Women *(1981),* The Other Side *(1989),* The Shadow Man *(1996),* Spending: A Utopian Divertimento *(1998),* Reflections on Geography and Identity *(2000), and* Pearl *(2005). "The Ghosts of Ellis Island" originally appeared in the* New York Times *in 1985.*

I once sat in a hotel in Bloomsbury[1] trying to have breakfast alone. A Russian with a habit of compulsively licking his lips asked if he could join me. I was afraid to say no; I thought it might be bad for détente. He explained to me that he was a linguist, and that he always liked to talk to Americans to see if he could make any connection between their speech and their ethnic background. When I told him about my mixed ancestry — my mother is Irish and Italian, my father a Lithuanian Jew — he began jumping up and down in his seat, rubbing his hands together, and licking his lips even more frantically:

---

[1]*Bloomsbury:* A section of London noted for its literary and cultural history. — EDS.

"Ah," he said, "so you are really somebody who comes from what is called the boiling pot of America." Yes, I told him, yes I was, but I quickly rose to leave. I thought it would be too hard to explain to him the relation of the boiling potters to the main course, and I wanted to get to the British Museum. I told him that the only thing I could think of that united people whose backgrounds, histories, and points of view were utterly diverse was that their people had landed at a place called Ellis Island.

I didn't tell him that Ellis Island was the only American landmark I'd ever visited. How could I describe to him the estrangement I'd always felt from the kind of traveler who visits shrines to America's past greatness, those rebuilt forts with muskets behind glass and sabers mounted on the walls and gift shops selling maple sugar candy in the shape of Indian headdresses, those reconstructed villages with tables set for fifty and the Paul Revere silver gleaming? All that Americana—Plymouth Rock, Gettysburg, Mount Vernon, Valley Forge—it all inhabits for me a zone of blurred abstraction with far less hold on my imagination than the Bastille or Hampton Court. I suppose I've always known that my uninterest in it contains a large component of the willed: I am American, and those places purport to be my history. But they are not mine.

Ellis Island is, though; it's the one place I can be sure my people are connected to. And so I made a journey there to find my history, like any Rotarian traveling in his Winnebago to Antietam to find his. I had become part of that humbling democracy of people looking in some site for a past that has grown unreal. The monument I traveled to was not, however, a tribute to some old glory. The minute I set foot upon the island I could feel all that it stood for: insecurity, obedience, anxiety, dehumanization, the terrified and careful deference of the displaced. I hadn't traveled to the Battery and boarded a ferry across from the Statue of Liberty to raise flags or breathe a richer, more triumphant air. I wanted to do homage to the ghosts.

I felt them everywhere, from the moment I disembarked and saw the   5
building with its high-minded brick, its hopeful little lawn, its ornamental cornices. The place was derelict when I arrived; it had not functioned for more than thirty years—almost as long as the time it had operated at full capacity as a major immigration center. I was surprised to learn what a small part of history Ellis Island had occupied. The main building was constructed in 1892, then rebuilt between 1898 and 1900 after a fire. Most of the immigrants who arrived during the latter half of the nineteenth century, mainly northern and western Europeans, landed not at Ellis Island but on the western tip of the Battery at Castle Garden, which had opened as a receiving center for immigrants in 1855.

By the 1880s the facilities at Castle Garden had grown scandalously inadequate. Officials looked for an island on which to build a new immigration center because they thought that on an island immigrants could be more easily protected from swindlers and quickly transported to railroad terminals in New Jersey. Bedloe's Island was considered, but New Yorkers were aghast at the idea of a "Babel" ruining their beautiful new treasure, "Liberty Enlightening the World." The statue's sculptor, Frédéric Auguste Bartholdi, reacted to the prospect of immigrants landing near his masterpiece in horror; he called it a "monstrous plan." So much for Emma Lazarus.[2]

Ellis Island was finally chosen because the citizens of New Jersey petitioned the federal government to remove from the island an old naval powder magazine that they thought dangerously close to the Jersey shore. The explosives were removed; no one wanted the island for anything. It was the perfect place to build an immigration center.

I thought about the island's history as I walked into the building and made my way to the room that was the center in my imagination of the Ellis Island experience: the Great Hall. It had been made real for me in the stark, accusing photographs of Louis Hine and others who took those pictures to make a point. It was in the Great Hall that everyone had waited — waiting, always, the great vocation of the dispossessed. The room was empty, except for me and a handful of other visitors and the park ranger who showed us around. I felt myself grow insignificant in that room, with its huge semicircular windows, its air, even in dereliction, of solid and official probity.

I walked in the deathlike expansiveness of the room's disuse and tried to think of what it might have been like, filled and swarming. More than sixteen million immigrants came through that room; approximately 250,000 were rejected. Not really a large proportion, but the implications for the rejected were dreadful. For some, there was nothing to go back to, or there was certain death; for others, who left as adventurers, to return would be to adopt in local memory the fool's role, and the failure's. No wonder that the island's history includes reports of three thousand suicides.

Sometimes immigrants could pass through Ellis Island in mere hours,   10
though for some the process took days. The particulars of the experience in the Great Hall were often influenced by the political events and attitudes on

---

[2]*Lazarus:* An American poet (1849–1887) who wrote the famous sonnet "The New Colossus," which appears at the base of the Statue of Liberty:

> Not like the brazen giant of Greek fame
> With conquering limbs astride from land to land;
> Here at our sea-washed, sunset gates shall stand
> A mighty woman with a torch, whose flame
> Is the imprisoned lightning, and her name
> Mother of Exiles. From her beacon-hand
> Glows world-wide welcome; her mild eyes command
> The air-bridged harbor that twin cities frame
> "Keep ancient lands, your storied pomp!" cries she
> With silent lips. "Give me your tired, your poor,
> Your huddled masses yearning to breathe free,
> The wretched refuse of your teeming shore.
> Send these, the homeless, tempest-tost to me,
> I lift my lamp beside the golden door!"
> —EDS.

the mainland. In the 1890s and the first years of the new century, when cheap labor was needed, the newly built receiving center took in its immigrants with comparatively little question. But as the century progressed, the economy worsened, eugenics became both scientifically respectable and popular, and World War I made American xenophobia seem rooted in fact.

Immigration acts were passed; newcomers had to prove, besides moral correctness and financial solvency, their ability to read. Quota laws came into effect, limiting the number of immigrants from southern and eastern Europe to less than 14 percent of the total quota. Intelligence tests were biased against all non-English-speaking persons and medical examinations became increasingly strict, until the machinery of immigration nearly collapsed under its own weight. The Second Quota Law of 1924 provided that all immigrants be inspected and issued visas at American consular offices in Europe, rendering the center almost obsolete.

On the day of my visit, my mind fastened upon the medical inspections, which had always seemed to me most emblematic of the ignominy and terror the immigrants endured. The medical inspectors, sometimes dressed in uniforms like soldiers, were particularly obsessed with a disease of the eyes called trachoma, which they checked for by flipping back the immigrants' top eyelids with a hook used for buttoning gloves—a method that sometimes resulted in the transmission of the disease to healthy people. Mothers feared that if their children cried too much, their red eyes would be mistaken for a symptom of the disease and the whole family would be sent home. Those immigrants suspected of some physical disability had initials chalked on their coats. I remembered the photographs

I'd seen of people standing, dumbstruck and innocent as cattle, with their manifest numbers hung around their necks and initials marked in chalk upon their coats: "E" for eye trouble, "K" for hernia, "L" for lameness, "X" for mental defects, "H" for heart disease.

I thought of my grandparents as I stood in the room; my seventeen-year-old grandmother, coming alone from Ireland in 1896, vouched for by a stranger who had found her a place as a domestic servant to some Irish who had done well. I tried to imagine the assault it all must have been for her; I've been to her hometown, a collection of farms with a main street—smaller than the athletic field of my local public school. She must have watched the New York skyline as the first- and second-class passengers were whisked off the gangplank with the most cursory of inspections while she was made to board a ferry to the new immigration center.

What could she have made of it—this buff-painted wooden structure with its towers and its blue slate roof, a place *Harper's Weekly* described as "a latter-day watering place hotel"? It would have been the first time she'd have heard people speaking something other than English. She would have mingled with people carrying baskets on their heads and eating foods unlike any she had ever seen—dark-eyed people, like the Sicilian she would marry ten years later, who came over with his family, responsible even then for his mother and sister. I don't know what they thought, my grandparents, for they were not expansive people, nor romantic; they didn't like to think of what they called "the hard times," and their trip across the ocean was the single adventurous act of lives devoted after landing to security, respectability, and fitting in.

What is the potency of Ellis Island for someone like me—an American, obviously, but one who has always felt that the country really belonged to the early settlers, that, as J. F. Powers wrote in "Morte D'Urban," it had been "handed down to them by the Pilgrims, George Washington and others, and that they were taking a risk in letting you live in it." I have never been the victim of overt discrimination; nothing I have wanted has been denied me because of the accidents of blood. But I suppose it is part of being an American to be engaged in a somewhat tiresome but always self-absorbing process of national definition. And in this process, I have found in traveling to Ellis Island an important piece of evidence that could remind me I was right to feel my differentness. Something had happened to my people on that island, a result of the eternal wrongheadedness of American protectionism and the predictabilities of simple greed. I came to the island, too, so I could tell the ghosts that I was one of them, and that I honored them—their stoicism, and their innocence, the fear that turned them inward, and their pride. I wanted to tell them that I liked them better than the Americans who made them pass through the Great Hall and stole their names and chalked their weaknesses in public on their clothing. And to tell the ghosts what I have always thought: that American history was a very classy party that was not much fun until they arrived, brought the good food, turned up the music, and taught everyone to dance.

The Reader's Presence

1. Gordon contrasts immigrant and mainstream American experiences, although nearly all present-day Americans have immigrant ancestry. How does she define *immigrant*? What imagery does she attach to the immigrant experience? How is this imagery made vivid for the reader? How do you think Gordon would wish a reader like herself to experience the essay? How do you think she would wish a mainstream American to experience the essay?

2. Gordon reveals little-known facts about the Statue of Liberty and Ellis Island. What symbolic meaning do these facts convey in terms of America's reception of immigrants? Ellis Island has since been refashioned into an impressive museum celebrating the history of immigrants in America. Does this development undercut or reinforce Gordon's opposition of official and hidden history?

3. Gordon's description of immigrants' contributions to American culture recalls Ralph Ellison's essay "What America Would Be Like without Blacks" (page 390). What sorts of contributions does Gordon credit immigrants with? In what ways are the two writers' visions of America as a "melting pot" similar? How do they differ?

Stephen Jay Gould

Sex, Drugs, Disasters, and the Extinction of Dinosaurs

Stephen Jay Gould (1941–2002) was professor of geology and zoology at Harvard and curator of invertebrate paleontology at Harvard's Museum of Comparative Zoology. He published widely on evolution and other topics and earned a reputation for making technical subjects readily comprehensible to lay readers without trivializing the material. His The Panda's Thumb *(1980) won the American Book Award, and* The Mismeasure of Man *(1981) won the National Book Critics Circle Award. Gould published more than one hundred articles in scientific journals, and he contributed to national magazines as well. "Sex, Drugs, Disasters, and the Extinction of Dinosaurs" appeared in* Discover *magazine in 1984. More recently, Gould wrote* Questioning the Millennium: A Rationalist's Guide to a*

Precisely Arbitrary Countdown *(1997),* Leonardo's Mountain of Clams and the Diet of Worms: Essays on Natural History *(1998),* Rocks of Ages: Science & Religion in the Fullness of Life *(1999),* The Lying Stones of Marrakesh *(2001), and* The Structure of Evolutionary Theory *(2001). Among many other honors and awards, he was a fellow of the National Science Foundation and the MacArthur Foundation. In 1999 Gould became president of the American Association for the Advancement of Science. John Updike comments that "Gould, in his scrupulous explication of [other scientists'] carefully wrought half-truths, abolishes the unnecessary distinction between the humanities and science, and honors the latter as a branch of humanistic thought, fallible and poetic."*

When asked if he found it difficult to write about complex scientific concepts in language that is accessible to general readers, Gould replied, "I don't see why it should be that difficult. . . . Every field has its jargon. I think scientists hide behind theirs perhaps more than people in other professions do — it's part of our mythology — but I don't think the concepts of science are intrinsically more difficult than the professional notions in any other field."

Science, in its most fundamental definition, is a fruitful mode of inquiry, not a list of enticing conclusions. The conclusions are the consequence, not the essence.

My greatest unhappiness with most popular presentations of science concerns their failure to separate fascinating claims from the methods that scientists use to establish the facts of nature. Journalists, and the public, thrive on controversial and stunning statements. But science is, basically, a way of knowing — in P. B. Medawar's apt words, "the art of the soluble." If the growing corps of popular science writers would focus on *how* scientists develop and defend those fascinating claims, they would make their greatest possible contribution to public understanding.

Consider three ideas, proposed in perfect seriousness to explain that greatest of all titillating puzzles — the extinction of dinosaurs. Since these three notions invoke the primally fascinating themes of our culture — sex, drugs, and violence — they surely reside in the category of fascinating claims. I want to show why two of them rank as silly speculation, while the other represents science at its grandest and most useful.

Science works with the testable proposals. If, after much compilation and scrutiny of data, new information continues to affirm a hypothesis, we may accept it provisionally and gain confidence as further evidence mounts. We can never be completely sure that a hypothesis is right, though we may be able to show with confidence that it is wrong. The best scientific hypotheses are also generous and expansive: They suggest extensions and implications that enlighten related, and even far distant, subjects. Simply consider how the idea of evolution has influenced virtually every intellectual field.

Useless speculation, on the other hand, is restrictive. It generates no testable hypothesis, and offers no way to obtain potentially refuting evidence. Please note that I am not speaking of truth or falsity. The speculation may well be true; still, if it provides, in principle, no material for

5

affirmation or rejection, we can make nothing of it. It must simply stand forever as an intriguing idea. Useless speculation turns in on itself and leads nowhere; good science, containing both seeds for its potential refutation and implications for more and different testable knowledge, reaches out. But, enough preaching. Let's move on to dinosaurs, and the three proposals for their extinction.

1. *Sex:* Testes function only in a narrow range of temperature (those of mammals hang externally in a scrotal sac because internal body temperatures are too high for their proper function). A worldwide rise in temperature at the close of the Cretaceous period caused the testes of dinosaurs to stop functioning and led to their extinction by sterilization of males.
2. *Drugs:* Angiosperms (flowering plants) first evolved toward the end of the dinosaurs' reign. Many of these plants contain psychoactive agents, avoided by mammals today as a result of their bitter taste. Dinosaurs had neither means to taste the bitterness nor livers effective enough to detoxify the substances. They died of massive overdoses.
3. *Disasters:* A large comet or asteroid struck the earth some 65 million years ago, lofting a cloud of dust into the sky and blocking sunlight, thereby suppressing photosynthesis and so drastically lowering world temperatures that dinosaurs and hosts of other creatures became extinct.

Before analyzing these three tantalizing statements, we must establish a basic ground rule often violated in proposals for the dinosaurs' demise. *There is no separate problem of the extinction of dinosaurs.* Too often we divorce specific events from their wider contexts and systems of cause and effect. The fundamental fact of dinosaur extinction is its synchrony with the demise of so many other groups across a wide range of habitats, from terrestrial to marine.

The history of life has been punctuated by brief episodes of mass extinction. A recent analysis by University of Chicago paleontologists Jack Sepkoski and Dave Raup, based on the best and most exhaustive tabulation of data ever assembled, shows clearly that five episodes of mass dying stand well above the "background" extinctions of normal times (when we consider all mass extinctions, large and small, they seem to fall in a regular 26-million-year cycle). The Cretaceous debacle, occurring 65 million years ago and separating the Mesozoic and Cenozoic eras of our geological time scale, ranks prominently among the five. Nearly all the marine plankton (single-celled floating creatures) died with geological suddenness; among marine invertebrates, nearly 15 percent of all families perished, including many previously dominant groups, especially the ammonites (relatives of squids in coiled shells). On land, the dinosaurs disappeared after more than 100 million years of unchallenged domination.

In this context, speculations limited to dinosaurs alone ignore the larger phenomenon. We need a coordinated explanation for a system of events that includes the extinction of dinosaurs as one component. Thus it makes little sense, though it may fuel our desire to view mammals as inevitable inheritors of the earth, to guess that dinosaurs died because small mammals ate their eggs (a perennial favorite among untestable speculations). It seems most unlikely that some disaster peculiar to dinosaurs befell these massive beasts—and that the debacle happened to strike just when one of history's five great dyings had enveloped the earth for completely different reasons.

The testicular theory, an old favorite from the 1940s, had its root in an interesting and thoroughly respectable study of temperature tolerances in the American alligator, published in the staid *Bulletin of the American Museum of Natural History* in 1946 by three experts on living and fossil reptiles—E. H. Colbert, my own first teacher in paleontology; R. B. Cowles; and C. M. Bogert.

The first sentence of their summary reveals a purpose beyond alligators: "This report describes an attempt to infer the reactions of extinct reptiles, especially the dinosaurs, to high temperatures as based upon reactions observed in the modern alligator." They studied, by rectal thermometry, the body temperatures of alligators under changing conditions of heating and cooling. (Well, let's face it, you wouldn't want to try sticking a thermometer under a 'gator's tongue.) The predictions under test go way back to an old theory first stated by Galileo in the 1630s—the unequal scaling of surfaces and volumes. As an animal, or an object, grows (provided its shape doesn't change), surface areas must increase more slowly than volumes—since surfaces get larger as length squared, while volumes increase much more rapidly, as length cubed. Therefore, small animals have high ratios of surface to volume, while large animals cover themselves with relatively little surface.

Among cold-blooded animals lacking any physiological mechanism for keeping their temperatures constant, small creatures have a hell of a time keeping warm—because they lose so much heat through their relatively large surfaces. On the other hand, large animals, with their relatively small surfaces, may lose heat so slowly that, once warm, they may maintain effectively constant temperatures against ordinary fluctuations of climate. (In fact, the resolution of the "hot-blooded dinosaur" controversy that burned so brightly a few years back may simply be that, while large dinosaurs possessed no physiological mechanism for constant temperature, and were not therefore warm-blooded in the technical sense, their large size and relatively small surface area kept them warm.)

Colbert, Cowles, and Bogert compared the warming rates of small and large alligators. As predicted, the small fellows heated up (and cooled down) more quickly. When exposed to a warm sun, a tiny 50-gram (1.76-ounce) alligator heated up one degree Celsius every minute and a half, while a large alligator, 260 times bigger at 13,000 grams (28.7 pounds), took seven and a half minutes to gain a degree. Extrapolating up to an adult 10-ton dinosaur,

10

they concluded that a one-degree rise in body temperature would take eighty-six hours. If large animals absorb heat so slowly (through their relatively small surfaces), they will also be unable to shed any excess heat gained when temperatures rise above a favorable level.

The authors then guessed that large dinosaurs lived at or near their optimum temperatures; Cowles suggested that a rise in global temperatures just before the Cretaceous extinction caused the dinosaurs to heat up beyond their optimal tolerance—and, being so large, they couldn't shed the unwanted heat. (In a most unusual statement within a scientific paper, Colbert and Bogert then explicitly disavowed this speculative extension of their empirical work on alligators.) Cowles conceded that this excess heat probably wasn't enough to kill or even to enervate the great beasts, but since testes often function only within a narrow range of temperature, he proposed that this global rise might have sterilized all the males, causing extinction by natural contraception.

The overdose theory has recently been supported by UCLA psychiatrist Ronald K. Siegel. Siegel has gathered, he claims, more than 2,000 records of animals who, when given access, administer various drugs to themselves—from a mere swig of alcohol to massive doses of the big H. Elephants will swill the equivalent of twenty beers at a time, but do not like alcohol in concentrations greater than 7 percent. In a silly bit of anthropocentric speculation, Siegel states that "elephants drink, perhaps, to forget . . . the anxiety produced by shrinking rangeland and the competition for food."

Since fertile imaginations can apply almost any hot idea to the extinction of dinosaurs, Siegel found a way. Flowering plants did not evolve until late in the dinosaurs' reign. These plants also produced an array of aromatic, amino-acid-based alkaloids—the major group of psychoactive agents. Most mammals are "smart" enough to avoid these potential poisons. The alkaloids simply don't taste good (they are bitter); in any case, we mammals have livers happily supplied with the capacity to detoxify them. But, Siegel speculates, perhaps dinosaurs could neither taste the bitterness nor detoxify the substances once ingested. He recently told members of the American Psychological Association: "I'm not suggesting that all dinosaurs OD'd on plant drugs, but it certainly was a factor." He also argued that death by overdose may help explain why so many dinosaur fossils are found in contorted positions. (Do not go gentle into that good night.)

Extraterrestrial catastrophes have long pedigrees in the popular literature of extinction, but the subject exploded again in 1979, after a long lull, when the father-son, physicist-geologist team of Luis and Walter Alvarez proposed that an asteroid, some 10 km in diameter, struck the earth 65 million years ago (comets, rather than asteroids, have since gained favor. Good science is self-corrective).

The force of such a collision would be immense, greater by far than the megatonnage of all the world's nuclear weapons. In trying to reconstruct a scenario that would explain the simultaneous dying of dinosaurs on land

and so many creatures in the sea, the Alvarezes proposed that a gigantic dust cloud, generated by particles blown aloft in the impact, would so darken the earth that photosynthesis would cease and temperatures drop precipitously. (Rage, rage against the dying of the light.) The single-celled photosynthetic oceanic plankton, with life cycles measured in weeks, would perish outright, but land plants might survive through the dormancy of their seeds (land plants were not much affected by the Cretaceous extinction, and any adequate theory must account for the curious pattern of differential survival). Dinosaurs would die by starvation and freezing; small, warm-blooded mammals, with more modest requirements for food and better regulation of body temperature, would squeak through. "Let the bastards freeze in the dark," as bumper stickers of our chauvinistic neighbors in sunbelt states proclaimed several years ago during the Northeast's winter oil crisis.

All three theories, testicular malfunction, psychoactive overdosing, and asteroidal zapping, grab our attention mightily. As pure phenomenology, they rank about equally high on any hit parade of primal fascination. Yet one represents expansive science, the others restrictive and untestable speculation. The proper criterion lies in evidence and methodology; we must probe behind the superficial fascination of particular claims.

How could we possibly decide whether the hypothesis of testicular frying is right or wrong? We would have to know things that the fossil record cannot provide. What temperatures were optimal for dinosaurs? Could they avoid the absorption of excess heat by staying in the shade, or in caves? At what temperatures did their testicles cease to function? Were late Cretaceous climates ever warm enough to drive the internal temperatures of dinosaurs close to this ceiling? Testicles simply don't fossilize, and how could we infer their temperature tolerances even if they did? In short, Cowles's hypothesis is only an intriguing speculation leading nowhere. The most damning statement against it appeared right in the conclusion of Colbert, Cowles, and Bogert's paper, when they admitted: "It is difficult to advance any definite arguments against the hypothesis." My statement may seem paradoxical—isn't a hypothesis really good if you can't devise any arguments against it? Quite the contrary. It is simply untestable and unusable.

Siegel's overdosing has even less going for it. At least Cowles extrapolated his conclusion from some good data on alligators. And he didn't completely violate the primary guideline of siting dinosaur extinction in the context of a general mass dying—for rise in temperature could be the root cause of a general catastrophe, zapping dinosaurs by testicular malfunction and different groups for other reasons. But Siegel's speculation cannot touch the extinction of ammonites or oceanic plankton (diatoms make their own food with good sweet sunlight; they don't OD on the chemicals of terrestrial plants). It is simply a gratuitous, attention-grabbing guess. It cannot be tested, for how can we know what dinosaurs tasted and what their livers could do? Livers don't fossilize any better than testicles.

The hypothesis doesn't even make any sense in its own context. Angiosperms were in full flower ten million years before dinosaurs went the

20

way of all flesh. Why did it take so long? As for the pains of a chemical death recorded in contortions of fossils, I regret to say (or rather I'm pleased to note for the dinosaurs' sake) that Siegel's knowledge of geology must be a bit deficient: muscles contract after death and geological strata rise and fall with motions of the earth's crust after burial—more than enough reason to distort a fossil's pristine appearance.

The impact story, on the other hand, has a sound basis in evidence. It can be tested, extended, refined, and, if wrong, disproved. The Alvarezes did not just construct an arresting guess for public consumption. They proposed their hypothesis after laborious geochemical studies with Frank Asaro and Helen Michael had revealed a massive increase of iridium in rocks deposited right at the time of extinction. Iridium, a rare metal of the platinum group, is virtually absent from indigenous rocks of the earth's crust; most of our iridium arrives on extraterrestrial objects that strike the earth.

The Alverez hypothesis bore immediate fruit. Based originally on evidence from two European localities, it led geochemists throughout the world to examine other sediments of the same age. They found abnormally high amounts of iridium everywhere—from continental rocks of the western United States to deep sea cores from the South Atlantic.

Cowles proposed his testicular hypothesis in the mid-1940s. Where has it gone since then? Absolutely nowhere, because scientists can do nothing with it. The hypothesis must stand as a curious appendage to a solid study of alligators. Siegel's overdose scenario will also win a few press notices and fade into oblivion. The Alvarezes' asteroid falls into a different category altogether, and much of the popular commentary has missed this essential distinction by focusing on the impact and its attendant results, and forgetting what really matters to a scientist—the iridium. If you talk just about asteroids, dust, and darkness, you tell stories no better and no more entertaining than fried testicles or terminal trips. It is the iridium—the source of testable evidence—that counts and forges the crucial distinction between speculation and science.

The proof, to twist a phrase, lies in the doing. Cowles's hypothesis has generated nothing in thirty-five years. Since its proposal in 1979, the Alvarez hypothesis has spawned hundreds of studies, a major conference, and attendant publications. Geologists are fired up. They are looking for iridium at all other extinction boundaries. Every week exposes a new wrinkle in the scientific press. Further evidence that the Cretaceous iridium represents extraterrestrial impact and not indigenous volcanism continues to accumulate. As I revise this essay in November 1984 (this paragraph will be out of date when the book is published),[1] new data include chemical "signatures" of other isotopes indicating unearthly provenance, glass spherules of a size and sort produced by impact and not by volcanic eruptions, and high-pressure varieties of silica formed (so far as we know) only under the tremendous shock of impact.

25

---

[1]*The Flamingo's Smile* (1985), in which Gould collected this essay.—EDS.

My point is simply this: Whatever the eventual outcome (I suspect it will be positive), the Alvarez hypothesis is exciting, fruitful science because it generates tests, provides us with things to do, and expands outward. We are having fun, battling back and forth, moving toward a resolution, and extending the hypothesis beyond its original scope.

As just one example of the unexpected, distant cross-fertilization that good science engenders, the Alvarez hypothesis made a major contribution to a theme that has riveted public attention in the past few months — so-called nuclear winter. In a speech delivered in April 1982, Luis Alvarez calculated the energy that a ten-kilometer asteroid would release on impact. He compared such an explosion with a full nuclear exchange and implied that all-out atomic war might unleash similar consequences.

This theme of impact leading to massive dust clouds and falling temperatures formed an important input to the decision of Carl Sagan and a group of colleagues to model the climatic consequences of nuclear holocaust. Full nuclear exchange would probably generate the same kind of dust cloud and darkening that may have wiped out the dinosaurs. Temperatures would drop precipitously and agriculture might become impossible. Avoidance of nuclear war is fundamentally an ethical and political imperative, but we must know the factual consequences to make firm judgments. I am heartened by a final link across disciplines and deep concerns — another criterion, by the way, of science at its best.[2] A recognition of the very phenomenon that made our evolution possible by exterminating the previously dominant dinosaurs and clearing a way for the evolution of large mammals, including us, might actually help to save us from joining those magnificent beasts in contorted poses among the strata of the earth.

The Reader's Presence

1. Although the title of Gould's essay focuses on the extinction of dinosaurs, his overriding interest is in demonstrating the way science works, and his purpose is to make that process fully accessible and understandable to the general public. Where does he lay out this central claim, and how does he demonstrate, clarify, and complicate it as his essay proceeds?

2. Reread Gould's essay, with special attention to his use of tone, diction, syntax, and metaphor. How does he use these compositional strategies to make information accessible to his readers? Point to passages where Gould uses the diction and syntax of a serious scientist. When — and with what effects — does his prose sound

---

[2]This quirky connection so tickles my fancy that I break my own strict rule about eliminating redundancies from [this essay]. . . .

more colloquial? Does his tone remain consistent throughout the essay? If not, when and how does it change? With what effects?

3. What distinctions does Gould draw among "testable proposals," "intriguing ideas," and "useless speculation"? What features of each does he identify? How does Gould encourage critical thinking in his reader? Compare his tactics to those of Malcolm Gladwell in "Big and Bad" (page 432). Where does each writer use humor to "translate" for the reader facts that might otherwise seem arcane?

Linda Hogan

Dwellings

The writer and educator Linda Hogan was born in Colorado in 1947. A member of the Chickasaw nation, she is active in Native American communities and in environmental politics. Hogan has published essays, plays, short stories, and many volumes of poetry, including most recently The Book of Medicines *(1993). Her novels* Mean Spirit *(1990),* Solar Storms *(1995), and* Power *(1998) have been celebrated for their complex and compelling representation of Native Americans. Hogan's interest in narrative and the natural environment is represented in the essay included here, which appears in her book* Dwellings: Reflections on the Natural World *(1995). Her most recent publications include* Intimate Nature: The Bond between Women and Animals *(1997), which she coedited, and a memoir,* The Woman Who Watches over the World *(2001). She has taught at the University of Minnesota and recently retired as a professor of English at the University of Colorado at Boulder.*

Hogan has said, "My writing comes from and goes back to the community, both the human and the global community. I am interested in the deepest questions, those of spirit, of shelter, of growth and movement toward peace and liberation, inner and outer."

Not far from where I live is a hill that was cut into by the moving water of a creek. Eroded this way, all that's left of it is a broken wall of earth that contains old roots and pebbles woven together and exposed. Seen from a distance, it is only a rise of raw earth. But up close it is something wonderful, a small cliff dwelling that looks almost as intricate and well made as those the Anasazi left behind when they vanished mysteriously centuries ago. This hill is a place that could be the starry skies at night turned inward into the thousand round holes where solitary bees have lived and died. It is a hill of tunneling rooms. At the mouths of some of the excavations, half-circles of clay beetle out like awnings shading a doorway. It is earth that was turned to clay in the mouths of the bees and spit out as they mined deeper into their dwelling places.

This place is where the bees reside at an angle safe from rain. It faces the southern sun. It is a warm and intelligent architecture of memory, learned by whatever memory lives in the blood. Many of the holes still contain gold husks of dead bees, their faces dry and gone, their flat eyes gazing out from death's land toward the other uninhabited half of the hill that is across the creek from the catacombs.

The first time I found the residence of the bees, it was dusty summer. The sun was hot, and land was the dry color of rust. Now and then a car rumbled along the dirt road and dust rose up behind it before settling back down on older dust. In the silence, the bees made a soft droning hum. They were alive then, and working the hill, going out and returning with pollen, in and out through the holes, back and forth between daylight and the cooler, darker regions of the inner earth. They were flying an invisible map through air, a map charted by landmarks, the slant of light, and a circling story they told one another about the direction of food held inside the center of yellow flowers.

Sitting in the hot sun, watching the small bees fly in and out around the hill, hearing the summer birds, the light breeze, I felt right in the world. I belonged there. I thought of my own dwelling places, those real and those imagined. Once I lived in a town called Manitou, which means "Great Spirit," and where hot mineral springwater gurgled beneath the streets and rose into open wells. I felt safe there. With the underground movement of water and heat a constant reminder of other life, of what lives beneath us, it seemed to be the center of the world.

A few years after that, I wanted silence. My daydreams were full of   5
places I longed to be, shelters and solitudes. I wanted a room apart from others, a hidden cabin to rest in. I wanted to be in a redwood forest with trees so tall the owls called out in the daytime. I daydreamed of living in a vapor cave a few hours away from here. Underground, warm, and moist, I thought it would be the perfect world for staying out of cold winter, for escaping the noise of living.

And how often I've wanted to escape to a wilderness where a human hand has not been in everything. But those were only dreams of peace, of comfort, of a nest inside stone or woods, a sanctuary where a dream or life wouldn't be invaded.

Years ago, in the next canyon west of here, there was a man who followed one of those dreams and moved into a cave that could only be reached by climbing down a rope. For years he lived there in comfort, like a troglodite. The inner weather was stable, never too hot, too cold, too wet, or too dry. But then he felt lonely. His utopia needed a woman. He went to town until he found a wife. For a while after the marriage, his wife climbed down the rope along with him, but before long she didn't want the mice scurrying about in the cave, or the untidy bats that wanted to hang from the stones of the ceiling. So they built a door. Because of the closed entryway, the temperature changed. They had to put in heat. Then the inner moisture of earth warped the door, so they had to have air-conditioning, and after that the earth wanted to go about life in its own way and it didn't give in to the people.

In other days and places, people paid more attention to the strong-headed will of earth. Once homes were built of wood that had been felled from a single region in a forest. That way, it was thought, the house would hold together more harmoniously, and the family of walls would not fall or lend themselves to the unhappiness or arguments of the inhabitants.

An Italian immigrant to Chicago, Aldo Piacenzi, built birdhouses that were dwellings of harmony and peace. They were the incredible spired shapes of cathedrals in Italy. They housed not only the birds, but also his memories, his own past. He painted them the watery blue of his Mediterranean, the wild rose of flowers in a summer field. Inside them was straw and the droppings of lives that layed eggs, fledglings who grew there. What places to inhabit, the bright and sunny birdhouses in dreary alleyways of the city.

One beautiful afternoon, cool and moist, with the kind of yellow   10
light that falls on earth in these arid regions, I waited for barn swallows to return from their daily work of food gathering. Inside the tunnel where they live, hundreds of swallows had mixed their saliva with mud and clay, much like the solitary bees, and formed nests that were perfect as a potter's bowl. At five in the evening, they returned all at once, a dark, flying shadow. Despite their enormous numbers and the crowding together of nests, they didn't pause for even a moment before entering the nests, nor did they crowd one another. Instantly they vanished into the nests. The tunnel went silent. It held no outward signs of life.
But I knew they were there, filled with the fire of living. And what a marriage of elements was in those nests. Not only mud's earth and water, the fire of sun and dry air, but even the elements contained one another. The bodies of prophets and crazy men were broken down in that soil.

I've noticed often how when a house is abandoned, it begins to sag. Without a tenant, it has no need to go on. If it were a person, we'd say it is depressed or lonely. The roof settles in, the paint cracks, the walls and floorboards warp and slope downward in their own natural ways, telling us that life must stay in everything as the world whirls and tilts and moves through boundless space.

One summer day, cleaning up after long-eared owls where I work at a rehabilitation facility for birds of prey, I was raking the gravel floor of a flight cage. Down on the ground, something looked like it was moving. I bent over to look into the pile of bones and pellets I'd just raked together. There, close to the ground, were two fetal mice. They were new to the planet, pink and hairless. They were so tenderly young. Their faces had swollen blue-veined eyes. They were nestled in a mound of feathers, soft as velvet, each one curled up smaller than an infant's ear, listening to the first sounds of earth. But the ants were biting them. They turned in agony, unable to pull away, not yet having the arms or legs to move, but feeling, twisting away from, the pain of the bites. I was horrified to see them bitten out of life that way. I dipped them in water, as if to take away the sting, and let the ants fall in the bucket. Then I held the tiny mice in the palm of my hand. Some of the ants were drowning in the water. I was trading one life for another, exchanging the lives of the ants for those of mice, but I hated their suffering, and hated even more that they had not yet grown to a life, and already they inhabited the miserable world of pain. Death and life feed each other. I know that.

Inside these rooms where birds are healed, there are other lives besides those of mice. There are fine gray globes the wasps have woven together, the white cocoons of spiders in a corner, the downward tunneling anthills. All these dwellings are inside one small walled space, but I think most about the mice. Sometimes the downy nests fall out of the walls where their mothers have placed them out of the way of their enemies. When one of the nests falls, they are so well made and soft, woven mostly from the chest feathers of birds. Sometimes the leg of a small quail holds the nest together like a slender cornerstone with dry, bent claws. The mice have adapted to life in the presence of their enemies, adapted to living in the thin wall between beak and beak, claw and claw. They move their nests often, as if a new rafter or wall will protect them from the inevitable fate of all our returns home to the deeper, wider nests of earth that houses us all.

One August at Zia Pueblo during the corn dance I noticed tourists   15
picking up shards of all the old pottery that had been made and broken there. The residents of Zia know not to take the bowls and pots left behind by the older ones. They know that the fragments of those earlier lives need to be smoothed back to earth, but younger nations, travelers from continents across the world who have come to inhabit this land, have little of their own to grow on. The pieces of earth that were formed into bowls, even on their way home to dust, provide the new people a lifeline to an unknown land, help them remember that they live in the old nest of earth.

It was in early February, during the mating season of the great horned owl. It was dusk, and I hiked up the back of a mountain to where I'd heard the owls a year before. I wanted to hear them again, the voices so tender, so deep, like a memory of comfort. I was halfway up the trail when I found a soft, round nest. It had fallen from one of the bare-branched trees. It was a delicate nest, woven together of feathers, sage, and strands of wild grass. Holding it in my hand in the rosy twilight, I noticed that a blue thread was entwined with the other gatherings there. I pulled at the thread a little, and then I recognized it. It was a thread from one of my skirts. It was blue cotton. It was the unmistakable color and shape of a pattern I knew. I liked it, that a thread of my life was in an abandoned nest, one that had held eggs and new life. I took the nest home. At home, I held it to the light and looked more closely. There, to my surprise, nestled into the gray-green sage, was a gnarl of black hair. It was also unmistakable. It was my daughter's hair, cleaned from a brush and picked up out in the sun beneath the maple tree, or the pit cherry where the birds eat from the overladen, fertile branches until only the seeds remain on the trees.

I didn't know what kind of nest it was, or who had lived there. It didn't matter. I thought of the remnants of our lives carried up the hill that way and turned into shelter. That night, resting inside the walls of our home, the world outside weighed so heavily against the thin wood of the house. The sloped roof was the only thing between us and the universe. Everything outside of our wooden boundaries seemed so large. Filled with the night's citizens, it all came alive. The world opened in the thickets of the dark. The wild grapes would soon ripen on the vines. The burrowing ones were emerging. Horned owls sat in treetops. Mice scurried here and there. Skunks, fox, the slow and holy porcupine, all were passing by this way. The young of the solitary bees were feeding on the pollen in the dark. The whole world was a nest on its humble tilt, in the maze of the universe, holding us.

The Reader's Presence

1. In each of the vignettes that make up this essay, Hogan contemplates the meaning of various dwellings. What are the specific characteristics of a dwelling place for Hogan? Who lives there? How does each dwelling suit and serve its inhabitants? Why does Hogan describe dwellings for animals as well as dwellings for humans? With what effect(s)? To what extent and in what ways do the two overlap? What are the advantages—and the disadvantages—of Hogan's having chosen to contemplate death as well as life in this essay about where we live? How would you characterize the vision of life, death, and the universe that emerges from this essay?

2. Reread carefully the story about the cave dweller and his wife told in paragraph 7. To what extent does Hogan encourage her readers to take the story literally? At what point does it begin to take on the qualities of myth or fable? Compare and contrast this story with the biblical story of Adam and Eve, and their fall from the Garden of Eden. To whom, or to what impulse(s), can each fall be attributed? How are women characterized in the respective stories?

How are the endings similar, and where do they diverge? Based on your comparative analysis of these stories, what inferences might you draw about the Native American and Judeo-Christian world-views?

3. Identify and discuss the various analogies Hogan draws throughout the essay. Where does she compare dwellings made by animals to human-made artifacts? human-made dwellings to natural phenomena? the animate to the inanimate? What are the effects of this interweaving of processes, objects, and species? In the following essay, John Hollander writes that "such representations of disorder as lists, paintings, photos, etc., all compromise the purity of true messiness by the verbal or visual order they impose on the confusion" ("Mess," see following selection). What form of order does Hogan's essay "impose" on the natural places in phenomena she discovers? Is "impose" the right word? If not, what verb would you substitute to describe Hogan's writing?

John Hollander

Mess

John Hollander (b. 1929) is one of the leading poets and literary scholars in the United States. Since his first book, Crackling of Thorns *(1958), he has published more than twenty collections of his poetry, including his more recent works,* The Poetry of Everyday Life *(1999),* Figurehead and Other Poems *(1999), and* Picture Window *(2003). He has also edited numerous anthologies, including* War Poems *(1999),* Sonnets: From Dante to the Present *(2001),* American Wits *(2003), and his latest,* Poetry for Young People: Animal Poems *(2004). His 1997 collection of literary criticism,* The Work of Poetry, *won the Robert Penn Warren–Cleanth Brooks award. After a decades-long teaching career, Hollander is now the Sterling Professor Emeritus English at Yale University. His poems and prose continue to appear regularly in the* New Yorker, *the* Partisan Review, *Esquire, and other magazines and journals. The essay "Mess" appeared in the* Yale Review *in 1995.*

Commenting on the experience of writing both poetry and prose, Hollander notes, "Ordinarily, the prose I write is critical or scholarly, where there is some occasion (a lecture to be given, a longish review to be done, etc.) to elicit the piece of writing. My most important writing is my poetry, which is not occasional in these ways. . . . This brief essay was generated more from within, like a poem, than most other prose of mine—nobody asked me to write it, but I felt impelled to observe something about one aspect of life that tends to get swept under the rug, as it were."

Mess is a state of mind. Or rather, messiness is a particular relation between the state of arrangement of a collection of things and a state of mind that contemplates it in its containing space. For example, X's mess may be Y's delight—sheer profusion, uncompromised by any apparent structure even in the representation of it. Or there may be some inner order or logic to A's mess that B cannot possibly perceive. Consider: someone—Alpha—rearranges all the books on Beta's library shelf, which have been piled or stacked, sometimes properly, sometimes not, but all in relevant sequence (by author and, within that, by date of publication), and rearranges them neatly, by size and color. Beta surveys the result, and can only feel, if not blurt out, "WHAT A MESS!" This situation often occurs with respect to messes of the workplace generally.

For there are many kinds of mess, both within walls and outside them: neglected gardens and the aftermath of tropical storms, and the indoor kinds of disorder peculiar to specific areas of our life with, and in and among, *things*. There are messes of one's own making, messes not even of one's own person, places, or things. There are personal states of mind about common areas of messiness—those of the kitchen, the bedroom, the bathroom, the salon (of whatever sort, from half a bed-sitter[1] to some grand public parlor), or those of personal appearance (clothes, hair, etc.). Then, for all those who are in any way self-employed or whose avocations are practiced in some private space—a workshop, a dark-room, a study or a studio—there is a mess of the workplace. It's not the most common kind of mess, but it's exemplary: the eye surveying it is sickened by the roller-coaster of scanning the scene. And, alas, it's the one I'm most afflicted with.

I know that things are really in a mess when—as about ninety seconds ago—I reach for the mouse on my Macintosh and find instead a thick layer of old envelopes, manuscript notes consulted three weeks ago, favorite pens and inoperative ones, folders used hastily and not replaced, and so forth. In order to start working, I brush these accumulated impedimenta aside, thus creating a new mess. But this is, worse yet, absorbed by the general condition of my study: piles of thin books and thick books, green volumes of the Loeb Classical Library and slimy paperbacks of ephemeral spy-thrillers, mostly used notebooks, bills paid and unpaid, immortal letters from beloved friends, unopened and untrashed folders stuffed with things that should be in various other folders, book-mailing envelopes, unanswered mail whose cries for help and attention are muffled by three months' worth of bank statements enshrouding them in the gloom of continued neglect. Even this fairly orderly inventory seems to simplify the confusion: in actuality, searching for a letter or a page of manuscript in this state of things

---

[1]*bed-sitter:* A combined bedroom and sitting room.—EDS.

involves crouching down with my head on one side and searching vertically along the outside of a teetering pile for what may be a thin, hidden layer of it.

Displacement, and lack of design, are obscured in the origins of our very word *mess*. The famous biblical "mess of red pottage" (lentil mush or dal) for which Esau sold his birthright wasn't "messy" in our sense (unless, of course, in the not very interesting case of Esau having dribbled it on his clothing). The word meant a serving of food, or a course in a meal: something *placed* in front of you (from the Latin *missis*, put or placed), hence "messmates" (dining companions) and ultimately "officers' mess" and the like. It also came to mean a dish of prepared mixed food—like an *olla podrida* or a minestrone—then by extension (but only from the early nineteenth century on) any hodge-podge: inedible, and outside the neat confines of a bowl or pot, and thus unpleasant, confusing, and agitating or depressing to contemplate. But for us, the association with food perhaps remains only in how much the state of mind of being messy is like that of being fat: for example, X says, "God, I'm getting gross! I'll have to diet!" Y, *really* fat, cringes on hearing this, and feels that for the slender X to talk that way is an obscenity. Similarly, X: "God, this place is a pigsty!" Y: (ditto). For a person prone to messiness, Cyril Connolly's celebrated observation about fat people is projected onto the world itself: inside every neat arrangement is a mess struggling to break out, like some kind of statue of chaos lying implicit in the marble of apparent organization.

In Paradise, there was no such thing as messiness. This was partly because unfallen, ideal life needed no supplemental *things*—objects of use and artifice, elements of any sort of technology. Thus there was nothing to leave lying around, messily or even neatly, by Adam and Eve—according to Milton—"at their savory dinner set / Of herbs and other country messes." But it was also because order, hence orderliness, was itself so natural that whatever bit of nature Adam and Eve might have been occupied with, or even using in a momentary tool-like way, flew or leapt or crept into place in some sort of reasonable arrangement, even as in our unparadised state things *fall* under the joyless tug of gravity. But messiness may seem to be an inevitable state of the condition of having so many *things*, precious or disposable, in one's life.

As I observed before, even to describe a mess is to impose order on it. The ancient Greek vision of primal chaos, even, was not *messy* in that it was pre-messy: there weren't any categories by which to define order, so that there could be no disorder—no nextness or betweenness, no above, below, here, there, and so forth. *"Let there be light"* meant "Let there be perception of something," and it was then that order became possible, and mess possibly implied. Now, a list or inventory is in itself an orderly literary form, and even incoherent assemblages of items fall too easily into some other kind of order: in *Through the Looking-Glass*, the Walrus's "Of shoes and ships, and sealing wax, / Of cabbages, and kings," is

5

given a harmonious structure by the pairs of alliterating words, and even by the half-punning association of "ships, [sailing] sealing wax." The wonderful catalogue in *Tom Sawyer* of the elements of what must have been, pocketed or piled on the ground, a mess of splendid proportions, is a poem of its own. The objects of barter for a stint of fence whitewashing (Tom, it will be remembered, turns *having* to do a chore into *getting* to do it by sheer con-man's insouciance) comprise

> twelve marbles, part of a jewsharp, a piece of blue bottle-glass to look through, a spool cannon, a key that wouldn't unlock anything, a frag-ment of chalk, a glass stopper of a decanter, a tin soldier, a couple of tadpoles, six fire-crackers, a kitten with only one eye, a brass door-knob, a dog collar—but no dog—the handle of a knife, four pieces of orange peel, and a dilapidated old window sash.

Thus such representations of disorder as lists, paintings, photos, etc., all compromise the purity of true messiness by the verbal or visual order they impose on the confusion. To get at the mess in my study, for exam-ple, a movie might serve best, alternately mixing mid-shot and zoom on a particular portion of the disaster, which would, in an almost fractal way, seem to be a mini-disaster of its own. There are even neatly convention-alized emblems of messiness that are, after all, all too neat: thus, whenever a movie wants to show an apartment or office that has been ransacked by Baddies (cop Baddies or baddy Baddies or whatever) in search of the Thing They Want, the designer is always careful to show at least one pic-ture on the wall hanging carefully askew. All this could possibly tell us about a degree of messiness is that the searchers were so messy (at an-other level of application of the term) in their technique that they violated their search agenda to run over to the wall and tilt the picture (very messy procedure indeed), or that, hastily leaving the scene to avoid detection, they nonetheless took a final revenge against the Occupant for not having the Thing on his or her premises, and tilted the picture in a fit of pique. And yet a tilted picture gives good cueing mileage: it can present a good bit of disorder at the expense of a minimum of misalignment, after all.

A meditation on mess could be endless. As I struggle to conclude this one, one of my cats regards me from her nest in and among one of the dis-aster areas that all surfaces in my study soon become. Cats disdain messes in several ways. First, they are proverbially neat about their shit and the condition of their fur. Second, they pick their way so elegantly among my piles of books, papers, and ancillary objects (dishes of paper clips, scissors, functional and dried-out pens, crumpled envelopes, outmoded postage stamps, boxes of slides and disks, staplers, glue bottles, tape dispensers— *you* know) that they cannot even be said to acknowledge the mess's exis-tence. The gray familiar creature currently making her own order out of a region of mess on my desk—carefully disposing herself around and over and among piles and bunches and stacks and crazily oblique layers and thereby reinterpreting it as natural landscape—makes me further despair until I realize that what she does with her body, I must do with my perception of this inevitable disorder—shaping its forms to the disorder and thereby shaping the disorder to its forms. She has taught me resignation.

The Reader's Presence

1. In the second sentence of his essay, Hollander defines "mess" as "a particular relation between the state of arrangement of a collection of things and a state of mind that contemplates it in its containing space." How would you paraphrase Hollander's definition? To what extent does his definition echo proverbs and traditional sayings such as "beauty is in the eye of the beholder"? What does Hollander's definition add to this kind of general insight about the observer? What role do "things" play in messiness, and what role is played by the person who contemplates them? Examine carefully the many observers mentioned in this essay, from the hypothetical X and Y in the first paragraph to the real cat in the final paragraph. What are their various reactions to the seeming disorder around them?

2. Hollander traces the origins of the word *mess* in paragraph 4. What is the connection between its original meaning and the meaning it took on "by extension" in the nineteenth century? According to Hollander, how does the state of mind of being messy correspond to the state of mind of being fat? He follows this association with yet another: the sculpture lying latent within the marble. Examine carefully—and then comment on—the way each analogy leads by association into the next and the effect of this series of associations.

3. Hollander's project is complicated by the fact that he has chosen to define a word that is enmeshed in his own writing process and product. How does the act of describing the "mess" on his desk (paragraph 3) alter the nature of the scene he describes? Is it, according to the author, even possible to do justice to a mess in written terms?

4. Consider the fluctuation between control and lack of control manifested not only in the subject of the essay but in the essay itself. Based on your analysis, how would you compare and contrast the degree of order in Hollander's study and in his writing? Is Hollander's essay a mess? Where are its messy passages? Why does Hollander find himself struggling to end the essay (paragraph 8)? Reread Jamaica Kincaid's essay, "Biography of a Dress" (page 175), in the light of Hollander's remarks. How does Kincaid contain or fail to contain the messiness of her memories? Are you bothered by or attracted to writing that is "tilted" or "misaligned"? Why?

Pico Iyer

Living in the Transit Lounge

Pico Iyer (b. 1957), travel writer, critic, and novelist, was born in Oxford, England, of Indian parents, raised in both his family's home in California and a boarding school in England, and educated at Oxford University and Harvard. Known for his travel writing, Iyer describes himself, somewhat ruefully, as "a mongrel" and a global soul among the many who exist in and between multiple cultures "and so fall in the cracks between them." Iyer's travel books include Video Night in Kathmandu *(1988),* The Lady and the Monk *(1991),* Falling off the Map *(1993),* Tropical Classical *(1997),* The Global Soul *(2000), and* Sun after Dark *(2004). He also edited* Best American Travel Writing 2004 *and co-edited* Salon.com's Wanderlust *(2000). He has written two novels,* Cuba and the Night *(1996) and* Abandon *(2003).*

Iyer has explained, "Writing should be an act of communication more than of mere self-expression—a telling of a story rather than a flourishing of skills. The less conscious one is of being 'a writer,' the better the writing." He first presented "Living in the Transit Lounge" as a talk at Yale University in January 1993. Versions of the essay have appeared in Harper's *and the* Utne Reader.

By the time I was nine, I was already used to going to school by trans-Atlantic plane, to sleeping in airports, to shuttling back and forth, three times a year, between my parents' (Indian) home in California and my boarding-school in England. Throughout the time I was growing up, I was never within 6,000 miles of the nearest relative—and came, therefore, to learn how to define relations in non-familial ways. From the time I was a teenager, I took it for granted that I could take my budget vacations (as I did) in Bolivia and Tibet, China and Morocco. It never seemed strange to me that a girl-friend might be half a world (or ten hours flying-time) away, that my closest friends might be on the other side of a continent or sea.

It was only recently that I realized that all these habits of mind and life would scarcely have been imaginable in my parents' youth; that the very facts and facilities that shape my world are all distinctly new developments, and mark me as a modern type.

It was only recently, in fact, that I realized that I am an example, perhaps, of an entirely new breed of people, a trans-continental tribe of wanderers that is multiplying as fast as IDD lines and IATA flights.[1] We

---

[1] *IDD lines and IATA flights:* International Direct Dialing telephone lines allow calls between countries without an operator's assistance. The International Air Transport Association is a trade group for the airline industry that offers frequent-flier programs and other amenities for travelers. —EDS.

are the Transit Loungers, forever heading to the Departure Gate, forever orbiting the world. We buy our interests duty-free, we eat our food on plastic plates, we watch the world through borrowed headphones. We pass through countries as through revolving doors, resident aliens of the world, impermanent residents of nowhere. Nothing is strange to us, and nowhere is foreign. We are visitors even in our own homes.

This is not, I think, a function of affluence so much as of simple circumstance. I am not, that is, a jet-setter pursuing vacations from Marbella to Phuket; I am simply a fairly typical product of a movable sensibility, living and working in a world that is itself increasingly small and increasingly mongrel. I am a multi-national soul on a multi-cultural globe where more and more countries are as polyglot and restless as airports. Taking planes seems as natural to me as picking up the phone, or going to school; I fold up my self and carry it round with me as if it were an overnight case.

The modern world seems increasingly made for people like me. I can plop myself down anywhere and find myself in the same relation of familiarity and strangeness: Lusaka, after all, is scarcely more strange to me than the foreigners' England in which I was born, the America where I am registered as an "alien," and the almost unvisited India that people tell me is my home. I can fly from London to San Francisco to Osaka and feel myself no more a foreigner in one place than another; all of them are just locations—pavilions in some intercontinental Expo—and I can work or live or love in any one of them. All have Holiday Inns, direct-dial phones, CNN and DHL. All have sushi and Thai restaurants, Kentucky Fried Chicken and Coke. My office is as close as the nearest FAX machine or modem. Roppongi is West Hollywood is Leblon.

This kind of life offers an unprecedented sense of freedom and mobility: tied down to nowhere, I can pick and choose among locations. Mine is the first generation that can go off to visit the Himalayas for a week, or sample life in the distant countries we have always dreamed about; ours is the first generation to be able to go to Kenya for a holiday to find our roots—or to find they are not there. At the lowest level, this new internationalism also means that I can get on a plane in Los Angeles, get off a few hours later in Jakarta, and check into a Hilton, and order a cheeseburger in English, and pay for it all with an American Express card. At the next level, it means that I can meet, in the Hilton coffee-shop, an Indonesian businessman who is as conversant as I am with Michael Kinsley and Magic Johnson and Madonna. At a deeper level, it means that I need never feel estranged. If all the world is alien to us, all the world is home.

I have learned, in fact, to love foreignness. In any place I visit, I have the privileges of an outsider: I am an object of interest, and even fascination; I am a person set apart, able to enjoy the benefits of the place without paying the taxes. And the places themselves seem glamorous to

5

me—romantic—as seen through foreign eyes: distance on both sides lends enchantment. Policemen let me off speeding tickets, girls want to hear the stories of my life, pedestrians will gladly point me to the nearest Golden Arches. Perpetual foreigners in the transit lounge, we enjoy a kind of diplomatic immunity; and, living off room service in our hotel rooms, we are never obliged to grow up, or even, really, to be ourselves.

We learn too the lesser skills of cosmopolitan life. We become relativists, sensitively aware that what goes down in Casablanca will not go down well in Cairo. We become analysts, able to see every place through an outsider's eyes, and even our homes through foreign spectacles. We become professional correspondents, adept at keeping up friendships through the mail, our affinities and sympathies scattered across all borders.

We learn, indeed, to exult in the blessings of belonging to what feels like a whole new race. It is a race, as Salman Rushdie says, of "people who root themselves in ideas rather than places, in memories as much as in material things; people who have been obliged to define themselves—because they are so defined by others—by their otherness; people in whose deepest selves strange fusions occur, unprecedented unions between what they were and where they find themselves." We learn to enjoy the fruits of international co-productions—Bertolucci movies, Peter Brook plays, Derek Walcott poems. All of us are international co-productions these days, global villages on two legs. All of us flaunt the United Colors of Benetton, with our English shoes, Japanese watches, and American terms. And when people argue that our very notion of wonder is eroded, that alienness itself is as seriously endangered as the wilderness, that more and more of the world is turning into a single synthetic monoculture, I am not worried: a Japanese version of a French fashion is something new, I say, not quite Japanese and not truly French. Comme des Garçons hybrids are the artform of the time.

And yet, sometimes, I stop myself and think. What kind of heart is   10 being produced by these new changes? And must I always be a None of the Above? When the stewardess comes down the aisle with disembarkation forms, what do I fill in? Am I an Asian-American? Even though I feel not very Asian and not at all American? An Indian American? An ambiguous term in any case, not least for one who has never lived in India, and lives in America only because it feels so little like home. My passport says one thing, my face another; my accent contradicts my eyes. Place of Residence, Final Destination, even Marital Status are not much easier to fill in; usually I just tick "Other."

And beneath all the boxes, where do we place ourselves? How does one fix a moving object on a map? I am not an exile, really, nor an immigrant; not deracinated, I think, any more than I am rooted. I have not fled the oppression of war, nor found ostracism in the places where I do alight; I scarcely feel severed from a home I have scarcely known. Is "citizen of the world" enough to comfort me? And does "feeling at home anywhere" make it easier to sleep at night?

Alienation, we are taught from kindergarten, is the condition of the time. This is the century of exiles and refugees, of boat people and statelessness; the time when traditions have been abolished, and men become closer to machines. This is the century of estrangement: more than a third of all Afghans live outside Afghanistan; the second city of the Khmers is a refugee camp; the second tongue of Belfast is Chinese. The very notion of nation-states is outdated; many of us are as cross-hatched within as Beirut.

To understand the modern state, we are often told, we must read Naipaul,[2] and see how people estranged from their cultures mimic people estranged from their roots. Naipaul is the definitive modern traveler in part because he is the definitive symbol of modern rootlessness; his singular qualification for his wanderings is not his stamina, nor his bravado, nor his love of exploration—it is, quite simply, his congenital displacement. Here is a man who was a foreigner at birth, a citizen of an exiled community set down on a colonized island. Here is a man for whom every arrival is enigmatic, a man without a home—except for an India to which he stubbornly returns, only to be reminded of his distance from it. The strength of Naipaul is the poignancy of Naipaul: the poignancy of a wanderer who tries to go home, but is not taken in, and is accepted by another home only so long as he admits that he's a lodger there.

There is, however, another way of apprehending foreignness, and that is the way of Nabokov.[3] In him we seen an avid cultivation of the novel: he collects foreign worlds with a conoisseur's delight, he sees foreign words as toys to play with, and exile as the state of kings. This touring aristocrat can even relish the pleasures of low culture precisely because they are the things that his own high culture lacks: the motel and the summer camp, the roadside attraction and the hot fudge sundae. I recognize in Naipaul a European's love for America rooted in America's very youthfulness and heedlessness and ahistoricity; I recognize in him the sense that the newcomer's viewpoint may be the one most conducive to bright ardor (a sixteen-year-old may be infinitely more interesting to a forty-year-old than to a fellow teenager). The hideous suburb that looks so vulgar from afar becomes a little warmer when one's in the thick of it. Unfamiliarity, in any form, breeds content.

Nabokov shows us that if nowhere is home, everywhere is. That 15 instead of taking alienation as our natural state, we can feel partially

---

[2]*Naipaul:* V. S. Naipaul (b. 1932), a noted British novelist who was born and raised in an Indian Community in Trinidad.—EDS.

[3]*Nabokov:* The great novelist Vladimir Nabokov (1899–1977) once described his own complex background as follows: "I am an American writer, born in Russia and educated in England, where I studied French literature, before spending fifteen years in Germany." The author of *Lolita* (1955) emigrated to the United States in 1940 and later became an American citizen.—EDS.

adjusted everywhere. That the outsider at the feast does not have to sit in the corner alone, taking notes; he can plunge into the pleasures of his new home with abandon.

We airport-hoppers can, in fact, go through the world as through a house of wonders, picking up something at every stop, and taking the whole globe as our playpen, or our supermarket (and even if we don't go to the world, the world will increasingly come to us: just down the street, almost wherever we are, are nori and salsa, tiramisu and *naan*). We don't have a home, we have a hundred homes. And we can mix and match as the situation demands. "Nobody's history is my history," Kazuo Ishiguro,[4] a great spokesman for the privileged homeless, once said to me, and then went on, "Whenever it was convenient for me to become very Japanese, I could become very Japanese, and then, when I wanted to drop it, I would just become this ordinary Englishman." Instantly, I felt a shock of recognition: I have a wardrobe of selves from which to choose. And I savor the luxury of being able to be an Indian in Cuba (where people are starving for yoga and Tagore), or an American in Thailand; to be an Englishman in New York.

And so we go on circling the world, six miles above the ground, displaced from Time, above the clouds, with all our needs attended to. We listen to announcements given in three languages. We confirm our reservations at every stop. We disembark at airports that are self-sufficient communities, with hotels, gymnasia and places of worship. At customs we have nothing to declare but ourselves.

But what is the price we pay for all of this? I sometimes think that this mobile way of life is as novel as high-rises, or the video monitors that are re-wiring our consciousness. And even as we fret about the changes our progress wreaks in the air and on the airwaves, in forests and on streets, we hardly worry about the changes it is working in ourselves, the new kind of soul that is being born out of a new kind of life. Yet this could be the most dangerous development of all, and not only because it is the least examined.

For us in the Transit Lounge, disorientation is as alien as affiliation. We become professional observers, able to see the merits and deficiencies of anywhere, to balance our parents' viewpoints with their enemies' position. Yes, we say, of course it's terrible, but look at the situation from Saddam's point of view. I understand how you feel, but the Chinese had their own cultural reasons for Tiananmen Square. Fervor comes to seem to us the most foreign place of all.

Seasoned experts at dispassion, we are less good at involvement, or   20
suspensions of disbelief; at, in fact, the abolition of distance. We are masters

[4]*Ishiguro:* The Japanese-born Kazuo Ishiguro (b. 1954) moved to Great Britain at the age of five. His books include such award-winning novels as *A Pale View of Hills* (1982) and *The Remains of the Day* (1988).—EDS.

of the aerial perspective, but touching down becomes more difficult. Unable to get stirred by the raising of a flag, we are sometimes unable to see how anyone could be stirred. I sometimes think that this is how Rushdie,[5] the great analyst of this condition, somehow became its victim. He had juggled homes for so long, so adroitly, that he forgot how the world looks to someone who is rooted—in country or belief. He had chosen to live so far from affiliation that he could no longer see why people choose affiliation in the first place. Besides, being part of no society means one is accountable to no one, and need respect no laws outside one's own. If single-nation people can be fanatical as terrorists, we can end up ineffectual as peacekeepers.

We become, in fact, strangers to belief itself, unable to comprehend many of the rages and dogmas that animate (and unite) people. Conflict itself seems inexplicable to us sometimes, simply because partisanship is; we have the agnostic's inability to retrace the steps of faith. I could not begin to fathom why some Moslems would think of murder after hearing about *The Satanic Verses*: yet sometimes I force myself to recall that it is we, in our floating skepticism, who are the exceptions, that in China and Iran, in Korea and Peru, it is not so strange to give up one's life for a cause.

We end up, then, like non-aligned nations, confirming our reservations at every step. We tell ourselves, self-servingly, that nationalism breeds monsters, and choose to ignore the fact that internationalism breeds them too. Ours is not the culpability of the assassin, but of the bystander who takes a snapshot of the murder. Or, when the revolution breaks out, hops on the next plane out.

In any case, the issues, in the Transit Lounge, are passing; a few hours from now, they'll be a thousand miles away. Besides, this is a foreign country, we have no interests here. The only thing we have to fear are hijackers—passionate people with beliefs.

Sometimes, though, just sometimes, I am brought up short by symptoms of my condition. They are not major things, but they are peculiar ones, and ones that would not have been so common fifty years ago. I have never bought a house of any kind, and my ideal domestic environment, I sometimes tell friends (with a shudder) is a hotel-room. I have never voted, or ever wanted to vote, and I eat in restaurants three times a day. I have never supported a nation (in the Olympic Games, say), or represented "my country" in anything. I refer to everyone in the third person, and seldom use the first person plural. Even my name is weirdly international, because my "real name" is one that makes sense only in the home where I have never lived.

---

[5]***Rushdie:*** After the publication of Salman Rushdie's novel *The Satanic Verses* (1988), its author Salman Rushdie (b. 1947), a British novelist born in India, was forced into hiding when the Iranian leader the Ayatollah Khomeini ordered his execution.—EDS.

I choose to live in America in part, I think, because it feels more
alien the longer I stay there (and is, of all places, the one most made up
of aliens and, to that extent, accommodating to them). I love being in
Japan because it reminds me, at every turn, of my foreignness. When I
want to see if any place is home, I must subject the candidates to a battery of tests. Home is the place of which one has memories but no expectations.

If I have any deeper home, it is, I suppose, in English. My language is
the house I carry round with me as a snail his shell; and in my lesser moments I try to forget that mine is not the language spoken in America, or
even, really, by any member of my family.

Yet even here, I find, I cannot place my accent, or reproduce it as I can
the tones of others. And I am so used to modifying my English inflections
according to whom I am talking to—an American, an Englishman, a vil-
lager in Nepal, a receptionist in Paris—that I scarcely know what kind of
voice I have.

I wonder, sometimes, if this new kind of non-affiliation may not be
alien to something fundamental in the human state. The refugee at least
harbors passionate feelings about the world he has left—and generally
seeks to return there; the exile at least is propelled by some kind of strong
emotion away from the old country and towards the new—indifference
is not an exile emotion. But what does the Transit Lounger feel? What are
the issues that we would die for? What are the passions that we would
live for?

Airports are among the only sites in public life where emotions are
hugely sanctioned, in block capitals. We see people weep, shout, kiss in
airports; we see them at the furthest edges of excitement and exhaustion.
Airports are privileged spaces where we can see the primal states writ
large—fear, recognition, hope. But there are some of us, perhaps, sitting
at the Departure Gate, boarding-passes in hand, watching the destinations
ticking over, who feel neither the pain of separation nor the exultation of
wonder; who alight with the same emotions with which we embarked; who
go down to the baggage carousel and watch our lives circling, circling, circling, waiting to be claimed.

The Reader's Presence

1. According to Iyer, what innovations and technology have brought
   about the "transcontinental tribe of wanderers"? What are the
   benefits of this lifestyle? What are the drawbacks?

2. Who is the "we" that Iyer refers to throughout the essay? What
   traits or characteristics do these people share? To what extent do
   they make up a community?

3. Transit loungers, Iyer explains, "become, in fact, strangers to belief itself, unable to comprehend many of the rages and dogmas that animate (and unite) people" (paragraph 21). Iyer suggests a world increasingly split between people without particular loyalties to cultures or homelands and those closely tied to place and culture. How does that idea resonate in Karen Armstrong's "Is a Holy War Inevitable?" (page 335)? What might be the advantages and disadvantages of having strong religious or cultural beliefs? What might be the advantages and disadvantages of feeling disconnected from a particular culture?

Sebastian Junger

Colter's Way

Sebastian Junger (b. 1962) is the author of the best-selling book The Perfect Storm *(1997). The book brought him instant recognition and was made into a feature film in 2000. Drawn to real-life adventure stories and situations tinged with danger, Junger prefers journalism to writing books: "It's a more exciting job, and it feels more relevant," he says. "And it was one of several reasons that after* The Perfect Storm, *I didn't write another book." His articles have appeared in such publications as* Vanity Fair, Outside, American Heritage, Michigan Quarterly Review, *and the* New York Times Magazine. *He has also contributed to* Men's Journal *and co-edited its anthology* Wild Stories *(2002).*

"Colter's Way" appears in Fire *(2001), a collection of Junger's articles about people in extreme situations—from the war in Kosovo to the fire-ravaged forests of Idaho.*

Late in the summer of 1808 two fur trappers named John Colter and John Potts decided to paddle up the Missouri River, deep into Blackfeet territory, to look for beaver. Colter had been there twice before; still, they couldn't have picked a more dangerous place. The area, now known as Montana, was blank wilderness, and the Blackfeet had been implacably hostile to white men ever since their first contact with Lewis and Clark several years earlier. Colter and Potts were working for a fur trader named Manuel Lisa, who built a fort at the confluence of the Yellowstone and Bighorn rivers. One morning in mid-August they loaded up their canoes, shoved off into the Yellowstone, and started paddling north.

Colter was the better known of the two men. Tall, lean, and a wicked shot, he had spent more time in the wilderness than probably any white man alive — first as a hunter on the Lewis and Clark Expedition, then two more years guiding and trapping along the Yellowstone. The previous winter he'd set out alone, with nothing but a rifle, a buffalo-skin blanket, and a thirty-pound pack, to complete a several-month trek through what is now Montana, Idaho, and Wyoming. He saw steam geysers in an area near present-day Cody, Wyoming, that was later dubbed Colter's Hell by disbelievers. Within weeks of arriving back at Lisa's fort in the spring of 1808, he headed right back out again, this time up to the Three Forks area of Montana, where he'd been with Lewis and Clark almost three years earlier. His trip was cut short when he was shot in the leg during a fight with some Blackfeet, and he returned to Lisa's fort to let the wound heal. No sooner was he better, though, than he went straight back to Three Forks, this time with John Potts. The two men quickly amassed almost a ton of pelts, but every day they spent in Blackfeet territory was pushing their luck. Finally, sometime in the fall, their luck ran out.

As they paddled the Jefferson River, five hundred Blackfeet Indians suddenly swarmed toward them along the bank. Potts grabbed his rifle and killed one of them with a single shot, but he may have done that just to spare himself a slow death; the Blackfeet immediately shot him so full of arrows that "he was made a riddle of," as Colter put it. Colter surrendered and was stripped naked. One of the Blackfeet asked whether he was a good runner. Colter had the presence of mind to say no, so the Blackfeet told him he could run for his life; when they caught him, they would kill him. Naked, unarmed, and given a head start of only a couple of hundred yards, Colter started to run.

He was, as it turned out, a good runner — very good. He headed for the Madison River, six miles away, and by the time he was halfway there, he'd already outdistanced every Blackfoot except one. His pursuer was carrying a spear, and Colter spun around unexpectedly, wrestled it away from him, and killed him with it. He kept running until he got to the river, dived in, and hid inside a logjam until the Blackfeet got tired of looking for him. He emerged after nightfall, swam several miles downstream, then clambered out and started walking. Lisa's fort was nearly two hundred miles away. He arrived a week and a half later, his feet in shreds.

Clearly, Colter was a man who sought risk. After two brutal years with   5
Lewis and Clark, all it took was a chance encounter with a couple of itinerant trappers for Colter to turn around and head back into Indian territory. And the following summer — after three straight years in the wild — Manuel Lisa convinced him to do the same thing. Even Colter's narrow escape didn't scare him off; soon after recovering from his ordeal, he returned to the Three Forks area to retrieve his traps and had to flee from the Blackfeet once again. And in April 1810 he survived another Blackfeet attack on a new stockade at Three Forks, an attack that left five men dead. Finally

Colter had had enough. He traveled down the Missouri and reached St. Louis by the end of May. He married a young woman and settled on a farm near Dundee, Missouri. Where the Blackfeet had failed, civilization succeeded: He died just two years later.

Given the trajectory of Colter's life, one could say that the wilderness was good for him, kept him alive. It was there that he functioned at the outer limits of his abilities, a state that humans have always thrived on. "Dangers . . . seemed to have for him a kind of fascination," another fur trapper who knew Colter said. It must have been while under the effect of that fascination that Colter felt most alive, most potent. That was why he stayed in the wilderness for six straight years; that was why he kept sneaking up to Three Forks to test his skills against the Blackfeet.

Fifty years later, whalers in New Bedford, Massachusetts, would find themselves unable to face life back home and — as miserable as they were — would sign up for another three years at sea. A hundred years after that, American soldiers at the end of their tours in Vietnam would realize they could not go back to civilian life and would volunteer for one more stint in hell.

"Their shirts and breeches of buckskin or elkskin had many patches sewed on with sinews, were worn thin between patches, were black from many campfires, and greasy from many meals," writes historian Bernard De Voto about the early trappers. "They were threadbare and filthy, they smelled bad, and any Mandan had lighter skin. They gulped rather than ate the tripes of buffalo. They had forgotten the use of chairs. Words and phrases, mostly obscene, of Nez Percé, Clatsop, Mandan, Chinook came naturally to their tongues."

None of these men had become trappers against his will; to one degree or another, they'd all volunteered for the job. However rough it was, it must have looked better than the alternative, which was — in one form or another — an uneventful life passed in society's embrace. For people like Colter, the one thing more terrifying than having something bad happen must have been to have nothing happen at all.

Modern society, of course, has perfected the art of having nothing happen at all. There is nothing particularly wrong with this except that for vast numbers of Americans, as life has become staggeringly easy, it has also become vaguely unfulfilling. Life in modern society is designed to eliminate as many unforeseen events as possible, and as inviting as that seems, it leaves us hopelessly underutilized. And that is where the idea of "adventure" comes in. The word comes from the Latin *adventura*, meaning "what must happen." An adventure is a situation where the outcome is not entirely within your control. It's up to fate, in other words. It should be pointed out that people whose lives are inherently dangerous, like coal miners or steelworkers, rarely seek "adventure." Like most things, danger ceases to be interesting as soon as you have no choice in the matter. For the rest of us, threats to our safety and comfort have been so completely wiped out that we have to go out of our way to create them.

About ten years ago a young rock climber named Dan Osman started free-soloing—climbing without a safety rope—on cliffs that had stymied some of the best climbers in the country. Falling was not an option. At about the same time, though, he began falling on purpose, jumping off cliffs tethered not by a bungee cord but by regular climbing rope. He found that if he calculated the arc of his fall just right, he could jump hundreds of feet and survive. Osman's father, a policeman, told a journalist named Andrew Todhunter, "Doing the work that I do, I have faced death many, many, many times. When it's over, you celebrate the fact that you're alive, you celebrate the fact that you have a family, you celebrate the fact that you can breathe. Everything, for a few instants, seems sweeter, brighter, louder. And I think this young man has reached a point where his awareness of life and living is far beyond what I could ever achieve."

Todhunter wrote a book about Osman called *Fall of the Phantom Lord*. A few months after the book came out, Osman died on a twelve-hundred-foot fall in Yosemite National Park. He had rigged up a rope that would allow him to jump off Leaning Tower, but after more than a dozen successful jumps by Osman and others, the rope snapped and Osman plummeted to the ground.

Colter of course would have thought Osman was crazy—risk your life for no good reason at all?—but he certainly would have understood the allure. Every time Colter went up to Three Forks, he was in effect free-soloing. Whether he survived or not was entirely up to him. No one was going to save him; no one was going to come to his aid. It's the oldest game in the world—and perhaps the most compelling.

The one drawback to modern adventuring, however, is that people can mistake it for something it's not. The fact that someone can free-solo a sheer rock face or balloon halfway around the world is immensely impressive, but it's not strictly necessary. And because it's not necessary, it's not heroic. Society would continue to function quite well if no one ever climbed another mountain, but it would come grinding to a halt if roughnecks stopped working on oil rigs. Oddly, though, it's the mountaineers who are heaped with glory, not the roughnecks, who have a hard time even getting a date in an oil town. A roughneck who gets crushed tripping pipe or a fire fighter who dies in a burning building has, in some ways, died a heroic death. But Dan Osman did not; he died because he voluntarily gambled with his life and lost. That makes him brave—unspeakably brave—but nothing more. Was his life worth the last jump? Undoubtedly not. Was his life worth living without those jumps? Apparently not. The task of every person alive is to pick a course between those two extremes.

I have only once been in a situation where everything depended on   15
me—my own version of Colter's run. It's a ludicrous comparison except that for the age that I was, the stakes seemed every bit as high. When I was eleven, I went skiing for a week with a group of boys my age, and late one afternoon when we had nothing to do, we walked off into the pine forests around the resort. The snow was very deep, up to our waists in places, and

we wallowed through slowly, taking turns breaking trail. After about half an hour, and deep into the woods now, we crested a hill and saw a small road down below us. We waited a few minutes, and sure enough, a car went by. We all threw snowballs at it. A few minutes later another one went by, and we let loose another volley.

Our snowballs weren't hitting their mark, so we worked our way down closer to the road and put together some really dense, heavy iceballs — ones that would throw like a baseball and hit just as hard. Then we waited, the woods getting darker and darker, and finally in the distance we heard the heavy whine of an eighteen-wheeler downshifting on a hill. A minute later it barreled around the turn, and at the last moment we all heaved our iceballs. Five or six big white splats blossomed on the windshield. That was followed by the ghastly yelp of an air brake.

It was a dangerous thing to do, of course: The driver was taking an icy road very fast, and the explosion of snow against his wind-shield must have made him jump right out of his skin. We didn't think of that, though; we just watched in puzzlement as the truck bucked to a stop. And then the driver's side door flew open and a man jumped out. And everyone started to run.

I don't know why he picked me, but he did. My friends scattered into the forest, no one saying a word, and when I looked back, the man was after me. He was so angry that strange grunts were coming out of him. I had never seen an adult that enraged. I ran harder and harder, but to my amazement, he just kept coming. We were all alone in the forest now, way out of earshot of my friends; it was just a race between him and me. I knew I couldn't afford to lose it; the man was too crazy, too determined, and there was no one around to intervene. I was on my own. *Adventura* — what must happen will happen.

Before I knew it, the man had drawn to within a few steps of me. Neither of us said a word; we just wallowed on through the snow, each engaged in our private agonies. It was a slow-motion race with unimaginable consequences. We struggled on for what seemed like miles but in reality was probably only a few hundred yards; the deep snow made it seem farther. In the end I outlasted him. He was a strong man, but he spent his days behind the wheel of a truck — smoking, no doubt — and he was no match for a terrified kid. With a groan of disgust he finally stopped and doubled over, swearing at me between breaths.

I kept running. I ran until his shouts had died out behind me and I couldn't stand up anymore, and then I collapsed in the snow. It was completely dark and the only sounds were the heaving of the wind through the trees and the liquid slamming of my heart. I lay there until I was calm, and then I got up and slowly made my way back to the resort. It felt as if I'd been someplace very far away and had come back to a world of tremendous frivolity and innocence. It was all lit up, peals of laughter coming from the bar, adults hobbling back and forth in ski boots and brightly colored parkas. "I've just come back from some other place," I thought. "I've just come back from some other place these people don't even know exists." 20

The Reader's Presence

1. What are the terms that define adventure for Junger? What does he suggest modern adventure lacks in comparison to the hardships the settlers endured? Why, according to Junger, do modern Americans seek adventure so much?

2. How does Junger's own example of adventure compare to John Colter's and Dan Osman's? To what extent does it fit his definition of adventure? Why do you think he chose to include his own experience? In your view, does the fact that he ends with his own anecdote strengthen or weaken Junger's essay?

3. "I have only once been in a situation where everything depended on me," writes Junger. What was at stake in Junger's adventure? Read Henry Louis Gates Jr.'s essay "Rope Burn" (page 153), in which his experience hinges on putting his life completely in someone else's hands. What does each man think is gained from these experiences? How are they similar? How are they different?

Stephen King

Everything You Need to Know about Writing Successfully — in Ten Minutes

Stephen King was born in 1947 in Portland, Maine. He began writing stories early in his life, but it was his discovery of a box of horror and science fiction novels in the attic of his aunt's house that made him decide to pursue a career as a writer. He published his first short stories in pulp horror magazines while in high school. After graduating from the University of Maine at Orono in 1970, King, while working at a low-paying job in a laundry, began writing his first novel, Carrie (1974). Carrie was followed by thirty-six more best-sellers, including half a dozen works written under the pen name Richard Bachman, as well as five short story collections and nine screenplays. His critically acclaimed work of nonfiction, On Writing (2000), the source of the following essay, was completed while he was recovering painfully from a much-publicized accident.

Stephen King has commented that, as a creative writer, he always hopes for "that element of inspiration which lifts you past the point where the characters are just you, where you do achieve something transcendental and the people are really people in the story."

I. THE FIRST INTRODUCTION

That's right. I know it sounds like an ad for some sleazy writers' school, but I really am going to tell you everything you need to pursue a successful and financially rewarding career writing fiction, and I really am going to do it in ten minutes, which is exactly how long it took me to learn. It will actually take you twenty minutes or so to read this article, however, because I have to tell you a story, and then I have to write a second introduction. But these, I argue, should not count in the ten minutes.

II. THE STORY, OR, HOW STEPHEN KING LEARNED TO WRITE

When I was a sophomore in high school, I did a sophomoric thing which got me in a pot of fairly hot water, as sophomoric didoes often do. I wrote and published a small satiric newspaper called *The Village Vomit*. In this little paper I lampooned a number of teachers at Lisbon (Maine) High School, where I was under instruction. These were not very gentle lampoons; they ranged from the scatological to the downright cruel.

Eventually, a copy of this paper found its way into the hands of a faculty member, and since I had been unwise enough to put my name on it (a fault, some critics would argue, of which I have still not been entirely cured), I was brought into the office. The sophisticated satirist had by that time reverted to what he really was: a fourteen-year-old kid who was shaking in his boots and wondering if he was going to get a suspension . . . what we called a "three-day vacation" in those dim days of 1964.

I wasn't suspended. I was forced to make a number of apologies—they were warranted, but they tasted like dog-dirt in my mouth—and spent a week in detention hall. And the guidance counselor arranged what he no doubt thought of as a more constructive channel for my talents. This was a job—contingent upon the editor's approval—writing sports for the Lisbon Enterprise, a twelve-page weekly of the sort with which any small-town resident will be familiar. This editor was the man who taught me everything I know about writing in ten minutes. His name was John Gould—not the famed New England humorist or the novelist who wrote *The Greenleaf Fires*, but a relative of both, I believe.

He told me he needed a sports writer, and we could "try each other out," if I wanted.

I told him I knew more about advanced algebra than I did sports.

Gould nodded and said, "You'll learn."

I said I would at least try to learn. Gould gave me a huge roll of yellow paper and promised me a wage of 1/2 [cts.] per word. The first two pieces I wrote had to do with a high school basketball game in which a member of my school team broke the Lisbon High scoring record. One of these pieces was a straight piece of reportage. The second was a feature article.

5

I brought them to Gould the day after the game, so he'd have them for the paper, which came out Fridays. He read the straight piece, made two minor corrections, and spiked it. Then he started in on the feature piece with a large black pen and taught me all I ever needed to know about my craft. I wish I still had the piece,—it deserves to be framed, editorial corrections and all—but I can remember pretty well how it went and how it looked when he had finished with it. Here's an example:

> Last night, in the ~~well-loved~~ gymnasium of Lisbon High School, partisans and Jay Hills fans alike were stunned by an athletic performance unequalled in school history: Bob Ransom, ~~known as Bullet Bob for both his size and accuracy,~~ scored thirty-seven points. Yes, you heard me right. ~~Plus~~ he did it with grace, and speed...and with an odd courtesy as well, committing only two personal fouls in his ~~knight-like~~ quest for a record which has eluded Lisbon ~~thinclads~~ (players) since ~~the years of Korea~~ (1953)...

When Gould finished marking up my copy in the manner I have indicated above, he looked up and must have seen something on my face. I think he must have thought it was horror, but it was not: It was revelation.   10

"I only took out the bad parts, you know," he said. "Most of it's pretty good."

"I know," I said, meaning both things; yes, most of it was good, and yes, he had only taken out the bad parts. "I won't do it again."

"If that's true," he said, "you'll never have to work again. You can do this for a living."

Then he threw back his head and laughed.

And he was right: I am doing this for a living, and as long as I can   15
keep on, I don't expect ever to have to work again.

III. THE SECOND INTRODUCTION

All of what follows has been said before. If you are interested enough in writing to be a purchaser of this magazine [*Writer*], you will have either heard or read all (or almost all) of it before. Thousands of writing courses are taught across the United States each year; seminars are convened; guest lecturers talk, then answer questions, and it all boils down to what follows.

I am going to tell you these things again because often people will only listen—really listen—to someone who makes a lot of money doing the thing he's talking about. This is sad but true. And I told you the story above not to make myself sound like a character out of a Horatio Alger novel but to make a point: I saw, I listened, and I learned. Until that day in John Gould's little office, I had been writing first drafts of stories that might run 2,500 words. The second drafts were apt to run 3,300 words. Following that day, my 2,500-word first drafts became 2,200-word second drafts. And two years after that, I sold the first one.

So here it is, with all the bark stripped off. It'll take ten minutes to read, and you can apply it right away . . . if you listen.

IV. EVERYTHING YOU NEED TO KNOW ABOUT WRITING SUCCESSFULLY

1. Be talented

This, of course, is the killer. What is talent? I can hear someone shouting, and here we are, ready to get into a discussion right up there with "What is the meaning of life?" for weighty pronouncements and total uselessness. For the purposes of the beginning writer, talent may as well be defined as eventual success—publication and money. If you wrote something for which someone sent you a check, if you cashed the check and it didn't bounce, and if you then paid the light bill with the money, I consider you talented.

Now some of you are really hollering. Some of you are calling me one   20 crass money-fixated creep. Nonsense. Worse than nonsense, off the subject. We're not talking about good or bad here. I'm interested in telling you how to get your stuff published, not in critical judgments of who's good or bad. As a rule, the critical judgments come after the check's been spent, anyway. I have my own opinions, but most times I keep them to myself. People who are published steadily and are paid for what they are writing may be either saints or trollops, but they are clearly reaching a great many someones who want what they have. Ergo, they are communicating. Ergo, they are talented. The biggest part of writing successfully is being talented, and in the context of marketing, the only bad writer is one who doesn't get paid. If you're not talented, you won't succeed. And if you're not succeeding, you should know when to quit.

When is that? I don't know. It's different for each writer. Not after six rejection slips, certainly, nor after sixty. But after six hundred? Maybe. After six thousand? My friend, after six thousand pinks, it's time you tried painting or computer programming.

Further, almost every aspiring writer knows when he is getting warmer—you start getting little jotted notes on your rejection slips, or personal letters . . . maybe a commiserating phone call. It's lonely out there in the cold, but there are encouraging voices . . . unless there is nothing in your words that warrants encouragement. I think you owe it to yourself to skip as much of the self-illusion as possible. If your eyes are open, you'll know which way to go . . . or when to turn back.

2. Be neat

Type. Double-space. Use a nice heavy white paper. If you've marked your manuscript a lot, do another draft.

3. Be self-critical

If you haven't marked up your manuscript a lot, you did a lazy job. Only God gets things right the first time. Don't be a slob.

4. Remove every extraneous word

You want to get up on a soapbox and preach? Fine. Get one, and try   25
your local park. You want to write for money? Get to the point. And if you remove the excess garbage and discover you can't find the point, tear up what you wrote and start all over again . . . or try something new.

5. Never look at a reference book while doing a first draft

You want to write a story? Fine. Put away your dictionary, your encyclopedias, your *World Almanac*, and your thesaurus. Better yet, throw your thesaurus into the wastebasket. The only things creepier than a thesaurus are those little paperbacks college students too lazy to read the assigned novels buy around exam time. Any word you have to hunt for in a thesaurus is the wrong word. There are no exceptions to this rule. You think you might have misspelled a word? O.K., so here is your choice: Either look it up in the dictionary, thereby making sure you have it right—and breaking your train of thought and the writer's trance in the bargain—or just spell it phonetically and correct it later. Why not? Did you think it was going to go somewhere? And if you need to know the largest city in Brazil and you find you don't have it in your head, why not write in Miami, or Cleveland? You can check it . . . but later. When you sit down to write, write. Don't do anything else except go to the bathroom, and only do that if it absolutely cannot be put off.

6. Know the markets

Only a dimwit would send a story about giant vampire bats surrounding a high school to *McCall's*. Only a dimwit would send a tender story about a mother and daughter making up their differences on

Christmas Eve to *Playboy* . . . but people do it all the time. I'm not exaggerating; I have seen such stories in the slush piles of the actual magazines. If you write a good story, why send it out in an ignorant fashion? Would you send your kid out in a snowstorm dressed in Bermuda shorts and a tank top? If you like science fiction, read science fiction novels and magazines. If you want to write mysteries, read the magazines. And so on. It isn't just a matter of knowing what's right for the present story; you can begin to catch on, after a while, to overall rhythms, editorial likes and dislikes, a magazine's slant. Sometimes your reading can influence the next story, and create a sale.

7. Write to entertain

Does this mean you can't write "serious fiction"? It does not. Somewhere along the line pernicious critics have invested the American reading and writing public with the idea that entertaining fiction and serious ideas do not overlap. This would have surprised Charles Dickens, not to mention Jane Austen, John Steinbeck, William Faulkner, Bernard Malamud, and hundreds of others. But your serious ideas must always serve your story, not the other way around. I repeat: If you want to preach, get a soapbox.

8. Ask yourself frequently, "Am I having fun?"

The answer needn't always be yes. But if it's always no, it's time for a new project or a new career.

9. How to evaluate criticism

Show your piece to a number of people—ten, let us say. Listen carefully to what they tell you. Smile and nod a lot. Then review what was said very carefully. If your critics are all telling you the same thing about some facet of your story—a plot twist that doesn't work, a character who rings false, stilted narrative, or half a dozen other possibles—change it. It doesn't matter if you really like that twist or that character; if a lot of people are telling you something is wrong with your piece, it is. If seven or eight of them are hitting on that same thing, I'd still suggest changing it. But if everyone—or even most everyone—is criticizing something different, you can safely disregard what all of them say.

10. Observe all rules for proper submission

Return postage, self-addressed envelope, etc.

11. An agent? Forget it. For now.

Agents get 10 percent to 15 percent of monies earned by their clients. Fifteen percent of nothing is nothing. Agents also have to pay the rent. Beginning writers do not contribute to that or any other necessity of life. Flog your stories around yourself. If you've done a novel, send around query letters to publishers, one by one, and follow up with sample chapters and/or the complete manuscript. And remember Stephen King's First Rule of Writers and Agent, learned by bitter personal experience: You don't need one until you're making enough for someone to steal . . . and if you're making that much, you'll be able to take your pick of good agents.

12. If it's bad, kill it

When it comes to people, mercy killing is against the law. When it comes to fiction, it is the law.

That's everything you need to know. And if you listened, you can write everything and anything you want. Now I believe I will wish you a pleasant day and sign off.

My ten minutes are up.   35

The Reader's Presence

1. Why does King include sections 1–3, even though they are not part of the "ten minutes"? What does the first introduction actually introduce? the second? How effectively does section II work with section IV? For example, how many rules did King learn when John Gould edited his story? Which rules does he break in his own essay? Why do you think he breaks them?

2. King is best known for writing horror novels, stories that scare people. What fears does he play on throughout this essay? How does he go about setting up suspenseful situations? What does he do to frighten people in this essay? If the rules are monsters, which ones do you think are the most frightening? Why?

3. By King's definition, a talented author is one who has been paid for his or her writing. Pick an author in this collection whom you consider talented and evaluate him or her according to King's rules. How successful should this writer be according to King? What other rules of success does the writer's essay suggest should be added to King's list?

4. King's essay represents an approach to an ongoing debate between money and art. Signalled by terms like *practicality* and *popularity*,

the money side holds that you should write to make money. Signalled by phrases like *art for art's sake* or *selling out* the art side holds that you should write to please yourself. George Orwell represents another approach to this debate when he lists "four great motives for writing" (page 544). Read Orwell's essay and determine how well each of the motives would lead to the kind of successful writing that King imagines. For example, how well—or how poorly—does Orwell's desire to "share an experience which one feels is valuable" (page 544) lead to King's "eventual success—publication and money" (paragraph 19)?

Maxine Hong Kingston

No Name Woman

Maxine Hong Kingston (b. 1940) won the National Book Critics Circle Award for nonfiction with her first book, The Woman Warrior: Memoirs of a Girlhood among Ghosts *(1976). "No Name Woman" is the opening chapter of this book, which* Time *magazine named one of the top ten nonfiction works of the 1970s. Her other works include* China Men *(1980), which won the American Book Award;* Trip Master Monkey: His Fake Book *(1988), a picaresque novel; and* To Be a Poet *(2002), a collection of her lectures and verse. A manuscript entitled* The Fourth Book of Peace *was destroyed, along with her home and all of her possessions, in a 1991 Oakland–Berkeley fire, but Kingston started over and published* The Fifth Book of Peace *in 2003. Kingston's writing often blurs the distinction between fiction and nonfiction. Her narratives blend autobiography, history, myth, and legend, drawing on the stories she remembers from her childhood in the Chinese American community of Stockton, California. Kingston's essays, stories, and poems also appear in numerous magazines, and she received the 1997 National Medal for the Humanities. In 2004, she retired as a senior lecturer for creative writing at the University of California, Berkeley.*

Kingston has said that before writing The Woman Warrior, *"My life as a writer had been a long struggle with pronouns. For 30 years I wrote in the first person singular. At a certain point I was thinking that I was self-centered and egotistical, solipsistic, and not very developed as a human being, nor as an artist, because I could only see from this one point of view." She began to write in the third person because "I thought I had to overcome this self-centeredness." As she wrote her third novel, Kingston experienced the disappearance of her authorial voice.*

"I feel that this is an artistic as well as psychological improvement on my part. Because I am now a much less selfish person."

"You must not tell anyone," my mother said, "what I am about to tell you. In China your father had a sister who killed herself. She jumped into the family well. We say that your father has all brothers because it is as if she had never been born.

"In 1924 just a few days after our village celebrated seventeen hurry-up weddings—to make sure that every young man who went 'out on the road' would responsibly come home—your father and his brothers and your grandfather and his brothers and your aunt's new husband sailed for America, the Gold Mountain. It was your grandfather's last trip. Those lucky enough to get contracts waved good-bye from the decks. They fed and guarded the stowaways and helped them off in Cuba, New York, Bali, Hawaii. 'We'll meet in California next year,' they said. All of them sent money home.

"I remember looking at your aunt one day when she and I were dressing; I had not noticed before that she had such a protruding melon of a stomach. But I did not think, 'She's pregnant,' until she began to look like other pregnant women, her shirt pulling and the white tops of her black pants showing. She could not have been pregnant, you see, because her husband had been gone for years. No one said anything. We did not discuss it. In early summer she was ready to have the child, long after the time when it could have been possible.

"The village had also been counting. On the night the baby was to be born the villagers raided our house. Some were crying. Like a great saw, teeth strung with lights, files of people walked zigzag across our land, tearing the rice. Their lanterns doubled in the disturbed black water, which drained away through the broken bunds. As the villagers closed in, we could see that some of them, probably men and women we knew well, wore white masks. The people with long hair hung it over their faces. Women with short hair made it stand up on end. Some had tied white bands around their foreheads, arms, and legs.

"At first they threw mud and rocks at the house. Then they threw eggs and began slaughtering our stock. We could hear the animals scream their deaths—the roosters, the pigs, a last great roar from the ox. Familiar wild heads flared in our night windows; the villagers encircled us. Some of the faces stopped to peer at us, their eyes rushing like searchlights. The hands flattened against the panes, framed heads, and left red prints.

"The villagers broke in the front and the back doors at the same time, even though we had not locked the doors against them. Their knives dripped with the blood of our animals. They smeared blood on the doors and walls. One woman swung a chicken, whose throat she had slit, splattering blood in red arcs about her. We stood together in the middle of our house, in the family hall with the pictures and tables of the ancestors around us, and looked straight ahead.

5

"At that time the house had only two wings. When the men came back we would build two more to enclose our courtyard and a third one to begin a second courtyard. The villagers pushed through both wings, even your grandparents' rooms, to find your aunt's, which was also mine until the men returned. From this room a new wing for one of the younger families would grow. They ripped up her clothes and shoes and broke her combs, grinding them underfoot. They tore her work from the loom. They scattered the cooking fire and rolled the new weaving in it. We could hear them in the kitchen breaking our bowls and banging the pots. They overturned the great waist-high earthenware jugs; duck eggs, pickled fruits, vegetables burst out and mixed in acrid torrents. The old woman from the next field swept a broom through the air and loosed the spirits-of-the-broom over our heads. 'Pig.' 'Ghost.' 'Pig,' they sobbed and scolded while they ruined our house.

"When they left, they took sugar and oranges to bless themselves. They cut pieces from the dead animals. Some of them took bowls that were not broken and clothes that were not torn. Afterward we swept up the rice and sewed it back up into sacks. But the smells from the spilled preserves lasted. Your aunt gave birth in the pigsty that night. The next morning when I went up for the water, I found her and the baby plugging up the family well.

"Don't let your father know that I told you. He denies her. Now that you have started to menstruate, what happened to her could happen to you. Don't humiliate us. You wouldn't like to be forgotten as if you had never been born. The villagers are watchful."

Whenever she had to warn us about life, my mother told stories that ran like this one, a story to grow up on. She tested our strength to establish realities. Those in the emigrant generations who could not reassert brute survival died young and far from home. Those of us in the first American generations have had to figure out how the invisible world the emigrants built around our childhoods fit in solid America.

The emigrants confused the gods by diverting their curses, misleading them with crooked streets and false names. They must try to confuse their offspring as well, who, I suppose, threaten them in similar ways — always trying to get things straight, always trying to name the unspeakable. The Chinese I know hide their names; sojourners take new names when their lives change and guard their real names with silence.

Chinese-Americans, when you try to understand what things in you are Chinese, how do you separate what is peculiar to childhood, to poverty, insanities, one family, your mother who marked your growing with stories, from what is Chinese? What is Chinese tradition and what is the movies?

If I want to learn what clothes my aunt wore, whether flashy or ordinary, I would have to begin, "Remember Father's drowned-in-the-well sister?" I cannot ask that. My mother has told me once and for all the useful parts. She will add nothing unless powered by Necessity, a riverbank that guides her life. She plants vegetable gardens rather than lawns; she carries the odd-shaped tomatoes home from the fields and eats food left for the gods.

Whenever we did frivolous things, we used up energy; we flew high kites. We children came up off the ground over the melting cones our parents brought home from work and the American movie on New Year's Day—*Oh, You Beautiful Doll* with Betty Grable one year, and *She Wore a Yellow Ribbon* with John Wayne another year. After the one carnival ride each, we paid in guilt; our tired father counted his change on the dark walk home.

Adultery is extravagance. Could people who hatch their own chicks and eat the embryos and the heads for delicacies and boil the feet in vinegar for party food, leaving only the gravel, eating even the gizzard lining— could such people engender a prodigal aunt? To be a woman, to have a daughter in starvation time was a waste enough. My aunt could not have been the lone romantic who gave up everything for sex. Women in the old China did not choose. Some man had commanded her to lie with him and be his secret evil. I wonder whether he masked himself when he joined the raid on her family.

Perhaps she encountered him in the fields or on the mountain where the daughters-in-law collected fuel. Or perhaps he first noticed her in the marketplace. He was not a stranger because the village housed no strangers. She had to have dealings with him other than sex. Perhaps he worked an adjoining field, or he sold her the cloth for the dress she sewed and wore. His demand must have surprised, then terrified her. She obeyed him; she always did as she was told.

When the family found a young man in the next village to be her husband, she stood tractably beside the best rooster, his proxy, and promised before they met that she would be his forever. She was lucky that he was her age and she would be the first wife, an advantage secure now. The night she first saw him, he had sex with her. Then he left for America. She had almost forgotten what he looked like. When she tried to envision him, she only saw the black and white face in the group photograph the men had had taken before leaving.

The other man was not, after all, much different from her husband. They both gave orders: she followed. "If you tell your family, I'll beat you. I'll kill you. Be here again next week." No one talked sex, ever. And she might have separated the rapes from the rest of living if only she did not have to buy her oil from him or gather wood in the same forest. I want her fear to have lasted just as long as rape lasted so that the fear could have been contained. No drawn-out fear. But women at sex hazarded birth and hence lifetimes. The fear did not stop but permeated everywhere. She told the man, "I think I'm pregnant." He organized the raid against her.

On nights when my mother and father talked about their life back home, sometimes they mentioned an "outcast table" whose business they still seemed to be settling, their voices tight. In a commensal tradition, where food is precious, the powerful older people made wrongdoers eat

15

alone. Instead of letting them start separate new lives like the Japanese, who could become samurais and geishas, the Chinese family, faces averted but eyes glowering sideways, hung on to the offenders and fed them left-overs. My aunt must have lived in the same house as my parents and eaten at an outcast table. My mother spoke about the raid as if she had seen it, when she and my aunt, a daughter-in-law to a different household, should not have been living together at all. Daughters-in-law lived with their husbands' parents, not their own; a synonym for marriage in Chinese is "taking a daughter-in-law." Her husband's parents could have sold her, mortgaged her, stoned her. But they had sent her back to her own mother and father, a mysterious act hinting at disgraces not told me. Perhaps they had thrown her out to deflect the avengers.

She was the only daughter; her four brothers went with her father, hus-   20
band, and uncles "out on the road" and for some years became western men. When the goods were divided among the family, three of the brothers took land, and the youngest, my father, chose an education. After my grandparents gave their daughter away to her husband's family, they had dispensed all the adventure and all the property. They expected her alone to keep the traditional ways, which her brothers, now among the barbarians, could fumble without detection. The heavy, deep-rooted women were to maintain the past against the flood, safe for returning. But the rare urge west had fixed upon our family, and so my aunt crossed boundaries not de-lineated in space.

The work of preservation demands that the feelings playing about in one's guts not be turned into action. Just watch their passing like cherry blossoms. But perhaps my aunt, my forerunner, caught in a slow life, let dreams grow and fade and after some months or years went toward what persisted. Fear at the enormities of the forbidden kept her desires delicate, wire and bone. She looked at a man because she liked the way the hair was tucked behind his ears, or she liked the question-mark line of a long torso curving at the shoulder and straight at the hip. For warm eyes or a soft voice or a slow walk—that's all—a few hairs, a line, a brightness, a sound, a pace, she gave up family. She offered us up for a charm that vanished with tiredness, a pigtail that didn't toss when the wind died. Why, the wrong lighting could erase the dearest thing about him.

It could very well have been, however, that my aunt did not take sub-tle enjoyment of her friend, but, a wild woman, kept rollicking company. Imagining her free with sex doesn't fit, though. I don't know any women like that, or men either. Unless I see her life branching into mine, she gives me no ancestral help.

To sustain her being in love, she often worked at herself in the mir-ror, guessing at the colors and shapes that would interest him, changing them frequently in order to hit on the right combination. She wanted to look back.

On a farm near the sea, a woman who tended her appearance reaped a reputation for eccentricity. All the married women blunt-cut their hair

in flaps about their ears or pulled it back in tight buns. No nonsense.
Neither style blew easily into heart-catching tangles. And at their weddings they displayed themselves in their long hair for the last time. "It
brushed the back of my knees," my mother tells me. "It was braided, and
even so, it brushed the backs of my knees."

At the mirror my aunt combed individuality into her bob. A bun could   25
have been contrived to escape into black streamers blowing in the wind or
in quiet wisps about her face, but only the older women in our picture
album wear buns. She brushed her hair back from her forehead, tucking
the flaps behind her ears. She looped a piece of thread, knotted into a circle between her index fingers and thumbs, and ran the double strand
across her forehead. When she closed her fingers as if she were making a
pair of shadow geese bite, the string twisted together catching the little
hairs. Then she pulled the thread away from her skin, ripping the hairs out
neatly, her eyes watering from the needles of pain. Opening her fingers,
she cleaned the thread, then rolled it along her hairline and the tops of the
eyebrows. My mother did the same to me and my sisters and herself. I
used to believe that the expression "caught by the short hairs" meant a
captive held with a depilatory string. It especially hurt at the temples, but
my mother said we were lucky we didn't have to have our feet bound
when we were seven. Sisters used to sit on their beds and cry together, she
said, as their mothers or their slave removed the bandages for a few minutes each night and let the blood gush back into their veins. I hope that
the man my aunt loved appreciated a smooth brow, that he wasn't just a
tits-and-ass man.

Once my aunt found a freckle on her chin, at a spot that the almanac
said predestined her for unhappiness. She dug it out with a hot needle and
washed the wound with peroxide.

More attention to her looks than these pullings of hairs and pickings
at spots would have caused gossip among the villagers. They owned work
clothes and good clothes, and they wore good clothes for feasting the new
seasons. But since a woman combing her hair hexes beginnings, my aunt
rarely found an occasion to look her best. Women looked like great sea
snails—the corded wood, babies, and laundry they carried were the
whorls on their backs. The Chinese did not admire a bent back; goddesses
and warriors stood straight. Still there must have been a marvelous freeing of beauty when a worker laid down her burden and stretched and
arched.

Such commonplace loveliness, however, was not enough for my aunt.
She dreamed of a lover for the fifteen days of New Year's, the time for
families to exchange visits, money, and food. She plied her secret comb.
And sure enough she cursed the year, the family, the village, and herself.

Even as her hair lured her imminent lover, many other men looked at
her. Uncles, cousins, nephews, brothers would have looked, too, had they
been home between journeys. Perhaps they had already been restraining

their curiosity, and they left, fearful that their glances, like a field of nesting birds, might be startled and caught. Poverty hurt, and that was their first reason for leaving. But another, final reason for leaving the crowded house was the never-said.

She may have been unusually beloved, the precious only daughter,   30
spoiled and mirror-gazing because of the affection the family lavished on her. When her husband left, they welcomed the chance to take her back from the in-laws; she could live like the little daughter for just a while longer. There are stories that my grandfather was different from other people, "crazy ever since the little Jap bayoneted him in the head." He used to put his naked penis on the dinner table, laughing. And one day he brought home a baby girl, wrapped up inside his brown western-style greatcoat. He had traded one of his sons, probably my father, the youngest, for her. My grandmother made him trade back. When he finally got a daughter of his own, he doted on her. They must have all loved her, except perhaps my father, the only brother who never went back to China, having once been traded for a girl.

Brothers and sisters, newly men and women, had to efface their sexual color and present plain miens. Disturbing hair and eyes, a smile like no other, threatened the ideal of five generations living under one roof. To focus blurs, people shouted face to face and yelled from room to room. The immigrants I know have loud voices, unmodulated to American tones even after years away from the village where they called their friendships out across the fields. I have not been able to stop my mother's screams in public libraries or over telephones. Walking erect (knees straight, toes pointed forward, not pigeon-toed, which is Chinese-feminine) and speaking in an inaudible voice, I have tried to turn myself American-feminine. Chinese communication was loud, public. Only sick people had to whisper. But at the dinner table, where the family members came nearest one another, no one could talk, not the outcasts nor any eaters. Every word that falls from the mouth is a coin lost. Silently they gave and accepted food with both hands. A preoccupied child who took his bowl with one hand got a sideways glare. A complete moment of total attention is due everyone alike. Children and lovers have no singularity here, but my aunt used a secret voice, a separate attentiveness.

She kept the man's name to herself throughout her labor and dying; she did not accuse him that he be punished with her. To save her inseminator's name she gave silent birth.

He may have been somebody in her own household, but intercourse with a man outside the family would have been no less abhorrent. All the village were kinsmen, and the titles shouted in loud country voices never let kinship be forgotten. Any man within visiting distance would have been neutralized as a lover — "brother," "younger brother," "older brother" — 115 relationship titles. Parents researched birth charts probably not so much to assure good fortune as to circumvent incest in a population that has but one hundred surnames. Everybody has eight million relatives. How useless then sexual mannerisms, how dangerous.

As if it came from an atavism deeper than fear, I used to add "brother" silently to boys' names. It hexed the boys, who would or would not ask me to dance, and made them less scary and as familiar and deserving of benevolence as girls.

But, of course, I hexed myself also — no dates. I should have stood up,   35 both arms waving, and shouted out across libraries, "Hey, you! Love me back." I had no idea, though, how to make attraction selective, how to control its direction and magnitude. If I made myself American-pretty so that the five or six Chinese boys in the class fell in love with me, everyone else — the Caucasian, Negro, and Japanese boys — would too. Sisterliness, dignified and honorable, made much more sense.

Attraction eludes control so stubbornly that whole societies designed to organize relationships among people cannot keep order, not even when they bind people to one another from childhood and raise them together. Among the very poor and the wealthy, brothers married their adopted sisters, like doves. Our family allowed some romance, paying adult brides' prices and providing dowries so that their sons and daughters could marry strangers. Marriage promises to turn strangers into friendly relatives — a nation of siblings.

In the village structure, spirits shimmered among the live creatures, balanced and held in equilibrium by time and land. But one human being flaring up into violence could open up a black hole, a maelstrom that pulled in the sky. The frightened villagers, who depended on one another to maintain the real, went to my aunt to show her a personal, physical representation of the break she made in the "roundness." Misallying couples snapped off the future, which was to be embodied in true offspring. The villagers punished her for acting as if she could have a private life, secret and apart from them.

If my aunt had betrayed the family at a time of large grain yields and peace, when many boys were born, and wings were being built on many houses, perhaps she might have escaped such severe punishment. But the men — hungry, greedy, tired of planting in dry soil, cuckolded — had been forced to leave the village in order to send food-money home. There were ghost plagues, bandit plagues, wars with the Japanese, floods. My Chinese brother and sister had died of an unknown sickness. Adultery, perhaps only a mistake during good times, became a crime when the village needed food.

The round moon cakes and round doorways, the round tables of graduated size that fit one roundness inside another, round windows and rice bowls — these talismans had lost their power to warn this family of the law: A family must be whole, faithfully keeping the descent line by having sons to feed the old and the dead who in turn look after the family. The villagers came to show my aunt and lover-in-hiding a broken house. The villagers were speeding up the circling of events because she was too shortsighted to see that her infidelity had already harmed the village, that waves of consequences would return unpredictably, sometimes in disguise, as now, to hurt her. This roundness had to be made coin-sized so that she would see its circumference: Punish her at the birth of her baby. Awaken her to the inexorable. People who refused fatalism because they could invent small resources insisted on culpability. Deny accidents and wrest fault from the stars.

After the villagers left, their lanterns now scattering in various directions toward home, the family broke their silence and cursed her. "Aiaa, we're going to die. Death is coming. Death is coming. Look what you've done. You've killed us. Ghost! Dead Ghost! Ghost! You've never been born." She ran out into the fields, far enough from the house so that she could no longer hear their voices, and pressed herself against the earth, her own land no more. When she felt the birth coming, she thought that she had been hurt. Her body seized together. "They've hurt me too much," she thought. "This is gall, and it will kill me." With forehead and knees against the earth, her body convulsed and then relaxed. She turned on her back, lay on the ground. The black well of sky and stars went out and out forever; her body and her complexity seemed to disappear. She was one of the stars, a bright dot in blackness, without home, without a companion, in eternal cold and silence. An agoraphobia rose in her, speeding higher and higher, bigger and bigger; she would not be able to contain it; there would be no end to fear.

Flayed, unprotected against space, she felt pain return, focusing her body. This pain chilled her—a cold, steady kind of surface pain. Inside, spasmodically, the other pain, the pain of the child, heated her. For hours she lay on the ground, alternately body and space. Sometimes a vision of normal comfort obliterated reality: She saw the family in the evening gambling at the dinner table, the young people massaging their elders' backs. She saw them congratulating one another, high joy on the mornings the rice shoots came up. When these pictures burst, the stars drew yet further apart. Black space opened.

She got to her feet to fight better and remembered that old-fashioned women gave birth in their pigsties to fool the jealous, pain-dealing gods, who do not snatch piglets. Before the next spasms could stop her, she ran to the pigsty, each step a rushing out into emptiness. She climbed over the fence and knelt in the dirt. It was good to have a fence enclosing her, a tribal person alone.

Laboring, this woman who had carried her child as a foreign growth that sickened her every day, expelled it at last. She reached down to touch the hot, wet, moving mass, surely smaller than anything human, and could feel that it was human after all—fingers, toes, nails, nose. She pulled it up on to her belly, and it lay curled there, butt in the air, feet precisely tucked one under the other. She opened her loose shirt and buttoned the child inside. After resting, it squirmed and thrashed and she pushed it up to her breast. It turned its head this way and that until it found her nipple. There, it made little snuffling noises. She clenched her teeth at its preciousness, lovely as a young calf, a piglet, a little dog.

She may have gone to the pigsty as a last act of responsibility: She would protect this child as she had protected its father. It would look after her soul, leaving supplies on her grave. But how would this tiny child without family find her grave when there would be no marker for her anywhere, neither in the earth nor the family hall? No one would give her a family hall name. She had taken the child with her into the wastes. At its birth the two of them had felt the same raw pain of separation, a wound that only the family pressing tight could close. A child with no descent line would not soften her life but only trail after her, ghostlike, begging her to give it purpose. At dawn the villagers on their way to the fields would stand around the fence and look.

Full of milk, the little ghost slept. When it awoke, she hardened her   45
breasts against the milk that crying loosens. Toward morning she picked up the baby and walked to the well.

Carrying the baby to the well shows loving. Otherwise abandon it. Turn its face into the mud. Mothers who love their children take them along. It was probably a girl; there is some hope of forgiveness for boys.

"Don't tell anyone you had an aunt. Your father does not want to hear her name. She has never been born." I have believed that sex was unspeakable and words so strong and fathers so frail that "aunt" would do my father mysterious harm. I have thought that my family, having settled among immigrants who had also been their neighbors in the ancestral land, needed to clean their name, and a wrong word would incite the kinspeople even here. But there is more to this silence: They want me to participate in her punishment. And I have.

In the twenty years since I heard this story I have not asked for details nor said my aunt's name; I do not know it. People who comfort the dead can also chase after them to hurt them further—a reverse ancestor worship. The real punishment was not the raid swiftly inflicted by the villagers, but the family's deliberately forgetting her. Her betrayal so maddened them, they saw to it that she would suffer forever, even after death. Always hungry, always needing, she would have to beg food from other ghosts, snatch and steal it from those whose living descendants give them gifts. She would have to fight the ghosts massed at crossroads for the buns a few thoughtful citizens leave to decoy her away from village and home so that the ancestral spirits could feast unharassed. At peace, they could act like gods, not ghosts, their descent lines providing them with paper suits and dresses, spirit money, paper houses, paper automobiles, chicken, meat, and rice into eternity—essences delivered up in smoke and flames, steam and incense rising from each rice bowl. In an attempt to make the Chinese care for people outside the family, Chairman Mao encourages us now to give our paper replicas to the spirits of outstanding soldiers and workers, no matter whose ancestors they may be. My aunt remains forever hungry. Goods are not distributed evenly among the dead.

My aunt haunts me — her ghost drawn to me because now, after fifty years of neglect, I alone devote pages of paper to her, though not origamied into houses and clothes. I do not think she always means me well. I am telling on her, and she was a spite suicide, drowning herself in the drinking water. The Chinese are always very frightened of the drowned one, whose weeping ghost, wet hair hanging and skin bloated, waits silently by the water to pull down a substitute.

The Reader's Presence

1. Kingston's account of her aunt's life and death is a remarkable blend of fact and speculation. Consider the overall structure of "No Name Woman." How many versions of the aunt's story do we hear? Where, for example, does the mother's story end? Where does the narrator's begin? Which version do you find more compelling? Why? What does the narrator mean when she says that her mother's stories "tested our strength to establish realities" (paragraph 10)?

2. The narrator's version of her aunt's story is replete with such words and phrases as *perhaps* and *It could very well have been.* The narrator seems far more speculative about her aunt's life than her mother is. At what point does the narrator raise doubts about the veracity of her mother's version of the aunt's story? What purpose does the mother espouse in telling the aunt's story? Is it meant primarily to express family lore? to issue a warning? Point to specific passages to verify your response. What is the proposed moral of the story? Is that moral the same for the mother as for the narrator? Explain.

3. What line does Kingston draw between the two cultures represented in the story: between the mother, a superstitious, cautious Chinese woman, and the narrator, an American-born child trying to "straighten out" her mother's confusing story? How does the narrator resolve the issue by thinking of herself as neither Chinese nor American, but as Chinese American? How does she imagine her relationship to her distant aunt? Compare Kingston's depiction of relationships across generations and cultures to those in N. Scott Momaday's "The Way to Rainy Mountain" (page 510) and to those in Richard Rodriguez's "Aria: A Memoir of a Bilingual Childhood" (page 239). How does language feature in each writer's family? How do problems of comprehension become occasions for creative play in each essay?

THE WRITER AT WORK

Maxine Hong Kingston on Writing for Oneself

In the fire that raged through the Oakland, California, hills in 1991, Maxine Hong Kingston lost, along with her entire house, all her copies of a work in progress. In the following interview conducted by Diane Simmons at Kingston's new home in 1997, the writer discusses how the fire and the loss of her work have transformed her attitude toward her own writing. Confronted with a similar loss (whether the work was on paper or hard drive), most authors would try to recapture as best they could what they had originally written. Why do you think Kingston wants to avoid that sort of recovery? The following exchange is from the opening of that long interview, which appeared in a literary periodical, the Crab Orchard Review *(Spring/Summer 1998). Diane Simmons is the author of* Maxine Hong Kingston *(New York: Twayne Publishers, 1999).*

I began by asking Ms. Kingston to talk about the book that was lost, and where she was going with her recent work.

Kingston: In the book that I lost in the fire, I was working on an idea of finding the book of peace again. There was a myth that there were three lost books of peace and so I was going to find the book of peace for our time. I imagine that it has to do with how to wage peace on earth and that there would be tactics on how to wage peace and how to stop war. I see that the books of war are popular; they are taught in the military academies; they're translated into all different languages. They [are used to] help corporate executives succeed in business. And people don't even think about the books of peace; people don't even know about them. I'm the only one that knows about it.

And so I was writing this and that was what was burned in the fire. What I'm working on now I'm calling *The Fifth Book of Peace*. I'm not recalling and remembering what I had written. To me it's the pleasure of writing to be constantly discovering, going into the new. To recall word by word what I had written before sounds like torture and agony for me. I know I can do it, I'm sure I can do it if I want to. One of my former students volunteered to hypnotize me so I could recall, but that seemed so wrong to me.

Simmons: How much was lost?

Kingston: About 200 written, rewritten pages, so it was very good. 5 But I had wanted to rewrite it again and I think to recall word by word would freeze me into a version and I didn't want to do that.

Simmons: Is the book you are working on now the same project, the same version?

Kingston: Yes, but it is not the same words. It's not the same story. It's the same idea that I want to work on peace. At one point I called it the global novel. But since then I've been thinking of it as a book of peace. And the one big difference is the Book of Peace was a work of fiction. I was imagining fictional characters. But after the fire I wanted to use writing for my personal self. I wanted to write directly what I was thinking and feeling, not imagining fictional other people. I wanted to write myself. I wanted to write in the way I wrote when I was a child which is to say my deepest feelings and thoughts as they could come out in a personal way and not for public consumption. It's not even for other people to read but for myself, to express myself, and it doesn't matter whether this would be published. I don't even want to think about publication or readers, but this is for my own expression of my own suffering or agony.

Simmons: You've said that that's how you wrote in the beginning.

Kingston: I always begin like that. I always have to begin like that. Getting back to the roots of language in myself. It's almost like diary writing which is not for others.

Simmons: You don't mean that you don't want other people to read   10
it necessarily.

Kingston: That's not a consideration. I don't want to think about any of that. I think of this as going back to a primitive state of what writing is for me, which is that I am finding my own voice again.

Simmons: Was it lost?

Kingston: Well, I started not to think about it anymore. After a while I had such an effective public voice, from childhood to now, I had found it and I had created it.

Simmons: Where do we see that public voice?

Kingston: The public voice is the voice that's in all my books.   15

Simmons: Even *Woman Warrior*?

Kingston: Yes. All my works. That is a public voice. What I mean by the private, personal voice is what I write when I'm trying to figure out things, what I write that's just for me. I get to be the reader and nobody else gets to read this. For years now I have not written in that way. I usually don't write diaries as an adult and so after the fire I needed to get to that again. I had forgotten about it.

Simmons: You are going back to before *Woman Warrior*, to before being a writer.

Kingston: Yes. Before being a writer who publishes.

Simmons: Why do you think the fire caused you to turn away from   20
fiction?

Kingston: At the same time my father died; he died a few weeks before the fire. At that time I felt I'd lost a lot. So I wanted to say what I felt about all that, about all my losses. And I don't see that as writing for publication. I see that as writing for myself, to put into words my losses. And so I started there, and wrote and wrote and wrote. But as I was writing, it became some of the things I was thinking in the book that burned; those would come into the writing, and then of course I go back to that very *id* basic place. I'm old enough and civilized enough now so that the sentences and the words that come out are very elegant, very good, very crafted. I don't return to a place that's not crafted anymore. So all this stuff that I wrote down is going to be part of *The Fifth Book of Peace*.

Abraham Lincoln

Gettysburg Address

Abraham Lincoln (1809–1865), the sixteenth president of the United States, led the country through a bloody civil war in which one side "would make war rather than let the nation survive; and the other would accept war rather than let it perish." During his presidency, Lincoln, who is still widely admired as both a political figure and a writer, wrote notable documents such as the Emancipation Proclamation and several poignant and moving speeches, including the Gettysburg Address.

Four months after the Battle of Gettysburg, Lincoln joined in a dedication of a national cemetery on the battlefield. The Gettysburg Address, delivered on November 19, 1863, would become one of the most famous—and shortest—speeches given by a U.S. president. The text that follows has been widely accepted as the "final" version of the Gettysburg Address. It comes from the "Bliss copy" of the speech—the fifth and final version of the text that Lincoln copied out by hand, probably sometime in early 1864.

For more on Abraham Lincoln, see page 501.

Four score and seven years ago our fathers brought forth on this continent, a new nation, conceived in Liberty, and dedicated to the proposition that all men are created equal.

Now we are engaged in a great civil war, testing whether that nation, or any nation so conceived and so dedicated, can long endure. We are met on a great battle-field of that war. We have come to dedicate a portion of that field, as a final resting place for those who here gave their lives that that nation might live. It is altogether fitting and proper that we should do this.

But, in a larger sense, we can not dedicate—we can not consecrate—we can not hallow—this ground. The brave men, living and dead, who struggled here, have consecrated it, far above our poor power to add or detract. The world will little note, nor long remember what we say here, but it can never forget what they did here. It is for us the living, rather, to be dedicated here to the unfinished work which they who fought here have thus far so nobly advanced. It is rather for us to be here dedicated to the great task remaining before us—that from these honored dead we take increased devotion to that cause for which they gave the last full measure of devotion—that we here highly resolve that these dead shall not have died in vain—that this nation, under God, shall have a new birth of freedom—and that government of the people, by the people, for the people, shall not perish from the earth.

The Reader's Presence

1. What historical event does Lincoln refer to at the beginning and end of the Gettysburg Address? Why do you think he chose to place this information in a position of such prominence? Why is this event relevant to the dedication of a cemetery?

2. Consider Lincoln's strategy of repetition. What phrases and sentence structures does he repeat? What is the effect of the repetition? Read the speech aloud. Do you find the repetition more or less effective when the words are spoken? Why?

3. Read Lincoln's Second Inaugural Address (page 501). In these two speeches, how does Lincoln speak of the Civil War? Do you think he uses his discussion of the war for different purposes in the Gettysburg Address and in the Second Inaugural Address? Why or why not? What do you see as the purpose of each speech?

THE WRITER AT WORK

Abraham Lincoln's Hay Draft of the Gettysburg Address

Two of the five surviving versions of the Gettysburg Address in Lincoln's own handwriting were written down just before or just after he gave the speech on November 19, 1863. Scholars disagree about whether one of these two drafts—known as the "Nicolay Draft" and the "Hay Draft"—might have been the pages Lincoln read from on the field at Gettysburg; both drafts differ somewhat from contemporary accounts of the speech that the president delivered that day. Both also differ from the final "Bliss copy" that has become the standard version of the Gettysburg Address (see previous page).

The images on the following pages show the pages of the Hay Draft of the Gettysburg Address, the second version that Lincoln wrote. Note the additions and changes Lincoln has made to this draft of his speech. Compare this version, written very close to the time of the speech's delivery, with the final version made several months later. As the fame of the Gettysburg Address continued to grow, Lincoln kept revising the words for an increasingly wide audience that had not been present to hear him speak. What do Lincoln's continuing revisions suggest about his hopes for this text? Which version do you find more compelling?

Four score and seven years ago our fathers brought forth, upon this continent, a new nation, conceived in Liberty, and dedicated to the proposition that all men are created equal.

Now we are engaged in a great civil war, testing whether that nation, or any nation, so conceived, and so dedicated, can long endure. We are met here on a great battle-field of that war. We have come to dedicate a portion of it as a final resting place for those who here gave their lives that that nation might live. It is altogether fitting and proper that we should do this.

But in a larger sense we can not dedicate— we can not consecrate— we can not hallow this ground. The brave men, living and dead, who struggled here, have consecrated it far above our poor power to add or detract. The world will little note, nor long remember, what we say here, but can never forget what they did here. It is for us, the living, rather to be dedicated here to the unfinished work which they have, thus far, so nobly carried on. It is rather for us to be here dedicated to the great task remaining before us—that from these honored dead we take increased devotion to that cause for which they here gave the last full measure of devotion—that we here highly resolve that these dead shall not have died in vain; that this nation shall have a new birth of freedom, and that this government of the people, by the people, for the people, shall not perish from the earth.

Abraham Lincoln

Second Inaugural Address

Abraham Lincoln (1809–1865) was elected to a second term as President of the United States shortly before the end of the Civil War. On the occasion of his second inaugural on March 4, 1865, Lincoln gave a well-known address remarkable for its lack of bitterness toward either his political opponents or the Confederate South. Just over a month later, on April 15, 1865, he was assassinated.

For more on Abraham Lincoln, see page 498.

Fellow Countrymen:

At this second appearing to take the oath of the presidential office, there is less occasion for an extended address than there was at the first. Then a statement, somewhat in detail, of a course to be pursued, seemed fitting and proper. Now, at the expiration of four years, during which public declarations have been constantly called forth on every point and phase of the great contest which still absorbs the attention, and engrosses the energies of the nation, little that is new could be presented. The progress of our arms, upon which all else chiefly depends, is as well known to the public as to myself; and it is, I trust, reasonably satisfactory and encouraging to all. With high hope for the future, no prediction in regard to it is ventured.

On the occasion corresponding to this four years ago, all thoughts were anxiously directed to an impending civil-war. All dreaded it—all sought to avert it. While the inaugural address was being delivered from this place, devoted altogether to *saving* the Union without war, insurgent agents were in the city seeking to *destroy* it without war—seeking to dissolve the Union, and divide effects, by negotiation. Both parties deprecated war; but one of them would *make* war rather than let the nation survive; and the other would *accept* war rather than let it perish. And the war came.

One eighth of the whole population were colored slaves, not distributed generally over the Union, but localized in the Southern part of it. These slaves constituted a peculiar and powerful interest. All knew that this interest was, somehow, the cause of the war. To strengthen, perpetuate, and extend this interest was the object for which the insurgents would rend the Union, even by war; while the Government claimed no right to do more than to restrict the territorial enlargement of it. Neither party expected for the war, the magnitude, or the duration, which it has already attained. Neither anticipated that the *cause* of the conflict might cease with, or even before, the conflict itself should cease. Each looked

Lincoln delivering his Second Inaugural Address

for an easier triumph, and a result less fundamental and astounding. Both read the same Bible, and pray to the same God; and each invokes His aid against the other. It may seem strange that any men should dare to ask a just God's assistance in wringing their bread from the sweat of other men's faces; but let us judge not that we be not judged. The prayers of both could not be answered; that of neither has been answered fully. The Almighty has His own purposes. "Woe unto the world because of offenses! for it must needs be that offenses come; but woe to that man by whom the offense cometh!" If we shall suppose that American Slavery is one of those offenses which, in the providence of God, must needs come, but which, having continued through His appointed time, He now wills to remove, and that He gives to both North and South, this terrible war, as the woe due to those by whom the offense came, shall we discern therein any departure from those divine attributes which the believers in a Living God always ascribe to Him? Fondly do we hope — fervently do we pray — that this mighty scourge of war may speedily pass away. Yet, if God wills that it continue, until all the wealth piled by the bond-man's two hundred and fifty years of unrequited toil shall be sunk, and until every drop of blood drawn with the lash, shall be paid by another drawn with the sword, as was said three thousand years ago, so still it must be said "the judgments of the Lord, are true and righteous altogether."

With malice toward none; with charity for all; with firmness in the right, 5 as God gives us to see the right, let us strive on to finish the work we are in; to bind up the nation's wounds; to care for him who shall have borne the battle, and for his widow, and his orphan — to do all which may achieve and cherish a just, and a lasting peace, among ourselves, and with all nations.

The Reader's Presence

1. How does Lincoln characterize the views of slavery before the Civil War held by the North and the South? What role does he suggest God has played in the conflict?

2. Analyze the perspective Lincoln adopts in this speech. Where does he use "I" and for what effect? Where does he use "we"? How do you think he defines "we" here?

3. Three selections in this book cover more than two hundred years in the tradition of American rhetoric. Thomas Jefferson's "Declaration of Independence" (page 711) dates from 1776, followed by Lincoln's Second Inaugural Address in 1865, and finally Martin Luther King Jr.'s landmark "I Have a Dream" speech (page 723) from 1963. What conventions of rhetoric are consistent across the centuries? What changes do you note over the years? How might personal style, audience, or subject matter account for the differences among these selections?

H. L. Mencken

The Hills of Zion

H. L. Mencken (1880–1956) was one of the early twentieth century's most influential writers and thinkers. Notorious for his sharp wit and all-too-honest criticism of anything or anyone that smacked of pretension, ignorance, or hypocrisy, Mencken became, as his biographer William Manchester has noted, "the self-appointed policeman of our moral and political standards." The H. L. Mencken Writing Award is still presented annually to the newspaper columnist whose commentary best exemplifies Mencken's spirit.

Mencken started as a reporter for the Baltimore Herald *at nineteen and just seven years later was appointed its editor-in-chief. He soon became the best-known editor and newspaperman in the business, covering some of the period's most controversial stories, including the famous 1925 Scopes "Monkey" Trial in Dayton, Tennessee, which challenged Darwinism and the teaching of evolution. Mencken wrote "The Hills of Zion" from Tennessee for the* Baltimore Evening Sun *"on a roaring hot sunday afternoon in a Chattanooga hotel room, naked above the waist and with only a pair of BVDs below." The piece was later collected in his book* Prejudices *(1926). He viewed the trial as a "circus"; as biographer Douglas C. Stenerson has said, "Mencken was moved to indignation by the discrepancy between the realities he observed about him and his vision of the kind of art, ethics, and personal behavior a society composed exclusively of truth-seekers and artists would produce."*

It was hot weather when they tried the infidel Scopes at Dayton, Tenn., but I went down there very willingly, for I was eager to see something of evangelical Christianity as a going concern. In the big cities of the Republic, despite the endless efforts of consecrated men, it is laid up with a wasting disease. The very Sunday-school superintendents, taking jazz from the stealthy radio, shake their fire-proof legs; their pupils, moving into adolescence, no longer respond to the proliferating hormones by enlisting for missionary service in Africa, but resort to necking instead. Even in Dayton, I found, though the mob was up to do execution upon Scopes, there was a strong smell of antinomianism.[1] The nine churches of the village were all half empty on Sunday, and weeds choked their yards. Only two or three of the resident pastors managed to sustain themselves by their ghostly science; the rest had to take orders for mail-order pantaloons or work in the adjacent strawberry fields; one, I heard, was a barber. On the courthouse green a score of sweating theologians debated the darker passages of Holy Writ day and night, but I soon found that they were all volunteers, and that the

[1]*antinomianism:* A theological belief that because salvation comes solely through faith and grace, a Christian therefore has no obligation to obey the law or any moral code.—Eds.

Book sale in Dayton, Tennessee, 1925

local faithful, while interested in their exegesis as an intellectual exercise, did not permit it to impede the indigenous debaucheries. Exactly twelve minutes after I reached the village I was taken in tow by a Christian man and introduced to the favorite tipple of the Cumberland Range: half corn liquor and half Coca-Cola. It seemed a dreadful dose to me, but I found that the Dayton illuminati got it down with gusto, rubbing their tummies and rolling their eyes. I include among them the chief local proponents of the Mosaic cosmogony. They were all hot for Genesis, but their faces were far too florid to belong to teetotalers, and when a pretty girl came tripping down the main street, which was very often, they reached for the places where their neckties should have been with all the amorous enterprise of movie actors. It seemed somehow strange.

An amiable newspaper woman of Chattanooga, familiar with those uplands, presently enlightened me. Dayton, she explained, was simply a great capital like any other. That is to say, it was to Rhea county what Atlanta was to Georgia or Paris to France. That is to say, it was predominantly epicurean and sinful. A country girl from some remote valley of the county, coming into town for her semi-annual bottle of Lydia Pinkham's Vegetable Compound,[2] shivered on approaching Robinson's drug-store quite as a country girl from up-State New York might shiver

---

[2]*Lydia Pinkham's Vegetable Compound:* A patent medicine that went on the market in 1875, advertising itself as a cure for the "female complaint." After the passage of The Pure Food and Drug Act in 1906, it was disclosed that the highly popular product contained 15 percent alcohol. Mencken expected his readers to know that fact. —EDS.

on approaching the Metropolitan Opera House. In every village lout she saw a potential white-slaver. The hard sidewalks hurt her feet. Temptations of the flesh bristled to all sides of her, luring her to Hell. This newspaper woman told me of a session with just such a visitor, holden a few days before. The latter waited outside one of the town hot-dog and Coca-Cola shops while her husband negotiated with a hardware merchant across the street. The newspaper woman, idling along and observing that the stranger was badly used by the heat, invited her to step into the shop for a glass of Coca-Cola. The invitation brought forth only a gurgle of terror. Coca-Cola, it quickly appeared, was prohibited by the country lady's pastor, as a levantine and Hell-sent narcotic. He also prohibited coffee and tea—and pies! He had his doubts about white bread and boughten meat. The newspaper woman, interested, inquired about ice-cream. It was, she found, not specifically prohibited, but going into a Coca-Cola shop to get it would be clearly sinful. So she offered to get a saucer of it, and bring it out to the sidewalk. The visitor vacillated—and came near being lost. But God saved her in the nick of time. When the newspaper woman emerged from the place she was in full flight up the street. Later on her husband, mounted on a mule, overtook her four miles out the mountain pike.

This newspaper woman, whose kindness covered city infidels as well as Alpine Christians, offered to take me back in the hills to a place where the old-time religion was genuinely on tap. The Scopes jury, she explained, was composed mainly of its customers, with a few Dayton sophisticates added to leaven the mass. It would thus be instructive to climb the heights and observe the former at their ceremonies. The trip, fortunately, might be made by automobile. There was a road running out of Dayton to Morgantown, in the mountains to the westward, and thence beyond. But foreigners, it appeared, would have to approach the sacred grove cautiously, for the upland worshipers were very shy, and at the first sight of a strange face they would adjourn their orgy and slink into the forest. They were not to be feared, for God had long since forbidden them to practise assassination, or even assault, but if they were alarmed a rough trip would go for naught. So, after dreadful bumpings up a long and narrow road, we parked our car in a little woodpath a mile or two beyond the tiny village of Morgantown, and made the rest of the approach on foot, deployed like skirmishers. Far off in a dark, romantic glade a flickering light was visible, and out of the silence came the rumble of exhortation. We could distinguish the figure of the preacher only as a moving mote in the light: it was like looking down the tube of a dark-field microscope. Slowly and cautiously we crossed what seemed to be a pasture, and then we stealthily edged further and further. The light now grew larger and we could begin to make out what was going on. We went ahead on all fours, like snakes in the grass.

From the great limb of a mighty oak hung a couple of crude torches of the sort that car inspectors thrust under Pullman cars when a train pulls in at night. In the guttering glare was the preacher, and for a while we could see no one else. He was an immensely tall and thin mountaineer in blue jeans, his collarless shirt open at the neck and his hair a tousled mop. As he preached he paced up and down under the smoking flambeaux, and at each turn he thrust his arms into the air and yelled "Glory to God!" We crept nearer in the shadow of the cornfield, and began to hear more of his discourse. He was preaching on the Day of Judgment. The high kings of the earth, he roared, would all fall down and die; only the sanctified would stand up to receive the Lord God of Hosts. One of these kings he mentioned by name, the king of what he called Greece-y. The king of Greece-y, he said, was doomed to Hell. We crawled forward a few more yards and began to see the audience. It was seated on benches ranged round the preacher in a circle. Behind him sat a row of elders, men and women. In front were the younger folk. We crept on cautiously, and individuals rose out of the ghostly gloom. A young mother sat suckling her baby, rocking as the preacher paced up and down. Two scared little girls hugged each other, their pigtails down their backs. An immensely huge mountain woman, in a gingham dress, cut in one piece, rolled on her heels at every "Glory to God!" To one side, and but half visible, was what appeared to be a bed. We found afterward that half a dozen babies were asleep upon it.

The preacher stopped at last, and there arose out of the darkness a   5
woman with her hair pulled back into a little tight knot. She began so quietly that we couldn't hear what she said, but soon her voice rose resonantly and we could follow her. She was denouncing the reading of books. Some wandering book agent, it appeared, had come to her cabin and tried to sell her a specimen of his wares. She refused to touch it. Why, indeed, read a book? If what was in it was true, then everything in it was already in the Bible. If it was false, then reading it would imperil the soul. This syllogism from the Caliph Omar complete, she sat down. There followed a hymn, led by a somewhat fat brother wearing silver-rimmed country spectacles. It droned on for half a dozen stanzas, and then the first speaker resumed the floor. He argued that the gift of tongues was real and that education was a snare. Once his children could read the Bible, he said, they had enough. Beyond lay only infidelity and damnation. Sin stalked the cities. Dayton itself was a Sodom. Even Morgantown had begun to forget God. He sat down, and a female aurochs in gingham got up. She began quietly, but was soon leaping and roaring, and it was hard to follow her. Under cover of the turmoil we sneaked a bit closer.

A couple of other discourses followed, and there were two or three hymns. Suddenly a change of mood began to make itself felt. The last hymn ran longer than the others, and dropped gradually into a monotonous, unintelligible chant. The leader beat time with his book. The faithful broke out with exultations. When the singing ended there was a brief palaver that we could not hear, and two of the men moved a bench into the circle of light directly under the flambeaux. Then a half-grown girl emerged from the darkness and threw herself upon it. We noticed with astonishment that she had bobbed hair. "This sister," said the leader, "has asked for prayers." We moved a bit closer. We could now see faces plainly, and hear every word. At a signal all the faithful crowded up to the bench and began to pray — not in unison, but each for himself. At another they all fell on their knees, their arms over the penitent. The leader kneeled facing us, his head alternately thrown back dramatically or buried in his hands. Words spouted from his lips like bullets from a machine-gun— appeals to God to pull the penitent back out of Hell, defiances of the demons of the air, a vast impassioned jargon of apocalyptic texts. Sud- denly he rose to his feet, threw back his head and began to speak in the tongues— blub-blub-blub, gurgle-gurgle-gurgle. His voice rose to a higher register. The climax was a shrill, inarticulate squawk, like that of a man throttled. He fell headlong across the pyramid of supplicants.

From the squirming and jabbering mass a young woman gradually de- tached herself—a woman not uncomely, with a pathetic homemade cap on her head. Her head jerked back, the veins of her neck swelled, and her fists went to her throat as if she were fighting for breath. She bent backward until she was like half a hoop. Then she suddenly snapped forward. We caught a flash of the whites of her eyes. Presently her whole body began to be convulsed—great throes that began at the shoulders and ended at the hips. She would leap to her feet, thrust her arms in air, and then hurl herself upon the heap. Her praying flattened out into a mere delirious caterwauling. I describe the thing discreetly, and as a strict behaviorist. The lady's subjec- tive sensations I leave to infidel pathologists, privy to the works of Ellis, Freud and Moll. Whatever they were, they were obviously not painful, for they were accompanied by vast heavings and gurglings of a joyful and even ecstatic nature. And they seemed to be contagious, too, for soon a second penitent, also female, joined the first, and then came a third, and a fourth, and a fifth. The last one had an extraordinary violent attack. She began with mild enough jerks of the head, but in a moment she was bounding all over the place, like a chicken with its head cut off. Every time her head came up a stream of hosannas would issue out of it. Once she collided with a dark, un- dersized brother, hitherto silent and stolid. Contact with her set him off as if he had been kicked by a mule. He leaped into the air, threw back his head, and began to gargle as if with a mouthful of BB shot. Then he loosed one tremendous, stentorian sentence in the tongues, and collapsed.

By this time the performers were quite oblivious to the profane universe and so it was safe to go still closer. We left our hiding and came up to the lit- tle circle of light. We slipped into the vacant seats on one of the rickety benches. The heap of mourners was directly before us. They bounced into us as they cavorted. The smell that they radiated, sweating there in that obscene heap, half suffocated us. Not all of them, of course, did the thing in the grand manner. Some merely moaned and rolled their eyes. The female ox in gingham flung her great bulk on the ground and jabbered an unintelligible prayer. One of the men, in the intervals between fits, put on his spectacles and read his Bible. Beside me on the bench sat the young mother and her baby. She suckled it through the whole orgy, obviously fascinated by what was going on, but never venturing to take any hand in it. On the bed just outside the light the half a dozen other babies slept peacefully. In the shad- ows, suddenly appearing and as suddenly going away, were vague figures, whether of believers or of scoffers I do not know. They seemed to come and go in couples. Now and then a couple at the ringside would step out and vanish into the black night. After a while some came back, the males looking somewhat sheepish. There was whispering outside the circle of vision. A couple of Model T Fords lurched up the road, cutting holes in the darkness with their lights. Once someone out of sight loosed a bray of laughter.

All this went on for an hour or so. The original penitent, by this time, was buried three deep beneath the heap. One caught a glimpse, now and then, of her yellow bobbed hair, but then she would vanish again. How she breathed down there I don't know; it was hard enough six feet away, with a strong five-cent cigar to help. When the praying brothers would rise up for a bout with the tongues their faces were streaming with perspiration. The fat harridan in gingham sweated like a longshoreman. Her hair got loose and fell down over her face. She fanned herself with her skirt. A powerful old gal she was, plainly equal in her day to a bout with obstetrics and a week's washing on the same morning, but this was worse than a week's washing. Finally, she fell into a heap, breathing in great, convulsive gasps.

Finally, we got tired of the show and returned to Dayton. It was nearly eleven o'clock—an immensely late hour for those latitudes—but the whole town was still gathered in the courthouse yard, listening to the disputes of theologians. The Scopes trial had brought them in from all directions. There was a friar wearing a sandwich sign announcing that he was the Bible champion of the world. There was a Seventh Day Adventist arguing that Clarence Darrow was the beast with seven heads and ten horns described in Revelation xiii, and that the end of the world was at hand. There was an evangelist made up like Andy Gump, with the news that atheists in Cincinnati were preparing to descend upon Dayton, hang the eminent Judge Raulston, and burn the town. There was an ancient who maintained that no Catholic could be a Christian. There was the eloquent Dr. T. T. Martin, of Blue Mountain, Miss., come to town with a truck-load of torches and hymn-books to put Darwin in his place. There was a singing brother bellowing apocalyptic hymns. There was William Jennings Bryan, followed everywhere by a gaping crowd. Dayton was having a roaring time. It was better than the circus. But the note of devotion was simply not there; the Daytonians, after listening a while, would slip away to Robinson's drug-store to regale themselves with Coca-Cola, or to the lobby of the Aqua Hotel, where the learned Raulston sat in state, judicially picking his teeth. The real religion was not present. It began at the bridge over the town creek, where the road makes off for the hills.

10

The Reader's Presence

1. What examples of hypocrisy does Mencken give in his description of the town of Dayton? Do you agree that the people he describes behave hypocritically? Does anyone he meets escape criticism? If so, why? If not, why not?

2. Who might be Mencken's intended audience? How do you think his original readers might have reacted to this piece? Do you think the article should have presented a more objective and balanced account of the events Mencken witnessed? Why or why not?

3. Compare Mencken's account of the revival meeting to Langston Hughes's personal account of being "saved" at a revival at age thirteen (page 162). How does Mencken's satirical account as an outsider differ in tone and diction from Hughes's more personal account as an insider? How does each writer's perspective shape the way he describes the revival?

N. Scott Momaday

The Way to Rainy Mountain

N. Scott Momaday (b. 1934) was born on a Kiowa Indian reservation in Oklahoma and grew up surrounded by the cultural traditions of his people. He has taught at the University of California, Berkeley; Stanford University; Columbia University; and Princeton University. He now teaches at the University of Arizona, where he has been since 1982. His first novel, House Made of Dawn *(1968), won a Pulitzer Prize. The author of poetry and autobiography, Momaday has edited a collection of Kiowa oral literature. His most recent publications include* Ancestral Voice: Conversations with N. Scott Momaday *(1989),* The Ancient Child *(1989),* In the Presence of the Sun: Stories and Poems *(1991),* Circle of Wonder: A Native American Christmas Story *(1994),* The Man Made of Words: Essays, Stories, Passages *(1997), and* In the Bear's House *(1999). "The Way to Rainy Mountain" appears as the introduction to the book of that name, published in 1969.*

Momaday thinks of himself as a storyteller. When asked to compare his written voice with his speaking voice, he replied, "My physical voice is something that bears on my writing in an important way. I listen to what I write. I work with it until it is what I want it to be in my hearing. I think that the voice of my writing is very much like the voice of my speaking. And I think in both cases it's distinctive. At least, I mean for it to be. I think that most good writers have individual voices, and that the best writers are those whose voices are most distinctive — most recognizably individual."

A single knoll rises out of the plain in Oklahoma, north and west of the Wichita Range. For my people, the Kiowas, it is an old landmark, and they gave it the name Rainy Mountain. The hardest winter in the world is there. Winter brings blizzards, hot tornadic winds arise in the spring, and in summer the prairie is an anvil's edge. The grass turns brittle and brown, and it cracks beneath your feet. There are green belts along the rivers and creeks, linear groves of hickory and pecan, willow and witch hazel. At a distance in July or August, the steaming foliage seems almost to writhe in fire. Great green and yellow grasshoppers are everywhere in the tall grass, popping up like corn to sting the flesh, and tortoises crawl about on the red earth, going nowhere in the plenty of time. Loneliness is an aspect of the land. All things in the plain are isolate; there is no confusion of objects in the eye, but *one* hill or *one* tree or *one* man. To look upon that landscape in the early morning, with the sun at your back, is to lose the sense of proportion. Your imagination comes to life, and this, you think, is where Creation was begun.

I returned to Rainy Mountain in July. My grandmother had died in the spring, and I wanted to be at her grave. She had lived to be very old and at last infirm. Her only living daughter was with her when she died, and I was told that in death her face was that of a child.

I like to think of her as a child. When she was born, the Kiowas were living the last great moment of their history. For more than a hundred years they had controlled the open range from the Smoky Hill River to the Red, from the headwaters of the Canadian to the fork of the Arkansas and Cimarron. In alliance with the Comanches, they had ruled the whole of the southern Plains. War was their sacred business, and they were among the finest horsemen the world has ever known. But warfare for the Kiowas was pre-eminently a matter of disposition rather than of survival, and they never understood the grim, unrelenting advance of the U.S. Cavalry. When at last, divided and ill-provisioned, they were driven onto the Staked Plains in the cold rains of autumn, they fell into panic. In Palo Duro Canyon they abandoned their crucial stores to pillage and had nothing then but their lives. In order to save themselves, they surrendered to the soldiers of Fort Sill and were imprisoned in the old stone corral that now stands as a military museum. My grandmother was spared the humiliation of those high gray walls by eight or ten years, but she must have known from birth the affliction of defeat, the dark brooding of old warriors.

Her name was Aho, and she belonged to the last culture to evolve in North America. Her forebears came down from the high country in western Montana nearly three centuries ago. They were a mountain people, a mysterious tribe of hunters whose language has never been positively classified in any major group. In the late seventeenth century they began a long migration to the south and east. It was a journey toward the dawn, and it led to a golden age. Along the way the Kiowas were befriended by the Crows, who gave them the culture and religion of the Plains. They acquired horses, and their ancient nomadic spirit was suddenly free of the ground. They acquired Tai-me, the sacred Sun Dance doll, from that moment the object and symbol of their worship, and so shared in the divinity of the sun. Not least, they acquired the sense of destiny, therefore courage and pride. When they entered upon the southern Plains they had been transformed. No longer were they slaves to the simple necessity of survival; they were a lordly and dangerous society of fighters and thieves, hunters and priests of the sun. According to their origin myth, they entered the world through a hollow log. From one point of view, their migration was the fruit of an old prophecy, for indeed they emerged from a sunless world.

Although my grandmother lived out her long life in the shadow of   5
Rainy Mountain, the immense landscape of the continental interior lay like memory in her blood. She could tell of the Crows, whom she had never seen, and of the Black Hills, where she had never been. I wanted to see in reality what she had seen more perfectly in the mind's eye, and traveled fifteen hundred miles to begin my pilgrimage.

Yellowstone, it seemed to me, was the top of the world, a region of deep lakes and dark timber, canyons and waterfalls. But, beautiful as it is, one might have the sense of confinement there. The skyline in all directions is close at hand, the high wall of the woods and deep cleavages of shade. There is a perfect freedom in the mountains, but it belongs to the eagle and the elk, the badger and the bear. The Kiowas reckoned their stature by the distance they could see, and they were bent and blind in the wilderness.

Descending eastward, the highland meadows are a stairway to the plain. In July the inland slope of the Rockies is luxuriant with flax and buckwheat, stonecrop and larkspur. The earth unfolds and the limit of the land recedes. Clusters of trees, and animals grazing far in the distance, cause the vision to reach away and wonder to build upon the mind. The sun follows a longer course in the day, and the sky is immense beyond all comparison. The great billowing clouds that sail upon it are shadows that move upon the grain like water, dividing light. Farther down, in the land of the Crows and Blackfeet, the plain is yellow. Sweet clover takes hold of the hills and bends upon itself to cover and seal the soil. There the Kiowas paused on their way; they had come to the place where they must change their lives. The sun is at home on the plains. Precisely there does it have the certain character of a god. When the Kiowas came to the land of the Crows, they could see the dark lees of the hills at dawn across the Bighorn River, the profusion of light on the grain shelves, the oldest deity ranging after the solstices. Not yet would they veer southward to the caldron of the land that lay below; they must wean their blood from the northern winter and hold the mountains a while longer in their view. They bore Tai-me in procession to the east.

A dark mist lay over the Black Hills, and the land was like iron. At the top of the ridge I caught sight of Devil's Tower upthrust against the gray sky as if in the birth of time the core of the earth had broken through its crust and the motion of the world was begun. There are things in nature that engender an awful quiet in the heart of man; Devil's

Tower is one of them. Two centuries ago, because they could not do otherwise, the Kiowas made a legend at the base of the rock. My grandmother said:

> Eight children were there at play, seven sisters and their brother. Suddenly the boy was struck dumb; he trembled and began to run upon his hands and feet. His fingers became claws, and his body was covered with fur. Directly there was a bear where the boy had been. The sisters were terrified; they ran, and the bear ran after them. They came to the stump of a great tree, and the tree spoke to them. It bade them climb upon it, and as they did so it began to rise into the air. The bear came to kill them, but they were just beyond its reach. It reared against the tree and scored the bark all around with its claws. The seven sisters were borne into the sky, and they became the stars of the Big Dipper.

From that moment, and so long as the legend lives, the Kiowas have kinsmen in the night sky. Whatever they were in the mountains, they could be no more. However tenuous their well-being, however much they had suffered and would suffer again, they had found a way out of the wilderness.

My grandmother had a reverence for the sun, a holy regard that now is all but gone out of mankind. There was a wariness in her, and an ancient awe. She was a Christian in her later years, but she had come a long way about, and she never forgot her birthright. As a child she had been to the Sun Dances; she had taken part in those annual rites, and by them she had learned the restoration of her people in the presence of Tai-me. She was about seven when the last Kiowa Sun Dance was held in 1887 in the Washita River above Rainy Mountain Creek. The buffalo were gone. In order to consummate the ancient sacrifice—to impale the head of a buffalo bull upon the medicine tree—a delegation of old men journeyed into Texas, there to beg and barter for an animal from the Goodnight herd. She was ten when the Kiowas came together for the last time as a living Sun Dance culture. They could find no buffalo; they had to hang an old hide from the sacred tree. Before the dance could begin, a company of soldiers rode out from Fort Sill under orders to disperse the tribe. Forbidden without cause the essential act of their faith, having seen the wild herds slaughtered and left to rot upon the ground, the Kiowas backed away forever from the medicine tree. That was July 20, 1890, at the great bend of the Washita. My grandmother was there. Without bitterness, and for as long as she lived, she bore a vision of deicide.

Now that I can have her only in memory, I see my grandmother in   10
the several postures that were peculiar to her: standing at the wood stove on a winter morning and turning meat in a great iron skillet; sitting at the south window, bent above her beadwork, and afterwards, when her vision failed, looking down for a long time into the fold of her hands; going out upon a cane, very slowly as she did when the weight

of age came upon her; praying. I remember her most often at prayer. She made long, rambling prayers out of suffering and hope, having seen many things. I was never sure that I had the right to hear, so exclusive were they of all mere custom and company. The last time I saw her she prayed standing by the side of her bed at night, naked to the waist, the light of a kerosene lamp moving upon her dark skin. Her long, black hair, always drawn and braided in the day, lay upon her shoulders and against her breasts like a shawl. I do not speak Kiowa, and I never understood her prayers, but there was something inherently sad in the sound, some merest hesitation upon the syllables of sorrow. She began in a high and descending pitch, exhausting her breath to silence; then again and again—and always the same intensity of effort, of something that is, and is not, like urgency in the human voice. Transported so in the dancing light among the shadows of her room, she seemed beyond the reach of time. But that was illusion; I think I knew then that I should not see her again.

Houses are like sentinels in the plain, old keepers of the weather watch. There, in a very little while, wood takes on the appearance of great age. All colors wear soon away in the wind and rain, and then the wood is burned gray and the grain appears and the nails turn red with rust. The windowpanes are black and opaque; you imagine there is nothing within, and indeed there are many ghosts, bones given up to the land. They stand here and there against the sky, and you approach them for a longer time than you expect. They belong in the distance; it is their domain.

Once there was a lot of sound in my grandmother's house, a lot of coming and going, feasting and talk. The summers there were full of excitement and reunion. The Kiowas are a summer people; they abide the cold and keep to themselves, but when the season turns and the land becomes warm and vital they cannot hold still; an old love of going returns upon them. The aged visitors who came to my grandmother's house when I was a child were made of lean and leather, and they bore themselves upright. They wore great black hats and bright ample shirts that shook in the wind. They rubbed fat upon their hair and wound their braids with strips of colored cloth. Some of them painted their faces and carried the scars of old and cherished enmities. They were an old council of warlords, come to remind and be reminded of who they were. Their wives and daughters served them well. The women might indulge themselves; gossip was at once the mark and compensation of their servitude. They made loud and elaborate talk among themselves, full of jest and gesture, fright and false alarm. They went abroad in fringed and flowered shawls, bright beadwork and German silver. They were at home in the kitchen, and they prepared meals that were banquets.

There were frequent prayer meetings, and great nocturnal feasts. When I was a child I played with my cousins outside, where the lamplight fell upon the ground and the singing of the old people rose up around us and carried away into the darkness. There were a lot of good things to eat, a lot of laughter and surprise. And afterwards, when the quiet returned, I lay down with my grandmother and could hear the frogs away by the river and feel the motion of the air.

Now there is a funeral silence in the rooms, the endless wake of some final word. The walls have closed in upon my grandmother's house. When I returned to it in mourning, I saw for the first time in my life how small it was. It was late at night, and there was a white moon, nearly full. I sat for a long time on the stone steps by the kitchen door. From there I could see out across the land; I could see the long row of trees by the creek, the low light upon the rolling plains, and the stars of the big dipper. Once I looked at the moon and caught sight of a strange thing. A cricket had perched upon the handrail, only a few inches away from me. My line of vision was such that the creature filled the moon like a fossil. It had gone there, I thought, to live and die, for there, of all places, was its small definition made whole and eternal. A warm wind rose up and purled like the longing within me.

The next morning I awoke at dawn and went out on the dirt road to 15 Rainy Mountain. It was already hot, and the grasshoppers began to fill the air. Still, it was early in the morning, and the birds sang out of the shadows. The long yellow grass on the mountain shone in the bright light, and a scissortail hied above the land. There, where it ought to be, at the end of a long and legendary way, was my grandmother's grave. Here and there on the dark stones were ancestral names. Looking back once, I saw the mountain and came away.

The Reader's Presence

1. Momaday tells several stories in this selection, including the history of the Kiowa people, the story of his grandmother's life and death, the story of his homecoming, and the legend of Devil's Tower. How does each story overlap and intertwine with the others? What forces compel the telling or creation of each story? What needs do the stories satisfy? Look, for example, at the legend related in paragraph 8. The Kiowas made this legend "because they could not do otherwise." Why could they have not done otherwise? How does this embedded legend enhance and complicate the other stories Momaday tells here?

2. From the beginning of this essay, Momaday sets his remarks very firmly in space and then in time. Discuss the importance of physical space in this essay. Why does Momaday take the journey to Rainy Mountain—a fifteen-hundred-mile "pilgrimage" (paragraph 5)? Why does he say that his grandmother's vision of this landscape is more perfect than his, even though she has never

actually seen the landscape he travels? Consider the many remarks about perspective, and change of perspective, that he includes, as well as his remarks on proportion. What significance
does he attach to these remarks? More generally, consider the temporal journeys that run parallel to the spatial journeys: the Kiowas'
"journey toward the dawn [that] led to a golden age" (paragraph 4)
and Momaday's own journeys that he relates in the essay. How
would you characterize the sense of space and time and the relation between the two that are conveyed in this essay?

3. In the interview quoted in the introductory note to this selection, Momaday talks about capturing his speaking voice in his
   writing. What are some of the phrases and passages that make
   you hear his distinctive voice as you read? Point to—and
   analyze—specific words and phrases to discuss how he creates
   the effect he is aiming for. Compare Momaday's voice to
   Zora Neale Hurston's in "How It Feels to Be Colored Me"
   (page 166) and to Calvin Trillin's in "A Traditional Family"
   (page 576). What common techniques do these writers use to
   make their prose appealing to the reader's ear?

Azar Nafisi

Reading Lolita *in Tehran*

*Azar Nafisi (b. 1950) was raised in Tehran, Iran, and educated in England
and the United States. Having returned to Iran in the 1970s to teach English literature, she experienced firsthand the revolution and its aftermath, when strict Islamic
religious codes were imposed; the harshest restrictions were placed on women.
Nafisi has said that "before the revolution I had an image of myself as a woman,
as a writer, as an academician, as a person with a set of values." Afterward, even
the smallest public gestures were forbidden, from kissing her husband in public to
shaking hands with a colleague. Fearing she would "become someone who was a
stranger to herself," Nafisi resigned her university position in 1995 and for two
years took a group of her best students "underground" for weekly discussions of
Western authors, including Vladimir Nabokov, the author of* Lolita *and the subject of Nafisi's scholarly work.*

*"Unfortunately you have to be deprived of something in order to understand
its worth," Nafisi told an interviewer. "I think if a civilization or a culture does
not take its own works of literature seriously it goes downhill. You need imagination in order to imagine a future that doesn't exist."*

Nafisi left Iran with her family in 1997. She is currently a visiting fellow at the Foreign Policy Institute of the Johns Hopkins University School of Advanced International Studies and the director of the Dialogue Project, an education and policy initiative for the development of democracy and human rights in the Muslim world. This essay, adapted from Nafisi's memoir Reading Lolita in Tehran *(2003), first appeared in the* Chronicle of Higher Education.

In the fall of 1995, after resigning from my last academic post, I decided to indulge myself and fulfill a dream. I chose seven of my best and most committed students and invited them to come to my home every Thursday morning to discuss literature. They were all women — to teach a mixed class in the privacy of my home was too risky, even if we were discussing harmless works of fiction.

For nearly two years, almost every Thursday morning, rain or shine, they came to my house, and almost every time, I could not get over the shock of seeing them shed their mandatory veils and robes and burst into color. When my students came into that room, they took off more than their scarves and robes. Gradually, each one gained an outline and a shape, becoming her own inimitable self. Our world in that living room with its window framing my beloved Elburz Mountains became our sanctuary, our self-contained universe, mocking the reality of black-scarved, timid faces in the city that sprawled below.

The theme of the class was the relationship between fiction and reality. We would read Persian classical literature, such as the tales of our own lady of fiction, Scheherazade, from *A Thousand and One Nights*, along with Western classics — *Pride and Prejudice, Madame Bovary, Daisy Miller, The Dean's December*, and *Lolita*, the work of fiction that perhaps most resonated with our lives in the Islamic Republic of Iran. For the first time in many years, I felt a sense of anticipation that was not marred by tension: I would not need to go through the tortuous rituals that had marked my days when I taught at the university — rituals governing what I was forced to wear, how I was expected to act, the gestures I had to remember to control.

Life in the Islamic Republic was as capricious as the month of April, when short periods of sunshine would suddenly give way to showers and storms. It was unpredictable: The regime would go through cycles of some tolerance, followed by a crackdown. Now, in the mid-1990s, after a period of relative calm and so-called liberalization, we had again entered a time of hardships. Universities had once more become the targets of attack by the cultural purists, who were busy imposing stricter sets of laws, going so far as to segregate men and women in classes and punishing disobedient professors.

The University of Allameh Tabatabai, where I had been teaching   5
since 1987, had been singled out as the most liberal university in Iran. It was rumored that someone in the Ministry of Higher Education had asked, rhetorically, if the faculty at Allameh thought they lived in Switzerland.

Switzerland had somehow become a byword for Western laxity. Any program or action that was deemed un-Islamic was reproached with a mocking reminder that Iran was by no means Switzerland.

The pressure was hardest on the students. I felt helpless as I listened to their endless tales of woe. Female students were being penalized for running up the stairs when they were late for classes, for laughing in the hallways, for talking to members of the opposite sex. One day Sanaz had barged into class near the end of the session, crying. In between bursts of tears, she explained that she was late because the female guards at the door, finding a blush in her bag, had tried to send her home with a reprimand.

Why did I stop teaching so suddenly? I had asked myself this question many times. Was it the declining quality of the university? The ever-increasing indifference among the remaining faculty members and students? The daily struggle against arbitrary rules and restrictions?

I often went over in my mind the reaction of the university officials to my letter of resignation. They had harassed and limited me in all manner of ways, monitoring my visitors, controlling my actions, refusing my long-overdue tenure; and when I resigned, they infuriated me by suddenly commiserating and by refusing to accept my resignation. The students had threatened to boycott classes, and it was of some satisfaction to me to find out later that despite threats of reprisals, they in fact did boycott my replacement. Everyone thought I would break down and eventually return. It took two more years before they finally accepted my resignation.

Teaching in the Islamic Republic, like any other vocation, was subservient to politics and subject to arbitrary rules. Always, the joy of teaching was marred by diversions and considerations forced on us by the regime—how well could one teach when the main concern of university officials was not the quality of one's work but the color of one's lips, the subversive potential of a single strand of hair? Could one really concentrate on one's job when what preoccupied the faculty was how to excise the word "wine" from a Hemingway story, when they decided not to teach Brontë because she appeared to condone adultery?

In selecting students for study in my home, I did not take into consideration their ideological or religious backgrounds. Later, I would count it as the class's great achievement that such a mixed group, with different and at times conflicting backgrounds, personal as well as religious and social, remained so loyal to its goals and ideals. One reason for my choice of these particular girls was the peculiar mixture of fragility and courage I sensed in them. They were what you would call loners, who did not belong to any particular group or sect. I admired their ability to survive not despite but in some ways because of their solitary lives. 10

One of the first books we read was Nabokov's *Invitation to a Beheading.* Nabokov creates for us in this novel not the actual physical pain and torture of a totalitarian regime but the nightmarish quality of living in an atmosphere of perpetual dread. Cincinnatus C. is frail, he is passive, he is a hero without knowing or acknowledging it: He fights with his instincts, and his acts of writing are his means of escape. He is a hero because he refuses to become like all the rest.

We formed a special bond with Nabokov despite the difficulty of his prose. This went deeper than our identification with his themes. His novels are shaped around invisible trapdoors, sudden gaps that constantly pull the carpet from under the reader's feet. They are filled with mistrust of what we call everyday reality, an acute sense of that reality's fickleness and frailty. There was something, both in his fiction and in his life, that we instinctively related to and grasped, the possibility of a boundless freedom when all options are taken away.

Nabokov used the term "fragile unreality" to explain his own state of exile; it also describes our existence in the Islamic Republic of Iran. We lived in a culture that denied any merit to literary works, considering them important only when they were handmaidens to something seemingly more urgent—namely, ideology. This was a country where all gestures, even the most private, were interpreted in political terms. The colors of my head scarf or my father's tie were symbols of Western decadence and imperialist tendencies. Not wearing a beard, shaking hands with members of the opposite sex, clapping or whistling in public meetings, were likewise considered Western and therefore decadent, part of the plot by imperialists to bring down our culture.

Our class was shaped within this context. There, in that living room, we rediscovered that we were also living, breathing human beings; and no matter how repressive the state became, no matter how intimidated and frightened we were, like Lolita we tried to escape and to create our own little pockets of freedom. And, like Lolita, we took every opportunity to flaunt our insubordination: by showing a little hair from under our scarves, insinuating a little color into the drab uniformity of our appearances, growing our nails, falling in love, and listening to forbidden music.

How can I create this other world outside the room? I have no choice 15 but to appeal to your imagination. Let's imagine one of the girls, say Sanaz, leaving my house, and let us follow her from there to her final destination. She says her goodbyes and puts on her black robe and scarf over her orange shirt and jeans, coiling her scarf around her neck to cover her huge gold earrings. She directs wayward strands of hair under the scarf, puts her notes into her large bag, straps it on over her shoulder, and walks out into the hall. She pauses for a moment on top of the stairs to put on thin, lacy, black gloves to hide her nail polish.

We follow Sanaz down the stairs, out the door, and into the street. You might notice that her gait and her gestures have changed. It is in her best interest not to be seen, not to be heard or noticed. She doesn't walk upright, but bends her head toward the ground and doesn't look at passers-by. She walks quickly and with a sense of determination. The streets of Tehran and other Iranian cities are patrolled by militia, who ride in white Toyota patrols—four gun-carrying men and women, sometimes followed by a minibus. They are called the Blood of God. They patrol the streets to make sure that women like Sanaz wear their veils properly, do not wear makeup, do not walk in public with men who are not their fathers, brothers, or husbands. If she gets on a bus, the seating is segregated. She must enter through the rear door and sit in the back seats, allocated to women.

You might well ask, What is Sanaz thinking as she walks the streets of Tehran? How much does this experience affect her? Most probably, she tries to distance her mind as much as possible from her surroundings. Perhaps she is thinking of her distant boyfriend and the time when she will meet him in Turkey. Does she compare her own situation with her mother's when she was the same age? Is she angry that women of her mother's generation could walk the streets freely, enjoy the company of the opposite sex, join the police force, become pilots, live under laws that were among the most progressive in the world regarding women? Does she feel humiliated by the new laws, by the fact that after the revolution, the age of marriage was lowered from eighteen to nine, that stoning became once more the punishment for adultery and prostitution?

In the course of nearly two decades, the streets have been turned into a war zone, where young women who disobey the rules are hurled into patrol cars, taken to jail, flogged, fined, forced to wash the toilets and humiliated—and, as soon as they leave, they go back and do the same thing. Is she aware, Sanaz, of her own power? Does she realize how dangerous she can be when her every stray gesture is a disturbance to public safety? Does she think how vulnerable are the Revolutionary Guards, who for over eighteen years have patrolled the streets of Tehran and have had to endure young women like herself, and those of other generations, walking, talking, showing a strand of hair just to remind them that they have not converted?

These girls had both a real history and a fabricated one. Although they came from very different backgrounds, the regime that ruled them had tried to make their personal identities and histories irrelevant. They were never free of the regime's definition of them as Muslim women.

Take the youngest in our class, Yassi. There she is, in a photograph I have of the students, with a wistful look on her face. She is bending her head to one side, unsure of what expression to choose. She is wearing a thin white-and-gray scarf, loosely tied at the throat—a perfunctory homage to her family's strict religious background. Yassi was a freshman who audited my graduate courses in my last year of teaching. She felt intimidated by the older students, who, she thought, by virtue of their seniority, were blessed not only with greater knowledge and a better command of English but also with more wisdom. Although she understood the most difficult texts better than many of the graduate students, and although she read the texts more dutifully and with more pleasure than most, she felt secure only in her terrible sense of insecurity.

About a month after I had decided privately to leave Allameh Tabatabai, Yassi and I were standing in front of the green gate at the entrance of the university. What I remember most distinctly about the university now is that green gate. I owe my memory of that gate to Yassi: She mentioned it in one of her poems. The poem is called "How Small Are the Things That I Like." In it, she describes her favorite objects—an orange backpack, a colorful coat, a bicycle just like her cousin's—and she also describes how much she likes to enter the university through the green gate. The gate appears in this poem, and in some of her other writings, as a magical entrance into the forbidden world of all the ordinary things she had been denied in life.

Yet that green gate was closed to her, and to all my girls. Next to the gate there was a small opening with a curtain hanging from it. Through this opening all the female students went into a small, dark room to be inspected. Yassi would describe later what was done to her in this room: "I would first be checked to see if I have the right clothes: the color of my coat, the length of my uniform, the thickness of my scarf, the form of my shoes, the objects in my bag, the visible traces of even the mildest makeup, the size of my rings and their level of attractiveness, all would be checked before I could enter the campus of the university, the same university in which men also study. And to them the main door, with its immense portals and emblems and flags, is generously open."

In the sunny intimacy of our encounter that day, I asked Yassi to have an ice cream with me. We went to a small shop, where, sitting opposite each other with two tall *cafés glacés* between us, our mood changed. We became, if not somber, quite serious. Yassi came from an enlightened religious family that had been badly hurt by the revolution. They felt the Islamic Republic was a betrayal of Islam rather than its assertion. At the start of the revolution, Yassi's mother and older aunt joined a progressive Muslim women's group that, when the new government started to crack down on its former supporters, was forced to go underground. Yassi's mother and aunt went into hiding for a long time. This aunt had four daughters, all older than Yassi, all of whom in one way or another supported an opposition group that was popular with young religious Iranians. They were all but one arrested, tortured, and jailed. When they were released, every one of them married within a year. They married almost haphazardly, as if to negate their former rebellious selves. Yassi felt that they had survived the jail but could not escape the bonds of traditional marriage.

To me, Yassi was the real rebel. She did not join any political group or organization. As a teenager she had defied family traditions and, in the face of strong opposition, had taken up music. Listening to any form of nonreligious music, even on the radio, was forbidden in her family, but Yassi forced her will. Her rebellion did not stop there: She did not marry the right suitor at the right time and instead insisted on leaving her hometown, Shiraz, to go to college in Tehran. Now she lived partly with her older sister and husband and partly in the home of an uncle with fanatical religious leanings. The university, with its low academic standards, its shabby morality, and its ideological limitations, had been a disappointment to her.

What could she do? She did not believe in politics and did not want   25
to marry, but she was curious about love. That day, she explained why all the normal acts of life had become small acts of rebellion and political insubordination to her and to other young people like her. All her life she was shielded. She was never let out of sight; she never had a private corner in which to think, to feel, to dream, to write. She was not allowed to meet any young men on her own. Her family not only instructed her on how to behave around men, but seemed to think they could tell her how she should feel about them as well. What seems natural to someone like you, she said, is so strange and unfamiliar to me.

Again she repeated that she would never get married. She said that for her a man always existed in books, that she would spend the rest of her life with Mr. Darcy[1]—even in the books, there were few men for her. What was wrong with that? She wanted to go to America, like her uncles, like me. Her mother and her aunts had not been allowed to go, but her uncles were given the chance. Could she ever overcome all the obstacles and go to America? Should she go to America? She wanted me to advise her; they all wanted that. But what could I offer her, she who wanted so much more from life than she had been given?

There was nothing in reality that I could give her, so I told her instead about Nabokov's "other world." I asked her if she had noticed how in most of Nabokov's novels, there was always the shadow of another world, one that was attainable only through fiction. It is this world that prevents his heroes and heroines from utter despair, that becomes their refuge in a life that is consistently brutal.

Take *Lolita*. This was the story of a twelve-year-old girl who had nowhere to go. Humbert had tried to turn her into his fantasy, into his dead love, and he had destroyed her. The desperate truth of Lolita's story is not the rape of a twelve-year-old by a dirty old man but the confiscation of one individual's life by another. We don't know what Lolita would have become if Humbert had not engulfed her. Yet the novel, the finished work, is hopeful, beautiful even, a defense not just of beauty but of life, ordinary everyday life, all the normal pleasures that Lolita, like Yassi, was deprived of.

Warming up and suddenly inspired, I added that, in fact, Nabokov had taken revenge against our own solipsizers; he had taken revenge on the Ayatollah Khomeini and those like him. They had tried to shape others according to their own dreams and desires, but Nabokov, through his portrayal of Humbert, had exposed all solipsists who take over other people's

---

[1]**Mr. Darcy:** The leading male character in Jane Austen's classic novel *Pride and Prejudice* (1813). —EDS.

lives. She, Yassi, had much potential; she could be whatever she wanted to be—a good wife or a teacher and poet. What mattered was for her to know what she wanted.

I want to emphasize that we were not Lolita, the Ayatollah was not Humbert, and this republic was not what Humbert called his princedom by the sea. *Lolita* was not a critique of the Islamic Republic, but it went against the grain of all totalitarian perspectives.

At some point, the truth of Iran's past became as immaterial to those who had appropriated it as the truth of Lolita's is to Humbert. It became immaterial in the same way that Lolita's truth, her desires and life, must lose color before Humbert's one obsession, his desire to turn a twelve-year-old unruly child into his mistress.

This is how I read Lolita. Again and again as we discussed Lolita in that class, our discussions were colored by my students' hidden personal sorrows and joys. Like tear stains on a letter, these forays into the hidden and the personal shaded all our discussions of Nabokov.

Humbert never possesses his victim; she always eludes him, just as objects of fantasy are always simultaneously within reach and inaccessible. No matter how they may be broken, the victims will not be forced into submission.

This was on my mind one Thursday evening after class, as I was looking at the diaries my girls had left behind, with their new essays and poems. At the start of our class, I had asked them to describe their image of themselves. They were not ready then to face that question, but every once in a while I returned to it and asked them again. Now, as I sat curled up on the love seat, I looked at dozens of pages of their recent responses.

I have one of these responses in front of me. It belongs to Sanaz, who handed it in shortly after a recent experience in jail, on trumped-up morality charges. It is a simple drawing in black and white, of a naked girl, the white of her body caught in a black bubble. She is crouched in an almost fetal position, hugging one bent knee. Her other leg is stretched out behind her. Her long, straight hair follows the same curved line as the contour of her back, but her face is hidden. The bubble is lifted in the air by a giant bird with long black talons. What interests me is a small detail: the girl's hand reaches out of the bubble and holds on to the talon. Her subservient nakedness is dependent on that talon, and she reaches out to it.

The drawing immediately brought to my mind Nabokov's statement in his famous afterword to *Lolita*, about how the "first little throb of Lolita" went through him in 1939 or early 1940, when he was ill with a severe attack of intercostal neuralgia. He recalls that "the initial shiver of inspiration was somehow prompted by a newspaper story about an ape in the Jardin des Plantes, who, after months of coaxing by a scientist, produced the first drawing ever charcoaled by an animal: this sketch showed the bars of the poor creature's cage."

30

35

The two images, one from the novel and the other from reality, reveal a terrible truth. Its terribleness goes beyond the fact that in each case an act of violence has been committed. It goes beyond the bars, revealing the victim's proximity and intimacy with its jailer. Our focus in each is on the delicate spot where the prisoner touches the bar, on the invisible contact between flesh and cold metal.

Most of the other students expressed themselves in words. Manna saw herself as fog, moving over concrete objects, taking on their form but never becoming concrete herself. Yassi described herself as a figment. Nassrin, in one response, gave me the *Oxford English Dictionary*'s definition of the word "paradox." Implicit in almost all of their descriptions was the way they saw themselves in the context of an outside reality that prevented them from defining themselves clearly and separately.

Manna had once written about a pair of pink socks for which she was reprimanded by the Muslim Students' Association. When she complained to a favorite professor, he started teasing her about how she had already ensnared and trapped her man, Nima, and did not need the pink socks[2] to entrap him further.

These students, like the rest of their generation, were different from   40
my generation in one fundamental aspect. My generation complained of a loss, the void in our lives that was created when our past was stolen from us, making us exiles in our own country. Yet we had a past to compare with the present; we had memories and images of what had been taken away. But my girls spoke constantly of stolen kisses, films they had never seen, and the wind they had never felt on their skin. This generation had no past. Their memory was of a half-articulated desire, something they never had. It was this lack, their sense of longing for the ordinary, taken-for-granted aspects of life, that gave their words a certain luminous quality akin to poetry.

I had asked my students if they remembered the dance scene in *Invitation to a Beheading*: The jailer invites Cincinnatus to a dance. They begin a waltz and move out into the hall. In a corner they run into a guard: "They described a circle near him and glided back into the cell, and now Cincinnatus regretted that the swoon's friendly embrace had been so brief." This movement in circles is the main movement of the novel. As long as he accepts the sham world the jailers impose upon him, Cincinnatus will remain their prisoner and will move within the circles of their creation. The worst crime committed by totalitarian mind-sets is that they force their citizens, including their victims, to become complicit in their crimes. Dancing with your jailer, participating in your own execution, that is an act of utmost brutality. My students witnessed it in show trials on television and enacted it every time they went out into the streets dressed as they were told to dress. They had not become part of the crowd who

[2]See Marjane Satrapi's "The Socks" on page 259.—EDS.

watched the executions, but they did not have the power to protest them, either.

The only way to leave the circle, to stop dancing with the jailer, is to find a way to preserve one's individuality, that unique quality which evades description but differentiates one human being from the other. That is why, in their world, rituals—empty rituals—become so central.

There was not much difference between our jailers and Cincinnatus's executioners. They invaded all private spaces and tried to shape every gesture, to force us to become one of them, and that in itself is another form of execution.

In the end, when Cincinnatus is led to the scaffold, and as he lays his head on the block, in preparation for his execution, he repeats the magic mantra: "by myself." This constant reminder of his uniqueness, and his attempts to write, to articulate and create a language different from the one imposed upon him by his jailers, saves him at the last moment, when he takes his head in his hands and walks away toward voices that beckon him from that other world, while the scaffold and all the sham world around him, along with his executioner, disintegrate.

The Reader's Presence

1. What does literature represent to Nafisi's students? How do the young women's experiences in Iran shape their interpretations and understandings of Nabokov?

2. Why is Cincinnatus's execution a metaphor Nafisi's students can relate to? What is the meaning of Cincinnatus's mantra "by myself"? How does Cincinnatus "save" himself in the end? Is this ending hopeful for Nafisi's students? Why or why not?

3. The strict moral regulations imposed by the Islamic regime are, Nafisi suggests, motivated by fear. When picturing her student Sanaz on the street, Nafisi asks, "Does she realize how dangerous she can be when her every stray gesture is a disturbance to public safety?" (paragraph 18). How is the education of women a potential threat to public safety in Iran? Read Sherman Alexie's "The Joy of Reading and Writing: Superman and Me" (page 73). How does he characterize his education as subversive? Who is threatened by his learning?

Danielle Ofri

SAT

Danielle Ofri (b. 1965) demonstrates that it is possible to be a productive writer while pursuing a busy life or career. The possessor of both an M.D. and a Ph.D., she is an attending physician at Bellevue Hospital and assistant professor of medicine at New York University School of Medicine. She is also editor-in-chief and co-founder of the Bellevue Literary Review *and the associate chief editor of the award-winning medical textbook* The Bellevue Guide to Outpatient Medicine. *Her essays have appeared in the* New York Times, *the* Los Angeles Times, Best American Essays, Best American Science Writing, *the* New England Journal of Medicine, *the* Missouri Review, Tikkun, *the* Journal of the American Medical Association, *and the* Lancet. *Her Web site, MedicalProse.com, explores the relationship between literature and medicine. A frequent guest on National Public Radio, Ofri lives in New York City with her husband and two children.*

Her first collection, Singular Intimacies: Becoming a Doctor at Bellevue *(2003), was described by physician/author Perri Klass as "a beautiful book about souls and bodies, sadness and healing at a legendary hospital." Abraham Verghese praises Ofri as "perceptive, unafraid, and willing to probe her own motives as well as those of others. This is what it takes for a good physician to arrive at the truth, and these same qualities make her an essayist of the first order." A New* York Times *profile reports, "To Dr. Ofri every patient's history is a mystery story, a narrative that unfolds full of surprises, exposing the vulnerability at the human core." Her second collection,* Incidental Findings: Lessons from My Patients in the Art of Medicine, *from which the essay "SAT" was taken, appeared in 2005.*

"Nemesio Rios?" I called out to the crowded waiting room of our medical clinic. I'd just finished a long stint attending on the wards and I was glad to be back to the relatively sane life of the clinic. "Nemesio Rios?" I called out again.

"Yuh," came a grunt, as a teenaged boy in baggy jeans with a ski hat pulled low over his brow hoisted himself up. He sauntered into my office and slumped into the plastic chair next to my desk.

"What brings you to the clinic today?"

He shrugged. "Feel all right, but they told me to come today," he said, slouching lower into the chair, his oversize sweatshirt reaching nearly to his knees. The chart said he'd been in the ER two weeks ago for a cough.

"How about a regular checkup?" He shrugged again. His eyes were 5 deep brown, tucked deep beneath his brow.

Past medical history? None. Past surgical history? None. Meds? None. Allergies? None. Family history? None.

"Where were you born?" I asked, wanting to know his nationality.

"Here."

"Here in New York?"

"Yeah, in this hospital."   10

"A Bellevue baby!" I said with a grin, noticing that his medical record number had only six digits (current numbers had nine digits). "A genuine Bellevue baby."

There was a small smile, but I could see him working hard to suppress it. "My mom's from Mexico."

"Have you ever been there?" I asked, curious.

"You sound like my mom." He rolled his eyes. "She's always trying to get me to go. She's over there right now visiting her sisters."

"You don't want to go visit?"   15

"Mexico? Just a bunch of corrupt politicians." Nemesio shifted his unlaced sneakers back and forth on the linoleum floor, causing a dull screech each time.

I asked about his family. In a distracted voice, as though he'd been through this a million times before, he told me that he was the youngest of eight, but now that his sister got married, it was only he and his mother left in the house. I asked about his father.

"He lives in Brooklyn." Nemesio poked his hand in and out of the pocket of his sweatshirt. "He's all right, I guess, but he drinks a lot," he said, his voice trailing off. "Doesn't do anything stupid, but he drinks."

"Are you in school now?"

"Me?" he said, his voice perking up for the first time from his base-   20
line mumble. "I'm twenty. I'm done! Graduated last year."

"What are you doing now?"

"Working in a kitchen. It's all right, I guess."

"Any thoughts about college?"

"You sound like my cousin in Connecticut. He's in some college there and he's always bugging me about going to college. But I'm lazy. No one to kick my lazy butt."

"What do you want to do when you grow up?"   25

"What I *really* want to do? I want to play basketball." He gave a small laugh. "But they don't take five-foot-seven guys in the NBA."

"Anything else besides basketball?"

He thought for a minute. "Comics. I like to draw comics. I guess I could be an artist that draws comics." His eye caught the tiny Monet poster I'd taped above the examining table. "That's pretty cool, that painting."

"There are a lot of great art schools here in New York." My comment floated off into empty space. We were silent for a few minutes. I made a few notes in the chart.

"That stuff about peer pressure is a bunch of crap," he said abruptly,   30
forcefully, sitting up in his chair, speaking directly toward the poster in front of him.

I leaned closer toward Nemesio, trying to figure out what this sudden outburst was related to. But he continued, staring straight forward, lecturing at the empty room, as if I weren't there.

"Anyone who tells you they do something because of peer pressure is full of crap." He was even more animated now, even angry. "People always asking me to do stuff, but I can make my own mind up." His hands came out of his sweatshirt pocket and began gesticulating in the air. "My brother and his friends, they're always drinking beer. But I don't like the taste of it. I don't believe in peer pressure."

Speech ended, Nemesio settled back into his chair, resumed his slouched posture, and repositioned his hands into his pockets. Then he glanced up at the ceiling and added quietly, almost wistfully, "But if beer tasted like apple juice, I might be drinking it every day."

He was quiet for a few minutes. One hand slid out of his pocket and started fiddling with the zipper on his sweatshirt.

Without warning he swiveled in his chair to face me directly, his   35
whole body leaning into my desk. "You ever face peer pressure, Doc?"

His eyes were right on mine, and I was caught off guard by this sudden shift in his voice and body language. I felt unexpectedly on the spot. Who does he see? I wondered. Do I represent the older generation or the medical profession or women or non-Hispanic whites? Or all of the above?

Nemesio refused to let my gaze wander off his. He demanded an answer to his question, and our doctor–patient encounter had obviously taken an abrupt turn. I could tell that a lot was riding on my answer, though I wasn't sure what exactly was at stake. Did he need me to provide a reassuring societal answer about how bad drugs are? Or did he need me to identify with him, to say that I've been where he's been, even if that was not exactly the truth?

"Yes," I said, after debating in my head for a moment, trying to think of something sufficiently potent to satisfy the question but not so sordid as to embarrass myself. "I have."

He stared at me, waiting for me to continue. His eyes looked younger and younger.

"In my first year of college," I said. "In the very first week. Everyone   40
was sitting in the stairwell and they were passing a joint around. Everyone took a drag. When it came to me I hesitated. I wasn't really interested in smoking, but everyone else was doing it."

"So what did you do?"

"I didn't want anyone to think I was a little kid, so I took a drag too."

"Did you like it?"

"No, I just hacked and coughed. I didn't even *want* the stupid joint to begin with, and I couldn't believe I was doing it just because everyone else was."

"That peer pressure is crap." Nemesio stated it as a fact and then   45
sank back into his seat.

"You're right. It is. It took me a little while to figure that out."

He pushed the ski hat back from his brow a few inches. "In my high school there was this teacher that was always on my case. She was always bugging me to study and take the tests. What a pain in the butt she was." He pulled the hat all the way off. "But now there's no one around to kick my lazy butt. I could get to college easy, but I'm just lazy."

My mind wandered back to a crisp autumn day in my second month of medical school. Still overwhelmed by the pentose-phosphate shunt and other minutiae of biochemistry, our Clinical Correlation group—led by two fourth-year students—promised us first-year students a taste of clinical medicine.

The CC student leaders had obtained permission for a tour of the New York City medical examiner's office. All suspicious death—murders, suicides, and the like—were investigated here.

The autumn sun dazzled against the bright turquoise bricks of the ME   50
building, which stood out in sharp contrast to the gray concrete buildings lining First Avenue. We congregated on the steps, endeavoring to look nonchalant.

The security guard checked our ID cards as well as our letter of entry. We followed him through the metal detector, down the whitewashed concrete hallway, into the unpainted service elevator with a hand-pulled metal grate.

We stared at our sneakers as the elevator lurched downward. It creaked past several floors and landed with a jolt. Out we spilled, gingerly, onto the raw concrete floor. Our first stop was the morgue. The cavernous walk-in refrigerator was icy and silent. There was a Freon smell, the kind I recalled from the frozen food departments in grocery stores. As a child, when I went shopping with my mother I used to lean into the bins of ice cream and frozen waffles and inhale that curiously appealing, vaguely sweet, chemical fragrance. But here the odor was intensified—magnified by the rigid chill and bleak soundlessness of the room.

Nine naked corpses lay on shelves, their wizened bodies covered with skin that glowed a ghastly green from the low-wattage fluorescent lights. These were the unclaimed bodies, mostly elderly men found on the streets. The ones that were never identified, never claimed by relatives. The ones that were sent next door to the medical school. These were the subjects of our first-year anatomy course.

From there we were herded into the autopsy room. Loosely swinging doors delivered us into a shock of cacophonous noise and harsh bright lights. We stumbled into each other, a discombobulated mass at the entranceway, blinking to adjust from the stark silence of the morgue. The autopsy room was long and rectangular. The high ceilings and brisk yellow walls lent an odd air of cheeriness. Seven metal tables lay parallel in the center. Six of them were surrounded by groups of pathology residents performing autopsies. The residents wore long rubber gloves and industrial-strength aprons. The sound of their voices and their clanking instruments echoed in the room.

The only body I had ever opened was my cadaver in anatomy lab,   55
which was preserved in formaldehyde and completely dried out. I'd never actually seen blood. In the autopsy room there was blood everywhere. Residents were handling organs—weighing hearts, measuring kidneys, taking samples from livers—then replacing them in the open corpses. Their aprons were spotted with scarlet streaks. Blood streamed down the troughs that surrounded each table.

It was disgusting, but I wasn't nauseated. These bodies didn't look like people anymore. It was more like a cattle slaughterhouse: cows and pigs lined up to be transformed into sterile packages of cellophane-wrapped chopped meat. The slaughterhouse that compelled you to vow lifetime vegetarianism, a resolve that lasted only until the next barbecue with succulent, browned burgers that looked nothing like the disemboweled carcasses you'd seen earlier.

Then I spied the last table, the only one without a sea of activity around it. Lying on the metal table was a young boy who didn't look older than twelve. He was wearing new Nikes and one leg of his jeans was rolled up to the knee. His bright red basketball jersey was pushed up, revealing a smooth brown chest. He looked as if he were sleeping.

I tiptoed closer. Could he really be dead? There was not a mark on his body. Every part was in its place. His clothes were crisp and clean. There was no blood, no dirt, no sign of struggle. He wasn't anything like the gutted carcasses on the other tables. His expression was serene, his face without blemish. His skin was plump. He was just a beautiful boy sleeping.

I wanted to rouse him, to tell him to get out of this house of death, quick, before the rubber-aproned doctors got to him. There is still time, I wanted to say. Get out while you can!

I leaned over his slender, exposed, adolescent chest. I peered closer.   60
There, just over his left nipple, was a barely perceptible hole. Smaller than the tip of my little finger. A tiny bullet hole.

I stared at that hole. That ignominious hole. That hole that stole this boy's life. I wanted to rewind the tape, to give him a chance to dodge six inches to the right. That's all he'd need—just six inches. Who would balk over six inches?

Somebody pulled on my arm. Time to go.

For months after my visit to the medical examiner's office, I had nightmares. But they weren't about bloody autopsies or refrigerated corpses. I dreamt only about the boy, that beautiful, untouched, intact boy. The one who'd had the misfortune to fall asleep in the autopsy room.

At night, he would creep into my bed. On the street, I could feel his breath on the back of my neck. In the library, while I battled the Krebs cycle and the branches of the trigeminal nerve, he would slip silently into the pages of my book. His body was so perfect, so untouched.

Except for that barely perceptible hole.   65

Now I looked at Nemesio Rios sitting before me; his beautiful body adrift in the uncertainty of adolescence, made all the rockier by the unfair burdens of urban poverty. Research has shown that health status and life expectancy are directly correlated with socioeconomic status and earning power. Whether this is related to having health insurance, or simply to having more knowledge to make healthier lifestyle choices, there is no doubt that being poor is bad for your health.

As I scribbled in his chart, an odd thought dawned on me: the best thing that I, as a physician, could recommend for Nemesio's long-term health would be to take the SAT and get into college. Too bad I couldn't just write a prescription for that.

"Have you taken the SAT yet?" I asked Nemesio.

"Nah. I can't stand U.S. history. What's the point of knowing U.S. history?"

I twisted my stethoscope around my finger. "Ever hear of McCarthy?"   70
He shrugged. "Yeah, maybe."

"McCarthy tried to intimidate people to turn in their friends and coworkers. Anyone who might believe differently from him. I'd hate to see that part of U.S history repeated."

He nodded slowly. "Yeah, I guess. I wouldn't want nobody to tell me what to think. That peer pressure is crap."

"Besides," I added, "there's no U.S. history on the SAT."

Nemesio turned toward me, his eyes opened wide. "Yeah? No U.S.   75
history?" His cheeks were practically glowing.

"No history. Just math and English."

"Wow," he said. "No U.S. history. That's pretty cool." His tone of voice changed abruptly as his gaze plummeted to the floor. "But damn, I can't remember those fractions and stuff."

"Sure you can," I said. "It's all the same from high school. If you review it, it'll all come back to you."

In medical school, I had taught an SAT prep course on the weekends to help pay my living expenses. For kids in more affluent neighborhoods, these courses were standard. But it didn't seem fair, because for Nemesio, his health depended on it.

"Listen," I said. "I'll make you a deal. You go out and buy one of   80
those SAT review books and bring it to our next appointment. I bet we can brush you up on those fractions."

He shifted in his seat and I could just detect a hint of a swagger in his torso. "Okay, Doc. I'll take you on."

Nemesio stood up to go and then turned quickly back to me. "College ain't so bad, but what I really want is to play basketball."

Now it was my turn to nod. "There's nothing like a good ballgame. I played point guard in college."

"You? You even shorter than me."

"That's why I had to find another career."   85

He grinned. "You and me both." Nemesio put his ski hat on and pulled it carefully down over his forehead. Then he slouched out the door.

Nemesio and I met three times over the next two months. While my stethoscope and blood pressure cuff sat idle, we reviewed algebra, analogies, geometry, and reading comprehension. With only a little prodding, Nemesio was able to recall what he had learned in high school. And he thought it was "really cool" when I showed him the tricks and shortcuts that I recalled from the SAT prep course.

I lost touch with Nemesio after that. Many days I thought about him, wondering how things turned out. If this were a movie, he'd score a perfect 1600 and be off to Princeton on full scholarship. But Harlem isn't Hollywood, and the challenges in real life are infinitely more complex. I don't know if Nemesio ever got into college—any college—or if he even took the SAT exam. But he did learn a bit more about fractions, and I learned a bit more about the meaning of preventative medicine. At the end of each visit, I would face the clinic billing sheet. The top fifty diagnoses were listed—the most common and important medical issues, according to Medicaid, that faced our patients. I scrutinized them each time, because I was required to check one off, to check off Nemesio Rios's most salient medical diagnosis and treatment, to identify the most pressing issues for his health, to categorize the medical interventions deemed necessary for this patient's well-being, otherwise the clinic wouldn't get reimbursed.

SAT prep was not among them.

The Reader's Presence

1. Ofri uses dialogue extensively throughout the essay. What are the effects of this choice? How would the essay be different if she had not used her patient's own words?

2. Why does Ofri juxtapose the material about Nemesio Rios with the material about her experiences in the morgue? Is the fact that Ofri does not reveal the outcome of Nemesio's story disturbing? Does this uncertainty make the essay more or less believable? Why?

3. Ofri argues that continuing his education is the best step her patient can take to safeguard his health. Do you agree? Read John Taylor Gatto's "Against School" (page 688). Does Gatto's argument apply to a case like that of Ofri's young patient? Why or why not?

George Orwell

Politics and the English Language

During his lifetime, George Orwell was well known for the political positions he laid out in his essays. The events that inspired Orwell to write his essays have long since passed, but his writing continues to be read and enjoyed. Orwell demonstrates that political writing need not be narrowly topical—it can speak to enduring issues and concerns. He suggested as much in 1946 when he wrote, "What I have most wanted to do throughout the past ten years is to make political writing into an art. My starting point is always a feeling of partisanship, a feeling of injustice. . . . But I could not do the work of writing a book, or even a long magazine article, if it were not also an aesthetic experience." "Politics and the English Language" appears in Shooting an Elephant and Other Essays *(1950).*

For more information about Orwell, see page 221.

Most people who bother with the matter at all would admit that the English language is in a bad way, but it is generally assumed that we cannot by conscious action do anything about it. Our civilization is decadent and our language—so that argument runs—must inevitably share in the general collapse. It follows that any struggle against the abuse of language is a sentimental archaism, like preferring candles to electric light or hansom cabs to airplanes. Underneath this lies the half-conscious belief that language is a natural growth and not an instrument which we shape for our own purposes.

Now, it is clear that the decline of a language must ultimately have political and economic causes: It is not due simply to the bad influence of this or that individual writer. But an effect can become a cause, reinforcing the original cause and producing the same effect in an intensified form, and so on indefinitely. A man may take to drink because he feels himself to be a failure, and then fail all the more completely because he drinks. It is rather the same thing that is happening to the English language. It becomes ugly and inaccurate because our thoughts are foolish, but the slovenliness of our language makes it easier for us to have foolish thoughts. The point is that the process is reversible. Modern English, especially written English, is full of bad habits which spread by imitation and which can be avoided if one is willing to take the necessary trouble. If one gets rid of these habits one can think more clearly, and to think clearly is a necessary first step towards political regeneration: so that the fight against bad English is not frivolous and is not the exclusive concern of professional writers. I will come back to this presently, and I hope that by that time the meaning of what I have said here will have become clearer. Meanwhile, here are five specimens of the English language as it is now habitually written.

These five passages have not been picked out because they are especially bad—I could have quoted far worse if I had chosen—but because they illustrate various of the mental vices from which we now suffer. They are a little below the average, but are fairly representative samples. I number them so that I can refer back to them when necessary:

(1) I am not, indeed, sure whether it is true to say that the Milton who once seemed not unlike a seventeenth-century Shelley had not become, out of an experience ever more bitter in each year, more alien [*sic*] to the founder of that Jesuit sect which nothing could induce him to tolerate.
>   Professor Harold Laski (*Essay in Freedom of Expression*).

(2) Above all, we cannot play ducks and drakes with a native battery of idioms which prescribes such egregious collections of vocals as the Basic *put up with* for *tolerate* or *put at a loss* for *bewilder*.
>   Professor Lancelot Hogben (*Interglossa*).

(3) On the one side we have the free personality: By definition it is not neurotic, for it has neither conflict nor dream. Its desires, such as they are, are transparent, for they are just what institutional approval keeps in the forefront of consciousness; another institutional pattern would alter their number and intensity; there is little in them that is natural, irreducible, or culturally dangerous. But *on the other side*, the social bond itself is nothing but the mutual reflection of these self-secure integrities. Recall the definition of love. Is not this the very picture of a small academic? Where is there a place in this hall of mirrors for either personality or fraternity?
>   Essay on psychology in *Politics* (New York).

(4) All the "best people" from the gentlemen's clubs, and all the frantic fascist captains, united in common hatred of Socialism and bestial horror of the rising tide of the mass revolutionary movement, have turned to acts of provocation, to foul incendiarism, to medieval legends of poisoned wells, to legalize their own destruction of proletarian organizations, and rouse the agitated petty-bourgeoisie to chauvinistic fervor on behalf of the fight against the revolutionary way out of the crisis.
>   Communist pamphlet.

(5) If a new spirit *is* to be infused into this old country, there is one thorny and contentious reform which must be tackled, and that is the humanization and galvanization of the B.B.C. Timidity here will bespeak cancer and atrophy of the soul. The heart of Britain may be sound and of strong beat, for instance, but the British lion's roar at present is like that of Bottom in Shakespeare's *Midsummer Night's Dream*—as gentle as any sucking dove. A virile new Britain cannot continue indefinitely to be traduced in the eyes or rather ears, of the world by the effete languors of Langham Place, brazenly masquerading as "standard English." When the

Voice of Britain is heard at nine o'clock, better far and infinitely less ludicrous to hear aitches honestly dropped than the present priggish, inflated, inhibited, school-ma'amish arch braying of blameless bashful mewing maidens!

Letter in Tribune.

Each of these passages has faults of its own, but, quite apart from avoidable ugliness, two qualities are common to all of them. The first is staleness of imagery: The other is lack of precision. The writer either has a meaning and cannot express it, or he inadvertently says something else, or he is almost indifferent as to whether his words mean anything or not. This mixture of vagueness and sheer incompetence is the most marked characteristic of modern English prose, and especially of any kind of political writing. As soon as certain topics are raised, the concrete melts into the abstract and no one seems able to think of turns of speech that are not hackneyed: Prose consists less and less of *words* chosen for the sake of their meaning, and more and more of *phrases* tacked together like the sections of a prefabricated hen-house. I list below, with notes and examples, various of the tricks by means of which the work of prose-construction is habitually dodged:

Dying Metaphors. A newly invented metaphor assists thought by 5 evoking a visual image, while on the other hand a metaphor which is technically "dead" (e.g., *iron resolution*) has in effect reverted to being an ordinary word and can generally be used without loss of vividness. But in between these two classes there is a huge dump of worn-out metaphors which have lost all evocative power and are merely used because they save people the trouble of inventing phrases for themselves. Examples are: *Ring the changes on, take up the cudgels for, toe the line, ride roughshod over, stand shoulder to shoulder with, play into the hands of, no axe to grind, grist to the mill, fishing in troubled waters, rift within the lute, on the order of the day, Achilles' heel, swan song, hotbed.* Many of these are used without knowledge of their meaning (what is a "rift," for instance?), and incompatible metaphors are frequently mixed, a sure sign that the writer is not interested in what he is saying. Some metaphors now current have been twisted out of their original meaning without those who use them even being aware of the fact. For example, *toe the line* is sometimes written *tow the line.* Another example is *the hammer and the anvil,* now always used with the implication that the anvil gets the worst of it. In real life it is always the anvil that breaks the hammer, never the other way about: A writer who stopped to think what he was saying would be aware of this, and would avoid perverting the original phrase.

Operators or Verbal False Limbs. These save the trouble of picking out appropriate verbs and nouns, and at the same time pad each sentence with extra syllables which give it an appearance of symmetry. Characteristic phrases are *render inoperative, militate against, make contact with, be subjected to, give rise to, give grounds for, have the effect of, play a leading part (role) in, make itself felt, take effect, exhibit a tendency to, serve the purpose of, etc., etc.* The keynote is the elimination of simple verbs. Instead of being a single word, such as *break, stop, spoil, mend, kill*, a verb becomes a *phrase*, made up of a noun or adjective tacked on to some general-purpose verb such as *prove, serve, form, play, render*. In addition, the passive voice is wherever possible used in preference to the active, and noun constructions are used instead of gerunds (*by examination of* instead of *by examining*). The range of verbs is further cut down by means of the *-ize* and *de-* formation, and the banal statements are given an appearance of profundity by means of the *not un-* formation. Simple conjunctions and prepositions are replaced by such phrases as *with respect to, having regard to, the fact that, by dint of, in view of, in the interests of, on the hypothesis that*; and the ends of sentences are saved from anticlimax by such resounding commonplaces as *greatly to be desired, cannot be left out of account, a development to be expected in the near future, deserving of serious consideration, brought to a satisfactory conclusion*, and so on and so forth.

Pretentious Diction. Words like *phenomenon, element, individual* (as noun), *objective, categorical, effective, virtual, basic, primary, promote, constitute, exhibit, exploit, utilize, eliminate, liquidate*, are used to dress up simple statements and give an air of scientific impartiality to biased judgments. Adjectives like *epoch-making, epic, historic, unforgettable, triumphant, age-old, inevitable, inexorable, veritable*, are used to dignify the sordid processes of international politics, while writing that aims at glorifying war usually takes on an archaic color, its characteristic words being: *realm, throne, chariot, mailed fist, trident, sword, shield, buckler, banner, jackboot, clarion*. Foreign words and expressions such as *cul de sac, ancien régime, deus ex machina, mutatis mutandis, status quo, gleichschaltung, weltanschauung*, are used to give an air of culture and elegance. Except for the useful abbreviations *i.e., e.g.*, and *etc.*, there is no real need for any of the hundreds of foreign phrases now current in English. Bad writers, and especially scientific, political, and sociological writers, are nearly always haunted by the notion that Latin or Greek words are grander than Saxon ones, and unnecessary words like *expedite, ameliorate, predict, extraneous, deracinated, clandestine, subaqueous*, and hundreds of others constantly gain ground from their Anglo-Saxon opposite numbers.[1] The jargon peculiar to Marxist writing (*hyena, hangman, cannibal, petty bourgeois, these gentry, lackey, flunkey, mad dog, White Guard, etc.*) consists largely

---

[1]An interesting illustration of this is the way in which the English flower names which were in use till very recently are being ousted by Greek ones, *snapdragon* becoming *antirrhinum*, *forget-me-not* becoming *myosotis*, etc. It is hard to see any practical reason for this change of fashion: It is probably due to an instinctive turning away from the more homely word and a vague feeling that the Greek word is scientific.

of words and phrases translated from Russian, German, or French; but the normal way of coining a new word is to use a Latin or Greek root with the appropriate affix and, where necessary, the *-ize* formation. It is often easier to make up words of this kind (*deregionalize, impermissible, extramarital, nonfragmentary*, and so forth) than to think up the English words that will cover one's meaning. The result, in general, is an increase in slovenliness and vagueness.

Meaningless Words. In certain kinds of writing, particularly in art criticism and literary criticism, it is normal to come across long passages which are almost completely lacking in meaning.[2] Words like *romantic, plastic, values, human, dead, sentimental, natural, vitality*, as used in art criticism, are strictly meaningless, in the sense that they not only do not point to any discoverable object, but are hardly ever expected to do so by the reader. When one critic writes, "The outstanding feature of Mr. X's work is its living quality," while another writes, "The immediately striking thing about Mr. X's work is its peculiar deadness," the reader accepts this as a simple difference of opinion. If words like *black* and *white* were involved, instead of the jargon words *dead* and *living*, he would see at once that language was being used in an improper way. Many political words are similarly abused. The word *Fascism* has now no meaning except in so far as it signifies "something not desirable." The words *democracy, socialism, freedom, patriotic, realistic, justice*, have each of them several different meanings which cannot be reconciled with one another. In the case of a word like *democracy*, not only is there no agreed definition, but the attempt to make one is resisted from all sides. It is almost universally felt that when we call a country democratic we are praising it: Consequently the defenders of every kind of regime claim that it is a democracy, and fear that they might have to stop using the word if it were tied down to any one meaning. Words of this kind are often used in a consciously dishonest way. That is, the person who uses them has his own private definition, but allows his hearer to think he means something quite different. Statements like *Marshal Pétain*[3] *was a true patriot, The Soviet Press is the freest in the world, The Catholic Church is opposed to persecution*, are almost always made with intent to deceive. Other words used in variable meanings, in most cases more or less dishonestly, are: *class, totalitarian, science, progressive, reactionary, bourgeois, equality.*

[2]Example: "Comfort's catholicity of perception and image, strangely Whitmanesque in range, almost the exact opposite in aesthetic compulsion, continues to evoke that trembling atmospheric accumulative hinting at a cruel, an inexorably serene timelessness. . . . Wrey Gardiner scores by aiming at simple bull's-eyes with precision. Only they are not so simple, and through this contented sadness runs more than the surface bitter-sweet of resignation." (*Poetry Quarterly*.)

[3]*Pétain:* Henri Philippe Pétain was a World War I French military hero who served as chief of state in France from 1940 to 1945, after France surrendered to Germany. A controversial figure, Pétain was regarded by some to be a patriot who had sacrificed himself for his country, while others considered him to be a traitor. He was sentenced to life imprisonment in 1945, the year before Orwell wrote his essay.—EDS.

Now that I have made this catalogue of swindles and perversions, let me give another example of the kind of writing that they lead to. This time it must of its nature be an imaginary one. I am going to translate a passage of good English into modern English of the worst sort. Here is a well-known verse from *Ecclesiastes*:

> I returned and saw under the sun, that the race is not to the swift, nor the battle to the strong, neither yet bread to the wise, nor yet riches to men of understanding, nor yet favor to men of skill; but time and chance happeneth to them all.

Here it is in modern English:

> Objective consideration of contemporary phenomena compels the conclusion that success or failure in competitive activities exhibits no tendency to be commensurate with innate capacity, but that a considerable element of the unpredictable must invariably be taken into account.

This is a parody, but not a very gross one. Exhibit (3), above, for instance, contains several patches of the same kind of English. It will be seen that I have not made a full translation. The beginning and ending of the sentence follow the original meaning fairly closely, but in the middle the concrete illustrations—race, battle, bread—dissolve into the vague phrase "success or failure in competitive activities." This had to be so, because no modern writer of the kind I am discussing—no one capable of using phrases like "objective consideration of contemporary phenomena"—would ever tabulate his thoughts in that precise and detailed way. The whole tendency of modern prose is away from concreteness. Now analyze these two sentences a little more closely. The first contains forty-nine words but only sixty syllables, and all its words are those of everyday life. The second contains thirty-eight words of ninety syllables: Eighteen of its words are from Latin roots, and one from Greek. The first sentence contains six vivid images, and only one phrase ("time and chance") that could be called vague. The second contains not a single fresh, arresting phrase, and in spite of its ninety syllables it gives only a shortened version of the meaning contained in the first. Yet without a doubt it is the second kind of sentence that is gaining ground in modern English. I do not want to exaggerate. This kind of writing is not yet universal, and outcrops of simplicity will occur here and there in the worst-written page. Still, if you or I were told to write a few lines on the uncertainty of human fortunes, we should probably come much nearer to my imaginary sentences than to the one from *Ecclesiastes*.

As I have tried to show, modern writing at its worst does not consist in picking out words for the sake of their meaning and inventing images in order to make the meaning clearer. It consists in gumming together long strips of words which have already been set in order by someone else, and making the results presentable by sheer humbug. The attraction of this way of writing is that it is easy. It is easier—even quicker once you have the habit—to say *In my opinion it is a not unjustifiable assumption that* than to say *I think*. If you use ready-made phrases, you not only don't have to hunt about for words; you also don't have to bother with the rhythms of your sentences, since these phrases are generally so arranged as to be more or less euphonious. When you are composing in a hurry—when you are dictating to a stenographer, for instance, or making a public speech—it is natural to fall into a pretentious, Latinized style. Tags like *a consideration which we should do well to bear in mind* or *a conclusion to which all of us would readily assent* will save many a sentence from coming down with a bump. By using stale metaphors, similes, and idioms, you save much mental effort, at the cost of leaving your meaning vague, not only for your reader but for yourself. This is the significance of mixed metaphors. The sole aim of a metaphor is to call up a visual image. When these images clash—as in *The Fascist octopus has sung its swan song, the jackboot is thrown into the melting pot*—it can be taken as certain that the writer is not seeing a mental image of the objects he is naming; in other words he is not really thinking. Look again at the examples I gave at the beginning of this essay. Professor Laski (1) uses five negatives in fifty-three words. One of these is superfluous, making nonsense of the whole passage, and in addition there is the slip—*alien* for akin—making further nonsense, and several avoidable pieces of clumsiness which increase the general vagueness. Professor Hogben (2) plays ducks and drakes with a battery which is able to write prescriptions, and, while disapproving of the everyday phrase *put up with*, is unwilling to look *egregious* up in the dictionary and see what it means; (3), if one takes an uncharitable attitude towards it, is simply meaningless: Probably one could work out its intended meaning by reading the whole of the article in which it occurs. In (4), the writer knows more or less what he wants to say, but an accumulation of stale phrases chokes him like tea leaves blocking a sink. In (5), words and meaning have almost parted company. People who write in this manner usually have a general emotional meaning—they dislike one thing and want to express solidarity with another—but they are not interested in the detail of what they are saying. A scrupulous writer, in every sentence that he writes, will ask himself at least four questions, thus: What am I trying to say? What words will express it? What image or idiom will make it clearer? Is this image fresh enough to have an effect? And he will probably ask himself two more: Could I put it more shortly? Have I said anything that is avoidably ugly? But you are not obliged to go to all this trouble. You can shirk it by simply throwing your mind open and letting the ready-made phrases come crowding in. They will construct your sentences for you—even think your thoughts for you, to a certain extent—and at need they will perform the important service of partially concealing your meaning even from yourself. It is at this point that the special connection between politics and the debasement of language becomes clear.

In our time it is broadly true that political writing is bad writing. Where it is not true, it will generally be found that the writer is some kind of rebel, expressing his private opinions and not a "party line." Orthodoxy, of whatever color, seems to demand a lifeless, imitative style. The political dialects to be found in pamphlets, leading articles, manifestos, White Papers, and the speeches of under-secretaries do, of course, vary from party to party, but they are all alike in that one almost never finds in them a fresh, vivid, home-made turn of speech. When one watches some tired hack on the platform mechanically repeating the familiar phrases—*bestial atrocities, iron heel, bloodstained tyranny, free peoples of the world, stand shoulder to shoulder*—one often has a curious feeling that one is not watching a live human being but some kind of dummy: a feeling which suddenly becomes stronger at moments when the light catches the speaker's spectacles and turns them into blank discs which seem to have no eyes behind them. And this is not altogether fanciful. A speaker who uses that kind of phraseology has gone some distance towards turning himself into a machine. The appropriate noises are coming out of his larynx, but his brain is not involved as it would be if he were choosing his words for himself. If the speech he is making is one that he is accustomed to make over and over again, he may be almost unconscious of what he is saying, as one is when one utters the responses in church. And this reduced state of consciousness, if not indispensable, is at any rate favorable to political conformity.

In our time, political speech and writing are largely the defense of the indefensible. Things like the continuance of British rule in India, the Russian purges and deportations, the dropping of the atom bombs on Japan, can indeed be defended, but only by arguments which are too brutal for most people to face, and which do not square with the professed aims of political parties. Thus political language has to consist largely of euphemism, question-begging, and sheer cloudy vagueness. Defenseless villages are bombarded from the air, the inhabitants driven out into the countryside, the cattle machine-gunned, the huts set on fire with incendiary bullets: This is called *pacification*. Millions of peasants are robbed of their farms and sent trudging along the roads with no more than they can carry: This is called *transfer of population* or *rectification of frontiers*. People are imprisoned for years without trial, or shot in the back of the neck or sent to die of scurvy in Arctic lumber camps:[4] This is called *elimination of unreliable elements*. Such phraseology is needed if one wants to name things without calling up mental pictures of them. Consider for instance some comfortable English professor defending Russian totalitarianism. He cannot say outright, "I believe in killing off your opponents when you get good results by doing so." Probably, therefore, he will say something like this:

"While freely conceding that the Soviet régime exhibits certain features which the humanitarian may be inclined to deplore, we must, I think, agree that a certain curtailment of the right to political opposition is an unavoidable concomitant of transitional periods, and that the rigors

---

[4]***People . . . camps:*** Though Orwell is decrying all totalitarian abuse of language, his examples are mainly pointed at the Soviet purges under Joseph Stalin.—EDS.

which the Russian people have been called upon to undergo have been amply justified in the sphere of concrete achievement."

The inflated style is itself a kind of euphemism. A mass of Latin words falls upon the facts like soft snow, blurring the outlines and covering up all the details. The great enemy of clear language is insincerity. When there is a gap between one's real and one's declared aims, one turns as it were instinctively to long words and exhausted idioms, like a cuttlefish squirting out ink. In our age there is no such thing as "keeping out of politics." All issues are political issues, and politics itself is a mass of lies, evasions, folly, hatred, and schizophrenia. When the general atmosphere is bad, language must suffer. I should expect to find—this is a guess which I have not sufficient knowledge to verify—that the German, Russian, and Italian languages have all deteriorated in the last ten or fifteen years, as a result of dictatorship.

But if thought corrupts language, language can also corrupt thought. A bad usage can spread by tradition and imitation, even among people who should and do know better. The debased language that I have been discussing is in some ways very convenient. Phrases like *a not unjustifiable assumption, leaves much to be desired, would serve no good purpose, a consideration which we should do well to bear in mind*, are a continuous temptation, a packet of aspirins always at one's elbow. Look back through this essay, and for certain you will find that I have again and again committed the very faults I am protesting against. By this morning's post I have received a pamphlet dealing with conditions in Germany. The author tells me that he "felt impelled" to write it. I open it at random, and here is almost the first sentence that I see: "(The Allies) have an opportunity not only of achieving a radical transformation of Germany's social and political structure in such a way as to avoid a nationalistic reaction in Germany itself, but at the same time of laying the foundations of a co-operative and unified Europe." You see, he "feels impelled" to write—feels, presumably, that he has something new to say—and yet his words, like cavalry horses answering the bugle, group themselves automatically into the familiar dreary pattern. The invasion of one's mind by ready-made phrases (*lay the foundations, achieve a radical transformation*) can only be prevented if one is constantly on guard against them, and every such phrase anaesthetizes a portion of one's brain.

I said earlier that the decadence of our language is probably curable. Those who deny this would argue, if they produced an argument at all, that language merely reflects existing social conditions, and that we cannot influence its development by any direct tinkering with words and constructions. So far as the general tone or spirit of a language goes, this may be true, but it is not true in detail. Silly words and expressions have often disappeared, not through any evolutionary process but owing to the conscious action of a minority. Two recent examples were *explore every avenue* and *leave no stone unturned*, which were killed by the jeers of a few journalists. There is a long list of flyblown metaphors which could similarly be got rid of if enough people would interest themselves in the jobs; and it should also be possible to laugh the *not un-* formation out of existence,[5] to reduce the amount of Latin and Greek in the average sentence, to drive out foreign phrases and strayed scientific words, and, in general, to make pretentiousness unfashionable. But all these are minor points. The defense of the English language implies more than this, and perhaps it is best to start by saying what it does *not* imply.

To begin with it has nothing to do with archaism, with the salvaging of obsolete words and turns of speech, or with the setting up of a "standard English" which must never be departed from. On the contrary, it is especially concerned with the scrapping of every word or idiom which has outworn its usefulness. It has nothing to do with correct grammar and syntax, which are of no importance so long as one makes one's meaning clear, or with the avoidance of Americanisms, or with having what is called a "good prose style." On the other hand it is not concerned with fake simplicity and the attempt to make written English colloquial. Nor does it even imply in every case preferring the Saxon word to the Latin one, though it does imply using the fewest and shortest words that will cover one's meaning. What is above all needed is to let the meaning choose the word, and not the other way about. In prose, the worst thing one can do with words is to surrender to them. When you think of a concrete object, you think wordlessly, and then, if you want to describe the thing you have been visualizing you probably hunt about till you find the exact words that seem to fit. When you think of something abstract you are more inclined to use words from the start, and unless you make a conscious effort to prevent it, the existing dialect will come rushing in and do the job for you, at the expense of blurring or even changing your meaning. Probably it is better to put off using words as long as possible and get one's meaning as clear as one can through pictures or sensations. Afterwards one can choose—not simply *accept*—the phrases that will best cover the meaning, and then switch round and decide what impression one's words are likely to make on another person. This last effort of the mind cuts out all stale or mixed images, all prefabricated phrases, needless repetitions, and humbug and vagueness generally. But one can often be in doubt about the effect of a word or a phrase, and one needs rules that one can rely on when instinct fails. I think the following rules will cover most cases:

(i)   Never use a metaphor, simile, or other figure of speech which you are used to seeing in print.

(ii)   Never use a long word where a short one will do.

(iii) If it is possible to cut a word out, always cut it out.

(iv)   Never use the passive where you can use the active.

---

[5]One can cure oneself of the *not un-* formation by memorizing this sentence: *A not un-black dog was chasing a not unsmall rabbit across a not ungreen field.*

(v) Never use a foreign phrase, a scientific word, or a jargon word if you can think of an everyday English equivalent.

(vi) Break any of these rules sooner than say anything outright barbarous.

These rules sound elementary, and so they are, but they demand a deep change in attitude in anyone who has grown used to writing in the style now fashionable. One could keep all of them and still write bad English, but one could not write the kind of stuff that I quoted in those five specimens at the beginning of this article.

I have not here been considering the literary use of language, but merely language as an instrument for expressing and not for concealing or preventing thought. Stuart Chase and others have come near to claiming that all abstract words are meaningless, and have used this as a pretext for advocating a kind of political quietism. Since you don't know what Fascism is, how can you struggle against Fascism? One need not swallow such absurdities as these, but one ought to recognize that the present political chaos is connected with the decay of language, and the one can probably bring about some improvement by starting at the verbal end. If you simplify your English, you are freed from the worst follies of orthodoxy. You cannot speak any of the necessary dialects, and when you make a stupid remark its stupidity will be obvious, even to yourself. Political language—and with variations this is true of all political parties, from Conservatives to Anarchists—is designed to make lies sound truthful and murder respectable, and to give an appearance of solidity to pure wind. One cannot change this all in a moment, but one can at least change one's own habits, and from time to time one can even, if one jeers loudly enough, send some worn-out and useless phrase—some *jackboot, Achilles' heel, hotbed, melting pot, acid test, veritable inferno,* or other lump of verbal refuse—into the dustbin where it belongs.

The Reader's Presence

1. What characteristics of Orwell's own writing demonstrate his six rules for writing good prose? Can you identify five examples in which Orwell practices what he preaches? Can you identify any moments when he seems to slip?

2. Note that Orwell does not provide *positive* examples of political expression. Why do you think this is so? Is Orwell implying that all political language—regardless of party or position—is corrupt? From this essay can you infer his political philosophy? Explain your answer.

3. Look carefully at Orwell's five examples of bad prose. Would you have identified this writing as "bad" if you had come across it in your college reading? Compare Orwell's list of rules for writing, and the ideas expressed in paragraph 16, to Langston Hughes's

How to Be a Bad Writer (in Ten Easy Lessons) (page 165). How does each writer use humor to persuade the reader of the serious effects of writing badly? What does each writer seem to think is at stake in how one writes?

THE WRITER AT WORK

George Orwell on the Four Reasons for Writing

As the preceding essay shows, George Orwell spent much time considering the art of writing. He believed it was of the utmost political importance to write clearly and accurately. In the following passage from another essay, "Why I Write," Orwell considers a more fundamental aspect of writing: the reasons behind why people write at all. You may observe that he doesn't list the reason most college students write — to respond to an assignment. Why do you think he omitted assigned writing? Can you think of other motives he doesn't take into account?

Putting aside the need to earn a living, I think there are four great motives for writing, at any rate for writing prose. They exist in different degrees in every writer, and in any one writer the proportions will vary from time to time, according to the atmosphere in which he is living. They are:

1. Sheer egoism. Desire to seem clever, to be talked about, to be remembered after death, to get your own back on grown-ups who snubbed you in childhood, etc., etc. It is humbug to pretend that this is not a motive, and a strong one. Writers share this characteristic with scientists, artists, politicians, lawyers, soldiers, successful businessmen — in short, with the whole top crust of humanity. The great mass of human beings are not acutely selfish. After the age of thirty they abandon individual ambition — in many cases, indeed, they almost abandon the sense of being individuals at all — and live chiefly for others, or are simply smothered under drudgery. But there is also the minority of gifted, willful people who are determined to live their own lives to the end, and writers belong in this class. Serious writers, I should say, are on the whole more vain and self-centered than journalists, though less interested in money.

2. Aesthetic enthusiasm. Perception of beauty in the external world, or, on the other hand, in words and their right arrangement. Pleasure in the impact of one sound on another, in the firmness of good prose or the rhythm of a good story. Desire to share an experience which one feels is valuable and ought not to be missed. The aesthetic motive is very feeble in a lot of writers, but even a pamphleteer or a writer of textbooks will have pet words and phrases which appeal to him for non-utilitarian reasons; or he may feel strongly about typography, width of margins, etc. Above the level of a railway guide, no book is quite free from aesthetic considerations.

3. Historical impulse. Desire to see things as they are, to find out true facts and store them up for the use of posterity.

4. Political purpose—using the word "political" in the widest possible sense. Desire to push the world in a certain direction, to alter other people's idea of the kind of society that they should strive after. Once again, no book is genuinely free from political bias. The opinion that art should have nothing to do with politics is itself a political attitude.

5

Katha Pollitt
Why Boys Don't Play with Dolls

Katha Pollitt was born in 1949 in New York City and is considered one of the leading poets of her generation. Her 1982 collection of poetry, Antarctic Traveller, *won a National Book Critics Circle Award. Her poetry has received many other honors and has appeared in the* Atlantic *and the* New Yorker. *Pollitt also writes essays, and she has gained a reputation for incisive analysis and persuasive argument. She contributes reviews, essays, and social commentary to numerous national publications, many of which are collected in* Reasonable Creatures *(1994). Her 2001 book,* Subject to Debate: Sense and Dissents on Women, Politics, and Culture, *draws on her twice-monthly column in the* Nation, *where she has been a writer, associate editor, and columnist for more than twenty-five years. "Why Boys Don't Play with Dolls" appeared in the* New York Times Magazine *in 1995.*

Pollitt thinks of writing poems and political essays as two distinct endeavors. "What I want in a poem—one that I read or one that I write—is not an argument, it's not a statement, it has to do with language.... There isn't that much political poetry that I find I even want to read once, and almost none that I would want to read again."

It's twenty-eight years since the founding of NOW, and boys still like trucks and girls still like dolls. Increasingly, we are told that the source of these robust preferences must lie outside society—in prenatal hormonal influences, brain chemistry, genes—and that feminism has reached its natural limits. What else could possibly explain the love of preschool girls for party dresses or the desire of toddler boys to own more guns than Mark from Michigan.[1]

---

[1] *Mark from Michigan:* Mark Koernke, a former right-wing talk-show host who supports the militia movement's resistance to federal government. —EDS.

True, recent studies claim to show small cognitive differences between the sexes: he gets around by orienting himself in space, she does it by remembering landmarks. Time will tell if any deserve the hoopla with which each is invariably greeted, over the protests of the researchers themselves. But even if the results hold up (and the history of such research is not encouraging), we don't need studies of sex-differentiated brain activity in reading, say, to understand why boys and girls still seem so unalike.

The feminist movement has done much for some women, and something for every woman, but it has hardly turned America into a playground free of sex roles. It hasn't even got women to stop dieting or men to stop interrupting them.

Instead of looking at kids to "prove" that differences in behavior by sex are innate, we can look at the ways we raise kids as an index to how unfinished the feminist revolution really is, and how tentatively it is embraced even by adults who fully expect their daughters to enter previously male-dominated professions and their sons to change diapers.

I'm at a children's birthday party. "I'm sorry," one mom silently   5
mouths to the mother of the birthday girl, who has just torn open her present—Tropical Splash Barbie. Now, you can love Barbie or you can hate Barbie, and there are feminists in both camps. But *apologize* for Barbie? Inflict Barbie, against your own convictions, on the child of a friend you know will be none too pleased?

Every mother in that room had spent years becoming a person who had to be taken seriously, not least by herself. Even the most attractive, I'm willing to bet, had suffered over her body's failure to fit the impossible American ideal. Given all that, it seems crazy to transmit Barbie to the next generation. Yet to reject her is to say that what Barbie represents—being sexy, thin, stylish—is unimportant, which is obviously not true, and children know it's not true.

Women's looks matter terribly in this society, and so Barbie, however ambivalently, must be passed along. After all, there are worse toys. The Cut and Style Barbie styling head, for example, a grotesque object intended to encourage "hair play." The grown-ups who give that probably apologize, too.

How happy would most parents be to have a child who flouted sex conventions? I know a lot of women, feminists, who complain in a comical, eyeball-rolling way about their sons' passion for sports: the ruined weekends, obnoxious coaches, macho values. But they would not think of discouraging their sons from participating in this activity they find so foolish. Or do they? Their husbands are sports fans, too, and they like their husbands a lot.

Could it be that even sports-resistant moms see athletics as part of manliness? That if their sons wanted to spend the weekend writing up their diaries, or reading, or baking, they'd find it disturbing? Too antisocial? Too lonely? Too gay?

Theories of innate differences in behavior are appealing. They let parents off the hook—no small recommendation in a culture that holds moms, and sometimes even dads, responsible for their children's every misstep on the road to bliss and success.

They allow grown-ups to take the path of least resistance to the dominant culture, which always requires less psychic effort, even if it means more actual work: just ask the working mother who comes home exhausted and nonetheless finds it easier to pick up her son's socks than make him do it himself. They let families buy for their children, without *too* much guilt, the unbelievably sexist junk that the kids, who have been watching commercials since birth, understandably crave.

But the thing that theories do most of all is tell adults that the *adult* world—in which moms and dads still play by many of the old rules even as they question and fidget and chafe against them—is the way it's supposed to be. A girl with a doll and a boy with a truck "explain" why men are from Mars and women are from Venus, why wives do housework and husbands just don't understand.

The paradox is that the world of rigid and hierarchical sex roles evoked by determinist theories is already passing away. Three-year-olds may indeed insist that doctors are male and nurses female, even if their own mother is a physician. Six-year-olds know better. These days, something like half of all medical students are female, and male applications to nursing school are inching upward. When tomorrow's three-year-olds play doctor, who's to say how they'll assign the roles?

With sex roles, as in every area of life, people aspire to what is possible, and conform to what is necessary. But these are not fixed, especially today. Biological determinism may reassure some adults about their present, but it is feminism, the ideology of flexible and converging sex roles, that fits our children's future. And the kids, somehow, know this.

That's why, if you look carefully, you'll find that for every kid who   15
fits a stereotype, there's another who's breaking one down. Sometimes it's the same kid—the boy who skateboards *and* takes cooking in his after-school program; the girl who collects stuffed animals *and* A-pluses in science.

Feminists are often accused of imposing their "agenda" on children. Isn't that what adults always do, consciously and unconsciously? Kids aren't born religious, or polite, or kind, or able to remember where they put their sneakers. Inculcating these behaviors, and the values behind them, is a tremendous amount of work, involving many adults. We don't have a choice, really, about *whether* we should give our children messages about what it means to be male and female—they're bombarded with them from morning till night.

The question, as always, is what do we want those messages to be?

The Reader's Presence

1. Pollitt notes in her opening paragraph that "it's twenty-eight years since the founding of NOW, and boys still like trucks and girls still like dolls." What does Pollitt identify as the competing theories to explain these differences between boys and girls? Which theory does Pollitt prefer, and how does she express her support of it?

2. As you reread the essay, consider carefully the role of the media in upholding the status quo with regard to differentiated roles for girls and boys. As you develop a response to this question, examine carefully both the media directed principally to children and the media targeted at adults. In the latter category, for instance, Pollitt refers to the media version of scientific research studies into gender differences (paragraph 2) and alludes to popular books that discuss the differences between men and women, such as *Men Are from Mars, Women Are from Venus*, and *You Just Don't Understand* (paragraph 12). Drawing on Pollitt's essay and on your own experience, identify—and discuss—the specific social responsibilities you would like to see America's mass media take more seriously.

3. How would you characterize Pollitt's stance toward today's parents? What are some of the reasons she gives to explain parents' choices and actions? Consider Pollitt's argument in the light of Bernard Cooper's essay "A Clack of Tiny Sparks: Remembrances of a Gay Boyhood" (page 121). How does Cooper's account of his parents' attitudes compare with Pollitt's portrait of parents? Do a similar comparative reading of Pollitt's polemic and Adrienne Rich's portrait of her parents in "Split at the Root: An Essay on Jewish Identity" (page 228). What general points about childrearing can you draw from the contrasts and commonalities between the essays? How does parenting figure in the transmission of beliefs and practices in America, according to these authors?

Joe Sacco

Through Other Eyes

Joe Sacco (b. 1960), who calls himself "a really good cartoonist who does journalism," was born in Malta, raised in Australia, and later emigrated to the United States. Graduating with a degree in journalism from the University of Oregon in 1981, Sacco lived for some time in Germany and then traveled to the Middle East as a "comics journalist" to document the lives of Palestinians living in the Gaza Strip. His comics from this period were collected as Palestine *(1996), for which Sacco won the American Book Award. He later traveled to Bosnia to chronicle the deadly conflict among Serbs, Croats, and Muslims in comic books including* Safe Area Goražde *(2000),* The Fixer *(2003), and his latest,* War's End *(2005).*

Describing his commitment to his unique combination of comic art and journalism, Sacco told an interviewer, "I am interested in what people care about, what they think about, and this gives me an ability to enter the world they live in." The following selection from Palestine *takes place after Sacco has spent considerable time living among Palestinian refugees; in "Through Other Eyes," his encounter with two Israeli women helps him enter their quite different world.*

The Reader's Presence

1. How do Sacco's views of the Old City and the market differ from those of Naomi and Paula? Do you think the women's fears of going to the market are rational? Why or why not? Does Sacco find their fears reasonable at the beginning? Does his opinion change?

2. Sacco includes himself as a character in all of his journalistic comics. Do you think this makes his journalism less objective? Would you prefer more objective coverage of the events in "Through Other Eyes"? Why or why not?

3. Examine the way that Sacco portrays himself and Paula in the market. Then look at the portion of Marjane Satrapi's "The Socks" in which the police arrive at the party (pages 268–270). How does each graphic writer describe the chaos and fear of the scene? How are the portrayals similar and different?

THE GRAPHIC WRITER AT WORK

Kristian Williams on *The Case for Comics Journalism*

Joe Sacco draws comics—or graphic novels, as serious examples of the genre are commonly called—but he is also a journalist. Unlike many more traditional journalists, however, he is a character in his own books and so clearly a part of the stories he covers. In this excerpt from "The Case for Comics Journalism," an article published in the Columbia Journalism Review *in 2005, Kristian Williams examines how work like Sacco's can provide the "voice and meaning" that many readers long to find in news stories.*

Of course, comic-book journalists face many of the same difficulties as those working in more conventional media—questions of bias, unreliable sources, language barriers, and ethical dilemmas. But their strategies for resolving them are quite different from those of standard newspaper reporting or broadcast journalism.

In *Palestine: In the Gaza Strip*, Joe Sacco remembers a conversation with two Israeli women. One asks, "Shouldn't you be seeing our side of the story, too?"

He reflects: "And what can I say? . . . standing there with two girls from Tel Aviv, it occurs to me that I have seen the Israelis, but through Palestinian eyes—that Israelis were mainly soldiers and settlers to me now, too."

He invites one of his new friends to the Arab market, to show her the Palestine he has seen. Instead, he discovers that walking beside an Israeli, surrounded by Palestinians, her fear is contagious. The Palestinians, who have been so kind to him, whom he has lived among for weeks, suddenly appear strange and hostile. Sacco feels himself near to panic. It is an enlightening moment. However briefly, he does see the conflict from the other side, and he realizes that the Israeli experience is not just about seizing land and conducting raids, but also about the quiet tension — the trepidation of a young woman walking through the market. Such ambivalence fits well with the complexities of the Palestinian territories.

Sacco recognizes that his perspective has been limited, perhaps even   5 compromised, by his immersion into Palestinian life. More traditional correspondents covering the Israeli–Palestinian conflict might have the same insight, but are largely unable to deal with it in their stories. Sacco, meanwhile, does not deny the reality of what he has seen, or try to balance it by staying with settlers or embedding with the Israeli Defense Forces. Nor does he apologize for his views, even with their blind spots and contradictions. Instead, he shows us what he has learned — including those elements that frustrate any easy conclusions. "What I've seen before my eyes," Sacco tells me, "isn't often balanced."

In comics journalism, more so perhaps than in any other medium, the reporter's role is consistently emphasized. He is often present, not merely as a voice or a talking head, but as a moral viewpoint and as a participant in the events described. "You become part of a story if you're a journalist," Sacco says. "I mean, you can try to write yourself out of it, but you become involved. I think it's more honest to show that your involvement affects people."

As the reporter comes into focus, we see that he is not a neutral conduit for news and information, but a person like ourselves — a fallible human being, vulnerable to bias and ignorance and error. By acknowledging his own humanity, the writer can encourage the reader to think critically about what he or she reads.

Comics are well suited to that role because of the inherent narrative properties of the medium. They are not merely illustrated stories, or pictures matched with commentary. Instead, the narrative relies on both the words and the pictures; meaning is produced by the interaction of image and text. Yet each element remains to some degree independent of the other. For this reason, and because several sets of text-image blocks can appear side by side on the same page, comics are well suited to represent the fragmentation of experience during crisis, or the incommensurable views of opposing sides in the midst of conflict, or the kaleidoscopic chaos of a desert carnival like Burning Man.

Moreover, by mixing written words and images, comics have the inherent ability to juxtapose a literal retelling and artistic symbolism, or conversely, symbolic language and representational imagery. . . .

The independence of the words and the pictures allows for an overlay   10 of subjective and objective storytelling. Tensions between the written word and the image can be used to highlight uncertainties, ambiguities, and ironies that other media might inadvertently play down or deliberately ignore.

All of this suggests, simply, that comics open possibilities for journalists that are less available in other media. And perhaps more importantly, they add to the options available to readers, who have lately demonstrated a hunger for voice and meaning in news coverage. Witness the proliferation of blogs and the continued popularity of zines. Like zines and blogs, comics drop the pretense of detachment and emphasize perspective. Furthermore, comics are visually engaging and famously easy to understand. They are, as Sacco says, "inviting. It looks like an easy read." After all, as everyone knows, even kids read comic books.

Eric Schlosser

Why McDonald's Fries Taste So Good

Eric Schlosser is a correspondent for the Atlantic. *His articles and essays about contemporary America have won numerous journalistic honors and awards, including a National Magazine Award for an article he wrote on marijuana. His latest collection of essays,* Reefer Madness: Sex, Drugs, and Cheap Labor in the American Black Market *(2003), examines the country's underground economy.* Fast Food Nation: The Dark Side of the All-American Meal *(2001), Schlosser's controversial and influential first book, prompted a reexamination of practices in the meat-processing industry.*

Of writing Fast Food Nation, *Schlosser said, "I care about the literary aspects of the book. I tried to make it as clear as possible, and make it an interesting thing to read, but I sacrificed some of that, ultimately, in order to get this out to people and let them know what's going on."*

The french fry was "almost sacrosanct for me," Ray Kroc, one of the founders of McDonald's, wrote in his autobiography, "its preparation a ritual to be followed religiously." During the chain's early years french fries were made from scratch every day. Russet Burbank potatoes were peeled, cut into shoestrings, and fried in McDonald's kitchens. As the chain expanded nationwide, in the mid-1960s, it sought to cut labor costs, reduce the number of suppliers, and ensure that its fries tasted the same at every restaurant. McDonald's began switching to frozen french fries in 1966—and few customers noticed the difference. Nevertheless, the change had a profound effect on the nation's agriculture and diet. A familiar food had been transformed into a highly processed industrial commodity. McDonald's fries now come from huge manufacturing plants that can peel, slice, cook, and freeze two million pounds of potatoes a day. The rapid expansion of McDonald's and the popularity of its low-cost, mass-produced fries changed the way Americans eat. In 1960 Americans consumed an average of about eighty-one pounds of fresh potatoes and four pounds of frozen french fries. In 2000 they consumed an average of about fifty pounds of fresh potatoes and thirty pounds of frozen fries. Today McDonald's is the largest buyer of potatoes in the United States.

The taste of McDonald's french fries played a crucial role in the chain's success—fries are much more profitable than hamburgers—and was long praised by customers, competitors, and even food critics. James Beard loved McDonald's fries. Their distinctive taste does not stem from the kind of potatoes that McDonald's buys, the technology that processes them, or the restaurant equipment that fries them: other chains use Russet Burbanks, buy their french fries from the same large processing companies, and have similar fryers in their restaurant kitchens. The taste of a french fry is largely determined by the cooking oil. For decades McDonald's cooked its french fries in a mixture of about seven percent cottonseed oil and 93 percent beef tallow. The mixture gave the fries their unique flavor—and more saturated beef fat per ounce than a McDonald's hamburger.

In 1990, amid a barrage of criticism over the amount of cholesterol in its fries, McDonald's switched to pure vegetable oil. This presented the company with a challenge: how to make fries that subtly taste like beef without cooking them in beef tallow. A look at the ingredients in McDonald's french fries suggests how the problem was solved. Toward the end of the list is a seemingly innocuous yet oddly mysterious phrase: "natural flavor." That ingredient helps to explain not only why the fries taste so good but also why most fast food—indeed, most of the food Americans eat today—tastes the way it does.

Open your refrigerator, your freezer, your kitchen cupboards, and look at the labels on your food. You'll find "natural flavor" or "artificial flavor" in just about every list of ingredients. The similarities between these two broad categories are far more significant than the differences. Both are man-made additives that give most processed food most of its taste. People usually buy a food item the first time because of its packaging or appearance. Taste usually determines whether they buy it again. About 90 percent of the money that Americans now spend on food goes to buy processed food. The canning, freezing, and dehydrating techniques used in processing destroy most of food's flavor—and so a vast industry has arisen in the United States to make processed food palatable. Without this flavor industry today's fast food would not exist. The names of the leading American fast-food chains and their best-selling menu items have become embedded in our popular culture and famous worldwide. But few people can name the companies that manufacture fast food's taste.

The flavor industry is highly secretive. Its leading companies will not   5
divulge the precise formulas of flavor compounds or the identities of clients. The secrecy is deemed essential for protecting the reputations of beloved brands. The fast-food chains, understandably, would like the public to believe that the flavors of the food they sell somehow originate in their restaurant kitchens, not in distant factories run by other firms. A McDonald's french fry is one of countless foods whose flavor is just a component in a complex manufacturing process. The look and the taste of what we eat now are frequently deceiving—by design.

THE FLAVOR CORRIDOR

The New Jersey Turnpike runs through the heart of the flavor industry, an industrial corridor dotted with refineries and chemical plants. International Flavors & Fragrances (IFF), the world's largest flavor company, has a manufacturing facility off Exit 8A in Dayton, New Jersey; Givaudan, the world's second-largest flavor company, has a plant in East Hanover. Haarmann & Reimer, the largest German flavor company, has a plant in Teterboro, as does Takasago, the largest Japanese flavor company. Flavor Dynamics has a plant in South Plainfield; Frutarom is in North Bergen; Elan Chemical is in Newark. Dozens of companies manufacture flavors in the corridor between Teaneck and South Brunswick. Altogether the area produces about two thirds of the flavor additives sold in the United States.

The IFF plant in Dayton is a huge pale-blue building with a modern office complex attached to the front. It sits in an industrial park, not far from a BASF plastics factory, a Jolly French Toast factory, and a plant that manufactures Liz Claiborne cosmetics. Dozens of tractor-trailers were parked at the IFF loading dock the afternoon I visited, and a thin cloud of steam floated from a roof vent. Before entering the plant, I signed a nondisclosure form, promising not to reveal the brand names of foods that contain IFF flavors. The place reminded me of Willy Wonka's chocolate factory. Wonderful smells drifted through the hallways, men and women in neat white lab coats cheerfully went about their work, and hundreds of little glass bottles sat on laboratory tables and shelves. The bottles contained powerful but fragile flavor chemicals, shielded from light by brown glass and round white caps shut tight. The long chemical names on the little white labels were as mystifying to me as medieval Latin. These odd-sounding things would be mixed and poured and turned into new substances, like magic potions.

I was not invited into the manufacturing areas of the IFF plant, where, it was thought, I might discover trade secrets. Instead I toured various laboratories and pilot kitchens, where the flavors of well-established brands are tested or adjusted, and where whole new flavors are created. IFF's snack-and-savory lab is responsible for the flavors of potato chips, corn chips, breads, crackers, breakfast cereals, and pet food. The confectionary lab devises flavors for ice cream, cookies, candies, toothpastes, mouth-washes, and antacids. Everywhere I looked, I saw famous, widely advertised products sitting on laboratory desks and tables. The beverage lab was full of brightly colored liquids in clear bottles. It comes up with flavors for popular soft drinks, sports drinks, bottled teas, and wine coolers, for all-natural juice drinks, organic soy drinks, beers, and malt liquors. In one pilot kitchen I saw a dapper food technologist, a middle-aged man with an elegant tie beneath his crisp lab coat, carefully preparing a batch of cookies with white frosting and pink-and-white sprinkles. In another pilot kitchen I saw a pizza oven, a grill, a milk-shake machine, and a french fryer identical to those I'd seen at innumerable fast-food restaurants.

In addition to being the world's largest flavor company, IFF manufactures the smells of six of the ten best-selling fine perfumes in the United States, including Estée Lauder's Beautiful, Clinique's Happy, Lancôme's Trésor, and Calvin Klein's Eternity. It also makes the smells of household products such as deodorant, dishwashing detergent, bath soap, shampoo, furniture polish, and floor wax. All these aromas are made through essentially the same process: the manipulation of volatile chemicals. The basic science behind the scent of your shaving cream is the same as that governing the flavor of your TV dinner.

"NATURAL" AND "ARTIFICIAL"

Scientists now believe that human beings acquired the sense of taste as   10
a way to avoid being poisoned. Edible plants generally taste sweet, harmful ones bitter. The taste buds on our tongues can detect the presence of half a dozen or so basic tastes, including sweet, sour, bitter, salty, astringent, and umami, a taste discovered by Japanese researchers—a rich and full sense of deliciousness triggered by amino acids in foods such as meat, shellfish, mushrooms, potatoes, and seaweed. Taste buds offer a limited means of detection, however, compared with the human olfactory system, which can perceive thousands of different chemical aromas. Indeed, "flavor" is primarily the smell of gases being released by the chemicals you've just put in your mouth. The aroma of a food can be responsible for as much as 90 percent of its taste.

The act of drinking, sucking, or chewing a substance releases its volatile gases. They flow out of your mouth and up your nostrils, or up the passageway in the back of your mouth, to a thin layer of nerve cells called the olfactory epithelium, located at the base of your nose, right between your eyes. Your brain combines the complex smell signals from your olfactory epithelium with the simple taste signals from your tongue, assigns a flavor to what's in your mouth, and decides if it's something you want to eat.

A person's food preferences, like his or her personality, are formed during the first few years of life, through a process of socialization. Babies innately prefer sweet tastes and reject bitter ones; toddlers can learn to enjoy hot and spicy food, bland health food, or fast food, depending on what the people around them eat. The human sense of smell is still not fully understood. It is greatly affected by psychological factors and expectations. The mind focuses intently on some of the aromas that surround us and filters out the overwhelming majority. People can grow accustomed to bad smells or good smells; they stop noticing what once seemed overpowering. Aroma and memory are somehow inextricably linked. A smell can suddenly evoke a long-forgotten moment. The flavors of childhood foods seem to leave an indelible mark, and adults often return to them, without always knowing why. These "comfort foods" become a source of pleasure and reassurance—a fact that fast-food chains use to their advantage. Childhood memories of Happy Meals, which come with french fries, can translate into frequent adult visits to McDonald's. On average, Americans now eat about four servings of french fries every week.

The human craving for flavor has been a largely unacknowledged and unexamined force in history. For millennia royal empires have been built, unexplored lands traversed, and great religions and philosophies forever changed by the spice trade. In 1492 Christopher Columbus set sail to find seasoning. Today the influence of flavor in the world marketplace is no less decisive. The rise and fall of corporate empires—of soft-drink companies, snack-food companies, and fast-food chains—is often determined by how their products taste.

The flavor industry emerged in the mid-nineteenth century, as processed foods began to be manufactured on a large scale. Recognizing the need for flavor additives, early food processors turned to perfume companies that had long experience working with essential oils and volatile aromas. The great perfume houses of England, France, and the Netherlands produced many of the first flavor compounds. In the early part of the twentieth century Germany took the technological lead in flavor production, owing to its powerful chemical industry. Legend has it that a German scientist discovered methyl anthranilate, one of the first artificial flavors, by accident while mixing chemicals in his laboratory. Suddenly the lab was filled with the sweet smell of grapes. Methyl anthranilate later became the chief flavor compound in grape Kool-Aid. After World War II much of the perfume industry shifted from Europe to the United States, settling in New York City near the garment district and the fashion houses. The flavor industry came with it, later moving to New Jersey for greater plant capacity. Man-made flavor additives were used mostly in baked goods, candies, and sodas until the 1950s, when sales of processed food began to soar. The invention of gas chromatographs and mass spectrometers—machines capable of detecting volatile gases at low levels—vastly increased the number of flavors that could be synthesized. By the mid-1960s flavor companies were churning out compounds to supply the taste of Pop Tarts, Bac-Os, Tab, Tang, Filet-O-Fish sandwiches, and literally thousands of other new foods.

The American flavor industry now has annual revenues of about $1.4   15 billion. Approximately 10,000 new processed-food products are introduced every year in the United States. Almost all of them require flavor additives. And about nine out of ten of these products fail. The latest flavor innovations and corporate realignments are heralded in publications such as *Chemical Market Reporter, Food Chemical News, Food Engineering*, and *Food Product Design*. The progress of IFF has mirrored that of the flavor industry as a whole. IFF was formed in 1958, through the merger of two small companies. Its annual revenues have grown almost fifteenfold since the early 1970s, and it currently has manufacturing facilities in twenty countries.

Today's sophisticated spectrometers, gas chromatographs, and headspace-vapor analyzers provide a detailed map of a food's flavor components, detecting chemical aromas present in amounts as low as one part per billion. The human nose, however, is even more sensitive. A nose can detect aromas present in quantities of a few parts per trillion—an amount equivalent to about 0.000000000003 percent. Complex aromas, such as those of coffee and roasted meat, are composed of volatile gases from nearly a thousand different chemicals. The smell of a strawberry arises from the interaction of about 350 chemicals that are present in minute amounts. The quality that people seek most of all in a food—flavor—is usually present in a quantity too infinitesimal to be measured in traditional culinary terms such as ounces or teaspoons. The chemical that provides the dominant flavor of bell pepper can be tasted in amounts as low as 0.02 parts per billion; one drop is sufficient to add flavor to five average-size swimming pools. The flavor additive usually comes next to last in a processed food's list of ingredients and often costs less than its packaging. Soft drinks contain a larger proportion of flavor additives than most products. The flavor in a twelve-ounce can of Coke costs about half a cent.

The color additives in processed foods are usually present in even smaller amounts than the flavor compounds. Many of New Jersey's flavor companies also manufacture these color additives, which are used to make processed foods look fresh and appealing. Food coloring serves many of the same decorative purposes as lipstick, eye shadow, mascara—and is often made from the same pigments. Titanium dioxide, for example, has proved to be an especially versatile mineral. It gives many processed candies, frostings, and icings their bright white color; it is a common ingredient in women's cosmetics; and it is the pigment used in many white oil paints and house paints. At Burger King, Wendy's, and McDonald's coloring agents have been added to many of the soft drinks, salad dressings, cookies, condiments, chicken dishes, and sandwich buns.

Studies have found that the color of a food can greatly affect how its taste is perceived. Brightly colored foods frequently seem to taste better than bland-looking foods, even when the flavor compounds are identical. Foods that somehow look off-color often seem to have off tastes. For thousands of years human beings have relied on visual cues to help determine what is edible. The color of fruit suggests whether it is ripe, the color of meat whether it is rancid. Flavor researchers sometimes use colored lights to modify the influence of visual cues during taste tests. During one experiment in the early 1970s people were served an oddly tinted meal of steak and french fries that appeared normal beneath colored lights. Everyone thought the meal tasted fine until the lighting was changed. Once it became apparent that the steak was actually blue and the fries were green, some people became ill.

The federal Food and Drug Administration does not require companies to disclose the ingredients of their color or flavor additives so long as all the chemicals in them are considered by the agency to be GRAS ("generally recognized as safe"). This enables companies to maintain the secrecy of their formulas. It also hides the fact that flavor compounds often contain more ingredients than the foods to which they give taste. The phrase "artificial strawberry flavor" gives little hint of the chemical wizardry and manufacturing skill that can make a highly processed food taste like strawberries.

A typical artificial strawberry flavor, like the kind found in a Burger 20 King strawberry milk shake, contains the following ingredients: amyl acetate, amyl butyrate, amyl valerate, anethol, anisyl formate, benzyl acetate, benzyl isobutyrate, butyric acid, cinnamyl isobutyrate, cinnamyl valerate, cognac essential oil, diacetyl, dipropyl ketone, ethyl acetate, ethyl amyl ketone, ethyl butyrate, ethyl cinnamate, ethyl heptanoate, ethyl heptylate, ethyl lactate, ethyl methylphenylglycidate, ethyl nitrate, ethyl propionate, ethyl valerate, heliotropin, hydroxyphenyl-2-butanone (10 percent solution in alcohol), α-ionone, isobutyl anthranilate, isobutyl butyrate, lemon essential oil, maltol, 4-methylacetophenone, methyl anthranilate, methyl benzoate, methyl cinnamate, methyl heptine carbonate, methyl naphthyl ketone, methyl salicylate, mint essential oil, neroli essential oil, nerolin, neryl isobutyrate, orris butter, phenethyl alcohol, rose, rum ether, γ-undecalactone, vanillin, and solvent.

Although flavors usually arise from a mixture of many different volatile chemicals, often a single compound supplies the dominant aroma. Smelled alone, that chemical provides an unmistakable sense of the food. Ethyl-2-methyl butyrate, for example, smells just like an apple. Many of today's highly processed foods offer a blank palette: whatever chemicals are added to them will give them specific tastes. Adding methyl-2-pyridyl ketone makes something taste like popcorn. Adding ethyl-3-hydroxy butanoate makes it taste like marshmallow. The possibilities are now almost limitless. Without affecting appearance or nutritional value, processed foods could be made with aroma chemicals such as hexanal (the smell of freshly cut grass) or 3-methyl butanoic acid (the smell of body odor).

The 1960s were the heyday of artificial flavors in the United States. The synthetic versions of flavor compounds were not subtle, but they did not have to be, given the nature of most processed food. For the past twenty years food processors have tried hard to use only "natural flavors" in their products. According to the FDA, these must be derived entirely from natural sources—from herbs, spices, fruits, vegetables, beef, chicken, yeast, bark, roots, and so forth. Consumers prefer to see natural flavors on a label, out of a belief that they are more healthful. Distinctions between artificial and natural flavors can be arbitrary and somewhat absurd, based more on how the flavor has been made than on what it actually contains.

"A natural flavor," says Terry Acree, a professor of food science at Cornell University, "is a flavor that's been derived with an out-of-date technology." Natural flavors and artificial flavors sometimes contain exactly the same chemicals, produced through different methods. Amyl acetate, for example, provides the dominant note of banana flavor. When it is distilled from bananas with a solvent, amyl acetate is a natural flavor. When it is produced by mixing vinegar with amyl alcohol and adding sulfuric acid as a catalyst, amyl acetate is an artificial flavor. Either way it smells and tastes the same. "Natural flavor" is now listed among the ingredients of everything from Health Valley Blueberry Granola Bars to Taco Bell Hot Taco Sauce.

A natural flavor is not necessarily more healthful or purer than an artificial one. When almond flavor—benzaldehyde—is derived from natural sources, such as peach and apricot pits, it contains traces of hydrogen cyanide, a deadly poison. Benzaldehyde derived by mixing oil of clove and amyl acetate does not contain any cyanide. Nevertheless, it is legally considered an artificial flavor and sells at a much lower price. Natural and artificial flavors are now manufactured at the same chemical plants, places that few people would associate with Mother Nature.

A TRAINED NOSE AND A POETIC SENSIBILITY

The small and elite group of scientists who create most of the flavor 25 in most of the food now consumed in the United States are called "flavorists." They draw on a number of disciplines in their work: biology, psychology, physiology, and organic chemistry. A flavorist is a chemist with a trained nose and a poetic sensibility. Flavors are created by blending scores of different chemicals in tiny amounts—a process governed by scientific principles but demanding a fair amount of art. In an age when delicate aromas and microwave ovens do not easily co-exist, the job of the flavorist is to conjure illusions about processed food and, in the words of one flavor company's literature, to ensure "consumer likeability." The flavorists with whom I spoke were discreet, in keeping with the dictates of their trade. They were also charming, cosmopolitan, and ironic. They not only enjoyed fine wine but could identify the chemicals that give each grape its unique aroma. One flavorist compared his work to composing music. A well-made flavor compound will have a "top note" that is often followed by a "dry-down" and a "leveling-off," with different chemicals responsible for each stage. The taste of a food can be radically altered by minute changes in the flavoring combination. "A little odor goes a long way," one flavorist told me.

In order to give a processed food a taste that consumers will find appealing, a flavorist must always consider the food's "mouthfeel" — the unique combination of textures and chemical interactions that affect how the flavor is perceived. Mouthfeel can be adjusted through the use of various fats, gums, starches, emulsifiers, and stabilizers. The aroma chemicals in a food can be precisely analyzed, but the elements that make up mouthfeel are much harder to measure. How does one quantify a pretzel's hardness, a french fry's crispness? Food technologists are now conducting basic research in rheology, the branch of physics that examines the flow and deformation of materials. A number of companies sell sophisticated devices that attempt to measure mouthfeel. The TA.XT2i Texture Analyzer, produced by the Texture Technologies Corporation, of Scarsdale, New York, performs calculations based on data derived from as many as 250 separate probes. It is essentially a mechanical mouth. It gauges the most-important rheological properties of a food — bounce, creep, breaking point, density, crunchiness, chewiness, gumminess, lumpiness, rubberiness, springiness, slipperiness, smoothness, softness, wetness, juiciness, spreadability, springback, and tackiness.

Some of the most important advances in flavor manufacturing are now occurring in the field of biotechnology. Complex flavors are being made using enzyme reactions, fermentation, and fungal and tissue cultures. All the flavors created by these methods — including the ones being synthesized by fungi — are considered natural flavors by the FDA. The new enzyme-based processes are responsible for extremely true-to-life dairy flavors. One company now offers not just butter flavor but also fresh creamy butter, cheesy butter, milky butter, savory melted butter, and super-concentrated butter flavor, in liquid or powder form. The development of new fermentation techniques, along with new techniques for heating mixtures of sugar and amino acids, have led to the creation of much more realistic meat flavors.

The McDonald's Corporation most likely drew on these advances when it eliminated beef tallow from its french fries. The company will not reveal the exact origin of the natural flavor added to its fries. In response to inquiries from *Vegetarian Journal*, however, McDonald's did acknowledge that its fries derive some of their characteristic flavor from "an animal source." Beef is the probable source, although other meats cannot be ruled out. In France, for example, fries are sometimes cooked in duck fat or horse tallow.

Other popular fast foods derive their flavor from unexpected ingredients. McDonald's Chicken McNuggets contain beef extracts, as does Wendy's Grilled Chicken Sandwich. Burger King's BK Broiler Chicken Breast Patty contains "natural smoke flavor." A firm called Red Arrow

Products specializes in smoke flavor, which is added to barbecue sauces, snack foods, and processed meats. Red Arrow manufactures natural smoke flavor by charring sawdust and capturing the aroma chemicals released into the air. The smoke is captured in water and then bottled, so that other companies can sell food that seems to have been cooked over a fire.

The Vegetarian Legal Action Network recently petitioned the FDA to   30
issue new labeling requirements for foods that contain natural flavors. The group wants food processors to list the basic origins of their flavors on their labels. At the moment vegetarians often have no way of knowing whether a flavor additive contains beef, pork, poultry, or shellfish. One of the most widely used color additives—whose presence is often hidden by the phrase "color added"—violates a number of religious dietary restrictions, may cause allergic reactions in susceptible people, and comes from an unusual source. Cochineal extract (also known as carmine or carminic acid) is made from the desiccated bodies of female *Dactylopius coccus Costa*, a small insect harvested mainly in Peru and the Canary Islands. The bug feeds on red cactus berries, and color from the berries accumulates in the females and their unhatched larvae. The insects are collected, dried, and ground into a pigment. It takes about 70,000 of them to produce a pound of carmine, which is used to make processed foods look pink, red, or purple. Dannon strawberry yogurt gets its color from carmine, and so do many frozen fruit bars, candies, and fruit fillings, and Ocean Spray pink-grapefruit juice drink.

In a meeting room at IFF, Brian Grainger let me sample some of the company's flavors. It was an unusual taste test—there was no food to taste. Grainger is a senior flavorist at IFF, a soft-spoken chemist with graying hair, an English accent, and a fondness for understatement. He could easily be mistaken for a British diplomat or the owner of a West End brasserie with two Michelin stars. Like many in the flavor industry, he has an Old World, old-fashioned sensibility. When I suggested that IFF's policy of secrecy and discretion was out of step with our mass-marketing, brand-conscious, self-promoting age, and that the company should put its own logo on the countless products that bear its flavors, instead of allowing other companies to enjoy the consumer loyalty and affection inspired by those flavors, Grainger politely disagreed, assuring me that such a thing would never be done. In the absence of public credit or acclaim, the small and secretive fraternity of flavor chemists praise one another's work. By analyzing the flavor formula of a product, Grainger can often tell which of his counterparts at a rival firm devised it. Whenever he walks down a supermarket aisle, he takes a quiet pleasure in seeing the well-known foods that contain his flavors.

Grainger had brought a dozen small glass bottles from the lab. After he opened each bottle, I dipped a fragrance-testing filter into it—a long white strip of paper designed to absorb aroma chemicals without producing off notes. Before placing each strip of paper in front of my nose, I closed my eyes. Then I inhaled deeply, and one food after another was conjured from the glass bottles. I smelled fresh cherries, black olives, sautéed onions, and shrimp. Grainger's most remarkable creation took me by surprise. After closing my eyes, I suddenly smelled a grilled hamburger. The aroma was uncanny, almost miraculous—as if someone in the room were flipping burgers on a hot grill. But when I opened my eyes, I saw just a narrow strip of white paper and a flavorist with a grin.

The Reader's Presence

1. What do McDonald's french fries have to do with Schlosser's primary aim in this selection? Why does he feature them in the title and use them in the opening to the essay? Why, in your opinion, didn't he use a different example?

2. Describe Schlosser's attitude toward "natural" and "artificial" flavoring. Does he think one is superior to the other? How critical does he appear toward food additives in general? Do you read his essay as a condemnation of fast food? How does his account of his laboratory visit color your response? Overall, were his laboratory experiences positive or negative? Explain what in his account makes you feel one way or the other.

3. Compare and contrast Schlosser's investigative techniques with those of James Fallows (page 416), Amy Cunningham (page 355), or Malcolm Gladwell (page 432). How does each writer establish a question to investigate, provoke your interest in the issue, gather information, and conduct the investigation? How important are sources and interviews? What information about sources and interviews is omitted from the essays?

Charles Simic

The Life of Images

Charles Simic (b. 1938) grew up in Belgrade, Yugoslavia (now Serbia), during World War II. He immigrated to the United States with his family when he was sixteen years old and became a naturalized citizen in 1971. "Being one of the millions of displaced persons made an impression on me. In addition to my own little story of bad luck, I heard plenty of others. I'm still amazed by all the vileness and stupidity I witnessed in my life," he says. Since his first volume of poetry, What the Grass Says *(1967), Simic has published more than sixty books and has won numerous awards, including the Pulitzer Prize in Poetry for* The World Doesn't End *(1989) and a MacArthur Foundation "genius grant." His book* Walking the Black Cat *(1996) was a finalist for the National Book Award for poetry;* The Voice at 3:00 A.M. *was nominated for the National Book Award and the* Los Angeles Times *Book Award in 2003. Simic's latest collection of poetry is* My Noiseless Entourage *(2005). He is a noted translator of French, Serbian, Croatian, Macedonian, and Slovenian poetry, and his own work has also been translated into many languages. A professor of English at the University of New Hampshire in Durham since 1973, he also contributes frequently to magazines and journals, including the* Harvard Review, *in which his essay "The Life of Images" was published in 2003.*

When asked what he found hardest to write about, Simic replied, "Everything is hard to write about. Many of my shortest and seemingly simple poems took years to get right. I tinker with most of my poems even after publication. I expect to be revising in my coffin as it is being lowered into the ground."

In one of Berenice Abbott's[1] photographs of the Lower East Side, I recall a store sign advertising *Silk Underwear*. Underneath, there was the additional information about "reasonable prices for peddlers." How interesting, I thought. Did someone carry a suitcase full of ladies' underwear and try to peddle them on some street corner farther uptown? Or did he ring doorbells in apartment buildings and offer them to housewives? I imagine the underwear came in many different sizes, so he may have had to carry two suitcases. The peddler was most likely an immigrant and had difficulty making himself understood. What he wanted was for the lady of the house to feel how soft the silk was but she either did not understand him or she had other reasons for hesitating. She wore a house robe, her hair was loose as if she just got out of bed, so she was embarrassed to

[1]***Abbott:*** A photographer (1898–1991) who is noted for her concentration on New York City. Combining artistry with documentary brilliance, her work ranks her among major American photographers. She wrote many articles on photography, and her best-known book is the one Simic refers to, *Changing New York* (1939). —EDS.

touch the undies draped over his extended hand. Then she finally did touch them.

The reason photographs live in my memory is that the city I continue to roam is rich with such visual delights. Everyone who does this is taking imaginary snapshots. For all I know my face, briefly glimpsed in a crowd, may live on in someone else's memory. The attentive eye makes the world mysterious. Some men or a woman going about their business seventy years ago either caught sight of a camera pointed at them or they passed by oblivious. It was like hide and seek. They thought they had concealed themselves in plain view and the camera found them out. It showed something even they did not know they were hiding. Often people had the puzzled look of someone who had volunteered to assist a hypnotist on a stage and awakened to the sound of the audience's applause.

I'm looking at the long-torn-down Second Avenue "El" at the intersection of Division Street and Bowery in another Abbott photograph. The date is April 24, 1936. It seems like a nice day, for the sunlight streams through the tracks and iron scaffold of the elevated train, making patterns of shadow and light on the sidewalk below. As far as I can make out, the street on both sides is lined with stores selling cheap furs. The entire area was for years a bargain hunter's paradise. My father knew a fellow in his office, an elderly, impeccably dressed man, who claimed that he did all his shopping on Orchard and Hester Streets, where he never paid more than five dollars for a suit. What interests me the most in this photograph is the shadowy couple under the El with their backs turned to us. She's willowy and taller than he is, as if she were a model or a salesgirl in one of these shops. They have drawn close together as if talking over something very important, or why would they otherwise stop like that in the middle of the street? The way this woman in a long skirt carries herself gives me the impression that she is young. Not so the man. With one hand casually resting on a post and his other stuck in his pocket, he appears confident, even brash. It's the way they stand together that suggests to me that they are not casual acquaintances. Most likely they work in the same neighborhood, but there is something else going on between them too. She seems very interested in what he is saying now. No one else in view pays them any attention. The fellow standing on the sidewalk in front of the Beauty Fur Shop looks off into the distance where a portly young man with glasses wearing an open overcoat over a three-piece suit is coming into view. He has just had lunch and is glancing idly at the shop windows as he strolls lazily back to the office. He is too young to be the boss, so he must be the son or the son-in-law of one of the store owners. Except for the couple who elude identification, there is nothing unusual here. A photograph such as this one, where time has stopped on an ordinary scene full of innuendoes, partakes of the infinite.

I cannot look long at any old photograph of the city without hearing some music in the background. The moment that happens, I'm transported

into the past so vividly no one can convince me that I did not live in that moment. I have heard just about every recording of popular music and jazz made between 1920 and 1950. This is probably the most esoteric knowledge I possess. It's easier to talk to people about Tibetan Buddhism, Arab poetry in Medieval Spain or Russian icons, than about Helen Kane, Annette Hanshaw, and Ethel Waters. Or how about some Boswell Sisters or Joe Venuti and his Blue Four, Red McKenzie and his Mound City Blue Blowers, Ted Lewis and his Orchestra playing "Egyptian Ella"? It scares me how much of that music is in my head. I have friends who cannot believe that I can enjoy both Mahler's symphonies and Coleman Hawkins. Young Ella Fitzgerald singing "If That's What You're Thinking, You're Wrong" with Chick Webb's band would be just right for Abbott's shadowy couple.

Can one experience nostalgia for a time and place one did not know? I   5 believe so. You could put me in solitary with Abbott's photograph of "Blossom Restaurant"[2] and I wouldn't notice the months pass away as I

---

[2]***"Blossom Restaurant":*** Abbott's photograph of the restaurant, at 103 Bowery, was taken on October 3, 1935.—EDS.

studied the menu chalked on the blackboard at its entrance. The prices, of course, are incredibly low, but that's secondary. The dishes enumerated here are what fascinates me. No one eats that kind of food today. Rare Mongolian, Patagonian, and Afghan specialties are procurable in New York, but not lamb oxtail stew, boiled beef, or even stuffed peppers. The ethnic makeup of the city has changed in the last thirty years. Most of the luncheonettes in 1950s and 1960s served samplings of German, Hungarian, and Jewish cuisine. Pea and bean soup, stuffed cabbage, corned beef and boiled potatoes, and veal cutlets were to be found regularly on the menu, together with the usual assortment of sandwiches. On every table, and all along the counter, there were containers stocked with dill pickles and slices of raw onion. The portions were enormous. A cheap dish like franks and kraut would stuff you for the rest of the day. I subsisted for years on soups and chowders cooked by a Greek in a greasy spoon on East 8th Street. They gave you two thick slices of rye bread and butter with the soup and all the pickles you could eat. After that, I could hardly keep my eyes open for the rest of the day.

Abbott's photograph of the Blossom restaurant front also includes the barbershop next door with its own price list. Does a tonsorial establishment anywhere in this country still offer electric massage? The gadget, which resembled contraptions from a horror film, was a mesh of spring coils and electric wires. Once the juice was turned on, the machine squirmed and shook for a minute or two over the customer's scalp, supposedly providing a stimulating, healthful, up-to-date treatment, while he sat back in the chair pretending to be absorbed in some article in the *Police Gazette*.[3] That ordeal was followed by a few sprinkles of strong-smelling cologne from a large bottle and a dusting of talcum powder on the freshly-shaved neck.

The worst haircut I ever had in my life was at a barber college at the Union Square subway station. "Learn Barbering and make Money," the sign said. It was the cheapest haircut in town. But, before I realized what was happening, the apprentice barber had cut off all my hair with clippers except for a tuft right up in front. The kid was clearly a hair fashion visionary decades ahead of his time, but back then I was in total panic. I rushed immediately across the street into Klein's department store and found a beret, which I wore pulled down over my ears for the next six weeks. The problem was that it was summer, hot and humid as it usually is in New York. I also wore dark glasses to give the impression that I was simply affecting the appearance of a jazz musician. I saw both Dizzy Gillespie and Thelonius Monk similarly decked out, but they tended to make their appearance only after dark, while I had to go to work in the morning in the storeroom of a publishing company where everyone who saw me burst out laughing. Lunch was a hassle too. The customers at adjoining tables snickered and the waitress who knew me well gave me a puzzled look as she brought me my sandwich. I always held unpopular opinions and was not afraid to voice them, but to have people stare at me because I had a funny haircut or wore a necktie of some outrageous hue was something I had no stomach for.

"My place is no bigger than a closet," a woman said to her companion on the street the other day as they rushed past me, and I saw it instantly with its clutter of furniture and its piles of clothes on the bed and the floor. Dickinson's "Madonna dim" came to mind and I did not even take a good look at her before she was lost in the crowd. No sooner has one seen an interesting face in the street than one gives it a biography. Through a small window in her room, the evening casts its first shadow on a blank wall where the outline of a picture that once hung there is still visible. She is not home yet, but there is a small bird in the cage waiting for her and so am I.

Mr. Nobody is what I call the man in the subway. I catch sight of him from time to time. He has labored all his life to make himself inconspicuous in dress and manner and has nearly succeeded. He sits in the far corner in his gray hat, gray moustache, pale collapsing cheeks, and empty, watery eyes, staring off into space while the subway train grinds along and the overhead lights go out briefly and return to find us puzzled, looking up from newspapers at each other sitting there. Even more odd than these

---

[3]*Police Gazette:* A century-old men's periodical that featured sensational news items and risqué photographs. It was especially popular in barbershops. — EDS.

searching looks we give strangers are the times when we catch someone doing the same to us. They see me as I truly am, one imagines, wanting both to run away from them and to ask what it is they see.

Today dozens of people are sunning themselves on park benches, sitting close together with eyes shut as if making a collective wish. An old mutt who has done a lot of thinking and sighing in his life lies at their feet, eyeing a rusty pigeon take wing as I pass by. The enigma of the ordinary—that's what makes old photographs so poignant. An ancient streetcar in sepia color. A few men holding on to their hats on a windy day. They hurry with their faces averted except for one befuddled old fellow who has stopped and is looking over his shoulder at what we cannot see, but where, we suspect, we ourselves will be coming into view someday, as hurried and ephemeral as any one of them.

The Reader's Presence

1. Consider the process Simic goes through when looking at a photograph. How does he make sense of the image? What does he add to it? What conclusions does he come to about the value of photography?

2. How does Simic move between interpreting the historic photographs by Berenice Abbott and interpreting scenes from his daily life in New York City? What does one have to do with the other? Does Simic read faces on the street or scenes in the city in the same way that he reads Abbott's photographs? Why or why not?

3. Discussing one of Abbott's photographs of daily life, Simic observes: "A photograph such as this one, where time has stopped on an ordinary scene full of innuendos, partakes of the infinite" (paragraph 3). Read Zadie Smith's "Scenes from the Smith Family Christmas" (page 278) and look at the accompanying photograph. Does it "partake of the infinite"? What stories does each writer use the photograph to tell? What do Simic's and Smith's stories share?

Calvin Trillin

A Traditional Family

The journalist, critic, novelist, and humorist Calvin Trillin was born in Kansas City in 1935, but has lived in New York City for many years. He works as a staff writer at the New Yorker *and contributes to many other magazines, including the* Atlantic, Harper's, Life, *and the* Nation. *Trillin is especially well known for his nonfiction. His magazine columns are collected in* Uncivil Liberties *(1982),* With All Disrespect: More Uncivil Liberties *(1985),* If You Can't Say Something Nice *(1987), and* Enough's Enough *(1990); Trillin has also published a series of very popular books dealing with food and eating. In* American Fried *(1974) he paints a revealing portrait of American life through his discussion of regional and national eating habits. His love of traveling and eating in the company of his wife Alice also led him to write* Alice, Let's Eat *(1978),* Third Helpings *(1983), and* Travels with Alice *(1989). More recently Trillin has forsworn the temptation to eat for a living and has taken his keen sense of humor to the stage in one-man shows. "A Traditional Family" is excerpted from his book* Too Soon to Tell *(1995); his other recent publications include* Deadline Poet: My Life as a Doggerelist *(1994),* Messages from My Father *(1996),* Family Man *(1998),* Tepper Isn't Going Out *(2001),* Feeding a Yen *(2003), and* Obliviously on He Sails: The Bush Administration in Rhyme *(2004).*

When asked to describe the process he goes through when writing factual as opposed to imaginative columns, Trillin replied, "In a nonfiction piece . . . you really have to carry around a lot of baggage. You have what happened, your understanding of what happened, what you want to get across about what happened, all kinds of burdens of being fair to whatever sides there are. The facts are terribly restricting." Trillin typically writes at least four drafts of nonfiction articles, but finds that imaginative writing is less predictable. When writing his humor columns, for example, "it's a much less rigid system than that of writing nonfiction. Sometimes it only takes two drafts; sometimes it takes five."

I just found out that our family is no longer what the Census Bureau calls a traditional American family, and I want everyone to know that this is not our fault.

We now find ourselves included in the statistics that are used constantly to show the lamentable decline of the typical American household from something like Ozzie and Harriet and the kids to something like a bunch of kooks and hippies.

I want everyone to know right at the start that we are not kooks. Oh sure, we have our peculiarities, but we are not kooks. Also, we are not hippies. We have no children named Goodness. I am the first one to admit that reasonable people may differ on how to characterize a couple of my veteran sportcoats, and there may have been a remark or two passed in the neighborhood from time to time about the state of our front lawn. But no one has ever seriously suggested that we are hippies.

In fact, most people find us rather traditional. My wife and I have a marriage certificate, although I can't say I know exactly where to put my hands on it right at the moment. We have two children. We have a big meal on Christmas. We put on costumes at Halloween. (What about the fact that I always wear an ax murderer's mask on Halloween? That happens to be one of the peculiarities.) We make family decisions in the traditional American family way, which is to say the father is manipulated by the wife and the children. We lose a lot of socks in the wash. At our house, the dishes are done and the garbage is taken out regularly — after the glass and cans and other recyclable materials have been separated out. We're not talking about a commune here.

So why has the Census Bureau begun listing us with households that consist of, say, the ex-stepchild of someone's former marriage living with someone who is under the mistaken impression that she is the aunt of somebody or other? Because the official definition of a traditional American family is two parents and one or more children under age eighteen. Our younger daughter just turned nineteen. Is that our fault?

As it happens, I did everything in my power to keep her from turning nineteen. When our daughters were about two and five, I decided that they were the perfect age, and I looked around for some sort of freezing process that might keep them there. I discovered that there was no such freezing process on the market. Assuming, in the traditional American way, that the technology would come along by and by, I renewed my investigation several times during their childhoods — they always seemed to be at the perfect age — but the freezing process never surfaced. Meanwhile, they kept getting older at what seemed to me a constantly accelerating rate. Before you could say "Zip up your jacket," the baby turned nineteen. What's a parent to do?

Ask for an easement. That's what a parent's to do. When I learned about the Census Bureau's definition of a traditional family — it was mentioned in an Associated Press story about how the latest census shows the traditional family declining at a more moderate pace than "the rapid and destabilizing rate" at which it declined between 1970 and 1980 — it occurred to me that we could simply explain the situation to the Census Bureau and ask that an exception be made in our case.

I realize that the Census Bureau would probably want to send out an inspector. I would acknowledge to him that our daughters are more or less away from home, but remind him that we have been assured by more experienced parents that we can absolutely count on their return. I would take the position, in other words, that we are just as traditional as any American family, just slightly undermanned at the moment — like a hockey team that has a couple of guys in the penalty box but is still a presence on the ice. We could show the official our Christmas tree decorations and our Halloween costumes and a lot of single socks. We might, in the traditional American way, offer him a cup of coffee and a small bribe.

I haven't decided for sure to approach the Census Bureau. For one thing, someone might whisper in the inspector's ear that I have been heard to refer to my older daughter's room—the room where we now keep the exercise bike—as "the gym," and that might take some explaining. Also, I haven't discussed the matter with my wife. I would, of course, abide by her wishes. It's traditional.

The Reader's Presence

1. According to Trillin, how does the Census Bureau define "a traditional American family"? How does Trillin discover that his family would no longer be included in the Census Bureau's statistical compilations about "traditional" American families? Why does his family no longer satisfy the Census Bureau's criteria? What does Trillin try to do about this "problem"?

2. What characteristics of his family's behavior does Trillin identify as "traditional"? Examine the effect(s) of Trillin's verb choices. What patterns do you notice? What other patterns do you notice that he has woven into his word choices? When—and how— does Trillin poke fun at himself and the members of his family? To what extent does his humor depend on irony? on wit? Point to specific words and phrases to support your response.

3. When—and how—does Trillin use gender and familial stereotypes to reinforce the points he makes? Compare his light piece to the far more serious essay by David Mamet about his "new, cobbled-together family" who live in a new suburban development ("The Rake," page 209). How do both writers play with the reader's sense of the normative or the ideal? Can you imagine a comic version of Mamet's essay, and a serious version of Trillin's? If so, what might they look like?

Barbara Tuchman

"This Is the End of the World": The Black Death

Barbara Tuchman (1912–1989) was an acclaimed historian who was noted for writing historical accounts in a literary style. Believing that most historians alienate their readers by including minute details and by ignoring the elements of well-written prose, Tuchman hoped to engage a broad audience with a well-told narrative. As she explained during a speech at the National Portrait Gallery in 1978, "I want the reader to turn the page and keep on turning to the end. . . . This is accomplished only when the narrative moves steadily ahead, not when it comes to a weary standstill, overloaded with every item uncovered in the research." Tuchman, a 1933 Radcliffe College graduate, never received formal training as a historian but developed an ability to document history early in her career while working as a research assistant for the Institute of Pacific Relations, a writer for the Nation, *a foreign correspondent during the Spanish Civil War, and an editor for the Office of War Information during World War II. Tuchman earned critical attention when her third book,* The Zimmermann Telegram, *became a best-seller in 1958. She received a Pulitzer Prize for* The Guns of August (1962), *a description of the early days of World War I, and for* Stilwell and the American Experience in China, 1911–1945, *a biographical account of Joseph Warren Stilwell, an American military officer during China's shift from feudalism to communism. Other books include* The Proud Tower: A Portrait of the World before the War, 1890–1914 (1966); A Distant Mirror: The Calamitous Fourteenth Century (1978), *from which* " 'This Is the End of the World': The Black Death" *is taken; and* The March of Folly: From Troy to Vietnam (1984).*

In October 1347, two months after the fall of Calais,* Genoese trading ships put into the harbor of Messina in Sicily with dead and dying men at the oars. The ships had come from the Black Sea port of Caffa (now Feodosiya) in the Crimea, where the Genoese maintained a trading post. The diseased sailors showed strange black swellings about the size of an egg or an apple in the armpits and groin. The swellings oozed blood and pus and were followed by spreading boils and black blotches on the skin from internal bleeding. The sick suffered severe pain and died quickly within five days of the first symptoms. As the disease spread, other symptoms of continuous fever and spitting of blood appeared instead of the swellings or buboes. These victims coughed and sweated heavily and died even more quickly, within three days or less, sometimes in 24 hours. In both types everything

---

fall of Calais: After a year-long siege, Calais, a town in France, surrendered to Edward III, king of England and self-declared king of France. —Eds.

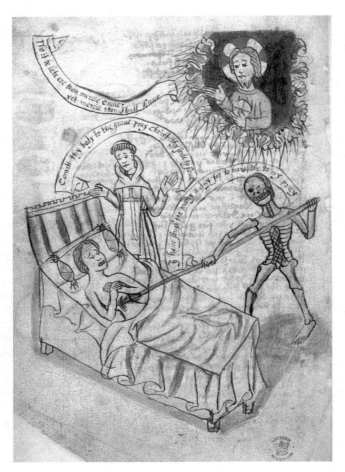

*Plague victim receiving last rites, from a fifteenth-century col-
lection of English religious texts*

that issued from the body—breath, sweat, blood from the buboes and
lungs, bloody urine, and blood-blackened excrement—smelled foul. Depression and despair accompanied the physical symptoms, and before the
end "death is seen seated on the face."[1]

The disease was bubonic plague, present in two forms: one that infected the bloodstream, causing the buboes and internal bleeding, and
was spread by contact; and a second, more virulent pneumonic type that
infected the lungs and was spread by respiratory infection. The presence
of both at once cause the high mortality and speed of contagion. So
lethal was the disease that cases were known of persons going to bed
well and dying before they woke, of doctors catching the illness at a bedside and dying before the patient. So rapidly did it spread from one to
another that to a French physician, Simon de Covino, it seemed as if one

sick person "could infect the whole world."[2] The malignity of the pestilence appeared more terrible because its victims knew no prevention and no remedy.

The physical suffering of the disease and its aspect of evil mystery were expressed in a strange Welsh lament[3] which saw "death coming into our midst like black smoke, a plague which cuts off the young, a rootless phantom which has no mercy for fair countenance. Woe is me of the shilling in the armpit! It is seething, terrible . . . a head that gives pain and causes a loud cry . . . a painful angry knob . . . Great is its seething like a burning cinder . . . a grievous thing of ashy color." Its eruption is ugly like the "seeds of black peas, broken fragments of brittle sea-coal . . . the early ornaments of black death, cinders of the peelings of the cockle weed, a mixed multitude, a black plague like halfpence, like berries. . . ."

Rumors of a terrible plague supposedly arising in China and spreading through Tartary (Central Asia) to India and Persia, Mesopotamia, Syria, Egypt, and all of Asia Minor had reached Europe in 1346. They told of a death toll so devastating that all of India was said to be depopulated, whole territories covered by dead bodies, other areas with no one left alive. As added up by Pope Clement VI at Avignon, the total of reported dead reached 23,840,000. In the absence of a concept of contagion, no serious alarm was felt in Europe until the trading ships brought their black burden of pestilence into Messina while other infected ships from the Levant carried it to Genoa and Venice.

By January 1348 it penetrated France via Marseille, and North 5 Africa via Tunis. Shipborne along coasts and navigable rivers, it spread westward from Marseille through the ports of Languedoc to Spain and northward up the Rhône to Avignon, where it arrived in March. It reached Narbonne, Montpellier, Carcassonne, and Toulouse between February and May, and at the same time in Italy spread to Rome and Florence and their hinterlands. Between June and August it reached Bordeaux, Lyon, and Paris, spread to Burgundy and Normandy, and crossed the Channel from Normandy into southern England. From Italy during the same summer it crossed the Alps into Switzerland and reached eastward to Hungary.

In a given area the plague accomplished its kill within four to six months and then faded, except in the larger cities, where, rooting into the close-quartered population, it abated during the winter, only to reappear in the spring and rage for another six months.

In 1349 it resumed in Paris, spread to Picardy, Flanders, and the Low Countries, and from England to Scotland and Ireland as well as to Norway, where a ghost ship with a cargo of wool and a dead crew drifted offshore until it ran aground near Bergen. From there the plague passed into Sweden, Denmark, Prussia, Iceland, and as far as Greenland. Leaving a strange pocket of immunity in Bohemia, and Russia unattacked until 1351, it had passed from most of Europe by mid-1350. Although the mortality rate was erratic, ranging from one fifth in some places to nine tenths or almost total elimination in others, the overall estimate of modern demographers has settled—for the area extending from India to Iceland—around the same figure expressed in Froissart's casual words: "a third of the world died." His estimate, the common one at the time, was not an inspired guess but a borrowing of St. John's figure for mortality from plague in Revelation, the favorite guide to human affairs of the Middle Ages.

A third of Europe would have meant about 20 million deaths. No one knows in truth how many died. Contemporary reports were an awed impression, not an accurate count. In crowded Avignon, it was said, 400 died daily; 7,000 houses emptied by death were shut up; a single graveyard received 11,000 corpses in six weeks; half the city's inhabitants reportedly died, including 9 cardinals or one third of the total, and 70 lesser prelates. Watching the endlessly passing death carts, chroniclers let normal exaggeration take wings and put the Avignon death toll at 62,000 and even at 120,000 although the city's total population was probably less than 50,000.

When graveyards filled up, bodies at Avignon were thrown into the Rhône until mass burial pits were dug for dumping the corpses. In London in such pits corpses piled up in layers until they overflowed. Everywhere reports speak of the sick dying too fast for the living to bury. Corpses were dragged out of homes and left in front of doorways. Morning light revealed new piles of bodies. In Florence the dead were gathered up by the Compagnia della Misericordia—founded in 1244 to care for the sick—whose members wore red robes and hoods masking the face except for the eyes. When their efforts failed, the dead lay putrid in the streets for days at a time. When no coffins were to be had, the bodies were laid on boards, two or three at once, to be carried to graveyards or common pits. Families dumped their own relatives into the pits, or buried them so hastily and thinly "that dogs dragged them forth and devoured their bodies."[4]

Amid accumulating death and fear of contagion, people died without last rites and were buried without prayers, a prospect that terrified the last hours of the stricken. A bishop in England gave permission to laymen to make confession to each other as was done by the Apostles, "or if no man is present then even to a woman,"[5] and if no priest could be found to administer extreme unction, "then faith must suffice." Clement VI found it necessary to grant remissions of sin to all who died of the plague because so many were unattended by priests. "And no bells tolled,"[6] wrote a chronicler of Siena, "and nobody wept no matter what his loss because almost everyone expected death. . . . And people said and believed, 'This is the end of the world.' "

In Paris, where the plague lasted through 1349, the reported death rate was 800 a day, in Pisa 500, in Vienna 500 to 600. The total dead in Paris numbered 50,000 or half the population. Florence, weakened by the famine of 1347, lost three to four fifths of its citizens, Venice two thirds,

Hamburg and Bremen, though smaller in size, about the same proportion. Cities, as centers of transportation, were more likely to be affected than villages, although once a village was infected, its death rate was equally high. At Givry, a prosperous village in Burgundy of 1,200 to 1,500 people, the parish register records 615 deaths in the space of fourteen weeks, compared to an average of thirty deaths a year in the previous decade.[7] In three villages of Cambridgeshire, manorial records show a death rate of 47 percent, 57 percent, and in one case 70 percent.[8] When the last survivors, too few to carry on, moved away, a deserted village sank back into the wilderness and disappeared from the map altogether, leaving only a grass-covered ghostly outline to show where mortals once had lived.

In enclosed places such as monasteries and prisons, the infection of one person usually meant that of all, as happened in the Franciscan convents of Carcassonne and Marseille, where every inmate without exception died. Of the 140 Dominicans at Montpellier only seven survived. Petrarch's brother Gherardo, member of a Carthusian monastery, buried the prior and 34 fellow monks one by one, sometimes three a day, until he was left alone with his dog and fled to look for a place that would take him in.[9] Watching every comrade die, men in such places could not but wonder whether the strange peril that filled the air had not been sent to exterminate the human race. In Kilkenny, Ireland, Brother John Clyn of the Friars Minor, another monk left alone among dead men, kept a record of what had happened lest "things which should be remembered perish with time and vanish from the memory of those who come after us."[10] Sensing "the whole world, as it were, placed within the grasp of the Evil One," and waiting for death to visit him too, he wrote, "I leave parchment to continue this work, if perchance any man survive and any of the race of Adam escape this pestilence and carry on the work which I have begun." Brother John, as noted by another hand, died of the pestilence, but he foiled oblivion.

The largest cities of Europe, with populations of about 100,000, were Paris and Florence, Venice and Genoa. At the next level, with more than 50,000, were Ghent and Bruges in Flanders, Milan, Bologna, Rome, Naples, and Palermo, and Cologne. London hovered below 50,000 the only city in England except York with more than 10,000. At the level of 20,000 to 50,000 were Bordeaux, Toulouse, Montpellier, Marseille, and Lyon in France, Barcelona, Seville, and Toledo in Spain, Siena, Pisa, and other secondary cities in Italy, and the Hanseatic trading cities of the Empire. The plague raged through them all, killing anywhere from one third to two thirds of their inhabitants. Italy, with a total population of 10 to 11 million, probably suffered the heaviest toll. Following the Florentine bankruptcies, the crop failures and workers' riots of 1346–47, the revolt of Cola di Rienzi that plunged Rome into anarchy, the plague came as the peak of successive calamities. As if the world were indeed in the grasp of the Evil One, its first appearance on the European mainland in January 1348 coincided with a fearsome earthquake that carved a path of wreckage from Naples up to Venice. Houses collapsed, church towers toppled, villages were crushed, and the destruction reached as far as Germany and Greece. Emotional response, dulled by horrors, underwent a kind of atrophy epitomized by the chronicler who wrote, "And in these days was burying without sorrowe and wedding without friendschippe."[11]

In Siena, where more than half the inhabitants died of the plague, work was abandoned on the great cathedral, planned to be the largest in the world, and never resumed, owing to loss of workers and master masons and "the melancholy and grief" of the survivors. The cathedral's truncated transept still stands in permanent witness to the sweep of death's scythe. Agnolo di Tura, a chronicler of Siena, recorded the fear of contagion that froze every other instinct. "Father abandoned child, wife husband, one brother another," he wrote, "for this plague seemed to strike through the breath and sight.[12] And so they died. And no one could be found to bury the dead for money or friendship. . . . And I, Angolo di Tura, called the Fat, buried my five children with my own hands, and so did many others likewise."

There were many to echo his account of inhumanity and few to balance it, for the plague was not the kind of calamity that inspired mutual help. Its loathsomeness and deadliness did not herd people together in mutual distress, but only prompted their desire to escape each other. "Magistrates and notaries refused to come and make the wills of the dying," reported a Franciscan friar of Piazza in Sicily;[13] what was worse, "even the priests did not come to hear their confessions."[14] A clerk of the Archbishop of Canterbury reported the same of English priests who "turned away from the care of their benefices from fear of death." Cases of parents deserting children and children their parents were reported across Europe from Scotland to Russia.[15] The calamity chilled the hearts of men, wrote Boccaccio* in his famous account of the plague in Florence that serves as introduction to the *Decameron*. "One man shunned another . . . kinsfolk held aloof, brother was forsaken by brother, oftentimes husband by wife; nay, what is more, and scarcely to be believed, fathers and mothers were found to abandon their own children to their fate, untended, unvisited as if they had been strangers." Exaggeration and literary pessimism were common in the fourteenth century, but the Pope's physician, Guy de Chauliac, was a sober, careful observer who reported the same phenomenon: "A father did not visit his son, nor the son his father. Charity was dead."[16]

Yet not entirely. In Paris, according to the chronicler Jean de Venette, the nuns of the Hôtel Dieu or municipal hospital, "having no fear of death, tended the sick with all sweetness and humility."[17] New nuns repeatedly

15

Giovanni Boccaccio (1313–1375): Italian writer best known for his collection of stories about the Black Death, *The Decameron*. —EDS.

took the places of those who died, until the majority "many times renewed by death now rest in peace with Christ as we may piously believe."

When the plague entered northern France in July 1348, it settled first in Normandy and, checked by winter, gave Picardy a deceptive interim until the next summer. Either in mourning or warning, black flags were flown from church towers of the worst-stricken villages of Normandy. "And in that time," wrote a monk of the abbey of Fourcarment, "the mortality was so great among the people of Normandy that those of Picardy mocked them."[18] The same unneighborly reaction was reported of the Scots, separated by a winter's immunity from the English. Delighted to hear of the disease that was scourging the "southrons," they gathered forces for an invasion, "laughing at their enemies." Before they could move, the savage mortality fell upon them too, scattering some in death and the rest in panic to spread the infection as they fled.

In Picardy in the summer of 1349 the pestilence penetrated the castle of Coucy to kill Enguerrand's* mother, Catherine, and her new husband.[19] Whether her nine-year-old son escaped by chance or was perhaps living elsewhere with one of his guardians is unrecorded. In nearby Amiens, tannery workers, responding quickly to losses in the labor force, combined to bargain for higher wages.[20] In another place villagers were seen dancing to drums and trumpets, and on being asked the reason, answered that, seeing their neighbors die day by day while their village remained immune, they believed they could keep the plague from entering "by the jollity that is in us. That is why we dance."[21] Further north in Tournai on the border of Flanders, Gilles li Muisis, Abbot of St. Martin's, kept one of the epidemic's most vivid accounts. The passing bells rang all day and all night, he recorded, because sextons were anxious to obtain their fees while they could. Filled with the sound of mourning, the city became oppressed by fear, so that the authorities forbade the tolling of bells and the wearing of black and restricted funeral services to two mourners. The silencing of funeral bells and of criers' announcements of deaths was ordained by most cities. Siena imposed a fine on the wearing of mourning clothes by all except widows.

Flight was the chief recourse of those who could afford it or arrange it. The rich fled to their country places like Boccaccio's young patricians of Florence, who settled in a pastoral palace "removed on every side from the roads" with "wells of cool water and vaults of rare wines." The urban poor died in their burrows, "and only the stench of their bodies informed neighbors of their death." That the poor were more heavily afflicted than the rich was clearly remarked at the time, in the north as in the south. A Scottish chronicler, John of Fordun, stated flatly that the pest "attacked especially the meaner sort and common people—seldom the magnates."[22] Simon de Covino of Montpellier made the same observation.[23] He ascribed

---

Castle . . . Enguerrand: Enguerrand de Coucy is the historical figure on whom Tuchman focuses in her account of the fourteenth century. — EDS.

it to the misery and want and hard lives that made the poor more susceptible, which was half the truth. Close contact and lack of sanitation was the
unrecognized other half. It was noticed too that the young died in greater
proportion than the old; Simon de Covino compared the disappearance of
youth to the withering of flowers in the fields.[24]

In the countryside peasants dropped dead on the roads, in the fields,   20
in their houses. Survivors in growing helplessness fell into apathy, leaving
ripe wheat uncut and livestock untended. Oxen and asses, sheep and
goats, pigs and chickens ran wild and they too, according to local reports,
succumbed to the pest. English sheep, bearers of the precious wool, died
throughout the country. The chronicler Henry Knighton, canon of Leices-
ter Abbey, reported 5,000 dead in one field alone, "their bodies so corrupted by the plague that neither beast nor bird would touch them," and
spreading an appalling stench.[25] In the Austrian Alps wolves came down
to prey upon sheep and then, "as if alarmed by some invisible warning,
turned and fled back into the wilderness."[26] In remote Dalmatia bolder
wolves descended upon a plague-stricken city and attacked human survivors. For want of herdsmen, cattle strayed from place to place and died
in hedgerows and ditches. Dogs and cats fell like the rest.[27]

The dearth of labor held a fearful prospect because the fourteenth
century lived close to the annual harvest both for food and for next year's
seed. "So few servants and laborers were left," wrote Knighton, "that no
one knew where to turn for help." The sense of a vanishing future created
a kind of dementia of despair. A Bavarian chronicler of Neuberg on the
Danube recorded that "Men and women . . . wandered around as if
mad" and let their cattle stray "because no one had any inclination to
concern themselves about the future."[28] Fields went uncultivated, spring
seed unsown. Second growth with nature's awful energy crept back over
cleared land, dikes crumbled, salt water reinvaded and soured the lowlands. With so few hands remaining to restore the work of centuries, people felt, in Walsingham's words, that "the world could never again regain
its former prosperity."[29]

Though the death rate was higher among the anonymous poor, the
known and the great died too. King Alfonso XI of Castile was the only
reigning monarch killed by the pest, but his neighbor King Pedro of
Aragon lost his wife, Queen Leonora, his daughter Marie, and a niece in
the space of six months. John Cantacuzene, Emperor of Byzantium, lost
his son. In France the lame Queen Jeanne and her daughter-in-law Bonne
de Luxemburg, wife of the Dauphin,* both died in 1349 in the same
phase that took the life of Enguerrand's mother. Jeanne, Queen of
Navarre, daughter of Louis X, was another victim. Edward III's second
daughter, Joanna, who was on her way to marry Pedro, the heir of Castile,
died in Bordeaux. Women appear to have been more vulnerable than
men, perhaps because, being more housebound, they were more exposed

---

Dauphin: The eldest son of a French king and presumably heir to the throne. — EDS.

to fleas. Boccaccio's mistress Fiammetta, illegitimate daughter of the King of Naples, died, as did Laura, the beloved—whether real or fictional—of Petrarch. Reaching out to us in the future, Petrarch cried, "Oh happy posterity who will not experience such abysmal woe and will look upon our testimony as a fable."[30]

In Florence Giovanni Villani, the great historian of his time, died at 68 in the midst of an unfinished sentence: "... *e dure questo pistolenza fino a* ... (in the midst of this pestilence there came to an end ...)."[31] Siena's master painters, the brothers Ambrogio and Pietro Lorenzetti, whose names never appear after 1348, presumably perished in the plague, as did Andrea Pisano, architect and sculptor of Florence. William of Ockham and the English mystic Richard Rolle of Hampole both disappear from mention after 1349. Francisco Datini, merchant of Prato, lost both his parents and two siblings. Curious sweeps of mortality afflicted certain bodies of merchants in London. All eight wardens of the Company of Cutters, all six wardens of the Hatters, and four wardens of the Goldsmiths died before July 1350. Sir John Pulteney, master draper and four times Mayor of London, was a victim, likewise Sir John Montgomery, Governor of Calais.

Among the clergy and doctors the mortality was naturally high because of the nature of their professions. Out of 24 physicians in Venice, 20 were said to have lost their lives in the plague, although, according to another account, some were believed to have fled or to have shut themselves up in their houses.[32] At Montpellier, site of the leading medieval medical school, the physician Simon de Covino reported that, despite the great number of doctors, "hardly one of them escaped."[33] In Avignon, Guy de Chauliac confessed that he performed his medical visits only because he dared not stay away for fear of infamy, but "I was in continual fear."[34] He claimed to have contracted the disease but to have cured himself by his own treatment; if so, he was one of the few who recovered.

Clerical mortality varied with rank. Although the one-third toll of cardinals reflects the same proportion as the whole, this was probably due to their concentration in Avignon. In England, in strange and almost sinister procession, the Archbishop of Canterbury, John Stratford, died in August 1348, his appointed successor died in May 1349, and the next appointee three months later, all three within a year. Despite such weird vagaries, prelates in general managed to sustain a higher survival rate than the lesser clergy. Among bishops the deaths have been estimated at about one in twenty. The loss of priests, even if many avoided their fearful duty of attending the dying, was about the same as among the population as a whole.

Government officials, whose loss contributed to the general chaos, found, on the whole, no special shelter. In Siena four of the nine members of the governing oligarchy died, in France one third of the royal notaries, in Bristol 15 out of the 52 members of the Town Council or almost one third. Tax-collecting obviously suffered, with the result that Philip VI was unable to collect more than a fraction of the subsidy granted him by the Estates in the winter of 1347–48.

Lawlessness and debauchery accompanied the plague as they had during the great plague of Athens of 430 B.C., when according to Thucydides, men grew bold in the indulgence of pleasure: "For seeing how the rich died in a moment and those who had nothing immediately inherited their property, they reflected that life and riches were alike transitory and they resolved to enjoy themselves while they could."[35] Human behavior is timeless. When St. John had his vision of plague in Revelation, he knew from some experience or race memory that those who survived "repented not of the work of their hands. . . . Neither repented they of their murders, nor of their sorceries, nor of their fornication, nor of their thefts."

Ignorance of the cause augmented the sense of horror. Of the real carriers, rats and fleas, the fourteenth century had no suspicion, perhaps because they were so familiar. Fleas, though a common household nuisance, are not once mentioned in contemporary plague writings, and rats only incidentally, although folklore commonly associated them with pestilence. The legend of the Pied Piper arose from an outbreak of 1284. The actual plague bacillus, *Pasturella pestis*, remained undiscovered for another 500 years. Living alternately in the stomach of the flea and the bloodstream of the rat who was the flea's host, the bacillus in its bubonic form was transferred to humans and animals by the bite of either rat or flea. It traveled by virtue of *Rattus rattus*, the small medieval black rat that lived on ships, as well as by the heavier brown or sewer rat. What precipitated the turn of the bacillus from innocuous to virulent form is unknown, but the occurrence is now believed to have taken place not in China but somewhere in central Asia and to have spread along the caravan routes. Chinese origin was a mistaken notion of the fourteenth century based on real but belated reports of huge death tolls in China from drought, famine, and pestilence which have since been traced to the 1330s, too soon to be responsible for the plague that appeared in India in 1346.[36]

The phantom enemy had no name. Called the Black Death only in later recurrences, it was known during the first epidemic simply as the Pestilence or Great Mortality. Reports from the East, swollen by fearful imaginings, told of strange tempests and "sheets of fire" mingled with huge hailstones that "slew almost all," or a "vast rain of fire" that burned up men, beasts, stones, trees, villages, and cities.[37] In another version, "foul blasts of wind" from the fires carried the infection to Europe "and now as some suspect it cometh round the seacoast." Accurate observation in this case could not make the mental jump to ships and rats because no idea of animal- or insect-borne contagion existed.

The earthquake was blamed for releasing sulfurous and foul fumes   30 from the earth's interior, or as evidence of a titanic struggle of planets and oceans causing waters to rise and vaporize until fish died in masses and corrupted the air. All these explanations had in common a factor of poisoned air, of miasmas and thick, stinking mists traced to every kind of natural or imagined agency from stagnant lakes to malign conjunction of the planets, from the hand of the Evil One to the wrath of God. Medical thinking, trapped in the theory of astral influences, stressed air as the communicator of disease, ignoring sanitation or visible carriers. The existence of two carriers confused the trail, the more so because the flea could live and travel independently of the rat for as long as a month and, if infected by the particularly virulent septicemic form of the bacillus, could infect humans without reinfecting itself from the rat. The simultaneous presence of the pneumonic form of the disease, which was indeed communicated through the air, blurred the problem further.

The mystery of the contagion was "the most terrible of all the terrors," as an anonymous Flemish cleric in Avignon wrote to a correspondent in Bruges. Plagues had been known before, from the plague of Athens (believed to have been typhus) to the prolonged epidemic of the sixth century A.D., to the recurrence of sporadic outbreaks in the twelfth and thirteenth centuries, but they had left no accumulated store of understanding.[38] That the infection came from contact with the sick or with their houses, clothes, or corpses was quickly observed but not comprehended. Gentile da Foligno, renowned physician of Perugia and doctor of medicine at the universities of Bologna and Padua, came close to respiratory infection when he surmised that poisonous material was "communicated by means of air breathed out and in."[39] Having no idea of microscopic carriers, he had to assume that the air was corrupted by planetary influences. Planets, however, could not explain the ongoing contagion. The agonized search for an answer gave rise to such theories as transference by sight. People fell ill, wrote Guy de Chauliac, not only by remaining with the sick but "even by looking at them." Three hundred years later Joshua Barnes, the seventeenth century biographer of Edward III, could write that the power of infection had entered into beams of light and "darted death from the eyes."

Doctors struggling with the evidence could not break away from the terms of astrology, to which they believed all human physiology was subject. Medicine was the one aspect of medieval life, perhaps because of its links with the Arabs, not shaped by Christian doctrine. Clerics detested astrology, but could not dislodge its influence. Guy de Chauliac, physician to three popes in succession, practiced in obedience to the zodiac. While his *Cirurgia* was the major treatise on surgery of its time, while he understood the use of anesthesia made from the juice of opium, mandrake, or hemlock, he nevertheless prescribed bleeding and purgatives by the planets and divided chronic from acute diseases on the basis of one being under the rule of the sun and the other of the moon.

In October 1348 Philip VI asked the medical faculty of the University of Paris for a report on the affliction that seemed to threaten human survival.[40] With careful thesis, antithesis, and proofs, the doctors ascribed it to a triple conjunction of Saturn, Jupiter, and Mars in the fortieth degree of Aquarius said to have occurred on March 20, 1345. They acknowledged, however, effects "whose cause is hidden from even the most highly trained intellects." The verdict of the masters of Paris became the official version.

Borrowed, copied by scribes, carried abroad, translated from Latin into various vernaculars, it was everywhere accepted, even by the Arab physicians of Cordova and Granada, as the scientific if not the popular answer. Because of the terrible interest of the subject, the translations of the plague tracts stimulated use of national languages. In that one respect, life came from death.

To the people at large there could be but one explanation—the wrath of God. Planets might satisfy the learned doctors, but God was closer to the average man. A scourge so sweeping and unsparing without any visible cause could only be seen as Divine punishment upon mankind for its sins. It might even be God's terminal disappointment in his creature. Matteo Villani compared the plague to the Flood in ultimate purpose and believed he was recording "the extermination of mankind."[41] Efforts to appease Divine wrath took many forms, as when the city of Rouen ordered that everything that could anger God, such as gambling, cursing, and drinking, must be stopped.[42] More general were the penitent processions authorized at first by the Pope, some lasting as long as three days, some attended by as many as 2,000, which everywhere accompanied the plague and helped to spread it.

The Triumph of Death, *from a fifteenth-century Catalan fresco*

Barefoot in sackcloth, sprinkled with ashes, weeping, praying, tearing   35
their hair, carrying candles and relics, sometimes with ropes around their
necks or beating themselves with whips, the penitents wound through the
streets, imploring the mercy of the Virgin and saints at their shrines. In a
vivid illustration for the *Très Riches Heures* of the Duc de Berry, the Pope
is shown in a penitent procession attended by four cardinals in scarlet
from hat to hem. He raises both arms in supplication to the angel on top
of the Castel Sant'Angelo, while white-robed priests bearing banners and
relics in golden cases turn to look as one of their number, stricken by the
plague, falls to the ground, his face contorted with anxiety. In the rear, a
gray-clad monk falls beside another victim already on the ground as the
townspeople gaze in horror. (Nominally the illustration represents a sixth
century plague in the time of Pope Gregory the Great, but as medieval
artists made no distinction between past and present, the scene is shown as
the artist would have seen it in the fourteenth century.) When it became
evident that these processions were sources of infection, Clement VI had to
prohibit them.

In Messina, where the plague first appeared, the people begged the
Archbishop of neighboring Catania to lend them the relics of St. Agatha.[43]
When the Catanians refused to let the relics go, the Archbishop dipped them
in holy water and took the water himself to Messina, where he carried it in
a procession with prayers and litanies through the streets. The demonic,
which shared the medieval cosmos with God, appeared as "demons in the
shape of dogs" to terrify the people. "A black dog with a drawn sword in
his paws appeared among them, gnashing his teeth and rushing upon them
and breaking all the silver vessels and lamps and candlesticks on the altars
and casting them hither and thither. . . . So the people of Messina, terrified
by this prodigious vision, were all strangely overcome by fear."

The apparent absence of earthly cause gave the plague a supernatural
and sinister quality. Scandinavians believed that a Pest Maiden emerged
from the mouth of the dead in the form of a blue flame and flew through
the air to infect the next house.[44] In Lithuania the Maiden was said to wave
a red scarf through the door or window to let in the pest. One brave man,
according to legend, deliberately waited at his open window with drawn
sword and, at the fluttering of the scarf, chopped off the hand. He died of
his deed, but his village was spared and the scarf long preserved as a relic in
the local church.

Beyond demons and superstition the final hand was God's. The Pope
acknowledged it in a Bull* of September 1348, speaking of the "pestilence
with which God is afflicting the Christian people." To the Emperor John
Cantacuzene it was manifest that a malady of such horrors, stenches, and
agonies, and especially one bringing the dismal despair that settled upon
its victims before they died, was not a plague "natural" to mankind but "a

---

Bull: A formal papal document. — EDS.

chastisement from Heaven."[45] To Piers Plowman "these pestilences were for pure sin."[46]

The general acceptance of this view created an expanded sense of guilt, for if the plague were punishment there had to be terrible sin to have occasioned it. What sins were on the fourteenth century conscience? Primarily greed, the sin of avarice, followed by usury, worldliness, adultery, blasphemy, falsehood, luxury, irreligion. Giovanni Villani, attempting to account for the cascade of calamity that had fallen upon Florence, concluded that it was retribution for the sins of avarice and usury that oppressed the poor. Pity and anger about the condition of the poor, especially victimization of the peasantry in war, was often expressed by writers of the time and was certainly on the conscience of the century. Beneath it all was the daily condition of medieval life, in which hardly an act or thought, sexual, mercantile, or military, did not contravene the dictates of the Church. Mere failure to fast or attend mass was sin. The result was an underground lake of guilt in the soul that the plague now tapped.

That the mortality was accepted as God's punishment may explain in   40
part the vacuum of comment that followed the Black Death. An investigator has noticed that in the archives of Périgord references to the war are innumerable, to the plague few. Froissart mentions the great death but once, Chaucer gives it barely a glance. Divine anger so great that it contemplated the extermination of man did not bear close examination.

NOTES

1. "Death Is Seen Seated": Simon de Covino, q. Campbell, 80.
2. "Could Infect the World": q. Gasquet, 41.
3. Welsh Lament: q. Ziegler, 190.
4. "Dogs Dragged Them Forth": Agnolo di Tura, q. Ziegler, 58.
5. "Or if No Man Is Present": Bishop of Bath and Wells, q. Ziegler, 125.
6. "No Bells Tolled": Agnolo di Tura, q. Schevill, *Siena*, 211. The same observation was made by Gabriel de Muisis, notary of Piacenza, q. Crawford, 113.
7. Givry Parish Register: Renouard, 111.
8. Three Villages of Cambridgeshire: Saltmarsh.
9. Petrarch's Brother: Bishop, 273.
10. Brother John Clyn: q. Ziegler, 195.
11. Apathy; "And in These Days": q. Deaux, 143, citing only "an old northern chronicle."
12. Agnolo di Tura, "Father Abandoned Child": q. Ziegler, 58.
13. "Magistrates and Notaries": q. Deaux, 49.
14. English Priests Turned Away: Ziegler, 261.
15. Parents Deserting Children: Hecker, 30.
16. Guy de Chauliac, "A Father": q. Gasquet, 50–51.
17. Nuns of the Hotel Dieu: *Chron. Jean de Venette*, 49.
18. Picards and Scots Mock Mortality of Neighbors: Gasquet, 53, and Ziegler, 198.
19. Catherine de Coucy: *L'Art de verifier*, 237.
20. Amiens Tanners: Gasquet, 57.
21. "By the Jollity That Is in Us": *Grandes Chrons.*, VI, 486–87.
22. John of Fordun: q. Ziegler, 199.
23. Simon de Covino on the Poor: Gasquet, 42.
24. On Youth: Cazelles, *Peste*.
25. Knighton on Sheep: q. Ziegler, 175.

26. Wolves of Austria and Dalmatia: ibid., 84, 111.
27. Dogs and Cats: Muisis, q. Gasquet, 44, 61.
28. Bavarian Chronicler of Neuberg: q. Ziegler, 84.
29. Walsingham, "The World Could Never": Denifle, 273.
30. "Oh Happy Posterity": q. Ziegler, 45.
31. Giovanni Villani, "*e dure questo*": q. Snell, 334.
32. Physicians of Venice: Campbell, 98.
33. Simon de Covino: ibid., 31.
34. Guy de Chauliac, "I Was in Fear": q. Thompson, *Ec. and Soc.*, 379.
35. Thucydides: q. Crawfurd, 30–31.
36. Chinese Origin: Although the idea of Chinese origin is still being repeated (e.g., by William H. McNeill, *Plagues and People*, New York, 1976, 161–63), it is disputed by L. Carrington Goodrich of the Association for Asian Studies, Columbia Univ., in letters to the author of 18 and 26 October 1973. Citing contemporary Chinese and other sources, he also quotes Dr. George A. Perera of the College of Physicians and Surgeons, an authority on communicable diseases, who "agrees with me that the spaces between epidemics in China (1334), Semirechyé (1338–9) and the Mediterranean basin (1347–9) seem too long for the first to be responsible for the last."
37. Reports from the East: Barnes, 432; Coulton, *Black Death*, 9–11.
38. Anonymous Flemish Cleric, "Most Terrible": His correspondence was edited in the form of a chronicle by De Smet, in *Recueil des chroniques de Flandres*, III, q. Ziegler, 22.
39. Gentile da Foligno, "Communicated by air": Campbell, 38.
40. Report of the University of Paris: Hecker, 51–53; Campbell, 15.
41. M. Villani, "Extermination of Mankind": q. Meiss, *Painting . . . After the Black Death*, 66.
42. Rouen Prohibits Gambling: Nohl, 74.
43. At Messina, Demons Like Dogs: Coulton, *Black Death*, 22–27.
44. Pest Maiden: Ziegler, 85.
45. Cantacuzene: Barnes, 435.
46. Piers Plowman, "Pure Sin": B text, V, 13.

BIBLIOGRAPHY

L'Art de verifier les dates des faits historiques, par un Religieux de la Congregation de St. Maur, vol. XII. Paris, 1818.
Barnes, Joshua, *The History of Edward III*. Cambridge, 1688.
Campbell, Anna M., *The Black Death and Men of Learning*. Columbia University Press, 1931.
Chronicle of Jean de Venette. Trans. Jean Birdsall. Ed. Richard A. Newhall. Columbia University Press, 1853.
Crawfurd, Raymond, *Plague and Pestilence in Literature and Art*. Oxford, 1914.
Coulton, G. G., *The Black Death*. London, 1929.
Deaux, George, *The Black Death, 1347*. London, 1969.
Denifle, Henri, *La Désolation des églises, monastères et hôpitaux en France pendant la guerre de cent ans*, vol. I. Paris, 1899.
Gasquet, Francis Aidan, Abbot, *The Black Death of 1348 and 1349*, 2nd ed. London, 1908.
Grandes Chroniques de France, vol. VI (to 1380). Ed. Paulin Paris. Paris, 1838.
Hecker, J. F. C., *The Epidemics of the Middle Ages*. London, 1844.
Meiss, Millard, *Painting in Florence and Siena After the Black Death*. Princeton, 1951.
Nohl, Johannes, *The Black Death: A Chronicle of the Plague Compiled from Contemporary Sources*. Trans. C. H. Clarke. London, 1971.
Saltmarsh, John, "Plague and Economic Decline in England in the Latter Middle Ages," *Cambridge Historical Journal*, vol. VII, no. 1, 1941.
Schevill, Ferdinand, *History of Florence*. New York, 1961.
Snell, Frederick, *The Fourteenth Century*. Edinburgh, 1899.
Thompson, James Westfall, *Economic and Social History of Europe in the Later Middle Ages*. New York, 1931.
Ziegler, Philip, *The Black Death*. New York, 1969. (The best modern study.)

The Reader's Presence

1. History is a form of story. Which elements of Tuchman's account
    seem to pertain to pure fact, and which to storytelling? Events are
    related in an objective tone. Is the writer's approval or disapproval
    ever evident? If so, where and in what ways?

2. This piece is drawn from a book titled *A Distant Mirror: The
    Calamitous Fourteenth Century*. In what ways does Tuchman's
    account suggest that fourteenth-century behaviors reflect our be-
    haviors today?

3. At times Tuchman recounts history in the aggregate; at times she
    traces history through a specific figure. Find a few instances of this
    latter technique. Why might she have chosen to augment the gen-
    eral with the particular and vice-versa? What is the effect of this
    technique on the reader?

4. "Ignorance of the cause augmented the sense of horror," Tuch-
    man writes of the fourteenth-century plague (paragraph 28), but
    her statement can be taken as universally true. Use Tuchman's in-
    sight to sharpen your perception of the emotions expressed in
    Michihiko Hachiya's journal ("From *Hiroshima Diary*," page 34)
    and in Don DeLillo's essay ("In the Ruins of the Future," page
    361). How does each of these writers respond to problems of un-
    speakable horror? How do their approaches to narrating disaster
    compare?

Sherry Turkle

How Computers Change the Way We Think

Sherry Turkle (b. 1948) is Abby Rockefeller Mauzé Professor of the Social Studies of Science and Technology at the Massachusetts Institute of Technology. She is also the founder and current director of the MIT Initiative on Technology and Self, a research and education center concerned with the "subjective side of technology" and focused on the way technological change—particularly computers and the Internet—affects humans. A clinical psychologist, she has published a number of books including The Second Self: Computers and the Human Spirit *(1984),* Psychoanalytic Politics: Jacques Lacan and Freud's French Revolution *(1992), and* Life on the Screen: Identity in the Age of the Internet *(1995).*

Turkle sees computer-mediated reality as having the potential "to create a kind of crisis about the simulated and the real. The notion of what it is to live in a culture of simulation—how much of that counts as real experience and how much of that is discounted—is going to become more and more in the forefront of what people think and talk about, because so much experience is going to be about not being there." Her piece "How Computers Change the Way We Think" appeared in the Chronicle of Higher Education *in 2004.*

The tools we use to think change the ways in which we think. The invention of written language brought about a radical shift in how we process, organize, store, and transmit representations of the world. Although writing remains our primary information technology, today when we think about the impact of technology on our habits of mind, we think primarily of the computer.

My first encounters with how computers change the way we think came soon after I joined the faculty at the Massachusetts Institute of Technology in the late 1970s, at the end of the era of the slide rule and the beginning of the era of the personal computer. At a lunch for new faculty members, several senior professors in engineering complained that the transition from slide rules to calculators had affected their students' ability to deal with issues of scale. When students used slide rules, they had to insert decimal points themselves. The professors insisted that that required students to maintain a mental sense of scale, whereas those who relied on calculators made frequent errors in orders of magnitude. Additionally, the students with calculators had lost their ability to do "back of the envelope" calculations, and with that, an intuitive feel for the material.

That same semester, I taught a course in the history of psychology. There, I experienced the impact of computational objects on students' ideas about their emotional lives. My class had read Freud's essay on slips of the tongue, with its famous first example: The chairman of a parliamentary session opens a meeting by declaring it closed. The students discussed how Freud interpreted such errors as revealing a person's mixed emotions. A computer-science major disagreed with Freud's approach. The mind, she argued, is a computer. And in a computational dictionary—like we have in the human mind—"closed" and "open" are designated by the same symbol, separated by a sign for opposition. "Closed" equals "minus open." To substitute "closed" for "open" does not require the notion of ambivalence or conflict.

"When the chairman made that substitution," she declared, "a bit was dropped; a minus sign was lost. There was a power surge. No problem."

The young woman turned a Freudian slip into an information-processing error. An explanation in terms of meaning had become an explanation in terms of mechanism.   5

Such encounters turned me to the study of both the instrumental and the subjective sides of the nascent computer culture. As an ethnographer and psychologist, I began to study not only what the computer was doing *for* us, but what it was doing *to* us, including how it was changing the way we see ourselves, our sense of human identity.

In the 1980s, I surveyed the psychological effects of computational objects in everyday life—largely the unintended side effects of people's tendency to project thoughts and feelings onto their machines. In the 20 years since, computational objects have become more explicitly designed to have emotional and cognitive effects. And those "effects by design" will become even stronger in the decade to come. Machines are being designed to serve explicitly as companions, pets, and tutors. And they are introduced in school settings for the youngest children.

Today, starting in elementary school, students use e-mail, word processing, computer simulations, virtual communities, and PowerPoint software. In the process, they are absorbing more than the content of what appears on their screens. They are learning new ways to think about what it means to know and understand.

What follows is a short and certainly not comprehensive list of areas where I see information technology encouraging changes in thinking. There can be no simple way of cataloging whether any particular change is good or bad. That is contested terrain. At every step we have to ask, as educators and citizens, whether current technology is leading us in directions that serve our human purposes. Such questions are not technical; they are social, moral, and political. For me, addressing that subjective side of computation is one of the more significant challenges for the next decade of information technology in higher education. Technology does not determine change, but it encourages us to take certain directions. If we make those directions clear, we can more easily exert human choice.

Thinking about privacy. Today's college students are habituated to   10
a world of online blogging, instant messaging, and Web browsing that
leaves electronic traces. Yet they have had little experience with the
right to privacy. Unlike past generations of Americans, who grew up
with the notion that the privacy of their mail was sacrosanct, our children are accustomed to electronic surveillance as part of their daily
lives.

I have colleagues who feel that the increased incursions on privacy
have put the topic more in the news, and that this is a positive change.
But middle-school and high-school students tend to be willing to provide
personal information online with no safeguards, and college students
seem uninterested in violations of privacy and in increased governmental and commercial surveillance. Professors find that students do not
understand that in a democracy, privacy is a right, not merely a privilege. In ten years, ideas about the relationship of privacy and government will require even more active pedagogy. (One might also hope that
increased education about the kinds of silent surveillance that technology makes possible may inspire more active political engagement with
the issue.)

Avatars or a self? Chat rooms, role-playing games, and other technological venues offer us many different contexts for presenting ourselves online. Those possibilities are particularly important for adolescents because
they offer what Erik Erikson described as a moratorium, a time out or safe
space for the personal experimentation that is so crucial for adolescent
development. Our dangerous world—with crime, terrorism, drugs, and
AIDS—offers little in the way of safe spaces. Online worlds can provide
valuable spaces for identity play.

But some people who gain fluency in expressing multiple aspects of
self may find it harder to develop authentic selves. Some children who
write narratives for their screen avatars may grow up with too little experience of how to share their real feelings with other people. For those who
are lonely yet afraid of intimacy, information technology has made it possible to have the illusion of companionship without the demands of friendship.

From powerful ideas to PowerPoint. In the 1970s and early 1980s,
some educators wanted to make programming part of the regular curriculum for K–12 education. They argued that because information technology carries ideas, it might as well carry the most powerful ideas that
computer science has to offer. It is ironic that in most elementary schools
today, the ideas being carried by information technology are not ideas
from computer science like procedural thinking, but more likely to be
those embedded in productivity tools like PowerPoint presentation software.

PowerPoint does more than provide a way of transmitting content. It   15
carries its own way of thinking, its own aesthetic—which not surprisingly

shows up in the aesthetic of college freshmen. In that aesthetic, presentation becomes its own powerful idea.

To be sure, the software cannot be blamed for lower intellectual standards. Misuse of the former is as much a symptom as a cause of the latter. Indeed, the culture in which our children are raised is increasingly a culture of presentation, a corporate culture in which appearance is often more important than reality. In contemporary political discourse, the bar has also been lowered. Use of rhetorical devices at the expense of cogent argument regularly goes without notice. But it is precisely because standards of intellectual rigor outside the educational sphere have fallen that educators must attend to how we use, and when we introduce, software that has been designed to simplify the organization and processing of information.

In "The Cognitive Style of PowerPoint" (Graphics Press, 2003), Edward R. Tufte suggests that PowerPoint equates bulleting with clear thinking. It does not teach students to begin a discussion or construct a narrative. It encourages presentation, not conversation. Of course, in the hands of a master teacher, a PowerPoint presentation with few words and powerful images can serve as the jumping-off point for a brilliant lecture. But in the hands of elementary-school students, often introduced to PowerPoint in the third grade, and often infatuated with its swooshing sounds, animated icons, and flashing text, a slide show is more likely to close down debate than open it up.

Developed to serve the needs of the corporate boardroom, the software is designed to convey absolute authority. Teachers used to tell students that clear exposition depended on clear outlining, but presentation software has fetishized the outline at the expense of the content.

Narrative, the exposition of content, takes time. PowerPoint, like so much in the computer culture, speeds up the pace.

Word processing vs. thinking. The catalog for the Vermont Country   20
Store advertises a manual typewriter, which the advertising copy says "moves at a pace that allows time to compose your thoughts." As many of us know, it is possible to manipulate text on a computer screen and see how it looks faster than we can think about what the words mean.

Word processing has its own complex psychology. From a pedagogical point of view, it can make dedicated students into better writers because it allows them to revise text, rearrange paragraphs, and experiment with the tone and shape of an essay. Few professional writers would part with their computers; some claim that they simply cannot think without their hands on the keyboard. Yet the ability to quickly fill the page, to see it before you can think it, can make bad writers even worse.

A seventh grader once told me that the typewriter she found in her mother's attic is "cool because you have to type each letter by itself. You have to know what you are doing in advance or it comes out a mess." The idea of thinking ahead has become exotic.

Taking things at interface value. We expect software to be easy to use, and we assume that we don't have to know how a computer works. In the early 1980s, most computer users who spoke of transparency meant that, as with any other machine, you could "open the hood" and poke around. But only a few years later, Macintosh users began to use the term when they talked about seeing their documents and programs represented by attractive and easy-to-interpret icons. They were referring to an ability to make things work without needing to go below the screen surface. Paradoxically, it was the screen's opacity that permitted that kind of transparency. Today, when people say that something is transparent, they mean that they can see how to make it work, not that they know how it works. In other words, transparency means epistemic opacity.

The people who built or bought the first generation of personal computers understood them down to the bits and bytes. The next generation of operating systems were more complex, but they still invited that old-time reductive understanding. Contemporary information technology encourages different habits of mind. Today's college students are already used to taking things at (inter)face value; their successors in 2014 will be even less accustomed to probing below the surface.

Simulation and its discontents. Some thinkers argue that the new opacity is empowering, enabling anyone to use the most sophisticated technological tools and to experiment with simulation in complex and creative ways. But it is also true that our tools carry the message that they are beyond our understanding. It is possible that in daily life, epistemic opacity can lead to passivity.

I first became aware of that possibility in the early 1990s, when the first generation of complex simulation games were introduced and immediately became popular for home as well as school use. SimLife teaches the principles of evolution by getting children involved in the development of complex ecosystems; in that sense it is an extraordinary learning tool. During one session in which I played SimLife with Tim, a 13-year-old, the screen before us flashed a message: "Your orgot is being eaten up." "What's an orgot?" I asked. Tim didn't know. "I just ignore that," he said confidently. "You don't need to know that kind of stuff to play."

For me, that story serves as a cautionary tale. Computer simulations enable their users to think about complex phenomena as dynamic, evolving systems. But they also accustom us to manipulating systems whose core assumptions we may not understand and that may not be true.

We live in a culture of simulation. Our games, our economic and political systems, and the ways architects design buildings, chemists envisage molecules, and surgeons perform operations all use simulation technology. In ten years the degree to which simulations are embedded in every area of life will have increased exponentially. We need to develop a new form of media literacy: readership skills for the culture of simulation.

We come to written text with habits of readership based on centuries of civilization. At the very least, we have learned to begin with the journalist's traditional questions: who, what, when, where, why, and how. Who wrote these words, what is their message, why were they written, and how are they situated in time and place, politically and socially? A central project for higher education during the next ten years should be creating programs in information-technology literacy, with the goal of teaching students to interrogate simulations in much the same spirit, challenging their built-in assumptions.

Despite the ever-increasing complexity of software, most computer   30
environments put users in worlds based on constrained choices. In other words, immersion in programmed worlds puts us in reassuring environments where the rules are clear. For example, when you play a video game, you often go through a series of frightening situations that you escape by mastering the rules—you experience life as a reassuring dichotomy of scary and safe. Children grow up in a culture of video games, action films, fantasy epics, and computer programs that all rely on that familiar scenario of almost losing but then regaining total mastery: There is danger. It is mastered. A still-more-powerful monster appears. It is subdued. Scary. Safe.

Yet in the real world, we have never had a greater need to work our way out of binary assumptions. In the decade ahead, we need to rebuild the culture around information technology. In that new sociotechnical culture, assumptions about the nature of mastery would be less absolute. The new culture would make it easier, not more difficult, to consider life in shades of gray, to see moral dilemmas in terms other than a battle between Good and Evil. For never has our world been more complex, hybridized, and global. Never have we so needed to have many contradictory thoughts and feelings at the same time. Our tools must help us accomplish that, not fight against us.

Information technology is identity technology. Embedding it in a culture that supports democracy, freedom of expression, tolerance, diversity, and complexity of opinion is one of the next decade's greatest challenges. We cannot afford to fail.

When I first began studying the computer culture, a small breed of highly trained technologists thought of themselves as "computer people." That is no longer the case. If we take the computer as a carrier of a way of knowing, a way of seeing the world and our place in it, we are all computer people now.

The Reader's Presence

1. Reread the example that Turkle uses to open her essay. Does the young woman's reinterpretation of a Freudian slip show that computers can change the way we think? Does it show a change in the way we think of ourselves? Why or why not?

2. Turkle advocates critical dialogue about the consequences of technology, emphasizing that these "questions are not technical; they are social, moral, and political" (paragraph 9). What are the social, moral, and political consequences that Turkle speaks of? Which concern her most and why? Do you share her concerns?

3. What is Turkle's opinion of the changes she outlines? Does she present them uncritically or does she place value on certain ways of thinking and being? Compare Turkle's essay to Ellen Ullman's "The Museum of Me" (below). How do the two writers differ in their responses to the changes that technology engenders? What examples from Turkle's essay support Ullman's argument? Do you think the two writers view technology in different or similar ways? Why?

Ellen Ullman

The Museum of Me

Ellen Ullman (b. 1950), writer, computer programmer, and technology consultant, entered "computerdom" in the 1970s, just when business computing was breaking wide open. "I've always written," she told an interviewer. "I'm from an older generation of programmers. For the most part, we did not come out of engineering (which was a much later development)." Ullman's experiences have shaped her unique perspective on the upsides and downsides of technology and its affect on human interaction. Close to the Machine: Technophilia and Its Discontents *(1997) is Ullman's account of her life in "cyberculture" as a programmer running her own business out of a live-in office loft in San Francisco. Ullman turned that experience into fiction in her first novel,* The Bug *(2003). Ullman contributes to such periodicals and media outlets as* Harper's, Wired, *and* Salon.com *and has been a frequent guest technology commentator for National Public Radio. Her essays have appeared in numerous anthologies.*

Ullman has argued that "today's success-dream seems to be about a house far away, not needing to be in crowded places, communicating with the world electronically. It's a suburbanized ideal of happiness, I think. It seeks a privatized, frictionless life." In "The Museum of Me," Ullman decries the concept that people "do not even want a shared experience."

Years ago, before the Internet as we know it had come into existence—
I think it was around Christmas, in 1990—I was at friend's house, where
her nine-year-old son and his friend were playing the video game that was

the state of the art at the time, Sonic the Hedgehog. They jumped around in front of the TV and gave off the sort of rude noises boys tend to make when they're shooting at things in a video game, and after about half an hour they stopped and tried to talk about what they'd just been doing. The dialogue went something like this:

"I wiped out at that part with the ladders."

"Ladders? What ladders?"

"You know, after the rooms."

"Oh, you mean the stairs?"   5

"No, I think they were ladders. I remember, because I died there twice."

"I never killed you around any ladders. I killed you where you jump down off this wall."

"Wall? You mean by the gates of the city?"

"Are there gates around the city? I always called it the castle."

The boys muddled along for several more minutes, making them-   10
selves more confused as they went. Finally they gave up trying to talk about their time with Sonic the Hedgehog. They just looked at each other and shrugged.

I didn't think about the two boys and Sonic again until I watched my clients try out the World Wide Web. By then it was 1995, the Internet as we know it was beginning to exist, but the two women who worked for my client, whom I'd just helped get online, had never before connected to the Internet or surfed the Web. They took to it instantly, each disappearing into nearly an hour of obsessive clicking, after which they tried to talk about it:

"It was great! I clicked that thing and went to this place. I don't remember its name."

"Yeah. It was a link. I clicked here and went there."

"Oh, I'm not sure it was a link. The thing I clicked was a picture of the library."

"Was it the library? I thought it was a picture of City Hall."   15

"Oh, no. I'm sure it was the library."

"No, City Hall. I'm sure because of the dome."

"Dome? Was there a dome?"

Right then I remembered Sonic and the two boys; my clients, like the two boys, had experienced something pleasurable and engaging, and they very much wanted to talk about it—talking being one of the primary ways human beings augment their pleasure. But what had happened to them, each in her own electronic world, resisted description. Like the boys, the two women fell into verbal confusion. How could they speak coherently about a world full of little wordless pictograms, about trails that led off in all directions, of idle visits to virtual places chosen on a whim-click?

Following hyperlinks on the Web is like the synaptic drift of dreams,   20
a loosening of intention, the mind associating freely, an experience that can be compelling or baffling or unsettling, or all of those things at once.

And like dreams, the experience of the Web is intensely private, charged with immanent meaning for the person inside the experience, but often confusing or irrelevant to someone else.

At the time, I had my reservations about the Web, but not so much about the private, dreamlike state it offered. Web surfing seemed to me not so much antisocial as asocial, an adventure like a video game or pinball, entertaining, sometimes interesting, sometimes a trivial waste of time; but in a social sense it seemed harmless, since only the person engaged in the activity was affected.

Something changed, however, not in me but in the Internet and the Web and in the world, and the change was written out in person-high letters on a billboard on the corner of Howard and New Montgomery streets in San Francisco. It was the fall of 1998. I was walking toward Market Street one afternoon when I saw it, a background of brilliant sky blue, with writing on it in airy white letters, which said: *now the world really does revolve around you*. The letters were lowercase, soft-edged, spaced irregularly, as if they'd been skywritten over a hot August beach and were already drifting off into the air. The message they left behind was a child's secret wish, the ultimate baby-world narcissism we are all supposed to abandon when we grow up: the world really does revolve around me.

What was this billboard advertising? Perfume? A resort? There was nothing else on it but the airy, white letters, and I had to walk right up to it to see a URL written at the bottom; it was the name of a company that makes semi-conductor equipment, machinery used by companies like Intel and AMD to manufacture integrated circuits. Oh, chips, I thought. Computers. Of course. What other subject produces such hyperbole? Who else but someone in the computer industry could make such a shameless appeal to individualism?

The billboard loomed over the corner for the next couple of weeks. Every time I passed it, its message irritated me more. It bothered me the way the "My Computer" icon bothers me on the Windows desktop, baby names like "My Yahoo" and "My Snap"; my, my, my; two-year-old talk; infantilizing and condescending.

But there was something more disturbing about this billboard, and I tried to figure out why, since it simply was doing what every other piece of advertising does: whispering in your ear that there is no one like you in the entire world, and what we are offering is for you, special you, and you alone. What came to me was this: Toyota, for example, sells the idea of a special, individual buyer ("It's not for everyone, just for you"), but chip makers, through the medium of the Internet and the World Wide Web, are creating the actual infrastructure of an individualized marketplace. 25

What had happened between 1995, when I could still think of the Internet as a private dream, and the appearance of that billboard in 1998 was the near-complete commercialization of the Web. And that commercialization had proceeded in a very particular and single-minded way: by attempting to isolate the individual within a sea of economic activity. Through a process known as "disintermediation," producers have worked to remove the expert intermediaries, agents, brokers, middlemen, who until now have influenced our interactions with the commercial world. What bothered me about the billboard, then, was that its message was not merely hype but the reflection of a process that was already under way: an attempt to convince the individual that a change currently being visited upon him or her is a good thing, the purest form of self, the equivalent of freedom. The world really does revolve around you.

In Silicon Valley, in Redmond, Washington, the home of Microsoft, and in the smaller silicon alleys of San Francisco and New York, "disintermediation" is a word so common that people shrug when you try to talk to them about it. Oh, disintermediation, that old thing. Everyone already knows about that. It has become accepted wisdom, a process considered inevitable, irrefutable, good.

I've long believed that the ideas embedded in technology have a way of percolating up and outward into the nontechnical world at large, and that technology is made by people with intentions and, as such, is not neutral. In the case of disintermediation, an explicit and purposeful change is being visited upon the structure of the global marketplace. And in a world so dominated by markets, I don't think I go too far in saying that this will affect the very structure of reality, for the Net is no longer simply a zone of personal freedoms, a pleasant diversion from what we used to call "real life"; it has become an actual marketplace that is changing the nature of real life itself.

Removal of the intermediary. All those who stand in the middle of a transaction, whether financial or intellectual: out! Brokers and agents and middlemen of every description: good-bye! Travel agents, real-estate agents, insurance agents, stockbrokers, mortgage brokers, consolidators, and jobbers, all the scrappy percentniks who troll the bywaters of capitalist exchange—who needs you? All those hard-striving immigrants climbing their way into the lower middle class through the penny-ante deals of capitalism, the transfer points too small for the big guys to worry about—find yourself some other way to make a living. Small retailers and store clerks, salespeople of every kind—a hindrance, idiots, not to be trusted. Even the professional handlers of intellectual goods, anyone who sifts through information, books, paintings, knowledge, selecting and summing up: librarians, book reviewers, curators, disc jockeys, teachers, editors, analysts—why trust anyone but yourself to make judgments about what is more or less interesting, valuable, authentic, or worthy of your attention? No one, no professional interloper, is supposed to come between you and your desires, which, according to this idea, are nuanced, difficult to communicate, irreducible, unique.

The Web did not cause disintermediation, but it is what we call an "enabling technology": a technical breakthrough that takes a difficult task   30 and makes it suddenly doable, easy; it opens the door to change, which then comes in an unconsidered, breathless rush.

We are living through an amazing experiment: an attempt to construct a capitalism without salespeople, to take a system founded upon the need to sell ever greater numbers of goods to ever growing numbers of people, and to do this without the aid of professional distribution channels — without buildings, sidewalks, shops, luncheonettes, street vendors, buses, trams, taxis, other women in the fitting room to tell you how you look in something and to help you make up your mind, without street people panhandling, Santas ringing bells at Christmas, shop women with their perfect makeup and elegant clothes, fashionable men and women strolling by to show you the latest look — in short, an attempt to do away with the city in all its messy stimulation, to abandon the agora for home and hearth, where it is safe and everything can be controlled.

The first task in this newly structured capitalism is to convince consumers that the services formerly performed by myriad intermediaries are useless or worse, that those commissioned brokers and agents are incompetent, out for themselves, dishonest. And the next task is to glorify the notion of self-service. Where companies once vied for your business by telling you about their courteous people and how well they would serve you — "Avis, We Try Harder" — their job now is to make you believe that only you can take care of yourself. The lure of personal service that was dangled before the middle classes, momentarily making us all feel almost as lucky as the rich, is being withdrawn. In the Internet age, under the pressure of globalized capitalism and its slimmed-down profit margins, only the very wealthy will be served by actual human beings. The rest of us must make do with Web pages, and feel happy about it.

One evening while I was watching television, I looked up to see a commercial that seemed to me to be the most explicit statement of the ideas implicit in the disintermediated universe. I gaped at it, because usually such ideas are kept implicit, hidden behind symbols. But this commercial was like the sky-blue billboard: a shameless and naked expression of the Web world, a glorification of the self, at home, alone.

It begins with a drone, a footstep in a puddle, then a ragged band pulling a dead car through the mud — road warriors with bandanas around their foreheads carrying braziers. Now we see rafts of survivors floating before the ruins of a city, the sky dark, red-tinged, as if fires were burning all around us, just over the horizon. Next we are outside the dead city's library, where stone lions, now coated in gold and come to life, rear up in despair. Inside the library, red-coated Fascist guards encircle the readers at the table. A young girl turns a page, loudly, and the guards say, "Shush!" in time to their march-step. We see the title of the book the girl is reading: *Paradise Lost*. The bank, too, is a scene of ruin. A long line snakes outside it in a dreary rain. Inside, the teller is a man with a white, spectral face, who gazes upon a black spider that is slowly crawling up his window. A young woman's face ages right before us, and in response, in ridicule, the bank guard laughs. The camera now takes us up over the roofs of this post-apocalyptic city. Lightning crashes in the dark, red-tinged sky. On a telephone pole, where the insulators should be, are skulls.

Cut to a cartoon of emerald-green grass, hills, a Victorian house with   35
a white picket fence and no neighbors. A butterfly flaps above it. What a relief this house is after the dreary, dangerous, ruined city. The door to this charming house opens, and we go in to see a chair before a computer screen. Yes, we want to go sit in that chair, in that room with candy-orange walls. On the computer screen, running by in teasing succession, are pleasant virtual reflections of the world outside: written text, a bank check, a telephone pole, which now signifies our connection to the world. The camera pans back to show a window, a curtain swinging in the breeze, and our sense of calm is complete. We hear the Intel-Inside jingle, which sounds almost like chimes. Cut to the legend: Packard Bell. Wouldn't you rather be at home?

In sixty seconds, this commercial communicates a worldview that reflects the ultimate suburbanization of existence: a retreat from the friction of the social space to the supposed idyll of private ease. It is a view that depends on the idea that desire is not social, not stimulated by what others want, but generated internally, and that the satisfaction of desires is not dependent upon other persons, organizations, structures, or governments. It is a profoundly libertarian vision, and it is the message that underlies all the mythologizing about the Web: the idea that the civic space is dead, useless, dangerous. The only place of pleasure and satisfaction is your home. You, home, family; and beyond that, the world. From the intensely private to the global, with little in between but an Intel processor and a search engine.

In this sense, the ideal of the Internet represents the very opposite of democracy, which is a method for resolving differences in a relatively orderly manner through the mediation of unavoidable civil associations. Yet there can be no notion of resolving differences in a world where each person is entitled to get exactly what he or she wants. Here all needs and desires are equally valid and equally powerful. I'll get mine and you'll get yours; there is no need for compromise and discussion. I don't have to tolerate you, and you don't have to tolerate me. No need for messy debate and the whole rigmarole of government with all its creaky, bothersome structures. There's no need for any of this, because now that we have the World Wide Web the problem of the pursuit of happiness has been solved! We'll each click for our individual joys, and our only dispute may come if something doesn't get delivered on time. Wouldn't you really rather be at home?

But who can afford to stay at home? Only the very wealthy or a certain class of knowledge worker can stay home and click. On the other side of this ideal of work-anywhere freedom (if indeed it is freedom never to be away from work) is the reality that somebody had to make the thing you ordered with a click. Somebody had to put it in a box, do the paperwork, carry it to you. The reality is a world divided not only between the haves and have-nots but between the ones who get to stay home and everyone else, the ones who deliver the goods to them.

The Net ideal represents a retreat not only from political life but also from culture — from that tumultuous conversation in which we try to talk to one another about our shared experiences. As members of a culture, we see the same movie, read the same book, hear the same string quartet. Although it is difficult for us to agree on what we might have seen, read, or heard, it is out of that difficult conversation that real culture arises. Whether or not we come to an agreement or understanding, even if some decide that understanding and meaning are impossible, we are still sitting around the same campfire.

But the Web as it has evolved is based on the idea that we do not even 40 want a shared experience. The director of San Francisco's Museum of Modern Art once told an audience that we no longer need a building to house works of art; we don't need to get dressed, go downtown, walk from room to room among crowds of other people. Now that we have the Web, we can look at anything we want whenever we want, and we no longer need him or his curators. "You don't have to walk through *my* idea of what's interesting to look at," he said to a questioner in the audience named Bill. "On the Web," said the director, "you can create the museum of Bill."

And so, by implication, there can be the museums of George and Mary and Helene. What then will this group have to say to one another about art? Let's say the museum of Bill is featuring early Dutch masters, the museum of Mary is playing video art, and the museum of Helene is displaying French tapestries. In this privatized world, what sort of "cultural" conversation can there be? What can one of us possibly say to another about our experience except, "Today I visited the museum of me, and I liked it."

The Reader's Presence

1. Examine the closing example in the essay, the "museum of me" featured in the title. How does the "museum of me" serve as an extended metaphor for virtual life? What is lost in experiencing culture on the Web? What is gained? What conclusion does Ullman draw about the possible effects of the Web on our society?

2. Ullman sees parallels between suburban living and the Internet and characterizes both as rooted in a desire to escape. Do you agree that people use the Internet to withdraw from "real life"? Why or why not?

3. Compare Ullman's more recent report on the effects of the Internet to William Gibson's 1996 essay "The Net Is a Waste of Time" (page 696). In what ways does the Internet that Gibson describes sound like what Ullman has experienced? How has the Internet today evolved from what Gibson describes? Do you think that Ullman would agree with Gibson's depiction of the Internet's meaning?

Marie Winn

TV Addiction

Born in 1936 in Prague, Czechoslovakia, Marie Winn came to the United States with her family in 1939. After receiving her education at Radcliffe College and Columbia University, Winn became a freelance writer specializing in children's literature. In addition to having written more than a dozen books for children or for parents and teachers of children, she has contributed to the New York Times, *the* New York Times Book Review, *and the* Wall Street Journal. *Her publications include* Children without Childhood *(1983),* Unplugging the Plug-In Drug *(1987), and* Redtails in Love: A Wildlife Drama in Central Park *(1998). "TV Addiction" is from* The Plug-In Drug: Television, Children and the Family *(originally published in 1977). The twenty-fifth anniversary edition,* The Plug-In Drug: Television, Computers and Family Life *(2002), adds the latest technological "addictions": video games, toys, and baby-accessible television.*

The word "addiction" is often used loosely and wryly in conversation. People will refer to themselves as "mystery-book addicts" or "cookie addicts." E. B. White wrote of his annual surge of interest in gardening: "We are hooked and are making an attempt to kick the habit." Yet nobody really believes that reading mysteries or ordering seeds by catalogue is serious enough to be compared with addictions to heroin or alcohol. In these cases the word "addiction" is used jokingly to denote a tendency to overindulge in some pleasurable activity.

People often refer to being "hooked on TV." Does this, too, fall into the lighthearted category of cookie eating and other pleasures that people pursue with unusual intensity? Or is there a kind of television viewing that falls into the more serious category of destructive addiction?

Not unlike drugs or alcohol, the television experience allows the participant to blot out the real world and enter into a pleasurable and passive mental state. To be sure, other experiences, notably reading, also provide a temporary respite from reality. But it's much easier to stop reading and return to reality than to stop watching television. The entry into another world offered by reading includes an easily accessible return ticket. The entry via television does not. In this way television viewing, for those vulnerable to addiction, is more like drinking or taking drugs—once you start it's hard to stop.

Just as alcoholics are only vaguely aware of their addiction, feeling that they control their drinking more than they really do ("I can cut it out any time I want—I just like to have three or four drinks before dinner"), many people overestimate their control over television watching. Even as they put off other activities to spend hour after hour watching television, they feel they could easily resume living in a different, less passive style. But somehow or other while the television set is present in their homes, it just stays on. With television's easy gratifications available, those other activities seem to take too much effort.

A heavy viewer (a college English instructor) observes: 5

> I find television almost irresistible. When the set is on, I cannot ignore it. I can't turn it off. I feel sapped, will-less, enervated. As I reach out to turn off the set, the strength goes out of my arms. So I sit there for hours and hours.

Self-confessed television addicts often feel they "ought" to do other things—but the fact that they don't read and don't plant their garden or sew or crochet or play games or have conversations means that those activities are no longer as desirable as television viewing. In a way, the lives of heavy viewers are as unbalanced by their television "habit" as drug addicts' or alcoholics' lives. They are living in a holding pattern, as it were, passing up the activities that lead to growth or development or a sense of accomplishment. This is one reason people talk about their television viewing so ruefully, so apologetically. They are aware that it is an unproductive experience, that by any human measure almost any other endeavor is more worthwhile.

It is the adverse effect of television viewing on the lives of so many people that makes it feel like a serious addiction. The television habit distorts the sense of time. It renders other experiences vague and curiously unreal while taking on a greater reality for itself. It weakens relationships by reducing and sometimes eliminating normal opportunities for talking, for communicating.

And yet television does not satisfy, else why would the viewer continue to watch hour after hour, day after day? "The measure of health," wrote the psychiatrist Lawrence Kubie, "is flexibility . . . and especially the freedom to cease when sated." But heavy television viewers can never be sated with their television experiences. These do not provide the true nourishment that satiation requires, and thus they find that they cannot stop watching.

The Reader's Presence

1. How does Winn characterize addiction? How does she apply that characterization to television watching? Do you think watching television is a genuine addiction, similar to addiction to drugs, alcohol, or tobacco? Why or why not?

2. Does Winn rely more heavily on evidence or opinion for her argument? Is her methodology convincing? What evidence do you find most persuasive?

3. Winn describes the feeling of powerlessness over television that some viewers experience. Compare Winn's description of television's effects to Sherry Turkle's assertion in "How Computers Change the Way We Think" (page 595) that "our tools carry the message that they are beyond our understanding" and that this "opacity can lead to passivity" (paragraph 25). What does Turkle say computer users take at face value? Is this effect significantly different from the powerlessness Winn describes, or are the effects of computers and television similar, in your view? Is either effect dangerous? Why or why not?

Tom Wolfe

Hooking Up

Tom Wolfe (b. 1931) grew up in Richmond, Virginia, and graduated from Washington and Lee University. He received his doctorate in American studies from Yale University and began a career as a reporter, eventually writing for such papers as the New York Herald Tribune and the Washington Post. His writing has also appeared in New York magazine, Harper's, and Esquire, where he has been a contributing editor since 1977. Writer, journalist, and social and cultural critic, Wolfe continues to be an arbiter (and satirist) of American cultural trends. His books The Kandy-Kolored Tangerine-Flake Streamline Baby (1965), The Electric Kool-aid Acid Test (1968), The Pump House Gang (1969), and Radical Chic and Mau Mauing the Flak Catchers (1970) were models of a flamboyant style known as "New Journalism." Wolfe's best-selling work of "extended" journalism, The Right Stuff (1979), won the American Book Award and National Book Critics Circle Award. His three novels, The Bonfire of the Vanities (1982), A Man in Full (1998), and I Am Charlotte Simmons (2004), contain the same blend of well-researched documentary journalism, entertainment, and realistic detail as his nonfiction work. Wolfe received the 2003 Chicago Tribune *Literary Prize for lifetime achievement.*

Wolfe has argued, "A novel of psychological depth without social depth isn't worth an awful lot because we are all individuals caught in an enormous web that consists of other people. It is in the social setting that the psychological battles take place." "Hooking Up: What Life Was Like at the Turn of the Second Millennium: An American's World" is from Wolfe's 2000 book of the same name, a combination of fiction, memoir, and cultural and social observation.

By the year 2000, the term "working class" had fallen into disuse in the United States, and "proletariat" was so obsolete it was known only to a few bitter old Marxist academics with wire hair sprouting out of their ears. The average electrician, air-conditioning mechanic, or burglar-alarm repairman lived a life that would have made the Sun King[1] blink. He spent his vacations in Puerto Vallarta, Barbados, or St. Kitts. Before dinner he would be out on the terrace of some resort hotel with his third wife, wearing his Ricky Martin cane-cutter shirt open down to the sternum, the better to allow his gold chains to twinkle in his chest hairs. The two of them would have just ordered a round of Quibel sparkling water, from the state of West Virginia, because by 2000 the once-favored European sparkling waters Perrier and San Pellegrino seemed so tacky.

European labels no longer held even the slightest snob appeal except among people known as "intellectuals," whom we will visit in a moment. Our typical mechanic or tradesman took it for granted that things European were second-rate. Aside from three German luxury automobiles — the Mercedes-Benz, the BMW, and the Audi — he regarded European-manufactured goods as mediocre to shoddy. On his trips abroad, our electrician, like any American businessman, would go to superhuman lengths to avoid being treated in European hospitals, which struck him as little better than those in the Third World. He considered European hygiene so primitive that to receive an injection in a European clinic voluntarily was sheer madness.

Indirectly, subconsciously, his views perhaps had to do with the fact that his own country, the United States, was now the mightiest power on earth, as omnipotent as Macedon under Alexander the Great, Rome under Julius Caesar, Mongolia under Genghis Khan, Turkey under Mohammed II, or Britain under Queen Victoria. His country was so powerful, it had begun to invade or rain missiles upon small nations in Europe, Africa, Asia, and the Caribbean for no other reason than that their leaders were lording it over their subjects at home.

Our air-conditioning mechanic had probably never heard of Saint-Simon,[2] but he was fulfilling Saint-Simon's and the other nineteenth-century

---

[1]*the Sun King:* Louis XIV, king of France (1638–1715), known for his absolutism and ostentation. — EDS.

[2]*Saint-Simon:* A French aristocrat, Henri de Saint-Simon (1760–1825) founded one of the most influential socialist programs of the nineteenth century. — EDS.

utopian socialists' dreams of a day when the ordinary workingman would have the political and personal freedom, the free time and the wherewithal to express himself in any way he saw fit and to unleash his full potential. Not only that, any ethnic or racial group—*any*, even recent refugees from a Latin country—could take over the government of any American city, if they had the votes and a modicum of organization. Americans could boast of a freedom as well as a power unparalleled in the history of the world.

Our typical burglar-alarm repairman didn't display one erg of chau-   5
vinistic swagger, however. He had been numbed by the aforementioned "intellectuals," who had spent the preceding eighty years being indignant over what a "puritanical," "repressive," "bigoted," "capitalistic," and "fascist" nation America was beneath its democratic façade. It made his head hurt. Besides, he was too busy coping with what was known as the "sexual revolution." If anything, "sexual revolution" was rather a prim term for the lurid carnival actually taking place in the mightiest country on earth in the year 2000. Every magazine stand was a riot of bare flesh, rouged areolae, moistened crevices, and stiffened giblets: boys with girls, girls with girls, boys with boys, bare-breasted female bodybuilders, so-called boys with breasts, riding backseat behind steroid-gorged bodybuilding bikers, naked except for *cache-sexes* and Panzer helmets, on huge chromed Honda or Harley-Davidson motorcycles.

But the magazines were nothing compared with what was offered on an invention of the 1990s, the Internet. By 2000, an estimated 50 percent of all hits, or "log-ons," were at Web sites purveying what was known as "adult material." The word "pornography" had disappeared down the memory hole along with "proletariat." Instances of marriages breaking up because of Web-sex addiction were rising in number. The husband, some fifty-two-year-old MRI technician or systems analyst, would sit in front of the computer for twenty-four or more hours at a stretch. Nothing that the wife could offer him in the way of sexual delights or food could compare with the one-handing he was doing day and night as he sat before the PC and logged on to such images as a girl with bare breasts and a black leather corset standing with one foot on the small of a naked boy's back, brandishing a whip.

In 1999, the year before, this particular sexual kink—sadomasochism—had achieved not merely respectability but high chic, and the word "perversion" had become as obsolete as "pornography" and "proletariat." Fashion pages presented the black leather and rubber paraphernalia as style's cutting edge. An actress named Rene Russo blithely recounted in the Living section of one of America's biggest newspapers how she had consulted a former dominatrix named Eva Norvind, who maintained a dungeon replete with whips and chains and assorted baffling leather masks, chokers, and cuffs, in order to prepare for a part as an aggressive, self-obsessed agent provocateur in *The Thomas Crown Affair*, Miss Russo's latest movie.

"Sexy" was beginning to replace "chic" as the adjective indicating what was smart and up-to-the-minute. In the year 2000, it was standard practice for the successful chief executive officer of a corporation to shuck his wife of two to three decades' standing for the simple reason that her subcutaneous packing was deteriorating, her shoulders and upper back were thickening like a shot-putter's — in short, she was no longer sexy. Once he set up the old wife in a needlepoint shop where she could sell yarn to her friends, he was free to take on a new wife, a "trophy wife," preferably a woman in her twenties, and preferably blond, as in an expression from that time, a "lemon tart." What was the downside? Was the new couple considered radioactive socially? Did people talk *sotto voce*, behind the hand, when the tainted pair came by? Not for a moment. All that happened was that everybody got on the cell phone or the Internet and rang up or E-mailed one another to find out the spelling of the new wife's first name, because it was always some name like Serena and nobody was sure how to spell it. Once that was written down in the little red Scully & Scully address book that was so popular among people of means, the lemon tart and her big CEO catch were invited to all the parties, as though nothing had happened.

Meanwhile, sexual stimuli bombarded the young so incessantly and intensely they were inflamed with a randy itch long before reaching puberty. At puberty the dams, if any were left, burst. In the nineteenth century, entire shelves used to be filled with novels whose stories turned on the need for women, such as Anna Karenina or Madame Bovary, to remain chaste or to maintain a façade of chastity. In the year 2000, a Tolstoy or a Flaubert[3] wouldn't have stood a chance in the United States. From age thirteen, American girls were under pressure to maintain a façade of sexual experience and sophistication. Among girls, "virgin" was a term of contempt. The old term "dating" — referring to a practice in which a boy asked a girl out for the evening and took her to the movies or dinner — was now deader than "proletariat" or "pornography" or "perversion." In junior high school, high school, and college, girls headed out in packs in the evening, and boys headed out in packs, hoping to meet each other fortuitously. If they met and some girl liked the looks of some boy, she would give him the nod, or he would give her the nod, and the two of them would retire to a halfway-private room and "hook up."

"Hooking up" was a term known in the year 2000 to almost every 10 American child over the age of nine, but to only a relatively small percentage of their parents, who, even if they heard it, thought it was being used in the old sense of "meeting" someone. Among the children, hooking up was always a sexual experience, but the nature and extent of what they did could vary widely. Back in the twentieth century, American girls had used

---

[3] *a Tolstoy or a Flaubert:* The Russian novelist Leo Tolstoy published *Anna Karenina* between 1874 and 1876; the French novelist Gustave Flaubert published *Madame Bovary* in 1865.—EDS.

baseball terminology. "First base" referred to embracing and kissing; "second base" referred to groping and fondling and deep, or "French," kissing, commonly known as "heavy petting"; "third base" referred to fellatio, usually known in polite conversation by the ambiguous term "oral sex"; and "home plate" meant conception-mode intercourse, known familiarly as "going all the way." In the year 2000, in the era of hooking up, "first base" meant deep kissing ("tonsil hockey"), groping, and fondling; "second base" meant oral sex; "third base" meant going all the way; and "home plate" meant learning each other's names.

Getting to home plate was relatively rare, however. The typical Filofax entry in the year 2000 by a girl who had hooked up the night before would be: "Boy with black Wu-Tang T-shirt and cargo pants: O, A, 6." Or "Stupid cock diesel" — slang for a boy who was muscular from lifting weights — "who kept saying, 'This is a cool deal': TTC, 3." The letters referred to the sexual acts performed (e.g., TTC for "that thing with the cup"), and the Arabic number indicated the degree of satisfaction on a scale of 1 to 10.

In the year 2000, girls used "score" as an active verb indicating sexual conquest, as in: "The whole thing was like very sketchy, but I scored that diesel who said he was gonna go home and caff up [drink coffee in order to stay awake and study] for the psych test." In the twentieth century, only boys had used "score" in that fashion, as in: "I finally scored with Susan last night." That girls were using such a locution points up one of the ironies of the relations between the sexes in the year 2000.

The continuing vogue of feminism had made sexual life easier, even insouciant, for men. Women had been persuaded that they should be just as active as men when it came to sexual advances. Men were only too happy to accede to the new order, since it absolved them of all sense of responsibility, let alone chivalry. Men began to adopt formerly feminine attitudes when the subject of marriage came up, pleading weakness and indecisiveness, as in: "I don't know; I'm just not ready yet" or "Of course I love you, but like, you know, I start weirding out when I try to focus on it."

With the onset of puberty, males were able to get sexual enjoyment so easily, so casually, that junior high schools as far apart geographically and socially as the slums of the South Bronx and Washington's posh suburbs of Arlington and Talbot County, Virginia, began reporting a new discipline problem. Thirteen- and fourteen-year-old girls were getting down on their knees and fellating boys in corridors and stairwells during the two-minute break between classes. One thirteen-year-old in New York, asked by a teacher how she could do such a thing, replied: "It's nasty, but I need to satisfy my man." Nasty was an aesthetic rather than a moral or hygienic judgment. In the year 2000, boys and girls did not consider fellatio to be a truely sexual act, any more than tonsil hockey. It was just "fooling around." The President of the United States at the time used to have a twenty-two-year-old girl, an unpaid volunteer in the presidential palace, the White House, come around to his office for fellatio. He later testified under oath that he had never "had sex" with her. Older Americans tended to be shocked, but junior-high-school, high-school, and college students understood completely what he was saying and wondered what on earth all the fuss was about. The two of them had merely been on second base, hooking up.

Teenage girls spoke about their sex lives to total strangers without the least embarrassment or guile. One New York City newspaper sent out a man-on-the-street interviewer with the question: "How did you lose your virginity?" Girls as well as boys responded without hesitation, posed for photographs, and divulged their name, age, and the neighborhood where they lived.

Stains and stigmas of every kind were disappearing where sex was concerned. Early in the twentieth century the term "cohabitation" had referred to the forbidden practice of a man and woman living together before marriage. In the year 2000, nobody under forty had ever heard of the word, since cohabitation was now the standard form of American courtship. For parents over forty, one of the thornier matters of etiquette concerned domestic bed assignments. When your son or daughter came home for the weekend with the live-in consort, did you put the two of them in the same bedroom, which would indicate implicit approval of the discomforting fait accompli? Or did you put them in different bedrooms and lie awake, rigid with insomnia, fearful of hearing muffled footfalls in the hallway in the middle of the night?

Putting them in different rooms was a decidedly old-fashioned thing to do; and in the year 2000, thanks to the feverish emphasis on sex and sexiness, nobody wanted to appear old, let alone old-fashioned. From the city of Baltimore came reports of grandmothers having their eyebrows, tongues, and lips pierced with gold rings in order to appear younger, since body-piercing was a popular fashion among boys and girls in their teens and early twenties. Expectant mothers were having their belly buttons pierced with gold rings so that the shapelessness of pregnancy would not make them feel old. An old man who had been a prominent United States senator and a presidential candidate, emerged from what he confessed to have been a state of incapacity to go on television to urge other old men to take a drug called Viagra to free them from what he said was one of the scourges of modern times, the disease that dared not speak its name: impotence. He dared not speak it, either. He called it "E.D.," for erectile dysfunction. Insurance companies were under pressure to classify impotence in old men as a disease and to pay for treatment.

In the late nineteenth and early twentieth centuries, old people in America had prayed, "Please, God, don't let me look poor." In the year 2000, they prayed, "Please, God, don't let me look old." Sexiness was equated with youth, and youth ruled. The most widespread age-related disease was not senility but juvenility. The social ideal was to look twenty-three and dress thirteen. All over the country, old men and women were dressing casually at every opportunity, wearing jeans, luridly striped sneakers, shorts, T-shirts, polo shirts, jackets, and sweaters, heedless of how such clothes revealed every sad twist, bow, hump, and webbed-up vein clump of their superannuated bodies. For that matter, in the year 2000, people throughout American society were inverting norms of dress that had persisted for centuries, if not millennia. Was the majesty of America's global omnipotence reflected in the raiments of the rich and prominent? Quite the opposite. In the year 2000, most American billionaires—and the press no longer took notice of men worth a mere $500 million or $750 million—lived in San Jose and Santa Clara Counties, California, an area known nationally, with mythic awe, as the Silicon Valley, the red-hot center of the computer and Internet industries. In 1999, the Internet industry alone had produced fourteen new billionaires. The Valley's mythology was full of the sagas of young men who had gone into business for themselves, created their own companies straight out of college, or, better still, had dropped out of college to launch their "start-ups," as these new digital-age enterprises were known. Such were the new "Masters of the Universe," a term coined in the eighties to describe the (mere) megamillionaires spawned by Wall Street during a boom in the bond business. By comparison with the Valley's boy billionaires, the Wall Streeters, even though they were enjoying a boom in the stock market in the year 2000, seemed slow and dreary. Typically, they graduated from college, worked for three years as number-crunching donkeys in some large investment-banking firm, went off to business school for two years to be certified as Masters of Business Administration, then returned to some investment-banking firm and hoped to start making some real money by the age of thirty. The stodginess of such a career was symbolized by the stodginess of their dress. Even the youngest of them dressed like old men: the dark blah suit, the light blah shirt, the hopelessly "interesting" Hermès tie . . . Many of them even wore silk braces.

The new Masters of the Universe turned all that upside down. At Il Fornaio restaurant in Palo Alto, California, where they gathered to tell war stories and hand out business cards at breakfast, the billionaire founders of the new wonder corporations walked in the door looking like well-pressed, well-barbered beachcombers, but beachcombers all the same. They wore khakis, boating moccasins (without socks), and ordinary cotton shirts with the cuffs rolled up and the front unbuttoned to the navel, and that was it. You could tell at a glance that a Silicon Valley billionaire carried no cell phone, Palm Pilot, HP-19B calculator, or RIM pager—he had people who did that for him. Having breakfast with him at Il Fornaio would be a vice president whose net worth was $100 or $200 million. He would be dressed just like the founder, except that he would also be wearing a sport jacket. Why? So that he could carry . . . the cell phone, the Palm Pilot, the HP-19B calculator, and the RIM pager, which received E-mail and felt big as a brick. But why not an attaché case? Because that was what old-fashioned businessmen Back East carried. Nobody would be caught dead at Il Fornaio carrying an attaché

case. The Back East attaché case was known scornfully as "the leather
lunch pail."

When somebody walked into Il Fornaio wearing a suit and tie, he   20
was likely to be mistaken for a maître d'. In the year 2000, as in prior
ages, service personnel, such as doormen, chauffeurs, waiters, and maître
d's, were expected to wear the anachronistic finery of bygone eras. In Silicon Valley, wearing a tie was a mark of shame that indicated you were
everything a Master of the Universe was not. Gradually, it would dawn
on you. The poor devil in the suit and tie held one of those lowly but necessary executive positions, in public or investor relations, in which one
couldn't avoid dealing with Pliocene old parties from . . . Back East.

Meanwhile, back East, the sons of the old rich were deeply involved
in inverted fashions themselves. One of the more remarkable sights in
New York City in the year 2000 was that of some teenage scion of an
investment-banking family emerging from one of the forty-two Good
Buildings, as they were known. These forty-two buildings on Manhattan's East Side contained the biggest, grandest, stateliest apartments ever
constructed in the United States, most of them on Park and Fifth Avenues. A doorman dressed like an Austrian Army colonel from the year
1870 holds open the door, and out comes a wan white boy wearing a
baseball cap sideways; an outsized T-shirt, whose short sleeves fall below
his elbows and whose tail hangs down over his hips; baggy cargo pants
with flapped pockets running down the legs and a crotch hanging below
his knees, and yards of material pooling about his ankles, all but obscur-
ing the Lugz sneakers. This fashion was deliberately copied from the
"homeys" — black youths on the streets of six New York slums, Harlem,
the South Bronx, Bedford-Stuyvesant, Fort Greene, South Ozone Park,
and East New York. After passing the doorman, who tipped his visored
officer's hat and said "Good day," the boy walked twenty feet to a waiting sedan, where a driver with a visored officer's hat held open a rear
door.

What was one to conclude from such a scene? The costumes said it
all. In the year 2000, the sons of the rich, the very ones in line to inherit
the bounties of the all-powerful United States, were consumed by a fear
of being envied. A German sociologist of the period, Helmut Schoeck,
said that "fear of being envied" was the definition of guilt. But if so, guilt
about what? So many riches, so much power, such a dazzling array of advantages? American superiority in all matters of science, economics, industry, politics, business, medicine, engineering, social life, social justice,
and, of course, the military was total and indisputable. Even Europeans
suffering the pangs of wounded chauvinism looked on with awe at the
brilliant example the United States had set for the world as the third millennium began. And yet there was a cloud on the millennial horizon.

America had shown the world the way in every area save one. In matters intellectual and artistic, she remained an obedient colony of Europe.
American architecture had never recovered from the deadening influence of

the German Bauhaus[4] movement of the twenties. American painting and sculpture had never recovered from the deadening influence of various theory-driven French movements, beginning with Cubism early in the twentieth century. In music, the early-twentieth-century innovations of George Gershwin, Aaron Copland, Duke Ellington, and Ferde Grofé had been swept away by the abstract, mathematical formulas of the Austrian composer Arnold Schoenberg. Schoenberg's influence had faded in the 1990s, but the damage had been done. The American theater had never recovered from the Absurdism of Samuel Beckett, Bertolt Brecht, and Luigi Pirandello.

But, above all, there was the curious case of American philosophy — which no longer existed. It was as if Emerson, Charles Peirce, William James, and John Dewey had never lived. The reigning doctrine was deconstruction, whose hierophants were two Frenchmen, Michel Foucault and Jacques Derrida. They began with a hyperdilation of a pronouncement of Nietzsche's to the effect that there can be no absolute truth, merely many "truths," which are the tools of various groups, classes, or forces. From this, the deconstructionists proceeded to the doctrine that language is the most insidious tool of all. The philosopher's duty was to deconstruct the language, expose its hidden agendas, and help save the victims of the American "Establishment": women, the poor, nonwhites, homosexuals, and hardwood trees.

Oddly, when deconstructionists required appendectomies or bypass   25
surgery or even a root-canal job, they never deconstructed medical or dental "truth," but went along with whatever their board-certified, profit-oriented surgeons proclaimed was the last word.

Confused and bored, our electrician, our air-conditioning mechanic, and our burglar-alarm repairman sat down in the evening and watched his favorite TV show (*The Simpsons*), played his favorite computer game (*Tony Hawk's Pro Skater*) with the children, logged on to the Internet, stayed up until 2 A.M. planning a trip to this fabulous-sounding resort just outside Bangkok, then "crashed" (went to bed exhausted), and fell asleep faster than it takes to tell it, secure in the knowledge that the sun would once more shine blessedly upon him in the morning. It was the year 2000.

The Reader's Presence

1. Wolfe makes frequent reference to how language has changed, pointing out defunct terms or newly coined phrases. What words does Wolfe say have been redefined or replaced? What are the connotations of the defunct term, and what is lost or gained with a new word?

---

[4]***Bauhaus:*** A school of industrial design and architecture that developed in Germany during the early twentieth century. — Eds.

2. Examine Wolfe's tone throughout the essay. How does he approach his subject? Where does he uses humor, and for what purpose? Where does he use hyperbole (overstatement) and why?

3. Wolfe presents his cultural observations from a distance and without explicit commentary. Compare Wolfe's approach to H. L. Mencken's in "The Hills of Zion" (page 504). What similarities and differences do you see in terms of tone, diction, perspective, and purpose?

Virginia Woolf
The Death of the Moth

One of the most important writers of the twentieth century, Virginia Woolf (1882–1941) explored innovations in indirect narration and the impressionistic use of language that are now considered hallmarks of the modern novel and continue to influence novelists on both sides of the Atlantic. Together with her husband, Leonard Woolf, she founded the Hogarth Press, which published many experimental works that have now become classics, including her own. A central figure in the Bloomsbury group of writers, Woolf established her reputation with the novels Mrs. Dalloway *(1925),* To the Lighthouse *(1927), and* The Waves *(1931). The feminist movement has helped to focus attention on her work, and Woolf's nonfiction has provided the basis for several important lines of argument in contemporary feminist theory.* A Room of One's Own *(1929),* Three Guineas *(1938), and* The Common Reader *(1938) are the major works of nonfiction published in Woolf's lifetime; posthumously, her essays have been gathered together in* The Death of the Moth *(1942) (where the essay reprinted here appears) and in the four-volume* Collected Essays *(1967).*

Reflecting on her own writing life, Woolf wrote, "The novelist — it is his distinction and his danger — is terribly exposed to life. . . . He can no more cease to receive impressions than a fish in mid-ocean can cease to let the water rush through his gills." To turn those impressions into writing, Woolf maintained, requires solitude and the time for thoughtful selection. Given tranquility, a writer can, with effort, discover art in experience. "There emerges from the mist something stark, formidable and enduring, the bone and substance upon which our rush of indiscriminating emotion was founded."

For more on Virginia Woolf, see page 66.

Moths that fly by day are not properly to be called moths; they do not excite that pleasant sense of dark autumn nights and ivy-blossom which the commonest yellow-underwing asleep in the shadow of the curtain never fails to rouse in us. They are hybrid creatures, neither gay like butterflies nor somber like their own species. Nevertheless the present specimen, with his narrow hay-colored wings, fringed with a tassel of the same color, seemed to be content with life. It was a pleasant morning, mid-September, mild, benignant, yet with a keener breath than that of the summer months. The plough was already scoring the field opposite the window, and where the share had been, the earth was pressed flat and gleamed with moisture. Such vigor came rolling in from the fields and the down beyond that it was difficult to keep the eyes strictly turned upon the book. The rooks too were keeping one of their annual festivities; soaring round the tree tops until it looked as if a vast net with thousands of black knots in it had been cast up into the air; which, after a few moments sank slowly down upon the trees until every twig seemed to have a knot at the end of it. Then, suddenly, the net would be thrown into the air again in a wider circle this time, with the utmost clamor and vociferation, as though to be thrown into the air and settle slowly down upon the tree tops were a tremendously exciting experience.

The same energy which inspired the rooks, the ploughmen, the horses, and even, it seemed, the lean bare-backed downs, sent the moth fluttering from side to side of his square of the windowpane. One could not help watching him. One, was, indeed, conscious of a queer feeling of pity for him. The possibilities of pleasure seemed that morning so enormous and so various that to have only a moth's part in life, and a day moth's at that, appeared a hard fate, and his zest in enjoying his meager opportunities to the full, pathetic. He flew vigorously to one corner of his compartment, and after waiting there a second, flew across to the other. What remained for him but to fly to a third corner and then to a fourth? That was all he could do, in spite of the size of the downs, the width of the sky, the far-off smoke of houses, and the romantic voice, now and then, of a steamer out at sea. What he could do he did. Watching him, it seemed as if a fiber, very thin but pure, of the enormous energy of the world had been thrust into his frail and diminutive body. As often as he crossed the pane, I could fancy that a thread of vital light became visible. He was little or nothing but life.

Yet, because he was so small, and so simple a form of the energy that was rolling in at the open window and driving its way through so many narrow and intricate corridors in my own brain and in those of other human beings, there was something marvelous as well as pathetic about him. It was as if someone had taken a tiny bead of pure life and decking it as lightly as possible with down and feathers, had set it dancing and zigzagging to show us the true nature of life. Thus displayed one could not get over the strangeness of it. One is apt to forget all about life, seeing it humped and bossed and garnished and cumbered so that it has to move with the greatest circumspection and dignity. Again, the thought of all that life might have been had he been born in any other shape caused one to view his simple activities with a kind of pity.

After a time, tired by his dancing apparently, he settled on the window ledge in the sun, and, the queer spectacle being at an end, I forgot about him. Then, looking up, my eye was caught by him. He was trying to resume his dancing, but seemed either so stiff or so awkward that he could only flutter to the bottom of the windowpane; and when he tried to fly across it he failed. Being intent on other matters I watched these futile attempts for a time without thinking, unconsciously waiting for him to resume his flight, as one waits for a machine, that has stopped momentarily, to start again without considering the reason of its failure. After perhaps a seventh attempt he slipped from the wooden ledge and fell, fluttering his wings, on to his back on the windowsill. The helplessness of his attitude roused me. It flashed upon me that he was in difficulties; he could no longer raise himself; his legs struggled vainly. But, as I stretched out a pencil, meaning to help him to right himself, it came over me that the failure and awkwardness were the approach of death. I laid the pencil down again.

The legs agitated themselves once more. I looked as if for the enemy   5
against which he struggled. I looked out of doors. What had happened there? Presumably it was midday, and work in the fields had stopped. Stillness and quiet had replaced the previous animation. The birds had taken themselves off to feed in the brooks. The horses stood still. Yet the power was there all the same, massed outside, indifferent, impersonal, not attending to anything in particular. Somehow it was opposed to the little hay-colored moth. It was useless to try to do anything. One could only watch the extraordinary efforts made by those tiny legs against an oncoming doom which could, had it chosen, have submerged an entire city, not merely a city, but masses of human beings; nothing, I knew had any chance against death. Nevertheless after a pause of exhaustion the legs fluttered again. It was superb this last protest, and so frantic that he succeeded at last in righting himself. One's sympathies, of course, were all on the side of life. Also, when there was nobody to care or to know, this gigantic effort on the part of an insignificant little moth, against a power of such magnitude, to retain what no one else valued or desired to keep, moved one strangely. Again, somehow, one saw life, a pure bead. I lifted the pencil again, useless though I knew it to be. But even as I did so, the unmistakable tokens of death showed themselves. The body relaxed, and instantly grew stiff. The struggle was over. The insignificant little creature now knew death. As I looked at the dead moth, this minute wayside triumph of so great a force over so mean an antagonist filled me with wonder. Just as life had been strange a few minutes before, so death was now as strange. The moth having righted himself now lay most decently and uncomplainingly composed. O yes, he seemed to say, death is stronger than I am.

The Reader's Presence

1. Woolf calls her essay "The Death of *the* Moth" rather than "The Death of *a* Moth." Describe what difference this makes. What quality does the definite article add to the essay?

2. Reread the essay, paying special attention not to the moth but to the writer. What presence does Woolf establish for herself in the essay? How does the act of writing itself get introduced? Of what significance is the pencil? Can you discover any connection between the essay's subject and its composition? Can you find any connection between this essay and the author's ideas about the writing process in *A Writer's Diary* (page 66)?

3. Reread Woolf's concluding paragraph and paragraph 11 of George Orwell's "Shooting an Elephant" (page 221). How do the passages compare on the level of physical detail? How vivid is the death of each creature? Reread the paragraphs again, paying special attention to point of view. How do the writers implicate themselves in the deaths they witness? How do they appeal to the reader? Is the reader made into an "innocent bystander" or is he or she more intimately involved? If so, how does this intimacy come about?

Part IV

Argumentative Writing: Contending with Issues

James Agee

America, Look at Your Shame!

James Agee (1909–1955) was a poet, journalist, novelist, and film critic during his relatively short career. However, recognition of his wide-ranging literary accomplishments came mostly after his death; at that time, many of his published works were out of print. His autobiographical novel, Death in the Family, *published posthumously, won the Pulitzer Prize in 1957, and within a few years nearly everything Agee had ever written was again available. Among his works are a collection of poems,* Permit Me Voyage *(1934); a novel,* The Morning Watch *(1951); the screenplay for John Huston's* The African Queen *(1951); film criticism, collected most recently in* Agee on Film *(2000); and what many critics believe to be his most lasting contribution,* Let Us Now Praise Famous Men *(1941), a groundbreaking collaboration with photographer Walker Evans documenting rural America during the Great Depression of the 1930s.*

A photograph from a front-page story about a brutal race riot in Detroit during World War II stirred Agee to write "America, Look at Your Shame!" in 1943. The manuscript has only recently been discovered and reprinted in Oxford American. *In it, Agee excoriates Americans for their actions at home while simultaneously confronting his own complicity in the country's racism.*

I keep remembering those photographs of the Detroit race riots[1] which appeared in *PM*.[2] Pages of them, and that typically *PM* headline, all over their front page.

AMERICA,

LOOK AT

YOUR

SHAME!

[1]**Detroit race riots:** The race riots that began in Detroit on June 20, 1943, resulted from rising tensions between the city's black population, crowded into a segregated ghetto, and whites, many of whom had migrated from the South to work in area defense plants. —EDS.

[2]**PM:** A liberal daily newspaper in New York City. —EDS.

That disgusted me, as their headlines so often do, but as I looked at the photographs I got a good deal of respect for the paper in spite of everything. Then I realized that with a few exceptions *PM* had cornered the photographs. They were unavailable to any other paper. That was as perfect and typical a low as I had ever seen them touch. I wanted to write them. Or to do them as much damage as I possibly could. The liberals and the left. They had never shown themselves up better.

Look at your shame, indeed.

There was one in particular, that I couldn't get out of my head; one of the less violent of them. It was the one which particularly showed that there were white people who were not only horrified by the riots but

June 20, 1943. PM documents the violence that afternoon in Detriot.

brave enough to do all they could for the Negroes. It showed two young men. They were holding up a terribly bleeding Negro man between them, and they looked at the camera as if they were at bay before a crowd of rioters, as perhaps they were not. The mixture of emotions on their faces was almost unbearable to keep looking at: almost a nausea of sympathy for the hurt man and for the whole situation; a kind of terror which all naturally unviolent people must feel in the middle of violence; absolute self-forgetfulness; a terrific, accidental look of bearing testimony — a sort of gruesome, over-realistic caricature; which was rather, really, the source of those attendant saints or angels who communicate with the world outside the picture in great paintings of crucifixions and exalted agonies.

The thing that made it so particularly powerful to me was that both these young men, one of them especially, so far as you could judge by study, were of a sort which is often somewhat sneered at, by most bad people and by many pretty good ones: rather humbly "artistic," foureffish people, of whom you might think that any emotion they felt would be tainted, at least, with fancy sentimentality.

It made me ashamed of every such reflex of easy classification and dismissal as I have ever felt — the more ashamed, because I had to wonder whether, in such a situation, I would have been capable of that self-forgetfulness and courage. It made me half-ashamed to keep looking at them, for that matter, as I had been doing again on that afternoon I am especially thinking of now. I care a great deal for such photographs; they do more, in certain ways, than any other art can. But there is also, in proportion to its best use, something criminal and indecent about the camera; and there is a great load of guilt on the eye that eats what it has predigested.

On this particular afternoon, which was the Sunday after the riots, I was up on East 92nd Street seeing a friend of mine, a photographer, and we spent quite a bit of the afternoon looking through things he had clipped and a few I had brought along. I had not seen my friend at leisure for a long time and we had a particularly good afternoon of it, in which the photograph I am speaking of turned up powerfully but casually, and moved off to become a sort of tinge in the back of the mind. By the end of the afternoon I had the unusual, gay sort of good opinion of myself, my friend, photography and what my senses could enjoy, which you are liable to get out of whiskey and easy pleasure if work causes the latter to turn up seldom enough. By the time I left to go downtown for supper, I was at the high point just short of where intoxication begins to droop into clumsiness or melancholy; and the minute I was outdoors the streets, in the very beautiful late of afternoon weather, improved, that if it can be improved, with the feeling of being alone for a little while, and with the sharp, tender enjoyment of a city I am ordinarily tired in.

At 91st Street, on York Avenue, I got on an 86th Street crosstown bus and sat far forward on the right. It started nearly empty, and filled up

"Brave lads, these Detroiters—when it's 10 or more to one," read the PM
caption printed with this photograph on June 23, 1943.

rather quickly; I did not much notice when, or with whom, because I was
looking out a great deal through the front and side windows, especially as
soon as the bus swung west onto 86th Street and the street and the bus
were filled with the low, bright sunlight. It was a light so gay, generous and
beautiful, it was almost as if it tasted of champagne and smelled of strawberries, hay and fresh butter. What it smelled of more, of course, was carbon monoxide, which can also be a festal sort of smell, when everything is
right, and was now; and the edges of the hundreds of doors and windows,
along the street, were cut in a blue-gold, clean compound of sunlight,
monoxide and stone. I watched all the people, puddling and straggling
along the walks, and as usual, wondered which were the Hitchcock[3] agents
and which were the harmless, and what might be going on in each mind as
they thought, if they did, of what was happening to Hitler and his idea and
his people, over where it was dark now, and they were counting their losses
in the East, and giving out modified reports in the middle, and staggering
under the bombers from the west. In an easy insensitive way, I began to be
very sorry for all those people caught in the hopeless middle; even for
Hitler and his damned idea, so monstrous except that they already
seemed so hopeless.

---

[3]*Hitchcock:* Sir Alfred Hitchcock (1899–1980), British film director of well-known es-
pionage movies. Agee was a noted film reviewer. — EDS.

Around me, I realized the bus was thicker and thicker with people, some standing, some packed on the seats, all swaying, pleasant and patient-seeming in the green and gold light which filled the bus. Across the aisle were some sailors, sitting, their faces very young and very red, in their very white uniforms. Halfway back in the bus were some young soldiers; the same quality of variegated physical perfection and of almost indecent cleanness, which so few civilians ever seem to have — like so many priests, or Sunday babies, or little girls in bride-of-heaven regalia, but even more likable; dumb, very likely, cruel, very possibly, developed and perfected for something I feel no trust in; yet about the best thing that ever turns up in human life. I liked them a great deal, and all my doubts of it cleared; I might not be perfectly sure what I wanted, but I was no longer personally sorry that within a week I was coming up for induction; I was almost glad; and if I were taken, many things could be worse. One of them, very possibly, would be to come out the other end of the war, still a virginal civilian.

I liked them still better as I watched them and began to hear them. I   10
specially noticed one quite strong young sailor, just across from me; a big boy, bigger than I am, a little; and because his eyes and his face had a good deal in them which as a child I used to fear, and have always been shy of, I now liked him particularly well. It was the sort of face which only turns up, so far as I know, in the South — heavy jaw, a slightly thin yet ornate mouth, powerful nose, blue-white, reckless, brutal eyes. I knew the voice just as well, and the special, rather crazy kind of bravery; they made me feel at once as isolated and as matchlessly at home as if I were back in the South again. Nearly all these boys, it turned out, were Southerners, the soldiers as well as the sailors, and the loud large sailor and the loudest and littlest of the soldiers were just finding this out about each other. One was from Atlanta; the other knew Atlanta very well. They began testing each other out on street names and bars, then on people, which did not go quite so well, and now and then the others chimed in with a wisecrack or an exclamation more simpleminded. They were happy as hell to run into each other like this — not even Viennese refugees can lay it on so thick, and enjoy it so much, as Southerners when they meet by surprise in an alien atmosphere. They were drunk, about as drunk as I was, and that helped; but they would have leaned on their dialects like trimming ship in a yacht-race, even if they were sober. It is a very special speech, as unattractive to most Northerners as it is dear to natives, and I will not try to reproduce it here, beyond suggesting that its special broadenings, lifts, twangs and elisions, even if you didn't know the idiom by heart, which I do, were as charming and miraculous as if, in the same New York bus, a couple of Parsees had saluted each other according to their own language and ritual.

A part of it, of course, was that they were basically insecure; it was insecurity and the Southerner's incomparable, almost pathic pride, as well as love of country and loneliness, and the aching contempt for the North, which made them so spectacular, made so many Northerners on the bus look warm, cold or uneasy accordingly, and made the young sailors and soldiers begin to vocalize about the niggers on the bus and the God damned niggers in this f—ing town and the f—ing niggers all over the whole God damned f—in' Nawth. The word cut across my solar plexus like a cold knife, and the whole bus, except for those two voices and the comments of their friends, was suddenly almost exploded by an immensely thick quietness. I glanced very quickly back; one of the soldiers met my eyes with eyes like hot iron, and two seats behind him sat a Negro (it is a word I dislike, but most of the others are still worse); sat a colored man of perhaps fifty, in nickel-rimmed glasses, a carefully starched white shirt, and a serge suit, managing so to use his eyes that you could see only the nickel rims and the lenses.

The flailing voices went on and on, more and more fanciful, naked and cruel, and though I was listening with great care for every word, and heard every word, I was also so occupied that I heard very little, and remember almost nothing, now. It was all the old, ugly routines; what we wouldn't do to Boy son of a bitchin nigguh that tuck a seat by a white woman if we was in Atlanta; dey would; get a Nawthun nigguh down deah, you'd see what dey'd do; yaanh, reckin *dey'd* see thang a tyew. Three any ovem tried it, black rapin bastuhds; but there was very little of this I heard, because I was too sick to hear much, and too busy. I was trying to think what to do and what to say. I had, repeatedly, a very clear image of the moment I would get up, draw a standee aside, and hit the big young sailor who was, after all, very little bigger than me, as hard as I could on his bright, shaven jaw. I also had, repeatedly, the exact image of what would happen then. Singlehanded, that boy could tear me to pieces; what the crowd of them could do was a little beyond my imagination. I had the image of looking him in the eye; various ways, in fact, of looking him in the eye. One was the cold, controlled rage which is occasionally used to pick a fight and which my kind more occasionally uses to bring a sexual quarrel or an intellectual argument as near to nature as we are likely to go. One was the more-in-sorrow-than-in-anger look which is liable to compound some genuineness of feeling with plagiarisms from photographs of Lincoln and paintings of Veronica's veil;[4] it is occasionally used, and effective, when somebody else's neurosis goes wild, but unless you are too good a human being to know you are using it, there is no uglier or more abject device of blackmail. One, worst of them all, was the blank eye which commits itself to nothing. But none of these, it was easy to see, were of any use unless I was ready to back them up physically, and I could hear, just as clearly as I could visualize, the phonograph-records of talk they would bring on; nigger-lover is the favorite word. I was also trying to think what to say; for I know from the past—and might have known by some of the Detroit photographs if I had thought of them just then—that their kind of talk and even action is sometimes completely

---

[4]*Veronica's veil:* In Catholic tradition, a veil used by a Jerusalem woman named Veronica to wipe sweat from Jesus's face on his walk to crucifixion.—EDS.

quieted by the right kind of talking, and better quieted then into sullenness; quieted into deep abashment. I have a friend, a small and elderly man, who would have brought that effect almost instantly. But his size and his age would have been a part of it; still more, his perfect self-forgetfulness, his unquestioning intrepidity. I was neither small nor elderly, nor self-forgetful, nor intrepid, nor singlehearted in any one of my perceptions or emotions; I was simply fumbling at words and knowledges: Look here. What are you fighting this war about. I know how you feel, I know you're from the South, I'm from the South myself, I know (I may be, but the way I say it makes it a lie). Things are different there, and all this you see here goes against every way you believe is right. But you've got to get used to it. You've got to know it. This is one of the main things this war is about (is it? is it?). If it isn't about this we might as well not be fighting it at all (we might as well not, indeed). You'll ask me where I've got any right to tell you what you're fighting for. I'm not even in uniform. I'm not I know but I'll be in one soon — next week (will I? do I want to be?). But that's not the point anyhow (this is falling apart). Anyone on this bus has got a right to know the point and to tell it to you, white or black (I sound like a Tennessee senator; race, creed and *co*luh), we've got to make this a free country where every human being can be well with every other human being, regardless of race, creed or color, we've got to make it a world like that. I don't believe you mean the harm you say, honestly, but you've got to realize it, you might as well be fighting for Hitler as to fight for this country feeling the way you do.

It was all so much cotton-batting on my tongue. I couldn't gather a phrase of it together and make it mean anything, even to myself. Talking to them, talking for the corroboration of most of the bus, unable to talk in my own language because my own language would mean nothing even if I could use it with enough belief to make it mean something to me. All the hopeless, bland, advertising-copy claims of the Four Freedoms was running in my head; all the undersupplying of the Chinese; all the talk of the "magnificent courage" of the Red Army, and all the Rice Krispies which took the place of a second front; all the Bryn Mawr girls, planning to police postwar Europe; all the *PM* articles and the Wallace[5] speeches and the slogans; I cannot know to this day with how much justice they undermined me, and with how much cowardice. I only know I could not believe a word I said; and had images of saying it and having the hell beaten out of me, and other images of saying it with effect; and other images of a fight which could be stopped by cops who are as much a phobia to me as rats; and others of modest and of carefully worded and of modestly rhetorical statements by myself, repeated in the press; a small yet not wholly undistinguished instant in the history of the world's long Fight for Freedom; that hit me with self-disgust like a blow in the belly; and I noticed that the big sailor was now standing, and an elderly Negro woman had his seat.

[5]*Wallace:* Henry Wallace (1888–1965), Progressive party leader and vice president under President Franklin Delano Roosevelt from 1941 to 1945. —Eds.

Whether he had stood rather than sit beside her, or out of an instant genuine courtesy, quickly repented, or out of mock courtesy, I could not tell from anything he was saying; and this still further perplexed me. If his motives were the first or the third, then it was more than even I could bear, not to fight him; if he had felt one moment of reflex courtesy, I felt friendliness towards him in spite of all he was now saying. I listened hard, to learn, and could not make out. One reason I could not make out was that I was also listening to the woman. She was talking very little, and crying a little, and telling him, and the whole bus, that he ought to be ashamed, talking that way. People never done him no harm. Ain't your skin that make the difference, it's how you feel inside. Ought to be ashamed. Just might bout's well be Hitluh, as a white man from the South. Wearing a sailor's uniform. Fighting for your country. Ought to be ashamed.

There was an immense relaxation in the quiet through the whole bus;   15
but not in me. I caught the eye, at that moment, of a man about my age, in one of the longways seats across the aisle. He was dressed in a brown, Sunday-looking suit. He may have been a Jew, and more certainly would have described himself, without self-consciousness or satire, as "an intellectual." We looked at each other and a queer, sick smile took one corner of his face, and I felt in my own cheeks that tickling, uncontrollable, nauseating smile which is so liable to seize my face when I tell one close friend disastrous news of another.

I remembered the photograph in *PM*, and looked sternly at the floor, with my cheek twitching.

That evening I told of the whole thing, as honestly as I could, to several people who were down for drinks. They were quite shocked by it, and seemed also rather favorably stirred by my honesty. That embarrassed me a good deal, but not as painfully as I wish it might have, and I found their agreement that they would have done the same almost as revolting as my own performance in the doing of it, and in the telling.

So now I am telling it to you.

The Reader's Presence

1. Agee expresses many contradictory feelings throughout the essay as he reflects on the incident on the bus. What are the internal conflicts he presents? What is the external conflict? To what extent are the conflicts resolved by the end of the essay? Why do you think Agee makes a distinction in the last lines between telling his friends and telling the audience about the incident?

2. What does Agee's inaction on the bus suggest about what it took for the men in the *PM* photographs to help strangers in the Detroit riots? After he left the bus, do you think Agee would have thought differently about those men? Why or why not?

3. Although Agee's tone is confessional and regretful, to what extent does he prescribe a model for appropriate action for the situation? Compare Agee's act of "witnessing" to Toi Derricotte's in "From *The Black Notebooks*" (page 17). In what sense are these essays a critique of the writer's own behavior? To what extent are the writers criticizing a racist system?

Dorothy Allison

This Is Our World

Dorothy Allison (b. 1949) was born in Greenville, South Carolina, and received an M.A. in anthropology from the New School for Social Research in New York City. A versatile writer, Allison has published poems, short stories, essays, and novels. Her first collection of short stories, Trash *(1988), won the Lambda Book Award for the best work of lesbian fiction. She gained mainstream attention with her first novel,* Bastard out of Carolina *(1992), which was a finalist for the National Book Award. Her most recent novel,* Cavedweller *(1998), is an epic tale about the lives of four women in a small town in Georgia. "Good storytellers learn which parts to throw out and which parts to sharpen, to drop all the subsets and get to the point," Allison says. She contributes to many periodicals, including* Harper's, *the* New York Times, Village Voice, *and* Southern Exposure. *"This Is Our World" first appeared in the summer 1998 issue of* DoubleTake, *a magazine featuring creative writing and photography.*

The first painting I ever saw up close was at a Baptist church when I was seven years old. It was a few weeks before my mama was to be baptized. From it, I took the notion that art should surprise and astonish, and hopefully make you think something you had not thought until you saw it. The painting was a mural of Jesus at the Jordan River done on the wall behind the baptismal font. The font itself was a remarkable creation—a swimming pool with one glass side set into the wall above and behind the pulpit so that ordinarily you could not tell the font was there, seeing only the painting of Jesus. When the tank was flooded with water, little lights along the bottom came on, and anyone who stepped down the steps seemed to be walking past Jesus himself and descending into the Jordan River. Watching baptisms in that tank was like watching movies at the drive-in, my cousins had told me. From the moment the deacon walked us around the church, I knew what my cousin had meant. I could not take my eyes off the painting or the glass-fronted tank. It looked every moment as if Jesus were about to come alive, as if he were about to step out onto the water of the river. I think the way I stared at the painting made the deacon nervous.

The deacon boasted to my mama that there was nothing like that baptismal font in the whole state of South Carolina. It had been designed, he told her, by a nephew of the minister—a boy who had gone on to build a shopping center out in New Mexico. My mama was not sure that someone who built shopping centers was the kind of person who should have been designing baptismal fonts, and she was even more uncertain about the steep steps by Jesus' left hip. She asked the man to let her practice going up and down, but he warned her it would be different once the water poured in.

"It's quite safe though," he told her. "The water will hold you up. You won't fall."

I kept my attention on the painting of Jesus. He was much larger than I was, a little bit more than life-size, but the thick layer of shellac applied to protect the image acted like a magnifying glass, making him seem larger still. It was Jesus himself that fascinated me, though. He was all rouged and pale and pouty as Elvis Presley. This was not my idea of the son of God, but I liked it. I liked it a lot.

"Jesus looks like a girl," I told my mama.   5

She looked up at the painted face. A little blush appeared on her cheekbones, and she looked as if she would have smiled if the deacon were not frowning so determinedly. "It's just the eyelashes," she said. The deacon nodded. They climbed back up the stairs. I stepped over close to Jesus and put my hand on the painted robe. The painting was sweaty and cool, slightly oily under my fingers.

"I liked that Jesus," I told my mama as we walked out of the church. "I wish we had something like that." To her credit, Mama did not laugh.

"If you want a picture of Jesus," she said, "we'll get you one. They have them in nice frames at Sears." I sighed. That was not what I had in mind. What I wanted was a life-size, sweaty painting, one in which Jesus looked as hopeful as a young girl—something other-worldly and peculiar, but kind of wonderful at the same time. After that, every time we went to church I asked to go up to see the painting, but the baptismal font was locked tight when not in use.

The Sunday Mama was to be baptized, I watched the minister step down into that pool past the Son of God. The preacher's gown was tailored with little weights carefully sewn into the hem to keep it from rising up in the water. The water pushed up at the fabric while the weights tugged it down. Once the minister was all the way down into the tank, the robe floated up a bit so that it seemed to have a shirred ruffle all along the bottom. That was almost enough to pull my eyes away from the face of Jesus, but not quite. With the lights on in the bottom of the tank, the eyes of the painting seemed to move and shine. I tried to point it out to my sisters, but they were uninterested. All they wanted to see was Mama.

Mama was to be baptized last, after three little boys, and their gowns   10
had not had any weights attached. The white robes floated up around
their necks so that their skinny boy bodies and white cotton underwear
were perfectly visible to the congregation. The water that came up above
the hips of the minister lapped their shoulders, and the shortest of the
boys seemed panicky at the prospect of gulping water, no matter how
holy. He paddled furiously to keep above the water's surface. The water
started to rock violently at his struggles, sweeping the other boys off their
feet. All of them pumped their knees to stay upright and the minister, realizing how the scene must appear to the congregation below, speeded up
the baptismal process, praying over and dunking the boys at high speed.

Around me the congregation shifted in their seats. My little sister slid
forward off the pew, and I quickly grabbed her around the waist and
barely stopped myself from laughing out loud. A titter from the back of
the church indicated that other people were having the same difficulty
keeping from laughing. Other people shifted irritably and glared at the
noisemakers. It was clear that no matter the provocation, we were to pretend nothing funny was happening. The minister frowned more fiercely
and prayed louder. My mama's friend Louise, sitting at our left, whispered a soft "Look at that" and we all looked up in awe. One of the
hastily blessed boys had dog-paddled over to the glass and was staring
out at us, eyes wide and his hands pressed flat to the glass. He looked as
if he hoped someone would rescue him. It was too much for me. I began
to giggle helplessly, and not a few of the people around me joined in. Impatiently the minister hooked the boy's robe, pulled him back, and
pushed him toward the stairs.

My mama, just visible on the staircase, hesitated briefly as the sodden
boy climbed up past her. Then she set her lips tightly together, and reached
down and pressed her robe to her thighs. She came down the steps slowly,
holding down the skirt as she did so, giving one stern glance to the two
boys climbing past her up the steps, and then turning her face deliberately
up to the painting of Jesus. Every move she made communicated resolution and faith, and the congregation stilled in respect. She was baptized
looking up stubbornly, both hands holding down that cotton robe while
below, I fought so hard not to giggle, tears spilled down my face.

Over the pool, the face of Jesus watched solemnly with his pink,
painted cheeks and thick, dark lashes. For all the absurdity of the event,
his face seemed to me startlingly compassionate and wise. That face understood fidgety boys and stubborn women. It made me want the painting even more, and to this day I remember it with longing. It had the
weight of art, that face. It had what I am sure art is supposed to have—
the power to provoke, the authority of a heartfelt vision.

I imagine the artist who painted the baptismal font in that Baptist
church so long ago was a man who did not think himself much of an
artist. I have seen paintings like his many times since, so perhaps he

worked from a model. Maybe he traced that face off another he had seen in some other church. For a while, I tried to imagine him a character out of a Flannery O'Connor[1] short story, a man who traveled around the South in the fifties painting Jesus wherever he was needed, giving the Son of God the long lashes and pink cheeks of a young girl. He would be the kind of man who would see nothing blasphemous in painting eyes that followed the congregation as they moved up to the pulpit to receive a blessing and back to the pews to sit chastened and still for the benediction. Perhaps he had no sense of humor, or perhaps he had one too refined for intimidation. In my version of the story, he would have a case of whiskey in his van, right behind the gallon containers of shellac and buried notebooks of his own sketches. Sometimes, he would read thick journals of art criticism while sitting up late in cheap hotel rooms and then get roaring drunk and curse his fate.

"What I do is wallpaper," he would complain. "Just wallpaper." But   15
the work he so despised would grow more and more famous as time passed. After his death, one of those journals would publish a careful consideration of his murals, calling him a gifted primitive. Dealers would offer little churches large sums to take down his walls and sell them as installations to collectors. Maybe some of the churches would refuse to sell, but grow uncomfortable with the secular popularity of the paintings. Still, somewhere there would be a little girl like the girl I had been, a girl who would dream of putting her hand on the cool, sweaty painting while the Son of God blinked down at her in genuine sympathy. Is it a sin, she would wonder, to put together the sacred and the absurd? I would not answer her question, of course. I would leave it, like the art, to make everyone a little nervous and unsure.

I love black-and-white photographs, and I always have. I have cut photographs out of magazines to paste in books of my own, bought albums at yard sales, and kept collections that had one or two images I wanted near me always. Those pictures tell me stories — my own and others, scary stories sometimes, but more often simply everyday stories, what happened in that place at that time to those people. The pictures I collect leave me to puzzle out what I think about it later. Sometimes, I imagine my own life as a series of snapshots taken by some omniscient artist who is just keeping track — not interfering or saying anything, just capturing the moment for me to look back at it again later. The eye of God, as expressed in a Dorothea Lange or Wright Morris.[2] This is the way it is, the photograph says, and I nod my head in appreciation. The power of art is in that nod of appreciation, though sometimes I puzzle nothing out, and

---

[1]*Flannery O'Connor:* For an example of her fiction, see page 942. — Eds.
[2]*Dorothea Lange or Wright Morris:* Lange (1895–1965) was an American photographer known for her depictions of rural poverty. Morris (1910–1998) was a prominent midwestern novelist also known for his photography; he often published books that combined text and photographs. — Eds.

the nod is more a shrug. No, I do not understand this one, but I see it. I take it in. I will think about it. If I sit with this image long enough, this story, I have the hope of understanding something I did not understand before. And that, too, is art, the best art.

My friend Jackie used to call my photographs sentimental. I had pinned them up all over the walls of my apartment, and Jackie liked a few of them but thought on the whole they were better suited to being tucked away in a book. On her walls, she had half a dozen bright prints in bottle-cap metal frames, most of them bought from Puerto Rican artists at street sales when she was working as a taxi driver and always had cash in her pockets. I thought her prints garish and told her so when she made fun of my photographs.

"They remind me of my mama," she told me. I had only seen one photograph of Jackie's mother, a wide-faced Italian matron from Queens with thick, black eyebrows and a perpetual squint.

"She liked bright colors?" I asked.

Jackie nodded. "And stuff you could buy on the street. She was always buying stuff off tables on the street, saying that was the best stuff. Best prices. Cheap skirts that lost their dye after a couple of washes, shoes with cardboard insoles, those funky little icons, weeping saints and long-faced Madonnas. She liked stuff to be really colorful. She painted all the ceilings in our apartment red and white. Red-red and white-white. Like blood on bone."

I looked up at my ceiling. The high tin ceiling was uniformly bloody when I moved in, with paint put on so thick, I could chip it off in lumps. I had climbed on stacks of boxes to paint it all cream white and pale blue.

"The Virgin's colors," Jackie told me. "You should put gold roses on the door posts."

"I'm no artist," I told her.

"I am," Jackie laughed. She took out a pencil and sketched a leafy vine above two of my framed photographs. She was good. It looked as if the frames were pinned to the vine. "I'll do it all," she said, looking at me to see if I was upset.

"Do it," I told her. 25

Jackie drew lilies and potato vines up the hall while I made tea and admired the details. Around the front door she put the Virgin's roses and curious little circles with crosses entwined in the middle. "It's beautiful," I told her.

"A blessing," she told me. "Like a bit of magic. My mama magic." Her face was so serious, I brought back a dish of salt and water, and we blessed the entrance. "Now the devil will pass you by," she promised me.

I laughed, but almost believed.

For a few months last spring I kept seeing an ad in all the magazines that showed a small child high in the air dropping toward the upraised arms of a waiting figure below. The image was grainy and distant. I could not tell if the child was laughing or crying. The copy at the bottom of the page read: "Your father always caught you."

"Look at this," I insisted the first time I saw the ad. "Will you look at   30
this?"

A friend of mine took the magazine, looked at the ad, and then up into my shocked and horrified face.

"They don't mean it that way," she said.

I looked at the ad again. They didn't mean it that way? They meant it innocently? I shuddered. It was supposed to make you feel safe, maybe make you buy insurance or something. It did not make me feel safe. I dreamed about the picture, and it was not a good dream.

I wonder how many other people see that ad the way I do. I wonder how many other people look at the constant images of happy families and make wry faces at most of them. It's as if all the illustrators have television sitcom imaginations. I do not believe in those families. I believe in the exhausted mothers, frightened children, numb and stubborn men. I believe in hard-pressed families, the child huddled in fear with his face hidden, the father and mother confronting each other with their emotions hidden, dispassionate passionate faces, and the unsettling sense of risk in the baby held close to that man's chest. These images make sense to me. They are about the world I know, the stories I tell. When they are accompanied by wry titles or copy that is slightly absurd or unexpected, I grin and know that I will puzzle it out later, sometimes a lot later.

I think that using art to provoke uncertainty is what great writing   35
and inspired images do most brilliantly. Art should provoke more questions than answers and, most of all, should make us think about what we rarely want to think about at all. Sitting down to write a novel, I refuse to consider if my work is seen as difficult or inappropriate or provocative. I choose my subjects to force the congregation to look at what they try so stubbornly to pretend is not happening at all, deliberately combining the horribly serious with the absurd or funny, because I know that if I am to reach my audience I must first seduce their attention and draw them into the world of my imagination. I know that I have to lay out my stories, my difficult people, each story layering on top of the one before it with care and craft, until my audience sees something they had not expected. Frailty—stubborn, human frailty—that is what I work to showcase. The wonder and astonishment of the despised and ignored, that is what I hope to find in art and in the books I write—my secret self, my vulnerable and embattled heart, the child I was and the woman I have become, not Jesus at the Jordan but a woman with only her stubborn memories and passionate convictions to redeem her.

"You write such mean stories," a friend once told me. "Raped girls, brutal fathers, faithless mothers, and untrustworthy lovers—meaner than the world really is, don't you think?"

I just looked at her. Meaner than the world really is? No. I thought about showing her the box under my desk where I keep my clippings. Newspaper stories and black-and-white images—the woman who drowned her children, the man who shot first the babies in her arms and then his wife, the teenage boys who led the three-year-old away along the train track, the homeless family recovering from frostbite with their eyes glazed and indifferent while the doctor scowled over their shoulders. The world is meaner than we admit, larger and more astonishing. Strength appears in the most desperate figures, tragedy when we have no reason to expect it. Yes, some of my stories are fearful, but not as cruel as what I see in the world. I believe in redemption, just as I believe in the nobility of the despised, the dignity of the outcast, the intrinsic honor among misfits, pariahs, and queers. Artists—those of us who stand outside the city gates and look back at a society that tries to ignore us—we have an angle of vision denied to whole sectors of the sheltered and indifferent population within. It is our curse and our prize, and for everyone who will tell us our work is mean or fearful or unreal, there is another who will embrace us and say with tears in their eyes how wonderful it is to finally feel as if someone else has seen their truth and shown it in some part as it should be known.

"My story," they say. "You told my story. That is me, mine, us." And it is.

We are not the same. We are a nation of nations. Regions, social classes, economic circumstances, ethical systems, and political convictions—all separate us even as we pretend they do not. Art makes that plain. Those of us who have read the same books, eaten the same kinds of food as children, watched the same television shows, and listened to the same music, we believe ourselves part of the same nation—and we are continually startled to discover that our versions of reality do not match. If we were more the same, would we not see the same thing when we look at a painting? But what is it we see when we look at a work of art? What is it we fear will be revealed? The artist waits for us to say. It does not matter that each of us sees something slightly different. Most of us, confronted with the artist's creation, hesitate, stammer, or politely deflect the question of what it means to us. Even those of us from the same background, same region, same general economic and social class, come to "art" uncertain, suspicious, not wanting to embarrass ourselves by revealing what the work provokes in us. In fact, sometimes we are not sure. If we were to reveal what we see in each painting, sculpture, installation, or little book, we would run the risk of exposing our secret selves, what we know and what we fear we do not know, and of course incidentally what it is we truly fear. Art is the Rorschach test for all of us, the projective hologram of our secret lives. Our emotional and intellectual lives are laid bare. Do you like hologram roses? Big, bold, brightly painted canvases? Representational art? Little boxes with tiny figures posed precisely? Do you dare say what it is you like?

For those of us born into poor and working-class families, these are   40
not simple questions. For those of us who grew up hiding what our home
life was like, the fear is omnipresent—particularly when that home life
was scarred by physical and emotional violence. We know if we say anything about what we see in a work of art we will reveal more about ourselves than the artist. What do you see in this painting, in that one? I see a
little girl, terrified, holding together the torn remnants of her clothing. I
see a child, looking back at the mother for help and finding none. I see a
mother, bruised and exhausted, unable to look up for help, unable to believe anyone in the world will help her. I see a man with his fists raised,
hating himself but making those fists tighter all the time. I see a little girl,
uncertain and angry, looking down at her own body with hatred and contempt. I see that all the time, even when no one else sees what I see. I
know I am not supposed to mention what it is I see. Perhaps no one else
is seeing what I see. If they are, I am pretty sure there is some cryptic
covenant that requires that we will not say what we see. Even when looking at an image of a terrified child, we know that to mention why that
child might be so frightened would be a breach of social etiquette. The
world requires that such children not be mentioned, even when so many
of us are looking directly at her.

There seems to be a tacit agreement about what it is not polite to
mention, what it is not appropriate to portray. For some of us, that polite
behavior is set so deeply we truly do not see what seems outside that tacit
agreement. We have lost the imagination for what our real lives have
been or continue to be, what happens when we go home and close the
door on the outside world. Since so many would like us to never mention
anything unsettling anyway, the impulse to be quiet, the impulse to deny
and pretend, becomes very strong. But the artist knows all about that impulse. The artist knows that it must be resisted. Art is not meant to be polite, secret, coded, or timid. Art is the sphere in which that impulse to hide
and lie is the most dangerous. In art, transgression is holy, revelation a
sacrament, and pursuing one's personal truth the only sure validation.

Does it matter if our art is canonized, if we become rich and successful, lauded and admired? Does it make any difference if our pictures become popular, our books made into movies, our creations win awards?
What if we are the ones who wind up going from town to town with our
notebooks, our dusty boxes of prints or Xeroxed sheets of music, never
acknowledged, never paid for our work? As artists, we know how easily
we could become a Flannery O'Connor character, reading those journals
of criticism and burying our faces in our hands, staggering under the
weight of what we see that the world does not. As artists, we also know
that neither worldly praise not critical disdain will ultimately prove the
worth of our work.

Some nights I think of that sweating, girlish Jesus above my mother's
determined features, those hands outspread to cast benediction on those
giggling uncertain boys, me in the congregation struck full of wonder and

love and helpless laughter. If no one else ever wept at that image, I did. I wished the artist who painted that image knew how powerfully it touched me, that after all these years his art still lives inside me. If I can wish for anything for my art, that is what I want—to live in some child forever—and if I can demand anything of other artists, it is that they attempt as much.

The Reader's Presence

1. You may have heard the old advice to writers—"say what you're going to say, say it, and then say what you've said." How does the structure of Allison's argument diverge from this rule? How does the essay begin? Where is her argument first explicitly stated? How is it developed?

2. What is the relation between the painting of Jesus and Allison's argument? Does the scene of her mother's baptism serve merely as an interesting anecdote, or can it be tied in some way to the questions she raises regarding the function and value of art? To what extent do Allison's personal stories contribute to or detract from her central argument? In what ways?

3. Pay close attention to Allison's ideas about the role of the artist (see especially paragraphs 35, 37, and 41). In paragraph 37 she says, "Artists—those of us who stand outside the city gates and look back at a society that tries to ignore us—we have an angle of vision denied to whole sectors of the sheltered and indifferent population within." Does Allison see the artist's position in society as privileged? Why or why not? Compare her sense of artistic mission ("trangression," "revelation," "personal truth," paragraph 41) to that of Gloria Anzaldúa in "How to Tame a Wild Tongue" (page 324). What is the place of beauty in each writer's understanding of art?

Edwidge Danticat

We Are Ugly, but We Are Here

Edwidge Danticat was born in Port-au-Prince, Haiti, in 1969 and was raised to the age of twelve by her aunt, finally joining her family in Brooklyn, New York, in 1981. She earned a B.A. from Barnard College and an M.F.A. from Brown University in 1993, and one year later published her reworked M.F.A. thesis, the critically acclaimed Breath, Eyes, Memory *(1994). She followed this novel with a collection of short stories about the Haitian experience,* Krik? Krak! *(1995) and another novel,* The Farming of Bones *(1998), which is set on the Caribbean island of Hispaniola in 1937, when hostilities between Haiti and the Dominican Republic exploded into a bloody massacre. Her latest novel,* The Dew Breaker *(2004), explores the terrible history of a Haitian torturer—a "dew breaker"—and the lives of his victims.*

Danticat, who is regarded as one of the best young authors in the United States, has won a Pushcart Short Story Prize and, in 1995, was a finalist for the National Book Award. She confesses to drawing her subject material from her native country's "rich landscape of memory." Her writing is often praised for its lushness and its appeal to the senses, but it also deals honestly with poverty, violence, and the political history of Haiti. Recently, Danticat edited two anthologies, Beacon Best of 2000 *and* The Butterfly's Way: Voices from the Haitian Diaspora *(2001). She has also written* After the Dance: A Walk through Carnival in Jacmel *(2002), her account of the people and the lush color of Haiti's Carnival; and two works for young people,* Behind the Mountains *(2002) and* Anacaona, Golden Flower: Haiti, 1490 *(2005). "We Are Ugly, but We Are Here" was originally published in the* Caribbean Writer *in 1996.*

One of the first people murdered on our land was a queen. Her name was Anacaona and she was an Arawak Indian. She was a poet, dancer, and even a painter. She ruled over the western part of an island so lush and green that the Arawaks called it Ayiti—land on high. When the Spaniards came from across the seas to look for gold, Anacaona was one of their first victims. She was raped and killed and her village pillaged. Anacaona's land is now the poorest country in the Western hemisphere, a place of continuous political unrest. Thus, for some, it is easy to forget that this land was the first Black Republic, home to the first people of African descent to uproot slavery and create an independent nation in 1804.

I was born under Haiti's dictatorial Duvalier regime. When I was four, my parents left Haiti to seek a better life in the United States. I must admit that their motives were more economic than political. But as anyone who knows Haiti will tell you, economics and politics are very intrinsically related in Haiti. Who is in power determines to a great extent whether or not people will eat.

I am twenty-six years old now and have spent more than half of my life in the United States. My most vivid memories of Haiti involve incidents that once represented the general situation there. In Haiti, there are a lot of "blackouts," sudden power failures. At those times, you can't read or study or watch TV, so you sit around a candle and listen to stories from the elders in the house. My grandmother was an old country woman who always felt displaced in the city of Port-au-Prince—where we lived—and had nothing but her patched-up quilts and her stories to console her. She was the one who told me about Anacaona. I used to share a room with her. I was in the room when she died. She was over a hundred years old. She died with her eyes wide open and I was the one who closed her eyes. I still miss the countless mystical stories that she told us. However, I accepted her death very easily because during my childhood death was always around us.

As a little girl, I attended more than my share of funerals. My uncle and legal guardian was a Baptist minister and his family was expected to attend every funeral he presided over. I went to all the funerals he presided over. I went to all the funerals in the same white lace dress. Perhaps it was because I attended so many funerals that I have such a strong feeling that death is not the end, that the people we bury are going off to live somewhere else. But at the same time, they will always be hovering around to watch over us and guide us through our journeys.

When I was eight, my uncle's brother-in-law went on a long journey to cut cane in the Dominican Republic. He came back, deathly ill. I remember his wife twirling feathers inside his nostrils and rubbing black pepper on his upper lip to make him sneeze. She strongly believed that if he sneezed, he would live. At night, it was my job to watch the sky above the house for signs of falling stars. In Haitian folklore, when a star falls out of the sky, it means someone will die. A star did fall out of the sky and he did die.

I have memories of Jean Claude "Baby Doc" Duvalier[1] and his wife, racing by in their Mercedes Benz and throwing money out of the window to the very poor children in our neighborhood. The children nearly killed each other trying to catch a coin or a glimpse of Baby Doc. One Christmas, they announced on the radio that the first lady, Baby Doc's wife, was giving away free toys at the palace. My cousins and I went and were nearly killed in the mob of children who flooded the palace lawns.

All of this now brings many questions buzzing to my head. Where was really my place in all of this? What was my grandmother's place? What is the legacy of the daughters of Anacaona? What do we all have left to remember, the daughters of Haiti?

Watching the news reports, it is often hard to tell whether there are real living and breathing women in conflict-stricken places like Haiti. The

5

---

[1]***Duvalier:*** Born in 1951, Jean-Claude "Baby Doc" Duvalier assumed the presidency of Haiti upon the death of his father, François "Papa Doc" Duvalier, in 1971 and ruled until he was forced into exile in 1986.—Eds.

evening news broadcasts only allow us a brief glimpse of presidential coups, rejected boat people, and sabotaged elections. The women's stories never manage to make the front page. However they do exist.

Today, I know women who, when the soldiers came to their homes in Haiti, would tell their daughters to lie still and play dead. I once met a woman whose sister was shot in her pregnant stomach because she was wearing a t-shirt with an "anti-military image." I know a mother who was arrested and beaten for working with a pro-democracy group. Her body remains laced with scars where the soldiers put out their cigarettes on her flesh. At night, this woman still smells the ashes of the cigarette butts that were stuffed lit inside her nostrils. In the same jail cell, she watched as paramilitary "attachés" raped her fourteen-year-old daughter at gun point. When mother and daughter took a tiny boat to the United States, the mother had no idea that her daughter was pregnant. Nor did she know that the child had gotten the HIV virus from one of the paramilitary men who had raped her. The grandchild—the offspring of the rape—was named Anacaona, after the queen, because that family of women is from the same region where Anacaona was murdered. The infant Anacaona has a face which no longer shows any trace of indigenous blood; however, her story echoes back to the first flow of blood on a land that has seen much more than its share.

There is a Haitian saying which might upset the aesthetic images of   10
most women. *Nou led, Nou la*, it says. We are ugly, but we are here. This saying makes a deeper claim for poor Haitian women than maintaining beauty, be it skin deep or otherwise. For most of us, what is worth celebrating is the fact that we are here, that we—against all the odds—exist. To the women who might greet each other with this saying when they meet along the countryside, the very essence of life lies in survival. It is always worth reminding our sisters that we have lived yet another day to answer the roll call of an often painful and very difficult life. It is in this spirit that to this day a woman remembers to name her child Anacaona, a name which resonates both the splendor and agony of a past that haunts so many women.

When they were enslaved, our foremothers believed that when they died their spirits would return to Africa, most specifically to a peaceful land we call *Guinen*, where gods and goddesses live. The women who came before me were women who spoke half of one language and half another. They spoke the French and Spanish of their captors mixed in with their own African language. These women seemed to be speaking in tongues when they prayed to their old gods, the ancient African spirits. Even though they were afraid that their old deities would no longer understand them, they invented a new language—our Kreyòl— with which to describe their new surroundings, a language from which colorful phrases blossomed to fit the desperate circumstances. When these women greeted each other, they found themselves speaking in codes.

—How are we today, Sister?

—I am ugly, but I am here.

These days, many of my sisters are greeting each other away from the homelands where they first learned to speak in tongues. Many have made it to other shores, after traveling endless miles on the high seas, on rickety boats that almost took their lives. Two years ago, a mother jumped into the sea when she discovered that her baby daughter had died in her arms on a journey which they had hoped would take them to a brighter future. Mother and child, they sank to the bottom of an ocean which already holds millions of souls from the middle passage—the holocaust of the slave trade—that is our legacy. That woman's sacrifice moved then-deposed Haitian President Jean Bertrand Aristide to the brink of tears. However, like the rest of us, he took comfort in the past sacrifices that were made for all of us, so that we could be here.

The past is full of examples when our foremothers and forefathers   15 showed such deep trust in the sea that they would jump off slave ships and let the waves embrace them. They too believed that the sea was the beginning and the end of all things, the road to freedom and their entrance to *Guinen*. These women have been part of the very construction of my being ever since I was a little girl. Women like my grandmother who had taught me the story of Anacaona, the queen.

My grandmother believed that if a life is lost, then another one springs up replanted somewhere else, the next life even stronger than the last. She believed that no one really dies as long as someone remembers, someone who will acknowledge that this person had—in spite of everything—been here. We are part of an endless circle, the daughters of Anacaona. We have stumbled, but have not fallen. We are ill-favored, but we still endure. Every once in a while, we must scream this as far as the wind can carry our voices: We are ugly, but we are here! And here to stay.

The Reader's Presence

1. Danticat begins the essay with the story of Anacaona. How is Anacaona characterized? Where does this legend reappear in the essay? What relation does it bear to the essay's message of hope and strength? What sort of hope and strength does the figure of Anacaona represent?

2. Danticat describes daily existence in Haiti: funerals, folk medicine, money thrown from a car. What tones does the writer use in evoking these scenes of her homeland? What moods do those tones convey? How might the essay's title tie into these everyday scenarios?

3. The saying that Danticat puts at the center of her essay epitomizes for her a profound truth about Haitian women. What is the truth? How are words themselves linked for Danticat to survival, "the

very essence of life" (paragraph 10)? How is storytelling linked to
endurance? Whose endurance? Read "The Socks" by Marjane
Satrapi (page 259). What does Satrapi's illustrated description of
events in Iran indicate about her views of the connection between
art and survival under a harsh regime? How are Danticat's and
Satrapi's narratives similar? How are they different?

THE WRITER AT WORK

Edwidge Danticat on Becoming a Writer

*As the previous selection shows, Edwidge Danticat is a writer concerned
deeply with Haitian legend and legacy. These concerns, especially when combined
with her political ideals, have been the chief stimulus for her writing. In the following brief interview that appeared in* Essence *magazine (May 1996), Danticat
discusses how she became a writer and the motives that have inspired and guided
her career. In an earlier "Writer at Work" selection, George Orwell (page 544)
outlines what he believes are the chief motives for why people write. How closely
do you think Danticat's motives conform to Orwell's list? Does she offer any reasons for writing that you think should be added to Orwell's outline?*

While I was growing up, most of the writers I knew were either in
hiding, missing, or dead. We were living under the brutal Duvalier dictatorship in Haiti, and silence was the law of the land. I learned that code
of silence early on. It was as real as the earth beneath our feet, which was
full of blood of martyrs, among them many novelists, poets, journalists,
and playwrights who had criticized our government.

Writing was a dangerous activity. Perhaps it was that danger that attracted me, the feeling of doing a high-wire act between stretching the
limits of silence and telling the whole truth.

Even though I now live in a country where people are not persecuted
for their words, I still feel as though I am always balancing between the
personal dangers of writing and the comfort and healing it offers me.

I write to communicate with my ancestors, to explore the truth of
their lives and to link it to my own. When I write, I think of my foremothers, who as Zora Neale Hurston[1] observed, were considered "the mules of
the earth." I think of wives who were separated from their husbands by
poverty and political violence, children who lived off other people's trash,
mothers and daughters, fathers and sons, all linked by centuries of pillage
and slaughter. These men and women sacrificed their own enjoyment and
pleasures so that the next generation—my generation—would have a
voice and a future.

---

[1]For more on Zora Neale Hurston, see page 166.—EDS.

I wrote my first short story when I was nine years old, on a few white   5
pages folded to form a tiny notebook. The story was about a little girl
who was visited every night by a clan of women just like the overburdened and underappreciated creatures who were part of my own lineage.

When I moved to the United States at age twelve, I was temporarily
floating between languages—Creole and English—so I stopped writing for
a while. At fourteen I was asked by a New York City–based newspaper,
New Youth Connections, to write about my experiences as a new immigrant. I wrote a short essay about adapting to my new life in Brooklyn,
and my public writing career began.

People often ask me, "How can I become a writer?" In response I tell
them the story of a Haitian painter I know. He is a very poor man who
often gives up food to buy materials to paint with. He lives in a worn-out
house in a slum. He never shows his paintings, and you have to fight him
to buy one from him.

One day while in his studio, pleading with him to sell me a piece, I
asked him, "Why create anything if you won't put it out there for the
world to see and enjoy?"

To that he replied, "I don't do this for the world. I do it because I
have no choice. I do it to save my life."

Now when I write, I realize that I'm writing to save my life. I write to   10
unearth all those things that scare me, to reach those places in my soul
that may seem remote and dark to others. I write to preserve my sanity
and to honor the sacrifices made by all those who came before me. The
way I figure, it's a privilege just to be given a voice to speak and to be
heard. God and the universe will take care of the rest.

Jared Diamond

The Ends of the World as We Know Them

*Pulitzer-prize–winning author Jared Diamond (b. 1937) is a physiologist, ecol-
ogist, and science writer known for his ability to make serious science accessible to a
general audience. Diamond received his Ph.D. from Cambridge University and has
been on the UCLA faculty since 1966, currently serving as professor of geography
and physiology at the School of Medicine. A recipient of many prestigious awards,*

he won the 1999 National Medal of Science for his work in the fields of evolutionary biology and conservation biology. He has done extensive fieldwork in South America, Africa, Indonesia, Australia, and New Guinea and written more than five hundred scholarly papers on evolutionary physiology, ecology, and ornithology.

Diamond's books include Why Is Sex Fun? *(1975);* The Third Chimpanzee *(1991), for which he was awarded the* Los Angeles Times *Book Prize and the* Science *Book Prize;* Guns, Germs, and Steel *(1997), for which he won the 1997 Pulitzer Prize for nonfiction; and his latest book,* Collapse *(2004), a historical analysis of the fates of societies faced with environmental or political catastrophe. He is a frequent contributor to such magazines as* Discover, Natural History, *and* Nature; *his essays are found in publications including the* Atlantic *and the* New York Times, *which published "The Ends of the World as We Know Them" on January 1, 2005.*

New Year's weekend traditionally is a time for us to reflect, and to make resolutions based on our reflections. In this fresh year, with the United States seemingly at the height of its power and at the start of a new presidential term, Americans are increasingly concerned and divided about where we are going. How long can America remain ascendant? Where will we stand ten years from now, or even next year?

Such questions seem especially appropriate this year. History warns us that when once-powerful societies collapse, they tend to do so quickly and unexpectedly. That shouldn't come as much of a surprise: peak power usually means peak population, peak needs, and hence peak vulnerability. What can be learned from history that could help us avoid joining the ranks of those who declined swiftly? We must expect the answers to be complex, because historical reality is complex: while some societies did indeed collapse spectacularly, others have managed to thrive for thousands of years without major reversal.

When it comes to historical collapses, five groups of interacting factors have been especially important: the damage that people have inflicted on their environment; climate change; enemies; changes in friendly trading partners; and the society's political, economic and social responses to these shifts. That's not to say that all five causes play a role in every case. Instead, think of this as a useful checklist of factors that should be examined, but whose relative importance varies from case to case.

For instance, in the collapse of the Polynesian society on Easter Island[1] three centuries ago, environmental problems were dominant, and climate change, enemies and trade were insignificant; however, the latter three factors played big roles in the disappearance of the medieval Norse colonies on Greenland. Let's consider two examples of declines stemming from different mixes of causes: the falls of classic Maya civilization and of Polynesian settlements on the Pitcairn Islands.

---

[1]*Easter Island:* Remote South Pacific island known for giant Moai statues, which were toppled during a period of decline for the Rapa Nui people there. — EDS.

Maya Native Americans of the Yucatan Peninsula and adjacent parts   5
of Central America developed the New World's most advanced civilization
before Columbus. They were innovators in writing, astronomy, architecture and art. From local origins around 2,500 years ago, Maya societies
rose especially after the year A.D. 250, reaching peaks of population and
sophistication in the late eighth century.

Thereafter, societies in the most densely populated areas of the southern Yucatan underwent a steep political and cultural collapse: between
760 and 910, kings were overthrown, large areas were abandoned, and at
least 90 percent of the population disappeared, leaving cities to become
overgrown by jungle. The last known date recorded on a Maya monument by their so-called Long Count calendar corresponds to the year 909.
What happened?

A major factor was environmental degradation by people: deforestation, soil erosion and water management problems, all of which resulted
in less food. Those problems were exacerbated by droughts, which may have
been partly caused by humans themselves through deforestation. Chronic
warfare made matters worse, as more and more people fought over less and
less land and resources.

Why weren't these problems obvious to the Maya kings, who could
surely see their forests vanishing and their hills becoming eroded? Part of
the reason was that the kings were able to insulate themselves from problems afflicting the rest of society. By extracting wealth from commoners,
they could remain well fed while everyone else was slowly starving.

What's more, the kings were preoccupied with their own power
struggles. They had to concentrate on fighting one another and keeping
up their images through ostentatious displays of wealth. By insulating
themselves in the short run from the problems of society, the elite merely
bought themselves the privilege of being among the last to starve.

Whereas Maya societies were undone by problems of their own mak-   10
ing, Polynesian societies on Pitcairn and Henderson Islands in the tropical
Pacific Ocean were undone largely by other people's mistakes. Pitcairn,
the uninhabited island settled in 1790 by the *H.M.S. Bounty* mutineers,
had actually been populated by Polynesians 800 years earlier. That society, which left behind temple platforms, stone and shell tools and huge
garbage piles of fish and bird and turtle bones as evidence of its existence,
survived for several centuries and then vanished. Why?

In many respects, Pitcairn and Henderson are tropical paradises, rich
in some food sources and essential raw materials. Pitcairn is home to Southeast Polynesia's largest quarry of stone suited for making adzes, while
Henderson has the region's largest breeding seabird colony and its only
nesting beach for sea turtles. Yet the islanders depended on imports from
Mangareva Island, hundreds of miles away, for canoes, crops, livestock
and oyster shells for making tools.

Unfortunately for the inhabitants of Pitcairn and Henderson, their Man-
garevan trading partner collapsed for reasons similar to those underlying the

Maya decline: deforestation, erosion and warfare. Deprived of essential imports in a Polynesian equivalent of the 1973 oil crisis, the Pitcairn and Henderson societies declined until everybody had died or fled.

The Maya and the Henderson and Pitcairn Islanders are not alone, of course. Over the centuries, many other societies have declined, collapsed or died out. Famous victims include the Anasazi in the American Southwest, who abandoned their cities in the twelfth century because of environmental problems and climate change, and the Greenland Norse, who disappeared in the fifteenth century because of all five interacting factors on the checklist. There were also the ancient Fertile Crescent societies, the Khmer at Angkor Wat, the Moche society of Peru—the list goes on.

But before we let ourselves get depressed, we should also remember that there is another long list of cultures that have managed to prosper for lengthy periods of time. Societies in Japan, Tonga, Tikopia, the New Guinea Highlands and Central and Northwest Europe, for example, have all found ways to sustain themselves. What separates the lost cultures from those that survived? Why did the Maya fail and the shogun succeed?

Half of the answer involves environmental differences: geography   15
deals worse cards to some societies than to others. Many of the societies that collapsed had the misfortune to occupy dry, cold or otherwise fragile environments, while many of the long-term survivors enjoyed more robust and fertile surroundings. But it's not the case that a congenial environment guarantees success: some societies (like the Maya) managed to ruin lush environments, while other societies—like the Incas, the Inuit, Icelanders and desert Australian Aborigines—have managed to carry on in some of the earth's most daunting environments.

The other half of the answer involves differences in a society's responses to problems. Ninth-century New Guinea Highland villagers, sixteenth-century German landowners, and the Tokugawa shoguns of seventeenth-century Japan all recognized the deforestation spreading around them and solved the problem, either by developing scientific reforestation (Japan and Germany) or by transplanting tree seedlings (New Guinea). Conversely, the Maya, Mangarevans and Easter Islanders failed to address their forestry problems and so collapsed.

Consider Japan. In the 1600s, the country faced its own crisis of deforestation, paradoxically brought on by the peace and prosperity following the Tokugawa shoguns' military triumph that ended 150 years of civil war. The subsequent explosion of Japan's population and economy set off rampant logging for construction of palaces and cities, and for fuel and fertilizer.

The shoguns responded with both negative and positive measures. They reduced wood consumption by turning to light-timbered construction, to fuel-efficient stoves and heaters, and to coal as a source of energy. At the same time, they increased wood production by developing and carefully managing plantation forests. Both the shoguns and the Japanese peasants took a long-term view: the former expected to pass on their power to their children, and the latter expected to pass on their land. In addition, Japan's isolation at the time made it obvious that the country would have to depend on its own resources and couldn't meet its needs by pillaging other countries. Today, despite having the highest human population density of any large developed country, Japan is more than seventy percent forested.

There is a similar story from Iceland. When the island was first settled by the Norse around 870, its light volcanic soils presented colonists with unfamiliar challenges. They proceeded to cut down trees and stock sheep as if they were still in Norway, with its robust soils. Significant erosion ensued, carrying half of Iceland's topsoil into the ocean within a century or two. Icelanders became the poorest people in Europe. But they gradually learned from their mistakes, over time instituting stocking limits on sheep and other strict controls, and establishing an entire government department charged with landscape management. Today, Iceland boasts the sixth-highest per-capita income in the world.

What lessons can we draw from history? The most straightforward: take environmental problems seriously. They destroyed societies in the past, and they are even more likely to do so now. If 6,000 Polynesians with stone tools were able to destroy Mangareva Island, consider what six billion people with metal tools and bulldozers are doing today. Moreover, while the Maya collapse affected just a few neighboring societies in Central America, globalization now means that any society's problems have the potential to affect anyone else. Just think how crises in Somalia, Afghanistan and Iraq have shaped the United States today.

Other lessons involve failures of group decision-making. There are many reasons why past societies made bad decisions, and thereby failed to solve or even to perceive the problems that would eventually destroy them. One reason involves conflicts of interest, whereby one group within a society (for instance, the pig farmers who caused the worst erosion in medieval Greenland and Iceland) can profit by engaging in practices that damage the rest of society. Another is the pursuit of short-term gains at the expense of long-term survival, as when fishermen overfish the stocks on which their livelihoods ultimately depend.

History also teaches us two deeper lessons about what separates successful societies from those heading toward failure. A society contains a built-in blueprint for failure if the elite insulates itself from the consequences of its actions. That's why Maya kings, Norse Greenlanders and Easter Island chiefs made choices that eventually undermined their societies. They themselves did not begin to feel deprived until they had irreversibly destroyed their landscape.

Could this happen in the United States? It's a thought that often occurs to me here in Los Angeles, when I drive by gated communities, guarded by private security patrols, and filled with people who drink bottled water, depend on private pensions, and send their children to private schools. By doing these things, they lose the motivation to support the police force, the municipal water supply, Social Security and public schools. If conditions deteriorate too much for poorer people, gates will not keep the rioters out. Rioters eventually burned the palaces of Maya kings and tore down the statues of Easter Island chiefs; they have also already threatened wealthy districts in Los Angeles twice in recent decades.

In contrast, the elite in seventeenth-century Japan, as in modern Scandinavia and the Netherlands, could not ignore or insulate themselves from broad societal problems. For instance, the Dutch upper class for hundreds of years has been unable to insulate itself from the Netherlands' water management problems for a simple reason: the rich live in the same drained lands below sea level as the poor. If the dikes and pumps keeping out the sea fail, the well-off Dutch know that they will drown along with everybody else, which is precisely what happened during the floods of 1953.

The other deep lesson involves a willingness to re-examine long-held   25
core values, when conditions change and those values no longer make sense. The medieval Greenland Norse lacked such a willingness: they continued to view themselves as transplanted Norwegian pastoralists, and to despise the Inuit as pagan hunters, even after Norway stopped sending trading ships and the climate had grown too cold for a pastoral existence. They died off as a result, leaving Greenland to the Inuit. On the other hand, the British in the 1950s faced up to the need for a painful reappraisal of their former status as rulers of a world empire set apart from Europe. They are now finding a different avenue to wealth and power, as part of a united Europe.

In this New Year, we Americans have our own painful reappraisals to face. Historically, we viewed the United States as a land of unlimited plenty, and so we practiced unrestrained consumerism, but that's no longer viable in a world of finite resources. We can't continue to deplete our own resources as well as those of much of the rest of the world.

Historically, oceans protected us from external threats; we stepped back from our isolationism only temporarily during the crises of two world wars. Now, technology and global interconnectedness have robbed us of our protection. In recent years, we have responded to foreign threats largely by seeking short-term military solutions at the last minute.

But how long can we keep this up? Though we are the richest nation on earth, there's simply no way we can afford (or muster the troops) to intervene in the dozens of countries where emerging threats lurk—particularly when each intervention these days can cost more than $100 billion and require more than 100,000 troops.

A genuine reappraisal would require us to recognize that it will be far less expensive and far more effective to address the underlying problems of public health, population and environment that ultimately cause threats to us to emerge in poor countries. In the past, we have regarded foreign aid as either charity or as buying support; now, it's an act of self-interest to preserve our own economy and protect American lives.

Do we have cause for hope? Many of my friends are pessimistic when   30
they contemplate the world's growing population and human demands
colliding with shrinking resources. But I draw hope from the knowledge
that humanity's biggest problems today are ones entirely of our own
making. Asteroids hurtling at us beyond our control don't figure high on
our list of imminent dangers. To save ourselves, we don't need new technology: we just need the political will to face up to our problems of population and the environment.

I also draw hope from a unique advantage that we enjoy. Unlike any
previous society in history, our global society today is the first with the
opportunity to learn from the mistakes of societies remote from us in
space and in time. When the Maya and Mangarevans were cutting down
their trees, there were no historians or archaeologists, no newspapers or
television, to warn them of the consequences of their actions. We, on the
other hand, have a detailed chronicle of human successes and failures at
our disposal. Will we choose to use it?

The Reader's Presence

1. What societies does Diamond use as examples? How does he suggest that the fates of historical societies relate to the survival of
   modern societies like our own? Do you agree with his views about
   the factors that will be important for our society's survival? Why
   or why not?

2. What connections does Diamond make between choices made in
   modern American society and in defunct cultures of the past?
   What does he suggest is going wrong in American culture that
   could adversely affect our society's future? Does he leave out anything that you consider an important factor in the survival of the
   United States as a society?

3. Read "Worried? Us?" by Bill McKibben (page 763). How does his
   argument about the importance of concern for the environment
   compare with Diamond's? Which essay do you find more compelling? Why?

Annie Dillard

Living Like Weasels

Annie Dillard (b. 1945) was awarded the Pulitzer Prize for general nonfiction in 1974 for Pilgrim at Tinker Creek, *which she describes (borrowing from Henry David Thoreau) as "a meteorological journal of the mind." She graduated from Hollins College in 1967;* Tinker Creek *is nearby. She has also published poetry in* Tickets for a Prayer Wheel *(1975) and* Mornings like This: Found Poems *(1995), literary theory in* Living by Fiction *(1982), essays in* Teaching a Stone to Talk *(1982) and* For the Time Being *(1999), and autobiography in* An American Childhood *(1987). Dillard published her first novel,* The Living, *in 1992, and* The Annie Dillard Reader *appeared in 1994. From 1973 to 1982 she served as contributing editor to* Harper's *magazine, and since 1979 she has taught creative writing at Wesleyan University. "Living Like Weasels" appears in her book* Teaching a Stone to Talk.*

In her 1997 essay "Advice to Young Writers," Dillard argues, "Don't use any extra words. A sentence is a machine; it has a job to do. An extra word in a sentence is like a sock in a machine."

A weasel is wild. Who knows what he thinks? He sleeps in his underground den, his tail draped over his nose. Sometimes he lives in his den for two days without leaving. Outside, he stalks rabbits, mice, muskrats, and birds, killing more bodies than he can eat warm, and often dragging the carcasses home. Obedient to instinct, he bites his prey at the neck, either splitting the jugular vein at the throat or crunching the brain at the base of the skull, and he does not let go. One naturalist refused to kill a weasel who was socketed into his hand deeply as a rattlesnake. The man could in no way pry the tiny weasel off, and he had to walk half a mile to water, the weasel dangling from his palm, and soak him off like a stubborn label.

And once, says Ernest Thompson Seton[1] — once, a man shot an eagle out of the sky. He examined the eagle and found the dry skull of a weasel fixed by the jaws to his throat. The supposition is that the eagle had pounced on the weasel and the weasel swiveled and bit as instinct taught him, tooth to neck, and nearly won. I would like to have seen that eagle from the air a few weeks or months before he was shot. Was the whole weasel still attached to his feathered throat, a fur pendant? Or did the eagle eat what he could reach, gutting the living weasel with his talons before his breast, bending his beak, cleaning the beautiful airborne bones?

---

[1]*Ernest Thompson Seton* (1860–1946): American author and naturalist who founded the wildlife organization upon which the Boy Scout movement was later patterned. — Eds.

I have been reading about weasels because I saw one last week. I startled a weasel who startled me, and we exchanged a long glance.

Near my house in Virginia is a pond—Hollins Pond. It covers two acres of bottomland near Tinker Creek with six inches of water and six thousand lily pads. There is a fifty-five mph highway at one end of the pond, and a nesting pair of wood ducks at the other. Under every bush is a muskrat hole or a beer can. The far end is an alternating series of fields and woods, fields and woods, threaded everywhere with motorcycle tracks—in whose bare clay wild turtles lay eggs.

One evening last week at sunset, I walked to the pond and sat on a downed log near the shore. I was watching the lily pads at my feet tremble and part over the thrusting path of a carp. A yellow warbler appeared to my right and flew behind me. It caught my eye; I swiveled around—and the next instant, inexplicably, I was looking down at a weasel, who was looking up at me.

Weasel! I'd never seen one wild before. He was ten inches long, thin as a curve, a muscled ribbon, brown as fruitwood, soft-furred, alert. His face was fierce, small and pointed as a lizard's; he would have made a good arrowhead. There was just a dot of chin, maybe two brown hairs' worth, and then the pure white fur began that spread down his underside. He had two black eyes I didn't see, any more than you see a window.

The weasel was stunned into stillness as he was emerging from beneath an enormous shaggy wild rose bush four feet away. I was stunned into stillness twisted backward on the tree trunk. Our eyes locked, and someone threw away the key.

Our look was as if two lovers, or deadly enemies, met unexpectedly on an overgrown path when each had been thinking of something else: a clearing blow to the gut. It was also a bright blow to the brain, or a sudden beating of brains, with all the charge and intimate grate of rubbed balloons. It emptied our lungs. It felled the forest, moved the fields, and drained the pond; the world dismantled and tumbled into that black hole of eyes. If you and I looked at each other that way, our skulls would split and drop to our shoulders. But we don't. We keep our skulls.

He disappeared. This was only last week, and already I don't remember what shattered the enchantment. I think I blinked, I think I retrieved my brain from the weasel's brain, and tried to memorize what I was seeing, and the weasel felt the yank of separation, the careening splashdown into real life and the urgent current of instinct. He vanished under the wild rose. I waited motionless, my mind suddenly full of data and my spirit with pleadings, but he didn't return.

Please do not tell me about "approach-avoidance conflicts." I tell you I've been in that weasel's brain for sixty seconds, and he was in mine. Brains are private places, muttering through unique and secret tapes—but the weasel and I both plugged into another tape simultaneously, for a sweet and shocking time. Can I help it if it was a blank?

What goes on in his brain the rest of the time? What does a weasel think about? He won't say. His journal is tracks in clay, a spray of feathers, mouse blood and bone: uncollected, unconnected, loose-leaf, and blown.

I would like to learn, or remember, how to live. I come to Hollins Pond not so much to learn how to live as, frankly, to forget about it. That is, I don't think I can learn from a wild animal how to live in particular — shall I suck warm blood, hold my tail high, walk with my footprints precisely over the prints of my hands? — but I might learn something of mindlessness, something of purity of living in the physical senses and the dignity of living without bias or motive. The weasel lives in necessity and we live in choice, hating necessity and dying at the last ignobly in its talons. I would like to live as I should, as the weasel lives as he should. And I suspect that for me the way is like the weasel's: open to time and death painlessly, noticing everything, remembering nothing, choosing the given with a fierce and pointed will.

I missed my chance. I should have gone for the throat. I should have lunged for that streak of white under the weasel's chin and held on, held on through mud and into the wild rose, held on for a dearer life. We could live under the wild rose wild as weasels, mute and uncomprehending. I could very calmly go wild. I could live two days in the den, curled, leaning on mouse fur, sniffing bird bones, blinking, licking, breathing musk, my hair tangled in the roots of grasses. Down is a good place to go, where the mind is single. Down is out, out of your ever-loving mind and back to your careless senses. I remember muteness as a prolonged and giddy fast, where every moment is a feast of utterance received. Time and events are merely poured, unremarked, and ingested directly, like blood pulsed into my gut through a jugular vein. Could two live that way? Could two live under the wild rose, and explore by the pond, so that the smooth mind of each is as everywhere present to the other, and as received and as unchallenged, as falling snow?

We could, you know. We can live any way we want. People take vows of poverty, chastity, and obedience — even of silence — by choice. The thing is to stalk your calling in a certain skilled and supple way, to locate the most tender and live spot and plug into that pulse. This is yielding, not fighting. A weasel doesn't "attack" anything; a weasel lives as he's meant to, yielding at every moment to the perfect freedom of single necessity.

I think it would be well, and proper, and obedient, and pure, to   15
grasp your one necessity and not let it go, to dangle from it limp wherever it takes you. Then even death, where you're going no matter how you live, cannot you part. Seize it and let it seize you up aloft even, till your eyes burn out and drop; let your musky flesh fall off in shreds, and

let your very bones unhinge and scatter, loosened over fields, over fields and woods, lightly, thoughtless, from any height at all, from as high as eagles.

The Reader's Presence

1. Dillard begins her essay with two documented accounts of weasels, presumably drawn from her reading. What do these accounts have in common? How do they establish the dominant characteristic of weasels and the theme of the essay?

2. "Our eyes locked," Dillard says in describing her encounter with the weasel. Why is this an appropriate image? How does the idea of "locking" run through the essay? She also uses the word *wild*. How does she characterize the wild? Could the wild be thought of differently, and in what ways?

3. Dillard's understanding of wild animals suggests a high degree of empathy on her part. Does she give the impression that her wish to live like a weasel is sincere? If not, what is the significance of this hypothetical argument? How does Dillard's sense of what she can learn from animals (in paragraph 14 especially) compare to Linda Hogan's in "Dwellings" (page 456)? Might Hogan agree with Dillard's distinction between animals (who live "in necessity") and humans (who live "in choice")? What might each writer think her writing can do for the reader?

THE WRITER AT WORK

Annie Dillard on the Writing Life

One of the nation's outstanding nonfiction writers—who prefers to think of herself as an "all-purpose writer" rather than an essayist—Annie Dillard is also a prominent creative writing teacher at Wesleyan University. Dillard once said that a commitment to writing is "like living any dedicated life." How is this idea reflected in the following excerpt from her book The Writing Life *(1989)? What is it that Dillard believes drives the creative artist and writer? Does her tough-minded advice apply only to artistic expression? In what other areas of human activity or expression might it also apply?*

Push it. Examine all things intensely and relentlessly. Probe and search each object in a piece of art. Do not leave it, do not course over it, as if it were understood, but instead follow it down until you see it in the mystery of its own specificity and strength. Giacometti's drawings and paintings show his bewilderment and persistence. If he had not acknowledged his bewilderment, he would not have persisted. A twentieth-century master of drawing, Rico Lebrun, taught that "the draftsman must aggress; only by persistent assault will the live image capitulate and give up its secret to an unrelenting line." Who but an artist fierce to know—not fierce to seem to know—would suppose that a live image possessed a secret? The artist is willing to give all his or her strength and life to probing with blunt instruments those same secrets no one can describe in any way but with those instruments' faint tracks.

Admire the world for never ending on you—as you would admire an opponent, without taking your eyes from him, or walking away.

One of the few things I know about writing is this: spend it all, shoot it, play it, lose it, all, right away, every time. Do not hoard what seems good for a later place in the book, or for another book; give it, give it all, give it now. The impulse to save something good for a better place later is the signal to spend it now. Something more will arise for later, something better. These things fill from behind, from beneath, like well water. Similarly, the impulse to keep to yourself what you have learned is not only shameful, it is destructive. Anything you do not give freely and abundantly becomes lost to you. You open your safe and find ashes.

After Michelangelo died, someone found in his studio a piece of paper on which he had written a note to his apprentice, in the handwriting of his old age: "Draw, Antonio, draw, Antonio, draw and do not waste time."

W. E. B. Du Bois

Of Our Spiritual Strivings

William Edward Burghardt Du Bois (1868–1963) was a scholar, social scientist, political activist, and leading figure in the early years of the movement to win equal rights for African Americans. Born and raised in Great Barrington, Massachusetts, he went to Tennessee to attend Fisk University, a liberal arts institution founded to educate former slaves. He later earned a Ph.D. in history from Harvard University. His dissertation, "The Suppression of the African Slave Trade to the United States of America, 1638–1870," was published as No. 1 in the Harvard Historical Series *and stands as a clear indication not only of the extraordinary quality of his scholarship but also of his life's work to come. As one biographer wrote, "All of his efforts were geared toward gaining equal treatment for black people in a world dominated by whites and toward marshaling and presenting evidence to refute the myths of racial inferiority." Trained as a sociologist, Du Bois documented the oppression of the people of the African diaspora, work that helped shape one of his most influential and lasting books,* The Souls of Black Folk *(1903), in which "Of Our Spiritual Strivings" appears. The book was a radical new approach to issues of race and a sharp break from the more moderate views of Booker T. Washington and other African American intellectuals of the time.*

Du Bois helped to establish the National Association for the Advancement of Colored People (NAACP) in 1909 and served as director of research and editor of its influential magazine, The Crisis. *He grew disillusioned with the NAACP's moderate policies and with the capitalist system in the United States and turned to more radical strategies for breaking down racial barriers, even joining the Communist Party. In 1960, he left the United States and became a citizen of Ghana, where he died in 1963 on the eve of the landmark civil rights march in Washington, D.C. (For more on the march, see page 723.)*

Du Bois wrote twenty-one books, edited fifteen more, and published more than one hundred essays and articles. His books include two novels, The Quest of the Silver Fleece *(1911) and* Dark Princess *(1928); a collection of essays and poetry,* Darkwater: Voices from Within the Veil *(1920); and two histories,* The Negro *(1915) and* The Gift of Black Folk *(1924). The centennial of the publication of* The Souls of Black Folk *was honored with celebrations all over the United States in 2003 — a testament to Du Bois's work and lasting influence.*

> O water, voice of my heart, crying in the sand,
>   All night long crying with a mournful cry,
> As I lie and listen, and cannot understand
>   The voice of my heart in my side or the voice of the sea,
> O water, crying for rest, is it I, is it I?
>   All night long the water is crying to me.
>
> Unresting water, there shall never be rest
>   Till the last moon droop and the last tide fail,
> And the fire of the end begin to burn in the west;
>   And the heart shall be weary and wonder and cry like the sea,
> All life long crying without avail,
>   As the water all night long is crying to me.
>
> —Arthur Symons

Between me and the other world there is ever an unasked question: unasked by some through feelings of delicacy; by others through the difficulty of rightly framing it. All, nevertheless, flutter round it. They approach me in a half-hesitant sort of way, eye me curiously or compassionately, and then, instead of saying directly, How does it feel to be a problem? they say, I

---

[1]A portion of the African American spiritual "Nobody Knows the Trouble I've Seen." — EDS.

know an excellent colored man in my town; or, I fought at Mechanicsville;[2] or, Do not these Southern outrages make your blood boil? At these I smile, or am interested, or reduce the boiling to a simmer, as the occasion may require. To the real question, How does it feel to be a problem? I answer seldom a word.

And yet, being a problem is a strange experience, — peculiar even for one who has never been anything else, save perhaps in babyhood and in Europe. It is in the early days of rollicking boyhood that the revelation first bursts upon one, all in a day, as it were. I remember well when the shadow swept across me. I was a little thing, away up in the hills of New England, where the dark Housatonic winds between Hoosac and Taghkanic to the sea. In a wee wooden schoolhouse, something put it into the boys' and girls' heads to buy gorgeous visiting-cards — ten cents a package — and exchange. The exchange was merry, till one girl, a tall newcomer, refused my card, — refused it peremptorily, with a glance. Then it dawned upon me with a certain suddenness that I was different from the others; or like, mayhap, in heart and life and longing, but shut out from their world by a vast veil. I had thereafter no desire to tear down that veil, to creep through; I held all beyond it in common contempt, and lived above it in a region of blue sky and great wandering shadows. That sky was bluest when I could beat my mates at examination-time, or beat them at a foot-race, or even beat their stringy heads. Alas, with the years all this fine contempt began to fade; for the worlds I longed for, and all their dazzling opportunities, were theirs, not mine. But they should not keep these prizes, I said; some, all, I would wrest from them. Just how I would do it I could never decide: by reading law, by healing the sick, by telling the wonderful tales that swam in my head, — some way. With other black boys the strife was not so fiercely sunny: their youth shrunk into tasteless sycophancy, or into silent hatred of the pale world about them and mocking distrust of everything white; or wasted itself in a bitter cry, Why did God make me an outcast and a stranger in mine own house? The shades of the prison-house closed round about us all: walls strait and stubborn to the whitest, but relentlessly narrow, tall, and unscalable to sons of night who must plod darkly on in resignation, or beat unavailing palms against the stone, or steadily, half hopelessly, watch the streak of blue above.

After the Egyptian and Indian, the Greek and Roman, the Teuton and Mongolian, the Negro is a sort of seventh son, born with a veil,[3] and gifted with second-sight in this American world, — a world which yields him no true self-consciousness, but only lets him see himself through the revelation of the other world. It is a peculiar sensation, this double-consciousness, this sense of always looking at one's self through the eyes of others, of measuring

---

[2]*Mechanicsville:* A Civil War battle. — EDS.

[3]*seventh son, born with a veil:* Seventh sons of seventh sons and children born with cauls, or membranes, over their faces are believed in some folk traditions to have psychic powers. — EDS.

one's soul by the tape of a world that looks on in amused contempt and pity. One ever feels his two-ness,—an American, a Negro; two souls, two thoughts, two unreconciled strivings; two warring ideals in one dark body, whose dogged strength alone keeps it from being torn asunder.

The history of the American Negro is the history of this strife,—this longing to attain self-conscious manhood, to merge his double self into a better and truer self. In this merging he wishes neither of the older selves to be lost. He would not Africanize America, for America has too much to teach the world and Africa. He would not bleach his Negro soul in a flood of white Americanism, for he knows that Negro blood has a message for the world. He simply wishes to make it possible for a man to be both a Negro and an American, without being cursed and spit upon by his fellows, without having the doors of Opportunity closed roughly in his face.

This, then, is the end of his striving: to be a co-worker in the kingdom of culture, to escape both death and isolation, to husband and use his best powers and his latent genius. These powers of body and mind have in the past been strangely wasted, dispersed, or forgotten. The shadow of a mighty Negro past flits through the tale of Ethiopia the Shadowy and of Egypt the Sphinx. Throughout history, the powers of single black men flash here and there like falling stars, and die sometimes before the world has rightly gauged their brightness. Here in America, in the few days since Emancipation, the black man's turning hither and thither in hesitant and doubtful striving has often made his very strength to lose effectiveness, to seem like absence of power, like weakness. And yet it is not weakness,—it is the contradiction of double aims. The double-aimed struggle of the black artisan—on the one hand to escape white contempt for a nation of mere hewers of wood and drawers of water, and on the other hand to plough and nail and dig for a poverty-stricken horde—could only result in making him a poor craftsman, for he had but half a heart in either cause. By the poverty and ignorance of his people, the Negro minister or doctor was tempted toward quackery and demagogy; and by the criticism of the other world, toward ideals that made him ashamed of his lowly tasks. The would-be black *savant* was confronted by the paradox that the knowledge his people needed was a twice-told tale to his white neighbors, while the knowledge which would teach the white world was Greek to his own flesh and blood. The innate love of harmony and beauty that set the ruder souls of his people a-dancing and a-singing raised but confusion and doubt in the soul of the black artist; for the beauty revealed to him was the soul-beauty of a race which his larger audience despised, and he could not articulate the message of another people. This waste of double aims, this seeking to satisfy two unreconciled ideals, has wrought sad havoc with the courage and faith and deeds of ten thousand thousand people,—has sent them often wooing false gods and invoking false means of salvation, and at times has even seemed about to make them ashamed of themselves.

Away back in the days of bondage they thought to see in one divine event the end of all doubt and disappointment; few men ever worshipped

Freedom with half such unquestioning faith as did the American Negro for two centuries. To him, so far as he thought and dreamed, slavery was indeed the sum of all villainies, the cause of all sorrow, the root of all prejudice; Emancipation was the key to a promised land of sweeter beauty than ever stretched before the eyes of wearied Israelites. In song and exhortation swelled one refrain — Liberty; in his tears and curses the God he implored had Freedom in his right hand. At last it came, — suddenly, fearfully, like a dream. With one wild carnival of blood and passion came the message in his own plaintive cadences: —

> "Shout, O children!
> Shout, you're free!
> For God has bought your liberty!"[4]

Years have passed away since then, — ten, twenty, forty; forty years of national life, forty years of renewal and development, and yet the swarthy spectre sits in its accustomed seat at the Nation's feast. In vain do we cry to this our vastest social problem: —

> "Take any shape but that, and my firm nerves
> Shall never tremble!"[5]

The Nation has not yet found peace from its sins; the freedman has not yet found in freedom his promised land. Whatever of good may have come in these years of change, the shadow of a deep disappointment rests upon the Negro people, — a disappointment all the more bitter because the unattained ideal was unbounded save by the simple ignorance of a lowly people.

The first decade was merely a prolongation of the vain search for freedom, the boon that seemed ever barely to elude their grasp, — like a tantalizing will-o'-the wisp, maddening and misleading the headless host. The holocaust of war, the terrors of the Ku-Klux Klan, the lies of carpet-baggers,[6] the disorganization of industry, and the contradictory advice of friends and foes, left the bewildered serf with no new watchword beyond the old cry for freedom. As the time flew, however, he began to grasp a new idea. The ideal of liberty demanded for its attainment powerful means, and these the Fifteenth Amendment gave him.[7] The ballot, which before he had looked upon as a visible sign of freedom, he now regarded as the chief means of gaining and perfecting the liberty with which war had partially endowed him. And why not? Had not votes made war and

---

[4]Lines from an early nineteenth-century spiritual. — EDS.

[5]Lines from William Shakespeare's *Macbeth*, Act III, scene IV, in which Macbeth reacts to seeing a ghost. — EDS.

[6]*carpetbaggers:* Northerners seeking political or financial gain by traveling to the post–Civil War South. — EDS.

[7]*Fifteenth Amendment:* A constitutional amendment, ratified in 1870, preventing a U.S. citizen's right to vote from being "denied or abridged . . . on account of race, color, or previous condition of servitude." — EDS.

emancipated millions? Had not votes enfranchised the freedmen? Was anything impossible to a power that had done all this? A million black men started with renewed zeal to vote themselves into the kingdom. So the decade flew away, the revolution of 1876 came,[8] and left the half-free serf weary, wondering, but still inspired. Slowly but steadily, in the following years, a new vision began gradually to replace the dream of political power,—a powerful movement, the rise of another ideal to guide the unguided, another pillar of fire by night after a clouded day. It was the ideal of "book-learning"; the curiosity, born of compulsory ignorance, to know and test the power of the cabalistic letters of the white man, the longing to know. Here at last seemed to have been discovered the mountain path to Canaan; longer than the highway of Emancipation and law, steep and rugged, but straight, leading to heights high enough to overlook life.

Up the new path the advance guard toiled, slowly, heavily, doggedly; only those who have watched and guided the faltering feet, the misty minds, the dull understandings, of the dark pupils of these schools know how faithfully, how piteously, this people strove to learn. It was weary work. The cold statistician wrote down the inches of progress here and there, noted also where here and there a foot had slipped or some one had fallen. To the tired climbers, the horizon was ever dark, the mists were often cold, the Canaan was always dim and far away. If, however, the vistas disclosed as yet no goal, no resting-place, little but flattery and criticism, the journey at least gave leisure for reflection and self-examination; it changed the child of Emancipation to the youth with dawning self-consciousness, self-realization, self-respect. In those sombre forests of his striving his own soul rose before him, and he saw himself,—darkly as through a veil; and yet he saw in himself some faint revelation of his power, of his mission. He began to have a dim feeling that, to attain his place in the world, he must be himself, and not another. For the first time he sought to analyze the burden he bore upon his back, that dead-weight of social degradation partially masked behind a half-named Negro problem. He felt his poverty; without a cent, without a home, without land, tools, or savings, he had entered into competition with rich, landed, skilled neighbors. To be a poor man is hard, but to be a poor race in a land of dollars is the very bottom of hardships. He felt the weight of his ignorance,—not simply of letters, but of life, of business, of the humanities; the accumulated sloth and shirking and awkwardness of decades and centuries shackled his hands and feet. Nor was his burden all poverty and ignorance. The red stain of bastardy, which two centuries of systematic legal defilement of Negro women had stamped upon his race, meant not only the loss of ancient African chastity, but also the hereditary weight of

---

[8]*revolution of 1876:* A political reaction in the South against rights granted to African Americans after the Civil War.—EDS.

a mass of corruption from white adulterers, threatening almost the obliteration of the Negro home.

A people thus handicapped ought not to be asked to race with the   10
world, but rather allowed to give all its time and thought to its own social problems. But alas! while sociologists gleefully count his bastards and his prostitutes, the very soul of the toiling, sweating black man is darkened by the shadow of a vast despair. Men call the shadow prejudice, and learnedly explain it as the natural defence of culture against barbarism, learning against ignorance, purity against crime, the "higher" against the "lower" races. To which the Negro cries Amen! and swears that to so much of this strange prejudice as is founded on just homage to civilization, culture, righteousness, and progress, he humbly bows and meekly does obeisance. But before that nameless prejudice that leaps beyond all this he stands helpless, dismayed, and well-nigh speechless; before that personal disrespect and mockery, the ridicule and systematic humiliation, the distortion of fact and wanton license of fancy, the cynical ignoring of the better and the boisterous welcoming of the worse, the all-pervading desire to inculcate disdain for everything black, from Toussaint[9] to the devil,—before this there rises a sickening despair that would disarm and discourage any nation save that black host to whom "discouragement" is an unwritten word.

But the facing of so vast a prejudice could not but bring the inevitable self-questioning, self-disparagement, and lowering of ideals which ever accompany repression and breed in an atmosphere of contempt and hate. Whisperings and portents came borne upon the four winds: Lo! we are diseased and dying, cried the dark hosts; we cannot write, our voting is vain; what need of education, since we must always cook and serve? And the Nation echoed and enforced this self-criticism, saying: Be content to be servants, and nothing more; what need of higher culture for half-men? Away with the black man's ballot, by force or fraud,—and behold the suicide of a race! Nevertheless, out of the evil came something of good,— the more careful adjustment of education to real life, the clearer perception of the Negroes' social responsibilities, and the sobering realization of the meaning of progress.

So dawned the time of *Sturm und Drang*:[10] storm and stress today rocks our little boat on the mad waters of the world-sea; there is within and without the sound of conflict, the burning of body and rending of soul; inspiration strives with doubt, and faith with vain questionings. The bright ideals of the past,—physical freedom, political power, the training of brains and the training of hands,—all these in turn have waxed and waned, until even the last grows dim and overcast. Are they all wrong,—all false? No, not that, but each alone was over-simple and incomplete,—the

---

[9]*Toussaint:* Toussaint L'Ouverture (c. 1743–1803) led a slave rebellion in Haiti that resulted in the country's independence. — EDS.

[10]*Sturm und Drang:* German for "storm and stress." — EDS.

dreams of a credulous race-childhood, or the fond imaginings of the other world which does not know and does not want to know our power. To be really true, all these ideals must be melted and welded into one. The training of the schools we need today more than ever,—the training of deft hands, quick eyes and ears, and above all the broader, deeper, higher culture of gifted minds and pure hearts. The power of the ballot we need in sheer self-defence,—else what shall save us from a second slavery? Freedom, too, the long-sought, we still seek,—the freedom of life and limb, the freedom to work and think, the freedom to love and aspire. Work, culture, liberty,—all these we need, not singly but together, not successively but together, each growing and aiding each, and all striving toward that vaster ideal that swims before the Negro people, the ideal of human brotherhood, gained through the unifying ideal of Race; the ideal of fostering and developing the traits and talents of the Negro, not in opposition to or contempt for other races, but rather in large conformity to the greater ideals of the American Republic, in order that some day on American soil two world-races may give each to each those characteristics both so sadly lack. We the darker ones come even now not altogether empty-handed: there are today no truer exponents of the pure human spirit of the Declaration of Independence than the American Negroes; there is no true American music but the wild sweet melodies of the Negro slave; the American fairy tales and folk-lore are Indian and African; and, all in all, we black men seem the sole oasis of simple faith and reverence in a dusty desert of dollars and smartness. Will America be poorer if she replace her brutal dyspeptic blundering with lighthearted but determined Negro humility? or her coarse and cruel wit with loving jovial good-humor? or her vulgar music with the soul of the Sorrow Songs?

Merely a concrete test of the underlying principles of the great republic is the Negro Problem, and the spiritual striving of the freedmen's sons is the travail of souls whose burden is almost beyond the measure of their strength, but who bear it in the name of an historic race, in the name of this the land of their fathers' fathers, and in the name of human opportunity.

And now what I have briefly sketched in large outline let me on coming pages tell again in many ways, with loving emphasis and deeper detail, that men may listen to the striving in the souls of black folk.

The Reader's Presence

1. Du Bois opens with a quotation from the English poet Arthur Symons, followed by a bar of music from the African American spiritual "Nobody Knows the Trouble I've Seen." What is the effect of opening the essay with these two epigraphs? Where else

does Du Bois refer to spirituals? How do spirituals relate to his theme of striving?

2. Du Bois states, "It is a peculiar sensation, this double-consciousness, this sense of always looking at one's self through the eyes of others, of measuring one's soul by the tape of a world that looks on in amused contempt and pity" (paragraph 3). What does Du Bois mean by "double-consciousness"? How did "double-consciousness" come about? What does Du Bois identify as its advantages?

3. Du Bois uses religious terms and imagery throughout the essay. Do you think this enhances his message? Why or why not? Read Abraham Lincoln's "Second Inaugural Address" (page 501). Are the purposes for which Lincoln uses religious imagery similar to or different from Du Bois's purposes for using such imagery? Why?

Gregg Easterbrook

The Myth of Fingerprints

Gregg Easterbrook was educated at Colorado College and Northwestern University, earning an M.A. in journalism in 1977 and quickly gaining a national reputation for his investigative reporting. He is a contributing editor of the Atlantic; *a senior editor of the* New Republic; *the* "Tuesday Morning Quarterback" *sports columnist for* Slate; *and a frequent contributor to the* New York Times, *the* Washington Post, *the* Los Angeles Times, *and the* New Yorker. *He is a visiting fellow at the Brookings Institution and the author of many books including* A Moment on the Earth: The Coming Age of Environmental Optimism *(1996),* Beside Still Waters: Searching for Meaning in an Age of Doubt *(1998),* Tuesday Morning Quarterback *(2001), and* The Progress Paradox: How Life Gets Better While People Feel Worse *(2003). He is also the author of two novels,* This Magic Moment *(1987) and* The Here and Now *(2002). "The Myth of Fingerprints" first appeared in the July 2000 issue of the* New Republic.

False convictions have been an important story this year [2000]. The reason? Genetic testing. So far, DNA tests have shown that at least sixty-eight people imprisoned by state and federal courts—including some sent to death row (though none executed)—were innocent. As a result, criminal defense lawyers Barry Scheck and Peter Neufeld are spearheading a national drive to make the tests available to thousands of inmates. They have dubbed their campaign the Innocence Project — creating the impression that DNA tests will serve mainly to exonerate.

In fact, genetic evidence will serve mainly to lock people up. In England, where DNA fingerprinting was invented and has been in widespread use for a decade, law enforcement agencies have already used genetic evidence to solve some 70,000 cases. In the fairly near future, a standard item in the trunks of American police cruisers — perhaps even on each officer's belt — may be a DNA analyzer. As a suspect is arrested, police will quickly swipe the inside of his cheek with a cotton swab and pop the results into the scanner. Within minutes the machine will produce a stream of data describing the suspect's unique genetic structure. The data will be uploaded to state or national DNA databases to determine whether the suspect's DNA matches that of blood, sweat, semen, or similar bodily fluids found at the scene of unsolved crimes around the nation. Such a procedure will be good for public safety and make our legal system more just, but in the long run it will be exactly the opposite of an "innocence project" — it will result in a steady stream of inmates about whose guilt we can be almost entirely certain.

The most striking effect of genetic fingerprinting may be on capital punishment, with some opponents suggesting that DNA exonerations could shift the debate in their favor. They're probably mistaken. Of the four people on Texas's death row who have been granted extra DNA testing, three have been executed anyway when genetic evidence either failed to clear them or confirmed their guilt. The fourth, Ricky McGinn, last month received a stay of execution from Governor George W. Bush so he too could be extended the tests — and they reportedly help support his conviction as well. The two big laboratories that process DNA tests, Cellmark Diagnostics and Forensic Science Associates, have exonerated an estimated 40 percent of the inmates whose "post-conviction" genetic evidence they have reviewed, but the other 60 percent have had their guilt confirmed — and what's being reviewed here is the genetic evidence from those with the strongest claims of mistaken conviction.

During the next few years, post-conviction DNA testing will analyze the evidence of death-row inmates convicted before genetic fingerprinting became practical, and some innocent people will surely be freed. But over time — as the system works through the backlog of those tried before genetic analysis was common — the test's main effect will be to increase society's confidence that the man or woman being strapped to the death gurney really did commit the crime. There are two basic arguments against capital punishment: that it is inherently wrong and that it might be used against the wrong person. Death-penalty opponents have been placing more and more emphasis in recent months on the second — precisely the one genetic fingerprinting will undermine.

DNA testing is not the first anti-crime device touted as infallible. Similar claims were made for fingerprinting, also developed in England, when

5

it was introduced at the end of the nineteenth century. But criminals learned to wear gloves or to wipe the crime scene clean. What's more, because fingerprints don't readily convert into the kind of digital data that can be rapidly accessed and shared by police — searching files for a print match is laborious and expensive — regular fingerprints may solve one particular crime but are not usually much help in matching a suspect to others.

Genetic fingerprinting, however, may really allow close-to-infallible identification. In the early '80s, English geneticist Alec Jeffreys realized that the "markers" on human chromosomes — short, structural areas of the genome — are unique from person to person, except for identical twins. Jeffreys developed a test that converts gene markers into a readout similar to a bar code, which can be easily loaded into computers. Not only has the Jeffreys test proved extremely reliable in identifying individuals, but, because it generates a digital result, computers can cross-reference one genetic fingerprint with thousands or millions of others, quickly and cheaply linking suspects to past crimes.

In recent years, DNA-fingerprinting technology has advanced to the point that, rather than requiring a good sample of blood or semen — which often meant securing warrants to jab suspects with needles — a speck of sweat or a swab from the inside of the mouth will do the trick. A test of mitochondrial DNA — which, while not unique to each individual, tells whether the DNA comes from a particular family's maternal line — can even be conducted on a strand of hair or "degraded" blood and bodily fluid samples that have been kept in storage. The cost of DNA fingerprinting has also dropped dramatically, from about $5,000 when the tests were first developed to about $100 for the newest versions, and is still falling.

Though very reliable, DNA fingerprinting won't solve every crime. It is useful mainly for what might be called intimate violent crimes, in which the perpetrator struggles with the victim and leaves behind blood, semen, or something else testable. (In the recent controversy over Bush's execution of Gary Graham, for instance, genetic evidence was moot — the victim was shot from a distance, leaving nothing of the killer's to test.) At other times, DNA in itself may neither exculpate nor damn. A hair from the murderer of Ricky McGinn's twelve-year-old stepdaughter was found on her corpse, for instance, and a DNA test is believed to show that this hair came from either McGinn or a close maternal relative of his. So, although a prosecutor could not convict McGinn on the DNA evidence alone, it could be a critical component of a larger case.

While there is currently no way to beat a DNA test, that could change, especially if criminals grow more careful with bodily fluids — say, abandoning knives for guns shot from afar. And people won't be researching biotech just to cure diseases — perhaps some enterprising chemist will invent a pill that scrambles the genetic markers in sweat and semen. But for now, at least, genetic fingerprinting is just shy of fool-proof.

For that reason, it is vital that DNA testing be used to exonerate   10
the innocent. There are two main questions about genetic evidence: whether people convicted before such tests were available can reopen their cases for post-conviction DNA reviews and whether genetic finger-printing should become a standard element of new arrests, as it already is in England.

Today only a few states, among them New York and Illinois, unam-biguously grant those already imprisoned access to additional DNA testing. Courts have traditionally put strict deadlines on how long after convic-tion someone can introduce new evidence, in part because experience teaches that the longer ago something happened, the easier it is to find someone willing to commit perjury about it. Prosecutors traditionally fight requests for post-conviction testing, too—which is shortsighted, since a false conviction not only imprisons an innocent person but lets the real perpetrator go free. The Justice Department recommends that post-conviction testing be allowed when it could prove "actual" innocence but not permitted in cases built on claims of technicalities or reversible error. This would be a substantial improvement, and a bill offered by Senator Patrick Leahy of Vermont would basically make it law.

Many states have compiled DNA databases and are scanning them to see if evidence from tested suspects matches evidence from unsolved cases. Virginia, which has enacted a law requiring convicted felons to submit to DNA analysis, now has about 120,000 DNA samples on record. It has al-ready found 177 matches between suspects and genetic material at the scenes of past crimes. This June, Virginia detectives took the gene markers of a man convicted of robbing a local gas station and ran them through the state database; they matched the DNA fingerprint to blood found and stored after a horribly gruesome—and until then unsolved—1992 mur-der. The gas-station robber was promptly arrested for the murder as well.

Yet, for routine police work, many states actually forbid DNA finger-printing or, nonsensically, allow it only after crimes of extreme violence—as though violent criminals should be caught but not mere thieves or carjackers. Leahy's bill, or something like it, would make genetic evidence more standard and also establish a national databank: had the accused murderer in the 1992 Virginia case robbed a gas station in another state and given his DNA sample there instead, Virginia detectives might never have found him. Fighting efforts to more effectively use genetic evidence is the American Civil Liberties Union, which is lobbying against testing laws on the grounds that chromosome material deserves privacy protection be-cause it might reveal such things as sexual orientation.

Why a murderer has a right to sexual privacy (or any kind of privacy) isn't clear, but in any case the ACLU claim evinces confusion about what

Jeffreys-style DNA tests can show. The "markers" analyzed in police tests constitute only a small, structural part of the genome. Just as a traditional fingerprint doesn't tell you anything about the suspect's personality—it just tells you about the shape of his or her finger ridges—genetic markers don't reveal anything about IQ or disease disposition or sexual orientation. Analyzing such complex traits, assuming it can be done at all, would require far more sophisticated tests, along the lines of the years-long human genome initiative. Perhaps someday there will be a quick, cheap test that gives police personal information derived from genes; that may be a reason to enact legal safeguards. . . . For now, the main reason the ACLU seems to fear DNA fingerprinting is that it works.

And that should give death-penalty opponents pause as well. Ex-   15
panded use of DNA evidence will free a few death-row innocents, which would be a blessing. But the new technology will also make society much more confident that those receiving their last meals really are guilty of a mortal sin. Suspicions that the innocent are being executed will not grow stronger as DNA testing spreads—they will grow weaker. And so opponents of capital punishment will lose the offensive they have claimed in recent months. They will be forced back to their real argument, the one that technology can't undermine: the inherent wickedness of execution itself.

The Reader's Presence

1. Who does Easterbrook think should be subject to mandatory DNA testing? According to him, why should these people be tested? Do you agree or disagree that mandatory genetic testing can "exonerate the innocent" (paragraph 10)? Why?

2. What is Easterbrook's position on the death penalty? In what ways does his position on this issue influence his position on mandatory DNA testing? How does he relate the two issues? Who do you think would be more likely to support Easterbrook's ideas about DNA testing: an innocent person falsely accused of a crime or a guilty person who was rightly accused of a crime? Explain why.

3. Like Easterbrook, the essayist Lewis Thomas ("On Cloning a Human Being," page 833) takes on an issue of science and tries to convince the reader to share his point of view. Compare the arguments made by these two essayists. What strategies do the authors use to convince you? What evidence do they introduce and how do they present it? How do they deal with possible objections? What would you say were "fair" argumentative strategies in the respective essays? Unfair? What, in particular, do you think makes one author more effective than the other?

Barbara Ehrenreich
Family Values

Barbara Ehrenreich (b. 1941) wrote some of her first articles and books on the inefficiency and inhumanity of the American health care system. In Complaints and Disorders: The Sexual Politics of Sickness *(coauthored with Deirdre English, 1973) she critiques the unjust and unequal treatment women receive in the medical system. She has written more than a dozen books, among them* The Hearts of Men: American Dreams and the Flight from Commitment *(1983);* The Worst Years of Our Lives: Irreverent Notes from a Decade of Greed *(1990), from which "Family Values" is taken; and* Kipper's Game *(1993). Ehrenreich is a contributing editor at the* Progressive *and the* Nation, *and her essays also appear regularly in magazines as varied as* Radical America, Time, Vogue, *and the* New York Times Magazine. *Her most recent books are* The Snarling Citizen: Essays *(1995),* Blood Rites: Origins and History of the Passions of War *(1997), and* Nickel and Dimed: On (Not) Getting By in America *(2001).*

Asked whether she writes in different voices for the alternative and the mainstream press, Ehrenreich replied, "I don't think it's really a different voice. . . . Obviously I assume more political sympathy for my views if I'm writing for Z or the Guardian *in England or the* Nation *than* Time, *but it might be the exact basic argument." She added, "An essay is like a little story, a short story, and I will obsess about what is the real point, what are the real connections, a long time before I ever put finger to keyboard."*

Sometime in the eighties, Americans had a new set of "traditional values" installed. It was part of what may someday be known as the "Reagan renovation," that finely balanced mix of cosmetic refinement and moral coarseness which brought $200,000 china to the White House dinner table and mayhem to the beleaguered peasantry of Central America. All of the new traditions had venerable sources. In economics, we borrowed from the Bourbons; in foreign policy, we drew on themes fashioned by the nomad warriors of the Eurasian steppes. In spiritual matters, we emulated the braying intolerance of our archenemies and esteemed customers, the Shi'ite fundamentalists.

A case could be made, of course, for the genuine American provenance of all these new "traditions." We've had our own robber barons, military adventures, and certainly more than our share of enterprising evangelists promoting ignorance and parochialism as a state of grace. From the vantage point of the continent's original residents, or, for example, the captive African laborers who made America a great agricultural power, our "traditional values" have always been bigotry, greed, and belligerence, buttressed by wanton appeals to a God of love.

The kindest—though from some angles most perverse—of the era's new values was "family." I could have lived with "flag" and "faith" as neotraditional values—not happily, but I could have managed—until "family" was press-ganged into joining them. Throughout the eighties, the winning political faction has been aggressively "profamily." They have invoked "the family" when they trample on the rights of those who hold actual families together, that is, women. They have used it to justify racial segregation and the formation of white-only, "Christian" schools. And they have brought it out, along with flag and faith, to silence any voices they found obscene, offensive, disturbing, or merely different.

Now, I come from a family—was raised in one, in fact—and one salubrious effect of right-wing righteousness has been to make me hew ever more firmly to the traditional values of my own progenitors. These were not people who could be accused of questionable politics or ethnicity. Nor were they members of the "liberal elite" so hated by our current conservative elite. They were blue-eyed, Scotch-Irish Democrats. They were small farmers, railroad workers, miners, shopkeepers, and migrant farm workers. In short, they fit the stereotype of "real" Americans; and their values, no matter how unpopular among today's opinion-shapers, are part of America's tradition, too. To my mind, of course, the finest part.

But let me introduce some of my family, beginning with my father, who   5
was, along with my mother, the ultimate source of much of my radicalism, feminism, and, by the standards of the eighties, all-around bad attitude.

One of the first questions in a test of mental competency is "Who is the president of the United States?" Even deep into the indignities of Alzheimer's disease, my father always did well on that one. His blue eyes would widen incredulously, surprised at the neurologist's ignorance, then he would snort in majestic indignation, "Reagan, that dumb son of a bitch." It seemed to me a good deal—two people tested for the price of one.

Like so many of the Alzheimer's patients he came to know, my father enjoyed watching the president on television. Most programming left him impassive, but when the old codger came on, his little eyes twinkling piggishly above the disciplined sincerity of his lower face, my father would lean forward and commence a wickedly delighted cackle. I think he was prepared, more than the rest of us, to get the joke.

But the funniest thing was Ollie North. For an ailing man, my father did a fine parody. He would slap his hand over his heart, stare rigidly at attention, and pronounce, in his deepest bass rumble, "God Bless Am-ar-ica!" I'm sure he couldn't follow North's testimony—who can honestly say that they did?—but the main themes were clear enough in pantomime: the watery-eyed patriotism, the extravagant self-pity, the touching servility toward higher-ranking males. When I told my father that many people considered North a hero, a representative of the finest American traditions, he scowled and swatted at the air. Ollie North was the kind of man my father had warned me about, many years ago, when my father was the smartest man on earth.

My father had started out as a copper miner in Butte, Montana, a tiny mountain city famed for its bars, its brawls, and its distinctly un-servile work force. In his view, which remained eagle-sharp even after a stint of higher education, there were only a few major categories of human beings. There were "phonies" and "decent" people, the latter group having hardly any well-known representative outside of Franklin Delano Roosevelt and John L. Lewis, the militant and brilliantly eloquent leader of the miners' union. "Phonies," however, were rampant, and, for reasons I would not understand until later in life, could be found clustered especially thick in the vicinity of money or power.

Well before he taught me other useful things, like how to distinguish   10
fool's gold, or iron pyrite, from the real thing, he gave me some tips on the detection of phonies. For one thing, they broadened the *e* in "America" to a reverent *ahh*. They were the first to leap from their seats at the playing of "The Star Spangled Banner," the most visibly moved participants in any prayer. They espoused clean living and admired war. They preached hard work and paid for it with nickels and dimes. They loved their country above all, but despised the low-paid and usually invisible men and women who built it, fed it, and kept it running.

Two other important categories figured in my father's scheme of things. There were dumb people and smart ones: a distinction which had nothing to do with class or formal education, the dumb being simply all those who were taken in by the phonies. In his view, dumbness was rampant, and seemed to increase in proportion to the distance from Butte, where at least a certain hard-bodied irreverence leavened the atmosphere. The best prophylactic was to study and learn all you could, however you could, and, as he adjured me over and over: always ask *why*.

Finally, there were the rich and the poor. While poverty was not seen as an automatic virtue—my parents struggled mightily to escape it—wealth always carried a presumption of malfeasance. I was instructed that, in the presence of the rich, it was wise to keep one's hand on one's wallet. "Well," my father fairly growled, "how do you think they got their money in the first place?"

It was my mother who translated these lessons into practical politics. A miner's daughter herself, she offered two overarching rules for comportment: never vote Republican and never cross a union picket line. The pinnacle of her activist career came in 1964, when she attended the Democratic Convention as an alternate delegate and joined the sit-in staged by civil rights leaders and the Mississippi Freedom Democratic Party. This was not the action of a "guilt-ridden" white liberal. She classified racial prejudice along with superstition and other manifestations of backward thinking, like organized religion and overcooked vegetables. The worst thing she could find to say about a certain in-law was that he was a Republican and a churchgoer, though when I investigated these charges later in life, I was relieved to find them baseless.

My mother and father, it should be explained, were hardly rebels. The values they imparted to me had been "traditional" for at least a generation before my parents came along. According to my father, the first great steps out of mental passivity had been taken by his maternal grandparents, John Howes and Mamie O'Laughlin Howes, sometime late in the last century. You might think their rebellions small stuff, but they provided our family with its "myth of origins" and a certain standard to uphold.

I knew little about Mamie O'Laughlin except that she was raised as a   15
Catholic and ended up in western Montana sometime in the 1880s. Her father, very likely, was one of those itinerant breadwinners who went west to prospect and settled for mining. At any rate, the story begins when her father lay dying, and Mamie dutifully sent to the next town for a priest. The message came back that the priest would come only if twenty-five dollars was sent in advance. This being the West at its wildest, he may have been justified in avoiding house calls. But not in the price, which was probably more cash than my great-grandmother had ever had at one time. It was on account of its greed that the church lost the souls of Mamie O'Laughlin and all of her descendents, right down to the present time. Futhermore, whether out of filial deference or natural intelligence, most of us have continued to avoid organized religion, secret societies, astrology, and New Age adventures in spiritualism.

As the story continues, Mamie O'Laughlin herself lay dying a few years later. She was only thirty-one, the mother of three small children, one of them an infant whose birth, apparently, led to a mortal attack of pneumonia. This time, a priest appeared unsummoned. Because she was too weak to hold the crucifix, he placed it on her chest and proceeded to administer the last rites. But Mamie was not dead yet. She pulled herself together at the last moment, flung the crucifix across the room, fell back, and died.

This was my great-grandmother. Her husband, John Howes, is a figure of folkloric proportions in my memory, well known in Butte many decades ago as a powerful miner and a lethal fighter. There are many stories about John Howes, all of which point to a profound inability to accept authority in any of its manifestations, earthly or divine. As a young miner, for example, he caught the eye of the mine owner for his skill at handling horses. The boss promoted him to an aboveground driving job, which was a great career leap for the time. Then the boss committed a foolish and arrogant error. He asked John to break in a team of horses for his wife's carriage. Most people would probably be flattered by such a request, but not in Butte, and certainly not John Howes. He declared that he was no man's servant, and quit on the spot.

Like his own wife, John Howes was an atheist or, as they more likely put it at the time, a freethinker. He, too, had been raised as a Catholic—on a farm in Ontario—and he, too, had had a dramatic, though somehow less glorious, falling out with the local clergy. According to legend, he once abused his position as an altar boy by urinating, covertly of course, in the holy water. This so enhanced his enjoyment of the Easter communion service that he could not resist letting a few friends in on the secret. Soon the priest found out and young John was defrocked as an altar boy and condemned to eternal damnation.

The full weight of this transgression hit a few years later, when he became engaged to a local woman. The priest refused to marry them and forbade the young woman to marry John anywhere, on pain of excommunication. There was nothing to do but head west for the Rockies, but not before settling his score with the church. According to legend, John's last act in Ontario was to drag the priest down from his pulpit and slug him, with his brother, presumably, holding the scandalized congregation at bay.

I have often wondered whether my great-grandfather was caught up   20
in the radicalism of Butte in its heyday: whether he was an admirer of Joe Hill, Big Bill Haywood, or Mary "Mother" Jones,[1] all of whom passed through Butte to agitate, and generally left with the Pinkertons[2] on their tails. But the record is silent on this point. All I know is one last story about him, which was told often enough to have the ring of another "traditional value."

According to my father, John Howes worked on and off in the mines after his children were grown, eventually saving enough to buy a small plot of land and retire to farming. This was his dream, anyway, and a powerful one it must have been for a man who had spent so much of his life underground in the dark. So he loaded up a horse-drawn cart with all his money and belongings and headed downhill, toward Montana's eastern plains. But along the way he came to an Indian woman walking with a baby in her arms. He offered her a lift and ascertained, pretty easily, that she was destitute. So he gave her his money, all of it, turned the horse around, and went back to the mines.

Far be it from me to interpret this gesture for my great-grandfather, whom I knew only as a whiskery, sweat-smelling, but straight-backed old man in his eighties. Perhaps he was enacting his own uncompromising version of Christian virtue, even atoning a little for his youthful offenses to the faithful. But at another level I like to think that this was one more gesture of defiance of the mine owners who doled out their own dollars

---

[1]*Joe Hill . . . Jones:* Joe Hill (1879–1915), a writer of popular protest songs, was executed for murder in 1915 after a trial that many, including President Woodrow Wilson, believed suspicious; Big Bill Haywood (1869–1928) was president of the Western Federation of Miners during Colorado's bloody labor wars; Mary "Mother" Jones (1830–1930), the "Miner's Angel," was for decades a legendary union organizer as well as a lecturer for the Socialist Party of American and contributor to the founding of the International Workers of the World. — EDS.

[2]*Pinkertons:* Employees of the Pinkerton National Detective Agency, founded in 1850, were frequently hired to thwart strikes, sometimes violently. — EDS.

so grudgingly—a way of saying, perhaps, that whatever they had to offer, he didn't really need all that much.

So these were the values, sanctified by tradition and family loyalty, that I brought with me to adulthood. Through much of my growing-up, I thought of them as some mutant strain of Americanism, an idiosyncracy which seemed to grow rarer as we clambered into the middle class. Only in the sixties did I begin to learn that my family's militant skepticism and odd-ball rebelliousness were part of a much larger stream of American dissent. I discovered feminism, the antiwar movement, the civil rights movement. I learned that millions of Americans, before me and around me, were "smart" enough, in my father's terms, to have asked "Why?"—and, beyond that, the far more radical question, "Why not?"

These are also the values I brought into the Reagan-Bush era, when all the dangers I had been alerted to as a child were suddenly realized. The "phonies" came to power on the strength, aptly enough, of a professional actor's finest performance. The "dumb" were being led and abetted by low-life preachers and intellectuals with expensively squandered educations. And the rich, as my father predicted, used the occasion to dip deep into the wallets of the desperate and the distracted.

It's been hard times for a traditionalist of my persuasion. Long-standing moral values—usually claimed as "Judeo-Christian" but actually of much broader lineage—were summarily tossed, along with most familiar forms of logic. We were told, at one time or another, by the president or his henchpersons, that trees cause pollution, that welfare causes poverty, and that a bomber designed for mass destruction may be aptly named the *Peacemaker.* "Terrorism" replaced missing children to become our national bugaboo and—simultaneously—one of our most potent instruments of foreign policy. At home, the poor and the middle class were shaken down, and their loose change funneled blithely upwards to the already overfed.   25

Greed, the ancient lubricant of commerce, was declared a wholesome stimulant. Nancy Reagan observed the deep recession of '82 and '83 by redecorating the White House, and continued with this Marie Antoinette theme while advising the underprivileged, the alienated, and the addicted to "say no." Young people, mindful of their elders' Wall Street capers, abandoned the study of useful things for finance banking and other occupations derived, ultimately, from three-card monte. While the poor donned plastic outerware and cardboard coverings, the affluent ran nearly naked through the streets, working off power meals of goat cheese, walnut oil, and crème fraîche.

Religion, which even I had hoped would provide a calming influence and reminder of mortal folly, decided to join the fun. In an upsurge of piety, millions of Americans threw their souls and their savings into evangelical empires designed on the principle of pyramid scams. Even the sleazy downfall of our telemessiahs—caught masturbating in the company of ten-dollar prostitutes or fornicating in their Christian theme parks—did not discourage the faithful. The unhappily pregnant were mobbed as "baby-killers"; sexual nonconformists—gay and lesbian—were denounced as "child molesters"; atheists found themselves lumped with "Satanists," Communists, and consumers of human flesh.

Yet somehow, despite it all, a trickle of dissent continued. There were homeless people who refused to be shelved in mental hospitals for the crime of poverty, strikers who refused to join the celebration of unions in faraway countries and scabs at home, women who insisted that their lives be valued above those of accidental embryos, parents who packed up their babies and marched for peace, students who protested the ongoing inversion of normal, nursery-school-level values in the name of a more habitable world.

I am proud to add my voice to all these. For dissent is also a "traditional value," and in a republic founded by revolution, a more deeply native one than smug-faced conservatism can ever be. Feminism was practically invented here, and ought to be regarded as one of our proudest exports to the world. Likewise, it tickles my sense of patriotism that Third World insurgents have often borrowed the ideas of our own African-American movement. And in what ought to be a source of shame to some and pride to others, our history of labor struggle is one of the hardest-fought and bloodiest in the world.

No matter that patriotism is too often the refuge of scoundrels. Dissent, rebellion, and all-around hell-raising remain the true duty of patriots.   30

The Reader's Presence

1. Do you believe, with Ehrenreich, that different periods in American history have carried different social values? Why or why not? What is your impression of the 1980s, and what sources have you derived this impression from? How does Ehrenreich characterize the 1980s? What elements of 1980s culture does she recall in supporting her claims?

2. One catch phrase frequently heard during Ehrenreich's radical college years was "the personal is political." In what ways were Ehrenreich's father's personal principles political, in her view? How does Ehrenreich's use of her father as a model make the personal political and the political personal? Does this intermingling of the personal and the political undermine or enhance her larger argument? Why?

3. Ehrenreich uses her own impressions and experience as evidence in her argument. How might the essay read if it were argued in more objective terms (historical facts, statistics, etc.)? What sorts of examples does she use to make her point? Can you think of examples contrary to hers (counterexamples)? Contrast the type of evidence used by Ehrenreich with that used by Calvin Trillin ("A Traditional Family," page 576).

Nora Ephron

The Boston Photographs

Nora Ephron (b. 1941) started her writing career as a reporter for the New York Post, *and since then has written for numerous magazines, including* New York, McCall's, *and* Cosmopolitan. *Ephron's collections of essays on popular culture include* Wall Flower at the Orgy *(1970),* Crazy Salad *(1975), and* Scribble, Scribble: Notes on the Media *(1978). The essay "The Boston Photographs" appeared originally in* Esquire *in 1975. She also wrote the screenplays for* Silkwood *(with Alice Arlen),* When Harry Met Sally, *and* Sleepless in Seattle. *In 1992 she directed her first movie,* This Is My Life, *written with her sister Delia Ephron; since then she has directed the films* Michael *(1996),* You've Got Mail *(1998), and* Lucky Numbers *(2000). Her most recent books are* Heartburn *(1983) and* Nora Ephron Collected *(1991).*

When Nora Ephron spoke at Wellesley College Commencement in 1979, she told the largely female audience, "We were sent off into a college environment that expected us to grow up to be soothing women. . . . We were to spend our lives making nice." Ephron believes that the world needs more troublemakers. In "The Boston Photographs," she makes a bold argument for publishing disturbing and controversial photographs.

"I made all kinds of pictures because I thought it would be a good rescue shot over the ladder . . . never dreamed it would be anything else. . . . I kept having to move around because of the light set. The sky was bright and they were in deep shadow. I was making pictures with a motor drive and he, the fire fighter, was reaching up and, I don't know, everything started falling. I followed the girl down taking pictures . . . I made three or four frames. I realized what was going on and I completely turned around, because I didn't want to see her hit."

You probably saw the photographs. In most newspapers, there were three of them. The first showed some people on a fire escape — a fireman, a woman and a child. The fireman had a nice strong jaw and looked very brave. The woman was holding the child. Smoke was pouring from the building behind them. A rescue ladder was approaching, just a few feet away, and the fireman had one arm around the woman and one arm reaching out toward the ladder. The second picture showed the fire escape slipping off the building. The child had fallen on the escape and seemed about to slide off the edge. The woman was grasping desperately at the legs of the fireman, who had managed to grab the ladder. The third picture showed the woman and child in midair, falling to the ground. Their arms and legs were outstretched, horribly distended. A potted plant was falling too. The caption said that the woman, Diana Bryant, nineteen, died in the fall. The child landed on the woman's body and lived.

678

The pictures were taken by Stanley Forman, thirty, of the *Boston Herald American*. He used a motor-driven Nikon F set a 1/250, f5.6-S. Because of the motor, the camera can click off three frames a second. More than four hundred newspapers in the United States alone carried the photographs; the tear sheets from overseas are still coming in. The *New York Times* ran them on the first page of its second section; a paper in south Georgia gave them nineteen columns; the *Chicago Tribune*, the *Washington Post* and the *Washington Star* filled almost half their front pages, the *Star* under a somewhat redundant headline that read: SENSATIONAL PHOTOS OF RESCUE ATTEMPT THAT FAILED.

The photographs are indeed sensational. They are pictures of death in action, of that split second when luck runs out, and it is impossible to look at them without feeling their extraordinary impact and remembering, in an almost subconscious way, the morbid fantasy of falling, falling off a building, falling to one's death. Beyond that, the pictures are classics, old-fashioned but perfect examples of photojournalism at its most spectacular. They're throwbacks, really, fire pictures, 1930s tabloid shots; at the same time they're technically superb and thoroughly modern—the sequence could not have been taken at all until the development of the motor-driven camera some sixteen years ago.

Most newspaper editors anticipate some reader reaction to photographs like Forman's; even so, the response around the country was enormous, and almost all of it was negative. I have read hundreds of the letters that were printed in letters-to-the-editor sections, and they repeat the same points. "Invading the privacy of death." "Cheap sensationalism." "I thought I was reading the *National Enquirer*." "Assigning the agony of a human being in terror of imminent death to the status of a side-show act." "A tawdry way to sell newspapers." The *Seattle Times* received sixty letters and calls; its managing editor even got a couple of them at home. A reader wrote the *Philadelphia Inquirer*: "*Jaws* and *Towering Inferno* are playing downtown; don't take business away from people who pay good money to advertise in your own paper." Another reader wrote the *Chicago Sun-Times*: "I shall try to hide my disappointment that Miss Bryant wasn't wearing a skirt when she fell to her death. You could have had some award-winning photographs of her underpants as her skirt billowed over her head, you voyeurs." Several newspaper editors wrote columns defending the pictures: Thomas Keevil of the *Costa Mesa* (California) *Daily Pilot* printed a ballot for readers to vote on whether they would have printed the pictures; Marshall L. Stone of Maine's *Bangor Daily News*, which refused to print the famous assassination picture of the Vietcong prisoner in Saigon,[1] claimed that the Boston pictures showed the dangers of fire escapes and raised questions

---

[1]*famous assassination picture . . . in Saigon:* A 1968 photograph by Eddie Adams of the Associated Press showed Saigon's chief of police executing a prisoner with a pistol; the photograph helped turn American opinion against the war. —EDS.

about slumlords. (The burning building was a five-story brick apartment
house on Marlborough Street in the Back Bay section of Boston.)

For the last five years, the *Washington Post* has employed various journalists as ombudsmen, whose job is to monitor the paper on behalf of the
public. The *Post*'s current ombudsman is Charles Seib, former managing
editor of the *Washington Star*; the day the Boston photographs appeared,
the paper received over seventy calls in protest. As Seib later wrote in a column about the pictures, it was "the largest reaction to a published item that
I have experienced in eight months as the *Post*'s ombudsman. . . .

"In the *Post*'s newsroom, on the other hand, I found no doubts, no
second thoughts . . . the question was not whether they should be printed
but how they should be displayed. When I talked to editors . . . they used
words like 'interesting' and 'riveting' and 'gripping' to describe them. The
pictures told of something about life in the ghetto, they said (although the
neighborhood where the tragedy occurred is not a ghetto, I am told).
They dramatized the need to check on the safety of fire escapes. They dramatically conveyed something that had happened, and that is the business
we're in. They were news. . . .

"Was publication of that [third] picture a bow to the same taste for
the morbidly sensational that makes gold mines of disaster movies? Most
papers will not print the picture of a dead body except in the most unusual
circumstances. Does the fact that the final picture was taken a millisecond
before the young woman died make a difference? Most papers will not

print a picture of a bare female breast. Is that a more inappropriate subject
for display than the picture of a human being's last agonized instant of
life?" Seib offered no answers to the questions he raised, but he went on to
say that although as an editor he would probably have run the pictures, as
a reader he was revolted by them.

In conclusion, Seib wrote: "Any editor who decided to print those
pictures without giving at least a moment's thought to what purpose they
served and what their effect was likely to be on the reader should ask another question: Have I become so preoccupied with manufacturing a
product according to professional traditions and standards that I have
forgotten about the consumer, the reader?"

It should be clear that the phone calls and letters and Seib's own   10
reaction were occasioned by one factor alone: the death of the woman.
Obviously, had she survived the fall, no one would have protested; the
pictures would have had a completely different impact. Equally obviously, had the child died as well—or instead—Seib would undoubtedly
have received ten times the phone calls he did. In each case, the pictures
would have been exactly the same—only the captions, and thus the responses, would have been different.

But the questions Seib raises are worth discussing—though not exactly for the reasons he mentions. For it may be that the real lesson of the
Boston photographs is not the danger that editors will be forgetful of reader
reaction, but that they will continue to censor pictures of death precisely
because of that reaction. The protests Seib fielded were really a variation
on an old theme—and we saw plenty of it during the Nixon-Agnew
years—the "Why doesn't the press print the good news?" argument. In
this case, of course, the objections were all dressed up and cleverly disguised as righteous indignation about the privacy of death. This is a form
of puritanism that is often justifiable; just as often it is merely puritanical.

Seib takes it for granted that the widespread though fairly recent
newspaper policy against printing pictures of dead bodies is a sound one;
I don't know that it makes any sense at all. I recognize that printing pictures of corpses raises all sorts of problems about taste and titillation and
sensationalism; the fact is, however, that people die. Death happens to be
one of life's main events. And it is irresponsible—and more than that,
inaccurate—for newspapers to fail to show it, or to show it only when an
astonishing set of photos comes in over the Associated Press wire. Most
papers covering fatal automobile accidents will print pictures of mangled
cars. But the significance of fatal automobile accidents is not that a
great deal of steel is twisted but that people die. Why not show it? That's
what accidents are about. Throughout the Vietnam war, editors were reluctant to print atrocity pictures. Why *not* print them? That's what that
war was about. Murder victims are almost never photographed; they are
granted their privacy. But their relatives are relentlessly pictured on their
way in and out of hospitals and morgues and funerals.

I'm not advocating that newspapers print these things in order to
teach their readers a lesson. The *Post* editors justified their printing of the

Boston pictures with several arguments in that direction; every one of them is irrelevant. The pictures don't show anything about slum life; the incident could have happened anywhere, and it did. It is extremely unlikely that anyone who saw them rushed out and had his fire escape strengthened. And the pictures were not news—at least they were not national news. It is not news in Washington, or New York, or Los Angeles that a woman was killed in a Boston fire. The only newsworthy thing about the pictures is that they were taken. They deserve to be printed because they are great pictures, breathtaking pictures of something that happened. That they disturb readers is exactly as it should be: that's why photojournalism is often more powerful than written journalism.

The Reader's Presence

1. At what point does Ephron's argument begin to emerge? How does she present information about the photographs? Why do you think she chooses to structure her argument as she does?

2. How does Ephron refute newspapers' justifications for printing the photographs? What might she argue should be the purpose of photojournalism? Do you agree with this purpose? Why or why not?

3. "Death happens to be one of life's main events," Ephron writes in paragraph 12, arguing that the photographs are important although they are "not news." How does knowing that the woman died in the fall affect the viewer's feelings about the photographs? Read "Last Letters Home" by Marine Staff Sergeant Aaron Dean White, Army Pfc. Diego Fernando Rincon, and Army Specialist Brett T. Christian (page 55). How does knowing about the deaths of these soldiers change the letters' impact on a reader? Do you see similar impulses behind the decisions to publish the Boston photographs and to publish the soldiers' letters? Why or why not?

Paul Fussell

A Well-Regulated Militia

A well-established English professor who taught at Rutgers University before accepting a distinguished professorship at the University of Pennsylvania in 1983, Paul Fussell (b. 1924) did not successfully break with academic prose until he tired of writing what he was "supposed to write." After twenty years of writing critical works such as Poetic Meter and Poetic Form *(1965) and* The Rhetorical World of Augustan Humanism *(1965), Fussell published his first work of nonfiction for a general audience.* The Great War and Modern Memory *(1975) won the National Book Award and the National Book Critics Circle Award and received wide critical acclaim for its examination of how World War I changed what Frank Kermode called "the texture of our culture." Fussell continued to touch upon the subject of war in his subsequent books,* Abroad: British Literary Traveling between the Wars *(1980) and* The Boy Scout Handbook and Other Observations *(1982). Fussell then wrote* Class: A Guide through the American Status System *(1983) and edited* The Norton Book of Travel *(1987). Fussell returned to his favorite subject in his collection of essays* Thank God for the Atom Bomb and Other Essays *(1988), from which this selection is taken. His other publications include* Bad, or The Dumbing of America *(1991),* The Anti-Egoist: Kingsley Amis, Man of Letters *(1994),* Doing Battle: The Making of a Skeptic *(1996),* Uniforms *(2002), and* The Boys' Crusade: The American Infantry in Northwestern Europe, 1944–1945 *(2003).*

In the spring Washington swarms with high school graduating classes. They come to the great pulsating heart of the Republic—which no one has yet told them is Wall Street—to be impressed by the White House and the Capitol and the monuments and the Smithsonian and the space capsules. Given the state of public secondary education, I doubt if many of these young people are at all interested in language and rhetoric, and I imagine few are fascinated by such attendants of power and pressure as verbal misrepresentation and disingenuous quotation. But any who are can profit from a stroll past the headquarters of the National Rifle Association of America, its slick marble façade conspicuous at 1600 Rhode Island Avenue, NW.

There they would see an entrance flanked by two marble panels offering language, and language more dignified and traditional than that customarily associated with the Association's gun-freak constituency, with its T-shirts reading GUNS, GUTS, AND GLORY ARE WHAT MADE AMERICA GREAT and its belt buckles proclaiming I'LL GIVE UP MY GUN WHEN THEY PRY MY COLD DEAD FINGERS FROM AROUND IT. The marble panel on the right reads, "The right of the people to keep and bear arms shall not be infringed," which sounds familiar. So familiar that the student naturally expects the left-hand panel to honor the principle of symmetry by presenting the first half of the quotation, namely: "A well-regulated Militia, being necessary to the security of a free state, . . ." But looking to the left, the inquirer discovers not that clause at all but rather this lame list of NRA functions and specializations: "Firearms Safety Education. Marksmanship Training. Shooting for Recreation." It's as if in presenting its well-washed, shiny public face the NRA doesn't want to remind anyone of the crucial dependent clause of the Second Amendment, whose latter half alone it is so fond of invoking to urge its prerogatives. (Some legible belt buckles of members retreat further into a seductive vagueness, reading only, "Our American Heritage: the Second Amendment.") We infer that for the Association, the less emphasis on the clause about the militia, the better. Hence its pretence on the front of its premises that the quoted main clause is not crucially dependent on the now unadvertised subordinate clause — indeed, it's meaningless without it.

Because flying .38- and .45-caliber bullets rank close to cancer, heart disease, and AIDS as menaces to public health in this country, the firearm lobby, led by the NRA, comes under liberal attack regularly, and with special vigor immediately after an assault on some conspicuous person like Ronald Reagan or John Lennon. Thus the *New Republic*, in April 1981, deplored the state of things but offered as a solution only the suggestion that the whole Second Amendment be perceived as obsolete and amended out of the Constitution. This would leave the NRA with not a leg to stand on.

But here as elsewhere a better solution would be not to fiddle with the Constitution but to take it seriously, the way we've done with the First Amendment, say, or with the Thirteenth, the one forbidding open and avowed slavery. And by taking the Second Amendment seriously I mean taking it literally. We should "close read" it and thus focus lots of attention on the grammatical reasoning of its two clauses. This might shame the NRA into pulling the dependent clause out of the closet, displaying it on its façade, and accepting its not entirely pleasant implications. These could be particularized in an Act of Congress providing:

(1) that the Militia shall now, after these many years, be "well-regulated," as the Constitution requires.

(2) that any person who has chosen to possess at home a gun of any kind, and who is not a member of the police or the military or an appropriate government agency, shall be deemed to have enrolled automatically in the Militia of the United States. Members of the Militia, who will be issued identifying badges, will be organized in units of battalion, company, or platoon size representing counties, towns, or boroughs. If they bear arms while not proceeding to or from scheduled exercises of the Militia, they will be punished "as a court martial may direct."

(3) that any gun owner who declines to join the regulated Militia may opt out by selling his firearms to the federal government for $1,000 each. He will sign an undertaking that if he ever again owns firearms he will be considered to have enlisted in the Militia.

(4) that because the Constitution specifically requires that the Militia shall be "well regulated," a regular training program, of the sort familiar to all who have belonged to military units charged with the orderly management of small arms, shall be instituted. This will require at least eight hours of drill each Saturday at some convenient field or park, rain or shine or snow or ice. There will be weekly supervised target practice (separation from the service, publicly announced, for those who can't hit a barn door). And there will be ample practice in digging simple defense works, like foxholes and trenches, as well as necessary sanitary installations like field latrines and straddle trenches. Each summer there will be a six-week

bivouac (without spouses), and this, like all the other exercises, will be under the close supervision of long-service noncommissioned officers of the United States Army and the Marine Corps. On bivouac, liquor will be forbidden under extreme penalty, but there will be an issue every Friday night of two cans of 3.2 beer, and feeding will follow traditional military lines, the cuisine consisting largely of shit-on-a-shingle, sandwiches made of bull dick (baloney) and choke-ass (cheese), beans, and fatty pork. On Sundays and holidays, powdered eggs for breakfast. Chlorinated water will often be available, in Lister Bags. Further obligatory exercises designed to toughen up the Militia will include twenty-five-mile hikes and the negotiation of obstacle courses. In addition, there will be instruction of the sort appropriate to other lightly armed, well-regulated military units: in map-reading, the erection of double-apron barbed-wire fences, and the rudiments of military courtesy and the traditions of the Militia, beginning with the Minute Men. Per diem payments will be made to those participating in these exercises.

(5) that since the purpose of the Militia is, as the Constitution says, to safeguard "the security of a free state," at times when invasion threatens (perhaps now the threat will come from Nicaragua, national security no longer being menaced by North Vietnam) all units of the Militia will be trucked to the borders for the duration of the emergency, there to remain in field conditions (here's where the practice in latrine-digging pays off) until Congress declares that the emergency has passed. Congress may also order the Militia to perform other duties consistent with its constitutional identity as a regulated volunteer force: for example, flood and emergency and disaster service (digging, sandbag filling, rescuing old people); patrolling angry or incinerated cities; or controlling crowds at large public events like patriotic parades, motor races, and professional football games.

(6) that failure to appear for these scheduled drills, practices, bivouacs, and mobilizations shall result in the Militiaperson's dismissal from the service and forfeiture of badge, pay, and firearm.

Why did the Framers of the Constitution add the word *bear* to the phrase "keep and bear arms?" Because they conceived that keeping arms at home implied the public obligation to bear them in a regulated way for "the security of" not a private household but "a free state." If interstate bus fares can be regulated, it is hard to see why the Militia can't be, especially since the Constitution says it must be. The *New Republic* has recognized that "the Second Amendment to the Constitution clearly connects the right to bear arms to the eighteenth-century national need to raise a militia." But it goes on: "That need is now obsolete, and so is the amendment." And it concludes: "If the only way this country can get control of firearms is to amend the Constitution, then it's time for Congress to get the process under way."

5

I think not. Rather, it's time not to amend Article II of the Bill of Rights (and Obligations) but to read it, publicize it, embrace it, and enforce it. That the Second Amendment stems from concerns that can be stigmatized as "eighteenth-century" cuts little ice. The First Amendment stems precisely from such concerns, and no one but Yahoos wants to amend it. Also "eighteenth-century" is that lovely bit in Section 9 of Article I forbidding any "Title of Nobility" to be granted by the United States. That's why we've been spared Lord Annenberg and Sir Leonard Bernstein, Knight.[1] Thank God for the eighteenth century, I say. It understood not just what a firearm is and what a Militia is. It also understood what "well regulated" means. It knew how to compose a constitutional article and it knew how to read it. And it assumed that everyone, gun lobbyists and touring students alike, would understand and correctly quote it. Both halves of it.

The Reader's Presence

1. Here is the Second Amendment of the Bill of Rights: "A well-regulated Militia being necessary to the security of a free state, the right of the people to keep and bear arms shall not be infringed." Why does Fussell point out that the first part of the amendment does not appear on the marble façade of the National Rifle Association headquarters in Washington, D.C.? Why does he believe that the first half of the amendment is crucial to a correct understanding of the second half? Do you agree? Can you think of an alternative interpretation?

2. Though he is a proponent of gun control, why doesn't Fussell believe the Second Amendment should be repealed or revised? In what ways does his interpretation preserve the Second Amendment? Do you think the National Rifle Association would endorse Fussell's proposal? Do you think it would support any aspects of it? Explain.

3. Fussell's argument turns on rereading a familiar (and in his eyes, misunderstood) text, rather than modifying it. What does Fussell mean when he says that we should "close read" the Second Amendment? How does a basic analysis of grammar and syntax support his point? What does he mean when he writes that "verbal misrepresentation and disingenuous quotation" are "attendants of power and pressure" (paragraph 1)? What might George Orwell say about Fussell's essay in light of his comments in "Politics and the English Language" (page 533)? Do Fussell and Orwell share certain assumptions? If so, what are they?

[1]*Lord Annenberg . . . Knight:* Walter H. Annenberg (1908–2002) was a controversial billionaire publisher, known both for his philanthropy and for using his publications for direct personal or political ends; Leonard H. Bernstein (1918–1990) was a massively influential composer whose many works include the score for *West Side Story.* —EDS.

John Taylor Gatto

Against School

"I've taught public school for twenty-six years but I just can't do it any-more," began an impassioned op-ed piece published in the Wall Street Journal *in 1991. Its author, John Taylor Gatto (b. 1935), continued, "I've come slowly to understand what it is I really teach: A curriculum of confusion, class position, ar-bitrary justice, vulgarity, rudeness, disrespect for privacy, indifference to quality, and utter dependency. I teach how to fit into a world I don't want to live in." With the headline "I May Be a Teacher but I'm Not an Educator," the essay set off a fierce debate among parents, teachers, and politicians about the system of public education in the United States. It also launched Gatto's career as a speaker, consultant, and writer.*

After graduating from Columbia University, Gatto worked as a scriptwriter, songwriter, and ad writer; drove a cab; sold hot dogs; and finally, began a distin-guished career as a schoolteacher. He was recognized as New York City Teacher of the Year for three years running. In 1991, the year he resigned in protest from his position as a seventh-grade teacher at the Booker T. Washington School in New York City, he was named New York State Teacher of the Year. He has edited and written many books on education, including The Exhausted School *(1993),* Dumbing Us Down *(1992),* A Different Kind of Teacher *(2000), and* Un-derground History of American Education *(2001). His essay "Against School" first appeared in* Harper's *magazine in 2001.*

I taught for thirty years in some of the worst schools in Manhattan, and in some of the best, and during that time I became an expert in bore-dom. Boredom was everywhere in my world, and if you asked the kids, as I often did, *why* they felt so bored, they always gave the same answers: They said the work was stupid, that it made no sense, that they already knew it. They said they wanted to be doing something real, not just sit-ting around. They said teachers didn't seem to know much about their subjects and clearly weren't interested in learning more. And the kids were right: their teachers were every bit as bored as they were.

Boredom is the common condition of schoolteachers, and anyone who has spent time in a teachers' lounge can vouch for the low energy, the whining, the dispirited attitudes, to be found there. When asked why *they* feel bored, the teachers tend to blame the kids, as you might expect. Who wouldn't get bored teaching students who are rude and interested only in grades? If even that. Of course, teachers are themselves products of the same twelve-year compulsory school programs that so thoroughly bore their students, and as school personnel they are trapped inside struc-tures even more rigid than those imposed upon the children. Who, then, is to blame?

We all are. My grandfather taught me that. One afternoon when I was seven I complained to him of boredom, and he batted me hard on the head. He told me that I was never to use that term in his presence again, that if I was bored it was my fault and no one else's. The obligation to amuse and instruct myself was entirely my own, and people who didn't know that were childish people, to be avoided if possible. Certainly not to be trusted. That episode cured me of boredom forever, and here and there over the years I was able to pass on the lesson to some remarkable student. For the most part, however, I found it futile to challenge the official notion that boredom and childishness were the natural state of affairs in the classroom. Often I had to defy custom, and even bend the law, to help kids break out of this trap.

The empire struck back, of course; childish adults regularly conflate opposition with disloyalty. I once returned from a medical leave to discover that all evidence of my having been granted the leave had been purposely destroyed, that my job had been terminated, and that I no longer possessed even a teaching license. After nine months of tormented effort I was able to retrieve the license when a school secretary testified to witnessing the plot unfold. In the meantime my family suffered more than I care to remember. By the time I finally retired in 1991, I had more than enough reason to think of our schools — with their long-term, cell-block–style, forced confinement of both students and teachers — as virtual factories of childishness. Yet I honestly could not see *why* they had to be that way. My own experience had revealed to me what many other teachers must learn along the way, too, yet keep to themselves for fear of reprisal: if we wanted to we could easily and inexpensively jettison the old, stupid structures and help kids *take* an education rather than merely *receive* a schooling. We could encourage the best qualities of youthfulness — curiosity, adventure, resilience, the capacity for surprising insight — simply by being more flexible about time, texts, and tests, by introducing kids to truly competent adults, and by giving each student what autonomy he or she needs in order to take a risk every now and then.

But we don't do that. And the more I asked why not, and persisted in thinking about the "problem" of schooling as an engineer might, the more I missed the point: What if there is no "problem" with our schools? What if they are the way they are, so expensively flying in the face of common sense and long experience in how children learn things, not because they are doing something wrong but because they are doing something right? Is it possible that George W. Bush accidentally spoke the truth when he said we would "leave no child behind"? Could it be that our schools are designed to make sure not one of them ever really grows up?

5

Do we really need school? I don't mean education, just forced schooling: six classes a day, five days a week, nine months a year, for twelve years. Is this deadly routine really necessary? And if so, for what? Don't hide behind reading, writing, and arithmetic as a rationale, because two million happy homeschoolers have surely put that banal justification to rest. Even if they hadn't, a considerable number of well-known Americans never went through the twelve-year wringer our kids currently go through, and they turned out all right. George Washington, Benjamin Franklin, Thomas Jefferson, Abraham Lincoln? Someone taught them, to be sure, but they were not products of a school *system*, and not one of them was ever "graduated" from a secondary school. Throughout most of American history, kids generally didn't go to high school, yet the unschooled rose to be admirals, like Farragut; inventors, like Edison; captains of industry, like Carnegie and Rockefeller; writers, like Melville and Twain and Conrad; and even scholars, like Margaret Mead.[1] In fact, until pretty recently people who reached the age of thirteen weren't looked upon as children at all. Ariel Durant, who co-wrote an enormous, and very good, multivolume history of the world with her husband, Will, was happily married at fifteen, and who could reasonably claim that Ariel Durant was an uneducated person? Unschooled, perhaps, but not uneducated.

We have been taught (that is, schooled) in this country to think of "success" as synonymous with, or at least dependent upon, "schooling," but historically that isn't true in either an intellectual or a financial sense. And plenty of people throughout the world today find a way to educate themselves without resorting to a system of compulsory secondary schools that all too often resemble prisons. Why, then, do Americans confuse education with just such a system? What exactly is the purpose of our public schools?

Mass schooling of a compulsory nature really got its teeth into the United States between 1905 and 1915, though it was conceived of much earlier and pushed for throughout most of the nineteenth century. The reason given for this enormous upheaval of family life and cultural traditions was, roughly speaking, threefold:

1) To make good people.
2) To make good citizens.
3) To make each person his or her personal best.

These goals are still trotted out today on a regular basis, and most of us accept them in one form or another as a decent definition of public education's mission, however short schools actually fall in achieving them. But we are dead wrong. Compounding our error is the fact that the national literature holds numerous and surprisingly consistent statements of compulsory schooling's true purpose. We have, for example, the great

---

[1]*Margaret Mead:* Mead (1901–1978) became the most famous anthropologist in the world, best known for *Coming of Age in Samoa* (1928), a book that analyzed cultural influence on adolescence. —EDS.

H. L. Mencken,[2] who wrote in *The American Mercury* for April 1924 that the aim of public education is not

> to fill the young of the species with knowledge and awaken their intelligence. . . . Nothing could be further from the truth. The aim . . . is simply to reduce as many individuals as possible to the same safe level, to breed and train a standardized citizenry, to put down dissent and originality. That is its aim in the United States . . . and that is its aim everywhere else.

Because of Mencken's reputation as a satirist, we might be tempted to dismiss this passage as a bit of hyperbolic sarcasm. His article, however, goes on to trace the template for our own educational system back to the now vanished, though never to be forgotten, military state of Prussia. And although he was certainly aware of the irony that we had recently been at war with Germany, the heir to Prussian thought and culture, Mencken was being perfectly serious here. Our educational system really is Prussian in origin, and that really is cause for concern.

The odd fact of a Prussian provenance for our schools pops up again   10 and again once you know to look for it. William James alluded to it many times at the turn of the century. Orestes Brownson, the hero of Christopher Lasch's 1991 book, *The True and Only Heaven*, was publicly denouncing the Prussianization of American schools back in the 1840s. Horace Mann's "Seventh Annual Report" to the Massachusetts State Board of Education in 1843 is essentially a paean to the land of Frederick the Great and a call for its schooling to be brought here. That Prussian culture loomed large in America is hardly surprising, given our early association with that utopian state. A Prussian served as Washington's aide during the Revolutionary War, and so many German-speaking people had settled here by 1795 that Congress considered publishing a German-language edition of the federal laws. But what shocks is that we should so eagerly have adopted one of the very worst aspects of Prussian culture: an educational system deliberately designed to produce mediocre intellects, to hamstring the inner life, to deny students appreciable leadership skills, and to ensure docile and incomplete citizens—all in order to render the populace "manageable."

It was from James Bryant Conant—president of Harvard for twenty years, WWI poison-gas specialist, WWII executive on the atomic-bomb project, high commissioner of the American zone in Germany after WWII, and truly one of the most influential figures of the twentieth century— that I first got wind of the real purposes of American schooling. Without Conant, we would probably not have the same style and degree of standardized testing that we enjoy today, nor would we be blessed with gargantuan high schools that warehouse 2,000 to 4,000 students at a time,

---

[2]For more on H. L. Mencken, see page 504.

like the famous Columbine High in Littleton, Colorado. Shortly after I retired from teaching I picked up Conant's 1959 book-length essay, *The Child the Parent and the State*, and was more than a little intrigued to see him mention in passing that the modern schools we attend were the result of a "revolution" engineered between 1905 and 1930. A revolution? He declines to elaborate, but he does direct the curious and the uninformed to Alexander Inglis's 1918 book, *Principles of Secondary Education*, in which "one saw this revolution through the eyes of a revolutionary."

Inglis, for whom a lecture in education at Harvard is named, makes it perfectly clear that compulsory schooling on this continent was intended to be just what it had been for Prussia in the 1820s: a fifth column into the burgeoning democratic movement that threatened to give the peasants and the proletarians a voice at the bargaining table. Modern, industrialized, compulsory schooling was to make a sort of surgical incision into the prospective unity of these underclasses. Divide children by subject, by age-grading, by constant rankings on tests, and by many other more subtle means, and it was unlikely that the ignorant mass of mankind, separated in childhood, would ever re-integrate into a dangerous whole.

Inglis breaks down the purpose—the *actual* purpose—of modern schooling into six basic functions, any one of which is enough to curl the hair of those innocent enough to believe the three traditional goals listed earlier:

1) The *adjustive* or *adaptive* function. Schools are to establish fixed habits of reaction to authority. This, of course, precludes critical judgment completely. It also pretty much destroys the idea that useful or interesting material should be taught, because you can't test for *reflexive* obedience until you know whether you can make kids learn, and do, foolish and boring things.

2) The *integrating* function. This might well be called "the conformity function," because its intention is to make children as alike as possible. People who conform are predictable, and this is of great use to those who wish to harness and manipulate a large labor force.

3) The *diagnostic and directive* function. School is meant to determine each student's proper social role. This is done by logging evidence mathematically and anecdotally on cumulative records. As in "your permanent record." Yes, you do have one.

4) The *differentiating* function. Once their social role has been "diagnosed," children are to be sorted by role and trained only so far as their destination in the social machine merits—and not one step further. So much for making kids their personal best.

5) The *selective* function. This refers not to human choice at all but to Darwin's theory of natural selection as applied to what he called "the favored races." In short, the idea is to help things

along by consciously attempting to improve the breeding stock. Schools are meant to tag the unfit—with poor grades, remedial placement, and other punishments—clearly enough that their peers will accept them as inferior and effectively bar them from the reproductive sweepstakes. That's what all those little humiliations from first grade onward were intended to do: wash the dirt down the drain.

6) The *propaedeutic* function. The societal system implied by these rules will require an elite group of caretakers. To that end, a small fraction of the kids will quietly be taught how to manage this continuing project, how to watch over and control a population deliberately dumbed down and declawed in order that government might proceed unchallenged and corporations might never want for obedient labor.

That, unfortunately, is the purpose of mandatory public education in this country. And lest you take Inglis for an isolated crank with a rather too cynical take on the educational enterprise, you should know that he was hardly alone in championing these ideas. Conant himself, building on the ideas of Horace Mann and others, campaigned tirelessly for an American school system designed along the same lines. Men like George Peabody, who funded the cause of mandatory schooling throughout the South, surely understood that the Prussian system was useful in creating not only a harmless electorate and a servile labor force but also a virtual herd of mindless consumers. In time a great number of industrial titans came to recognize the enormous profits to be had by cultivating and tending just such a herd via public education, among them Andrew Carnegie and John D. Rockefeller.

There you have it. Now you know. We don't need Karl Marx's conception of a grand warfare between the classes to see that it is in the interest of complex management, economic or political, to dumb people down, to demoralize them, to divide them from one another, and to discard them if they don't conform. Class may frame the proposition, as when Woodrow Wilson, then president of Princeton University, said the following to the New York City School Teachers Association in 1909: "We want one class of persons to have a liberal education, and we want another class of persons, a very much larger class, of necessity, in every society, to forgo the privileges of a liberal education and fit themselves to perform specific difficult manual tasks." But the motives behind the disgusting decisions that bring about these ends need not be class-based at all. They can stem purely from fear, or from the by now familiar belief that "efficiency" is the paramount virtue, rather than love, liberty, laughter, or hope. Above all, they can stem from simple greed.

There were vast fortunes to be made, after all, in an economy based on mass production and organized to favor the large corporation rather

15

than the small business or the family farm. But mass production required mass consumption, and at the turn of the twentieth century most Americans considered it both unnatural and unwise to buy things they didn't actually need. Mandatory schooling was a godsend on that count. School didn't have to train kids in any direct sense to think they should consume nonstop, because it did something even better: it encouraged them not to think at all. And that left them sitting ducks for another great invention of the modern era—marketing.

Now, you needn't have studied marketing to know that there are two groups of people who can always be convinced to consume more than they need to: addicts and children. School has done a pretty good job of turning our children into addicts, but it has done a spectacular job of turning our children into children. Again, this is no accident. Theorists from Plato to Rousseau to our own Dr. Inglis knew that if children could be cloistered with other children, stripped of responsibility and independence, encouraged to develop only the trivializing emotions of greed, envy, jealousy, and fear, they would grow older but never truly grow up. In the 1934 edition of his once well-known book *Public Education in the United States*, Ellwood P. Cubberley detailed and praised the way the strategy of successive school enlargements had extended childhood by two to six years, and forced schooling was at that point still quite new. This same Cubberley—who was dean of Stanford's School of Education, a textbook editor at Houghton Mifflin, and Conant's friend and correspondent at Harvard—had written the following in the 1922 edition of his book *Public School Administration*: "Our schools are . . . factories in which the raw products (children) are to be shaped and fashioned. . . . And it is the business of the school to build its pupils according to the specifications laid down."

It's perfectly obvious from our society today what those specifications were. Maturity has by now been banished from nearly every aspect of our lives. Easy divorce laws have removed the need to work at relationships; easy credit has removed the need for fiscal self-control; easy entertainment has removed the need to learn to entertain oneself; easy answers have removed the need to ask questions. We have become a nation of children, happy to surrender our judgments and our wills to political exhortations and commercial blandishments that would insult actual adults. We buy televisions, and then we buy the things we see on the television. We buy computers, and then we buy the things we see on the computer. We buy $150 sneakers whether we need them or not, and when they fall apart too soon we buy another pair. We drive SUVs and believe the lie that they constitute a kind of life insurance, even when we're upside-down in them. And, worst of all, we don't bat an eye when Ari Fleischer[3] tells us to "be careful what you

---

[3]*Ari Fleischer:* White House Press Secretary under President George W. Bush from 2001 to 2003.—EDS.

say," even if we remember having been told somewhere back in school that America is the land of the free. We simply buy that one too. Our schooling, as intended, has seen to it.

Now for the good news. Once you understand the logic behind modern schooling, its tricks and traps are fairly easy to avoid. School trains children to be employees and consumers; teach your own to be leaders and adventurers. School trains children to obey reflexively; teach your own to think critically and independently. Well-schooled kids have a low threshold for boredom; help your own to develop an inner life so that they'll never be bored. Urge them to take on the serious material, the *grown-up* material, in history, literature, philosophy, music, art, economics, theology—all the stuff schoolteachers know well enough to avoid. Challenge your kids with plenty of solitude so that they can learn to enjoy their own company, to conduct inner dialogues. Well-schooled people are conditioned to dread being alone, and they seek constant companionship through the TV, the computer, the cell phone, and through shallow friendships quickly acquired and quickly abandoned. Your children should have a more meaningful life, and they can.

First, though, we must wake up to what our schools really are: laboratories of experimentation on young minds, drill centers for the habits and attitudes that corporate society demands. Mandatory education serves children only incidentally; its real purpose is to turn them into servants. Don't let your own have their childhoods extended, not even for a day. If David Farragut could take command of a captured British warship as a preteen, if Thomas Edison could publish a broadsheet at the age of twelve, if Ben Franklin could apprentice himself to a printer at the same age (then put himself through a course of study that would choke a Yale senior today), there's no telling what your own kids could do. After a long life, and thirty years in the public school trenches, I've concluded that genius is as common as dirt. We suppress our genius only because we haven't yet figured out how to manage a population of educated men and women. The solution, I think, is simple and glorious. Let them manage themselves. 20

The Reader's Presence

1. Would you agree with Gatto that compulsory schooling has the effect of creating conformity and obedience to authority? Why or why not? To what extent does schooling attempt to form citizens? To what extent are students trained to be consumers?

2. Gatto makes a distinction between "education" and "schooling." What is significant about this distinction? What are the consequences of conflating the two?

3. Gatto argues that compulsory schooling can effectively prevent students from becoming independent thinkers. Read Joseph Epstein's "The Perpetual Adolescent" (page 396). Do you think Epstein would agree that schooling is at least partly responsible for resistance to adulthood? Do you agree? Why or why not?

William Gibson

The Net Is a Waste of Time

William Gibson was born in 1948 in Conway, South Carolina, and now lives with his wife and children in Vancouver, British Columbia. Since Gibson coined the term cyberspace and used it in his 1984 Neuromancer—*a debut novel that won all three major science fiction awards (the Hugo, Nebula, and Philip K. Dick awards)—he has been the foremost practitioner of the "cyberpunk" genre. Gibson's other novels include* Count Zero *(1986),* Mona Lisa Overdrive *(1988),* Virtual Light *(1993),* Idoru *(1999), and* All Tomorrow's Parties *(1999). He has also written a screenplay,* Johnny Mnemonic *(1995), and an episode of the television show* The X-Files. *Gibson is known for writing slowly and for being somewhat reclusive. Although he believes "most social change is technology-driven," until recently he did not have an e-mail address. (Today, however, he has his own Web site and blog.)*

The essay "The Net Is a Waste of Time" first appeared in the New York Times Magazine *in 1996.*

I coined the word "cyberspace" in 1981 in one of my first science fiction stories and subsequently used it to describe something that people insist on seeing as a sort of literary forerunner of the Internet. This being so, some think it remarkable that I do not use E-mail. In all truth, I have avoided it because I am lazy and enjoy staring blankly into space (which is also the space where novels come from) and because unanswered mail, e- or otherwise, is a source of discomfort.

But I have recently become an avid browser of the World Wide Web. Some people find this odd. My wife finds it positively perverse. I, however, scent big changes afoot, possibilities that were never quite as manifest in earlier incarnations of the Net.

I was born in 1948. I can't recall a world before television, but I know I must have experienced one. I do, dimly, recall the arrival of a piece of brown wooden furniture with sturdy Bakelite knobs and a screen no larger than the screen on this Powerbook.

Initially there was nothing on it but "snow," and then the nightly advent of a targetlike device called "the test pattern," which people actually gathered to watch.

Today I think about the test pattern as I surf the Web. I imagine that the   5 World Wide Web and its modest wonders are no more than the test pattern for whatever the twenty-first century will regard as its equivalent medium. Not that I can even remotely imagine what that medium might actually be.

In the age of wooden television in the South where I grew up, leisure involved sitting on screened porches, smoking cigarettes, drinking iced tea, engaging in conversation and staring into space. It might also involve fishing.

Sometimes the Web does remind me of fishing. It never reminds me of conversation, although it can feel a lot like staring into space. "Surfing the Web" (as dubious a metaphor as "the information highway") is, as a friend of mind has it, "like reading magazines with the pages stuck together." My wife shakes her head in dismay as I patiently await the downloading of some Japanese Beatles fan's personal catalogue of bootlegs. "But it's from Japan!" She isn't moved. She goes out to enjoy the flowers in her garden.

I stay in. Hooked. Is this leisure—this browsing, randomly linking my way through these small patches of virtual real-estate—or do I somehow imagine that I am performing some more dynamic function? The content of the Web aspires to absolute variety. One might find anything there. It is like rummaging in the forefront of the collective global mind. Somewhere, surely, there is a site that contains . . . everything we have lost?

The finest and most secret pleasure afforded new users of the Web rests in submitting to the search engine of Alta Vista the names of people we may not have spoken aloud in years. Will she be here? Has he survived unto this age? (She isn't there. Someone with his name has recently posted to a news group concerned with gossip about soap stars.) What is this casting of the nets of identity? Do we engage here in something of a tragic seriousness?

In the age of wooden television, media were there to entertain, to sell   10 an advertiser's product, perhaps to inform. Watching television, then, could indeed be considered a leisure activity. In our hypermediated age, we have come to suspect that watching television constitutes a species of work. Post-industrial creatures of an information economy, we increasingly sense that accessing media is what we do. We have become terminally self-conscious. There is no such thing as simple entertainment. We watch ourselves watching. We watch ourselves watching Beavis and Butthead, who are watching rock videos. Simply to watch, without the buffer of irony in place, might reveal a fatal naïveté.

But that is our response to aging media like film and television, survivors from the age of wood. The Web is new, and our response to it has not yet hardened. That is a large part of its appeal. It is something half-formed, growing. Larval. It is not what it was six months ago; in another six months it will be something else again. It was not planned; it simply happened, is happening. It is happening the way cities happened. It *is* a city.

Toward the end of the age of wooden televisions the futurists of the Sunday supplements announced the advent of the "leisure society." Technology would leave us less and less to do in the Marxian sense of yanking the levers of production. The challenge, then, would be to fill our days with meaningful, healthful, satisfying activity. As with most products of an earlier era's futurism, we find it difficult today to imagine the exact coordinates from which this vision came. In any case, our world does not offer us a surplus of leisure. The word itself has grown somehow suspect, as quaint and vaguely melancholy as the battered leather valise in a Ralph Lauren window display. Only the very old or the economically disadvantaged (provided they are not chained to the schedules of their environment's more demanding addictions) have a great deal of time on their hands. To be successful, apparently, is to be chronically busy. As new technologies search out and lace over every interstice in the net of global communication, we find ourselves with increasingly less excuse for . . . slack.

And that, I would argue, is what the World Wide Web, the test pattern for whatever will become the dominant global medium, offers us. Today, in its clumsy, larval, curiously innocent way, it offers us the opportunity to waste time, to wander aimlessly, to daydream about the countless other lives, the other people, on the far sides of however many monitors in that postgeographical meta-country we increasingly call home. It will probably evolve into something considerably less random, and less fun—we seem to have a knack for that—but in the meantime, in its gloriously unsorted Global Ham[1] Television Postcard Universes phase, surfing the Web is a procrastinator's dream. And people who see you doing it might even imagine you're working.

The Reader's Presence

1. Of what importance is the age of television to Gibson's point about the World Wide Web? Why is television an "aging" medium? In what ways does he believe the Web differs from television?

2. How does Gibson reach his conclusion that the best thing about the Web is that it "offers us the opportunity to waste time" (paragraph 13)? Why is that an advantage of this new "global medium"? Go back through the essay and explain how Gibson establishes the grounds for his conclusion.

---

[1] *Global Ham:* Ham radio is amateur radio with mostly local or personal applications, its operators licensed by the government but forbidden to broadcast to the general public. — EDS.

3. Read Gibson's essay in conjunction with Marie Winn's "TV Addiction" (see page 608). Do you find any similarities between the way these two writers describe television? Winn was writing before the Internet had become a household reality. Does her description of television support Gibson's argument? Would you say that people are no longer addicted to television but are addicted now to the Internet?

Vicki Hearne

What's Wrong with Animal Rights

Vicki Hearne (1946–2001) had a unique career as a poet, author, and animal trainer, and taught creative writing at Yale University and at the University of California. She published three volumes of poetry, Nervous Horses *(1980),* In the Absence of Horses *(1983), and* The Parts of Light *(1994). Hearne was known for her ability to train aggressive dogs (particularly pit bull terriers), and she wrote an account of her experiences in* Bandit: Dossier of a Dangerous Dog *(1991). Her other books include* Adam's Task: Calling Animals by Name *(1987),* The White German Shepherd *(1988), and* Animal Happiness *(1994). "What's Wrong with Animal Rights" was originally published in* Harper's *in 1991 and was selected for* The Best American Essays 1992.

Not all happy animals are alike. A Doberman going over a hurdle after a small wooden dumbbell is sleek, all arcs of harmonious power. A basset hound cheerfully performing the same exercise exhibits harmonies of a more lugubrious nature. There are chimpanzees who love precision the way musicians or fanatical housekeepers or accomplished hypochondriacs do; others for whom happiness is a matter of invention and variation — chimp vaudevillians. There is a rhinoceros whose happiness, as near as I can make out, is in needing to be trained every morning, all over again, or else he "forgets" his circus routine, and in this you find a clue to the slow, deep, quiet chuckle of his happiness and to the glory of the beast. Happiness for Secretariat is in his ebullient bound, that joyful length of stride. For the draft horse or the weight-pull dog, happiness is of a different shape, more awesome and less obviously intelligent. When the pulling horse is at its most intense, the animal goes into himself, allocating all of the educated power that organizes his desire to dwell in fierce and

delicate intimacy with that power, leans into the harness, and MAKES
THAT SUCKER MOVE.

If we are speaking of human beings and use the phrase "animal happiness," we tend to mean something like "creature comforts." The emblems of this are the golden retriever rolling in the grass, the horse with his
nose deep in the oats, the kitty by the fire. Creature comforts are important to animals—"Grub first, then ethics" is a motto that would describe
many a wise Labrador retriever, and I have a pit bull named Annie whose
continual quest for the perfect pillow inspires her to awesome feats. But
there is something more to animals, a capacity for satisfactions that come
from work in the fullest sense—what is known in philosophy and in this
country's Declaration of Independence as "happiness." This is a sense of
personal achievement, like the satisfaction felt by a good wood-carver or a
dancer or a poet or an accomplished dressage horse. It is a happiness that,
like the artist's must come from something within the animal, something
trainers call "talent." Hence, it cannot be imposed on the animal. But it is
also something that does not come *ex nihilo*. If it had not been a fairly ordinary thing, in one part of the world, to teach young children to play the
pianoforte, it is doubtful that Mozart's music would exist.

Happiness is often misunderstood as a synonym for pleasure or as an
antonym for suffering. But Aristotle associated happiness with ethics—
codes of behavior that urge us toward the sensation of getting it right, a
kind of work that yields the "click" of satisfaction upon solving a problem
or surmounting an obstacle. In his *Ethics*, Aristotle wrote, "If happiness is
activity in accordance with excellence, it is reasonable that it should be in
accordance with the highest excellence." Thomas Jefferson identified the
capacity for happiness as one of the three fundamental rights on which all
others are based: "life, liberty, and the pursuit of happiness."

I bring up this idea of happiness as a form of work because I am an
animal trainer, and work is the foundation of the happiness a trainer and
an animal discover together. I bring up these words also because they
cannot be found in the lexicon of the animal-rights movement. This absence accounts for the uneasiness toward the movement of most people,
who sense that rights advocates have a point but take it too far when they
liberate snails or charge that goldfish at the county fair are suffering. But
the problem with the animal-rights advocates is not that they take it too
far; it's that they've got it all wrong.

Animal rights are built upon a misconceived premise that rights were   5
created to prevent us from unnecessary suffering. You can't find an animal-
rights book, video, pamphlet, or rock concert in which someone doesn't
mention the Great Sentence, written by Jeremy Bentham in 1789. Arguing
in favor of such rights, Bentham wrote: "The question is not, Can they
reason? nor, can they *talk*? but, can they suffer?"

The logic of the animal-rights movement places suffering at the icono-
graphic center of a skewed value system. The thinking of its proponents—
given eerie expression in a virtually sado-pornographic sculpture of a

tortured monkey that won a prize for its compassionate vision—has collapsed into a perverse conundrum. Today the loudest voices calling for—demanding—the destruction of animals are the humane organizations. This is an inevitable consequence of the apotheosis of the drive to relieve suffering: death is the ultimate release. To compensate for their contradictions, the humane movement has demonized, in this century and the last, those who made animal happiness their business: veterinarians, trainers, and the like. We think of Louis Pasteur as the man whose work saved you and me and your dog and cat from rabies, but antivivisectionists of the time claimed that rabies increased in areas where there were Pasteur Institutes.

An anti-rabies public relations campaign mounted in England in the 1880s by the Royal Society for the Prevention of Cruelty to Animals and other organizations led to orders being issued to club any dog found not wearing a muzzle. England still has her cruel and unnecessary law that requires an animal to spend six months in quarantine before being allowed loose in the country. Most of the recent propaganda about pit bulls—the crazy claim that they "take hold with their front teeth while they chew away with their rear teeth" (which would imply, incorrectly, that they have double jaws)—can be traced to literature published by the Humane Society of the United States during the fall of 1987 and earlier. If your neighbors want your dog or horse impounded and destroyed because he is a nuisance—say the dog barks, or the horse attracts flies—it will be the local Humane Society to whom your neighbors turn for action.

In a way, everyone has the opportunity to know that the history of the humane movement is largely a history of miseries, arrests, prosecutions, and death. The Humane Society is the pound, the place with the decompression chamber or the lethal injections. You occasionally find worried letters about this in Ann Landers's column.

Animal-rights publications are illustrated largely with photographs of two kinds of animals—"Helpless Fluff" and "Agonized Fluff," the two conditions in which some people seem to prefer their animals, because any other version of an animal is too complicated for propaganda. In the introduction to his book *Animal Liberation*, Peter Singer[1] says somewhat smugly that he and his wife have no animals and, in fact, don't much care for them. This is offered as evidence of his objectivity and ethical probity. But it strikes me as an odd, perhaps, obscene underpinning for an ethical project that encourages university and high school students to cherish their ignorance of, say, great bird dogs as proof of their devotion to animals.

I would like to leave these philosophers behind, for they are inept   10
connoisseurs of suffering who might revere my Airedale for his capacity to scream when subjected to a blowtorch but not for his wit and courage, not for his natural good manners that are a gentle rebuke to ours. I want

[1]For more on Peter Singer, see page 800.—EDS.

to celebrate the moment not long ago when, at his first dog show, my Airedale, Drummer, learned that there can be a public place where his work is respected. I want to celebrate his meticulousness, his happiness upon realizing at the dog show that no one would swoop down upon him and swamp him with the goo-goo excesses known as the "teddy-bear complex" but that people actually got out of his way, gave him room to work. I want to say, "There can be a six-and-a-half-month-old puppy who can care about accuracy, who can be fastidious, and whose fastidiousness will be a foundation for courage later." I want to say, "Leave my puppy alone!"

I want to leave the philosophers behind, but I cannot, in part because the philosophical problems that plague academicians of the animal-rights movement are illuminating. They wonder, do animals have rights or do they have interests? Or, if these rightists lead particularly unexamined lives, they dismiss that question as obvious (yes, of course animals have rights, prima facie) and proceed to enumerate them, James Madison style. This leads to the issuance of bills of rights—the right to an environment, the right not to be used in medical experiments—and other forms of trivialization.

The calculus of suffering can be turned against the philosophers of festering flesh, even in the case of food animals, or exotic animals who perform in movies and circuses. It is true that it hurts to be slaughtered by man, but it doesn't hurt nearly as much as some of the cunningly cruel arrangements meted out by "Mother Nature." In Africa, 75 percent of the lions cubbed do not survive to the age of two. For those who make it to two, the average age at death is ten years. Asali, the movie and TV lioness, was still working at age twenty-one. There are fates worse than death, but twenty-one years of a close working relationship with Hubert Wells, Asali's trainer, is not one of them. Dorset sheep and polled Herefords would not exist at all were they not in a symbiotic relationship with human beings.

A human being living in the "wild"—somewhere, say, without the benefits of medicine and advanced social organization—would probably have a life expectancy of from thirty to thirty-five years. A human being living in "captivity"—in, say, a middle-class neighborhood of what the Centers for Disease Control call a Metropolitan Statistical Area—has a life expectancy of seventy or more years. For orangutans in the wild in Borneo and Malaysia, the life expectancy is thirty-five years; in captivity, fifty years. The wild is not a suffering-free zone or all that frolicsome a location.

The questions asked by animal-rights activists are flawed, because they are built on the concept that the origin of rights is in the avoidance of suffering rather than in the pursuit of happiness. The question that needs to be asked—and that will put us in closer proximity to the truth—is not, do they have rights? or, what are those rights? but rather, what is a right?

Rights originate in committed relationships and can be found, both 15 intact and violated, wherever one finds such relationships—in social compacts, within families, between animals, and between people and non-human animals. This is as true when the nonhuman animals in question are lions or parakeets as when they are dogs. It is my Airedale whose excellencies have my attention at the moment, so it is with reference to him that I will consider the question, what is a right?

When I imagine situations in which it naturally arises that A defends or honors or respects B's rights, I imagine situations in which the relationship between A and B can be indicated with a possessive pronoun. I might say, "Leave her alone, she's my daughter" or "That's what she wants, and she is my daughter. I think I am bound to honor her wants." Similarly, "Leave her alone, she's my mother." I am more tender of the happiness of my mother, my father, my child, than I am of other people's family members; more tender of my friends' happinesses than your friends' happinesses, unless you and I have a mutual friend.

Possession of a being by another has come into more and more disrepute, so that the common understanding of one person possessing another is slavery. But the important detail about the kind of possessive pronoun that I have in mind is reciprocity: if I have a friend, she has a friend. If I have a daughter, she has a mother. The possessive does not bind one of us while freeing the other; it cannot do that. Moreover, should the mother reject the daughter, the word that applies is "disown." The form of disowning that most often appears in the news is domestic violence. Parents abuse children; husbands batter wives.

Some cases of reciprocal possessives have built-in limitations, such as "my patient / my doctor" or "my student / my teacher" or "my agent / my client." Other possessive relations are extremely limited but still remarkably binding: "my neighbor" and "my country" and "my president."

The responsibilities and the ties signaled by reciprocal possession typically are hard to dissolve. It can be as difficult to give up an enemy as to give up a friend, and often the one becomes the other, as though the logic of the possessive pronoun outlasts the forms it chanced to take at a given moment, as though we were stuck with one another. In these bindings, nearly inextricable, are found the origin of our rights. They imply a possessiveness but also recognize an acknowledgment by each side of the other's existence.

The idea of democracy is dependent on the citizens' having knowledge of the government; that is, realizing that the government exists and knowing how to claim rights against it. I know this much because I get mail from the government and see its "representatives" running about in uniforms. Whether I actually have any rights in relationship to the government is less clear, but the idea that I do is symbolized by the right to vote. I obey the government, and, in theory, it obeys me, by counting my ballot, reading the *Miranda* warning to me, agreeing to be bound by the Constitution. My friend obeys me as I obey her; the government "obeys" me to some extent, and, to a different extent, I obey it.

What kind of thing can my Airedale, Drummer, have knowledge of? He can know that I exist and through that knowledge can claim his happinesses, with varying degrees of success, both with me and against me. Drummer can also know about larger human or dog communities than the one that consists only of him and me. There is my household—the other dogs, the cats, my husband. I have had enough dogs on campuses to know that he can learn that Yale exists as a neighborhood or village. My older dog, Annie, not only knows that Yale exists but can tell Yalies from townies, as I learned while teaching there during labor troubles.

Dogs can have elaborate conceptions of human social structures, and even of something like their rights and responsibilities within them, but these conceptions are never elaborate enough to construct a rights relationship between a dog and the state, or a dog and the Humane Society. Both of these are concepts that depend on writing and memoranda, officers in uniform, plaques and seals of authority. All of these are literary constructs, and all of them are beyond a dog's ken, which is why the mail carrier who doesn't also happen to be a dog's friend is forever an intruder—this is why dogs bark at mailmen.

It is clear enough that natural rights relations can arise between people and animals. Drummer, for example, can insist, "Hey, let's go outside and do something!" if I have been at my computer several days on end. He can both refuse to accept various of my suggestions and tell me when he fears for his life—such as the time when the huge, white flapping flag appeared out of nowhere, as it seemed to him, on the town green one evening when we were working. I can (and do) say to him either, "Oh, you don't have to worry about that" or, "Uh oh, you're right, Drum, that guy looks dangerous." Just as the government and I—two different species of organism—have developed improvised ways of communicating, such as the vote, so Drummer and I have worked out a number of ways to make our expressions known. Largely through obedience, I have taught him a fair amount about how to get responses from me. Obedience is reciprocal; you cannot get responses from a dog to whom you do not respond accurately. I have enfranchised him in a relationship to me by educating him, creating the conditions by which he can achieve a certain happiness specific to a dog, maybe even specific to an Airedale, inasmuch as this same relationship has allowed me to plumb the happiness of being a trainer and writing this article.

Instructions in this happiness are given terms that are alien to a culture in which liver treats, fluffy windup toys, and miniature sweaters are confused with respect and work. Jack Knox, a sheepdog trainer originally from Scotland, will shake his crook at a novice handler who makes a promiscuous move to praise a dog, and will call out in his Scottish accent, "Eh! Eh! Get back, get BACK! Ye'll no be abusin' the dogs like that in my clinic." America is a nation of abused animals. Knox says, because we are always swooping at them with praise, "no gi'ing them their freedom." I am reminded of Rainer Maria Rilke's account in which the Prodigal Son leaves—has to leave—because everyone loves him, even the dogs love him, and he has no path to the delicate and fierce truth of himself. Unconditional praise and love, in Rilke's story, disenfranchise us, distract us from what truly excites our interest.

In the minds of some trainers and handlers, praise is dishonesty.   25
Paradoxically, it is a kind of contempt for animals that masquerades as a

reverence for helplessness and suffering. The idea of freedom means that you do not, at least not while Jack Knox is nearby, helpfully guide your dog through the motions of, say, herding over and over—what one trainer calls "explainy-wainy." This is rote learning. It works tolerably well on some handlers, because people have vast unconscious minds and can store complex preprogrammed behaviors. Dogs, on the other hand, have almost no unconscious minds, so they can learn only by thinking. Many children are like this until educated out of it.

If I tell my Airedale to sit and stay on the town green, and someone comes up and burbles, "What a pretty thing you are," he may break his stay to go for a caress. I pull him back and correct him for breaking. Now he holds his stay because I have blocked his way to movement but not because I have punished him. (A correction blocks one path as it opens another for desire to work; punishment blocks desire and opens nothing.) He holds his stay now, and—because the stay opens this possibility of work, new to a heedless young dog—he watches. If the person goes on talking, and isn't going to gush with praise, I may heel Drummer out of his stay and give him an "Okay" to make friends. Sometimes something about the person makes Drummer feel that reserve is in order. He responds to an insincere approach by sitting still, going down into himself, and thinking, "This person has no business pawing me. I'll sit very still, and he will go away." If the person doesn't take the hint from Drummer, I'll give the pup a little backup by saying. "Please don't pet him, he's working," even though he was not under any command.

The pup reads this, and there is a flicker of a working trust now stirring in the dog. Is the pup grateful? When the stranger leaves, does he lick my hand, full of submissive blandishments? This one doesn't. This one says nothing at all, and I say nothing much to him. This is a working trust we are developing, not a mutual congratulation society. My backup is praise enough for him; the use he makes of my support is praise enough for me.

Listening to a dog is often praise enough. Suppose it is just after dark and we are outside. Suddenly there is a shout from the house. The pup and I both look toward the shout and then toward each other: "What do you think?" I don't so much as cock my head, because Drummer is growing up, and I want to know what he thinks. He takes a few steps toward the house, and I follow. He listens again and comprehends that it's just Holly, who at fourteen is much given to alarming cries and shouts. He shrugs at me and goes about his business. I say nothing. To praise him for this performance would make about as much sense as praising a human being for the same thing. Thus:

A. What's that?

B. I don't know. [Listens] Oh, it's just Holly.

A. What a goooooood human being!

B. Huh?

This is one small moment in a series of like moments that will culminate in an Airedale who on a Friday will have the discrimination and confidence required to take down a man who is attacking me with a knife and on Saturday clown and play with the children at the annual Orange Empire Dog Club Christmas party.

People who claim to speak for animal rights are increasingly devoted   30
to the idea that the very keeping of a dog or a horse or a gerbil or a lion is in and of itself an offense. The more loudly they speak, the less likely they are to be in a rights relation to any given animal, because they are spending so much time in airplanes or transmitting fax announcements of the latest Sylvester Stallone anti-fur rally. In a 1988 *Harper's* forum, for example, Ingrid Newkirk, the national director of People for the Ethical Treatment of Animals, urged that domestic pets be spayed and neutered and ultimately phased out. She prefers, it appears, wolves—and wolves someplace else—to Airedales and, by a logic whose interior structure is both emotionally and intellectually forever closed to Drummer, claims thereby to be speaking for "animal rights."

She is wrong. I am the only one who can own up to my Airedale's inalienable rights. Whether or not I do it perfectly at any given moment is no more refutation of this point than whether I am perfectly my husband's mate at any given moment refutes the fact of marriage. Only people who know Drummer, and whom he can know, are capable of this relationship. PETA and the Humane Society and the ASPCA and the Congress and NOW—as institutions—do have the power to affect my ability to grant rights to Drummer but are otherwise incapable of creating conditions or laws or rights that would increase his happiness. Only Drummer's owner has the power to obey him—to obey who he is and what he is capable of—deeply enough to grant him his rights and open up the possibility of happiness.

The Reader's Presence

1. Hearne writes from an "expert" perspective as an animal trainer. Suppose she were not an expert. How would that change your reading of her argument?

2. Hearne takes issue both with the common definition of "animal," protesting that not all animals are alike, and with the common notion of "happiness" as comfort (paragraphs 1 and 2). How do questions of these definitions form the basis of her argument? Is it possible to disagree with Hearne's definitions and still support her overall argument, or vice-versa? Why or why not?

3. Throughout her essay, Hearne attends to the political dimensions of her argument. In paragraph 20, for example, she introduces "the idea of democracy" and in the final paragraph she refers to her "Airedale's inalienable rights." Find other such examples.

How does Hearne incorporate American political history into her essay? Do you find her allusion to slavery (paragraph 17) persuasive? necessary? Compare Hearne's ideas about dogs to Annie Dillard's understanding of wild animals in "Living Like Weasels" (page 654). Is Dillard's essay as philosophical as Hearne's? as political? as poetical? How does each essay address the reader? What are their respective goals?

Langston Hughes

Liberals Need a Mascot

Between 1950 and 1965, Langston Hughes (1902–1967) wrote a column for the Chicago Defender *featuring a fictional character called Jesse B. Simple. Simple—an unsophisticated everyman, as his name suggests—expressed his down-to-earth opinions on numerous subjects of the time. Simple proved so popular that Hughes published three books of stories about him,* Simple Speaks His Mind *(1950),* Simple Takes a Wife *(1953), and* Simple Stakes a Claim *(1957), which became a Broadway musical,* Simply Heavenly, *that year. "Liberals Need a Mascot" appeared in a 2004 collection,* The Return of Simple, *made up of previously unpublished and out-of-print works.*

For more on Hughes, see page 162.

"Just what is a liberal?" asked Simple.

"Well, as nearly as I can tell, a liberal is a nice man who acts decently toward people, talks democratically, and often is democratic in his personal life, but does not stand up very well in action when some real social issue like Jim Crow[1] comes up."

"Like my boss," said Simple, "who is always telling me he believes in equal rights and I am the most intelligent Negro he ever saw—and I deserve a better job. I say, 'Why don't you give it to me, then?' And he says, 'Unfortunately, I don't have one for you.'

" 'But ever so often you hire new white men that ain't had the experience of me and I have to tell them what to do, though they are over me. How come that?'

---

[1]*Jim Crow:* First enacted in the late nineteenth century, Jim Crow laws allowed racial segregation, restricted voting rights based on race, and denied many African Americans the kinds of jobs, education, and housing available to whites. The passage of the Civil Rights Act of 1964 and the Voting Rights Act of 1965 ended the Jim Crow era of legal discrimination.—Eds.

" 'Well,' he says, 'the time just ain't ripe.' Is that what a liberal is?"   5
asked Simple.

"That's just about what a liberal is," I said.

"Also a liberal sets back in them nice air-cooled streamlined coaches
on the trains down South, while I ride up front in a hot old Jim Crow
car," said Simple. "Am I right?"

"You are just about right," I said. "All the liberals I ever heard of
ride with white folks when they go down South, not with us, yet they deplore Jim Crow."

"Do liberals have an animal?" asked Simple.

"What do you mean, do liberals have an animal?"   10

"The Republicans have an elephant, Democrats have a jackass," said
Simple. "I mean, what does the liberals have?"

"I do not know," I said, "since they are not a political party. But if
they were, what animal do you think they ought to have?"

"An ostrich," said Simple.

"Why an ostrich?" I demanded.

"Ain't you never seen an ostrich?" said Simple. "Old ostrich sticks his   15
head in the sand whenever he don't want to look at anything. But he leaves
his hind parts bare for anybody to kick him square in his caboose. An ostrich
is just like nice white folks who can smile at me so sweet as long as I am
working and sweating and don't ask for nothing. Soon as I want a promotion
or a raise in pay, down go their heads in the sand and they cannot see their
way clear. 'The time ain't ripe.' And if I insist, they will have the boss man
put me dead out in the street so they can't see me. Is that what a liberal is?"

"Could be," I said, "except that an ostrich is a bird that does not
sing, and a liberal can sing very sweetly."

"An elephant don't talk," said Simple, "but they are always making
him talk in them cartoons where he represents the Republicans. So I do
not see why an ostrich can't sing."

"I didn't mean sing literally," I said. "What I really meant was talk,
use platitudes, make speeches."

"This ostrich of mine can make speeches," said Simple. "He can pull
his head out of the sand and say, 'I see a new day ahead for America! I
see the democratic dawn of equal rights for all! I see . . . '

"Whereupon, I will say, 'Can you see me?'   20

"And that ostrich will say, 'Indeed, my dark friend, democracy cannot overlook you.'

"I will say, 'Then help me get an apartment in that city-built tax-free
insurance project where nobody but white folks can live.'

"That ostrich will say, 'Excuse me!' And stick his head right back
down in the sand. Then I will haul off and try to kick his daylights out.
And Mr. Big Dog will say, 'Shame on you, trying to embarrass a friend of
the Negro race.'

"I will say, 'Embarrass nothing! I am trying to break his carcass!
Only thing, it is too high up for my foot to reach.' That is another trouble
with liberals," said Simple. "They are always too high to reach."

"They're well-to-do, man. That's why liberals don't have to worry 25
about colored folks."

"Then gimme an animal whose hips is closer to the ground," said
Simple.

The Reader's Presence

1. What characteristics does Jesse B. Simple seem to exhibit in this selection? What ideas does Hughes use Simple to express? Are these
   views more or less effective coming from a fictional character? Why?

2. How does Simple define *liberal*? Does Hughes seem to agree or
   disagree with his definition? How can you tell? Is the mascot Simple chooses appropriate, given the definition he presents? Why or
   why not?

3. What point does Hughes make about race relations in the United
   States in the 1950s and early 1960s? Read Randall Kennedy's
   "Blind Spot" (page 721). What does Kennedy's discussion of
   racial profiling and its relation to affirmative action suggest about
   how attitudes toward race have—and have not—changed since
   Hughes wrote these pieces?

Langston Hughes
That Word Black

*Langston Hughes (1902–1967) created the plain-speaking character Jesse B.
Simple for a newspaper column that ran in the* Chicago Defender *from 1950 to
1965. Like "Liberals Need a Mascot" (page 707), this column, "That* Word *Black,"
appeared in a 2004 collection,* The Return of Simple.*

For more on Hughes, see page 162.

"This evening," said Simple, "I feel like talking about the word *black*."

"Nobody's stopping you, so go ahead. But what you really ought to
have is a soap-box out on the corner of 126th and Lenox where the rest
of the orators hang out."

"They expresses some good ideas on that corner," said Simple, "but
for my ideas I do not need a crowd. Now, as I were saying, the word *black*,

white folks have done used that word to mean something bad so often until now when the N.A.A.C.P. asks for civil rights for the black man, they think they must be bad. Looking back into history, I reckon it all started with a *black* cat meaning bad luck. Don't let one cross your path!

"Next, somebody got up a *blacklist* on which you get if you don't vote right. Then when lodges come into being, the folks they didn't want in them got *blackballed*. If you kept a skeleton in your closet, you might get *blackmailed*. And everything bad was *black*. When it came down to the unlucky ball on the pool table, the eight-rock, they made it the *black* ball. So no wonder there ain't no equal rights for the *black* man."

"All you say is true about the odium attached to the word *black*," I   5
said. "You've even forgotten a few. For example, during the war if you bought something under the table, illegally, they said you were trading on the *black* market. In Chicago, if you're a gangster, the *Black Hand Society* may take you for a ride. And certainly if you don't behave yourself, your family will say you're a *black* sheep. Then, if your mama burns a *black* candle to change the family luck, they call it *black* magic."

"My mama never did believe in voodoo, so she did not burn no black candles," said Simple.

"If she had, that would have been a *black* mark against her."

"Stop talking about my mama. What I want to know is, where do white folks get off calling everything bad *black*? If it is a dark night, they say it's *black* as hell. If you are mean and evil, they say you got a *black* heart. I would like to change all that around and say that the people who Jim Crow me have got a *white* heart. People who sell dope to children have got a *white* mark against them. And all the white gamblers who were behind the basketball fix are the *white* sheep of the sports world. God knows there was few, if any, Negroes selling stuff on the black market during the war, so why didn't they call it the *white* market? No, they got to take me and my color and turn it into everything *bad*. According to white folks, black is bad.

"Wait till my day comes! In my language, bad will be *white*. Blackmail will be *white*mail. Black cats will be good luck, and *white* cats will be bad. If a white cat crosses your path, look out! I will take the black ball for the cue ball and let the *white* ball be the unlucky eight-rock. And on my blacklist — which will be a *white*list then — I will put everybody who ever Jim Crowed me from Rankin to Hitler, Talmadge to Malan,[1] South Carolina to South Africa.

"I am black. When I look in the mirror, I see myself, daddy-o, but I   10
am not ashamed. God made me. He also made F.D.,[2] dark as he is. He

<hr />

[1]*Rankin . . . Malan:* John Elliott Rankin (1882–1960) was a U.S. representative from Mississippi from 1921 to 1953 and champion of white supremacy; Herman Eugene Talmadge (1913–2002) was the governor of Georgia from 1948 to 1955, a U.S. senator from 1956 to 1980, and a strong opponent of school desegregation; Daniel François Malan (1874–1959) was prime minister of South Africa from 1948 to 1954 and the first to segregate the country by imposing apartheid. — EDS.

[2]*F.D.:* Simple's "dark-black young cousin," Franklin D. Roosevelt Brown, who appears in other sketches. — EDS.

did not make us no badder than the rest of the folks. The earth is black and all kinds of good things comes out of the earth. Everything that grows comes up out of the earth. Trees and flowers and fruit and sweet potatoes and corn and all that keeps mens alive comes right up out of the earth—good old black earth. Coal is black and it warms your house and cooks your food. The night is black, which has a moon, and a million stars, and is beautiful. Sleep is black, which gives you rest, so you wake up feeling good. I am black. I feel very good this evening.

"What is wrong with black?"

The Reader's Presence

1. What point is Hughes making about the importance of language in this essay? How much difference do the connotations Simple lists for *black* make in the way you perceive the meaning of the word? Why?

2. Consider the fairness—or unfairness—of Simple's charge that the word *black* creates a negative impression of African Americans. How effective is his argument? Why?

3. Read Michiko Kakutani's "The Word Police" (page 716). How might she respond to Simple's discussion of the word *black*? Are the politically correct terms she discusses the natural outgrowth of sensitivity to the potential negative connotations of words—such as the word Simple is discussing? Why or why not?

Thomas Jefferson
The Declaration of Independence

Thomas Jefferson (1743–1826) was born and raised in Virginia and attended William and Mary College. After being admitted to the bar, he entered politics and served in the Virginia House of Burgesses and the Continental Congress of 1775. During the Revolutionary War he was elected governor of Virginia, and after independence was appointed special minister to France and later secretary of state. As the nation's third president he negotiated the Louisiana Purchase. Of all his accomplishments as an inventor, architect, diplomat, scientist, and politician, Jefferson counted his work in designing the University of Virginia among the most important, along with his efforts to establish separation of church and state and the composition of the Declaration of Independence.

In May and June 1776, the Continental Congress had been vigorously debating the dangerous idea of independence and felt the need to issue a document that clearly pointed out the colonial grievances against Great Britain. A committee was appointed to "prepare a declaration" that would summarize the specific reasons for colonial discontent. The committee of five included Thomas Jefferson, Benjamin Franklin, and John Adams. Jefferson, who was noted for his skills in composition and, as Adams put it, "peculiar felicity of expression," was chosen to write the first draft. The assignment took Jefferson about two weeks, and he submitted the draft first to the committee, which made a few verbal alterations, and then on June 28 to Congress, where, after further alterations mainly relating to slavery, it was finally approved on July 4, 1776.

Jefferson claims to have composed the document without research, working mainly from ideas he felt were commonly held at the time. As Jefferson recalled many years later, he drafted the document as "an appeal to the tribunal of the world" and hoped "to place before mankind the common sense of the subject, in terms so plain and firm as to command their assent." He claims that "neither aiming at originality of principle or sentiment . . . it was intended to be an expression of the American mind, and to give to that expression the proper tone and spirit called for by the occasion."

When in the Course of human events, it becomes necessary for one people to dissolve the political bands which have connected them with another, and to assume among the Powers of the earth, the separate and equal station to which the Laws of Nature and of Nature's God entitle them, a decent respect to the opinions of mankind requires that they should declare the causes which impel them to the separation.

We hold these truths to be self-evident, that all men are created equal, that they are endowed by their Creator with certain inalienable Rights, that among these are Life, Liberty and the pursuit of Happiness. That to secure these rights, Governments are instituted among Men, deriving their just powers from the consent of the governed. That whenever any Form of Government becomes destructive of these ends, it is the Right of the People to alter or to abolish it, and to institute new Government, laying its foundation on such principles and organizing its powers in such form, as to them shall seem most likely to effect their Safety and Happiness. Prudence, indeed, will dictate that Governments long established should not be changed for light and transient causes; and accordingly all experience hath shown, that mankind are more disposed to suffer, while evils are sufferable, than to right themselves by abolishing the forms to which they are accustomed. But when a long train of abuses and usurpations, pursuing invariably the same Object evinces a design to reduce them under absolute Despotism, it is their right, it is their duty, to throw off such Government, and to provide new Guards for their future security. — Such has been the patient sufferance of these Colonies; and such is now the necessity which constrains them to alter their former Systems of Government. The history of the present King of Great Britain is a history of repeated injuries and usurpations, all having in direct object the establishment of an absolute Tyranny over these States. To prove this, let Facts be submitted to a candid world.

He has refused his Assent to Laws, the most wholesome and necessary for the public good.

He has forbidden his Governors to pass Laws of immediate and pressing importance, unless suspended in their operation till his Assent should be obtained; and when so suspended, he has utterly neglected to attend to them.

He has refused to pass other laws for the accommodation of large 5 districts of people, unless those people would relinquish the right of Representation in the Legislature, a right inestimable to them and formidable to tyrants only.

He has called together legislative bodies at places unusual, uncomfortable, and distant from the depository of their Public Records, for the sole purpose of fatiguing them into compliance with his measures.

He has dissolved Representative Houses repeatedly, for opposing with manly firmness his invasions on the rights of the people.

He has refused for a long time, after such dissolutions, to cause others to be elected; whereby the Legislative Powers, incapable of Annihilation, have returned to the People at large for their exercise; the State remaining in the mean time exposed to all the dangers of invasion from without, and convulsions within.

He has endeavoured to prevent the population of these States;[1] for that purpose obstructing the Laws for Naturalization of Foreigners; refusing to pass others to encourage their migration hither, and raising the conditions of new Appropriations of Lands.

He has obstructed the Administration of Justice, by refusing his As- 10 sent to Laws for establishing Judiciary Powers.

He has made Judges dependent on his Will alone, for the tenure of their offices, and the amount and payment of their salaries.

He has erected a multitude of New Offices, and sent hither swarms of Officers to harass our People, and eat out their substance.

He has kept among us, in times of peace, Standing Armies without the Consent of our legislature.

He has affected to render the Military independent of and superior to the Civil Power.

He has combined with others to subject us to a jurisdiction foreign to 15 our constitution, and unacknowledged by our laws; giving his Assent to their acts of pretended Legislation:

For quartering large bodies of armed troops among us:

---

[1]*prevent the population of these States:* This meant limiting emigration to the Colonies, thus controlling their growth. —EDS.

For protecting them, by a mock Trial, from Punishment for any Murders which they should commit on the Inhabitants of these States:

For cutting off our Trade with all parts of the world:

For imposing taxes on us without our Consent:

For depriving us in many cases, of the benefits of Trial by Jury: 20

For transporting us beyond Seas to be tried for pretended offenses:

For abolishing the free System of English Laws in a neighbouring Province, establishing therein an Arbitrary government, and enlarging its Boundaries so as to render it at once an example and fit instrument for introducing the same absolute rule into these Colonies:

For taking away our Charters, abolishing our most valuable Laws, and altering fundamentally the Forms of our Governments:

For suspending our own Legislatures, and declaring themselves invested with Power to legislate for us in all cases whatsoever.

He has abdicated Government here, by declaring us out of his Protec-   25
tion and waging War against us.

He has plundered our seas, ravaged our Coasts, burnt our towns, and destroyed the lives of our people.

He is at this time transporting large armies of foreign mercenaries to compleat the works of death, desolation and tyranny, already begun with circumstances of Cruelty & perfidy scarcely paralleled in the most barbarous ages, and totally unworthy of the Head of a civilized nation.

He has constrained our fellow Citizens taken Captive on the high Seas to bear Arms against their Country, to become the executioners of their friends and Brethren, or to fall themselves by their Hands.

He has excited domestic insurrections amongst us, and has endeavoured to bring on the inhabitants of our frontiers, the merciless Indian Savages, whose known rule of warfare, is an undistinguished destruction of all ages, sexes and conditions.

In every stage of these Oppressions We have Petitioned for Read-   30
dress in the most humble terms: Our repeated Petitions have been answered only by repeated injury. A Prince, whose character is thus marked by every act which may define a Tyrant, is unfit to be the ruler of a free People.

Nor have We been wanting in attention to our British brethren. We have warned them from time to time of attempts by their legislature to extend an unwarrantable jurisdiction over us. We have reminded them of the circumstances of our emigration and settlement here. We have appealed to their native justice and magnanimity, and we have conjured them by the ties of our common kindred to disavow these usurpations, which, would inevitably interrupt our connections and correspondence. They too have been deaf to the voice of justice and of consanguinity. We must, therefore, acquiesce in the necessity, which denounces our Separation, and hold them, as we hold the rest of mankind, Enemies in War, in Peace Friends.

We, therefore, the Representatives of the United States of America, in General Congress, Assembled, appealing to the Supreme Judge of the world for the rectitude of our intentions, do in the Name, and by Authority of the good People of these Colonies, solemnly publish and declare, That these United Colonies are, and of Right ought to be Free and Independent States, that they are Absolved from all Allegiance to the British Crown, and that all political connection between them and the State of Great Britain, is and ought to be totally dissolved; and that as Free and Independent States, they have full Power to levy War, conclude Peace, contract Alliances, establish Commerce, and to do all other Acts and Things which Independent States may of right do. And for the support of this Declaration, with a firm reliance on the Protection of Divine Providence, we mutually pledge to each other our Lives, our Fortunes and our sacred Honor.

The Reader's Presence

1. How does Jefferson seem to define *independence?* Whom does the definition include? Whom does it exclude? How does Jefferson's definition of independence differ from your own? It has been pointed out that Jefferson disregards "interdependence." Can you formulate an argument contrary to Jefferson's?

2. Examine the Declaration's first sentence. Who is the speaker here? What is the effect of the omniscient tone of the opening? Why does the first paragraph have no personal pronouns or references to specific events? What might Jefferson's argument stand to gain in generalizing the American situation?

3. As in classical epics and the Bible, Jefferson frequently relies on the rhetorical devices of repetition and lists. What is the effect of such devices? Can you find another essay in this anthology that relies on similar strategies? What do these essays have in common? What sets them apart? Paul Fussell refers to "the Framers of the Constitution" in his essay on the right to bear arms ("A Well-Regulated Militia," page 683). "Thank God for the eighteenth century," Fussell writes (paragraph 6), following an appreciation of the phraseology and the spirit of the Second Amendment to the Bill of Rights. What about the Declaration strikes you as representative of eighteenth-century ideas and language? Do you share Fussell's opinion about the continuing applicability of such texts?

Michiko Kakutani

The Word Police

Michiko Kakutani (b. 1955) graduated from Yale University in 1976 and then worked as a reporter at the Washington Post *and a staff writer for* Time. *In 1979 she joined the cultural news department of the* New York Times *and has been the paper's senior book critic since 1983. She received the 1998 Pulitzer Prize for her "passionate, intelligent writing on books and contemporary literature." Kakutani has also published a collection of interviews,* The Poet at the Piano *(1988). "The Word Police" appeared in the* New York Times *in January 1993.*

This month's inaugural festivities, with their celebration, in Maya Angelou's words, of "humankind"—"the Asian, the Hispanic, the Jew / The African, the Native American, the Sioux, / The Catholic, the Muslim, the French, the Greek / The Irish, the Rabbi, the Priest, the Sheik, / The Gay, the Straight, the Preacher, / The privileged, the homeless, the Teacher"— constituted a kind of official embrace of multiculturalism and a new politics of inclusion.

The mood of political correctness, however, has already made firm inroads into popular culture. Washington boasts a store called Politically Correct that sells pro-whale, anti-meat, ban-the-bomb T-shirts, bumper stickers, and buttons, as well as a local cable television show called "Politically Correct Cooking" that features interviews in the kitchen with representatives from groups like People for the Ethical Treatment of Animals.

The Coppertone suntan lotion people are planning to give their long-time cover girl, Little Miss (Ms.?) Coppertone, a male equivalent, Little Mr. Coppertone. And even Superman (Superperson?) is rumored to be returning this spring, reincarnated as four ethnically diverse clones: an African-American, an Asian, a Caucasian and a Latino.

Nowhere is this P.C. mood more striking than in the increasingly noisy debate over language that has moved from university campuses to the country at large—a development that both underscores Americans' puritanical zeal for reform and their unwavering faith in the talismanic power of words.

Certainly no decent person can quarrel with the underlying impulse behind political correctness: a vision of a more just, inclusive society in which racism, sexism, and prejudice of all sorts have been erased. But the methods and fervor of the self-appointed language police can lead to a rigid orthodoxy—and unintentional self-parody—opening the movement to the scorn of conservative opponents and the mockery of cartoonists and late-night television hosts.

5

It's hard to imagine women earning points for political correctness by saying "ovarimony" instead of "testimony"—as one participant at the recent Modern Language Association convention was overheard to suggest. It's equally hard to imagine people wanting to flaunt their lack of prejudice by giving up such words and phrases as "bull market," "kaiser roll," "Lazy Susan," and "charley horse."

Several books on bias-free language have already appeared, and the 1991 edition of the *Random House Webster's College Dictionary* boasts an appendix titled "Avoiding Sexist Language." The dictionary also includes such linguistic mutations as "womyn" (women, "used as an alternative spelling to avoid the suggestion of sexism perceived in the sequence m-e-n") and "waitron" (a gender-blind term for waiter or waitress).

Many of these dictionaries and guides not only warn the reader against offensive racial and sexual slurs, but also try to establish and enforce a whole new set of usage rules. Take, for instance, *The Bias-Free Word Finder, a Dictionary of Nondiscriminatory Language* by Rosalie Maggio (Beacon Press)—a volume often indistinguishable, in its meticulous solemnity, from the tongue-in-cheek *Official Politically Correct Dictionary and Handbook* put out last year by Henry Beard and Christopher Cerf (Villard Books). Ms. Maggio's book supplies the reader intent on using kinder, gentler language with writing guidelines as well as a detailed listing of more than 5,000 "biased words and phrases."

Whom are these guidelines for? Somehow one has a tough time picturing them replacing *Fowler's Modern English Usage* in the classroom, or being adopted by the average man (sorry, individual) in the street.

The "pseudogeneric 'he,'" we learn from Ms. Maggio, is to be avoided 10 like the plague, as is the use of the word "man" to refer to humanity. "Fellow," "king," "lord" and "master" are bad because they're "male-oriented words," and "king," "lord" and "master" are especially bad because they're also "hierarchical, dominator society terms." The politically correct lion becomes the "monarch of the jungle," new-age children play "someone on the top of the heap," and the "Mona Lisa" goes down in history as Leonardo's "acme of perfection."

As for the word "black," Ms. Maggio says it should be excised from terms with a negative spin: she recommends substituting words like "mouse" for "black eye," "ostracize" for "blackball," "payola" for "blackmail" and "outcast" for "black sheep." Clearly, some of these substitutions work better than others: somehow the "sinister humor" of Kurt Vonnegut or *Saturday Night Live* doesn't quite make it; nor does the "denouncing" of the Hollywood 10.

For the dedicated user of politically correct language, all these rules can make for some messy moral dilemmas. Whereas "battered wife" is a gender-biased term, the gender-free term "battered spouse," Ms. Maggio notes, incorrectly implies "that men and women are equally battered."

On one hand, say Francine Wattman Frank and Paula A. Treichler in their book *Language, Gender, and Professional Writing* (Modern Language

Association), "he or she" is an appropriate construction for talking about an individual (like a jockey, say) who belongs to a profession that's predominantly male—it's a way of emphasizing "that such occupations are not barred to women or that women's concerns need to be kept in mind." On the other hand, they add, using masculine pronouns rhetorically can underscore ongoing male dominance in those fields, implying the need for change.

And what about the speech codes adopted by some universities in recent years? Although they were designed to prohibit students from uttering sexist and racist slurs, they would extend, by logic, to blacks who want to use the word "nigger" to strip the term of its racist connotations, or homosexuals who want to use the word "queer" to reclaim it from bigots.

In her book, Ms. Maggio recommends applying bias-free usage   15 retroactively: she suggests paraphrasing politically incorrect quotations, or replacing "the sexist words or phrases with ellipsis dots and/or bracketed substitutes," or using "*sic*" "to show that the sexist words come from the original quotation and to call attention to the fact that they are incorrect."

Which leads the skeptical reader of *The Bias-Free Word Finder* to wonder whether "All the King's Men" should be retitled "All the Ruler's People"; "Pet Sematary," "Animal Companion Graves"; "Birdman of Alcatraz," "Birdperson of Alcatraz"; and "The Iceman Cometh," "The Ice Route Driver Cometh"?

Will making such changes remove the prejudice in people's minds? Should we really spend time trying to come up with non-male-based alternatives to "Midas touch," "Achilles' heel," and "Montezuma's revenge"? Will tossing out Santa Claus—whom Ms. Maggio accuses of reinforcing "the cultural male-as-norm system"—in favor of Belfana, his Italian female alter ego, truly help banish sexism? Can the avoidance of "violent expressions and metaphors" like "kill two birds with one stone," "sock it to 'em" or "kick an idea around" actually promote a more harmonious world?

The point isn't that the excesses of the word police are comical. The point is that their intolerance (in the name of tolerance) has disturbing implications. In the first place, getting upset by phrases like "bullish on America" or "the City of Brotherly Love" tends to distract attention from the real problems of prejudice and injustice that exist in society at large, turning them into mere questions of semantics. Indeed, the emphasis currently put on politically correct usage has uncanny parallels with the academic movement of deconstruction—a method of textual analysis that focuses on language and linguistic pyrotechnis—which has become firmly established on university campuses.

In both cases, attention is focused on surfaces, on words and metaphors; in both cases, signs and symbols are accorded more importance than content. Hence, the attempt by some radical advocates to remove *The Adventures of Huckleberry Finn* from curriculums on the grounds that Twain's use of the word "nigger" makes the book a racist text— never mind the fact that this American classic (written in 1884) depicts the spiritual kinship achieved between a white boy and a runaway slave, never mind the fact that the "nigger" Jim emerges as the novel's most honorable, decent character.[1]

Ironically enough, the P.C. movement's obsession with language is accompanied by a strange Orwellian willingness to warp the meaning of words by placing them under a high-powered ideological lens. For instance, the *Dictionary of Cautionary Words and Phrases*—a pamphlet issued by the University of Missouri's Multicultural Management Program to help turn "today's journalists into tomorrow's multicultural newsroom managers"—warns that using the word "articulate" to describe members of a minority group can suggest the opposite, "that 'those people' are not considered well educated, articulate and the like."

The pamphlet patronizes minority groups, by cautioning the reader against using the words "lazy" and "burly" to describe any member of such groups; and it issues a similar warning against using words like "gorgeous" and "petite" to describe women.

As euphemism proliferates with the rise of political correctness, there is a spread of the sort of sloppy, abstract language that Orwell said is "designed to make lies sound truthful and murder respectable, and to give an appearance of solidity to pure wind." "Fat" becomes "big boned" as "differently sized"; "stupid" becomes "exceptional"; "stoned" becomes "chemically inconvenienced."

Wait a minute here! Aren't such phrases eerily reminiscent of the euphemisms coined by the government during Vietnam and Watergate? Remember how the military used to speak of "pacification," or how President Richard M. Nixon's press secretary, Ronald L. Ziegler, tried to get away with calling a lie an "inoperative statement"?

Calling the homeless "the underhoused" doesn't give them a place to live; calling the poor "the economically marginalized" doesn't help them pay the bills. Rather, by playing down their plight, such language might even make it easier to shrug off the seriousness of their situation.

Instead of allowing free discussion and debate to occur, many gung-ho advocates of politically correct language seem to think that simple suppression of a word or concept will magically make the problem disappear. In the *Bias-Free Word Finder*, Ms. Maggio entreats the reader not to perpetuate the negative stereotype of Eve. "Be extremely cautious in referring to the biblical Eve," she writes; "this story has profoundly contributed to negative attitudes toward women throughout history, largely because of misogynistic and patriarchal interpretations that labeled her evil, inferior, and seductive."

The story of Bluebeard, the rake (whoops!—the libertine) who killed his seven wives, she says, is also to be avoided, as is the biblical story of Jezebel. Of Jesus Christ, Ms. Maggio writes: "There have been few individuals in history as completely androgynous as Christ, and it does his message a disservice to overinsist on his maleness." She doesn't give the

---

[1]For another view of *Huckleberry Finn*, see page 815.—EDS.

reader any hints on how this might be accomplished; presumably, one is supposed to avoid describing him as the Son of God.

Of course the P.C. police aren't the only ones who want to proscribe what people should say or give them guidelines for how they may use an idea; Jesse Helms and his supporters are up to exactly the same thing when they propose to patrol the boundaries of the permissible in art. In each case, the would-be censor aspires to suppress what he or she finds distasteful — all, of course, in the name of the public good.

In the case of the politically correct, the prohibition of certain words, phrases and ideas is advanced in the cause of building a brave new world free of racism and hate, but this vision of harmony clashes with the very ideals of diversity and inclusion that the multicultural movement holds dear, and it's purchased at the cost of freedom of expression and freedom of speech.

In fact, the utopian world envisioned by the language police would be bought at the expense of the ideas of individualism and democracy articulated in "The Gettysburg Address": "Fourscore and seven years ago our fathers brought forth on this continent a new nation, conceived in liberty and dedicated to the proposition that all men are created equal."

Of course, the P.C. police have already found Lincoln's words hopelessly "phallocentric." No doubt they would rewrite the passage: "Fourscore and seven years ago our foremothers and forefathers brought forth on this continent a new nation, formulated with liberty, and dedicated to the proposition that all humankind is created equal."   30

The Reader's Presence

1. Kakutani begins by dissecting what she sees as a current state of affairs. What kinds of words does she use to describe this state of affairs? Is she merely stating the facts or beginning her argument? Kakutani uses the word *police* (paragraph 5) to describe those who would alter the English language. What does this word imply? Is it justified?

2. The author humorously cites rather awkward word substitutions from *The Bias-Free Word Finder*. Is this example sufficient and fair as evidence? Does mockery strengthen or weaken Kakutani's case?

3. One writer mentioned in Kakutani's essay suggests that people should avoid using expressions that include the word *black* and that have negative connotations (paragraph 11). How does Kakutani seem to feel about this suggestion? Read "That Word *Black*" by Langston Hughes (page 709). What does Hughes's character Simple say about the same subject? How much difference do you see between Hughes's apparent position on the word *black* and Kakutani's?

Randall Kennedy

Blind Spot

Randall Kennedy (b. 1954) attended Princeton University and Yale Law School. Early in his legal career, he clerked for such notable figures as U.S. Supreme Court Justice Thurgood Marshall. He joined the faculty at Harvard University Law School in 1984, where he continues to teach today. Known widely for his nuanced views on racial issues, he has written three books on the subject, Race, Crime, and the Law *(1997), which received a Robert F. Kennedy Book Award in 1998;* Nigger: The Strange Career of a Troublesome Word *(2002); and* Interracial Intimacies: Sex, Marriage, Identity, and Adoption *(2003). He serves on the editorial boards of the* Nation *and the* American Prospect, *and he contributes many articles to publications including the* Atlantic, Dissent, Time, *the* New Republic, *and the* Wall Street Journal. *He has also published widely in scholarly journals. "Blind Spot" was first published in the* Atlantic *in April 2002.*

Kennedy's works attempt a dispassionate perspective on issues related to race in America, but he is acutely aware of the sensitivity of his chief subject. In an article for the Nation, *he quoted W. E. B. Du Bois's statement, "The problem of the twentieth century is the problem of the color line." (For more on Du Bois, see page 658.) "Despite all that has changed," Kennedy wrote, "his words remain a challenge for the twenty-first."*

What is one to think about "racial profiling"? Confusion abounds about what the term even means. It should be defined as the policy or practice of using race as a factor in selecting whom to place under special surveillance: If police officers at an airport decide to search Passenger A because he is twenty-five to forty years old, bought a first-class ticket with cash, is flying cross-country, and is apparently of Arab ancestry, Passenger A has been subjected to racial profiling. But officials often prefer to define racial profiling as being based *solely* on race; and in doing so they are often seeking to preserve their authority to act against a person *partly* on the basis of race. Civil rights activists, too, often define racial profiling as solely race-based; but their aim is to arouse their followers and to portray law-enforcement officials in as menacing a light as possible.

The problem with defining racial profiling in the narrow manner of these strange bedfellows is that doing so obfuscates the real issue confronting Americans. Exceedingly few police officers, airport screeners, or other authorities charged with the task of foiling or apprehending criminals act solely on the basis of race. Many, however, act on the basis of intuition, using race along with other indicators (sex, age, patterns of past conduct) as a guide. The difficult question, then, is not whether the authorities ought to be allowed to act against individuals on the basis of race alone; almost everyone would disapprove of that. The difficult question is whether they ought to be allowed to use race *at all* in schemes of surveillance. If, indeed, it is used, the action amounts to racial discrimination. The extent of the discrimination may be relatively small when race is only one factor among many, but even a little racial discrimination should require lots of justification.

The key argument in favor of racial profiling, essentially, is that taking race into account enables the authorities to screen carefully and at less expense those sectors of the population that are more likely than others to contain the criminals for whom officials are searching. Proponents of this theory stress that resources for surveillance are scarce, that the dangers to be avoided are grave, and that reducing these dangers helps everyone—including, sometimes especially, those in the groups subjected to special scrutiny. Proponents also assert that it makes good sense to consider whiteness if the search is for Ku Klux Klan assassins, blackness if the search is for drug couriers in certain locales, and Arab nationality or ethnicity if the search is for agents of al Qaeda.

Some commentators embrace this position as if it were unassailable, but under U.S. law racial discrimination backed by state power is presumptively illicit. This means that supporters of racial profiling carry a heavy burden of persuasion. Opponents rightly argue, however, that not much rigorous empirical proof supports the idea of racial profiling as an effective tool of law enforcement. Opponents rightly contend, also, that alternatives to racial profiling have not been much studied or pursued. Stressing that racial profiling generates clear harm (for example, the fear, resentment, and alienation felt by innocent people in the profiled group), opponents of racial profiling sensibly question whether compromising our hard-earned principle of anti-discrimination is worth merely speculative gains in overall security.

A notable feature of this conflict is that champions of each position frequently embrace rhetoric, attitudes, and value systems that are completely at odds with those they adopt when confronting another controversial instance of racial discrimination—namely, affirmative action. Vocal supporters of racial profiling who trumpet the urgency of communal needs when discussing law enforcement all of a sudden become fanatical individualists when condemning affirmative action in college admissions and the labor market. Supporters of profiling, who are willing to impose what amounts to a racial tax on profiled groups, denounce as betrayals of "color blindness" programs that require racial diversity. A similar turnabout can be seen on the part of many of those who support affirmative action. Impatient with talk of communal needs in assessing racial profiling, they very often have no difficulty with subordinating the interests of individual white candidates to the purported good of the whole. Opposed to race consciousness in policing, they demand race consciousness in deciding whom to admit to college or select for a job.

The racial-profiling controversy—like the conflict over affirmative action—will not end soon. For one thing, in both cases many of the contestants are animated by decent but contending sentiments. Although exasperating, this is actually good for our society; and it would be even better if participants in the debates acknowledged the simple truth that their adversaries have something useful to say.

The Reader's Presence

1. How does Kennedy define racial profiling at the beginning of the essay? What is the benefit of presenting a "correct" definition? What other definitions does Kennedy reject and why? Consider the advantage of defining your terms in a debate. What advantage does Kennedy's definition give him?

2. What is the "blind spot" Kennedy refers to in the title? Why does he propose that both sides of the debate examine that "blind spot"?

3. Read Brent Staples's "Just Walk on By" (page 283). To what extent is Staples's experience an example of racial profiling? What other factors might influence the way women judge him on the street? Do you think Staples would agree with Kennedy's view of racial profiling? What might the women say about their need to assess risk and judge their safety?

Martin Luther King Jr.

I Have a Dream

Martin Luther King Jr. (1929–1968) was born in Atlanta, Georgia, and after training for the ministry became pastor of the Dexter Avenue Baptist Church in Montgomery, Alabama. In 1956 he was elected president of the Montgomery Improvement Association, the group that organized a transportation boycott in response to the arrest of Rosa Parks. King later became president of the Southern Christian Leadership Conference, and under his philosophy of nonviolent direct action he led marches and protests throughout the South, to Chicago, and to Washington, D.C. In 1963 King delivered his most famous speech, "I Have a Dream," before 200,000 people in front of the Lincoln Memorial in Washington, D.C., and in 1964 he was awarded the Nobel Peace Prize. King was assassinated on April 3, 1968, in Memphis, Tennessee.

King was a masterful orator and a powerful writer. Along with his many speeches, King wrote several books, including Why We Can't Wait *(1963),* Where

Do We Go from Here: Chaos or Community? *(1967),* The Measure of a Man *(1968), and* Trumpet of Conscience *(1968).*
For more on Martin Luther King Jr., see page 738.

Five score years ago, a great American, in whose symbolic shadow we stand, signed the Emancipation Proclamation.[1] This momentous decree came as a great beacon light of hope to millions of Negro slaves who had been seared in the flames of withering injustice. It came as a joyous daybreak to end the long night of captivity.

But one hundred years later, we must face the tragic fact that the Negro is still not free. One hundred years later, the life of the Negro is still sadly crippled by the manacles of segregation and the chains of discrimination. One hundred years later, the Negro lives on a lonely island of poverty in the midst of a vast ocean of material prosperity. One hundred years later, the Negro is still languishing in the corners of American society and finds himself an exile in his own land. So we have come here today to dramatize an appalling condition.

In a sense we have come to our nation's Capitol to cash a check. When the architects of our republic wrote the magnificent words of the Constitution and the Declaration of Independence, they were signing a promissory note to which every American was to fall heir. This note was a promise that all men would be guaranteed the unalienable rights of life, liberty, and the pursuit of happiness.

It is obvious today that America has defaulted on this promissory note insofar as her citizens of color are concerned. Instead of honoring this sacred obligation, America has given the Negro people a bad check; a check which has come back marked "insufficient funds." But we refuse to believe that the bank of justice is bankrupt. We refuse to believe that there are insufficient funds in the great vaults of opportunity of this nation. So we have come to cash this check — a check that will give us upon demand the riches of freedom and the security of justice. We have also come to this hallowed spot to remind America of the fierce urgency of *now.* This is no time to engage in the luxury of cooling off or to take the tranquilizing drug of gradualism. *Now* is the time to make real the promises of Democracy. *Now* is the time to rise from the dark and desolate valley of segregation to the sunlit path of racial justice. *Now* is the time to open the doors of opportunity to all of God's children. *Now* is the time to lift our nation from the quicksands of racial injustice to the solid rock of brotherhood.

It would be fatal for the nation to overlook the urgency of the mo-   5
ment and to underestimate the determination of the Negro. This sweltering summer of the Negro's legitimate discontent will not pass until there is an invigorating autumn of freedom and equality. 1963 is not an end, but a beginning. Those who hope that the Negro needed to blow off

---

[1]*Emancipation Proclamation:* Abraham Lincoln signed the Emancipation Proclamation that officially freed the slaves in 1863. — EDS.

steam and will now be content will have a rude awakening if the nation returns to business as usual. There will be neither rest nor tranquility in America until the Negro is granted his citizenship rights. The whirlwinds of revolt will continue to shake the foundations of our nation until the bright day of justice emerges.

But there is something I must say to my people who stand on the warm threshold which leads into the palace of justice. In the process of gaining our rightful place we must not be guilty of wrongful deeds. Let us not seek to satisfy our thirst for freedom by drinking from the cup of bitterness and hatred. We must forever conduct our struggle on the high plane of dignity and discipline. We must not allow our creative protest to degenerate into physical violence. Again and again we must rise to the majestic heights of meeting physical force with soul force. The marvelous new militancy which has engulfed the Negro community must not lead us to a distrust of all white people, for many of our white brothers, as evidenced by their presence here today, have come to realize that their destiny is tied up with our destiny and their freedom is inextricably bound to our freedom. We cannot walk alone.

And as we walk, we must make the pledge that we shall march ahead. We cannot turn back. There are those who are asking the devotees of civil rights, "When will you be satisfied?" We can never be satisfied as long as the Negro is the victim of the unspeakable horrors of police brutality. We can never be satisfied as long as our bodies, heavy with the fatigue of travel, cannot gain lodging in the motels of the highways and the hotels of the cities. We cannot be satisfied as long as the Negro's basic mobility is from a smaller ghetto to a larger one. We can never be satisfied as long as a Negro in Mississippi cannot vote and a Negro in New York believes he has nothing for which to vote. No, no, we are not satisfied, and we will not be satisfied until justice rolls down like waters and righteousness like a mighty stream.

I am not unmindful that some of you have come here out of great trials and tribulations. Some of you have come fresh from narrow jail cells. Some of you have come from areas where your quest for freedom left you battered by the storms of persecution and staggered by the winds of police brutality. You have been the veterans of creative suffering. Continue to work with the faith that unearned suffering is redemptive.

Go back to Mississippi, go back to Alabama, go back to South Carolina, go back to Georgia, go back to Louisiana, go back to the slums and ghettoes of our northern cities, knowing that somehow this situation can and will be changed. Let us not wallow in the valley of despair.

I say to you today, my friends, that in spite of the difficulties and frustrations of the moment I still have a dream. It is a dream deeply rooted in the American dream.

I have a dream that one day this nation will rise up and live out the true meaning of its creed: "We hold these truths to be self-evident; that all men are created equal."[2]

---

[2]From the Declaration of Independence by Thomas Jefferson (page 711). — Eds.

I have a dream that one day on the red hills of Georgia the sons of former slaves and the sons of former slaveowners will be able to sit down together at the table of brotherhood.

I have a dream that the state of Mississippi, a desert state sweltering with the heat of injustice and oppression, will be transformed into an oasis of freedom and justice.

I have a dream that my four little children will one day live in a nation where they will not be judged by the color of their skin but by the content of their character.

I have a dream today.   15

I have a dream that the state of Alabama, whose governor's[3] lips are presently dripping with the words of interposition and nullification, will be transformed into a situation where little black boys and black girls will be able to join hands with little white boys and white girls and walk together as sisters and brothers.

I have a dream today.

I have a dream that one day every valley shall be exalted, every hill and mountain shall be made low, the rough places will be made plain, and the crooked places will be made straight, and the glory of the Lord shall be revealed, and all flesh shall see it together.

This is our hope. This is the faith with which I return to the South. With this faith we will be able to hew out of the mountain of despair a stone of hope. With this faith we will be able to transform the jangling discords of our nation into a beautiful symphony of brotherhood. With this faith we will be able to work together, to pray together, to struggle together, to go to jail together, to stand up for freedom together, knowing that we will be free one day.

This will be the day when all of God's children will be able to sing   20 with new meaning.

> My country, 'tis of thee
> Sweet land of liberty,
>   Of thee I sing:
> Land where my fathers died,
> Land of the pilgrims' pride,
> From every mountainside
>   Let freedom ring.

And if America is to be a great nation this must become true. So let freedom ring from the prodigious hilltops of New Hampshire. Let freedom ring from the mighty mountains of New York. Let freedom ring from the heightening Alleghenies of Pennsylvania!

Let freedom ring from the snowcapped Rockies of Colorado!

---

[3]*governor's:* The governor of Alabama in 1963 was segregationist George Wallace (1919–1998), who eventually came to support integration and equal rights for African Americans. — EDS.

Let freedom ring from the curvaceous peaks of California!
But not only that; let freedom ring from Stone Mountain of Georgia!
Let freedom ring from Lookout Mountain of Tennessee! 25
Let freedom ring from every hill and molehill of Mississippi. From every mountainside, let freedom ring.

When we let freedom ring, when we let it ring from every village and every hamlet, from every state and every city, we will be able to speed up that day when all of God's children, black men and white men, Jews and Gentiles, Protestants and Catholics, will be able to join hands and sing in the words of the old Negro spiritual, "Free at last! free at last! thank God almighty, we are free at last!"

The Reader's Presence

1. How does King use familiar concepts and phrases from American democracy to create his message? What are some examples? How does he use repetition? How does he use rhythm? What are the effects of his rhetoric?

2. Make a list of the metaphors King uses throughout the speech. What connotations do they bring? What reccurring themes does he draw on for his metaphors? How do metaphors help extend the meanings of the words he describes?

3. Read Ho Che Anderson's graphic representation of King's "I Have a Dream" speech, which follows this piece. How does Anderson represent King as a speaker and leader? How does the juxtaposition of images and words influence your perception of the event?

THE GRAPHIC WRITER AT WORK

Ho Che Anderson on *I Have a Dream*

Ho Che Anderson (b. 1970) was born in the United Kingdom and raised in Canada, where he lives today. He has authored a number of graphic "comix" including Young Hoods in Love *(1994),* I Want to Be Your Dog *(1996), and, in collaboration with Wilfred Santiago, the series* Pop Life *(1998). His biographical trilogy,* King *(Volumes I–III), illustrates the life of Martin Luther King Jr. from his birth to his assassination. Anderson's complex rendering of the 1963 civil rights march on Washington, D.C., during which Dr. King delivered his most famous speech, "I Have a Dream," is excerpted from* King, *Volume II (2002). The first volume,* King *(1992), won a 1995 Parent's Choice Award;* King, *Volume III, was published in 2003.*

Martin Luther King Jr.

Letter from Birmingham Jail

Martin Luther King Jr. (1929–1968), one of the nation's best-known civil rights activists, led protests across the South in the years before the passage of the Civil Rights Act of 1964. He was arrested in 1960 for sitting at a whites-only lunch counter in Greensboro, North Carolina, and in 1962 he was jailed in Albany, Georgia. On April 12, 1963, King was again arrested, this time in Birmingham, Alabama, for demonstrating without a permit. He served eleven days in jail. While there, he wrote "Letter from Birmingham Jail" in response to a letter from eight clergymen who argued against King's acts of civil disobedience. The letter was published in King's book Why We Can't Wait *(1963).*

Many of King's writings, including the letter printed here and the famous "I Have a Dream" speech (see page 723), are designed to educate his audiences and inspire them to act. "Through education we seek to break down the spiritual barriers to integration," he said, and "through legislation and court orders we seek to break down the physical barriers to integration. One method is not a substitute for the other, but a meaningful and necessary supplement."

For more on Martin Luther King Jr., see page 723.

MARTIN LUTHER KING JR.
Birmingham City Jail
April 16, 1963

Bishop C. C. J. CARPENTER
Bishop JOSEPH A. DURICK
Rabbi MILTON L. GRAFMAN
Bishop PAUL HARDIN

Bishop NOLAN B. HARMON
The Rev. GEORGE M. MURRAY
The Rev. EDWARD V. RAMAGE
The Rev. EARL STALLINGS

My dear Fellow Clergymen,

While confined here in the Birmingham City Jail, I came across your recent statement calling our present activities "unwise and untimely." Seldom, if ever, do I pause to answer criticism of my work and ideas. If I sought to answer all of the criticisms that cross my desk, my secretaries would be engaged in little else in the course of the day and I would have no time for constructive work. But since I feel that you are men of genuine good will and your criticisms are sincerely set forth, I would like to answer your statement in what I hope will be patient and reasonable terms.

I think I should give the reason for my being in Birmingham, since you have been influenced by the argument of "outsiders coming in." I have the honor of serving as president of the Southern Christian Leadership Conference, an organization operating in every Southern state with headquarters in Atlanta, Georgia. We have some eighty-five affiliate organizations all across the South—one being the Alabama Christian Movement for Human Rights. Whenever necessary and possible we share staff, educational, and financial resources with our affiliates. Several months ago our local affiliate here in Birmingham invited us to be on call to engage in a nonviolent direct action program if such were deemed necessary. We readily consented and when the hour came we lived up to our promises. So I am here, along with several members of my staff, because we were invited here. I am here because I have basic organizational ties here. Beyond this, I am in Birmingham because injustice is here. Just as the eighth century prophets left their little villages and carried their "thus saith the Lord" far beyond the boundaries of their home town, and just as the Apostle Paul left his little village of Tarsus and carried the gospel of Jesus Christ to practically every hamlet and city of the Graeco-Roman world, I too am compelled to carry the gospel of freedom beyond my particular home town. Like Paul, I must constantly respond to the Macedonian call for aid.

Moreover, I am cognizant of the interrelatedness of all communities and states. I cannot sit idly by in Atlanta and not be concerned about what happens in Birmingham. Injustice anywhere is a threat to justice everywhere. We are caught in an inescapable network of mutuality tied in a single garment of destiny. Whatever affects one directly affects all indirectly. Never again can we afford to live with the narrow, provincial "outside agitator" idea. Anyone who lives inside the United States can never be considered an outsider anywhere in this country.

You deplore the demonstrations that are presently taking place in Birmingham. But I am sorry that your statement did not express a similar concern for the conditions that brought the demonstrations into being. I am sure that each of you would want to go beyond the superficial social analyst who looks merely at effects, and does not grapple with underlying causes. I would not hesitate to say that it is unfortunate that so-called demonstrations are taking place in Birmingham at this time, but I would say in more emphatic terms it is even more unfortunate that the white power structure of this city left the Negro community with no other alternative.

In any nonviolent campaign there are four basic steps: (1) collection of the facts to determine whether injustices are alive; (2) negotiation; (3) self-purification; and (4) direct action. We have gone through all of these steps in Birmingham. There can be no gainsaying of the fact that racial injustice engulfs this community. Birmingham is probably the most thoroughly segregated city in the United States. Its ugly record of police brutality is known in every section of this country. Its unjust treatment of Negroes in the courts is a notorious reality. There have been more unsolved bombings of Negro homes and churches in Birmingham than any city in this nation. These are the hard, brutal, and unbelievable facts. On the basis of these conditions Negro leaders sought to negotiate with the city fathers. But the political leaders consistently refused to engage in good faith negotiation.

Then came the opportunity last September to talk with some of the leaders of the economic community. In these negotiating sessions certain promises were made by the merchants—such as the promise to remove the humiliating racial signs from the stores. On the basis of these promises Rev. Shuttlesworth and the leaders of the Alabama Christian Movement for Human Rights agreed to call a moratorium on any type of demonstrations. As the weeks and months unfolded we realized that we were the victims of a broken promise. The signs remained. As in so many experiences of the past we were confronted with blasted hopes, and the dark shadow of a deep disappointment settled upon us. So we had no alternative except that of preparing for direct action, whereby we would present our very bodies as a means of laying our case before the conscience of the local and national community. We were not unmindful of the difficulties involved. So we decided to go through a process of self-purification. We started having workshops on nonviolence and repeatedly asked ourselves the questions, "Are you able to accept blows without retaliating?" "Are you able to endure the ordeals of jail?"

We decided to set our direct action program around the Easter season, realizing that with the exception of Christmas, this was the largest shopping period of the year. Knowing that a strong economic withdrawal program would be the by-product of direct action, we felt that this was the best time to bring pressure on the merchants for the needed changes. Then it occurred to us that the March election was ahead, and so we speedily decided to postpone action until after election day. When we discovered that Mr. Connor[1] was in the run-off, we decided again to postpone so that the demonstrations could not be used to cloud the issues. At this time we agreed to begin our nonviolent witness the day after the run-off.

This reveals that we did not move irresponsibly into direct action. We too wanted to see Mr. Connor defeated; so we went through postponement after postponement to aid in this community need. After this we felt that direct action could be delayed no longer.

You may well ask, "Why direct action? Why sit-ins, marches, etc.? Isn't negotiation a better path?" You are exactly right in your call for negotiation. Indeed, this is the purpose of direct action. Nonviolent direct action seeks to create such a crisis and establish such creative tension that a community that has constantly refused to negotiate is forced

---

[1]*Mr. Connor:* Eugene "Bull" Connor and Albert Boutwell ran for mayor of Birmingham, Alabama, in 1963. Although Boutwell, the more moderate candidate, was declared the winner, Connor, the city commissioner of public safety, refused to leave office, claiming that he had been elected to serve until 1965. While the issue was debated in the courts, Connor was on the street ordering the police to use force to suppress demonstrations against segregation. —EDS.

to confront the issue. It seeks so to dramatize the issue that it can no longer be ignored. I just referred to the creation of tension as a part of the work of the nonviolent resister. This may sound rather shocking. But I must confess that I am not afraid of the word tension. I have earnestly worked and preached against violent tension, but there is a type of constructive nonviolent tension that is necessary for growth. Just as Socrates felt that it was necessary to create a tension in the mind so that individuals could rise from the bondage of myths and half-truths to the unfettered realm of creative analysis and objective appraisal, we must see the need of having nonviolent gadflies to create the kind of tension in society that will help men rise from the dark depths of prejudice and racism to the majestic heights of understanding and brotherhood. So the purpose of the direct action is to create a situation so crisis-packed that it will inevitably open the door to negotiation. We, therefore, concur with you in your call for negotiation. Too long has our beloved Southland been bogged down in the tragic attempt to live in monologue rather than dialogue.

One of the basic points in your statement is that our acts are un- 10 timely. Some have asked, "Why didn't you give the new administration time to act?" The only answer that I can give to this inquiry is that the new administration must be prodded about as much as the outgoing one before it acts. We will be sadly mistaken if we feel that the election of Mr. Boutwell will bring the millennium to Birmingham. While Mr. Boutwell is much more articulate and gentle than Mr. Connor, they are both segregationists dedicated to the task of maintaining the status quo. The hope I see in Mr. Boutwell is that he will be reasonable enough to see the futility of massive resistance to desegregation. But he will not see this without pressure from the devotees of civil rights. My friends, I must say to you that we have not made a single gain in civil rights without determined legal and nonviolent pressure. History is the long and tragic story of the fact that privileged groups seldom give up their privileges voluntarily. Individuals may see the moral light and voluntarily give up their unjust posture; but as Reinhold Niebuhr[2] has reminded us, groups are more immoral than individuals.

We know through painful experience that freedom is never voluntarily given by the oppressor; it must be demanded by the oppressed. Frankly I have never yet engaged in a direct action movement that was "well timed," according to the timetable of those who have not suffered unduly from the disease of segregation. For years now I have heard the word "Wait!" It rings in the ear of every Negro with a piercing familiarity. This "wait" has almost always meant "never." It has been a tranquilizing thaliodomide, relieving the emotional stress for a moment, only to give

---

[2]**Niebuhr:** Protestant theologian (1892–1971) best known for attempts to relate Christianity to modern politics. — EDS.

birth to an ill-formed infant of frustration. We must come to see with the distinguished jurist of yesterday that "justice too long delayed is justice denied." We have waited for more than three hundred and forty years for our constitutional and God-given rights. The nations of Asia and Africa are moving with jet-like speed toward the goal of political independence, and we still creep at horse and buggy pace toward the gaining of a cup of coffee at a lunch counter.

I guess it is easy for those who have never felt the stinging darts of segregation to say wait. But when you have seen vicious mobs lynch your mothers and fathers at will and drown your sisters and brothers at whim; when you have seen hate-filled policemen curse, kick, brutalize, and even kill your black brothers and sisters with impunity; when you see the vast majority of your twenty million Negro brothers smothering in an air-tight cage of poverty in the midst of an affluent society; when you suddenly find your tongue twisted and your speech stammering as you seek to explain to your six-year-old daughter why she can't go to the public amusement park that has just been advertised on television, and see tears welling up in her little eyes when she is told that Funtown is closed to colored children, and see the depressing clouds of inferiority begin to form in her little mental sky, and see her begin to distort her little personality by unconsciously developing a bitterness toward white people; when you have to concoct an answer for a five-year-old son asking in agonizing pathos: "Daddy, why do white people treat colored people so mean?"; when you take a cross country drive and find it necessary to sleep night after night in the uncomfortable corners of your automobile because no motel will accept you; when you are humiliated day in and day out by nagging signs reading "white" men and "colored"; when your first name becomes "nigger" and your middle name becomes "boy" (however old you are) and your last name becomes "John," and when your wife and mother are never given the respected title "Mrs."; when you are harried by day and haunted by night by the fact that you are a Negro, living constantly at tip-toe stance never quite knowing what to expect next, and plagued with inner fears and outer resentments; when you are forever fighting a degenerating sense of "nobodiness";—then you will understand why we find it difficult to wait. There comes a time when the cup of endurance runs over, and men are no longer willing to be plunged into an abyss of injustice where they experience the bleakness of corroding despair. I hope, sirs, you can understand our legitimate and unavoidable impatience.

You express a great deal of anxiety over our willingness to break laws. This is certainly a legitimate concern. Since we so diligently urge people to obey the Supreme Court's decision of 1954 outlawing segregation in the public schools, it is rather strange and paradoxical to find us consciously breaking laws. One may well ask, "How can you advocate breaking some laws and obeying others?" The answer is found in the fact that there are two types of laws. There are *just* laws and there are *unjust* laws. I would be the first to advocate obeying just laws. One has not only a legal but moral responsibility to obey just laws. Conversely, one has a moral responsibility to disobey unjust laws. I would agree with Saint Augustine that "An unjust law is no law at all."

Now what is the difference between the two? How does one determine when a law is just or unjust? A just law is a man-made code that squares with the moral law or the law of God. An unjust law is a code that is out of harmony with the moral law. To put it in the terms of Saint Thomas Aquinas, an unjust law is a human law that is not rooted in eternal and natural law. Any law that uplifts human personality is just. Any law that degrades human personality is unjust. All segregation statutes are unjust because segregation distorts the soul and damages the personality. It gives the segregator a false sense of superiority and the segregated a false sense of inferiority. To use the words of Martin Buber, the great Jewish philosopher, segregation substitutes an "I-it" relationship for the "I-thou" relationship, and ends up relegating persons to the status of things. So segregation is not only politically, economically, and sociologically unsound, but it is morally wrong and sinful. Paul Tillich[3] has said that sin is separation. Isn't segregation an existential expression of man's tragic separation, an expression of his awful estrangement, his terrible sinfulness? So I can urge men to obey the 1954 decision of the Supreme Court[4] because it is morally right, and I can urge them to disobey segregation ordinances because they are morally wrong.

Let us turn to a more concrete example of just and unjust laws. An unjust law is a code that a majority inflicts on a minority that is not binding on itself. This is *difference* made legal. On the other hand a just law is a code that a majority compels a minority to follow that it is willing to follow itself. This is *sameness* made legal.

Let me give another explanation. An unjust law is a code inflicted upon a minority which that minority had no part in enacting or creating because they did not have the unhampered right to vote. Who can say the legislature of Alabama which set up the segregation laws was democratically elected? Throughout the state of Alabama all types of conniving methods are used to prevent Negroes from becoming registered voters and there are some counties without a single Negro registered to vote despite the fact that the Negro constitutes a majority of the population. Can any law set up in such a state be considered democratically structured?

These are just a few examples of unjust and just laws. There are some instances when a law is just on its face but unjust in its application. For instance, I was arrested Friday on a charge of parading without a permit.

---

[3]*Tillich* (1886–1965): Theologian and philosopher. — Eds.
[4]*1954 decision of the Supreme Court: Brown v. Board of Education,* the case in which the Supreme Court ruled racial segregation in the nation's public schools unconstitutional. — Eds.

Now there is nothing wrong with an ordinance which requires a permit for a parade, but when the ordinance is used to preserve segregation and to deny citizens the First Amendment privilege of peaceful assembly and peaceful protest, then it becomes unjust.

I hope you can see the distinction I am trying to point out. In no sense do I advocate evading or defying the law as the rabid segregationist would do. This would lead to anarchy. One who breaks an unjust law must do it *openly, lovingly* (not hatefully as the white mothers did in New Orleans when they were seen on television screaming "nigger, nigger, nigger") and with a willingness to accept the penalty. I submit that an individual who breaks a law that conscience tells him is unjust, and willingly accepts the penalty by staying in jail to arouse the conscience of the community over its injustice, is in reality expressing the very highest respect for law.

Of course there is nothing new about this kind of civil disobedience. It was seen sublimely in the refusal of Shadrach, Meshach, and Abednego to obey the laws of Nebuchadnezzar because a higher moral law was involved. It was practiced superbly by the early Christians who were willing to face hungry lions and the excruciating pain of chopping blocks, before submitting to certain unjust laws of the Roman Empire. To a degree academic freedom is a reality today because Socrates practiced civil disobedience.

We can never forget that everything Hitler did in Germany was   20
"legal" and everything the Hungarian freedom fighters[5] did in Hungary was "illegal." It was "illegal" to aid and comfort a Jew in Hitler's Germany. But I am sure that, if I had lived in Germany during that time, I would have aided and comforted my Jewish brothers even though it was illegal. If I lived in a communist country today where certain principles dear to the Christian faith are suppressed, I believe I would openly advocate disobeying those antireligious laws.

I must make two honest confessions to you, my Christian and Jewish brothers. First I must confess that over the last few years I have been gravely disappointed with the white moderate. I have almost reached the regrettable conclusion that the Negroes' great stumbling block in the stride toward freedom is not the White Citizens' "Counciler" or the Ku Klux Klanner, but the white moderate who is more devoted to "order" than to justice; who prefers a negative peace which is the absence of tension to a positive peace which is the presence of justice; who constantly says "I agree with you in the goal you seek, but I can't agree with your methods of direct action"; who paternalistically feels that he can set the timetable for another man's freedom; who lives by the myth of time and who constantly advises the Negro to wait until a "more convenient season."

[5] *Hungarian freedom fighters:* Those who fought in the unsuccessful 1956 revolt against Soviet oppression. — EDS.

Shallow understanding from people of good will is more frustrating than absolute misunderstanding from people of ill will. Lukewarm acceptance is much more bewildering than outright rejection.

I had hoped that the white moderate would understand that law and order exist for the purpose of establishing justice, and that when they fail to do this they become the dangerously structured dams that block the flow of social progress. I had hoped that the white moderate would understand that the present tension in the South is merely a necessary phase of the transition from an obnoxious negative peace, where the Negro passively accepted his unjust plight, to a substance-filled positive peace, where all men will respect the dignity and worth of human personality. Actually, we who engage in nonviolent direct action are not the creators of tension. We merely bring to the surface the hidden tension that is already alive. We bring it out in the open where it can be seen and dealt with. Like a boil that can never be cured as long as it is covered up but must be opened with all its pus-flowing ugliness to the natural medicines of air and light, injustice must likewise be exposed, with all of the tension its exposing creates, to the light of human conscience and the air of national opinion before it can be cured.

In your statement you asserted that our actions, even though peaceful, must be condemned because they precipitate violence. But can this assertion be logically made? Isn't this like condemning the robbed man because his possession of money precipitated the evil act of robbery? Isn't this like condemning Socrates because his unswerving commitment to truth and his philosophical delvings precipitated the misguided popular mind to make him drink the hemlock? Isn't this like condemning Jesus because His unique God consciousness and never-ceasing devotion to His will precipitated the evil act of crucifixion? We must come to see, as federal courts have consistently affirmed, that it is immoral to urge an individual to withdraw his efforts to gain his basic constitutional rights because the quest precipitates violence. Society must protect the robbed and punish the robber.

I had also hoped that the white moderate would reject the myth of time. I received a letter this morning from a white brother in Texas which said: "All Christians know that the colored people will receive equal rights eventually, but is it possible that you are in too great of a religious hurry? It has taken Christianity almost 2000 years to accomplish what it has. The teachings of Christ take time to come to earth." All that is said here grows out of a tragic misconception of time. It is the strangely irrational notion that there is something in the very flow of time that will inevitably cure all ills. Actually time is neutral. It can be used either destructively or constructively. I am coming to feel that the people of ill will have used time much more effectively than the people of good will. We will have to repent in this generation not merely for the vitriolic words and actions of the bad people, but for the appalling silence of the good people. We must come to see that human progress never rolls in on wheels of inevitability. It comes through the tireless efforts and persistent work of men willing to be co-workers with God, and without this hard work time itself becomes an ally of the forces of social stagnation.

We must use time creatively, and forever realize that the time is always   25 ripe to do right. Now is the time to make real the promise of democracy, and transform our pending national elegy into a creative psalm of brotherhood. Now is the time to lift our national policy from the quicksand of racial injustice to the solid rock of human dignity.

You spoke of our activity in Birmingham as extreme. At first I was rather disappointed that fellow clergymen would see my nonviolent efforts as those of the extremist. I started thinking about the fact that I stand in the middle of two opposing forces in the Negro community. One is a force of complacency made up of Negroes who, as a result of long years of oppression, have been so completely drained of self-respect and a sense of "somebodiness" that they have adjusted to segregation, and of a few Negroes in the middle class who, because of a degree of academic and economic security, and because at points they profit by segregation, have unconsciously become insensitive to the problems of the masses. The other force is one of bitterness and hatred and comes perilously close to advocating violence. It is expressed in the various black nationalist groups that are springing up over the nation, the largest and best known being Elijah Muhammad's Muslim movement.[6] This movement is nourished by the contemporary frustration over the continued existence of racial discrimination. It is made up of people who have lost faith in America, who have absolutely repudiated Christianity, and who have concluded that the white man is an incurable "devil." I have tried to stand between these two forces saying that we need not follow the "do-nothing-ism" of the complacent or the hatred and despair of the black nationalist. There is the more excellent way of love and nonviolent protest. I'm grateful to God that, through the Negro church, the dimension of nonviolence entered our struggle. If this philosophy had not emerged I am convinced that by now many streets of the South would be flowing with floods of blood. And I am further convinced that if our white brothers dismiss us as "rabble rousers" and "outside agitators"—those of us who are working through the channels of nonviolent direct action—and refuse to support our nonviolent efforts, millions of Negroes, out of frustration and despair, will seek solace and security in black nationalist ideologies, a development that will lead inevitably to a frightening racial nightmare.

Oppressed people cannot remain oppressed forever. The urge for freedom will eventually come. This is what has happened to the American Negro. Something within has reminded him of his birthright of freedom;

---

[6]*Elijah Muhammad's Muslim movement:* Led by Elijah Muhammad, the Black Muslims opposed integration and promoted the creation of a black nation within the United States.—Eds.

something without has reminded him that he can gain it. Consciously and unconsciously, he has been swept in by what the Germans call the *Zeitgeist,*[7] and with his black brothers of Africa, and his brown and yellow brothers of Asia, South America, and the Caribbean, he is moving with a sense of cosmic urgency toward the promised land of racial justice. Recognizing this vital urge that has engulfed the Negro community, one should readily understand public demonstrations. The Negro has many pent-up resentments and latent frustrations. He has to get them out. So let him march sometime; let him have his prayer pilgrimages to the city hall; understand why he must have sit-ins and freedom rides. If his repressed emotions do not come out in these nonviolent ways, they will come out in ominous expressions of violence. This is not a threat; it is a fact of history. So I have not said to my people, "Get rid of your discontent." But I have tried to say that this normal and healthy discontent can be channeled through the creative outlet of nonviolent direct action. Now this approach is being dismissed as extremist. I must admit that I was initially disappointed in being so categorized.

But as I continued to think about the matter I gradually gained a bit of satisfaction from being considered an extremist. Was not Jesus an extremist in love? "Love your enemies, bless them that curse you, pray for them that despitefully use you." Was not Amos[8] an extremist for justice — "Let justice roll down like waters and righteousness like a mighty stream." Was not Paul an extremist for the gospel of Jesus Christ — "I bear in my body the marks of the Lord Jesus." Was not Martin Luther an extremist — "Here I stand; I can do none other so help me God." Was not John Bunyan[9] an extremist — "I will stay in jail to the end of my days before I make a butchery of my conscience." Was not Abraham Lincoln an extremist — "This nation cannot survive half slave and half free." Was not Thomas Jefferson an extremist — "We hold these truths to be self-evident, that all men are created equal." So the question is not whether we will be extremist but what kind of extremist will we be. Will we be extremists for hate or will we be extremists for love? Will we be extremists for the preservation of injustice — or will we be extremists for the cause of justice? In that dramatic scene on Calvary's hill three men were crucified. We must never forget that all three were crucified for the same crime — the crime of extremism. Two were extremists for immorality, and thus fell below their environment. The other, Jesus Christ, was an extremist for love, truth, and goodness, and thereby rose above His environment. So, after all, maybe the South, the nation, and the world are in dire need of creative extremists.

---

[7] *Zeitgeist:* A German word meaning "spirit of the time." — EDS.
[8] *Amos:* Prophet who preached against false worship and immorality. — EDS.
[9] *John Bunyan:* Puritan author (1628–1688) of *Pilgrim's Progress.* — EDS.

I had hoped that the white moderate would see this. Maybe I was too optimistic. Maybe I expected too much. I guess I should have realized that few members of a race that has oppressed another race can understand or appreciate the deep groans and passionate yearnings of those that have been oppressed, and still fewer have the vision to see that injustice must be rooted out by strong, persistent, and determined action. I am thankful, however, that some of our white brothers have grasped the meaning of this social revolution and committed themselves to it. They are still all too small in quantity, but they are big in quality. Some like Ralph McGill, Lillian Smith, Harry Golden, and James Dabbs have written about our struggle in eloquent, prophetic, and understanding terms. Others have marched with us down nameless streets of the South. They have languished in filthy, roach-infested jails, suffering the abuse and brutality of angry policemen who see them as "dirty nigger lovers." They, unlike so many of their moderate brothers and sisters, have recognized the urgency of the moment and sensed the need for powerful "action" antidotes to combat the disease of segregation.

Let me rush on to mention my other disappointment. I have been so   30
greatly disappointed with the white Church and its leadership. Of course there are some notable exceptions. I am not unmindful of the fact that each of you has taken some significant stands on this issue. I commend you, Rev. Stallings, for your Christian stand on this past Sunday, in welcoming Negroes to your worship service on a nonsegregated basis. I commend the Catholic leaders of this state for integrating Springhill College several years ago.

But despite these notable exceptions I must honestly reiterate that I have been disappointed with the Church. I do not say that as one of those negative critics who can always find something wrong with the Church. I say it as a minister of the gospel, who loves the Church; who was nurtured in its bosom; who has been sustained by its spiritual blessings and who will remain true to it as long as the cord of life shall lengthen.

I had the strange feeling when I was suddenly catapulted into the leadership of the bus protest in Montgomery[10] several years ago that we would have the support of the white Church. I felt that the white ministers, priests, and rabbis of the South would be some of our strongest allies. Instead, some have been outright opponents, refusing to understand the freedom movement and misrepresenting its leaders; all too many others have been more cautious than courageous and have remained silent behind the anesthetizing security of stained glass windows.

---

[10]*bus protest in Montgomery:* After Rosa Parks was arrested on December 1, 1955, in Montgomery, Alabama, for refusing to give her seat on a bus to a white male passenger, a bus boycott began, which lasted nearly one year and was supported by nearly all of the city's black residents. —EDS.

In spite of my shattered dreams of the past, I came to Birmingham with the hope that the white religious leadership of the community would see the justice of our cause and, with deep moral concern, serve as the channel through which our just grievances could get to the power structure. I had hoped that each of you would understand. But again I have been disappointed.

I have heard numerous religious leaders of the South call upon their worshippers to comply with a desegregation decision because it is the law, but I have longed to hear white ministers say follow this decree because integration is morally right and the Negro is your brother. In the midst of blatant injustices inflicted upon the Negro, I have watched white churches stand on the sideline and merely mouth pious irrelevancies and sanctimonious trivialities. In the midst of a mighty struggle to rid our nation of racial and economic injustice, I have heard so many ministers say, "Those are social issues with which the Gospel has no real concern," and I have watched so many churches commit themselves to a completely other-worldly religion which made a strange distinction between body and soul, the sacred and the secular.

So here we are moving toward the exit of the twentieth century with a religious community largely adjusted to the status quo, standing as a tail-light behind other community agencies rather than a headlight leading men to higher levels of justice.

I have travelled the length and breadth of Alabama, Mississippi, and all the other Southern states. On sweltering summer days and crisp autumn mornings I have looked at her beautiful churches with their spires pointing heavenward. I have beheld the impressive outlay of her massive religious education buildings. Over and over again I have found myself asking: "Who worships here? Who is their God? Where were their voices when the lips of Governor Barnett[11] dripped with words of interposition and nullification? Where were they when Governor Wallace[12] gave the clarion call for defiance and hatred? Where were their voices of support when tired, bruised, and weary Negro men and women decided to rise from the dark dungeons of complacency to the bright hills of creative protest?"

Yes, these questions are still in my mind. In deep disappointment, I have wept over the laxity of the Church. But be assured that my tears have been tears of love. There can be no deep disappointment where there is not deep love. Yes, I love the Church; I love her sacred walls. How could I do otherwise? I am in the rather unique position of being the son, the grandson, and the great grandson of preachers. Yes, I see the Church as the body of Christ. But, oh! How we have blemished and

35

---

[11]*Governor Barnett:* Ross R. Barnett, governor of Mississippi from 1960 to 1964.—EDS.
[12]*Governor Wallace:* George C. Wallace served as governor of Alabama from 1963 to 1966, 1971 to 1979, and 1983 to 1987.—EDS.

scarred that body through social neglect and fear of being nonconformists.

There was a time when the Church was very powerful. It was during
that period when the early Christians rejoiced when they were deemed
worthy to suffer for what they believed. In those days the Church was
not merely a thermometer that recorded the ideas and principles of popular opinion; it was a thermostat that transformed the mores of society.
Wherever the early Christians entered a town the power structure got
disturbed and immediately sought to convict them for being "disturbers
of the peace" and "outside agitators." But they went on with the conviction that they were a "colony of heaven" and had to obey God rather
than man. They were small in number but big in commitment. They
were too God-intoxicated to be "astronomically intimidated." They
brought an end to such ancient evils as infanticide and gladiatorial
contest.

Things are different now. The contemporary Church is so often a weak,
ineffectual voice with an uncertain sound. It is so often the arch-supporter
of the status quo. Far from being disturbed by the presence of the
Church, the power structure of the average community is consoled by the
Church's silent and often vocal sanction of things as they are.

But the judgment of God is upon the Church as never before. If   40
the Church of today does not recapture the sacrificial spirit of the early
Church, it will lose its authentic ring, forfeit the loyalty of millions, and
be dismissed as an irrelevant social club with no meaning for the twentieth century. I am meeting young people every day whose disappointment
with the Church has risen to outright disgust.

Maybe again I have been too optimistic. Is organized religion too inextricably bound to the status quo to save our nation and the world?
Maybe I must turn my faith to the inner spiritual Church, the church
within the Church, as the true *ecclesia*[13] and the hope of the world. But
again I am thankful to God that some noble souls from the ranks of organized religion have broken loose from the paralyzing chains of conformity
and joined us as active partners in the struggle for freedom. They have left
their secure congregations and walked the streets of Albany, Georgia, with
us. They have gone through the highways of the South on torturous rides
for freedom. Yes, they have gone to jail with us. Some have been kicked
out of their churches and lost the support of their bishops and fellow ministers. But they have gone with the faith that right defeated is stronger than
evil triumphant. These men have been the leaven in the lump of the race.
Their witness has been the spiritual salt that has preserved the true meaning of the Gospel in these troubled times. They have carved a tunnel of
hope through the dark mountain of disappointment.

---

[13]*ecclesia:* The Latin word for church. —Eds.

I hope the Church as a whole will meet the challenge of this decisive hour. But even if the Church does not come to the aid of justice, I have no despair about the future. I have no fear about the outcome of our struggle in Birmingham, even if our motives are presently misunderstood. We will reach the goal of freedom in Birmingham and all over the nation, because the goal of America is freedom. Abused and scorned though we may be, our destiny is tied up with the destiny of America. Before the pilgrims landed at Plymouth, we were here. Before the pen of Jefferson etched across the pages of history the majestic words of the Declaration of Independence, we were here. For more than two centuries our foreparents labored in this country without wages; they made cotton "king"; and they built the homes of their masters in the midst of brutal injustice and shameful humiliation — and yet out of a bottomless vitality they continued to thrive and develop. If the inexpressible cruelties of slavery could not stop us, the opposition we now face will surely fail. We will win our freedom because the sacred heritage of our nation and the eternal will of God are embodied in our echoing demands.

I must close now. But before closing I am impelled to mention one other point in your statement that troubled me profoundly. You warmly commended the Birmingham police force for keeping "order" and "preventing violence." I don't believe you would have so warmly commended the police force if you had seen its angry violent dogs literally biting six unarmed, nonviolent Negroes. I don't believe you would so quickly commend the policemen if you would observe their ugly and inhuman treatment of Negroes here in the city jail; if you would watch them push and curse old Negro women and young Negro girls; if you would see them slap and kick old Negro men and young Negro boys; if you will observe them, as they did on two occasions, refuse to give us food because we wanted to sing our grace together. I'm sorry that I can't join you in your praise for the police department.

It is true that they have been rather disciplined in their public handling of the demonstrators. In this sense they have been rather publicly "nonviolent." But for what purpose? To preserve the evil system of segregation. Over the last few years I have consistently preached that nonviolence demands that the means we use must be as pure as the ends we seek. So I have tried to make it clear that it is wrong to use immoral means to attain moral ends. But now I must affirm that it is just as wrong, or even more so, to use moral means to preserve immoral ends. Maybe Mr. Connor and his policemen have been rather publicly nonviolent, as Chief Pritchett[14]

---

[14]***Chief Pritchett:*** Pritchett served as police chief in Albany, Georgia, during nonviolent demonstrations in 1961 and 1962. Chief Pritchett responded to the nonviolent demonstrations with nonviolence, refusing to allow his officers to physically or verbally abuse the demonstrators. — EDS.

was in Albany, Georgia, but they have used the moral means of nonviolence to maintain the immoral end of flagrant racial injustice. T. S. Eliot has said that there is no greater treason than to do the right deed for the wrong reason.

I wish you had commended the Negro sit-inners and demonstrators   45
of Birmingham for their sublime courage, their willingness to suffer, and their amazing discipline in the midst of the most inhuman provocation. One day the South will recognize its real heroes. They will be the James Merediths,[15] courageously and with a majestic sense of purpose, facing jeering and hostile mobs and the agonizing loneliness that characterizes the life of the pioneer. They will be old, oppressed, battered Negro women, symbolized in a seventy-two year old woman of Montgomery, Alabama, who rose up with a sense of dignity and with her people decided not to ride the segregated buses, and responded to one who inquired about her tiredness with ungrammatical profundity: "My feets is tired, but my soul is rested." They will be young high school and college students, young ministers of the gospel and a host of the elders, courageously and nonviolently sitting in at lunch counters and willingly going to jail for conscience sake. One day the South will know that when these disinherited children of God sat down at lunch counters they were in reality standing up for the best in the American dream and the most sacred values in our Judeo-Christian heritage, and thus carrying our whole nation back to great wells of democracy which were dug deep by the founding fathers in the formulation of the Constitution and the Declaration of Independence.

Never before have I written a letter this long (or should I say a book?). I'm afraid that it is much too long to take your precious time. I can assure you that it would have been much shorter if I had been writing from a comfortable desk, but what else is there to do when you are alone for days in the dull monotony of a narrow jail cell other than write long letters, think strange thoughts, and pray long prayers?

If I have said anything in this letter that is an overstatement of the truth and is indicative of an unreasonable impatience, I beg you to forgive me. If I have said anything in this letter that is an understatement of the truth and is indicative of my having a patience that makes me patient with anything less than brotherhood, I beg God to forgive me.

I hope this letter finds you strong in the faith. I also hope that circumstances will soon make it possible for me to meet each of you, not as an integrationist or a civil rights leader, but as a fellow clergyman and a Christian brother. Let us all hope that the dark clouds of racial prejudice

---

[15]*James Merediths:* Under the protection of federal marshals and the National Guard in 1962, James Meredith was the first black man to enroll at the University of Mississippi. — Eds.

will soon pass away and the deep fog of misunderstanding will be lifted from our fear-drenched communities and in some not too distant tomorrow the radiant stars of love and brotherhood will shine over our great nation with all of their scintillating beauty.

> *Yours for the cause of*
> *Peace and Brotherhood*
> MARTIN LUTHER KING JR.

The Reader's Presence

1. King wrote this letter in response to the eight clergymen identified at the beginning of the letter, a group who had declared that the civil rights activities of King and his associates were "unwise and untimely." What does King gain by characterizing his "Fellow Clergymen" as "men of genuine good will," whose criticisms are "sincerely set forth"? What evidence can you point to in King's letter to verify the claim that his audience extends far beyond the eight clergymen he explicitly addresses? Comment on the overall structure of King's letter. What principle of composition underpins the structure of his response?

2. King establishes the tone of his response to the criticisms of the clergymen at the end of the opening paragraph: "I would like to answer your statement in what I hope will be patient and reasonable terms." As you reread his letter, identify specific words and phrases—as well as argumentative strategies—that satisfy these criteria that King imposes on himself. In what specific sense does King use the word *hope* here? As you reread his letter, point to each subsequent reference to hope. How does King emphasize the different meanings and connotations of the word as he unfolds his argument?

3. This letter has the ring of the oratory for which King was widely known and justly praised. Read passages aloud and note the ways that King appeals to his reader's ear (for example, with the balanced clauses of many of his sentences). In paragraph 42, King notes that "our destiny is tied up with the destiny of America" and repeats the refrain "we were here," speaking of the essential place of African Americans in the making of American freedom. How does King enlarge the scope of his political vision in this paragraph? How does he relate the 1963 crisis of African American oppression to the founding of the American republic? How do the cadences of King's prose help to make his point?

Compare King's letter to Edwidge Danticat's essay about the suffering and survival of Haitan women, "We Are Ugly, but We Are Here" (page 642). How do these writers instill hope into their writing?

THE WRITER AT WORK

Martin Luther King Jr. on Self-Importance

In the following piece, the famous African American political leader expresses his profound mistrust of the individual voice that rises above those for whom that voice speaks. In this, as in so many respects, King joins a long tradition of wrestling with the question of how to reconcile one's own creativity with the larger—and vastly more important—word and mission of God. King's spiritual mission was, of course, a social vision as well: that of racial equality in America. In speaking for those who believed with him in the possibility of making this dream a reality, King drew upon his consummate skills as a preacher, orator, and organizer. Throughout his short public life (spanning only twelve years, ending with his assassination on April 4, 1968, in Memphis, Tennessee), King struggled with the competing claims of personal celebrity and of the community he so forcefully represented. How do King's ideas about representation (standing for and speaking on behalf of others) resonate with the ideas of other notable Americans included in this anthology, for example, Thomas Jefferson (page 711), Malcolm X (page 194), and Abraham Lincoln (pages 498, 501)?

Would you allow me to share a personal experience with you this morning? And I say it only because I think it has bearing on this message. One of the problems that I have to face and even fight every day is this problem of self-centeredness, this tendency that can so easily come to my life now that I'm something special, that I'm something important. Living over the past year, I can hardly go into any city or any town in this nation where I'm not lavished with hospitality by peoples of all races and of all creeds. I can hardly go anywhere to speak in this nation where hundreds and thousands of people are not turned away because of lack of space. And then after speaking, I often have to be rushed out to get away from the crowd rushing for autographs. I can hardly walk the street in any city of this nation where I'm not confronted with people running up on the street, "Isn't this Reverend King of Alabama?" Living under this it's easy, it's a dangerous tendency that I will come to feel that I'm something special, that I stand somewhere in this universe because of my ingenuity and that I'm important, that I can walk around life with a type of arrogance because of an importance that I have. And one of the prayers that I pray to God every day is: "O God, help me to see my self in my true perspective. Help me, O God, to see that I'm just a symbol of a movement. Help me to see that I'm the victim of what the Germans call a *Zeitgeist* and that something was getting ready to happen in history; history was ready for it. And that a boycott would have taken place in Montgomery, Alabama, if I had never come to Alabama. Help me to realize that I'm where I am because of the forces of history and because of the fifty thousand Negroes of Alabama who will never get their names in the papers and in the headline. O God, help me to see that where I stand today, I stand because others helped me to stand there and because the forces of history projected me there. And this movement would have come in history even if M. L. King had never been born." And when we come to see that, we stand with humility. This is the prayer I pray to God every day, "Lord help me to see M. L. King as M. L. King in his true perspective." Because if I don't see that, I will become the biggest fool in America.

Laura Kipnis

Against Love

Laura Kipnis is a cultural theorist, author, and videographer whose work blends academic theory, social criticism, and witty analysis, all "richly informed by her post-marxist, post-structuralist, post-feminist, post-everything sense of humor," according to a recent biography. She is the author of Ecstasy Unlimited *(1993), a collection of essays and videoscripts;* Bound and Gagged: Pornography and the Politics of Fantasy in America *(1996); and* Against Love: A Polemic *(2003). Kipnis's video essays — including* Ecstasy Unlimited: The Interpenetrations of Sex and Capital *(1985),* A Man's Woman *(1988), and* Marx: The Video *(1990) — have been screened in such venues as the Museum of Modern Art, the American Film Institute, and the Whitney Museum. Kipnis has also written essays and reviews for* Slate, *the* Village Voice, Harper's, Critical Inquiry, Wide Angle, *and the* New York Times Magazine, *where "Against Love" appeared in 2001.*

Kipnis's work has evolved over time, shifting from what was once a strictly academic tone to her more recent playful and casual style. In an interview with the editor of the Minnesota Review, *she admits that she has developed a growing interest in "creativity" over "theory." She explains, "I trace it back to my art school origins. I started as a painter, actually, and there's something about the writing I've been doing lately which has gotten really intricate and worked over,*

that reminds me of my origins as a painter. I've started to write in a painterly
way, dabbing at it, endlessly revising."

Kipnis currently teaches radio, television, and film at Northwestern Univer-
sity in Evanston, Illinois. In a discussion of Against Love *in 2001, Kipnis pointed*
out that "the voice isn't precisely 'me,' it's some far more vivacious and playful
version of me. It's a polemic, so there are certain questions I don't have to ad-
dress, or complications I don't have to go into. I can be completely irresponsible.
I love it."

Love is, as we know, a mysterious and controlling force. It has vast
power over our thoughts and life decisions. It demands our loyalty, and
we, in turn, freely comply. Saying no to love isn't simply heresy; it is
tragedy—the failure to achieve what is most essentially human. So deeply
internalized is our obedience to this most capricious despot that artists
create passionate odes to its cruelty, and audiences seem never to tire of
the most deeply unoriginal mass spectacles devoted to rehearsing the litany
of its torments, fixating their very beings on the narrowest glimmer of its
fleeting satisfactions.

Yet despite near total compliance, a buzz of social nervousness attends the subject. If a society's lexicon of romantic pathologies reveals its
particular anxieties, high on our own list would be diagnoses like "inability to settle down" or "immaturity," leveled at those who stray from
the norms of domestic coupledom either by refusing entry in the first place
or, once installed, pursuing various escape routes: excess independence,
ambivalence, "straying," divorce. For the modern lover, "maturity" isn't a
depressing signal of impending decrepitude but a sterling achievement, the
sine qua non of a lover's qualifications to love and be loved.

This injunction to achieve maturity—synonymous in contemporary usage with thirty-year mortgages, spreading waistlines and
monogamy—obviously finds its raison d'être in modern love's central
anxiety, that structuring social contradiction the size of the San Andreas
Fault: namely, the expectation that romance and sexual attraction can
last a lifetime of coupled togetherness despite much hard evidence to the
contrary.

Ever optimistic, heady with love's utopianism, most of us eventually
pledge ourselves to unions that will, if successful, far outlast the desire
that impelled them into being. The prevailing cultural wisdom is that even
if sexual desire tends to be a short-lived phenomenon, "mature love" will
kick in to save the day when desire flags. The issue that remains unad-
dressed is whether cutting off other possibilities of romance and sexual
attraction for the more muted pleasures of mature love isn't similar to
voluntarily amputating a healthy limb: a lot of anesthesia is required and
the phantom pain never entirely abates. But if it behooves a society to
convince its citizenry that wanting change means personal failure or
wanting to start over is shameful or simply wanting more satisfaction

than what you have is an illicit thing, clearly grisly acts of self-mutilation will be required.

There hasn't always been quite such optimism about love's longevity.   5
For the Greeks, inventors of democracy and a people not amenable to being pushed around by despots, love was a disordering and thus prefer-ably brief experience. During the reign of courtly love, love was illicit and usually fatal. Passion meant suffering: the happy ending didn't yet exist in the cultural imagination. As far as togetherness as an eternal ideal, the 12th-century advice manual "De Amore et Amoris Remedio" ("On Love and the Remedies of Love") warned that too many opportunities to see or chat with the beloved would certainly decrease love.

The innovation of happy love didn't even enter the vocabulary of ro-mance until the 17th century. Before the 18th century—when the family was primarily an economic unit of production rather than a hothouse of Oedipal tensions—marriages were business arrangements between families; participants had little to say on the matter. Some historians consider roman-tic love a learned behavior that really only took off in the late 18th century along with the new fashion for reading novels, though even then affection between a husband and wife was considered to be in questionable taste.

Historians disagree, of course. Some tell the story of love as an eter-nal and unchanging essence; others, as a progress narrative over stifling social conventions. (Sometimes both stories are told at once; consistency isn't required.) But has modern love really set us free? Fond as we are of projecting our own emotional quandaries back through history, constru-ing vivid costume dramas featuring medieval peasants or biblical courte-sans sharing their feelings with the post-Freudian savvy of lifelong analysands, our amatory predecessors clearly didn't share all our particu-lar aspirations about their romantic lives.

We, by contrast, feel like failures when love dies. We believe it could be otherwise. Since the cultural expectation is that a state of coupled perma-nence is achievable, uncoupling is experienced as crisis and inadequacy— even though such failures are more the norm than the exception.

As love has increasingly become the center of all emotional expression in the popular imagination, anxiety about obtaining it in sufficient quantities—and for sufficient duration—suffuses the population. Every-one knows that as the demands and expectations on couples escalated, so did divorce rates. And given the current divorce statistics (roughly 50 per-cent of all marriages end in divorce), all indications are that whomever you love today—your beacon of hope, the center of all your optimism—has a good chance of becoming your worst nightmare tomorrow. (Of course, that 50 percent are those who actually leave their unhappy marriages and not a particularly good indication of the happiness level or nightmare potential of those who remain.) Lawrence Stone, a historian of marriage, suggests—rather jocularly, you can't help thinking—that today's rising divorce rates are just a modern technique for achieving what was once taken care of far more efficiently by early mortality.

Love may or may not be a universal emotion, but clearly the social   10 forms it takes are infinitely malleable. It is our culture alone that has dedicated itself to allying the turbulence of romance and the rationality of the long-term couple, convinced that both love and sex are obtainable from one person over the course of decades, that desire will manage to sustain itself for thirty or forty or fifty years and that the supposed fate of social stability is tied to sustaining a fleeting experience beyond its given life span.

Of course, the parties involved must "work" at keeping passion alive (and we all know how much fun that is), the presumption being that even after living in close proximity to someone for a historically unprecedented length of time, you will still muster the requisite desire to achieve sexual congress on a regular basis. (Should passion fizzle out, just give up sex. Lack of desire for a mate is never an adequate rationale for "looking elsewhere.") And it is true, many couples do manage to perform enough psychic retooling to reshape the anarchy of desire to the confines of the marriage bed, plugging away at the task year after year (once a week, same time, same position) like diligent assembly-line workers, aided by the occasional fantasy or two to help get the old motor to turn over, or keep running, or complete the trip. And so we have the erotic life of a nation of workaholics: if sex seems like work, clearly you're not working hard enough at it.

But passion must not be allowed to die! The fear—or knowledge—that it does shapes us into particularly conflicted psychological beings, perpetually in search of prescriptions and professional interventions, regardless of cost or consequence. Which does have its economic upside, at least. Whole new sectors of the economy have been spawned, with massive social investment in new technologies from Viagra to couples' porn: capitalism's Lourdes[1] for dying marriages.

There are assorted low-tech solutions to desire's dilemmas too. Take advice. In fact, take more and more advice. Between print, airwaves and the therapy industry, if there were any way to quantify the G.N.P. in romantic counsel, it would be a staggering number. Desperate to be cured of love's temporality, a love-struck populace has molded itself into an advanced race of advice receptacles, like some new form of miracle sponge that can instantly absorb many times its own body weight in wetness.

Inexplicably, however, a rebellious breakaway faction keeps trying to leap over the wall and emancipate themselves, not from love itself—unthinkable!—but from love's domestic confinements. The escape routes are well trodden—love affairs, midlife crises—though strewn with the

---

[1]*Lourdes:* Notre Dame de Lourdes in France has been a site of Catholic pilgrimage ever since a fourteen-year-old girl reportedly received a vision there in 1858.—EDS.

left-behind luggage of those who encountered unforeseen obstacles along the way (panic, guilt, self-engineered exposures) and beat self-abashed retreats to their domestic gulags, even after pledging body and soul to new-found loves in the balmy utopias of nondomesticated romances. Will all the adulterers in the audience please stand up? You know who you are. Don't be embarrassed! Adulterers aren't just "playing around." These are our home-grown closet social theorists, because adultery is not just a referendum on the sustainability of monogamy; it is a veiled philosophical discussion about the social contract itself. The question on the table is this "How much renunciation of desire does society demand of us, versus the degree of gratification it provides?" Clearly, the adulterer's answer, following a long line of venerable social critics, would be, "Too much."

But what exactly is it about the actual lived experience of modern domestic love that would make flight such a compelling option for so many? Let us briefly examine those material daily life conditions.

Fundamentally, to achieve love and qualify for entry into that realm of salvation and transcendence known as the couple (the secular equivalent of entering a state of divine grace), you must *be* a lovable person. And what precisely does being lovable entail? According to the tenets of modern love, it requires an advanced working knowledge of the intricacies of *mutuality*.

Mutuality means recognizing that your partner has needs and being prepared to meet them. This presumes, of course, that the majority of those needs can and should be met by one person. (Question this, and you question the very foundations of the institution. So don't.) These needs of ours run deep, a tangled underground morass of ancient, gnarled roots, looking to ensnarl any hapless soul who might accidentally trod upon their outer radices.

Still, meeting those needs is the most effective way to become the object of another's desire, thus attaining intimacy, which is required to achieve the state known as psychological maturity. (Despite how closely it reproduces the affective conditions of our childhoods, since trading compliance for love is the earliest social lesson learned; we learn it in our cribs.)

You, in return, will have your own needs met by your partner in matters large and small. In practice, many of these matters turn out to be quite small. Frequently, it is the tensions and disagreements over the minutiae of daily living that stand between couples and their requisite intimacy. Taking out the garbage, tone of voice, a forgotten errand — these are the rocky shoals upon which intimacy so often founders.

Mutuality requires *communication*, since in order to be met, these needs must be expressed. (No one's a mind reader, which is not to say that many of us don't expect this quality in a mate. Who wants to keep having to tell someone what you need?) What you need is for your mate to understand you — your desires, your contradictions, your unique sensitivities, what irks you. (In practice, that means what about your mate irks you.)

You, in turn, must learn to understand the mate's needs. This means being willing to hear what about yourself irks your mate. Hearing is not a simple physiological act performed with the ears, as you will learn. You may think you know how to *hear*, but that doesn't mean that you know how to *listen*.

With two individuals required to coexist in enclosed spaces for extended periods of time, domesticity requires substantial quantities of compromise and adaptation simply to avoid mayhem. Yet with the post-Romantic ideal of unconstrained individuality informing our most fundamental ideas of the self, this can prove a perilous process. Both parties must be willing to jettison whatever aspects of individuality might prove irritating while being simultaneously allowed to retain enough individuality to feel their autonomy is not being sacrificed, even as it is being surgically excised.

Having mastered mutuality, you may now proceed to *advanced intimacy*. Advanced intimacy involves inviting your partner "in" to your most interior self. Whatever and wherever our "inside" is, the widespread—if somewhat metaphysical—belief in its existence (and the related belief that whatever is in there is dying to get out) has assumed a quasi-medical status. Leeches once served a similar purpose. Now we "express our feelings" in lieu of our fluids because everyone knows that those who don't are far more prone to cancer, ulcers or various dire ailments.

With love as our culture's patent medicine, prescribed for every ill (now even touted as a necessary precondition for that other great American obsession, longevity), we willingly subject ourselves to any number of arcane procedures in its quest. "Opening up" is required for relationship health, so lovers fashion themselves after doctors wielding long probes to penetrate the tender regions. Try to think of yourself as one big orifice: now stop clenching and relax. If the procedure proves uncomfortable, it just shows you're not open enough. Psychotherapy may be required before sufficient dilation can be achieved: the world's most expensive lubricant.

Needless to say, this opening-up can leave you feeling quite vulnerable, lying there psychically spread-eagled and shivering on the examining table of your relationship. (A favored suspicion is that your partner, knowing exactly where your vulnerabilities are, deliberately kicks you there—one reason this opening-up business may not always feel as pleasant as advertised.) And as anyone who has spent much time in—or just in earshot of—a typical couple knows, the "expression of needs" is often the Trojan horse of intimate warfare, since expressing needs means, by definition, that one's partner has thus far failed to meet them.

In any long-term couple, this lexicon of needs becomes codified over time into a highly evolved private language with its own rules. Let's call this couple grammar. Close observation reveals this as a language composed of   25 one recurring unit of speech: the interdiction—highly nuanced, mutually imposed commands and strictures extending into the most minute areas of household affairs, social life, finances, speech, hygiene, allowable idiosyncrasies and so on. From bathroom to bedroom, car to kitchen, no aspect of coupled life is not subject to scrutiny, negotiation and codes of conduct.

A sample from an inexhaustible list, culled from interviews with numerous members of couples of various ages, races and sexual orientations:

You can't leave the house without saying where you're going. You can't not say what time you'll return. You can't go out when the other person feels like staying at home. You can't be a slob. You can't do less than 50 percent of the work around the house, even if the other person wants to do 100 percent more cleaning than you find necessary or even reasonable. You can't leave the dishes for later, load them the way that seems best to you, drink straight from the carton or make crumbs. You can't leave the bathroom door open—it's offensive. You can't leave the bathroom door closed—your partner needs to get in. You can't not shave your underarms or legs. You can't gain weight. You can't watch soap operas. You can't watch infomercials or the pregame show or Martha Stewart. You can't eat what you want—goodbye Marshmallow Fluff; hello tofu meatballs. You can't spend too much time on the computer. And stay out of those chat rooms. You can't take risks, unless they are agreed-upon risks, which somewhat limits the concept of "risk." You can't make major purchases alone, or spend money on things the other person considers excesses. You can't blow money just because you're in a bad mood, and you can't be in a bad mood without being required to explain it. You can't begin a sentence with "You always. . . ." You can't begin a sentence with "I never. . . ." You can't be simplistic, even when things are simple. You can't say what you really think of that outfit or color combination or cowboy hat. You can't be cynical about things the other person is sincere about. You can't drink without the other person counting your drinks. You can't have the wrong laugh. You can't bum cigarettes when you're out because it embarrasses your mate, even though you've explained the unspoken fraternity between smokers. You can't tailgate, honk or listen to talk radio in the car. And so on. The specifics don't matter. What matters is that the operative word is "can't."

Thus is love obtained.

Certainly, domesticity offers innumerable rewards: companionship, child-rearing convenience, reassuring predictability and many other benefits too varied to list. But if love has power over us, domesticity is its enforcement wing: the iron dust mop in the velvet glove. The historian Michel Foucault[2] has argued that modern power made its mark on the

---

[2]***Michel Foucault:*** French philosopher and historian (1926–1984), who questioned assumptions about the constitution of power and knowledge.—Eds.

world by inventing new types of enclosures and institutions, places like factories, schools, barracks, prisons and asylums, where individuals could be located, supervised, processed and subjected to inspection, order and the clock. What current social institution is more enclosed than modern intimacy? What offers greater regulation of movement and time, or more precise surveillance of body and thought, to a greater number of individuals?

Of course, it is your choice—as if any of us could really choose not   30
to desire love or not to feel like hopeless losers should we fail at it. We moderns are beings yearning to be filled, yearning to be overtaken by love's mysterious power. We prostrate ourselves at love's portals, like social strivers waiting at the rope line outside some exclusive club hoping to gain admission and thereby confirm our essential worth. A life without love lacks an organizing narrative. A life without love seems so barren, and it might almost make you consider how empty the rest of the world is, as if love were vital plasma and everything else just tap water.

Exchanging obedience for love comes naturally—after all, we all were once children whose survival depended on the caprices of love. And there you have the template for future intimacies. If you love me, you'll do what I want—or need, or demand—and I'll love you in return. We all become household dictators, petty tyrants of the private sphere, who are, in our turn, dictated to.

And why has modern love developed in such a way as to maximize submission and minimize freedom, with so little argument about it? No doubt a citizenry schooled in renouncing desire instead of imagining there could be something more would be, in many respects, advantageous. After all, wanting more is the basis for utopian thinking, a path toward dangerous social demands, even toward imagining the possibilities for altogether different social arrangements. But if the most elegant forms of social control are those that came packaged in the guise of individual needs and satisfactions, so wedded to the individual psyche that any opposing impulse registers as the anxiety of unlovability, who needs a soldier on every corner? We are more than happy to police ourselves and those we love and call it living happily ever after. Perhaps a secular society needed another metaphysical entity to subjugate itself to after the death of God, and love was available for the job. But isn't it a little depressing to think we are somehow incapable of inventing forms of emotional life based on anything other than subjugation?

The Reader's Presence

1. How does Kipnis reevaluate the meaning of adultery and mid-life crises? What sort of evidence are these phenomena, in her opinion?

2. What elements of Kipnis's writing mark this essay as a scholarly argument? Do you agree that it is also a "polemic," as the subtitle of her book indicates? Is it more effective as a scholarly argument or as a polemic? Why?

3. Kipnis suggests that society benefits from convincing its populace to marry and that people have been brainwashed into believing that these long-term arrangements are natural. What benefits does society gain from long-term relationships? What, in Kipnis's opinion, do individuals give up? Read John Gatto's "Against School" (page 688). What, according to his argument, does the individual lose in submitting to compulsory schooling? Who, according to Gatto, benefits from it?

Bill McKibben

Worried? Us?

Bill McKibben (b. 1960) advocates human behavior toward Earth that is "sound and elegant and civilized and respectful of community." Born in Palo Alto, California, and raised in Massachusetts, he now lives with his family in New York's Adirondack Mountains. After graduating from Harvard University in 1982, McKibben immediately went to work as a writer, and later editor, at the New Yorker, *where he wrote more than four hundred articles for the magazine's "Talk of the Town" column. His essays, reporting, and criticism appear regularly in publications such as the* Atlantic, Harper's, *the* New York Review of Books, *the* New York Times, Natural History, Orion, Rolling Stone, *and* Outside. *McKibben is currently a visiting scholar of environmental studies at Middlebury College in Vermont.*

McKibben's 1989 book, The End of Nature, *sounded one of the earliest alarms about global warming and catalyzed an international debate on the issue that is still ongoing. His long list of books catalogues his concerns about the health of our global ecosystem, particularly the relationship between humanity and nature and the impact of our consumer society on both. His books include* The Age of Missing Information *(1992),* Hope, Human and Wild *(1995),* Maybe One: A Personal and Environmental Argument for Single-Child Families *(1998),* Long Distance *(2000),* Enough: Staying Human in an Engineered Age (2003), *and his latest,* Wandering Home (2005).

In a 1999 interview, McKibben discussed the competing visions of what is good for people and the planet on which we live: "The market forces pushing

convenience, individualism, and comfort are still stronger than the attraction of
community, fellowship, and connection with the natural world. . . . What we call
the environmental crisis is really a crisis of desire. We're losing the battle to offer
people an alternative set of things to desire."
      McKibbens's essay "Worried? Us?" asks why, in the face of mainstream sci-
entific evidence to the contrary, so many people continue to ignore the threat of
global warming. It was first published in Granta *in 2003.*

For fifteen years now, some small percentage of the world's scientists
and diplomats and activists has inhabited one of those strange dreams
where the dreamer desperately needs to warn someone about something
bad and imminent; but somehow, no matter how hard he shouts, the
other person in the dream—standing smiling, perhaps, with his back to
an oncoming train—can't hear him. This group, this small percentage,
knows that the world is about to change more profoundly than at any
time in the history of human civilization. And yet, so far, all they have
achieved is to add another line to the long list of human problems—people
think about "global warming" in the way they think about "violence on
televison" or "growing trade deficits," as a marginal concern to them, if a
concern at all. Enlightened governments make smallish noises and negotiate smallish treaties; enlightened people look down on America for its
blind piggishness. Hardly anyone, however, has fear in their guts.

Why? Because, I think, we are fatally confused about time and space.
Though we know that our culture has placed our own lives on a demonic
fast-forward, we imagine that the earth must work on some other
timescale. The long slow accretion of epochs—the Jurassic, the Cretaceous, the Pleistocene—lulls us into imagining that the physical world offers us an essentially stable background against which we can run our
race. Humbly, we believe that the world is big and that we are small. This
humility is attractive, but also historic and no longer useful. In the world
as we have made it, the opposite is true. Each of us is big enough, for example, to produce our own cloud of carbon dioxide. As a result, we—
our cars and our industry—have managed to raise the atmospheric level
of carbon dioxide, which had been stable at 275 parts per million
throughout human civilization, to about 380 parts per million, a figure
that is climbing by one and a half parts per million each year. This increase began with the Industrial Revolution in the eighteenth century, and
it has been accelerating ever since. The consequence, if we take a median
from several respectable scientific projections, is that the world's temperature will rise by five degrees Fahrenheit (roughly two and a half degrees
Celsius) over the next hundred years, to make it hotter than it has been
for 400 million years. At some level, these are the only facts worth knowing about our earth.

Fifteen years ago, it was a hypothesis. Those of us who were convinced that the earth was warming fast were a small minority. Science

was skeptical, but set to work with rigour. Between 1988 and 1995, scientists drilled deep into glaciers, took core samples from lake bottoms, counted tree rings, and, most importantly, refined elaborate computer models of the atmosphere. By 1995, the almost impossibly contentious world of science had seen enough. The world's most distinguished atmospheric chemists, physicists and climatologists, who had organized themselves into a large collective called the Intergovernmental Panel on Climate Change, made their pronouncement: "The balance of evidence suggests that there is a discernible human influence on global climate." In the eight years since, science has continued to further confirm and deepen these fears, while the planet itself has decided, as it were, to peer-review their work with a succession of ominously hot years (1998 was the hottest ever, with 2002 trailing by only a few hundredths of a degree). So far humanity has raised the planet's temperature by about one degree Fahrenheit, with most of that increase happening after 1970 — from about fifty-nine degrees Fahrenheit, where it had been stuck since the first cities rose and the first crops grew, to about sixty degrees. Five more degrees in the offing, as I have said, but already we understand, with an almost desperate clarity, how finely balanced our world has been. One degree turns out to be a lot. In the cryosphere — the frozen portions of the planet's surface — glaciers are everywhere in rapid retreat (spitting out Bronze Age hunter-gatherers). The snows of Kilimanjaro are set to become the rocks of Kilimanjaro by 2015. Montana's Glacier National Park is predicted to lose its last glaciers by 2030. We know how thick Arctic ice is — we know it because Cold War nuclear-powered submarines needed the information for their voyages under the ice cap. When the data was declassified in the waning days of the Clinton administration, it emerged that Arctic ice was forty per cent thinner than it had been forty years before. *Perma*frost is melting. Get it?

"Global warming" can be a misleading phrase — the temperature is only the signal that extra solar radiation is being trapped at the earth's surface. That extra energy drives many things: wind-speeds increase, a reflection of the increasing heat-driven gradients between low and high pressure; sea level starts to rise, less because of melting ice caps than because warm air holds more water vapor than cold; hence evaporation increases and with it drought, and then, when the overloaded clouds finally part, deluge and flood. Some of these effects are linear. A recent study has shown that rice fertility drops by ten per cent for each degree Celsius that the temperature rises above thirty degrees Celsius during the rice plant's flowering. At forty degrees Celsius, rice fertility drops to zero. But science has come to understand that some effects may not follow such a clear progression. To paraphrase Orwell, we may all be hot, but some will be hotter than others. If the Gulf Stream fails because of Arctic melting, some may, during some seasons, even be colder.

The success of the scientific method underlines the failure of the political method. It is clear what must happen — the rapid conversion of our energy system from fossil to renewable fuels. And it is clear that it could happen—much of the necessary technology is no longer quixotic, no longer the province of backyard tinkerers. And it is also clear that it isn't happening. Some parts of Europe have made material progress— Denmark has built great banks of windmills. Some parts of Europe have made promises—the United Kingdom thinks it can cut its carbon emissions by sixty per cent by 2050. But China and India are still building power plants and motorways, and the United States has made it utterly clear that nothing will change soon. When Bill Clinton was President he sat by while American civilians traded up from cars to troop-transport vehicles; George Bush has not only rejected the Kyoto treaty,[1] he has ordered the Environmental Protection Agency to replace "global warming" with the less ominous "climate change," and issued a national energy policy that foresees ever more drilling, refining and burning. Under it, American carbon emissions will grow another forty per cent in the next generation.

As satisfying as it is to blame politicians, however, it will not do. Politicians will follow the path of least resistance. So far there has not been a movement loud or sustained enough to command political attention. Electorates demand economic prosperity—more of it—above all things. Gandhianism, the political philosophy that restricts material need, is now only a memory even in the country of its birth. And our awareness that the world will change in every aspect, should we be so aware, is muted by the future tense, even though that future isn't far away, so near in fact that preventing global warming is a lost cause—all we can do now is to try to keep it from getting utterly out of control.

This is a failure of imagination, and in this way a literary failure. Global warming has still to produce an Orwell or a Huxley, a Verne or a Wells, a *Nineteen Eighty-Four* or a *War of the Worlds*, or in film any equivalent of *On The Beach*[2] or *Doctor Strangelove*. It may never do so. It may be that because—fingers crossed—we have escaped our most recent fear, nuclear annihilation via the Cold War, we resist being scared all over again. Fear has its uses, but fear on this scale seems to be disabling, paralysing. Anger has its uses too, but the rage of anti-globalization demonstrators has yet to do more than alienate majorities. Shame sends a

---

[1]*Kyoto treaty:* A treaty drawn up in 1997 with the aim of reducing worldwide emissions of greenhouse gases. President George W. Bush withdrew it from U.S. consideration in 2001.—EDS.

[2]*Huxley . . . On the Beach:* Aldous Huxley (1894–1963), author of the dystopian novel *Brave New World* (1932); Jules Verne (1828–1905), French speculative and science fiction writer, author of *Journey to the Center of the Earth* (1864) and *20,000 Leagues under the Sea* (1870); H. G. Wells (1866–1946), British author of *Island of Dr. Moreau* (1896) and *War of the Worlds* (1898); *On the Beach*, a 1959 film based on a 1957 novel of the same name by Australian writer Nevil Shute, about a group waiting for inevitable death by radiation after a nuclear war.—EDS.

few Americans shopping for small cars, but on the whole America, now the exemplar to the world, is very nearly unshameable.

My own dominant feeling has always been sadness. In 1989, I published *The End of Nature*, the first book for a lay audience about global warming. Half of it was devoted to explaining the science, the other half to my unease. It seemed, and still seems, to me that humanity has intruded into and altered every part of the earth (or very nearly) with our habits and economies. Thoreau once said that he could walk half an hour from his home in Concord, Massachusetts, and come to a place where no man stood from one year to the next, and "there consequently politics are not, for politics are but the cigar smoke of a man." Now that cigar smoke blows everywhere.

Paradoxically, the world also seems more lonely. Everything else exists at our sufferance. Biologists guess that the result of a rapid warming will be the greatest wave of extinction since the last asteroid crashed into the earth. Now we are the asteroid. The notion that we live in a God-haunted world is harder to conjure up. God rebuked Job: "Were you there when I wrapped the ocean in clouds . . . and set its boundaries, saying, 'Here you may come but no farther. Here shall your proud waves break . . . Who gathers up the stormclouds, slits them and pours them out?' " Job, and everyone else until our time, had the sweet privilege of shutting up in the face of that boast—it was clearly God or gravity or some force other than us. But as of about 1990 we can answer back, because we set the sea level now, and we run the storm systems. The excretion of our economy has become the most important influence on the planet we were born into. We're what counts.

Our ultimate sadness lies in the fact that we know that this is not a pre-ordained destiny; it isn't fate. New ways of behaving, of getting and spending, can still change the future: there is, as the religious evangelist would say, still time, though not much of it, and a miraculous conversion is called for—Americans in the year 2000 produced fifteen per cent more carbon dioxide than they had ten years before.

The contrast between two speeds is the key fact of our age: between the pace at which the physical world is changing and the pace at which human society is reacting to this change. In history, if it exists, we shall be praised or damned.

The Reader's Presence

1. How does McKibben use his opening metaphor to explain his attitude toward the conversation about global warming? What is his tone in the opening paragraph? How would you explain the tone of the title? By the end of the essay, how has his tone changed?

2. What does McKibben say in the essay to support his case that global warming is a major threat to our survival? How does he establish himself as a credible expert on the subject?

3. Compare McKibben's essay to Ian Frazier's "All-Consuming Patriotism" (page 422). Does Frazier's analysis of American culture explain the reluctance of Westerners to take global warming seriously? Why or why not? How might Frazier's theory on the relationship between government and its citizens explain the stance of the United States on environmental policies?

Martha Nussbaum

Can Patriotism Be Compassionate?

Martha Nussbaum (b. 1947) received her B.A. from New York University and her Ph.D. from Harvard, and has taught at Harvard, Brown, and Oxford universities. She has published many books, including The Fragility of Goodness: Luck and Ethics in Greek Tragedy and Philosophy *(1986/2001),* Love's Knowledge: Essays on Philosophy and Literature *(1990),* Upheavals of Thought: The Intelligence of Emotions *(2001),* Hiding from Humanity: Disgust, Shame, and the Law *(2004), and, with co-editor Cass R. Sunstein,* Animal Rights: Current Debates and New Directions *(2004). This essay first appeared in the* Nation *in December 2001.*

The Ernst Freund Distinguished Professor at the University of Chicago, Nussbaum teaches in the law school, the philosophy department, the divinity school, and the classics department. She has said that, in order to act ethically on the global stage, it is necessary to cultivate "the ability to imagine what it might be like to be in the shoes of someone who's different from yourself."

In the aftermath of September 11, we have all experienced strong emotions for our country: fear, outrage, grief, astonishment. Our media portray the disaster as a tragedy that has happened to our nation, and that is how we very naturally see it. So too the ensuing war: It is called "America's New War," and most news reports focus on the meaning of events for us and our nation. We think these events are important because they concern us—not just human lives, but American lives. In one way, the crisis has expanded our imaginations. We find ourselves feeling sympathy for many people who did not even cross our minds before: New

York firefighters, that gay rugby player who helped bring down the fourth plane, bereaved families of so many national and ethnic origins. We even sometimes notice with a new attention the lives of Arab-Americans among us, or feel sympathy for a Sikh taxi driver who complains about customers who tell him to go home to "his country," even though he came to the United States as a political refugee from Punjab. Sometimes our compassion even crosses that biggest line of all, the national boundary. Events have led many Americans to sympathize with the women and girls of Afghanistan, for example, in a way that many feminists had been trying to get people to do for a long time, without success.

All too often, however, our imaginations remain oriented to the local; indeed, this orientation is implicit in the unusual level of our alarm. The world has come to a stop in a way that it never has for Americans when disaster has befallen human beings in other places. Floods, earthquakes, cyclones—and the daily deaths of thousands from preventable malnutrition and disease—none of these typically make the American world come to a standstill, none elicit a tremendous outpouring of grief and compassion. The plight of innocent civilians in the current war evokes a similarly uneven and flickering response.

And worse: Our sense that the "us" is all that matters can easily flip over into a demonizing of an imagined "them," a group of outsiders who are imagined as enemies of the invulnerability and the pride of the all-important "us." Just as parents' compassion for their own children can all too easily slide into an attitude that promotes the defeat of other people's children, so too with patriotism: Compassion for our fellow Americans can all too easily slide over into an attitude that wants America to come out on top, defeating or subordinating other peoples or nations. Anger at the terrorists themselves is perfectly appropriate; so is the attempt to bring them to justice. But "us versus them" thinking doesn't always stay focused on the original issue; it too easily becomes a general call for American supremacy, the humiliation of "the other."

One vivid example of this slide took place at a baseball game I went to at Chicago's Comiskey Park, the first game played there after September 11—and a game against the Yankees, so there was a heightened awareness of the situation of New York and its people. Things began well, with a moving ceremony commemorating the firefighters who had lost their lives and honoring local firefighters who had gone to New York afterward to help out. There was even a lot of cheering when the Yankees took the field, a highly unusual transcendence of local attachments. But as the game went on and the beer flowed, one heard, increasingly, "U-S-A, U-S-A," echoing the chant from the 1980 Olympic hockey match in which the United States defeated Russia. This chant seemed to express a wish for America to defeat, abase, humiliate its enemies. Indeed, it soon became a general way of expressing the desire to crush one's enemies, whoever they were. When the umpire made a bad call that went against the Sox, the same group in the stands turned to him, chanting "U-S-A."

In other words, anyone who crosses us is evil, and should be crushed. It's not surprising that Stoic philosopher and Roman emperor Marcus Aurelius, trying to educate himself to have an equal respect for all human beings, reported that his first lesson was "not to be a fan of the Greens or Blues at the races, or the light-armed or heavy-armed gladiators at the Circus."

Compassion is an emotion rooted, probably, in our biological her-   5
itage. (Although biologists once portrayed animal behavior as egoistic, primatologists by now recognize the existence of altruistic emotion in apes, and it may exist in other species as well.) But this history does not mean that compassion is devoid of thought. In fact, as Aristotle argued long ago, human compassion standardly requires three thoughts: that a serious bad thing has happened to someone else; that this bad event was not (or not entirely) the person's own fault; and that we ourselves are vulnerable in similar ways. Thus compassion forms a psychological link between our own self-interest and the reality of another person's good or ill. For that reason it is a morally valuable emotion — when it gets things right. Often, however, the thoughts involved in the emotion, and therefore the emotion itself, go astray, failing to link people at a distance to ones' own current possibilities and vulnerabilities. (Rousseau said that kings don't feel compassion for their subjects because they count on never being human, subject to the vicissitudes of life.) Sometimes, too, compassion goes wrong by getting the seriousness of the bad event wrong: Sometimes, for example, we just don't take very seriously the hunger and illness of people who are distant from us. These errors are likely to be built into the nature of compassion as it develops in childhood and then adulthood: We form intense attachments to the local first, and only gradually learn to have compassion for people who are outside our own immediate circle. For many Americans, that expansion of moral concern stops at the national boundary.

Most of us are brought up to believe that all human beings have equal worth. At least the world's major religions and most secular philosophies tell us so. But our emotions don't believe it. We mourn for those we know, not for those we don't know. And most of us feel deep emotions about America, emotions we don't feel about India or Russia or Rwanda. In and of itself, this narrowness of our emotional lives is probably acceptable and maybe even good. We need to build outward from meanings we understand, or else our moral life would be empty of urgency. Aristotle long ago said, plausibly, that the citizens in Plato's ideal city, asked to care for all citizens equally, would actually care for none, since care is learned in small groups with their more intense attachments. Reading Marcus Aurelius bears this out: The project of weaning his imagination from its intense erotic attachments to the familial and the local gradually turns into the rather alarming project of weaning his heart from deep investment in the world. He finds that the only way to be utterly evenhanded is to cultivate a kind of death within life, seeing all people as distant and shadowlike, "vain images in a procession." If we want our life with others to contain strong passions—for justice in a world of injustice, for aid in a world where many go without what they need—we would do well to begin, at least, with our familiar strong emotions toward family, city and country. But concern should not stop with these local attachments.

Americans, unfortunately, are prone to such emotional narrowness. So are all people, but because of the power and geographical size of America, isolationism has particularly strong roots here. When at least some others were finding ways to rescue the Jews during the Holocaust, America's inactivity and general lack of concern were culpable, especially in proportion to American power. It took Pearl Harbor to get us even to come to the aid of our allies. When genocide was afoot in Rwanda, our own sense of self-sufficiency and invulnerability stopped us from imagining the Rwandans as people who might be us; we were therefore culpably inactive toward them. So too in the present situation. Sometimes we see a very laudable recognition of the interconnectedness of all peoples, and of the fact that we must join forces with people in all nations to defeat terrorists and bring them to justice. At other times, however, we see simplifying slogans ("America Fights Back") that portray the situation in terms of a good "us" crusading against an evil "them"—failing to acknowledge, for instance, that people in all nations have strong reasons to oppose terrorism, and that the fight has many active allies.

Such simplistic thinking is morally wrong, because it encourages us to ignore the impact of our actions on innocent civilians and to focus too little on the all-important project of humanitarian relief. It is also counterproductive. We now understand, or ought to, that if we had thought more about support for the educational and humanitarian infrastructure of Pakistan, for example, funding good local nongovernmental organizations there the way several European nations have done in India, young people in Pakistan might possibly have been educated in a climate of respect for religious pluralism, the equality of women and other values that we rightly prize instead of having fundamentalist *madrassahs*[1] as their only educational option. Our policy in South Asia has exhibited for many years a gross failure of imagination and sympathy; we basically thought in terms of cold war values, ignoring the real lives of people to whose prospects our actions could make a great difference. Such crude thinking is morally obtuse; it is also badly calculated to advance any good cause we wish to embrace, in a world where all human lives are increasingly interdependent.

Compassion begins with the local. But if our moral natures and our emotional natures are to live in any sort of harmony, we must find devices

---

[1]*madrassahs:* A group of buildings used for teaching Islamic theology and religious law, typically including a mosque.—Eds.

through which to extend our strong emotions—and our ability to imagine the situation of others—to the world of human life as a whole. Since compassion contains thought, it can be educated. We can take this disaster as occasion for narrowing our focus, distrusting the rest of the world, and feeling solidarity with Americans alone. Or we can take it as an occasion for expansion of our ethical horizons. Seeing how vulnerable our great country is, we can learn something about the vulnerability that all human beings share, about what it is like for distant others to lose those they love to a disaster not of their own making, whether it is hunger or flood or war.

Because human beings find the meaning of life in attachments that   10
are local, we should not ask of people that they renounce patriotism, any more than we now ask them to renounce the love of their parents and children. But we typically do ask parents not to try to humiliate or thwart other people's children, and we work (at least sometimes) for schools that develop the abilities of all children, that try to make it possible for everyone to support themselves and find rewarding work. So too with the world: We may love our own nation most, but we should also strive for a world in which the capacities of human beings will not be blighted by hunger or misogyny or lack of education—or by being in the vicinity of a war one has not caused. We should therefore demand an education that does what it can to encourage the understanding of human predicaments—and also to teach children to recognize the many obstacles to that pursuit, the many pitfalls of the self-centered imagination as it tries to be just. There are hopeful signs in the present situation, particularly in attempts to educate the American public about Islam, about the histories of Afghanistan and Pakistan, and about the situation and attitudes of Arab-Americans in this country. But we need to make sure these educational efforts are consistent and systematic, not just fear-motivated responses to an immediate crisis.

Our media and our systems of education have long given us far too little information about lives outside our borders, stunting our moral imaginations. The situation of America's women and its racial, ethnic, and sexual minorities has to some extent worked its way into curricula at various levels, and into our popular media. We have done less well with parts of the world that are unfamiliar. This is not surprising, because such teaching requires a lot of investment in new curricular initiatives, and such television programming requires a certain temporary inattention to the competition for ratings. But we now know that we live in a complex, interconnected world, and we know our own ignorance. As Socrates said, this is at least the beginning of progress. At this time of national crisis we can renew our commitment to the equal worth of humanity, demanding media, and schools, that nourish and expand our imaginations by presenting non-American lives as deep, rich, and compassion-worthy. "Thus from our weakness," said Rousseau of such an education, "our fragile happiness is born." Or, at least, it might be born.

The Reader's Presence

1. Evaluate the validity of Nussbaum's claim that becoming compassionate requires an "expansion of our ethical horizons" (paragraph 9) by looking at the instances where she sees a lack of compassion. For each instance, how would you expand people's horizons? According to Nussbaum, what conditions are necessary to make people feel compassionate? Which do you think would work? Which wouldn't? Why and why not?

2. Beginning with a twenty-first-century United States's perspective, Nussbaum expands and contracts her temporal focus several times. For example, she talks about recent events (a baseball game) and then immediately switches to a discussion of Aristotle's argument about compassion. By writing this way, she broadens the "emotional narrowness" which she feels constricts America. In what other ways does she try to broaden our horizons? In how many other ways does she contract and expand her focus? Which ways create compassion most effectively? Why?

3. While Nussbaum discusses the post–9/11 mindset in relation to compassion, Gerald Early, in "Fear and Fate in America" (page 372), discusses the role of fear. Are lack of compassion and fear intertwined in relation to Americans' reactions to September 11, 2001? Why or why not?

Bertrand Russell

Why I Am Not a Christian

Mathematician, philosopher, logician, and social critic, Bertrand Russell (1872–1970) was born in England and is regarded as one of the greatest thinkers of modern times. Russell was an extremely prolific and influential writer, and his books, many of them highly readable, include Principia Mathematica, *a three-volume set published in 1910, 1912, and 1913;* Marriage and Morals *(1929); A* History of Western Philosophy *(1945);* Why I Am Not a Christian *(1957); and* The Autobiography of Bertrand Russell *(3 vols.: 1967–69). Russell was also known for his outspoken views on pacifism, advocacy of free love, and criticism of American foreign policy. "Why I Am Not a Christian," one of his most famous essays, was delivered as a lecture in 1927 to the National Secular Society.*

As your Chairman has told you, the subject about which I am going to speak to you tonight is "Why I Am Not a Christian." Perhaps it would be as well, first of all, to try to make out what one means by the word *Christian*. It is used these days in a very loose sense by a great many people. Some people mean no more by it than a person who attempts to live a good life. In that sense I suppose there would be Christians in all sects and creeds; but I do not think that that is the proper sense of the word, if only because it would imply that all the people who are not Christians—all the Buddhists, Confucians, Mohammedans, and so on—are not trying to live a good life. I do not mean by a Christian any person who tries to live decently according to his lights. I think that you must have a certain amount of definite belief before you have a right to call yourself a Christian. The word does not have quite such a full-blooded meaning now as it had in the times of St. Augustine and St. Thomas Aquinas. In those days, if a man said that he was a Christian it was known what he meant. You accepted a whole collection of creeds which were set out with great precision, and every single syllable of those creeds you believed with the whole strength of your convictions.

WHAT IS A CHRISTIAN?

Nowadays it is not quite that. We have to be a little more vague in our meaning of Christianity. I think, however, that there are two different items which are quite essential to anybody calling himself a Christian. The first is one of a dogmatic nature—namely, that you must believe in God and immortality. If you do not believe in those two things, I do not think that you can properly call yourself a Christian. Then, further than that, as the name implies, you must have some kind of belief about Christ. The Mohammedans, for instance, also believe in God and in immortality, and yet they would not call themselves Christians. I think you must have at the very lowest the belief that Christ was, if not divine, at least the best and wisest of men. If you are not going to believe that much about Christ, I do not think you have any right to call yourself a Christian. Of course, there is another sense, which you find in *Whitaker's Almanack* and in geography books, where the population of the world is said to be divided into Christians, Mohammedans, Buddhists, fetish worshipers, and so on; and in that sense we are all Christians. The geography books count us all in, but that is a purely geographical sense, which I suppose we can ignore. Therefore I take it that when I tell you why I am not a Christian I have to tell you two different things: first, why I do not believe in God and in immortality; and, secondly, why I do not think that Christ was the best and wisest of men, although I grant him a very high degree of moral goodness.

But for the successful efforts of unbelievers in the past, I could not take so elastic a definition of Christianity as that. As I said before, in olden days it had a much more full-blooded sense. For instance, it included the belief in hell. Belief in eternal hell-fire was an essential item of Christian belief until pretty recent times. In this country, as you know, it ceased to be an essential item because of a decision of the Privy Council, and from that decision the Archbishop of Canterbury and the Archbishop of York dissented; but in this country our religion is settled by Act of Parliament, and therefore the Privy Council was able to override their Graces and hell was no longer necessary to a Christian. Consequently I shall not insist that a Christian must believe in hell.

THE EXISTENCE OF GOD

To come to this question of the existence of God: It is a large and serious question, and if I were to attempt to deal with it in any adequate manner I should have to keep you here until Kingdom Come, so that you will have to excuse me if I deal with it in a somewhat summary fashion. You know, of course, that the Catholic Church has laid it down as a dogma that the existence of God can be proved by the unaided reason. That is a somewhat curious dogma, but it is one of their dogmas. They had to introduce it because at one time the freethinkers adopted the habit of saying that there were such and such arguments which mere reason might urge against the existence of God, but of course they knew as a matter of faith that God did exist. The arguments and the reasons were set out at great length, and the Catholic Church felt that they must stop it. Therefore they laid it down that the existence of God can be proved by the unaided reason and they had to set up what they considered were arguments to prove it. There are, of course, a number of them, but I shall take only a few.

THE FIRST CAUSE ARGUMENT

Perhaps the simplest and easiest to understand is the argument of the   5
First Cause. (It is maintained that everything we see in this world has a cause, and as you go back in the chain of causes further and further you must come to a First Cause, and to that First Cause you give the name of God.) That argument, I suppose, does not carry very much weight nowadays, because, in the first place, cause is not quite what it used to be. The philosophers and the men of science have got going on cause, and it has not anything like the vitality it used to have; but, apart from that, you can see that the argument that there must be a First Cause is one that cannot have any validity. I may say that when I was a young man and was debating these questions very seriously in my mind, I for a long time accepted the argument of the First Cause, until one day, at the age of eighteen, I read John Stuart Mill's *Autobiography*, and I there found this

sentence: "My father taught me that the question 'Who made me?' cannot be answered, since it immediately suggests the further question 'Who made God?'" That very simple sentence showed me, as I still think, the fallacy in the argument of the First Cause. If everything must have a cause, then God must have a cause. If there can be everything without a cause, it may just as well be the world as God, so that there cannot be any validity in that argument. It is exactly of the same nature as the Hindu's view that the world rested upon an elephant and the elephant rested upon a tortoise; and when they said, "How about the tortoise?" the Indian said, "Suppose we change the subject." The argument is really no better than that. There is no reason why the world could not have come into being without a cause; nor, on the other hand, is there any reason why it should not have always existed. There is no reason to suppose that the world had a beginning at all. The idea that things must have a beginning is really due to the poverty of our imagination. Therefore, perhaps, I need not waste any more time upon the argument about the First Cause.

THE NATURAL LAW ARGUMENT

Then there is a very common argument from natural law. That was a favorite argument all through the eighteenth century, especially under the influence of Sir Isaac Newton and his cosmogony. People observed the planets going around the sun according to the law of gravitation, and they thought that God had given a behest to these planets to move in that particular fashion, and that was why they did so. That was, of course, a convenient and simple explanation that saved them the trouble of looking any further for explanations of the law of gravitation. Nowadays we explain the law of gravitation in a somewhat complicated fashion that Einstein has introduced. I do not propose to give you a lecture on the law of gravitation, as interpreted by Einstein, because that again would take some time; at any rate, you no longer have the sort of natural law that you had in the Newtonian system, where, for some reason that nobody could understand, nature behaved in a uniform fashion. We now find that a great many things we thought were natural laws are really human conventions. You know that even in the remotest depths of stellar space there are still three feet to a yard. That is, no doubt, a very remarkable fact, but you would hardly call it a law of nature. And a great many things that have been regarded as laws of nature are of that kind. On the other hand, where you can get down to any knowledge of what atoms actually do, you will find they are much less subject to law than people thought, and that the laws at which you arrive are statistical averages of just the sort that would emerge from chance. There is, as we all know, a law that if you throw dice you will get double sixes only about once in thirty-six times, we do not regard that as evidence that the fall of the dice is regulated by design; on the contrary, if the double sixes came every time we should think that there was design. The laws of nature are of that sort as regards a great many of them. They are statistical averages such as would emerge from the laws of chance; and that makes this whole business of natural law much less impressive than it formerly was. Quite apart from that, which represents the momentary state of science that may change tomorrow, the whole idea that natural laws imply a lawgiver is due to a confusion between natural and human laws. Human laws are behests commanding you to behave a certain way, in which way you may choose to behave, or you may choose not to behave; but natural laws are a description of how things do in fact behave, and being a mere description of what they in fact do, you cannot argue that there must be somebody who told them to do that, because even supposing that there were, you are then faced with the question "Why did God issue just those natural laws and no others?" If you say that he did it simply from his own good pleasure, and without any reason, you then find that there is something which is not subject to law, and so your train of natural law is interrupted. If you say, as more orthodox theologians do, that in all the laws which God issues he had a reason for giving those laws rather than others—the reason, of course, being to create the best universe, although you would never think it to look at it—if there were a reason for the laws which God gave, then God himself was subject to law, and therefore you do not get any advantage by introducing God as an intermediary. You have really a law outside and anterior to the divine edicts, and God does not serve your purpose, because he is not the ultimate lawgiver. In short, this whole argument about natural law no longer has anything like the strength that it used to have. I am traveling on in time in my review of the arguments. The arguments that are used for the existence of God change their character as time goes on. They were at first hard intellectual arguments embodying certain quite definite fallacies. As we come to modern times they become less respectable intellectually and more and more affected by a kind of moralizing vagueness.

THE ARGUMENT FROM DESIGN

The next step in this process brings us to the argument from design. You all know the argument from design: Everything in the world is made just so that we can manage to live in the world, and if the world was ever so little different, we could not manage to live in it. That is the argument from design. It sometimes takes a rather curious form; for instance, it is argued that rabbits have white tails in order to be easy to shoot. I do not know how rabbits would view that application. It is an easy argument to parody. You all know Voltaire's remark, that obviously the nose was designed to be such as to fit spectacles. That sort of parody has turned out to be not nearly so wide of the mark as it might have seemed in the eighteenth century, because since the time of Darwin we understand much better why living creatures are adapted to their environment. It is not that their environment was made to be suitable to them but that they grew to be suitable to it, and that is the basis of adaptation. There is no evidence of design about it.

When you come to look into this argument from design, it is a most astonishing thing that people can believe that this world, with all the things that are in it, with all its defects, should be the best that omnipotence and omniscience have been able to produce in millions of years. I really cannot believe it. Do you think that, if you were granted omnipotence and omniscience and millions of years in which to perfect your world, you could produce nothing better than the Ku Klux Klan or the Fascists? Moreover, if you accept the ordinary laws of science, you have to suppose that human life and life in general on this planet will die out in due course: It is a stage in the decay of the solar system; at a certain stage of decay you get the sort of conditions of temperature and so forth which are suitable to protoplasm, and there is life for a short time in the life of the whole solar system. You see in the moon the sort of thing to which the earth is tending—something dead, cold, and lifeless.

I am told that that sort of view is depressing, and people will sometimes tell you that if they believed that, they would not be able to go on living. Do not believe it; it is all nonsense. Nobody really worries much about what is going to happen millions of years hence. Even if they think they are worrying much about that, they are really deceiving themselves. They are worried about something much more mundane, or it may merely be a bad digestion; but nobody is really seriously rendered unhappy by the thought of something that is going to happen to this world millions and millions of years hence. Therefore, although it is of course a gloomy view to suppose that life will die out—at least I suppose we may say so, although sometimes when I contemplate the things that people do with their lives I think it is almost a consolation—it is not such as to render life miserable. It merely makes you turn your attention to other things.

THE MORAL ARGUMENTS FOR DEITY

Now we reach one stage further in what I shall call the intellectual descent that the Theists have made in their argumentations, and we come to what are called the moral arguments for the existence of God. You all know, of course, that there used to be in the old days three intellectual arguments for the existence of God, all of which were disposed of by Immanuel Kant in the *Critique of Pure Reason*; but no sooner had he disposed of those arguments than he invented a new one, a moral argument, and that quite convinced him. He was like many people: In intellectual matters he was skeptical, but in moral matters he believed implicitly in the maxims that he had imbibed at his mother's knee. That illustrates what

10

the psychoanalysts so much emphasize—the immensely stronger hold upon us that our very early associations have than those of later times.

Kant, as I say, invented a new moral argument for the existence of God, and that in varying forms was extremely popular during the nineteenth century. It has all sorts of forms. One form is to say that there would be no right or wrong unless God existed. I am not for the moment concerned with whether there is a difference between right and wrong, or whether there is not: That is another question. The point I am concerned with is that, if you are quite sure there is a difference between right and wrong, you are then in this situation: Is that difference due to God's fiat or is it not? If it is due to God's fiat, then for God himself there is no difference between right and wrong, and it is no longer a significant statement to say that God is good. If you are going to say, as theologians do, that God is good, you must then say that right and wrong have some meaning which is independent of God's fiat, because God's fiats are good and not bad independently of the mere fact that he made them. If you are going to say that, you will then have to say that it is not only through God that right and wrong came into being, but that they are in their essence logically anterior to God. You could, of course, if you liked, say that there was a superior deity who gave orders to the God who made this world, or could take up the line that some of the gnostics took up—a line which I often thought was a very plausible one—that as a matter of fact this world that we know was made by the devil at a moment when God was not looking. There is a good deal to be said for that, and I am not concerned to refute it.

THE ARGUMENT FOR THE REMEDYING OF INJUSTICE

Then there is another very curious form of moral argument, which is this: They say that the existence of God is required in order to bring justice into the world. In the part of this universe that we know there is great injustice, and often the good suffer, and often the wicked prosper, and one hardly knows which of those is the more annoying; but if you are going to have justice in the universe as a whole you have to suppose a future life to redress the balance of life here on earth. So they say that there must be a God, and there must be heaven and hell in order that in the long run there may be justice. That is a very curious argument. If you looked at the matter from a scientific point of view, you would say, "After all, I know only this world. I do not know about the rest of the universe, but so far as one can argue at all on probabilities one would say that probably this world is a fair sample, and if there is injustice here the odds are that there is injustice elsewhere also." Supposing you got a crate of oranges that you opened, and you found all the top layer of oranges bad, you would not argue, "The underneath ones must be good, so as to redress the balance." You would say, "Probably the whole lot is a bad consignment"; and that is really what a scientific person would argue about the universe. He would say, "Here we find in this world a great deal of injustice, and so far as that goes that is a reason for supposing that justice does not rule in the world; and therefore so far as it goes it affords a moral argument against deity and not in favor of one." Of course I know that the sort of intellectual arguments that I have been talking to you about are not what really moves people. What really moves people to believe in God is not any intellectual argument at all. Most people believe in God because they have been taught from early infancy to do it, and that is the main reason.

Then I think that the next most powerful reason is the wish for safety, a sort of feeling that there is a big brother who will look after you. That plays a very profound part in influencing people's desire for a belief in God.

THE CHARACTER OF CHRIST

I now want to say a few words upon a topic which I often think is not quite sufficiently dealt with by Rationalists, and that is the question whether Christ was the best and the wisest of men. It is generally taken for granted that we should all agree that that was so. I do not myself. I think that there are a good many points upon which I agree with Christ a great deal more than the professing Christians do. I do not know that I could go with Him all the way, but I could go with Him much further than most professing Christians can. You will remember that He said, "Resist not evil: But whosoever shall smite thee on thy right cheek, turn to him the other also." That is not a new precept or a new principle. It was used by Lao-tse and Buddha some 500 or 600 years before Christ, but it is not a principle which as a matter of fact Christians accept. I have no doubt that the present Prime Minister,[1] for instance, is a most sincere Christian, but I should not advise any of you to go and smite him on one cheek. I think you might find that he thought this text was intended in a figurative sense.

Then there is another point which I consider excellent. You will re-   15
member that Christ said, "Judge not lest ye be judged." That principle I do not think you would find was popular in the law courts of Christian countries. I have known in my time quite a number of judges who were very earnest Christians, and none of them felt that they were acting contrary to Christian principles in what they did. Then Christ says, "Give to him that asketh of thee, and from him that would borrow of thee turn not thou away." That is a very good principle. Your Chairman has reminded you that we are not here to talk politics, but I cannot help observing that the last general election was fought on the question of how desirable it

---

[1]*present Prime Minister:* Stanley Baldwin (1867–1947). — EDS.

was to turn away from him that would borrow of thee, so that one must assume that the Liberals and Conservatives of this country are composed of people who do not agree with the teaching of Christ, because they certainly did very emphatically turn away on that occasion.

Then there is one other maxim of Christ which I think has a great deal in it, but I do not find that it is very popular among some of our Christian friends. He says, "If thou wilt be perfect, go and sell that which thou hast, and give to the poor." That is a very excellent maxim, but, as I say, it is not much practiced. All these, I think, are good maxims, although they are a little difficult to live up to. I do not profess to live up to them myself; but then, after all, it is not quite the same thing as for a Christian.

DEFECTS IN CHRIST'S TEACHING

Having granted the excellence of these maxims, I come to certain points in which I do not believe that one can grant either the superlative wisdom or the superlative goodness of Christ as depicted in the Gospels; and here I may say that one is not concerned with the historical question. Historically it is quite doubtful whether Christ ever existed at all, and if He did we do not know anything about Him, so that I am not concerned with the historical question, which is a very difficult one. I am concerned with Christ as He appears in the Gospels, taking the Gospel narrative as it stands, and there one does find some things that do not seem to be very wise. For one thing, He certainly thought that His second coming would occur in clouds of glory before the death of all the people who were living at that time. There are a great many texts that prove that. He says, for instance, "Ye shall not have gone over the cities of Israel till the Son of Man be come." Then He says, "There are some standing here which shall not taste death till the Son of Man comes into His kingdom"; and there are a lot of places where it is quite clear that He believed that His second coming would happen during the lifetime of many then living. That was the belief of His earlier followers, and it was the basis of a good deal of His moral teaching. When He said, "Take no thought for the morrow," and things of that sort, it was very largely because He thought that the second coming was going to be very soon, and that all ordinary mundane affairs did not count. I have, as a matter of fact, known some Christians who did believe that the second coming was imminent. I knew a parson who frightened his congregation terribly by telling them that the second coming was very imminent indeed, but they were much consoled when they found that he was planting trees in his garden. The early Christians did really believe it, and they did abstain from such things as planting trees in their gardens, because they did accept from Christ the belief that the second coming was imminent. In that respect, clearly He was not so wise as some other people have been, and He was certainly not superlatively wise.

THE MORAL PROBLEM

Then you come to moral questions. There is one very serious defect to my mind in Christ's moral character, and that is that He believed in hell. I do not myself feel that any person who is really profoundly human can believe in everlasting punishment. Christ certainly as depicted in the Gospels did believe in everlasting punishment, and one does find repeatedly a vindictive fury against those people who would not listen to His preaching—an attitude which is not uncommon with preachers, but which does somewhat detract from superlative excellence. You do not, for instance, find that attitude in Socrates. You find him quite bland and urbane toward the people who would not listen to him; and it is, to my mind, far more worthy of a sage to take that line than to take the line of indignation. You probably all remember the sort of things that Socrates was saying when he was dying, and the sort of things that he generally did say to people who did not agree with him.

You will find that in the Gospels Christ said, "Ye serpents, ye generation of vipers, how can ye escape the damnation of hell." That was said to people who did not like His preaching. It is not really to my mind quite the best tone, and there are a great many of these things about hell. There is, of course, the familiar text about the sin against the Holy Ghost: "Whosoever speaketh against the Holy Ghost it shall not be forgiven him neither in this World nor in the world to come." That text has caused an unspeakable amount of misery in the world, for all sorts of people have imagined that they have committed the sin against the Holy Ghost, and thought that it would not be forgiven them either in this world or in the world to come. I really do not think that a person with a proper degree of kindliness in his nature would have put fears and terrors of that sort into the world.

Then Christ says, "The Son of Man shall send forth His angels, and they shall gather out of His kingdom all things that offend, and them which do iniquity, and shall cast them into a furnace of fire; there shall be wailing and gnashing of teeth"; and He goes on about the wailing and gnashing of teeth. It comes in one verse after another, and it is quite manifest to the reader that there is a certain pleasure in contemplating wailing and gnashing of teeth, or else it would not occur so often. Then you all, of course, remember about the sheep and the goats; how at the second coming He is going to divide the sheep from the goats, and He is going to say to the goats, "Depart from me, ye cursed, into everlasting fire." He continues, "And these shall go away into everlasting fire." Then He says again, "If thy hand offend thee, cut it off; it is better for thee to enter into life maimed, than having two hands to go into hell, into the fire that never shall be quenched; where the worm dieth not and the fire is not quenched." He repeats that again and again also. I must say that I think all this doctrine, that hell-fire is a punishment for sin, is a doctrine of cruelty. It is a doctrine that put cruelty

20

into the world and gave the world generations of cruel torture; and the Christ of the Gospels, if you could take Him as His chroniclers represent Him, would certainly have to be considered partly responsible for that.

There are other things of less importance. There is the instance of the Gadarene swine, where it certainly was not very kind to the pigs to put the devils into them and make them rush down the hill to the sea. You must remember that He was omnipotent, and He could have made the devils simply go away; but He chose to send them into the pigs. Then there is the curious story of the fig tree, which always rather puzzled me. You remember what happened about the fig tree. "He was hungry; and seeing a fig tree afar off having leaves, He came if haply He might find anything thereon; and when He came to it He found nothing but leaves, for the time of figs was not yet. And Jesus answered and said unto it: 'No man eat fruit of thee hereafter for ever' . . . and Peter . . . saith unto Him: 'Master, behold the fig tree which thou cursedst is withered away.' " This is a very curious story, because it was not the right time of year for figs, and you really could not blame the tree. I cannot myself feel that either in the matter of wisdom or in the matter of virtue Christ stands quite as high as some other people known to history. I think I should put Buddha and Socrates above Him in those respects.

THE EMOTIONAL FACTOR

As I said before, I do not think that the real reason why people accept religion has anything to do with argumentation. They accept religion on emotional grounds. One is often told that it is a very wrong thing to attack religion, because religion makes men virtuous. So I am told; I have not noticed it. You know, of course, the parody of that argument in Samuel Butler's book, *Erewhon Revisited*. You will remember that in *Erewhon* there is a certain Higgs who arrives in a remote country, and after spending some time there he escapes from that country in a balloon. Twenty years later he comes back to that country and finds a new religion in which he is worshipped under the name of the "Sun Child," and it is said that he ascended into heaven. He finds that the Feast of the Ascension is about to be celebrated, and he hears Professors Hanky and Panky say to each other that they never set eyes on the man Higgs, and they hope they never will; but they are the high priests of the religion of the Sun Child. He is very indignant, and he comes up to them, and he says, "I am going to expose all this humbug and tell the people of Erewhon that it was only I, the man Higgs, and I went up in a balloon." He was told, "You must not do that, because all the morals of this country are bound round this myth, and if they once know that you did not ascend into heaven they will all become wicked"; and so he is persuaded of that and he goes quietly away.

That is the idea — that we should all be wicked if we did not hold to the Christian religion. It seems to me that the people who have held to it have been for the most part extremely wicked. You find this curious fact, that the more intense has been the religion of any period and the more profound has been the dogmatic belief, the greater has been the cruelty and the worse has been the state of affairs. In the so-called ages of faith, when men really did believe the Christian religion in all its completeness, there was the Inquisition, with its tortures; there were millions of unfortunate women burned as witches; and there was every kind of cruelty practiced upon all sorts of people in the name of religion.

You find as you look around the world that every single bit of progress in humane feeling, every improvement in the criminal law, every step toward the diminution of war, every step toward better treatment of the colored races, or every mitigation of slavery, every moral progress that there has been in the world, has been consistently opposed by the organized churches of the world. I say quite deliberately that the Christian religion, as organized in its churches, has been and still is the principal enemy of moral progress in the world.

HOW THE CHURCHES HAVE RETARDED PROGRESS

You may think that I am going too far when I say that that is still 25
so. I do not think that I am. Take one fact. You will bear with me if I mention it. It is not a pleasant fact, but the churches compel one to mention facts that are not pleasant. Supposing that in this world that we live in today an inexperienced girl is married to a syphilitic man; in that case the Catholic Church says, "This is an indissoluble sacrament. You must endure celibacy or stay together. And if you stay together, you must not use birth control to prevent the birth of syphilitic children." Nobody whose natural sympathies have not been warped by dogma, or whose moral nature was not absolutely dead to all sense of suffering, could maintain that it is right and proper that that state of things should continue.

That is only an example. There are a great many ways in which, at the present moment, the church, by its insistence upon what it chooses to call morality, inflicts upon all sorts of people undeserved and unnecessary suffering. And of course, as we know, it is in its major part an opponent still of progress and of improvement in all the ways that diminish suffering in the world, because it has chosen to label as morality a certain narrow set of rules of conduct which have nothing to do with human happiness; and when you say that this or that ought to be done because it would make for human happiness, they think that has nothing to do with the matter at all. "What has human happiness to do with morals? The object of morals is not to make people happy."

FEAR, THE FOUNDATION OF RELIGION

Religion is based, I think, primarily and mainly upon fear. It is partly the terror of the unknown and partly, as I have said, the wish to feel that you have a kind of elder brother who will stand by you in all your troubles and disputes. Fear is the basis of the whole thing—fear of the mysterious, fear of defeat, fear of death. Fear is the parent of cruelty, and therefore it is no wonder if cruelty and religion have gone hand in hand. It is because fear is at the basis of those two things. In this world we can now begin a little to understand things, and a little to master them by help of science, which has forced its way step by step against the Christian religion, against the churches, and against the opposition of all the old precepts. Science can help us to get over this craven fear in which mankind has lived for so many generations. Science can teach us, and I think our own hearts can teach us, no longer to look around for imaginary supports, no longer to invent allies in the sky, but rather to look to our own efforts here below to make this world a fit place to live in, instead of the sort of place that the churches in all these centuries have made it.

WHAT WE MUST DO

We want to stand upon our own feet and look fair and square at the world—its good facts, its bad facts, its beauties, and its ugliness; see the world as it is and be not afraid of it. Conquer the world by intelligence and not merely by being slavishly subdued by the terror that comes from it. The whole conception of God is a conception derived from the ancient Oriental despotisms. It is a conception quite unworthy of free men. When you hear people in church debasing themselves and saying that they are miserable sinners, and all the rest of it, it seems contemptible and not worthy of self-respecting human beings. We ought to stand up and look the world frankly in the face. We ought to make the best we can of the world, and if it is not so good as we wish, after all it will still be better than what these others have made of it in all these ages. A good world needs knowledge, kindliness, and courage; it does not need a regretful hankering after the past or a fettering of the free intelligence by the words uttered long ago by ignorant men. It needs a fearless outlook and a free intelligence. It needs hope for the future, not looking back all the time toward a past that is dead, which we trust will be far surpassed by the future that our intelligence can create.

The Reader's Presence

1. Summarize Russell's first and second paragraphs, each in one sentence. In a third sentence, describe and evaluate his strategy in

opening with these paragraphs. What might be Russell's intention? What tone does Russell use in pursuing his points? Is this an expected tone for the subject matter? Does Russell's tone enhance or undermine the seriousness of his argument?

2. How does Russell characterize the "First Cause" argument? Is this how its originators are likely to have characterized it? Can you understand the original argument from Russell's version of it? What sense of Russell's perspective do you gain from his "reading" of the original argument? What sort of audience do you think Russell was addressing? Why?

3. Russell's essay is, among other things, a review of arguments on behalf of Christianity, each of which he carefully dismantles. Russell also devotes several pages to the figure of Christ—his character, his maxims, his moral stature, and his wisdom. The climax of his essay, however, may be his critique of the church: "I say quite deliberately that the Christian religion, *as organized in its churches*, has been and still is the principal enemy of moral progress in the world" (paragraph 24, emphasis added). Both Russell and Martin Luther King Jr. were pacifists. Compare Russell's use of Christ and the church to the way King uses both in his "Letter from Birmingham Jail" (page 738). King's letter is not, strictly speaking, a defense of Christianity, but how might you read it as a response to Russell's polemic?

Scott Russell Sanders

The Men We Carry in Our Minds

Scott Russell Sanders (b. 1945) writes in a variety of genres: science fiction, realistic fiction, folktales, children's stories, essays, and historical novels. In all his work, however, he is concerned with the ways in which people live in communities. Some of his books include The Paradise of Bombs *(1987), from which "The Men We Carry in Our Minds" is taken;* Staying Put: Making a Home in a Restless World *(1993);* Here Comes the Mystery Man *(1993);* Writing from the Center *(1995);* Hunting for Hope: A Father's Journey *(1998);* The Country of Language *(1999); and* Bad Man Ballad *(2004). Sanders contributes to both literary and popular magazines. He is a professor of English at Indiana University.*

Sanders has said, "I believe that a writer should be a servant of language, community, and nature. Language is the creation and sustenance of community .... My writing is driven by a deep regard for particular places and voices, persons and tools, plants and animals, for human skills and stories. . . . If my writing does not help my neighbors to live more alertly, pleasurably, or wisely, then it is worth little."

"This must be a hard time for women," I say to my friend Anneke. "They have so many paths to choose from, and so many voices calling them."

"I think it's a lot harder for men," she replies.

"How do you figure that?"

"The women I know feel excited, innocent, like crusaders in a just cause. The men I know are eaten up with guilt."

We are sitting at the kitchen table drinking sassafras tea, our hands 5 wrapped around the mugs because this April morning is cool and drizzly. "Like a Dutch morning," Anneke told me earlier. She is Dutch herself, a writer and midwife and peacemaker, with the round face and sad eyes of a woman in a Vermeer painting who might be waiting for the rain to stop, for a door to open. She leans over to sniff a sprig of lilac, pale lavender, that rises from a vase of cobalt blue.

"Women feel such pressure to be everything, do everything," I say. "Career, kids, art, politics. Have their babies and get back to the office a week later. It's as if they're trying to overcome a million years' worth of evolution in one lifetime."

"But we help one another. We don't try to lumber on alone, like so many wounded grizzly bears, the way men do." Anneke sips her tea. I gave her the mug with the owls on it, for wisdom. "And we have this deep-down sense that we're in the *right*—we've been held back, passed over, used—while men feel they're in the wrong. Men are the ones who've been discredited, who have to search their souls."

I search my soul. I discover guilty feelings aplenty—toward the poor, the Vietnamese, Native Americans, the whales, an endless list of debts—a guilt in each case that is as bright and unambiguous as a neon sign. But toward women I feel something more confused, a snarl of shame, envy, wary tenderness, and amazement. This muddle troubles me. To hide my unease I say, "You're right, it's tough being a man these days."

"Don't laugh." Anneke frowns at me, mournful-eyed, through the sassafras steam. "I wouldn't be a man for anything. It's much easier being the victim. All the victim has to do is break free. The persecutor has to live with his past."

How deep is that past? I find myself wondering after Anneke has left. 10 How much of an inheritance do I have to throw off? Is it just the beliefs I breathed in as a child? Do I have to scour memory back through father and grandfather? Through St. Paul? Beyond Stonehenge and into the twilit caves? I'm convinced the past we must contend with is deeper even than speech. When I think back on my childhood, on how I learned to see men and women, I have a sense of ancient, dizzying depths. The back roads of Tennessee and Ohio where I grew up were probably closer, in their sexual patterns, to the campsites of Stone Age hunters than to the genderless cities of the future into which we are rushing.

The first men, besides my father, I remember seeing were black convicts and white guards, in the cottonfield across the road from our farm on the outskirts of Memphis. I must have been three or four. The prisoners wore dingy gray-and-black zebra suits, heavy as canvas, sodden with sweat. Hatless, stooped, they chopped weeds in the fierce heat, row after row, breathing the acrid dust of boll-weevil poison. The overseers wore dazzling white shirts and broad shadowy hats. The oiled barrels of their shotguns flashed in the sunlight. Their faces in memory are utterly blank. Of course those men, white and black, have become for me an emblem of racial hatred. But they have also come to stand for the twin poles of my early vision of manhood—the brute toiling animal and the boss.

When I was a boy, the men I knew labored with their bodies. They were marginal farmers, just scraping by, or welders, steelworkers, carpenters; they swept floors, dug ditches, mined coal, or drove trucks, their forearms ropy with muscle; they trained horses, stoked furnaces, built tires, stood on assembly lines wrestling parts onto cars and refrigerators. They got up before light, worked all day long whatever the weather, and when they came home at night they looked as though somebody had been whipping them. In the evenings and on weekends they worked on their own places, tilling gardens that were lumpy with clay, fixing broken-down cars, hammering on houses that were always too drafty, too leaky, too small.

The bodies of the men I knew were twisted and maimed in ways visible and invisible. The nails of their hands were black and split, the hands tattooed with scars. Some had lost fingers. Heavy lifting had given many of them finicky backs and guts weak from hernias. Racing against conveyor belts had given them ulcers. Their ankles and knees ached from years of standing on concrete. Anyone who had worked for long around machines was hard of hearing. They squinted, and the skin of their faces was creased like the leather of old work gloves. There were times, studying them, when I dreaded growing up. Most of them coughed, from dust or cigarettes, and most of them drank cheap wine or whiskey, so their eyes looked bloodshot and bruised. The fathers of my friends always seemed older than the mothers. Men wore out sooner. Only women lived into old age.

As a boy I also knew another sort of men, who did not sweat and break down like mules. They were soldiers, and so far as I could tell they scarcely worked at all. During my early school years we lived on a military base, an arsenal in Ohio, and every day I saw GIs in the guardshacks, on the stoops of barracks, at the wheels of olive drab Chevrolets. The chief fact of their lives was boredom. Long after I left the Arsenal I came to recognize the sour smell the soldiers gave off as that of souls in limbo. They were all waiting—for wars, for transfers, for leaves, for promotions, for the end of their hitch—like so many braves waiting for the hunt to begin. Unlike the warriors of older tribes, however, they would have no say about when the battle would start or how it would be waged. Their waiting was broken only when they practiced for war. They fired guns at targets, drove tanks across the churned-up fields of the military reservation, set off bombs in the wrecks of old fighter planes. I knew this was all play. But I also felt certain that when the hour for killing arrived, they would kill. When the real shooting started, many of them would die. This was what soldiers were *for*, just as a hammer was for driving nails.

Warriors and toilers: those seemed, in my boyhood vision, to be the 15
chief destinies for men. They weren't the only destinies, as I learned from having a few male teachers, from reading books, and from watching television. But the men on television—the politicians, the astronauts, the generals, the savvy lawyers, the philosophical doctors, the bosses who gave orders to both soldiers and laborers—seemed as remote and unreal to me as the figures in tapestries. I could no more imagine growing up to become one of these cool, potent creatures than I could imagine becoming a prince.

A nearer and more hopeful example was that of my father, who had escaped from a red-dirt farm to a tire factory, and from the assembly line to the front office. Eventually he dressed in a white shirt and tie. He carried himself as if he had been born to work with his mind. But his body, remembering the earlier years of slogging work, began to give out on him in his fifties, and it quit on him entirely before he turned sixty-five. Even such a partial escape from man's fate as he had accomplished did not seem possible for most of the boys I knew. They joined the army, stood in line for jobs in the smoky plants, helped build highways. They were bound to work as their fathers had worked, killing themselves or preparing to kill others.

A scholarship enabled me not only to attend college, a rare enough feat in my circle, but even to study in a university meant for the children of the rich. Here I met for the first time young men who had assumed from birth that they would lead lives of comfort and power. And for the first time I met women who told me that men were guilty of having kept all the joys and privileges of the earth for themselves. I was baffled. What privileges? What joys? I thought about the maimed, dismal lives of most of the men back home. What had they stolen from their wives and daughters? The right to go five days a week, twelve months a year, for thirty or forty years to a steel mill or a coal mine? The right to drop bombs and die in war? The right to feel every leak in the roof, every gap in the fence, every cough in the engine, as a wound they must mend? The right to feel, when the lay-off comes or the plant shuts down, not only afraid but ashamed?

I was slow to understand the deep grievances of women. This was because, as a boy, I had envied them. Before college, the only people I had ever known who were interested in art or music or literature, the only ones who read books, the only ones who ever seemed to enjoy a sense of ease and grace were the mothers and daughters. Like the menfolk, they fretted about money, they scrimped and made-do. But, when the pay stopped coming in, they were not the ones who had failed. Nor did they have to go to war, and that seemed to me a blessed fact. By comparison with the narrow, ironclad days of fathers, there was an expansiveness, I thought, in the days of mothers. They went to see neighbors, to shop in town, to run errands at school, at the library, at church. No doubt, had I looked harder at their lives, I would have envied them less. It was not my fate to become a woman, so it was easier for me to see the graces. Few of them held jobs outside the home, and those who did filled thankless roles as clerks and waitresses. I didn't see, then, what a prison a house could be, since houses seemed to me brighter, handsomer places than any factory. I did not realize—because such things were never spoken of—how often women suffered from men's bullying. I did learn about the wretchedness of abandoned wives, single mothers, widows; but I also learned about the wretchedness of lone men. Even then I could see how exhausting it was for a mother to cater all day to the needs of young children. But if I had been asked, as a boy, to choose between tending a baby and tending a machine, I think I would have chosen the baby. (Having now tended both, I know I would choose the baby.)

So I was baffled when the women at college accused me and my sex of having cornered the world's pleasures. I think something like my bafflement has been felt by other boys (and by girls as well) who grew up in dirt-poor farm country, in mining country, in black ghettos, in Hispanic barrios, in the shadows of factories, in Third World nations—any place where the fate of men is as grim and bleak as the fate of women. Toilers and warriors. I realize now how ancient these identities are, how deep the tug they exert on men, the undertow of a thousand generations. The miseries I saw, as a boy, in the lives of nearly all men I continue to see in the lives of many—the body-breaking toil, the tedium, the call to be tough, the humiliating powerlessness, the battle for a living and for territory.

When the women I met at college thought about the joys and privi- 20
leges of men, they did not carry in their minds the sort of men I had known in my childhood. They thought of their fathers, who were bankers, physicians, architects, stockbrokers, the big wheels of the big cities. These fathers rode the train to work or drove cars that cost more than any of my childhood houses. They were attended from morning to night by female helpers, wives, and nurses and secretaries. They were never laid off, never short of cash at month's end, never lined up for welfare. These fathers made decisions that mattered. They ran the world.

The daughters of such men wanted to share in this power, this glory. So did I. They yearned for a say over their future, for jobs worthy of their abilities, for the right to live at peace, unmolested, whole. Yes, I thought, yes yes. The difference between me and these daughters was that they saw me, because of my sex, as destined from birth to become like their fathers, and therefore as an enemy to their desires. But I knew better. I wasn't an enemy, in fact or in feeling. I was an ally. If I had known, then, how to tell them so, would they have believed me? Would they now?

The Reader's Presence

1. Sanders begins the essay by jumping directly into a conversation (paragraphs 1–9). What initial effect does this conversation have on the reader? What does Sanders want you to think of him as you read the dialogue? How does he move from the conversation to the body of the essay (paragraphs 10 and following)? How might you describe the transition? Does Sanders's voice change at paragraph 10? Does Sanders return to Anneke's distinction between the victim and the persecutor (end of paragraph 9)? If so, how? Finally, how do you understand the opening dialogue by the end of the essay, having encountered the full passion of Sanders's beliefs about his legacy of masculinity?

2. Consider the title of the essay. Why does Sanders use the word *carry*? What image does the word convey? How is that image reinforced throughout the essay?

3. Sanders's essay is as much about class as it is about gender. Discuss the roles of privation and privilege, of physical labor and higher education in the essay. Sanders is in many respects a compatriot of Dorothy Allison; the two writers share a strong sense of the ethical responsibility of the artist. Reread Allison's essay "This Is Our World" (page 633) and Sanders's thoughts about writing that follow, and compare the two writers' understanding of their roles as writers in American society. How do class issues enter into each essay?

THE WRITER AT WORK

Scott Russell Sanders on Writing Essays

The well-known American essayist Scott Russell Sanders is also a professor of English at Indiana University and the author of several novels, short story collections, and books of criticism. In the following passage from "The Singular First Person," which was originally delivered as a keynote talk at an academic conference on the essay at Seton Hall University in 1988, Sanders argues for the relevance of essay writing in a society that increasingly relies on abstract and formulaic language. If you compare this passage with the style of argument Sanders makes in the preceding essay, you will see that he is a writer who practices what he preaches. He also raises an interesting question about the difference between essays and fiction that you might consider when reading the stories in Part V: Do essayists put more of themselves at risk than novelists and short story writers?

The essay is a haven for the private, idiosyncratic voice in an era of anonymous babble. Like the blandburgers served in their millions along our highways, most language served up in public these days is textureless, tasteless mush. On television, over the phone, in the newspaper, wherever humans bandy words about, we encounter more and more abstractions, more empty formulas. Think of the pablum ladled out by politicians. Think of the fluffy white bread of advertising. Think, Lord help us, of committee reports. In contrast, the essay remains stubbornly concrete and particular: it confronts you with an oil-smeared toilet at the Sunoco station, a red vinyl purse shaped like a valentine heart, a bow-legged dentist hunting deer with an elephant gun. As Orwell forcefully argued,[1] and as dictators seem to agree, such a bypassing of abstractions, such an insistence on the concrete, is a politically subversive act. Clinging to this door, that child, this grief, following the zigzag motions of an inquisitive mind, the essay renews language and clears trash from the springs of thought. A century and a half ago, Emerson called on a new generation of writers to cast off the hand-me-down rhetoric of the day, to "pierce this rotten diction and fasten words again to visible things." The essayist aspires to do just that.

As if all these virtues were not enough to account for a renaissance of this protean genre, the essay has also taken over some of the territory abdicated by contemporary fiction. Pared down to the brittle bones of plot, camouflaged with irony, muttering in brief sentences and grade-school vocabulary, today's fashionable fiction avoids disclosing where the author stands on anything. Most of the trends in the novel and short story over the past twenty years have led away from candor—toward satire, artsy jokes, close-lipped coyness, metafictional hocus-pocus, anything but a direct statement of what the author thinks and feels. If you hide behind enough screens, no one will ever hold you to an opinion or demand from you a coherent vision or take you for a charlatan.

The essay is not fenced round by these literary inhibitions. You may speak without disguise of what moves and worries and excites you. In fact, you had better speak from a region pretty close to the heart, or the reader will detect the wind of phoniness whistling through your hollow phrases. In the essay you may be caught with your pants down, your ignorance and sentimentality showing, while you trot recklessly about on one of your hobbyhorses. You cannot stand back from the action, as Joyce instructed us to do, and pare your fingernails. You cannot palm off your cockamamie notions on some hapless character. If the words you put down are foolish, everyone knows precisely who the fool is.

[1]See "Politics and the English Language," page 533.—EDS.

To our list of the essay's contemporary attractions we should add the perennial ones of verbal play, mental adventure, and sheer anarchic high spirits. The writing of an essay is like finding one's way through a forest without being quite sure what game you are chasing, what landmark you are seeking. You sniff down one path until some heady smell tugs you in a new direction, and then off you go, dodging and circling, lured on by the songs of unfamiliar birds, puzzled by the tracks of strange beasts, leaping from stone to stone across rivers, barking up one tree after another. Much of the pleasure in writing an essay—and, when the writing is any good, the pleasure in reading it—comes from this dodging and leaping, this movement of the mind. It must not be idle movement, however, if the essay is to hold up; it must be driven by deep concerns. The surface of a river is alive with lights and reflections, the breaking of foam over rocks, but beneath that dazzle it is going somewhere. We should expect as much from an essay: the shimmer and play of mind on the surface and in the depths a strong current.

Leslie Marmon Silko

In the Combat Zone

Poet, novelist, screenwriter, and storyteller Leslie Marmon Silko (b. 1948) is of mixed heritage, part Pueblo Indian, part Mexican, and part white. She was raised on the Laguna Pueblo and educated at the University of New Mexico, where she now teaches English. Her publications include a montage of stories, legends, poems, and photographs called Storyteller *(1981), several works of fiction, the screenplay for Marlon Brando's film* Black Elks, *an illustrated autobiographical narrative called* Sacred Water Narratives and Pictures *(1993), and* Yellow Woman and a Beauty of the Spirit: Essays on Native American Life Today *(1996). Her more recent works include* Love Poem and Slim Man Canyon *(1999) and a novel* Gardens in the Dunes *(1999). Her work has been extensively anthologized and published in magazines and journals. "In the Combat Zone" appeared in* Hungry Mind Review *in 1995. In 1981, Silko was awarded a MacArthur Fellowship prize for her writing. She has taught in New Mexico, Alaska, and Arizona and holds academic appointments at both the Universities of New Mexico and Arizona.*

When asked by an interviewer why she writes, she replied, "I don't know what I know until it comes out in narrative." Speaking specifically of the process of composing her novel Almanac of the Dead *(1991), she said, "It's like a do-it-yourself psychoanalysis. It's sort of dangerous to be a novelist . . . you're working with language and all kinds of things can escape with the words of a narrative."*

Women seldom discuss our wariness or the precautions we take after dark each time we leave the apartment, car, or office to go on the most brief errand. We take for granted that we are targeted as easy prey by muggers, rapists, and serial killers. This is our lot as women in the United States. We try to avoid going anywhere alone after dark, although economic necessity sends women out night after night. We do what must be done, but always we are alert, on guard, and ready. We have to be aware of persons walking on the sidewalk behind us; we have to pay attention to others who board an elevator we're on. We try to avoid all staircases and deserted parking garages when we are alone. Constant vigilance requires considerable energy and concentration seldom required of men.

I used to assume that most men were aware of this fact of women's lives, but I was wrong. They may notice our reluctance to drive at night to the convenience store alone, but they don't know or don't want to know the experience of a woman out alone at night. Men who have been in combat know the feeling of being a predator's target, but it is difficult for men to admit that we women live our entire lives in a combat zone. Men have the power to end violence against women in the home, but they feel helpless to protect women from violent strangers. Because men feel guilt and anger at their inability to shoulder responsibility for the safety of their wives, sisters, and daughters, we don't often discuss random acts of violence against women.

When we were children, my sisters and I used to go to Albuquerque with my father. Sometimes strangers would tell my father it was too bad that he had three girls and no sons. My father, who has always preferred the company of women, used to reply that he was glad to have girls and not boys, because he might not get along as well with boys. Furthermore, he'd say, "My girls can do anything your boys can do, and my girls can do it better." He had in mind, of course, shooting and hunting.

When I was six years old, my father took me along as he hunted deer; he showed me how to walk quietly, to move along, and then to stop and listen carefully before taking another step. A year later, he traded a pistol for a little single shot .22 rifle just my size.

He took me and my younger sisters down to the dump by the river   5 and taught us how to shoot. We rummaged through the trash for bottles and glass jars; it was great fun to take aim at a pickle jar and watch it shatter. If the Rio San Jose had water running in it, we threw bottles for moving targets in the muddy current. My father told us that a .22 bullet can travel a mile, so we had to be careful where we aimed. The river was a good place because it was below the villages and away from the houses; the high clay riverbanks wouldn't let any bullets stray. Gun safety was drilled into us. We were cautioned about other children whose parents might not teach them properly; if we ever saw another child with a gun, we knew to get away. Guns were not toys. My father did not approve of BB guns because they were classified as toys. I had a .22 rifle when I was seven years old. If I felt like shooting, all I had to do was tell my parents where I was going, take my rifle and a box of .22 shells and go. I was never tempted to shoot at birds or animals because whatever was killed had to be eaten. Now, I realize how odd this must seem; a seven-year-old with a little .22 rifle and a box of ammunition, target shooting alone at the river. But that was how people lived at Laguna when I was growing up; children were given responsibilities from an early age.

Laguna Pueblo people hunted deer for winter meat. When I was thirteen, I carried George Pearl's saddle carbine, a .30–30, and hunted deer for the first time. When I was fourteen, I killed my first mule deer buck with one shot through the heart.

Guns were for target shooting and guns were for hunting, but also I knew that Grandma Lily carried a little purse gun with her whenever she drove alone to Albuquerque or Los Lunas. One night my mother and my grandmother were driving the fifty miles from Albuquerque to Laguna down Route 66 when three men in a car tried to force my grandmother's car off the highway. Route 66 was not so heavily traveled as Interstate 40 is now, and there were many long stretches of highway where no other car passed for minutes on end. Payrolls at the Jackpile Uranium Mine were large in the 1950s, and my mother or my grandmother had to bring home thousands from the bank in Albuquerque to cash the miners' checks on paydays.

After that night, my father bought my mother a pink nickel-plated snub-nose .22 revolver with a white bone grip. Grandma Lily carried a tiny Beretta as black as her prayer book. As my sisters and I got older, my father taught us to handle and shoot handguns, revolvers mostly, because back then, semiautomatic pistols were not as reliable—they frequently jammed. I will never forget the day my father told us three girls that we never had to let a man hit us or terrorize us because no matter how big and strong the man was, a gun in our hand equalized all differences of size and strength.

Much has been written about violence in the home and spousal abuse. I wish to focus instead on violence from strangers toward women because this form of violence terrifies women more, despite the fact that most women are murdered by a spouse, relative, fellow employee, or next-door neighbor, not a stranger. Domestic violence kills many more women and children than strangers kill, but domestic violence also follows more predictable patterns and is more familiar: He comes home drunk and she knows what comes next. A good deal of the terror of a stranger's attack comes from its suddenness and unexpectedness. Attacks by strangers occur with enough frequency that battered women and children often cite their fears of such attacks as reasons for remaining in abusive domestic situations. They fear the violence they imagine strangers will inflict on them more than they fear the abusive home. More than one feminist has pointed out that rapists and serial killers help keep the patriarchy securely in place.

An individual woman may be terrorized by her spouse, but women   10 are not sufficiently terrorized that we avoid marriage. Yet many women I know, including myself, try to avoid going outside of their homes alone after dark. Big deal, you say; well, yes, it is a big deal since most lectures, performances, and films are presented at night; so are dinners and other social events. Women out alone at night who are assaulted by strangers are put on trial by public opinion: Any woman out alone after dark is asking for trouble. Presently, for millions of women of all socioeconomic backgrounds, sundown is lockdown. We are prisoners of violent strangers.

Daylight doesn't necessarily make the streets safe for women. In the early 1980s, a rapist operated in Tucson in the afternoon near the University of Arizona campus. He often accosted two women at once, forced them into residential alleys, then raped each one with a knife to her throat and forced the other to watch. Afterward the women said that part of the horror of their attack was that all around them, everything appeared normal. They could see people inside their houses and cars going down the street—all around them life was going on as usual while their lives were being changed forever.

The afternoon rapist was not the only rapist in Tucson at that time; there was the prime-time rapist, the potbellied rapist, and the apologetic rapist all operating in Tucson in the 1980s. The prime-time rapist was actually two men who invaded comfortable foothills homes during television prime time when residents were preoccupied with television and eating dinner. The prime-time rapists terrorized entire families; they raped the women and sometimes they raped the men. Family members were forced to go to automatic bank machines to bring back cash to end the ordeal. Potbelly rapist and apologetic rapist need little comment, except to note that the apologetic rapist was good looking, well educated, and smart enough to break out of jail for one last rape followed by profuse apologies and his capture in the University of Arizona library. Local papers recounted details about Tucson's last notorious rapist, the red bandanna rapist. In the late 1970s, this rapist attacked more than twenty women over a three-year period, and Tucson police were powerless to stop him. Then one night, the rapist broke into a midtown home where the lone resident, a woman, shot him four times in the chest with a .38 caliber revolver.

In midtown Tucson, on a weekday afternoon, I was driving down Campbell Avenue to the pet store. Suddenly the vehicle behind me began to weave into my lane, so I beeped the horn politely. The vehicle swerved back to its lane, but then in my rearview mirror I saw the small late-model truck change lanes and begin to follow my car very closely. I drove a few blocks without looking in the rearview mirror, but in my sideview mirror I saw the compact truck was right behind me. OK. Some motorists stay upset for two or three blocks, some require ten blocks or more to recover their senses. Stoplight after stoplight, when I glanced into the rearview mirror I saw the man—in his early thirties, tall, white, brown hair, and dark glasses. This guy must not have a job if he has the time to follow me for miles—oh, ohhh! No beast more dangerous in the U.S.A. than an unemployed white man.

At this point I had to make a decision: Do I forget about the trip to the pet store and head for the police station downtown, four miles away? Why should I have to let this stranger dictate my schedule for the afternoon? The man might dare to follow me to the police station, but by the time I reach the front door of the station, he'd be gone. No crime was committed; no Arizona law forbids tailgating someone for miles or for turning into a parking lot behind them. What could the police do? I had no license plate number to report because Arizona requires only one license plate, on the rear bumper of the vehicle. Anyway, I was within a block of the pet store where I knew I could get help from the pet store owners. I would feel better about this incident if it was not allowed to ruin my trip to the pet store.

The guy was right on my rear bumper; if I'd had to stop suddenly for   15
any reason, there'd have been a collision. I decide I will not stop even if he does ram into the rear of my car. I study this guy's face in my rearview mirror; six feet two inches tall, 175 pounds, medium complexion, short hair, trimmed moustache. He thinks he can intimidate me because I am a woman, five feet five inches tall, 140 pounds. But I am not afraid, I am furious. I refuse to be intimidated. I won't play his game. I can tell by the face I see in the mirror this guy has done this before, he enjoys using his truck to menace lone women.

I keep thinking he will quit, or he will figure that he's scared me enough, but he seems to sense that I am not afraid. It's true. I am not afraid because years ago my father taught my sisters and me that we did not have to be afraid. He'll give up when I turn into the parking lot outside the pet store, I think. But I watch in my rearview mirror; he's right on my rear bumper. As his truck turns into the parking lot behind my car, I reach over and open the glove compartment. I take out the holster with my .38 special and lay it on the car seat beside me.

I turned my car into a parking spot so quickly that I was facing my stalker who had momentarily stopped his truck and was watching me. I slid the .38 out of its holster onto my lap. I watched the stranger's face, trying to determine whether he would jump out of his truck with a baseball bat or gun and come after me. I felt calm. No pounding heart or rapid breathing. My early experience deer hunting had prepared me well. I did not panic because I felt I could stop him if he tried to harm me. I was in no hurry. I sat in the car and waited to see what choice my stalker would make. I looked directly at him without fear because I had my .38 and I was ready to use it. The expression on my face must have been unfamiliar to him; he was used to seeing terror in the eyes of the women he followed. The expression on my face communicated a warning: If he approached the car window, I'd kill him.

He took a last look at me then sped away. I stayed in my car until his truck disappeared in the traffic of Campbell Avenue.

I walked into the pet store shaken. I had felt able to protect myself throughout the incident, but it left me emotionally drained and exhausted. The stranger had only pursued me—how much worse to be battered or raped.

Years before, I was unarmed the afternoon that two drunken deer   20 hunters threatened to shoot me off my horse with razor-edged hunting arrows from fiberglass crossbows. I was riding a colt on a national park trail near my home in the Tucson Mountains. These young white men in their late twenties were complete strangers who might have shot me if the colt had not galloped away erratically bucking and leaping—a moving target too difficult for the drunken bow hunters to aim at. The colt brought me to my ranch house where I called the county sheriff's office and the park ranger. I live in a sparsely populated area where my nearest neighbor is a quarter-mile away. I was afraid the men might have followed me back to my house so I took the .44 magnum out from under my pillow and strapped it around my waist until the sheriff or park ranger arrived. Forty-five minutes later, the park ranger arrived; the deputy sheriff arrived fifteen minutes after him. The drunken bow hunters were apprehended on the national park and arrested for illegally hunting; their bows and arrows were seized as evidence for the duration of bow hunting season. In southern Arizona that is enough punishment; I didn't want to take a chance of stirring up additional animosity with these men because I lived alone then; I chose not to make a complaint about their threatening words and gestures. I did not feel that I backed away by not pressing charges; I feared that if I pressed assault charges against these men, they would feel that I was challenging them to all-out war. I did not want to have to kill either of them if they came after me, as I thought they might. With my marksmanship and my .243 caliber hunting rifle from the old days, I am confident that I could stop idiots like these. But to have to take the life of another person is a terrible experience I will always try to avoid.

It isn't height or weight or strength that make women easy targets; from infancy women are taught to be self-sacrificing, passive victims. I was taught differently. Women have the right to protect themselves from death or bodily harm. By becoming strong and potentially lethal individuals, women destroy the fantasy that we are sitting ducks for predatory strangers.

In a great many cultures, women are taught to depend on others, not themselves, for protection from bodily harm. Women are not taught to defend themselves from strangers because fathers and husbands fear the consequences themselves. In the United States, women depend on the courts and the police, but as many women have learned the hard way, the police cannot be outside your house twenty-four hours a day. I don't want more police. More police on the streets will not protect women. A few policemen are rapists and killers of women themselves; their uniforms and squad cars give them an advantage. No, I will be responsible for my own safety, thank you.

Women need to decide who has the primary responsibility for the health and safety of their bodies. We don't trust the State to manage our reproductive organs, yet most of us blindly trust that the State will protect us (and our reproductive organs) from predatory strangers. One look at the rape and murder statistics for women (excluding domestic incidents) and it is clear that the government FAILS to protect women from the violence of strangers. Some may cry out for a "stronger" State, more police, mandatory sentences, and swifter executions. Over the years we have seen the U.S. prison population become the largest in the world, executions take place every week now, inner-city communities are occupied by the National Guard, and people of color are harassed by police, but guess what? A woman out alone, night or day, is confronted with more danger of random violence from strangers than ever before. As the U.S. economy continues "to downsize," and the good jobs disappear forever, our urban and rural landscapes will include more desperate, angry men with nothing to lose.

Only women can put a stop to the "open season" on women by strangers. Women are TAUGHT to be easy targets by their mothers, aunts, and grandmothers, who themselves were taught that "a woman doesn't kill" or "a woman doesn't learn how to use a weapon." Women must learn how to take aggressive action individually, apart from the police and the courts.

Presently, twenty-one states issue permits to carry concealed weapons;   25 most states require lengthy gun safety courses and a police security check before issuing a permit. Inexpensive but excellent gun safety and self-defense courses designed for women are also available from every quality gun dealer who hopes to sell you a handgun at the end of the course. Those who object to firearms need trained companion dogs or collectives of six or more women to escort one another day and night. We must destroy the myth that women are born to be easy targets.

The Reader's Presence

1. What does Silko mean by a "combat zone"? What is the origin of the term? How does she apply it to women's experiences? Do you think the term is applicable? What behavior does the term legitimize? Why do you think she concentrates on violence from strangers instead of domestic violence?

2. Why do you think Silko introduces stories about hunting experiences? In what ways do those experiences shape her background? Do you think they have shaped her present attitude? How do the experiences help reinforce her point about gun ownership? In what ways do they make her more qualified to speak on the issue?

3. In her opening two paragraphs, Silko describes the precautions women take in public every day, of which men are often ignorant. Read Brent Staples's "Just Walk on By" (page 283), which details his experiences of being stereotyped as a threat. How do you think Staples and Silko might discuss this idea of safety? Does Staples show himself to be aware of women's safety concerns? Why or why not? What might Silko say in response to Staples's feelings about "being perceived as dangerous"?

Peter Singer

The Singer Solution to World Poverty

Peter Singer, born in Melbourne, Australia, in 1946, has had a long career as the dean of the animal rights movement and is one of today's most controversial contemporary philosophers. He has taught at the University of Colorado at Boulder and the University of California at Irvine and is now the DeCamp Professor of Bioethics at Princeton University's Center for Human Values. His book Animal Liberation, *first published in 1975 and reprinted many times since, has become a basic sourcebook for animal rights activists. His* Practical Ethics *(1979) is one of the most widely recognized works of applied ethics. He has also written* Rethinking Life and Death, *which received an award from the National Book Council in 1995. In 2000 Singer published* Writings on an Ethical Life *and* A Darwinian Left: Politics, Evolution, and Cooperation, *which argues that the left should replace Marx with Darwin. Among Singer's recent books are* One World: The Ethics of Globalization *(2002),* Pushing Time Away: My Grandfather and the Tragedy of Jewish Vienna *(2003), and* President of Good and Evil: The Ethics of George W. Bush *(2004). "The Singer Solution to World Poverty" was first published in the* New York Times *in September 1999.*

A reviewer of Writings on an Ethical Life *commented: "Singer argues that value judgments should be matters of rational scrutiny and not matters of taste about which argument is futile. . . . For Singer, living ethically is living a meaningful life. It is a life that makes a difference in the world. It is a life that reduces the sum total of suffering."*

In the Brazilian film *Central Station*, Dora is a retired schoolteacher who makes ends meet by sitting at the station writing letters for illiterate people. Suddenly she has an opportunity to pocket $1,000. All she has to do is persuade a homeless nine-year-old boy to follow her to an address she has been given. (She is told he will be adopted by wealthy foreigners.) She delivers the boy, gets the money, spends some of it on a television set, and settles down to enjoy her new acquisition. Her neighbor spoils the fun, however, by telling her that the boy was too old to be adopted—he will be killed and his organs sold for transplantation. Perhaps Dora knew this all along, but after her neighbor's plain speaking, she spends a troubled night. In the morning Dora resolves to take the boy back.

Suppose Dora had told her neighbor that it is a tough world, other people have nice new TVs too, and if selling the kid is the only way she can get one, well, he was only a street kid. She would then have become, in the eyes of the audience, a monster. She redeems herself only by being prepared to bear considerable risks to save the boy.

At the end of the movie, in cinemas in the affluent nations of the world, people who would have been quick to condemn Dora if she had not rescued the boy go home to places far more comfortable than her apartment. In fact, the average family in the United States spends almost one-third of its income on things that are no more necessary to them than Dora's new TV was to her. Going out to nice restaurants, buying new clothes because the old ones are no longer stylish, vacationing at beach resorts—so much of our income is spent on things not essential to the preservation of our lives and health. Donated to one of a number of charitable agencies, that money could mean the difference between life and death for children in need.

All of which raises a question: In the end, what is the ethical distinction between a Brazilian who sells a homeless child to organ peddlers and an American who already has a TV and upgrades to a better one—knowing that the money could be donated to an organization that would use it to save the lives of kids in need?

Of course, there are several differences between the two situations 5 that could support different moral judgments about them. For one thing, to be able to consign a child to death when he is standing right in front of you takes a chilling kind of heartlessness; it is much easier to ignore an appeal for money to help children you will never meet. Yet for a utilitarian philosopher like myself—that is, one who judges whether acts are right or wrong by their consequences—if the upshot of the American's failure to donate the money is that one more kid dies on the streets of a Brazilian city, then it is, in some sense, just as bad as selling the kid to the organ peddlers. But one doesn't need to embrace my utilitarian ethic to see that, at the very least, there is a troubling incongruity in being so quick to condemn Dora for taking the child to the organ peddlers while, at the same time, not regarding the American consumer's behavior as raising a serious moral issue.

In his 1996 book, *Living High and Letting Die*, the New York University philosopher Peter Unger presented an ingenious series of imaginary examples designed to probe our intuitions about whether it is wrong to live well without giving substantial amounts of money to help people who are hungry, malnourished, or dying from easily treatable illnesses like diarrhea. Here's my paraphrase of one of these examples:

Bob is close to retirement. He has invested most of his savings in a very rare and valuable old car, a Bugatti, which he has not been able to insure. The Bugatti is his pride and joy. In addition to the pleasure he gets from driving and caring for his car, Bob knows that its rising market value means that he will always be able to sell it and live comfortably after retirement. One day when Bob is out for a drive, he parks the Bugatti near the end of a railway siding and goes for a walk up the track. As he does so, he sees that a runaway train, with no one aboard, is running down the railway track. Looking farther down the track, he sees the small figure of a child very likely to be killed by the runaway train. He can't stop the train and the child is too far away to warn of the danger, but he can throw a switch that will divert the train down the siding where his Bugatti is parked. Then nobody will be killed—but the train will destroy his Bugatti. Thinking of his joy in owning the car and the financial security it represents, Bob decides not to throw the switch. The child is killed. For many years to come, Bob enjoys owning his Bugatti and the financial security it represents.

Bob's conduct, most of us will immediately respond, was gravely wrong. Unger agrees. But then he reminds us that we, too, have opportunities to save the lives of children. We can give to organizations like Unicef or Oxfam America. How much would we have to give one of these organizations to have a high probability of saving the life of a child threatened by easily preventable diseases? (I do not believe that children are more worth saving than adults, but since no one can argue that children have brought their poverty on themselves, focusing on them simplifies the issues.) Unger called up some experts and used the information they provided to offer some plausible estimates that include the cost of raising money, administrative expenses, and the cost of delivering aid where it is most needed. By his calculation, $200 in donations would help a sickly two-year-old transform into a healthy six-year-old—offering safe passage through childhood's most dangerous years. To show how practical philosophical argument can be, Unger even tells his readers that they can easily donate funds by using their credit card and calling one of these toll-free numbers: (800) 367-5437 for Unicef; (800) 693-2687 for Oxfam America.

Now you, too, have the information you need to save a child's life. How should you judge yourself if you don't do it? Think again about Bob and his Bugatti. Unlike Dora, Bob did not have to look into the eyes of the child he was sacrificing for his own material comfort. The child was a complete stranger to him and too far away to relate to in an intimate, personal way. Unlike Dora, too, he did not mislead the child or initiate the chain of events imperiling him. In all these respects, Bob's situation resembles that of people able but unwilling to donate to overseas aid and differs from Dora's situation.

If you still think that it was very wrong of Bob not to throw the switch that would have diverted the train and saved the child's life, then it is hard to see how you could deny that it is also very wrong not to send money to one of the organizations listed above. Unless, that is, there is some morally important difference between the two situations that I have overlooked.

Is it the practical uncertainties about whether aid will really reach the people who need it? Nobody who knows the world of overseas aid can doubt that such uncertainties exist. But Unger's figure of $200 to save a child's life was reached after he had made conservative assumptions about the proportion of the money donated that will actually reach its target.

One genuine difference between Bob and those who can afford to donate to overseas aid organizations but don't is that only Bob can save the child on the tracks, whereas there are hundreds of millions of people who can give $200 to overseas aid organizations. The problem is that most of them aren't doing it. Does this mean that it is all right for you not to do it?

Suppose that there were more owners of priceless vintage cars—Carol, Dave, Emma, Fred, and so on, down to Ziggy—all in exactly the same situation as Bob, with their own siding and their own switch, all sacrificing the child in order to preserve their own cherished car. Would that make it all right for Bob to do the same? To answer this question affirmatively is to endorse follow-the-crowd ethics—the kind of ethics that led many Germans to look away when the Nazi atrocities were being committed. We do not excuse them because others were behaving no better.

We seem to lack a sound basis for drawing a clear moral line between Bob's situation and that of any reader of this article with $200 to spare who does not donate it to an overseas aid agency. These readers seem to be acting at least as badly as Bob was acting when he chose to let the runaway train hurtle toward the unsuspecting child. In the light of this conclusion, I trust that many readers will reach for the phone and donate that $200. Perhaps you should do it before reading further.

Now that you have distinguished yourself morally from people who put their vintage cars ahead of a child's life, how about treating yourself and your partner to dinner at your favorite restaurant? But wait. The money you will spend at the restaurant could also help save the lives of children overseas! True, you weren't planning to blow $200 tonight, but if you were to give up dining out just for one month, you would easily save that amount. And what is one month's dining out, compared to a child's life? There's the rub. Since there are a lot of desperately needy children in the world, there will always be another child whose life you could save for another $200. Are you therefore obliged to keep giving until you have nothing left? At what point can you stop?

Hypothetical examples can easily become farcical. Consider Bob. How far past losing the Bugatti should he go? Imagine that Bob had got his foot stuck in the track of the siding, and if he diverted the train, then before it rammed the car it would also amputate his big toe. Should he still throw the switch? What if it would amputate his foot? His entire leg?

As absurd as the Bugatti scenario gets when pushed to extremes, the point it raises is a serious one: Only when the sacrifices become very significant indeed would most people be prepared to say that Bob does nothing wrong when he decides not to throw the switch. Of course, most people could be wrong; we can't decide moral issues by taking opinion polls. But consider for yourself the level of sacrifice that you would demand of Bob, and then think about how much money you would have to give away in order to make a sacrifice that is roughly equal to that. It's almost certainly much, much more than $200. For most middle-class Americans, it could easily be more like $200,000.

Isn't it counterproductive to ask people to do so much? Don't we run the risk that many will shrug their shoulders and say that morality, so conceived, is fine for saints but not for them? I accept that we are unlikely to see, in the near or even medium-term future, a world in which it is normal for wealthy Americans to give the bulk of their wealth to strangers. When it comes to praising or blaming people for what they do, we tend to use a standard that is relative to some conception of normal behavior. Comfortably off Americans who give, say, 10 percent of their income to overseas aid organizations are so far ahead of most of their equally comfortable fellow citizens that I wouldn't go out of my way to chastise them for not doing more. Nevertheless, they should be doing much more, and they are in no position to criticize Bob for failing to make the much greater sacrifice of his Bugatti.

At this point various objections may crop up. Someone may say: "If every citizen living in the affluent nations contributed his or her share I wouldn't have to make such a drastic sacrifice, because long before such levels were reached, the resources would have been there to save the lives of all those children dying from lack of food or medical care. So why should I give more than my fair share?" Another, related objection is that the government ought to increase its overseas aid allocations, since that would spread the burden more equitably across all taxpayers.

Yet the question of how much we ought to give is a matter to be decided in the real world—and that, sadly, is a world in which we know that most people do not, and in the immediate future will not, give substantial amounts to overseas aid agencies. We know, too, that at least in the next year, the United States government is not going to meet even the very modest United Nations–recommended target of 0.7 percent of gross national product; at the moment it lags far below that, at 0.09 percent, not even half of Japan's 0.22 percent or a tenth of Denmark's 0.97 percent. Thus, we know that the money we can give beyond that theoretical "fair share" is still going to save lives that would otherwise be lost. While

20

the idea that no one need do more than his or her fair share is a powerful one, should it prevail if we know that others are not doing their fair share and that children will die preventable deaths unless we do more than our fair share? That would be taking fairness too far.

Thus, this ground for limiting how much we ought to give also fails. In the world as it is now, I can see no escape from the conclusion that each one of us with wealth surplus to his or her essential needs should be giving most of it to help people suffering from poverty so dire as to be life-threatening. That's right: I'm saying that you shouldn't buy that new car, take that cruise, redecorate the house, or get that pricey new suit. After all, a $1,000 suit could save five children's lives.

So how does my philosophy break down in dollars and cents? An American household with an income of $50,000 spends around $30,000 annually on necessities, according to the Conference Board, a nonprofit economic research organization. Therefore, for a household bringing in $50,000 a year, donations to help the world's poor should be as close as possible to $20,000. The $30,000 required for necessities holds for higher incomes as well. So a household making $100,000 could cut a yearly check for $70,000. Again, the formula is simple: Whatever money you're spending on luxuries, not necessities, should be given away.

Now, evolutionary psychologists tell us that human nature just isn't sufficiently altruistic to make it plausible that many people will sacrifice so much for strangers. On the facts of human nature, they might be right, but they would be wrong to draw a moral conclusion from those facts. If it is the case that we ought to do things that, predictably, most of us won't do, then let's face that fact head-on. Then, if we value the life of a child more than going to fancy restaurants, the next time we dine out we will know that we could have done something better with our money. If that makes living a morally decent life extremely arduous, well, then that is the way things are. If we don't do it, then we should at least know that we are failing to live a morally decent life — not because it is good to wallow in guilt but because knowing where we should be going is the first step toward heading in that direction.

When Bob first grasped the dilemma that faced him as he stood by that railway switch, he must have thought how extraordinarily unlucky he was to be placed in a situation in which he must choose between the life of an innocent child and the sacrifice of most of his savings. But he was not unlucky at all. We are all in that situation.

The Reader's Presence

1. How convincing do you find Singer's hypothetical examples, such as Bob and his uninsured Bugatti? Do you think the examples support his basic argument or weaken it? Explain your response.

2. In paragraph 5, Singer defines a utilitarian philosopher as one who "judges whether acts are right or wrong by their consequences." Can you think of utilitarian solutions other than Singer's to the problems of world poverty? For example, would population control methods that drastically reduced the number of impoverished children born into the world also be a utilitarian solution? Would donations to organizations that fund population control be more effective than charitable donations that directly assist children? If Singer's solution were adopted and more and more children were assisted, would that eventually encourage higher birth rates and thus worsen the very problem Singer wants to solve?

3. Consider Singer's essay in conjunction with Jonathan Swift's classic satirical essay on poverty, "A Modest Proposal" (page 825). In what ways does Swift's essay also take a utilitarian position? How do you think Swift would react to Singer's solution to world poverty?

Lauren Slater

The Trouble with Self-Esteem

Lauren Slater (b. 1962) began her writing career after earning a doctorate in clinical psychology from Boston University. Her first book, Welcome to My Country: A Therapist's Memoir of Madness *(1996), tells the stories of some of the patients she treated over the course of her eleven-year career. She is perhaps best known, however, for her accounts of her own mental illness and recovery,* Prozac Diary *(1998) and* Lying: A Metaphorical Memoir *(2000). Discussing the difference between writing about her patients and about herself, Slater explains, "I think I found it easier to write about other people, about patients, because I could portray the enormity and dignity of their suffering without risking self-absorption, or blatant narcissism. In writing about myself, I feel much more constricted. I worry about solipsism, shortsightedness, self-aggrandizement, self-denigration, and all the other treacherous territories that come with the fascinating pursuit of autobiography."*

Slater has also published numerous books combining scientific research, a professional's perspective, and personal experience, including Love Works like This *(2002),* Opening Skinner's Box: Great Psychological Experiments of the Twentieth Century *(2004), and* Blue beyond Blue *(2005). She has contributed pieces to the* New York Times, Harper's, Elle, *and* Nerve, *and her essays are found in numerous anthologies including* Best American Essays *of 1994 and 1997,* Best American Science Writing 2002, *and* Best American Magazine Writing 2002. *Her essay "The Trouble with Self-Esteem" appeared in the* New York Times Magazine *in 2002.*

Take this test:

1. On the whole I am satisfied with myself.
2. At times I think that I am no good at all.
3. I feel that I have a number of good qualities.
4. I am able to do things as well as most other people.
5. I feel I do not have much to be proud of.
6. I certainly feel useless at times.
7. I feel that I am a person of worth, at least the equal of others.
8. I wish I could have more respect for myself.
9. All in all, I am inclined to feel that I am a failure.
10. I take a positive attitude toward myself.

Devised by the sociologist Morris Rosenberg, this questionnaire is one of the most widely used self-esteem assessment scales in the United States. If your answers demonstrate solid self-regard, the wisdom of the social sciences predicts that you are well adjusted, clean and sober, basically lucid, without criminal record and with some kind of college cum laude under your high-end belt. If your answers, on the other hand, reveal some inner shame, then it is obvious: you were, or are, a teenage mother; you are prone to social deviance; and if you don't drink, it is because the illicit drugs are bountiful and robust.

It has not been much disputed, until recently, that high self-esteem — defined quite simply as liking yourself a lot, holding a positive opinion of your actions and capacities — is essential to well-being and that its opposite is responsible for crime and substance abuse and prostitution and murder and rape and even terrorism. Thousands of papers in psychiatric and social-science literature suggest this, papers with names like "Characteristics of Abusive Parents: A Look At Self-Esteem" and "Low Adolescent Self-Esteem Leads to Multiple Interpersonal Problems." In 1990, David Long published "The Anatomy of Terrorism," in which he found that hijackers and suicide bombers suffer from feelings of worthlessness and that their violent, fluorescent acts are desperate attempts to bring some inner flair to a flat mindscape.

This all makes so much sense that we have not thought to question it. The less confidence you have, the worse you do; the more confidence you have, the better you do; and so the luminous loop goes round. Based on our beliefs, we have created self-esteem programs in schools in which the main objective is, as Jennifer Coon-Wallman, a psychotherapist based in Boston, says, "to dole out huge heapings of praise, regardless of actual accomplishment." We have a National Association for Self-Esteem with about a thousand members, and in 1986, the State Legislature of California founded the "California Task Force to Promote Self-Esteem and Personal and Social Responsibility." It was galvanized by Assemblyman John Vasconcellos, who fervently believed that by raising his citizens' self-concepts, he could divert drug abuse and all sorts of other social ills.

It didn't work.

In fact, crime rates and substance abuse rates are formidable, right   5 along with our self-assessment scores on paper-and-pencil tests. (Whether these tests are valid and reliable indicators of self-esteem is a subject worthy of inquiry itself, but in the parlance of social-science writing, it goes "beyond the scope of this paper.") In part, the discrepancy between high self-esteem scores and poor social skills and academic acumen led researchers like Nicholas Emler of the London School of Economics and Roy Baumeister of Case Western Reserve University to consider the unexpected notion that self-esteem is overrated and to suggest that it may even be a culprit, not a cure.

"There is absolutely no evidence that low self-esteem is particularly harmful," Emler says. "It's not at all a cause of poor academic performance; people with low self-esteem seem to do just as well in life as people with high self-esteem. In fact, they may do better, because they often try harder." Baumeister takes Emler's findings a bit further, claiming not only that low self-esteem is in most cases a socially benign if not beneficent condition but also that its opposite, high self-regard, can maim and even kill. Baumeister conducted a study that found that some people with favorable views of themselves were more likely to administer loud blasts of ear-piercing noise to a subject than those more tepid, timid folks who held back the horn. An earlier experiment found that men with high self-esteem were more willing to put down victims to whom they had administered electric shocks than were their low-level counterparts.

Last year alone there were three withering studies of self-esteem released in the United States, all of which had the same central message: people with high self-esteem pose a greater threat to those around them than people with low self-esteem and feeling bad about yourself is not the cause of our country's biggest, most expensive social problems. The research is original and compelling and lays the groundwork for a new, important kind of narrative about what makes life worth living—if we choose to listen, which might be hard. One of this country's most central tenets, after all, is the pursuit of happiness, which has been strangely joined to the pursuit of self-worth. Shifting a paradigm is never easy. More than 2,000 books offering the attainment of self-esteem have been published; educational programs in schools designed to cultivate self-esteem continue to proliferate, as do rehabilitation programs for substance abusers that focus on cognitive realignment with self-affirming statements like, "Today I will accept myself for who I am, not who I wish I were." I have seen therapists tell their sociopathic patients to say "I adore myself" every day or to post reminder notes on their kitchen cabinets and above their toilet-paper dispensers, self-affirmations set side by side with waste.

Will we give these challenges to our notions about self-esteem their due or will the research go the way of the waste? "Research like that is seriously flawed," says Stephen Keane, a therapist who practices in Newburyport, Mass. "First, it's defining self-esteem according to very conventional and problematic masculine ideas. Second, it's clear to me that many violent men, in particular, have this inner shame; they find out early in life they're not going to measure up, and they compensate for it with fists. We need, as men, to get to the place where we can really honor and expand our natural human grace."

Keane's comment is rooted in a history that goes back hundreds of years, and it is this history that in part prevents us from really tussling with the insights of scientists like Baumeister and Emler. We have long held in this country the Byronic[1] belief that human nature is essentially good or graceful, that behind the sheath of skin is a little globe of glow to be harnessed for creative uses. Benjamin Franklin, we believe, got that glow, as did Joseph Pulitzer and scads of other, lesser, folks who eagerly caught on to what was called, in the 19th century, "mind cure."

Mind cure augurs New Age healing, so that when we lift and look at 10 the roots, New Age is not new at all. In the 19th century, people fervently believed that you were what you thought. Sound familiar? Post it above your toilet paper. You are what you think. What you think. What you think. In the 1920's, a French psychologist, Émile Coué, became all the rage in this country; he proposed the technique of autosuggestion and before long had many citizens repeating, "Day by day in every way I am getting better and better."

But as John Hewitt says in his book criticizing self-esteem, it was maybe Ralph Waldo Emerson more than anyone else who gave the modern self-esteem movement its most eloquent words and suasive philosophy. Emerson died more than a century ago, but you can visit his house in Concord, Mass., and see his bedroom slippers cordoned off behind plush velvet ropes and his eyeglasses, surprisingly frail, the frames of thin gold, the ovals of shine, perched on a beautiful desk. It was in this house that Emerson wrote his famous transcendentalist essays like "On Self-Reliance," which posits that the individual has something fresh and authentic within and that it is up to him to discover it and nurture it apart from the corrupting pressures of social influence. Emerson never mentions "self-esteem" in his essay, but his every word echoes with the self-esteem movement of today, with its romantic, sometimes silly and clearly humane belief that we are special, from head to toe.

---

[1]**Byronic:** After the English poet George Gordon, Lord Byron (1788–1824). —EDS.

Self-esteem, as a construct, as a quasi religion, is woven into a tradition that both defines and confines us as Americans. If we were to deconstruct self-esteem, to question its value, we would be, in a sense, questioning who we are, nationally and individually. We would be threatening our self-esteem. This is probably why we cannot really assimilate research like Baumeister's or Emler's; it goes too close to the bone and then threatens to break it. Imagine if you heard your child's teacher say, "Don't think so much of yourself." Imagine your spouse saying to you, "You know, you're really not so good at what you do." We have developed a discourse of affirmation, and to deviate from that would be to enter another arena, linguistically and grammatically, so that what came out of our mouths would be impolite at best, unintelligible at worst.

Is there a way to talk about the self without measuring its worth? Why, as a culture, have we so conflated the two quite separate notions — a) self and b) worth? This may have as much to do with our entrepreneurial history as Americans, in which everything exists to be improved, as it does, again, with the power of language to shape beliefs. How would we story the self if not triumphantly, redemptively, enhanced from the inside out? A quick glance at amazon.com titles containing the word "self" shows that a hefty percentage also have -improvement or -enhancement tucked into them, oftentimes with numbers — something like 101 ways to improve your self-esteem or 503 ways to better your outlook in 60 days or 604 ways to overcome negative self-talk. You could say that these titles are a product of a culture, or you could say that these titles and the contents they sheathe shape the culture. It is the old argument: do we make language or does language make us? In the case of self-esteem, it is probably something in between, a synergistic loop-the-loop.

On the subject of language, one could, of course, fault Baumeister and Emler for using "self-esteem" far too unidimensionally, so that it blurs and blends with simple smugness. Baumeister, in an attempt at nuance, has tried to shade the issue by referring to two previously defined types: high *unstable* self-esteem and high *well-grounded* self-esteem. As a psychologist, I remember once treating a murderer, who said, "The problem with me, Lauren, is that I'm the biggest piece of [expletive] the world revolves around." He would have scored high on a self-esteem inventory, but does he really "feel good" about himself? And if he doesn't really feel good about himself, then does it not follow that his hidden low, not his high, self-esteem leads to violence? And yet as Baumeister points out, research has shown that people with overt low self-esteem aren't violent, so why would low self-esteem cause violence only when it is hidden? If you follow his train of thinking, you could come up with the sort of silly conclusion that covert low self-esteem causes aggression, but overt low self-esteem does not, which means concealment, not cockiness, is the real culprit. That makes little sense.

"The fact is," Emler says, "we've put antisocial men through every self-esteem test we have, and there's *no* evidence for the old psychodynamic   15 concept that they secretly feel bad about themselves. These men are racist or violent because they don't feel bad *enough* about themselves." Baumeister and his colleagues write: "People who believe themselves to be among the top 10 percent on any dimension may be insulted and threatened whenever anyone asserts that they are in the 80th or 50th or 25th percentile. In contrast, someone with lower self-esteem who regards himself or herself as being merely in the top 60 percent would only be threatened by the feedback that puts him or her at the 25th percentile. . . . In short, the more favorable one's view of oneself, the greater the range of external feedback that will be perceived as unacceptably low."

Perhaps, as these researchers are saying, pride really is dangerous, and too few of us know how to be humble. But that is most likely not the entire reason why we are ignoring flares that say, "Look, sometimes self-esteem can be bad for your health." There are, as always, market forces, and they are formidable. The psychotherapy industry, for instance, would take a huge hit were self-esteem to be re-examined. After all, psychology and psychiatry are predicated upon the notion of the self, and its enhancement is the primary purpose of treatment. I am by no means saying mental health professionals have any conscious desire to perpetuate a perhaps simplistic view of self-esteem, but they are, we are (for I am one of them, I confess), the "cultural retailers" of the self-esteem concept, and were the concept to falter, so would our pocketbooks.

Really, who would come to treatment to be taken down a notch? How would we get our clients to pay to be, if not insulted, at least uncomfortably challenged? There is a profound tension here between psychotherapy as a business that needs to retain its customers and psychotherapy as a practice that has the health of its patients at heart. Mental health is not necessarily a comfortable thing. Because we want to protect our patients and our pocketbooks, we don't always say this. The drug companies that underwrite us never say this. Pills take you up or level you out, but I have yet to see an advertisement for a drug of deflation.

If you look at psychotherapy in other cultures, you get a glimpse into the obsessions of our own. You also see what a marketing fiasco we would have on our hands were we to dial down our self-esteem beliefs. In Japan, there is a popular form of psychotherapy that does not focus on the self and its worth. This psychotherapeutic treatment, called Morita, holds as its central premise that neurotic suffering comes, quite literally, from extreme self-awareness. "The most miserable people I know have been self-focused," says David Reynolds, a Morita practitioner in Oregon. Reynolds writes, "Cure is not defined by the alleviation of discomfort or the attainment of some ideal state (which is impossible) but by taking constructive action in one's life which helps one to live a full and meaningful existence and not be ruled by one's emotional state."

Morita therapy, which emphasizes action over reflection, might have some trouble catching on here, especially in the middle-class West, where folks would be hard pressed to garden away the 50-minute hour. That's what Morita patients do; they plant petunias and practice patience as they wait for them to bloom.

Like any belief system, Morita has its limitations. To detach from feelings carries with it the risk of detaching from their significant signals, which carry important information about how to act: reach out, recoil. But the current research on self-esteem does suggest that we might benefit, if not fiscally than at least spiritually, from a few petunias on the Blue Cross bill. And the fact that we continue, in the vernacular, to use the word "shrink" to refer to treatment means that perhaps unconsciously we know we sometimes need to be taken down a peg.   20

Down to . . . what? Maybe self-control should replace self-esteem as a primary peg to reach for. I don't mean to sound puritanical, but there is something to be said for discipline, which comes from the word "disciple," which actually means to comprehend. Ultimately, self-control need not be seen as a constriction; restored to its original meaning, it might be experienced as the kind of practiced prowess an athlete or an artist demonstrates, muscles not tamed but trained, so that the leaps are powerful, the spine supple and the energy harnessed and shaped.

There are therapy programs that teach something like self-control, but predictably they are not great moneymakers and they certainly do not attract the bulk of therapy consumers, the upper middle class. One such program, called Emerge, is run by a psychologist named David Adams in a low-budget building in Cambridge, Mass. Emerge's clients are mostly abusive men, 75 percent of them mandated by the courts. "I once did an intake on a batterer who had been in psychotherapy for three years, and his violence wasn't getting any better," Adams told me. "I said to him, 'Why do you think you hit your wife?' He said to me, 'My therapist told me it's because I don't feel good about myself inside.'" Adams sighs, then laughs. "We believe it has *nothing* to do with how good a man feels about himself. At Emerge, we teach men to evaluate their behaviors honestly and to interact with others using empathy and respect." In order to accomplish these goals, men write their entire abuse histories on 12-by-12 sheets of paper, hang the papers on the wall and read them. "Some of the histories are so long, they go all around the room," Adams says. "But it's a powerful exercise. It gets a guy to really concretely *see*." Other exercises involve having the men act out the abuse with the counselor as the victim. Unlike traditional "suburban" therapies, Emerge is under no pressure to keep its customers; the courts do that for them. In return, they are free to pursue a path that has to do with "balanced confrontation," at the heart of which is critical reappraisal and self— no, not esteem— responsibility.

While Emerge is for a specific subgroup of people, it might provide us with a model for how to reconfigure treatment— and maybe even life— if we do decide the self is not about how good it feels but how well it does, in work and love. Work and love. That's a phrase fashioned by Freud himself, who once said the successful individual is one who has achieved meaningful work and meaningful love. Note how separate this sentence is from the notion of self. We blame Freud for a lot of things, but we can't blame that cigar-smoking Victorian for this particular cultural obsession. It was Freud, after all, who said that the job of psychotherapy was to turn neurotic suffering into ordinary suffering. Freud never claimed we should be happy, and he never claimed confidence was the key to a life well lived.

I remember the shock I had when I finally read this old analyst in his native tongue. English translations of Freud make him sound maniacal, if not egomaniacal, with his bloated words like id, ego and superego. But in the original German, id means under-I, ego translates into I and superego is not super-duper but, quite simply, over-I. Freud was staking a claim for a part of the mind that watches the mind, that takes the global view in an effort at honesty. Over-I. I can see. And in the seeing, assess, edit, praise and prune. This is self-appraisal, which precedes self-control, for we must first know both where we flail and stumble, and where we are truly strong, before we can make disciplined alterations. Self-appraisal. It has a certain sort of rhythm to it, does it not? Self-appraisal may be what Baumeister and Emler are actually advocating. If our lives are stories in the making, then we must be able to edit as well as advertise the text. Self-appraisal. If we say self-appraisal again and again, 101 times, 503 times, 612 times, maybe we can create it. And learn its complex arts.

The Reader's Presence

1. How does Slater establish her credibility? Identify techniques, words, phrases, and evidence that enhance your view of her as an expert. What makes establishing credibility especially important in this essay?

2. In Slater's opinion, how is self-esteem tied to American identity? What have Americans invested in the idea of self-esteem? What might be lost if self-esteem were no longer seen as valuable?

3. In refuting the idea that self-esteem is highly valuable, Slater honestly addresses what would be threatened by such a change in perspective. How does Slater address each of these threats? Compare Slater's technique of arguing against a widely accepted ideal to Laura Kipnis's argument in "Against Love" (page 755) and John Gatto's in "Against School" (page 688). Which argument(s) do you find most convincing? Why?

THE WRITER AT WORK

Lauren Slater on Writing Groups

Many professional writers find it stimulating and inspiring to share their work with friends and colleagues. They prefer to do this while the writing is in progress so they can discover problems they haven't anticipated, take note of alternate directions they might pursue, or simply obtain a "gut reaction" from a supportive audience. For Slater, a key advantage of working with a writing group is the impetus provided by a dialogue: "You feel like you're really involved in a dialogue as opposed to a monologue. I do better in engaging in dialogues." These comments on writing groups are part of an interview Slater did with Alys Culhane that appeared in the creative nonfiction journal Fourth Genre *in spring 2005.*

Culhane: I recently read that your writing group is integral to your writing process. Is this so? And if so, what's its history?

Slater: It's been quite critical. I was 24 when I started working with this group and I've just turned 40. My writing group has shortened or abolished the state between writer and reader. It can be weeks on end that you are writing, and when you send something out, weeks on end before you hear anything back. But you can bring something to group, and people will hear it right away. This provides a real impetus. You feel like you're really involved in a dialogue as opposed to a monologue. I do better in engaging in dialogues.

Culhane: Why do you think this is?

Slater: Probably everything I write is kind of a co-construction of what I think and what other people think and I just don't see myself as being someone who's pulling ideas out of her own head. I dialogue with people, with books, with pictures, with everything—the world is always giving me things and I'm always taking them and turning them over. I often feel like a quilt maker—and the members of my writing group have, in a way, provided me with ways of thinking about a design and given me some of the squares. So have other friends, other writers, other books. I'm a very derivative writer and I rely heavily on other texts.

Culhane: Can you provide a specific instance where a reliance upon other texts appears in your work?

Slater: Yes. I just finished a book of fairy tales, *Blue Beyond Blue*. In this book I take established fairy tales and established fairy-tale characters and tell the story of Snow White through the eyes of the stepmother, Hansel and Gretel through the eyes of the witch.

Culhane: How has the structure of your writing group changed over time?

Slater: It's always been very loose. There's been considerable discussion about life issues that have changed over the years, from getting a boyfriend, to having breast cancer, to having kids or not having kids; the issues have changed as we've changed. In terms of structure, we have always followed the same set of "rules." We convene around 8:30 P.M. every Thursday night. We eat. We talk. At around about 11 P.M. we start to read our work. We stay for as long as it takes for everyone who has work to read it. After a person is finished reading, we go around the room and give our own comments on the piece. When this is done, we plunge into a discussion. We're all very tired on Fridays.

Culhane: Now after many years of sharing your writing with the same people do you find that you anticipate their response when you're writing?

Slater: Yes. For example, to some degree I know that one person is going to feel that a particular, say, meditative or internal beginning is slow because her writing style favors very action-oriented scenes. Others are more partial to memoir, or to fiction. Some of us adhere to the "Show, Don't Tell" rule whereas others are more likely to analyze and interpret.

Culhane: Do you anticipate their specific responses?

Slater: Yes. As a writer, what I'm really looking for is a very visceral kind of response; I take visceral reactions much more to heart than studious ones. I ask myself, did they connect with this piece, does it resonate? What I should do with this paragraph or that paragraph isn't an issue to me.

Jane Smiley

Say It Ain't So, Huck

Pulitzer-prize–winning author Jane Smiley (b. 1949) has written more than a dozen works of fiction as well as many nonfiction pieces on topics ranging from politics to horses, from marriage to Barbie, and from farming to Wall Street. Born in Los Angeles and raised in St. Louis, Smiley attended Vassar College and the University of Iowa, where she earned an M.F.A. from the Iowa Writers' Workshop and a Ph.D. in English. In 1981, she joined the faculty at Iowa State University in Ames and taught there until 1996. The Midwest provided the setting for a number of her novels including her first, Barn Blind *(1980);* A Thousand Acres *(1991), for which she was awarded the 1992 Pulitzer Prize; and* Moo *(1995), a send-up of agriculture/land grant colleges much like the one at which she taught. Though she sometimes describes herself as a "comic writer," much of her fiction deals with families and their desperate attempts to connect with one another and to stay together.*

Other influences have extended the breadth of her writing and changed its direction. As she told an interviewer, winning the Pulitzer was nice, but it didn't change her life. "It made me famous, but . . . becoming a mother at 43, buying a horse at 42, that changed my life." Smiley's affinity for horses shows up in her novels The All-True Travels and Adventures of Lidie Newton *(1998) and* Horse Heaven *(2000), and in a number of nonfiction books including* A Year at the Races *(2004). Smiley has contributed articles to countless magazines and publications, including* Vogue, *the* New Yorker, Practical Horseman, *the* New York Times Magazine, *the* Nation, *and* Harper's, *in which the essay, "Say It Ain't So, Huck," appeared in 1996.*

So I broke my leg. Doesn't matter how — since the accident I've heard plenty of broken-leg tales, and, I'm telling you, I didn't realize that walking down the stairs, walking down hills, dancing in high heels, or stamping your foot on the brake pedal could be so dangerous. At any rate, like numerous broken-legged intellectuals before me, I found the prospect of three months in bed in the dining room rather seductive from a book-reading point of view, and I eagerly got started. Great novels piled up on my table, and right at the top was *The Adventures of Huckleberry Finn*, which, I'm embarrassed to admit, I hadn't read since junior high school. The novel took me a couple of days (it was longer than I had remembered), and I closed the cover stunned. Yes, stunned. Not, by any means, by the artistry of the book but by the notion that this is the novel all American literature grows out of, that this is a great novel, that this is even a serious novel.

Although Huck had his fans at publication, his real elevation into the pantheon was worked out early in the Propaganda Era, between 1948 and 1955, by Lionel Trilling, Leslie Fiedler, T. S. Eliot, Joseph Wood Krutch,[1] and some lesser lights, in the introductions to American and British editions of the novel and in such journals as *Partisan Review* and *The New York Times Book Review*. The requirements of Huck's installation rapidly revealed themselves: the failure of the last twelve chapters (in which Huck finds Jim imprisoned on the Phelps plantation and Tom Sawyer is reintroduced and elaborates a cruel and unnecessary scheme for Jim's liberation) had to be diminished, accounted for, or forgiven; after that, the novel's special qualities had to be placed in the context first of other American novels (to their detriment) and then of world literature. The best bets here seemed to be Twain's style and the river setting, and the critics invested accordingly: Eliot, who had never read the novel as a boy, traded on his own childhood beside the big river, elevating Huck to the Boy, and the Mississippi to the River God, therein finding the sort of mythic resonance that he admired. Trilling liked the river god idea, too, though he didn't bother to capitalize it. He also thought

---

[1]*Lionel Trilling . . . Krutch:* Influential literary critics who considered *The Adventures of Huckleberry Finn* a classic. — EDS.

that Twain, through Huck's lying, told truths, one of them being (I kid you not) that "something . . . had gone out of American life after the [Civil War], some simplicity, some innocence, some peace." What Twain himself was proudest of in the novel—his style—Trilling was glad to dub "not less than definitive in American literature. The prose of *Huckleberry Finn* established for written prose the virtues of American colloquial speech. . . . He is the master of the style that escapes the fixity of the printed page, that sounds in our ears with the immediacy of the heard voice, the very voice of unpretentious truth." The last requirement was some quality that would link Huck to other, though "lesser," American novels such as Herman Melville's *Moby-Dick*, that would possess some profound insight into the American character. Leslie Fiedler obligingly provided it when he read homoerotic attraction into the relationship between Huck and Jim, pointing out the similarity of this to such other white man–dark man friendships as those between Ishmael and Queequeg in *Moby-Dick* and Natty Bumppo and Chingachgook in James Fenimore Cooper's *Last of the Mohicans*.

The canonization proceeded apace: great novel (Trilling, 1950), greatest novel (Eliot, 1950), world-class novel (Lauriat Lane Jr., 1955). Sensible naysayers, such as Leo Marx,[2] were lost in the shuffle of propaganda. But, in fact, *The Adventures of Huckleberry Finn* has little to offer in the way of greatness. There is more to be learned about the American character *from* its canonization than *through* its canonization.

Let me hasten to point out that, like most others, I don't hold any grudges against Huck himself. He's just a boy trying to survive. The villain here is Mark Twain, who knew how to give Huck a voice but didn't know how to give him a novel. Twain was clearly aware of the story's difficulties. Not finished with having revisited his boyhood in *Tom Sawyer*, Twain conceived of a sequel and began composition while still working on *Tom Sawyer*'s page proofs. Four hundred pages into it, having just passed Cairo and exhausted most of his memories of Hannibal and the upper Mississippi, Twain put the manuscript aside for three years. He was facing a problem every novelist is familiar with: his original conception was beginning to conflict with the implications of the actual story. It is at this point in the story that Huck and Jim realize two things: they have become close friends, and they have missed the Ohio River and drifted into what for Jim must be the most frightening territory of all—down the river, the very place Miss Watson was going to sell him to begin with. Jim's putative savior, Huck, has led him as far astray as a slave can go, and the farther they go, the worse it is going to be for him. Because the Ohio was not Twain's territory, the fulfillment

[2]***Marx:*** Leo Marx (b. 1919) is one of the best-known figures in postwar American Studies. —EDS.

of Jim's wish would necessarily lead the novel away from the artistic integrity that Twain certainly sensed his first four hundred pages possessed. He found himself writing not a boy's novel, like *Tom Sawyer*, but a man's novel, about real moral dilemmas and growth. The patina of nostalgia for a time and place, Missouri in the 1840s (not unlike former President Ronald Reagan's nostalgia for his own boyhood, when "Americans got along"), had been transformed into actual longing for a timeless place of friendship and freedom, safe and hidden, on the big river. But the raft had floated Huck and Jim, and their author with them, into the truly dark heart of the American soul and of American history: slave country.

Twain came back to the novel and worked on it twice again, once   5
to rewrite the chapters containing the feud between the Grangerfords and the Shepherdsons, and later to introduce the Duke and the Dauphin. It is with the feud that the novel begins to fail, because from here on the episodes are mere distractions from the true subject of the work: Huck's affection for and responsibility to Jim. The signs of this failure are everywhere, as Jim is pushed to the side of the narrative, hiding on the raft and confined to it, while Huck follows the Duke and the Dauphin onshore to the scenes of much simpler and much less philosophically taxing moral dilemmas, such as fraud. Twain was by nature an improviser, and he was pleased enough with these improvisations to continue. When the Duke and the Dauphin finally betray Jim by selling him for forty dollars, Huck is shocked, but the fact is neither he nor Twain has come up with a plan that would have saved Jim in the end. Tom Sawyer does that.

Considerable critical ink has flowed over the years in an attempt to integrate the Tom Sawyer chapters with the rest of the book, but it has flowed in vain. As Leo Marx points out, and as most readers sense intuitively, once Tom reappears, "[m]ost of those traits which made [Huck] so appealing a hero now disappear. . . . It should be added at once that Jim doesn't mind too much. The fact is that he has undergone a similar transformation. On the raft he was an individual, man enough to denounce Huck when Huck made him the victim of a practical joke. In the closing episode, however, we lose sight of Jim in the maze of farcical invention." And the last twelve chapters are boring, a sure sign that an author has lost the battle between plot and theme and is just filling in the blanks.

As with all bad endings, the problem really lies at the beginning, and at the beginning of *The Adventures of Huckleberry Finn* neither Huck nor Twain takes Jim's desire for freedom at all seriously; that is, they do not accord it the respect that a man's passion deserves. The sign of this is that not only do the two never cross the Mississippi to Illinois, a free state, but they hardly even consider it. In both *Tom Sawyer* and *Huckleberry Finn*, the Jackson's Island scenes show that such a crossing, even in secret, is both possible and routine, and even though it would present legal difficulties for an escaped slave, these would certainly pose no more hardship than locating the mouth of the Ohio and then finding passage up it. It is true that there could have been slave catchers in pursuit (though the novel ostensibly takes place in the 1840s and the Fugitive Slave Act was not passed until 1850), but Twain's moral failure, once Huck and Jim link up, is never even to account for their choice to go down the river rather than across it. What this reveals is that for all his lip service to real attachment between white boy and black man, Twain really saw Jim as no more than Huck's sidekick, homoerotic or otherwise. All the claims that are routinely made for the book's humanitarian power are, in the end, simply absurd. Jim is never autonomous, never has a vote, always finds his purposes subordinate to Huck's, and, like every good sidekick, he never minds. He grows ever more passive and also more affectionate as Huck and the Duke and the Dauphin and Tom (and Twain) make ever more use of him for their own purposes. But this use they make of him is not supplementary; it is integral to Twain's whole conception of the novel. Twain thinks that Huck's affection is a good enough reward for Jim.

The sort of meretricious critical reasoning that has raised Huck's paltry good intentions to a "strategy of subversion" (David L. Smith) and a "convincing indictment of slavery" (Eliot) precisely mirrors the same sort of meretricious reasoning that white people use to convince themselves that they are not "racist." If Huck *feels* positive toward Jim, and *loves* him, and *thinks* of him as a man, then that's enough. He doesn't actually have to act in accordance with his feelings. White Americans always think racism is a feeling, and they reject it or they embrace it. To most Americans, it seems more honorable and nicer to reject it, so they do, but they almost invariably fail to understand that how they *feel* means very little to black Americans, who understand racism as a way of structuring American culture, American politics, and the American economy. To invest *The Adventures of Huckleberry Finn* with "greatness" is to underwrite a very simplistic and evasive theory of what racism is and to promulgate it, philosophically, in schools and the media as well as in academic journals. Surely the discomfort of many readers, black and white, and the censorship battles that have dogged *Huck Finn* in the last twenty years are understandable in this context. No matter how often the critics "place in context" Huck's use of the word "nigger," they can never excuse or fully hide the deeper racism of the novel—the way Twain and Huck use Jim because they really don't care enough about his desire for freedom to let that desire change their plans. And to give credit to Huck suggests that the only racial insight Americans of the nineteenth or twentieth century are capable of is a recognition of the obvious—that blacks, slave and free, are human.

Ernest Hemingway, thinking of himself, as always, once said that all American literature grew out of *Huck Finn*. It undoubtedly would have been better for American literature, and American culture, if our literature had grown out of one of the best-selling novels of all time, another American work of the nineteenth century, *Uncle Tom's Cabin*, which for its portrayal of an array of thoughtful, autonomous, and passionate black characters leaves *Huck Finn* far behind. *Uncle Tom's Cabin* was published in 1852, when Twain was seventeen, still living in Hannibal and contributing to his brother's newspapers, still sympathizing with the South, nine years before his abortive career in the Confederate Army. *Uncle Tom's Cabin* was the most popular novel of its era, universally controversial. In 1863, when Harriet Beecher Stowe visited the White House, Abraham Lincoln condescended to remark to her, "So this is the little lady who made this great war."

The story, familiar to most nineteenth-century Americans, either   10
through the novel or through the many stage adaptations that sentimentalized Stowe's work, may be sketched briefly: A Kentucky slave, Tom, is sold to pay off a debt to a slave trader, who takes him to New Orleans. On the boat trip downriver, Tom is purchased by the wealthy Augustine St. Clare at the behest of his daughter, Eva. After Eva's death, and then St. Clare's, Tom is sold again, this time to Simon Legree, whose remote plantation is the site of every form of cruelty and degradation. The novel was immediately read and acclaimed by any number of excellent judges: Charles Dickens, George Eliot, Leo Tolstoy, George Sand—the whole roster of nineteenth-century liberals whose work we read today and try to persuade ourselves that *Huck Finn* is equal to. English novelist and critic Charles Kingsley thought *Uncle Tom's Cabin* the best novel ever written. These writers honored Stowe's book for all its myriad virtues. One of these was her adept characterization of a whole world of whites and blacks who find themselves gripped by slavery, many of whose names have entered the American language as expressions—not only Uncle Tom himself but Simon Legree and, to a lesser extent, little Eva and the black child Topsy. The characters appear, one after another, vivified by their attitudes, desires, and opinions as much as by their histories and their fates. Surely Augustine St. Clare, Tom's owner in New Orleans, is an exquisite portrayal of a humane but indecisive man, who knows what he is doing but not how to stop it. Surely Cassy, a fellow slave whom Tom meets on the Legree plantation, is one of the great angry women in all of literature—not only bitter, murderous, and nihilistic but also intelligent and enterprising. Surely the midlife spiritual journey of Ophelia St. Clare, Augustine's Yankee cousin, from self-confident ignorance to affectionate understanding is most convincing, as is Topsy's parallel journey from ignorance and self-hatred to humanity. The ineffectual Mr. Shelby and his submissive, and subversive, wife; the slave trader Haley; Tom's wife, Chloe; Augustine's wife, Marie; Legree's overseers, Sambo and Quimbo—good or evil, they all live.

As for Tom himself, we all know what an "Uncle Tom" is, except we don't. The popular Uncle Tom sucks up to the master and exhibits bovine patience. The real Uncle Tom is both a realist and a man of deep principle. When he is sold by Mr. Shelby in Kentucky, he knows enough of Shelby's affairs to know that what his master asserts is true: it's Tom who must go or the whole estate will be sold off for debt, including Tom's wife and three children. Later, on the Legree estate, his religious faith tells him that the greatest danger he finds there is not to his life but to his soul. His logic is impeccable. He holds fast to his soul, in the face of suffering, in a way that even nonbelievers like myself must respect. In fact, Tom's story eerily prefigures stories of spiritual solace through deep religious belief that have come out of both the Soviet Gulag and the Nazi concentration camp in the same way that the structure of power on Legree's plantation, and the suffering endured there, forecasts and duplicates many stories of recent genocides.

The power of *Uncle Tom's Cabin* is the power of brilliant analysis married to great wisdom of feeling. Stowe never forgets the logical end of any relationship in which one person is the subject and the other is the object. No matter how the two people feel, or what their intentions are, the logic of the relationship is inherently tragic and traps both parties until the false subject/object relationship is ended. Stowe's most oft-repeated and potent representation of this inexorable logic is the forcible separation of family members, especially of mothers from children. Eliza, faced with the sale of her child, Harry, escapes across the breaking ice of the Ohio River. Lucy, whose ten-month-old is sold behind her back, kills herself. Prue, who has been used for breeding, must listen to her last child cry itself to death because her mistress won't let her save it; she falls into alcoholism and thievery and is finally whipped to death. Cassy, prefiguring a choice made by one of the characters in Toni Morrison's *Beloved*, kills her last child so that it won't grow up in slavery. All of these women have been promised something by their owners—love, education, the privilege and joy of raising their children—but, owing to slavery, all of these promises have been broken. The grief and despair these women display is no doubt what T. S. Eliot was thinking of when he superciliously labeled *Uncle Tom's Cabin* "sensationalist propaganda," but, in fact, few critics in the nineteenth century ever accused Stowe of making up or even exaggerating such stories. One group of former slaves who were asked to comment on Stowe's depiction of slave life said that she had failed to portray the very worst, and Stowe herself was afraid that if she told some of what she had heard from escaped slaves and other informants during her eighteen years in Cincinnati, the book would be too dark to find any readership at all.

Stowe's analysis does not stop with the slave owners and traders, or with the slaves themselves. She understands perfectly that slavery is an economic system embedded in America as a whole, and she comments ironically on Christian bankers in New York whose financial dealings result in the sale of slaves, on Northern politicians who promote the capture of escaped slaves for the sake of the public good, on ministers of churches who give the system a Christian stamp of approval. One of Stowe's most skillful techniques is her method of weaving a discussion of slavery into the dialogue of her characters. Especially interesting is a conversation Mark Twain could have paid attention to. Augustine St. Clare and his abolitionist cousin, Ophelia, are discussing his failure to act in accordance with his feelings of revulsion against slavery. After entertaining Ophelia's criticisms for a period, Augustine points out that Ophelia herself is personally disgusted by black people and doesn't like to come into contact with them. He says, "You would think no harm in a child's caressing a large dog, even if he was black . . . custom with us does what Christianity ought to do, — obliterates the feeling of personal prejudice." When Ophelia takes over the education of Topsy, a child who has suffered a most brutal previous upbringing, she discovers that she can do nothing with her until she takes her, literally, to her bosom. But personal relationships do not mitigate the evils of slavery; Ophelia makes sure to give Topsy her freedom.

Stowe also understands that the real root of slavery is that it is profitable as well as customary. Augustine and his brother live with slavery because it is the system they know and because they haven't the imagination to live without it. Simon Legree embraces slavery because he can make money from it and because it gives him even more absolute power over his workers than he could find in the North or in England.

The very heart of nineteenth-century American experience and literature, the nature and meaning of slavery, is finally what Twain cannot face in *The Adventures of Huckleberry Finn*. As Jim and Huck drift down Twain's beloved river, the author finds himself nearing what must have been a crucial personal nexus: how to reconcile the felt memory of boyhood with the cruel implications of the social system within which that boyhood was lived. He had avoided this problem for the most part in *Tom Sawyer*: slaves hardly impinge on the lives of Tom and the other boys. But once Twain allows Jim a voice, this voice must speak in counterpoint to Huck's voice and must raise issues that cannot easily be resolved, either personally or culturally. Harriet Beecher Stowe, New Englander, daughter of Puritans and thinkers, active in the abolitionist movement and in the effort to aid and educate escaped slaves, had no such personal conflict when she sat down to write *Uncle Tom's Cabin*. Nothing about slavery was attractive to her either as a New Englander or as a resident of Cincinnati for almost twenty years. Her lack of conflict is apparent in the clarity of both the style and substance of the novel.

Why, then, we may ask, did *Uncle Tom's Cabin*, for all its power and popularity, fail to spawn American literature? Fail, even, to work as a model for how to draw passionate, autonomous, and interesting black literary characters? Fail to keep the focus of the American literary imagination on the central dilemma of the American experience: race? Part of the reason is certainly that the public conversation about race and slavery that had been a feature of antebellum American life fell silent after the Civil War. Perhaps the answer is to be found in *The Adventures of Huckleberry Finn*: everyone opted for the ultimate distraction, lighting out for the territory. And the reason is to be found in *Uncle Tom's Cabin*: that's where the money was.

But so what? These are only authors, after all, and once a book is published the author can't be held accountable for its role in the culture. For that we have to blame the citizens themselves, or their teachers, or *their* teachers, the arbiters of critical taste. In "Melodramas of Beset Manhood: How Theories of American Fiction Exclude Women Authors," the scholar Nina Baym has already detailed how the canonization of a very narrow range of white, Protestant, middle-class male authors (Twain, Hawthorne, Melville, Emerson, etc.) has misrepresented our literary life — first by defining the only worthy American literary subject as "the struggle of the individual against society [in which] the essential quality of America comes to reside in its unsettled wilderness and the opportunities that such a wilderness offers to the individual as the medium on which he may inscribe, unhindered, his own destiny and his own nature," and then by casting women, and especially women writers (specialists in the "flagrantly bad best-seller," according to Leslie Fiedler), as the enemy. In such critical readings, all other themes and modes of literary expression fall out of consideration as "un-American." There goes *Uncle Tom's Cabin*, there goes Edith Wharton,[3] there goes domestic life as a subject, there go almost all the best-selling novelists of the nineteenth century and their readers, who were mostly women. The real loss, though, is not to our literature but to our culture and ourselves, because we have lost the subject of how the various social groups who may not escape to the wilderness are to get along in society; and, in the case of *Uncle Tom's Cabin*, the hard-nosed, unsentimental dialogue about race that we should have been having since before the Civil War. Obviously, *Uncle Tom's Cabin* is no more the last word on race relations than *The Brothers Karamazov* or *David Copperfield* is on any number of characteristically Russian or English themes and social questions. Some of Stowe's ideas about inherent racial characteristics (whites: cold, heartless; blacks: naturally religious and warm) are bad and have been exploded. One of her solutions to the American racial conflicts that she foresaw, a colony in Africa, she later repudiated. Nevertheless, her views about many issues were brilliant, and her heart was wise. She gained the

---

[3]**Wharton:** Author (1862–1937) of *Ethan Frome* (1911) and *The Age of Innocence* (1920). —EDS.

respect and friendship of many men and women of goodwill, black and white, such as Frederick Douglass, the civil-rights activist Mary Church Terrill, the writer and social activist James Weldon Johnson, and W.E.B. Du Bois. What she did was find a way to talk about slavery and family, power and law, life and death, good and evil, North and South. She truly believed that all Americans together had to find a solution to the problem of slavery in which all were implicated. When her voice, a courageously public voice—as demonstrated by the public arguments about slavery that rage throughout *Uncle Tom's Cabin*—fell silent in our culture and was replaced by the secretive voice of Huck Finn, who acknowledges Jim only when they are alone on the raft together out in the middle of the big river, racism fell out of the public world and into the private one, where whites think it really is but blacks know it really isn't.

Should *Huckleberry Finn* be taught in the schools? The critics of the Propaganda Era laid the groundwork for the universal inclusion of the book in school curriculums by declaring it great. Although they predated the current generation of politicized English professors, this was clearly a political act, because the entry of *Huck Finn* into classrooms sets the terms of the discussion of racism and American history, and sets them very low: all you have to do to be a hero is acknowledge that your poor sidekick is human; you don't actually have to act in the interests of his humanity. Arguments about censorship have been regularly turned into nonsense by appeals to Huck's "greatness." Moreover, so much critical thinking has gone into defending Huck so that he *can* be great, so that American literature can be found different from and maybe better than Russian or English or French literature, that the very integrity of the critical enterprise has been called into question. That most readers intuitively reject the last twelve chapters of the novel on the grounds of tedium or triviality is clear from the fact that so many critics have turned themselves inside out to defend them. Is it so mysterious that criticism has failed in our time after being so robust only a generation ago? Those who cannot be persuaded that *The Adventures of Huckleberry Finn* is a great novel have to draw *some* conclusion.

I would rather my children read *Uncle Tom's Cabin*, even though it is far more vivid in its depiction of cruelty than *Huck Finn*, and this is because Stowe's novel is clearly and unmistakably a tragedy. No whitewash, no secrets, but evil, suffering, imagination, endurance, and redemption—just like life. Like little Eva, who eagerly but fearfully listens to the stories of the slaves that her family tries to keep from her, our children want to know what is going on, what has gone on, and what we intend to do about it. If "great" literature has any purpose, it is to help us face up to our responsibilities instead of enabling us to avoid them once again by lighting out for the territory.

The Reader's Presence

1. What aspects of *Huckleberry Finn* does Smiley criticize? What is the basis of her argument that the book does not deserve its exalted reputation? What standards does she use to judge the novel?

2. Why does Smiley think that *Huckleberry Finn* was wrongly canonized? Why does she believe that *Uncle Tom's Cabin* was passed by?

3. In "What America Would Be Like without Blacks" (page 390), Ralph Ellison offers a much more positive critique of *Huckleberry Finn*. What underlying assumptions do Ellison and Smiley make that allow them to reach such different conclusions about Twain's novel? Which position do you find more convincing? Why?

Jonathan Swift

A Modest Proposal

For Preventing the Children of Poor People in Ireland from Being a Burden to Their Parents or Country, and for Making Them Beneficial to the Public

Jonathan Swift (1667–1745) was born and raised in Ireland, the son of English parents. He was ordained an Anglican priest, and although as a young man he lived a literary life in London, he was appointed against his wishes to be dean of St. Patrick's Cathedral in Dublin. Swift wrote excellent poetry but is remembered principally for his essays and political pamphlets, most of which were published under pseudonyms. Swift received payment for only one work in his entire life, Gulliver's Travels *(1726), for which he earned £200. Swift's political pamphlets were very influential in his day; among other issues, he spoke out against English exploitation of the Irish. Some of Swift's more important publications include* A Tale of a Tub *(1704),* The Importance of the Guardian Considered *(1713),* The Public Spirit of the Whigs *(1714), and* A Modest Proposal *(1729).*

Writing to his friend Alexander Pope, Swift commented that "the chief end I propose to my self in all my labors is to vex the world rather than divert it, and if

I could compass that design without hurting my own person or Fortune I would
be the most Indefatigable writer you have ever seen."

It is a melancholy object to those who walk through this great town[1]
or travel in the country, when they see the streets, the roads, and cabin
doors, crowded with beggars of the female sex, followed by three, four,
or six children, all in rags and importuning every passenger for an alms.
These mothers instead of being able to work for their honest livelihood,
are forced to employ all their time in strolling to beg sustenance for their
helpless infants: who as they grow up either turn thieves for want of
work, or leave their dear native country to fight for the pretender in
Spain,[2] or sell themselves to the Barbadoes.[3]

I think it is agreed by all parties that this prodigious number of children in the arms, or on the backs, or at the heels of their mothers, and
frequently of their fathers, is in the present deplorable state of the kingdom a very great additional grievance; and, therefore, whoever could find
out a fair, cheap, and easy method of making these children sound, useful
members of the commonwealth, would deserve so well of the public as to
have his statute set up for a preserver of the nation.

But my intention is very far from being confined to provide only for
the children of professed beggars; it is of a much greater extent, and shall
take in the whole number of infants at a certain age who are born of parents in effect as little able to support them as those who demand our charity in the streets.

As to my own part, having turned my thoughts for many years
upon this important subject, and maturely weighed the several schemes
of our projectors,[4] I have always found them grossly mistaken in their
computation. It is true, a child just dropped from its dam may be supported by her milk for a solar year, with little other nourishment; at
most not above the value of 2s.,[5] which the mother may certainly get, or
the value in scraps, by her lawful occupation of begging; and it is
exactly at one year old that I propose to provide for them in such a
manner as instead of being a charge upon their parents or the parish, or
wanting food and raiment for the rest of their lives, they shall on the
contrary contribute to the feeding, and partly to the clothing, of many
thousands.

---

[1]*this great town:* Dublin. — EDS.

[2]*pretender in Spain:* James Stuart (1688–1766); exiled in Spain, he laid claim to the
English crown and had the support of many Irishmen who had joined an army hoping to restore him to the throne. — EDS.

[3]*the Barbadoes:* Inhabitants of the British colony in the Caribbean where Irishmen emigrated to work as indentured servants in exchange for their passage. — EDS.

[4]*projectors:* Planners. — EDS.

[5]*2s.:* Two shillings; in Swift's time one shilling was worth less than twenty-five cents.
Other monetary references in the essay are to pounds sterling ("£"), pence ("d."), a crown,
and a groat. A pound consisted of twenty shillings; a shilling of twelve pence; a crown was
five shillings; a groat was worth a few cents. — EDS.

There is likewise another great advantage in my scheme, that it will prevent those voluntary abortions, and that horrid practice of women murdering their bastard children, alas! too frequent among us! sacrificing the poor innocent babes I doubt more to avoid the expense than the shame, which would move tears and pity in the most savage and inhuman breast.

The number of souls in this kingdom being usually reckoned one million and a half, of these I calculate there may be about 200,000 couple whose wives are breeders; from which number I subtract 30,000 couple who are able to maintain their own children (although I apprehend there cannot be so many, under the present distress of the kingdom); but this being granted, there will remain 170,000 breeders. I again subtract 50,000 for those women who miscarry, or whose children die by accident or disease within the year. There only remain 120,000 children of poor parents annually born. The question therefore is, how this number shall be reared and provided for? which, as I have already said, under the present situation of affairs, is utterly impossible by all the methods hitherto proposed. For we can neither employ them in handicraft or agriculture; we neither build houses (I mean in the country) nor cultivate land; they can very seldom pick up a livelihood by stealing, till they arrive at six years old, except where they are of towardly parts,[6] although I confess they learn the rudiments much earlier; during which time they can, however, be properly looked upon only as probationers; as I have been informed by a principal gentleman in the county of Cavan, who protested to me that he never knew above one or two instances under the age of six, even in a part of the kingdom so renowned for the quickest proficiency in that art.

I am assured by our merchants, that a boy or a girl before twelve years old is no salable commodity; and even when they come to this age they will not yield above 3£. or 3£. 2s. 6d. at most on the exchange; which cannot turn to account either to the parents or kingdom, the charge of nutriment and rags having been at least four times that value.

I shall now therefore humbly propose my own thoughts, which I hope will not be liable to the least objection.

I have been assured by a very knowing American of my acquaintance in London, that a young healthy child well nursed is at a year old a most delicious, nourishing, and wholesome food, whether stewed, roasted, baked, or broiled; and I make no doubt that it will equally serve in a fricassee or a ragout.[7]

I do therefore humbly offer it to public consideration that of the 120,000 children already computed, 20,000 may be reserved for breed,

---

[6]*towardly parts:* Natural abilities. —Eds.
[7]*ragout:* A stew. —Eds.

whereof only one-fourth part to be males; which is more than we allow to sheep, black cattle, or swine; and my reason is, that these children are seldom the fruits of marriage, a circumstance not much regarded by our savages; therefore one male will be sufficient to serve four females. That the remaining 100,000 may, at a year old, be offered in sale to the persons of quality and fortune through the kingdom; always advising the mother to let them suck plentifully in the last month, so as to render them plump and fat for a good table. A child will make two dishes at an entertainment for friends; and when the family dines alone, the fore and hind quarter will make a reasonable dish, and seasoned with a little pepper or salt will be very good boiled on the fourth day, especially in winter.

I have reckoned upon a medium that a child just born will weigh 12 pounds, and in a solar year, if tolerably nursed, will increase to 28 pounds.

I grant this food will be somewhat dear, and therefore very proper for landlords, who, as they have already devoured most of the parents, seem to have the best title to the children.

Infants' flesh will be in season throughout the year, but more plentiful in March, and a little before and after: for we are told by a grave author, an eminent French physician,[8] that fish being a prolific diet, there are more children born in Roman Catholic countries about nine months after Lent than at any other season; therefore, reckoning a year after Lent, the markets will be more glutted than usual, because the number of popish infants is at least three to one in this kingdom: and therefore it will have one other collateral advantage, by lessening the number of papists among us.

I have already computed the charge of nursing a beggar's child (in which list I reckon all cottagers, laborers, and four-fifths of the farmers) to be about 2s. per annum, rags included; and I believe no gentleman would repine to give 10s. for the carcass of a good fat child, which, as I have said, will make four dishes of excellent nutritive meat, when he has only some particular friend or his own family to dine with him. Thus the squire will learn to be a good landlord, and grow popular among the tenants; the mother will have 8s. net profit, and be fit for work till she produces another child.

Those who are more thrifty (as I must confess the times require) may flay the carcass; the skin of which artificially[9] dressed will make admirable gloves for ladies, and summer boots for fine gentlemen.

15

---

[8]*French physician:* François Rabelais (c. 1494–1553), the great Renaissance humanist and author of the comic masterpiece *Gargantua and Pantagruel*. Swift is being ironic in calling Rabelais "grave." —EDS.
[9]*artificially:* Artfully. —EDS.

As to our city of Dublin, shambles[10] may be appointed for this purpose in the most convenient parts of it, and butchers we may be assured will not be wanting: although I rather recommend buying the children alive, and dressing them hot from the knife as we do roasting pigs.

A very worthy person, a true lover of his country, and whose virtues I highly esteem, was lately pleased in discoursing on this matter to offer a refinement upon my scheme. He said that many gentlemen of this kingdom, having of late destroyed their deer, he conceived that the want of venison might be well supplied by the bodies of young lads and maidens, not exceeding fourteen years of age nor under twelve; so great a number of both sexes in every country being now ready to starve for want of work and service; and these to be disposed of by their parents, if alive, or otherwise by their nearest relations. But with due deference to so excellent a friend and so deserving a patriot, I cannot be altogether in his sentiments; for as to the males, my American acquaintance assured me from frequent experience that their flesh was generally tough and lean, like that of our schoolboys by continual exercise, and their taste disagreeable; and to fatten them would not answer the charge. Then as to the females, it would, I think, with humble submission be a loss to the public, because they soon would become breeders themselves: and besides, it is not improbable that some scrupulous people might be apt to censure such a practice (although indeed very unjustly), as a little bordering upon cruelty; which, I confess, has always been with me the strongest objection against any project, how well soever intended.

But in order to justify my friend, he confessed that this expedient was put into his head by the famous Psalmanazar[11] a native of the island Formosa, who came from thence to London about twenty years ago: and in conversation told my friend, that in his country when any young person happened to be put to death, the executioner sold the carcass to persons of quality as a prime dainty; and that in his time the body of a plump girl of fifteen, who was crucified for an attempt to poison the emperor, was sold to his imperial majesty's prime minister of state, and other great mandarins of the court, in joints from the gibbet, at 400 crowns. Neither indeed can I deny, that if the same use were made of several plump young girls in this town, who without one single groat to their fortunes cannot stir abroad without a chair,[12] and appear at the playhouse and assemblies in foreign fineries which they never will pay for, the kingdom would not be the worse.

[10]*shambles:* Slaughterhouses. — Eds.
[11]*Psalmanazar:* George Psalmanazar (c. 1679–1763) was a Frenchman who tricked London society into believing he was a native of Formosa (now Taiwan). — Eds.
[12]*a chair:* A sedan chair in which one is carried about. — Eds.

Some persons of a desponding spirit are in great concern about the vast number of poor people, who are aged, diseased, or maimed, and I have been desired to employ my thoughts what course may be taken to ease the nation of so grievous an encumbrance. But I am not in the least pain upon that matter, because it is very well known that they are every day dying and rotting by cold and famine, and filth and vermin, as fast as can be reasonably expected. And as to the young laborers, they are now in as hopeful condition: They cannot get work, and consequently pine away for want of nourishment, to a degree that if at any time they are accidentally hired to common labor, they have not strength to perform it; and thus the country and themselves are happily delivered from the evils to come.

I have too long digressed, and therefore shall return to my subject. I think the advantages by the proposal which I have made are obvious and many, as well as of the highest importance.   20

For first, as I have already observed, it would greatly lessen the number of papists, with whom we are yearly overrun, being the principal breeders of the nation as well as our most dangerous enemies; and who stay at home on purpose to deliver the kingdom to the Pretender, hoping to take their advantage by the absence of so many good Protestants, who have chosen rather to leave their country than stay at home and pay tithes against their conscience to an Episcopal curate.

Secondly, The poor tenants will have something valuable of their own, which by law may be made liable to distress[13] and help to pay their landlord's rent, their corn and cattle being already seized, and money a thing unknown.

Thirdly, Whereas the maintenance of 100,000 children from two years old and upward, cannot be computed at less that 10s. a-piece per annum, the nation's stock will be thereby increased £50,000 per annum, beside the profit of a new dish introduced to the tables of all gentlemen of fortune in the kingdom who have any refinement in taste. And the money will circulate among ourselves, the goods being entirely of our own growth and manufacture.

Fourthly, The constant breeders beside the gain of 8s. sterling per annum by the sale of their children, will be rid of the charge of maintaining them after the first year.

Fifthly, This food would likewise bring great custom to taverns,   25
where the vintners will certainly be so prudent as to procure the best receipts[14] for dressing it to perfection, and consequently have their houses frequented by all the fine gentlemen, who justly value themselves upon their knowledge in good eating; and a skilful cook who understands how to oblige his guests, will contrive to make it as expensive as they please.

---

[13]*distress:* Seizure for payment of debt. —Eds.
[14]*receipts:* Recipes. —Eds.

Sixthly, This would be a great inducement to marriage, which all wise nations have either encouraged by rewards or enforced by laws and penalties. It would increase the care and tenderness of mothers toward their children, when they were sure of a settlement for life to the poor babes, provided in some sort by the public, to their annual profit instead of expense. We should see an honest emulation among the married women, which of them would bring the fattest child to the market. Men would become as fond of their wives during the time of their pregnancy as they are now of their mares in foal, their cows in calf, their sows when they are ready to farrow; nor offer to beat or kick them (as is too frequent a practice) for fear of a miscarriage.

Many other advantages might be enumerated. For instance, the addition of some thousand carcasses in our exportation of barreled beef, the propagation of swine's flesh, and improvement in the art of making good bacon, so much wanted among us by the great destruction of pigs, too frequent at our table; which are no way comparable in taste or magnificence to a well-grown, fat, yearling child, which roasted whole will make a considerable figure at a lord mayor's feast or any other public entertainment. But this and many others I omit, being studious of brevity.

Supposing that 1,000 families in this city would be constant customers for infants' flesh, besides others who might have it at merry-meetings, particularly at weddings and christenings, I compute that Dublin would take off annually about 20,000 carcasses; and the rest of the kingdom (where probably they will be sold somewhat cheaper) the remaining 80,000.

I can think of no one objection that will possibly be raised against this proposal unless it should be urged that the number of people will be thereby much lessened in the kingdom. This I freely own, and it was indeed one principal design in offering it to the world. I desire the reader will observe, that I calculate my remedy for this one individual kingdom of Ireland and for no other that ever was, is, or I think ever can be upon earth. Therefore let no man talk to me of other expedients: of taxing our absentees at 5s. a pound: of using neither clothes nor household furniture except what is of our own growth and manufacture: of utterly rejecting the materials and instruments that promote foreign luxury: of curing the expensiveness of pride, vanity, idleness, and gaming in our women: of introducing a vein of parsimony, prudence, and temperance: of learning to love our country, in the want of which we differ even from Laplanders and the inhabitants of Topinamboo:[15] of quitting our animosities and factions, nor acting any longer like the Jews, who were murdering one another at the very moment their city was taken:[16] of being a little cautious

[15]*Laplanders and the inhabitants of Topinamboo:* Lapland is the area of Scandinavia above the Arctic Circle; Topinamboo, in Brazil, was known in Swift's time for the savagery of its tribes. — EDS.

[16]*was taken:* A reference to the Roman seizure of Jerusalem (A.D. 70). — EDS.

not to sell our country and conscience for nothing: of teaching landlords to have at least one degree of mercy toward their tenants: lastly, of putting a spirit of honesty, industry, and skill into our shopkeepers; who, if a resolution could now be taken to buy only our native goods, would immediately unite to cheat and exact upon us in the price the measure, and the goodness, nor could ever yet be brought to make one fair proposal of just dealing, though often and earnestly invited to it.

Therefore I repeat, let no man talk to me of these and the like expedi-   30
ents, till he has at least some glimpse of hope that there will be ever some hearty and sincere attempt to put them in practice.

But as to myself, having been wearied out for many years with offering vain, idle, visionary thoughts, and at length utterly despairing of success, I fortunately fell upon this proposal; which, as it is wholly new, so it has something solid and real, of no expense and little trouble, full in our own power, and whereby we can incur no danger in disobliging England. For this kind of commodity will not bear exportation, the flesh being of too tender a consistence to admit a long continuance in salt, although perhaps I could name a country which would be glad to eat up our whole nation without it.

After all, I am not so violently bent upon my own opinion as to reject any offer proposed by wise men, which shall be found equally innocent, cheap, easy, and effectual. But before something of that kind shall be advanced in contradiction to my scheme, and offering a better, I desire the author or authors will be pleased maturely to consider two points. First, as things now stand, how they will be able to find food and raiment for 100,000 useless mouths and backs. And secondly, there being a round million of creatures in human figure throughout this kingdom, whose subsistence put into a common stock would leave them in debt 2,000,000£. sterling, adding those who are beggars by profession to the bulk of farmers, cottagers, and laborers, with the wives and children who are beggars in effect; I desire those politicians who dislike my overture, and may perhaps be so bold as to attempt an answer, that they will first ask the parents of these mortals, whether they would not at this day think it a great happiness to have been sold for food at a year old in the manner I prescribe, and thereby have avoided such a perpetual scene of misfortunes as they have since gone through by the oppression of landlords, the impossibility of paying rent without money or trade, the want of common sustenance, with neither house nor clothes to cover them from the inclemencies of the weather, and the most inevitable prospect of entailing the like or greater miseries upon their breed for ever.

I profess, in the sincerity of my heart, that I have not the least personal interest in endeavoring to promote this necessary work, having no other motive than the public good of my country, by advancing our trade, providing for infants, relieving the poor, and giving some pleasure to the rich. I have no children by which I can propose to get a single penny; the youngest being nine years old, and my wife past childbearing.

The Reader's Presence

1. Consider Swift's title. In what sense is the proposal "modest"? What is modest about it? What synonyms would you use for *modest* that appear in the essay? In what sense is the essay a "proposal"? Does it follow any format that resembles a proposal? What aspects of its language seem to resemble proposal writing?

2. For this essay Swift invents a speaker, an unnamed, fictional individual who "humbly" proposes a plan to relieve poverty in Ireland. What attitudes and beliefs in the essay do you attribute to the speaker? Which do you attribute to Swift, the author? Having considered two authors (the speaker of the proposal and Swift), now consider two readers — the reader the speaker imagines and the reader Swift imagines. How do these two readers differ? Reread the final paragraph of the essay from the perspective of each of these readers. How do you think each reader is expected to respond?

3. In the introductory comment Swift is quoted as wanting "to vex the world rather than divert it" with his writing. Where in the essay do you find Swift most vexing? How does he attempt to provoke the reader's outrage? Where does the first, most visceral indication of the speaker's plan appear? Does he heighten the essay's effect after this point? If so, where and how? How does Swift mount a serious political argument in the midst of such hyperbole? Read "Against Love" by Laura Kipnis (page 755). How does she use hyperbole or satire in the presentation of her argument? Does she make a serious point? Why or why not?

Lewis Thomas

On Cloning a Human Being

Lewis Thomas (1913–1993) was trained as a physician and scientist, but his intellectual curiosity and his publications took him far beyond the practice of medicine. In 1971 he became a regular contributor to the New England Journal of Medicine, *writing a column called "Notes of a Biology Watcher." Several of these essays are collected in* The Lives of a Cell *(1974), which explores the many ways in which organisms relate to one another for their mutual benefit. Joyce Carol Oates praised this book, saying that it "anticipates the kind of writing that will appear more and more frequently, as scientists take on the language of poetry in order to communicate human truths too mysterious for old-fashioned common sense."*

Thomas also published The Medusa and the Snail: More Notes of a Biology Watcher *(1979), from which "On Cloning a Human Being" is taken. His later books expanded the range of his investigations into natural and social processes and include* Late Night Thoughts on Listening to Mahler's Ninth Symphony *(1984) and a collection of essays on language,* Et Cetera, Et Cetera: Notes of a Word Watcher *(1990).*

Thomas wrote this essay in the late 1970s, long before cloning living creatures became a scientific actuality.

It is now theoretically possible to recreate an identical creature from any animal or plant, from the DNA contained in the nucleus of any somatic cell. A single plant root-tip cell can be teased and seduced into conceiving a perfect copy of the whole plant; a frog's intestinal epithelial cell possesses the complete instructions needed for a new, same frog. If the technology were further advanced, you could do this with a human being, and there are now startled predictions all over the place that this will in fact be done, someday, in order to provide a version of immortality for carefully selected, especially valuable people.

The cloning of humans is on most of the lists of things to worry about from Science, along with behavior control, genetic engineering, transplanted heads, computer poetry, and the unrestrained growth of plastic flowers.

Cloning is the most dismaying of prospects, mandating as it does the elimination of sex with only a metaphoric elimination of death as compensation. It is almost no comfort to know that one's cloned, identical surrogate lives on, especially when the living will very likely involve edging one's real, now aging self off to the side, sooner or later. It is hard to imagine anything like filial affection or respect for a single, unmated nucleus; harder still to think of one's new, self-generated self as anything but an absolute, desolate orphan. Not to mention the complex interpersonal relationship involved in raising one's self from infancy, teaching the language, enforcing discipline, instilling good manners and the like. How would you feel if you became an incorrigible juvenile delinquent by proxy, at the age of fifty-five?

The public questions are obvious. Who is to be selected, and on what qualifications? How to handle the risks of misused technology, such as self-determined cloning by the rich and powerful but socially objectionable, or the cloning by governments of dumb, docile masses for the world's work? What will be the effect on all the uncloned rest of us of human sameness? After all, we've accustomed ourselves through hundreds of millennia to the continual exhilaration of uniqueness; each of us is totally different, in a fundamental sense, from all the other four billion.

Selfness is an essential fact of life. The thought of human nonselfness, precise sameness, is terrifying, when you think about it.

Well, don't think about it, because it isn't a probable possibility, not   5
even as a long shot for the distant future, in my opinion. I agree that you might clone some people who would look amazingly like their parental cell donors, but the odds are that they'd be almost as different as you or me, and certainly more different than any of today's identical twins.

The time required for the experiment is only one of the problems, but a formidable one. Suppose you wanted to clone a prominent, spectacularly successful diplomat, to look after the Middle East problems of the distant future. You'd have to catch him and persuade him, probably not very hard to do, and extirpate a cell. But then you'd have to wait for him to grow up through embryonic life and then for at least forty years more, and you'd have to be sure all observers remained patient and unmeddlesome through his unpromising, ambiguous childhood and adolescence.

Moreover, you'd have to be sure of recreating his environment, perhaps down to the last detail. "Environment" is a word which really means people, so you'd have to do a lot more cloning than just the diplomat himself.

This is a very important part of the cloning problem, largely overlooked in our excitement about the cloned individual himself. You don't have to agree all the way with B. F. Skinner[1] to acknowledge that the environment does make a difference, and when you examine what we really mean by the word "environment" it comes down to other human beings. We use euphemisms and jargon for this, like "social forces," "cultural influences," even Skinner's "verbal community," but what is meant is the dense crowd of nearby people who talk to, listen to, smile or frown at, give to, withhold from, nudge, push, caress, or flail out at the individual. No matter what the genome says, these people have a lot to do with shaping a character. Indeed, if all you had was the genome, and no people around, you'd grow a sort of vertebrate plant, nothing more.

So, to start with, you will undoubtedly need to clone the parents. No question about this. This means the diplomat is out, even in theory, since you couldn't have gotten cells from both his parents at the time when he was himself just recognizable as an early social treasure. You'd have to limit the list of clones to people already certified as sufficiently valuable for the effort, with both parents still alive. The parents would need cloning and, for consistency, their parents as well. I suppose you'd also need the usual informed-consent forms, filled out and signed, not easy to get if I know parents, even harder for grandparents.

But this is only the beginning. It is the whole family that really influ-   10
ences the way a person turns out, not just the parents, according to current psychiatric thinking. Clone the family.

---

[1] **B. F. Skinner** (1904–1990): One of America's most well-known behavioral psychologists. His most famous book, *Walden II*, is a fictional account of a community run by his behaviorist principles. — EDS.

Then what? The way each member of the family develops has already been determined by the environment set around him, and this environment is more people, people outside the family, schoolmates, acquaintances, lovers, enemies, car-pool partners, even, in special circumstances, peculiar strangers across the aisle on the subway. Find them, and clone them.

But there is no end to the protocol. Each of the outer contacts has his own surrounding family, and his and their outer contacts. Clone them all.

To do the thing properly, with any hope of ending up with a genuine duplicate of a single person, you really have no choice. You must clone the world, no less.

We are not ready for an experiment of this size, nor, I should think, are we willing. For one thing, it would mean replacing today's world by an entirely identical world to follow immediately, and this means no new, natural, spontaneous, random, chancy children. No children at all, except for the manufactured doubles of those now on the scene. Plus all those identical adults, including all of today's politicians, all seen double. It is too much to contemplate.

Moreover, when the whole experiment is finally finished, fifty years   15
or so from now, how could you get a responsible scientific reading on the outcome? Somewhere in there would be the original clonee, probably lost and overlooked, now well into middle age, but everyone around him would be precise duplicates of today's everyone. It would be today's same world, filled to overflowing with duplicates of today's people and their same, duplicated problems, probably all resentful at having had to go through our whole thing all over, sore enough at the clonee to make endless trouble for him, if they found him.

And obviously, if the whole thing were done precisely right, they would still be casting about for ways to solve the problem of universal dissatisfaction, and sooner or later they'd surely begin to look around at each other, wondering who should be cloned for his special value to society, to get us out of all this. And so it would go, in regular cycles, perhaps forever.

I once lived through a period when I wondered what Hell could be like, and I stretched my imagination to try to think of a perpetual sort of damnation. I have to confess, I never thought of anything like this.

I have an alternative suggestion, if you're looking for a way out. Set cloning aside, and don't try it. Instead, go in the other direction. Look for ways to get mutations more quickly, new variety, different songs. Fiddle around, if you must fiddle, but never with ways to keep things the same, no matter who, not even yourself. Heaven, somewhere ahead, has got to be a change.

The Reader's Presence

1. As a biologist, Thomas writes as an "expert." How would you read this essay differently if it were written by a nonscientist, reasoning

through common sense rather than inside knowledge of the subject? What sort of audience does Thomas appear to be writing for? What sorts of fears does he address? What is his general argument?

2. Thomas concludes with advice pertinent both to genetic engineering and life in general. How does Thomas link cellular and greater human concerns? Is this leap from biology to everyday life convincing? Why or why not? Does it undermine or enhance Thomas's authority?

3. In paragraphs 6–12 Thomas outlines a hypothetical scenario that quickly becomes ridiculous. What is the effect of such exaggeration? Why might Thomas have pursued this technique? How does it compare, in tone and effect, to what precedes this section? Can you compare Thomas's essay to Jonathan Swift's "A Modest Proposal" (page 825)? Is Thomas's essay more usefully compared with Stephen Jay Gould's "Sex, Drugs, Disasters, and the Extinction of Dinosaurs" (page 448)? How does each of these three essayists use scientific evidence (or the simulation thereof) to support his argument? To what extent is each writer describing a situation and/or staking a claim?

Sojourner Truth

And Ain't I a Woman?

Sojourner Truth was born Isabella Baumfree in New York, circa 1797. After being liberated from slavery by the New York State Emancipation Act of 1827, she lived briefly in New York, working as a domestic servant. She took the name Sojourner Truth as a sign of her religious vocation and soon became famous as a wandering preacher, spellbinding crowds wherever she spoke. Eventually she joined the abolitionist movement and lectured on her experiences as a slave before white audiences throughout the North. She became friendly with the major abolitionists of the era, including Harriet Beecher Stowe, who called her "the Libyan sibyl." She lived for many years in Florence, Massachusetts, and in the 1850s relocated to Battle Creek, Michigan, where she spent the rest of her life. During the Civil War she helped to raise relief funds for escaped slaves and to gather supplies for black volunteer regiments. In 1864, she was received warmly at the White House by President Abraham Lincoln. Sojourner Truth's autobiography, The Narrative of Sojourner Truth *(narrated to Olive Gilbert), was published in 1850.*

She died in 1883. "And Ain't I a Woman?" is a speech she gave at the Women's Rights Convention in 1851.

The leaders of the movement trembled on seeing a tall, gaunt black woman in a gray dress and white turban, surmounted with an uncouth sun-bonnet, march deliberately into the church, walk with the air of a queen up the aisle, and take her seat upon the pulpit steps. A buzz of disapprobation was heard all over the house, and there fell on the listening ear, "An abolition affair!" "Woman's rights and niggers!" "I told you so!" . . .

I chanced on that occasion to wear my first laurels in public life as president of the meeting. At my request order was restored, and the business of the Convention went on. Morning, afternoon, and evening exercises came and went. Through all these sessions old Sojourner, quiet and reticent as the "Lybian Statue," sat crouched against the wall on the corner of the pulpit stairs, her sun-bonnet shading her eyes, her elbows on her knees, her chin resting upon her broad, hard palms. At intermission she was busy selling the "Life of Sojourner Truth," a narrative of her own strange and adventurous life. Again and again, timorous and trembling ones came to me and said, with earnestness, "Don't let her speak, Mrs. Gage, it will ruin us. Every newspaper in the land will have our cause mixed up with abolition and niggers, and we shall be utterly denounced." My only answer was, "We shall see when the time comes."

The second day the work waxed warm. Methodist, Baptist, Episcopal, Presbyterian, and Universalist ministers came in to hear and discuss the resolutions presented. One claimed superior rights and privileges for man, on the ground of "superior intellect"; another, because of the "manhood of Christ; if God had desired the equality of woman, He would have given some token of His will through the birth, life, and death of the Saviour." Another gave us a theological view of the "sin of our first mother."

There were very few women in those days who dared to "speak in meeting"; and the august teachers of the people were seemingly getting the better of us, while the boys in the galleries, and the sneerers among the pews, were hugely enjoying the discomfiture, as they supposed, of the "strong-minded." Some of the tender-skinned friends were on the point of losing dignity, and the atmosphere betokened a storm. When, slowly from her seat in the corner rose Sojourner Truth, who, till now, had scarcely lifted her head. "Don't let her speak!" gasped half a dozen in my ear. She moved slowly and solemnly to the front, laid her old bonnet at her feet, and turned her great speaking eyes to me. There was a hissing sound of disapprobation above and below. I rose and announced "Sojourner Truth," and begged the audience to keep silence for a few moments.

The tumult subsided at once, and every eye was fixed on this almost   5
Amazon form, which stood nearly six feet high, head erect, and eyes piercing the upper air like one in a dream. At her first word there was a profound hush. She spoke in deep tones, which, though not loud, reached

every ear in the house, and away through the throng at the doors and windows.

"Wall, chilern, whar dar is so much racket dar must be somethin' out o' kilter. I tink dat 'twixt de niggers of de Souf and de womin at de Norf, all talkin' 'bout rights, de white men will be in a fix pretty soon. But what's all dis here talkin' 'bout?

"Dat man ober dar say dat womin needs to be helped into carriages, and lifted ober ditches, and to hab de best place everywhar. Nobody eber helps me into carriages, or ober mud-puddles, or gibs me any best place!" And raising herself to her full height, and her voice to a pitch like rolling thunder, she asked, "And a'n't I a woman? Look at me! Look at my arm! (and she bared her right arm to the shoulder, showing her tremendous muscular power). I have ploughed, and planted, and gathered into barns, and no man could head me! And a'n't I a woman? I could work as much and eat as much as a man—when I could get it—and bear de lash as well! And a'n't I a woman? I have borne thirteen chilern, and seen 'em mos' all sold off to slavery, and when I cried out with my mother's grief, none but Jesus heard me! And a'n't I a woman?

"Den dey talks 'bout dis ting in de head; what dis dey call it?" ("Intellect," whispered some one near.) "Dat's it, honey. What's dat got to do wid womin's rights or nigger's rights? If my cup won't hold but a pint, and yourn holds a quart, wouldn't ye be mean not to let me have my little half-measure full?" And she pointed her significant finger, and sent a keen glance at the minister who had made the argument. The cheering was long and loud.

"Den dat little man in black dar, he say women can't have as much rights as men, 'cause Christ wan't a woman! Whar did your Christ come from?" Rolling thunder couldn't have stilled that crowd, as did those deep, wonderful tones, as she stood there with outstretched arms and eyes of fire. Raising her voice still louder, she repeated, "Whar did your Christ come from? From God and a woman! Man had nothin' to do wid Him." Oh, what a rebuke that was to that little man.

Turning again to another objector, she took up the defense of Mother Eve. I can not follow her through it all. It was pointed, and witty, and solemn; eliciting at almost every sentence deafening applause; and she ended by asserting: "If de fust woman God ever made was strong enough to turn de world upside down all alone, dese women togedder (and she glanced her eye over the platform) ought to be able to turn it back, and get it right side up again! And now dey is asking to do it, de men better let 'em." Long-continued cheering greeted this. " 'Bleeged to ye for hearin' on me, and now ole Sojourner han't got nothin' more to say."

10

Amid roars of applause, she returned to her corner, leaving more than one of us with streaming eyes, and hearts beating with gratitude. She had taken us up in her strong arms and carried us safely over the slough of difficulty turning the whole tide in our favor. I have never in my life seen anything like the magical influence that subdued the mobbish spirit of the day, and turned the sneers and jeers of an excited crowd into notes of respect and admiration. Hundreds rushed up to shake hands with her, and congratulate the glorious old mother, and bid her God-speed on her mission of "testifyin' agin concerning the wickedness of this 'ere people."

The Reader's Presence

1. Imagine yourself as the two men whom Truth directly addresses: "[that] man over there" and "[that] little man in black" (paragraphs 7 and 9). Continue the conversation. What might each one have said in reply to her points? How would she have responded? In developing your dialogue, focus on maintaining Truth's style and rhythm as much as possible. How convincing was your version of the dialogue? What was the most difficult challenge you faced in making her voice sound "right"? What was the easiest aspect of recreating her voice?

2. Truth was illiterate when she spoke at the Women's Rights Convention in 1851. Recollecting the speech in 1863—twelve years later—the convention's president, Frances Gage, wrote what has become the official version of Truth's words. Reread the speech carefully. What indications do you find that the speech has been changed from spoken language to written word? How do these changes affect the overall meaning of the speech? In answering this question, think about what has been left out of the written version (for example, facial expressions, gestures, tone). What has been added (for example, punctuation, asides)? Do you think the changes make the speech more powerful and successful, or less powerful? How?

3. Why has Truth's speech continued to be popular for over 150 years? Examine another selection that is dated from at least 20 years ago, such as Martin Luther King Jr.'s "Letter from Birmingham Jail" (page 738) or Thomas Jefferson's "Declaration of Independence" (page 711). What characteristics do the selections share? How do the pieces continue to be relevant to a world very different from the world in which they were written? What indications do you find that the essays are past their time? How long do you think the essays will continue to be important? Why?

Scott Turow

To Kill or Not to Kill

Author and attorney Scott Turow (b. 1949) began as a writer, switched to law, and then combined the two into a successful career as both practicing lawyer and best-selling novelist. After graduating from Amherst in 1970, Turow received a fellowship to the Stanford University Creative Writing Center and taught creative writing there until 1975. He then began reevaluating his choices. "I became convinced that one could not make a living in the U.S. writing serious fiction," he says. "I was never terribly bitter about that. I didn't see why the world had an obligation to support novelists." He entered Harvard Law School and, after receiving his law degree in 1978, returned to his hometown of Chicago to work as both prosecutor and defense counsel with the United States District Attorney's office. In all of his writings, Turow has taken advantage of his insider's knowledge of the legal system. He published an autobiographical narrative, One L: An Inside Account of Life in the First Year at Harvard Law School *(1977), which was followed by a series of widely reviewed, highly regarded legal thrillers:* Presumed Innocent *(1987),* The Burden of Proof *(1990),* Pleading Guilty *(1993),* The Laws of Our Fathers *(1996),* Personal Injuries *(1999), and* Reversible Errors *(2002). Turow also contributes stories, articles, and reviews to many newspapers and literary journals.*

In addition to chairing the Illinois Executive Ethics Commission, Turow is a partner in the Chicago law firm Sonnenschein Nath and Rosenthal, where he specializes in white-collar criminal litigation. He also does extensive pro-bono criminal work; in 1995 he won the reversal of a murder conviction of an innocent man on death row. Ultimate Punishment: A Lawyer's Reflections on Dealing with the Death Penalty *(2003) is based on his work on behalf of death-row inmates and his term on the Illinois Commission on Capital Punishment. In the book and in the following essay, "To Kill or Not to Kill," which appeared in the* New Yorker *in 2003, Turow attempts to come to terms with the moral and ethical dilemma posed by capital punishment.*

When Joseph Hartzler, a former colleague of mine in the United States attorney's office in Chicago, was appointed the lead prosecutor in the trial of Timothy McVeigh, the Oklahoma City bomber, he remarked that McVeigh was headed for Hell, no matter what. His job, Hartzler said, was simply to speed up the delivery. That was also the attitude evinced by the prosecutors vying to be first to try the two Beltway sniper suspects.[1] Given the fear and fury the multiple shootings inspired, it wasn't surprising that polls showed that Americans favored imposing what

---

[1] *Beltway sniper suspects:* The Beltway snipers, John Allen Muhammad and Lee Boyd Malvo, randomly killed ten people and wounded three more in and around Washington, D.C., during a three-week period in 2002. —EDS.

Attorney General [John] Ashcroft referred to as the "ultimate sanction." Yet despite the retributive wrath that the public seems quick to visit on particular crimes, or criminals, there has also been, in recent years, growing skepticism about the death-penalty system in general. A significant number of Americans question both the system's over-all fairness and, given the many cases in which DNA evidence has proved that the wrong person was convicted of a crime, its ability to distinguish the innocent from the guilty.

Ambivalence about the death penalty is an American tradition. When the Republic was founded, all the states, following English law, imposed capital punishment. But the humanistic impulses that favored democracy led to questions about whether the state should have the right to kill the citizens upon whose consent government was erected. Jefferson was among the earliest advocates of restricting executions. In 1846, Michigan became the first American state to outlaw capital punishment, except in the case of treason, and public opinion has continued to vacillate on the issue. Following the Second World War and the rise and fall of a number of totalitarian governments, Western European nations began abandoning capital punishment, but their example is of limited relevance to us, since our murder rate is roughly four times the rate in Europe. One need only glance at a TV screen to realize that murder remains an American preoccupation, and the concomitant questions of how to deal with it challenge contending strains in our moral thought, pitting Old Testament against New, retribution against forgiveness.

I was forced to confront my own feelings about the death penalty as one of fourteen members of a commission appointed by Governor George Ryan of Illinois to recommend reforms of the state's capital-punishment system. In the past twenty-five years, thirteen men who spent time on death row in Illinois have been exonerated, three of them in 1999. Governor Ryan declared a moratorium on executions in January, 2000, and five weeks later announced the formation of our commission. We were a diverse group: two sitting prosecutors; two sitting public defenders; a former Chief Judge of the Federal District Court; a former U.S. senator; three women; four members of racial minorities; prominent Democrats and Republicans. Twelve of us were lawyers, nine with experience as defense attorneys and eleven — including William Martin, who won a capital conviction against the mass murderer Richard Speck, in 1967 — with prosecutorial backgrounds. Roberto Ramírez, a Mexican-American immigrant who built a successful janitorial business, knew violent death at first hand. His father was murdered, and his grandfather shot and killed the murderer. Governor Ryan gave us only one instruction. We were to determine what reforms, if any, would make application of the death penalty in Illinois fair, just, and accurate. In March, 2000, during the press conference at which members of the commission were introduced, we were asked who among us opposed capital punishment. Four people raised their hands. I was not one of them.

For a long time, I referred to myself as a death-penalty agnostic, although in the early seventies, when I was a student, I was reflexively against capital punishment. When I was an assistant U.S. attorney, from 1978 to 1986, there was no federal death penalty. The Supreme Court declared capital-punishment statutes unconstitutional in 1972, and although the Court changed its mind in 1976, the death penalty did not become part of federal law again until 1988. However, Illinois had reinstated capital punishment in the mid-seventies, and occasionally my colleagues became involved in state-court murder prosecutions. In 1984, when my oldest friend in the office, Jeremy Margolis, secured a capital sentence against a two-time murderer named Hector Reuben Sanchez, I congratulated him. I wasn't sure what I might do as a legislator, but I had come to accept that some people are incorrigibly evil and I knew that I could follow the will of the community in dealing with them, just as I routinely accepted the wisdom of the RICO statute[2] and the mail-fraud and extortion laws it was my job to enforce.

My first direct encounter with a capital prosecution came in 1991.   5
I was in private practice by then and had published two successful novels, which allowed me to donate much of my time as a lawyer to pro-bono work. One of the cases I was asked to take on was the appeal of Alejandro (Alex) Hernandez, who had been convicted of a notorious kidnapping, rape, and murder. In February, 1983, a ten-year-old girl, Jeanine Nicarico, was abducted from her home in a suburb of Chicago, in DuPage County. Two days later, Jeanine's corpse, clad only in a nightshirt, was found by hikers in a nearby nature preserve. She had been blindfolded, sexually assaulted several times, and then killed by repeated blows to the head. More than forty law-enforcement officers formed a task force to hunt down the killer, but by early 1984 the case had not been solved, and a heated primary campaign was under way for the job of state's attorney in DuPage County. A few days before the election, three men — Alex Hernandez, Rolando Cruz, and Stephen Buckley — were indicted.

The incumbent lost the election anyway, to a local lawyer, Jim Ryan, who took the case to trial in January, 1985. (Ryan later became the attorney general of Illinois, a position he is about to relinquish.) The jury deadlocked on Buckley, but both Hernandez and Cruz were convicted and sentenced to death. There was no physical evidence against either of them — no blood, semen, fingerprints, or other forensic proof. The state's case consisted solely of each defendant's statements, a contradictory maze of mutual accusations and demonstrable falsehoods. By the time the case reached me, seven years after the men were arrested, the charges against Buckley had been dropped and the Illinois Supreme Court had reversed the original convictions of Hernandez and Cruz and ordered separate

---

[2]*RICO statute:* The "Racketeer Influenced and Corrupt Organization Act" passed in 1970. — Eds.

retrials. In 1990, Cruz was condemned to death for a second time. Hernandez's second trial ended with a hung jury, but at a third trial, in 1991, he was convicted and sentenced to eighty years in prison.

Hernandez's attorneys made a straightforward pitch to me: their client, who has an I.Q. of about 75, was innocent. I didn't believe it. And, even if it was true, I couldn't envision persuading a court to overturn the conviction a second time. Illinois elects its state-court judges, and this was a celebrated case: "the case that broke Chicago's heart" was how it was sometimes referred to in the press. Nevertheless, I read the brief that Lawrence Marshall, a professor of law at Northwestern University, had filed in behalf of Cruz, and studied the transcripts of Hernandez's trials. After that, there was no question in my mind. Alex Hernandez was innocent.

In June, 1985, another little girl, Melissa Ackerman, had been abducted and murdered in northern Illinois. Like Jeanine Nicarico, she was kidnapped in broad daylight, sexually violated, and killed in a wooded area. A man named Brian Dugan was arrested for the Ackerman murder, and, in the course of negotiating for a life sentence, he admitted that he had raped and killed Jeanine Nicarico as well.

The Illinois State Police investigated Dugan's admissions about the Nicarico murder and accumulated a mass of corroborating detail. Dugan was not at work the day the girl disappeared, and a church secretary, working a few blocks from the Nicarico home, recalled a conversation with him. A tire print found where Jeanine's body was deposited matched the tires that had been on Dugan's car. He knew many details about the crime that had never been publicly revealed, including information about the interior of the Nicarico home and the blindfold applied to Jeanine.

Nevertheless, the DuPage County prosecutors refused to accept Dugan's confession. Even after Cruz's and Hernandez's second convictions were overturned in the separate appeals that Larry Marshall and I argued, and notwithstanding a series of DNA tests that excluded Cruz and Hernandez as Jeanine Nicarico's sexual assailant, while pointing directly at Dugan, the prosecutors pursued the cases. It was only after Cruz was acquitted in a third trial, late in 1995, that both men were finally freed.   10

Capital punishment is supposed to be applied only to the most heinous crimes, but it is precisely those cases which, because of the strong feelings of repugnance they evoke, most thoroughly challenge the detached judgment of all participants in the legal process — police, prosecutors, judges, and juries. The innocent are often particularly at risk. Most defendants charged with capital crimes avoid the death penalty by reaching a plea bargain, a process that someone who is innocent is naturally reluctant to submit to. Innocent people tend to insist on a trial, and when they get it the jury does not include anyone who will refuse on principle to impose a death sentence. Such people are barred from juries in capital cases by a Supreme Court decision, Witherspoon v. Illinois, that, some scholars believe, makes the juries more conviction-prone. In Alex Hernandez's third

trial, the evidence against him was so scant that the DuPage County
state's attorney's office sought an outside legal opinion to determine
whether it could get the case over the bare legal threshold required to go
to a jury. Hernandez was convicted anyway, although the trial judge refused to impose a death sentence, because of the paucity of evidence.

A frightened public demanding results in the aftermath of a ghastly
crime also places predictable pressures on prosecutors and police, which
can sometimes lead to questionable conduct. Confronted with the evidence of Brian Dugan's guilt, the prosecutors in Hernandez's second trial
had tried to suggest that he and Dugan could have committed the crime
together, even though there was no proof that the men knew each other.
Throughout the state's case, the prosecutors emphasized a pair of shoe
prints found behind the Nicarico home, where a would-be burglar—i.e.,
Hernandez—could have looked through a window. Following testimony
that Hernandez's shoe size was about 7, a police expert testified that the
shoe prints were "about size 6." Until he was directly cross-examined, the
expert did not mention that he was referring to a woman's size 6, or that
he had identified the tread on one of the prints as coming from a
woman's shoe, a fact he'd shared with the prosecutor, who somehow
failed to inform the defense.

This kind of overreaching by the prosecution occurred frequently. A
special grand jury was convened after Cruz and Hernandez were freed.
Three former prosecutors and four DuPage County police officers were
indicted on various counts, including conspiring to obstruct justice. They
were tried and—as is often the case when law-enforcement officers are
charged with overzealous execution of their duties—acquitted, although
the county subsequently reached a multimillion-dollar settlement in a civil
suit brought by Hernandez, Cruz, and their onetime co-defendant,
Stephen Buckley. Despite assertions by DuPage County prosecutors that
Jeanine Nicarico's killer deserves to die, Brian Dugan has never been
charged with her murder, although Joseph Birkett, the state's attorney for
the county, admitted in November that new DNA tests prove Dugan's
role with "scientific certainty." In the past, Birkett had celebrated the ac-
quittal of his colleagues on charges of conspiring to obstruct justice and
had attacked the special prosecutor who'd brought the charges. He continues to make public statements suggesting that Cruz and Hernandez
might be guilty. An ultimately unsuccessful attempt was made to demote
the judge who acquitted Cruz, and last year, when the judge resigned
from the bench, he had to pay for his own going-away party. In the
meantime, the prosecutor who tried to incriminate Alex Hernandez with
the print from a woman's shoe is now Chief Judge in DuPage County.

If these are the perils of the system, why have a death penalty? Many
people would answer that executions deter others from committing murder, but I found no evidence that convinced me. For example, Illinois,
which has a death penalty, has a higher murder rate than the neighboring

state of Michigan, which has no capital punishment but roughly the same racial makeup, income levels, and population distribution between cities and rural areas. In fact, in the last decade the murder rate in states without the death penalty has remained consistently lower than in the states that have had executions. Surveys of criminologists and police chiefs show that substantial majorities of both groups doubt that the death penalty significantly reduces the number of homicides.

Another argument—that the death penalty saves money, because it   15 avoids the expense of lifetime incarceration—doesn't hold up, either, when you factor in the staggering costs of capital litigation. In the United States in 2000, the average period between conviction and execution was eleven and a half years, with lawyers and courts spewing out briefs and decisions all that time.

The case for capital punishment that seemed strongest to me came from the people who claim the most direct benefit from an execution: the families and friends of murder victims. The commission heard from survivors in public hearings and in private sessions, and I learned a great deal in these meetings. Death brought on by a random element like disease or a tornado is easier for survivors to accept than the loss of a loved one through the conscious will of another human being. It was not clear to me at first what survivors hoped to gain from the death of a murderer, but certain themes emerged. Dora Larson has been a victims'-rights advocate for nearly twenty years. In 1979, her ten-year-old daughter was kidnapped, raped, and strangled by a fifteen-year-old boy who then buried her in a grave he had dug three days earlier. "Our biggest fear is that someday our child's or loved one's killer will be released," she told the commission. "We want these people off the streets so that others might be safe." A sentence of life without parole should guarantee that the defendant would never repeat his crime, but Mrs. Larson pointed out several ways in which a life sentence poses a far greater emotional burden than an execution. Because her daughter's killer was under eighteen, he was ineligible for the death penalty. "When I was told life, I thought it was life," Larson said to us. "Then I get a letter saying our killer has petitioned the governor for release."

Victims' families talk a lot about "closure," an end to the legal process that will allow them to come to final terms with their grief. Mrs. Larson and others told us that families frequently find the execution of their lost loved one's killer a meaningful emotional landmark. A number of family members of the victims of the Oklahoma City bombing expressed those sentiments after they watched Timothy McVeigh die. The justice the survivors seek is the one embedded in the concept of restitution: the criminal ought not to end up better off than his victim. But the national victims'-rights movement is so powerful that victims have become virtual proprietors of the capital system, leading to troubling inconsistencies. For instance, DuPage County has long supported the Nicarico family's adamant wish for a death sentence for Jeanine's killer, but the virtually identical murder of Melissa Ackerman resulted in a life term with no possibility of parole for Brian Dugan, because Melissa's parents preferred a quick resolution. It makes no more sense to let victims rule the capital process than it would to decide what will be built on the World Trade Center site solely according to the desires of the survivors of those killed on September 11th. In a democracy, no minority, even people whose losses scour our hearts, should be entitled to speak for us all.

Governor Ryan's commission didn't spend much time on philosophical debates, but those who favored capital punishment tended to make one argument again and again: sometimes a crime is so horrible that killing its perpetrator is the only just response. I've always thought death-penalty proponents have a point when they say that it denigrates the profound indignity of murder to punish it in the same fashion as other crimes. These days, you can get life in California for your third felony, even if it's swiping a few videotapes from a Kmart. Does it vindicate our shared values if the most immoral act imaginable, the unjustified killing of another human being, is treated the same way? The issue is not revenge or retribution, exactly, so much as moral order. When everything is said and done, I suspect that this notion of moral proportion—ultimate punishment for ultimate evil—is the reason most Americans continue to support capital punishment.

This places an enormous burden of precision on the justice system, however. If we execute the innocent or the undeserving, then we have undermined, not reinforced, our sense of moral proportion. The prosecution of Alex Hernandez demonstrated to me the risks to the innocent. A case I took on later gave me experience with the problematic nature of who among the guilty gets selected for execution. One afternoon, I had assembled a group of young lawyers in my office to discuss pro-bono death-penalty work when, by pure coincidence, I found a letter in my in-box from a man, Christopher Thomas, who said he'd been convicted of first-degree murder and sentenced to death, even though none of the four eyewitnesses to the crime who testified had identified him. We investigated and found that the letter was accurate—in a sense. None of the eyewitnesses had identified Thomas. However, he had two accomplices, both of whom had turned against him, and Thomas had subsequently confessed three different times, the last occasion on videotape.

According to the various accounts, Chris Thomas—who is black, and was twenty-one at the time of the crime—and his two pals had run out of gas behind a strip mall in Waukegan, Illinois. They were all stoned, and they hatched a plan to roll somebody for money. Rafael Gasgonia, a thirty-nine-year-old Filipino immigrant, was unfortunate enough to step out for a smoke behind the photo shop where he worked as a delivery driver. The three men accosted him. Thomas pointed a gun at his head, and when a struggle broke out Thomas fired once, killing Gasgonia instantly.

I was drawn to Chris Thomas's case because I couldn't understand how a parking-lot stickup gone bad had ended in a death sentence. But

20

after we studied the record, it seemed clear to us that Thomas, like a lot of other defendants, was on death row essentially for the crime of having the wrong lawyers. He had been defended by two attorneys under contract to the Lake County public defender's office. They were each paid thirty thousand dollars a year to defend a hundred and three cases, about three hundred dollars per case. By contract, one assignment had to be a capital case. The fiscal year was nearly over, and neither of the contract lawyers had done his capital work, so they were assigned to Thomas's case together. One of them had no experience of any kind in death-penalty cases; the other had once been standby counsel for a man who was defending himself.

In court, we characterized Thomas's defense as all you would expect for six hundred dollars. His lawyers seemed to regard the case as a clear loser at trial and, given the impulsive nature of the crime, virtually certain to result in a sentence other than death. They did a scanty investigation of Thomas's background for the sentencing hearing, an effort that was hindered by the fact that the chief mitigation witness, Thomas's aunt, who was the closest thing to an enduring parental figure in his life, had herself been prosecuted on a drug charge by one of the lawyers during his years as an assistant state's attorney. As a result, Thomas's aunt distrusted the lawyers, and, under her influence, Chris soon did as well. He felt screwed around already, since he had confessed to the crime and expressed remorse, and had been rewarded by being put on trial for his life. At the sentencing hearing, Thomas took the stand and denied that he was guilty, notwithstanding his many prior confessions. The presiding judge, who had never before sentenced anybody to death, gave Thomas the death penalty.

In Illinois, some of this could not happen now. The Capital Litigation Trust Fund has been established to pay for an adequate defense, and the state Supreme Court created a Capital Litigation trial bar, which requires lawyers who represent someone facing the death penalty to be experienced in capital cases. Nonetheless, looking over the opinions in the roughly two hundred and seventy capital appeals in Illinois, I was struck again and again by the wide variation in the seriousness of the crimes. There were many monstrous offenses, but also a number of garden-variety murders. And the feeling that the system is an unguided ship is only heightened when one examines the first-degree homicides that have resulted in sentences other than death. Thomas was on death row, but others from Lake County—a man who had knocked a friend unconscious and placed him on the tracks in front of an oncoming train, for instance, and a mother who had fed acid to her baby—had escaped it.

The inevitable disparities between individual cases are often enhanced by social factors, like race, which plays a role that is not always well understood. The commission authorized a study that showed that in Illinois, you are more likely to receive the death penalty if you are white—two and a half times as likely. One possible reason is that in a racially divided society whites tend to associate with, and thus to murder, other whites. And choosing a white victim makes a murderer three and a half times as likely to be punished by a death sentence as if he'd killed someone who was black. (At least in Illinois, blacks and whites who murdered whites were given a death sentence at essentially the same rate, which has not always been true in other places.)

Geography also matters in Illinois. You are five times as likely to get   25
a death sentence for first-degree murder in a rural area as you are in Cook County, which includes Chicago. Gender seems to count, too. Capital punishment for slaying a woman is imposed at three and half times the rate for murdering a man. When you add in all the uncontrollable variables — who the prosecutor and the defense lawyer are, the nature of the judge and the jury, the characteristics of the victim, the place of the crime — the results reflect anything but a clearly proportionate morality.

And execution, of course, ends any chance that a defendant will acknowledge the claims of the morality we seek to enforce. More than three years after my colleagues and I read Chris Thomas's letter, a court in Lake County resentenced him to a hundred years in prison, meaning that, with good behavior, he could be released when he is seventy-one. He wept in court and apologized to the Gasgonia family for what he had done.

Supporters of capital punishment in Illinois, particularly those in law enforcement, often use Henry Brisbon as their trump card. Get rid of the death penalty, they say, and what do you do about the likes of Henry?

On the night of June 3, 1973, Brisbon and three "rap partners" (his term) forced several cars off I-57, an interstate highway south of Chicago. Brisbon made a woman in one of the cars disrobe, and then he discharged a shotgun in her vagina. He compelled a young couple to lie down in a field together, instructed them to "make this your last kiss," and shot both of them in the back. His role in these crimes was uncovered only years later, when he confessed to an inmate working as a law librarian in the penitentiary where he was serving a stretch for rape and armed robbery. Because the I-57 killings occurred shortly after the Supreme Court declared capital punishment unconstitutional, Brisbon was not eligible for the death penalty. He was given a sentence of one thousand to three thousand years in prison, probably the longest term ever imposed in Illinois.

In October, 1978, eleven months after the sentencing, Brisbon murdered again. He placed a homemade knife to the throat of a guard to subdue him, then went with several inmates to the cell of another prisoner and stabbed him repeatedly. By the time Brisbon was tried again, in early 1982, Illinois had restored capital punishment, and he was sentenced to death. The evidence in his sentencing hearings included proof of yet another murder Brisbon had allegedly committed prior to his imprisonment, when he placed a shotgun against the face of a store clerk and blew him away. He had accumulated more than two hundred disciplinary violations while he was incarcerated, and had played a major role in the violent takeover of Stateville prison, in September, 1979. Predictably, the death sentence did not markedly improve Brisbon's conduct. In the years since he was first condemned, he has been accused of a number of serious assaults on guards, including a stabbing, and he severely injured another inmate when he threw a thirty-pound weight against his skull.

Brisbon is now held at the Tamms Correctional Center, a "super-max" facility that houses more than two hundred and fifty men culled from an Illinois prison population of almost forty-five thousand. Generally speaking, Tamms inmates are either gang leaders or men with intractable discipline problems. I wanted to visit Tamms, hoping that it would tell me whether it is possible to incapacitate people like Brisbon, who are clearly prone to murder again if given the opportunity.   30

Tamms is situated near the southern most point of Illinois, farther south than parts of Kentucky. The Mississippi, a wide body of cloacal brown, floods the nearby lowlands, creating a region of green marshes along orange sandstone bluffs. Tamms stands at the foot of one of those stone outcroppings, on a vast, savannalike grassland. The terms of confinement are grim. Inmates are permitted no physical contact with other human beings. Each prisoner is held twenty-three hours a day inside a seven-by-twelve-foot block of preformed concrete that has a single window to the outside, roughly forty-two by eighteen inches, segmented by a lateral steel bar. The cell contains a stainless-steel fixture housing a toilet bowl and a sink and a concrete pallet over which a foam mattress is laid. The front of the cell has a panel of punch-plate steel pierced by a network of half-inch circles, almost like bullet holes, that permit conversation but prevent the kind of mayhem possible when prisoners can get their hands through the bars. Once a day, an inmate's door is opened by remote control, and he walks down a corridor of cells to an outdoor area, twelve by twenty-eight feet, surrounded by thirteen-foot-high concrete walls, with a roof over half of it for shelter from the elements. For an hour, a prisoner may exercise or just breathe fresh air. Showers are permitted on a similar remote-control basis, for twenty minutes, several times a week.

In part because the facility is not full, incarceration in Tamms costs about two and a half times as much as the approximately twenty thousand dollars a year that is ordinarily spent on an inmate in Illinois, but the facility has a remarkable record of success in reducing disciplinary infractions and assaults. George Welborn, a tall, lean man with a full head of graying hair, a mustache, and dark, thoughtful eyes, was the warden of Tamms when I visited. I talked to him for much of the day, and toward the end asked if he really believed that he could keep Brisbon from killing again. Welborn, who speaks with a southern-Illinois twang, was an assistant warden at Stateville when Brisbon led the inmate uprising there, and he testified against him in the proceedings that resulted in his death sentence. He took his time with my question, but answered, guardedly, "Yes."

I was permitted to meet Brisbon, speaking with him through the punch-plate from the corridor in front of his cell. He is a solidly built

African-American man of medium height, somewhat bookish-looking, with heavy glasses. He seemed quick-witted and amiable, and greatly amused by himself. He had read all about the commission, and he displayed a letter in which, many years ago, he had suggested a moratorium on executions. He had some savvy predictions about the political impediments to many potential reforms of the capital system.

"Henry is a special case," Welborn said to me later, when we spoke on the phone. "I would be foolish to say I can guarantee he won't kill anyone again. I can imagine situations, God forbid . . . But the chances are minimized here." Still, Welborn emphasized, with Brisbon there would never be any guarantees.

I had another reason for wanting to visit Tamms. Illinois's execution   35
chamber is now situated there. Unused for more than two years because of Governor Ryan's moratorium, it remains a solemn spot, with the sterile feel of an operating theatre in a hospital. The execution gurney, where the lethal injection is administered, is covered by a crisp sheet and might even be mistaken for an examining table except for the arm paddles that extend from it and the crisscrossing leather restraints that strike a particularly odd note in the world of Tamms, where virtually everything else is of steel, concrete, or plastic.

Several years ago, I attended a luncheon where Sister Helen Prejean, the author of "Dead Man Walking," delivered the keynote address. The daughter of a prominent lawyer, Sister Helen is a powerful orator. Inveighing against the death penalty, she looked at the audience and repeated one of her favorite arguments: "If you really believe in the death penalty, ask yourself if you're willing to inject the fatal poison." I thought of Sister Helen when I stood in the death chamber at Tamms. I felt the horror of the coolly contemplated ending of the life of another human being in the name of the law. But if John Wayne Gacy, the mass murderer who tortured and killed thirty-three young men, had been on that gurney, I could, as Sister Helen would have it, have pushed the button. I don't think the death penalty is the product of an alien morality, and I respect the right of a majority of my fellow-citizens to decide that it ought to be imposed on the most horrific crimes.

The members of the commission knew that capital punishment would not be abolished in Illinois anytime soon. Accordingly, our formal recommendations, many of which were made unanimously, ran to matters of reform. Principal among them was lowering the risks of convicting the innocent. Several of the thirteen men who had been on death row and were then exonerated had made dubious confessions, which appeared to have been coerced or even invented. We recommended that all interrogations of suspects in capital cases be videotaped. We also proposed altering lineup procedures, since eyewitness testimony has proved to be far less trustworthy than I ever thought while I was a prosecutor. We urged that courts provide pretrial hearings to determine the reliability of jailhouse snitches, who have surfaced often in Illinois's capital cases, testifying to supposed confessions in exchange for lightened sentences.

To reduce the seeming randomness with which some defendants appear to end up on death row, we proposed that the twenty eligibility criteria for capital punishment in Illinois be trimmed to five: multiple murders, murder of a police officer or firefighter, murder in a prison, murder aimed at hindering the justice system, and murder involving torture. Murders committed in the course of another felony, the eligibility factor used in Christopher Thomas's case, would be eliminated. And we urged the creation of a statewide oversight body to attempt to bring more uniformity to the selection of death-penalty cases.

To insure that the capital system is something other than an endless maze for survivors, we recommended guaranteed sentences of life with no parole when eligible cases don't result in the death penalty. And we also outlined reforms aimed at expediting the post-conviction review and clemency processes.

Yet our proposals sidestepped the ultimate question. One fall day, 40 Paul Simon, the former U.S. senator who was one of the commission's chairs and is a longtime foe of the death penalty, forced us to vote on whether Illinois should have a death penalty at all. The vote was an expression of sentiment, not a formal recommendation. What was our best advice to our fellow-citizens, political realities aside? By a narrow majority, we agreed that capital punishment should not be an option.

I admit that I am still attracted to a death penalty that would be applied to horrendous crimes, or that would provide absolute certainty that the likes of Henry Brisbon would never again satisfy their cruel appetites. But if death is available as a punishment, the furious heat of grief and rage that these crimes inspire will inevitably short-circuit any capital system. Now and then, we will execute someone who is innocent, while the fundamental equality of each survivor's loss creates an inevitable emotional momentum to expand the categories for death-penalty eligibility. Like many others who have wrestled with capital punishment, I have changed my mind often, driven back and forth by the errors each position seems to invite. Yet after two years of deliberation, I seem to have finally come to rest. When Paul Simon asked whether Illinois should have a death penalty, I voted no.

The Reader's Presence

1. At the end of the introductory section of the essay, Turow concludes by stating that four people on the Illinois committee were against the death penalty. "I was not one of them," he states. How does this statement structure the progression of his argument?

How is this statement bookended at the end of the essay? What effect does this technique have on you as a reader?

2. Turow begins his essay by mentioning two high-profile convicted murderers—Timothy McVeigh and the Beltway sniper. How does opening with these extreme cases serve Turow's argument? Does it help or hurt his case to present two cases that many Americans would be more likely to use to justify capital punishment?

3. Read "The Witches of Salem Village" by Kai Erikson (page 406). For what crimes were people sentenced to death in Salem? How did some who were convicted of witchcraft escape the death penalty? Does Turow's argument indicate that the application of the death penalty in twenty-first-century America is still arbitrary and unjust? Why or why not?

Mark Twain

Corn-pone Opinions

Mark Twain, the pseudonym of Samuel Clemens (1835–1910), was a master satirist, journalist, novelist, orator, and steamboat pilot. He grew up in Hannibal, Missouri, a frontier setting that appears in different forms in several of his novels, most notably in his masterpiece Adventures of Huckleberry Finn *(1869). His satirical eye spared very few American political or social institutions including slavery, and for this reason, as well as because it violated conventional standards of taste,* Huckleberry Finn *created a minor scandal when it was published. Nonetheless, with such books as* The Innocents Abroad *(1869),* Roughing It *(1872),* The Adventures of Tom Sawyer *(1876), and* The Prince and the Pauper *(1882), Twain secured himself a position as one of the most popular authors in American history. Twain built his career upon his experiences in the western states and his travels in Europe and the Middle East, but he eventually settled in Hartford, Connecticut. His last years were spent as one of the most celebrated public speakers and social figures in the United States.*

Reflecting upon the experience of writing, Twain once wrote in his notebook, "The time to begin writing an article is when you have finished it to your satisfaction. By that time you begin to clearly and logically perceive what it is that you really want to say."

"Corn-pone Opinions" was found in Mark Twain's papers after his death and first published in 1923 in Europe and Elsewhere, *edited by Albert Bigelow Paine.*

Fifty years ago, when I was a boy of fifteen and helping to inhabit a Missourian village on the banks of the Mississippi, I had a friend whose society was very dear to me because I was forbidden by my mother to partake of it. He was a gay and impudent and satirical and delightful young black man—a slave—who daily preached sermons from the top of his master's woodpile, with me for sole audience. He imitated the pulpit style of the several clergymen of the village, and did it well, and with fine passion and energy. To me he was a wonder. I believed he was the greatest orator in the United States and would some day be heard from. But it did not happen; in the distribution of rewards he was overlooked. It is the way, in this world.

He interrupted his preaching, now and then, to saw a stick of wood; but the sawing was a pretense—he did it with his mouth; exactly imitating the sound the bucksaw makes in shrieking its way through the wood. But it served its purpose; it kept his master from coming out to see how the work was getting along. I listened to the sermons from the open window of a lumber room at the back of the house. One of his texts was this:

"You tell me whar a man gits his corn pone,[1] en I'll tell you what his 'pinions is."

I can never forget it. It was deeply impressed upon me. By my mother. Not upon my memory, but elsewhere. She had slipped in upon me while I was absorbed and not watching. The black philosopher's idea was that a man is not independent, and cannot afford views which might interfere with his bread and butter. If he would prosper, he must train with the majority; in matters of large moment, like politics and religion, he must think and feel with the bulk of his neighbors, or suffer damage in his social standing and in his business prosperities. He must restrict himself to corn-pone opinions—at least on the surface. He must get his opinions from other people; he must reason out none for himself; he must have no first-hand views.

I think Jerry was right, in the main, but I think he did not go far   5
enough.

1. It was his idea that a man conforms to the majority view of his locality by calculation and intention.

This happens, but I think it is not the rule.

2. It was his idea that there is such a thing as a first-hand opinion; an original opinion; an opinion which is coldly reasoned out in a man's head, by a searching analysis of the facts involved, with the heart unconsulted, and the jury room closed against outside influences. It may be that such an opinion has been born somewhere, at some time or other, but I suppose it got away before they could catch it and stuff it and put it in the museum.

---

[1] *Corn pone:* Southern expression that dates from the mid-nineteenth century for a simple corn bread or muffin; *pone* comes from a Native American word for something baked.—Eds.

I am persuaded that a coldly-thought-out and independent verdict upon a fashion in clothes, or manners, or literature, or politics, or religion, or any other matter that is projected into the field of our notice and interest, is a most rare thing — if it has indeed ever existed.

A new thing in costume appears — the flaring hoopskirt, for example —   10
and the passers-by are shocked, and the irreverent laugh. Six months later everybody is reconciled; the fashion has established itself; it is admired, now, and no one laughs. Public opinion resented it before, public opinion accepts it now, and is happy in it. Why? Was the resentment reasoned out? Was the acceptance reasoned out? No. The instinct that moves to conformity did the work. It is our nature to conform; it is a force which not many can successfully resist. What is its seat? The inborn requirement of self-approval. We all have to bow to that; there are no exceptions. Even the woman who refuses from first to last to wear the hoopskirt comes under that law and is its slave; she could not wear the skirt and have her own approval; and that she *must* have, she cannot help herself. But as a rule our self-approval has its source in but one place and not elsewhere — the approval of other people. A person of vast consequences can introduce any kind of novelty in dress and the general world will presently adopt it — moved to do it, in the first place, by the natural instinct to passively yield to that vague something recognized as authority, and in the second place by the human instinct to train with the multitude and have its approval. An empress introduced the hoopskirt, and we know the result. A nobody introduced the bloomer, and we know the result. If Eve should come again, in her ripe renown, and reintroduce her quaint styles — well, we know what would happen. And we should be cruelly embarrassed, along at first.

The hoopskirt runs its course and disappears. Nobody reasons about it. One woman abandons the fashion; her neighbor notices this and follows her lead; this influences the next woman; and so on and so on, and presently the skirt has vanished out of the world, no one knows how nor why, nor cares, for that matter. It will come again, by and by and in due course will go again.

Twenty-five years ago, in England, six or eight wine glasses stood grouped by each person's plate at a dinner party, and they were used, not left idle and empty; to-day there are but three or four in the group, and the average guest sparingly uses about two of them. We have not adopted this new fashion yet, but we shall do it presently. We shall not think it out; we shall merely conform, and let it go at that. We get our notions and habits and opinions from outside influences; we do not have to study them out.

Our table manners, and company manners, and street manners change from time to time, but the changes are not reasoned out; we merely notice and conform. We are creatures of outside influences; as a rule we do not think, we only imitate. We cannot invent standards that will stick; what we mistake for standards are only fashions, and perishable. We may continue to admire them, but we drop the use of them. We notice this in literature. Shakespeare is a standard, and fifty years ago we used to write tragedies which we couldn't tell from—from somebody else's; but we don't do it any more, now. Our prose standard, three quarters of a century ago, was ornate and diffuse; some authority or other changed it in the direction of compactness and simplicity, and conformity followed, without argument. The historical novel starts up suddenly, and sweeps the land. Everybody writes one, and the nation is glad. We had historical novels before; but nobody read them, and the rest of us conformed— without reasoning it out. We are conforming in the other way, now, because it is another case of everybody.

The outside influences are always pouring in upon us, and we are always obeying their orders and accepting their verdicts. The Smiths like the new play; the Joneses go to see it, and they copy the Smith verdict. Morals, religions, politics, get their following from surrounding influences and atmospheres, almost entirely; not from study, not from thinking. A man must and will have his own approval first of all, in each and every moment and circumstance of his life—even if he must repent of a self-approved act the moment after its commission, in order to get his self-approval *again*: but, speaking in general terms, a man's self-approval in the large concerns of life has its source in the approval of the peoples about him, and not in a searching personal examination of the matter. Mohammedans are Mohammedans because they are born and reared among that sect, not because they have thought it out and can furnish sound reasons for being Mohammedans; we know why Catholics are Catholics; why Presbyterians are Presbyterians; why Baptists are Baptists; why Mormons are Mormons; why thieves are thieves; why monarchists are monarchists; why Republicans are Republicans and Democrats, Democrats. We know it is a matter of association and sympathy, not reasoning and examination; that hardly a man in the world has an opinion upon morals, politics, or religion which he got otherwise than through his associations and sympathies. Broadly speaking, there are none but corn-pone opinions. And broadly speaking, corn-pone stands for self-approval. Self-approval is acquired mainly from the approval of other people. The result is conformity. Sometimes conformity has a sordid business interest—the bread-and-butter interest—but not in most cases, I think. I think that in the majority of cases it is unconscious and not calculated; that it is born of the human being's natural yearning to stand well with his fellows and have their inspiring approval and praise—a yearning which is commonly so strong and so insistent that it cannot be effectually resisted, and must have its way.

A political emergency brings out the corn-pone opinion in fine force   15 in its two chief varieties—the pocketbook variety, which has its origin in self-interest, and the bigger variety, the sentimental variety—the one which can't bear to be outside the pale; can't bear to be in disfavor; can't endure the averted face and the cold shoulder; wants to stand well with his friends, wants to be smiled upon, wants to be welcome, wants to hear the precious words, "*He's* on the right track!" Uttered, perhaps by an ass, but still an ass of high degree, an ass whose approval is gold and diamonds to a smaller ass, and confers glory and honor and happiness, and membership in the herd. For these gauds many a man will dump his lifelong principles into the street, and his conscience along with them. We have seen it happen. In some millions of instances.

Men think they think upon great political questions, and they do; but they think with their party, not independently; they read its literature, but not that of the other side; they arrive at convictions, but they are drawn from a partial view of the matter in hand and are of no particular value. They swarm with their party, they feel with their party, they are happy in their party's approval; and where the party leads they will follow, whether for right and honor, or through blood and dirt and a mush of mutilated morals.

In our late canvass half of the nation passionately believed that in silver lay salvation, the other half as passionately believed that that way lay destruction. Do you believe that a tenth part of the people, on either side, had any rational excuse for having an opinion about the matter at all? I studied that mighty question to the bottom—came out empty. Half of our people passionately believe in high tariff, the other half believe otherwise. Does this mean study and examination, or only feeling? The latter, I think. I have deeply studied that question, too—and didn't arrive. We all do no end of feeling, and we mistake it for thinking. And out of it we get an aggregation which we consider a boon. Its name is Public Opinion. It is held in reverence. It settles everything. Some think it the Voice of God.

The Reader's Presence

1. "Corn pone" was a dish eaten, in Twain's time, by poor Southerners. How might this image of a lowly, common foodstuff be tied to the opinions of Twain's commonsense slave "philosopher"? What is Twain's position on Jerry's everyday wisdom? What sort of audience does Twain appear to be writing for? How does Twain "translate" Jerry's statement?

2. Twain agrees with Jerry's statement, but feels he "did not go far enough." How do Twain's opinions differ from Jerry's? How does Twain use Jerry's opinions, starting in paragraph 9, to launch his own? Twain does not return to Jerry in the essay. How does the dramatic technique of ending the essay with topics far from those with which it was begun affect your reading of it?

3. About ten years after Samuel Clemens was born in Missouri, the New England philosopher Ralph Waldo Emerson wrote an essay called "Self-Reliance" in which he sharply criticized *his* fellow

Americans' tendency toward conformism. "If I know your sect," he wrote, "I anticipate your argument." How does Twain invoke the ideal of self-reliance? Twain calls Jerry's mode of oratory a kind of "pulpit style"; Emerson, too, was a preacher whose essays loosely resemble sermons. What does Twain's essay have in common with the structure of a traditional sermon? Compare the essay to that of another preacher, Martin Luther King Jr.'s "Letter from Birmingham Jail" (page 738). Why might Twain, a deeply irreverent writer, participate in the American sermon tradition? What is the effect of this "sermon" on you as reader? Is Twain's essay as sharp a piece of oratory as King's? How does it appeal to the reader's ear?

Gore Vidal

Drugs

Gore Vidal (b. 1925), author, playwright, screenwriter, essayist, and reviewer, is known for his satirical observations, acerbic wit, and eloquence. He is a prolific author of more than twenty books, including The City and the Pillar *(1948),* Myra Breckinridge *(1968),* Myron *(1974),* Palimpsest: A Memoir *(1995), and* The Smithsonian Institution *(1998). Among Vidal's irreverent historical novels are* Julian *(1964),* Burr *(1973),* 1876 *(1976),* Lincoln *(1984), and* The Golden Age *(2000). His best-known dramatic work is* Visit to a Small Planet *(1957), which was made into a movie. Vidal has published collections of his writings in* The Essential Gore Vidal *(1999),* Gore Vidal, Sexually Speaking *(1999), and* The Last Empire *(2001). His latest work is* Imperial America *(2004).* Conversations with Gore Vidal, *a series of interviews, was published in 2005. The essay "Drugs" originally appeared in 1970 as an editorial in the* New York Times *and was later included in his book* Homage to Daniel Shays: Collected Essays 1952–1972 *(1972).*

It is possible to stop most drug addiction in the United States within a very short time. Simply make all drugs available and sell them at cost. Label each drug with a precise description of what effect—good and bad—the drug will have on the taker. This will require heroic honesty. Don't say that marijuana is addictive or dangerous when it is neither, as millions of people know—unlike "speed," which kills most unpleasantly, or heroin, which is addictive and difficult to kick.

For the record, I have tried—once—almost every drug and liked none, disproving the popular Fu Manchu theory that a single whiff of opium will enslave the mind. Nevertheless many drugs are bad for certain people to take and they should be told why in a sensible way.

Along with exhortation and warning, it might be good for our citizens to recall (or learn for the first time) that the United States was the creation of men who believed that each man has the right to do what he wants with his own life as long as he does not interfere with his neighbor's pursuit of happiness. (That his neighbor's idea of happiness is persecuting others does confuse matters a bit.)

This is a startling notion to the current generation of Americans. They reflect a system of public education which has made the Bill of Rights, literally, unacceptable to a majority of high school graduates (see the annual Purdue reports) who now form the "silent majority"—a phrase which that underestimated wit Richard Nixon took from Homer, who used it to describe the dead.

Now one can hear the warning rumble begin: If everyone is allowed to take drugs everyone will and the GNP will decrease, the Commies will stop us from making everyone free, and we shall end up a race of zombies, passively murmuring "groovy" to one another. Alarming thought. Yet it seems most unlikely that any reasonably sane person will become a drug addict if he knows in advance what addiction is going to be like.   5

Is everyone reasonably sane? No. Some people will always become drug addicts just as some people will always become alcoholics, and it is just too bad. Every man, however, has the power (and should have the legal right) to kill himself if he chooses. But since most men don't, they won't be mainliners either. Nevertheless, forbidding young people things they like or think they might enjoy only makes them want those things all the more. This psychological insight is, for some mysterious reason, perennially denied our governors.

It is a lucky thing for the American moralist that our country has always existed in a kind of time-vacuum: We have no public memory of anything that happened before last Tuesday. No one in Washington today recalls what happened during the years alcohol was forbidden to the people by a Congress that thought it had a divine mission to stamp out Demon Rum— launching, in the process, the greatest crime wave in the country's history, causing thousands of deaths from bad alcohol, and creating a general (and persisting) contempt among the citizenry for the laws of the United States.

The same thing is happening today. But the government has learned nothing from past attempts at prohibition, not to mention repression.

Last year when the supply of Mexican marijuana was slightly curtailed by the Feds, the pushers got the kids hooked on heroin and deaths increased dramatically, particularly in New York. Whose fault? Evil men like the Mafiosi? Permissive Dr. Spock? Wild-eyed Dr. Leary?[1] No.

---

[1] **Dr. Leary:** Timothy Leary (1926–1996) was a lecturer in psychology at Harvard and a noted proponent of psychedelic drugs who urged young Americans in the late 1960s to "tune in, turn on, drop out." —EDS.

The government of the United States was responsible for those   10
deaths. The bureaucratic machine has a vested interest in playing cops
and robbers. Both the Bureau of Narcotics and the Mafia want strong
laws against the sale and use of drugs because if drugs are sold at cost
there would be no money in it for anyone.

If there was no money in it for the Mafia, there would be no friendly
playground pushers, and addicts would not commit crimes to pay for the
next fix. Finally, if there was no money in it, the Bureau of Narcotics would
wither away, something they are not about to do without a struggle.

Will anything sensible be done? Of course not. The American people
are as devoted to the idea of sin and its punishment as they are to making
money — and fighting drugs is nearly as big a business as pushing them.
Since the combination of sin and money is irresistible (particularly to the
professional politician), the situation will only grow worse.

The Reader's Presence

1. Writing in 1970, Vidal admits to having tried "almost every
   drug." What might the impact of such an admission by a public
   figure have been at that time? Would the impact be the same
   today? What sort of audience might Vidal's piece be directed to?
   Does his admission seem casual or calculated? Does it strengthen
   or weaken his argument? Why?

2. In paragraph 5, Vidal constructs a hypothetical scenario of what
   would happen if drugs were not illegal. Does he endorse or mock
   this scenario? Whose opinion does he seem to be representing? What
   sorts of words does he use to describe a drug-addicted world? Does
   his use of humor enhance or undermine his argument?

3. Vidal asserts that the U.S. government profits from drug sales and
   prosecution, and he links the government to organized crime. He
   argues, finally, that drugs will continue to be a problem in this society as long as Americans are "devoted" to making money: For
   all their dangers, drugs are big business. How does Vidal support
   these claims? What is his view of the American people? How does
   it compare to Martha Nussbaum's portrait of American compassion in "Can Patriotism Be Compassionate?" (page 768)? Cite
   specific examples from each text.

John Edgar Wideman

The Night I Was Nobody

John Edgar Wideman was born in 1941 in Washington, D.C., and grew up in Homewood, a Pittsburgh ghetto. Much of his fiction is set in Homewood or neighborhoods like it, and it explores issues facing the black urban poor in America. He has published more than a dozen books, including Brothers and Keepers *(1984), a memoir that focuses on his brother Robby; the novel* Philadelphia Fire *(1990);* The Stories of John Edgar Wideman *(1992);* Fatheralong: A Meditation on Fathers and Sons, Race and Society *(1994); and* Hoop Roots *(2001), a memoir about his obsession with basketball. Wideman's most recent work includes* The Island: Martinique *(2003) and* God's Gym *(2005), his first collection of short stories in more than a decade. Wideman has been honored with numerous awards and prizes, including the Lannan Literary Fellowship for Fiction (1991) and a MacArthur Fellowship (1993–98). Wideman was a Rhodes scholar at Oxford University (1963) and a Kent fellow at the University of Iowa Writing Workshop (1966). Currently he is affiliated with the University of Massachusetts at Amherst and lectures at colleges all over the United States. He is also an athlete and a member of the Philadelphia Big Five Basketball Hall of Fame. "The Night I Was Nobody" appeared in* Speak My Name: Black Men on Masculinity and the American Dream *(1995).*

When Wideman lived in Cheyenne and taught at the University of Wyoming (1975–1986), an interviewer inquired whether he felt a distance between his life and his fiction. "My particular imagination has always worked well in a kind of exile," he responded. "It fits the insider-outsider view I've always had. It helps to write away from the center of action."

On July 4th, the fireworks day, the day for picnics and patriotic speeches, I was in Clovis, New Mexico, to watch my daughter, Jamila, and her team, the Central Massachusetts Cougars, compete in the Junior Olympics Basketball national tourney. During our ten-day visit to Clovis the weather had been bizarre. Hailstones as large as golf balls. Torrents of rain flooding streets hubcap deep. Running through the pelting rain from their van to a gym, Jamila and several teammates cramming through a doorway had looked back just in time to see a funnel cloud touch down a few blocks away. Continuous sheet lightning had shattered the horizon, crackling for hours night and day. Spectacular, off-the-charts weather flexing its muscles, reminding people what little control they had over their lives.

Hail rat-tat-tatting against our windshield our first day in town wasn't exactly a warm welcome, but things got better fast. Clovis people were glad to see us and the mini-spike we triggered in the local economy. Hospitable, generous, our hosts lavished upon us the same hands-on affection and attention to detail that had transformed an unpromising place in the middle of nowhere into a very livable community.

On top of all that, the Cougars were kicking butt, so the night of July 3rd I wanted to celebrate with a frozen margarita. I couldn't pry anybody else away from "Bubba's," the movable feast of beer, chips, and chatter the adults traveling with the Cougars improvised nightly in the King's Inn Motel parking lot, so I drove off alone to find one perfect margarita.

Inside the door of Kelley's Bar and Lounge I was flagged by a guy collecting a cover charge and told I couldn't enter wearing my Malcolm X hat. I asked why; the guy hesitated, conferred for a moment with his partner, then declared that Malcolm X hats were against the dress code. For a split second I thought it might be that *no* caps were allowed in Kelley's. But the door crew and two or three others hanging around the entranceway all wore the billed caps ubiquitous in New Mexico, duplicates of mine, except theirs sported the logos of feed stores and truck stops instead of a silver X.

What careened through my mind in the next couple of minutes is essentially unsayable but included scenes from my own half-century of life as a black man, clips from five hundred years of black/white meetings on slave ships, auction blocks, plantations, basketball courts, in the Supreme Court's marble halls, in beds, back alleys and back rooms, kisses and lynch ropes and contracts for millions of dollars so a black face will grace a cereal box. To tease away my anger I tried joking with folks in other places. Hey, Spike Lee. That hat you gave me on the set of the Malcolm movie in Cairo ain't legal in Clovis.

But nothing about these white guys barring my way was really funny. Part of me wanted to get down and dirty. Curse the suckers. Were they prepared to do battle to keep me and my cap out? Another voice said, Be cool. Don't sully your hands. Walk away and call the cops or a lawyer. Forget these chumps. Sue the owner. Or should I win hearts and minds? Look, fellas, I understand why the X on my cap might offend or scare you. You probably don't know much about Malcolm. The incredible metamorphoses of his thinking, his soul. By the time he was assassinated he wasn't a racist, didn't advocate violence. He was trying to make sense of America's impossible history, free himself, free us from the crippling legacy of race hate and oppression.

While all the above occupied my mind, my body, on its own, had assumed a gunfighter's vigilance, hands ready at sides, head cocked, weight poised, eyes tight and hard on the doorkeeper yet alert to anything stirring on the periphery. Many other eyes, all in white faces, were checking out the entranceway, recognizing the ingredients of a racial incident. Hadn't they witnessed Los Angeles going berserk on their TV screens just a couple months ago? That truck driver beaten nearly to death in the street, those packs of black hoodlums burning and looting? Invisible lines were being drawn in the air, in the sand, invisible chips bristled on shoulders.

The weather again. Our American racial weather, turbulent, unchanging in its changeability, its power to rock us and stun us and smack us from our routines and tear us apart as if none of our cities, our pieties, our promises, our dreams, ever stood a chance of holding on. The racial weather. Outside us, then suddenly, unforgettably, unforgivingly inside, reminding us of what we've only pretended to have forgotten. Our limits, our flaws. The lies and compromises we practice to avoid dealing honestly with the contradictions of race. How dependent we are on luck to survive—*when* we survive—the racial weather.

One minute you're a person, the next moment somebody starts treating you as if you're not. Often it happens just that way, just that suddenly. Particularly if you are a black man in America. Race and racism are a force larger than individuals, more powerful than law or education or government or the church, a force able to wipe these institutions away in the charged moments, minuscule or mountainous, when black and white come face to face. In Watts in 1965,[1] or a few less-than-glorious minutes in Clovis, New Mexico, on the eve of the day that commemorates our country's freedom, our inalienable right as a nation, as citizens, to life, liberty, equality, the pursuit of happiness, those precepts and principles that still look good on paper but are often as worthless as a sheet of newspaper to protect you in a storm if you're a black man at the wrong time in the wrong place.

None of this is news, is it? Not July 3rd in Clovis, when a tiny misfire   10 occurred, or yesterday in your town or tomorrow in mine? But haven't we made progress? Aren't things much better than they used to be? Hasn't enough been done?

We ask the wrong questions when we look around the see a handful of fabulously wealthy black people, a few others entering the middle classes. Far more striking than the positive changes are the abiding patterns and assumptions that have not changed. Not all black people are mired in social pathology, but the bottom rung of the ladder of opportunity (and the space *beneath* the bottom rung) is still defined by the color of the people trapped there—and many *are* still trapped there, no doubt about it, because their status was inherited, determined generation after generation by blood, by color. Once, all black people were legally excluded from full participation in the mainstream. Then fewer. Now only some. But the mechanisms of disenfranchisement that originally separated African Americans from other Americans persist, if not legally, then in the apartheid mind-set, convictions and practices of the majority. The seeds sleep but don't die. Ten who suffer from exclusion today can become ten thousand tomorrow. Racial weather can change that quickly.

How would the bouncer have responded if I'd calmly declared, "This is a free country, I can wear any hat I choose"? Would he thank me for standing up for our shared birthright? Or would he have to admit, if pushed, that American rights belong only to *some* Americans, white Americans?

We didn't get that far in our conversation. We usually don't. The girls' faces pulled me from the edge—girls of all colors, sizes, shapes, gritty kids bonding through hard clean competition. Weren't these guys

---

[1]*Watts in 1965:* In August of 1965, a police traffic stop provoked six days of rioting in which thirty-four people died in the Watts neighborhood of Los Angeles.—Eds.

who didn't like my X cap kids too? Who did they think I was? What did
they think they were protecting? I backed out, backed down, climbed in
my car and drove away from Kelley's. After all, I didn't want Kelley's. I
wanted a frozen margarita and a mellow celebration. So I bought plenty
of ice and the ingredients for a margarita and rejoined the festivities at
Bubba's. Everybody volunteered to go back with me to Kelley's, but I didn't
want to spoil the victory party, taint our daughters' accomplishments,
erase the high marks Clovis had earned hosting us.

But I haven't forgotten what happened in Kelley's. I write about it
now because this is my country, the country where my sons and daughter
are growing up, and your daughters and sons, and the crisis, the affliction, the same ole, same ole waste of life continues across the land, the
nightmarish weather of racism, starbursts of misery in the dark.

The statistics of inequality don't demonstrate a "black crisis"—that   15
perspective confuses cause and victim, solutions and responsibility. When
the rain falls, it falls on us all. The bad news about black men—that they die
sooner and more violently than white men, are more ravaged by unemploy-
ment and lack of opportunity, are more exposed to drugs, disease, broken
families, and police brutality, more likely to go to jail than college, more
cheated by the inertia and callousness of a government that represents and
protects the most needy the least—this is not a "black problem," but a *national* shame affecting us all. Wrenching ourselves free from the long nightmare of racism will require collective determination, countless individual
acts of will, gutsy, informed, unselfish. To imagine the terrible cost of not
healing ourselves, we must first imagine how good it would feel to be healed.

The Reader's Presence

1. The incident Wideman recounts in this essay takes place on the eve
   of July Fourth, "the fireworks day, the day for picnics and patriotic
   speeches" (paragraph 1). Look closely at the modifiers he chooses
   to describe the Fourth of July. Given the events that took place in
   Clovis that night, comment on the significance of each phrase.
   How else might he have described this holiday, and why might he
   have intentionally discarded those descriptions? Identify—and comment on the effectiveness of—other moments in the essay when
   Wideman refers to the Fourth of July in related themes.

2. An extended metaphor of weather runs through this essay. Trace the
   analogy through the comparisons and contrasts Wideman makes or
   implies. In what specific ways, for instance, are the townsfolk described in paragraph 2 like or unlike the weather? How does this
   change as the essay progresses? How does racism resemble and differ from the weather? Given this guiding metaphor, does Wideman
   leave his reader with much hope for an end to racism?

3. Wideman's Malcolm X hat is the object that sparks the inciting incident of the essay. The hat, Wideman tells his reader, was a gift from director Spike Lee during the making of the film *Malcolm X* in 1992. Wideman's allusion to the famous African American leader, Malcolm X, is not trivial. What does Malcolm X's "presence" in the essay do for Wideman's argument? Compare Wideman's essay to the excerpt from Malcolm X's autobiography included in this anthology ("Homeboy," page 194). How do these authors express their emotions about racism? How does each writer employ vernacular language (everyday speech), and to what effects? How does each of them justify the recording of their experiences for others to read? Compare how the two discuss ideas of rage, violence, shame, and hope.

Terry Tempest Williams
The Clan of One-Breasted Women

The environmentalist and writer Terry Tempest Williams (b. 1953) lives in Utah, where she is active in the movement to expand federally protected wilderness areas. She has been a professor of English at the University of Utah and naturalist-in-residence at the Utah Museum of Natural History. In Refuge: An Unnatural History of Family and Place *(1991), she documents the epidemic of cancer caused by nuclear weapons tested in Utah during the 1950s and meditates upon the meaning of this tragedy for her family. "The Clan of One-Breasted Women" appears in* Refuge. *Her first book,* Pieces of a White Shell: A Journey to Navajoland *(1984), received a Southwest Book Award. Other books include* Coyote's Canyon *(1989),* An Unspoken Hunger: Stories from the Field *(1994),* Desert Quartet *(1995),* Leap *(2000), and* Red: Passion and Patience in the Desert *(2001). She also coedited* Testimony: Writers of the West Speak on Behalf of Utah Wilderness *(1996),* New Genesis: Mormons Writing on the Environment *(1999), and* The Open Space of Democracy *(2005).*

Reflecting upon her motivation for writing about her personal experience with cancer, Williams notes, "Perhaps I am telling this story in an attempt to heal myself, to confront what I do not know, to create a path for myself with the idea that 'memory is the only way home.' "

I belong to a Clan of One-Breasted Women. My mother, my grandmothers, and six aunts have all had mastectomies. Seven are dead.

The two who survive have just completed rounds of chemotherapy and radiation.

I've had my own problems: two biopsies for breast cancer and a small tumor between my ribs diagnosed as a "borderline malignancy."

This is my family history.

Most statistics tell us that breast cancer is genetic, hereditary, with rising percentages attached to fatty diets, childlessness, or becoming pregnant after thirty. What they don't say is that living in Utah may be the greatest hazard of all.

We are a Mormon family with roots in Utah since 1847. The "word   5
of wisdom" in my family aligned us with good foods—no coffee, no tea, tobacco, or alcohol. For the most part, our women were finished having their babies by the time they were thirty. And only one faced breast cancer prior to 1960. Traditionally, as a group of people, Mormons have a low rate of cancer.

Is our family a cultural anomaly? The truth is, we didn't think about it. Those who did, usually the men, simply said, "bad genes." The women's attitude was stoic. Cancer was part of life. On February 16, 1971, the eve of my mother's surgery, I accidentally picked up the telephone and overheard her ask my grandmother what she could expect.

"Diane, it is one of the most spiritual experiences you will ever encounter."

I quietly put down the receiver.

Two days later, my father took my brothers and me to the hospital to visit her. She met us in the lobby in a wheelchair. No bandages were visible. I'll never forget her radiance, the way she held herself in a purple velvet robe, and how she gathered us around her.

"Children, I am fine. I want you to know I felt the arms of God   10
around me."

We believed her. My father cried. Our mother, his wife, was thirty-eight years old.

A little over a year after Mother's death, Dad and I were having dinner together. He had just returned from St. George, where the Tempest Company was completing the gas lines that would service southern Utah. He spoke of his love for the country, the sandstoned landscape, bareboned and beautiful. He had just finished hiking the Kolob trail in Zion National Park. We got caught up in reminiscing, recalling with fondness our walk up Angel's Landing on his fiftieth birthday and the years our family had vacationed there.

Over dessert, I shared a recurring dream of mine. I told my father that for years, as long as I could remember, I saw this flash of light in the night in the desert—that this image had so permeated my being that I could not venture south without seeing it again, on the horizon, illuminating buttes and mesas.

"You did see it," he said.

"Saw what?"   15

"The bomb. The cloud. We were driving home from Riverside, California. You were sitting on Diane's lap. She was pregnant. In fact, I remember the day, September 7, 1957. We had just gotten out of the Service. We were driving north, past Las Vegas. It was an hour or so before dawn, when this explosion went off. We not only heard it, but felt it. I thought the oil tanker in front of us had blown up. We pulled over and suddenly, rising from the desert floor, we saw it, clearly, this golden-stemmed cloud, the mushroom. The sky seemed to vibrate with an eerie pink glow. Within a few minutes, a light ash was raining on the car."

I stared at my father.

"I thought you knew that," he said. "It was a common occurrence in the fifties."

It was at this moment that I realized the deceit I had been living under. Children growing up in the American Southwest, drinking contaminated milk from contaminated cows, even from the contaminated breasts of their mothers, my mother—members, years later, of the Clan of One-Breasted Women.

It is a well-known story in the Desert West, "The Day We Bombed 20 Utah," or more accurately, the years we bombed Utah: above ground atomic testing in Nevada took place from January 27, 1951 through July 11, 1962. Not only were the winds blowing north covering "low-use segments of the population" with fallout and leaving sheep dead in their tracks but the climate was right. The United States of the 1950s was red, white, and blue. The Korean War was raging. McCarthyism[1] was rampant. Ike[2] was it, and the cold war was hot. If you were against nuclear testing, you were for a communist regime.

Much has been written about this "American nuclear tragedy." Public health was secondary to national security. The Atomic Energy Commissioner, Thomas Murray, said, "Gentlemen, we must not let anything interfere with this series of tests, nothing."

Again and again, the American public was told by its government, in spite of burns, blisters, and nausea, "It has been found that the tests may be conducted with adequate assurance of safety under conditions prevailing at the bombing reservations." Assuaging public fears was simply a matter of public relations. "Your best action," an Atomic Energy Commission booklet read, "is not to be worried about fallout." A news release typical of the times stated, "We find no basis for concluding that harm to any individual has resulted from radioactive fallout."

On August 30, 1979, during Jimmy Carter's presidency, a suit was filed, *Irene Allen v. The United States of America.* Mrs. Allen's case was the first on an alphabetical list of twenty-four test cases, representative of

[1]*McCarthyism:* The practice of publicizing accusations of political disloyalty or subversion without sufficient regard to evidence. Associated with Senator Joseph McCarthy (1908–1957).—EDs.

[2]*Ike:* President Dwight D. Eisenhower (1890–1969) was known as "Ike."—EDs.

nearly twelve hundred plaintiffs seeking compensation from the United States government for cancers caused by nuclear testing in Nevada.

Irene Allen lived in Hurricane, Utah. She was the mother of five children and had been widowed twice. Her first husband, with their two oldest boys, had watched the tests from the roof of the local high school. He died of leukemia in 1956. Her second husband died of pancreatic cancer in 1978.

In a town meeting conducted by Utah Senator Orrin Hatch, shortly   25
before the suit was filed, Mrs. Allen said, "I am not blaming the government, I want you to know that, Senator Hatch. But I thought if my testimony could help in any way so this wouldn't happen again to any of the generations coming up after us . . . I am happy to be here this day to bear testimony of this."

God-fearing people. This is just one story in an anthology of thousands.

On May 10, 1984, Judge Bruce S. Jenkins handed down his opinion. Ten of the plaintiffs were awarded damages. It was the first time a federal court had determined that nuclear tests had been the cause of cancers. For the remaining fourteen test cases, the proof of causation was not sufficient. In spite of the split decision, it was considered a landmark ruling. It was not to remain so for long.

In April 1987, the Tenth Circuit Court of Appeals overturned Judge Jenkins's ruling on the ground that the United States was protected from suit by the legal doctrine of sovereign immunity, a centuries-old idea from England in the days of absolute monarchs.

In January 1988, the Supreme Court refused to review the Appeals Court decision. To our court system it does not matter whether the United States government was irresponsible, whether it lied to its citizens, or even that citizens died from the fallout of nuclear testing. What matters is that our government is immune: "The King can do no wrong."

In Mormon culture, authority is respected, obedience is revered, and   30
independent thinking is not. I was taught as a young girl not to "make waves" or "rock the boat."

"Just let it go," Mother would say. "You know how you feel, that's what counts."

For many years, I have done just that—listened, observed, and quietly formed my own opinions, in a culture that rarely asks questions because it has all the answers. But one by one, I have watched the women in my family die common, heroic deaths. We sat in waiting rooms hoping for good news, but always receiving the bad. I cared for them, bathed their scarred bodies, and kept their secrets. I watched beautiful women become bald as Cytoxan, cisplatin, and Adriamycin were injected into their veins. I held their foreheads as they vomited green-black bile, and I shot them with morphine when the pain became inhuman. In the end, I witnessed their last peaceful breaths, becoming a midwife to the rebirth of their souls.

The price of obedience has become too high.

The fear and inability to question authority that ultimately killed rural communities in Utah during atmospheric testing of atomic weapons is the same fear I saw in my mother's body. Sheep. Dead sheep. The evidence is buried.

I cannot prove that my mother, Diane Dixon Tempest, or my grandmothers, Lettie Romney Dixon and Kathryn Blackett Tempest, along with my aunts developed cancer from nuclear fallout in Utah. But I can't prove they didn't. 35

My father's memory was correct. The September blast we drove through in 1957 was part of Operation Plumbbob, one of the most intensive series of bomb tests to be initiated. The flash of light in the night in the desert, which I had always thought was a dream, developed into a family nightmare. It took fourteen years, from 1957 to 1971, for cancer to manifest in my mother—the same time, Howard L. Andrews, an authority in radioactive fallout at the National Institutes of Health, says radiation cancer requires to become evident. The more I learn about what it means to be a "downwinder," the more questions I drown in.

What I do know, however, is that as a Mormon woman of the fifth generation of Latter-day Saints, I must question everything, even if it means losing my faith, even if it means becoming a member of a border tribe among my own people. Tolerating blind obedience in the name of patriotism or religion ultimately takes our lives.

When the Atomic Energy Commission described the country north of the Nevada Test Site as "virtually uninhabited desert terrain," my family and the birds at Great Salt Lake were some of the "virtual uninhabitants."

One night, I dreamed women from all over the world circled a blazing fire in the desert. They spoke of change, how they hold the moon in their bellies and wax and wane with its phases. They mocked the presumption of even-tempered beings and made promises that they would never fear the witch inside themselves. The women danced wildly as sparks broke away from the flames and entered the night sky as stars.

And they sang a song given to them by Shoshone grandmothers: 40

Ah ne nah, nah	Consider the rabbits
nin nah nah—	How gently they walk on the earth—
ah ne nah, nah	Consider the rabbits
nin nah nah—	How gently they walk on the earth—
Nyaga mutzi	We remember them
oh ne nay—	We can walk gently also—
Nyaga mutzi	We remember them
oh ne nay	We can walk gently also

The women danced and drummed and sang for weeks, preparing themselves for what was to come. They would reclaim the desert for the sake of their children, for the sake of the land.

A few miles downwind from the fire circle, bombs were being tested. Rabbits felt the tremors. Their soft leather pads on paws and feet recognized the shaking sands, while the roots of mesquite and sage were smoldering. Rocks were hot from the inside out and dust devils hummed unnaturally. And each time there was another nuclear test, ravens watched the desert heave. Stretch marks appeared. The land was losing its muscle.

The women couldn't bear it any longer. They were mothers. They had suffered labor pains but always under the promise of birth. The red hot pains beneath the desert promised death only, as each bomb became a stillborn. A contract had been made and broken between human beings and the land. A new contract was being drawn by the women, who understood the fate of the earth as their own.

Under the cover of darkness, ten women slipped under a barbed-wire fence and entered the contaminated country. They were trespassing. They walked toward the town of Mercury, in moonlight, taking their cues from coyote, kit fox, antelope squirrel, and quail. They moved quietly and deliberately through the maze of Joshua trees. When a hint of daylight appeared they rested, drinking tea and sharing their rations of food. The women closed their eyes. The time had come to protest with the heart, that to deny one's genealogy with the earth was to commit treason against one's soul.

At dawn, the women draped themselves in mylar, wrapping long streamers of silver plastic around their arms to blow in the breeze. They wore clear masks, that became the faces of humanity. And when they arrived at the edge of Mercury, they carried all the butterflies of a summer day in their wombs. They paused to allow their courage to settle.

The town that forbids pregnant women and children to enter because of radiation risks was asleep. The women moved through the streets as winged messengers, twirling around each other in slow motion, peeking inside homes and watching the easy sleep of men and women. They were astonished by such stillness and periodically would utter a shrill note or low cry just to verify life. 45

The residents finally awoke to these strange apparitions. Some simply stared. Others called authorities, and in time, the women were apprehended by wary soldiers dressed in desert fatigues. They were taken to a white, square building on the edge of Mercury. When asked who they were and why they were there, the women replied, "We are mothers and we have come to reclaim the desert for our children."

The soldiers arrested them. As the ten women were blindfolded and handcuffed, they began singing:

> *You can't forbid us everything*
> *You can't forbid us to think —*
> *You can't forbid our tears to flow*
> *And you can't stop the songs that we sing.*

The women continued to sing louder and louder, until they heard the voices of their sisters moving across the mesa:

Ah ne nah, nah
nin nah nah —
Ah ne nah, nah
nin nah nah —
Nyaga mutzi
oh ne nay —
Nyaga mutzi
oh ne nay —

"Call for reinforcements," one soldier said.

"We have," interrupted one woman, "we have — and you have no idea of our numbers."

I crossed the line at the Nevada Test Site and was arrested with nine other Utahns for trespassing on military lands. They are still conducting nuclear tests in the desert. Ours was an act of civil disobedience. But as I walked toward the town of Mercury, it was more than a gesture of peace. It was a gesture on behalf of the Clan of One-Breasted Women.

As one officer cinched the handcuffs around my wrists, another   50
frisked my body. She found a pen and a pad of paper tucked inside my left boot.

"And these?" she asked sternly.

"Weapons," I replied.

Our eyes met. I smiled. She pulled the leg of my trousers back over my boot.

"Step forward, please," she said as she took my arm.

We were booked under an afternoon sun and bused to Tonopah,   55
Nevada. It was a two-hour ride. This was familiar country. The Joshua trees standing their ground had been named by my ancestors, who believed they looked like prophets pointing west to the Promised Land. These were the same trees that bloomed each spring, flowers appearing like white flames in the Mojave. And I recalled a full moon in May, when Mother and I had walked among them, flushing out mourning doves and owls.

The bus stopped short of town. We were released.

The officials thought it was a cruel joke to leave us stranded in the desert with no way to get home. What they didn't realize was that we were home, soul-centered and strong, women who recognized the sweet smell of sage as fuel for our spirits.

The Reader's Presence

1. Paragraph 3 reads, "This is my family history." Which parts of Williams's essay are particular to her family, and what do they

add to the larger social history of her time and place? How does her family's religion, Mormonism, play into the family history? What does she gain by drawing on the earlier spiritual tradition of the Shoshones, which is rooted in the same geographical area? What other "families," besides her nuclear and extended family, might Williams belong to?

2. Examine carefully—and discuss in detail—the roles of dream and reality in this essay. Characterize the power of each. Consider also the relationship between dream and nightmare. How do you read the "dream" Williams recounts in paragraph 39 and following? Characterize the relationship between that dream and the "civil disobedience" she recounts in the following section (paragraph 49 and following).

3. Consider the role of language in Williams's essay. Do you see instances of what might be termed "Orwellian doublespeak"? If so, where? What effects is Williams trying to achieve? Does she successfully use pen and paper as "weapons," as she says is her intention? Why or why not? Read George Orwell's "Politics and the English Language" (page 533). Would you expect Orwell to approve or disapprove of the political purposes to which Williams puts language? Why?

Howard Zinn

Stories Hollywood Never Tells

Howard Zinn (b. 1922), professor emeritus of political science at Boston University, is known both for his active involvement in the civil rights and peace movements and for his scholarship. He has published scores of books that reflect the issues of their times yet remain in print, demonstrating their continuing relevance. A sampling includes The Southern Mystique *(1964);* Vietnam: The Logic of Withdrawal *(1967);* Disobedience and Democracy: Nine Fallacies on Law and Order *(1968);* The Politics of History *(1970);* A People's History of the United States: 1492 to the Present *(1980), which has sold more than a million copies;* Declarations of Independence *(1990);* The Zinn Reader: Writings on Disobedience and Democracy *(1997);* Howard Zinn on History *(2000);* Three Strikes: Stories of American Labor *(2001); and* Artists in Times of War *(2003). His most recent book,* Voices of a People's History of the United States *(2004), is a companion to* A People's History. *The essay "Stories Hollywood Never Tells," adapted from* Artists in Times of War, *was published in the* Sun *in 2004.*

Zinn has also written plays, a musical, and an autobiography, You Can't Be Neutral on a Moving Train *(1994). Zinn continues to write, travel, and lecture, and he is a frequent contributor to such magazines as the* Nation *and the* Progressive.

Zinn has argued that perseverence in the face of opposition is essential: "I am totally confident not that the world will get better, but that we should not give up the game before all the cards have been played. The metaphor is deliberate; life is a gamble. Not to play is to foreclose any chance of winning. To play, to act, is to create at least a possibility of changing the world."

However hateful they may be sometimes, I have always loved the movies. When I began reading and studying history, I kept coming across incidents and events that led me to think, *Wow, what a movie this would make.* I would look to see if a movie had been made about it, but I'd never find one. It took me a while to realize that Hollywood isn't going to make movies like the ones I imagined. Hollywood isn't going to make movies that are class-conscious, or antiwar, or conscious of the need for racial equality or gender equality.

I wondered about this. It seemed to me that the people in Hollywood didn't all get together in a room and decide, "We're going to do just this kind of film and not the other kind of film." Yet it's not just an oversight or an accident, either. Leon Trotsky once used an expression to describe events that are not accidents, and are not planned deliberately, but are something in between. He called this the "natural selection of accidents," in which, if there's a certain structure to a situation, then these "accidents" will inevitably happen, whether anyone plans them or not. It seems that the structure of Hollywood is such that it will not produce the kinds of films that I imagined. It's a structure where money and profit are absolutely the first consideration: before art, before aesthetics, before human values.

When you consider the films about war that have come out of Hollywood—and there have been hundreds and hundreds, maybe even thousands—they almost always glorify military heroism. We need to think about telling the story of war from a different perspective.

Let's take one of our most popular wars to begin with: the Revolutionary War. How can you speak against the Revolutionary War, right? But to tell the story of the American Revolution, not from the standpoint of the schoolbooks, but from the standpoint of war as a complex phenomenon intertwined with moral issues, we must acknowledge not just that Americans were oppressed by the English, but that some Americans were oppressed by other Americans. For instance, American Indians did not rush to celebrate the victory of the colonists over England, because for them it meant that the line that the British had drawn to limit westward expansion in the Proclamation of 1763 would now be obliterated. The colonists would be free to move west into Indian lands.

John Adams, one of the Founding Fathers and a revolutionary leader,   5
estimated that one-third of the colonists supported the American Revolution, one-third were opposed, and one-third were neutral. It would be interesting to tell the story of the American Revolution from the viewpoint of an ordinary workingman who hears the Declaration of Independence read to him from a balcony in Boston, promising freedom and equality and so on, and immediately is told that rich men can get out of service by paying several hundred dollars. This man then joins the army, despite his misgivings, despite his own feelings of being oppressed—not just by the British, but by the leaders of the colonial world—because he is promised some land. But as the war progresses and he sees the mutilations and the killing, he becomes increasingly disaffected. There's no place in society where class divisions are more clear-cut than in the military, and he sees that the officers are living in splendor while the ordinary enlisted men don't have any clothes or shoes, aren't being paid, and are being fed slop. So he joins the mutineers.

In the Revolutionary War, there were two mutinies against Washington's army: the mutiny of the Pennsylvania Line, and the mutiny of the New Jersey Line. Let's say our workingman joins the Pennsylvania Line, and they march on the Continental Congress, but eventually are surrounded by Washington's army, and several of their former comrades are forced to shoot several of the mutineers. Then this soldier, embittered by what he's seen, gets out of the army and gets some land in western Massachusetts. After the war is over, he becomes part of Shays' Rebellion, in which a group of small farmers rebel against the rich men who control the legislature in Boston and who are imposing heavy taxes on them, taking away their land and farms. The farmers, many of them Revolutionary War veterans, surround the courthouses and refuse to let the auctioneer go in to auction off their farms. The militia is called out to suppress them, and the militia also goes over to their side. Finally an army is raised by the moneyed class in Boston to suppress Shays' Rebellion.

I have never seen Hollywood tell this kind of story. If you know of a film that has been made about it, I wish you'd tell me so that we could have a celebration of that rare event.

Wars are more complicated than the simple good-versus-evil scenario presented to us in our history books and our culture. Wars are not simply conflicts of one people against another; wars always involve class differences within each side, and victory is very often not shared by everybody, but only among a few. The people who fight the wars are not the people who benefit from the wars.

I think somebody should make a new movie about the Mexican War. I haven't seen one that tells how the Mexican War started, or how the president of the United States deceived the American people. I know it's surprising to hear that a president would willfully deceive the people of the United States, but this was one of those rare cases. President James Polk told Americans that Mexican troops had fired at our troops on U.S. soil. Really the fighting broke out on disputed soil that both Mexico and the U.S. had claimed. The war had been planned in advance by the Polk administration, because it coveted this beautiful territory of the Southwest.

It would be interesting to tell that story from the viewpoint of an ordinary soldier, who sees the mayhem and the bloodshed as the army moves into Mexico and destroys town after town. More and more U.S. soldiers grow disaffected from the war, and as they make their final march toward Mexico City, General Scott wakes up one morning to discover that half his army has deserted. 10

It would be interesting, too, to tell the story from the point of view of one of the Massachusetts volunteers who comes back at the end of the war and is invited to a victory celebration. When the commander of the Massachusetts volunteers gets up to speak, he is booed off the platform by the surviving half of his men, who resent what happened to their comrades in the war and who wonder what they were fighting for. I should tell you: this really happened.

The film could also include a scene after the war in which the U.S. Army is moving to suppress a rebellion in Santa Fe, because mostly Mexicans still live there. The army marches through the streets of Santa Fe, and all the townspeople go into their houses and close the shutters. The army is met by total silence, an expression of how the population feels about this great American victory.

Another little story about the Mexican War is the tale of the deserters. Many of those who volunteered to fight in the Mexican War did so for the same reason that people volunteer for the military today: they were desperately poor and hoped that their fortunes would improve as a result of enlisting. During the Mexican War, some of these volunteers were recent Irish immigrants. When these immigrant soldiers saw what was being done to the people of Mexico, a number of them deserted and went over to the Mexican side. They formed their own battalion, which they called St. Patrick's Battalion, or the San Patricio Battalion, and they fought for the Mexicans.

It's not easy to make the Spanish-American War look like a noble enterprise — though of course Hollywood can do anything. The war has gotten a certain amount of attention, because of the heroism of Theodore Roosevelt and his Rough Riders, but not a lot. In the history textbooks, the Spanish-American War is called "a splendid little war." It lasted three months. We fought it to free the Cubans, because we're always going to war to free somebody. We expelled the Spaniards from Cuba, but we didn't expel ourselves, and the United States in effect took over Cuba after the war. One grievance we have against Fidel Castro is that he ended U.S. control of Cuba. We're certainly not against him simply because he's a dictator. We've never had anything against dictators in general.

I remember learning in school that, as a result of the Spanish-American   15
War, we somehow took over the Philippines, but I never knew the details.
When you look into it, you'll find that the Spanish-American War lasted
three months; the Philippine War lasted for years and was a brutal,
bloody suppression of the Filipino movement for independence. In many
ways, it was a precursor of the Vietnam War, in terms of the atrocities
committed by the U.S. Army. Now, that's a story that has never been
told.

Black American soldiers in the Philippines soon began to identify more
with the Filipinos than with their fellow white Americans. While these black
soldiers were fighting to suppress the Filipinos, they also were hearing from
relatives about the lynchings and race riots in their hometowns. They
were hearing about black people being killed in large numbers — and here
they were, fighting against a nonwhite people on behalf of the United
States government. A number of black soldiers deserted and went over to
fight with the Filipinos.

In 1906, when the Philippine War was supposedly over — but really
the U.S. Army was still suppressing pockets of rebellion — there was a
massacre. That's the only way to describe it. The Moros are inhabitants
of a southern island in the Philippines. The army swooped down and an-
nihilated a Moro village of six hundred men, women, and children — all
of whom were unarmed. Every last one of them was killed. Mark Twain
wrote angrily about this. He was especially angry about the fact that President Theodore Roosevelt sent a letter of congratulations to the military
commander who had ordered this atrocity, saying it was a great military
victory. Have you ever seen a movie in which Theodore Roosevelt was
presented as a racist? As an imperialist? As a supporter of massacres?
And there he is, up on Mount Rushmore. I've had the thought: *A hammer, a chisel*. But no, it wouldn't do.

War needs to be presented on film in such a way as to encourage the
population simply to say no to war. We need a film about those heroic
Americans who protested World War I. When you look at them, you see
socialists, pacifists, and just ordinary people who saw the stupidity of entering a war that was taking the lives of ten million people in Europe.
You see Emma Goldman, the feminist and anarchist, who went to prison
for opposing the draft and the war. You see Helen Keller. Every film
about Helen Keller concentrates on the fact that she was disabled. I've
never seen a film in which Helen Keller is presented as what she was: a
radical, a socialist, an antiwar agitator. You also see Kate Richards
O'Hare, a socialist who was put in jail for opposing World War I. There
is a story from her time in prison that would make a great scene in a
movie: The prisoners are stifling for lack of air, and O'Hare takes a book
that she's been reading, reaches through the bars, and hurls the book
through a skylight to let the air in. All the prisoners applaud and cheer.

I have to acknowledge that there have been a few antiwar films made
about World War I. *All Quiet on the Western Front* is an extraordinary

film. I recently wrote an article comparing it to *Saving Private Ryan*. Despite the mayhem, *Saving Private Ryan* was essentially a glorification of war, whereas *All Quiet on the Western Front* expresses a diamond-clear antiwar sentiment.

What about the many films devoted to World War II, the "good war"? 20 When Studs Terkel did his oral history of World War II, he called it *The "Good War,"* with quotation marks around *Good War*. In that war, we fought against a terrible evil—fascism—but our own atrocities multiplied as the war went on, culminating in the bombings of Hiroshima and Nagasaki. I have not seen a Hollywood film about the bombing of Hiroshima. The closest we've come to a movie that deals with our bombing of civilian populations was the film version of Kurt Vonnegut's book *Slaughterhouse-Five*, about the bombing of Dresden, Germany, and that was a rarity.

Films about the Civil War tend to focus on the famous battles, like Gettysburg, Fredericksburg, and Bull Run. The Civil War is, again, one of our "good wars"—the slaves were freed because of it—but it is not that simple. There is the class element of who was and who was not drafted, who paid substitutes, who made huge amounts of money off the war. And then there is what happened to the Indians. In the midst of the Civil War, while the armies were fighting in the South, another part of the Union Army was out west, destroying Indian settlements and taking over Indian land. In 1864, not long after the Emancipation Proclamation, the U.S. Army was in Colorado attacking an Indian village, killing hundreds of men, women, and children at Sand Creek, in one of the worst Indian massacres in American history. This massacre occurred during the war to end slavery. In the years of the Civil War, more land was taken from the Indians than in any other comparable period in history.

There's a lot of historical work to be done, a lot of films that need to be made. There are so many class struggles in the U.S. that could be dealt with in movies. We've seen movies that deal with working-class people, but it's always some individual who rises up out of his or her situation and "makes it" in society. Stories of Americans who organize and get together to oppose the powers that hold them down have been very rare.

The American political system and the revered and celebrated Constitution of the United States do not grant any economic rights to the American people. We very often forget that the Constitution gives political rights but not economic rights. If you are not wealthy, then your political rights are limited, even though they are guaranteed on paper in the Constitution. The freedom of speech is granted there, but how much free speech you have depends on how much money and what access to resources you have. The Declaration of Independence talks about the right to life, liberty, and the pursuit of happiness. But how can you have life, liberty, and the pursuit of happiness if you don't have food, housing, and healthcare?

Working people throughout history have had to organize, struggle, go on strike, declare boycotts, and face the police and the army. They have had to do it themselves, against the opposition of government, in order to win the eight-hour workday and other slight improvements to their working conditions. A great film remains to be made about the Haymarket Affair of 1886, which was part of the struggle for the eight-hour work-day. The Haymarket Affair culminated in the execution of four anarchists who were charged with planting a bomb, though in the end nobody ever found out who really had planted it.

The great railroad strike of 1894 tied up the railway system of   25
the United States, and all the power of the army and the courts had to be brought against the striking workers. Eugene Debs, who organized the railroad workers, has never been the central figure in a movie. He was sent to prison for opposing World War I, and he made such an impression on his fellow prisoners that, when he was released, the warden let all the inmates out into the yard, and they applauded as Debs was granted his freedom.

I've met someone who is actually writing a script about the Lawrence textile strike of 1912, a magnificent episode in American history, because the striking workers won. It was a multicultural strike. A working population that spoke twelve different languages got together and defied the textile companies and the police, who were sent to the railroad station to prevent the children of the workers from leaving town. Police literally attacked the women and children at the station, because the company

Engraving depicting the 1886 Haymarket Riot

wanted to starve out the strikers, and that would be less likely to happen if their children were safe. But the strikers held out, and with the help of the Industrial Workers of the World, they finally won.

Then there's the Ludlow Massacre, which took place during the Colorado coal strike of 1913–14, one of the most bitter, bloody, dramatic strikes in American history. The workers were up against the Rockefeller interests. (It's not easy to make an unflattering film about the Rockefellers.) One of the strike's leaders was Mother Jones, an eighty-three-year-old woman who had previously organized textile workers in West Virginia and Pennsylvania. That's another story that should be told. There were kids working in the textile mills at the age of eleven and twelve. Mother Jones led these children on a march from Pennsylvania to Oyster Bay, New York, where President Theodore Roosevelt was on summer vacation. They stood there outside the resort with signs that

Immigrant women striking in Lawrence, Massachusetts, 1912

said, WE WANT TIME TO PLAY. Has there ever been a film made about that?

We've had films on Christopher Columbus,[1] but I don't know of any film that shows Columbus as what he was: a man ruled by the capitalist ethic. Columbus and the Spaniards were killing people for gold. The Catholic priest Bartolomé de Las Casas was an eyewitness. He exposed what was going on, and a remarkable debate took place before the Royal Commission of Spain in 1650. The debate was between las Casas and Sepulveda, another priest, who argued that the Indians were not human and therefore you could do anything you wanted to them.

There's also the story of the Trail of Tears—the expulsion of the Cherokees from the Southeast. Andrew Jackson, one of our national heroes, signed the order to expel them. That was ethnic cleansing on a large scale: the march across the continent, the U.S. Army driving the Indians from their homeland to a little space in Oklahoma that was then called "Indian Territory." When oil was later discovered there, the Indian population was once again evicted. Of the sixteen thousand people who marched westward, four thousand died on the march, while the U.S. Army pushed them, and the U.S. president extolled what happened.

Of course someone should finally tell the story of black people in the United States from a black person's point of view. We've had a number of films about the civil-rights movement from white points of view. *The Long Walk Home* (1991) tells the story of the Montgomery bus boycott from Sissy Spacek's point of view. *Mississippi Burning* (1988) is about the murder of three civil-rights workers in Mississippi in 1964. The FBI agents are the heroes of the film, but every person who was in Mississippi in 1964—my wife and I were both there at the time—knew that the FBI was the enemy. The FBI was watching people being beaten and not doing anything about it. The FBI was silent and absent when people needed protection against murderers. In this Hollywood film, they become heroes. We need the story of the civil-rights movement told from the viewpoint of black people.

Of course, many good movies and wonderful documentaries have been made. Michael Moore's film *Roger and Me*, which has been seen by tens of millions of people, is a remarkable success story. So the possibilities do exist to practice a kind of guerrilla warfare and make films outside of the Hollywood establishment.

If such films are made—about war, about class conflict, about the history of governmental lies, about broken treaties and official violence—if those stories reach the public, we might produce a new generation. As a teacher, I'm not interested in just reproducing class after class of graduates who will get out, become successful, and take their obedient places in the slots that society has prepared for them. What we must do—whether

[1]For more on Columbus, see page 13.—EDS.

we teach or write or make films—is educate a new generation to do this very modest thing: change the world.

The Reader's Presence

1. Explain what Zinn means by the "natural selection of accidents" preventing true depictions of war, class, and race from appearing in films. Do you agree that Hollywood's structure works against such depictions? Why or why not?

2. Reading the essay, who did you imagine Zinn's audience to be? How sympathetic to his argument would you expect them to be? What evidence can you find for your answers?

3. Zinn says, "Stories of Americans who organize and get together to oppose the powers that hold them down have been very rare" in Hollywood (paragraph 22), but he presents examples to indicate that such stories have appeared again and again throughout American history. In "Family Values" (page 671), Barbara Ehrenreich argues that too few Americans recognize the kind of progressive views espoused for generations in her family as "traditional American values." What "American values" would Zinn and Ehrenreich be likely to share? Do you see these values as traditional? as important? Why or why not?

Part V

The Voices of Fiction: Eight Short Stories

Sherman Alexie

This Is What It Means to Say Say Phoenix, Arizona

Sherman Alexie's short story "This Is What It Means to Say Phoenix, Arizona" appears in The Lone Ranger and Tonto Fistfight in Heaven *(1993). Alexie has said, "Most of my heroes are just decent people. Decency is rare and underrated. I think my writing is somehow just about decency." Victor and Thomas, two "decent people" in this story, are also characters in Alexie's first screenplay. The film,* Smoke Signals, *premiered at the 1998 Sundance Film Festival, where it won the Audience Award and the Filmmakers Trophy. Alexie describes the film as "a very basic story, a road trip/buddy movie about a lost father. . . ." The narrative structure, as he has pointed out, appears "in everything from the Bible to the* Iliad *and the* Odyssey."*

For additional information on Sherman Alexie, see page 73.

Just after Victor lost his job at the BIA,[1] he also found out that his father had died of a heart attack in Phoenix, Arizona. Victor hadn't seen his father in a few years, only talked to him on the telephone once or twice, but there still was a genetic pain, which was soon to be pain as real and immediate as a broken bone.

Victor didn't have any money. Who does have money on a reservation, except the cigarette and fireworks salespeople? His father had a savings account waiting to be claimed, but Victor needed to find a way to get to Phoenix. Victor's mother was just as poor as he was, and the rest of his family didn't have any use at all for him. So Victor called the Tribal Council.

"Listen," Victor said. "My father just died. I need some money to get to Phoenix to make arrangements."

---

[1]*BIA:* Bureau of Indian Affairs, an agency that has historically often been at odds with the tribes it was created to administer. —Eds.

"Now, Victor," the council said. "You know we're having a difficult time financially."

"But I thought the council had special funds set aside for stuff like this."   5

"Now, Victor, we do have some money available for the proper return of tribal members' bodies. But I don't think we have enough to bring your father all the way back from Phoenix."

"Well," Victor said. "It ain't going to cost all that much. He had to be cremated. Things were kind of ugly. He died of a heart attack in his trailer and nobody found him for a week. It was really hot, too. You get the picture."

"Now, Victor, we're sorry for your loss and the circumstances. But we can really only afford to give you one hundred dollars."

"That's not even enough for a plane ticket."

"Well, you might consider driving down to Phoenix."   10

"I don't have a car. Besides, I was going to drive my father's pickup back up here."

"Now, Victor," the council said. "We're sure there is somebody who could drive you to Phoenix. Or is there somebody who could lend you the rest of the money?"

"You know there ain't nobody around with that kind of money."

"Well, we're sorry, Victor, but that's the best we can do."

Victor accepted the Tribal Council's offer. What else could he do? So he signed the proper papers, picked up his check, and walked over to the Trading Post to cash it.   15

While Victor stood in line, he watched Thomas Builds-the-Fire standing near the magazine rack, talking to himself. Like he always did. Thomas was a storyteller that nobody wanted to listen to. That's like being a dentist in a town where everybody has false teeth.

Victor and Thomas Builds-the-Fire were the same age, had grown up and played in the dirt together. Ever since Victor could remember, it was Thomas who always had something to say.

Once, when they were seven years old, when Victor's father still lived with the family, Thomas closed his eyes and told Victor this story: "Your father's heart is weak. He is afraid of his own family. He is afraid of you. Late at night he sits in the dark. Watches the television until there's nothing but that white noise. Sometimes he feels like he wants to buy a motorcycle and ride away. He wants to run and hide. He doesn't want to be found."

Thomas Builds-the-Fire had known that Victor's father was going to leave, knew it before anyone. Now Victor stood in the Trading Post with a one-hundred-dollar check in his hand, wondering if Thomas knew that Victor's father was dead, if he knew what was going to happen next.

Just then Thomas looked at Victor, smiled, and walked over to him.   20

"Victor, I'm sorry about your father," Thomas said.

"How did you know about it?" Victor asked.

"I heard it on the wind. I heard it from the birds. I felt it in the sunlight. Also, your mother was just in here crying."

"Oh," Victor said and looked around the Trading Post. All the other Indians stared, surprised that Victor was even talking to Thomas. Nobody talked to Thomas anymore because he told the same damn stories over and over again. Victor was embarrassed, but he thought that Thomas might be able to help him. Victor felt a sudden need for tradition.

"I can lend you the money you need," Thomas said suddenly. "But   25
you have to take me with you."

"I can't take your money," Victor said. "I mean, I haven't hardly talked to you in years. We're not really friends anymore."

"I didn't say we were friends. I said you had to take me with you."

"Let me think about it."

Victor went home with his one hundred dollars and sat at the kitchen table. He held his head in his hands and thought about Thomas Builds-the-Fire, remembered little details, tears and scars, the bicycle they shared for a summer, so many stories.

Thomas Builds-the-Fire sat on the bicycle, waited in Victor's yard. He   30
was ten years old and skinny. His hair was dirty because it was the Fourth of July.

"Victor," Thomas yelled. "Hurry up. We're going to miss the fireworks."

After a few minutes, Victor ran out of his house, jumped the porch railing, and landed gracefully on the sidewalk.

"And the judges award him a 9.95, the highest score of the summer," Thomas said, clapped, laughed.

"That was perfect, cousin," Victor said. "And it's my turn to ride the bike."

Thomas gave up the bike and they headed for the fairgrounds. It was   35
nearly dark and the fireworks were about to start.

"You know," Thomas said. "It's strange how us Indians celebrate the Fourth of July. It ain't like it was *our* independence everybody was fighting for."

"You think about things too much," Victor said. "It's just supposed to be fun. Maybe Junior will be there."

"Which Junior? Everybody on this reservation is named Junior."

And they both laughed.

The fireworks were small, hardly more than a few bottle rockets and   40
a fountain. But it was enough for two Indian boys. Years later, they would need much more.

Afterwards, sitting in the dark, fighting off mosquitoes, Victor turned to Thomas Builds-the-Fire.

"Hey," Victor said. "Tell me a story."

Thomas closed his eyes and told this story: "There were these two Indian boys who wanted to be warriors. But it was too late to be warriors in the old way. All the horses were gone. So the two Indian boys stole a car and drove to the city. They parked the stolen car in front of the police station and then hitchhiked back home to the reservation. When they got back, all their friends cheered and their parents' eyes shone with pride. *You were very brave*, everybody said to the two Indian boys. *Very brave*."

"Ya-hey," Victor said. "That's a good one. I wish I could be a warrior."

"Me, too," Thomas said.   45

They went home together in the dark, Thomas on the bike now, Victor on foot. They walked through shadows and light from the street-lamps.

"We've come a long ways," Thomas said. "We have outdoor lighting."

"All I need is the stars," Victor said. "And besides, you still think about things too much."

They separated then, each headed for home, both laughing all the way.

Victor sat at his kitchen table. He counted his one hundred dollars   50
again and again. He knew he needed more to make it to Phoenix and back. He knew he needed Thomas Builds-the-Fire. So he put his money in his wallet and opened the front door to find Thomas on the porch.

"Ya-hey, Victor," Thomas said. "I knew you'd call me."

Thomas walked into the living room and sat down on Victor's favorite chair.

"I've got some money saved up," Thomas said. "It's enough to get us down there, but you have to get us back."

"I've got this hundred dollars," Victor said. "And my dad had a savings account I'm going to claim."

"How much in your dad's account?"   55

"Enough. A few hundred."

"Sounds good. When we leaving?"

When they were fifteen and had long since stopped being friends, Victor and Thomas got into a fistfight. That is, Victor was really drunk and beat Thomas up for no reason at all. All the other Indian boys stood around and watched it happen. Junior was there and so were Lester, Seymour, and a lot of others. The beating might have gone on until Thomas was dead if Norma Many Horses hadn't come along and stopped it.

"Hey, you boys," Norma yelled and jumped out of her car. "Leave him alone."

If it had been someone else, even another man, the Indian boys   60
would've just ignored the warnings. But Norma was a warrior. She was powerful. She could have picked up any two of the boys and smashed their skulls together. But worse than that, she would have dragged them all over to some tipi and made them listen to some elder tell a dusty old story.

The Indian boys scattered, and Norma walked over to Thomas and picked him up.

"Hey, little man, are you okay?" she asked.

Thomas gave her a thumbs up.

"Why they always picking on you?"

Thomas shook his head, closed his eyes, but no stories came to him, 65
no words or music. He just wanted to go home, to lie in his bed and let
his dreams tell his stories for him.

Thomas Builds-the-Fire and Victor sat next to each other in the airplane, coach section. A tiny white woman had the window seat. She was
busy twisting her body into pretzels. She was flexible.

"I have to ask," Thomas said, and Victor closed his eyes in embarrassment.

"Don't," Victor said.

"Excuse me, miss," Thomas asked. "Are you a gymnast or something?"

"There's no something about it," she said. "I was first alternate on 70
the 1980 Olympic team."

"Really?" Thomas asked.

"Really."

"I mean, you used to be a world-class athlete?" Thomas asked.

"My husband still thinks I am."

Thomas Builds-the-Fire smiled. She was a mental gymnast, too. She 75
pulled her leg straight up against her body so that she could've kissed her
kneecap.

"I wish I could do that," Thomas said.

Victor was ready to jump out of the plane. Thomas, that crazy Indian
storyteller with ratty old braids and broken teeth, was flirting with a beautiful Olympic gymnast. Nobody back home on the reservation would ever
believe it.

"Well," the gymnast said. "It's easy. Try it."

Thomas grabbed at his leg and tried to pull it up into the same position as the gymnast. He couldn't even come close, which made Victor and
the gymnast laugh.

"Hey," she asked. "You two are Indian, right?" 80

"Full-blood," Victor said.

"Not me," Thomas said. "I'm half magician on my mother's side and
half clown on my father's."

They all laughed.

"What are your names?" she asked.

"Victor and Thomas." 85

"Mine is Cathy. Pleased to meet you all."

The three of them talked for the duration of the flight. Cathy the
gymnast complained about the government, how they screwed the 1980
Olympic team by boycotting.

"Sounds like you all got a lot in common with Indians," Thomas said.

Nobody laughed.

After the plane landed in Phoenix and they had all found their way to   90
the terminal, Cathy the gymnast smiled and waved good-bye.

"She was really nice," Thomas said.

"Yeah, but everybody talks to everybody on airplanes," Victor said.
"It's too bad we can't always be that way."

"You always used to tell me I think too much," Thomas said. "Now
it sounds like you do."

"Maybe I caught it from you."

"Yeah."   95

Thomas and Victor rode in a taxi to the trailer where Victor's father
died.

"Listen," Victor said as they stopped in front of the trailer. "I never
told you I was sorry for beating you up that time."

"Oh, it was nothing. We were just kids and you were drunk."

"Yeah, but I'm still sorry."

"That's all right."   100

Victor paid for the taxi and the two of them stood in the hot Phoenix
summer. They could smell the trailer.

"This ain't going to be nice," Victor said. "You don't have to go in."

"You're going to need help."

Victor walked to the front door and opened it. The stink rolled out
and made them both gag. Victor's father had lain in that trailer for a week
in hundred-degree temperatures before anyone found him. And the only
reason anyone found him was because of the smell. They needed dental
records to identify him. That's exactly what the coroner said. They needed
dental records.

"Oh, man," Victor said. "I don't know if I can do this."   105

"Well, then don't."

"But there might be something valuable in there."

"I thought his money was in the bank."

"It is. I was talking about pictures and letters and stuff like that."

"Oh," Thomas said as he held his breath and followed Victor into   110
the trailer.

When Victor was twelve, he stepped into an underground wasp nest.
His foot was caught in the hole, and no matter how hard he struggled, Vic-
tor couldn't pull free. He might have died there, stung a thousand times, if
Thomas Builds-the-Fire had not come by.

"Run," Thomas yelled and pulled Victor's foot from the hole. They
ran then, hard as they ever had, faster than Billy Mills,[2] faster than Jim
Thorpe,[3] faster than the wasps could fly.

---

[2]*Billy Mills (b. 1938):* An Oglala Lakota (Sioux), he was the only American to win an
Olympic gold medal in the 10,000-meter race—at the 1964 Tokyo Olympic Games.—EDS.
[3]*Jim Thorpe (1887–1953):* A member of the Sac and Fox tribe and acclaimed to be the
greatest athlete of the twentieth century. He won gold medals in the pentathlon and decathlon
in the 1912 Olympic games and played both professional football and baseball.—EDS.

Victor and Thomas ran until they couldn't breathe, ran until it was cold and dark outside, ran until they were lost and it took hours to find their way home. All the way back, Victor counted his stings.

"Seven," Victor said. "My lucky number."

Victor didn't find much to keep in the trailer. Only a photo album and   115
a stereo. Everything else had that smell stuck in it or was useless anyway.

"I guess this is all," Victor said. "It ain't much."

"Better than nothing," Thomas said.

"Yeah, and I do have the pickup."

"Yeah," Thomas said, "it's in good shape."

"Dad was good about that stuff."   120

"Yeah, I remember your dad."

"Really?" Victor asked. "What do you remember?"

Thomas Builds-the-Fire closed his eyes and told this story: "I remember when I had this dream that told me to go to Spokane, to stand by the Falls in the middle of the city and wait for a sign. I knew I had to go there but I didn't have a car. Didn't have a license. I was only thirteen. So I walked all the way, took me all day, and I finally made it to the Falls. I stood there for an hour waiting. Then your dad came walking up. *What the hell are you doing here?* he asked me. I said, *Waiting for a vision.* Then your father said, *All you're going to get here is mugged.* So he drove me over to Denny's, bought me dinner, and then drove me home to the reservation. For a long time I was mad because I thought my dreams had lied to me. But they didn't. Your dad was my vision. *Take care of each other* is what my dreams were saying. *Take care of each other.*"

Victor was quiet for a long time. He searched his mind for memories of his father, found the good ones, found a few bad ones, added it all up, and smiled.

"My father never told me about finding you in Spokane," Victor said.   125

"He said he wouldn't tell anybody. Didn't want me to get in trouble. But he said I had to watch out for you as part of the deal."

"Really?"

"Really. Your father said you would need the help. He was right."

"That's why you came down here with me, isn't it?" Victor asked.

"I came because of your father."   130

Victor and Thomas climbed into the pickup, drove over to the bank, and claimed the three hundred dollars in the savings account.

Thomas Builds-the-Fire could fly.

Once, he jumped off the roof of the tribal school and flapped his arms like a crazy eagle. And he flew. For a second, he hovered, suspended above all the other Indian boys who were too smart or too scared to jump.

"He's flying," Junior yelled, and Seymour was busy looking for the trick wires or mirrors. But it was real. As real as the dirt when Thomas lost altitude and crashed to the ground.

He broke his arm in two places.   135

"He broke his wing," Victor chanted, and the other Indian boys joined in, made it a tribal song.

"He broke his wing, he broke his wing, he broke his wing," all the Indian boys chanted as they ran off, flapping their wings, wishing they could fly, too. They hated Thomas for his courage, his brief moment as a bird. Everybody has dreams about flying. Thomas flew.

One of his dreams came true for just a second, just enough to make it real.

Victor's father, his ashes, fit in one wooden box with enough left over to fill a cardboard box.

"He was always a big man," Thomas said.   140

Victor carried part of his father and Thomas carried the rest out to the pickup. They set him down carefully behind the seats, put a cowboy hat on the wooden box and a Dodgers cap on the cardboard box. That's the way it was supposed to be.

"Ready to head back home?" Victor asked.

"It's going to be a long drive."

"Yeah, take a couple days, maybe."

"We can take turns," Thomas said.   145

"Okay," Victor said, but they didn't take turns. Victor drove for sixteen hours straight north, made it halfway up Nevada toward home before he finally pulled over.

"Hey, Thomas," Victor said. "You got to drive for a while."

"Okay."

Thomas Builds-the-Fire slid behind the wheel and started off down the road. All through Nevada, Thomas and Victor had been amazed at the lack of animal life, at the absence of water, of movement.

"Where is everything?" Victor had asked more than once.   150

Now when Thomas was finally driving they saw the first animal, maybe the only animal in Nevada. It was a long-eared jackrabbit.

"Look," Victor yelled. "It's alive."

Thomas and Victor were busy congratulating themselves on their discovery when the jackrabbit darted out into the road and under the wheels of the pickup.

"Stop the goddamn car," Victor yelled, and Thomas did stop, backed the pickup to the dead jackrabbit.

"Oh, man, he's dead," Victor said as he looked at the squashed   155
animal.

"Really dead."

"The only thing alive in this whole state and we just killed it."

"I don't know," Thomas said, "I think it was suicide."

Victor looked around the desert, sniffed the air, felt the emptiness and loneliness, and nodded his head.

"Yeah," Victor said, "it had to be suicide."   160

"I can't believe this," Thomas said. "You drive for a thousand miles and there ain't even any bugs smashed on the windshield. I drive for ten seconds and kill the only living thing in Nevada."

"Yeah," Victor said. "Maybe I should drive."

"Maybe you should."

Thomas Builds-the-Fire walked through the corridors of the tribal school by himself. Nobody wanted to be anywhere near him because of all those stories. Story after story.

Thomas closed his eyes and this story came to him: "We are all given 165
one thing by which our lives are measured, one determination. Mine are the stories which can change or not change the world. It doesn't matter which as long as I continue to tell the stories. My father, he died on Okinawa in World War II, died fighting for this country, which had tried to kill him for years. My mother, she died giving birth to me, died while I was still inside her. She pushed me out into the world with her last breath. I have no brothers or sisters. I have only my stories which came to me before I even had the words to speak. I learned a thousand stories before I took my first thousand steps. They are all I have. It's all I can do."

Thomas Builds-the-Fire told his stories to all those who would stop and listen. He kept telling them long after people had stopped listening.

Victor and Thomas made it back to the reservation just as the sun was rising. It was the beginning of a new day on earth, but the same old shit on the reservation.

"Good morning," Thomas said.

"Good morning."

The tribe was waking up, ready for work, eating breakfast, reading 170
the newspaper, just like everybody else does. Willene LeBret was out in her garden wearing a bathrobe. She waved when Thomas and Victor drove by.

"Crazy Indians made it," she said to herself and went back to her roses.

Victor stopped the pickup in front of Thomas Builds-the-Fire's HUD house. They both yawned, stretched a little, shook dust from their bodies.

"I'm tired," Victor said.

"Of everything," Thomas added.

They both searched for words to end the journey. Victor needed to 175
thank Thomas for his help, for the money, and make the promise to pay it all back.

"Don't worry about the money," Thomas said. "It don't make any difference anyhow."

"Probably not, enit?"

"Nope."

Victor knew that Thomas would remain the crazy storyteller who talked to dogs and cars, who listened to the wind and pine trees. Victor knew that he couldn't really be friends with Thomas, even after all that had happened. It was cruel but it was real. As real as the ashes, as Victor's father, sitting behind the seats.

"I know how it is," Thomas said. "I know you ain't going to treat me   180 any better than you did before. I know your friends would give you too much shit about it."

Victor was ashamed of himself. Whatever happened to the tribal ties, the sense of community? The only real thing he shared with anybody was a bottle and broken dreams. He owed Thomas something, anything.

"Listen," Victor said and handed Thomas the cardboard box which contained half of his father. "I want you to have this."

Thomas took the ashes and smiled, closed his eyes, and told this story: "I'm going to travel to Spokane Falls one last time and toss these ashes into the water. And your father will rise like a salmon, leap over the bridge, over me, and find his way home. It will be beautiful. His teeth will shine like silver, like a rainbow. He will rise, Victor, he will rise."

Victor smiled.

"I was planning on doing the same thing with my half," Victor said.   185 "But I didn't imagine my father looking anything like a salmon. I thought it'd be like cleaning the attic or something. Like letting things go after they've stopped having any use."

"Nothing stops, cousin," Thomas said. "Nothing stops."

Thomas Builds-the-Fire got out of the pickup and walked up his driveway. Victor started the pickup and began the drive home.

"Wait," Thomas yelled suddenly from his porch. "I just got to ask one favor."

Victor stopped the pickup, leaned out the window, and shouted back. "What do you want?"

"Just one time when I'm telling a story somewhere, why don't you   190 stop and listen?" Thomas asked.

"Just once?"

"Just once."

Victor waved his arms to let Thomas know that the deal was good. It was a fair trade, and that was all Victor had ever wanted from his whole life. So Victor drove his father's pickup toward home while Thomas went into his house, closed the door behind him, and heard a new story come to him in the silence afterwards.

The Reader's Presence

1. Thomas is portrayed as an outcast in the community, "a story-teller that nobody wanted to listen to." What stories does Thomas tell? Why are they unpopular with listeners? What do Thomas's stories have to do with his role as an outcast?

2. Describe Victor's state of mind and place in life at the beginning of the story. What is he like? What has happened to him? Compare this Victor to Victor as he appears at the end of the story. Has he changed? Do you think that he will change in the future? Why or why not?

3. Compare the characters of Thomas and Victor to Alexie's description in "The Joy of Reading and Writing: Superman and Me" (page 73) of the children on the Spokane Indian Reservation of his youth. What characteristics does Thomas share with the children Alexie describes (including himself as a boy)? What characteristics does Victor share with them? How are Alexie's fictional reservation and the people who live there like — and unlike — the reservation and people he describes in his essay?

Raymond Carver

The Bath

Raymond Carver (1938–1988) is best known for his tightly crafted, spare, and often grim short stories. In fact, his mastery of dialogue and his fine eye for detail have made his collections of short stories best-sellers in the United States and abroad. These collections include Will You Please Be Quiet, Please? *(1976);* What We Talk about When We Talk about Love *(1981), in which "The Bath" can be found;* Cathedral *(1984); and* Where I'm Calling From *(1988). Carver worked and reworked his stories, even after they were published. Another version of "The Bath" was later published in* Cathedral; *this later story, called "A Small Good Thing," won the 1983 O. Henry Award. In 1993 Robert Altman made the critically acclaimed film* Short Cuts *based on a number of Carver's short stories.*

Describing the process of writing fiction, Carver says, "I never start with an idea. I always see something. I start with an image, a cigarette being put out in a jar of mustard, for instance, or the remains, the wreckage, of a dinner left on the table. Pop cans in the fireplace, that sort of thing. And a feeling goes with that. And that feeling seems to transport me back to that particular time and place, and the ambience of time. But it is the image, and the emotion that goes with that image — that's what's important."

For more information on Raymond Carver, see page 103.

Saturday afternoon the mother drove to the bakery in the shopping center. After looking through a loose-leaf binder with photographs of cakes taped onto the pages, she ordered chocolate, the child's favorite.

The cake she chose was decorated with a spaceship and a launching pad under a sprinkling of white stars. The name SCOTTY would be iced on in green as if it were the name of the spaceship.

The baker listened thoughtfully when the mother told him Scotty would be eight years old. He was an older man, this baker, and he wore a curious apron, a heavy thing with loops that went under his arms and around his back and then crossed in front again where they were tied in a very thick knot. He kept wiping his hands on the front of the apron as he listened to the woman, his wet eyes examining her lips as she studied the samples and talked.

He let her take her time. He was in no hurry.

The mother decided on the spaceship cake, and then she gave the baker her name and her telephone number. The cake would be ready Monday morning, in plenty of time for the party Monday afternoon. This was all the baker was willing to say. No pleasantries, just this small exchange, the barest information, nothing that was not necessary.

Monday morning, the boy was walking to school. He was in the   5
company of another boy, the two boys passing a bag of potato chips back and forth between them. The birthday boy was trying to trick the other boy into telling what he was going to give in the way of a present.

At an intersection, without looking, the birthday boy stepped off the curb, and was promptly knocked down by a car. He fell on his side, his head in the gutter, his legs in the road moving as if he were climbing a wall.

The other boy stood holding the potato chips. He was wondering if he should finish the rest or continue on to school.

The birthday boy did not cry. But neither did he wish to talk anymore. He would not answer when the other boy asked what it felt like to be hit by a car. The birthday boy got up and turned back for home, at which time the other boy waved good-bye and headed off for school.

The birthday boy told his mother what had happened. They sat together on the sofa. She held his hands in her lap. This is what she was doing when the boy pulled his hands away and lay down on his back.

Of course, the birthday party never happened. The birthday boy was   10
in the hospital instead. The mother sat by the bed. She was waiting for the boy to wake up. The father hurried over from his office. He sat next to the mother. So now the both of them waited for the boy to wake up. They waited for hours, and then the father went home to take a bath.

The man drove home from the hospital. He drove the streets faster than he should. It had been a good life till now. There had been work, fatherhood, family. The man had been lucky and happy. But fear made him want a bath.

He pulled into the driveway. He sat in the car trying to make his legs work. The child had been hit by a car and he was in the hospital, but he was going to be all right. The man got out of the car and went up to the door. The dog was barking and the telephone was ringing. It kept ringing while the man unlocked the door and felt the wall for the light switch.

He picked up the receiver. He said, "I just got in the door!"

"There's a cake that wasn't picked up."

This is what the voice on the other end said.   15

"What are you saying?" the father said.

"The cake," the voice said. "Sixteen dollars."

The husband held the receiver against his ear, trying to understand. He said, "I don't know anything about it."

"Don't hand me that," the voice said.

The husband hung up the telephone. He went into the kitchen and   20
poured himself some whiskey. He called the hospital.

The child's condition remained the same.

While the water ran into the tub, the man lathered his face and shaved. He was in the tub when he heard the telephone again. He got himself out and hurried through the house, saying, "Stupid, stupid," because he wouldn't be doing this if he'd stayed where he was in the hospital. He picked up the receiver and shouted, "Hello!"

The voice said, "It's ready."

The father got back to the hospital after midnight. The wife was sitting in the chair by the bed. She looked up at the husband and then she looked back at the child. From an apparatus over the bed hung a bottle with a tube running from the bottle to the child.

"What's this?" the father said.   25

"Glucose," the mother said.

The husband put his hand to the back of the woman's head.

"He's going to wake up," the man said.

"I know," the woman said.

In a little while the man said, "Go home and let me take over."   30

She shook her head. "No," she said.

"Really," he said. "Go home for a while. You don't have to worry. He's sleeping, is all."

A nurse pushed open the door. She nodded to them as she went to the bed. She took the left arm out from under the covers and put her fingers on the wrist. She put the arm back under the covers and wrote on the clipboard attached to the bed.

"How is he?" the mother said.

"Stable," the nurse said. Then she said, "Doctor will be in again   35
shortly."

"I was saying maybe she'd want to go home and get a little rest," the man said. "After the doctor comes."

"She could do that," the nurse said.

The woman said, "We'll see what the doctor says." She brought her hand up to her eyes and leaned her head forward.

The nurse said, "Of course."

The father gazed at his son, the small chest inflating and deflating   40
under the covers. He felt more fear now. He began shaking his head. He
talked to himself like this. The child is fine. Instead of sleeping at home,
he's doing it here. Sleep is the same wherever you do it.

The doctor came in. He shook hands with the man. The woman got
up from the chair.

"Ann," the doctor said and nodded. The doctor said, "Let's just see
how he's doing." He moved to the bed and touched the boy's wrist. He
peeled back an eyelid and then the other. He turned back the covers
and listened to the heart. He pressed his fingers here and there on the
body. He went to the end of the bed and studied the chart. He noted
the time, scribbled on the chart, and then he considered the mother and the
father.

This doctor was a handsome man. His skin was moist and tan. He
wore a three-piece suit, a vivid tie, and on his shirt were cufflinks.

The mother was talking to herself like this. He has just come from
somewhere with an audience. They gave him a special medal.

The doctor said, "Nothing to shout about, but nothing to worry   45
about. He should wake up pretty soon." The doctor looked at the boy
again. "We'll know more after the tests are in."

"Oh, no," the mother said.

The doctor said, "Sometimes you see this."

The father said, "You wouldn't call this a coma, then?"

The father waited and looked at the doctor.

"No, I don't want to call it that," the doctor said. "He's sleeping. It's   50
restorative. The body is doing what it has to do."

"It's a coma," the mother said. "A kind of coma."

The doctor said, "I wouldn't call it that."

He took the woman's hands and patted them. He shook hands with
the husband.

The woman put her fingers on the child's forehead and kept them
there for a while. "At least he doesn't have a fever," she said. Then she
said, "I don't know. Feel his head."

The man put his fingers on the boy's forehead. The man said, "I   55
think he's supposed to feel this way."

The woman stood there awhile longer, working her lip with her
teeth. Then she moved to her chair and sat down.

The husband sat in the chair beside her. He wanted to say something
else. But there was no saying what it should be. He took her hand and put
it in his lap. This made him feel better. It made him feel he was saying
something. They sat like that for a while, watching the boy, not talking.
From time to time he squeezed her hand until she took it away.

"I've been praying," she said.

"Me too," the father said. "I've been praying too."

A nurse came back in and checked the flow from the bottle.   60

A doctor came in and said what his name was. This doctor was wearing loafers.

"We're going to take him downstairs for more pictures," he said. "And we want to do a scan."

"A scan?" the mother said. She stood between this new doctor and the bed.

"It's nothing," he said.

"My God," she said.   65

Two orderlies came in. They wheeled a thing like a bed. They unhooked the boy from the tube and slid him over onto the thing with wheels.

It was after sunup when they brought the birthday boy back out. The mother and father followed the orderlies into the elevator and up to the room. Once more the parents took up their places next to the bed.

They waited all day. The boy did not wake up. The doctor came again and examined the boy again and left after saying the same things again. Nurses came in. Doctors came in. A technician came in and took blood.

"I don't understand this," the mother said to the technician.

"Doctor's orders," the technician said.   70

The mother went to the window and looked out at the parking lot. Cars with their lights on were driving in and out. She stood at the window with her hands on the sill. She was talking to herself like this. We're into something now, something hard.

She was afraid.

She saw a car stop and a woman in a long coat get into it. She made believe she was that woman. She made believe she was driving away from here to someplace else.

The doctor came in. He looked tanned and healthier than ever. He went to the bed and examined the boy. He said, "His signs are fine. Everything's good."

The mother said, "But he's sleeping."   75

"Yes," the doctor said.

The husband said, "She's tired. She's starved."

The doctor said, "She should rest. She should eat. Ann," the doctor said.

"Thank you," the husband said.

He shook hands with the doctor and the doctor patted their shoulders and left.   80

"I suppose one of us should go home and check on things," the man said. "The dog needs to be fed."

"Call the neighbors," the wife said. "Someone will feed him if you ask them to."

She tried to think who. She closed her eyes and tried to think anything at all. After a time she said, "Maybe I'll do it. Maybe if I'm not here watching, he'll wake up. Maybe it's because I'm watching that he won't."

"That could be it," the husband said.

"I'll go home and take a bath and put on something clean," the woman said.

"I think you should do that," the man said.

She picked up her purse. He helped her into her coat. She moved to the door, and looked back. She looked at the child, and then she looked at the father. The husband nodded and smiled.

She went past the nurses' station and down to the end of the corridor, where she turned and saw a little waiting room, a family in there, all sitting in wicker chairs, a man in a khaki shirt, a baseball cap pushed back on his head, a large woman wearing a housedress, slippers, a girl in jeans, hair in dozens of kinky braids, the table littered with flimsy wrappers and styrofoam and coffee sticks and packets of salt and pepper.

"Nelson," the woman said. "Is it about Nelson?"

The woman's eyes widened.

"Tell me now, lady," the woman said. "Is it about Nelson?"

The woman was trying to get up from her chair. But the man had his hand closed over her arm.

"Here, here," the man said.

"I'm sorry," the mother said. "I'm looking for the elevator. My son is in the hospital. I can't find the elevator."

"Elevator is down that way," the man said, and he aimed a finger in the right direction.

"My son was hit by a car," the mother said. "But he's going to be all right. He's in shock now, but it might be some kind of coma too. That's what worries us, the coma part. I'm going out for a little while. Maybe I'll take a bath. But my husband is with him. He's watching. There's a chance everything will change when I'm gone. My name is Ann Weiss."

The man shifted in his chair. He shook his head.

He said, "Our Nelson."

She pulled into the driveway. The dog ran out from behind the house. He ran in circles on the grass. She closed her eyes and leaned her head against the wheel. She listened to the ticking of the engine.

She got out of the car and went to the door. She turned on lights and put on water for tea. She opened a can and fed the dog. She sat down on the sofa with her tea.

The telephone rang.

"Yes!" she said. "Hello!" she said.

"Mrs. Weiss," a man's voice said.

"Yes," she said. "This is Mrs. Weiss. Is it about Scotty?" she said.

"Scotty," the voice said. "It is about Scotty," the voice said. "It has 105
to do with Scotty, yes."

The Reader's Presence

1. What information does the omniscient point of view provide that would be unavailable if the story were told by the mother? by the father? How does the inclusion of this information affect the story?

2. In the hospital scenes, what clues does Carver give to the woman's feelings? How do her dialogue, her actions, and the things she notices indicate her emotional state?

3. What information does the story not provide that you might have expected it to? Why do you think Carver chose to tell this story about events affecting a family in such minimal detail? Read Carver's essay "My Father's Life" (page 103). What similarities does the nonfiction piece share with the short story? What details does Carver leave out of the essay? Why do you think he made these choices?

Nathaniel Hawthorne
Young Goodman Brown

Nathaniel Hawthorne (1804–1864) was born on July 4 in Salem, Massachusetts, into a family that had lived in Salem for generations. His great-grandfather, John Hathorne—the w was added to the family name later—was one of the seven magistrates judging the Salem witch trials of 1692–93. Hathorne and the other magistrates were responsible for examining and sentencing defendants, nineteen of whom were hanged before the hysteria came to an end. (For more on the Salem witch trials, see page 406.) The distressing history of Nathaniel Hawthorne's Puritan family and hometown provided fertile ground for his novels and short stories, many of which—like "Young Goodman Brown"—are set in and around Salem. His most famous and enduring works include two novels, The Scarlet Letter *(1850) and* The House of the Seven Gables *(1851), and three noted short-story collections,* Twice-Told Tales *(1837),* The Great Stone Face, and Other Tales of the White Mountains *(1877), and* Mosses from an Old Manse *(1846), in which "Young Goodman Brown" first appeared.*

Young Goodman[1] Brown came forth at sunset into the street at Salem village; but put his head back, after crossing the threshold, to exchange a parting kiss with his young wife. And Faith, as the wife was aptly named, thrust her own pretty head into the street, letting the wind play with the pink ribbons of her cap while she called to Goodman Brown.

"Dearest heart," whispered she, softly and rather sadly, when her lips were close to his ear, "prithee put off your journey until sunrise and sleep in your own bed to-night. A lone woman is troubled with such dreams and such thoughts that she's afeared of herself sometimes. Pray tarry with me this night, dear husband, of all nights in the year."

"My love and my Faith," replied young Goodman Brown, "of all nights in the year, this one night must I tarry away from thee. My journey, as thou callest it, forth and back again, must needs be done 'twixt now and sunrise. What, my sweet, pretty wife, dost thou doubt me already, and we but three months married?"

"Then God bless you!" said Faith, with the pink ribbons; "and may you find all well when you come back."

"Amen!" cried Goodman Brown. "Say thy prayers, dear Faith, and   5
go to bed at dusk, and no harm will come to thee."

So they parted; and the young man pursued his way until, being about to turn the corner by the meeting-house, he looked back and saw the head of Faith still peeping after him with a melancholy air, in spite of her pink ribbons.

"Poor little Faith!" thought he, for his heart smote him. "What a wretch am I to leave her on such an errand! She talks of dreams, too. Methought as she spoke there was trouble in her face, as if a dream had warned her what work is to be done to-night. But no, no; 'twould kill her to think it. Well, she's a blessed angel on earth; and after this one night I'll cling to her skirts and follow her to heaven."

With this excellent resolve for the future, Goodman Brown felt himself justified in making more haste on his present evil purpose. He had taken a dreary road, darkened by all the gloomiest trees of the forest, which barely stood aside to let the narrow path creep through, and closed immediately behind. It was all as lonely as could be; and there is this peculiarity in such a solitude, that the traveller knows not who may be concealed by the innumerable trunks and the thick boughs overhead; so that with lonely footsteps he may yet be passing through an unseen multitude.

"There may be a devilish Indian behind every tree," said Goodman Brown to himself; and he glanced fearfully behind him as he added, "What if the devil himself should be at my very elbow!"

His head being turned back, he passed a crook of the road, and, look-   10
ing forward again, beheld the figure of a man, in grave and decent attire, seated at the foot of an old tree. He arose at Goodman Brown's approach and walked onward side by side with him.

---

[1]*Goodman:* Mr.—EDS.

"You are late, Goodman Brown," said he. "The clock of the Old South was striking as I came through Boston, and that is full fifteen minutes agone."

"Faith kept me back a while," replied the young man, with a tremor in his voice, caused by the sudden appearance of his companion, though not wholly unexpected.

It was now deep dusk in the forest, and deepest in that part of it where these two were journeying. As nearly as could be discerned, the second traveller was about fifty years old, apparently in the same rank of life as Goodman Brown, and bearing a considerable resemblance to him, though perhaps more in expression than features. Still they might have been taken for father and son. And yet, though the elder person was as simply clad as the younger, and as simple in manner too, he had an indescribable air of one who knew the world, and who would not have felt abashed at the governor's dinner table or in King William's court, were it possible that his affairs should call him thither. But the only thing about him that could be fixed upon as remarkable was his staff, which bore the likeness of a great black snake, so curiously wrought that it might almost be seen to twist and wriggle itself like a living serpent. This, of course, must have been an ocular deception, assisted by the uncertain light.

"Come, Goodman Brown," cried his fellow-traveller, "this is a dull pace for the beginning of a journey. Take my staff, if you are so soon weary."

"Friend," said the other, exchanging his slow pace for a full stop, 15 "having kept covenant by meeting thee here, it is my purpose now to return whence I came. I have scruples touching the matter thou wot'st of."

"Sayest thou so?" replied he of the serpent, smiling apart. "Let us walk on, nevertheless, reasoning as we go; and if I convince thee not thou shalt turn back. We are but a little way in the forest yet."

"Too far! too far!" exclaimed the goodman, unconsciously resuming his walk. "My father never went into the woods on such an errand, nor his father before him. We have been a race of honest men and good Christians since the days of the martyrs;[2] and shall I be the first of the name of Brown that ever took this path and kept—"

"Such company, thou wouldst say," observed the elder person, interpreting his pause. "Well said, Goodman Brown! I have been as well acquainted with your family as with ever a one among the Puritans; and that's no trifle to say. I helped your grandfather, the constable, when he lashed the Quaker woman so smartly through the streets of Salem; and it was I that brought your father a pitch-pine knot, kindled at my own hearth, to set fire to an Indian village, in King Philip's war.[3] They were my good friends, both; and many a pleasant walk have we had along this

---

[2]*days of the martyrs:* Queen Mary I of England, a Catholic, ordered the executions of three hundred Protestants during her reign (1553–1558).—Eds.

[3]*King Philip's war:* In 1675–76, hostilities between settlers in New England and Chief Metacomset, called "King Philip" by the colonists, resulted in the deadliest war (proportionate to population) in American history.—Eds.

path, and returned merrily after midnight. I would fain be friends with you for their sake."

"If it be as thou sayest," replied Goodman Brown, "I marvel they never spoke of these matters; or, verily, I marvel not, seeing that the least rumor of the sort would have driven them from New England. We are a people of prayer, and good works to boot, and abide no such wickedness."

"Wickedness or not," said the traveller, with the twisted staff, "I have   20
a very general acquaintance here in New England. The deacons of many a church have drunk the communion wine with me; the selectmen of divers towns make me their chairman; and a majority of the Great and General Court are firm supporters of my interest. The governor and I, too—But these are state secrets."

"Can this be so?" cried Goodman Brown, with a stare of amazement at his undisturbed companion. "Howbeit, I have nothing to do with the governor and council; they have their own ways, and are no rule for a simple husbandman like me. But, were I to go on with thee, how should I meet the eye of that good old man, our minister, at Salem village? Oh, his voice would make me tremble both Sabbath day and lecture day."

Thus far the elder traveller had listened with due gravity; but now burst into a fit of irrepressible mirth, shaking himself so violently that his snake-like staff actually seemed to wriggle in sympathy.

"Ha! ha! ha!" shouted he again and again; then composing himself, "Well, go on, Goodman Brown, go on; but, prithee, don't kill me with laughing."

"Well, then, to end the matter at once," said Goodman Brown, considerably nettled, "there is my wife, Faith. It would break her dear little heart; and I'd rather break my own."

"Nay, if that be the case," answered the other, "e'en go thy ways,   25
Goodman Brown. I would not for twenty old women like the one hobbling before us that Faith should come to any harm."

As he spoke he pointed his staff at a female figure on the path, in whom Goodman Brown recognized a very pious and exemplary dame, who had taught him his catechism in youth, and was still his moral and spiritual adviser, jointly with the minister and Deacon Gookin.

"A marvel, truly, that Goody Cloyse should be so far in the wilderness at nightfall," said he. "But with your leave, friend, I shall take a cut through the woods until we have left this Christian woman behind. Being a stranger to you, she might ask whom I was consorting with and whither I was going."

"Be it so," said his fellow-traveller. "Betake you to the woods, and let me keep the path."

Accordingly the young man turned aside, but took care to watch his companion, who advanced softly along the road until he had come within a staff's length of the old dame. She, meanwhile, was making the best of her way, with singular speed for so aged a woman, and mumbling some indistinct words—a prayer, doubtless—as she went. The traveller put forth his staff and touched her withered neck with what seemed the serpent's tail.

"The devil!" screamed the pious old lady.

"Then Goody Cloyse knows her old friend?" observed the traveller, confronting her and leaning on his writhing stick.

"Ah, forsooth, and is it your worship indeed?" cried the good dame. "Yea, truly is it, and in the very image of my old gossip, Goodman Brown, the grandfather of the silly fellow that now is. But—would your worship believe it?—my broomstick hath strangely disappeared, stolen, as I suspect, by that unhanged witch, Goody Cory, and that, too, when I was all anointed with the juice of smallage and cinquefoil and wolf's bane"—

"Mingled with fine wheat and the fat of a new-born babe," said the shape of old Goodman Brown.

"Ah, your worship knows the recipe," cried the old lady, cackling aloud. "So, as I was saying, being all ready for the meeting, and no horse to ride on, I made up my mind to foot it; for they tell me there is a nice young man to be taken into communion to-night. But now your good worship will lend me your arm, and we shall be there in a twinkling."

"That can hardly be," answered her friend. "I may not spare you my arm, Goody Cloyse; but here is my staff, if you will."

So saying, he threw it down at her feet, where, perhaps, it assumed life, being one of the rods which its owner had formerly lent to the Egyptian magi. Of this fact, however, Goodman Brown could not take cognizance. He had cast up his eyes in astonishment, and, looking down again, beheld neither Goody Cloyse nor the serpentine staff, but his fellow-traveller alone, who waited for him as calmly as if nothing had happened.

"That old woman taught me my catechism," said the young man; and there was a world of meaning in this simple comment.

They continued to walk onward, while the elder traveller exhorted his companion to make good speed and persevere in the path, discoursing so aptly that his arguments seemed rather to spring up in the bosom of his auditor than to be suggested by himself. As they went, he plucked a branch of maple to serve for a walking stick, and began to strip it of the twigs and little boughs, which were wet with evening dew. The moment his fingers touched them they became strangely withered and dried up as with a week's sunshine. Thus the pair proceeded, at a good free pace, until suddenly, in a gloomy hollow of the road, Goodman Brown sat himself down on the stump of a tree and refused to go any farther.

"Friend," said he, stubbornly, "my mind is made up. Not another step will I budge on this errand. What if a wretched old woman do choose to go to the devil when I thought she was going to heaven: is that any reason why I should quit my dear Faith and go after her?"

"You will think better of this by and by," said his acquaintance, composedly. "Sit here and rest yourself a while; and when you feel like moving again, there is my staff to help you along."

Without more words, he threw his companion the maple stick, and was as speedily out of sight as if he had vanished into the deepening gloom. The young man sat a few moments by the roadside, applauding himself greatly, and thinking with how clear a conscience he should meet the minister in his morning walk, nor shrink from the eye of good old Deacon Gookin. And what calm sleep would be his that very night, which was to have been spent so wickedly, but so purely and sweetly now, in the arms of Faith! Amidst these pleasant and praiseworthy meditations, Goodman Brown heard the tramp of horses along the road, and deemed it advisable to conceal himself within the verge of the forest, conscious of the guilty purpose that had brought him thither, though now so happily turned from it.

On came the hoof tramps and the voices of the riders, two grave old voices, conversing soberly as they drew near. These mingled sounds appeared to pass along the road, within a few yards of the young man's hiding-place; but, owing doubtless to the depth of the gloom at that particular spot, neither the travellers nor their steeds were visible. Though their figures brushed the small boughs by the wayside, it could not be seen that they intercepted, even for a moment, the faint gleam from the strip of bright sky athwart which they must have passed. Goodman Brown alternately crouched and stood on tiptoe, pulling aside the branches and thrusting forth his head as far as he durst without discerning so much as a shadow. It vexed him the more, because he could have sworn, were such a thing possible, that he recognized the voices of the minister and Deacon Gookin, jogging along quietly, as they were wont to do, when bound to some ordination or ecclesiastical council. While yet within hearing, one of the riders stopped to pluck a switch.

"Of the two, reverend sir," said the voice like the deacon's, "I had rather miss an ordination dinner than to-night's meeting. They tell me that some of our community are to be here from Falmouth and beyond, and others from Connecticut and Rhode Island, besides several of the Indian powwows, who, after their fashion, know almost as much deviltry as the best of us. Moreover, there is a goodly young woman to be taken into communion."

"Mighty well, Deacon Gookin!" replied the solemn old tones of the minister. "Spur up, or we shall be late. Nothing can be done, you know, until I get on the ground."

The hoofs clattered again; and the voices, talking so strangely in the empty air, passed on through the forest, where no church had ever been gathered, nor solitary Christian prayed. Whither, then, could these holy men be journeying so deep into the heathen wilderness? Young Goodman Brown caught hold of a tree for support, being ready to sink down on the ground, faint and overburdened with the heavy sickness of his heart. He looked up to the sky, doubting whether there really was a heaven above him. Yet there was the blue arch, and the stars brightening in it. 45

"With heaven above and Faith below, I will yet stand firm against the devil!" cried Goodman Brown.

While he still gazed upward into the deep arch of the firmament and had lifted his hands to pray, a cloud, though no wind was stirring, hurried across the zenith and hid the brightening stars. The blue sky was still visible, except directly overhead, where this black mass of cloud was sweeping swiftly northward. Aloft in the air, as if from the depths of the cloud, came a confused and doubtful sound of voices. Once the listener fancied that he could distinguish the accents of towns-people of his own, men and women, both pious and ungodly, many of whom he had met at the communion table, and had seen others rioting at the tavern. The next moment, so indistinct were the sounds, he doubted whether he had heard aught but the murmur of the old forest, whispering without a wind. Then came a stronger swell of those familiar tones, heard daily in the sunshine at Salem village, but never until now from a cloud of night. There was one voice, of a young woman, uttering lamentations, yet with an uncertain sorrow, and entreating for some favor, which, perhaps, it would grieve her to obtain; and all the unseen multitude, both saints and sinners, seemed to encourage her onward.

"Faith!" shouted Goodman Brown, in a voice of agony and desperation; and the echoes of the forest mocked him, crying, "Faith! Faith!" as if bewildered wretches were seeking her all through the wilderness.

The cry of grief, rage, and terror was yet piercing the night, when the unhappy husband held his breath for a response. There was a scream, drowned immediately in a louder murmur of voices, fading into far-off laughter, as the dark cloud swept away, leaving the clear and silent sky above Goodman Brown. But something fluttered lightly down through the air and caught on the branch of a tree. The young man seized it, and beheld a pink ribbon.

"My Faith is gone!" cried he, after one stupefied moment. "There is no good on earth; and sin is but a name. Come, devil; for to thee is this world given." 50

And, maddened with despair, so that he laughed loud and long, did Goodman Brown grasp his staff and set forth again, at such a rate that he seemed to fly along the forest path rather than to walk or run. The road grew wilder and drearier and more faintly traced, and vanished at length, leaving him in the heart of the dark wilderness, still rushing onward with the instinct that guides mortal man to evil. The whole forest was peopled with frightful sounds—the creaking of the trees, the howling of wild beasts, and the yell of Indians; while sometimes the wind tolled like a distant church bell, and sometimes gave a broad roar around the traveller, as if all Nature were laughing him to scorn. But he was himself the chief horror of the scene, and shrank not from its other horrors.

"Ha! ha! ha!" roared Goodman Brown when the wind laughed at him. "Let us hear which will laugh loudest. Think not to frighten me with your deviltry. Come witch, come wizard, come Indian powwow, come devil himself, and here comes Goodman Brown. You may as well fear him as he fears you."

In truth, all through the haunted forest there could be nothing more frightful than the figure of Goodman Brown. On he flew among the black pines, brandishing his staff with frenzied gestures, now giving vent to an inspiration of horrid blasphemy, and now shouting forth such laughter as set all the echoes of the forest laughing like demons around him. The fiend in his own shape is less hideous than when he rages in the breast of man. Thus sped the demoniac on his course, until, quivering among the trees, he saw a red light before him, as when the felled trunks and branches of a clearing have been set on fire, and throw up their lurid blaze against the sky, at the hour of midnight. He paused, in a lull of the tempest that had driven him onward, and heard the swell of what seemed a hymn, rolling solemnly from a distance with the weight of many voices. He knew the tune; it was a familiar one in the choir of the village meeting-house. The verse died heavily away, and was lengthened by a chorus, not of human voices, but of all the sounds of the benighted wilderness pealing in awful harmony together. Goodman Brown cried out, and his cry was lost to his own ear by its unison with the cry of the desert.

In the interval of silence he stole forward until the light glared full upon his eyes. At one extremity of an open space, hemmed in by the dark wall of the forest, arose a rock, bearing some rude, natural resemblance either to an altar or a pulpit, and surrounded by four blazing pines, their tops aflame, their stems untouched, like candles at an evening meeting. The mass of foliage that had overgrown the summit of the rock was all on fire, blazing high into the night and fitfully illuminating the whole field. Each pendent twig and leafy festoon was in a blaze. As the red light arose and fell, a numerous congregation alternately shone forth, then disappeared in shadow, and again grew, as it were, out of the darkness, peopling the heart of the solitary woods at once.

"A grave and dark-clad company," quoth Goodman Brown.   55

In truth they were such. Among them, quivering to and fro between gloom and splendor, appeared faces that would be seen next day at the council board of the province, and others which, Sabbath after Sabbath, looked devoutly heavenward, and benignantly over the crowded pews, from the holiest pulpits in the land. Some affirm that the lady of the governor was there. At least there were high dames well known to her, and wives of honored husbands, and widows, a great multitude, and ancient maidens, all of excellent repute, and fair young girls, who trembled lest their mothers should espy them. Either the sudden gleams of light flashing over the obscure field bedazzled Goodman Brown, or he recognized a score of the church members of Salem village famous for their especial sanctity. Good old Deacon Gookin had arrived, and waited at the skirts of that venerable saint, his revered pastor. But, irreverently consorting with these grave, reputable, and pious people, these elders of the church, these chaste dames and dewy virgins, there were men of dissolute lives and women of spotted fame, wretches given over to all mean and filthy vice, and suspected even of horrid crimes. It was strange to see that the good shrank not from the wicked, nor were the sinners abashed by the saints. Scattered also among their pale-faced enemies were the Indian priests, or powwows, who had often scared their native forest with more hideous incantations than any known to English witchcraft.

"But where is Faith?" thought Goodman Brown; and, as hope came into his heart, he trembled.

Another verse of the hymn arose, a slow and mournful strain, such as the pious love, but joined to words which expressed all that our nature can conceive of sin, and darkly hinted at far more. Unfathomable to mere mortals is the lore of fiends. Verse after verse was sung; and still the chorus of the desert swelled between like the deepest tone of a mighty organ; and with the final peal of that dreadful anthem there came a sound, as if the roaring wind, the rushing streams, the howling beasts, and every other voice of the unconcerted wilderness were mingling and according with the voice of guilty man in homage to the prince of all. The four blazing pines threw up a loftier flame, and obscurely discovered shapes and visages of horror on the smoke wreaths above the impious assembly. At the same moment the fire on the rock shot redly forth and formed a glowing arch above its base, where now appeared a figure. With reverence be it spoken, the figure bore no slight similitude, both in garb and manner, to some grave divine of the New England churches.

"Bring forth the converts!" cried a voice that echoed through the field and rolled into the forest.

At the word, Goodman Brown stepped forth from the shadow of the trees and approached the congregation, with whom he felt a loathful brotherhood by the sympathy of all that was wicked in his heart. He could have well-nigh sworn that the shape of his own dead father beckoned him to advance, looking downward from a smoke wreath, while a woman, with dim features of despair, threw out her hand to warn him back. Was it his mother? But he had no power to retreat one step, nor to resist, even in thought, when the minister and good old Deacon Gookin seized his arms and led him to the blazing rock. Thither came also the slender form of a veiled female, led between Goody Cloyse, that pious teacher of the catechism, and Martha Carrier,[4] who had received the devil's promise to be queen of hell. A rampant hag was she. And there stood the proselytes beneath the canopy of fire.

"Welcome, my children," said the dark figure, "to the communion of your race. Ye have found thus young your nature and your destiny. My children, look behind you!"

They turned; and flashing forth, as it were, in a sheet of flame, the fiend worshippers were seen; the smile of welcome gleamed darkly on every visage.

"There," resumed the sable form, "are all whom ye have reverenced from youth. Ye deemed them holier than yourselves, and shrank from

---

[4]***Martha Carrier:*** a Salem woman hanged as a witch in 1692. —EDS.

your own sin, contrasting it with their lives of righteousness and prayerful aspirations heavenward. Yet here are they all in my worshipping assembly. This night it shall be granted you to know their secret deeds: how hoary-bearded elders of the church have whispered wanton words to the young maids of their households; how many a woman, eager for widows' weeds, has given her husband a drink at bedtime and let him sleep his last sleep in her bosom; how beardless youths have made haste to inherit their fathers' wealth; and how fair damsels — blush not, sweet ones — have dug little graves in the garden, and bidden me, the sole guest, to an infant's funeral. By the sympathy of your human hearts for sin ye shall scent out all the places — whether in church, bed-chamber, street, field, or forest — where crime has been committed, and shall exult to behold the whole earth one stain of guilt, one mighty blood spot. Far more than this. It shall be yours to penetrate, in every bosom, the deep mystery of sin, the fountain of all wicked arts, and which inexhaustibly supplies more evil impulses than human power — than my power at its utmost — can make manifest in deeds. And now, my children, look upon each other."

They did so; and, by the blaze of the hell-kindled torches, the wretched man beheld his Faith, and the wife her husband, trembling before that unhallowed altar.

"Lo, there ye stand, my children," said the figure, in a deep and solemn tone, almost sad with its despairing awfulness, as if his once angelic nature could yet mourn for our miserable race. "Depending upon one another's hearts, ye had still hoped that virtue were not all a dream. Now are ye undeceived. Evil is the nature of mankind. Evil must be your only happiness. Welcome again, my children, to the communion of your race." 65

"Welcome," repeated the fiend worshippers, in one cry of despair and triumph.

And there they stood, the only pair, as it seemed, who were yet hesitating on the verge of wickedness in this dark world. A basin was hollowed, naturally, in the rock. Did it contain water, reddened by the lurid light? or was it blood? or, perchance, a liquid flame? Herein did the shape of evil dip his hand and prepare to lay the mark of baptism upon their foreheads, that they might be partakers of the mystery of sin, more conscious of the secret guilt of others, both in deed and thought, than they could now be of their own. The husband cast one look at his pale wife, and Faith at him. What polluted wretches would the next glance show them to each other, shuddering alike at what they disclosed and what they saw!

"Faith! Faith!" cried the husband, "look up to heaven, and resist the wicked one."

Whether Faith obeyed he knew not. Hardly had he spoken when he found himself amid calm night and solitude, listening to a roar of the wind which died heavily away through the forest. He staggered against the rock, and felt it chill and damp; while a hanging twig, that had been all on fire, besprinkled his cheek with the coldest dew.

The next morning young Goodman Brown came slowly into the   70
street of Salem village, staring around him like a bewildered man. The
good old minister was taking a walk along the graveyard to get an appetite for breakfast and meditate his sermon, and bestowed a blessing, as
he passed, on Goodman Brown. He shrank from the venerable saint as if
to avoid an anathema. Old Deacon Gookin was at domestic worship, and
the holy words of his prayer were heard through the open window.
"What God doth the wizard pray to?" quoth Goodman Brown. Goody
Cloyse, that excellent old Christian, stood in the early sunshine at her
own lattice, catechizing a little girl who had brought her a pint of morning's milk. Goodman Brown snatched away the child as from the grasp of
the fiend himself. Turning the corner by the meeting-house, he spied the
head of Faith, with the pink ribbons, gazing anxiously forth, and bursting
into such joy at sight of him that she skipped along the street and almost
kissed her husband before the whole village. But Goodman Brown looked
sternly and sadly into her face, and passed on without a greeting.

Had Goodman Brown fallen asleep in the forest and only dreamed a
wild dream of a witch-meeting?

Be it so if you will; but, alas! it was a dream of evil omen for young
Goodman Brown. A stern, a sad, a darkly meditative, a distrustful, if not
a desperate man did he become from the night of that fearful dream. On
the Sabbath day, when the congregation were singing a holy psalm, he
could not listen because an anthem of sin rushed loudly upon his ear and
drowned all the blessed strain. When the minister spoke from the pulpit
with power and fervid eloquence, and, with his hand on the open Bible,
of the sacred truths of our religion, and of saint-like lives and triumphant
deaths, and of future bliss or misery unutterable, then did Goodman
Brown turn pale, dreading lest the roof should thunder down upon the
gray blasphemer and his hearers. Often, awakening suddenly at midnight,
he shrank from the bosom of Faith; and at morning or eventide, when the
family knelt down at prayer, he scowled and muttered to himself, and
gazed sternly at his wife, and turned away. And when he had lived long,
and was borne to his grave a hoary corpse, followed by Faith, an aged
woman, and children and grandchildren, a goodly procession, besides
neighbors not a few, they carved no hopeful verse upon his tombstone,
for his dying hour was gloom.

The Reader's Presence

1. What effect does the story's setting have on the reader? Why are
   the time and place important? What does this story suggest about
   Goodman Brown's state of mind?

2. What details does Hawthorne provide about the appearance and
   behavior of the companion who accompanies Goodman Brown?

What do these details imply about the companion's identity? Why is his appearance "not wholly unexpected" (paragraph 12)?

3. Read "The Witches of Salem Village" by Kai Erikson (page 406). How does this background information affect your understanding of what is happening in Hawthorne's story? Is Goodman Brown imagining things in the forest? Does it matter whether what he sees there is real? Why or why not?

Gish Jen

Who's Irish?

Gish Jen (b. 1956), a second-generation Chinese American, writes fiction that is a collage of her Chinese roots and her very American upbringing. Her collection of short stories, Who's Irish? *(1999), was described by* Kirkus Reviews *as a "sharp-eyed debut collection . . . examining American life from a foreigner's perspective." A prolific writer of short stories, her work has appeared in the* New Yorker, *the* Atlantic, *the* New Republic, *the* Los Angeles Times, *and the* New York Times, *as well as in numerous textbooks and anthologies, including* The Best American Short Stories of the Century, *edited by John Updike. She has received grants and awards from the Guggenheim Foundation, the Bunting Institute, the National Endowment for the Arts, the American Academy of Arts and Sciences, and the Lannan Foundation.*

Jen argues that understanding one's own culture involves more than just a "huge, public embracing of ethnic roots." She says, "I think that anybody who is interested in their identity would do well to learn about the place they grew up in, and learn about its culture. We make ourselves in this country; even people who are racial and ethnic minorities transform themselves."

For additional information on Gish Jen, see page 171.

In China, people say mixed children are supposed to be smart, and definitely my granddaughter Sophie is smart. But Sophie is wild, Sophie is not like my daughter Natalie, or like me. I am work hard my whole life, and fierce besides. My husband always used to say he is afraid of me, and in our restaurant, busboys and cooks all afraid of me too. Even the gang members come for protection money, they try to talk to my husband. When I am there, they stay away. If they come by mistake, they pretend they are come to eat. They hide behind the menu, they order a lot of food.

They talk about their mothers. Oh, my mother have some arthritis, need to take herbal medicine, they say. Oh, my mother getting old, her hair all white now.

I say, Your mother's hair used to be white, but since she dye it, it become black again. Why don't you go home once in a while and take a look? I tell them, Confucius say a filial son knows what color his mother's hair is.

My daughter is fierce too, she is vice president in the bank now. Her new house is big enough for everybody to have their own room, including me. But Sophie take after Natalie's husband's family, their name is Shea. Irish. I always thought Irish people are like Chinese people, work so hard on the railroad, but now I know why the Chinese beat the Irish. Of course, not all Irish are like the Shea family, of course not. My daughter tell me I should not say Irish this, Irish that.

How do you like it when people say the Chinese this, the Chinese that, she say.

You know, the British call the Irish heathen, just like they call the Chinese, she say.

You think the Opium War[1] was bad, how would you like to live right next door to the British, she say.

And that is that. My daughter have a funny habit when she win an argument, she take a sip of something and look away, so the other person is not embarrassed. So I am not embarrassed. I do not call anybody anything either. I just happen to mention about the Shea family, an interesting fact: four brothers in the family, and not one of them work. The mother, Bess, have a job before she got sick, she was executive secretary in a big company. She is handle everything for a big shot, you would be surprised how complicated her job is, not just type this, type that. Now she is a nice woman with a clean house. But her boys, every one of them is on welfare, or so-called severance pay, or so-called disability pay. Something. They say they cannot find work, this is not the economy of the fifties, but I say, Even the black people doing better these days, some of them live so fancy, you'd be surprised. Why the Shea family have so much trouble? They are white people, they speak English. When I come to this country, I have no money and do not speak English. But my husband and I own our restaurant before he die. Free and clear, no mortgage. Of course, I understand I am just lucky, come from a country where the food is popular all over the world. I understand it is not the Shea family's fault they come from a country where everything is boiled. Still, I say.

5

---

[1]*Opium War:* In the early nineteenth century, Great Britain bought raw opium from India and imported it into China in exchange for tea, silk, and porcelain. When China banned the importation of opium in 1839, Great Britain attacked with gunboats, demanding that the opium imports be permitted to continue. The Chinese defeat was formalized with the Treaty of Nanking in 1842, which ceded Hong Kong to Britain and granted many concessions to British traders. —EDS.

She's right, we should broaden our horizons, say one brother, Jim, at Thanksgiving. Forget about the car business. Think about egg rolls.

Pad thai, say another brother, Mike. I'm going to make my fortune in pad thai. It's going to be the new pizza.

I say, You people too picky about what you sell. Selling egg rolls not   10
good enough for you, but at least my husband and I can say, We made it. What can you say? Tell me. What can you say?

Everybody chew their tough turkey.

I especially cannot understand my daughter's husband John, who has no job but cannot take care of Sophie either. Because he is a man, he say, and that's the end of the sentence.

Plain boiled food, plain boiled thinking. Even his name is plain boiled: John. Maybe because I grew up with black bean sauce and hoisin sauce and garlic sauce, I always feel something is missing when my son-in-law talk.

But, okay: so my son-in-law can be man, I am baby-sitter. Six hours a day, same as the old sitter, crazy Amy, who quit. This is not so easy, now that I am sixty-eight, Chinese age almost seventy. Still, I try. In China, daughter take care of mother. Here it is the other way around. Mother help daughter, mother ask, Anything else I can do? Otherwise daughter complain mother is not supportive. I tell daughter, We do not have this word in Chinese, *supportive*. But my daughter too busy to listen, she has to go to meeting, she has to write memo while her husband go to the gym to be a man. My daughter say otherwise he will be depressed. Seems like all his life he has this trouble, depression.

No one wants to hire someone who is depressed, she say. It is impor-   15
tant for him to keep his spirits up.

Beautiful wife, beautiful daughter, beautiful house, oven can clean itself automatically. No money left over, because only one income, but lucky enough, got the baby-sitter for free. If John lived in China, he would be very happy. But he is not happy. Even at the gym things go wrong. One day, he pull a muscle. Another day, weight room too crowded. Always something.

Until finally, hooray, he has a job. Then he feel pressure.

I need to concentrate, he say. I need to focus.

He is going to work for insurance company. Salesman job. A paycheck, he say, and at least he will wear clothes instead of gym shorts. My daughter buy him some special candy bars from the health-food store. They say THINK! on them, and are supposed to help John think.

John is a good-looking boy, you have to say that, especially now that   20
he shave so you can see his face.

I am an old man in a young man's game, say John.

I will need a new suit, say John.

This time I am not going to shoot myself in the foot, say John.

Good, I say.

She means to be supportive, my daughter say. Don't start the send   25
her back to China thing, because we can't.

Sophie is three years old American age, but already I see her nice Chinese side swallowed up by her wild Shea side. She looks like mostly Chinese.
Beautiful black hair, beautiful black eyes. Nose perfect size, not so flat looks
like something fell down, not so large looks like some big deal got stuck in
wrong face. Everything just right, only her skin is a brown surprise to John's
family. So brown, they say. Even John say it. She never goes in the sun, still
she is that color, he say. Brown. They say, Nothing the matter with brown.
They are just surprised. So brown. Nattie is not that brown, they say. They
say, It seems like Sophie should be a color in between Nattie and John.
Seems funny, a girl named Sophie Shea be brown. But she is brown, maybe
her name should be Sophie Brown. She never go in the sun, still she is that
color, they say. Nothing the matter with brown. They are just surprised.
   The Shea family talk is like this sometimes, going around and around
like a Christmas-tree train.
   Maybe John is not her father, I say one day, to stop the train. And
sure enough, train wreck. None of the brothers ever say the word *brown*
to me again.
   Instead, John's mother, Bess, say, I hope you are not offended.
   She say, I did my best on those boys. But raising four boys with no   30
father is no picnic.
   You have a beautiful family, I say.
   I'm getting old, she say.
   You deserve a rest, I say. Too many boys make you old.
   I never had a daughter, she say. You have a daughter.
   I have a daughter, I say. Chinese people don't think a daughter is so   35
great, but you're right. I have a daughter.
   I was never against the marriage, you know, she say. I never thought
John was marrying down. I always thought Nattie was just as good as
white.
   I was never against the marriage either, I say. I just wonder if they
look at the whole problem.
   Of course you pointed out the problem, you are a mother, she say.
And now we both have a granddaughter. A little brown granddaughter,
she is so precious to me.
   I laugh. A little brown granddaughter, I say. To tell you the truth, I
don't know how she came out so brown.
   We laugh some more. These days Bess need a walker to walk. She   40
take so many pills, she need two glasses of water to get them all down.
Her favorite TV show is about bloopers, and she love her bird feeder. All
day long, she can watch that bird feeder, like a cat.
   I can't wait for her to grow up, Bess say. I could use some female
company.

Too many boys, I say.

Boys are fine, she say. But they do surround you after a while.

You should take a break, come live with us, I say. Lots of girls at our house.

Be careful what you offer, say Bess with a wink. Where I come from,   45
people mean for you to move in when they say a thing like that.

Nothing the matter with Sophie's outside, that's the truth. It is inside
that she is like not any Chinese girl I ever see. We go to the park, and this
is what she does. She stand up in the stroller. She take off all her clothes
and throw them in the fountain.

Sophie! I say. Stop!

But she just laugh like a crazy person. Before I take over as baby-sitter,
Sophie has that crazy-person sitter, Amy the guitar player. My daughter
thought this Amy very creative—another word we do not talk about in
China. In China, we talk about whether we have difficulty or no difficulty.
We talk about whether life is bitter or not bitter. In America, all day long,
people talk about creative. Never mind that I cannot even look at this Amy,
with her shirt so short that her belly button showing. This Amy think Sophie should love her body. So when Sophie take off her diaper, Amy laugh.
When Sophie run around naked, Amy say she wouldn't want to wear a diaper either. When Sophie go *shu-shu* in her lap, Amy laugh and say there are
no germs in pee. When Sophie take off her shoes, Amy say bare feet is best,
even the pediatrician say so. That is why Sophie now walk around with no
shoes like a beggar child. Also why Sophie love to take off her clothes.

Turn around! say the boys in the park. Let's see that ass!

Of course, Sophie does not understand. Sophie clap her hands, I am   50
the only one to say, No! This is not a game.

It has nothing to do with John's family, my daughter say. Amy was
too permissive, that's all.

But I think if Sophie was not wild inside, she would not take off her
shoes and clothes to begin with.

You never take off your clothes when you were little, I say. All
my Chinese friends had babies, I never saw one of them act wild like that.

Look, my daughter say. I have a big presentation tomorrow.

John and my daughter agree Sophie is a problem, but they don't know   55
what to do.

You spank her, she'll stop, I say another day.

But they say, Oh no.

In America, parents not supposed to spank the child.

It gives them low self-esteem, my daughter say. And that leads to
problems later, as I happen to know.

My daughter never have big presentation the next day when the sub-   60
ject of spanking come up.

I don't want you to touch Sophie, she say. No spanking, period.

Don't tell me what to do, I say.

I'm not telling you what to do, say my daughter. I'm telling you how I feel.

I am not your servant, I say. Don't you dare talk to me like that.

My daughter have another funny habit when she lose an argument. She spread out all her fingers and look at them, as if she like to make sure they are still there.

My daughter is fierce like me, but she and John think it is better to explain to Sophie that clothes are a good idea. This is not so hard in the cold weather. In the warm weather, it is very hard.

Use your words, my daughter say. That's what we tell Sophie. How about if you set a good example.

As if good example mean anything to Sophie. I am so fierce, the gang members who used to come to the restaurant all afraid of me, but Sophie is not afraid.

I say, Sophie, if you take off your clothes, no snack.

I say, Sophie, if you take off your clothes, no lunch.

I say, Sophie, if you take off your clothes, no park.

Pretty soon we are stay home all day, and by the end of six hours she still did not have one thing to eat. You never saw a child stubborn like that.

I'm hungry! she cry when my daughter come home.

What's the matter, doesn't your grandmother feed you? My daughter laugh.

No! Sophie say. She doesn't feed me anything!

My daughter laugh again. Here you go, she say.

She say to John, Sophie must be growing.

Growing like a weed, I say.

Still Sophie take off her clothes, until one day I spank her. Not too hard, but she cry and cry, and when I tell her if she doesn't put her clothes back on I'll spank her again, she put her clothes back on. Then I tell her she is good girl, and give her some food to eat. The next day we go to the park and, like a nice Chinese girl, she does not take off her clothes.

She stop taking off her clothes, I report. Finally!

How did you do it? my daughter ask.

After twenty-eight years experience with you, I guess I learn something, I say.

It must have been a phase, John say, and his voice is suddenly like an expert.

His voice is like an expert about everything these days, now that he carry a leather briefcase, and wear shiny shoes, and can go shopping for a new car. On the company, he say. The company will pay for it, but he will be able to drive it whenever he want.

A free car, he say. How do you like that.

It's good to see you in the saddle again, my daughter say. Some of your family patterns are scary.

At least I don't drink, he say. He say, And I'm not the only one with scary family patterns.

That's for sure, say my daughter.

Everyone is happy. Even I am happy, because there is more trouble with Sophie, but now I think I can help her Chinese side fight against her wild side. I teach her to eat food with fork or spoon or chopsticks, she cannot just grab into the middle of a bowl of noodles. I teach her not to play with garbage cans. Sometimes I spank her, but not too often, and not too hard.

Still, there are problems. Sophie like to climb everything. If there is a   90
railing, she is never next to it. Always she is on top of it. Also, Sophie like to hit the mommies of her friends. She learn this from her playground best friend, Sinbad, who is four. Sinbad wear army clothes every day and like to ambush his mommy. He is the one who dug a big hole under the play structure, a foxhole he call it, all by himself. Very hardworking. Now he wait in the foxhole with a shovel full of wet sand. When his mommy come, he throw it right at her.

Oh, it's all right, his mommy say. You can't get rid of war games, it's part of their imaginative play. All the boys go through it.

Also, he like to kick his mommy, and one day he tell Sophie to kick his mommy too.

I wish this story is not true.

Kick her, kick her! Sinbad say.

Sophie kick her. A little kick, as if she just so happened was swinging   95
her little leg and didn't realize that big mommy leg was in the way. Still I spank Sophie and make Sophie say sorry, and what does the mommy say?

Really, it's all right, she say. It didn't hurt.

After that, Sophie learn she can attack mommies in the playground, and some will say, Stop, but others will say, Oh, she didn't mean it, especially if they realize Sophie will be punished.

This is how, one day, bigger trouble come. The bigger trouble start when Sophie hide in the foxhole with that shovel full of sand. She wait, and when I come look for her, she throw it at me. All over my nice clean clothes.

Did you ever see a Chinese girl act this way?

Sophie! I say. Come out of there, say you're sorry.   100

But she does not come out. Instead, she laugh. Naaah, naah-na, naaa-naaa, she say.

I am not exaggerate: millions of children in China, not one act like this.

Sophie! I say. Now! Come out now!

But she know she is in big trouble. She know if she come out, what will happen next. So she does not come out. I am sixty-eight, Chinese age almost seventy, how can I crawl under there to catch her? Impossible. So I yell, yell, yell, and what happen? Nothing. A Chinese mother would help, but American mothers, they look at you, they shake their head, they go home. And, of course, a Chinese child would give up, but not Sophie.

I hate you! she yell. I hate you, Meanie!   105
Meanie is my new name these days.

Long time this goes on, long long time. The foxhole is deep, you cannot
see too much, you don't know where is the bottom. You cannot hear too
much either. If she does not yell, you cannot even know she is still there or
not. After a while, getting cold out, getting dark out. No one left in the
playground, only us.

Sophie, I say. How did you become stubborn like this? I am go home
without you now.

I try to use a stick, chase her out of there, and once or twice I hit her,
but still she does not come out. So finally I leave. I go outside the gate.

Bye-bye! I say. I'm go home now.   110

But still she does not come out and does not come out. Now it is dinner time, the sky is black. I think I should maybe go get help, but how can
I leave a little girl by herself in the playground? A bad man could come. A
rat could come. I go back in to see what is happen to Sophie. What if she
have a shovel and is making a tunnel to escape?

Sophie! I say.
No answer.
Sophie!

I don't know if she is alive. I don't know if she is fall asleep down   115
there. If she is crying, I cannot hear her.

So I take the stick and poke.

Sophie! I say. I promise I no hit you. If you come out, I give you a lol-
lipop.

No answer. By now I worried. What to do, what to do, what to do? I
poke some more, even harder, so that I am poking and poking when my
daughter and John suddenly appear.

What are you doing? What is going on? say my daughter.
Put down that stick! say my daughter.   120
You are crazy! say my daughter.

John wiggle under the structure, into the foxhole, to rescue Sophie.
She fell asleep, say John the expert. She's okay. That is one big hole.
Now Sophie is crying and crying.

Sophia, my daughter say, hugging her. Are you okay, peanut? Are you   125
okay?

She's just scared, say John.
Are you okay? I say too. I don't know what happen, I say.
She's okay, say John. He is not like my daughter, full of questions.
He is full of answers until we get home and can see by the lamplight.

Will you look at her? he yell then. What the hell happened?
Bruises all over her brown skin, and a swollen-up eye.   130
You are crazy! say my daughter. Look at what you did! You are crazy!
I try very hard, I say.
How could you use a stick? I told you to use your words!
She is hard to handle, I say.

She's three years old! You cannot use a stick! say my daughter.   135
She is not like any Chinese girl I ever saw, I say.
I brush some sand off my clothes. Sophie's clothes are dirty too, but at least she has her clothes on.
Has she done this before? ask my daughter. Has she hit you before?
She hits me all the time, Sophie say, eating ice cream.
Your family, say John.   140
Believe me, say my daughter.

A daughter I have, a beautiful daughter. I took care of her when she could not hold her head up. I took care of her before she could argue with me, when she was a little girl with two pigtails, one of them always crooked. I took care of her when we have to escape from China, I took care of her when suddenly we live in a country with cars everywhere, if you are not careful your little girl get run over. When my husband die, I promise him I will keep the family together, even though it was just two of us, hardly a family at all.

But now my daughter take me around to look at apartments. After all, I can cook, I can clean, there's no reason I cannot live by myself, all I need is a telephone. Of course, she is sorry. Sometimes she cry, I am the one to say everything will be okay. She say she have no choice, she doesn't want to end up divorced. I say divorce is terrible, I don't know who invented this terrible idea. Instead of live with a telephone, though, surprise, I come to live with Bess. Imagine that. Bess make an offer and, sure enough, where she come from, people mean for you to move in when they say things like that. A crazy idea, go to live with someone else's family, but she like to have some female company, not like my daughter, who does not believe in company. These days when my daughter visit, she does not bring Sophie. Bess say we should give Nattie time, we will see Sophie again soon. But seems like my daughter have more presentation than ever before, every time she come she have to leave.

I have a family to support, she say, and her voice is heavy, as if soaking wet. I have a young daughter and a depressed husband and no one to turn to.

When she say no one to turn to, she mean me.   145
These days my beautiful daughter is so tired she can just sit there in a chair and fall asleep. John lost his job again, already, but still they rather hire a baby-sitter than ask me to help, even they can't afford it. Of course, the new baby-sitter is much younger, can run around. I don't know if Sophie these days is wild or not wild. She call me Meanie, but she like to kiss me too, sometimes. I remember that every time I see a child on TV. Sophie like to grab my hair, a fistful in each hand, and then kiss me smack on the nose. I never see any other child kiss that way.

The satellite TV has so many channels, more channels than I can count, including a Chinese channel from the Mainland and a Chinese channel from Taiwan, but most of the time I watch bloopers with Bess. Also, I watch the bird feeder—so many, many kinds of birds come. The Shea sons hang around all the time, asking when will I go home, but Bess tell them, Get lost.

She's a permanent resident, say Bess. She isn't going anywhere.

Then she wink at me, and switch the channel with the remote control.

Of course, I shouldn't say Irish this, Irish that, especially now I am become honorary Irish myself, according to Bess. Me! Who's Irish? I say, and she laugh. All the same, if I could mention one thing about some of the Irish, not all of them of course, I like to mention this: Their talk just stick. I don't know how Bess Shea learn to use her words, but sometimes I hear what she say a long time later. *Permanent resident. Not going anywhere.* Over and over I hear it, the voice of Bess.

The Reader's Presence

1. The grandmother complains that Sophie "is not like any Chinese girl I ever see" (paragraph 46). How does Sophie defy her grandmother's expectations of what a Chinese girl should be? What are the different expectations for a child's behavior in the United States and in China, according to this story?

2. Why do you think Jen chooses to allow the grandmother's tactics of spanking and scolding to work on Sophie at first? How does the author's choice affect the reader's perception of the family conflict?

3. Like every other detail in a story, names are carefully chosen by the writer. Read Jen's essay "Name Dropping" (page 171). In it, she reflects: "Names matter to us; and as for whether the world cares, I think it does much more than it realizes." How do the names in "Who's Irish?" add to our understanding of Jen's characters? What is the significance of the names Jen chooses?

Jamaica Kincaid

Girl

Jamaica Kincaid became a professional writer almost by accident. Living in New York City *in the 1970s, she befriended one of the staff writers at the* New Yorker *and began to accompany him as he conducted research for the "Talk of the Town" section. Before long, she discovered that she could write and that her writing impressed the editors of the magazine. When her first piece of nonfiction was published, Kincaid remembers, "That is when I realized what my writing was. My writing was the thing that I thought. Not something else. Just what I thought." After working as a staff writer at the* New Yorker *for four years, she began to turn to fiction. "Girl" is the first piece of fiction she published; it appeared in the* New Yorker *in 1978.*

For more information on Jamaica Kincaid, see page 175.

Wash the white clothes on Monday and put them on the stone heap; wash the color clothes on Tuesday and put them on the clothesline to dry; don't walk barehead in the hot sun; cook pumpkin fritters in very hot sweet oil; soak your little clothes right after you take them off; when buying cotton to make yourself a nice blouse, be sure that it doesn't have gum on it, because that way it won't hold up well after a wash; soak salt fish overnight before you cook it; is it true that you sing benna[1] in Sunday School?; always eat your food in such a way that it won't turn someone else's stomach; on Sundays try to walk like a lady and not like the slut you are so bent on becoming; don't sing benna in Sunday School; you mustn't speak to wharf-rat boys, not even to give directions; don't eat fruits on the street—flies will follow you; *but I don't sing benna on Sundays at all and never in Sunday School;* this is how to sew on a button; this is how to make a buttonhole for the button you have just sewed on; this is how to hem a dress when you see the hem coming down and so to prevent yourself from looking like the slut I know you are so bent on becoming; this is how you iron your father's khaki shirt so that it doesn't have a crease; this is how you iron your father's khaki pants so that they don't have a crease; this is how you grow okra—far from the house, because okra tree harbors red ants; when you are growing dasheen,[2] make sure it gets plenty of water or else it makes your throat itch when you are eating it; this is how you sweep a corner; this is how you sweep a whole house; this is how you sweep a yard; this is how you smile to someone you don't like too much; this is how you smile to someone you don't like at all; this is how you smile to someone you like completely; this is how you set a table for tea; this is how you set a table for dinner; this is how you set a table for dinner with an important guest; this is how you set a table for lunch; this is how you set a table for breakfast; this is how to behave in the presence of men who don't know you very well, and this way they won't recognize immediately the slut I have warned you against becoming; be sure to wash every day, even if it is with your own spit; don't squat down to play marbles—you are not a boy, you know; don't pick people's flowers—you might catch something; don't throw stones at blackbirds, because it might not be a blackbird at all; this is how to make

---

[1]*benna:* Popular calypso-like music. —EDS.
[2]*dasheen:* A starchy vegetable. —EDS.
[3]*doukona:* Cornmeal. —EDS.

a bread pudding; this is how to make doukona;[3] this is how to make pepper pot; this is how to make a good medicine for a cold; this is how to make a good medicine to throw away a child before it even becomes a child; this is how to catch a fish; this is how to throw back a fish you don't like, and that way something bad won't fall on you; this is how to bully a man; this is how a man bullies you; this is how to love a man, and if this doesn't work there are other ways, and if they don't work don't feel too bad about giving up; this is how to spit up in the air if you feel like it, and this is how to move quick so that it doesn't fall on you; this is how to make ends meet; always squeeze bread to make sure it's fresh; *but what if the baker won't let me feel the bread?*; you mean to say that after all you are really going to be the kind of woman who the baker won't let near the bread?

The Reader's Presence

1. Whose voice dominates this story? To whom is the monologue addressed? What effect(s) does the speaker seek to have on the listener? Where does the speaker appear to have acquired her values? Categorize the kinds of advice you find in the story. Identify sentences in which one category of advice merges into another. How are the different kinds of advice alike, and to what extent are they contradictory?

2. "Girl" speaks only two lines, both of which are italicized. In each case, what prompts her to speak? What is the result? Stories generally create the expectation that at least one main character will undergo a change. What differences, if any, do you notice between her first and second lines of dialogue (and the replies she elicits), differences that might suggest that such a change has taken place? If so, in whom? Analyze the girl's character based not only on what she says but on what she hears (if one can assume that this monologue was not delivered all in one sitting, but is rather the distillation of years' worth of advice, as heard by the girl).

3. Consider the role of gender in this story. What gender stereotypes are perpetuated by the main speaker? Look not only at the stereotypes that affect women, but also at those that define the roles of men. What can you infer about the males, who remain behind the scenes? Read Kincaid's "Biography of a Dress" (page 175). Do the essay and the photograph that accompanies it suggest how Kincaid's mother may have perceived gender roles? How does Kincaid say that she responded as a child to the role her mother wants her to play? How does she suggest she has responded to this role as an adult?

THE WRITER AT WORK

Jamaica Kincaid on *Girl*

> *To many readers, "Girl" appears to be an odd and confusing short story. It's far shorter than most published stories and consists almost entirely of a monologue spoken by a mother to her daughter. Readers may wonder: "What makes this a story?" In the following passage from an interview with Jamaica Kincaid, Allan Varda asks the author some questions about this intriguing little story and discovers behind its composition a larger agenda that we might not perceive from a single reading. Do Kincaid's answers to Varda's questions help you better understand what's happening in the story? In what ways? After considering the story and interview, you also might want to turn (or return) to Kincaid's essay, "Biography of a Dress" (see page 175) and see how they enhance its autobiographical and social significance.*

AV: There is a litany of items in "Girl" from a mother to her daughter about what to do and what *not* to do regarding the elements of being "a nice young lady." Is this the way it was for you and other girls in Antigua?

JK: In a word, yes.

AV: Was that good or bad?

JK: I don't think it's the way I would tell my daughter, but as a mother I would tell her what I think would be best for her to be like. This mother in "Girl" was really just giving the girl an idea about the things she would need to be a self-possessed woman in the world.

AV: But you didn't take your mother's advice?   5

JK: No, because I had other ideas on how to be a self-possessed woman in the world. I didn't know that at the time. I only remember these things. What the mother in the story sees as aids to living in the world, the girl might see as extraordinary oppression, which is one of the things I came to see.

AV: Almost like she's Mother England.

JK: I was just going to say that. I've come to see that I've worked through the relationship of the mother and the girl to a relationship between Europe and the place that I'm from, which is to say, a relationship between the powerful and the powerless. The girl is powerless and the mother is powerful. The mother shows her how to be in the world, but at the back of her mind she thinks she never will get it. She's deeply skeptical that this child could ever grow up to be a self-possessed woman and in the end she reveals her skepticism; yet even within the skepticism is, of course, dismissal and scorn. So it's not unlike the relationship between the conquered and the conqueror.

Joyce Carol Oates

Where Are You Going, Where Have You Been?

Novelist, playwright, poet, essayist, and critic Joyce Carol Oates (b. 1938) is rarely described without the word "prolific." Over a four-decade-long writing career, she has written some fifty novels, more than a dozen plays, and scores of short stories. "Ideas for fiction come to me in the way of numerous tributaries flowing into a single rushing river," she has said. "No individual tributary is explicable other than in terms of its place in the larger stream."

Oates's short story "Where Are You Going, Where Have You Been?" first appeared in 1966 and has been anthologized frequently since. She has said that the idea came from a magazine piece she saw—but never finished reading—about a "thrill killer" in Tucson, Arizona. "Where Are You Going, Where Have You Been?" was the basis for the film Smooth Talk *in 1985.*

For more information on Joyce Carol Oates, see page 215.

For Bob Dylan

Her name was Connie. She was fifteen and she had a quick nervous giggling habit of craning her neck to glance into mirrors, or checking other people's faces to make sure her own was all right. Her mother, who noticed everything and knew everything and who hadn't much reason any longer to look at her own face, always scolded Connie about it. "Stop gawking at yourself, who are you? You think you're so pretty?" she would say. Connie would raise her eyebrows at these familiar complaints and look right through her mother, into a shadowy vision of herself as she was right at that moment: she knew she was pretty and that was everything. Her mother had been pretty once too, if you could believe those old snapshots in the album, but now her looks were gone and that was why she was always after Connie.

"Why don't you keep your room clean like your sister? How've you got your hair fixed—what the hell stinks? Hair spray? You don't see your sister using that junk."

Her sister June was twenty-four and still lived at home. She was a secretary in the high school Connie attended, and if that wasn't bad enough—with her in the same building—she was so plain and chunky and steady that Connie had to hear her praised all the time by her mother and her mother's sisters. June did this, June did that, she saved money and helped clean the house and cooked and Connie couldn't do a thing, her mind was all filled with trashy daydreams. Their father was away at work most of the time and when he came home he wanted supper and he read

925

the newspaper at supper and after supper he went to bed. He didn't bother talking much to them, but around his bent head Connie's mother kept picking at her until Connie wished her mother was dead and she herself was dead and it was all over. "She makes me want to throw up sometimes," she complained to her friends. She had a high, breathless, amused voice which made everything she said a little forced, whether it was sincere or not.

There was one good thing: June went places with girl friends of hers, girls who were just as plain and steady as she, and so when Connie wanted to do that her mother had no objections. The father of Connie's best girl friend drove the girls the three miles to town and left them off at a shopping plaza, so that they could walk through the stores or go to a movie, and when he came to pick them up again at eleven he never bothered to ask what they had done.

They must have been familiar sights, walking around that shopping   5 plaza in their shorts and flat ballerina slippers that always scuffed the sidewalk, with charm bracelets jingling on their thin wrists; they would lean together to whisper and laugh secretly if someone passed by who amused or interested them. Connie had long dark blond hair that drew anyone's eye to it, and she wore part of it pulled up on her head and puffed out and the rest of it she let fall down her back. She wore a pullover jersey blouse that looked one way when she was at home and another way when she was away from home. Everything about her had two sides to it, one for home and one for anywhere that was not home: her walk that could be childlike and bobbing, or languid enough to make anyone think she was hearing music in her head, her mouth which was pale and smirking most of the time, but bright and pink on these evenings out, her laugh which was cynical and drawling at home—"Ha, ha, very funny"—but high-pitched and nervous anywhere else, like the jingling of the charms on her bracelet.

Sometimes they did go shopping or to a movie, but sometimes they went across the highway, ducking fast across the busy road, to a drive-in restaurant where older kids hung out. The restaurant was shaped like a big bottle, though squatter than a real bottle, and on its cap was a revolving figure of a grinning boy who held a hamburger aloft. One night in midsummer they ran across, breathless with daring, and right away someone leaned out a car window and invited them over, but it was just a boy from high school they didn't like. It made them feel good to be able to ignore him. They went up through the maze of parked and cruising cars to the bright-lit, fly-infested restaurant, their faces pleased and expectant as if they were entering a sacred building that loomed out of the night to give them what haven and what blessing they yearned for. They sat at the counter and crossed their legs at the ankles, their thin shoulders rigid with excitement and listened to the music that made everything so good: the music was always in the background like music at a church service, it was something to depend upon.

A boy named Eddie came in to talk with them. He sat backwards on his stool, turning himself jerkily around in semi-circles and then stopping and turning again, and after a while he asked Connie if she would like something to eat. She said she did and so she tapped her friend's arm on her way out—her friend pulled her face up into a brave droll look—and Connie said she would meet her at eleven, across the way. "I just hate to leave her like that," Connie said earnestly, but the boy said that she wouldn't be alone for long. So they went out to his car and on the way Connie couldn't help but let her eyes wander over the windshields and faces all around her, her face gleaming with the joy that had nothing to do with Eddie or even this place; it might have been the music. She drew her shoulders up and sucked in her breath with the pure pleasure of being alive, and just at that moment she happened to glance at a face just a few feet from hers. It was a boy with shaggy black hair, in a convertible jalopy painted gold. He stared at her and then his lips widened into a grin. Connie slit her eyes at him and turned away, but she couldn't help glancing back and there he was still watching her. He wagged a finger and laughed and said, "Gonna get you, baby," and Connie turned away again without Eddie noticing anything.

She spent three hours with him, at the restaurant where they ate hamburgers and drank Cokes in wax cups that were always sweating, and then down an alley a mile or so away, and when he left her off at five to eleven only the movie house was still open at the plaza. Her girl friend was there, talking with a boy. When Connie came up the two girls smiled at each other and Connie said, "How was the movie?" and the girl said, "*You* should know." They rode off with the girl's father, sleepy and pleased, and Connie couldn't help but look at the darkened shopping plaza with its big empty parking lot and its signs that were faded and ghostly now, and over at the drive-in restaurant where cars were still circling tirelessly. She couldn't hear the music at this distance.

Next morning June asked her how the movie was and Connie said, "So-so."

She and that girl and occasionally another girl went out several times a week that way, and the rest of the time Connie spent around the house—it was summer vacation—getting in her mother's way and thinking, dreaming, about the boys she met. But all the boys fell back and dissolved into a single face that was not even a face, but an idea, a feeling, mixed up with the urgent insistent pounding of the music and the humid night air of July. Connie's mother kept dragging her back to the daylight by finding things for her to do or saying suddenly, "What's this about the Pettinger girl?"

And Connie would say nervously, "Oh, her. That dope." She always drew thick clear lines between herself and such girls, and her mother was simple and kindly enough to believe her. Her mother was so simple, Connie thought, that it was maybe cruel to fool her so much. Her mother went scuffling around the house in old bedroom slippers and complained over the telephone to one sister about the other, then the other called up and the two of them complained about the third one. If June's name was mentioned her mother's tone was approving, and if Connie's name was

10

mentioned it was disapproving. This did not really mean she disliked Connie and actually Connie thought that her mother preferred her to June because she was prettier, but the two of them kept up a pretense of exasperation, a sense that they were tugging and struggling over something of little value to either of them. Sometimes, over coffee, they were almost friends, but something would come up—some vexation that was like a fly buzzing suddenly around their heads—and their faces went hard with contempt.

One Sunday Connie got up at eleven—none of them bothered with church—and washed her hair so that it could dry all day long, in the sun. Her parents and sister were going to a barbecue at an aunt's house and Connie said no, she wasn't interested, rolling her eyes, to let mother know just what she thought of it. "Stay home alone then," her mother said sharply. Connie sat out back in a lawn chair and watched them drive away, her father quiet and bald, hunched around so that he could back the car out, her mother with a look that was still angry and not at all softened through the windshield, and in the back seat poor old June all dressed up as if she didn't know what a barbecue was, with all the running yelling kids and the flies. Connie sat with her eyes closed in the sun, dreaming and dazed with the warmth about her as if this were a kind of love, the caresses of love, and her mind slipped over onto thoughts of the boy she had been with the night before and how nice he had been, how sweet it always was, not the way someone like June would suppose but sweet, gentle, the way it was in movies and promised in songs; and when she opened her eyes she hardly knew where she was, the back yard ran off into weeds and a fenceline of trees and behind it the sky was perfectly blue and still. The asbestos "ranch house" that was now three years old startled her—it looked small. She shook her head as if to get awake.

It was too hot. She went inside the house and turned on the radio to drown out the quiet. She sat on the edge of her bed, barefoot, and listened for an hour and a half to a program called XYZ Sunday Jamboree, record after record of hard, fast, shrieking songs she sang along with, interspersed by exclamations from "Bobby King": "An' look here you girls at Napoleon's—Son and Charley want you to pay real close attention to this song coming up!"

And Connie paid close attention herself, bathed in a glow of slow-pulsed joy that seemed to rise mysteriously out of the music itself and lay languidly about the airless little room, breathed in and breathed out with each gentle rise and fall of her chest.

After a while she heard a car coming up the drive. She sat up at once,   15 startled, because it couldn't be her father so soon. The gravel kept crunching all the way in from the road—the driveway was long—and Connie ran to the window. It was a car she didn't know. It was an open jalopy, painted a bright gold that caught the sun opaquely. Her heart began to pound and her fingers snatched at her hair, checking it, and she whispered "Christ. Christ," wondering how bad she looked. The car came to a stop at the side door and the horn sounded four short taps as if this were a signal Connie knew.

She went into the kitchen and approached the door slowly, then hung out the screen door, her bare toes curling down off the step. There were two boys in the car and now she recognized the driver: he had shaggy, shabby black hair that looked crazy as a wig and he was grinning at her.

"I ain't late, am I?" he said.

"Who the hell do you think you are?" Connie said.

"Toldja I'd be out, didn't I?"

"I don't even know who you are."   20

She spoke sullenly, careful to show no interest or pleasure, and he spoke in a fast bright monotone. Connie looked past him to the other boy, taking her time. He had fair brown hair, with a lock that fell onto his forehead. His sideburns gave him a fierce, embarrassed look, but so far he hadn't even bothered to glance at her. Both boys wore sunglasses. The driver's glasses were metallic and mirrored everything in miniature.

"You wanta come for a ride?" he said.

Connie smirked and let her hair fall loose over one shoulder.

"Don'tcha like my car? New paint job," he said. "Hey."

"What?"   25

"You're cute."

She pretended to fidget, chasing flies away from the door.

"Don'tcha believe me, or what?" he said.

"Look, I don't even know who you are," Connie said in disgust.

"Hey, Ellie's got a radio, see. Mine's broke down." He lifted his   30
friend's arm and showed her the little transistor the boy was holding, and now Connie began to hear the music. It was the same program that was playing inside the house.

"Bobby King?" she said.

"I listen to him all the time. I think he's great."

"He's kind of great," Connie said reluctantly.

"Listen, that guy's *great*. He knows where the action is."

Connie blushed a little, because the glasses made it impossible for her   35
to see just what this boy was looking at. She couldn't decide if she liked him or if he was just a jerk, and so she dawdled in the doorway and wouldn't come down or go back inside. She said, "What's all that stuff painted on your car?"

"Can'tcha read it?" He opened the door very carefully, as if he was afraid it might fall off. He slid out just as carefully, planting his feet firmly on the ground, the tiny metallic world in his glasses slowing down like gelatine hardening and in the midst of it Connie's bright green blouse. "This here is my name, to begin with," he said. ARNOLD FRIEND was written in tar-like black letters on the side, with a drawing of a round grinning face that reminded Connie of a pumpkin, except it wore sunglasses. "I wanta introduce myself, I'm Arnold Friend and that's my real name and I'm gonna be your friend, honey, and inside the car's Ellie

Oscar, he's kinda shy." Ellie brought his transistor up to his shoulder and balanced it there. "Now these numbers are a secret code, honey," Arnold Friend explained. He read off the numbers 33, 19, 17 and raised his eyebrows at her to see what she thought of that, but she didn't think much of it. The left rear fender had been smashed and around it was written, on the gleaming gold background: DONE BY CRAZY WOMAN DRIVER. Connie had to laugh at that. Arnold Friend was pleased at her laughter and looked up at her. "Around the other side's a lot more—you wanta come and see them?"

"No."

"Why not?"

"Why should I?"

"Don'tcha wanta see what's on the car? Don'tcha wanta go for a ride?"   40

"I don't know."

"Why not?"

"I got things to do."

"Like what?"

"Things."   45

He laughed as if she had said something funny. He slapped his thighs. He was standing in a strange way, leaning back against the car as if he were balancing himself. He wasn't tall, only an inch or so taller than she would be if she came down to him. Connie liked the way he was dressed, which was the way all of them dressed: tight faded jeans stuffed into black, scuffed boots, a belt that pulled his waist in and showed how lean he was, and a white pull-over shirt that was a little soiled and showed the hard small muscles of his arms and shoulders. He looked as if he probably did hard work, lifting and carrying things. Even his neck looked muscular. And his face was a familiar face, somehow: the jaw and chin and cheeks slightly darkened, because he hadn't shaved for a day or two, and the nose long and hawk-like, sniffing as if she were a treat he was going to gobble up and it was all a joke.

"Connie, you ain't telling the truth. This is your day set aside for a ride with me and you know it," he said, still laughing. The way he straightened and recovered from his fit of laughing showed that it had been all fake.

"How do you know what my name is?" she said suspiciously.

"It's Connie."

"Maybe and maybe not."   50

"I know my Connie," he said, wagging his finger. Now she remembered him even better, back at the restaurant, and her cheeks warmed at the thought of how she sucked in her breath just at the moment she passed him—how she must have looked to him. And he had remembered her. "Ellie and I come out here especially for you," he said. "Ellie can sit in back. How about it?"

"Where?"

"Where what?"

"Where're we going?"

He looked at her. He took off the sunglasses and she saw how pale   55
the skin around his eyes was, like holes that were not in shadow but instead in light. His eyes were like chips of broken glass that catch the light
in an amiable way. He smiled. It was as if the idea of going for a ride
somewhere, to some place, was a new idea to him.

"Just for a ride, Connie sweetheart."

"I never said my name was Connie," she said.

"But I know what it is. I know your name and all about you, lots of
things," Arnold Friend said. He had not moved yet but stood still leaning
back against the side of his jalopy. "I took a special interest in you, such a
pretty girl, and found out all about you like I know your parents and sister are gone somewheres and I know where and how long they're going
to be gone, and I know who you were with last night, and your best
friend's name is Betty. Right?"

He spoke in a simple lilting voice, exactly as if he were reciting the
words to a song. His smile assured her that everything was fine. In the car
Ellie turned up the volume on his radio and did not bother to look around
at them.

"Ellie can sit in the back seat," Arnold Friend said. He indicated his   60
friend with a casual jerk of his chin, as if Ellie did not count and she
could not bother with him.

"How'd you find out all that stuff?" Connie said.

"Listen: Betty Schultz and Tony Fitch and Jimmy Pettinger and Nancy
Pettinger," he said, in a chant. "Raymond Stanley and Bob Hutter—"

"Do you know all those kids?"

"I know everybody."

"Look, you're kidding. You're not from around here."   65

"Sure."

"But—how come we never saw you before?"

"Sure you saw me before," he said. He looked down at his boots, as
if he were a little offended. "You just don't remember."

"I guess I'd remember you," Connie said.

"Yeah?" He looked up at this, beaming. He was pleased. He began   70
to mark time with the music from Ellie's radio, tapping his fists lightly
together. Connie looked away from his smile to the car, which was
painted so bright it almost hurt her eyes to look at it. She looked at that
name, ARNOLD FRIEND. And up at the front fender was an expression
that was familiar—MAN THE FLYING SAUCERS. It was an expression kids had used the year before, but didn't use this year. She looked at
it for a while as if the words meant something to her that she did not yet
know.

"What're you thinking about? Huh?" Arnold Friend demanded.
"Not worried about your hair blowing around in the car, are you?"

"No."

"Think I maybe can't drive good?"

"How do I know?"

"You're a hard girl to handle. How come?" he said. "Don't you know I'm your friend? Didn't you see me put my sign in the air when you walked by?"

"What sign?"

"My sign." And he drew an X in the air, leaning out toward her. They were maybe ten feet apart. After his hand fell back to his side the X was still in the air, almost visible. Connie let the screen door close and stood perfectly still inside it, listening to the music from her radio and the boy's blend together. She stared at Arnold Friend. He stood there so stiffly relaxed, pretending to be relaxed, with one hand idly on the door handle as if he were keeping himself up that way and had no intention of ever moving again. She recognized most things about him, the tight jeans that showed his thighs and buttocks and the greasy leather boots and the tight shirt, and even that slippery friendly smile of his, that sleepy dreamy smile that all the boys used to get across ideas they didn't want to put into words. She recognized all this and also the singsong way he talked, slightly mocking, kidding, but serious and a little melancholy, and she recognized the way he tapped one fist against the other in homage to the perpetual music behind him. But all these things did not come together.

She said suddenly, "Hey, how old are you?"

His smile faded. She could see then that he wasn't a kid, he was much older—thirty, maybe more. At this knowledge her heart began to pound faster.

"That's a crazy thing to ask. Can'tcha see I'm your own age?"

"Like hell you are."

"Or maybe a coupla years older, I'm eighteen."

"Eighteen?" she said doubtfully.

He grinned to reassure her and lines appeared at the corners of his mouth. His teeth were big and white. He grinned so broadly his eyes became slits and she saw how thick the lashes were, thick and black as if painted with a black tar-like material. Then he seemed to become embarrassed, abruptly, and looked over his shoulder at Ellie. "*Him*, he's crazy," he said. "Ain't he a riot, he's a nut, a real character." Ellie was still listening to the music. His sunglasses told nothing about what he was thinking. He wore a bright orange shirt unbuttoned halfway to show his chest, which was a pale, bluish chest and not muscular like Arnold Friend's. His shirt collar was turned up all around and the very tips of the collar pointed out past his chin as if they were protecting him. He was pressing the transistor radio up against his ear and sat there in a kind of daze, right in the sun.

"He's kinda strange," Connie said.

"Hey, she says you're kinda strange! Kinda strange!" Arnold Friend cried. He pounded on the car to get Ellie's attention. Ellie turned for the first time and Connie saw with shock that he wasn't a kid either—he had a fair, hairless face, cheeks reddened slightly as if the veins grew too close to the surface of his skin, the face of a forty-year-old baby. Connie felt a wave of dizziness rise in her at this sight and she stared at him as if waiting for something to change the shock of the moment, make it all right again. Ellie's lips kept shaping words, mumbling along with the words blasting his ear.

"Maybe you two better go away," Connie said faintly.

"What? How come?" Arnold Friend cried. "We come out here to take you for a ride. It's Sunday." He had the voice of the man on the radio now. It was the same voice, Connie thought. "Don'tcha know it's Sunday all day and honey, no matter who you were with last night today you're with Arnold Friend and don't you forget it!—Maybe you better step out here," he said, and this last was in a different voice. It was a little flatter, as if the heat was finally getting to him.

"No. I got things to do."

"Hey."   90

"You two better leave."

"We ain't leaving until you come with us."

"Like hell I am—"

"Connie, don't fool around with me. I mean—I mean, don't fool *around*," he said, shaking his head. He laughed incredulously. He placed his sunglasses on top of his head, carefully, as if he were indeed wearing a wig, and brought the stems down behind his ears. Connie stared at him, another wave of dizziness and fear rising in her so that for a moment he wasn't even in focus but was just a blur, standing there against his gold car, and she had the idea that he had driven up the driveway all right but had come from nowhere before that and belonged nowhere and that everything about him and even the music that was so familiar to her was only half real.

"If my father comes and sees you—"   95

"He ain't coming. He's at a barbecue."

"How do you know that?"

"Aunt Tillie's. Right now they're—uh—they're drinking. Sitting around," he said vaguely, squinting as if he were staring all the way to town and over to Aunt Tillie's back yard. Then the vision seemed to clear and he nodded energetically. "Yeah. Sitting around. There's your sister in a blue dress, huh? And high heels, the poor sad bitch—nothing like you, sweetheart! And your mother's helping some fat woman with the corn, they're cleaning the corn—husking the corn—"

"What fat woman?" Connie cried.

"How do I know what fat woman. I don't know every goddamn fat   100 woman in the world!" Arnold Friend laughed.

"Oh, that's Mrs. Hornby.... Who invited her?" Connie said. She felt a little light-headed. Her breath was coming quickly.

"She's too fat. I don't like them fat. I like them the way you are, honey," he said, smiling sleepily at her. They stared at each other for a while, through the screen door. He said softly, "Now what you're going to do is this: you're going to come out that door. You're going to sit up front with me and Ellie's going to sit in the back, the hell with Ellie, right? This isn't Ellie's date. You're my date. I'm your lover, honey."

"What? You're crazy—"

"Yes, I'm your lover. You don't know what that is but you will," he said. "I know that too. I know all about you. But look: it's real nice and you couldn't ask for nobody better than me, or more polite. I always keep my word. I'll tell you how it is, I'm always nice at first, the first time. I'll hold you so tight you won't think you have to try to get away or pretend anything because you'll know you can't. And I'll come inside you where it's all secret and you'll give in to me and you'll love me—"

"Shut up! You're crazy!" Connie said. She backed away from the door. 105 She put her hands against her ears as if she'd heard something terrible, something not meant for her. "People don't talk like that, you're crazy," she muttered. Her heart was almost too big now for her chest and its pumping made sweat break out all over her. She looked out to see Arnold Friend pause and then take a step toward the porch lurching. He almost fell. But, like a clever drunken man, he managed to catch his balance. He wobbled in his high boots and grabbed hold of one of the porch posts.

"Honey?" he said. "You still listening?"

"Get the hell out of here!"

"Be nice, honey. Listen."

"I'm going to call the police—"

He wobbled again and out of the side of his mouth came a fast spat 110 curse, an aside not meant for her to hear. But even this "Christ!" sounded forced. Then he began to smile again. She watched this smile come, awkward as if he were smiling from inside a mask. His whole face was a mask, she thought wildly, tanned down onto his throat but then running out as if he had plastered make-up on his face but had forgotten about his throat.

"Honey—? Listen, here's how it is. I always tell the truth and I promise you this: I ain't coming in that house after you."

"You better not! I'm going to call the police if you—if you don't—"

"Honey," he said, talking right through her voice, "honey, I'm not coming in there but you are coming out here. You know why?"

She was panting. The kitchen looked like a place she had never seen before, some room she had run inside but which wasn't good enough, wasn't going to help her. The kitchen window had never had a curtain, after three years, and there were dishes in the sink for her to do—probably—and if you ran your hand across the table you'd probably feel something sticky there.

"You listening, honey? Hey?" 115

"—going to call the police—"

"Soon as you touch the phone I don't need to keep my promise and can come inside. You won't want that."

She rushed forward and tried to lock the door. Her fingers were shaking. "But why lock it," Arnold Friend said gently, talking right into her face. "It's just a screen door. It's just nothing." One of his boots was at a strange angle, as if his foot wasn't in it. It pointed out to the left, bent at the ankle. "I mean, anybody can break through a screen door and glass and wood and iron or anything else if he needs to, anybody at all and specially Arnold Friend. If the place got lit up with a fire, honey, you'd come runnin' out into my arms, right into my arms an' safe at home—like you knew I was your lover and'd stopped fooling around, I don't mind a nice shy girl but I don't like no fooling around." Part of those words were spoken with a slight rhythmic lilt, and Connie somehow recognized them— the echo of a song from last year, about a girl rushing into her boy friend's arms and coming home again—

Connie stood barefoot on the linoleum floor, staring at him. "What do you want?" she whispered.

"I want you," he said.   120

"What?"

"Seen you that night and thought, that's the one, yes sir. I never needed to look any more."

"But my father's coming back. He's coming to get me. I had to wash my hair first—" She spoke in a dry, rapid voice, hardly raising it for him to hear.

"No, your daddy is not coming and yes, you had to wash your hair and you washed it for me. It's nice and shining and all for me. I thank you, sweetheart," he said, with a mock bow, but again he almost lost his balance. He had to bend and adjust his boots. Evidently his feet did not go all the way down; the boots must have been stuffed with something so that he would seem taller. Connie stared out at him and behind him at Ellie in the car, who seemed to be looking off toward Connie's right, into nothing. Then Ellie said, pulling the words out of the air one after another as if he were just discovering them, "You want me to pull out the phone?"

"Shut your mouth and keep it shut," Arnold Friend said, his face red 125
from bending over or maybe from embarrassment because Connie had seen his boots. "This ain't none of your business."

"What—what are you doing? What do you want?" Connie said. "If I call the police they'll get you, they'll arrest you—"

"Promise was not to come in unless you touch that phone, and I'll keep that promise," he said. He resumed his erect position and tried to force his shoulders back. He sounded like a hero in a movie, declaring something important. He spoke too loudly and it was as if he were speaking to someone behind Connie. "I ain't made plans for coming in that house where I don't belong but just for you to come out to me, the way you should. Don't you know who I am?"

"You're crazy," she whispered. She backed away from the door but did not want to go into another part of the house, as if this would give him permission to come through the door. "What do you . . . You're crazy, you. . . ."

"Huh? What're you saying, honey?"

Her eyes darted everywhere in the kitchen. She could not remember   130
what it was, this room.

"This is how it is, honey: you come out and we'll drive away, have a nice ride. But if you don't come out we're gonna wait till your people come home and then they're all going to get it."

"You want that telephone pulled out?" Ellie said. He held the radio away from his ear and grimaced, as if without the radio the air was too much for him.

"I toldja shut up, Ellie," Arnold Friend said, "you're deaf, get a hearing aid, right? Fix yourself up. This little girl's no trouble and's gonna be nice to me, so Ellie keep to yourself, this ain't your date—right? Don't hem in on me, don't hog, don't crush, don't bird dog, don't trail me," he said in a rapid, meaningless voice, as if he were running through all the expressions he'd learned but was no longer sure which one of them was in style, then rushing on to new ones, making them up with his eyes closed. "Don't crawl under my fence, don't squeeze in my chipmunk hole, don't sniff my glue, suck my pop-sicle, keep your own greasy fingers on yourself!" He shaded his eyes and peered in at Connie, who was backed against the kitchen table. "Don't mind him, honey, he's just a creep. He's a dope. Right? I'm the boy for you and like I said, you come out here nice like a lady and give me your hand, and nobody else gets hurt, I mean, your nice old bald-headed daddy and your mummy and your sister in her high heels. Because listen: why bring them in this?"

"Leave me alone," Connie whispered.

"Hey, you know that old woman down the road, the one with the   135
chickens and stuff—you know her?"

"She's dead!"

"Dead? What? You know her?" Arnold Friend said.

"She's dead—"

"Don't you like her?"

"She's dead—she's—she isn't here any more—"   140

"But don't you like her, I mean, you got something against her? Some grudge or something?" Then his voice dipped as if he were conscious of rudeness. He touched the sunglasses on top of his head as if to make sure they were still there. "Now you be a good girl."

"What are you going to do?"

"Just two things, or maybe three," Arnold Friend said. "But I promise it won't last long and you'll like me that way you get to like people you're close to. You will. It's all over for you here, so come on out. You don't want your people in any trouble, do you?"

She turned and bumped against a chair or something, hurting her leg, but she ran into the back room and picked up the telephone. Something roared in her ear, a tiny roaring, and she was so sick with fear that she could do nothing but listen to it—the telephone was clammy and very heavy and her fingers groped down to the dial but were too weak to touch it. She began to scream into the phone, into the roaring. She cried out, she cried for her mother, she felt her breath start jerking back and forth in her lungs as if it were something Arnold Friend was stabbing her with again and again with no tenderness. A noisy sorrowful wailing rose all about her and she was locked inside it the way she was locked inside this house.

After a while she could hear again. She was sitting on the floor, with   145 her wet back against the wall.

Arnold Friend was saying from the door, "That's a good girl. Put the phone back."

She kicked the phone away from her.

"No, honey. Pick it up. Put it back right."

She picked it up and put it back. The dial tone stopped.

"That's a good girl. Now you come outside."   150

She was hollow with what had been fear but what was now just an emptiness. All that screaming had blasted it out of her. She sat, one leg cramped under her, and deep inside her brain was something like a pinpoint of light that kept going and would not let her relax. She thought, I'm not going to see my mother again. She thought, I'm not going to sleep in my bed again. Her bright green blouse was all wet.

Arnold Friend said, in a gentle-loud voice that was like a stage voice, "The place where you came from ain't there any more, and where you had in mind to go is cancelled out. This place you are now— inside your daddy's house—is nothing but a cardboard box I can knock down any time. You know that and always did know it. You hear me?"

She thought, I have got to think. I have got to know what to do.

"We'll go out to a nice field, out in the country here where it smells so nice and it's sunny," Arnold Friend said. "I'll have my arms tight around you so you won't need to try to get away and I'll show you what love is like, what it does. The hell with this house! It looks solid all right," he said. He ran a fingernail down the screen and the noise did not make Connie shiver, as it would have the day before. "Now put your hand on your heart, honey. Feel that? That feels solid too but we know better. Be nice to me, be sweet like you can because what else is there for a girl like you but to be sweet and pretty and give in?—and get away before her people get back?"

She felt her pounding heart. Her hand seemed to enclose it. She   155 thought for the first time in her life that it was nothing that was hers, that belonged to her, but just a pounding, living thing inside this body that wasn't really hers either.

"You don't want them to get hurt," Arnold Friend went on. "Now get up, honey. Get up all by yourself."

She stood.

"Now turn this way. That's right. Come over to me—Ellie, put that away, didn't I tell you? You dope. You miserable creepy dope," Arnold Friend said. His words were not angry but only part of an incantation. The incantation was kindly. "Now come out through the kitchen to me honey and let's see a smile, try it, you're a brave sweet little girl and now they're eating corn and hotdogs cooked to bursting over an outdoor fire, and they don't know one thing about you and never did and honey you're better than them because not a one of them would have done this for you."

Connie felt the linoleum under her feet; it was cool. She brushed her hair back out of her eyes. Arnold Friend let go of the post tentatively and opened his arms for her, his elbows pointing in toward each other and his wrists limp, to show that this was an embarrassed embrace and a little mocking, he didn't want to make her self-conscious.

She put out her hand against the screen. She watched herself push the 160 door slowly open as if she were back safe somewhere in the other doorway, watching this body and this head of long hair moving out into the sunlight where Arnold Friend waited.

"My sweet little blue-eyed girl," he said in a half-sung sigh that had nothing to do with her brown eyes but was taken up just the same by the vast sunlit reaches of the land behind him and on all sides of him—so much land that Connie had never seen before and did not recognize except to know that she was going to it.

The Reader's Presence

1. Oates describes Connie as having "two sides . . . , one for home and one for anywhere that was not home" (paragraph 5). What are the differences between the two sides? In what ways does Arnold Friend also seem to have two sides? How are these characters alike? How are they different?

2. Compare the ending of this story to the conclusion of Raymond Carver's "The Bath" (page 895). What do you think happens after each story ends? Why do you think Carver and Oates made the decision to end the story without discussing how the characters' situations will resolve? Does the ending increase or decrease each story's emotional tension? Why?

3. Read Oates's "District School #7, Niagara County, New York" (page 215). How does Oates describe her own youth? How does she characterize adults—family members, her teacher, the writers whose books she enjoyed? What does Oates seem to have felt about adulthood? How would you characterize Connie's relationship with adults?

THE WRITER AT WORK

Joyce Carol Oates on *Smooth Talk:*
Short Story into Film

Joyce Carol Oates's "Where Are You Going, Where Have You Been?" has been described as "a study in the peril that lurks beneath the surface of everyday life." In 1985, Joyce Chopra directed a film, Smooth Talk, *with a screenplay by Tom Cole based on Oates's story. The film continues after the story ends, giving viewers an unexpectedly optimistic glimpse of Connie's fate.* Smooth Talk *won the Grand Jury Prize at the Sundance Film Festival in 1986. The following article appeared in the* New York Times *in 1986. Does Oates's original conception of the story fit with your expectations of what might happen to Connie? Does considering a happy ending—or at least an ending without tragedy—make a difference in your view of the story as a whole?*

Some years ago in the American Southwest there surfaced a tabloid psychopath known as "The Pied Piper of Tucson." I have forgotten his name, but his specialty was the seduction and occasional murder of teen-aged girls. He may or may not have had actual accomplices, but his bizarre activities were known among a circle of teenagers in the Tucson area; for some reason they kept his secret, deliberately did not inform parents or police. It was this fact, not the fact of the mass murderer himself, that struck me at the time. And this was a pre-Manson time, early or mid-1960s.

The Pied Piper mimicked teenagers in their talk, dress, and behavior, but he was not a teenager—he was a man in his early thirties. Rather short, he stuffed rags in his leather boots to give himself height. (And sometimes walked unsteadily as a consequence: did none among his admiring constituency notice?) He charmed his victims as charismatic psychopaths have always charmed their victims, to the bewilderment of others who fancy themselves free of all lunatic attractions. The Pied Piper of Tucson: a trashy dream, a tabloid archetype, sheer artifice, comedy, cartoon—surrounded, however improbably, and finally tragically by real people. You think that, if you look twice, he won't be there. But there he is.

I don't remember any longer where I first read about this Pied Piper—very likely in *Life* Magazine. I do recall deliberately not reading the full article because I didn't want to be distracted by too much detail. It was not after all the mass murderer himself who intrigued me, but the disturbing fact that a number of teenagers—from "good" families—aided and abetted his crimes. This is the sort of thing authorities and responsible citizens invariably call "inexplicable" because they can't find explanations for it. *They* would not have fallen under this maniac's spell, after all.

An early draft of my short story "Where Are You Going, Where Have You Been?"—from which the film *Smooth Talk* was adapted by Joyce Chopra and Tom Cole—had the rather too explicit title "Death and the Maiden." It was cast in a mode of fiction to which I am still partial—indeed, every third or fourth story of mine is probably in this mode—"realistic allegory," it might be called. It is Hawthornean, romantic, shading into parable. Like the medieval German engraving from which my title was taken, the story was minutely detailed yet clearly an allegory of the fatal attractions of death (or the devil). An innocent young girl is seduced by way of her own vanity; she mistakes death for erotic romance of a particularly American/trashy sort.

In subsequent drafts the story changed its tone, its focus, its language, its title. It became "Where Are You Going, Where Have You Been?" Written at a time when the author was intrigued by the music of Bob Dylan, particularly the hauntingly elegiac song "It's All Over Now, Baby Blue," it was dedicated to Bob Dylan. The charismatic mass murderer drops into the background and his innocent victim, a fifteen-year-old, moves into the foreground. She becomes the true protagonist of the tale, courting and being courted by her fate, a self-styled 1950s pop figure, alternately absurd and winning. There is no suggestion in the published story that "Arnold Friend" has seduced and murdered other young girls, or even that he necessarily intends to murder Connie. Is his interest "merely" sexual? (Nor is there anything about the complicity of other teenagers. I saved that yet more provocative note for a current story, "Testimony.") Connie is shallow, vain, silly, hopeful, doomed—but capable nonetheless of an unexpected gesture of heroism at the story's end. Her smooth-talking seducer, who cannot lie, promises her that her family will be unharmed if she gives herself to him; and so she does. The story ends abruptly at the point of her "crossing over." We don't know the nature of her sacrifice, only that she is generous enough to make it.

In adapting a narrative so spare and thematically foreshortened as "Where Are You Going, Where Have You Been?" film director Joyce Chopra and screenwriter Tom Cole were required to do a good deal of filling in, expanding, inventing. Connie's story becomes lavishly, and lovingly, textured; she is not an allegorical figure so much as a "typical" teen-aged girl (if Laura Dern, spectacularly good-looking, can be so defined). Joyce Chopra, who has done documentary films on contemporary teenage culture and, yet more authoritatively, has an adolescent daughter of her own, creates in *Smooth Talk* a vivid and absolutely believable world for Connie to inhabit. Or worlds: as in the original story there is Connie-at-home, and there is Connie-with-her-friends. Two fifteen-year-old girls, two finely honed styles, two voices, sometimes but not often overlapping. It is one of the marvelous visual features of the film that we *see* Connie and her friends transform themselves, once they are safely free of parental observation. The girls claim their true identities in the neighborhood shopping mall. What freedom, what joy!

Smooth Talk is, in a way, as much Connie's mother's story as it is Connie's; its center of gravity, its emotional nexus, is frequently with the mother—warmly and convincingly played by Mary Kay Place. (Though the mother's sexual jealousy of her daughter is slighted in the film.) Connie's ambiguous relationship with her affable, somewhat mysterious father (well played by Levon Helm) is an excellent touch: I had thought, subsequent to the story's publication, that I should have built up the father, suggesting, as subtly as I could, an attraction there paralleling the attraction Connie feels for her seducer, Arnold Friend. And Arnold Friend himself— "A. Friend" as he says—is played with appropriately overdone sexual swagger by Treat Williams, who is perfect for the part; and just the right age. We see that Arnold Friend isn't a teenager even as Connie, mesmerized by his presumed charm, does not seem to *see* him at all. What is so difficult to accomplish in prose—nudging the reader to look over the protagonist's shoulder, so to speak—is accomplished with enviable ease in film.

Treat Williams as Arnold Friend is supreme in his very awfulness, as, surely, the original Pied Piper of Tucson must have been. (Though no one involved in the film knew about the original source.) Mr. Williams flawlessly impersonates Arnold Friend as Arnold Friend impersonates—is it James Dean? James Dean regarding himself in mirrors, doing James Dean impersonations? That Connie's fate is so trashy is in fact her fate.

What is outstanding in Joyce Chopra's *Smooth Talk* is its visual freshness, its sense of motion and life; the attentive intelligence the director has brought to the semi-secret world of the American adolescent—shopping mall flirtations, drive-in restaurant romances, highway hitchhiking, the fascination of rock music played very, very loud. (James Taylor's music for the film is wonderfully appropriate. We hear it as Connie hears it; it is the music of her spiritual being.) Also outstanding, as I have indicated, and numerous critics have noted, are the acting performances. Laura Dern is so dazzlingly right as "my" Connie that I may come to think I modeled the fictitious girl on her, in the way that writers frequently delude themselves about motions of causality.

My difficulties with *Smooth Talk* have primarily to do with my   10 chronic hesitation—about seeing/hearing work of mine abstracted from its contexture of language. All writers know that language is their subject; quirky word choices, patterns of rhythm, enigmatic pauses, punctuation marks. Where the quick scanner sees "quick" writing, the writer conceals nine tenths of the iceberg. Of course we all have "real" subjects, and we will fight to the death to defend those subjects, but beneath the tale-telling it is the tale-telling that grips us so very fiercely. The writer works in a single dimension, the director works in three. I assume they are professionals to their fingertips; authorities in their medium as I am an authority (if I am) in mine. I would fiercely defend the placement of a semicolon in one of my novels but I would probably have deferred in the end to Joyce Chopra's decision to reverse the story's conclusion, turn it upside down, in a sense, so that the film ends not with death, not with a sleepwalker's crossing over to her fate, but upon a scene of reconciliation, rejuvenation.

A girl's loss of virginity, bittersweet but not necessarily tragic. Not today. A girl's coming-of-age that involves her succumbing to, but then rejecting, the "trashy dreams" of her pop teenage culture. "Where Are You Going, Where Have You Been?" defines itself as allegorical in its conclusion: Death and Death's chariot (a funky souped-up convertible) have come for the Maiden. Awakening is, in the story's final lines, moving out into the sunlight where Arnold Friend waits:

> "My sweet little blue-eyed girl," he said in a half-sung sigh that had nothing to do with [Connie's] brown eyes but was taken up just the same by the vast sunlit reaches of the land behind him and on all sides of him—so much land that Connie had never seen before and did not recognize except to know that she was going to it.

—a conclusion impossible to transfigure into film.

Flannery O'Connor

A Good Man Is Hard to Find

Flannery O'Connor (1925–1964) was born in Savannah, Georgia, the only child of devout Catholic parents. At the age of thirteen, O'Connor moved with her parents to her mother's ancestral home in Milledgeville, Georgia, after her father became terminally ill with lupus. In 1945 she received an A.B. degree from Georgia State College for Women, where she contributed regularly to the school's literary magazine. While earning an M.F.A. from the Writers' Workshop at the University of Iowa, O'Connor published her first short story, "The Geranium," in 1946. After graduation O'Connor was a resident at Yaddo, an artists' retreat in New York, and lived in New York City and in Connecticut until 1951, when she was diagnosed with lupus and returned to Georgia for treatment. She and her mother moved a short distance from Milledgeville to their family farm, Andalusia, where O'Connor lived until her death at the age of thirty-nine, raising peafowl, painting, and writing daily. During her short yet distinguished life, O'Connor published two novels, Wise Blood *(1952) and* The Violent Bear It Away *(1960), and a collection of short stories,* A Good Man Is Hard to Find *(1955), the title story of which appears here. A book of essays,* Mystery and Manners *(1969); two other short story collections,* Everything That Rises Must Converge *(1965) and* The Complete Stories of Flannery O'Connor *(1971), winner of a National Book Award; and a collection of letters,* The Habit of Being *(1979), were published posthumously.*

The grandmother didn't want to go to Florida. She wanted to visit some of her connections in east Tennessee and she was seizing at every chance to change Bailey's mind. Bailey was the son she lived with, her only boy. He was sitting on the edge of his chair at the table, bent over the orange sports section of the *Journal*. "Now look here, Bailey," she said, "see here, read this," and she stood with one hand on her thin hip and the other rattling the newspaper at his bald head. "Here this fellow that calls himself The Misfit is aloose from the Federal Pen and headed toward Florida and you read here what it says he did to these people. Just you read it. I wouldn't take my children in any direction with a criminal like that aloose in it. I couldn't answer to my conscience if I did."

Bailey didn't look up from his reading so she wheeled around then and faced the children's mother, a young woman in slacks, whose face was as broad and innocent as a cabbage and was tied around with a green head-kerchief that had two points on the top like a rabbit's ears. She was sitting on the sofa, feeding the baby his apricots out of a jar. "The children have been to Florida before," the old lady said. "You all ought to take them somewhere else for a change so they would see different parts of the world and be broad. They never have been to east Tennessee."

The children's mother didn't seem to hear her but the eight-year-old boy, John Wesley, a stocky child with glasses, said, "If you don't want to go to Florida, why dontcha stay at home?" He and the little girl, June Star, were reading the funny papers on the floor.

"She wouldn't stay at home to be queen for a day," June Star said without raising her yellow head.

"Yes and what would you do if this fellow, The Misfit, caught you?" 5
the grandmother asked.

"I'd smack his face," John Wesley said.

"She wouldn't stay at home for a million bucks," June Star said. "Afraid she'd miss something. She has to go everywhere we go."

"All right, Miss," the grandmother said. "Just remember that the next time you want me to curl your hair."

June Star said her hair was naturally curly.

The next morning the grandmother was the first one in the car, ready 10
to go. She had her big black valise that looked like the head of a hippopotamus in one corner, and underneath it she was hiding a basket with Pitty Sing, the cat, in it. She didn't intend for the cat to be left alone in the house for three days because he would miss her too much and she was afraid he might brush against one of the gas burners and accidentally asphyxiate himself. Her son, Bailey, didn't like to arrive at a motel with a cat.

She sat in the middle of the back seat with John Wesley and June Star on either side of her. Bailey and the children's mother and the baby sat in front and they left Atlanta at eight forty-five with the mileage on the car at 55890. The grandmother wrote this down because she thought it would be interesting to say how many miles they had been when they got back. It took them twenty minutes to reach the outskirts of the city.

The old lady settled herself comfortably, removing her white cotton gloves and putting them up with her purse on the shelf in front of the back window. The children's mother still had on slacks and still had her head tied up in a green kerchief, but the grandmother had on a navy blue straw sailor hat with a bunch of white violets on the brim and a navy blue dress with a small white dot in the print. Her collars and cuffs were white organdy trimmed with lace and at her neckline she had pinned a purple spray of cloth violets containing a sachet. In case of an accident, anyone seeing her dead on the highway would know at once that she was a lady.

She said she thought it was going to be a good day for driving, neither too hot nor too cold, and she cautioned Bailey that the speed limit was fifty-five miles an hour and that the patrolmen hid themselves behind billboards and small clumps of trees and sped out after you before you had a chance to slow down. She pointed out interesting details of the scenery: Stone Mountain; the blue granite that in some places came up to both sides of the highway; the brilliant red clay banks slightly streaked with purple; and the various crops that made rows of green lace-work on the ground. The trees were full of silver-white sunlight and the meanest of them sparkled. The children were reading comic magazines and their mother had gone back to sleep.

"Let's go through Georgia fast so we won't have to look at it much," John Wesley said.

"If I were a little boy," said the grandmother, "I wouldn't talk about 15 my native state that way. Tennessee has the mountains and Georgia has the hills."

"Tennessee is just a hillbilly dumping ground," John Wesley said, "and Georgia is a lousy state too."

"You said it," June Star said.

"In my time," said the grandmother, folding her thin veined fingers, "children were more respectful of their native states and their parents and everything else. People did right then. Oh look at the cute little pickaninny!" she said and pointed to a Negro child standing in the door of a shack. "Wouldn't that make a picture, now?" she asked and they all turned and looked at the little Negro out of the back window. He waved.

"He didn't have any britches on," June Star said.

"He probably didn't have any," the grandmother explained. "Little 20 niggers in the country don't have things like we do. If I could paint, I'd paint that picture," she said.

The children exchanged comic books.

The grandmother offered to hold the baby and the children's mother passed him over the front seat to her. She set him on her knee and bounced him and told him about the things they were passing. She rolled her eyes and screwed up her mouth and stuck her leathery thin face into his smooth bland one. Occasionally he gave her a faraway smile. They passed a large cotton field with five or six graves fenced in the middle of it, like a small island. "Look at the graveyard!" the grandmother said, pointing it out. "That was the old family burying ground. That belonged to the plantation."

"Where's the plantation?" John Wesley asked.

"Gone With the Wind," said the grandmother. "Ha. Ha."

When the children finished all the comic books they had brought, they opened the lunch and ate it. The grandmother ate a peanut butter sandwich and an olive and would not let the children throw the box and the paper napkins out the window. When there was nothing else to do they played a game by choosing a cloud and making the other two guess what shape it suggested. John Wesley took one the shape of a cow and June Star guessed a cow and John Wesley said, no, an automobile, and June Star said he didn't play fair, and they began to slap each other over the grandmother.

The grandmother said she would tell them a story if they would keep quiet. When she told a story, she rolled her eyes and waved her head and was very dramatic. She said once when she was a maiden lady she had been courted by a Mr. Edgar Atkins Teagarden from Jasper, Georgia. She said he was a very good-looking man and a gentleman and that he brought her a watermelon every Saturday afternoon with his initials cut in it, E. A. T. Well, one Saturday, she said, Mr. Teagarden brought the watermelon and there was nobody at home and he left it on the front porch and returned in his buggy to Jasper, but she never got the watermelon, she said, because a nigger boy ate it when he saw the initials, E. A. T.! This story tickled John Wesley's funny bone and he giggled and giggled but June Star didn't think it was any good. She said she wouldn't marry a man that just brought her a watermelon on Saturday. The grandmother said she would have done well to marry Mr. Teagarden because he was a gentleman and had bought Coca-Cola stock when it first came out and that he had died only a few years ago, a very wealthy man.

They stopped at The Tower for barbecued sandwiches. The Tower was a part stucco and part wood filling station and dance hall set in a clearing outside of Timothy. A fat man named Red Sammy Butts ran it and there were signs stuck here and there on the building and for miles up and down the highway saying, TRY RED SAMMY'S FAMOUS BARBE-CUE. NONE LIKE FAMOUS RED SAMMY'S! RED SAM! THE FAT BOY WITH THE HAPPY LAUGH! A VETERAN! RED SAMMY'S YOUR MAN!

Red Sammy was lying on the bare ground outside The Tower with his head under a truck while a gray monkey about a foot high, chained to a small chinaberry tree, chattered nearby. The monkey sprang back into the tree and got on the highest limb as soon as he saw the children jump out of the car and run toward him.

Inside, The Tower was a long dark room with a counter at one end and tables at the other and dancing space in the middle. They all sat down at a board table next to the nickelodeon and Red Sam's wife, a tall burnt-brown woman with hair and eyes lighter than her skin, came and took their order. The children's mother put a dime in the machine and played "The Tennessee Waltz," and the grandmother said that tune always made her want to dance. She asked Bailey if he would like to dance but he only glared at her. He didn't have a naturally sunny disposition like she did and trips made him nervous. The grandmother's brown eyes were very bright. She swayed her head from side to side and pretended she was dancing in her chair. June Star said play something she could tap to so the children's mother put in another dime and played a fast number and June Star stepped out onto the dance floor and did her tap routine.

"Ain't she cute?" Red Sam's wife said, leaning over the counter. 30 "Would you like to come be my little girl?"

"No I certainly wouldn't," June Star said. "I wouldn't live in a broken-down place like this for a million bucks!" and she ran back to the table.

"Ain't she cute?" the woman repeated, stretching her mouth politely.

"Aren't you ashamed?" hissed the grandmother.

Red Sam came in and told his wife to quit lounging on the counter and hurry up with these people's order. His khaki trousers reached just to his hip bones and his stomach hung over them like a sack of meal swaying under his shirt. He came over and sat down at a table nearby and let out a combination sigh and yodel. "You can't win," he said. "You can't win," and he wiped his sweating red face off with a gray handkerchief. "These days you don't know who to trust," he said. "Ain't that the truth?"

"People are certainly not nice like they used to be," said the grand- 35 mother.

"Two fellers come in here last week," Red Sammy said, "driving a Chrysler. It was a old beat-up car, but it was a good one and these boys looked all right to me. Said they worked at the mill and you know I let them fellers charge the gas they bought? Now why did I do that?"

"Because you're a good man!" the grandmother said at once.

"Yes'm, I suppose so," Red Sam said as if he were struck with this answer.

His wife brought the orders, carrying the five plates all at once without a tray, two in each hand and one balanced on her arm. "It isn't a soul in this green world of God's that you can trust," she said. "And I don't count nobody out of that, not nobody," she repeated, looking at Red Sammy.

"Did you read about that criminal, The Misfit, that's escaped?" 40 asked the grandmother.

"I wouldn't be a bit surprised if he didn't attact this place right here," said the woman. "If he hears about it being here, I wouldn't be none surprised to see him. If he hears it's two cent in the cash register, I wouldn't be a tall surprised if he . . ."

"That'll do," Red Sam said. "Go bring these people their Co'-Colas," and the woman went off to get the rest of the order.

"A good man is hard to find," Red Sammy said. "Everything is getting terrible. I remember the day you could go off and leave your screen door unlatched. Not no more."

He and the grandmother discussed better times. The old lady said that in her opinion Europe was entirely to blame for the way things were now. She said the way Europe acted you would think we were made of money and Red Sam said it was no use talking about it, she was exactly right. The children ran outside into the white sunlight and looked at the monkey in the lacy chinaberry tree. He was busy catching fleas on himself and biting each one carefully between his teeth as if it were a delicacy.

They drove off again into the hot afternoon. The grandmother took   45
cat naps and woke up every few minutes with her own snoring. Outside of Toombsboro she woke up and recalled an old plantation that she had visited in this neighborhood once when she was a young lady. She said the house had six white columns across the front and that there was an avenue of oaks leading up to it and two little wooden trellis arbors on either side in front where you sat down with your suitor after a stroll in the garden. She recalled exactly which road to turn off to get to it. She knew that Bailey would not be willing to lose any time looking at an old house, but the more she talked about it, the more she wanted to see it once again and find out if the little twin arbors were still standing. "There was a secret panel in this house," she said craftily, not telling the truth but wishing that she were, "and the story went that all the family silver was hidden in it when Sherman[1] came through but it was never found . . ."

"Hey!" John Wesley said. "Let's go see it! We'll find it! We'll poke all the woodwork and find it! Who lives there? Where do you turn off at? Hey Pop, can't we turn off there?"

"We never have seen a house with a secret panel!" June Star shrieked. "Let's go to the house with the secret panel! Hey Pop, can't we go see the house with the secret panel!"

"It's not far from here, I know," the grandmother said. "It wouldn't take over twenty minutes."

Bailey was looking straight ahead. His jaw was as rigid as a horseshoe. "No," he said.

The children began to yell and scream that they wanted to see the   50
house with the secret panel. John Wesley kicked the back of the front seat and June Star hung over her mother's shoulder and whined desperately into her ear that they never had any fun even on their vacation, that they could never do what THEY wanted to do. The baby began to scream and John Wesley kicked the back of the seat so hard that his father could feel the blows in his kidney.

"All right!" he shouted and drew the car to a stop at the side of the road. "Will you all shut up? Will you all just shut up for one second? If you don't shut up, we won't go anywhere."

"It would be very educational for them," the grandmother murmured.

---

[1] **Sherman:** General William Tecumseh Sherman (1820–1891) was the Union general who captured Atlanta in 1864.—Eds.

"All right," Bailey said, "but get this: this is the only time we're going to stop for anything like this. This is the one and only time."

"The dirt road that you have to turn down is about a mile back," the grandmother directed. "I marked it when we passed.

"A dirt road," Bailey groaned.   55

After they had turned around and were headed toward the dirt road, the grandmother recalled other points about the house, the beautiful glass over the front doorway and the candle-lamp in the hall. John Wesley said that the secret panel was probably in the fireplace.

"You can't go inside this house," Bailey said. "You don't know who lives there."

"While you all talk to the people in front, I'll run around behind and get in a window," John Wesley suggested.

"We'll all stay in the car," his mother said.

They turned onto the dirt road and the car raced roughly along in a   60 swirl of pink dust. The grandmother recalled the times when there were no paved roads and thirty miles was a day's journey. The dirt road was hilly and there were sudden washes in it and sharp curves on dangerous embankments. All at once they would be on a hill, looking down over the blue tops of trees for miles around, then the next minute, they would be in a red depression with the dust-coated trees looking down on them.

"This place had better turn up in a minute," Bailey said, "or I'm going to turn around."

The road looked as if no one had traveled on it in months.

"It's not much farther," the grandmother said and just as she said it, a horrible thought came to her. The thought was so embarrassing that she turned red in the face and her eyes dilated and her feet jumped up, upsetting her valise in the corner. The instant the valise moved, the newspaper top she had over the basket under it rose with a snarl and Pitty Sing, the cat, sprang onto Bailey's shoulder.

The children were thrown to the floor and their mother, clutching the baby, was thrown out the door onto the ground; the old lady was thrown into the front seat. The car turned over once and landed right-side-up in a gulch off the side of the road. Bailey remained in the driver's seat with the cat — gray-striped with a broad white face and an orange nose — clinging to his neck like a caterpillar.

As soon as the children saw they could move their arms and legs, they   65 scrambled out of the car, shouting, "We've had an ACCIDENT!" The grandmother was curled up under the dashboard, hoping she was injured so that Bailey's wrath would not come down on her all at once. The horrible thought she had had before the accident was that the house she had remembered so vividly was not in Georgia but in Tennessee.

Bailey removed the cat from his neck with both hands and flung it out the window against the side of a pine tree. Then he got out of the car and started looking for the children's mother. She was sitting against the side of the red gutted ditch, holding the screaming baby, but she only had a cut down her face and a broken shoulder. "We've had an ACCI-DENT!" the children screamed in a frenzy of delight.

"But nobody's killed," June Star said with disappointment as the grandmother limped out of the car, her hat still pinned to her head but the broken front brim standing up at a jaunty angle and the violet spray hanging off the side. They all sat down in the ditch, except the children, to recover from the shock. They were all shaking.

"Maybe a car will come along," said the children's mother hoarsely.

"I believe I have injured an organ," said the grandmother, pressing her side, but no one answered her. Bailey's teeth were clattering. He had on a yellow sport shirt with bright blue parrots designed in it and his face was as yellow as the shirt. The grandmother decided that she would not mention that the house was in Tennessee.

The road was about ten feet above and they could see only the tops 70 of the trees on the other side of it. Behind the ditch they were sitting in there were more woods, tall and dark and deep. In a few minutes they saw a car some distance away on top of a hill, coming slowly as if the oc-cupants were watching them. The grandmother stood up and waved both arms dramatically to attract their attention. The car continued to come on slowly, disappeared around a bend and appeared again, moving even slower, on top of the hill they had gone over. It was a big black battered hearselike automobile. There were three men in it.

It came to a stop just over them and for some minutes, the driver looked down with a steady expressionless gaze to where they were sitting, and didn't speak. Then he turned his head and muttered something to the other two and they got out. One was a fat boy in black trousers and a red sweat shirt with a silver stallion embossed on the front of it. He moved around on the right side of them and stood staring, his mouth partly open in a kind of loose grin. The other had on khaki pants and a blue striped coat and a gray hat pulled down very low, hiding most of his face. He came around slowly on the left side. Neither spoke.

The driver got out of the car and stood by the side of it, looking down at them. He was an older man than the other two. His hair was just beginning to gray and he wore silver-rimmed spectacles that gave him a scholarly look. He had a long creased face and didn't have on any shirt or undershirt. He had on blue jeans that were too tight for him and was holding a black hat and a gun. The two boys also had guns.

"We've had an ACCIDENT!" the children screamed.

The grandmother had the peculiar feeling that the bespectacled man was someone she knew. His face was as familiar to her as if she had known him all her life but she could not recall who he was. He moved away from the car and began to come down the embankment, placing his feet carefully so that he wouldn't slip. He had on tan and white shoes and no socks, and his ankles were red and thin. "Good afternoon," he said. "I see you all had you a little spill."

"We turned over twice!" said the grandmother. 75

"Oncet," he corrected. "We seen it happen. Try their car and see will it run, Hiram," he said quietly to the boy with the gray hat.

"What you got that gun for?" John Wesley asked. "Whatcha gonna do with that gun?"

"Lady," the man said to the children's mother, "would you mind calling them children to sit down by you? Children make me nervous. I want all you all to sit down right together there where you're at."

"What are you telling US what to do for?" June Star asked.

Behind them the line of woods gaped like a dark open mouth. "Come   80
here," said their mother.

"Look here now," Bailey began suddenly, "we're in a predicament! We're in . . ."

The grandmother shrieked. She scrambled to her feet and stood staring. "You're The Misfit!" she said. "I recognized you at once!"

"Yes'm," the man said, smiling slightly as if he were pleased in spite of himself to be known, "but it would have been better for all of you, lady, if you hadn't of reckernized me."

Bailey turned his head sharply and said something to his mother that shocked even the children. The old lady began to cry and The Misfit reddened.

"Lady," he said, "don't you get upset. Sometimes a man says things   85
he don't mean. I don't reckon he meant to talk to you thataway."

"You wouldn't shoot a lady, would you?" the grandmother said and removed a clean handkerchief from her cuff and began to slap at her eyes with it.

The Misfit pointed the toe of his shoe into the ground and made a little hole and then covered it up again. "I would hate to have to," he said.

"Listen," the grandmother almost screamed, "I know you're a good man. You don't look a bit like you have common blood. I know you must come from nice people!"

"Yes mam," he said, "finest people in the world." When he smiled he showed a row of strong white teeth. "God never made a finer woman than my mother and my daddy's heart was pure gold," he said. The boy with the red sweat shirt had come around behind them and was standing with his gun at his hip. The Misfit squatted down on the ground. "Watch them children, Bobby Lee," he said. "You know they make me nervous." He looked at the six of them huddled together in front of him and he seemed to be embarrassed as if he couldn't think of anything to say. "Ain't a cloud in the sky," he remarked, looking up at it. "Don't see no sun but don't see no cloud neither."

"Yes, it's a beautiful day," said the grandmother. "Listen," she said,   90
"you shouldn't call yourself The Misfit because I know you're a good man at heart. I can just look at you and tell."

"Hush!" Bailey yelled. "Hush! Everybody shut up and let me handle this!" He was squatting in the position of a runner about to sprint forward but he didn't move.

"I pre-chate that, lady," The Misfit said and drew a little circle in the ground with the butt of his gun.

"It'll take a half a hour to fix this here car," Hiram called, looking over the raised hood of it.

"Well, first you and Bobby Lee get him and that little boy to step over yonder with you," The Misfit said, pointing to Bailey and John Wesley. "The boys want to ast you something," he said to Bailey. "Would you mind stepping back in them woods there with them?"

"Listen," Bailey began, "we're in a terrible predicament! Nobody realizes what this is," and his voice cracked. His eyes were as blue and intense as the parrots in his shirt and he remained perfectly still.

The grandmother reached up to adjust her hat brim as if she were going to the woods with him but it came off in her hand. She stood staring at it and after a second she let it fall on the ground. Hiram pulled Bailey up by the arm as if he were assisting an old man. John Wesley caught hold of his father's hand and Bobby Lee followed. They went off toward the woods and just as they reached the dark edge, Bailey turned and supporting himself against a gray naked pine trunk, he shouted, "I'll be back in a minute, Mamma, wait on me!"

"Come back this instant!" his mother shrilled but they all disappeared into the woods.

"Bailey Boy!" the grandmother called in a tragic voice but she found she was looking at The Misfit squatting on the ground in front of her. "I just know you're a good man," she said desperately. "You're not a bit common!"

"Nome, I ain't a good man," The Misfit said after a second as if he had considered her statement carefully, "but I ain't the worst in the world neither. My daddy said I was a different breed of dog from my brothers and sisters. 'You know,' Daddy said, 'it's some that can live their whole life out without asking about it and it's others has to know why it is, and this boy is one of the latters. He's going to be into everything!'" He put on his black hat and looked up suddenly and then away deep into the woods as if he were embarrassed again. "I'm sorry I don't have on a shirt before you ladies," he said, hunching his shoulders slightly. "We buried our clothes that we had on when we escaped and we're just making do until we can get better. We borrowed these from some folks we met," he explained.

"That's perfectly all right," the grandmother said. "Maybe Bailey has an extra shirt in his suitcase."

"I'll look and see terrectly," The Misfit said.

"Where are they taking him?" the children's mother screamed.

"Daddy was a card himself," The Misfit said. "You couldn't put anything over on him. He never got in trouble with the Authorities though. Just had the knack of handling them."

"You could be honest too if you'd only try," said the grandmother. "Think how wonderful it would be to settle down and live a comfortable life and not have to think about somebody chasing you all the time."

The Misfit kept scratching in the ground with the butt of his gun as if   105
he were thinking about it. "Yes'm, somebody is always after you," he murmured.

The grandmother noticed how thin his shoulder blades were just behind his hat because she was standing up looking down on him. "Do you
ever pray?" she asked.

He shook his head. All she saw was the black hat wiggle between his
shoulder blades. "Nome," he said.

There was a pistol shot from the woods, followed closely by another.
Then silence. The old lady's head jerked around. She could hear the wind
move through the tree tops like a long satisfied insuck of breath. "Bailey
Boy!" she called.

"I was a gospel singer for a while," The Misfit said. "I been most
everything. Been in the arm service, both land and sea, at home and abroad,
been twict married, been an undertaker, been with the railroads, plowed
Mother Earth, been in a tornado, seen a man burnt alive oncet," and
looked up at the children's mother and the little girl who were sitting close
together, their faces white and their eyes glassy; "I even seen a woman
flogged," he said.

"Pray, pray," the grandmother began, "pray, pray . . ."   110

"I never was a bad boy that I remember of," The Misfit said in an almost dreamy voice, "but somewheres along the line I done something
wrong and got sent to the penitentiary. I was buried alive," and he looked
up and held her attention to him by a steady stare.

"That's when you should have started to pray," she said. "What did
you do to get sent to the penitentiary that first time?"

"Turn to the right, it was a wall," The Misfit said, looking up again
at the cloudless sky. "Turn to the left, it was a wall. Look up it was a ceiling, look down it was a floor. I forget what I done, lady. I set there and
set there, trying to remember what it was I done and I ain't recalled it to
this day. Oncet in a while, I would think it was coming to me, but it never
come."

"Maybe they put you in by mistake," the old lady said vaguely.

"Nome," he said. "It wasn't no mistake. They had the papers on me."   115

"You must have stolen something," she said.

The Misfit sneered slightly. "Nobody had nothing I wanted," he said.
"It was a head-doctor at the penitentiary said what I had done was kill
my daddy but I known that for a lie. My daddy died in nineteen ought
nineteen of the epidemic flu and I never had a thing to do with it. He was
buried in the Mount Hopewell Baptist churchyard and you can go there
and see for yourself."

"If you would pray," the old lady said, "Jesus would help you."

"That's right," The Misfit said.

"Well then, why don't you pray?" she asked trembling with delight   120
suddenly.

"I don't want no hep," he said. "I'm doing all right by myself."

Bobby Lee and Hiram came ambling back from the woods. Bobby Lee was dragging a yellow shirt with bright blue parrots in it.

"Throw me that shirt, Bobby Lee," The Misfit said. The shirt came flying at him and landed on his shoulder and he put it on. The grandmother couldn't name what the shirt reminded her of. "No, lady," The Misfit said while he was buttoning it up, "I found out the crime don't matter. You can do one thing or you can do another, kill a man or take a tire off his car, because sooner or later you're going to forget what it was you done and just be punished for it."

The children's mother had begun to make heaving noises as if she couldn't get her breath. "Lady," he asked, "would you and that little girl like to step off yonder with Bobby Lee and Hiram and join your husband?"

"Yes, thank you," the mother said faintly. Her left arm dangled help- 125 lessly and she was holding the baby, who had gone to sleep, in the other. "Hep that lady up, Hiram," The Misfit said as she struggled to climb out of the ditch, "and Bobby Lee, you hold onto that little girl's hand."

"I don't want to hold hands with him," June Starr said. "He reminds me of a pig."

The fat boy blushed and laughed and caught her by the arm and pulled her off into the woods after Hiram and her mother.

Alone with The Misfit, the grandmother found that she had lost her voice. There was not a cloud in the sky nor any sun. There was nothing around her but woods. She wanted to tell him that he must pray. She opened and closed her mouth several times before anything came out. Finally she found herself saying, "Jesus, Jesus," meaning, Jesus will help you, but the way she was saying it, it sounded as if she might be cursing.

"Yes'm," the Misfit said as if he agreed. "Jesus thown everything off balance. It was the same case with Him as with me except He hadn't committed any crime and they could prove I had committed one because they had the papers on me. Of course," he said, "they never shown me my papers. That's why I sign myself now. I said long ago, you get you a signature and sign everything you do and keep a copy of it. Then you'll know what you done and you can hold up the crime to the punishment and see do they match and in the end you'll have something to prove you ain't been treated right. I call myself The Misfit," he said, "because I can't make what all I done wrong fit what all I gone through in punishment."

There was a piercing scream from the woods, followed closely by a 130 pistol report. "Does it seem right to you, lady, that one is punished a heap and another ain't punished at all?"

"Jesus!" the old lady cried. "You've got good blood! I know you wouldn't shoot a lady! I know you come from nice people! Pray! Jesus, you ought not to shoot a lady. I'll give you all the money I've got!"

"Lady," The Misfit said, looking beyond her far into the woods, "there never was a body that give the undertaker a tip."

There were two more pistol reports and the grandmother raised her head like a parched old turkey hen crying for water and called, "Bailey Boy, Bailey Boy!" as if her heart would break.

"Jesus was the only One that ever raised the dead." The Misfit continued, "and He shouldn't have done it. He thown everything off balance. If He did what He said, then it's nothing for you to do but thow away everything and follow Him, and if He didn't, then it's nothing for you to do but enjoy the few minutes you got left the best way you can—by killing somebody or burning down his house or doing some other meanness to him. No pleasure but meanness," he said and his voice had become almost a snarl.

"Maybe He didn't raise the dead," the old lady mumbled, not knowing what she was saying and feeling so dizzy that she sank down in the ditch with her legs twisted under her.　　135

"I wasn't there so I can't say He didn't," The Misfit said. "I wisht I had of been there," he said, hitting the ground with his fist. "It ain't right I wasn't there because if I had of been there I would of known. Listen lady," he said in a high voice, "if I had of been there I would of known and I wouldn't be like I am now." His voice seemed about to crack and the grandmother's head cleared for an instant. She saw the man's face twisted close to her own as if he was going to cry and she murmured, "Why you're one of my babies. You're one of my own children!" She reached out and touched him on the shoulder. The Misfit sprang back as if a snake had bitten him and shot her three times through the chest. Then he put his gun down on the ground and took off his glasses and began to clean them.

Hiram and Bobby Lee returned from the woods and stood over the ditch, looking down at the grandmother who half sat and half lay in a puddle of blood with her legs crossed under her like a child's and her face smiling up at the cloudless sky.

Without his glasses, The Misfit's eyes were red-rimmed and pale and defenseless-looking. "Take her off and thow her where you thown the others," he said, picking up the cat that was rubbing itself against his leg.

"She was a talker, wasn't she?" Bobby Lee said, sliding down the ditch with a yodel.

"She would of been a good woman," The Misfit said, "if it had been　140 somebody there to shoot her every minute of her life."

"Some fun!" Bobby Lee said.

"Shut up, Bobby Lee," The Misfit said. "It's no real pleasure in life."

The Reader's Presence

1. The grandmother is described only indirectly, through her words, actions, and interactions with others. Reread paragraphs 1–9. How does the grandmother appear to see herself? How do you see her? In what ways does the writer's "voice" influence your impression of the character?

2. What might the Misfit figure symbolize in relation to the grandmother and her family? Does his nickname have any significance? What sort of tone does O'Connor establish in the Misfit encounter? Is it eerie, comedic, or somewhere in between? Imagine the story as presented in a different tone; how would it differ? What does O'Connor's position on the characters and events appear to be? What clues in her approach lead you to your conclusion? (See also O'Connor's commentary on the story.)

3. In the "Writer at Work" that follows, O'Connor discusses the crucial action or gesture that makes a story work. "[I]t is probably some action, some gesture of a character that is unlike any other in the story, one which indicates where the real heart of the story lies. . . . It would be a gesture which somehow made contact with mystery" (paragraph 12). O'Connor locates this key moment in paragraph 136 of "A Good Man Is Hard to Find" (page 954), when the grandmother's "head cleared for an instant." Locate the crucial gesture or action in Raymond Carver's story "The Bath" (page 895) and in Sherman Alexie's story "This Is What It Means to Say Phoenix, Arizona" (page 885). Is O'Connor's description of such a gesture and its key role in "making a story hold up" applicable to stories by writers other than herself? Is "mystery" as important to Carver and to Alexie as it is to O'Connor?

THE WRITER AT WORK

Flannery O'Connor on Her Own Work

Flannery O'Connor's "A Good Man Is Hard to Find" ranks as one of American fiction's most durable short stories. It has been reprinted and analyzed in critical periodicals hundreds of times since it first appeared in 1953. Ten years after its first publication and shortly before her untimely death, O'Connor was invited to read the story at Hollins College in Virginia (now Hollins University), where she made the following remarks. Her comments on the story were then included in a collection of nonfiction published by her editor in 1969 under the very appropriate title "Mystery and Manners." As you consider the story, you may want to focus on these terms: mystery *and* manners. *How does each word describe an important aspect of the story? How are they interrelated? You should also consider the story from the perspective O'Connor herself provides in the following selection. Do you think her comments on her own story are critically persuasive? Did you come away from the story with a different sense of its significance? Do you think that what an author says about his or her own work must always be the final word?*

Last fall I received a letter from a student who said she would be "graciously appreciative" if I would tell her "just what enlightenment" I expected her to get from each of my stories. I suspect she had a paper to write. I wrote her back to forget about the enlightenment and just try to enjoy them. I knew that was the most unsatisfactory answer I could have given because, of course, she didn't want to enjoy them, she just wanted to figure them out.

In most English classes the short story has become a kind of literary specimen to be dissected. Every time a story of mine appears in a Freshman anthology, I have a vision of it, with its little organs laid open, like a frog in a bottle.

I realize that a certain amount of this what-is-the-significance has to go on, but I think something has gone wrong in the process when, for so many students, the story becomes simply a problem to be solved, something which you evaporate to get Instant Enlightenment.

A story really isn't any good unless it successfully resists paraphrase, unless it hangs on and expands in the mind. Properly, you analyze to enjoy, but it's equally true that to analyze with any discrimination, you have to have enjoyed already, and I think that the best reason to hear a story read is that it should stimulate that primary enjoyment.

I don't have any pretensions to being an Aeschylus or Sophocles and   5 providing you in this story with a cathartic experience out of your mythic background, though this story I'm going to read certainly calls up a good deal of the South's mythic background, and it should elicit from you a degree of pity and terror, even though its way of being serious is a comic one. I do think, though, that like the Greeks you should know what is going to happen in this story so that any element of suspense in it will be transferred from its surface to its interior.

I would be most happy if you had already read it, happier still if you knew it well, but since experience has taught me to keep my expectations along these lines modest, I'll tell you that this is the story of a family of six which, on its way driving to Florida, gets wiped out by an escaped convict who calls himself the Misfit. The family is made up of the Grandmother and her son, Bailey, and his children, John Wesley and June Star and the baby, and there is also the cat and the children's mother. The cat is named Pitty Sing, and the Grandmother is taking him with them, hidden in a basket.

Now I think it behooves me to try to establish with you the basis on which reason operates in this story. Much of my fiction takes its character from a reasonable use of the unreasonable, though the reasonableness of my use of it may not always be apparent. The assumptions that underlie this use of it, however, are those of the central Christian mysteries. These are assumptions to which a large part of the modern audience takes exception. About this I can only say that there are perhaps other ways than my own in which this story could be read, but none other by which it could have been written. Belief, in my own case anyway, is the engine that makes perception operate.

The heroine of this story, the Grandmother, is in the most significant position life offers the Christian. She is facing death. And to all appearances she, like the rest of us, is not too well prepared for it. She would like to see the event postponed. Indefinitely.

I've talked to a number of teachers who use this story in class and who tell their students that the Grandmother is evil, that in fact, she's a witch, even down to the cat. One of these teachers told me that his students, and particularly his Southern students, resisted this interpretation with a certain bemused vigor, and he didn't understand why. I had to tell him that they resisted it because they all had grandmothers or great-aunts just like her at home, and they knew, from personal experience, that the old lady lacked comprehension, but that she had a good heart. The Southerner is usually tolerant of those weaknesses that proceed from innocence, and he knows that a taste for self-preservation can be readily combined with the missionary spirit.

This same teacher was telling his students that morally the Misfit was 10 several cuts above the Grandmother. He had a really sentimental attachment to the Misfit. But then a prophet gone wrong is almost always more interesting than your grandmother, and you have to let people take their pleasures where they find them.

It is true that the old lady is a hypocritical old soul; her wits are no match for the Misfit's, nor is her capacity for grace equal to his; yet I think the unprejudiced reader will feel that the Grandmother has a special kind of triumph in this story which instinctively we do not allow to someone altogether bad.

I often ask myself what makes a story work, and what makes it hold up as a story, and I have decided that it is probably some action, some gesture of a character that is unlike any other in the story, one which indicates where the real heart of the story lies. This would have to be an action or a gesture which was both totally right and totally unexpected; it would have to be one that was both in character and beyond character; it would have to suggest both the world and eternity. The action or gesture I'm talking about would have to be on the anagogical level, that is, the level which has to do with the Divine life and our participation in it. It would be a gesture that transcended any neat allegory that might have been intended or any pat moral categories a reader could make. It would be a gesture which somehow made contact with mystery.

There is a point in this story where such a gesture occurs. The Grandmother is at last alone, facing the Misfit. Her head clears for an instant and she realizes, even in her limited way, that she is responsible for the man before her and joined to him by ties of kinship which have their roots deep in the mystery she has been merely prattling about so far. And at this point, she does the right thing, she makes the right gesture.

I find that students are often puzzled by what she says and does here, but I think myself that if I took out this gesture and what she says with it, I would have no story. What was left would not be worth your attention. Our age not only does not have a very sharp eye for the almost imperceptible intrusions of grace, it no longer has much feeling for the nature of the violences which precede and follow them. The devil's greatest wile, Baudelaire has said, is to convince us that he does not exist.

I suppose the reasons for the use of so much violence in modern fic-   15
tion will differ with each writer who uses it, but in my own stories I have found that violence is strangely capable of returning my characters to reality and preparing them to accept their moment of grace. Their heads are so hard that almost nothing else will do the work. This idea, that reality is something to which we must be returned at considerable cost, is one which is seldom understood by the casual reader, but it is one which is implicit in the Christian view of the world.

I don't want to equate the Misfit with the devil. I prefer to think that, however unlikely this may seem, the old lady's gesture, like the mustard-seed, will grow to be a great crow-filled tree in the Misfit's heart, and will be enough of a pain to him there to turn him into the prophet he was meant to become. But that's another story.

This story has been called grotesque, but I prefer to call it literal. A good story is literal in the same sense that a child's drawing is literal. When a child draws, he doesn't intend to distort but to set down exactly what he sees, and as his gaze is direct, he sees the lines that create motion. Now the lines of motion that interest the writer are usually invisible. They are lines of spiritual motion. And in this story you should be on the lookout for such things as the action of grace in the Grandmother's soul, and not for the dead bodies.

We hear many complaints about the prevalence of violence in modern fiction, and it is always assumed that this violence is a bad thing and meant to be an end in itself. With the serious writer, violence is never an end in itself. It is the extreme situation that best reveals what we are essentially, and I believe these are times when writers are more interested in what we are essentially than in the tenor of our daily lives. Violence is a force which can be used for good or evil, and among other things taken by it is the kingdom of heaven. But regardless of what can be taken by it, the man in the violent situation reveals those qualities least dispensable in his personality, those qualities which are all he will have to take into eternity with him; and since the characters in this story are all on the verge of eternity, it is appropriate to think of what they take with them. In any case, I hope that if you consider these points in connection with the story, you will come to see it as something more than an account of a family murdered on the way to Florida.

John Updike

A & P

"A&P" is one of nineteen stories from John Updike's 1962 collection titled Pigeon Feathers and Other Stories, *which appeared early in the writer's long and impressive career. In a 2001 interview, Updike commented on his goals as a writer and what he appreciates in other writing: "I've just tried to write in a way that would entertain and please me, if I were the reader . . . the kind of writer I'm attracted to is a writer who gives pleasure—the prose writer who does a little more than what is strictly called for to deliver the image or the facts. I'm not a very fast reader, so I like to open up a book and feel some whiff of poetry or of extra effort or of something inventive going on, so that even read backwards, a paragraph of prose will yield something to the sense." Updike has said humorously of his approach to reading: "My purpose in reading has ever secretly been not to come and judge but to come and steal."*

For Updike, his presence as a writer is inevitable: "You can't really control your writer's voice. It's a lot like your handwriting—you can't stop it. You can try to alter it, but it always comes out as you. My prose tends to come out as me . . ."

For more information on John Updike, see page 298.

In walks these three girls in nothing but bathing suits. I'm in the third checkout slot, with my back to the door, so I don't see them until they're over by the bread. The one that caught my eye first was the one in the plaid green two-piece. She was a chunky kid, with a good tan and a sweet broad soft-looking can with those two crescents of white just under it, where the sun never seems to hit, at the top of the backs of her legs. I stood there with my hand on a box of HiHo crackers trying to remember if I rang it up or not. I ring it up again and the customer starts giving me hell. She's one of these cash-register-watchers, a witch about fifty with rouge on her cheekbones and no eyebrows, and I know it made her day to trip me up. She'd been watching cash registers for fifty years and probably never seen a mistake before.

By the time I got her feathers smoothed and her goodies into a bag— she gives me a little snort in passing, if she'd been born at the right time they would have burned her over in Salem—by the time I get her on her way the girls had circled around the bread and were coming back, without a pushcart, back my way along the counters, in the aisle between the checkouts and the Special bins. They didn't even have shoes on. There was this chunky one, with the two-piece—it was bright green and the seams on the bra were still sharp and her belly was still pretty pale so I guessed she just got it (the suit)—there was this one, with one of those chubby berry-faces, the lips all bunched together under her nose, this one, and a tall one, with black hair that hadn't quite frizzed right, and one of these

959

sunburns right across under the eyes, and a chin that was too long—you know, the kind of girl other girls think is very "striking" and "attractive" but never quite makes it, as they very well know, which is why they like her so much—and then the third one, that wasn't quite so tall. She was the queen. She kind of led them, the other two peeking around and making their shoulders round. She didn't look around, not this queen, she just walked straight on slowly, on these long white prima-donna legs. She came down a little hard on her heels, as if she didn't walk in her bare feet that much, putting down her heels and then letting the weight move along to her toes as if she was testing the floor with every step, putting a little deliberate extra action into it. You never know for sure how girls' minds work (do you really think it's a mind in there or just a little buzz like a bee in a glass jar?) but you got the idea she had talked the other two into coming in here with her, and now she was showing them how to do it, walk slow and hold yourself straight.

She had on a kind of dirty-pink—beige maybe, I don't know—bathing suit with a little nubble all over it and, what got me, the straps were down. They were off her shoulders looped loose around the cool tops of her arms, and I guess as a result the suit had slipped a little on her, so all around the top of the cloth there was this shining rim. If it hadn't been there you wouldn't have known there could have been anything whiter than those shoulders. With the straps pushed off, there was nothing between the top of the suit and the top of her head except just *her*, this clean bare plane of the top of her chest down from the shoulder bones like a dented sheet of metal tilted in the light. I mean, it was more than pretty.

She had sort of oaky hair that the sun and salt had bleached, done up in a bun that was unraveling, and a kind of prim face. Walking into the A & P with your straps down, I suppose it's the only kind of face you *can* have. She held her head so high her neck, coming up out of those white shoulders, looked kind of stretched, but I didn't mind. The longer her neck was, the more of her there was.

She must have felt in the corner of her eye me and over my shoulder   5
Stokesie in the second slot watching, but she didn't tip. Not this queen. She kept her eyes moving across the racks, and stopped, and turned so slow it made my stomach rub the inside of my apron, and buzzed to the other two, who kind of huddled against her for relief, and then they all three of them went up the cat-and-dog-food-breakfast-cereal-macaroni-rice-raisins-seasonings-spreads-spaghetti-soft-drinks-crackers-and-cookies aisle. From the third slot I look straight up this aisle to the meat counter, and I watched them all the way. The fat one with the tan sort of fumbled with the cookies, but on second thought she put the package back. The sheep pushing their carts down the aisle—the girls were walking against the usual traffic (not that we have one-way signs or anything)—were pretty hilarious. You could see them, when Queenie's white shoulders dawned on them, kind of jerk, or hop, or hiccup, but their eyes snapped back to their own baskets and on

they pushed. I bet you could set off dynamite in an A & P and the people would by and large keep reaching and checking oatmeal off their lists and muttering "Let me see, there was a third thing, began with A, asparagus, no, ah, yes, applesauce!" or whatever it is they do mutter. But there was no doubt, this jiggled them. A few houseslaves in pin curlers even looked around after pushing their carts past to make sure what they had seen was correct.

You know, it's one thing to have a girl in a bathing suit down on the beach, where what with the glare nobody can look at each other much anyway, and another thing in the cool of the A & P, under the fluorescent lights, against all those stacked packages, with her feet paddling along naked over our checkerboard green-and-cream rubber-tile floor.

"Oh Daddy," Stokesie said beside me. "I feel so faint."

"Darling," I said. "Hold me tight." Stokesie's married, with two babies chalked up on his fuselage already, but as far as I can tell that's the only difference. He's twenty-two, and I was nineteen this April.

"Is it done?" he asks, the responsible married man finding his voice. I forgot to say he thinks he's going to be manager some sunny day, maybe in 1990 when it's called the Great Alexandrov and Petrooshki Tea Company or something.

What he meant was, our town is five miles from a beach, with a big summer colony out on the Point, but we're right in the middle of town, and the women generally put on a shirt or shorts or something before they get out of the car into the street. And anyway these are usually women with six children and varicose veins mapping their legs and nobody, including them, could care less. As I say, we're right in the middle of town, and if you stand at our front doors you can see two banks and the Congregational church and the newspaper store and three real-estate offices and about twenty-seven old freeloaders tearing up Central Street because the sewer broke again. It's not as if we're on the Cape, we're north of Boston and there's people in this town haven't seen the ocean for twenty years. 10

The girls had reached the meat counter and were asking McMahon something. He pointed, they pointed, and they shuffled out of sight behind a pyramid of Diet Delight peaches. All that was left for us to see was old McMahon patting his mouth and looking after them sizing up their joints. Poor kids, I began to feel sorry for them, they couldn't help it.

Now here comes the sad part of the story, at least my family says it's sad, but I don't think it's so sad myself. The store's pretty empty, it being Thursday afternoon, so there was nothing much to do except lean on the register and wait for the girls to show up again. The whole store was like a pinball machine and I didn't know which tunnel they'd come out of. After a while they come around out of the far aisle, around the light bulbs, records at discount of the Caribbean Six or Tony Martin Sings or some such gunk you wonder they waste the wax on, sixpacks of candy bars, and plastic toys done up in cellophane that fall apart when a kid looks at them anyway. Around they come, Queenie still leading the way, and holding a little gray jar in her hands. Slots Three through Seven are unmanned and I could see her wondering between Stokes and me, but Stokesie with his usual luck draws an old party in baggy gray pants who stumbles up with four giant cans of pineapple juice (what do these bums *do* with all that pineapple juice? I've often asked myself). So the girls come to me. Queenie puts down the jar and I take it into my fingers icy cold. Kingfish Fancy Herring Snacks in Pure Sour Cream: 49¢. Now her hands are empty, not a ring or a bracelet, bare as God made them, and I wonder where the money's coming from. Still with that prim look she lifts a folded dollar bill out of the hollow at the center of her nubbled pink top. The jar went heavy in my hand. Really, I thought that was so cute.

Then everybody's luck begins to run out. Lengel comes in from haggling with a truck full of cabbages on the lot and is about to scuttle into that door marked MANAGER behind which he hides all day when the girls touch his eye. Lengel's pretty dreary, teaches Sunday school and the rest, but he doesn't miss that much. He comes over and says, "Girls, this isn't the beach."

Queenie blushes, though maybe it's just a brush of sunburn I was noticing for the first time, now that she was so close. "My mother asked me to pick up a jar of herring snacks." Her voice kind of startled me, the way voices do when you see the people first, coming out so flat and dumb yet kind of tony, too, the way it ticked over "pick up" and "snacks." All of a sudden I slid right down her voice into the living room. Her father and the other men were standing around in ice-cream coats and bow ties and the women were in sandals picking up herring snacks on toothpicks off a big glass plate and they were all holding drinks the color of water with olives and sprigs of mint in them. When my parents have somebody over they get lemonade and if it's a real racy affair Schlitz in tall glasses with "They'll Do It Every Time" cartoons stenciled on.

"That's all right," Lengel said. "But this isn't the beach." His repeating this struck me as funny, as if it had just occurred to him, and he had been thinking all these years the A & P was a great big dune and he was the head lifeguard. He didn't like my smiling—as I say he doesn't miss much—but he concentrates on giving the girls that sad Sunday-school-superintendent stare.   15

Queenie's blush is no sunburn now, and the plump one in plaid, that I liked better from the back—a really sweet can—pipes up, "We weren't doing any shopping. We just came in for the one thing."

"That makes no difference," Lengel tells her, and I could see from the way his eyes went that he hadn't noticed she was wearing a two-piece before. "We want you decently dressed when you come in here."

"We *are* decent," Queenie says suddenly, her lower lip pushing, getting sore now that she remembers her place, a place from which the crowd that runs the A & P must look pretty crummy. Fancy Herring Snacks flashed in her very blue eyes.

"Girls, I don't want to argue with you. After this come in here with your shoulders covered. It's our policy." He turns his back. That's policy for you. Policy is what the kingpins want. What the others want is juvenile delinquency.

All this while, the customers had been showing up with their carts but, you know, sheep, seeing a scene, they had all bunched up on Stokesie, who shook open a paper bag as gently as peeling a peach, not wanting to miss a word. I could feel in the silence everybody getting nervous, most of all Lengel, who asks me, "Sammy, have you rung up their purchase?"

I thought and said "No" but it wasn't about that I was thinking. I go through the punches, 4, 9, GROC. TOT—it's more complicated than you think, and after you do it often enough, it begins to make a little song, that you hear words to, in my case "Hello (*bing*) there, you (*gung*) hap-py *pee*-pul (*splat*)!"—the *splat* being the drawer flying out. I uncrease the bill, tenderly as you may imagine, it just having come from between the two smoothest scoops of vanilla I had ever known were there, and pass a half and a penny into her narrow pink palm, and nestle the herrings in a bag and twist its neck and hand it over, all the time thinking.

The girls, and who'd blame them, are in a hurry to get out, so I say "I quit" to Lengel quick enough for them to hear, hoping they'll stop and watch me, their unsuspected hero. They keep right on going, into the electric eye; the door flies open and they flicker across the lot to their car, Queenie and Plaid and Big Tall Goony-Goony (not that as raw material she was so bad), leaving me with Lengel and a kink in his eyebrow.

"Did you say something, Sammy?"

"I said I quit."

"I thought you did."

"You didn't have to embarrass them."

"It was they who were embarrassing us."

I started to say something that came out "Fiddle-de-doo." It's a saying of my grandmother's, and I know she would have been pleased.

"I don't think you know what you're saying," Lengel said.

"I know you don't," I said. "But I do." I pull the bow at the back of my apron and start shrugging it off my shoulders. A couple customers that had been heading for my slot begin to knock against each other, like scared pigs in a chute.

Lengel sighs and begins to look very patient and old and gray. He's been a friend of my parents for years. "Sammy, you don't want to do this to your Mom and Dad," he tells me. It's true, I don't. But it seems to me that once you begin a gesture it's fatal not to go through with it. I fold the apron, "Sammy" stitched in red on the pocket, and put it on the counter, and drop the bow tie on top of it. The bow tie is theirs, if you've ever wondered. "You'll feel this for the rest of your life," Lengel says, and I know that's true, too, but remembering how he made the pretty girl blush makes me so scrunchy inside I punch the No Sale tab and the machine whirs "pee-pul" and the drawer splats out. One advantage to this scene taking place in summer, I can follow this up with a clean exit, there's no fumbling around getting your coat and galoshes, I just saunter into the electric eye in my white shirt that my mother ironed the night before, and the door heaves itself open, and outside the sunshine is skating around on the asphalt.

I look around for my girls, but they're gone, of course. There wasn't anybody but some young married screaming with her children about some candy they didn't get by the door of a powder-blue Falcon station wagon. Looking back in the big windows, over the bags of peat moss and aluminum lawn furniture stacked on the pavement, I could see Lengel in my place in the slot, checking the sheep through. His face was dark gray and his back stiff, as if he'd just had an injection of iron, and my stomach kind of fell as I felt how hard the world was going to be to me hereafter.

The Reader's Presence

1. The story is written in colloquial language. Reread the first two paragraphs. What does the narrator's style of expression convey about him? What effect does the narrator's style of expression have upon your reading of the story? Are you more, or less, inclined to believe his words? Suppose the same story were recounted in more conventional English. Would its meaning differ? If so, in what ways? How do you think Updike wishes the reader to view the narrator? Does Updike seem to agree, partially agree, or disagree with the narrator's point of view? What clues in the narrative lead you to your conclusion?

2. A great deal of the story hinges upon what the narrator doesn't know or say. Is the girls' attire the only issue in the confrontation? What other tensions are evident in the store and in the town? What impression of the situation do you glean "between the lines"? How does the writer convey information beyond the scope of what the narrator is able to articulate?

3. Updike's story presents a seemingly minor event at a supermarket as the catalyst for a major change in the narrator's life. "I felt how hard the world was going to be to me hereafter," Sammy says in the story's final sentence. How do the perceptions of the past, present, and future intersect in the story? How seriously do you take the narrator's grim view of his future? Read Updike's "At War with My Skin" (page 298). How do past, present, and future intersect in the essay? How does Updike's psoriasis serve as a catalyst? Do you think he is serious about all that he has done and become as a result of it? Why or why not?

Acknowledgments

Diane Ackerman, "We Are Our Words" from *Parade*, May 30, 2004. Copyright © 2004 by Diane Ackerman. All rights reserved. Reprinted by permission of *Parade* Publications and the William Morris Agency, LLC on behalf of the author.

James Agee, "America, Look at Your Shame!" from *Oxford American*, January/February 2003. Copyright © 2003 by James Agee. Reprinted with the permission of the Wylie Agency Inc.

Sherman Alexie, "The Joy of Reading and Writing: Superman and Me" from *The Most Wonderful Books*, edited by Michael Dorris and Emilie Buchwald. Copyright © 1997 by Milkweed Editions. Reprinted by permission of the author. "This Is What It Means to Say Phoenix, Arizona" from *The Lone Ranger and Tonto Fistfight in Heaven*. Copyright © 1993 by Sherman Alexie. Used by permission of Grove/Atlantic, Inc.

Dorothy Allison, "This Is Our World" from *DoubleTake* 13, Summer 1998. Copyright © 1998 by Dorothy Allison. Reprinted by permission of The Frances Goldin Agency, Inc.

Ho Che Anderson, "I Have a Dream" from *King* Volume 2. Copyright © 2002 by Ho Che Anderson. Reprinted courtesy of Fantagraphics Books.

Maya Angelou, "What's Your Name, Girl?" from *I Know Why the Caged Bird Sings* by Maya Angelou. Copyright © 1969 and renewed 1997 by Maya Angelou. Used by permission of Random House, Inc.

Gloria Anzaldúa, "How to Tame a Wild Tongue" from *Borderlands/La Frontera: The New Mestiza*. Copyright © 1987, 1999 by Gloria Anzaldúa. Reprinted by permission of Aunt Lute Books.

Karen Armstrong, "Is a Holy War Inevitable?" from *GQ*, January 2002. Copyright © 2002. Reproduced by permission of Felicity Bryan Literary Agency and the author.

James Baldwin, "Notes of a Native Son" from *Notes of a Native Son*. Copyright © 1955 and renewed 1983 by James Baldwin. Reprinted by permission of Beacon Press, Boston. "On Black English." Originally published as "If Black English Isn't a Language, Then Tell Me, What Is?" in *The New York Times*. Copyright © 1979 by James Baldwin. Collected in *The Price of the Ticket*, published by St. Martin's Press. Reprinted by arrangement with the James Baldwin Estate.

David Brooks, "People Like Us" from *The Atlantic Monthly*, September 2003. Reprinted by permission of the author.

Stephen L. Carter, "The Insufficiency of Honesty" from *Integrity*. Copyright © 1996 by Stephen L. Carter. Reprinted by permission of Basic Books, a member of Perseus Books, L.L.C.

Raymond Carver, "My Father's Life." Copyright © 1984 by Tess Gallagher. First appeared in *Esquire*. Reprinted by permission of International Creative Management, Inc. "The Bath" from *What We Talk About When We Talk About Love*. Copyright © 1981 by Raymond Carver. Used by permission of Alfred A. Knopf, a division of Random House, Inc.

Judith Ortiz Cofer, "Silent Dancing" and "On Memory and Personal Essays," which is excerpted from "Preface," are reprinted with permission from the publisher of *Silent Dancing: A Partial Remembrance of a Puerto-Rican Childhood* (Houston: Arte Público Press—University of Houston, 1990).

Christopher Columbus, "October 12–14, 1492" from *Journals and Other Documents on the Life of Christopher Columbus*, edited and translated by Samuel Eliot Morison. Copyright © 1963 by S. E. Morison. Reprinted by permission of Curtis Brown, Ltd.

Bernard Cooper, "A Clack of Tiny Sparks: Remembrances of a Gay Boyhood." Copyright © 1990 by *Harper's Magazine*. All rights reserved. Reproduced from the January '91 issue by special permission.

Amy Cunningham, "Why Women Smile." Copyright © 1993 by Amy Cunningham. First published in *Lear's* and edited by Nelson Aldrich. Reprinted by permission of the author.

Edwidge Danticat, "We Are Ugly, But We Are Here" from *The Caribbean Writer*, Summer 1996. Copyright © 1996 by Edwidge Danticat. "On Becoming a Writer" excerpted from an interview in *Essence*, May 1996. Copyright © 1996 by Edwidge Danticat. Both selections reprinted by permission of Edwidge Danticat and Aragi Inc.

Don DeLillo, "In the Ruins of the Future: Reflections on Terror, Loss and Time in the Shadow of September." Copyright © 2001 by Don DeLillo. First published in *Harper's Magazine*. Used by permission of the Wallace Literary Agency, Inc.

Toi Derricotte, "October" and "July" from *The Black Notebooks: An Interior Journey*. Copyright © 1997 by Toi Derricotte. Used by permission of W. W. Norton & Company, Inc.

Jared Diamond, "The Ends of the World as We Know Them" from *The New York Times*, January 1, 2005. Copyright © 2005 by The New York Times. Reprinted by permission.

Acknowledgments 967

Laura Kipnis, "Against Love" from *The New York Times Magazine*, October 14, 2001. Copyright © 2001 by Laura Kipnis. Reprinted by permission.

Nancy Mairs, "On Being a Cripple" from *Plain Text*. Copyright © 1986 by The Arizona Board of Regents. Reprinted by permission of the University of Arizona Press. "On Finding a Voice" from *Voice Lessons*. Copyright © 1994 by Nancy Mairs. Reprinted by permission of Beacon Press, Boston.

Malcolm X, "Homeboy" from *The Autobiography of Malcolm X* by Malcolm X and Alex Haley. Copyright © 1964 by Alex Haley and Malcolm X, copyright © 1965 by Alex Haley and Betty Shabazz. Used by permission of Random House, Inc.

David Mamet, "The Rake: A Few Scenes from My Childhood" from *The Cabin*. Copyright © 1992 by David Mamet. Used by permission of Vintage Books, a division of Random House, Inc.

Adam Mayblum, "The Price We Pay" from *DoubleTake Magazine*, Special Edition 2001. Copyright © 2001 by Adam Mayblum. Reprinted by permission of the author.

Bill McKibben, "Worried? Us?" from *Granta* 83. Reprinted by permission of the author.

N. Scott Momaday, "The Way to Rainy Mountain." Copyright © 1969, 1997 by the University of New Mexico Press. First published in *The Reporter*, January 26, 1967. Reprinted by permission of the University of New Mexico Press.

Azar Nafisi, "Reading *Lolita* in Tehran" from *The Chronicle of Higher Education*, April 25, 2003. Adapted from *Reading* Lolita *in Tehran*. Copyright © 2002 by Azar Nafisi. Used by permission of Random House, Inc.

Martha Nussbaum, "Can Patriotism Be Compassionate?" Copyright © 2001 by The Nation. Reprinted with permission from the December 17, 2001 issue of *The Nation*. For subscription information, call 1-800-333-8536. Portions of each week's *Nation* magazine can be accessed at http://www.thenation.com.

Joyce Carol Oates, "District School #7, Niagara County, New York" from *The Faith of a Writer*. Copyright © 2003 by The Ontario Review, Inc. Reprinted by permission of HarperCollins Publishers. "Where Are You Going, Where Have You Been?" Copyright © 1970 Ontario Review. Reprinted by permission of John Hawkins & Associates, Inc. "*Smooth Talk*: Short Story into Film" from *Woman Writer: Occasions and Opportunities*. Copyright © 1988 by The Ontario Review. Used by permission of Dutton, a division of Penguin Group (USA) Inc.

Flannery O'Connor, "A Good Man Is Hard to Find" from *A Good Man Is Hard to Find and Other Stories*. Copyright © 1953 by Flannery O'Connor and renewed 1981 by Regina O'Connor. Reprinted by permission of Harcourt, Inc. "On Her Own Work" excerpted from "A Reasonable Use of the Unreasonable" from *Mystery and Manners* by Flannery O'Connor. Copyright © 1969 by the Estate of Mary Flannery O'Connor. Reprinted by permission of Farrar, Straus and Giroux, LLC.

Danielle Ofri, "SAT" from *Incidental Findings*. Copyright © 2005 by Danielle Ofri. Reprinted by permission of Beacon Press, Boston.

George Orwell, "Shooting an Elephant" from *Shooting an Elephant and Other Essays*. In the US, copyright © 1950 by Sonia Brownell Orwell and renewed 1978 by Sonia Pitt-Rivers. In Canada, copyright © 1936 by George Orwell. "Politics and the English Language." In the US, copyright © 1946 by Sonia Brownell Orwell and renewed 1974 by Sonia Orwell. In Canada, copyright © 1946 by George Orwell. From *Shooting an Elephant and Other Essays*. "On the Four Reasons for Writing" excerpted from "Why I Write" from *Such, Such Were the Joys*. In the US, copyright © 1953 by Sonia Brownell Orwell and renewed 1981 by Mrs. George K. Perutz, Mrs. Miriam Gross, and Dr. Michael Dickson, Executors of the Estate of Sonia Brownell Orwell. In Canada, copyright © 1953 by George Orwell. All selections reprinted by permission of Harcourt, Inc., Bill Hamilton as the Literary Executor of the Estate of the Late Sonia Brownell Orwell, and Secker & Warburg Ltd.

Katha Pollitt, "Why Boys Don't Play with Dolls" from *The New York Times Magazine*, October 8, 1995. Copyright © 1995 by Katha Pollitt. Reprinted by permission of The New York Times.

Adrienne Rich, "Split at the Root: An Essay on Jewish Identity (abridged)" from *Blood, Bread, and Poetry: Selected Prose 1979–1985*. Copyright © 1986 by Adrienne Rich. Used by permission of the author and W. W. Norton & Company, Inc.

Richard Rodriguez, "Aria: A Memoir of a Bilingual Childhood." Copyright © 1980 by Richard Rodriguez. Originally appeared in *The American Scholar*. Reprinted by permission of Georges Borchardt, Inc., for the author. "On a Writer's Identity" excerpted from "Crossing Borders: An Interview with Richard Rodriguez" by Scott London, *The*

Barbara Tuchman, "'This Is the End of the World': The Black Death" from *A Distant Mirror*. Copyright © 1978 by Barbara W. Tuchman. Used by permission of Alfred A. Knopf, a division of Random House, Inc.

Sherry Turkle, "How Computers Change the Way We Think" from *The Chronicle of Higher Education*, January 30, 2004. Reprinted by permission of the author.

Scott Turow, "To Kill or Not to Kill" excerpted from "Annals of Law: To Kill or Not to Kill." First appeared in *The New Yorker*, January 6, 2003 and was later revised and published in the book *Ultimate Punishment* by Scott Turow. Copyright © 2003 by Scott Turow. Reprinted by permission of Farrar, Straus and Giroux, LLC.

Ellen Ullman, "The Museum of Me" from *Harper's Magazine*, May 2000. Reproduced courtesy of Ellen Ullman.

John Updike, "At War with My Skin" from *Self-Consciousness*. Copyright © 1989 by John Updike. "A & P" from *Pigeon Feathers and Other Stories*. Copyright © 1962 and renewed 1990 by John Updike. Both selections used by permission of Alfred A. Knopf, a division of Random House, Inc.

Gore Vidal, "Drugs." Copyright © 1970 by Gore Vidal. From *Homage to Daniel Shays: Collected Essays*. Used by permission of Random House, Inc.

Alice Walker, "Beauty: When the Other Dancer is the Self" from *In Search of Our Mothers' Gardens: Womanist Prose*. Copyright © 1983 by Alice Walker. Reprinted by permission of Harcourt, Inc.

Marine Staff Sergeant Aaron Dean White, Army Pfc. Diego Fernando Rincon, and Army Specialist Brett T. Christian, "Last Letters Home" from *Esquire*, February 2004. Reprinted by permission of Esquire Magazine, a division of Hearst Corp.

E. B. White, "Once More to the Lake" from *One Man's Meat*. Text copyright © 1941 by E. B. White. Copyright renewed. Reprinted by permission of Tilbury House, Publishers, Gardiner, Maine. "On the Essayist" from the Foreword to *Essays of E. B. White*. Copyright © 1977 by E. B. White. Reprinted by permission of HarperCollins Publishers.

John Edgar Wideman, "The Night I Was Nobody." Copyright © 1996 by John Edgar Wideman. Reprinted with the permission of the Wylie Agency Inc.

Kristian Williams, excerpt from "The Case for Comics Journalism" from *Columbia Journalism Review*, March/April 2005. Reprinted by permission of the author.

Terry Tempest Williams, "The Clan of One-Breasted Women" from *Refuge: An Unnatural History of Family and Place*. Copyright © 1991 by Terry Tempest Williams. Used by pemission of Pantheon Books, a division of Random House, Inc.

Marie Winn, "TV Addiction" excerpted from "Cookies or Heroin?" from *The Plug-In Drug, Revised and Updated 25th Anniversary Edition*. Copyright 1977, 1985, 2002 by Marie Winn Miller. Used by permission of Viking Penguin, a division of Penguin Group (USA).

Tom Wolfe, "Hooking Up" from *Hooking Up*. Copyright © 2000 by Tom Wolfe. Reprinted by permission of Farrar, Straus, and Giroux, LLC.

Virginia Woolf, "This Loose, Drifting Material of Life," "Chained to My Rock," and "They Get Closer Every Time" from *A Writer's Diary*. "The Death of the Moth" from *A Writer's Diary*. All selections copyright © 1954 by Leonard Woolf and renewed 1982 by Quentin Bell and Angelica Garnett. All selections reprinted by permission of Harcourt, Inc.

Howard Zinn, "Stories Hollywood Never Tells" from *The Sun*, July 2004. Reprinted with permission of Howard Zinn.

Art

49 © Art Chantry; **61** Photography Collection, Miriam and Ira D. Wallach Division of Art, Prints and Photographs, The New York Public Library, Astor, Lenox and Tilden Foundations; **140–150** PEANUTS © United Feature Syndicate, Inc.; **279** Photo courtesy of Zadie Smith c/o AP Watt Ltd.; **409** Library of Congress; **446** Photo by Lewis Hine, courtesy George Eastman House; **500–501** Library of Congress; **502** Library of Congress; **505** © Bettmann/CORBIS; **572** Photography Collection, Miriam and Ira D. Wallach Division of Art, Prints and Photographs, The New York Public Library, Astor, Lenox and Tilden Foundations; **573** Photography Collection, Miriam and Ira D. Wallach Division of Art, Prints and Photographs, The New York Public Library, Astor, Lenox and Tilden Foundations; **580** HIP/Art Resource, NY. British Library, London, Great Britain; **590** Scala, Art Resource, NY. Galleria Nazionale, Palermo, Italy; **626–628** Detroit Free Press; **680–681** © Stanley J. Forman, Pulitzer Prize Spot News, 1976; **878** Library of Congress; **879** Collection of Immigrant City Archives, Lawrence, Massachusetts.

Index of Authors and Titles